Buyer Power in EU Competition Law

Ignacio Herrera Anchustegui

Foreword by Dr. Albert Sánchez Graells

Para Papá.

contact@concurrences.com
www.concurrences.com

Printed in the United Kingdom

First Printing, October 2017
978-1-939007-24-7 (paperback)
978-1-939007-29-2 (e-book)

Cover and book design by Yves Buliard, www.yvesbuliard.fr
Layout implementation: Darlene Swanson, www.van-garde.com

ACKNOWLEDGEMENTS

At the beginning of your Ph.D. studies you are told that a dissertation in law – which now has evolved into a book - is the outcome of an individual piece of work. In my case, this has certainly not been the case. I have been fortunate to have encountered on this research journey exceptional human beings that have aided me in a way or another to reach this milestone. To all of you, thank you for your support, advice and suggestions.

I would like to express my gratitude to my supervisors *Ass. Professor Ronny Gjendemsjø* and *Prof. Erling Hjelmeng*. Their hands-off approach but their constant presence allowed me to develop as an independent researcher and their trust encouraged me to trust my own abilities. *Ronny* you have been an exceptional mentor, your support, criticism, advice and willingness to always listen to my lengthy monologs has been outstanding help. *Erling*, your criticism, advice, direct and to the critical points comments and motivation allowed me to reshape my ideas, ponder about what is important and what is not and challenge my own conceptions. To both of you, my most sincere *takk*, I will always be in debt.

This thesis would not have been possible without all the support I received from the Faculty of Law of the University of Bergen. There my thanks go first to *Prof. Ragna Aarli* and *Prof. Tore Lunde* for taking a 'gamble' with me when I applied for a Ph.D. position. I also would like to thank *Dean Prof. Asbjørn Strandbakken* and *Vice-Dean Prof. Berte-Elen Konow, Prof. Karl-Harald Søvig, Prof. Jørn Øyrehaugen Sunde, Prof. Sigrid Eskeland Schütz, Prof. Ernst Nordtveit,* and, *Prof. Eme. Kai Krüger* for their institutional and personal support.

Also, I would like to thank the members of the Competition and Market Law Research Group and the BECCLE 'crew'. The economic advice of *Prof. Tommy Gabrielsen, Prof. Lars Sørgard, Prof. Kurt Brekke*, and *Ass. Professor Bjørn Olav Johansen* has been instrumental. To my (senior) colleagues and friends *Prof. Christian Franklin, Prof. Halvard Fredriksen,* and *Post.doctoral Researcher Malgorzata Cyndecka,* thank you so much for including me in the team, switching to English during lunch time and coping with me. To the Ph.D., BECCLE gang: *Ingrid H. Barlund, Håvard Ormberg, Linda Midtun, Kristian Strømnes, Teis Lømo, Øyvind Røed, Simen Ulsaker, Håvard Sandvik* and *Timothy Wyndham*, thank you all for the great times, shared airplanes, read papers, graphs and patience with me. Also, I would like to thank my research assistants: *Agnieszka Bulat, Piotr Stanislawski* and *Anne-Kjersti Klingsheim* for the hard work, careful eye and patience.

This thesis would not have been possible without the very generous research grant by the *Norwegian Research Council*. I also am indebted to the *Meltzerfondet* for granting me during four years financial support to carry out parts of the research. *Tusen takk.*

Now the thanks travel across the Norwegian and North Sea to all of those that have helped me in this journey.

In the UK my thanks go to *Reader Albert Sánchez Graells* at Bristol University, who has been a mentor, an almost third supervisor, and of invaluable help in my research adventures. *Moltes gràcies*. Also, I want to express my gratitude to the members of the Centre for Competition Policy of the University of East Anglia, in particular to *Lecturer Sebastian Peyer, vielen Dank* for the support, motivation and 'Hitchcock' guidance, and *Prof. Morten Hviid* for your recommendations and allowing me to visit the CCP, *mange tak.*

In Germany and Luxembourg, I would also like to thank the Walter Eucken Institut research staff in Freiburg for allowing me to visit you and learn a great deal about Ordoliberalism. *Vielen Dank*! Also, I am very grateful to *Prof. Dr. Carl Baudenbacher*, *Dr. Philipp Speitler,* and *Michael-James Clifton, LL.M.*, at the EFTA Court for allowing me to visit them, *merci.*

In the US my gratitude goes to *Prof. Peter C. Carstensen* at the University of Wisconsin, *Prof. Daniel Gifford* at the University of Minnesota and *Prof. John B. Kirkwood* at Seattle University for their support, guidance, kindness and helping me navigating the US Antitrust waters.

In Spain I have been very fortunate to have the support and guidance of *Prof. Antonio Robles Martín-Laborda. Muchas gracias,* Antonio. Also, I would like to thank *Prof. Joxerramon Bengoetxea* for his advice, suggestions concerning ordoliberalism and legal theory, *eskerrik asko*. Lastly, I would like to thank *Prof. Fernando Cachafeiro* for allowing me to collaborate in an exciting project on food distribution and buyer power, *moitas grazas*.

In the Nordic countries I would like to thank the members of my PhD evaluation committee for their critical remarks, comments and suggestions. *Prof. Caroline Heide-Jørgensen, Prof. Lars Henriksson* and *Prof. Petri Kuoppamäki*. Thank you.

Also, I would like to express my gratitude to the members of the 2017 Concurrences PhD Award, *Catherine Prieto, Nicolas Petit, Sylvaine Poillot-Peruzzetto, Wouter Wils* and *Philippe Choné*, for having read my thesis and considered it worthy of this distinction. *Merci*.

Lastly, some personal thanks.

To *Christine Plaza-Falkner* all my thanks for her support, love, guidance and kindness. *Vielen herzlichen Dank*. I also want to thank *Eirik Talleraas* for his suggestion regarding "… how about a Ph.D. in Norway?", *tusen takk!* To my family in Donostia,

Jexux Arrizabalaga eta Marijose Egaña, mila esker. Also, my thanks go to my sister *María Isabel Herrera* who supported me and helped me with translations and proof-reading, *mil gracias!* In Norway, I would like to thank *Yngvild Beathe Olsen* for her support through the years, *takk*.

Also, a *muchas gracias con acento argentino* goes to my mentor and friend, *Prof. Adolfo Salgueiro* of my *alma mater*, the Andrés Bello Catholic University back home in Venezuela. Thank you for your support, kindness and letting me take my first academic steps as your assistant. I am in debt and grateful to you.

Finally, I would like to thank my parents. You are and have been my support, guide and inspiration. *Gracias, Mamá y Papá.*

Bergen, July 2017

Ignacio Herrera Anchustegui

FOREWORD

It is no exaggeration for Dr Herrera Anchustegui to say that, for the longest time and in the context of legal analysis, "buyer power has mostly been identified with monopsony power and simplified by assuming that its treatment should be symmetrical to, or the 'mirror image' of seller side cases, or opting for simplifications of the topic." However, it is a touch more challenging and may raise an eyebrow or two to claim that "treating buyer power fully economically and symmetrical to monopoly power is not the correct approach, nor is the way in which the Courts apply the law to it." The reader should, however, rest assured that Dr Herrera Anchustegui does not reach such critical conclusion on a whim, but rather as the result of a conscientious and minute analysis of virtually every case involving issues of buyer power under EU competition law.

In this book, Dr Herrera Anchustegui embarks on an ordoliberal and economically informed investigation of the treatment of buyer power in EU competition law with the aim of gaining a holistic view of both the concept and the policy interventions that emerge from past practice across all relevant areas of EU competition law: i.e. anticompetitive behaviour, abuse of dominance and merger control. The reader that follows him in this less than easy journey will be richly rewarded. The research in this book covers a gap in the literature that probably was not perceived as such because of the long shadow of the 'mirror image' mantra and the impression that buyer power issues were, by and large, a peculiar challenge of the supermarkets and agricultural sectors. Beyond those, and possibly one or two examples from regulated industries, even the most knowledgeable scholars and practitioners would need to rack their brains to recall contexts or cases where the competition law analysis rested on theories of harm built upon the exercise of buying power. They would probably also be surprised to read that Dr Herrera Anchustegui does not consider most of these cases to raise a *proper* competition law issue, and would (in keeping with his ordoliberal approach) rather redirect them to other areas of regulation of economic activity of a contractual nature. Therefore, this book offers the specialists an opportunity to reassess the received wisdom on the treatment of buyer power under EU competition law. It also offers readers approaching the topic for the first time an authoritative guide to navigate a difficult and, until now, relatively untrodden territory.

The book has many strengths, but also a curse for the author. One of its main strengths is that it lays out, in terms accessible to non-economists, a clear microeconomic understanding of the issues and challenges implicit in the design of a competition policy around buyer power. This is useful because it goes well-beyond the 'mirror image' mantra and makes the not minor effort of importing to the legal arena developments in industrial organisation research that can support a more nuanced approach to buyer power from a legal perspective. Another of the main strengths of the book is that it offers the reader insights at two different levels. At a micro level, the detailed assessment of cases on the basis of a clearly specified economic model offers new insights on past decisions and their implications. At a macro level, the study as a whole results in a valuable synthesis of concepts and regulatory interventions across the span of EU competition law and policy. Thus, the book gives the reader an opportunity to get both a good perspective on the topic and in-depth analysis of specific cases, which makes it equally relevant for scholars and practitioners.

A final strength I would stress is that the book is encyclopaedic and comprehensive, and that its structure, based on a functional approach to the exercise of buying power, is such as to allow it to grow in the future and over several further editions that incorporate future developments in law and policy. This places it in an exceptional position to become a reference point for scholars and practitioners active in competition law. Which brings me to the curse for the author. Given that this is an area that promises to continue expanding in the future, and that this study will help fuel a more vigorous enforcement of competition law in cases involving the exercise of buying power (in particular in non-consumer-facing markets), it seems that this book is not solely the pinnacle of a brilliant doctoral project, but also the start of a never-ending academic endeavour to influence, evaluate and reconsider law and policy in this area– to which Dr Herrera Anchustegui would do well to dedicate a significant part of his career. That said, *volenti non fit iniuria*.

Dr Albert Sánchez-Graells
Reader in Economic Law
University of Bristol Law School

TABLES OF LEGISLATION

TREATIES AND INTERNATIONAL CONVENTIONS

Treaty on European Union, consolidated version [2012] OJ C 326/13

Treaty on the Functioning of the European Union, consolidated version [2012] OJ C 326/47

Paris Convention for the Protection of Industrial Property of March 20, 1883, as revised at Brussels on December 14, 1900, at Washington on June 2, 1911, at The Hague on November 6, 1925, at London on June 2, 1934, at Lisbon on October 31, 1958, and at Stockholm on July 14, 1967, and as amended on September 28, 1979

Convention on the Organisation for Economic Co-operation and Development, Paris 14th December [1960]

EU/EEA LEGISLATION

Commission Regulation (EEC) No 1984/83 of 22 June 1983 on the application of Article 85 (3) of the Treaty to categories of exclusive purchasing agreements [1983] OJ L 173/5

Council Directive 93/13/EEC of 5 April 1993 on unfair terms in consumer contracts [1993] OJ L 95/29

Council Regulation (EC) No 1/2003 of 16 December 2002 on the implementation of the rules on competition laid down in Articles [101] and [102] of the Treaty [2003] OJ L 1/1

Directive 2004/18/EC of the European Parliament and of the Council of 31 March 2004 on the co-ordination of procedures for the award of public works contracts, public supply contracts and public service contracts [2004] OJ L 134/114

Council Regulation (EC) No 139/2004 of 20 January 2004 on the control of concentrations between undertakings (the EC Merger Regulation) [2004] OJ L 24/1

Directive 2005/29/EC of the European Parliament and of the Council of 11 May 2005 concerning unfair business-to-consumer commercial practices in the internal market and amending Council Directive 84/450/EEC, Directives 97/7/EC, 98/27/EC and 2002/65/EC of the European Parliament and of the Council and Regulation (EC) No 2006/2004 of the European Parliament and of the Council ('Unfair Commercial Practices Directive') [2005] OJ L 149/22

Commission Regulation (EU) No 330/2010 of 20 April 2010 on the application of Article 101(3) of the Treaty on the Functioning of the European Union to categories of vertical agreements and concerted practices [2010] OJ L 102/1

Protocol (No 3) on the Statute of the Court of Justice of the European Union [2010] OJ C 83/210

Directive 2011/7/EU of the European Parliament and of the Council of 16 February 2011 on combating late payment in commercial transactions [2011] OJ L 48/1

Directive 2011/83/EU of the European Parliament and of the Council of 25 October 2011 on consumer rights, amending Council Directive 93/13/EEC and Directive 1999/44/EC of the European Parliament and of the Council and repealing Council Directive 85/577/EEC and Directive 97/7/EC of the European Parliament and of the Council [2011] OJ L 304/64

Regulation (EU) No 261/2012 of the European Parliament and of the Council of 14 March 2012 amending Council Regulation (EC) No 1234/2007 as regards contractual relations in the milk and milk products sector [2012] OJ L 94/38

Rules of Procedure of the Court of Justice [2012] OJ L 265/1

Commission Regulation (EU) No 316/2014 of 21 March 2014 on the application of Article 101(3) of the Treaty on the Functioning of the European Union to categories of technology transfer agreements [2014] OJ L 93/17

Directive 2014/24/EU of the European Parliament and of the Council of 26 February 2014 on public procurement and repealing Directive 2004/18/EC [2014] OJ L 94/65

Directive 2014/23/EU of the European Parliament and of the Council of 26 February 2014 on the award of concession contracts [2014] OJ L 94/1

Directive 2014/25/EU of the European Parliament and of the Council of 26 February 2014 on procurement by entities operating in the water, energy, transport and postal services sectors and repealing Directive 2004/17/EC [2014] OJ L 94/243

EU/EEA MEMBER STATES LEGISLATION

Austrian Bundesgesetz gegen Kartelle und andere Wettbewerbsbeschränkungen (Kartellgesetz 2005 – KartG 2005) (zuletzt geändert durch das Bundesgesetz BGB1. I. Nr. 2/2008), *Austria*

Bundesgesetz vom 29. Juni 1977 zur Verbesserung der Nahversorgung und der Wettbewerbsbedingungen, *Austria*

Competition and Consumer (Industry Codes—Food and Grocery) Regulation 2015, Select Legislative Instrument No. 16, 2015, *Australia*

Act No. 395/2009 of 9 September 2009 on Significant Market Power in the Sale of Agricultural and Food Products and Abuse thereof, *Czech Republic*

Estonian Competition Act (as amended up to Act RT I, 23.02.2011, 3), *Estonia*

Ordinance 45-1483 of 30 June 1945, *France*

Loi n° 74-696 du 7 août 1974 relative à la radiodiffusion et à la television, *France*

Commercial Code, Legislative Section, Book IV Article L410-1 to L470-8, *France*

Competition Act (No 948/2011), last amended in 2014, *Finland*

Act against Restraints of Competition (Competition Act – GWB), last amended by the Article 5 of the Act of 21.07.2014 (Federal Law Gazette I, p. 1066), *Germany*

Law 146/1914 of January 27, 1914, on Unfair Competition, *Greece*

Law 3959/2011 - "Protection of Free Competition", *Greece*

The Competition Act (Act LVII of 1996), lastly amended in April 2010, *Hungary*

Act CLXIV of 2005 on Trade /competition law related provisions, *Hungary*

Legge 18 giugno 1998, n. 192, "Disciplina della subfornitura nelle attività produttive", Official Journa N. 143 of June 22, 1998, *Italy*

Latvian Competition Law, lastly amended in 2009, Section 13(2), *Latvia*

Law on Competition 23 March 1999 No VIII-1099 (As last amended on 22 March 2012 No XI-1937), *Lithuania*

Law on Prohibition of Unfair Business-To-Consumer Commercial Practices 21 December 2007 No X-1409, *Lithuania*

Law on Competition 23 March 1999 No Viii-1099 (As last amended on 22 March 2012 No XI-1937), *Lithuania*

Law No 19/2012 of 8 May, repealing Laws No 18/2003 of 11 June and No 39/2006 of 25 August, and makes the second amendment to Law No 2/99 of 13 January, *Portugal*

Law of Competition 21 of April 10th 1996, last reformed in 14 of February, 2012, *Romania*

Act No. 140/2010 Coll. on Unfair Terms in Business Contracts between Reseller and Supplier of Goods that are Foodstuffs, *Slovakia*

Unfair Competition Act, Ley 3/1991, de 10 de enero, de Competencia Desleal, Official Journal N. 10 of January 11, 1991, *Spain*

The sectoral Act on Better Functioning for the Food Retailing Markets, Ley 12/2013, de 2 de agosto, de medidas para mejorar el funcionamiento de la cadena alimentaria, Official Journal N. 185 of August 3, 2012, *Spain*

Competition Act, Ley 15/2007, de 3 de julio, de Defensa de la Competencia, Official Journa N. 159 of July 4, 2007, *Spain*

Competition Act, Ley Act 52/1999, of 28 December, amending Act 16/1989, of 17 July, *Spain*

Competition Act 1998, *United Kingdom*

LEGISLATION OF THE UNITED STATES OF AMERICA

The Capper–Volstead Act (P.L. 67-146), the Co-operative Marketing Associations Act (7 U.S.C. 291, 292), enacted February 18, 1922

The Clayton Antitrust Act of 1914 (Pub.L. 63–212, 38 Stat. 730, enacted October 15, 1914, codified at 15 U.S.C. §§ 12–27, 29 U.S.C. §§ 52–53)

The Code of Laws of the United States of America

The Federal Trade Commission Act of 1914, last amended and incorporating the U.S. SAFE WEB Act amendments of 2006, codified under Title 15, Chapter 2, Section of the U.S.C.

The Packers and Stockyards Act of 1921, codified under Section 7 U.S.C. Sections 181 to 229b

The Robinson–Patman Act of 1936 (or Anti-Price Discrimination Act, Pub. L. No. 74-692, 49 Stat. 1526 (codified at 15 U.S.C. § 13)

The Sherman Antitrust Act of 1890 (Sherman Act,[1] 26 Stat. 209, 15 U.S.C. §§ 1–7)

TABLE OF CASES, OPINIONS AND DECISIONS

JUDGMENTS BY THE EUROPEAN COURT OF JUSTICE

C-26/62 - *Van Gend en Loos v Administratie der Belastingen*, EU:C:1963:1 E.C.R. [1963] 00001

C-56/64 - *Consten and Grundig v Commission of the EEC*, EU:C:1966:41 E.C.R. [1966] 00429

C-56/65 - *Société Technique Minière v Maschinenbau Ulm*, EU:C:1966:38 E.C.R. [1966] 003377

C-23/67 - *Brasserie De Haecht v Wilkin Janssen*, EU:C:1967:54 E.C.R. [1967] 00525

C-24/67 - *Parke, Davis & Co. v Probel and Others*, EU:C:1968:11 E.C.R. [1968] 00081

C-5/69 - *Voelk v Vervaecke*, EU:C:1969:35 E.C.R. [1969] 00295

C-29/69 - *Stauder v Stadt Ulm*, EU:C:1969:57 E.C.R [1969] 00419

C-41/69 - *Chemiefarma v Commission*, EU:C:1970:71 E.C.R. [1970] 00661

C-54/69 - *Francolor v Commission*, EU:C:1972:75 E.C.R. [1972] 00851

C-40/70 - *Sirena v Eda*, EU:C:1971:18 E.C.R. [1971] 00069

C-6/72 - *Europemballage Corporation and Continental Can Company v Commission*, EU:C:1973:22

C-8/72 - *Vereeniging van Cementhandelaren v Commission*, EU:C:1972:84 E.C.R. [1972] 00977

Joined cases C-6/73 and C-7/73 *Istituto Chemioterapico Italiano and Commercial Solvents v Commission*, EU:C:1974:18 E.C.R. [1974] 00223

C-40/73 - *Suiker Unie and Others v Commission*, EU:C:1975:174 E.C.R. [1975] 01663

C-26/75 - *General Motors v Commission*, EU:C:1975:150

C-26/76 - *Metro v Commission*, EU:C:1977:167 [1977] 01875

C-27/76 - *United Brands v Commission*, EU:C:1978:22 E.C.R. [1978] 00207

C-85/76 - *Hoffmann-La Roche v Commission*, EU:C:1979:36 E.C.R. [1979] 00461

C-22/78 - *Hugin v Commission*, EU:C:1979:138 E.C.R. [1979] 01869

C-32/78 - *BMW Belgium v Commission*, EU:C:1979:191 E.C.R. [1979] 02435

C-61/80 - *Coöperatieve Stremsel- en Kleurselfabriek v Commission*, EU:C:1981:75 E.C.R. [1981] 00851

Joined cases C-100-103/80 *Musique Diffusion Française and Others v Commission*, EU:C:1983:158 E.C.R [1983] 01825

C-322/81 - *Michelin v Commission*, EU:C:1983:313 E.C.R. [1983] 03461

C-123/83 - *BNIC v Clair*, EU:C:1985:33 E.C.R. [1985] 00391

C-243/83 - *Binon v AMP*, EU:C:1985:284 E.C.R. [1985] 02015

C-298/83 - *CICCE v Commission*, EU:C:1985:150 E.C.R. [1985] 01105

C-42/84 - *Remia v Commission*, EU:C:1985:327 E.C.R. [1985] 02545

C-62/86 - *AKZO v Commission*, EU:C:1991:286 E.C.R. [1991] I-03359

C-66/86 - *Ahmed Saeed Flugreisen and Others v Zentrale zur Bekämpfung unlauteren Wettbewerbs*, EU:C:1989:140 E.C.R. [1989] 00803

C-246/86 - *Belasco and Others v Commission*, EU:C:1989:301 E.C.R. [1989] 02117

C-30/87 - *Bodson v Pompes funèbres des régions libérées*, EU:C:1988:225 E.C.R. [1988] 2479

C-55/87 - *Moksel v BALM*, EU:C:1988:377 E.C.R [1988] 03845

C-395/87 - *Tournier*, EU:C:1989:319 E.C.R [1989] 02521

C-215/88 - *Casa Fleischhandel v BALM*, EU:C:1989:331 E.C.R [1989] 02789

C-234/89 - *Delimitis v Henninger Bräu*, EU:C:1991:91 [1991] I-00935

C-41/90 - *Höfner and Elser*, EU:C:1991:161 [1991] I-01979

C-126/91 - *Schutzverband gegen Unwesen i.d. Wirtschaft v Rocher*, EU:C:1993:191 E.C.R. [1993] I-02361

Joined cases C-159/91 and C-160/91 *Poucet and Pistre v AGF and Cancava*, EU:C:1993:63 E.C.R. [1993] I-00637

C-250/92 - *Gøttrup-Klim and Others Grovvareforeninger v Dansk Landbrugs Grovvareselskab*, EU:C:1994:413 E.C.R. [1994] I-05641

C-319/93 - *Dijkstra and Others v Friesland (Frico Domo) Coöperatie and Others*, EU:C:1995:433 E.C.R. [1995] I-04471

C-399/93 - *Oude Luttikhuis and Others v Verenigde Coöperatieve Melkindustrie Coberco*, EU:C:1995:434 E.C.R. [1995] I-04515

Joined cases C-68/94 and C-30/95 - *France and Société commerciale des potasses and de l'azote and Entreprise minière and chimique v Commission*, EU:C:1998:148 E.C.R. [1998] I-01375

C-244/94 - *FFSA and Others v Ministère de l'Agriculture and de la Pêche*, EU:C:1995:392 E.C.R. [1995] I-04013

C-333/94 P - *Tetra Pak v Commission*, EU:C:1996:436 E.C.R. [1996] I-05951

C-185/95 P - *Baustahlgewebe v Commission*, EU:C:1998:608 E.C.R. [1998] I-08417

C-35/96 - *Commission v Italy*, EU:C:1998:303 [1998] I-03851

C-67/96 - *Albany*, EU:C:1999:430 E.C.R. [1999] I-05751

C-395/96 P - *Compagnie Maritime Belge Transports and Others v Commission*, EU:C:2000:132 E.C.R. [2000] I-01365

C-266/97 P - *VBA v VGB and Others*, EU:C:2000:171 E.C.R. [2000] I-02135

C-163/99 - *Portugal v Commission*, EU:C:2001:189 E.C.R. [2001] I-02613

Joined cases C-238/99 P, C-244/99 P, C-245/99 P, C-247/99 P, C-250/99 P to C-252/99 P and C-254/99 P *Limburgse Vinyl Maatschappij and Others v Commission*, EU:C:2002:582 E.C.R. [2002] I-08375

C-309/99 - *Wouters and Others*, EU:C:2001:390 E.C.R. [2002] I-01577

C-497/99 P - *Irish Sugar v Commission*, EU:C:2001:393 E.C.R. [2001] I-05333

C Joined cases C-204/00 P, C-205/00 P, C-211/00 P, C-213/00 P, C-217/00 P and C-219/00 P - *Aalborg Portland and Others v Commission*, EU:C:2004:6 [2004] I-00123

C-218/00 - *Cisal*, EU:C:2002:36 E.C.R [2002] I-00691

C-2/01 P - *BAI and Commission v Bayer*, EU:C:2004:2 E.C.R. [2004] I-00023

C-82/01 P - *Aéroports de Paris v Commission*, EU:C:2002:617 E.C.R. [2002] I-09297

Joined cases C-264/01, C-306/01, C-354/01 and C-355/01 *AOK-Bundesverband and Others*, EU:C:2004:150 [2004] I-02493

C-418/01 - *IMS Health*, EU:C:2004:257 E.C.R. [2004] I-05039

C-189/02 P - *Dansk Rørindustri and Others v Commission*, EU:C:2005:408 E.C.R [2005] I-05425

C-205/03 P - *FENIN v Commission*, EU:C:2006:453 E.C.R [2006] I-06295

C-95/04 P - *British Airways v Commission*, EU:C:2007:166 E.C.R. [2007] I-02331

C-279/06 - *CEPSA*, EU:C:2008:485 E.C.R. [2008] I-06681

C-413/06 P - *Bertelsmann and Sony Corporation of America v Impala*, EU:C:2008:392 E.C.R. [2008] I-04951

C-468/06 to C-478/06, *Sot. Lélos kai Sia v GlaxoSmithKline*, EU:C:2008:504 E.C.R. [2008] I-07139

C-501/06 P - *GlaxoSmithKline Services and Others v Commission and Others*, EU:C:2009:610 E.C.R. [2009] I-09291

C-52/07 - *Kanal 5 and TV 4*, EU:C:2008:703 E.C.R [2008] I-09275

Joined cases C-101/07 P and C-110/07 P *Coop de France bétail and viande v Commission*, EU:C:2008:741 E.C.R. [2008] I-10193

C-113/07 P - *Selex Sistemi Integrati v Commission*, EU:C:2009:191 E.C.R. [2009] I-02207

C-202/07 P - *France Télécom v Commission*, EU:C:2009:214 E.C.R. [2009] I-02369

C-209/07 - *Beef Industry Development and Barry Brothers*, EU:C:2008:643 E.C.R. [2008] I-08637

C-260/07 - *Pedro IV Servicios*, EU:C:2009:215 E.C.R. [2009] I-02437

C-350/07 - *Kattner Stahlbau*, EU:C:2009:127 E.C.R [2009] I-01513

C-441/07 P - *Commission v Alrosa*, EU:C:2010:377 E.C.R. [2010] I-05949

C-8/08 - *T-Mobile Netherlands and Others*, EU:C:2009:343 E.C.R. [2009] I-04529

C-280/08 P - *Deutsche Telekom v Commission*, EU:C:2010:603 E.C.R. [2010] I-09555

C-52/09 - *TeliaSonera Sverige*, EU:C:2011:83 E.C.R. [2011] I-00527

C-90/09 P - *General Química and Others v Commission*, EU:C:2011:21 E.C.R. [2011] I-00001

C-109/10 P - *Solvay v Commission*, EU:C:2011:686 E.C.R. [2011] I-10329

C-209/10 P - *Post Danmark*, EU:C:2012:172 [2012], published in the electronic Reports of Cases

C-389/10 P - *KME Germany and Others v Commission*, EU:C:2011:816 E.C.R. [2011] I-13125

C-457/10 P - *AstraZeneca v Commission*, EU:C:2012:770 [2012], published in the electronic Reports of Cases

C-549/10 P - *Tomra and Others v Commission*, EU:C:2012:221 [2012], published in the electronic Reports of Cases

C-138/11 - *Compass-Datenbank*, EU:C:2012:449 [2012], published in the electronic Reports of Cases

C-226/11 - *Expedia*, EU:C:2012:795 [2012] published in the electronic Reports

C-646/11 P - *3F v Commission*, EU:C:2013:36 [2013], published in the electronic Reports of Cases

C-295/12 P - *Telefónica and Telefónica de España v Commission*, EU:C:2014:2062 [2014] not yet published in the Courts Reports

C-67/13 P - *CB v Commission*, EU:C:2014:2204, [2014], not yet published in the Courts Reports

C-293/13 P - *Fresh Del Monte Produce v Commission and Commission / Fresh Del Monte Produce*, ECLI:EU:C:2015:416 [2015], Not yet published in the Courts reports

C-23/14 - *Post Danmark*, EU:C:2015:651 [2015], not yet published in the Courts Reports

C-185/14 - *EasyPay and Finance Engineering*, EU:C:2015:716 [2015], not yet published in the Courts Reports

C-373/14 P - *Toshiba Corporation v Commission*, EU:C:2016:26 [2016], not yet published in the Courts Report

C-357/14 P - *Electrabel and Dunamenti Erőmű v Commission*, EU:C:2015:642 [2015], not yet published in the Courts Report, para. 29-31

C-101/15 *Pilkington Group and Others v Commission*, EU:C:2016:631 [2016], not yet published in the Courts Report

OPINIONS OF ADVOCATES GENERAL

Opinion of Advocate General Slynn in C-123/83 - *BNIC v Clair*, EU:C:1984:300 [1985] 00391

Opinion of Advocate General Lenz in C-298/83 - *CICCE v Commission*, EU:C:1985:16 [1985]

Opinion of Advocate General Van Gerven in C-234/89 - *Delimitis v Henninger Bräu*, EU:C:1990:358 [1991] I-00935

Opinion of Advocate General Tesauro in C-250/92 - *Gøttrup-Klim and Others Grovvareforeninger v Dansk Landbrugs Grovvareselskab*, EU:C:1994:249 [1994]

Opinion of Advocate General Jacobs in C-67/96 – *Albany*, EU:C:1999:28 E.C.R. [1999] I-05751

Opinion of Advocate General Léger in C-309/99 - *Wouters and Others*, EU:C:2001:390 E.C.R. [2002] I-01577

Opinion of Advocate General Jacobs in Joined cases C-264/01, C-306/01, C-354/01 and C-355/01 *AOK-Bundesverband and Others*, EU:C:2003:304 [2003]

Opinion of Advocate General Sitx-Hackl in C-247/02 – *Sintesi*, EU:C:2004:399 E.C.R. [2004] I-09215

Opinion of Advocate General Jacobs in C-53/03 - *Syfait and Others (GlaxoSmithKline)*, EU:C:2004:673 E.C.R. [2005] I-04609

Opinion of Advocate General Poiares Maduro in C-205/03 P - *FENIN v Commission*, EU:C:2005:666 E.C.R.

Opinion of Advocate General Kokott in C-95/04 P - *British Airways v Commission*, EU:C:2006:133 E.C.R. [2007] I-02331

Opinion of Advocate General Trstenjak in C-209/07 - *Beef Industry Development and Barry Brothers*, EU:C:2008:467 E.C.R. [2008] I-08637

Opinion of Advocate General Kokott in C-441/07 P - *Commission v Alrosa*, ECLI:EU:C:2009:555

Opinion of Advocate General Kokott in C-8/08 - *T-Mobile Netherlands and Others*, EU:C:2009:110 E.C.R. [2009] I-04529

Opinion of Advocate General Kokott in C-109/10 P - *Solvay v Commission*, EU:C:2011:256 E.C.R. [2011] I-10329

Opinion of Advocate General Mengozzi in C-209/10 - *Post Danmark*, EU:C:2011:342 [2011], published in the electronic Reports of Cases

Opinion of Advocate General Wahl in C-67/13 P - *CB v Commission*, EU:C:2014:1958 [2014], not yet published on the Courts Reports

Opinion of Advocate General Kokott in C-23/14 - *Post Danmark*, EU:C:2015:343 [2015], not yet published

Opinion of Advocate General Wahl in C-413/14 P – *Intel Corporation Inc. v European Commission*, EU:C:2016:788 [2016], not yet published

JUDGMENTS BY THE GENERAL COURT

T-30/89 - *Hilti v Commission*, EU:T:1991:70 E.C.R. [1991] II-01439

T-51/89 - *Tetra Pak v Commission*, EU:T:1990:41 E.C.R. [1990] II-00309

Joined cases T-68/89, T-77/89 and T-78/89 *SIV and Others v Commission*, EU:T:1992:38 E.C.R. [1992] II-01403

T-145/89 - *Baustahlgewebe v Commission*, EU:T:1995:66 E.C.R. [1995] II-00987

T-83/91 - *Tetra Pak v Commission*, EU:T:1994:246 E.C.R. [1994] II-00755

T-17/93 - *Matra Hachette v Commission*, EU:T:1994:89 E.C.R. [1994] II-00595

Joined cases T-528/93, T-542/93, T-543/93 and T-546/93 *Métropole Télévision v Commission*, EU:T:1996:99 E.C.R. [1996]

T-77/94 – *VGB and Others v Commission*, EU:T:1997:70 E.C.R. [1997] II-00759

T-229/94 - *Deutsche Bahn v Commission*, EU:T:1997:155 E.C.R. [1997] II-01689

T-374/94 - *European Night Services and Others v Commission*, EU:T:1998:198 E.C.R. [1998] II-03141

T-86/95 - *Compagnie générale maritime and Others v Commission*, EU:T:2002:50 E.C.R [2002] II-01011

T-41/96 - *Bayer v Commission*, EU:T:2000:242 E.C.R. [2000] II-03383

T-22/97 - *Kesko v Commission*, EU:T:1999:327 E.C.R. [1999] II-03775

T-228/97 - *Irish Sugar v Commission*, EU:T:1999:246 E.C.R. [1999] II-02969

T-62/98 - *Volkswagen v Commission*, EU:T:2000:180 E.C.R. [2000] II-02707

T-65/98 - *Van den Bergh Foods v Commission*, EU:T:2003:281 E.C.R. [2003] II-04653

T-128/98 - *Aéroports de Paris v Commission*, EU:T:2000:290 E.C.R. [2000 II-03929]

Joined cases T-191/98, T-212/98 to T-214/98 *Atlantic Container Line and Others v Commission*, EU:T:2003:245 E.C.R. [2003] II-03275

T-202/98 - *Tate & Lyle and Others v Commission*, EU:T:2001:185 E.C.R. [2001] II-02035

T-17/99 - *KE KELIT v Commission*, EU:T:2002:73 E.C.R. [2002] II-01647

T-112/99 - *M6 and Others v Commission*, EU:T:2001:215 E.C.R. [2001] II-02459

T-131/99 - *Shaw and Falla v Commission*, EU:T:2002:83 E.C.R. [2002] II-02023

T-175/99 - *UPS Europe v Commission*, EU:T:2002:78 E.C.R [2002] II-01915

T-219/99 - *British Airways v Commission*, EU:T:2003:343 E.C.R. [2003] II-05917

T-231/99 - *Joynson v Commission*, EU:T:2002:84 E.C.R [2002] II-02085

T-319/99 - *Fenin v Commission*, EU:T:2003:50 E.C.R. [2003] II-00357

T-342/99 - *Airtours v Commission*, EU:T:2002:146 E.C.R. [2002] II-02585

T-44/00 - *Mannesmannröhren-Werke v Commission*, EU:T:2004:218 E.C.R. [2004] II-02223

T-213/00 - *CMA CGM and Others v Commission*, EU:T:2003:76 E.C.R. [2003] II-00913

T-342/00 - *Petrolessence and SG2R v Commission*, EU:T:2003:97 E.C.R. [2003] II-01161

T-57/01 - *Solvay v Commission*, EU:T:2009:519 E.C.R. [2009] II-04621

T-66/01 - *Imperial Chemical Industries v Commission*, EU:T:2010:255 E.C.R. [2010] II-02631

T-168/01 - *GlaxoSmithKline Services v Commission*, EU:T:2006:265 E.C.R [2006] II-02969

T-203/01 - *Michelin v Commission*, EU:T:2003:250 E.C.R. [2003] II-04071

T-210/01 - *General Electric v Commission*, EU:T:2005:456 E.C.R. [2005] II-05575

T-325/01 - *DaimlerChrysler v Commission*, EU:T:2005:322 E.C.R. [2005] II-03319

T-5/02 - *Tetra Laval v Commission*, EU:T:2002:264 E.C.R. [2002] II-04381

T-114/02 - *BaByliss v Commission*, EU:T:2003:100 E.C.R. [2003] II-01279

T-282/02 - *Cementbouw Handel & Industrie v Commission*, EU:T:2006:64 E.C.R. [2006] II-00319

Joined cases T-217/03 and T-245/03 *FNCBV and Others v Commission*, EU:T:2006:391 E.C.R. [2006] II-04987

T-271/03 - *Deutsche Telekom v Commission*, EU:T:2008:101 E.C.R. [2008] II-00477

T-340/03 - *France Télécom v Commission*, EU:T:2007:22 E.C.R. [2007] II-00107

T-419/03 - *Altstoff Recycling Austria v Commission*, EU:T:2011:102 E.C.R. [2011] II-00975

T-155/04 - *SELEX Sistemi Integrati v Commission*, EU:T:2006:387 E.C.R. [2006] II-04797

T-177/04 - *easyJet v Commission*, EU:T:2006:187 E.C.R. [2006] II-01931

T-201/04 - *Microsoft v Commission*, EU:T:2007:289 E.C.R. [2007] II-03601

T-301/04 - *Clearstream v Commission*, EU:T:2009:317 E.C.R. [2009] II-03155

T-464/04 - *Impala v Commission*, EU:T:2006:216 E.C.R. [2006] II-02289

T-321/05 - *AstraZeneca v Commission*, EU:T:2010:266 E.C.R. [2010] II-02805

T-446/05 - *Amann & Söhne and Cousin Filterie v Commission*, EU:T:2010:165 E.C.R. [2010] II-01255

T-155/06 - *Tomra Systems and Others v Commission*, EU:T:2010:370 E.C.R. [2010] II-04361

T-170/06 - *Alrosa v Commission*, EU:T:2007:220 E.C.R. [2007] II-02601

T-282/06 - *Sun Chemical Group and Others v Commission*, EU:T:2007:203 E.C.R. [2007] II-02149

T-357/06 - *Koninklijke Wegenbouw Stevin v Commission*, EU:T:2012:488, published in the electronic Reports of Cases

T-362/06 - *Ballast Nedam Infra v Commission*, EU:T:2012:492, published in the electronic Reports of Cases

T-336/07 - *Telefónica and Telefónica de España v Commission*, EU:T:2012:172 [2012], published in the electronic Reports of Cases

T-342/07 - *Ryanair v Commission*, EU:T:2010:280 E.C.R. [2010] II-03457

T-461/07 - *Visa Europe and Visa International Service v Commission*, EU:T:2011:181 E.C.R. [2011] II-01729

T-491/07 - *CB v Commission*, EU:T:2012:633, published in the electronic Reports of Cases

T-427/08 - *CEAHR v Commission*, EU:T:2010:517 E.C.R. [2010] II-05865

T-587/08 - *Fresh Del Monte Produce v Commission*, EU:T:2013:129 [2013] not yet reported in the Court Reports

T-72/09 - *Pilkington Group and Others v Commission*, EU:T:2014:1094 [2014], not yet published

T-286/09 - *Intel v Commission*, EU:T:2014:547 [2014], not yet published in the electronic Reports of Cases

T-519/09 - Toshiba v Commission, EU:T:2014:263 [2014], published in the electronic Reports of Cases

T-533/10 - *DTS Distribuidora de Televisión Digital v Commission*, EU:T:2014:629 [2014] not yet published in the electronic Reports of Cases

T-175/12 - *Deutsche Börse v Commission*, EU:T:2015:148 [2015], not yet published in the electronic Reports of Cases

EFTA COURT JUDGMENTS

E-15/10 - *Posten Norge AS v EFTA Surveillance Authority* [2012]

E-29/15 *Sorpa bs. v The Icelandic Competition Authority (Samkeppniseftirlitið)* [2016]

EU/EEA NATIONAL CASE LAW

Düsseldorf Appellate Court in Decision of 18 November 2015 *EDEKA/Plus-Übernahme* revoking a Decision B2-58/09 *Edeka Konditionenforderungen* - Verstoß gegen das "Anzapfverbot", 3 July 2014 by the Bundeskartellamt. *Germany*

German Federal Court, *Rossignol* [1975], BGH NJW 1976, 801, *Germany*

Vj-46/2001/13, Magyar Posta Rt. And Matáv Rt., of August 13, 2001, *Hungary*

JUDGMENTS BY THE SUPREME COURT OF THE UNITED STATES OF AMERICA

Swift & Co. v United States, 196 U.S. 375 (1905)

United States v Crescent Amusement Co., 323 U.S. 173 (1944)

American Tobacco Co. v United States, 328 U.S. 781 (1946)

Federal Trade Commission v Morton Salt Co., 334 U.S. 37 (1948)

United States v Griffith, 334 U.S. 100 (1948)

Mandeville Island Farms, Inc. v American Crystal Sugar Co., 334 U.S. 219 (1948)

Federal Trade Commission v Motion Picture Advertising Svc. Co., Inc., 344 U.S. 392 (1953)

Times-Picayune Publishing Co. v United States, 345 U.S. 594 (1953)

United States v E.I. du pont de Nemours & Co., 351 U.S. 377 (1956)

Silver v New York Stock Exchange 373 U.S. 341 (1963)

United States v Von's Grocery Co., 384 U.S. 270 (1966)

Federal Trade Commission v Procter & Gamble Co., 386 U.S. 568 (1967)

United States v Topco Associates, Inc., 405 U.S. 596 (1972)

Cantor v Detroit Edison Co., 428 U.S. 579 (1976)

Great Atlantic & Pacific Tea Co. v Federal Trade Commission, 440 U.S. 69 (1979)

Jefferson Cty. Pharm. Ass'n v Abbott Labs., 460 U.S. 150 (1983)

Northwest Wholesale Stationers, Inc. v Pacific Stationery Printing Co., 472 U.S. 284 (1985)

Cargill, Inc. v Monfort of Colorado, Inc., 479 U.S. 104 (1986)

United States v Trans-Missouri Freight Ass, 166 U.S. 290 (1987)

Bus. Electr. Corp. v Sharp Electr. Corp. 485 U.S. 717 (1988)

Atlantic Richfield Co. v USA Petroleum Co., 495 U.S. 238 340. (1990)

Eastman Kodak Company v Image Technical Services, Inc., et al. 504 U.S. 451 (1992)

Brooke Group Ltd. v Brown & Williamson Tobacco Corp., 509 U.S. 209 (1993)

Spectrum Sports, Inc. v McQuillan, 506 U.S. 447 (1993)

Cooper Indus. v Leatherman Tool Grp., 532 U.S. 424, 439–40 (2001)

Verizon Communications Inc., v Law Offices of Curtis v Trinko, LLP, 540 U.S. 398 (2004)

Weyerhaeuser Company, v Ross-Simmons Hardwood Lumber Company, Inc., in 127 S. Ct. 1069 (2007)

JUDGMENTS BY THE COURTS OF APPEAL OF THE UNITED STATES OF AMERICA

United States v Aluminim co. of America, 148 F.2d 416 (2nd Cir. 1945)

United States v Alcoa, 148 F.2d 416 (2nd Cir. 1945)

National Macaroni Manufacturers Association v Federal Trade Commission, 345 F2.d 421 (7th Cir. 1965)

Berkey Photo, Inc v Eastman Kodak Co., 603 F.2d 263, (2nd Cir. 1979)

Reid Bros. Logging Co. v Ketchikan Pulp Co., 699 F.2d 1292 (9th Cir. 1983)

Kartell v Blue Shield of Massachusetts, 749 F.2d 922 (1st Cir. 1984)

Vogel v American Society of Appraisers, 744 F.2d 598, (7th Cir. 1984)

Balmoral Cinema Inc., v Allied Artist Pictures Corp., 855 F.2d 313 (6th Cir. 1989)

Beef Indus. Antitrust Litig., 907 F.2d 510 (5th Cir. 1990)

United States v Brown University, 5 F. 3d 658 (3rd Cir.1993)

United States v Romer, 148 F.3d 359 (4th Cir. 1998)

Brookins v Int'l Motors Contest Ass'n, 219 F.3d 849, (8th Cir. 2000)

TOYS "R" US, INC. v Federal Trade Commission, 221 F.3d 928 (7th Cir. 2000)

Knevelbaard Dairies v Kraft Foods, Inc., 232 F.3d 979 (9th Cir. 2000)

Virgin Atlantic Airways Limited v British Airways Plc, 99-9402 (2nd Cir., 2001)

Confederated Tribes of Siletz Indians of Ore. v Weyerhaeuser Co., 411 F. 3d 1030, 10 (9th Cir. 2005)

West Penn Allegheny Health Sys., Inc. v UPMC, No. 09-4468 (3rd Cir. 2010)

JUDGMENTS BY THE DISTRICT COURTS OF THE UNITED STATES OF AMERICA

Virgin Atlantic Airways v British Airways Plc, 69 F.Supp. 2nd 571 (1999)

State v Kraft General Foods, Inc., 926 F. Supp. 321 (S.D.N.Y. 1995)

EUROPEAN COMMISSION DECISIONS

Commission Decision of 26 July 1976 relating to a proceeding under Article 85 of the EEC Treaty (IV/28.980 - *Pabst & Richarz/BNIA*) [1976] OJ L 231/24

Commission Decision of 9 July 1980 relating to a proceeding under Article 85 of the EEC Treaty (IV/27.958 *National Sulphuric Acid Association*) [1980] OJ L 260/24

Commission Decision of 17 December 1980 relating to a proceeding under Article 85 of the EEC Treaty (IV/29.869 - *Italian cast glass*) [1980] OJ L 383/19

Commission Decision of 15 December 1982 relating to a proceeding under Article 85 of the EEC Treaty (IV/29.883 - *AROW/BNIC*) [1982] OJ L 379/1

Commission Decision of 6 August 1984 relating to a proceeding under Article 85 of the EEC Treaty (IV/30.350 - *Zinc Producer Group*) [1984] OJ L 220/27

Commission Decision of 19 December 1984 relating to a proceeding under Article 85 of the EEC Treaty (IV/26.870 - *Aluminium imports from eastern Europe*) [1985] OJ L 92/1

Commission Decision of 18 July 1988 relating to a proceeding under Article 86 of the EEC Treaty (Case No IV/30.178 *Napier Brown - British Sugar*) [1988] OJ L 284/41

Commission Decision of 15 September 1989 relating to a proceeding under Article 85 of the EEC Treaty (IV/31.734 - *Film purchases by German television stations*) [1989] OJ L 284/36

Commission Decision of 19 December 1990 relating to a proceeding under Article 85 of the EEC Treaty (IV/33.133-A: *Soda-ash - Solvay, ICI*) [1991] OJ L 152/1

Commission Decision of 22 July 1992 relating to a proceeding under Council Regulation (EEC) No 4064/89 (Case No IV/M.190 - *Nestlé/Perrier*) [1992] OJ L 356/1

Commission Decision of 21 December 1993 relating to a proceeding pursuant to Article 86 of the EC Treaty (IV/34.689 - *Sea Containers v Stena Sealink - Interim measures*) [1994] OJ L 15/8

Commission Decision of 13 July 1994 relating to a proceeding under Article 85 of the EC Treaty (IV/C/33.833 - *Cartonboard*) [1994] OJ L 243/1

Commission Decision of 21 June 1994 declaring a concentration to be compatible with the common market and the functioning of the EEA Agreement (IV/M.430 - *Procter & Gamble/VP Schickedanz (II)*) [1994] OJ L 354/32

Commission Decision of 21 December 1993 relating to a proceeding pursuant to Article 86 of the EC Treaty (IV/34.689 - *Sea Containers v Stena Sealink - Interim measures*), [1994] OJ L 15/8

Commission Decision of 20 November 1996 declaring a concentration to be incompatible with the common market (Case No IV/M.784 - *Kesko/Tuko*) Council Regulation (EEC) No 4064/89 [1997] OJ L 110/53

Commission Decision of 30 July 1997 declaring a concentration compatible with the common market and the functioning of the EEA Agreement (Case No IV/M.877 - *Boeing/McDonnell Douglas*) [1997] OJ L 336/16

Commission Decision of 14 May 1997 relating to a proceeding pursuant to Article 86 of the EC Treaty (IV/34.621, 35.059/F-3 - *Irish Sugar plc*) [1997] OJ L 258/1

Commission Decision of 11 September 1997 declaring a concentration to be compatible with the common market and the functioning of the EEA Agreement (Case No IV/M.833 - *The Coca-Cola Company/Carlsberg A/S*) [1998] OJ L 145/41

Commission Decision of 30/07/1998 declaring a concentration to be compatible with the common market (Case No IV/M.1245 - *Valeo/ITT Industries*) [1998] OJ C 288/5

Commission Decision of 25 November 1998 declaring a concentration to be compatible with the common market and the functioning of the EEA Agreement (Case No IV/M.1225 - *Enso/Stora*) [1999] OJ L 254/9

Case IV.F.1/36.834- *FENIN*, document number SG(99) D/7040 [1999]

Commission Decision of 16 June 1999 relating to a proceeding pursuant to Article 81 of the EC Treaty (Case IV/35.992/F3 - *Scottish and Newcastle*) [1999] OJ L 186/28

Commission Decision of 16 June 1999 relating to a proceeding pursuant to Article 81 of the EC Treaty (Case IV/36.081/F3 — *Bass*) [1999] OJ L 186/1

Commission Decision of 3 February 1999 relating to proceedings under Council Regulation (EEC) No 4064/89 (Case No IV/M.1221 - *Rewe/Meinl*) [1999] OJ L 274/1

Commission Decision of 14 July 1999 relating to a proceeding under Article 82 of the EC Treaty (IV/D-2/34.780 - *Virgin/British Airways*) [2000] OJ L 30/1

Non-opposition to a notified concentration (Case COMP/M.1684 — *Carrefour/Promodès*) [2000] OJ C 164/5

Commission Decision of 31 January 2001 declaring a concentration to be incompatible with the common market and the functioning of the EEA Agreement (Case COMP/M.2097 *SCA/Metsä Tissue*) [2001] OJ L 57/1

Commission Decision of 11 October 2000 declaring a concentration to be compatible with the common market and the EEA Agreement (Case No COMP/M.1845 — *AOL/Time Warner*) [2001] OJ L 268/28

Commission Decision of 3 April 2001 declaring a concentration to be compatible with the common market and the functioning of the EEA Agreement (Case COMP/M.2139 — *Bombardier/ADtranz*) [2002] OJ L 69/50

Commission Decision of 13 December 2000 relating to a proceeding under Article 82 of the EC Treaty (COMP/33.133-D: *Soda-ash — ICI*) [2003] OJ L 10/33

Commission decision of 3 July 2001 declaring a concentration to be compatible with the common market and the functioning of the EEA Agreement (Case COMP/ JV.55 — *Hutchison/RCPM/ECT*) 1723) [2003] OJ L 223 1/31

Commission Decision of 2 April 2003 relating to a proceeding pursuant to Article 81 of the EC Treaty (Case COMP/C.38.279/F3 — *French beef*) [2003] OJ L 209/12

Commission Decision of 28 June 2000 declaring a concentration incompatible with the common market and the EEA Agreement (Case COMP/M.1741 — *MCI WorldCom/Sprint*) [2003] OJ L 300/1

Commission Decision of 23 July 2004 in case no. COMP/A.36.568/D3 – *Scandlines Sverige AB v Port of Helsingborg* [2004]

Commission Decision of 19 July 2004 declaring a concentration to be compatible with the common market and the functioning of the EEA Agreement (Case No COMP/M. 3333 - *Sony/BMG*) [2004] OJ L 62/30

Commission Decision of 3 July 2001 declaring a concentration to be incompatible with the common market and the EEA Agreement Case COMP/M.2220 — *General Electric/Honeywell* [2004] OJ L 48/1

Commission Decision of 17 October 2001 declaring a concentration to be incompatible with the common market and the functioning of the EEA Agreement (Case COMP/M.2187 — CVC/Lenzing) [2004] OJ L 82/20

Commission Decision of 2 September 2003 declaring a concentration to be compatible with the common market and the functioning of the EEA Agreement (Case COMP/M.3083 — GE/ Instrumentarium) [2004] OJ L 109/1

Commission Decision of 23 July 2004 in case no. COMP/A.36.570/D3 – *Sundbusserne v Port of Helsingborg* [2004]

Commission Decision of 21/12/2005 declaring a concentration to be compatible with the common market (Case No COMP/M.3968 - *Sovion/Südfleisch*) according to Council Regulation (EC) No 139/2004 [2005]

Non-opposition to a notified concentration (Case COMP/M.3732 — *Procter & Gamble/Gillette*) [2005] OJ C 239/6

Commission Decision of 20 October 2005 relating to a proceeding under Article 81(1) of the EC Treaty (Case COMP/C.38.281/B.2 — *Raw Tobacco Italy*) [2006] OJ L 353/45

Commission Decision of Non-opposition to a notified concentration M.4057 — *Korsnäs/Assidomän Cartonboard* [2006] OJ C 209/12

Commission Decision of 22 February 2006 relating to a proceeding pursuant to Article 82 of the EC Treaty and Article 54 of the EEA Agreement (Case COMP/B-2/38.381 — *De Beers*) [2006] OJ L 205/24

Non-opposition to a notified concentration (Case COMP/M.4300 — *Philips/Intermagnetics*) [2007] OJ C 123/1

Commission Decision declaring a concentration compatible with the common market and the functioning of the EEA Agreement (COMP/M.3333 — *Sony/BMG*), [2007], unabridged version

Commission Decision of 20 October 2004 relating to a proceeding under Article 81(1) of the EC Treaty (Case COMP/C.38.238/B.2) — *Raw tobacco — Spain* [2007] OJ L 102/14

Summary of Commission Decision of 29 March 2006 relating to a proceeding under Article 82 of the Treaty establishing the European Community and Article 54 of the EEA Agreement against Tomra Systems ASA, Tomra Europe AS, Tomra Systems BV, Tomra Systems GmbH, Tomra Butikksystemer AS, Tomra Systems AB and Tomra Leergutsysteme GmbH (Case COMP/E-1/38.113 — *Prokent/Tomra*) [2008] OJ C 219/11

Summary of Commission Decision of 10 May 2007 declaring a concentration compatible with the common market and the functioning of the EEA Agreement (Case COMP/M.4381 — *JCI/FIAMM*) [2009] OJ C 241/12

Summary of Commission Decision of 15 October 2008 relating to a proceeding under Article 81 of the EC Treaty (Case COMP/39.188 — *Bananas*) [2009] OJ C 189/12

Summary of Commission Decision of 1 October 2008 relating to a proceeding under Article 81 of the Treaty establishing the European Community and Article 53 of the EEA Agreement (Case COMP/C.39181 — *Candle Waxes*) [2009] OJ C 295/17

Summary of Commission Decision of 12 November 2008 relating to a proceeding under Article 81 of the Treaty establishing the European Community and Article 53 of the EEA Agreement (Case COMP/39.125 — *Car glass*) [2009] OJ C 173/13

Summary of Commission Decision of 17 December 2008 declaring a concentration compatible with the common market and the functioning of the EEA Agreement (Case COMP/M.5046 — *Friesland Foods/Campina*) [2009] OJ C 75/21

Summary of Commission Decision of 13 May 2009 relating to a proceeding under Article 82 of the EC Treaty and Article 54 of the EEA Agreement (Case COMP/C-3/37.990 — *Intel*) [2009] OJ C 227/13.

Summary of Commission Decision of 17 November 2010 declaring a concentration compatible with the internal market and the functioning of the EEA Agreement (Case COMP/M.5658 — *Unilever/Sara Lee Body Care*) [2012] OJ C 23/30

Summary of Commission Decision of 29 May 2013 declaring a concentration compatible with the internal market and the functioning of the EEA Agreement (Case COMP/M.6690 — *Syniverse/Mach*) [2014] OJ C 60/7

Summary of Commission Decision of 15 October 2014 relating to a proceeding under Article 102 of the Treaty on the Functioning of the European Union and Article 54 of the EEA Agreement (Case AT.39523 — *Slovak Telekom*) [2015] OJ C 314/7, unabridged version

EU/EEA DECISIONS BY NATIONAL COMPETITION AUTHORITIES

Decision No. 650/2008, Commission for the Protection of Competition, *Bulgaria*

Decision No 05-D-44 of 21 July 2005 *relative à des pratiques mises en œuvre par le groupe La Provence (anciennement dénommé Le Provençal) dans le secteur de la publicité dans la presse quotidienne régionale à Marseille,* Autorité de la Concurrence, *France*

Decision B2-58/09 *Edeka Konditionenforderungen* - Verstoß gegen das "Anzapfverbot", 3 July 2014 by the Bundeskartellamt, *Germany*

Decision 373/V/2007, Hellenic Competition Commission, *Greece*

Decision No. 2269/326 [2013], Authority for Consumers & Markets, *The Netherlands*

COM/15/02, The Reduction in Travel Agents' Commissions by Aer Lingus plc [2002], Competition and Consumer Protection Commission, *Ireland*

CA98/19/2002 *The Association of British Travel Agents and British Airways plc* [2002], Office of Fair Trading, *United Kingdom*

CA98/09/2003 *BetterCare Group Ltd/North & West Belfast Health & Social Services Trust* [2003], Office of Fair Trading, *United Kingdom*

TABLE OF EUROPEAN COMMISSION'S SOFT LAW

EUROPEAN COMMISSION COMMUNICATIONS AND GUIDANCE NOTICES

Commission Notice on the definition of relevant market for the purposes of Community competition law [1997] OJ C 372/5

Commission Notice — Guidelines on the applicability of Article 81 of the EC Treaty to horizontal cooperation agreements [2001] OJ C 3/2

Guidelines on the assessment of horizontal mergers under the Council Regulation on the control of concentrations between undertakings [2004] OJ C 31/5

Communication from the Commission - Guidelines on the application of Article 81(3) of the Treaty [2004] OJ C101/97

Commission Notice — Guidelines on the effect on trade concept contained in Articles 81 and 82 of the Treaty [2004] OJ C 101/81

Commission Notice on restrictions directly related and necessary to concentrations [2005] OJ C 56/24

Commission Notice on Immunity from fines and reduction of fines in cartel cases [2006] OJ C 298/17

Guidelines on the assessment of non-horizontal mergers under the Council Regulation on the control of concentrations between undertakings [2008] OJ C 265/6

Communication from the Commission — Guidance on the Commission's enforcement priorities in applying Article 82 of the EC Treaty to abusive exclusionary conduct by dominant undertakings [2009] OJ C 45/7

Guidelines on Vertical Restraints [2010] OJ C 130/1

Communication from the Commission — Guidelines on the applicability of Article 101 of the Treaty on the Functioning of the European Union to horizontal co-operation agreements [2011] OJ C 11/1

Communication from the Commission — Guidelines on the application of Article 101 of the Treaty on the Functioning of the European Union to technology transfer agreements [2014] OJ C 89/3

Commission staff working document - Guidance on restrictions of competition "by object" for the purpose of defining which agreements may benefit from the De Minimis Notice, acccompanying communication from the Commission - Notice on agreements of minor importance which do not appreciably restrict competition under Article 101(1) of the Treaty on the Functioning of the European Union (De Minimis Notice), [C(2014) 4136 final], Brussels, 25.6.2014, SWD (2014) 198 final

Communication from the Commission — Notice on agreements of minor importance which do not appreciably restrict competition under Article 101(1) of the Treaty on the Functioning of the European Union (De Minimis Notice), [2014] OJ C 291/1

ABBREVIATIONS

BATNA	Best Alternative to a Negotiated Agrement
BPI	Buyer Power Index
CBP	Coutervailing Buyer Power
CJEU	Court of Justice of the European Union
Commission	European Commission
Courts	The European Courts – The General Court and the Court of Justice of the European Union
ECLI	European Case Law Identifier
FTC	US Federal Trade Commission
HHI	Herfindahl-Hirschman Index
NCA	National Competition Authority
SCI	Supply Chain Initiative
UPPs	Unfair Purchasing Practices

TABLE OF FIGURES

TABLE OF CONTENTS

PART I

INTRODUCTION & METHODOLOGY

1

INTRODUCTION AND ANALYSIS FRAMEWORK

I. Object of the study

1. The topic of this study is the analysis *of buyer power and its treatment in EU competition law*. My contribution to the legal research is identifying, synthetizing, discussing, and evaluating the buyer power regulation in EU competition law and clarifying what buyer power is, how it is legally treated, and whether there is a consistent and coherent buyer power competition policy and legal regulation.

2. Buyer power represents the other side of competition law, focusing on buying conducts and how a buyer can exert its market power to the detriment of competition. This implies that I have shifted the traditional competition law focus on the protection of the market against the wrongdoings of *buyers* and not sellers. The concern about buyers' anti-competitive behaviour is not new and can be traced back to 1890 in the US with the Sherman Act's prohibition of monopsony power[1]. It is not until the mid-1990s, however, that buyer power concern, for both monopsony and bargaining power, started to become a topic of interest for competition academics and competition authorities alike. This interest is arguably due to the growing amount of economic research highlighting both the benefits and consequences of buyer power, and due to the

---

1 Raising this connection see, *inter alia*: Robert G. Harris and Thomas M. Jorde, 'Antitrust Market Definition: An Integrated Approach' 72 California Law Review (1984), 3, p.16-18; Gregory J Werden, 'Monopsony and The Sherman Act: Consumer Welfare in a New Light' 74 Antitrust Law Journal (2007); Damien Geradin, 'Loyalty Rebates after Intel: Time for the European Court of Justice to Overrule Hoffman-La Roche' 11 Journal of Competition Law & Economics (2015), 707.

rising importance of buyer-resellers in the different product and geographic markets and the increased concentration in purchasers' markets, such as in the case of food retailing[2].

3. As Korah and O'Sullivan held in 2002, "[f]rom thinking in both Europe and the USA, *it is clear that it is not easy to know what to do about buyer power*"[3]. This difficulty and the lack of clear guidance was my main motivation for studying this area of competition law. Buyer power is an interesting research topic because its welfare effects are ambiguous, which as Ezrachi puts it "raises challenging questions of policy and enforcement"[4], or, as Faull and Nikpay argue it, there are "two views of buyer power", a positive and a negative[5]. Also, because there is little research that deals with it from a legal perspective. In fact, it has even been called the "new kid on the block" by the American Antitrust Institute[6]. This welfare ambiguity has caused it to either being demonized – as in the case of monopsony power – or seen as mostly procompetitive in the instance of bargaining power. Also, in the legal circles, buyer power has mostly been identified with monopsony power and simplified by assuming that its treatment should be symmetrical to, or the 'mirror image' of seller side cases, or opting for simplifications of the topic[7]. Because of the uncertainty concerning its welfare effects, the scarce case law clarifying its regulation, and the scant academic legal literature addressing it, the time is ripe in legal academia to undertake a holistic study regarding the competitive effects and regulations of buyer power.

4. By studying buyer power, I analyze *two different purchasing patterns with different economic effects*; consequently, buyer power can be positive or negative for welfare, depending on the circumstances of the case and, particularly, whether the purchaser exercises monopsony or bargaining power: the two sub-types of buyer power discussed in this study.

---

2 Also highlighting this see, *inter alia:* A. Pera, Assessment of buyer power in recent investigations and mergers, in O. Gianni, Grippo & Partners (ed.), Legal Update: Antitrust, (2010), available at: http://www.gop.it/doc_pubblicazioni/40_hjv4kr3vun_eng.pdf; College of Europe and Centre for European Policy Studies, *The Impact of National Rules on Unilateral Conduct that Diverge from Article 102 of the Treaty of the Functioning of the European Union* (2012); Lars Henriksson, *Swedish National Report: The Grocery Retail Market in Sweden: Is Antitrust Efficiently Handling this Market?* (LIDC Congress, 2013); F.A.H. van Doorn, 'The Law and Economics of Buyer Power in EU Competition Policy' (Eleven International Publishing 2015), p. 13; Bundeskartellamt *Sektoruntersuchung: Lebensmitteleinzelhandel*, (2014); European Commission, *The Economic Impact of Modern Retail on Choice and Innovation in the EU Food Sector* (2014).

3 Valentine Korah and Denis O'Sullivan, *Distribution Agreements under the EC Competition Rules* (Hart Publishing 2002), p. 53.

4 Ezrachi A, *EU Competition Law: An Analytical Guide to the Leading Cases* (4th ed. edn, Hart 2014), p. 435.

5 Jonathan Faull and Ali Nikpay, *The EC Law of Competition* (Oxford University Press 1999), para. 6.300.

6 American Antitrust Institute, 'The New Kid on the Block: Buyer Power' in Albert A. Foer (ed), *The Next Antitrust Agenda: The American Antitrust Institute's Transition Report on Competition Policy to the 44th President of the United States* (American Antitrust Institute 2008), p. 95.

7 This is the general conclusion of another recent study dealing with buyer power in EU law, see: van Doorn.

5. *Monopsony power represents the negative aspect of buyer power and is the analogue reverse form of monopoly.* In a monopsony model the buyer pays a price that is below the competitive level by reducing the quantity it acquires. In welfare terms, this behaviour leads to an inefficient outcome in the upstream market because less goods and/or services are employed and it shifts profits from the seller to the buyer without adequate compensation[8]. Monopsony power, additionally, may or may not impact downstream consumers, depending on whether the buyer also has downstream market power or whether the demand withholding of goods shifts prices upwards. On the other hand, *bargaining power*, theory based on the work of Galbraith of countervailing power[9], *tends to be in most cases efficiency enhancing* as the buyer reduces the prices it pays without lowering the quantity of goods it purchases by means of resorting to its competitive advantage over the seller. What occurs in the upstream market is a transfer of profits from the seller to the buyer that neutralizes seller market power and drives prices towards, but not below, the competitive level. Additionally, the price reduction obtained by the buyer may be passed on in the downstream market to end consumers in the form of lower prices if there is competitive pressure. However, bargaining power can be welfare detrimental depending on the circumstances of the case, for example, if it is used to foreclose rival buyers or leveraged to, or from, another market to exploit suppliers or end consumers.

6. To analyze buyer power I have based my research on several assumptions which have an important influence on the project's delimitation and research questions. First, based on the case law of the Court of Justice of the European Union (CJEU), I assume that *purchasing is an economic activity* if the goods acquired are subsequently employed in a downstream economic activity. This rather restrictive approach to purchasing as an economic activity has created a *lacuna* regarding the competition law application to purchases carried out by contracting authorities under the scope of EU public procurement law to goods that are not subsequently used in an economic activity, pursuant to the *FENIN* and *Selex* economic activity doctrine[10]. I have discussed this lack of public buyer power competition law scrutiny in public procurement markets

---

8 For the sake of brevity and avoiding unnecessary repetition I employ in this study, unless noted otherwise, the term "goods" as encompassing both products, works and services.

9 John Kenneth Galbraith, *The Affluent Society & Other Writings 1952-1967: American Capitalism; The Great Crash, 1929; The Affluent Society; The New Industrial State.* (The Library of America 2010), p. 97-135.

10 Judgment of 11 July in *FENIN v Commission*, C-205/03 P, EU:C:2006:453; Judgment of 4 March 2003, *Fenin v Commission*, T-319/99, ECR, EU:T:2003:50; Judgment of 26 March 2009 in *Selex Sistemi Integrati v Commission*, C-113/07 P, EU:C:2009:191.

elsewhere, as this falls outside of the scope of this study[11]. Secondly, this study assumes *ab initio* that buyer power is under the scope of application of EU competition law if exercised by an undertaking. For this reason, I do not inquire as to whether there is a legislative gap concerning buyer power control, which was the research focus of van Doorn, but rather ask *what is the legal treatment given to buyer power*[12].

A. Research questions and structure of this study

7. In my study of buyer power treatment, I have centered my research on analyzing four main research questions: *What is and what ought to be understood in EU competition law by buyer power? What is the legal treatment given to the exertion of anticompetitive buyer power in EU competition law? Which theories of harm of buyer power abuse are there? What is the welfare standard employed for buyer power cases?*

8. In a broad perspective all these questions have a single aim: the identification, synthetization, and schematization of a *comprehensive and cross-sectional discussion of buyer power to determine what the legal regulation to buying conducts in EU competition law is.* This contribution is novel and valuable due to its approach, depth, scope, and the absence of academic works of a similar extent in the field. Also, although my study is focused mainly on EU competition law, part of my contribution is contrasting buyer power regulation in US antitrust law and the law of selected EU Member States (MS). I do this by also analyzing similar conducts and the legal treatment in those jurisdictions and contrasting the outcomes with the EU competition law solutions.

9. My research structure aims to answer these research questions by analyzing specific purchasing behaviours or 'theories of harm' that are relevant for competition law, its treatment by the case law (if any), and policy discussions concerning the adequacy of such treatment. I have decided not to explore buyer power from a structural perspective focused on a partial study of its regulation under Article 101, Article 102 TFEU and the EU Merger Control regime, as recently done by van Doorn[13]. Instead, have I opted *to analyze it from a cross-sectoral behavioural perspective, by focusing my research on purchasing conducts that are relevant to buyer power.*

---

11 Ignacio Herrera Anchustegui, 'Centralizing Public Procurement and Competitiveness in Directive 2014/24' 4 European Law Reporter (2015) 119; Albert Sánchez Graells and Ignacio Herrera Anchustegui, 'Revisiting the Concept of Undertaking from a Public Procurement Law Perspective - A Discussion on EasyPay and Finance Engineering' 37 European Competition Law Review (2016) 93; Albert Sánchez Graells and Ignacio Herrera Anchustegui, 'Impact of Public Procurement Aggregation on Competition. Risks, Rationale and Justification for the Rules in Directive 2014/24' in Patricia Valcárcel Fernández (ed), *Compra conjunta y demanda agregada en la contratación del sector público Un análisis jurídico y económico* (Thomson-Aranzadi 2016).

12 van Doorn.

13 Ibid.

10. The cross-sectional analysis of buyer power is conducted with independence from the 'competition law sector' they belong to, which allows me to compare the treatment of arguably similar economic conducts with their legal regulation, and determine whether the treatment given by the Commission and/or the Courts is consistent across all areas of EU competition law. In my opinion, the treatment of the same type of behaviour, regardless of the 'area' of competition law, should be as consistent and symmetrical as possible to ensure predictability, cohesiveness, and internal rationale. Also, from an economic standpoint, a homogenous treatment is justified because buyer power economics and its welfare effects do not drastically change depending on the area of competition law in which they take place, even though important differences exist depending on whether the conduct is actual or expected or if there is coordination among buyers. This, nevertheless, does not imply that this general cohesive approach to buyer power should not be adjusted to the situation at hand. My analysis shows that the Courts and the Commission apply EU competition law to buyer power consistently but adjust their approach according to the economic and regulatory nuances of agreements, unilateral behaviours or concentrations, as also occurs in selling side cases. Furthermore, such an approach allows me to minimize the description of the discussed cases and limit as much as possible repetition of economic concepts.

11. However, the cross-sectional nature of this research is ambitious and challenging because it requires readjustment and reinterpretation of many traditional competition law concepts that are employed in seller side cases but which are not the same for buyer cases. Also, the aim of producing a cross-sectional and holistic study of buyer power has resulted in this work being lengthy.

12. Based on this holistic and behavioural approach to buyer power, I have structured this as follows: Part I, which is comprised of chapter 1, serves as the introduction to my buyer power study, discusses the methodology I employ in the remainder of it, its justification, scope and delimitation.

13. Part II groups two background chapters of my research dealing with economic and policy aspects related to buyer power, which serve as the foundation for the understanding of the legal discussion. In chapter 2, I carry out a detailed analysis of buyer power economics by distinguishing monopsony from bargaining power as different expressions of buyer power, and examine their effect on welfare in the upstream and downstream markets. In chapter 3, I discuss buyer power through an ordoliberal lens and explain how I employ ordoliberalism as a competition policy benchmark to guide the analysis of buyer power regulation, as well as discuss the legal treatment given to it from both a *de lege lata* and *lege ferenda* perspectives.

14. Part III deals with the definition of relevant purchasing markets. To this end, I have divided it in two chapters inspired by a *dualistic approach* to buyer mar-

kets. The dualistic approach suggests that buyer market definition should go beyond a purely upstream focus (where purchasing takes place) and that also the competitiveness of the undertaking in the downstream market where it acts as a retailer must be assessed to fully capture the buyer power effects vis-à-vis suppliers, end consumers and rival undertakings. Chapter 4 deals with the relevant market definition by revisiting the 'hypothetical monopsonist test,' with a focus on product market definition. This is followed in chapter 5 by the methodology employed for the assessment of buyer market power by means of different tools and sources, its quantification and an examination of when buyer power substantially arises to become a competitive concern.

15. Part IV constitutes the core of this study. It discusses buyer power as a competitive concern anchored on theories of harm grouped on how buyer power is employed. Chapter 6 initiates the study of buyer power theories of harm, focusing on *buyer power exclusion* whenever market power is employed to the detriment of rival undertakings that compete in the upstream purchasing market, as buyers, or in the downstream market, as retailers. This exclusionary use of buyer power involves increasing a rival's cost with the aim of making it less efficient and therefore, less attractive for end consumers and suppliers alike, pushing them out of the market to gain unopposed buyer and/or seller power. Chapter 7 follows with a discussion of *buyer power in its exploitative form* by imposing low purchasing prices or withholding demand by either concerted or unilateral behaviour to extract supracompetitive profits. In this chapter, I also discuss the case of buying alliances and its distinction from buyer cartels as a positive expression of buyer power that does not exploit suppliers and has a beneficial effect on end consumers. This part concludes with another modality of buyer power exploitation centered on *unfair purchasing practices,* conducts that are commonly claimed to take place in food retailing markets. Chapter 8 questions the anti-competitive nature of unfair purchasing practices and discusses whether these conducts ought to be regulated by other legal disciplines, as they tend to constitute problems of bilateral equilibrium and contractual fairness. Also, my analysis looks into the different regulatory avenues outside EU competition law in the Community and national law to tackle this expression of buyer power.

16. Part V discusses buyer power from a seller's perspective by analyzing countervailing buyer power as a seller market power neutralizer, and considering how buyer power can be limited by suppliers. *Countervailing buyer power,* discussed in chapter 9, constitutes a 'positive' aspect of buyer power as it has the ability to neutralize opposing seller market power and preclude an undertaking from behaving independently from its competitors and exerting dominance, significantly impeding competition as the result of a concentration, or serving as an efficiency defense for the acceptance of an agreement among undertakings. In chapter 10, I deal with *buyer power limitation,* its compatibility with com-

petition law and the types of conduct suppliers employ to neutralize a buyer's ability to exercise market power against them, for instance, by setting price ceilings, establishing selling quotas, or granting fidelity rebates.

17. Part VI ends this study by discussing at large the findings of the study, paving the way towards a synthetization of an EU buyer power policy and signaling other areas ripe for further research.

B. Analysis structure

18. The different expressions of buyer power and the competitive issues generated by it are discussed in individual chapters following a similar structure. The chapters begin with a general discussion of the topic and the main economic intuition explaining the type of abuse to be discussed as a starting point of the analysis of the theories of harm and the legal regulation of them.

19. Then, I proceed to analyze the behaviour from the perspective of each of the cross-sectional areas of competition law: unilateral behaviour, concentrations and agreements. The discussion of the theories of harm is firstly structured in accordance to issues that are typical of unilateral behaviour, for several reasons. Buyer power problems are better illustrated through unilateral behaviour because the economic rationale of the conduct of a single undertaking is simpler and more intuitively appealing than coordinated behaviour, which is more complex and has implications in horizontal and vertical levels that are not always found in single undertaking conducts. Furthermore, dominance examples illustrate similar problems that may arise in concentration that may significantly affect effective competition. Also, most buyer power cases and theories of harm deal with unilateral exercise of buyer power as shown by the case law and the relatively fewer cases of buyers' cartels or buying alliances. Furthermore, buyer power effects tend to be of a vertical nature (buyer vs supplier) that "may lead to restrictive effects on competition on the purchasing and/or downstream selling market or markets, such as increased prices, reduced output, product quality or variety, or innovation, market allocation, or anti-competitive foreclosure of other possible purchasers"[14]. However, buyer power can also have horizontal effects in cases of coordination because it may be employed by buyers to reduce upstream and/or downstream competition[15]. The analysis of the practices and its legal treatment is made by a study of the relevant case law and Commission's practice and its discussion with other aspects of buyer power regulation.

---

14 Communication from the Commission — Guidelines on the applicability of Article 101 of the Treaty on the Functioning of the European Union to horizontal co-operation agreements [2011] OJ C 11/1, para. 200.

15 Communication from the Commission — Guidelines on the applicability of Article 101 of the Treaty on the Functioning of the European Union to horizontal co-operation agreements [2011] OJ C 11/1, para. 201.

20. Lastly, the chapters conclude with a discussion of the findings and evaluation of the treatment of buyer power, of the types of practices, the harm required to trigger the applicability of EU competition law, expressing the state of the law from a *de lege lata* perspective, and introducing interpretative or policy suggestions *de lege ferenda,* if any.

21. Also, and as a general rule, my analysis of buyer power is predominantly legal, but it does incorporate economics into the discussion through a method that I denominate an *economically informed legal analysis*[16], and which I discuss in detail in chapter 1, section §II.A. I firstly employ economic theory to define the implications of buyer power from a welfare-oriented perspective. This understanding of the buyer power economic implications is used to comprehend the competition effects of the conducts that are being evaluated on other market participants and competition as a process. Therefore, I resort to economics to illustrate the competitive problem (or benefit) posed by buyer power and to serve as a foundational ground for the discussion of the legal treatment given by the Courts and the Commission to these behaviours. In other words, my use of economic theory is subordinated to the law, implying that I use it to understand the factual problem that the law ought to solve. In this sense, I do not carry out a 'law & economics' analysis understood as either evaluating the law and case law from an economic perspective nor do I base my interpretation of the cases or *de lege ferenda* suggestions on pure welfare considerations.

22. Additionally, and related to my implementation of an economically informed legal analysis, I employ ordoliberalism as the competition school of thought that orients my evaluation and comparison of the legal treatment to buyer power, as discussed in chapter 1, section §II.C., and chapter 3. In a nutshell, ordoliberalism proposes the ordering of society, and in particular the market, by means of a pre-set of legal rules integrated in the economic constitution that aim to protect the competitive order and safeguard individual freedom and consumer welfare against the abuse of market power, public or private. I employ ordoliberalism as an analytical and benchmarking tool that allows me to compare and determine whether the case law and the reasoning of the Courts are in line with ordoliberal thinking or not, or whether they adopt a different competition policy line. I, however, do not discuss whether or not EU competition law or the EU buyer power regulation is or ought to be ordoliberal, as this is outside of my scope and would require a different legal methodology.

16 I would like to thank Albert Sánchez Graells for suggesting this term for the adopted methodology.

II. Methodology

23. For this research, I employ a research methodology that combines microeconomic and legal theory to carry out an *economically informed legal analysis* of the buyer power regulation, following an integrative approach to the study of economic regulation[17]. On the one hand, I employ *microeconomics and industrial organization* theory, to explain the economics behind buyer power, and to serve as a starting point for the legal analysis and to integrate[18] economic thinking when identifying and analyzing the different theories of harm I discuss — because legal economic research must be informed by economics[19]. This methodological choice provides an economically informed legal analysis – although not a 'law and economics' approach – to the interpretation and application of the law as I do not directly evaluate the economic consistency of the regulations nor suggest policy changes purely anchored on microeconomic models. On the other hand, I employ the legal doctrinal method with emphasis placed on teleological interpretation to identify the relevant cases, analyze, evaluate and discuss the current state of the law. The following sections discuss these choices in further detail.

A. An economically informed legal analysis for buyer power

24. Competition law is one of the economic regulatory pillars of the EU internal market[20]. Its goals are the promotion, protection and enforcement of the fundamental freedoms, societal welfare and economic efficiency[21]. Competition

---

17 Albert Sánchez Graells, *Public Procurement and the EU Competition Rules* (2nd edn, Hart 2015), p. 20.

18 National Academy of Sciences Institute of Medicine, and National Academy of Engineering, *Facilitating Interdisciplinary Research* (The National Academies Press 2004), p. 2; Maurice Adams, 'Doing What Doesn't Come Naturally. On the Distinctiveness of Comparative Law' in Mark Van Hoecke (ed), *Methodologies of legal research: which kind of method for what kind of discipline?* (Hart 2011), p. 237-240.

19 Sánchez Graells, [2015], 20. See discussing the role of economics in competition law, *inter alia*: Giorgio Monti, *EC Competition Law* (Cambridge University Press 2007), p. 1-6; Simon Bishop and Mike Walker, *The Economics of EC Competition Law: Concepts, Application and Measurement* (Sweet & Maxwell 2010), paras. 1-001 to 1-013; Alexander Italianer, *The Interplay Between Law and Economics* (8 December 2010); Gunnar Niels, Helen Jenkins and James Kavanagh, *Economics for Competition Lawyers* (Oxford University Press 2011), p. 2-6; Douglas H. Ginsburg and Eric M. Fraser, 'The Role of Economic Analysis in Competition Law' in R. Ian McEwin (ed), *Intellectual property, competition law and economics in Asia* (Hart 2011); Doris Hildebrand, *The Role of Economic Analysis in EU Competition Law: The European School* (Fourth Edition edn, Kluwer Law International 2016); Jorge Padilla, 'The Role of Economics in EU Competition Law: From Monti's Reform to the State Aid Modernization Package' 2-2016 Concurrences Review (2016) 1.

20 For literature dealing with European economic law and the role of the state in the market, see, *inter alia*, Nina Boeger, 'Book Review: The Regulation of the State in Competitive Markets in the EU by Erika Szyszczak' 33 European Law Review (2008) 442; Wolf Sauter and Harm Schepel, *State and Market in European Union Law: The Public and Private Spheres of the Internal Market Before the EU Courts* (Cambridge University Press 2009). For a general overview on the single market as an objective of the EU as a whole see Paul Craig and Gráinne De Búrca, *EU Law: Texts, Cases and Materials* (Oxford University Press 2011), p. 581-610.

21 Alison Jones and Brenda Sufrin, *EU Competition Law: Text, Cases and Materials* (Oxford University Press 2014), p. 1.

law regulates the behaviours of undertakings that carry out economic activity in the market and determines which conducts are allowed and which forbidden, depending on their perniciousness to market functioning. Its goals are preventing competition from being restricted, distorted or affected, and seeking to maximize economic welfare. As competition law's regulation is directly focused on economic conduct, a proper understanding of these behaviours' effects requires knowledge concerning microeconomics and the market functioning. Therefore, the study of competition law is an area ripe for legal and economic interdisciplinary research, and, as Bishop and Walker argue, "[t]he application of competition law cannot properly take place without regard to economic considerations"[22].

25. To this end, and mindful of my limitations as a non-economist, I have decided to resort to *an economically informed legal analysis,* an interdisciplinary method that employs economic knowledge to better understand the object of the legal regulation, the implications of the rules and the consequences of the outcomes of the case law for welfare. An economically informed legal analysis entails the employment of economic theory to conform legal analysis with the economic realities and market consequences of a decision. It does not, however, imply that *economics should be used with a normative effect*; this is, the legal decision-making being determined by the outcome of economic modeling or argumentations by itself and outside of the legal system as a whole. Instead, the answers to the research questions and the determination of the buyer power regulation are obtained through the analysis of the law with economics as an auxiliary tool used to guide the application of the law and improve the economic quality of the decision-making, but not to substitute the law by pure economics[23]. From my perspective, the use of microeconomics and industrial organization are auxiliary to the study and application of law, in the sense that they may influence the legislative drafting process and provide the judge with some essential knowledge to refer to when deciding a case. However, at least in my point of view, they are not the sole answer to legal problems.

26. This point requires further clarification. This study uses a qualitative interdisciplinary method incorporating an economic approach to law but does not employ either a 'law and economics' or 'behavioural economics and law' approach when analyzing the law[24]. *Law and economics* presupposes the use of economic theory, traditionally microeconomics, to predict human conduct in response to the law – for example, conduct changes under the influence of

---

22 Bishop and Walker, [2010], para. 1-002. See also on the importance of economics in EU competition law: Monti, [2007], p. 53-87.

23 Jan M. Smits, *What is Legal Doctrine? On the Aims and Methods of Legal-Dogmatic Research* (2015) 1.

24 For more on behavioral economics and law, see: J De Conninck, 'Behavioural Economics and Legal Research' in Mark Van Hoecke (ed), *Methodologies of legal research: which kind of method for what kind of discipline?* (Hart 2011), p. 257-275.

incentives – and also provides “a useful normative standard for evaluating law and policy”[25]. *Behavioural economics and law* provides explanations and predicts how humans will behave when making decisions based on the current status of the law or how they will behave if the law is changed[26]. These two methodologies take economic theory one step further than my economically informed legal approach does because they assume a construction of the legal rules anchored on economic theory and see economics as the guide to law, not as a supplement to it. On the other hand, in the economically informed legal analysis, the study, evaluation and bettering of EU competition law uses economic theory as a starting point to improve the legal regulation of buyer power, determine what the legal principles are, and to try to ensure that the legal regulation of purchasing behaviours is as economically sound and efficient as possible, within the goals and principles pursued by the EU competition law.

27. *The economically informed legal analysis, therefore, serves four purposes.* Firstly, understanding what buyer power is and its economic implications as a necessary starting point for a legal analysis of buying conducts. Secondly, the understanding of buying conducts allowed me to group different behaviours and classify them as either exploitative, exclusionary of seller-oriented exercises of buyer power. Thirdly, within each of the sub-types of buyer power exercise, I have identified economic theories of harm that are assessed through the legal treatment by the competition provisions, the case law and the Commission’s practice. Using theories of harm anchored on economic scenarios allows me to discuss buyer power in a holistic manner encompassing all competition law areas, without dividing economic conducts and effects into legal constructs. Fourthly, an understanding of buyer power effects allows me to assess which type of harm triggers competition intervention and the welfare standard that is protected as the outcome of the case law. The identification of which harm triggers competition intervention and which type of welfare is protected allows me to determine whether there is a consistent competition policy across the different theories of harm and types of conducts. Concerning the type of harm required to trigger the application of the law, my discussion aims to identify which standard is employed in EU competition law. In other words, whether EU buyer power regulation intervenes adopting a broad perspective even absent evidence of direct end downstream consumer harm towards the protection of the competitive process in either the upstream or downstream markets; or whether it resorts to a narrower approach in which competition law is triggered only upon direct end consumer harm[27].

---

25 Robert Cooter and Thomas Ulen, *Law & Economics* (Pearson 2008), p. 4.

26 De Conninck [2011], p. 258-266.

27 On the different welfare standards, see: Bishop and Walker, [2010], para. 2-001-2-019. See also in detail chapter 3, section §IV.C.

B. The use of economic theory

28. Following the discussion regarding the economically informed legal analysis, I have integrated economic theory in this study by means of a literature review on buyer power economics, in chapter 2. Here, I discuss the economic effects of monopsony and bargaining power from a static and dynamic perspective, as well as its impact on welfare. This analysis is made by a literature review focused on the main works that have been published over the last two decades, while not disregarding the seminal work of Galbraith, which has inspired theories of buyer (bargaining) power[28]. This literature review comprises recounting and analyzing economic theory and goes beyond a mere summary of it. One of the important remarks to be made concerning the economics of buyer power and its theorization is that most economic models studying buyer power deal with private buyers and not public buyers[29]. Also, these models tend to be based on an intermediate dealer that usually enjoys substantial upstream and downstream market power, as is the case, for example, with large food-retailers[30]. My study, however, does not carry out a sectoral analysis of any industry in particular and instead analyzes buyer power as a whole.

29. Finally, I resort to ordoliberalism as a benchmarking tool pertaining to the consistency and compatibility of buyer power regulation; I discuss this economic school of thought below.

---

28 Galbraith, [2010], p. 97-135.

29 A notable exception to this is the study made by Daniel Condon, 'Monopsony Power and the Market for Clergy: Some Evidence from the Census' 42 The Quarterly Review of Economics and Finance (2002) 889.

30 See, for example on food retailing: European Commission and others *Buyer Power and its Impact on Competition in the Food Retail Distribution Sector of the European Union*, (2000); UK Competition Commission *Supermarkets: A report on the Supply of Groceries from Multiple Stores in the United Kingdom*, London (2000); Paul W Dobson, 'Exploiting Buyer Power: Lessons from the British Grocery Trade' 72 Antitrust Law Journal (2004-2005) 529; S. Robson (Rob) Walton, 'Wal-Mart, Supplier-Partners, and the Buyer Power Issue' 72 Antitrust Law Journal (2004-2005) 509; Jorge Rodrigues, *Buyer Power and Pass-Through of Large Retailing Groups in the Portuguese Food Sector* (2006); Paul W. Dobson and Ratula Chakraborty, 'Buyer Power in the U.K. Groceries Market' 53 The Antitrust Bulletin (2008) 333; Oddgeir Hole, *Price Setting in the Swedish Grocery Market: Monopoly and Monopsony Market Forces* (2008); Paul Walter Dobson, 'Relationship Between Buyer and Seller power in Retailing: UK Supermarkets' in Bruce Lyons (ed), *Cases in European competition policy: the economic analysis* (Cambridge University Press 2009); Lehiaren Defentsarako Euskal Auzitegia / Tribunal Vasco de Defensa de la Competencia *Distribution of Daily Consumer Goods: Competition, Oligopoly and Tacit Collusion*, Vitoria-Gasteiz (April 2009); Bob Young, 'Supermarket Buyer Power' Competition Law Insight (2013) 13; Javier Berasategi, *Supermarket Power: Serving Consumers or Harming Competition* (2014); European Commission (2014); Bundeskartellamt *Summary of the Final Report of the Sector Inquiry into the Food Retail Sector*, (2014).

C. Comparing buyer power regulation with ordoliberal competition policy

30. The use of economics and the adoption of specific schools of economic thought have a considerable impact on the design, interpretation and evaluation of competition regulation, as well as affecting the ethical implications and moral choices of policy makers and academics[31]. Furthermore, competition policies and rules are based on different goals and premises, which are protected by the Courts in the application of the law and which shape the judgments' content through the legal language. The protection of these goals is usually obtained through the use of economic and legal arguments that academically support one argument or solution over another.

31. As part of my research, I have decided to *compare the regulation of buyer power in EU competition law and (to a limited extent) in the US antitrust with a buyer-power inspired ordoliberal competition policy*[32]. It is important to stress that this comparison does not intend to determine whether EU buyer power regulation is 'ordoliberal', but rather whether the buyer power regulation and the case law is compatible with this economic school of thought. Such an approach would require a different methodology and would answer different research questions than those which I investigate in this study. The use of ordoliberal competition as a comparison benchmark enables me to determine whether the case law and the Commission's practice are compatible with this economic school of thought or not, as regards buyer power. Also, employing ordoliberal competition policy as a benchmark tool gives my comparison and policy choices an academic background and justification.

32. There are several reasons that justify this methodological choice. A comparison of the EU regulation on buyer power with ordoliberalism is interesting and valuable because it allows determination of whether the current legal treatment is consistent in policy terms with this economic school of thought and opens the way for further research in this area. In particular, my comparison will try to determine whether EU buyer power regulation also seeks to protect the competitive process in the upstream and downstream markets and protect the economic freedom of rival buyers without the need for downstream consumer harm. Also, the comparison would allow me to determine the internal consistency of the case law across the different competition law areas, as an

---

31 For a general treatment of ethics in economics see: A. Dutt and C. Wilber, *Economics and Ethics: An Introduction* (Palgrave Macmillan UK 2010). See also: Walter J. Schultz, *The Moral Conditions of Economic Efficiency* (Cambridge University Press 2001), who puts forward that "efficient outcomes of market interaction cannot be achieved without a system of moral normative constraints for securing competitive behavior and a set of conventions for facilitating exchange, for coordinating supply and demand, and for internalizing certain types of externalities" p 1.

32 See for a somewhat similar methodology employed by Bovis to the analysis of public procurement rules under a method he has labeled as "[t]he ordoliberal approach to public procurement regulation" in Christopher Bovis, *The Law of EU Public Procurement* (2nd ed. edn, Oxford University Press 2015), paras. 1.20-1.62.

ordoliberal background grants me full scope with which to contrast the specific regulations against. Furthermore, this comparative analysis also permits me to contrast whether there is any policy tension among the EU institutions regarding buyer power; i.e. whether the Courts and the Commission have different enforcement and policy preferences, particularly regarding the type of harm required for competition intervention in buyer power cases. Also, resorting to ordoliberalism as a benchmarking tool provides the reader with the academic background information and assumptions that underpin my qualitative assessment of the case law and the Commission's practice. Furthermore, a comparison of the EU buyer power regulation with ordoliberal competition policy also enables me to contrast the outcomes with other competition policy schools — in particular the Chicago and Post-Chicago schools — and determine whether a different policy approach has an impact in the outcome of the cases. Lastly, a comparison with ordoliberal economic theory grants this study further novelty when compared to various other attempts to discuss buyer power regulation in EU competition law.

33. To carry out this comparison of EU buyer power regulation to ordoliberalism, I incorporated, in chapter 3, a discussion of ordoliberal competition policy and my interpretation of what an ordoliberally inspired buyer power competition policy implies. This comparison is incorporated by analyzing the outcome of the case law to ordoliberal theory and highlighting the congruence of the case law with it. As part of this analysis, I also discuss arguments that may explain the reasons why the Courts have decided to adopt their given approach from a competition policy perspective. My research visits to the University of Freiburg and the Walter Eucken Institute under the supervision of Professor Emeritus Viktor Vanberg and Professor Lars Feld were of invaluable help.

D. The legal analysis, a doctrinal work

34. The core of this work is the legal analysis of EU competition law regulation of buyer power by means of studying the relevant legal norms, the case law, soft law instruments and academic literature. This legal study will be carried out following the legal doctrinal method, as I describe in this sub-section. This qualitative legal method implies the use of the legal system as the subject of inquiry with its own hierarchy or norms and rules[33], and as the theoretical framework in which the research answers are to be found[34]. For this I have collected the pertinent legal material – by referring to the relevant legal

---

33 P. C. Westerman, 'Open or Autonomous? The Debate on legal Methodology as a Reflection of the Debate on Law' in Mark Van Hoecke (ed), *Methodologies of Legal Research: Which Kind of Method for what Kind of Discipline?* (Hart 2011), p. 90.

34 J. BM. Vranken, 'Methodology of Legal Doctrinal Research: A Comment on Westerman' in Mark Van Hoecke (ed), *Methodologies of legal research: which kind of method for what kind of discipline?* (Hart 2011), p. 113.

sources, interpreting the law following the legal rules of interpretation with a preference for a teleological approach, recourse to classical rules on legal construction of arguments, and principles of EU law.

35. I use the legal doctrinal method for the evaluation of buyer power regulation to determine both what the current state of the law is (*de lege lata*) and how it ought to be (*de lege ferenda*), in the case of inconsistencies, based on the law itself, economic theory and competition policy. This method comprises a systematic study of the regulation governing buyer power as an economic phenomenon, the content of such regulation, resolving its unclarities and creating a consistent and cohesive legal buyer power regulation[35]. The adoption of the legal method is justified because the focal point of my research is determining what the regulation of buyer power is, and, therefore, clarifying the state of the law.

36. Thus, the interpretation of the texts shall be based upon the hierarchy of norms, deductive reasoning and argumentation by analogy towards the systematization and rationalization of the current law on buyer power. In this sense, this study adopts an analytical posture when examining the law and resorts to qualitative analysis rather than any quantitative analysis of the law.

E. Citation and nomenclature

37. With the entry into force of the Lisbon Treaty, the Articles of the former EC Treaty have been renumbered[36]. The provisions dealing with the treatment of undertakings have remained identical in their content with minor terminology modifications and are now grouped under Title VII, Chapter 1, Section 1, in particular, Articles 101-109 TFEU. Consequently, and to facilitate the reading of this study, when discussing legislation and the case law I employ the post-TFEU numbering and re-number the original provisions in brackets, unless for some historical or contextual reason this is undesirable.

III. Project justification

38. Buyer power is an important topic that has received little attention by competition law academics, which leaves an important gap concerning what its legal treatment is and should be. Although EU competition rules are drafted in a 'neutral way', most of the case law, the research and the norms are oriented to seller side cases: the provision and not the purchase of goods. This study

---

35 Smits, p. 5.

36 The Treaty of the Functioning of the European Union and the Treaty of the European Union entered into force on December 1st, 2009.

rotates this approach and analyzes competition law from the other side of the walkway, with the buyer as the center of the discussion.

39. Despite the legal regulation gap, in the last decade buyer power has gained preponderance in the academic, political and institutional discourse partly due to modern retailing techniques and the increasing presence of intermediaries that acquire input and resell the same or the processed input in the downstream market. Because these powerful buyers also tend to have a large presence as sellers, suppliers may be dependent on then to reach end consumers and sell their goods. An example that depicts such a situation and which has been at the forefront of buyer power analysis is the case of food retailing where the good and evil of buyer power has been portrayed. This surge in practical importance has not been accompanied with sufficient legal research on buyer power. This legal gap is also pernicious from a legal perspective as competition regulators, the Courts, undertakings, the academic community, legislators, and the public in general have doubts regarding the treatment of buyer power and its regulation.

40. Also, the academic research that has been carried out so far tends to study buyer power from either a purely economic or legal perspective, albeit with an increasing trend towards interdisciplinary work. The existing research, nevertheless, has a sectoral or partialized focus, as few studies have dealt with buyer power as a whole or made inquiry regarding the existence of a buyer power doctrine in EU competition law. Also, I have identified two specific shortcomings of the research. Concerning legal studies, most research has simplified buyer power issues and approaches these as purely monopsony instances, suggesting a symmetrical treatment to seller market power cases. This has led to confusion among the legal community and to the myth that all buyer power cases are monopsony cases. The small amount of legal research that has been carried out in the field of bargaining power is partially due to the small amount of cases and also due to the economic complexity of the topic. In this study, I aim at clarifying this issue and clearly differentiating between monopsony and bargaining power as sub-expressions of buyer power that ought to be treated differently by the law because of their distinct welfare implications. Also, in my research I have found a lack of economic consensus regarding what the welfare effects of certain buyer power expressions are, and, accordingly, what the competition treatment of these should be.

41. Also, my study is justified because it paves the way towards further academic research in the field of buyer power and, in particular, a *de lege ferenda* study regarding the refinement and improvement of buyer power policies and regulation within and outside of EU competition law.

42. Consequently, and for the reasons stated, a general buyer power study in EU competition law is needed because, by drawing similarities and comparing

the differences in the treatment of the different buyer power expressions, it is possible to *synthetize and clarify the legal treatment of buying conducts in EU competition law*. This *de lege lata* clarification is needed to *provide legal certainty and predictability concerning the behaviour of buyers in competitive markets.*

IV. Delimitation

43. As part of my research, I have identified several areas related to buyer power regulation that I have decided to leave outside of the scope of my research due to their nature and specificity.

44. First, I have excluded a study of the *exercise of buyer power by contracting authorities under the scope of application of EU public procurement law, in particular central purchasing bodies*. According to the current case law, the status of the purchasing as an 'economic activity' of contracting authorities depends on the nature of the subsequent use they are given to. Therefore, not all purchasing carried out by contracting authorities is within the scope of EU competition law, and arguably most of it falls outside of it[37]. The problem of buyer power in public procurement is not a theoretical chimera; rather it may affect close to 19% of the GDP of the European Union[38], which may be exacerbated pursuant to the drive of procurement aggregation techniques in the 2014 public procurement directives, such as strengthening central pur-

37 See Judgment of 4 March 2003, *Fenin v Commission*, T-319/99, ECR, EU:T:2003:50, paras. 35-41; Judgment of 11 July in *FENIN v Commission*, C-205/03 P, EU:C:2006:453, paras. 25-27; Judgment of 26 March 2009 in *Selex Sistemi Integrati v Commission*, C-113/07 P, EU:C:2009:191; Judgment of 23 April 1991, *Höfner and Elser v Macrotron*, C-41/90, EU:C:1991:161; Judgment of 16 March 2004 in *AOK-Bundesverband and Others*, joined cases C-264/01, C-306/01, C-354/01 and C-355/01, EU:C:2004:150; Judgment of 18 June 1998, *Commission v Italy*, EU:C:1998:303. See also discussing the topic of economic activity: Judgment of 22 October 2015 in *EasyPay and Finance Engineering*, C-185/14, EU:C:2015:716; Judgment of 12 July 2012 in *Compass-Datenbank*, C-138/11, EU:C:2012:449 [2012], published in the electronic Reports of Cases; Judgment of 24 October 2002 in *Aéroports de Paris v Commission*, C-82/01 P, EU:C:2002:617. For some literature on this see, *inter alia*: Catriona Munro, 'Competition Law and Public Procurement: Two Sides of the Same Coin?' 6 Public Procurement Law Review (2006) 352; Erika Szyszczak, *The Regulation of the State in Competitive Markets in the EU* (Hart 2007); Mustafa T. Karayigit, 'Under the Triangle Rules of Competition, State Aid and Public Procurement: Public Undertakings Entrusted with the Operation of Services of General Economic Interest' 30 European Competition Law Review (2009) 542; Office of Fair Trading *Competition in Mixed Markets: Ensuring Competitive Neutrality*, (2010); Rainer Lindberg, 'Buying Exclusion in EU Competition Rules — Assessing Reasons and Consequences' 7 European Competition Journal (2011) 433; Carmen Estevan de Quesada, 'Competition and Transparency in Public Procurement Markets' 5 Public Procurement Law Review (2014) 229; Martin Farley and Nicolas Pourbaix, 'The EU Concessions Directive: Building (Toll) Bridges between Competition Law and Public Procurement?' Journal of European Competition Law & Practice (2014); Sánchez Graells, *Public Procurement and the EU Competition Rules* (2nd edn, Hart 2015); Sánchez Graells and Herrera Anchustegui 'Revisiting the Concept of Undertaking from a Public Procurement Law Perspective - A Discussion on EasyPay and Finance Engineering' (2016).

38 European Commission http://trade.ec.europa.eu/doclib/press/index.cfm?id=788; European Parliament. "Public procurement package: getting the best value for money". Press Release – Competition – 05/09/2013 on http://www.europarl.europa.eu/news/en/news-room/content/20130903IPR18507/html/Public-procurement-package-getting-the-best-value-for-money.

chasing bodies, framework agreements and dynamic purchasing systems[39]. These issues have been excluded because they would imply the integration of a different legal discipline and due to the likelihood that public purchasing patterns do not respond to the same economic incentives as private or profit-making buyers.

45. Second, I have excluded the question of whether EU competition law should promote the creation of bargaining power to foster economic efficiency and neutralize seller power, as this is an area for *de lege ferenda* research, which should be answered once there is sufficient certainty concerning bargaining power economic effects and their legal treatment. This approach has been commanded in the US by Kirkwood, who has suggested that there are three circumstances in which cartels that countervail seller or buyer market power may be considered lawful[40], and a more recent work which suggests using *public buyer power* to decrease the purchasing prices of medicines as part of the US healthcare system[41]. The flip-side of the argument is that allowing such exemptions jeopardizes the consistency of the system.

46. Third, I have excluded from the research the study of 'private labels' as an example of own store brands developed by retailers that decide to expand their line of business by either producing themselves or outsourcing goods to be sold to the end consumer[42]. Private labels are often associated with buyer power and unfair purchasing practices as the competitive pressure they exert on a supplier may increase a retailer's bargaining power upstream and its market share downstream. The impact and importance of private labels, however, is not a pure buyer power issue. More likely it is a topic of upstream integration or expansion, and it also adopts a sectoral approach. For these reasons, I

---

39 Directive 2014/24/EU of the European Parliament and of the Council of 26 February 2014 on public procurement and repealing Directive 2004/18/EC [2014] OJ L 94/65; Directive 2014/25/EU of the European Parliament and of the Council of 26 February 2014 on procurement by entities operating in the water, energy, transport and postal services sectors and repealing Directive 2004/17/EC [2014] OJ L 94/243. For a discussion of the aggregated demand techniques see, *inter alia*: Carina Risvig Hamer, 'Regular Purchases and Aggregated Procurement: The Changes in the new Public Procurement Directive Regarding Framework Agreements, Dynamic Purchasing Systems and Central Purchasing Bodies' 4 Public Procurement Law Review (2014) 201; Herrera Anchustegui (2015); Sánchez Graells, [2015]; Sánchez Graells and Herrera Anchustegui, 'Impact of Public Procurement Aggregation on Competition. Risks, Rationale and Justification for the Rules in Directive 2014/24' [2016].

40 John B. Kirkwood, 'Collusion to Control a Powerful Customer: Amazon, E-Books, and Antitrust Policy' 69 University of Miami Law Review (2014) 1.

41 John B Kirkwood, *Buyer Power and Healthcare Prices* (2015) 1.

42 For some literature dealing with private labels from a legal and economic perspective see: Alastair Gorrie, 'Competition Between Branded and Private Label Goods. Do Competition Concerns Arise when a Customer is also a Competitor?' 27 European Competition Law Review (2006) 217; Ariel Ezrachi and Ulf Bernitz (eds), *Private Labels, Brands and Competition Policy: The Changing Landscape of Retail Competition* (Oxford University Press 2009); Ariel Ezrachi, 'Unchallenged Market Power? The Tale of Supermarkets, Private labels and Competition Law' 33 World Competition (2010) 257; S. Meza and K. Sudhir, 'Do Private Labels Increase Retailer Bargaining Power?' 8 QME-Quant Mark Econ (2010) 333; Chris Doyle and Richard Murgatroyd, 'The Role of Private Labels in Antitrust' 7 Journal of Competition Law and Economics (2011) 631; Ariel Ezrachi and Koen De Jong, 'Buyer power, private labels and the welfare consequences of quality erosion' 33 European Competition Law Review (2012) 257; Wernhard Möschel, 'Market Definition with Branded Goods and Private Label Products' 35 European Competition Law Review (2014) 29.

have decided to exclude private labels from my analysis but recognize it is an area ripe for further legal research.

47. From a temporal perspective, I have chosen to delimit the scope of my research to all the relevant legal sources and academic published material available by *January 1st, 2017* to best reflect the state of the law up to that date.

48. Lastly, in this study I have tried to incorporate all the relevant literature, case law, and legislation available primarily in English, which represents, by far, the language in which the vast majority of relevant academic research has been done regarding buyer power. To a minor extent, I have also resorted to material available in other languages in which I have some linguistic proficiency: Spanish, German, French, Italian and Scandinavian languages.

PART II

BUYER POWER ECONOMICS AND ORDOLIBERAL BUYER POWER POLICY

2

BUYER POWER: MONOPSONY AND BARGAINING POWER, AN ECONOMIC APPROACH

I. Introduction

49. Understanding buyer power economics in its forms of monopsony and bargaining power is a pre-requisite to the analysis of buyer power treatment in EU competition law and policy. In this chapter, I discuss the economics of buying conducts by engaging in a literature review on the matter[43]. In conducting this economic analysis I detach from traditional approaches to buyer power that equate it with monopsony cases[44], or the view that buyer power cases are the mirror image of monopoly cases[45]. Also, I challenge the view that the only positive expression of buyer (bargaining power) is countervailing buyer power or that, as Vogel claimed back in 1998, the concept of buyer

43 Since the late 1990s and, particularly, during the first decade of the 21st century, the application of competition law to buyers has become a topic of interest for academics, legal practitioners, economists and businessmen and courts have seen an increase in buyer power cases being litigated. Arguably, the interest increase in this field has been generated by the emergence of powerful buyers in several economic sectors, among them being the most explored the food retailing. See, among others: OECD Policy Roundtables: Buying Power of Multiproduct Retailers, (1999); Commission and others (2000); Walton (2004-2005); Dobson (2004-2005); Warren S Grimes, 'Buyer Power and Retail Gatekeeper Power: Protecting Competition and The Atomistic Seller' 72 Antitrust Law Journal (2004-2005) 563; Dobson and Chakraborty (2008); Hole, [2008]; OECD Policy Roundtables: Monopsony and Buyer Power, (2009); Ezrachi and De Jong (2012).

44 The opinion of the Bundeskartellamt when stating "the simple monopsony model often does not adequately reflect the reality of procurement markets" is similar in this regard: in Bundeskartellamt *Buyer Power in Competition Law - Status and Perspectives,* Bonn (2008) 2, p. 2.

45 van Doorn; Peter C. Carstensen, 'Emerging Issues in Buyer Power Analysis' 3 Agriculture and Food Committee e-Bulleting, American Bar Association (2012) 2.

power is alien to the economic analysis of competition law[46]. Since the early 2000s there has been a surge in economic literature dealing with buyer power, which attempts to shed light on its competitive effects and that requires further analysis and synthetization.

50. I analyze the economics behind monopsony and bargaining power by reviewing the existing literature in industrial organization, albeit not doing original economic research, due to the scope of this study. My aim is to present a general theory on buyer power that can be resorted to as a guidance for most type of cases, neither anchored on the more common 'model-based', nor 'sectoral-based' approaches by synthetizing the economic state of the art. This general approach also corresponds with the holistic legal analysis I carry out regarding buyer power regulation as I aim to offer a "one-stop shop" of buyer power effects that guides the theories of harm in which the legal analysis is built. Furthermore, this chapter has been written with a legal audience in mind, which explains why I have decided to keep microeconomic modeling to the minimum, focusing on getting the main issues across without compromising the depth of the discussion.

51. My contribution, therefore, consists in clarifying that buyer power is an umbrella term covering monopsony and bargaining power effects, which, despite being connected to buyers, are very different in their nature and welfare effects. This distinction between them means that buyer power has ambiguous economic effects[47]. Furthermore, I contribute with an analysis of the situations in which monopsony and bargaining power arise by *discussing their sources* as well as their *economic effects on welfare*. As this chapter shows, however, in terms of such effects, there is no clear economic picture when it comes to buyer power among economists. In the case of monopsony, there is agreement among the literature that monopsony is an inefficient and anti-competitive purchasing behaviour because it decreases prices below the competitive level by withholding demand, generating an allocative welfare loss due the use of fewer resources[48]. Nevertheless, monopsony rarely occurs because it does not constitute an efficient buying conduct for the purchaser. The same clear cut answer, though, is not to be found regarding bargaining power effects that by and large tend to be welfare enhancing but depend not only on the upstream effects of the purchasing but also on its related downstream effects, which ought to be evaluated by means of a dualistic approach. These downstream effects are

---

46 Louis Vogel, 'Competition Law and Buying Power: The Case for a New Approach in Europe' 19 European Competition Law Review (1998) 4. Also supporting the view that competition economics neglected buyer power issues see: Bundeskartellamt '*Buyer Power in Competition Law - Status and Perspectives*' (2008) 1.

47 Horst Raff and Nicolas Schmitt, 'Buyer Power in International Markets' 79 Journal of International Economics (2009) 222, p. 223; Ioannis Kokkoris and Howard Shelanski, *EU Merger Control: A Legal and Economic Analysis* (Oxford University Press 2014) 408, p. 408.

48 Zhiqi Chen, 'Buyer power: Economic Theory and Antitrust Policy' 22 Research in Law and Economics (2007) 17.

connected to whether or not there is sufficient competition that forces the powerful buyer to pass on the benefits to end consumers in the form of lower prices, increased quantity and quality, and more variety. Furthermore, in the chapter I submit that whenever a powerful buyer is also a powerful retailer it enjoys of an *'hourglass shape'*[49] that increases the anti-competitive risks by a buying conduct. Lastly, a contribution of this chapter is also to remark upon the lack of economic consensus regarding the bargaining power effects, which further limits the ability to provide standard answers that can serve as legal guidance or evidence. This means that, from a legal perspective, the best alternative is to take a cautious approach to buyer (bargaining) power cases and, until further necessary economic analysis is carried out in the future[50], adopt a case-by-case assessment of conducts and effects.

52. In discussing buyer power economics, I have structured this chapter as follows. Section §II discusses buyer power as an umbrella concept covering both monopsony and bargaining power; section §III analyzes the economics of monopsony, presents a model to back up this theory and discusses its sources and the likelihood that it will appear in practice. In section §IV, I discuss the economics of bargaining power, its differences from monopsony and its sources. I then, in section §V, analyze the direct and price effects of buyer power, both in monopsony and bargaining power; while, in section §VI, I discuss the indirect effects of buyer power. Section §VII concludes with a summary of the findings.

II. Buyer power as an umbrella term for competition risks

53. In this study I employ buyer power as an umbrella term to describe two situations that represent different forms of buying and bargaining over purchasing prices: monopsony and bargaining (sensu stricto) power. The term *'buyer power'* has no generally accepted definition in the economic and legal literature and engulfs different types of purchasing strategies[51]. Authors use the

---

49 Term coined by the author.

50 Chris Doyle and Roman Inderst, 'Some Economics on the Treatment of Buyer Power in Antitrust' 28 European Competition Law Review (2007) 210.

51 Also highlighting this, see: Chen (2007) p. 19; Doyle and Inderst (2007) p. 211; Bundeskartellamt *Summary of the Final Report of the Sector Inquiry into the Food Retail Sector*, (2014), 1.

term to only express the idea of either monopsony[52], or bargaining power[53]; or to encapsulate both[54]. In my view, however, the imprecise use of the term has led to misunderstanding and confusion among, particularly but not exclusively, legal scholars.

54. This use of an umbrella term is not free from criticism; for instance, Carstensen argues that making a distinction between bargaining power and monopsony power is "not helpful"[55]. In my view, the distinction *is* helpful because, even though bargaining power may at times be anti-competitive, unlike monopsony power, its exercise tends to be welfare enhancing on most occasions.

55. Following Chen's definition, buyer power *lato sensu* is exerted when a buyer (or a coordinated group of them) is able to reduce purchasing prices in a profitable manner below the supplier's standard selling price. This price reduction can be obtained by either withholding purchases – monopsony – or through bilateral negotiations and pure competitive bargaining to reduce the suppli-

---

52 See using the term buyer power to refer to monopsony, *inter alia*: Manfred Neumann, *Competition Policy: History, Theory and Practice* (Edward Elgar 2001), p. 11 to 12; Grimes (2004-2005); Roger G Noll, '"Buyer Power" and Economic Policy' 72 Antitrust Law Journal (2004-2005) 589; Victor Chimienti, 'The Abuse of Dominance in the new Albanian Competition Act' 26 European Competition Law Review (2005) 151; Frances Dehtmers, 'Collective Dominance under EC Merger Control - After Airtours and the Introduction of Unilateral Effects is there still a Future for Collective Dominance?' 26 European Competition Law Review (2005) 638. See also using the term buyer power mainly referring to monopsony and oligopsony effect and, in my view, somewhat imprecisely to bargaining/countervailing power: David A. Hyman and William E. Kovacic, 'Monopoly, Monopsony, and Market Definition: An Antitrust Perspective on Market Concentration Among Health Insurers' 23 Health Affairs (2004), 25; Jonathan M. Jacobson, 'Monopsony 2013: Still Not Truly Symmetric' December 2013 The Antitrust Source (2013), 1; Robert O'Donoghue and A. Jorge Padilla, *The Law and Economics of Article 102 TFEU* (Hart 2013), p. 840; Mika Oinonen, 'The New 30% Rule: A Viable Solution to Detrimental Buyer Power in the Finnish Grocery Retail Sector?' 10 European Competition Journal (2014), 97.

53 See using the term buyer power to refer to bargaining power: Doyle and Inderst (2007); Paul W. Dobson and Roman Inderst, 'The Waterbed Effect: Where Buying and Selling Power Come Together' Wisconsin Law Review (2008) 331.

54 See, using buyer power as an umbrella term, *inter alia*: Commission and others (2000); Ioannis Kokkoris, 'Buyer Power Assessment in Competition Law: A Boon or a Menace?' 29 World Competition (2006), 139; Chen (2007); Paul W. Dobson and Roman Inderst, 'Differential Buyer Power and the Waterbed Effect: Do Strong Buyers Benefit or Harm Consumers?' 28 European Competition Law Review (2007), 393; Doyle and Inderst (2007); Peter C. Carstensen, 'Buyer Power and Merger Analysis–The Need for Different Metrics' (Workshop on Merger Enforcement held by the Antitrust Division and the Federal Trade Commission), 1; American Antitrust Institute [2008], 96; Dobson and Inderst (2008); OECD '*Policy Roundtables: Monopsony and Buyer Power*' (2009); Ioannis Kokkoris and Leanne Day, 'Buyer Power in UK Merger Control' 30 European Competition Law Review (2009), 176; Dennis W. Carlton and Mark Israel, 'Proper Treatment of Buyer Power in Merger Review' 39 Review of Industrial Organization (2011), 127; Ariel Ezrachi, 'Buying Alliances and Input Price Fixing: In Search of a European Enforcement Standard' 8 Journal of Competition Law and Economics (2012), 47; Ezrachi and De Jong (2012); John B Kirkwood, 'Powerful Buyers and Merger Enforcement' 92 Boston University Law Review (2012), 1485; European Competition Network, *ECN Activities in the Food Sector* (2012), para. 73; Lars Henriksson, *Countervailing Buyer Power in EU Antitrust Analysis* (October 17, 2012); Henriksson, *Swedish National Report: The Grocery Retail Market in Sweden: Is Antitrust Efficiently Handling this Market?* (2013); Ariel Ezrachi and Mark Williams, 'Competition Law and the Regulation of Buyer Power and Buyer Cartels in China and Hong Kong' 9 Asian Journal of Comparative Law (2013) 295; Bundeskartellamt '*Summary of the Final Report of the Sector Inquiry into the Food Retail Sector*' (2014); van Doorn, p. 76-84; Kirkwood (2014); Kokkoris and Shelanski, [2014] 407 to 441; Ezrachi [2014], p. 435; Dennis W. Carlton, Mary Coleman and Mark Israel, 'Buyer Power in Merger Review' in Roger D. Blair and D. Daniel Sokol (eds), *The Oxford Handbook of International Antitrust Economics*, Vol. 1 (Oxford University Press 2015), p. 530; Antonio Robles Martín-Laborda, 'La Cadena Alimentaria: Cuando el Poder de Mercado lo Tiene el Comprador' (2015) accessed 12.10.2015.

55 Peter C. Carstensen, 'Buyer Power and the Horizontal Merger Guidelines: Minor Progress on an Important Issue' 14 University of Pennsylvania Journal of Business Law (2012) 775, p. 788.

er's prices and obtain better contractual conditions[56]. In both cases, the buyer captures a higher share of surplus when negotiating with the supplier that, absent buyer power, would have been retained by the supplier[57]. These better terms and conditions, contrary to Grimes' view, can be the result of efficient outcomes, as occurs with bargaining power[58].

56. This proposed definition, however, only captures pricing effects of buyer power. Additionally, powerful buyers may also capture non-price contractual benefits such as, for example, slotting allowances, listing charges, preferential treatment, contribution to retail expenses, or transfer of contractual risks, benefits which are often associated with unfair purchasing practices and which I discuss at length in chapter 8[59]. The nature of the non-price benefits will largely depend on the industry and type of contract at hand as they will derive from the outcome of negotiation between parties that enjoy bargaining power and are usually the result of offers and counteroffers, as the Court of Appeals of Düsseldorf remarked[60].

57. Also in general, buyer power as a whole has two main sources: first, the existence of alternative suppliers that would allow the buyer to obtain better price conditions from the buyer, and second, each party's own bargaining skill. In sections §III and §IV of this chapter, I discuss the specific sources for each of the forms of buyer power.

58. However, monopsony and bargaining power are different types of buyer power. The *main difference between monopsony and bargaining* power lies in *whether there is a reduction of purchases – withholding effect – to affect the price paid by the buyer*[61]. For monopsony to exist, the purchasing conduct must unavoid-

---

56 Chen (2007), p. 19. Also following Chen's definition see: Kirkwood 'Powerful Buyers and Merger Enforcement' (2012), p. 1493. A similar definition is also used by Dobson in Dobson (2004-2005), p. 532; Dobson and Inderst (2007), p. 393.

57 Carlton and Israel (2011), p. 128.

58 To Grimes, buyer power is the ability of the buyer to "significantly influence the terms of a purchase for reasons other than efficiency", Grimes (2004-2005), p. 565. This holds true only for monopsony cases and not for bargaining power cases.

59 Dobson (2004-2005), p. 532; Alberto Pera and Valentina Bonfitto, 'Buyer Power in Anti-trust Investigations: A Review' 32 European Competition Law Review (2011) 414, p. 414; Oinonen (2014), p. 101.

60 Düsseldorf Appellate Court in Decision of 18 November 2015 *EDEKA/Plus-Übernahme* revoking a Decision B2-58/09 *Edeka Konditionenforderungen* - Verstoß gegen das "Anzapfverbot", 3 July 2014 by the Bundeskartellamt. Summary available at: http://www.olg-duesseldorf.nrw.de/behoerde/presse/Presse_aktuell/20151118_PM_Edeka/index.php. See the discussion of this case by the author in an invited entry in the blog "Competencia y Regulación" of Prof. Antonio Robles Martín-Laborda entitled "El Acuerdo DIA-EROSKI: Alianza compradora o cártel de compra?" (The DIA-EROSKI Agreement: Buying alliance or buyers cartel?)", http://derechocompetencia.blogspot.no/2015/12/el-acuerdo-dia-eroski-alianza.html.

61 This also appears to be the distinction used by the Commission to define what constitutes a monopsony practice, as stressed in the Horizontal Merger Guidelines where monopsony is linked to a withholding effect, see Guidelines on the assessment of horizontal mergers under the Council Regulation on the control of concentrations between undertakings [2004] OJ C 31/5, paras 61-63. See also remarking that buyer power (monopsony) may significantly impede competition when "it is likely to *lead to a reduction in output of the final products* or the foreclosure of competitors of the merged entity", Commission Decision of 21/12/2005 declaring a concentration to be compatible with the common market (Case No COMP/M.3968 - *Sovion/Südfleisch*) according to Council Regulation (EC) No 139/2004 [2005], para. 37 (emphasis added).

ably require a demand withholding effect (i.e. purchase less quantity), whereas in bargaining power cases, the reduction in purchasing price is obtained according to the negotiation strength of each party, where a redistribution of profit between buyers and sellers takes places leaving "nothing on the table" (i.e. there is less or no allocative efficiency loss), if parties resort to complex contracts using two-part tariffs, instead of linear pricing contracts.

59. This distinction is not shared by all legal scholars dealing with buyer power. For van Doorn, for instance, the main difference between monopsony and buyer power lies in the fact that monopsony power is only exercised against suppliers with no seller power, while bargaining power occurs among parties with market power[62]. This approach, however, overlooks the fact that a buyer with monopsony power could still withhold purchases, even if the supplier has seller market power when the supply curve is upward slopping to decrease the price it pays. Nevertheless, van Doorn also admits that for monopsony power to exist purchases must be withheld, while for bargaining power there is none[63].

60. Consequently, and to facilitate the understanding of the terminology, I will use term buyer power whenever I am referring to the two variants in a joint manner. And to refer to a particular expression of it I will refer to either monopsony or bargaining power.

61. One of the most relevant buyer power characteristics is that *its exercise will affect the upstream and downstream markets*, which, therefore, requires in my view a *dualistic approach to buyer power that captures both effects*[64]. In this study I define the *upstream market* as the market in which the buyer acquires the input it needs to offer a processed good or some service in a different market, by either transforming it or by consuming it. The *downstream market*, herein, is where the buyer offers its goods to its customers (which may or not be final consumers), as for example occurs when a supermarket buys processed milk from farmers (upstream market) and sells it to end consumers (downstream markets).

62. On the upstream market, buyer power affects the competitive conditions between the buyer, rival buyers and suppliers, and in particular the contractual conditions between the buyer and its supplier. Additionally, buyer power may indirectly affect, in positive or negative terms, market conditions in the downstream market and, therefore, have an impact on end consumers. For example,

62 van Doorn, p. 78.

63 Ibid, p. 78- 102.

64 Chen (2007), p. 20 Also remarking that buyer power is combined with seller market power, see: Korah and O'Sullivan, [2002], p. 46. See also stressing that monopsony causes inefficiency both in a consumer welfare and total welfare perspective: Roger D. Blair and John E. Lopatka, 'Predatory Buying and the Antitrust Laws' 2 Utah Law Review (2008) 415, p. 443-444.

buyer power problems in the upstream market may imply that competition among rival buyers and suppliers is adversely affected, with the consequence that there is a diminishment on innovation, quality of price competition intensity, that, in the medium and long run, would hurt consumers, even if there is no direct immediate downstream end consumer harm caused by the purchasing conduct.

63. Connected to this impact on upstream and downstream markets, buyer power problems are most likely to arise between parties that regularly trade between each other due the importance the buyer signifies for the supplier, precisely because the close connection between them; although not necessarily due to a powerful buyer having a monopolistic position as a retailer or as a buyer, as simplified by Faull and Nikpay[65]. This explains why buyer power not only may be used as with an exploitative aim vis-à-vis suppliers but can also act as an exclusionary device against rival buyers that may or may not compete as retailers in the same downstream market.

64. Furthermore, buyer power cases arise when the purchasing undertaking acquires an input, processes it and sells it as an output, acting as a retailer or middleman. Thus, in buyer-supplier situations there tends to be contractual relations of considerable length, with fairly frequent contact, and, on occasions, investment by the parties to meet the needs of their counterparts. The importance of the trade relationship among parties is an element that explains how buyer power is exercised among undertakings and why exploitative monopsony power tends to be a rare phenomenon.

65. From a legal perspective, *the exercise of both monopsony and bargaining power is under the scope of application of EU competition law*, as these conducts are capable of creating market inefficiencies, and affecting competitive conditions and 'competition as such' that may cause competitive harm to end consumers, rival buyers and suppliers alike. Furthermore, buyer power is a competition concern affecting all areas covered by EU competition law. It can be created an exerted by coordinated undertakings that join their purchasing efforts through buyer agreements or tacit coordination[66], or also exercised by a unilateral and dominant undertaking, or it can be the expected outcome of a merger among buying undertakings. However, the fact that buyer power is present in different areas of competition law does not mean that the economics of buyer power changes. In fact, from an economic perspective, buyer power remains largely the same in any of these different scenarios and this justifies a general approach to buyer power economics.

---

65 Jonathan Faull and Ali Nikpay, *The EC Law of Competition* (Oxford University Press 1999), para. 3-110.

66 Neumann, [2001], p. 156.

III. Monopsony, the model

66. The traditional or 'old'[67] angle given to buyer power issues is focused on the intuitively appealing but rather simplified monopsony model as one example of bargaining over purchasing prices inefficiently. Literature describes monopsony as the mirror image of monopoly[68]. This section shows that even though the figures are analogous, they are not entirely symmetrical[69]. I first present a discussion of the monopsony model, followed by an example illustrating the exercise of monopsony power. The section also discusses how monopsony arises and ends with a discussion of whether monopsony is problematic in reality.

67. According to the textbook microeconomic model[70], monopsony exists when there is a single buyer in the market enjoying substantial purchasing market power[71]. This sole buyer – or coordinated oligopsony[72] – could be facing a myriad of fringe suppliers[73], part of a highly competitive upstream market, in which none of them enjoys substantial market power, or facing a single supplier with substantial market power and could thus be in a bilateral monopoly

---

67 Using the term of "older literature" to refer to the discussion of buyer power as pure monopsony issues see: Bundeskartellamt '*Summary of the Final Report of the Sector Inquiry into the Food Retail Sector*' (2014), p. 9.

68 In my view, the use of this or similar expressions denotes the negative approach that is shown regarding monopsony situations by the relevant academic literature. Examples of such expressions are to be found in, for example: Blair and Lopatka (2008), p. 415; Capps, who also uses the expression "mirror image" when comparing monopsony to monopoly in Cory S. Capps, 'Buyer Power in Health Plan Mergers' 6 Journal of Competition Law and Economics (2009) 375, p. 376. The German and US reports to the OECD use the same term in OECD '*Policy Roundtables: Monopsony and Buyer Power*' (2009), respectively. Waterman uses the expression of "flip side" borrowing it from Carlton and Perloff when stating: "In a standard textbook treatment, monopsony is a flip side version of monopoly", in David Waterman, 'Local Monopsony and Free Riders' 8 Information Economics and Policy (1996) 337. A similar expression is used by the US Department of Justice and Federal Trade Commission *Horizontal Merger Guidelines* Washington D.C. (2010) 2, when stating: "[e]nhancement of market power by buyers, sometimes called 'monopsony power', has adverse effects comparable to enhancement of market power by sellers". In similar terms see: Steven C Salop, 'Anticompetitive Overbuying by Power Buyers' 72 Antitrust Law Journal (2004-2005) 669. See also, US Supreme Court case *Weyerhauser Co. v. Ross-Simmons Hardwood Lumber* part III. No.- 05-381, (549 U.S. 312 (2007)).

69 Jacobson (2013).

70 For example, see the treatment of the 'classic' monopsony model in microeconomics texts in, *inter alia*, James P. Quirk, *Intermediate Microeconomics* (Science Research Associates 1987) 358 to 362; Robert H. Frank and Amy Jocelyn Glass, *Microeconomics and Behavior* (McGraw-Hill 1999) 503 to 508; Hal R. Varian, *Intermediate Microeconomics: A Modern Approach* (W.W. Norton & Co. 2006) 471 to 474; B. Douglas Bernheim and Michael D. Whinston, *Microeconomics* (McGraw-Hill Irwin 2008) 648 to 652; Robert S. Pindyck and Daniel L. Rubinfeld, *Microeconomics* (Pearson Prentice Hall 2009) 373 to 381.

71 It should be noted that, for the Commission, a monopsony includes the situation in which the exercise of the market power is carried out by a group of coordinated buyers. In my opinion, such a figure corresponds, technically speaking, to a buyer's cartel or the situation of oligopsony. The Commission defined monopsony power, in a very broad manner, as a situation that "emerge[s] when a buyer, or a coordinated group of buyers such as a buying alliance, purchases a charge share of an upstream supplier's outputs that the suppliers ability to switch to alternatives quickly are eliminated. As a result, the monopsony buyer can obtain lower input prices or favourable contract terms, typically by withholding (or threatening to withhold) purchases". European Commission's contribution in OECD '*Policy Roundtables: Monopsony and Buyer Power*' (2009), p. 225.

72 The effects and analysis made here also apply to oligopsony cases. Similarly, see: Neumann, [2001], p. 154; Noll (2004-2005), p. 589; Chen (2007), p. 22.

73 Jonathan Parker and Adrian Majumdar, *UK Merger Control* (Hart 2011), p. 562.

situation[74]. Furthermore, monopsonist buyers can be found at any level of the production chain[75], although they are often retailing firms that compete in a downstream market[76].

68. In any of these situations, the buyer will exercise its buyer market power by withholding purchases (i.e. buying less)[77] to decrease the purchasing price it pays for a good below the competitive levels[78]. The price is set by the buyer fixing a purchasing price it is willing to pay for the input, *in a take-it or leave-it offer*[79], or by refusing to negotiate on price. In such a setting, the monopsonist becomes a price-maker[80], which negotiates based on quantity and/or price[81]. For the monopsonist withholding demand is profitable because it allows it to lower the market-wide purchasing prices[82] transferring profits

---

74 Noll (2004-2005), p. 602-606; OECD '*Policy Roundtables: Monopsony and Buyer Power*' (2009), p. 35-36. A bilateral monopoly takes place, in its simplest form, whenever a single supplier in the upstream market faces a single buyer who is also a monopolist in the downstream market. On a non-cooperative solution the welfare outcome depends on who has the lead in the negotiation by setting a price whereas the counterpart simply determines quantity. If it is the buyer, then the seller becomes a price taker and vice versa, see: ibid; Office of Fair Trading *Research Paper 16: The Welfare Consequences of the Exercise of Buyer Power,* (1998) para 5.3; Roger D. Blair and Jeffrey L. Harrison, *Monopsony in Law and Economics* (Cambridge University Press 2010) 126. However, such a solution does not maximize the profits for both parties and, therefore, they would rather enter into a negotiated agreement setting by jointly determining the optimal quantity and price terms and distributing the surplus, OECD '*Policy Roundtables: Monopsony and Buyer Power*' (2009), p. 35. In practice, however, the intersection will be given by the bargaining outcome among parties. Noll even goes further and claims that, because of this, non-cooperative bilateral monopolies "can probably never arise" in Noll (2004-2005) 602. Ideally, this occurs whenever marginal revenue downstream equals to marginal cost upstream. Also in a similar vein stressing that bilateral monopolies very rarely occur in practice, see Henriksson, *Countervailing Buyer Power in EU Antitrust Analysis*.

75 J. M. Jacobson and G. J. Dorman, 'Joint Purchasing, Monopsony and Antitrust' XXXVI The Antitrust Bulletin (1991) 1, p. 5.

76 American Bar Association, *Market Power Handbook: Competition Law and Economic Foundations* (ABA Section of Antitrust Law ed, 2012) 52, p. 52; O'Donoghue and Padilla, [2013] p. 840.

77 Salop labels such demand withholding practice as "underbuying", arguing that "[m]onopsony conduct involves 'underbuying' an input to profitably reduce its price", Salop (2004-2005), p. 672; see also using this term: P. Areeda, Herbert Hovenkamp and J. Solow, *Antitrust Law: An Analysis of Antitrust Principles and their Application* Vol. IIB (3rd edn, Wolters Kluwer 1995), p. 442.

78 A similar definition is provided by the OECD when stating: "[a]firm as monopsony power if its shares of purchases in the upstream input market is sufficiently large that it can cause the market price to fall by purchasing less and cause it to rise by purchasing more". Note, however, that it is stressed that monopsony under this definition can occur even if there is more than a single buyer in the market, in OECD '*Policy Roundtables: Monopsony and Buyer Power*' (2009), p. 9. As I describe infra in the competition regulation of monopsony, this purchasing price needs to be *below competitive levels* in order for it to be considered anticompetitive. See, for example the contribution of Canadian Competition Bureau as well as Germany's contribution in ibid, p. 142 and 176, respectively. See also: Andrew Gavil, William Kovacic and Jonathan Baker, *Antitrust Law in Perspective: Cases, Concepts and Problems in Competition Policy* (2nd edn, Thomson West 2008) 517 to 518, p. 517-518; Kirkwood (2014), p. 35.

79 Kirkwood 'Powerful Buyers and Merger Enforcement' (2012), p. 1501; Carstensen 'Buyer Power and the Horizontal Merger Guidelines: Minor Progress on an Important Issue' (2012), p. 796.

80 The main characteristic of both a monopolist and a monopsonist is that, in contrast to buyers and sellers in a competitive market, they are price makers instead of price takers. See, for instance: Bernheim and Whinston, [2008], p. 472. In contrast, see the concept of perfect competition and price taker in John P. Burkett, *Microeconomics: Optimization, Experiments, and Behavior* (Oxford University Press 2006), p. 60; OECD '*Policy Roundtables: Monopsony and Buyer Power*' (2009), p. 26.

81 Bundeskartellamt '*Summary of the Final Report of the Sector Inquiry into the Food Retail Sector*' (2014), p. 9.

82 This is, not only the monopsonist benefits from the reduction in price but it affects all other buyers. John B Kirkwood, 'Buyer Power and Exclusionary Conduct: Should Brooke Group Set the Standards for Buyer-Induced Price Discrimination and Predatory Bidding?' 72 Antitrust Law Journal (2004-2005) 625, p. 638.

from suppliers to the buyer[83], and which may lead to higher prices to end consumers due to scarcity[84].

69. Consequently, monopsony power generates a reduction of welfare due to loss of allocative efficiency because too few resources are employed[85]. As few resources are employed there are unrealized gains from additional trade[86]. This misallocation of resources holds irrespectively of the downstream market situation; this is: *monopsony is always inefficient*[87].

A. Isolation's supermarket

70. In order to clearly grasp the monopsony effects, I employ an example that illustrates this problem[88]. In a secluded town named Isolation, there is a sole supermarket. Isolation's Supermarket is the only buyer of agricultural goods produced by the local farmers who have no other alternative buyers as they are too far away from them, making transportation costs too high. Also, Isolation's Supermarket faces no possible competitors entering the market because the town is too remote and Isolation's Supermarket has also gained the reputation of being a fierce competitor when confronted by any kind of potential entrants, for instance by entering into predatory conducts. Additionally, Isolation's mayor, by means of an administrative decree, gave Isolation's Supermarket an exclusive license to operate in the town for the next 20 years. Hence, Isolation's Supermarket possesses a legal and a *de facto* monopoly as the sole food retailer in the town. Therefore, not only does it have buyer power but also it also has substantial seller market power.

71. The board of directors of Isolation's Supermarket behaves like a rational economic agent and pursues the maximization of the undertaking's profits as a buyer[89]. To do so, and following monopsony theory, they decide to exploit

---

83 OECD '*Policy Roundtables: Monopsony and Buyer Power*' (2009), p. 9. Note, however, that higher prices in a downstream market will only occur in the event the buyer uses the acquired input to produce goods and/or services that will be sold later on or offered in a downstream market. In principle, no higher prices in a downstream market will be generated if the input is acquired for inner consumption.

84 Competition Commission - UK *The Supply of Groceries in the UK Market Investigation*, London (2008), para. 9.68.

85 Blair and Harrison, [2010], p. 44. The same negative consequence is pointed out by the OECD in OECD '*Policy Roundtables: Monopsony and Buyer Power*' (2009), p. 9; Jacobson (2013), p. 2.

86 Office of Fair Trading '*Research Paper 16: The Welfare Consequences of the Exercise of Buyer Power*' (1998), p. 12.

87 Jacobson (2013), p. 3; Carlton, Coleman and Israel [2015], p. 531.

88 A somewhat similar case was handled by the European Commission in the *Friesland Foods/Campina* merger Decision, which involved the merger of two dairy cooperatives in the Netherlands for the collection of raw milk. See: Summary of Commission Decision of 17 December 2008 declaring a concentration compatible with the common market and the functioning of the EEA Agreement (Case COMP/M.5046 — *Friesland Foods/Campina*) [2009] OJ C 75/21. See discussing also this case: Ariel Ezrachi and Maria Ioannidou, 'Buyer Power in European Union Merger Control' 10 European Competition Journal (2014) 69, p. 80-81.

89 As Noll describes it: "[…] the motivation behind monopsony behavior is to transfer wealth in the form of economic rents from one side of the market to the other", Noll (2004-2005), p. 589.

their suppliers by offering a purchasing price that is below the competitive level, which allows them to reap extra profits as a buyer. Also, as there is no competition as a food retailer Isolation Supermarket can also exert seller market power to reap additional benefits vis-à-vis end consumers.

72. To exert monopsony power, the supply curve the buyer faces has to be upward sloping. This is to say, the more beef they buy, the more they have to pay for each additional unit; however, if they decide to restrict the amount they buy they are able to decrease the purchasing prices below the price set by the competitive level[90]. This ability to purchase beef below the competitive price is strengthened because beef is a perishable product: once a cow is killed for a portion of its beef the rest will have to be sold or it will go to waste. This puts farmers in almost a take-it-or-leave-it situation to minimize their loss[91].

73. To maximize Isolation's Supermarket profits the board decides to employ its buyer power by acquiring fewer kilos of beef than they would normally require, driving the purchasing price of all units down[92]. This practice affects both farmers and consumers alike. On the one hand, farmers must kill a cow even if they are only selling 70% of the meat, and end consumers have less quantity readily available for their own consumption, which – provided demand remains the same and there are no substitutes – will result in an upward rising price in the downstream market. Additionally, the local farmers have no alternative as they are presented with take-it-or-leave-it contract[93]. Either they offer their produce to Isolation's Supermarket or their beef will perish and, in the long run, they will be forced out of the farm business as they are unable to cover their costs[94].

74. As Isolation's Supermarket is a price maker, it can select any level of price combinations (p) depending of the amount of beef that will be purchased (b). However, the profit maximization strategy for the supermarket will be when the

---

90 As it will be explained further on, a requirement for monopsony power to occur is the existence of an upward-sloping supply curve, this is, the curve is convex in its form. If the supply curve is concave (downward-sloping) or flat, then the buyer cannot influence the prices he or she pays for the goods and/or services by reducing the amount he or she purchases.

91 Also considering the threat of purchase delay as a source of buyer power see: Guidelines on the assessment of horizontal mergers under the Council Regulation on the control of concentrations between undertakings [2004] OJ C 31/5, para. 65; Korah and O'Sullivan, [2002], p. 49; European Commission, *Study on the Legal Framework Covering Business-To-Business Unfair Trading Practices in the Retail Supply Chain* (2014), p. 28.

92 The monopsonist is aware of their powerful situation and, therefore, willingly decides to make use of their market power to maximize their profits. A similar view is expressed by Jacobson and Dorman when stating: "[t]he essence of monopsony is the firm's recognition that its own buying activities have an influence on the input price and that by altering its buying pattern the firm is able to enhance its profits at the expense of its suppliers", Jacobson and Dorman (1991), p. 6.

93 The Dutch Competition Authority uses the term "like it or lump it" contract for similar situations observed in two bargaining power cases related to insurance agreements between medical doctors and dentists. See The Netherlands contribution in OECD '*Policy Roundtables: Monopsony and Buyer Power*' (2009), p. 207-211.

94 This implies that the supply demand is inelastic. As will be explained infra, the elasticity of supply is a relevant factor for monopsony to exist. On this point, see Pindyck and Rubinfeld, [2009], p. 377-378.

marginal revenue from purchasing one kilo of beef equals the marginal cost that represents buying that same kilo of beef[95]. In terms of the representation of this effect on a graph (as shown below), the amount of kilos of beef to be purchased will be determined by the intersections of the demand curve with the marginal cost curve, therefore generating a price (Pm) and an amount of beef (Bm)[96]. By doing so, the supermarket reduces the prices paid for each kilo of beef due to the withholding effect. This is best seen with the following graph:

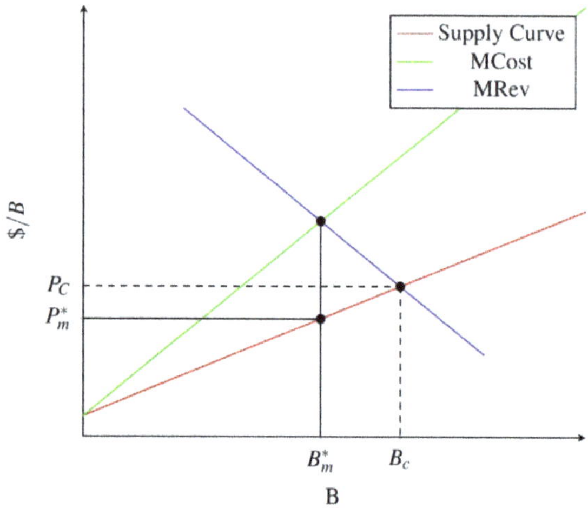

Figure 1: Isolation's Supermarket - Monopsony[97]

75. Consequently, Isolation's Supermarket purchases fewer kilos of beef in order to pay less and maximize profits while reducing its expenditure. For the buyer, this reduces costs when compared to a situation pre-monopsony, and under very specific circumstances it may increase societal welfare, if a Williamson tradeoff model is used[98].

---

95 Quirk, [1987], p. 359 and 377; Bernheim and Whinston, [2008], p. 472. Pyndick and Rubinfeld use a different terminology but to the same ends when stating that "the monopsonist purchases up to the point where marginal expenditure intersects marginal value", see Pindyck and Rubinfeld, [2009], p. 373-381; Blair and Harrison arrive at the same conclusion, employing different terminology, when stating: "[...] it will hire [labor] where the marginal factor cost (MFC) equals demand (D), which is the value of the marginal product", Blair and Harrison, [2010] 44, p. 44.

96 Roger D. Blair and D. Daniel Sokol, 'The Rule of Reason and the Goals of Antitrust: An Economic Approach' 78 Antitrust Law Journal (2012) 471, p. 493. Contrast this outcome with the 'standard outcome' in a perfectly competitive market in which the price to be paid by the buyer is represented by the intersections of the curves of supply and demand.

97 This graphic has been made based on Pindyck and Rubinfeld, [2009], p. 377-378.

98 From a welfare perspective, the gains originating from the cost reduction resulting from the monopsony exercise may under very strict circumstances offset the deadweight loss generated by the allocative inefficiency due to the lesser amount of goods purchased and, therefore, be welfare enhancing from a suppliers' perspective or even a total welfare perspective, in line with the Williamson tradeoff model: Oliver E. Williamson, 'Economies as an Antitrust Defense: The Welfare Tradeoffs' 58 The American Economic Review (1968) 18. I would like to thank Daniel J. Gifford for bringing this to my attention.

76. For Isolation's Supermarket, the monopsony gains are represented by the sum of A minus B (A – B), while the farmers' loss is represented by A plus C (A + C). This surplus is captured from the portion that, under competitive market circumstances, would have corresponded to the seller[99]. In sum, society is worse off by the sum of B + C, which is the deadweight loss generated by monopsony power[100]. Furthermore, the monopsony effect is detrimental for society, as there is an allocative efficiency loss due to the unused kilos of beef[101].

77. In contrast, a competitive market in which neither the seller nor the buyer has market power would lead to a very different outcome when compared to the monopsony situation. In this scenario, the supermarket would decide to purchase more kilos of beef (Bc) at the intersection of the supply and demand curves and, therefore, pay a higher price per kilo (Pc) and maximize social welfare[102], represented by the sum of consumer and producer surplus. Here, all factors are exploited to their maximum capacity, resulting in an efficient outcome thanks to the competitive pressure in which the buyer maximizes purchases in the upstream market leading to further sales in the downstream market, and which is equivalent to a state of competitive market equilibria and more resources are efficiently employed.

B. The conditions for monopsony power

78. Monopsony power can be exerted only if several conditions are present. In this section I discuss which of them must exist in order for monopsony to occur. One aspect found in my research is that there is no academic consensus when it comes to all these monopsony sources[103]. However, there is consensus regarding the following necessary conditions:

i) the existence of a sole buyer or few buyers (oligopsony);

ii) an upward sloping supply curve;

iii) an inelastic supply curve;

---

99 Jacobson and Dorman (1991), p. 5.

100 Section §V.A of the present chapter deals in detail with the negative welfare effects derived from monopsony power.

101 For a similar view, see Quirk, [1987], p. 360, who states that "[u]nder monopsony with an upward-sloping supply curve for the input, the price paid per unit of the input is lower that it would be under perfect competition, and fewer units are hired"; Blair and Sokol (2012), p. 493.

102 Blair and Harrison, [2010], p. 43.

103 For example in Office of Fair Trading '*Research Paper 16: The Welfare Consequences of the Exercise of Buyer Power*' (1998), para. 4.5, there is a reference to only three requirements, namely: upward sloping supply curve, high share on the purchase market, and barriers to entry to the market and not considering, at least explicitly, for example, the elasticity factor. On the other hand, Chen argues that the only condition necessary to exercise monopsony power in a detrimental way is that supply curves are upward sloping, see in Chen (2007), p. 22.

iv) economic rents to be extracted;[104]

v) little to no possibility of entry into the purchasing market by competitors.

79. Assessing the existence of these conditions is of importance from an enforcement perspective because absent these circumstances the case is unlikely to be that of a monopsony, but instead a case of bargaining power, with all the welfare effect implications this distinction has.

a. A sole buyer – or a group of a few buyers –with substantial market power

80. The "textbook" monopsony model is characterized by the presence of a sole buyer, however, it is possible that monopsony may arise as a consequence of coordination among buyers in a market that will now act as single entity[105]. As there are no other buyers to resort to, suppliers have no alternative sources of demand[106]. Therefore, market shares – which represent buyers' size – provide some indication of monopsony power, although other requirements are to be factored in. Conversely, when there are many competing buyers on the buying side of the market then they are unable to exert monopsony power, as the suppliers have alternative sources of demand[107].

b. An upward sloping supply curve

81. Monopsony additionally requires that the supply curve the buyer faces must be upward sloping or convex[108]. Due to scarcity factors, the intuition is that the more goods are purchased, the higher the price is to be paid or that there is presence of decreasing returns of scale. This implies that, with each additional purchase, the purchasing price of all the units of goods/services increases. Classic examples of industries with upward-slopping supply curves are labor markets and agriculture[109]. For instance, if Isolation's Supermarket buys 100

---

104 Noll (2004-2005), p. 592.

105 "There are three necessary conditions for the exertion of monopsony power: (1) the buyer or group of buyers must represent a substantial portion of total purchases in the market; (2) the supply curve must be upward sloping; and (3) there must be some barriers to entry into the buyers' market" Jacobson and Dorman (1991), p. 10. I, instead, prefer stating that the buyer(s) enjoys market power than rather limiting the requirement to sole market share as a purchaser.

106 As Blair and Harrison point out: "[t]here is no doubt that the market share of the large buyer is an important determinant of buyer power" in Blair and Harrison, [2010], p. 58. In similar terms, see Kokkoris, borrowing from the work of the Office of Fair Trading, when stating that it is a requirement that "[…] the buyers contribute to a substantial portion of purchases in the market" in Kokkoris (2006), p. 144; and see Office of Fair Trading '*Research Paper 16: The Welfare Consequences of the Exercise of Buyer Power*' (1998), para. 4.5.

107 Pindyck and Rubinfeld, [2009], p. 378.

108 For a general treatment of supply curves see, *inter alia,* Jagdish N. Sheth and Arun Sharma, 'Supplier Relationships: Emerging Issues and Challenges' 26 Industrial Marketing Management (1997) 91; Varian, [2006], p 5-6 and 383-422; Pindyck and Rubinfeld, [2009], p. 22-23 and 284-306. The supply curve in a market is formed by the sum of all the cost curves of all suppliers of an input as discussed by Jacobson (2013), p. 5.

109 Carstensen 'Emerging Issues in Buyer Power Analysis' (2012); Jacobson (2013), p. 6.

kilos of beef, it will pay a per unit price €10.25, but it if acquires 101 kilos then the unit price increases to €10.30[110].

82. Thanks to an upward sloping supply curve, a monopsonist is able to decrease the purchasing prices by acquiring a lesser amount of input from its suppliers[111]. If the supply curve is either flat or downward slopping, the monopsonist cannot exercise any influence in reducing the price as it will either remain constant and/or decrease in price when purchasing more units[112].

83. Jacobson and Dorman remark, nonetheless, that in practice upward sloping supply curves are not as common as flat supply curves as in many industries "increased production can be achieved at roughly constant per unit costs"[113]. Upward sloping supply curves may be present, for example, on increasing-costs industries in which the production costs increases as per each unit produced wherein the effect of diminishing returns dominate[114], or where labor is a key factor[115]. However, it is likely that upward slopping supply curves are more prevalent than as suggested by these authors.

c. *The supply curve must be inelastic*

84. Additionally, the supply curve must be inelastic[116]. For monopsony to be present the suppliers have little to no alternatives than selling to the monopsonist, even if the prices for the goods or services they trade have their selling price drastically reduced[117]. In other words, there are few alternative sources of de-

---

110 See the comparison to a flat or horizontal supply curve in Jacobson and Dorman (1991), p. 11. See also: Bernheim and Whinston, [2008], p. 472.

111 Varian, [2006], p. 648.

112 Supply curves can be flat or downward sloping in industries with positive economies of scale or where marginal costs are flat or decreasing, such as, for example, the case of constant-cost industries and decreasing cost industries, such as manufacturing markets, software or pharmaceuticals. See *inter alia*: F. M. Scherer and David Ross, *Industrial Market Structure and Economic Performance* (Houghton Mifflin 1990), p. 97-141. See also: Dennis W. Carlton and Jeffrey M. Perloff, *Modern Industrial Organization* (Pearson/Addison Wesley 2005), p. XXIII, 822 s.: ill. For a discussion on supply structures in industrial organization, see: Jeffrey Church and Roger Ware, *Industrial Organization: A Strategic Approach* (McGraw-Hill 2000), p. 22-25.

113 Jacobson and Dorman (1991), p. 12. More recently, Jacobson held that "[t]his is a condition that, although critical to monopsony analysis, does not always hold in the real world", in Jacobson (2013), p. 4. Cf this with Shea who argues that upward sloping supply curves are not that rare: John Shea, 'Do Supply Curves Slope Up?' 108 The Quarterly Journal of Economics (1993) 1.

114 Pindyck and Rubinfeld, [2009], p. 300-301.

115 Jacobson and Dorman (1991), p. 13.

116 The same view was expressed by the Canadian Competition Bureau when stating: "[…] monopsony includes within its meaning situations where supply is perfectly inelastic such that a decrease in price below competitive levels does not result in a decrease in output" in OECD '*Policy Roundtables: Monopsony and Buyer Power*' (2009), p. 142. Elasticity is the measure of the sensitivity of one variable (price) to another (supply). Elasticity describes the change that will occur when the price of a good/service, for instance beef, rises and whether people will purchase less, the same or more of it. Elasticity can be elastic or inelastic. A demand will be elastic, when after, say, an increase in price of beef, the demand drops substantially. Whereas, demand will be inelastic when the increase in price is not translated into a reduction of demand. For a detailed discussion on elasticity in competition law see: Bishop and Walker, [2010], para. 11-001 to 11-038; Niels, Jenkins and Kavanagh, [2011], p. 34-37.

117 Neumann, [2001], p. 12.

mand for the supplier, or there are no other uses for its product[118]. Going back to the Isolation's Supermarket example, the farmers are constrained to selling their produce to the supermarket, even with the reduction in purchasing prices, because there are no other demand sources for acquisition of the goods and, therefore there is an inelastic supply. Thanks to this need to sell at almost any price, the monopsonist can obtain the price reduction[119].

d. The existence of economic rents that can be extracted by the monopsonist

85. According to Noll, monopsony power can only exist when the supplier has supracompetitive rents that can be extracted, which implies a transfer of wealth from the supplier to the buyer[120]. Rents are necessary as their existence allows the buyer to gain surplus that would have otherwise been retained by the producer under normal market circumstances[121]. The transferred rent from the suppliers to the buyer can be observed in the Isolation Supermarket model by a portion of the A + C areas that are lost by the sellers and appropriated by the monopsonist.

e. Entry barriers to the buyer's side of the market

86. Lastly, monopsony demands the existence of entry barriers[122] to the buyer's market[123]. In their absence other buyers would enter the market or other current buyers would expand their capacity to extract the extraordinary monopsonistic gains, in a similar fashion to which entry would occur in a monopolistic market. The more alternative demand sources there are, the less chance buyers have of making the suppliers' curve inelastic and forcing the price reduction.

---

118 For a similar argument see the Canadian contribution in OECD '*Policy Roundtables: Monopsony and Buyer Power*' (2009), p. 142. Also see Hungary's contribution in ibid, p. 185; Pindyck and Rubinfeld, [2009], p. 378.

119 Pindyck and Rubinfeld, [2009], p. 377-378; Kirkwood (2014), p. 35.

120 For Noll, a rent is present in a determined market when "in the aggregate, suppliers of the product receive more revenues than are necessary to introduce them to provide the quantity of goods that is sold", Noll (2004-2005), p. 592

121 OECD '*Policy Roundtables: Monopsony and Buyer Power*' (2009), p. 21-22 and 27.

122 For a general treatment of entry barriers in competition law see *inter alia*: Richard Schmalensee, 'Economies of Scale and Barriers to Entry' 89 Journal of Political Economy (1981) 1228; Harold Demsetz, 'Barriers to Entry' 72 The American Economic Review (1982) 47; David T. Scheffman and Pablo T. Spiller, 'Buyers' Strategies, Entry Barriers, and Competition' 30 Economic Inquiry (1992) 418; David Harbord and Tom Hoehn, 'Barriers to Entry and Exit in European Competition Policy' 14 International Review of Law and Economics (1994) 411; Bishop and Walker, [2010], para. 3-020 to 3-030.

123 Jacobson and Dorman (1991), p. 10. See as well Office of Fair Trading '*Research Paper 16: The Welfare Consequences of the Exercise of Buyer Power*' (1998), para. 4.5.

C. Is monopsony power a problem likely to arise in practice?

87. Monopsony cases rarely occur in practice, especially over a considerable period of time,[124] an opinion also shared by Carlton, Coleman and Israel[125]. Due to this unlikelihood and the narrow conditions in which it appears, not only is monopsony said to be the 'older' approach to buyer power, but it is also no longer considered by some NCAs as a likely measurement of buyer power, as, "[t]he Agencies do not view a short-run reduction in the quantity purchased as the only, or best indicator, of whether a merger enhances buyer market power"[126]. These remarks are supported by my study, which confirms that withholding is a rare practice as confirmed by the case law and data collected by Competition Authorities[127].

88. There are several arguments that support this proposal of unlikelihood of monopsony cases. Firstly, if monopsony is employed to reduce purchasing prices below the seller's marginal costs, suppliers will slowly be forced out of the market, as their economic activity is no longer profitable (not even their costs are covered)[128]. Consequently, a rational buyer will not "squeeze" a reasonable amount of its suppliers because by doing so it will be left without the input that it requires to provide downstream its output for final consumers. This type of argument was employed by Advocate General Poiares Maduro in *FENIN v Commission*, stating that "[an] undertaking in a monopsonistic position has no interest in bringing such pressure to bear on its suppliers that they become obliged to leave the upstream market"[129]. However, the monopsonist can afford to squeeze some marginal suppliers out of the market as other more efficient suppliers will remain in it (even if their profitability decreases). Nevertheless,

---

124 See making this same point, the UK NCA decision CA98/09/2003 *BetterCare Group Ltd/North & West Belfast Health & Social Services Trust* [2003], para 56. For a concurrent opinion see: Kirkwood 'Powerful Buyers and Merger Enforcement' (2012), p. 1497-1500. Also remarking that monopsony in food retailer markets is unlikely to appear, see: Federal Trade Commission, *Report on the Federal Trade Commission Workshop on Slotting Allowances and Other Marketing Practices in the Grocery Industry* (2001): https://www.ftc.gov/sites/default/files/documents/reports/report-federal-trade-commission-workshop-slotting-allowances-and-other-marketing-practices-grocery/slottingallowancesreportfinal_0.pdf; Kirkwood (2014), p. 7; Antonio Buttà and Andrea Pezzoli, 'Buyer power and competition policy: from brick-and-mortar retailers to digital platforms ' 41 Economia E Politica Industriale (2014) 159, p. 160. Cf with the work of van Doorn which does not address this issue in: van Doorn.

125 Carlton, Coleman and Israel [2015], p. 531.

126 US Department of Justice and Federal Trade Commission, Horizontal Merger Guidelines (2010), p. 32.

127 According to the UK Competition Commission: "[h]owever, having reviewed industry cost structures, as well as recent purchasing patterns and retail prices, in the fresh fruit sector, we did not find any evidence to support a finding that demand withholding was taking place" in Competition Commission, UK (2008), para 9.69.

128 Hovenkamp expresses a similar idea when stating that: "[n]o supplier would stay in business if it were forced to sell to the monopsonist at a price lower than its average costs, and price would tend toward average cost in a competitive market", in Herbert Hovenkamp, *Federal Antitrust Policy: The Law of Competition and its Practice* (3rd edn, Thomson/West 2005), p. 14; O'Donoghue and Padilla, [2013], p. 841. However, not all suppliers will be forced out of the market at the same time, as suppliers have different costs curves. The suppliers that will be forced to exit the market first would be those whose marginal cost curve is the highest.

129 Opinion of Advocate General Poiares Maduro of 10 November 2005 in Judgment of 11 July in *FENIN v Commission*, C-205/03 P, EU:C:2005:666, para. 66.

as some suppliers leave the market, those remaining grow stronger and may be able to countervail the monopsony power of the large buyer in what becomes a neutralizing cycle.

89. Secondly, most buyers that may employ monopsony power would, instead, rather use bargaining power to maximize their purchases and reduce their input prices. This would lower the buyer's costs, which would allow it to increase its sales in the downstream market, which, taken as a whole, would imply a higher margin of profit compared to the monopsony profit it could otherwise obtain. In other terms, *monopsony is not the most profit maximizing conduct for a powerful buyer.*

90. Thirdly, exercise of monopsony power reduces the overall market price of the input – i.e. the reduction in price will also benefit other buyers and not only the price paid by the buyer. Hence, such a move, absent additional measures, such as imposing exclusive supply obligations, will not be particularly beneficial to the powerful buyer as noted by Kirkwood[130].

91. Lastly, the monopsony model is short sighted because it assumes that purchasing contracts are only negotiated based on quantity and on anonymous take-it-or-leave it offers, and that the price paid per unit remains static[131]. In practice, though, this is not the case as most contracts are usually the outcome of bilateral negotiations that take into account other factors beyond price and quality[132], and adopting two-part tariffs.

IV. Bargaining power

92. Bargaining power, or more strictly efficient bargaining power in opposition to inefficient monopsony power, is the "newer" approach to buyer power and *should be the focus of buyer power economics and legal regulation*[133]. As shown in this study, the competition law cases dealt with in EU competition law (and even those not covered by it, such as imposing 'unfair' purchasing conditions) largely tend to be bargaining power cases because *they do not involve demand withholding* and instead transfer profit from suppliers to

---

130 Kirkwood 'Buyer Power and Exclusionary Conduct: Should Brooke Group Set the Standards for Buyer-Induced Price Discrimination and Predatory Bidding?' (2004-2005), p. 638.

131 Carlton and Israel (2011), p. 129.

132 Bundeskartellamt '*Buyer Power in Competition Law - Status and Perspectives*' (2008), p. 2.

133 Bundeskartellamt '*Summary of the Final Report of the Sector Inquiry into the Food Retail Sector*' (2014), p. 9.

buyers through negotiations[134], more specifically by, for example, threatening to purchase less[135], withdrawing a benefit[136], or shifting demand to another supplier[137]. This allows the powerful buyer to obtain better conditions from its sellers than when compared to other buyers[138].

93. In this study, I employ bargaining power[139] as a concept that describes the strength in bilateral negotiations of a *buyer* vis-à-vis its supplier(s) that allows the purchaser to obtain better trading conditions and transfer supracompetitive profits from supplier to buyer, for example by receiving rebates or special preferential conditions[140]. These better purchasing conditions include price and non-price terms[141], unlike monopsony power that only includes a reduction in purchasing price[142].

94. In turn, these lower purchasing prices or non-price benefits may be *passed on to final consumers* – if the downstream market is competitive – who will benefit from the same or higher output with a lower price[143]. The more competitive the market downstream, the stronger the passing on effect to consumers is[144]. Thus, *prima facie, bargaining power is efficiency enhancing*[145] because it *countervails or neutralizes seller market power* driving prices closer to the competitive level, an effect firstly theorized by Galbraith[146].

---

134 See also stressing this: Doyle and Inderst (2007), p. 211; Dobson and Inderst (2008), p. 338-341; OECD '*Policy Roundtables: Monopsony and Buyer Power*' (2009), p. 21; Competition Commission, UK (2008), para. 9.2; Ezrachi and Williams (2013), p. 296.

135 OECD '*Policy Roundtables: Monopsony and Buyer Power*' (2009), p. 37.

136 Kirkwood 'Buyer Power and Exclusionary Conduct: Should Brooke Group Set the Standards for Buyer-Induced Price Discrimination and Predatory Bidding?' (2004-2005), p. 638-639; American Bar Association, [2012], p. 53-54.

137 Ezrachi and De Jong (2012), p. 257-258.

138 Kokkoris and Shelanski, [2014], p. 407.

139 Bargaining power, if present, can be exercised by any of the parties entering into bilateral negotiations. Due to the nature of this study, I will not discuss issues related to general bargaining theory or game theory that deal with sellers.

140 Dobson and Inderst (2007), p. 393; Dobson [2009], p. 115-116; Buttà and Pezzoli (2014).

141 Carlton, Coleman and Israel [2015], p. 533.

142 See also adopting such an approach: American Antitrust Institute [2008], p. 99.

143 "NCAs also agree that the exercise of buyer power can bring positive effects if competition among retailers exists in downstream markets and the lower purchasing costs achieved in procurement markets are passed to consumers in terms of lower prices." in European Competition Network (2012), para 253; Competition Commission, UK (2008), para 36. Pera reaches the same conclusion when stating that "[NCAs] have tended to downplay the anti-competitive effects of buyer power, unless it is associated with market power on the selling side: absence of such a market power compels retailers to transfer to consumers the preferential conditions they have obtained" in Alberto Pera, 'Assessment of Buyer Power in Recent Investigations and Mergers' (2010), available at: http://www.gop.it/doc_pubblicazioni/40_hjv4kr3vun_eng.pdf, p. 16.

144 Dobson and Inderst (2008), 340.

145 OECD '*Policy Roundtables: Monopsony and Buyer Power*' (2009), p. 43; European Competition Network (2012), para. 73.

146 The concept of countervailing power was first developed by Galbraith, in Galbraith, [2010], p. 97-135 Some authors use the term countervailing power as synonym for bargaining power, see *inter alia*: Chen (2007); Kirkwood 'Powerful Buyers and Merger Enforcement' (2012); Kirkwood (2014). Galbraith's idea of countervailing buyer power has become widely accepted wisdom by modern economists. For more, see: Lester C. Thurow, *Galbraith, John Kenneth*, Vol. II (John Eatwell, Murray Milgate and Peter Newman eds, The MacMillan Press Limited 1987), p. 455. See also: Bradley J. Ruffle, *Buyer Countervailing Power: A Survey of the Theory and Experimental Evidence* (2005) 6, p. 6.

95. Despite the ability to neutralize seller market power and generate efficiencies, not all exertions of bargaining power would be efficiency enhancing, particularly with regard to end consumers, as the passing on of the benefits in the form of lower purchasing prices depends on the competitiveness of the market where the buyer operates, particularly downstream[147], and the type of contract that buyers and suppliers enter into. As it will be discussed through this study, bargaining power can also be employed anti-competitively to exploit suppliers and/or exclude competitors and not benefit consumers[148].

96. Concerning the ways of exercising bargaining power, it is important to distinguish between two different forms of purchasing, depending on whether parties adopt a single or a two-part tariff or other type of complex contract, as the efficiency of these contracts and of bargaining power are different[149]. For both of these different bargaining forms, I operate with the same assumptions: a market in which there is a single buyer negotiating with a single supplier, and where the buyer is a monopolist downstream. Both of these modalities of bargaining have in common that the purchasing price is lowered towards the competitive level and the buyer is able to extract profits (rents) that otherwise would stay with the supplier.

97. In the first case, when parties adopt a *linear contract* (i.e.: only one form of pricing) the supplier will be incentivized to increase its selling price at a level above its marginal costs of production. On the other hand, the buyer will use its buyer bargaining power to decrease the purchasing price as close as possible to the supplier's marginal cost and obtain the largest amount of the contract's profit. As the prices for the goods are 'pushed down' by the buyer towards the supplier's marginal cost curve, buyer power is seen as beneficial because it reduces the prices closer to the competitive level. However, in this setting the outcome of the contract negotiation is *not fully efficient* as the buyer will seek to increase its prices, having an effect on the downstream prices set by the buyer to end consumers. Therefore, as prices are set above the supplier's marginal cost, there is a problem of *double marginalization*[150]. Another problem with this model is that parties would be unable to offer rebates based on quantity, as the contract is linear. These inefficiencies are offset, however if the buyer has all the bargaining power and is able to reduce the wholesale purchasing price to the point where it intersects the supplier's marginal cost.

---

147 Cf with Jacobson (2013).

148 European Competition Network (2012), para. 73. American Antitrust Institute [2008], p. 103.

149 See distinguishing the outcomes if there is single or two part tariff for bargaining power models: Chen (2007).

150 See stressing that if contracts in buyer power are not complex (i.e.: not having two part tariff structures), then issues of double marginalization arise: Zhiqi Chen, *Monopoly and Product Diversity: The Role of Retailer Countervailing Power* (2006, revised version) 1, p. 10; Roman Inderst and Christian Wey, 'Buyer Power and Supplier Incentives' 51 European Economic Review (2007), p. 650.

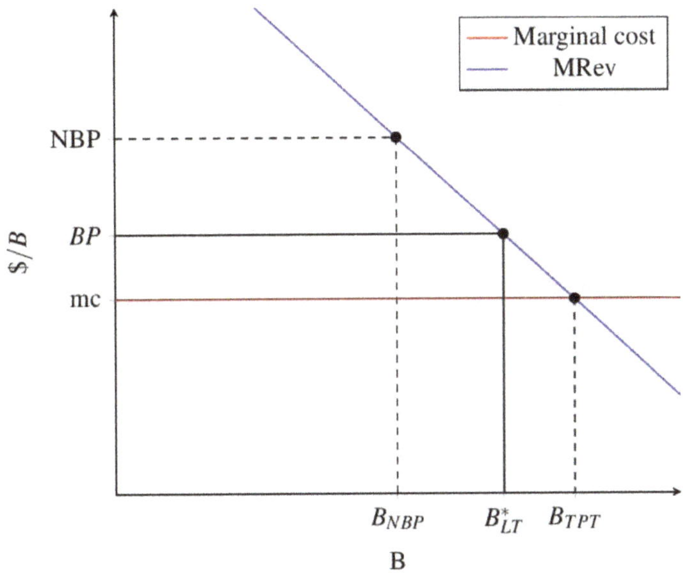

Figure 2: Bargaining Power - Linear Contract

98. A better outcome within bargaining models would be when the parties adopt a different strategy and enter into complex contracts employing *a two-part tariff* system in which they agree to set the wholesale purchasing price at the marginal cost level. In a narrow approach, *only this type of contracting between buyers and sellers would be fully efficient bargaining.* As remarked by Chen, this type of contract is efficient because "the use of two-part tariffs allows the undertakings to eliminate the double-marginalization problem, and, thus, in equilibrium the manufacturer and each retailer will set the contract terms in such a way to maximize their joint profit"[151]. In this case, what occurs is that after setting the wholesale price the parties to the contract will negotiate how profit will be distributed among them and the buyer uses its bargaining power to obtain a larger proportion of the share of the joint profits. Therefore, under this scenario bargaining power does not decrease the purchasing price paid, sensu stricto, like in the example of linear contracts, but indirectly the two-part tariff contract allows for the parties to agree to a price that is the equivalent to the marginal cost. Therefore, incidentally it does achieve the most optimal price reduction possible from the supplier to the buyer.

151 Chen, *Monopoly and Product Diversity: The Role of Retailer Countervailing Power* (2006, revised version), p. 10.

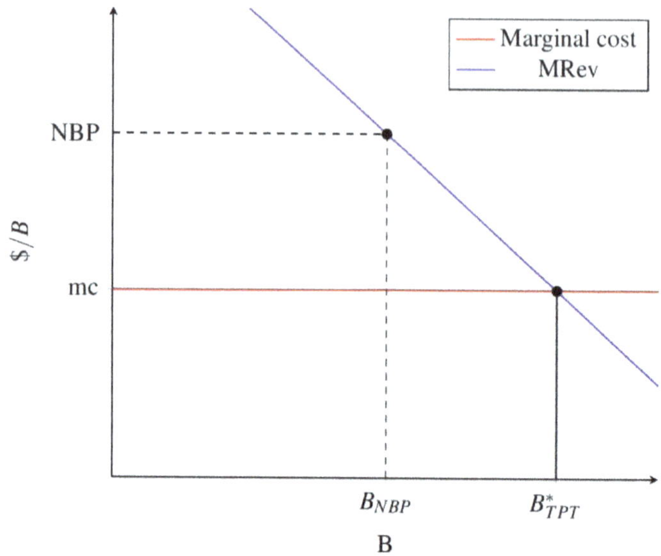

Figure 3: Bargaining Power – Two-Part Tariff Contract

99. This type of bargaining power is fully efficient when compared to the case of linear pricing contracts because it eliminates the double marginalization issue as the purchasing price is fixed at the marginal cost and neither the supplier nor the buyer increase their prices upstream and downstream, respectively, to cover that price increase. Furthermore, two-part tariff bargaining models allow for the parties to concede rebates, for example based on quantity, or other types of non-price concessions.

100. Another characteristic of bargaining power is that it only arises if sellers are reaping supracompetitive benefits (in the form of higher prices than the competitive level)[152]. In the absence of seller market power, the buyer would not be able to pressure its suppliers to price lower and closer to the competitive market price[153]. Hence, bargaining power acts as *countervailing power*[154] offsetting in whole or in part sellers' market power and leading to a competitive or quasi competitive outcome of setting prices[155], by forcing or agreeing with

152 Similarly, Kirkwood 'Buyer Power and Exclusionary Conduct: Should Brooke Group Set the Standards for Buyer-Induced Price Discrimination and Predatory Bidding?' (2004-2005), p. 639.

153 OECD '*Policy Roundtables: Monopsony and Buyer Power*' (2009), p. 26 and 43; Kirkwood (2014), p. 58.

154 Galbraith, [2010], p. 97-135. Some authors use the term countervailing power as synonym for bargaining power, see *inter alia*: Chen 'Buyer power: Economic Theory and Antitrust Policy' (2007); Kirkwood 'Powerful Buyers and Merger Enforcement' (2012); Kirkwood (2014).

155 Judgment of 15 December 1994 in *Gøttrup-Klim and Others Grovvareforeninger v Dansk Landbrugs Grovvareselskab*, C-250/92, EU:C:1994:413, para. 32; Kirkwood 'Buyer Power and Exclusionary Conduct: Should Brooke Group Set the Standards for Buyer-Induced Price Discrimination and Predatory Bidding?' (2004-2005), p. 640; OECD '*Policy Roundtables: Monopsony and Buyer Power*' (2009), p. 21; Kirkwood 'Powerful Buyers and Merger Enforcement' (2012), p. 1494.

suppliers to set wholesale prices as close or at their marginal costs. According to Galbraith's theory and as recently confirmed by Johansen, countervailing power arises naturally among suppliers and buyers as a *self-generating force* that keeps opposed market power in check for both buyers and suppliers by neutralizing it[156], without the need for government intervention[157].

101. Lastly, bargaining power is a dynamic concept in the sense that its intensity varies from moment to moment and contract to contract. A buying undertaking may enjoy a large degree of bargaining power, for example, when there is plenty of supply for a good due to excess production in the upstream market. For instance, this would be the case of a good year for the production of wheat to produce durum for pasta[158]. In such a situation, the buyer can argue that they have several alternative suppliers and there is plenty of wheat to be acquired and hence demand a lower purchasing price. However, the bargaining power of the same buyer when compared to the same seller can drastically change if poor climate or a disease have abnormally and unforeseeably affected the production of wheat. The buyer that a few months ago enjoyed substantial buyer power now has little, as it is the seller who will be able to choose its buyer due to scarcity. This dynamic feature of bargaining power is particularly important when discussing the imposition of unfair trade practices in chapter 8.

A. Distinguishing bargaining power from monopsony

102. Bargaining power differs from monopsony power in several important factors, despite them both representing different purchasing modalities that lower the prices paid by a buyer for their input. Firstly, *bargaining power benefits do not imply a withholding effect as monopsony does.* Instead, the benefits are achieved by seeking individual discounts based on negotiation strategies, as remarked by Inderst and Doyle[159]. Indeed, bargaining power incentivizes the buyer to acquire more units if it is able to lower its purchasing price, and thus, *increasing output*. Furthermore, unlike in the monopsony effect, these better terms or conditions will only improve the competitive conditions of the specific buyer while not affecting prices market-wide[160].

---

156 Bjørn Olav Johansen, *Buyer Power, Welfare and Public Policy* (University of Bergen 2012), p. 3.

157 Galbraith, [2010], p. 99; Brian Facey and Cassandra Brown, *Competition and Antitrust Laws in Canada* (Lexis Nexis 2013), p. 250.

158 This example is inspired by the US case *National Macaroni Manufacturers Association v. Federal Trade Commission,* 345 F2.d 421 (7th Cir. 1965).

159 Doyle and Inderst (2007), p. 212; also similarly American Bar Association, [2012], p. 53-54.

160 Supporting this view that bargaining power leads to individualized discounts see: European Commission and others (2000), p. 3; Doyle and Inderst (2007), p. 212; OECD '*Policy Roundtables: Monopsony and Buyer Power*' (2009), p. 37. See also claiming that generally bargaining power has effect only vis-à-vis the involved parties van Doorn, 97; Ezrachi and De Jong (2012).

103. Secondly, exercising bargaining power, unlike monopsony power, does not imply that the buyer becomes a price maker[161]. The price is 'bargained' between supplier and seller by entering into negotiations between buyer and seller, and not in anonymous deals like in the monopsony models, as also remarked by Ezrachi and De Jong[162].

104. Thirdly, bargaining power exercise does not always imply that the buyer forces suppliers to price *below* competitive levels as monopsony does[163]. As prices are still somewhat profitable, buyers are able to exercise bargaining power more often than monopsony power without squeezing suppliers out of the market[164].

105. Fourthly, unlike monopsony, in bargaining power cases there is likely to be more than one buyer, although in these situations there may be relatively few firms negotiating, whereby some of these may be relatively large compared to their rivals and enjoy a larger market share[165].

106. Lastly, parties will only trade if their outside option (i.e. buying from a different supplier or starting self-supply) is less profitable[166], unlike monopsony cases in which parties are forced to trade to minimize losses. Consequently, alternative sources of supply, as explained below, act as a competitive constraint to the seller, forcing them to offer equal or better terms to the buyer than those offered its competitors.

B. Sources of bargaining power

107. Different from the monopsony case, there is no standard microeconomic model for bargaining power, as this effect can be the result of several circumstances and takes place in complex negotiations inter partes. However, it is common for academic literature to propose specialized models pertaining to particular industries and even social situations[167]. These models offer different frameworks for explaining how buyers and sellers split the surplus generated

---

161 OECD '*Policy Roundtables: Monopsony and Buyer Power*' (2009), p. 21-26.

162 Ezrachi and De Jong (2012), p. 257.

163 Kirkwood 'Powerful Buyers and Merger Enforcement' (2012), p. 1494.

164 Kirkwood (2014), p. 7.

165 OECD '*Policy Roundtables: Monopsony and Buyer Power*' (2009), p. 37.

166 Doyle and Inderst (2007), p. 212.

167 For an example of bargaining power models see, *inter alia*: K. Kultti, 'About Bargaining Power' 69 Econ Lett (2000) 341; R. Inderst, 'Contract Design and Bargaining Power' 74 Econ Lett (2002) 171; L. P. Osterdal, 'Bargaining Power in Repeated Games' 49 Math Soc Sci (2005) 110; Doyle and Inderst (2007), p. 211-213; OECD '*Policy Roundtables: Monopsony and Buyer Power*' (2009), p. 37 to 39; Meza and Sudhir (2010); Shinn-Shyr Wang, Christian Rojas and Nathalie Lavoie, 'Buyer Market Power and Vertically Differentiated Retailers' (2010) <http://people.umass.edu/resec/workingpapers/documents/ResEcWorkingPaper2010-1.pdf>; R. Stenbacka and M. Tombak, 'Make and Buy: Balancing Bargaining Power' 81 J Econ Behav Organ (2012) 391.

from the purchase of goods or services[168]. In all these frameworks there is a constant: the more bargaining power the buyer is capable of exercising vis-à-vis the seller, the larger the surplus it will obtain for itself[169].

108. The ability to exercise bargaining power is anchored on the existence of sufficient sources that allow the buyer to exert competitive pressure on suppliers. In this section, I identify four sources of bargaining power[170] that serve as indicators for competition authorities and judges when evaluating a case to determine its existence and extent[171]. These sources of bargaining power are strongly connected with the assessment of buyer market power, as discussed in chapter 5, section §IV.

a. Buyer's size

109. In principle, the larger a buyer is – and consequently the more market share it has – the more bargaining power it will have. However, as pointed out by Dobson and Inderst, size alone may not necessarily imply the existence of bargaining power[172], particularly if the other side of the market is highly concentrated or other bargaining power sources are absent. However, market size – absolute and relative[173] – acts as a good proxy for enforcement agencies, as the sheer size of an undertaking has negotiation importance[174]. Nevertheless, bargaining power may also exist even if market shares are small because other sources, such as the degree of dependency and competition among suppliers grant bargaining power to the buyer[175].

110. There are several reasons why large market shares indicate the possibility of existence of bargaining power. Firstly, as stressed by Dobson and Inderst, the larger the market size, the more credible the threat of switching suppliers is[176]. In principle, and depending on the nature of the good purchased, the larger the buyer, the cheaper the switching costs per unit will be, and the greater the

168 OECD '*Policy Roundtables: Monopsony and Buyer Power*' (2009), p. 38.

169 Ibid.

170 Ibid, p. 39. Also suggesting that buyer power has several sources, including market concentration, high barriers to entry and strong cooperative alliances among buyers in European Competition Network (2012), para. 253.

171 In Czech Republic, according to the Article 3(2) of Act No. 395/2009 of 9 September 2009 on Significant Market Power in the Sale of Agricultural and Food Products and Abuse thereof 'significant market power' (bargaining power) is said to originate from the following sources: "market structure, barriers to entry, market share of the supplier and the buyer, their financial power, size of the customer's business network, and size and location of their individual stores".

172 Pierpaolo Battigalli, Chiara Fumagalli and Michele Polo, 'Buyer power and quality improvements' 61 Research in Economics (2007) 45, p. 47; Dobson and Inderst (2008), p. 339.

173 Ezrachi and De Jong (2012), p. 257; UK (2008), para. 96.

174 Doyle and Inderst (2007), p. 213; Dobson and Inderst (2008), p. 339.

175 Henriksson, *Countervailing Buyer Power in EU Antitrust Analysis*.

176 Dobson and Inderst (2007), p. 395. Supporting this view, see: OECD '*Policy Roundtables: Monopsony and Buyer Power*' (2009), p. 40.

incentives to invest in seeking potential suppliers[177]. Secondly, if a buyer is large enough it can sponsor entry of suppliers into the market[178], as has been recognized by the Commission in *Enso/Stora*[179]. Thirdly, a large buyer may represent a large portion of the total sales of a supplier[180]. This proportion of sales allows the determination of whether a supplier is in a *dependent* situation vis-à-vis the buyer and, hence, prone to give larger discounts[181]. The larger the quota the buyer represents for the supplier, the more it will be willing to give larger discounts to avoid losing the buyer as a client and reducing its profits[182]. Fourthly, large market shares may also be an indicator of lack of alternative sources of demand and, therefore, increased bargaining power.

111. However, mere size is not a credible source of bargaining power, as confirmed in *AstraZeneca v Commission*[183]. A buyer may have a large market share but little or no bargaining power if the supplier has alternative sources of demand or enjoys more bargaining power. In *AstraZeneca v Commission*, the position of the German state as a buyer of medicines for public healthcare systems lacked real bargaining power with which to neutralize the imposition of very high prices for particularly advance medicines as the demand curve was highly inelastic. The CJEU found that despite the fact that the buyer was a "monopsonist" (*rectius*, large buyer) the costs of medicines were inelastic because they were paid by the MS and products were innovative and a "must stock"[184]. Thus, size and market shares are a mere indication of bargaining power but not a definitive answer.

b. *Alternative sources of supply*

112. The more supply options, the more bargaining power a buyer has. Alternative sources of supply would be those undertakings that are not engaged by the buyer and have spare capacity to sell the input required in the market; i.e. other sellers offering substitute goods. Each supplier acts as a competitive constraint – supply side substitution – to its competitors for the capture of

---

177 OECD '*Policy Roundtables: Monopsony and Buyer Power*' (2009), p. 40.

178 Dobson and Inderst (2007), p. 395; OECD '*Policy Roundtables: Monopsony and Buyer Power*' (2009), p. 40.

179 Commission Decision of 25 November 1998 declaring a concentration to be compatible with the common market and the functioning of the EEA Agreement (Case No IV/M.1225 - *Enso/Stora*) [1999] OJ L 254/9, para. 92.

180 Doyle and Inderst (2007), p. 213.

181 Dobson and Inderst (2008), p. 339-340; OECD '*Policy Roundtables: Monopsony and Buyer Power*' (2009), p. 40; Pera and Bonfitto (2011), p. 414. See also raising the dependency argument but regarding monopsony and oligopsony, Oinonen (2014), p. 101. The topic of dependency is discussed at length in chapter 5, section §IV.C and chapter 8, section §VI.

182 Doyle and Inderst (2007), p. 213.

183 Judgment of 6 December 2012 in *AstraZeneca v Commission*, C-457/10 P, EU:C:2012:770, para. 170-182. See also: Judgment of 1 July 2010, *AstraZeneca v Commission*, T-321/05, ECR, EU:T:2010:266, para. 255-269.

184 Judgment of 6 December 2012 in *AstraZeneca v Commission*, C-457/10 P, EU:C:2012:770, para. 178-181.

demand. The more competition and number of suppliers there is, the better off the buyer will be vis-à-vis the sellers[185]. Indeed, if there are few alternative sources of supply there will be little supply side substitutability and the buyer will be mutually dependent on the seller.

c. Alternative sources of demand

113. The reverse of supply side substitutability is represented by demand side substitutability, this is, the amount of buyers competing for the input. The more buyers compete, the less bargaining power they will have, as suppliers have alternative buyers to resort to in case the offer made by a powerful buyer is not sufficiently profitable. Therefore, the more competitive the upstream market is, the less bargaining power a single undertaking has. However, if a buyer has substantial market power downstream because it faces little competition from other buyers then it will have more bargaining power[186]. Therefore, downstream conditions also play a role when determining the existence of substantial bargaining power.

d. Bargaining effectiveness

114. Lastly, the buyer's bargaining effectiveness is a source of bargaining power[187]. The OECD defines bargaining effectiveness as the ability to extract a larger share of the incremental surplus due to specific negotiation strategies or characteristics of the buyer[188]. For example, if the buyer is not financially constrained and has enough input in stock, diminishing the urgency of acquiring goods or services, then it will have more bargaining power. Also, the amount of market information that the buyer has increases its bargaining power, particularly in terms of asymmetric information possessed by suppliers[189]. This information will allow the buyer to accurately determine their other supply options and, thus, be less constrained by their current negotiation partner.

V. Direct buyer power effects

115. In this section, I present the direct welfare effects of monopsony and bargaining power in price and non-price terms, largely based on the *assumption that the buyer competes with the same rivals in the upstream market as buyers and the downstream market as retailers*. By direct buyer power effects, I mean

---

185 OECD '*Policy Roundtables: Monopsony and Buyer Power*' (2009), 40.

186 Ibid, p. 41.

187 Battigalli, Fumagalli and Polo (2007), p. 46.

188 OECD '*Policy Roundtables: Monopsony and Buyer Power*' (2009), p. 42.

189 Ibid, p. 41

those that take place between the buyer and its direct supplier and the buyer (as retailer) and its direct end consumers. Regarding the direct market effects, if they only compete in the upstream market then *the effects of buyer power on the downstream market vis-à-vis those rival buyers would have to be determined based on and influenced directly by the pure upstream effects*. More often than not, however, buyers compete with the same rivals both in the input and output market, which explains why the *focus of this section and literature is on the overall effect of buyer power in upstream and downstream market power*. Also, as buyer power affects downstream competitive conditions – in addition to generating competition effects among suppliers and buyers – it will have a direct welfare effect on consumer welfare, which also explains why the competitive concern of NCAs and Courts is also triggered when buyer power adversely affects consumer welfare.

116. Linked to this, it must be stressed that buyer power conducts have a *dual effect in the upstream and downstream market*, which requires a *dualistic approach to the analysis of buyer power cases*, in order to avoid under enforcement of the competition rules. These welfare effects of the expressions of buyer power pave the way for the legal discussion regarding the treatment of buyer power and suggestions towards a buyer competition policy in EU competition law.

A. Monopsony effects

117. Monopsony power is always inefficient because the withholding effect generates a deadweight loss and loss of allocative efficiency[190]. Also, the consequences in price terms for the final consumer are almost always inefficient because either the prices increase or remain unchanged, while never decreasing. In the following sections, I discuss the price and non-price effects of monopsony power.

118. Most of the monopsony models assume the use of a single-price strategy, as noted by Noll[191]. Whenever a buyer exercises monopsony power, it withholds demand by purchasing less goods[192], consequently, employing less resources than in a competitive market[193]. Withholding demand implies a reduction in allocative efficiency and a deadweight loss, as recognized by the

190 Chen 'Buyer power: Economic Theory and Antitrust Policy' (2007), p. 22; Kirkwood, also of this opinion proposes that cartels that counteract monopsony power should be allowed in US antitrust law because "[i]f the customer's power was monopsony power, no further proof would be required (as if the care was desirable), for counteracting monopsony power through the creation of supplier power is ordinarily procompetitive" in Kirkwood (2014), p. 7.

191 Noll (2004-2005), p. 594. A single price strategy is whenever each quantity purchased has the same price; the total price paid (T) will simply depend on unit price (p) per quantity (q): T= pxq.

192 Dobson (2004-2005), p. 345.

193 Commission and others (2000), p. 8; Noll (2004-2005), p. 595; Doyle and Inderst (2007), p. 211-212.

EU Commission in *Friesland Foods/Campina*[194]. *This inefficient outcome holds true even if the monopsonist faces perfect competition downstream*[195]. By withholding demand, the monopsonist transfers wealth from the suppliers to itself *but does not generate wealth*[196]. Additionally, due to the purchasing of less input, the amount of downstream goods will also be reduced, unless other perfect substitutes exist,[197] or there are alternative buyers. This scarcity of goods pushes the retail price up for the final consumers, unless there is compensation in supply by other buyers/retailers, as noted by van Doorn[198].

119. If instead of a linear tariff the monopsonist employs a two-part tariff, the negative welfare effects of monopsony power can be lessened, thereby reducing the welfare loss and allocative efficiency. To do so, Chen claims that parties ought to set non-linear pricing schemes (i.e. two-part tariffs or price discrimination) "to capture the lost profit opportunity embedded in the deadweight loss"[199].

120. In the case of an oligopsony, the welfare loss is said to be less than it is with a single monopsonist as "the final price is lower and the purchase price is higher [...] [c]orrespondingly, both profits and the welfare loss are lower", as remarked by Neumann[200]. The reason behind this slightly weaker negative effect is that there will be some degree of competition among the oligopsonists, particularly those not part of a collusive agreement[201]. However, if the oligopsony is the result of collusive monopsony, the effects will be as if they were a single monopsonist since buyers will coordinate to restrict purchases and lower prices[202].

121. This less pernicious impact does not imply that competition policy should see oligopsony outcomes as desirable or permitted. Agreements among buyers tending to reduce purchasing quantities and consequently price ought to be forbidden as object restrictions of competition in accordance with Article 101(1) (a) TFEU, and as discussed in chapter 7.

---

194 "It should be clarified whether the increased buying power of the notifying parties could have a detrimental effect on competition, by enabling the new entity to obtain lower prices from farmers by reducing its purchase of raw milk, which would in turn lead to lower output also in the downstream markets and thus harm consumer welfare", Summary of Commission Decision of 17 December 2008 declaring a concentration compatible with the common market and the functioning of the EEA Agreement (Case COMP/M.5046 — *Friesland Foods/Campina*) [2009] OJ C 75/21, taken from the unabridged version, para. 98; Chen 'Buyer power: Economic Theory and Antitrust Policy' (2007), p. 22; Ezrachi and De Jong (2012), p. 257; Ezrachi and Ioannidou (2014), p. 80-81.

195 Chen 'Buyer power: Economic Theory and Antitrust Policy' (2007) 22.

196 Werden (2007), p. 710.

197 Noll (2004-2005), p. 596-597.

198 van Doorn, p. 89.

199 Chen 'Buyer power: Economic Theory and Antitrust Policy' (2007), p. 28. See also: Noll (2004-2005), p. 603.

200 Neumann, [2001], p. 155. This assumes, however, that parties coordinate their behavior, but the same outcome – or slightly similar – holds even in the absence of coordination.

201 OECD '*Policy Roundtables: Monopsony and Buyer Power*' (2009), p. 31.

202 Office of Fair Trading '*Research Paper 16: The Welfare Consequences of the Exercise of Buyer Power*' (1998), p. 13; Commission and others (2000), p. 10.

122. In addition to the negative welfare effects produced by the monopsony exercise, its impact will depend on the market power of the undertaking in the upstream and downstream markets. If the undertaking has *substantial market power not only as a buyer but also as a seller*, a situation that I describe as the *hourglass shape*, the pernicious effects of monopsony are increased because there is higher likelihood of competitive harm for suppliers, rival buyers and end consumers. If the monopsonist lacks downstream market power then the competitive effects are circumscribed only to the upstream market (in the short term) affecting suppliers and rival buyers. In the following, I discuss these competitive effects and concerns.

a. *Monopsonist with upstream and downstream market power*

123. If the monopsonist also has substantial market power downstream, in addition to the inefficient outcome generated by monopsony power itself, prices in the downstream market for final consumers will be in addition higher as the undertaking will also raise selling prices above the competitive level for the output price obtaining both monopsony and monopoly profits[203]. When the monopsonist is also a monopolist it is known as a monemporist[204].

124. This dual competitive harm happens because by having market power upstream and downstream, its output level will be determined by its marginal costs. Hence, to reduce its marginal costs it will buy less units and, therefore, will also sell less units in the downstream market but at an even higher price, due to the lack of competition[205].

125. This argument was firstly raised by the Commission, when stating that, "if selling power is present in the downstream market, buyer power may be a means of strategically enhancing the former, with potentially adverse welfare effects"[206], and reiterated in the concentration assessment of *Rewe/Meinl* when holding that:

> The exercise of buyer power which leads to the securing of more favourable purchase deal is not to be considered *per se* detrimental to the economy as a whole. Especially where the supplier side is itself highly concentrated and powerful, buyers are faced with

---

203 See calling this phenomenon in overbuying cases "dual market power" Keith N. Hylton, *Weyerhaeuser, Predatory Bidding, and Error Costs* (2008), p. 1. See also: Neumann, [2001], p. 155; Werden (2007), p. 711; O'Donoghue and Padilla, [2013], p. 845; Buttà and Pezzoli (2014), p. 161.

204 The term 'monemporist' was firstly coined by Nicholls in 1941 in William H. Nicholls, *A Theoretical Analysis of Imperfect Competition with Special Application to the Agricultural Industries* (Iowa State College Press 1941); OECD '*Policy Roundtables: Monopsony and Buyer Power*' (2009) p. 30-31. In the case of a monemporist, the reduction in purchasing quantity will be even lower than in the case of a monopsonist. This is explained due to its profit maximizing function and its marginal costs downstream. In the downstream market, the monopsonist with substantial market power will find it more profitable to reduce the quantity of sales even further because its marginal costs are higher than they would be if it were not a monopolist, and higher than of a competitive firm.

205 Ezrachi and De Jong (2012).

206 Commission and others (2000), p. 33.

> effective competition in their own selling market and hence are compelled to pass on any savings to their own customers, buyer power can prevent monopoly or oligopoly profits from being earned on the supply side. *However, if the powerful buyer himself occupies in his selling market a strong position which is no longer kept sufficiently in check by the competition, any savings can no longer be expected to be passed on to customers*[207].

126. Also, the literature has recognized these pernicious effects, such as, for instance, O'Donoghue and Padilla, who argue that when the dominant buyer "also has power as a seller in the output market [...], it may be able to increase sale prices"[208] and there will be a "double reduction in the final supply, in which case the welfare effect is, unsurprisingly, worse than if only one of either monopoly or monopsony existed"[209].

127. The undertaking, then, acts as an *hourglass* that extracts additional profits from both the upstream suppliers and downstream consumers, leading to an inefficient outcome from both a consumer and a total welfare perspective[210]. Hence, the monopsonist not only generates an inefficient outcome in the upstream market by withholding purchases but can also raise the selling price of the output vis-à-vis final consumer by further reducing output. The closer the monopsonist is to become a monopolist, the worse the welfare effect[211]. Therefore, and also in line with Jacobson's view, the most competition concern should be placed on those monopsonists that fit the hourglass shape[212].

---

207 Commission Decision of 3 February 1999 relating to proceedings under Council Regulation (EEC) No 4064/89 (Case No IV/M.1221 - *Rewe/Meinl*) OJ L 274/1, para. 71 (emphasis added).

208 O'Donoghue and Padilla, [2013].

209 Ibid, p. 845.

210 OECD '*Policy Roundtables: Monopsony and Buyer Power*' (2009), p. 30-31. Also supporting this, see: Tribunal Vasco de la Competencia (April 2009), p. 138.

211 Office of Fair Trading '*Research Paper 16: The Welfare Consequences of the Exercise of Buyer Power*' (1998), p. 12-13; European Commission and others (2000), p. 8-9.

212 "Importantly, the Weyerhaeuser Court's heightened standard appears to favor the monopsonist about which we should be most concerned—the one with market power as a seller in the downstream market" in Jacobson (2013), p. 9-10.

128. The hourglass shape concept and the idea of this double anti-competitive concern is illustrated in the graph below.

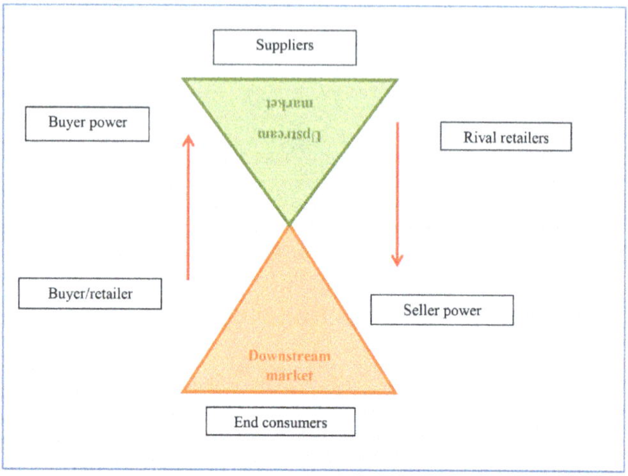

Figure 4: Hourglass Shape, Isolation's Supermarket

129. This dual concern when a monopsonist enjoys both market power upstream and downstream seems to have been taken into account or reflected by the Courts as a factor that has the potential to increase the anticompetitiveness of a buyer's conduct in buyer power cases in general, particularly in cases dealing with buyer power leverage, as occurred in *British Airways v Commission*[213], or in the US antitrust in *Confederated Tribes of Siletz Indians of Ore. v Weyerhaeuser Co.,* later on decided differently by the US supreme Court in *Weyerhaeuser Co. v Ross-Simmons Hardwood Lumber Co., Inc*[214]. Furthermore, the dual competitive risk posed by an hourglass shaped undertaking has been recognized by the Commission where the main concern seems to be placed on the wellbeing of end consumers[215].

---

213 In section §V.B of this shame chapter I discuss the hourglass shape effects for bargaining power cases.

214 *Confederated Tribes of Siletz Indians of Ore. v. Weyerhaeuser Co.*, 411 F. 3d 1030, 10 (9th Cir. 2005); *Weyerhaeuser Company, v. Ross-Simmons Hardwood Lumber Company, Inc.*, in 127 S. Ct. 1069 (2007). I discuss in detail this case in chapter 6, section §IV.

215 See for instance the Guidelines on Horizontal Agreements when stating: "[…] If downstream competitors purchase a significant part of their products together, their incentives for price competition on the selling market or markets may be considerably reduced. If the parties have a significant degree of market power […] on the selling market or markets, the lower purchase prices achieved by the joint purchasing arrangement are likely not to be passed on to consumers", Communication from the Commission — Guidelines on the applicability of Article 101 of the Treaty on the Functioning of the European Union to horizontal co-operation agreements [2011] OJ C 11/1, para. 201. Similarly, the hourglass shape problem was raised by the Commission in the previous horizontal cooperation guidelines when stating: "[…] lower purchasing costs resulting from the exercise of buying power cannot be seen as pro-competitive, if the purchasers together have power on the selling markets. In this case, the cost savings are probably not passed on to consumers", in Commission Notice Guidelines on the applicability of Article 81 of the EC Treaty to horizontal cooperation Agreements (2001/C 3/02), (OJ C 3/2 6.1.2001), para. 127. See also Guidelines on Vertical Restraints [2010] OJ C 130/1, para. 194.

130. This proposal of the hourglass shape undertaking is based on certain assumptions. Firstly, I assume that there is ratio 1:1 between the purchases in the upstream market and the sales in the downstream market, as the demand for the input is directly derived from the consumer demand for the output[216]. For example, such as when a supermarket buys 1,000 liters of processed milk to sell in the food retailing market the same 1,000 liters of processed milk to end consumers[217]. Secondly, I am assuming that for the hourglass undertaking there is no profit-maximizing rational behaviour other than not passing on the benefits to downstream consumers and receiving the monopsony profit.

131. The hourglass shape explains why certain conducts that appear irrational for a buyer may occur in practice; for instance, the case of predatory buying. If the undertaking not only enjoys substantial upstream but also downstream market power, it may incur a loss by paying more than it needs to secure input and foreclose rival buyers because it will recoup its loss by increasing retailing prices in the downstream market vis-à-vis end consumers[218], or by exercising monopsony power in the upstream market once other buyers have been foreclosed.

132. A counterargument against the exercise of monopsony and downstream market power is that an undertaking with downstream market power will be incentivized not to lower its purchases but instead increase them[219]. The problem with this argument is that, under the assumptions of a monopsony model, it would not hold because the supplier's marginal cost curve is always upward sloping. Therefore, the more units the buyer acquires, the higher the price it would have to pay. Hence, such an argument would be valid in cases where the supplier curve is flat or downward slopping such as instances of bargaining power that do not involve demand withholding to reduce the purchasing price, but not for monopsony cases.

---

216 Blair and Sokol (2012), p. 488.

217 See the concern of the Commission related to the supermarket sector in: European Competition Network (2012); Communication from the Commission to the European Parliament, the Council, the European Economic and Social Committee and the Committee of the Regions "Food prices in Europe", (2008) COM(2008) 821 final, available at: http://eur-lex.europa.eu/LexUriServ/LexUriServ.do?uri=COM:2008:0821:FIN:EN:PDF. In a Nordic perspective, see the concern due to the growing market concentration in the food retailing sector in Scandinavia and the Nordic Countries in the Faroese Danish, Finnish, Greenlandic, Icelandic, Norwegian and Swedish Competition Authorities, *Nordic Food Markets - A Taste for Competition* (2005): http://www.konkurransetilsynet.no/iKnowBase/Content/392450/NORDIC_FOOD_MARKETS.PDF. Also, the extinct UK Competition Commission published a report on supermarket retailing where one of the main issues was "the examination of circumstances when oligopolistic firms hold both buyer and seller power ([…]" in the Competition Commission, UK (2000). See also Dobson [2009]. Another example that the literature recognizes as a situation where the undertaking has monopsony power upstream and monopoly power downstream is that of health insurers in Hyman and Kovacic (2004), p. 25-28.

218 Jacobson (2013), p. 9. I would like to thank Bruno Jullien for his comments regarding this argument.

219 My attention to this argument was drawn by Albert Sánchez Graells, for which I thank him.

b. Monopsony and no substantial market power downstream

133. However, if the monopsonist has no substantial market power in the downstream market, then the harmful effects of monopsony power are mitigated or sometimes eliminated in terms of price and final quantity available for end consumers[220]. Yet, the upstream competitive harm vis-à-vis suppliers and other possible buyers remains, in the form of profit distribution, as well as the loss of allocative efficiency[221]. This could also have an adverse impact for end consumers in the downstream market because competition upstream would be weakened, leading to issues of dynamic inefficiency in the medium to long term.

134. As the monopsony conduct implies demand withholding this means that there will be less output of the good available for end consumers than there previously was, which may lead to an increase in price and loss of allocative welfare. However, if there are other buyers that can sell readily available substitutes for the monopsonized input in the downstream markets, these units sold of substitute goods/services will replace the quantities lost due to the monopsony effect[222]. These additional purchases may be the consequence of the lower market prices caused by the monopsony effect, which also benefit other buyers, as noted by Salop[223]. If the substitution is not perfect, the inefficient outcome will not be precluded but minimized because some end consumers are not satisfied.

135. If the compensation for the withheld units takes place, then it is possible to say that the downstream market price will not be affected because, as stressed by Areeda, Hovenkamp and Solow, "if the monopsonist resells in a competitive market, price and output in the output market will be unaffected by the exercise of monopsony power"[224]. This happens, for example, in the case of local input markets characterized by a single buyer but where the downstream market is broader: regional or national[225]. Consequently, in a perfect competition model, the monopsonist has to reduce its selling prices to the competitive level in order to not lose all of its sales to other more efficient sellers. Yet, this does not imply any additional benefits for consumers, just the standard competitive outcome[226].

---

220 Also stressing that when a monopsonist has no market power downstream, the negative consequences are less and, thus, should not be prohibited "per se" see Robles Martín-Laborda.

221 Jacobson (2013).

222 Ibid, p. 2-3.

223 Salop (2004-2005), p. 673.

224 Areeda, Hovenkamp and Solow, [1995], Volume IIB, ¶501, p. 109. Also remarking that absent downstream market power, monopsony exertion does not affect price downstream see: Ezrachi and De Jong, who claim that in such a situation, "the market for the output is competitive, the presence of a monopsony upstream is not likely to affect the price, since the monopsony is a 'price taker'", Ezrachi and De Jong (2012), p. 257. See also: Office of Fair Trading '*Research Paper 16: The Welfare Consequences of the Exercise of Buyer Power*' (1998), para. 4.13; Marius Schwartz, 'Should Antitrust Assess Buyer Market Power Differently than Seller Market Power?' (DOJ/FTC Workshop on Merger Enforcement), 1, p. 2; Oinonen (2014), p. 100.

225 OECD '*Policy Roundtables: Monopsony and Buyer Power*' (2009), p. 28.

226 Chen 'Buyer power: Economic Theory and Antitrust Policy' (2007), p. 28.

136. This moderate view regarding the limited effects of monopsony power, should there be no downstream competition, has been directly addressed by Advocate General Poiares Maduro, in arguing that:

> Thus, where a purchase is linked to the performance of non-economic functions, it may fall outside the scope of competition law. That conclusion is consistent with the economic theory according to which the existence of a *monopsony does not pose a serious threat to competition since it does not necessarily have any effect on the downstream market*[227].

137. However, these claims should not be interpreted as though there is no competitive harm. Consequently, a lenient approach to monopsony is under-inclusive and flawed[228]. It may not produce short term consumer harm, but if a broader perspective to buyer power is employed then there is still upstream harm (and total welfare diminishment) pursuant to the inefficient use of resources and loss of allocative efficiency[229]. Furthermore, if there are no substitutes or no other buyers that acquire the same input, the scarcity produced by the demand withholding will naturally push output prices upwards in the downstream market, compared to a non-monopsonistic upstream market. Nevertheless, this upward pricing pressure is not set by the monopsonist but by the competitive market itself.

B. Bargaining power effects

138. Unlike monopsony power, *the economic effects of bargaining power tend to be welfare enhancing* as they have a propensity to increase economic efficiency, improve supply conditions, reduce prices for end consumers, neutralize seller market power and increase welfare from both a consumer and total welfare perspective[230]. However, *bargaining power may also be detrimental for society*, particularly but not exclusively, if the powerful buyer also has substantial market power downstream – as in the *hourglass shape* – as it will not be forced to pass on the benefits of its bargaining power to consumers in the form of lower purchasing prices, or if the bargaining power is used to exclude rival buyers and/or exploit suppliers. Consequently, it is not possible to offer a clear-cut picture regarding bargaining power effects, although it is possible to offer some guidance to be employed on a case-by-case assessment[231].

---

227 Opinion of Advocate General Poiares Maduro of 10 November 2005 in Judgment of 11 July in *FENIN v Commission*, C-205/03 P, EU:C:2005:666, para. 66 (emphasis added).

228 See also criticizing Advocate General Poiares Maduro's opinion in *FENIN v Commission* and suggesting not to dismiss monopsony problems from the scrutiny of EU competition law see: van Doorn, p. 136.

229 OECD '*Policy Roundtables: Monopsony and Buyer Power*' (2009), p. 29; see also raising these issues Kirkwood (2014), p. 57, footnote 264.

230 For such a generalized view on the pro-competitiveness of bargaining power see, *inter alia*: Bundeskartellamt '*Summary of the Final Report of the Sector Inquiry into the Food Retail Sector*' (2014), p. 13; Dobson and Chakraborty (2008), p. 343; Henriksson, *Countervailing Buyer Power in EU Antitrust Analysis*; Kirkwood (2014), p. 7.

231 Ezrachi and De Jong (2012), p. 258.

139. As discussed in this chapter's section §II.D, the efficiency and the way that purchasing prices are reduced by means of bargaining power depends on the type of contract entered into by the parties. However, in this section, I discuss the potential positive and negative effects of bargaining power from a general perspective and conclude that, by and large, *bargaining power is usually beneficial from a welfare perspective,* particularly for end consumers if the price reductions are passed on owing to competitiveness in the involved markets. Nevertheless, a disclaimer must be made. Bargaining models and their effects are highly dependent on the assumptions made, including the type of contract at hand, the market structure, and other case-specific considerations. Therefore, any effort to present bargaining power effects in general, as I do in this section, is ambitious due to its scope, and should be understood as a guiding reference and not as a case-specific answer to each situation due to the sensitivity of bargaining power to the facts of the circumstance.

140. From a price perspective, bargaining power can potentially benefit players in the upstream and downstream market by increasing efficiencies and maximizing profit[232]. However, occasionally bargaining power can be limited to a transfer of wealth from suppliers to buyers, exploitative or not, for instance by the imposition of unfair trading practices[233], or may lead to a situation in which consumers are worse off, should the powerful buyer have market power downstream. Or more importantly, be used as an exclusionary device against upstream and/or downstream rivals.

a. *Buyer with bargaining power and facing a downstream competitive market*

141. If the buyer enjoys bargaining power but faces a competitive market downstream, this would maximize the bargaining power's welfare enhancing effects. In the upstream market, bargaining power *countervails* supplier's market power by pushing prices to the competitive level and neutralizing the suppliers' market power. In so doing, the supracompetitive benefits are no longer kept by the supplier and are transferred to the buyer, whom, in the downstream market, must pass them on to end consumers in the form of lower end consumer prices. In principle, this reduction in purchasing price is individual, as pointed out by Dobson and Chakraborty (i.e. it only benefits the buyer and its own end customers)[234]. Nevertheless, a spillover effect (the anti-waterbed effect) may mean that the reduction in purchasing price obtained by the powerful buyer may also benefit other buyers as discussed infra.

---

232 Also suggesting the generally efficiency enhancing nature and effects of the exercise of bargaining power see: UK (2008), para 9.4

233 European Commission *Tackling Unfair Trading Practices in the Business-to-Business food supply chain,* Strasbourg (2014), p. 2.

234 Dobson and Chakraborty (2008), p. 343.

142. In the downstream market, the price reduction derived from the bargaining power will be *passed on* to the final consumer due to competitive pressure exerted by rival retailers[235]. Consequently, when the downstream market is competitive there is less room for anti-competitive harm concerning bargaining power exertion, as remarked upon by the Commission's Guidelines on Vertical Restraints when dealing with exclusive supply[236], and as also noted by Korah and O'Sullivan[237]. As such, the powerful buyer acts as an agent for end consumers vis-à-vis suppliers in the attainment of lower prices and improved quality[238]. Unlike the upstream market, the lower prices benefit not only the buyer's end customers but *all end customers* as the reduction in price will spur competition among retailers encouraging efficient practices, innovation and improvement in the quality of the goods and/or services offered[239].

b. Buyer with bargaining power and downstream market power

143. This constitutes the scenario where bargaining power may trigger the most serious competition concerns as its exertion may generate anti-competitive effects without the passing on of the benefits. Bargaining power exercised by an *hourglass shaped* undertaking, a concept discussed in chapter 2, section §V.A.a, may lead to anti-competitive outcomes both in the upstream and downstream market[240], because this hourglass undertaking may employ aggressive tactics as a buyer and as a seller[241], which Kirkwood denominates a "self-reinforcing circle"[242].

---

235 See also, supporting this view in the short term, the report prepared by the Spanish NCA and discussed in European Competition Network (2012), para. 254; Dobson and Inderst (2007), p. 393; Dobson and Chakraborty (2008), p. 343; Ezrachi and De Jong (2012), p. 258.

236 "The importance of the buyer on the downstream market is however the factor which determines whether a competition problem may arise. *If the buyer has no market power downstream, then no appreciable negative effects for consumers can be expected*". Guidelines on Vertical Restraints [2010] OJ C 130/1, para. 194 (emphasis added).

237 Korah and O'Sullivan, [2002], p. 48.

238 Doyle and Inderst (2007), p. 215.

239 Ibid, p. 216; Dobson and Chakraborty (2008), p. 343.

240 Chen 'Buyer power: Economic Theory and Antitrust Policy' (2007), p. 36.

241 See Kirkwood's analysis with respect to the "e-Book" conspiracy and the position of Amazon as an hourglass shaped undertaking not exerting monopsony but bargaining power in Kirkwood (2014); see also: *United States of America v. Apple Inc., et al.*, 12 Civ. 2862 (DLC). The case was appealed before the Court of Appeals of the 2nd Circuit and upheld in *United States v. Apple, Inc.*, No. 13-3741 (2d Cir. 2015) and the US Supreme Court declined the petition for a writ of certiorari in *Apple v. United States*, U.S. Supreme Court, No. 15-565 (2016). In the EU the Commission also initiated an investigation concerning the cartel formed by suppliers of books and rendered the Summary of Commission Decision of 25 July 2013 relating to a proceeding under Article 101 of the Treaty on the Functioning of the European Union and Article 53 of the EEA Agreement (Case COMP/39.847/*E-BOOKS*) [2013] OJ C 378/25, in which a series of commitments were made binding to the book publishers for a period of 5 years, in which it was agreed to terminate the agency agreements and certain restraints when renegotiating their commercial arrangements for e-books were agreed to. See also remarking that there is no passing on buyer power efficiency whenever the buyer has downstream market power: Kirkwood 'Buyer Power and Exclusionary Conduct: Should Brooke Group Set the Standards for Buyer-Induced Price Discrimination and Predatory Bidding?' (2004-2005), 648.

242 Kirkwood (2014), p. 47.

144. In the downstream market, due to the lack of competition, the buyer is not forced to pass on the profit re-distribution from the supplier to the buyer to its end consumers and it would be able to retain the wealth transfer between the supplier to the buyer, in a two-part tariff contract[243]. In a linear tariff model, the buyer, even if a downstream monopolist will have to pass on some sort of price reduction to end consumers, although not all of it. Additionally, the powerful buyer will be able to discriminate in "favour of its own downstream operations and against potential downstream competitors" by leveraging market power from the input market to the downstream market, analogous to a price squeeze[244].

145. Furthermore, the powerful buyer may leverage its privileged downstream position vis-à-vis its suppliers, as it may sometimes act as a necessary trading partner or distribution vehicle that suppliers depend on to reach end consumers[245]. This allows the buyer to extract other rents and privileges from suppliers, such as imposing unfair purchasing practices[246].

146. Additionally, Chen remarks that if the market is oligopsonistic, buyers may find profitable "to raise the purchase prices they pay the suppliers and extract profits from the suppliers in the form of lump-sum payments" leading to a general increase in retail prices in the market as a whole[247].

147. In the upstream market, an *hourglass shaped* undertaking may abuse its bargaining power to stifle competition in the upstream and/or downstream market by excluding rivals buyers that may also compete as retailers[248]. In so doing, the undertaking will increase its rivals' costs to foreclose competitors[249] by, for example, leveraging its market power upstream to protect, strengthen or enhance its market position downstream, as discussed in *British Airways v Commission*[250]. Foreclosure may happen in several ways, for example by

---

243 Also of this opinion are: Chen 'Buyer power: Economic Theory and Antitrust Policy' (2007), p. 36; Kokkoris and Day (2009), p. 177; Ruffle, p. 19; Ezrachi (2012), p. 68; Ezrachi and De Jong (2012), p. 258.

244 Christopher Bellamy, Graham D. Child and P. M. Roth, *European Community Law of Competition* (Sweet & Maxwell 2001), para. 9-085; Christopher Bellamy and others, *European Union Law of Competition* (7th ed. edited by Vivien Rose, David Bailey. edn, Oxford University Press 2013), para. 10.113.

245 Commission Decision of 14 July 1999 relating to a proceeding under Article 82 of the EC Treaty (IV/D-2/34.780 - *Virgin/British Airways*) [2000] OJ L 30/1, para. 32 and 47.

246 Chen 'Buyer power: Economic Theory and Antitrust Policy' (2007), p. 36. The issue of dependence and unfair purchasing practices are discussed in detail in chapters 5 and 8, respectively.

247 Ibid.

248 Ibid.

249 "Buying power of the parties to the joint purchasing arrangement could be used to foreclose competing purchasers by limiting their access to efficient suppliers", Communication from the Commission — Guidelines on the applicability of Article 101 of the Treaty on the Functioning of the European Union to horizontal co-operation agreements [2011] OJ C 11/1, para. 203.

250 "BA is therefore wrong to deny that it is an obligatory business partner of travel agents established in the United Kingdom and to maintain that those agents have no actual need to sell BA tickets. BA's arguments are not capable of calling into question the finding, in recital 93 of the contested decision, that BA enjoys a particularly powerful position in relation to its nearest rivals *and* the largest travel agents." Judgment of 17 December 2003, *British Airways v Commission* of 17 December 2003, T-219/99, ECR, EU:T:2003:343, para. 121 (emphasis added).

entering into predatory overbuying[251], securing supply from the most efficient suppliers through exclusive purchasing agreements[252], or by imposing exclusive dealing clauses vis-à-vis suppliers or raising entry or exit barriers for other buyers. These conducts with foreclosure effects are discussed at length in chapter 6.

VI. Indirect buyer power effects

148. In this section, I discuss buyer power effects that go beyond the pure buyer-supplier-end consumer price effects of monopsony and bargaining power by looking at what the consequences of buyer power on the competitive conditions and third parties from a more dynamic perspective are. In particular, I deal with the waterbed and anti-waterbed effects, investment and innovation, quality and increased concentration and decreased variety. For all these cases, the discussion is centered around bargaining power, as, for the case of monopsony, the positive effects are non-existent and the risks for anti-competitive effects are increased.

A. The waterbed effect

149. The exercise of bargaining power may influence the price paid by other buyers vis-à-vis suppliers in a positive or a negative way. The 'waterbed effect' describes the situation that prevails whenever the purchasing prices for other buyers increase due to exertion of buyer power by a powerful rival. The waterbed effect is relative in the sense that its consequences will depend on the circumstances of the case and will impact each rival buyer (and suppliers) in a particular way[253]. Furthermore, the waterbed effect is anchored on models *assuming linear tariff* contracts as I discussed in chapter 2, section §IV.

150. There are *three theories behind the waterbed effect*: a mechanical explanation, bargaining power changes due to the upstream market structure, and market share shifting in the downstream market[254]. I discuss these theories in the following paragraphs[255].

---

251 Salop (2004-2005); Kirkwood 'Buyer Power and Exclusionary Conduct: Should Brooke Group Set the Standards for Buyer-Induced Price Discrimination and Predatory Bidding?' (2004-2005).

252 Thomas G. Krattenmaker and Steven C. Salop, 'Anticompetitive Exclusion: Raising Rivals' Costs to Achieve Power over Price' 96 The Yale Law Journal (1986) 209, p. 234.

253 Buttà and Pezzoli (2014), p. 163.

254 Dobson and Inderst (2007), p. 393-400; and Dobson and Inderst (2008), p. 343 to 350. See also: OECD '*Policy Roundtables: Monopsony and Buyer Power*' (2009), p. 25, and discussing these two alternative sources of the waterbed effect: Dobson and Chakraborty (2008), p. 344.

255 See also the analysis of these theories in Kirkwood 'Powerful Buyers and Merger Enforcement' (2012), p. 1544-1546; and OECD '*Policy Roundtables: Monopsony and Buyer Power*' (2009), p. 50-53.

151. The *mechanical explanation* of the waterbed effect depicts a situation in which the suppliers charge a higher price to the non-powerful buyers to recoup the lost profits on contracting with the powerful buyer[256]. This is the most intuitive but weakest explanation on how the waterbed effect works. From a different perspective, the exercise of bargaining power increases rival's input costs, which may lead to either competitors exiting the market or them increasing their prices downstream[257]. The outcome is that the powerful buyer will enjoy larger market power downstream as competitors exit the market or sell at retailer levels at higher prices and, in the long run, downstream prices as a whole will tend to rise[258]. Consequently, *the waterbed effect produces an exclusionary outcome over rivals that can lead to exploitative abuses in the medium/long term*. This mechanic waterbed explanation was recognized by the Commission in its Guidelines on the applicability of Article 81 of the EC Treaty to horizontal cooperation agreements, when stating:

> (…) the primary concerns in the context of buying power are that lower prices may not be passed on to customers further downstream and that it *may cause cost increases for the purchasers' competitors on* the selling markets because either suppliers *will try to recover price reductions* for one group of customers by *increasing prices for other customers or competitors* have less access to efficient suppliers[259].

152. However, the current Guidelines on Horizontal Agreements that replaced the former text depart from the mechanical approach to the waterbed effect[260]. It no longer makes references to any "recovering process" of lost profits while still maintaining that buyer power may lead "to restrictive effects on competition on the purchasing and/or downstream selling market or markets, such as increased prices […] [and] [b]uying power of the parties to the joint purchasing arrangement could be used to foreclose competing purchasers by limiting their access to efficient suppliers"[261].

---

256 This appears to have been the rationale of the now extinct UK Competition Commission when evaluating the price differentials paid by smaller supermarket retailers to suppliers in comparison with largest buyers in UK Competition Commission (2000), para. 2.451; see also: Dobson [2009], p. 122. Also using the mechanical effect explanation see, *inter alia*, Pera, p. 3; Carstensen 'Buyer Power and the Horizontal Merger Guidelines: Minor Progress on an Important Issue' (2012), p. 796, Dobson and Chakraborty (2008), p. 344; Oinonen (2014), p. 102.

257 OECD '*Policy Roundtables: Monopsony and Buyer Power*' (2009), p. 47.

258 Buttà and Pezzoli (2014), p. 163.

259 Commission Notice Guidelines on the applicability of Article 81 of the EC Treaty to horizontal cooperation Agreements (2001/C 3/02), (OJ C 3/2 6.1.2001), para. 126 (emphasis added), see also the same idea in para. 129 and para. 135.

260 See also stressing this fact: Jonathan Faull, Ali Nikpay and Deirdre Taylor, *The EU Law of Competition* (3rd ed. Oxford University Press 2014), para. 7.374.

261 Communication from the Commission — Guidelines on the applicability of Article 101 of the Treaty on the Functioning of the European Union to horizontal co-operation agreements [2011] OJ C 11/1, para. 203.

153. This departure from the mechanical approach by the Commission is welcomed as the theory has some pitfalls. Firstly, according to the intuition behind the mechanical waterbed effect, the increase in prices vis-à-vis other buyers is the consequence of wanting to recoup the discounts granted to the large buyer, and lost profit. This, nevertheless, does not explain why suppliers were not already charging a higher price to some buyers if this was foreseeable, even in the absence of the powerful buyer[262]. Nor does it account for why a discount to a buyer implies that the seller is forced to increase its selling prices to other buyers; if the deal with the powerful buyer is not good enough, the seller has other demand sources to sell its goods to. Secondly, assuming that if suppliers do not increase their output prices to other (weaker) buyers implies that suppliers will be forced to leave the upstream market as costs would not be profitable. In my view such argument may apply if the buyer exerts monopsony power on a take-it-or-leave-it basis, as it pays a purchasing price below the competitive level. However, if bargaining power is exerted or there are other alternative buyers, then suppliers would not sell at a loss.

154. The *upstream approach to the waterbed effect,* the second explanation of it by Dobson and Inderst, is based on the increase of market shares by a powerful retailer. A consequence of market power increase as a retailer is that the undertaking also enjoys a bargaining position that allows for obtaining better terms and conditions by leveraging its success from one market to another, and which affects upstream competition[263]. The improved bargaining position increases market concentration in the supplier's side as a natural response to avoid the transfer of profit from supplier to buyer. This can happen in two ways. Firstly, whenever the exercise of bargaining power leads to the exit of some suppliers that find the current market prices no longer profitable. Secondly, if the industry has barriers of entry but research and development of new products allows for the entry of newcomers, the exercise of bargaining power can prevent potential entry. In the long run, the increase of buyer market power will generate a trend to increase upstream concentration among suppliers, which now have more bargaining power[264]. Consequently, bargaining power effects upstream ought to distinguish between smaller suppliers (who will be worse off and may even disappear) and large suppliers, which will in the long run either be in the same situation or better off than before[265]. Also, in the long run, the buyers' bargaining power decreases, as now they will face suppliers with stronger bargaining positions themselves. Consequently, smaller buyers are also worse off than before the buyer exer-

262 Also raising a similar argument: Robles Martín-Laborda; Dobson and Inderst (2007), p. 397; Dobson and Inderst (2008), p. 342; Parker and Majumdar, [2011], p. 564-565; Kirkwood 'Powerful Buyers and Merger Enforcement' (2012), p. 1544.

263 Dobson and Inderst (2007), p. 397-398; and Dobson and Inderst (2008), p. 344.

264 Dobson [2009], p. 124.

265 Dobson and Inderst (2008), p. 344-345.

cised its bargaining power, as they will be less powerful and will have to pay more for the same quantity of goods as before.

155. In my view, this explanation of the waterbed effect by Dobson and Inderst is in line with the postulates of the countervailing theory of Galbraith, as market power tends to naturally grow to neutralize opposing market power[266]. Unlike Dobson and Inderst, to me, if this concentration is the consequence of countervailing power, the outcome in terms of price should be that of an equilibrium, such as in the cooperative bilateral monopoly model, and not a rise, assuming that quantity remains constant. Also, this presupposes that the buyer will squeeze suppliers or prevent their entry. Again, such behaviour appears to be lacking long-term rationale. A rational buyer would not pressure its suppliers in such a way if it wants to avoid a subsequent situation of market power neutralization. The buyer will be better served if more suppliers are present in the market as it grants it with more supplier side constraint and, thus, enhances its bargaining power.

156. The last theory regarding the waterbed effect is based on *a change of retailer's market shares*[267]. Dobson and Inderst submit that in this case the waterbed effect takes place due to the larger market shares obtained by the powerful buyer as a consequence of its more competitive offering in the downstream market[268]. As the buyer increases its sales and gains market share downstream thanks to its ability as a buyer to reduce its input costs, it is able to sell goods as a retailer at a lower price capturing demand from its competitors that are unable to offer the same lower prices. Smaller retailers are worse off as they will lose volume, customers and will receive less advantageous terms of supply, creating a waterbed effect[269]. This theory has two consequences. Firstly, prices in the downstream market will be – at least in the short term – lower for final consumers due to the passing on to end consumers. As acknowledged by Dobson and Inderst: "[t]he larger retailer can now lever its discounts into lower retail prices and/or better services and thereby obtain a larger share of the final market"[270]. Secondly, the theory seems to grant a protection that is broader than pure end consumer harm and aims to tackle anti-competitive effects on smaller retailers and weaker suppliers that may impact the competitive process, but can also be excessively protective of rival undertakings.

157. Summing up, *in its three variants the waterbed effect has negative implications for short and long term competition.* In the short term, the waterbed

266 Also noticing the influence of Galbraith's countervailing power theory see: Kirkwood 'Powerful Buyers and Merger Enforcement' (2012), p. 1544-1546.

267 See also the analysis of this type of waterbed effect in Buttà and Pezzoli (2014).

268 Dobson and Inderst (2008), p. 346-347.

269 Ibid, p. 347.

270 Ibid, p. 347.

effect increases rival buyer's costs and downstream retail prices. In the long run, as the powerful buyer is more efficient than its competitors, it captures their market share and has a foreclosing effect, weakening or eliminating downstream competition. This exclusionary effect was acknowledged by Commission firstly in *Kesko/Tuko*[271] and later in *Carrefour/Promodès*[272] as the "spiral effect"[273]. The spiral effect increases market concentration downstream, leading to a vicious circle of more retailer power and the capacity to later on reap monopoly profits from end consumers due to the creation of entry and exit barriers[274]. Concerning long-term effects on consumer prices, the increase in input costs for rival buyers also pushes retail prices upwards. However, rival buyer-retailers may not increase prices excessively as they could lose too much demand to the powerful buyer and eventually be foreclosed. Which of these negative effects predominates is ambiguous[275]. Nevertheless, and as remarked by Dobson, the spiral effect may also lead to a "virtuous circle"[276]. Once the spiral effect takes place, the retailer can benefit from further efficiency gains that allow it to further improve downstream market conditions and further decrease prices for end consumers[277].

B. The anti-waterbed effect

158. It is, however, disputed in economic literature that buyer power exertion generates a waterbed effect. It has been proposed that, in particular, bargaining power, can produce an 'anti-waterbed effect' as the discounts obtained by a powerful buyer may also benefit its rivals in the form of lower input prices[278]. The intuition behind this argument is that once a buyer has obtained a discount from a supplier, if known to other buyers, they will also try to obtain a discounted price[279]. As Dobson and Inderst submit, these spillover discounts are generated due to the "now lower margins that the supplier earns from con-

271 The Commission considered that the concentration would create an entity with too high a degree of buyer power leading suppliers to be dependent on the buyer, and also imposing too high entry barriers for potential competition. Commission Decision of 20 November 1996 declaring a concentration to be incompatible with the common market (Case No IV/M.784 - *Kesko/Tuko*) Council Regulation (EEC) No 4064/89 [1997] OJ L 110/53, taken from the unabridged version.

272 Non-opposition to a notified concentration (Case COMP/M.1684 — *Carrefour/Promodès*) [2000] OJ C 164/5, French public version, para. 45-46.

273 See discussing the spiral effect and its negative effects on competition: Alan Overd, 'Buyer Power' 22 European Competition Law Review (2001) 249, p. 250; Office of Fair Trading, *The Competitive Effects of Buyer Groups* (2007) para 1.74; Bundeskartellamt '*Buyer Power in Competition Law - Status and Perspectives*' (2008), p. 3; Dobson [2009], p. 122; Tribunal Vasco de la Competencia (April 2009), p. 139; Ezrachi and De Jong (2012), p. 258.

274 Faull and Nikpay, [1999], para. 4.154.

275 Dobson and Inderst (2007), p. 398; OECD '*Policy Roundtables: Monopsony and Buyer Power*' (2009), p. 50.

276 Dobson [2009], p. 122.

277 Ibid, p. 122-123.

278 The term "anti-waterbed effect" was firstly coined by Dobson and Inderst in: Dobson and Inderst (2007), p. 399.

279 Dobson and Inderst (2008), p. 353.

ducting business with the first retailer"[280]. Thus, giving successive discounts to other buyers becomes less costly for the supplier[281]. An alternative theory of the anti-waterbed effect was used by the Commission in *Enso/Stora* in which it explained this positive effect to other buyers as being in the interest of a seller under countervailing buyer pressure from a very large buyer to keep other customers in the market in order to avoid becoming dependent on a single demand source[282].

159. Furthermore, Dobson and Inderst argue that the anti-waterbed effect will be more dominant the more equal buyers are vis-à-vis suppliers. If there is a large difference in market size between buyers, then the waterbed effect dominates[283]. However, they also note that if suppliers are aware of the dominance of the waterbed effect they will be better off by securing the presence of other buyers and, therefore, will grant them discounts as well. The logic is that if the waterbed effect dominates then suppliers will have less demand sources and, in the long run, will face too powerful a buyer[284].

C. How should the waterbed effect be approached?

160. Pursuant to the discussion regarding the water and anti-waterbed effects and the lack of economic consensus, EU competition law should adopt a cautious approach to the topic, following a case-by-case assessment, as which of these effects dominates will depend on the circumstances of the conduct under analysis[285]. Furthermore, even if the waterbed effect dominates in the upstream market the effect for final consumers may be lower purchasing prices[286]. Consequently, I propose rejecting a hard and fast rule that equates bargaining power exercise to generating a waterbed effect.

161. Furthermore, in the assessment of the waterbed effect and the choice of a theory of harm it is important to disengage from employing the mechanic theory of the waterbed effect, which fortunately the Commission has stopped

280 Dobson and Inderst (2007), p. 399. Also supporting this argument of the supplier having an incentive to grant a lower purchasing price see: OECD '*Policy Roundtables: Monopsony and Buyer Power*' (2009), p. 50.

281 Dobson and Inderst (2008), p. 353.

282 Commission Decision of 25 November 1998 declaring a concentration to be compatible with the common market and the functioning of the EEA Agreement (Case No IV/M.1225 - *Enso/Stora*) [1999] OJ L 254/9, para 96.

283 Dobson and Inderst (2007), p. 399; Dobson and Inderst (2008), p. 353.

284 Dobson and Inderst (2007), p. 399; Dobson and Inderst (2008), p. 353.

285 Dobson and Inderst (2007), p. 399; OECD '*Policy Roundtables: Monopsony and Buyer Power*' (2009), p. 49-50; Buttà and Pezzoli (2014), p. 163.

286 OECD '*Policy Roundtables: Monopsony and Buyer Power*' (2009), p. 50.

using,[287] as it is not well grounded in economics. However, from a legal perspective, the outcome regarding the existence of the waterbed effect does not change based on which one of the three theories is employed, but the argument employed (if based on the mechanical effect) would be flawed. Lastly, in any case, in the assessment of the water and anti-waterbed effects, the emphasis ought to be placed on its effects in the short *and* long run both in the upstream and downstream market to fully capture the dual effect of buyer power in competition.

D. Buyer power effects on investment, innovation and dynamic efficiency

162. Part of the literature suggests that buyer power exertion may have deleterious consequences for supplier's incentives to invest and innovate generating a hold-up problem[288]. If buyer power is exploited, suppliers may be less incentivized to invest and innovate because the buyer is able to extract the extraordinary profits generated by better and more innovative goods and services that would otherwise have belonged to the supplier[289]. This could happen in retailing markets where the buyer power of large supermarkets may act as a disincentive for suppliers to invest and innovate in the production of newer and better products or increase output, leading to reduction of capacity, fewer products and lower quality[290].

163. The adverse effect on investment and innovation, according to Dobson et alia in a Commission's report, might increase if bargaining power is exercised against small suppliers[291], which is also the opinion of the Commission concerning abuse of bargaining power in food retailing[292]. However, as remarked by Inderst and Doyle, the argument submitting that buyer power stifles innovation overlooks the fact that a supplier's decision to invest depends on the

287 Commission Notice Guidelines on the applicability of Article 81 of the EC Treaty to horizontal cooperation Agreements (2001/C 3/02), (OJ C 3/2 6.1.2001), para. 126. Cf with the absence of the recoup effect in Commission — Guidelines on the applicability of Article 101 of the Treaty on the Functioning of the European Union to horizontal co-operation agreements [2011] OJ C 11/1, para. 200-204.

288 Supporting this see: European Commission and others (2000), p. 4; Noll (2004-2005), p. 612; Grimes (2004-2005), p. 566; Battigalli, Fumagalli and Polo (2007); Competition Commission UK (2008), para. 36; Dobson and Chakraborty (2008), p. 345; Peter C. Carstensen, 'Buyer Cartels Versus Buying Groups: Legal Distinctions, Competitive Realities, and Antitrust Policy' William & Mary Business Law Review (2010) 1, p. 33; Pera and Bonfitto (2011), p. 415-416; Pera, p. 3, available at http://www.gop.it/doc_pubblicazioni/40_hjv4kr3vun_eng.pdf; Kirkwood 'Powerful Buyers and Merger Enforcement' (2012); Alexander Italianer, *The Devil is in the Retail* (2 October 2014), p. 3; Buttà and Pezzoli (2014), p. 164.

289 Noll sets this explanation in a monopsony power situation in Noll (2004-2005), p. 612 and 621; see also: Dobson (2004-2005); Dobson and Chakraborty (2008), p. 345. See also suggesting investment problems caused by exercise of buyer power in healthcare markets: Kirkwood, *Buyer Power and Healthcare Prices*, 6.

290 Competition Commission, UK (2008), para 9.5. Concerning the quality issue see also: Dobson and Chakraborty (2008), p. 346; Ezrachi and De Jong (2012).

291 European Commission and others (2000), p. 38.

292 European Commission '*Tackling Unfair Trading Practices in the Business-to-Business food supply chain*' (2014), p. 12.

profit difference that would be obtained with or without the investment, and not on the overall level of profitability[293].

164. On the other hand, research shows that *bargaining power can increase innovation as it may incentivize suppliers and competitors to invest*[294]. In the case of rival buyers competing downstream, Dobson and Chakraborty argue that the exertion of bargaining power by a powerful buyer will force these competitors to invest to contest the price advantage of the powerful buyer and avoid being squeezed out of the market[295]. Additionally, a buyer with substantial market power could be willing to financially support the investments of a supplier as it could benefit from increased sales in the downstream market[296].

165. In the upstream market, suppliers facing a powerful buyer have an incentive to invest because by doing so they receive a larger fraction of the incremental profits generated by their investment. Also, if the investment decreases their marginal cost, it also reduces the value of outside supply options for the buyer and, therefore, reduces the buyer bargaining power[297], for current and future contracts.[298] Also, suppliers have an incentive to invest to increase their chances of securing a contract with other potential buyers in case a large customer decides to look for alternative suppliers and prevent becoming or being dependent on a single buyer[299].

166. Lastly, bargaining power may also spur investment by sponsoring the entry of new sources of supply[300]. This was recognized by the Commission in the *Enso/Stora* Decision[301]. In this case, the Commission considered that Tetra Pak had sufficient countervailing buyer power to neutralize the market power of the merging undertaking as it could sponsor the development of capacity of one of the other suppliers in the market *or sponsor entry of new undertakings to produce its input*[302].

---

293 Doyle and Inderst (2007), p. 217.

294 See also making a similar claim: Italianer, *The Devil is in the Retail*, p. 7; UK (2008), para. 9.4.

295 Dobson and Chakraborty (2008), p. 344.

296 Bundeskartellamt '*Buyer Power in Competition Law - Status and Perspectives*' (2008), p. 4.

297 Roman Inderst and Christian Wey, 'How Strong Buyers Spur Upstream Innovation' 524 DIW Berlin: Discussion Papers (2005), 1.

298 Chen 'Buyer power: Economic Theory and Antitrust Policy' (2007), p. 26; Kirkwood 'Powerful Buyers and Merger Enforcement' (2012), p. 1551.

299 Inderst and Wey 'Buyer Power and Supplier Incentives' (2007), p. 648.

300 Doyle and Inderst (2007), p. 216; Inderst and Wey 'Buyer Power and Supplier Incentives' (2007), p. 649. For a discussion of sponsoring of new entrants in public procurement markets see: Sánchez Graells and Herrera Anchustegui, 'Impact of Public Procurement Aggregation on Competition. Risks, Rationale and Justification for the Rules in Directive 2014/24' [2016], p. 135-136.

301 Commission Decision of 25 November 1998 declaring a concentration to be compatible with the common market and the functioning of the EEA Agreement (Case No IV/M.1225 - *Enso/Stora*) [1999] OJ L 254/9, para. 88.

302 Commission Decision of 25 November 1998 declaring a concentration to be compatible with the common market and the functioning of the EEA Agreement (Case No IV/M.1225 - *Enso/Stora*) [1999] OJ L 254/9, para. 92.

E. Buyer power effects on quality

167. Bargaining power can also create incentives to increase or to decrease quality. Battigalli, Fumagalli and Polo submit that buyer power negatively affects the incentives of suppliers to invest in quality improvements, particularly in the case of private labels,[303] and when investing in research and development is necessary for obtaining quality improvements[304]. As bargaining power extracts profits from suppliers, these will have little incentive to invest in maintaining and improving the quality of goods[305]. This has a negative impact on both the buyer and the end consumer that acquires the goods[306]. Similarly, Ezrachi and De Jong describe a situation in which the exercise of bargaining power affects output quality as suppliers are pressured "to sell at near loss"[307]. In their view, in some markets, such as food retailing, if the final consumer cannot easily detect the drop in quality, the supplier can increase profitability by reducing the quality of the goods it produces. Accordingly, they argue, the quality erosion is likely to neglect the positive effects of the bargaining power regarding the welfare gains in the form of lower purchasing prices and, therefore lead to a loss in welfare[308].

168. In my view, these theories on quality erosion may be criticized from several angles. Firstly, quality erosion may appear whenever there is little or no competition in the downstream market; however, in the presence of substantial downstream market competition it will be unlikely to exist. If the supplier diminishes the quality of the products, a rational buyer that faces competition in the downstream market will see how consumers and its customers – who are likely to notice the reduction in quality – will shift their demand to other (better) retailers. This, nevertheless, assumes a high degree of care from the consumer, and is debatable whether this is the case, particularly in unsophisticated markets, like day-to-day purchases. Furthermore, it is contrary to the interest of the powerful buyer that quality is eroded (even if difficult but not impossible to detect) and, therefore, the buyer is likely to set up quality control programs, as remarked by Dobson and Chakraborty[309]. Secondly, if the supplier increases quality it diminishes the bargaining power of its buyer, which would allow the supplier to gain a competitive advantage when nego-

303 Also stressing the effect of private labels increasing buyer power of food retailers see: European Competition Network (2012), para. 254; Bundeskartellamt '*Summary of the Final Report of the Sector Inquiry into the Food Retail Sector*' (2014), p. 5; Faull, Nikpay and Taylor, [2014], para. 5.888.

304 Battigalli, Fumagalli and Polo (2007). Also suggesting that quality erosion tends to take place in the presence of private labels see: Ezrachi and De Jong (2012).

305 Battigalli, Fumagalli and Polo (2007), p. 47. Similarly, see: Dobson and Chakraborty (2008), p. 344.

306 Their model consists of a monopolistic producer and two independent retailers that enter into all or none negotiations, Battigalli, Fumagalli and Polo (2007), p. 46.

307 Ezrachi and De Jong (2012), p. 258

308 Ibid, p. 259. In their work, Ezrachi and De Jong distinguish between two types of quality erosion: undetected and agreed quality erosion, by making a distinction regarding whether or not the buyer is aware of it.

309 Suggesting that bargaining power encourages setting up of quality control measures in the retail industry see: Dobson and Chakraborty (2008), p. 344.

tiating future contracts in better terms, and limiting the extraction of its rents. Thirdly, agreed quality erosion not only implies a risk of losing sales but also, if detected by competition authorities, being sanctioned due to entering into collusive practices prohibited by Article 101(1)(b) TFEU.

F. Buyer power effects on market concentration: variety and exclusion

169. Lastly, both the EU legislation and the Commission have raised a concern regarding the effect of buyer power leading to further concentration in the upstream and downstream markets due to the waterbed effect, and which is also consistent with the countervailing power theory of Galbraith. For instance, this was explicitly recognized regarding aggregated public procurement by the Recital 59 of the Directive 2014/24 on Public Procurement[310]. Also, recently, the Commission has raised concerns about the pernicious buyer power effects on small and medium enterprises in the food-retailing sector, as these small retailers and suppliers may be foreclosed and squeezed out of the market due to the imposition of unfair commercial practices arising from a substantial difference in bargaining power[311].

170. This negative effect on concentration due to the exercise of buyer power may take place in the upstream market as suppliers will look for strategies that increase their seller market power and negotiate terms and conditions that are more beneficial to their interest, neutralizing buyer bargaining power and making it more likely to merge or create commercial alliances. In the downstream market, if the powerful buyer passes on the bargaining benefits to end consumers in the form of lower retailing prices it will capture its competitor's demand – and will increase its market shares – unless these (smaller or less efficient) competitors offer either similar prices and/or better quality goods. Increased market concentration implies fewer competitors that may or may not be more efficient, and consequently less variety of goods or services[312].

171. A variety of similar concerns on the negative effects of buyer power on concentration and variety have been expressed by the US Federal Trade Commission in food retailing markets, pertaining to whenever the buyer acts

---

310 "[h]owever, the aggregation and centralisation of purchases should be carefully monitored in order to avoid excessive concentration of purchasing power and collusion, and to preserve transparency and competition, as well as market access opportunities for SMEs" Recital 59 Directive 2014/24/EU of the European Parliament and of the Council of 26 February 2014 on public procurement and repealing Directive 2004/18/EC [2014] OJ L 94/65. For a discussion of the concentration effect generated by aggregated purchasing in public procurement markets see: Herrera Anchustegui (2015); Sánchez Graells and Herrera Anchustegui [2016], p. 140-142.

311 European Commission '*Tackling Unfair Trading Practices in the Business-to-Business food supply chain*' (2014), p. 3.

312 Office of Fair Trading, *The Competitive Effects of Buyer Groups*, para. 7.13.

as a gate-keeper[313], and as also discussed by Kirkwood regarding e-books[314]. Furthermore, authors like Chen argue that buyer power, if exerted against a monopolist, will have a positive effect on reducing end consumer prices but will decrease further product diversity[315].

172. In contrast with these negative views regarding buyer power impact in concentration and variety, recent literature shows that buyer/retailer bargaining power does not decrease the variety of available goods or services or, if it does, not as much as seller market power does[316]. Gabrielsen and Johansen compare manufacturers in terms of selling market power and retailers with buyer market power and conclude that buyer power implies less exclusion and, therefore, allows for a greater variety of goods/services[317]. They conclude that authorities should refrain from restricting or eliminating bargaining power if they are concerned about product variety and price increases. Similarly, the former UK Office of Fair Trading held that the exercise of buyer power and its effects on variety are likely to be positive as "where downstream competition is effective, markets would typically respond to consumer desires for more diversity"[318].

173. The foregoing discussion leads to the question of whether competition policy ought to protect 'sufficient variety' and a 'healthy amount' of market players in the upstream and downstream market at the expense of short and medium-term efficiency and lower consumer prices. This is an area of buyer power economics and competition policy that is still ripe for further research.

VII. Conclusions

174. In this chapter, I have analyzed the economics behind buyer power and discussed its direct and indirect welfare effects. I submit that buyer power is an umbrella term encompassing monopsony and bargaining power, different expressions of buyer power with different effects, making it an ambiguous umbrella concept. Furthermore, buyer power has a *dual effect in competition.*

---

313 European Commission (2001), p. 58.

314 The evidence presented, however, did not support that buyer power induced a lack of variety of titles sold by Amazon, see the discussion in: Kirkwood (2014).

315 Zhiqi Chen, 'Monopoly and Product Diversity: The Role of Retailer Countervailing Power' 04-19 Carleton Economic Papers (2004), p. 21-22.

316 Tommy Staahl Gabrielsen and Bjørn Olav Johansen, 'Buyer Power and Exclusion in Vertically Related Markets' 38 International Journal of Industrial Organization (2015) 1; Office of Fair Trading, *The Competitive Effects of Buyer Groups*, para. 7.22-7.23. Cf this with the view of Chen who claims that manufacturer seller power reduces variety and that buyer bargaining power exacerbates this distortion in product diversity; thus retailer countervailing power is not an adequate solution to manufacturer selling power, in Chen 'Monopoly and Product Diversity: The Role of Retailer Countervailing Power' (2004).

317 Gabrielsen and Johansen (2015), p. 3.

318 Office of Fair Trading, *The Competitive Effects of Buyer Groups*, para. 7.23.

It will always impact the *upstream conditions* between rival buyers and suppliers, and it also *affect downstream conditions* when the buyer competes as a retailer with other rival buyers, and also having an impact in end consumer prices and non-price competition. Therefore, any buyer power policy that focuses exclusively in upstream or downstream harm would be under-inclusive and run the risk of not fully capturing buyer power effects. Consequently, and as discussed through this research, buyer power analysis should adopt a *dualistic approach* to its upstream and downstream welfare effects, so as to fully capture buyer power effects and avoid risks of under enforcement while aiming at not over-enforcing EU competition rules[319].

175. *Monopsony power is always inefficient* because fewer goods are purchased than otherwise would be the case in a competitive setting, paying a price below the competitive level, generating an allocative efficiency loss and a profit transfer from suppliers to the buyer. This inefficient outcome holds even if monopsony power might have little or no impact on end consumer prices because the monopsonist lacks downstream market power. Furthermore, monopsony power almost always has negative efficiency effects in terms of non-price conditions: it reduces innovation, investment, erodes quality and tends to increase market concentration upstream. Therefore, regarding monopsony power cases, it will be likely that a conduct that involves withholding purchases will restrict competition by object under Article 101 TFEU or by nature in cases of unilateral behaviour.

176. In turn, the *exercise of bargaining power tends to be welfare enhancing* as it reduces input prices by neutralizing opposed supplier market power without withholding demand. Furthermore, the price reduction may be passed on to end consumers in the form of lower prices if there is sufficient competition where the buyer operates as a retailer[320]. Additionally, bargaining power may have positive non-price effects, such as in the case of spurring investment and innovation, promoting quality and quality control, and limiting variety erosion from seller market power. However, bargaining power may also be exerted in an anti-competitive manner to exploit suppliers and exclude rivals buyers competing in the upstream and that, additionally but not necessarily, compete in the downstream market as retailers.

---

319 For literature dealing with Type I and II errors in competition and antitrust law see, *inter alia*: Maarten Pieter Schinkel and Jan Tuinstra, 'Imperfect Competition Law Enforcement' CeNDEF Working Paper No 04-07 (2004) 1; Monti, [2007], p. 16-18; T. Mäger and T. B. Paul, 'The Interaction of Public and Private Enforcement – The Calculation and Reconciliation of Fines and Damages in Europe and Germany' in K. Hüschelrath and H. Schweitzer (eds), *Public and Private Enforcement of Competition Law in Europe: Legal and Economic Perspectives* (Springer 2014), p. 77-104; David Lewis *Chilling Competition*, (http://www.comptrib.co.za/assets/Uploads/Speeches/lewis13.pdf).

320 This is also Kirkwood's view when stating that "the exercise of countervailing power (bargaining power) is frequently procompetitive, collusion (among sellers to eliminate it) should be allowed to offset it unless there is clear evidence of competitive harm" in Kirkwood (2014), p. 51. See also the views of Buttà and Pezzoli when stating "[b]uyer power (meaning bargaining power) is generally beneficial for final consumers and might even boost the productivity of upstream suppliers" in Buttà and Pezzoli (2014), p. 173.

177. This ambiguous buyer power effect on welfare implies that competition law *should steer away from an outdated and simplistic approach that sees buyer power cases as representations of monopsony power or only portraying the negative aspects of bargaining power*. Also, it ought to recognize the largely benign effect of bargaining power and, therefore, apply a more lenient treatment than when compared to monopsony cases. This, though, does not imply that bargaining power conducts should be outside the scope of competition law scrutiny[321]. Also, the lack of certainty makes difficult to offer a 'shortcut' in the form of a reliable framework to capture all cases of buyer power conducts. Even though these models have been proposed, they are difficult to apply due to the assumptions they are built on[322]. Another problem with this type of guidance for cases is that they are anchored on market structures and not conducts. The adoption of these form/structured based approaches to the application of the law may lead to the erroneous belief that what is forbidden is the existence of a 'form or shape' or type of market power distribution, when instead what is forbidden is the abuse of market power through conducts.

178. Further, I have analyzed the direct buyer power effects on prices and showed that, for both monopsony and bargaining power, whenever the buyer also enjoys substantial downstream market power, the risks of anti-competitive harm increase under the *hourglass shape* theory[323]. This happens because if the buyer has no competitive pressure to pass on the price reductions obtained due to its buyer power, it will keep the supra-competitive profits that have been transferred from the supplier while it also employs its market power downstream vis-à-vis end consumers. Also, as it has substantial downstream market power it can use this to reinforce its upstream position to the detriment of suppliers and, most importantly, other rival buyers.

179. Regarding indirect buyer power effects, the picture is less clear as there is no complete consensus as to whether buyer (bargaining) power has a positive effect regarding price for other buyers and suppliers (the waterbed effect), investment, quality or market concentration. This blurry picture makes it difficult to make generalizations that can easily be extrapolated to cases and used as rules of thumb. Therefore, a cautious approach to indirect buyer power effects should be adopted by analyzing the circumstances of the case and looking at the competition effects of the purchasing conduct, in particular when dealing with bargaining power exertion.

---

321 Also sharing this view see: van Doorn.

322 European Commission and others (2000); Chen 'Buyer power: Economic Theory and Antitrust Policy' (2007).

323 This is also the opinion of Korah and O'Sullivan when stating that "[i]f the emphasis is on protecting consumers, there should be concern only when there is insufficient competition downstream to ensure that the benefits of buyer power are passed on to buyers", in Korah and O'Sullivan, [2002], p. 53.

180. Summing up, an understanding of buyer power economics and an awareness of the limitations and lack of consensus in the economic literature regarding some of its effects is a necessary first step towards the legal analysis of buying conducts in line with the economically informed legal analysis adopted in this study. Furthermore, this chapter is of importance as in my analysis of the legal regulation as at times economic-based discussions are presented, which are based on these findings and which allow the reader to understand why certain arguments and positions are adopted.

3

BUYER POWER THROUGH AN ORDOLIBERAL LENS*

I. Introduction

181. Ordoliberal ideas, in particular the ideas of *Wettbewerbsordnung* and *Wettbewerbsfreiheit* – a system of ordered competition and freedom to compete have been, and still are, influential[324], in the historical development of the European integration idea, in particular regarding the creation of the internal market[325], and EU competition policy[326]. At its core, ordoliberal-

---

* A version of this chapter dealing with ordoliberalism as an economic policy and its history has been published in the Oslo Law Review as Ignacio Herrera Anchustegui, 'Competition Law through an Ordoliberal Lens' 2 Oslo Law Review (2015) 139. The version presented here, however, focuses only on the ordoliberal aspects regarding competition and buyer power policy, and which were not thoroughly discussed in the previously discussion in the published work.

324 See recently the Judgment of 6 October 2009 in *GlaxoSmithKline Services and Others v Commission and Others*, Joined cases C-501/06 P, C-513/06 P, C-515/06 P and C-519/06 P, EU:C:2009:610, para. 63. Also stressing the ordoliberal influence in such statement see: Peter Behrens, 'The "Consumer Choice" Paradigm in German Ordoliberalism and its Impact upon EU Competition Law' 1/14 Europa-Kolleg Hamburg Discussion Paper (2014) 1. See also the treatment of rebates in Judgment of 12 June 2014, *Intel v Commission*, T-286/09, ECR, EU:T:2014:547, and Judgment of 6 October 2015 in *Post Danmark*, C-23/14, EU:C:2015:651.

325 Karel Van Miert, 'The Future of European Competition Policy' (1998) <http://ec.europa.eu/competition/speeches/text/sp1998_042_en.html> accessed 6/11/2014; Alessandro Somma, 'Private Law as Biopolitics: Ordoliberalism, Social Market Economy, and the Public Dimension of Contract' 76 Law and Contemporary Problems (2013) 105, p. 105, who sees the influence of the "ordoliberal agenda" in EU matters as well as adopting measures through a rather not very democratic decision-making process.

326 Gerber goes even further in his defense of the influence of ordoliberal thinking in EU competition law when stating "[t]his ordoliberal creation (competition law) has evolved into the European concept of competition law, and without it the develop-ment of the European Community is unimaginable", in David J. Gerber, 'Constitutionalizing the Economy: German Neo-Liberalism, Competition Law and the "New" Europe' 42 The American Journal of Comparative Law (1994) 25, p. 49. See, *inter alia*, supporting this assertion: David J. Gerber, *Law and Competition in Twentieth Century Europe: Protecting Prometheus* (Oxford University Press 2001), in particular Chapter VII; Ian Rose and Cynthia Ngwe, 'The Ordoliberal Tradition in the European Union, Its Influence on Article 82 EC and the IBA's Comments on the Article 82 EC Discussion Paper' 3 Competition Law International (2007) 8, p. 8; Flavio Felice and Massimiliano Vatiero, 'Ordo and European Competition Law' <http://www.siecon.org/online/wp-content/uploads/2013/09/Felice-Vatiero.pdf>, last visited 11/12/2014; Liza Lovdahl Gormsen, 'The Conflict Between Economic Freedom and Consumer Welfare in the Modernisation of Article 82 EC' 3 European Competition Journal (2007) 329; Ekaterina Rousseva, *Rethinking Exclusionary Abuses in EU Competition Law* (Hart 2010), p. 26-32; Michal S. Gal, 'Abuse of Dominance - Exploitative Abuses' in Ioannis Lianos and Damien Geradin (eds), *Handbook on European competition law: enforcement and procedure* (Edward Elgar Pub. Ltd. 2013), p. 388 to 391.

ism – also known as the Freiburg School of Law and Economics or German neo-liberalism[327] – advocates for a state-regulated competitive process as a necessary instrument for the protection of individual economic freedom[328]. Ordoliberalism, however, is not just about competition policy – nor is it just about competition economics. Rather, it considers the competitive process as one of the pillars of a holistic political economy and societal order[329].

182. In this study, and as discussed in chapter 1, *I employ ordoliberalism as an economic policy that serves as a benchmark tool to contrast and criticize against the regulation of buyer power, but not to justify the efficiency or validity of legal rules*. To do so, the legislation, decisions and judgments will be analyzed from an ordoliberal perspective by highlighting whether they are in line with ordoliberal ideas or whether and how they depart from such a policy standing. Through this contrasting exercise, this study provides a new perspective and allows for an (e)valuation of the EU regime on buyer power, for comparisons to be drawn with US antitrust law on equivalent issues, and for the discussion of certain elements *de lege ferenda.* Furthermore, by analyzing buyer power from an ordoliberal perspective, I am able *to determine whether its treatment in EU competition law is in line, or perhaps, influenced by ordoliberal competition policy.*

183. Also, ordoliberalism is a well suited analytical benchmarking tool for an evaluation and analysis of buyer power because, as noted by Akman:

> the main concern of Eucken was 'complete competition', that is competition in which no firm in a market has power to coerce other firms in that market. If there is competition on the supply side, as well as on the demand side [...] then the market form of complete competition is achieved[330].

---

327 An alternative name is used by Peacock and Willgerodt who refer to the *Ordo-Kreis* (Ordo-Circle) as the group of scholars part of this trend of thought arguably because not all scholars following these teachings studied or taught at the University of Freiburg, in Alan Peacock and Hans Willgerodt, 'German Neo-Liberals and the Social Market Economy' in Alan Peacock and Hans Willgerodt (eds), *German Neo-Liberals and the Social Market Economy*, Vol. I (MacMillan 1989), p. 1-15. Although some refer to the Freiburg school as only covering economics, I put forth in this chapter that this competition policy school has been enriched by both legal and economic scholars in a multidisciplinary perspective. Also of this opinion is Kamecke who even goes forward and claims that "Eucken's theoretical approach contributed more to political economy than to economic theory, and so it would probably be long forgotten by now if it had not been taken up by lawyers and politicians in the German postwar area", Ulrich Kamecke, 'The Proper Scope of Government Viewed from an Ordoliberal Perspective: The Example of Competition Policy: Comment' 157 Journal of Institutional and Theoretical Economics (JITE) (2001) 23, p. 23.

328 Individual freedom in ordoliberal theory is understood as the freedom of entrepreneurship, namely "to engage in competition to seek gratification by means of voluntary exchange on free markets", as defined by Bonefeld in Werner Bonefeld, 'Freedom and the Strong State: On German Ordoliberalism' 17 New Political Economy (2012) 633, p. 638.

329 See the views of Müller-Armack when claiming that the competitive order must act in the framework of society as a whole in Alfred Müller-Armack, 'The Social Market Economy as an Economic and Social Order' 36 Review of Social Economy (1978) 325, p. 327. On the central topics of Ordoliberalism, see: Manfred E. Streit, 'Economic Order, Private Law and Public Policy - The Freiburg School of Law and Economics in Perspective' 148 Journal of Institutional and Theoretical Economics (JITE) (1992) 675.

330 Pinar Akman, *The Concept of Abuse in EU Competition Law: Law and Economic Approaches* (Hart 2012), p. 58.

184. Thus, *ordoliberalism looks at markets in a dualistic way: taking into account upstream and downstream markets and the full effects of a purchasing conduct*. Furthermore, ordoliberalism is consistent with the adoption of an economically informed legal analysis methodology employed in this work as it a school that combines legal and economic perspectives in an interdisciplinary manner by translating the economic language into law without becoming "law and economics"[331]. Lastly, ordoliberalism is a well-suited analytic instrument as it advocates for the regulation of market power in a holistic manner whenever it can curb the economic freedom of market participants, such as in the case of unfair purchasing practices that, in an ordoliberal perspective[332], ought to be regulated by competition norms *lato sensu*[333].

185. In this chapter, my aim, therefore, is to show how an ordoliberal competition policy addresses issue of buyer power so that the comparison between the current legal treatment and the regulation can be made in a way that allows the reader to determine the consistency – or otherwise – of the EU buyer power treatment to ordoliberal ideas.

186. In this sense, a disclaimer ought to be made. Although there is existing literature dealing with ordoliberalism and, in particular, the influence of ordoliberal thinking in the development of EU competition law, I adopt a different approach when discussing the ordoliberal perspective when dealing with buyer power. This chapter does not explore the influence of ordoliberal ideas in the historical development of the EU and its competition policy from a historical perspective; nor does it discuss ordoliberalism as an economic school at large as this is a topic that I have covered substantially elsewhere[334]. There are three reasons for this limitation. Firstly, there is already relevant literature written on the topic dealing *in extenso* with the influence (or lack thereof) of ordoliberalism in EU competition policy[335]. Secondly, embarking on such a task would be outside of the scope and topic of this study. Thirdly, and linked to the former, I employ ordoliberalism as an analytical tool for analysis of buyer power regulation and not the other way around; this is, ordoliberalism contributes to the analysis because it serves as a theoretical construct to compare the EU treatment to buyer power to, which in itself is a novel approach and methodological choice.

---

331 Viktor Vanberg, 'Freiburg School of Law and Economics' in Peter Newman (ed), *The New Palgrave Dictionary*, Vol. 2 (1998), p. 173

332 F Böhm, W Eucken and H Grossman-Doerth, 'The Ordo Manifesto of 1936' in Alan Peacock and Hans Willgerodt (eds), *Germany's Social Market Economy: Origins and Evolution* (MacMillan 1989), p. 24-25.

333 Gormsen, 'Article 82 EC: Where are We Coming From and Where are We Going to?' (2006), p. 10; Rainer Klump and Manuel Wörsdörfer, 'On the affiliation of phenomenology and ordoliberalism: Links between Edmund Husserl, Rudolf and Walter Eucken' 18 The European Journal of the History of Economic Thought (2011), p. 569.

334 Herrera Anchustegui 'Competition Law through an Ordoliberal Lens' (2015).

335 See the views of Akman who claims that ordoliberal ideas were not by and large incorporated in the drafting of Article 102 TFEU in Pinar Akman, 'Searching for the Long-Lost Soul of Article 82 EC' 29 Oxford Journal of Legal Studies (2009) 267; Akman, *The Concept of Abuse in EU Competition Law: Law and Economic Approaches* [2012], p. 55-105. See also Nazzini, [2011], p. 131-132.

187. I have organized the chapter as follows: section §II introduces ordoliberalism and its main components as an economic policy. Section §III discusses competition from an ordoliberal point of view by analyzing which goals are protected, different types of competition, the connection of ordoliberalism and the 'more economic approach', and the role of the state in competition enforcement. Section §IV constructs a buyer power policy from an ordoliberal perspective anchored on the general theory of the school to allow me to carry out the comparison of the regulation of buyer power with this theoretical construct. In this section, I discuss the sufficiency of the current EU competition law regime and its applicability, the need to adopt a dualistic approach to buyer power which, in turn, also implies adopting a broader welfare and harm standard to competition intervention in buyer power cases. Then, I discuss the leeway for protecting freedom to compete and distributive concerns within an ordoliberal competition policy *lato sensu*. Lastly, section §V concludes the chapter by summarizing the main findings and policy implications of a buyer power policy grounded on ordoliberal ideas.

II. Ordoliberalism in a nutshell

188. Ordoliberal ideas were born in Freiburg, Germany, in the late 1920s and early 1930s amidst the Great Depression of 1929, the rise of the Nazi regime to power[336], and the state-planned economics of the Soviet Union[337]. In the center of this social and political turmoil, ordoliberals suggested implementing a third way[338] between *laissez-faire* and central planning, promoting the existence of a strong state governing economic activity and freedom to compete[339]. Ordoliberalism, this third

---

336 Similarly, see Gerber (1994), p. 25; Matthew Cole, 'Ordoliberalism and its influence on EU tying law' 36 European Competition Law Review (2015) 255. Cf with Somma (2013), p. 110-111. For a discussion of Nazism from an ordoliberal perspective, see: Michel Foucault and others, *The Birth of Biopolitics: Lectures at the Collège de France, 1978-1979* (Palgrave Macmillan 2008), p. 109-115.

337 Also similarly, see Oliver Marc Hartwich, *Neoliberalism: The Genesis of a Political Swearword* (The Centre for Independent Studies (CIS) 2009) 1, p. 6-7. Interestingly, the birth of ordoliberalism coincided with the birth of Keynesianism.

338 Such was Rüstow's views on ordoliberalism, an economic ideology in between capitalism and communism, Alexander Rüstow, 'Zwischen Kapitalismus und Kommunismus' in Nils Goldschmidt and Michael Wohlgemuth (eds), *Grundtexte zur Freiburger Tradition der Ordnungsökonomik* (Mohr Siebeck 2008), p. 423–448. For Eucken "the number of organizational forms (of the economy and society), in which the modern economy *may be* ordered is very small", thus portraying his idea of ordoliberalism as an alternative way between capitalism and centrally planned economies in Walter Eucken, 'El Problema Político de la Ordenación' in Lucas Beltrán (ed), *La Economía de Mercado*, Vol I (Sociedad de Estudios y Publicaciones 1963), p. 79 (author's translation and emphasis in original). See also: J Wiseman, 'Social Policy and the Social Market Economy' in Alan Peacock and Hans Willgerodt (eds), *German Neo-Liberals and the Social Market Economy*, Vol I (MacMillan 1989), p. 162-163; Barry J. Rodger, 'Competition Policy, Liberalism and Globalization: A European Perspective' 6 Columbia Journal of European Law (2000) 289, p. 293; also using the term "third way": Gerber (1994), p. 35. Also of this view is Bonefeld when stating "[t]he ordoliberal idea of a social market economy has been seen as a progressive alternative beyond the left and right" and "they thus saw their neoliberalism as a third way in distinction to laissez-faire liberalism and collective forms of political economy", in Bonefeld (2012), p. 634; and similarly in Werner Bonefeld, 'German Neoliberalism and the Idea of a Social Market Economy: Free Economy and the Strong State' Journal of Social Sciences (2012) 139, p. 141. See also Foucault and others, [2008], p. 119-120.

339 Kamecke (2001), p. 24.

way between neo-liberalism and state-planned economy worked along the principles of preserving a large degree of *laissez-faire* while advocating the creation of "an institutional framework, which brings order to economic processes in a liberal atmosphere"[340]. This economic order is anchored on the "Freiburg Imperative"[341]: a societal system grounded on the regulation of the competitive order of market freedom, protection of private property and trust in the market-price system[342], in addition to institutional pillars governing other societal aspects of human life[343]. Out of these concepts, as expressed by Eucken, the competitive price system is the fundamental one as it ensures an efficient outcome and use of resources[344]. Eucken stated that achieving social order is necessary to direct society's economic life. Such ordering "consists in all the forms in which it is carried out the direction of daily economic process"[345], and the *Ordnung* ought to be dictated by the state, which imposes rules for the competitive process but respects individual freedom.

189. An ordoliberal society is based upon on what I have labeled the four central themes of ordoliberalism:[346]

i) *Ordnungsökonomik* – economic order – and economic freedom in the frame of an economic constitution;

ii) the social market economy;

iii) economic freedom; and

iv) *Wettbewerbspolitik* - competition policy[347].

190. Further, ordoliberal ideas have the law at the center of its thinking. The economic constitution, the creation of Böhm[348], is a political instrument that "defines the rules of the game under which economic activities can be carried out in the respective jurisdictions"[349], based on the ideas of a "private law

340 Taken from H.G. Grosskettler, 'Designing an Economic Order. The Contribution of the Freiburg School' in Donald A. Walker (ed), *Perspectives on the History of Economic Thought*, Vol II (1989) in Rodger (2000), p. 293. See also Neumann, [2001], p. 37.

341 Term coined by Alexander Ebner, 'The Intellectual Foundations of the Social Market Economy' 33 Journal of Economic Studies (2006) 206, p. 213.

342 Such as suppressing price controls as done by Erhard in Germany the 1950s.

343 Ebner (2006), p. 213; similarly, see Alan Peacock and Hans Willgerodt, 'German Liberalism and Economic Revival' in Alan Peacock and Hans Willgerodt (eds), *Germany's Social Market Economy: Origins and Evolution* (MacMillan 1989), p. 7.

344 Kamecke (2001), p. 24.

345 Eucken [1963], p. 36.

346 Herrera Anchustegui 'Competition Law through an Ordoliberal Lens' (2015), p. 145-152.

347 Streit (1992), p. 678.

348 J Tumlir, 'Franz Böhm and the Development of Economic-Constitutional Analysis' in Alan Peacock and Hans Willgerodt (eds), *German Neo-Liberals and the Social Market Economy*, Vol I (MacMillan 1989), p. 136.

349 Wolfgang Kerber and Viktor Vanberg, 'Constitutional Aspects of Party Autonomy and Its Limits - The Perspective of Constitutional Economics' in Stefan Grundmann, Wolfgang Kerber and Stephen Weatherhill (eds), *Party Autonomy and the Role of Information in the Internal Market* (2001), p. 53.

society", freedom of contract and voluntary transactions[350]. It sets positive and negative limits on state intervention in the economy in a normative sense, inspired in the legal traditions of the *Rechtsstaat*[351]. These rules aim at enhancing private cooperation, and as a result of this coordination, parties will then act in a competitive manner increasing their economic performance and efficiency, and preserving the competitiveness in society[352].

191. The concept of social market economy – *Soziale Marktwirtschaft* – is a key ordoliberal influence in the European project as it has been expressly incorporated in Article 3 TEU. This concept was firstly introduced by Müller-Armarck in 1946, who described it as "market freedom with social balance", meaning that it was possible to combine the productive prosperity of a capitalist driven economy with institutions and regulations guided by the pursuance of social justice[353]. In other words, it seeks to combine social balance with entrepreneurship and market competition to foster economic productivity[354]. The social market economy concept is anchored on three pillars:

i) a competition policy based on the system of *Ordnungsökonomie*;

ii) the abandonment of policies that unsystematically foster state interventionism;

iii) an economic policy based on the market economy in rejection to the central planned model[355].

192. Lastly, economic freedom is the other main pillar of the ordoliberal construct[356]. Such freedom is constituted and enforced by a set of rules which are part of the legal framework that "defines mutually compatible private domains within which individuals are free to act, protected from encroachment by other private law subjects as well as from government intervention"[357]. This understanding of economic freedom is closely linked with *the idea of freedom to compete*, a recurrent topic in EU competition law and buyer power

---

350 For the function of private law in ordoliberal thinking see: F. Böhm, 'Rule of Law in a Market Economy' in Alan Peacock and Hans Willgerodt (eds), *Germany's Social Market Economy: Origins and Evolution* (MacMillan 1989), p. 46-67; Tumlir [1989], p. 136; and Viktor Vanberg, 'Consumer Welfare, Total Welfare and Economic Freedom – On the Normative Foundations of Competition Policy' 09 Freiburger Diskussionspapiere zur Ordnungsökonomik (2009) 1, p. 10.

351 Gerber (1994), p. 46.

352 Somma (2013), p. 109.

353 Streit (1992), p. 696. In similar terms, see the view of Karel Van Miert, former European Commissioner for Competition in Van Miert; see also Ebner (2006), p. 215.

354 Ebner (2006), p. 216.

355 Müller-Armack (1978), p. 327-328.

356 Gormsen 'The Conflict Between Economic Freedom and Consumer Welfare in the Modernisation of Article 82 EC' (2007), p. 331; Akman, *The Concept of Abuse in EU Competition Law: Law and Economic Approaches* [2012], p. 55. On the views of the rule of the entrepreneur, see Böhm [1989], p. 58-62; also seeing ordoliberal freedom as freedom of entrepreneurship, see Bonefeld (2012), p. 633-656.

357 Vanberg 'Consumer Welfare, Total Welfare and Economic Freedom – On the Normative Foundations of Competition Policy' (2009), p. 8.

regulation, and which, as remarked by Eucken, the threat to economic freedom arises not only from state intervention but importantly also from private actors such as monopolists cartel or cartel members, making private persons dependent on modern private power structures[358]. In itself, protecting freedom as a goal has an economic value but it also captures other social considerations of non-economic content that, nevertheless, ought to be protected[359].

193. This ordoliberal economic freedom cannot be understood without the existence of a regulated competitive economic process. Ordoliberals saw competition as the tool through which not only economic freedom is expressed but also protected from abuse. The following sections, dealing with the conception of competition in an ordoliberal perspective and buyer power through an ordoliberal perspective, link freedom with competition as a process, and discuss analytical concepts that give content to the economic freedom.

III. Competition in an ordoliberal perspective

194. Ordoliberal competition is an indigenous European competition policy that differs from the Harvard and the Chicago schools[360]. Ordoliberalism represents a 'third way' competition policy that has as its main goal the protection of the freedom to compete – *Wettbewerbsfreiheit* – instead of the goal of achieving perfect or imperfect competition[361], or maximizing allocative efficiency[362]. It proposes a general competition policy as part of society's economic order based on competition law rather than advocating a micro-economic modelling for a case-by-case assessment, such as the neoclassical models applied

---

358 W Eucken, 'What Kind of Economic and Social System' in Alan Peacock and Hans Willgerodt (eds), *Germany's Social Market Economy: Origins and Evolution* (MacMillan 1989), p. 35.

359 Vanberg 'Consumer Welfare, Total Welfare and Economic Freedom – On the Normative Foundations of Competition Policy' (2009), p. 14.

360 Akman, *The Concept of Abuse in EU Competition Law: Law and Economic Approaches* [2012], p. 59; this also appears to be the view of Van Miert, former European Commissioner for Competition, when stating that "how much easier it was to convince people of the value of a strong competition policy if one talked the language of the Erhard-style social market economy rather than the language of the Chicago School", in Van Miert. For a short discussion on why ordoliberal competition policy differs from the Chicago School conception of competition see Wernhard Möschel, 'Competition Policy from an Ordo Point of View' in Alan Peacock and Hans Willgerodt (eds), *German Neo-Liberals and the Social Market Economy*, Vol I (MacMillan 1989), p. 147.

361 For more on the idea of "freedom to compete" see, *inter alia*: Erich Hoppmann, 'Workable Competition - The Development of an Idea on the Norm for the Policy of Competition' 13 Antitrust Bulletin (1968) 61; Vanberg 'Consumer Welfare, Total Welfare and Economic Freedom – On the Normative Foundations of Competition Policy' (2009); Caroline Heide-Jørgensen, 'The Relationship Between Article 101(1) TFEU and Article 101(3) TFEU' in Caroline Heide-Jørgensen and others (eds), *Aims and values in competition law* (DJØF Publ. 2013), p. 98-99; see also in this chapter's section §III.B where this issue is discussed at length.

362 The Chicago School claims that the sole goal of competition should be the maximization of allocative efficiency as discussed, for example in Richard A. Posner, *Antitrust Law: An Economic Perspective* (University of Chicago Press 1976), p. 163-170; Robert H. Bork, *The Antitrust Paradox: A Policy at War With Itself* (1978), p. 56-61. See very recently the Opinion of Advocate General Wahl of 20 October 2016 in *Intel Corporation v Commission*, C-413/14 P, EU:C:2016:788, arguing that formalistic approaches are wrong and outdated in EU competition law when it comes to abuse of dominance.

to competition law cases[363]. Paraphrasing Eucken, the aim of this competitive order is to provide the legal framework upon which the pursuit of individual freedom is restricted solely on the freedom of others[364].

195. Unlike industrial organization and welfaristic competition economics, the first group of ordoliberal scholars did not employ the language of mathematics to express their views. Such a method lacking the express use of mathematics has been qualified as "an unfashionable idiom [...] and they may be put forward with missionary zeal which is anathema to 'positive' economics"[365]. Arguably, this unusual methodology and lack of mathematical 'evidence' has caused competition economists to be wary of ordoliberal teachings and to see this trend of thought as mere politics or philosophy. Other authors, like Peacock and Willgerodt, argue that ordoliberalism is a "political economy unrelated to economic analysis"[366]. Such types of claims, however, forget the historical context of their ideas and the interdisciplinary language used by the ordoliberals to express their views in law and economics. Furthermore, the fact that non-technical language was used to express their economic ideas does not preclude the fact that these analytical concepts are indeed anchored on economic analysis. As stressed by Gerber:

> The foremost vehicle for ordoliberal influence in shaping thought in these areas has been *the new language it generated.* This language features both a new grammar and a significantly altered vocabulary. The grammar - i.e., the rules that structure the language - is based on the interplay of economic and legal ordering concepts. *Economic analysis supplies the rules necessary for the market to function effectively and thus provides the standards for most economic policy decisions*[367].

196. On the other hand, this lack of mathematical language probably partly accounts for why ordoliberal ideas have had a historical appeal for lawyers, and, in particular, judges as they tend to speak the language of the law, by which abstract concepts are given meaning through teleological interpretation.

---

363 For Lenel, an ordoliberal belonging to the "third wave", competition is just dealing with "a micro-economic task: it is to regulate the individual economic relationships in such a way that production is in line with consumers' wishes at the least possible cost", in H. O. Lenel, 'Evolution of the Social Market Economy' in Alan Peacock and Hans Willgerodt (eds), *German Neo-Liberals and the Social Market Economy*, Vol I (MacMillan 1989), p. 265.

364 Walter Eucken, *Grundsätze der Wirtschaftspolitik* (Mohr Siebeck 1952), p. 250.

365 Peacock and Willgerodt, 'Overall View of the German Liberal Movement' [1989], p. 3. Cf this with the view of Möschel who claims that ordoliberals did use economic models, such as the traditional model of perfect competition in Möschel [1989], p. 142. However, in my research, I have not found explicit (modern) economic modeling in the works reviewed, which does not imply that the models are implicit and taken into account to put forth their ideas

366 James S. Venit, 'Article 82: The Last Frontier - Fighting Fire With Fire?' 28 Fordham International Law Journal (2004) 1157, p. 1157. In this work, Venit does not make a direct reference to any of the works of ordoliberal thinkers and limits himself to include a single reference by Möschel describing the focal points of ordoliberalism.

367 Gerber (1994), p. 67 (emphasis added).

197. In the current section, I explore the ordoliberal conception of competition by analyzing the main postulates of this school of thought, identifying its aim, discussing the different types of competition and, finally, determining what ought to be the role of the state in the regulation of competition and as a competitor itself.

A. Understanding ordoliberal competition

198. The concepts of competition and freedom to compete – *Wettbewerbsordnung* and *Wettbewerbsfreiheit* – are central to ordoliberalism[368], and are considered by Peacock and Willgerodt to be the "most original feature of Ordo thinking on policy matters"[369]. For ordoliberals, competition is the necessary consequence of scarcity of goods. As such, it has an indispensable function of coordination and social organization[370]. The competitive order is the essence of the economy because it permits the effective functioning of the system[371]. Consequently, while there is no doubt that the competitive market system is the appropriate tool, it is for the economic constitution to determine in which legal terms competition is carried out so that competition can be effective and efficient[372], and for an ordoliberal competition policy, to control private and public market power to guarantee competition as process[373]. Unregulated competition, as advocated by classical liberalism, degenerates into abuse of market power that curbs economic freedom and destroys itself due to the accumulation of market power[374]. Competition's policy[375] role is to counteract this self-destructive tendency of market competition. Thus, ordoliberalism advocates for state-imposed economic regulation by means of competition laws. By adopting competition as the regulating system, ordoliberalism is a shift from the principle of exchange being the guiding principle of market organization[376].

---

368 Nils Goldschmidt and Arnold Berndt, 'Leonhard Miksch (1901–1950) A Forgotten Member of the Freiburg School' 64 American Journal of Economics and Sociology (2005) 973, p. 975; Foucault and others, [2008], p. 118-119.

369 Peacock and Willgerodt, 'Overall View of the German Liberal Movement' [1989], p. 9.

370 Müller-Armack (1978), p. 325-326.

371 Gerber (1994), p. 43.

372 Vanberg 'Consumer Welfare, Total Welfare and Economic Freedom – On the Normative Foundations of Competition Policy' (2009), p. 7; Peter Behrens, 'The "Consumer Choice" Paradigm in German Ordoliberalism and its Impact upon EU Competition Law' 1/14 Europa-Kolleg Hamburg Discussion Paper Series (2014), p. 12. Cf with the view of Akman who argues that for ordoliberalism economic efficiency is just "an indirect and derived goal; its results generally from the realization of individual freedom of action in a market system" in Akman, *The Concept of Abuse in EU Competition Law: Law and Economic Approaches* [2012], p. 58-60.

373 Streit (1992), p. 685. Cf with the view of Ludvig von Mises who sharply pointed out that as such, economic freedom does not exist and that "the market is free for as long as it does precisely what the government wants it to do", Ludwig von Mises, *Human Action* (4th edn, 1996), p. 723–724.

374 Peacock and Willgerodt, 'Overall View of the German Liberal Movement' [1989], p. 7.

375 For a discussion of the content of ordoliberalism as a competition policy see: Möschel [1989], p. 142.

376 Foucault and others, [2008], p. 118.

199. For Eucken, market power concentration, monopolies, cartels and centralized planning of the economy '*kill*' competition[377]. Therefore, free economic competition can only exist if it is organized by the state in accordance with liberal principles to prevent the abuse of economic power[378]. In other words, the invisible hand by itself is insufficient to secure proper competition, and a state-imposed order is required to avoid abuses of market power. This was also the stance of the former European Commissioner Van der Miert, who in 1997, quoting Ralf Dahrendorf, stated:

> Economic reforms are all very well. Privatisation, deregulation, releasing initiative are clearly important. Only market forces will in the end get the collapsed state economies out of the rut. But market forces not only have to be released, they also have to be contained by accepted and enforced rules of the game. The invisible hand is not sufficient. Like a football match it needs rules of the game and a referee. The market is not anarchy but a subtle construct of human ingenuity[379].

200. Furthermore, the competitive order has no value if excluded from the broader conception of the *Ordnungspolitik*[380]. The ordoliberal competition policy is part "of a framework of a general economic system"[381] and constitutes a key element of the development of the social market economy as part of the ordering of economic freedom[382]. It does so by focusing on the control and correction of price manipulation, maintaining the voluntariness of contracting[383], precluding market power abuse – by a sole entity or by a group of entities coordinating their behaviour – through an administrative "monopoly office" acting as a market police[384]. Regulated competition is a tool for the maintenance of economic order by preserving the market process as the foundational ground for social cohesion[385]. Also, the freedom to compete should not be restricted by legal rules grounded on inefficient economic grounds nor can it be left unregulated, as it would degenerate into unfair competition and social conflict

---

377 Walter Eucken, 'Técnica, Concentración y Ordenación de la Economía' in Lucas Beltrán (ed), *La Economía de Mercado*, Vol. I (1950), p. 151.

378 Somewhat similar is the view of Foucault who claims that for ordoliberals the state must govern for the market and not because of the market, Foucault and others, [2008], p. 121.

379 Van Miert.

380 Gerber (1994).

381 Möschel [1989], p. 154.

382 Cf with Vanberg, who in a slightly different manner, argues that protecting the freedom to compete is nothing else than protecting the individual freedom that is consecrated in a system of private law. Vanberg 'Consumer Welfare, Total Welfare and Economic Freedom – On the Normative Foundations of Competition Policy' (2009). See also: Christopher Townley, *Article 81 EC and the Public Policy* (Hart 2009), p. 214.

383 Kerber and Vanberg [2001], p. 64.

384 Rodger (2000), p. 293; Bonefeld (2012), p. 638. Rose and Ngwe go even further by stating that for the ordoliberals, the competitive process is an end in itself in Rose and Ngwe (2007), p. 8.

385 Ebner (2006), p. 213.

or *Vermachtung*[386]. Deciding whether "competition is restricted, whether competition is efficient or obstructive, whether or not price-cutting contradicts the principle of the system – all these issues *can only be decided by investigations conducted by economics* in the various states of the market"[387].

201. However, not all 'German-neoliberals' fully share this idea of an imposed competitive order. For Hayek, competition is a by-product of economic freedom of economic agents and it acts as a process of self-control of the players in a market performing economics activities[388]. In my view, competition ought to not be merely about self-control or naturally formed countervailing power[389]. For competition to exist there must also be legal rules in place, imposed by the state, which discipline the exercise of market power and can guarantee that the market conditions are kept healthy so that the self-controlling forces of the market can be effectively applied.

a. Competition and economic freedom as goals themselves

202. The goal of an ordoliberal competition policy is the protection of individual economic freedom to compete in the economic sphere and protecting competition as such[390]. By safeguarding the competitive process and economic freedom from abuse of private and public market power, the interests of consumers are satisfied and their wellbeing is guaranteed[391]. In the words of Böhm, protecting the system of price competition and ensuring a "fair system by which services or assets could be subject to voluntary exchange agreements to ensure equivalent payment" shields individuals from abusive market power

386 Rodger (2000), p. 294; Joachim Zweynert, 'How German is German Neo-Liberalism?' 26 Review of Austrian Economics (2013), p. 115.

387 Böhm, Eucken and Grossman-Doerth [1989], p. 24-25.

388 Hayek, unlike the first two waves of ordoliberals, distrusts competition regulation, even in its American variants, and would rather leave the market on its own as expressed by Möschel [1989], p. 153.

389 Felice and Vatiero, p. 8; also stating the rejection of ordoliberal theories concerning Galbraith's pure theories of self-regulating competition, see Peacock and Willgerodt, 'German Neo-Liberals and the Social Market Economy' [1989], p. 10; Möschel [1989], p. 147; Friedrich A. Lutz, 'Observations on the Problem of Monopolies' in A. Peacock and H. Willgerodt (eds), *Germany's Social Market Economy: Origins and Evolution* (MacMillan 1989), p. 168-170.

390 Supporting this view, see: Hoppmann (1968), p. 62; Möschel [1989], p. 146; Foucault and others, [2008], p. 120-121; Vanberg 'Consumer Welfare, Total Welfare and Economic Freedom – On the Normative Foundations of Competition Policy' (2009), p. 9. For non-ordoliberal views that also argue that the goal of competition should be the protection of economic process see: Werden (2007); Eleanor M. Fox, 'Against Goals' 81 Fordham Law Review (2013) 2157.

391 Vanberg, 'Freiburg School of Law and Economics' [1998], p. 176. See the view of the CJEU when stating that Article 102 TFEU "is not only aimed at practices which may cause damage to consumers directly, but also at those which are detrimental to them through their impact on an effective competition structure", recognizing the need for protecting competition as a process itself, in Judgment of 21 February 1973 in *Europemballage Corporation and Continental Can Company v Commission*, C-6/72, EU:C:1973:22, para. 26; See also: Opinion of Advocate General Stix-Hackl of 1 July 204 in *Sintesi*, C-247/02, EU:C:2004:399 E.C.R. [2004] I-09215, para. 34-40; Opinion of Advocate General Kokott of 23 February 2006 in Judgment of 15 March 2007 in *British Airways v Commission*, C-95/04 P, EU:C:2006:133, para. 125. Cf this with the view of Gerber who suggests that through complete competition in which no firm can coerce the behavior of others economic freedom is secured in Gerber (1994), p. 43.

that attempts to subjugate and exploit them[392]. Arguably, the ordoliberal proposition of promoting competition as a goal in itself has had a profound impact on EU competition policy which recognizes this goal, alongside the need to foster market integration, as its traditional aims[393].

203. However, not all scholars agree that ordoliberalism pursues protection of competition as a process. For instance, Kamecke holds that "Eucken *did not consider freedom of economic action as a value in itself.* As soon as freedom is in conflict with economic efficiency, he is willing to sacrifice the competitive market order in favor of some government action"[394]. To me, this argument is circular and misses the point that, for ordoliberals, economic freedom has positive and negative limits imposed by the law, and that by securing economic freedom, economic efficiency will follow as consequence of solving the competition's prisoner dilemma: how to act not to lose to your rivals' responses. Furthermore, Maier-Rigaud remarks that competition as a goal is a concept that has been advocated by German neoliberals and not only by early ordoliberals, with supporters such as Hayek, Hoppmann, Möschel and Vanberg, under different underlying assumptions[395]. What these different waves do have in common is the fear against state action and advocating for the protection of economic freedom[396]. This argument by Maier-Rigaud raises interesting issues, although it does miss the point that ordoliberalism is not only the work of the first or second wave of scholars but indeed a living economic policy that has evolved and, as it has, therefore, conceptions of the goal of competition policy have also changed. Furthermore, my research shows that conception of competition freedom as a goal was already present in the works of Eucken and Böhm.

204. Economic freedom and freedom to compete ought to be protected as they are

---

392 Böhm [1989], p. 58. Also stressing the "fairness element" regarding economic freedom see: Gal [2013], p. 389.

393 The goal of market integration was key in deciding that restrictions of parallel trade to consumers were in breach to Article 102 TFEU in Judgment of 16 September 2008 in *Sot. Lélos kai Sia v. GlaxoSmithKline*, joined cases C-468/06 to C-478/06, EU:C:2008:504 E.C.R. [2008] I-07139; see also: Judgment of 13 July 1966 in *Consten and Grundig v Commission* of the EEC, C-56/64, EU:C:1966:41; Guidelines on Vertical Restraints [2010] OJ C 130/1, para. 7. See also: Böhm [1989]; Massimo Motta, *Competition Policy: Theory and Practice* (Cambridge University Press 2006), p. 23; Okeoghene Odudu, 'The Wider Concerns of Competition Law' 30 Oxford Journal of Legal Studies (2010), p. 599-613; Ioannis Lianos, 'Some Reflections on the Question of the Goals of EU Competition Law' in Ioannis Lianos and Damien Geradin (eds), *Handbook on European competition law: enforcement and procedure* (Edward Elgar Pub. Ltd. 2013), p. 30 to 36; Ioannis Lianos, 'Some Reflections on the Question of the Goals of EU Competition Law' 3/2013 CLES Working Paper Series (2013) 1, p. 14-15; Heide-Jørgensen [2013], p. 97-98. Also in the US the protection of competition as such was, until the 'Antitrust Revolution' of the 1970s, an aim of US antitrust law as confirmed in *Federal Trade Commission v. Procter & Gamble Co.*, 386 U.S. 568 (1967), where the Supreme Court held that "[p]ossible economics cannot be used as a defense to illegality. Congress was aware that some mergers which lessen competition may also result in economics, but it struck the balance in favor of protecting competition".

394 Kamecke (2001), p. 27 (emphasis added).

395 F. Maier-Rigaud, 'On the normative foundations of competition law – efficiency, political freedom and the freedom to compete' in Daniel Zimmer (ed), *The Goals of Competition Law* (Edward Elgar 2012), p. 139-147.

396 Ibid, p. 145.

"public goods"[397] that derive from the preservation of individual freedom[398]. Consequently, the prime objective of an ordoliberal competition policy is the protection of the competitive process by setting a competitive standard of performance competition which implies adherence to the 'constitutional rules' and satisfies consumers' needs in accordance with the lawful capacities of undertakings and the securing of individual freedom[399]. *Provided the competitive process is protected and preserved, economic efficiency and social peace should follow*. In this sense, if freedom to compete is preserved, economic efficiency is a derived consequence because performance competition is allowed to naturally take place, which would lead towards economic progress[400]. Such freedom to compete, however, requires that economic players have equal legal standing and that economic activities are coordinated through voluntary contracting and exchange[401].

205. This conception of freedom to compete demands that private parties behave in accordance with a set of pre-existing rules enshrined in the economic constitution, which serves as a grantor and guarantor of such individual freedom[402]. For Vanberg, ordoliberalism ought to pursue the protection of freedom to compete to generate consumer welfare as a natural consequence. In his view, economic freedom would be violated if and/or when competition authorities prohibit a conduct allowed by the economic constitution or when they would allow it based on economic efficiency considerations but without a legal provision[403]. Therefore, economic efficiency arguments have to 'fit' the set of rules. Prima facie this argument can be seen as formalistic or void as it is the judge who defines what this economic freedom is. Nevertheless, the EU competition law system itself provides mechanisms that, if appropriately applied, solve the apparent contradiction, as is the case regarding Article 101(3) TFEU that allows for the consideration of economic efficiencies to trigger a legal exception to a conduct that would otherwise be prohibited.

b. Protecting competition as a process as economically efficient

206. Protecting the competitive process is economically efficient and desirable because it prevents society from playing the competition's prisoner dilemma because 'cheating' becomes illegal. Indeed, the competitive process mini-

---

397 Vanberg, 'Freiburg School of Law and Economics' [1998], p. 177. Supporting the view that for ordoliberal thought freedom to compete is the guiding goal of competition law, see Maier-Rigaud [2012], p. 135.

398 Similarly, Maier-Rigaud [2012], p. 136.

399 Möschel [1989], p. 142; Akman 'Searching for the Long-Lost Soul of Article 82 EC' (2009), p. 273.

400 This is the main idea expressed by Hoppmann concerning the ordoliberal approach to freedom to compete in Hoppmann (1968), p. 61-82.

401 Vanberg, 'Freiburg School of Law and Economics' [1998], p. 175.

402 Vanberg 'Consumer Welfare, Total Welfare and Economic Freedom – On the Normative Foundations of Competition Policy' (2009), p. 10.

403 Ibid, p. 10-11.

mizes two risks: the issue of cheating and the problem of under-competitive choices. Some actors will be tempted to circumvent the market's rules to obtain a benefit at the expense of the other players and the rest will then choose the under competitive option to protect themselves[404], which does not benefit society, to prevent such 'cheating'. This prisoner's dilemma is largely solved if the members of society adhere to a competitive *order* imposed by the state in accordance with the rule of law[405]. If the rules are properly designed, then lawful behaviour by economic players will produce an outcome that is economically efficient. Here lies the rational justification for an ordoliberal competition policy: it allows undertakings to escape the prisoner's dilemma and punishes those agents who deviate from the competitive outcome by cheating the rules[406].

207. Another explanation supporting the efficiency of competition as a goal in itself is that freedom to compete would be Pareto-efficient if "individual decisions have only a negligible influence on the market prices"[407]. Accordingly, market power will be kept in check such that any significant detrimental effect on market prices is avoided. Alternatively, absent truly 'free competition' then it would be possible to apply 'competition as if' to guide the behaviour of players[408]. I find the logic of this argument unsatisfactory. In practice, freedom to compete and efficient outcomes will not always coincide, for example, the freedom to compete will be dictated by the adoption of legal rules that by their nature might be sub-optimal from a welfare perspective. Also, to achieve a more efficient economic outcome, certain trading agreements and practices will be forbidden and economic freedom will therefore be limited, particularly if the decision to prohibit is taken *ex-post.* Here lies the fundamental issue of informing legal texts with appropriate economic foundations, the quid of a contemporary ordoliberal policy.

208. Consequently, in my view, the claims that protecting competition as a goal is economically unjustified – vis-à-vis "efficiency oriented" aims[409] – or that it protects "inefficient competitors which would conflict with the objective

---

404 Vanberg, 'Freiburg School of Law and Economics' [1998], p. 178.

405 Cf with the view expressed by Foucault when stating that "[...] competition and only competition can ensure economic rationality. How does it ensure economic rationality? Well, it ensures it through the formation of prices which, precisely to the extent that there is full and complete competition, can measure economic magnitudes and thus regulate choices", in Foucault and others, [2008], p. 119.

406 Vanberg, 'Freiburg School of Law and Economics' [1998], p. 178.

407 Kamecke (2001), p. 24.

408 For a discussion of the concept of "competition as if" see infra in this chapter 3, section §III.C, and also: Goldschmidt and Berndt (2005), p. 973-998. For the concept of workable competition see John M. Clark, *Competition as a Dynamic Process* (The Brookings Institution 1961).

409 For a general discussion on this topic, see: Maier-Rigaud [2012], p. 132-168.

of enhancing welfare", as perceived by Akman[410], or that "ordoliberalism is based on humanist values rather than efficiency or other purely economic concerns"[411] as argued by Gormsen, appear too absolute. These arguments seem to overstate the fact that, occasionally, ordoliberal goals might prevent undertakings from carrying out certain practices that could potentially be efficient in the short-term but, which, in a medium to long term dynamic efficiency setting could thwart competition. Although that could occur, as ordoliberalism may be prone to over-enforcement, the number of cases in which it would arise would be minor and justifiable, given the need for legal certainty and its own intrinsic value[412]. Furthermore, these criticisms are based on the (mis) understanding that securing economic freedom does not always coincide with fostering economic efficiency, from either a total or consumer perspective and it implies protecting inefficient undertakings[413]. Akman notes that ordoliberalism does not promote efficiency as an aim but as a result. This distinction, however, appears to me more dialectical than of practical importance, as for as long as the competitive process is free, the practical result is economic freedom and efficiency[414]. In other words, ordoliberalism does not advocate the protection of inefficient competitors, nor does it promote an excessive amount of market players[415], nor does it advocate the adoption of an interventionist industrial policy, even if occasionally protecting competition and economic freedom could shield some less efficient undertakings than the dominant firm from the market vagaries. Far from it: ordoliberalism promotes protecting 'competition as such' because it is economically efficient in the medium and long term, even if on occasion certain practices that could potentially be efficient in a short term and static sense are prohibited.

---

410 Akman 'Searching for the Long-Lost Soul of Article 82 EC' (2009), p. 268-269. In my view, one of the reasons why Akman might have such a different opinion lies on the fact that her research was limited to a few sources of the original works ordoliberal authors, particularly if in German, but rather based on existing literature in English language by mostly non-ordoliberal thinkers.

411 Gormsen 'The Conflict Between Economic Freedom and Consumer Welfare in the Modernisation of Article 82 EC' (2007), p. 334, and Liza Lovdahl Gormsen, *A Principled Approach to Abuse of Dominance in European Competition Law* (Cambridge University Press 2010) p. 42.

412 See raising a similar argument regarding the use of 'form-based approaches' in EU competition law: Wouter Wils, 'The Judgment of the EU General Court in *Intel* and the So-Called More Economic Approach to Abuse of Dominance' 37 World Competition (2014) 405.

413 Akman argues that, for ordoliberalism, economic efficiency is just "an indirect and derived goal; its results generally from the realization of individual freedom of action in a market system" in Akman, *The Concept of Abuse in EU Competition Law: Law and Economic Approaches* [2012], p. 56 and 60; see also: Akman 'Searching for the Long-Lost Soul of Article 82 EC' (2009), p. 276-277. Cf also Gormsen who argues that this protection "is linked to social justice and civil liberties, not to consumer welfare", in Gormsen 'The Conflict Between Economic Freedom and Consumer Welfare in the Modernisation of Article 82 EC' (2007), p. 334.

414 Akman 'Searching for the Long-Lost Soul of Article 82 EC' (2009), p. 275.

415 Markets have a finite number of market participants if efficiency is to be maximized and which it is conditioned by the minimum efficient scale; this may explain why certain markets are more concentrated than others. For a discussion see: Schmalensee (1981); Faull and Nikpay, [1999], para. 1.38.

B. Types of ordoliberal competition

209. Ordoliberalism distinguishes between two types of competition: performance and prevention competition. Performance competition[416] – *Leistungswettbewerb* – is the ability to obtain a competitive advantage by producing the best goods possible at the lowest price[417]. On the other hand, prevention competition is largely similar to what is modernly understood by exclusionary abuses in contemporary EU competition law. It aims at damaging the competitors' position without this implying that the undertaking has improved its competition capacity. Prevention competition also resembles the concept of *Behinderungswettbewerb,* coined by Nipperdey, as it describes competition that prevents a rival from performing at their best capacity[418]: it simply makes the competitor worse-off. Ordoliberalism aims to suppress prevention competition by forcing players to behave in accordance with pre-defined market rules.

C. Competition as if?

210. In connection with the limitation of the abuse of market power, an ordoliberal concept sometimes linked to interpretations made by the CJEU of Article 102 TFEU[419], and the doctrine of special responsibility[420] is the theory of "competition as if" developed by Miksch[421], a disciple of Eucken[422]. O'Donoghue and Padilla, mistakenly in my view, go as far as claiming that "ordoliberal thinking on the goal of competition law was based on notions of 'fairness' and that undertakings with market power should behave 'as if' there was effective competition"[423]. Competition 'as if' employs the legal competition framework in setting the 'standard conduct' a dominant undertaking ought to follow whenever acting in the market. This concept partly echoes the special

---

416 Gerber translates this concept in a slightly different manner and uses the term "performance competition" to represent a similar idea, see: Gerber (1994), p. 53; Gerber, [2001], p. 253. See also recognizing these two types of competition: Akman, *The Concept of Abuse in EU Competition Law: Law and Economic Approaches* [2012], p. 57.

417 Felice and Vatiero, p. 6.

418 Gerber (1994), p. 53.

419 See the analysis of Nazzini who concludes that there is no historical indication that the "as if" conduct was proposed when drafting the now Article 102 TFEU during the Rome Treaty negotiations in Nazzini, [2011], p. 132. Also see the comments of Robles Martín-Laborda concerning exploitative prices in Antonio Robles Martín-Laborda, *Exploitative Prices in European Competition Law* (2015), p. 3.

420 Rousseva, [2010], p. 31.

421 Gerber (1994), p. 52-53; Goldschmidt and Berndt (2005), p. 973-998.

422 Supporting this view, see: Gerber (1994), p. 52; Ebner (2006), p. 206-223; Gormsen 'Article 82 EC: Where are We Coming From and Where are We Going to?' (2006), p. 10; Rose and Ngwe (2007), p. 8. Cf with the view of Akman who claims that ordoliberal ideas and the concept of competition as if is "not the 'abuse' concept of the drafters of Article 82 EC since they were mainly concerned with the customers who dealt with the dominant undertakings, not their competitors", Akman 'Searching for the Long-Lost Soul of Article 82 EC' (2009), p. 276. See also: Anne C. Witt, 'The Commission's Guidance Paper on Abusive Exclusionary Conduct - More Radical than it Appears?' 35 European Law Review (2010) 214.

423 Robert O'Donoghue and A. Jorge Padilla, *The law and economics of Article 82 EC* (Hart 2006), p. 9.

responsibility doctrine of dominant undertakings, which imposes stricter limits on the freedom of an undertaking to act when compared to a non-dominant undertaking. In the words of the CJEU:

> an undertaking has a dominant position is not in itself a recrimination but simply means that, irrespective of the reasons for which it has such a dominant position, the undertaking concerned has a special responsibility not to allow its conduct to impair genuine undistorted competition on the common market[424].

211. By competing 'as if', undertakings have to behave as if they lack market power and being consistent with performance competition[425]. According to Gerber, this standard would not require governmental intervention as it is an objectively applicable measure, which provides a clear answer[426]. From this perspective, the concept of 'competition as if' appears to be formalistic and almost per se.

212. One of its main problems, however, is that 'competition as if' is an impractical concept because competition is a discovery process, to put it in Hayekian terms[427]. The competition authority would not always be able to anticipate how competition 'would have been' had parties been deprived of their market power. Furthermore, 'competition as if' opens the door to two different interpretations: should it be competition 'as if' undertakings had no substantial market power, or 'as if' there were perfect competition?[428] From another perspective, 'competition as if' is imprecise and promotes legal uncertainty. Nonetheless, Hayek's criticism of competition as a discovery process is a valid argument to *any* competition standard that does not employ a pure per se approach because any balancing act based on counterfactual evidence implies that the competition authority needs to foresee how ideal competition *would have been*.

213. Furthermore, the idea of 'competition as if' has also been criticized because it arguably contradicts economic freedom and, therefore, is not in accord with

---

424 Judgment of 9 November 1983 in *Michelin v Commission*, C-322/81, EU:C:1983:313, para. 57. This doctrine has been reiterated several times by the Courts with regard to cases related to buyer power exertion, such as in Judgment of 16 March 2000 in *Compagnie Maritime Belge Transports and Others v Commission*, C-395/96 P, EU:C:2000:132, para. 37; Judgment of 9 September 2010, *Tomra Systems and Others v Commission*, T-155/06, ECR, EU:T:2010:370, para. 207, Judgment of 17 December 2003, *British Airways v Commission* of 17 December 2003, T-219/99, ECR, EU:T:2003:343, para. 242; Judgment of 7 October 1999, *Irish Sugar v Commission*, T-228/97, ECR, EU:T:1999:246, para. 112; and in general cases, more recently in Judgment of 6 December 2012 in *AstraZeneca v Commission*, C-457/10 P, EU:C:2012:770, para. 105. See also Communication from the Commission — Guidance on the Commission's enforcement priorities in applying Article 82 of the EC Treaty to abusive exclusionary conduct by dominant undertakings [2009] OJ C 45/7, para. 1.

425 Gerber (1994), p. 52, and 65.

426 Ibid, p. 52-53.

427 For a brief discussion of competition as a discovery process see, Behrens 'The "Consumer Choice" Paradigm in German Ordoliberalism and its Impact upon EU Competition Law' (2014), p. 20.

428 The latter appears to be the opinion of Gerber in Gerber (1994), p. 52.

core ordoliberal ideas[429]. The base of this argument is that 'competition as if' implies that a dominant undertaking ought not to behave as if it had market power and has a "special responsibility" of observing a much higher degree of care than an undertaking which lacks substantial market power. Consequently, this standard imposes a limitation on economic freedom. I partially agree with this criticism but argue that imposing limits on the behaviour of a dominant undertaking does not contradict the precepts of ordoliberal economic freedom. What it does do is set negative limits to secure the protection of competition as such and prevent abuses of market power vis-à-vis consumers. Yet, I agree that a dominant undertaking should not be deprived of its right to exercise performance competition – *Leistungswettbewerb* – in accordance with the limits imposed by an ordoliberal competition law.

214. To conclude, I propose that contemporary ordoliberal competition policy should distance itself from the idea of 'competition as if' due to its deficiencies, and rather opt for setting clear competitive rules defining which types of behaviour ought to be captured by the *Missbrauchprinzip*.

D. Ordoliberalism, use of economics and the 'more economic approach'

215. In the last decade, the supporters of a 'more economic approach' to EU competition law have argued against ordoliberal ideas in an "attempt to replace the protection of the competitive process by a welfare maximization goal in stark contrast to an Ordoliberal conception"[430]. In this sense, some authors hold that an ordoliberal conception of competition law is outdated, formalistic, old fashioned or even utopian[431], and incompatible with the use of microeconomics and industrial organization within EU competition law, and the economically informed legal analysis methodology I employ in this study as discussed in chapter 1, section §II.C.

216. The proponents of such a view argue that EU competition policy (*rectius* the Commission's view on some aspects of EU competition policy)[432] has departed from an ordoliberal approach to adopt a 'more economic approach', which is less form-based and more effect-based, as also recently proposed by Advocate

429 Maier-Rigaud [2012], p. 146.

430 Kiran Klaus Patel and Heike Schweitzer (eds), *The Historical Foundations of EU Competition Law* (Oxford University Press 2013), p. 223; Giorgio Monti, 'EU Competition Law from Rome to Lisbon - Social Market Economy' in Caroline Heide-Jørgensen and others (eds), *Aims and Values in Competition Law* (DJØF Publ. 2013), p. 44-49.

431 Such is the opinion of Venit (2004), p. 1157-1178; see also: van Doorn, p. 19. Cf with the moderate opinion of Gerber who claims that some ordoliberal positions are obsolete whereas others are still valid in Gerber (1994), p. 75-83.

432 Behrens 'The "Consumer Choice" Paradigm in German Ordoliberalism and its Impact upon EU Competition Law' (2014).

General Wahl in his Opinion in *Intel Corporation v Commission*[433]. Put it differently, more "mathematic", which allegedly confers a presumption of scientific validity; however, these 'more economically informed' arguments may not always be as non-value laden or objective as is claimed, as also remarked by Wils[434]. Also, as stressed by Hayek, economic modeling cannot be tested in reality because competition is a 'discovery process' in which the facts of the case are the means by which the outcome of the situation is discovered[435].

217. Furthermore, these claims against ordoliberalism and its lack of 'economic depth' have arguably arisen from misrepresentations, lack of knowledge of ordoliberal ideas, or by recourse to the works of figures associated with ordoliberal thinking, but not core ordoliberals themselves, such as Röpke, Miksch and Müller-Armack. These authors advocate more extreme versions of political interventionism, social and distributive welfare concerns, and purely formalistic approaches to competition policy. It must be said that these ideas, however, do not represent the majoritarian view among ordoliberals. Also, the attacks against ordoliberalism are sometimes due to and confused by the less 'economically inclined' teleological interpretation of the law made by the Courts, whereby ordoliberal ideas can be confused with the legal reasoning, rather than objections against ordoliberalism itself[436].

218. I reject such extreme views, as an ordoliberal conception of competition law is more complex than pure formalisms or advocacy of excessive state interventionism. Furthermore, *ordoliberalism does not reject the use of economic insights to solve specific cases nor to improve the quality of legal standards and legislation*. In fact, the Ordoliberal School was a pioneer in integrating economic thinking into the application of law. Indeed, these positions overlook the fact that ordoliberal competition is part of an institutional economics policy with the aim of the achievement of societal order based on imposed rules governing the market, and not a microeconomic trend of competition economics or industrial organization[437].

219. In contrast, I put forth that an ordoliberal conception of competition policy is neither archaic, nor incompatible with the use of economic theory in the application of competition law. An ordoliberally-inspired EU competition policy

433 Opinion of Advocate General Wahl of 20 October 2016 in *Intel Corporation v Commission*, C-413/14 P, EU:C:2016:788.

434 Wils (2014), p. 412.

435 F.A. Hayek, 'Competition as a Discovery Procedure' in *New Studies in Philosophy, Politics, Economics and the History of Ideas* (University of Chicago Press 1978), p. 179.

436 See for example the criticism of Venit in Venit (2004), aimed at the lack of economic a serious economic assessment by the CJEU in the buyer power related case Judgment of 17 December 2003, *British Airways v Commission* of 17 December 2003, T-219/99, ECR, EU:T:2003:343, and the subsequent appeal in Judgment of 15 March 2007 in *British Airways v Commission*, C-95/04 P, EU:C:2007:166.

437 Vanberg 'Consumer Welfare, Total Welfare and Economic Freedom – On the Normative Foundations of Competition Policy' (2009), p. 13.

is not necessarily at odds with a more detailed microeconomic analysis of competition practices; to do so would indeed be archaic and simplistic. This approach does not preclude the use of economic expertise to refine the praxis of competition law in the assessment of cases and also to model and improve the legal regime.

220. However, ordoliberalism is not compatible with the advocates of a 'more economic approach' that argue for a departure from the rule of law by adopting a case-by-case assessment based on pure welfare considerations as a guiding policy instrument without the existence of more formal or structured rules defining the economic game[438]. In other words, I disagree with claiming that a case-by-case assessment based on pure welfare considerations without regard to some general rules can improve competition and provide legal uses with a fair degree of predictability[439]. If a more economic approach, however, is understood as advocating for the use of economic insights and in accordance and as allowed by the rules in place[440], then ordoliberalism agrees with such 'more economically informed' analysis of the cases. Consequently, an ordoliberal competition policy agrees with what Schweitzer and Patel have qualified as a "light" approach, suggesting a review of the established application of competition law to be in line with economic theory so that "EU competition (law) can be interpreted in a more concise and unerring manner"[441].

221. Furthermore, it is indeed possible to combine ordoliberalism as a competition policy with modern microeconomics and industrial organization, provided the *level of applications of economics within the law* is correctly understood. An ordoliberal inspired competition policy *shapes and sets the rules and aims of an institutional framework,* whereas a neo-classical microeconomic analysis of the cases is the *concrete application* of the competition policy[442]. By distinguishing these levels of application on a 'macro and micro' level, it is possible to introduce economic efficiency analysis when deciding specific

---

438 Somewhat similar is the view of Vanberg who claims that in an ordoliberal based system "competition policy cannot make the right of private law subjects to exercise such freedom contingent on how economic advisors assess the welfare effects in particular instances, and that welfare considerations can have their legitimate place only at the constitutional level where the rules of the economic game are chosen", ibid, p. 27. See also the opinion of Gormsen when stating that ordoliberal competition policy "is shaped by the rule of law rather than by ad hoc political decision-making", in Gormsen 'The Conflict Between Economic Freedom and Consumer Welfare in the Modernisation of Article 82 EC' (2007), p. 334.

439 See also: Vanberg 'Consumer Welfare, Total Welfare and Economic Freedom – On the Normative Foundations of Competition Policy' (2009), p. 24.

440 This is, the analysis under Article 101(3) TFEU and the interpretation by the CJEU concerning objective considerations regarding Article 102 TFEU.

441 Schweitzer and Patel distinguish three aspects of the 'more economic approach', one proposing changing the goals of EU competition law, another using economics to establish the relevant facts and decide accordingly, and the "light" version which advocates using modern economics to guide the application of the law. See more in Patel and Schweitzer [2013], p. 220. See also: Heike Schweitzer, 'Recent Developments in EU Competition Law (2006–2008): Single-Firm Dominance and the Interpretation of Article 82' 5 European Review of Contract Law (2009) 175.

442 Vanberg 'Consumer Welfare, Total Welfare and Economic Freedom – On the Normative Foundations of Competition Policy' (2009), p. 10.

cases through the interpretation of the competition rules that are applied to the concrete circumstance if such possibility is foreseen by the legislator or the judiciary, such as in the explicit case of Article 101(3) TFEU or as Article 102 TFEU has been interpreted by the Courts. This does not mean, though, that a case-by-case economic approach influences competition policy, but quite the opposite: it is competition policy that allows for a case-by-case economic assessment. As noted by Vanberg:

> The advocates of economic freedom and Leistungswettbewerb have no reason to deny that comparing the prospective welfare effects of alternative rules of the market game is an essential prerequisite in choosing an economic constitution, and that economics can provide an important service by informing about the working properties of potential alternative systems of rules. What they reject is the claim that a *'more economic approach' can help to improve competition policy* by informing about the specific welfare effects *in particular instances*[443].

222. Therefore, ordoliberalism is an economic school of thought that allows and advocates for the use of economic knowledge to guide the application of the law to guarantee, to the greatest extent possible, an economically coherent interpretation of law. However, ordoliberal ideas are not compatible with extreme views of the 'more economic approach' that advocate resorting to economic knowledge and pure case-by-case analysis without regard to the legal construction or the goals of protecting competition as a process and a degree of economic freedom. Also, such a conception is also in line with the economically informed legal analysis method.

E. The role of the state: limited role for administrative discretion

223. Ordoliberals endorse the idea of a strong state restraining competition forces and securing the social and political pre-requisites to secure individual economic freedom – represented by the right of property and freedom of contracting[444]– and which it is seen as the paramount value[445]. In other words, economic freedom needs to be restricted and protected by law from its unregulated exercise to guarantee its existence[446]. This strong state should act as market

443 Ibid, p. 19 (emphasis added).

444 Kerber and Vanberg [2001], p. 64.

445 Bonefeld (2012), p. 634 and 638.

446 Ibid, p. 639.

police[447] – *Marktpolizei* – and promote the idea of responsible entrepreneurship by intervening in society's social, ethical and normative frameworks[448].

224. The role of the state as a *Marktpolizei* presupposes the creation of a competition authority, the *Kartellamt*, with two roles. Firstly, it determines whenever there is a breach of the rules of the competitive game. Secondly, by sanctioning economic actors by their wrong-doing attempts, it aims at restoring the competitive game[449].

225. In practice, achieving freedom to compete requires laws limiting the influence of both private and public power in the sphere of individual economic freedom, by setting an institutional and legislative framework. These rules limit *ad-hoc* decision-making and administrative discretion[450]. Ordoliberalism prefers the adoption of a set of general clauses allowing or precluding behaviours – in a rather 'formalistic' or by nature manner – while also accepting exceptions for cases incompatible due to economic grounds with these rules of thumb. This rather 'formalistic' approach has been criticized for being simplistic and ungrounded on economic terms[451]. What the criticism fails to recognize is that ordoliberalism does not preclude deviating from the formal rule and it does in fact permit recourse to exceptions whenever the economic outcome of the practice is in conflict with text of the law. The key for the ordoliberal policy, then, is the adoption of rules within the economic constitution allowing for such exceptions and not a practice based on pure economic efficiency concerns and administrative discretion without a rule allowing for it. This leads to the problem of how the state and its organs can remain impartial in the selection of cases and application of competition law. Unfortunately, no theoretical answer can be readily provided, apart from stating that if the set of rules are clear, pre-established and 'neutral' then the *Marktpolizei* should remain independent and free from political and economic pressure. This is not always borne out in reality though; such an example can be found in the ordoliberal-inspired German Act Against Restraints of Competition, where the Federal Minister of Economics and Technology may overrule a decision by the Bundeskartellamt declaring the compatibility of a merger not only due to economic efficiencies but on the grounds that it is justified by "an overriding public interest"[452].

447 The idea of a "*Marktpolizei*" was proposed by Rüstow and the concept included, among other aspects, the idea of a competition enforcement agency. For more on the concept of market police see, *inter alia*, Hartwich, p. 17; Bonefeld (2012), p. 649; Somma (2013), p. 106.

448 Bonefeld (2012), p. 651.

449 Hartwich, p. 17.

450 Möschel [1989], p. 152.

451 Patel and Schweitzer [2013], p. 207.

452 §42.1. of the Act Against Restraints of Competition (2014) last amended by Article 5 of the Act of 21.07.2014 (Federal Law Gazette I, p.1066).

IV. Buyer power policy from an ordoliberal perspective

226. The exposition thus far presented paves the way for a discussion regarding how ordoliberalism looks at buyer power, allowing me to contrast its EU competition with an ordoliberal competition policy benchmark. To do so, specificities regarding the policy treatment of buyer power under an ordoliberal approach are discussed. Further, this section sets the competition policy foundation through which the current EU legislation is contrasted from an ordoliberal perspective, as discussed in the methodology chapter 1, section §II.C., and aims at identifying and constructing an ordoliberal buyer power policy benchmark inspired by this economic school of thought. With this economic benchmark clarified it is possible to analyze whether the content of the EU buyer power regulation, and also beyond the EU, from a legal and economic perspective, are similar – and to what extent – to an ordoliberal competition policy.

A. Need for buyer power specific regulation?

227. Ordoliberalism advocates for state intervention in the economic sphere by setting clear rules directing the competitive process to secure freedom of competition. These laws are incorporated as part of the "economic constitution" by means of a competition law. In line with this, an issue to clarify is whether *from an ordoliberal perspective there is a need for introducing a modification to EU competition law at a statutory level to deal with buyer power?*

228. I submit that the current provisions are adequate and broad enough to incorporate through teleological interpretation, an ordoliberally modelled buyer power regulation. Interestingly, albeit not surprisingly, this is the same conclusion van Doorn recently reached, and which was the main objective of his study, from a consumer welfare perspective, following a 'Chicagoan' approach, although admitting that a "pure consumer welfare standard" does not fit all buyer power cases[453]. What ordoliberalism demands, however, is an *economically informed* and *legally consistent* judicial treatment of buyer power. This is, the development of a clear, coherent, economically grounded and predictable body of EU case law that distinguishes between monopsony and bargaining power effects and defines which type of practices under certain circumstances are an expression of anticompetitive buyer market power. To facilitate this identification, I have studied buyer power problems anchored on theories of harm that may serve as guidance for courts, NCAs and practitioners to identify potentially dangerous expressions of buyer power. Lastly, in an ordoliberal setting, it would be ideal that it is the case law and not Commission's

453 van Doorn.

guidance notices the legal instrument making the distinction[454]. Nevertheless, non-binding guidance from the Commission is well received, as it can be more thorough, general, and analytical in comparison to a judicial decision.

229. I am aware of the difficulty of such task and also that it is unlikely that the Courts will soon develop such a comprehensive, economically informed and coherent body of case law. There are several reasons which are the grounds for this difficulty. Firstly, the random nature of cases discussed at a judicial level. Secondly, the infrequency with which buyer powers hitherto have been litigated before the Courts. Thirdly, it may be unlikely that the Courts will render judgments with a detailed and specified economic content for buyer power regulation, as it may appear that such a task involves the evaluation of complex economic matters that may fall outside its revision scope[455]. The task of incorporating the advocated dual legal treatment to buyer power and the different theories of harm, nevertheless, may also be carried out by the Commission and/or NCAs when dealing with specific cases, as part of its function is the evaluation of complex economic matters. It is, then, the Commission, aside from academic work, who in practice is likely to lead an economically coherent treatment of buyer power in EU competition law.

B. A differentiated general treatment for buyer power

230. This study proposes that monopsony and bargaining power effects must receive a differentiated treatment by EU competition law because their welfare effects are different. However, the rules covering buyer power as a whole, including monopsony and bargaining power effects, ought to be the same and applied uniformly *regardless of the type of anti-competitive behaviour* that the involved undertaking(s) has (or have) allegedly entered into. In other words, the proposed general regulation of buyer power should be applied in a consistent, coherent, comprehensive and uniform manner irrespective of the

---

454 The legal impact of such guiding tools is moderate; despite they have the power to bind the Commission as it is not free to depart from what it has stated in its notices based on the principle of legitimate expectations, the guidance notices do not have the value as a binding legal source.

455 In my view, not distinguishing between monopsony and bargaining power cases and not choosing the appropriate guiding theory of harm should be considered as a manifest error in appraisal. Also, the issue of the scope of judicial review has been subject to an interesting development and non-consistent case law. See: Eric Barbier de la Serre, 'Standard of Review in Competition Law Cases: Posten Norge and Beyond' in EFTA Court (ed), *The EEA and the EFTA Court: Decentred Integration* (Hart Publishing 2014). Some judgments, particularly older ones, claim that there is limited scope for reviewing complex economic matters. For these inconsistencies see, *inter alia*, claiming a reduced scope for judicial review: Judgment of 11 July 2007, *Alrosa v Commission*, T-170/06, ECR, EU:T:2007:220, para. 122; Judgment of 7 February 2004 in *Aalborg Portland and Others v Commission*, Joined cases C-204/00 P, C-205/00 P, C-211/00 P, C-213/00 P, C-217/00 P and C-219/00 P, EU:C:2004:6, para. 279; Judgment of 11 July 1985 in *Remia v Commission*, C-42/84, EU:C:1985:327, para. 34. For judgments arguing that the scope is larger see: Judgment of 8 December 2011 in *KME Germany and Others v Commission*, C-389/10 P, EU:C:2011:816, para. 121; and from an EFTA Court perspective see: E-15/10 - *Posten Norge AS v EFTA Surveillance Authority* [2012], para. 102, where it clearly stated that "the submission that the Court may intervene only if it considers a complex economic assessment of ESA to be manifestly wrong must be rejected".

typology of the case under investigation[456]. This, nevertheless, does not override the fact that the outcome of the application is likely to vary depending on whether the buyer power exerted is bargaining or monopsony power. In so doing, I reject the idea of adopting different buyer power policies or tailored made rules depending on the typology of the case faced by the NCA or Courts. This is further reinforced by the fact that ex-ante it would be difficult, without reviewing the facts of the case, to determine whether it is an exercise of monopsony or bargaining power.

231. A comprehensive and generalized buyer power policy applied across all typology of cases is consequent with the ordoliberal postulate of generalistic rules of uniform application of EU competition law. Additionally, this comprehensive generalized treatment is in-line with neoclassical literature discussing the models of buyer power. The different models do not distinguish between merger and abuse of dominance cases, for example. In microeconomic terms, by and large bargaining power will be bargaining power regardless of whether it was exercised by a single dominant undertaking or by a pool of undertakings acting as a sole entity in a joint exercise of buyer market power, even though the interactions between them do change.

232. Yet, I do propose acknowledging whether the case involves monopsony or bargaining power to orient the application of the general EU competition rules. It might appear to some that distinguishing between monopsony and bargaining power is a mere formalistic differentiation and that it ought to be left to the case-by-case assessment of welfare consequences. To a certain extent, the distinction is formalistic because predictable laws require different theoretical constructs to differentiate economic realities. This distinction is also economically fundamental because monopsony and buyer power are *different* phenomena.

233. To briefly recapitulate the proposals covered in chapter 2, sections §V and §VI, behaviours generating monopsony effects shall be treated as economically inefficient and undesirable whereas bargaining power effects should be treated as, almost always, procompetitive if the undertaking exerting it does not fit the hourglass model. On the one hand, monopsonistic practices among coordinated buyers are very likely to be assessed in their context and aim and be considered as *object restriction* of competition under Article 101 TFEU and monopsony power exerted by a dominant firm is also very likely to be in breach of Article 102 TFEU, as restricting purchases with the sole aim of reducing the purchasing price unduly distorts competition by itself and is virtually economically unjustifiable from both a consumer and total welfare perspective. Nonetheless, monopsony behaviour might not have negative welfare effects (or much less) if the purchasing method incorporates a

456 One of the aims of my analysis is to determine if this homogenous and coherent treatment applies in EU competition law to all types of buyer power cases.

two-part tariff model.

234. On the other hand, bargaining power practices will be in principle considered as pro-competitive, particularly if the buyer does not possess substantial market power in the downstream market where it carries out its subsequent economic activity. However, even in those circumstances, bargaining power might cause competition harm in the upstream market that affects the ability of buyers or suppliers to effectively compete and that, in the long run, are capable of harming end consumers by means of less intensity of competition and therefore higher prices, less innovation and quality. Furthermore, if the undertaking possesses substantial market power downstream then the competition authority must investigate the case in depth to determine whether bargaining power can be detrimental from a consumer welfare standard perspective, in addition to any kind of upstream anti-competitive effects. The key difference with monopsony, then is that, in principle, bargaining power would have the ability to reduce purchasing prices towards the competitive level and, therefore, be efficient in the instances of bargaining power with two-part tariff contracts, or at least more efficient than monopsony practices with linear contracts, as I discussed in chapter 2, section §IV. Because of this, bargaining power cases will tend to be effect based-restrictions of competition and requiring plenty of counterfactual analysis.

235. Lastly, by adopting a comprehensive and generalized buyer power theory, I deliberately opt for securing legal certainty and predictability of the cases at the expense, in the minority of them, of concrete justice. However, the proposed buyer power treatment is quite specific as it advocates determining the type of buyer power exertion, whether it is monopsony or bargaining power, to then assess the conduct's effects and, thus guide the application of the norms and the case outcome. Understood it as such, this generalized legal treatment of applying the same rules to buyer power does distinguish among the practical scenarios, in reality. The challenge, in any event, is the correct assessment of the case and the subsequent application of the appropriate derived rule.

C. Which welfare standard and which kind of harm triggers competition intervention in buyer power cases?

236. Welfare standards and the type of welfare which seeks to be maximized by competition is a fundamental matter for our discipline[457]. There are three basic ways of approaching this topic. On the one hand, we have *consumer welfare or surplus*, which is the difference between "the maximum amount that a consumer is willing to pay for a good and the amount that the consumer actually pays"[458]. For

457 Bishop and Walker, [2010], para. 2-017.

458 Pindyck and Rubinfeld, [2009].

instance, if a buyer values a kilo of beef at €19 but pays €17 there is a difference of 2 euros in its favor and this represents the surplus for that specific consumer. In more economic terms, the consumer welfare surplus is represented by an area under the demand curve but which happens to be above the set price[459]. Producer (supplier) surplus is defined reversely as the difference a supplier keeps between the price it is willing to sell a good for and the payment it has obtained. On economic terms, it is denoted as the area "above the marginal cost curve but below the price", or the excess of what goods were sold for[460]. Lastly, total surplus or social welfare is represented by the sum of both consumer and supplier surplus.

237. Opting for a type of welfare standard is relevant because it provides guidance to competition authorities when it comes to determining what type of surplus the chosen policy is aiming to maximize. However, in practice, the distinction is of less importance than it may seem because, for most cases, as remarked by Bishop and Walker, "maximising consumer welfare and maximising social welfare require the same outcomes"[461].

238. EU competition policy – arguably the Commission's[462] – seems to advocate for the adoption of a (short term) consumer welfare standard that triggers competition intervention based on end consumer harm[463]. With such an approach it is assumed that the competitive outcome should be to the benefit of consumers[464]. This, however and as noted by Orbach, is a "phrase of great rhe-

---

459 Bishop and Walker, [2010], para. 2-015.

460 Ibid, para. 2-015.

461 Ibid, para. 2-019.

462 See, *inter alia*, in the Commission's official documents different expressions advocating for the adoption of a consumer welfare standard: "[t]he objective of Article 81 is to protect competition on the market as a means of enhancing consumer welfare and of ensuring an efficient allocation of resources", Communication from the Commission - Guidelines on the application of Article 81(3) of the Treaty [2004] OJ C 101/97, para. 13; "[t]he objective of Article 101 is to ensure that undertakings do not use agreements – in this context, vertical agreements – to restrict competition on the market to the detriment of consumers" in Guidelines on Vertical Restraints [2010] OJ C 130/1, para. 7; "[e]ffective competition brings benefits to consumers, such as low prices, high quality products, a wide selection of goods and services, and innovation. Through its control of mergers, the Commission prevents mergers that would be likely to deprive customers of these benefits by significantly increasing the market power of firms" in Guidelines on the assessment of horizontal mergers under the Council Regulation on the control of concentrations between undertakings [2004] OJ C 31/5, para. 8; "[...] it is competition and not competitors, that should be protected. Ultimately, the aim is to avoid consumer harm", Philip Lowe, 'Consumer Welfare and Efficiency – New Guiding Principles of Competition Policy?' (13th International Conference on Competition and 14th European Competition Day); Neelie Kroes, 'The European Commission's Enforcement Priorities as Regards Exclusionary Abuses of Dominance - Current Thinking' 4 Competition Law International (2008) 5, p. 5. For some literature on the topic, see: Gormsen, [2010], p. 20 to 58; Svend Albæk, 'Consumer Welfare in EU Competition Policy' in Caroline Heide-Jørgensen and others (eds), *Aims and values in competition law* (DJØF Publ. 2013), p. 67-87; Behrens 'The "Consumer Choice" Paradigm in German Ordoliberalism and its Impact upon EU Competition Law' (2014). On why choosing a welfare standard matters see: Blair and Sokol (2012).

463 For Kaplow and Shavell the concept of welfare encompasses less than the broader concept of "well-being" or "utility" which in addition to pure economic profit for buyers and sellers also include more diffuse concepts such as fairness, aesthetic fulfillment, and so forth. Louis Kaplow and Steven Shavell, *Fairness Versus Welfare* (Harvard University Press 2002).

464 Cf with Bork who argues that economic efficiency should be the goal of competition law in Bork, [1978]. Blair and Sokol argue that despite he used the wording "consumer welfare" he meant in reality "total welfare" in Blair and Sokol (2012), p. 476. Also arguing that Bork's expression is confusing and meant aggregated welfare, see Carstensen 'Emerging Issues in Buyer Power Analysis' (2012), p. 4.

torical power" but diffuse content[465]. Nevertheless, to date, the Courts have not made any decision or pronouncement concerning which is the welfare standard adopted and pursued in EU competition law and policy. If anything, the Courts seem more eager to adopt a broad and diffuse standard of protecting competition as such and market structures, in general - as recently ratified by the CJEU in *Post Danmark II*[466]- and without necessary direct link to end consumer prices[467]. Further, in the case of some particular forms of buyer power exertion also showing concern for the wellbeing of weaker buyers and the upstream competitive conditions, as it is the case when dealing with countervailing buyer power as discussed *in extenso* in chapter 9, section §VIII[468], and concerning imposing minimum purchasing prices (discussed in chapter 10), price discrimination, and as shown at the Member State level concerning unfair trading practices vis-à-vis suppliers as discussed in chapter 8.

239. The discussion of the welfare standard advocated by ordoliberalism in general and for buyer power cases is interesting. Historically, the first wave of ordoliberals did not discuss welfare standards in the modern economic language[469]. In my research, I have found that, for an ordoliberal buyer power policy, the welfare standard employed is an '*aggregated consumer welfare standard*' that has been embedded, particularly, in the works of Böhm and Eucken as part of the concept of *Leistungswettbewerb,* and which takes into account consumer harm in the long run by focusing more on medium and long term consequences of a conduct and the fostering of dynamic efficiency rather than focusing on pure static short-term consumer surplus. More importantly, this standing further implies that an ordoliberal buyer power policy anchored on a dualistic treatment of buyer power cases implies that a broad harm standard must apply in buyer power cases; i.e. competition law intervention should not only be triggered whenever there is anti-competitive harm regarding end short term consumer surplus in the downstream market. The upstream market conditions and the medium and long term perspective matters as part of protecting competition as such and, to some extent, the market agents' economic freedom.

---

465 Barak Y. Orbach, 'The Antitrust Consumer Welfare Paradox' 7 Journal of Competition Law & Economics (2010) 133.

466 Judgment of 6 October 2015 in *Post Danmark*, C-23/14, EU:C:2015:651, para. 26.

467 Judgment of 4 June 2009 in *T-Mobile Netherlands and Others*, C-8/08, EU:C:2009:343, para. 39.

468 Cf with the position of the US Supreme Court in Antitrust matters, less concerned with the market structure or freedom to compete in the upstream market and more with end results when holding that "[l]ow prices benefit consumers regardless of how those prices are set, and so long as they are above predatory levels, they do not threaten competition" in *Atlantic Richfield Co. v. USA Petroleum Co.*, 495 U.S. 238 340. (1990), p. 340.

469 In the research carried I did not find an explicit reference by any of the ordoliberals of the first or second wave of the preferred welfare standard. Cf this with the views of Vanberg who considers that the debate should not be focused on which welfare standard to use but rather on the protection of economic freedom and the need to distinguish whether the discussion is to be centered at the constitutional level or at the sub-constitutional level of policy choices in Vanberg 'Consumer Welfare, Total Welfare and Economic Freedom – On the Normative Foundations of Competition Policy' (2009).

240. Indeed, in Böhm's view, the criterion distinguishing what qualifies as a permissible behaviour and what constitutes forbidden behaviour is *consumer interest.*[470] Yet this focus on the consumer interest seems to be overlooked or dismissed by the literature. For instance, Akman holds that "ordoliberal ideas are inconsistent with the 'consumer welfare' approach"[471]. In a similar fashion, Gormsen argues that protecting economic freedom and consumer welfare are incompatible, and that consumer welfare is not a motivation for economic freedom in the slightest degree[472]. Other views suggest that ordoliberalism supports total welfare standard "as the result of a truly competitive process", as expressed by Behrens[473], or that it supports a soft-total welfare standard and that it was an influential precedent for the position of the Chicago School in such matters[474]. However, firstly, for ordoliberalism, consumer welfare is not only a director of the decisions of economic actors but also the justifiable economic interest of economic activity. Secondly, holding, as Bonefeld seems to suggest, that ordoliberal ideas were influential in the development of the Chicago School is historically inaccurate as, even today, ordoliberal ideas are largely unknown – or misunderstood – in the English-speaking world[475].

241. Yet, the mid-way answer is true, and with some inner tensions as I discuss. The ordoliberal 'aggregated consumer welfare standard' is a compromise between the pure consumer welfare standard and a full total welfare standard that tries to strike a balance between consumer protection and protection of competition as a process. This compromise is reached by understanding that, for ordoliberalism, the consumer shall not only be the end consumer in the downstream market but also other consumers (buyers) in the competitive process, as well as suppliers vis-à-vis powerful buyers[476]. In addition, the protection of the consumer's interest should be medium/long-term oriented and not purely short-term driven[477], because protecting the competitive process

470 F. Böhm 'The Non-State ("Natural") Laws Inherent in a Competitive Economy' in W. Stützel, et alia (ed), *Standard Texts on the Social Market Economy* (1992), p. 107.

471 Akman 'Searching for the Long-Lost Soul of Article 82 EC' (2009), p. 268.

472 Gormsen 'The Conflict Between Economic Freedom and Consumer Welfare in the Modernisation of Article 82 EC' (2007), p. 330-331 and 343.

473 Behrens 'The "Consumer Choice" Paradigm in German Ordoliberalism and its Impact upon EU Competition Law' (2014), p. 27 to 32.

474 Such is the interpretation of Bonefeld of Foucault's view on ordoliberalism as *Vitalpolitik*, see: Bonefeld (2012), p. 633-656; Bonefeld (2012), p. 139-171.

475 Also stressing the fact that ordoliberal ideas have not been broadly published in English see: Behrens 'The "Consumer Choice" Paradigm in German Ordoliberalism and its Impact upon EU Competition Law' (2014), p. 17.

476 This compromised approach also appears to be the one taken by the CJEU in *Post Danmark II* when dealing with efficiencies defenses but not market harm when stating that "it is for the dominant undertaking to show that the efficiency gains likely to result from the conduct under consideration counteract any likely negative effects on competition *and* consumer welfare in the affected markets" in Judgment of 6 October 2015 in *Post Danmark*, C-23/14, EU:C:2015:651, para. 49, and see also para. 69 (emphasis added). See also stating that consumer is not only the final one Albæk [2013], p. 75.

477 Bundeskartellamt '*Buyer Power in Competition Law - Status and Perspectives*' (2008), p. 13. See discussing how to determine medium and long term welfare in dynamic efficiency terms: Vikas Kathuria, 'A Conceptual Framework to Identify Dynamic Efficiency' 11 European Competition Journal (2015) 319.

prevents harm to end consumers and reduction of their welfare. The focus is therefore on achieving dynamic efficiency that goes beyond pure static efficiency and in the consumer needs.

242. For Böhm, one of the characteristics of the private law society and ordoliberalism is that "not only is the *satisfaction of consumer needs* well above the average for the members of the wealthy class but also they are offered totally different possibilities of productive activity within society"[478]. He claims that consumer concerns are "the sole directly justifiable economic interest"[479]. Consequently, if the consumer's interest and satisfaction are the justifiable economic interest there is little doubt that the economic efficiency of a market behaviour shall be tested by using as a reference the wellbeing of consumers as a benchmark or reference tool[480]. Also, the concept of performance competition – *Leistungswettbewerb*[481] – recognizes consumer welfare standard as the yardstick tool for measuring the competitive outcome. The *Leistungswettbewerb* describes the idea of competition among undertakings for the production of better services and products for consumers[482]. In this regard, the market order seeks to assure "that the only road to business success is through the narrow gate of better performance in service of the consumer and not through many back doors of unfair and subversive competition"[483]. For Vanberg, employing the *Leistungswettbewerb* standard implies adopting rules that would make consumers' preferences the "ultimate controlling force in the process of production"[484]. Thus, ordoliberal thinking, without resorting to the same microeconomic language as contemporary competition economics, also advocates for an idea of "consumer sovereignty" with the aim of achieving consumer welfare.

243. On the other hand, nonetheless, the ordoliberal construct argues for a broader welfare approach because it pursues the protection of the competitive process, which implies a concern for the wellbeing of the competitive structures and the balancing of gains and losses among all parties, including suppliers vis-à-vis powerful buyers[485]. Hence, there is a balancing exercise to be made between protecting the wellbeing of consumer needs as advocated by Böhm

---

478 Böhm [1989], p, 59.

479 F. Böhm, 'The Non-State ("Natural") Laws Inherent in a Competitive Economy' in W. Stützel, et alia (ed), *Standard Texts on the Social Market Economy* (1992), p. 107.

480 For a thorough discussion of the ordoliberal ideas of "consumer choice" see: Behrens 'The "Consumer Choice" Paradigm in German Ordoliberalism and its Impact upon EU Competition Law' (2014).

481 As noted by Gerber, the concept of *Leistungswettbewerb* was firstly coined by Nipperdey – not an ordoliberal himself - in 1930 to distinguish the idea of performance competition that later evolved in the ordoliberal thinking to represent consumer's preference as the coordinator of the production process, Gerber (1994), p. 53.

482 Vanberg, 'Freiburg School of Law and Economics' [1998], p. 177.

483 Wilhelm Röpke, *A Humane Economy* (Third Edition edn, ISI Books 1998), p. 31.

484 Vanberg 'Consumer Welfare, Total Welfare and Economic Freedom – On the Normative Foundations of Competition Policy' (2009), p. 15.

485 Carstensen 'Buyer Cartels Versus Buying Groups: Legal Distinctions, Competitive Realities, and Antitrust Policy' (2010), p. 23.

and the competitive process. A focus anchored exclusively on short-term consumer welfare may lead to a "disproportionate focus on the selling side of the market and an under appreciation" of buyer power risks, which is at odds with the protection of the freedom to compete and competition as such[486]. This, however, should not be understood as advocating for the protection of inefficient undertakings that deserve no competition protection as this implies less efficient use of resources and welfare loss.

a. Which type of harm is needed to trigger the application of competition law?

244. Related to the former discussion comes the question of which type of harm or in which market must harm exist to trigger the application of competition law in buyer power cases. For ordoliberalism, and connected with the interest in protecting competition as a process and the economic freedom of market participants, *competition law intervention in buyer power cases is warranted even if there is no direct short term downstream end consumer harm,* because buyer power distortions in the upstream market adversely affect competition as such and the market participants' economic freedom[487].

245. This broader ordoliberal approach to the competition harm required to trigger the application of the law is of practical importance. A posture that advocates for triggering competition law only upon the existence of end consumer harm focuses its analysis on pure downstream competition considerations and, likely, purely static efficiency concerns[488]. According to such a perspective, if the buying conduct has no direct end consumer harm – regardless of the impact it might have in the competitive process in the upstream market – competition intervention would not be necessary. As I discuss through this study, such is the approach that is taken by most US Courts and US academics, and in Europe by the advocates of the 'more economic approach', including some recent soft law issued by the Commission.

246. Instead, a broader approach to competition harm implies that competition law will be applicable in buyer power cases whenever, in addition to the short-term wellbeing of end consumers, there is substantial and unjustified economic harm affecting the competitive structure and competition as such as well as the economic freedom and interests of all consumers and suppliers in the production chain in all involved markets. Furthermore, the analysis is not anchored on pure a static efficiency concern but rather the medium and long-term consequences *for the competitive structure upstream and downstream,*

486 Ibid p. 46. See also: Carstensen 'Emerging Issues in Buyer Power Analysis' (2012), p. 4.

487 "The buyer power cases are, overall, more consistent with the proposition that the concern of antitrust law is primarily with preserving and protecting the competitive process than with some specific economic theory of efficiency", Carstensen 'Emerging Issues in Buyer Power Analysis' (2012), p. 4.

488 See expressing concern about an excessive focus on static efficiency within the end consumer welfare: Bishop and Walker, [2010], para. 2-019.

as well as implications connected to economic freedom. This is so because a limited and economically justified protection of producers' interest against anti-competitive buyer power conducts is compatible with the protection of competition as such and efficiency, as remarked by Jones from a US antitrust law perspective[489]. Protecting competition as such, economic freedom and the competitive process serve consumers in the medium and long-term as market concentration is kept in check, markets are healthy and market power does not erode the benefits of the market economy.

247. A similar position to this compromised approach has been suggested recently by Kirkwood, who argues that:

> [t]he purpose of antitrust law – of competition law – is to combat conduct that *both diminishes competition and reduces consumer welfare*. For this reason, the fundamental goal of antitrust law is best described as protecting 'consumers from anticompetitive conduct – conduct that creates market power, transfers wealth from consumers to producers, and fails to provide consumers with compensating benefits[490].

248. This broader approach to competition intervention against abuses of buyer market power beyond strict downstream consumer harm is also consistent with the adoption of a dualistic approach to buyer power cases. It is so because by going further than triggering the application of the law based only on pure downstream effects on consumer welfare, *EU competition law will intervene whenever there are anticompetitive buyer power effects in all involved markets and when competition as such is distorted, fully capturing all buyer power effects.*

249. Another benefit of this broader approach to competition intervention anchored on harm to the competitive process is that it avoids risks of under enforcement in terms of a pure end consumer harm standard, because it captures instances where the anti-competitive effect occurs in the upstream market and which may not have an impact on the downstream market in the short-term or, also, simply because the undertakings only compete as buyers, but not as retailers.

250. This ordoliberal broader approach to the triggering of competition law intervention in buyer power cases whenever there is harm to the competitive structure, even if there is no evidence of a direct detriment to end consumer's conditions in the short run, also finds support in the EU case law. This is clearly seen, for instance in the CJEU Judgments in *T-Mobile Netherlands and*

---

489 William K Jones, 'Concerted Refusals to Deal and the Producer Interest in Antitrust' 50 Ohio State Law Journal (1989) 73, p. 89.

490 Kirkwood (2014), p. 30 (emphasis added).

Others[491] and also in *TeliaSonera Sverige*[492]. If the harm does affect the competitive structure and competition as such, then the ordoliberal broad welfare and harm approaches argue that such conduct does indeed warrant competition intervention, even if there is no short-term detriment to consumer conditions[493]. Such a broader solution taken by the Courts, and in line with ordoliberal postulates, is also the one applied in buyer power cases as I show in this study. In fact, this position is shared by Ezrachi and Ioannidou who argue that:

> [i]n the context of buyer power, most interesting are statements from the European Court which widen the goals of competition policy to include market structure and the process of competition. Such statements may support intervention even when buyer power does not directly harm consumers but does adversely affect upstream producers[494].

251. It must be stressed, however, *that not any type of upstream harm will trigger the application of competition law from an ordoliberal perspective*. There are some buyers and suppliers that when facing buyer market power would be 'excluded' not because the conduct is not economically justified, but because these undertakings are *not efficient* and for the market and competition as a whole they are better outside of the market, or because the 'exploitation' involves an issue of pure contractual profit distribution but not necessarily a harm to competition as I discuss in chapter 8. Intervention is warranted when upstream competition is endangered because there are cases of unjustified and spread exclusion, or when (efficient) suppliers are exploited in a way that forces them outside of the market. This could also happen whenever the exertion of buyer market power has an adverse impact in innovation, quality or product diversity in the medium and long term. In all these cases competition law is triggered because the harm to competition as such has the potential to harm end consumers in the medium and long term.

252. In this work, I will evaluate whether such a broad standard to trigger competition intervention as advocated by ordoliberal thinking is the one employed by the courts in Europe and the US, even if it is employed with the aim of protecting weaker buyers to avoid excessive market concentration that may have an impact in the competitive structure of the market[495].

---

491 Judgment of 4 June 2009 in *T-Mobile Netherlands and Others*, C-8/08, EU:C:2009:343, para. 36-37.

492 Judgment of 17 February 2011 in *TeliaSonera Sverige*, C-52/09, EU:C:2011:83, para. 22.

493 Bundeskartellamt '*Buyer Power in Competition Law - Status and Perspectives*' (2008), p. 13. Arguing that this posture can be derived from the EU case law in buyer power cases see also: Ezrachi and Ioannidou (2014), p. 73.

494 Ezrachi and Ioannidou (2014), p. 73.

495 Cf with *Atlantic Richfield Co. v. USA Petroleum Co.*, 495 U.S. 238 340. (1990), 340.

253. Consequently, and as a rule of thumb, as part of its ordoliberal buyer power policy, this study will employ an aggregated consumer welfare standard (as understood in this section) as a compromise concerning the protection of the consumer's interest and the competitive structure of the market. Furthermore, ordoliberalism takes a broader approach to the type of harm required in buyer power cases to trigger the application of EU competition not requiring for this the existence of direct short-term end consumer harm if there is substantial and unjustified harm to competition in the upstream market. I employ these two factors as the comparative thresholds to evaluate whether or not a behaviour is compatible with EU competition law and an ordoliberally inspired buyer power policy.

D. Freedom to compete

254. The ordoliberal understanding of competition as a process that allows for the achievement of economic freedom implies protection of the freedom of contract and voluntary transactions[496]. As expressed by Hoppmann, competition fosters individual initiative by allowing suppliers to freely determine which offer from which buyer they want to accept[497]. This implies that, for ordoliberalism, in terms of deciding whether to opt for a *short term* more economically efficient alternative that erodes a sufficient possibility of choice and undermines economic freedom (for example by limiting the amount of market players and thus substantially reducing variety), or a *short term* less economically efficient outcome that preserves sufficient possibility of choice for the individual, the latter would be the preferred option[498]. In other words, preserving freedom of choice is understood as 'economically efficient' in *a medium and long-term* perspective because it secures an arguably greater degree of economic freedom and voluntariness on contracting preventing the social *Vermachtung*. However, this view should not be taken to the extreme. Such a radical views are found among some authors linked with ordoliberalism, in particular in Röpke's conception of 'small is beautiful' by suggesting that undertakings ought to be of small and medium size as the concentration of market power is inherently evil[499]. I disagree with this extreme ordoliberal view as the law should not protect inefficiency or small/weaker undertakings for several reasons, including

496 Böhm, 'Rule of Law in a Market Economy' [1989], p. 46-67; Tumlir [1989], p. 136; and Vanberg 'Consumer Welfare, Total Welfare and Economic Freedom – On the Normative Foundations of Competition Policy' (2009), p. 10. Stressing the relation between freedom of choice and protecting the market structure see Behrens 'The "Consumer Choice" Paradigm in German Ordoliberalism and its Impact upon EU Competition Law' (2014), p. 23.

497 Hoppmann (1968), p. 62.

498 Peacock and Willgerodt, 'German Liberalism and Economic Revival' [1989], p. 7; Behrens 'The "Consumer Choice" Paradigm in German Ordoliberalism and its Impact upon EU Competition Law' (2014), p. 23.

499 Gerber (1994), p. 37. This also appears to be the view of O'Donoghue and Padilla when stating that "[t]his reflected a view that small and medium sized enterprises were important to consumer welfare and they should receive some protection from the excesses of market power", in O'Donoghue and Padilla, *The Law and Economics of Article 82 EC* [2006], p. 9.

the maximization of welfare. Further, this trend is only shared by a minority among ordoliberals, and it better represents the ideas of sociological liberalism, a connected but not ordoliberal school of thought.

255. When determining the appropriate degree of freedom of choice, medium and long-term efficiency considerations must be taken into account. Thus, a *proportionality or rule of reason test* ought to determine whether an efficient behaviour that significantly restricts choice or the economic freedom of rival undertakings is allowed or not as part of the analysis, but not the only part of the analysis. Otherwise protecting economic freedom and freedom of choice would be equivalent to protecting inefficient market players[500]. This also appears to be the position of Böhm and Eucken who would have sought a legislative solution that would not aim to protect small and inefficient undertakings from market dynamics, while not allowing a 'winner takes all situation' either. To paraphrase Böhm, the key lies in, recognizing competition as an instrument to satisfy consumer *needs* and *choice* in a medium and long-term perspective. The problem, of course, is striking the correct balance between freedom to compete, choice and economic efficiency.

256. This moderate view inclined towards some *protection of economic freedom appears to be the criterion adopted by the Courts regarding buyer power regulation in general,* and in particular in the case of countervailing buyer power and buyer power exclusion, as discussed in chapters 9 and 6, respectively, and the situation of positions of relative dominance and dependence under national laws when dealing with unfair purchasing practices, as discussed in chapter 8.

257. An argument against pursuing some protection of freedom to compete and choice as a goal in buyer power cases is that due to its abstract nature it is very difficult to measure in welfare terms or to implement the proportionality test suggested above, as it is difficult to balance the values of economic freedom and economic efficiency, or how valuable freedom is in welfare terms.

E. Redistributive concerns?

258. *Re-distributive concerns in competition policy* are the subject of an interesting debate within ordoliberalism, and it also plays a role in buyer power cases as I discuss when *dealing with exploitative unfair purchasing practices* in chapter 8.

---

500 Such is the opinion of Akman when claiming that: "Ordoliberalism protects the competitive process to achieve individual economic freedom and this can result in protecting inefficient competitors which would conflict with the objective of enhancing welfare" in Akman 'Searching for the Long-Lost Soul of Article 82 EC' (2009), p. 268-269.

259. In general, ordoliberals were interested in a society where welfare considerations and re-distribution of wealth are part of the economic and political system. As noted by Gerber, "[i]t is important to recognize that the deepest wellsprings of ordoliberal thought were humanist values rather than efficiency or other purely economic concerns"[501]. However, the *Wettweberbsordnung* may entail that some disparities in the distribution of wealth are based on each one's economic productivity. This, in turn, implies that those which are more productive are better off[502]. Further, an analysis of the work of Eucken highlights that economic freedom does not necessarily produce a fair outcome; it just tends to be economically efficient. In this sense, Eucken "calls for *redistributive measures* whenever the outcome of the market system is *socially unacceptable*"[503]. Ordoliberalism, then, advocates for a progressive tax system that balances the distortions produced by the competitive process[504] but outside competition law and policy.

260. The discussion, then, is not whether an ordoliberal society should possess wealth distribution mechanisms, but rather whether competition law should be the mechanism for such an end. For me the answer is clear: competition law should not be the tool used to re-distribute wealth[505]. The function of competition as a process ought to be the maximization of wealth so that other better-suited tools can redistribute the wealth within society.

261. In reviewing the ideas of first or second-wave ordoliberals, I have found no evidence to support a different interpretation than the one above, or suggesting that competition law should be (one of) the mechanism(s) used for wealth redistribution. This, nevertheless, is contradicted by the view of Peacock and Willgerodt, as they interpret ordoliberal competition policy as giving room for proposals that may even "include support for a redistribution of income which cannot be justified 'scientifically'. For instance, in this view it would not worry Ordo-liberals if anti-monopoly policy were to have both allocative and distributional effects, even if the latter cannot be objectively evaluated"[506].

262. I disagree with this interpretation of ordoliberal ideas that seek to employ competition law as a redistributive mechanism, a topic I deal with in extensor

501 Gerber (1994), p. 36 and identically in Gerber, [2001], p. 239.

502 Friedrich A. Lutz, 'Objeciones al Orden de la Competencia' in Lucas Beltrán (ed), *La Economía de Mercado*, vol I (Sociedad de Estudios y Publicaciones 1963), p. 268.

503 Kamecke (2001), p. 26 (emphasis added). Cf with Foucault in Foucault and others, [2008], p. 142-143, who claim that in ordoliberalism there is little to no room for distribution of wealth among individuals.

504 Lutz [1963], p. 274.

505 Christopher Townley, 'Is there (Still) room for Non-Economic Arguments in Article 101 TFEU Cases?' in Caroline Heide-Jørgensen and others (eds), *Aims and Values in Competition Law* (DJØF Publ. 2013), p. 115-180; also cf with Harris and Jorde (1984), who claim that in addition to efficiency, antitrust should seek procedural fairness and equity in profit distribution. See also: Heike Schweitzer, 'Competition Law and Public Policy: Reconsidering an Uneasy Relationship. The Example of Art. 81' LAW 2007/30 EUI Working Papers (2007) 1.

506 Peacock and Willgerodt, 'German Liberalism and Economic Revival' [1989], p. 7.

concerning unfair purchasing practices in chapter 8. Instead, I argue that in a *holistic* lato sensu ordoliberal oriented *competition policy* there should be room for redistributive mechanisms in-line with the Social Market Economy, but outside of *competition law – sensu stricto*[507]. In other words, other legal disciplines or administrative mechanisms - such as the application of a redistributive tax mechanism, labor law that sets working standards, and educational policies - are better suited tools for distributing the wealth generated by the competitive process, while competition law should be focused on fostering the economically efficient outcome that later on is to be distributed by other mechanisms. In short, EU competition law should be oriented towards achieving *welfare maximization*, not welfare distribution.

V. Conclusion

263. This chapter has discussed competition from an ordoliberal perspective in general, to then go on to identify and construct a theory explaining how ordoliberalism would regulate buyer power. As discussed in chapter 1, I employ ordoliberalism as a competition policy benchmark to contrast whether or not the current legislation in the EU – and partially the US – adopts a similar pattern in its regulation. And, in cases where there is divergence, then determine where this divergence lies and the reasons behind this. By adopting such an informed methodological choice, the evaluations and suggestions are internally coherent and testable against the theoretical background.

264. In my discussion, I have presented the key elements of competition in an ordoliberal perspective, particularly regarding the goals of the protection of competition as a process and as economically efficient. Furthermore, the chapter also shows how ordoliberalism offers an indigenous perspective to the analysis of this topic under a European competition policy that has shaped – and continues to shape – the law and practice of competition regulation. I also addressed issues regarding the views on different types of competition, as well as discussing whether or not 'competition as if' is an accepted ordoliberal standard. The section also dealt with the compatibility of ordoliberalism with the use of modern microeconomics and industrial organization theory and showed how ordoliberal competition is not against an interdisciplinary approach to either competition law application or theory. However, the application of economic knowledge should not replace the legal goals of EU competition policy and should be circumscribed to guiding case decision-making

---

507 See, *inter alia*, Joseph F. Brodley, 'The Economic Goals of Antitrust: Efficiency, Consumer Welfare, and Technological Progress' 62 New York University Law Review (1987) 1020; Motta, [2006], p. 18-22; Bishop and Walker, [2010], p. 4-8; Albert Sánchez Graells, *Public Procurement and the EU Competition Rules* (Hart 2011), p. 89-92.

and suggesting changes to the current legal standards and legal interpretations by the Courts. Therefore, using ordoliberal theory is not opposed to the economic analysis of the law and is consistent with my economically informed legal analysis.

265. This chapter has also embarked on a novel and ambitious aim of identifying and creating an ordoliberal general theory for the treatment of buyer power anchored on the general ordoliberal foundations that seek to protect competition as such, with the aim of achieving medium and long-term 'aggregated consumer welfare'. This broader welfare standard adequately fits buyer power because ordoliberalism seeks to control the exercise of market power either from buyers or sellers in the upstream and/or downstream market as it affects 'competition as such'.

266. Also, this policy construction has allowed me to determine that, under the current EU legislation, an ordoliberal competition policy does not require new specific provisions to control the exercise of buyer market power, as the current instruments are sufficiently applicable. Furthermore, the objective of ordoliberalism of installing a competitive market order and protecting competition as a process requires the adoption of a dualistic approach to buyer power: ordoliberalism will keep in check instances of the exercise of monopsony power and bargaining power, and it will also necessitate the scrutiny of buyer market power effects in both the upstream and downstream market. In connection with this, an ordoliberal approach to buyer power does not only seek to maximize short-term consumer welfare standard in a static sense and to only intervene in the presence of end consumer harm. Such approach is too narrow for an ordoliberal buyer power policy. Instead, my proposal is anchored on a dualistic approach to buyer power cases and the protection of competition as such and the market structure would adopt a broader aggregated consumer welfare standard, which aims to balance the interest of end consumers and other market participants to achieve consumer wellbeing in the medium and long term by protecting competition as such. This, in turn, implies that, for ordoliberalism, competition harm that occurs outside the downstream market vis-à-vis end consumers is still a source of concern and constitutes sufficient reason to intervene and sanction or prevent the wrongdoing because buyer power effects in the upstream market may also negatively impact the competitive process as a whole. Also, this chapter discusses to which extent the protection of freedom to compete and re-distribution are an issue of concern in terms of an ordoliberal treatment to buyer power. In these two cases, however, the general answer is that even if they are, competition law sensu stricto is not the most adequate tool to remedy these issues because other regulatory avenues are better suited to both re-distribute wealth and protect contractual freedom among undertakings.

267. In sum, an ordoliberal approach to buyer power, as laid out in this chapter, allows me to compare the current EU buyer power regulation against this benchmark to determine whether the existing treatment is consistent with an ordoliberal approach and the extent to which it is. This, furthermore, opens the way for a discussion of why and how the adopted solutions by the Courts and the Commission deviate from it. Finally, by resorting to ordoliberalism, an indigenous European competition policy, it is possible to create a sharp contrast to the buyer power regulation in the US antitrust system and see if the different policy schools that have arguably most influenced such different legal regimes reach different outcomes.

PART III

RELEVANT BUYING MARKETS

4

MARKET DEFINITION IN BUYER POWER CASES: REVISITING THE TRADITIONAL METHODOLOGIES

I. Introduction

268. EU competition law has not devoted particular attention to the development of a coherent and detailed methodology for defining buyer markets[508], instead, it has resorted to the mere reversal of selling-oriented market definition to evaluate purchasing-oriented cases. A suitable explanation for the lack of a buyer-oriented market definition methodology is twofold: the relatively few buyer power cases in EU competition law, and the lack of literature and discussion concerning the need for a specific buyer power market definition methodology. Consequently, attempts by competition agencies worldwide, including the Commission, and literature in general regarding the adoption of a proper methodology defining buyer markets are limited. In this section, *I propose revising the current market definition methodologies* for defining relevant purchasing markets. My central contribution is *the proposal of a dualistic approach to buyer's market definition* that fully captures buyer market power and its effects in the upstream and downstream markets by defining the market in which the buyer acquires its input and the market in which it sells its output.

269. The justification of this dualistic approach to buyer-market definition is that buyer power cases invariably have repercussions on the upstream *and* down-

508 A similar view is expressed by Füller when stating: "[t]he problems of seller power mirrored in buyer power: However, European practice has heretofore not yet developed a coherent concept for defining buyer markets", in J. Füller, Market Definition in Günther Hirsch, Frank Montag and Franz Jürgen Säcker, *Competition Law: European Community Practice and Procedure: Article-by-Article Commentary* (Sweet & Maxwell 2008), p. 449. See also: Carlton and Israel (2011); Buttà and Pezzoli (2014).

stream markets, as remarked upon by Steiner[509], or have a horizontal and vertical effect, as postulated by Buttà and Pezzoli[510]. Buyer power directly affects the competitive conditions between suppliers and buyers in the upstream market and may positively or negatively impact the downstream market and the relations between the buyer-retailer, its competitors and end consumers, as discussed in chapter 2[511].

270. Furthermore, there are other reasons that justify adopting a different approach to the definition of relevant buying markets and, therefore, revisiting the existing methodologies. As Carstensen expressed, buying markets and buyers' incentives differ from seller markets[512]. In a transaction the buyers are the ones deciding what, when, how much, how and from whom an input is bought, enjoying a discretionary power that sellers usually lack. This implies that a buyer (or several coordinated buyers) may enjoy substantial purchasing power (although not necessarily dominance) from smaller market shares compared to sellers[513], as reflected in the Commission's Decisions in *Rewe/Meinl*[514] *and Carrefour/Promodès*[515] dealing with risks of imposing unfair purchasing practices. Also, the product market definition and the market power assessment tools ought to take into account these differences, as, when the traditional seller-oriented metrics are merely reversed, the analysis may lead to the erroneous conclusion that substantial buyer power does not exist when in reality it does or vice versa.

271. In this chapter, I explore the concept of market definition from the perspective of a buyer and apply the dualistic approach proposal in order to aim at answering the following research sub-questions:

509 Robert L. Steiner, 'Vertical Competition, Horizontal Competition and Market Power' 53 The Antitrust Bulletin (2008) 251.

510 Cf with Buttà and Pezzoli (2014), p. 161, who name these effects vertical and horizontal.

511 Carstensen 'Buyer Power and the Horizontal Merger Guidelines: Minor Progress on an Important Issue' (2012).

512 Carstensen, 'Buyer Power and Merger Analysis–The Need for Different Metrics'; Peter C. Carstensen, 'Buyer Power, Competition Policy, and Antitrust: The Competitive Effects of Discrimination Among Suppliers' 53 The Antitrust Bulletin (2008) 271; Carstensen 'Buyer Cartels Versus Buying Groups: Legal Distinctions, Competitive Realities, and Antitrust Policy' (2010), p. 17; Carstensen 'Buyer Power and the Horizontal Merger Guidelines: Minor Progress on an Important Issue' (2012).

513 See also supporting this interpretation: Dobson (2004-2005); Pranvera Këllezi, 'Abuse below the Threshold of Dominance? Market Power, Market Dominance, and Abuse of Economic Dependence' in Mark-Oliver Mackenrodt, Beatriz Conde Gallego and Stefan Enchelmaier (eds), *Abuse of Dominant Position: New Interpretation, New Enforcement Mechanisms?* (Springer 2008), p. 83; Carstensen 'Buyer Cartels Versus Buying Groups: Legal Distinctions, Competitive Realities, and Antitrust Policy' (2010), p. 6; Buttà and Pezzoli (2014), p. 165.

514 Commission Decision of 3 February 1999 relating to proceedings under Council Regulation (EEC) No 4064/89 (Case No IV/M.1221 - *Rewe/Meinl*) OJ L 274/1, para. 101.

515 Non-opposition to a notified concentration (Case COMP/M.1684 — *Carrefour/Promodès*) [2000] OJ C 164/5, French public version, paras. 52-55.

i. *Is the definition of purchasing relevant markets different from seller-oriented cases?*

ii. *If this is the case, what is the source of the difference?*

iii. *Is it necessary to revisit the existing methodologies applicable to the definition of purchasing markets?*

iv. *If so, how; what does this revision consist of and how should buyer market power be defined?*

v. *What are the shortcomings of these methodologies?*

272. To address these issues, this chapter is organized as follows: section §II discusses the concept of market definition and its role in the different realms of EU competition law. Section §III contains my proposal of a dualistic market definition for purchasing markets and discusses what the methodology changes necessary to apply the dualistic approach to buyer-oriented cases are, going further than a mere reverse than the selling-oriented cases. In section §IV, the core of this chapter, I discuss how buyer product-market definition is carried out by revisiting the most important concepts, legal instruments and existing methodologies in the EU and abroad. Section §V concludes the chapter with a summary of the findings and sets the ground for a discussion of buyer market power assessment in chapter 5.

II. Market definition

273. Market definition is a tool that identifies and defines the boundaries of competition and the competitive relations between undertakings[516] by determining what the competitive constraints faced by undertakings involved in a competition case are[517]. Doing so facilitates the understanding of the case and allows for the determination of an undertaking's market power[518], and the assessment

516 Commission Notice on the definition of relevant market for the purposes of Community competition law [1997] OJ C 372/5, para. 2; see also Guidelines on the assessment of horizontal mergers under the Council Regulation on the control of concentrations between undertakings [2004] OJ C 31/5, para. 10. Also highlighting the characteristic of a tool see: Harris and Jorde (1984); Faull and Nikpay, [1999] para. 1.136; Jonathan B. Baker, 'Market Definition: An Analytical Overview' 74 Antitrust Law Journal (2007), 129; Dennis W. Carlton, 'Market Definition: Use and Abuse' 3 Competition Policy International (2007) 3; Füller in Hirsch, Montag and Säcker, [2008], p. 437.

517 Areeda, Hovenkamp and Solow, [1995], p. 225; Mika Oinonen, *Does EU Merger Control Discriminate Against Small Markets Companies?: Diagnosing the Argument with Conclusions* (Kluwer Law International 2010), p. 236; OECD, 'Policy Roundtables: Market Definition' (2012).

518 Commission Notice on the definition of relevant market for the purposes of Community competition law [1997] OJ C 372/5, para. 2; Massimo Motta, *Competition Policy: Theory and Practice* (Cambridge University Press 2004), p. 101; Carlton (2007), p. 5; Bellamy and others, [2013], para. 4.001; Richard Whish and David Bailey, *Competition law* (8th ed. edn, Oxford University Press 2015), p. 29; Louis Kaplow, 'Market Definition' in Roger D. Blair and D. Daniel Sokol (eds), *The Oxford Handbook of International Antitrust Economics*, Vol. 1 (Oxford University Press 2015), p. 345; European Commission *Market Definition in a Globalised World*, (2015), p. 1.

of the anti-competitive effects of the conduct under scrutiny[519]. Furthermore, market definitions can be applied regardless of the nature of the conduct; i.e.: they apply to buyer and seller oriented cases and are applicable across all areas of competition law, albeit with different degrees of relevance and minor adjustments between them.

274. Furthermore, the market definition methodology *follows a structural approach in EU competition law* where the relevant product and geographical markets are firstly defined, in order to then assess, the undertaking(s)'s market power and determine whether or not it is dominant, or the extent of combined its market power, or whether a concentration would lead to the creation or strengthening of a dominant position[520], as clarified by the CJEU in *Continental Can*[521], and consequently adopted by the Commission in its guidelines and case practice[522]. In the dualistic approach to buyer market power definition, this structural approach is maintained first by determining the product market, and then by determining the relevant geographical market. This successive methodological structure is to avoid undertakings switching to substitute products and other locations, as remarked by Crocioni[523].

275. In addition to the structural approach to market definition in EU competition law, authors like Jones and Sufrin, as well as Oinonen, have emphasized that the approach is also indirect[524]. I interpret this as implying that there are alternative methods to directly assess an undertaking's market power without first defining the relevant market. In the case of buyer power, the Buyer Power Index by Blair and Harrison[525], and Blair and Lopatka[526] represents such an approach and is discussed in chapter 5.

519 Gregory J. Werden, 'The Relevant Market: Possible and Productive' April 2014 Antitrust Law Journal Online (2014) 1.

520 Harris and Jorde (1984), p. 4; Faull and Nikpay, [1999], para. 1.128; Motta, *Competition Policy: Theory and Practice* [2004], p. 101; Roger J. Van den Bergh and Peter D. Camesasca, *European Competition Law and Economics: A Comparative Perspective* (Sweet & Maxwell 2006), p. 76; Franz Jürgen Säcker, *The Concept of the Relevant Product Market: Between Demand-Side Substitutability in Supply-Side Substitutability in Competition Law* (Peter Lang 2008), p. 13; C. J. Cook and C. S. Kerse, *EC Merger Control* (Sweet & Maxwell 2009), p. 216; Oinonen, [2010], p. 150; Niels, Jenkins and Kavanagh, [2011], p. 25; OECD 'Policy Roundtables: Market Definition' (2012), p. 26; Jones and Sufrin, [2014], p. 60.

521 Judgment of 21 February 1973 in *Europemballage Corporation and Continental Can Company v Commission*, C-6/72, EU:C:1973:22, para. 32.

522 Commission Notice on the definition of relevant market for the purposes of Community competition law [1997] OJ C 372/5.

523 Pietro Crocioni, 'The Hypothetical Monopolist Test: What it can and cannot tell you' 23 European Competition Law Review (2002), p. 355.

524 Oinonen, [2010], p. 153; Jones and Sufrin, [2014], p. 61.

525 Blair and Harrison, [2010], p. 54-67.

526 Blair and Lopatka (2008).

A. Market definition: scope of application and time focus

276. Market definition plays a role in all spheres of EU competition law, with major or minor importance, and with either a backward or forward-looking role, depending on the type of case. In the following, I briefly discuss the main differences in the analysis among the areas of EU competition law as this is also reflected in buyer power cases.

277. Concerning agreement cases, market definition plays a lesser role and the Commission may find an infringement of Article 101 TFEU without arriving at a full definition of the relevant market[527]. Practice shows that, in most instances, it is implicitly assumed that if the infringement is anti-competitive by object the market definition is not needed as neither a market power requirement nor anti-competitive effects ought to be proven if they are inferred from the conduct and its context, as it can be assumed that they exist, as confirmed by the CJEU in *Expedia*[528]. However, as confirmed by the CJEU in *CB v Commission*, in an object infringement the assessment must pay attention to the "content of its provisions, its objectives and the economic and legal context of which it forms a part", which implies a minimal economic assessment of the case, leaving the door open for an interpretation that requires a basic market definition[529]. Furthermore, also concerning anti-competitive agreements by object, the CJEU dismissed an allegation in *Toshiba* concerning the applicability of the geographical market and confirmed the General Court's finding that even if not active in the EEA geographic market (because the agreement shared markets) the undertaking was a competitor engaged in an agreement restrictive of competition by object and should have been fined, without this requiring a detailed relevant market analysis[530].

278. Nevertheless, with regard to agreements that may be anti-competitive *due to their effects*[531] a more detailed or a comprehensive market definition would be

527 Bellamy and others, [2013], para. 4.006.

528 Judgment of 13 December 2012 in *Expedia*, C-226/11, EU:C:2012:795, para. 35; Füller in Hirsch, Montag and Säcker, [2008], p. 440; also of this opinion is Vogel when stating "supervisory authorities traditionally consider that, by its mere existence, an agreement implies that the parties intend to coordinate or consolidate their monopoly power. So defining the relevant market is not as important in the law on restrictive agreements as it is for the rules of on dominant positions", Louis Vogel, *European Competition Law* (Law Lex 2012), p. 55; see also: Hanno Wollmann, 'Horizontal Restraints of Competition' in Günter Hirsch, Franz Montag and Franz Jürgen Säcker (eds), *Competition Law: European Community Practice and Procedure* (Thomson - Sweet & Maxwell 2008), p. 495. In US antitrust law the solution is somewhat similar, except for violations that are per se illegal, any other type of antitrust offence requires the plaintiff to plead and prove the relevant market; see for more: American Bar Association, *Market Definition in Antitrust* (American Bar Association ed, 2012), p.2.

529 Judgment of 11 September 2014 in *CB v Commission*, C-67/13 P, EU:C:2014:2204, para. 53; cf with Summary of Commission Decision of 1 October 2008 relating to a proceeding under Article 81 of the Treaty establishing the European Community and Article 53 of the EEA Agreement (Case COMP/C.39181 — *Candle Waxes*) [2009] OJ C 295/17, taken from the unabridged version, para. 279.

530 Judgment of 20 February 2016 in *Toshiba Corporation v Commission*, C-373/14, EU:C:2016:26; Judgment of 21 May 2014, *Toshiba v Commission*, T-519/09, ECR, EU:T:2014:263.

531 Whish and Bailey, *Competition law* [2015], p. 28.

made as the Commission must prove an appreciable or perceptible effect on trade between Member States, as demanded by the General Court in *Compagnie générale maritime and Others v Commission* and *European Night Services and Others v Commission*, and ratified by the CJEU in *Delimitis*[532]. The assessment, therefore, would have as it "sole purpose of defining the relevant market, in order to apply Article 101(1) TFEU, is to determine whether the agreement in question may harm trade between Member States and has as its object or effect the prevention, restriction or distortion of competition within the common market"[533]. Thus, in agreements anti-competitive by effects there is a broader role for market definition with regard to the extent of its economic consequences[534].

279. Concerning Article 101(3) TFEU as an efficiency defense, the relevant market definition is necessary to establish whether, in a given situation, the fourth condition laid down in Article 101(3) (b) TFEU is met, although not for the other three cumulative conditions[535].

280. In dominance cases, market definition is a prerequisite, as "before an abuse of a dominant position is ascertained, it is necessary to establish the existence of a dominant position in a given market, which presupposes that such a market has already been defined"[536]. Thus, dominance does not occur *in abstracto* but *in concreto*. Its purpose is determining whether the undertaking under investigation is dominant and is conducted for past and on-going conducts[537].

281. For concentration cases, "a proper definition market of the relevant market is

532 Judgment of 28 February 1991 in *Delimitis v Henninger Bräu*, C-234/89, EU:C:1991:91, para. 16, in which the CJEU requires determining the relevant market in the assessment of the compatibility of exclusive supply agreements with Article 101 TFEU; Judgment of 28 February 2002, *Compagnie générale maritime and Others v Commission*, T-86/95, ECR, EU:T:2002:50, para. 116; Judgment of 15 September 1998, *European Night Services and Others v Commission*, T-374/94, ECR, EU:T:1998:198, para. 93 and ss, where the General Court annulled the Commission's decision based on the absence of the analysis of the relevant market and the inclusion of the market shares of the involved undertaking; see also: Communication from the Commission — Guidelines on the applicability of Article 101 of the Treaty on the Functioning of the European Union to horizontal co-operation agreements [2011] OJ C 11/1, para. 43. In the literature, see: Lennart Ritter and W. David Braun, *European Competition Law: A Practitioner's Guide* (3rd edn, Kluwer Law International 2004), p. 24; Ivo Van Bael and Jean-François Bellis, *Competition Law of the European Community* (4th edn, Kluwer Law International 2005), p. 132. In US antitrust law some type of cartel cases courts require showing that the defendant has a certain amount of market power, see: Hovenkamp, [2005], p. 80.

533 Judgment of 27 September 2012, *Koninklijke Wegenbouw Stevin v Commission*, T-357/06, ECR, EU:T:2012:488, para. 135.

534 Judgment of 27 September 2012, *Koninklijke Wegenbouw Stevin v Commission*, T-357/06, ECR, EU:T:2012:488, para. 137; Judgment of 6 July 2000, *Volkswagen v Commission*, T-62/98, ECR, EU:T:2000:180, para. 230; Judgment of 8 July 2004, *Mannesmannröhren-Werke v Commission*, T-44/00, ECR, EU:T:2004:218, para. 132.

535 Judgment of 19 March 2003, *CMA CGM and Others v Commission*, T-213/00, ECR, EU:T:2003:76, para. 226; and ratified in Judgment of 27 September 2012, *Koninklijke Wegenbouw Stevin v Commission*, T-357/06, ECR, EU:T:2012:488, para. 138.

536 Judgment of 6 July 2000, *Volkswagen v Commission*, T-62/98, ECR, EU:T:2000:180, para. 230.

537 Niels, Jenkins and Kavanagh, [2011], p. 30. In US antitrust law for cases under the scope of Section 2 of the Sherman Antitrust Act 26 Stat. 209, 15 U.S.C., market definition is employed to determine the existence of market power; see: Carlton (2007), p. 3.

a necessary precondition for any assessment of the effect of a concentration in competition" as held by the CJEU in *Kali und Salz*[538], in order to identify in a systematic manner the immediate competitive constraints facing the merging entity[539], and to help determine its compatibility with the common market[540].

282. Unlike in the instances of agreements and dominance, *market definition in concentration cases is forward looking*[541] because it adopts a different time horizon[542]. The goal here is prospective given that it aims at predicting whether a proposed merger or acquisition is likely to significantly impede effective competition post-concentration as required by the Merger Control Regulation[543]. Extraordinarily, however, there may be dominance or agreement cases where the investigated conduct has been planned but not executed and where the analysis of its potential effects is also forward looking[544].

283. The fundamental distinction between prospective and retrospective analysis is the determination of the appropriate comparison price[545]. In retrospective cases, the analysis focuses on the 'but-for-price'[546], the price that would have prevailed in the conduct's absence[547]. Therefore, the Small but Significant and Non-Transitory Increase in Price test (SSNIP test) has to be compared to this 'as-if' price to avoid making the relevant market too large[548], and the

538 Judgment of 31 March 1998 in *France and Société commerciale des potasses and de l'azote and Entreprise minière and chimique v Commission*, Joined cases C-68/94 and C-30/95 EU:C:1998:148, para. 222 and 143; see reiterating this approach in a buyer power related case in Judgment of 28 June 2004, *Airtours v Commission*, T-342/99, ECR, EU:T:2002:146, para. 19.

539 Guidelines on the assessment of horizontal mergers under the Council Regulation on the control of concentrations between undertakings [2004] OJ C 31/5, para. 10.

540 Council Regulation (EC) No 139/2004 of 20 January 2004 on the control of concentrations between undertakings (the EC Merger Regulation) [2004] OJ L 24/1, Article 2.3; Guidelines on the assessment of horizontal mergers under the Council Regulation on the control of concentrations between undertakings [2004] OJ C 31/5, para. 1.

541 Niels, Jenkins and Kavanagh, [2011], p. 30.

542 "The different time horizon considered in each case might lead to the result that different geographic markets are defined for the same products depending on whether the Commission is examining a change in the structure of supply, such as a concentration or a cooperative joint venture, or examining issues relating to certain past behavior", Commission Notice on the definition of relevant market for the purposes of Community competition law [1997] OJ C 372/5, para. 12; also highlighting the different approach that market definition ought to employ depending on whether the harm is prospective or retrospective, see: Bellamy, Child and Roth, [2001], para. 6.094; Ritter and Braun, [2004], p. 25; Motta, *Competition Policy: Theory and Practice* [2004], p. 105; Baker (2007), p. 389; Cf with Vogel, [2012], p. 389.

543 Council Regulation (EC) No 139/2004 of 20 January 2004 on the control of concentrations between undertakings (the EC Merger Regulation) [2004] OJ L 24/1; see also stressing the fact that in mergers the market definition is forward looking: Judgment of 25 October 2002, *Tetra Laval v Commission*, T-5/02, ECR, EU:T:2002:264, para. 251; see a similar opinion in US antitrust law in Gavil, Kovacic and Baker, [2008], p. 491; on the assessment of present and future market power, see: Areeda, Hovenkamp and Solow, [1995], p. 235.

544 Also remarking upon this possibility is Carlton when expressing that "if the bad act has not yet taken effect, the current price can be used as the benchmark price", in Carlton (2007), p. 20.

545 Baker (2007), p. 159-160; Carlton (2007), p. 19.

546 The 'but-for-price' idea looks conceptually akin to the "competition as if" concept developed by Miksch and discussed in chapter 3, section §III.C.

547 Motta does not use the 'but-for-price' standard but rather the 'competitive price', which in my view is even more difficult to assess in practice, in Motta, *Competition Policy: Theory and Practice* [2004], p. 105.

548 Motta, *Competition Policy: Theory and Practice* [2004], p. 105.

difficulty lies in determining what the hypothetical price would have been[549]. In prospective cases, the analysis does not compare a hypothetical price, but takes into account the current prevailing price in the market[550], unless there are grounds to believe that after the concentration prices will likely be reduced. Also, prospective cases tend to adopt a broader market analysis because it takes into account future competitive conditions whereas retrospective analysis should not[551].

284. Despite these differences between past and future-oriented methodologies, particularly in concentration cases, the Guidelines on the Assessment of Horizontal Mergers under the Council Regulation on the Control of Concentrations between Undertakings (EU Horizontal Mergers Guidelines) refers to the Notice on Market Definition as the instrument guiding the methodology for defining the relevant market, as some considerations pertinent to the relevant markets "may also be of importance for the competitive assessment of the merger"[552].

III. Buyer power market definition: a dualistic approach

285. The majority of the market definition case law, soft law and literature refer to seller-oriented cases, with very little literature and guidance concerning the methodologies applicable to buying markets. Accordingly, I identified a gap in knowledge concerning buyer market definition.

286. I submit that the traditional seller-oriented methodologies need to be adjusted for the analysis of purchasing relevant markets to avoid shortcomings and erroneous results. This revision demands taking into account the structure of competition in purchasing markets to adjust the traditional approach to market definition and *consider the relation between upstream and downstream competition in buyer power cases*, as also remarked upon by the Basque

549 The case of the Cellophane fallacy is well known, regarding the conceptual error made by the US Supreme Court by overlooking the fact that firms that are already exercising market power may impose current prices that, if increased any further, would make the price increase unprofitable, in *United States v. E.I. du pont de Nemours & Co.*, 351 U.S. 377 [1956].

550 Baker (2007), p. 159.

551 Ritter and Braun, [2004], p. 25.

552 Guidelines on the assessment of horizontal mergers under the Council Regulation on the control of concentrations between undertakings [2004] OJ C 31/5, para. 10.

NCA, and by the work of Bedre-Defolie and Caprice when analyzing merger effects among buyers[553]. However, and following the case law, revisiting the buying market definition methodologies may not imply a total departure from the Commission's method of defining product and geographic markets as held in *British Airways v Commission* by the General Court[554].

287. In buyer power cases, and unlike as held by the US Supreme Court, not "all competitive effects are, by definition, horizontal"[555]. In fact, buyer power conducts tend to generate a combination of both vertical and horizontal effects in the upstream and downstream markets as the reflection of the economics of buyer power. Therefore, and following Carstensen's views, "buyer power analysis requires metrics that measure both power and effects grounded in the economic realities of the buying side of the market place"[556]. Otherwise, merely reversing seller side methodologies or omitting buyer power specificities will lead to errors when performing a market definition for a buying undertaking[557].

288. In spite of this, some buyer power literature focuses solely on one of the effects of buyer market power in the market definition phase by analyzing only the upstream effects[558]. In my view, this perspective is incomplete because as such the buyer power cases are mainly assessed as examples of monopsony power and the transfer of wealth between suppliers and buyers in a static setting, while leaving the buyer power effects on downstream competition unattended. Therefore, this approach overlooks those effects and the fact that buyer (bargaining) power may be beneficial because the price reductions obtained in the upstream market are passed on to end consumers downstream, or that it may also affect adversely downstream competition. Furthermore, a pure upstream market definition approach is inconsistent with the emphasis placed by the Commission, the US Courts and part of the literature concerning the type of harm and anti-competitive effects required in the downstream mar-

553 Tribunal Vasco de la Competencia (April 2009), p. 18; Özlem Bedre-Defolie and Stéphane Caprice, *Merger Efficiency and Welfare Implications of Buyer Power* (2011) p. 1.

554 Judgment of 17 December 2003, *British Airways v Commission* of 17 December 2003, T-219/99, ECR, EU:T:2003:343, paras. 89-117; see also remarking upon the buyer market definition orientation of the case: Jones and Sufrin, EU Competition Law: Text, Cases, and Materials [2011], p. 312-314.

555 *Bus. Electr. Corp. v. Sharp Electr. Corp.* 485 U.S. 717 (1988), p. 730.

556 Carstensen, 'Buyer Power and Merger Analysis–The Need for Different Metrics', p. 2; see also Carstensen 'Buyer Power and the Horizontal Merger Guidelines: Minor Progress on an Important Issue' (2012), p. 777-778.

557 See also the criticism by a report published by the Office of Fair Trading and elaborated by RBB Economics when stating that "[w]e would not advocate turning the hypothetical monopolist test on its head and attempting to define a market by applying a 'hypothetical buyer group test', i.e. asking whether a hypothetical buyer group could profitably sustain prices below competitive levels", in Office of Fair Trading, *The Competitive Effects of Buyer Groups* (2007) para 1.77.

558 Focusing mostly exclusively on the upstream market analysis see, *inter alia*: Ioannis Kokkoris, 'The Concept of Market Definition and the SSNIP Test in the Merger Appraisal' 26 European Competition Law Review (2005) 209; Kokkoris (2006); Bundeskartellamt *Buyer Power in Competition Law - Status and Perspectives,* Bonn (2008), p. 5; Blair and Harrison, [2010], p. 62; Kokkoris and Shelanski, [2014], p. 422-426. Areeda, Hovenkamp and Solow propose that "monopsony power can be estimated in the conventional antitrust way by defining a relevant buyer's market and then estimating the defendant's share of it", in Areeda, Hovenkamp and Solow, [1995], p. 53.

ket to trigger the application of competition law to buyer power abuse. This trend, however, seems to be changing and a dualistic approach to buyer power market definition is apparently gaining momentum[559].

A. The dualistic approach and its content

289. Following the previous discussion, I propose that the *relevant market definition of buyer power cases must be made in both the procurement market (upstream market) as well as in the retailer market (downstream market),* and not solely in the upstream market. This proposal comes as a synthetization of the case evolution as shown in the Commission's practice concerning merger assessments[560], the practice of some NCAs such as the *Bundeskartellamt* when dealing with abuse of economic dependence[561], the guidance and practice of the UK's NCA[562], my analysis of buyer power economics, and a review of the literature. My aim with this proposal is to improve the existing methodology by incorporating facets derived from buyer power economics and integrating the criticism of the literature.

290. A dual market definition implies using different methodologies when defining two interrelated markets[563], which, as noted by Dobson, is a complex exercise because it ought to consider the multiple contexts in which the undertaking operates[564]. However, unlike in the model proposed by Steiner, my approach does not imply a single market definition for both upstream and downstream markets, but *two different* but connected assessments: one for the upstream market and another for the downstream market[565]. Also, my dualistic approach

559 See the dual approach suggested by the OECD and the contribution of some of its MS when distinguishing between monopsony and bargaining power for a market definition in OECD (2012).

560 In *Sovion/Südfleisch* the Commission explicitly performed a market definition for the purchase of pigs and cattle and then proceeded to carry out a market definition concerning the sale of fresh meat to fully evaluate the buyer power effects of the proposed concentration in Commission Decision of 21/12/2005 declaring a concentration to be compatible with the common market (Case No COMP/M.3968 - *Sovion/Südfleisch*) according to Council Regulation (EC) No 139/2004 [2005]; see also: Commission Decision of 20 November 1996 declaring a concentration to be incompatible with the common market (Case No IV/M.784 - *Kesko/Tuko*) Council Regulation (EEC) No 4064/89 [1997] OJ L 110/53; Commission Decision of 3 February 1999 relating to proceedings under Council Regulation (EEC) No 4064/89 (Case No IV/M.1221 - *Rewe/Meinl*) OJ L 274/1; non-opposition to a notified concentration (Case COMP/M.1684 — *Carrefour/Promodès*) [2000] OJ C 164/5. See also remarking that in these cases "the European Commission stressed that due to the interconnection between input and output markets, the increase in buyer power could reinforce market power on the output market and this harm consumer welfare" in van Doorn, p. 167; Ezrachi and Ioannidou (2014), p. 76.

561 Bundeskartellamt, B2-58/09 *Edeka Konditionenforderungen* - Verstoß gegen das "Anzapfverbot", 3 July 2014. The decision was appealed and revoked by the Düsseldorf Appellate Court in the Decision of 18 November 2015 *EDEKA/Plus-Übernahme* due to errors concerning the determination of whether suppliers were dependent on its buyer – although not concerning the dualistic market analysis approach.

562 See the UK's Contribution, jointly prepared by the now extinct Competition Commission and Office of Fair Trading, in OECD '*Policy Roundtables: Monopsony and Buyer Power*' (2009), p. 229-243, and my discussion in chapter 4, section §IV.E.b.

563 Also noting the interrelation between markets in buyer power cases see: Pera, available at: http://www.gop.it/doc_pubblicazioni/40_hjv4kr3vun_eng.pdf.

564 Dobson [2009], p. 103.

565 Steiner (2008).

is a holistic proposal as it is suitable to all market definitions across all areas of EU competition law, rather than for specific type of cases[566].

291. My dualistic approach follows the structural methodology adopted by EU competition law. Firstly, the relevant purchasing and retailing markets will be determined in terms of product and geographic spheres, initially defining the upstream market and then the downstream market in succession. In this study, I only address the methodologies and problems related to the definition of the upstream markets because the methodology describing the market definition for a selling undertaking by applying the hypothetical monopolist test is well described in the literature and falls outside of the scope of this work[567].

292. Unlike traditional seller markets – in particular in the case of exploitative abuses – most buyer power cases involve an effect in the upstream (purchasing market) and the downstream (selling market) because the undertaking that acquires goods from its suppliers will sell or transform this input in its downstream market activity vis-à-vis a (most likely) final consumer[568]. This implies that buyer power market definition must analyze both the upstream and downstream markets to fully assess the market impact of the exercise of buyer power[569]. Once this analysis is carried out, competition authorities will evaluate whether the conduct under investigation involves an exercise of monopsony or bargaining power to then proceed to assess the extent of the undertaking's buyer market power and the behaviour's effect on competition.

293. However, the dualistic approach has to devote special consideration to the identity of the geographical and product markets evaluated as these might not necessarily coincide. For example, regarding geographical markets, the upstream market for the purchase of raw timber might be local, where a small producer competes with a multinational undertaking, while the downstream market is different because the local producer sells its output again locally while the multinational undertaking sells its goods in an international market. The same could arise from a product-oriented perspective: the input market is the same as undertakings compete in the purchasing of oil but in the downstream market they do not compete as they produce different derivatives: gas-

---

566 See also: Van Bael and Bellis, [2005], p. 147.

567 For some interesting discussions suggesting the adoption of other methodologies or revisiting the current ones see, *inter alia*: Simon Baker and Andrea Lofaro, 'Buyer power and the Enso/Stora decision' 21 European Competition Law Review (2000) 187; Crocioni (2002); Kokkoris (2005); John Vickers, 'Market Power in Competition Cases' 2 European Competition Journal (2006) 3; Adriaan ten Kate and Gunnar Niels, 'The Relevant Market: A Concept Still in Search of a Definition' 5 Journal of Competition Law and Economics (2009) 297; OECD *'Policy Roundtables: Market Definition'* (2012), p. 59-79.

568 Also supporting this view of the competitive risks in the upstream and downstream market in relation to purchasing agreements see: Carstensen 'Buyer Cartels Versus Buying Groups: Legal Distinctions, Competitive Realities, and Antitrust Policy' (2010); Ezrachi (2012), p. 66; Bundeskartellamt *Summary of the Final Report of the Sector Inquiry into the Food Retail Sector,* (2014).

569 Somewhat similarly and stressing the need to examine buyer power effects in the upstream and downstream market see: Pera, p. 16.

oline or plastic, for example. In these cases of lack of identity regarding the geographic or product spheres, the interrelation of the upstream and downstream market is less than when full identity exists, having an impact on the assessment of the instance and conducts, and may lead to instances in which the undertakings involved do not compete with each other[570]. Therefore, in such cases, the dualistic approach and interlink between upstream and downstream markets must be tailored to suit the facts.

B. Justification of the dualistic approach

294. The adoption of the dualistic approach in EU competition law is justified by economic and legal grounds and it is an adequate tool to be employed in buyer power cases as a whole because it fully captures both monopsony and bargaining power effects by looking at the market consequences both upstream and downstream. The rationale behind this is intuitive and, citing the OECD:

> if the buyer power comes from its gate keeping role, then what is more important than its shares of purchases in the upstream market is its *market power* and hence market share in the relevant downstream market. Identifying buyer power requires precise and careful market definition of the relevant downstream product and geographic markets to identify market power in distribution services provided by the buyer[571].

295. From an economic perspective, the dualistic approach to buyer power is justified because the incentives and economics of buying markets are different from selling-oriented markets. In buying markets the purchaser is the one that leads and makes the key decisions, as well as purchasing markets being different in respect to the fact that the buyer does not make a direct profit from acquiring goods whereas a seller does when selling a good[572]. Also, buyer power effects have implications in the upstream market and also affect the downstream market competitiveness and ultimately the end consumer[573], particularly, albeit not exclusively, if the undertaking possesses substantial downstream market power fitting the 'hourglass shape' as described in chapter 2, section

---

570 Cf with van Doorn that suggests that in cases of lack of geographical identity the markets are not related in van Doorn, p. 77.

571 OECD '*Policy Roundtables: Monopsony and Buyer Power*' (2009), p. 22.

572 Carstensen 'Buyer Power and the Horizontal Merger Guidelines: Minor Progress on an Important Issue' (2012), p. 791.

573 Chen, 'Buyer power: Economic Theory and Antitrust Policy' 22 Research in Law and Economics (2007), p. 20. Making a similar remark in the case of buyer cartels see: Carstensen 'Buyer Cartels Versus Buying Groups: Legal Distinctions, Competitive Realities, and Antitrust Policy' (2010), p. 11; also stressing this point for markets in the vertical chain see: Niels, Jenkins and Kavanagh, [2011], p. 92. In a US antitrust law perspective, it has been held that in the case of input markets, courts have explicitly considered the impact of downstream products in defining the upstream input market, see: American Bar Association, *Market Definition in Antitrust* [2012], p. 50; *Brookins v Int'l Motors Contest Ass'n*, 219 F.3d 849, (8th Cir. 2000), p. 853-854.

§V.A.a. This is because demand in the upstream purchasing market is usually derived from the demand for the final product[574].

296. *Furthermore, the dualistic approach captures all buyer power effects*. In the upstream market it is able to capture *exploitative effects* vis-à-vis suppliers in the form of unfairly low purchasing prices, to determine the effects of a buyers' cartel or capture unfair purchasing prices effects on suppliers, topics discussed in chapters 7 and 8. Also, a dual approach captures *exclusionary effects* in the upstream market between rivals that compete for the acquisition of an input as well as being able to capture whenever exclusion takes place or is strengthened in the downstream market when the rivals compete as retailers, as discussed in chapter 6. Also, the dualistic approach allows competition authorities to *identify and assess the effects of buyer power over end consumers in the downstream markets.*

297. Also, the dualistic approach allows authorities to determine if the buying undertaking fits the hourglass shape by using both upstream and downstream market power as a good indication of the possible welfare implications of buyer power exercise as discussed in chapter 2, section §V.

298. Additionally, from a legal perspective, the dualistic approach finds support in the current state of EU competition law. The General Court has tacitly recognized the need for a dualistic approach to buyer power cases in *British Airways v Commission*[575]. In this case, the General Court and later the CJEU confirmed that it was in breach of Article 102 TFEU the granting of loyalty enhancing supracompetitive bonuses from a buyer to its suppliers with the aim and effect of foreclosing its competitors in a related downstream market where they competed as providers of air passenger transport services[576]. The dualistic approach rationale for buyer power cases was supported as the General Court held that "competition law concentrates upon protecting the market structure from artificial distortions because by doing so the interests of the consumer in the medium to long term are best protected"[577]. It does so by taking into account the buyer power competitive effects in all markets in which the buying undertaking carries out its economic activity, especially since this was a case of market power leveraging from the upstream to the downstream market.

574 Niels, Jenkins and Kavanagh, [2011], p. 92; American Bar Association, *Market Definition in Antitrust* [2012], p. 51.

575 Judgment of 17 December 2003, *British Airways v Commission* of 17 December 2003, T-219/99, ECR, EU:T:2003:343; Judgment of 15 March 2007 in *British Airways v Commission*, C-95/04 P, EU:C:2007:166.

576 I discuss in detail the leverage of buyer power as an exclusionary form of buyer market power abuse in chapter 6, section §VII.

577 Judgment of 17 December 2003, *British Airways v Commission* of 17 December 2003, T-219/99, ECR, EU:T:2003:343, para. 264; see also Judgment of 21 February 1973 in *Europemballage Corporation and Continental Can Company v Commission*, C-6/72, EU:C:1973:22, para. 26.

299. More explicitly, however, has been the recognition of the need for a dualistic approach in the Merger Control Regulation when stressing the need for assessing the outcome of the operation in a holistic manner and taking into account constraints and consequences upstream and downstream market:

> […] [i]n making this appraisal, the Commission shall take into account:
>
> (a) the need to maintain and develop effective competition within the common market in view of, among other things, *the structure of all the markets concerned* and the actual or potential competition from undertakings located either within or outwith the Community
>
> (b) the *market position of the undertakings concerned* and their economic and financial power, *the alternatives available to suppliers and users*, their access to supplies or markets, any legal or other barriers to entry, *supply and demand trends* for the relevant goods and services, *the interests of the intermediate and ultimate consumers*, and the development of technical and economic progress provided that it is to consumers' advantage and does not form an obstacle to competition[578].

300. This recognition has also been integrated into the Commission's practice[579], as it is also reflected in some of the Commission's reports, which argue that "[i]t is important to take into consideration the two different dimensions of the retail sector [upstream buying and downstream retailing], in order to properly situate it in the broader supply chain and fully understand the role it plays in the European economy"[580].

301. However, the reception of the dualistic approach is timid when it comes to the Commission's soft law instruments. My analysis shows that when a dualist approach has been adopted, such as in the Guidelines on Horizontal Agreements[581], and the Commission Notice on Guidelines on Vertical

---

578 Council Regulation (EC) No 139/2004 of 20 January 2004 on the control of concentrations between undertakings (the EC Merger Regulation) [2004] OJ L 24/1, Article 2.1(a) and (b) (emphasis added).

579 Commission Decision of 3 February 1999 relating to proceedings under Council Regulation (EEC) No 4064/89 (Case No IV/M.1221 - *Rewe/Meinl*) OJ L 274/1, para. 76; see the opinion of Ezrachi and Ioannidou, who argue that in this case the Commission was required "to adjust its analysis of the relevant markets as the transaction on the buyer side affected both the downstream retail market as well as the upstream procurement market" in Ezrachi and Ioannidou (2014), p. 76.

580 European Commission, *The Economic Impact of Modern Retail on Choice and Innovation in the EU Food Sector* (2014), p. 45.

581 Communication from the Commission — Guidelines on the applicability of Article 101 of the Treaty on the Functioning of the European Union to horizontal co-operation agreements [2011] OJ C 11/1, paras. 197-199.

Restraints (Guidelines on Vertical Restraints)[582], the approach has *been a moderated but not a fully comprehensive one.*

302. In the Guidelines on Horizontal Agreements, the Commission correctly points out that a purchasing agreement – and in general buyer power – affects two markets: the purchasing market and the selling market[583]. According to the Commission, the definition of the relevant purchasing market is mandatory to assess the competitive effects in the upstream market power by following the principles described in the Notice on Market Definition and adopting the *Buyer's SSNIP test*, discussed below. It states that in addition to this market definition, "if parties are (...) competitors on one or more selling markets, those markets are also relevant for the assessment" and their definition ought to be made in accordance with the traditional methodologies, like as I put forward with the dualistic approach[584]. This partial approach by the Commission is a timid one because according to it the downstream analysis shall be made only whenever parties are competitors and is not necessary in the other circumstances. Precisely, to determine if parties are competitors, it is necessary to carry out some market definition and conclude in which markets undertakings compete. Furthermore, anti-competitive harm by buyers may have an impact on downstream consumers even if parties are not direct competitors in the downstream market, particularly in the medium to long-term. Indeed, it is sensible to think that if parties to a purchasing agreement are also competitors, the anti-competitive risks are increased due to a risk of coordination in the downstream market. However, in my view, *the dual approach and market definitions ought to be carried out even if parties are not direct competitors*, in order to take into account the related market structures. Therefore, the Guidelines on Horizontal Agreements provide a partial and limited improvement to the traditional approach to buyer power market definition. Yet, this is nevertheless insufficient, casuistic and not a general statement regarding all types of buyer power cases and it would be advisable for this to be the case.

303. Three other considerations justify the proposal for a dualistic approach to buyer market definition. First, dual market definitions are analogous to other multimarket definitions carried out in EU competition law. Clear examples

582 See the concern for the competitive effects upstream and downstream market power in the case of exclusive supply in the Guidelines on Vertical Restraints [2010] OJ C 130/1, para. 194; see also the dualistic approach concerning relevant market for calculating the 30% market share threshold under the Block Exemption Regulation in the Guidelines on Vertical Restraints [2010] OJ C 130/1 paras. 87-95; see also: Jochen Ehlers, 'Vertical Restraints' in Günter Hirsch, Franz Montag and Franz Jürgen Säcker (eds), *Competition Law: European Community Practice and Procedure* (Thomson - Sweet & Maxwell 2008) para. 2.3.073.

583 Communication from the Commission — Guidelines on the applicability of Article 101 of the Treaty on the Functioning of the European Union to horizontal co-operation agreements [2011] OJ C 11/1, para. 197.

584 Communication from the Commission — Guidelines on the applicability of Article 101 of the Treaty on the Functioning of the European Union to horizontal co-operation agreements [2011] OJ C 11/1, para. 199.

are as it was explicitly recognized in *Tetra Pak v Commission*[585], the dual measurement of the market share for the application of Article 3 of the Block Exemption Regulation in the upstream and downstream market[586], as well as in cases dealing with tying and bundling[587], refusals to deal[588], and aftermarkets[589]. When assessing these types of conducts, the Commission defines both the tying and the tied relevant markets as necessary pre-requisites[590]. Second, the adoption of an economically informed methodology is also another factor that is consistent and compatible with the suggestion of a dualistic and tailored buyer-oriented approach to buyer market power definition. Third, a dual market definition is in line with ordoliberal theory and the objective of protecting the competition as such and the competitive market structure, as recognized by the CJEU in *GlaxoSmithKline Services and Others v Commission and Others*[591], with similar arguments found in buyer merger cases, as noted by Ezrachi and Ioannidou[592], and a broader standard regarding buyer power anti-competitive harm as discussed in chapter 3, section §IV.

---

585 "Analysis of the markets in the milk-packaging sector thus shows that the four markets concerned, defined in the Decision, were indeed separate markets", Judgment of 6 October 1994, *Tetra Pak v Commission*, T-83/91, ECR, EU:T:1994:246, para. 73.

586 Article 3, Commission Regulation (EU) No 330/2010 of 20 April 2010 on the application of Article 101(3) of the Treaty on the Functioning of the European Union to categories of vertical agreements and concerted practices [2010] OJ L 102/1; Guidelines on Vertical Restraints [2010] OJ C 130/1, para. 88.

587 See for example: Judgment of 12 December 1991, *Hilti v Commission*, T-30/89, ECR, EU:T:1991:70, where the General Court found the existence of three product markets; Judgment of 17 September 2007, *Microsoft v Commission*, T-201/04, ECR, EU:T:2007:289, paras. 912-944, where the General Court concluded that operating system software and media players are separate products in different markets.

588 See, for example, stressing the ability of undertakings to affect two markets (and therefore also the need to evaluate them) in Commission Decision of 21 December 1993 relating to a proceeding pursuant to Article 86 of the EC Treaty (IV/34.689 - *Sea Containers v. Stena Sealink - Interim measures*) [1994] OJ L 15/8; see discussing the two interrelated markets that are evaluated sometimes as a single market in cases of refusal to deal/essential facilities: Temple-Lang J, 'The Principle of Essential Facilities in European Community Competition Law - The Position Since Bronner' (2000) 1 Journal of Network Industries 375, p. 378; Pitofsky R, Paterson D and Hooks J, 'The Essential Facilities Doctrine Under U.S. Antitrust Law' (2002-2003) 70 Antitrust Law Journal 443, p. 458-461.

589 Judgment of 31 May 1979 in *Hugin v Commission*, C-22/78, EU:C:1979:138, where the CJEU found the existence of separate markets for cash register machines, reparation services and aftermarkets for spare parts; Judgment of 15 December 2010, *CEAHR v Commission*, T-427/08, ECR, EU:T:2010:517, where the General Court decided that the manufacture and repair and maintenance service for luxury watches are separate markets and annulled the Commission Decision based on its erroneous finding on a sole market; and Judgment of 14 November 1996 in *Tetra Pak v Commission*, C-333/94 P, EU:C:1996:436, where it was discussed whether machinery for packing and cartons were related products.

590 Rose and Ngwe (2007), p. 11; see also: Nicolas Gauss and Alison Oldale, *Market Definition*, Vol. 5 (F. Enrique González-Díaz and Robbert Snelders eds, Claeys and Casteels 2013), para. 1.83.

591 "Secondly, it must be borne in mind that the Court has held that, like other competition rules laid down in the Treaty, Article 81 EC aims to protect not only the interests of competitors or of consumers, but also the structure of the market and, in so doing, competition as such", Judgment of 6 October 2009 in *GlaxoSmithKline Services and Others v Commission and Others*, Joined cases C-501/06 P, C-513/06 P, C-515/06 P and C-519/06 P, EU:C:2009:610, para. 63.

592 Ezrachi and Ioannidou (2014), p. 73.

IV. The relevant purchasing market

304. In this section, I discuss the current approaches to defining the relevant purchasing market by analyzing the most significant aspects contemplated in the different Commission's guidelines and other authoritative sources, as well as stressing the methodologies' shortcomings. Additionally, my analysis adopts a generalist perspective and is applicable to agreement, dominance and merger cases, unless explicitly stated otherwise. Also, I focus the discussion on the product market definition dimension and do not deal in extenso with the geographic market dimension, as the methodology is neither particularly relevant nor modified by my proposal of a dualistic approach for buyer power, and can follow the standard treatment given in seller-side cases[593].

A. Conceptualizing the relevant market

305. Defining the relevant market aims at identifying which products or services (product market) are close substitutes for one another within a geographical area in which conditions of competition are sufficiently homogeneous (geographic market) that other rival undertakings operate as a competitive constraint on the behaviour of suppliers and/or *buyers* of those goods[594]. It serves both to assess monopsony and bargaining power cases because it follows a similar approach as the framework upon which the investigation is constructed is the same. Furthermore, it also helps to determine which other undertakings are active in the market and are affected by the buying behaviour. Based on the relevant market findings, market size and market shares can be calculated owing to their sales/purchases of the relevant products in the relevant area[595] and therefore the undertaking(s)'s market power can be assessed[596].

306. The relevant market is usually defined by application of the hypothetical monopolist test – also known as the SSNIP test – based on the measurement of demand substitutability as the most common, but not exclusive approach[597]. Supply substitutability is also taken into account when it is timely and effective to do so[598]. The SSNIP test answers whether a market is a collection of specific goods in a particular geographic location such that a single undertaking would

593 For a general discussion of geographic market definition see, *inter alia*: Oinonen, [2010], p. 264-288; Richard A. Posner and William M. Landes, 'Market Power in Antitrust Case' 94 Harvard Law Review (1980) 937; for a short discussion of geographic market definition in buyer power cases dealing with food retailing see: Bundeskartellamt '*Sektoruntersuchung: Lebensmitteleinzelhandel*' (2014).

594 Motta, *Competition Policy: Theory and Practice* [2004], p. 102; Niels, Jenkins and Kavanagh, [2011], p. 29; Jones and Sufrin, *EU Competition Law: Text, Cases, and Materials* [2011], p. 63.

595 Commission Notice on the definition of relevant market for the purposes of Community competition law [1997] OJ C 372/5, para. 53; Bishop and Walker, [2010], para. 4-003.

596 Faull and Nikpay, [1999], para. 1.144; Oinonen, [2010], p. 296.

597 Crocioni (2002), p. 354; Säcker, [2008], p. 15-28 and 63-65; Niels, Jenkins and Kavanagh, [2011], p. 38.

598 Commission Notice on the definition of relevant market for the purposes of Community competition law [1997] OJ C 372/5, paras. 20-21.

be able to increase prices profitably for a considerable period of time[599]. As such, a relevant market is worth monopolizing because monopolization allows a price increase to be profitable[600]. However, the SSNIP test does not determine whether the undertaking(s) has had significant market power, is dominant or whether a concentration could significantly impede effective competition; this is left to market power assessment, which I discuss in chapter 5.

307. Several alternatives for a proper buyer-oriented market definition have been proposed in the soft law and literature. The majority of these have in common the adoption of a "hypothetical monopsonist test" – that I denominate *the Buyer's SSNIP test* – a modified version of the standard assessment. This implies that the analysis adopts the seller's point of view and asks what the competing uses for its output are, and which other channels or buyers will acquire its output rather than asking what products are substitutable for consumers[601]. As such, the emphasis is placed on whether suppliers have alternative distribution channels for their output or whether they face an inelastic supply curve[602]. The following paragraphs discuss and assess the different proposals incorporated in authoritative sources.

B. The Commission's view on Buying Market Definition

308. The methodology for defining the relevant market, including the *Buyer's SSNIP test*, in EU competition law has been mostly developed and incorporated in different Commission's Guidelines that have received the endorsement of the General Court[603]. Of special importance is the Commission Notice on the definition of the relevant market for the purposes of the Community competition law (Notice on Market Definition), published in 1997[604]. Due to the importance and the level of detail of the Notice on Market Definition, the remainder of this section discusses its content in extenso.

---

599 Motta, *Competition Policy: Theory and Practice* [2004], p. 102-103; Bishop and Walker, [2010], para. 4-005; OECD 'Policy Roundtables: Market Definition' (2012).

600 Bishop and Walker, [2010], paras. 4-005-006.

601 Bundeskartellamt '*Buyer Power in Competition Law - Status and Perspectives*' (2008), p. 5; Blair and Harrison, [2010], p. 62.

602 See chapter 2, section II.B for a discussion on the elasticity of supply.

603 "In order to evaluate the merits of the applicants' arguments, both in principle and in the specific circumstances of this case, it is necessary to place them in the theoretical framework adopted by the Commission in the Notice on market definition for the purposes of determining competitive constraints", Judgment of 1 July 2010, *AstraZeneca v Commission*, T-321/05, ECR, EU:T:2010:266, para. 86; see also: Judgment of 15 December 2010, *CEAHR v Commission*, T-427/08, ECR, EU:T:2010:517, para. 68-70; Judgment of 29 March 2012, *Telefónica and Telefónica de España v Commission*, T-336/07, ECR, EU:T:2012:172, para. 113; Judgment of 17 September 2007, *Microsoft v Commission*, T-201/04, ECR, EU:T:2007:289, para. 484; Judgment of 9 September 2009, *Clearstream v Commission*, T-301/04, ECR, EU:T:2009:317, para. 50.

604 Commission Notice on the definition of relevant market for the purposes of Community competition law [1997] OJ C 372/5.

309. The Notice on Market Definition is applicable to agreements, dominance and concentration cases, albeit with certain limitations[605]. It draws inspiration from the ideas developed by the case law and US antitrust experience when defining relevant markets[606], and provided EU competition law at the time with a 'modernized' and more economically influenced approach to market definition than before[607]. The Notice on Market Definition adopts the hypothetical monopolist test as the main methodology for defining the relevant market and clarifies the how the Commission defines the relevant markets in the enforcement of EU competition law. For buyer power cases, the Notice on Market Definition suggests the adoption of the reverse of the seller-side test (the *Buyer's SSNIP test*) and does not distinguish in terms of whether the test applies to monopsony and/or bargaining power cases.

310. Despite its longevity, the Notice on Market Definition has not been replaced and its main principles are still applied by the Commission and accepted by the Courts, although it has been partially updated by more specific and area-centered Commission communications[608]. The EU Horizontal Merger Guidelines make explicit reference to the Notice on Market Definition as the instrument providing guidance when defining the relevant market[609]. In the case of agreements between purchasing undertakings, the Guidelines on Horizontal Agreements provides an updated and detailed account of the methodology defining relevant purchasing markets when assessing purchasing agreements[610]. These other soft law instruments largely follow the principles described in the Notice on Market Definition but also updated it and adjust it

605 See para. 10 of the Guidelines on the assessment of horizontal mergers under the Council Regulation on the control of concentrations between undertakings [2004] OJ C 31/5, which refer to the Notice on Market Definition for guidance in the assessment of the competitive constraints faced by the merging entity. Also of this opinion are Cook and Kerse, [2009], p. 218; Jones and Sufrin, *EU Competition Law: Text, Cases and Materials* [2014], p. 65.

606 The SSNIP test was firstly incorporated in the US 1982 Merger Guidelines as "the market definition used by the Department can be stated formally as follows: 'a market consists of a group of products and an associated geographic area such that (and the absence of new entry) a hypothetical, unregulated firm that made all the sales of those products in that area could increase its profits through a small but significant and non-transitory increase in price (above prevailing or likely future levels)'", US Department of Justice Merger Guidelines [1982], footnote 6, available at: http://www.justice.gov/atr/hmerger/11248.htm; also highlighting the influence of US antitrust law experience and the approach "taken by antitrust authorities in the US" see: Jones and Sufrin, *EU Competition Law: Text, Cases and Materials* [2014], p. 67; Whish and Bailey, [2015], p. 27.

607 Jones and Sufrin, *EU Competition Law: Text, Cases and Materials* [2014], p. 65.

608 Communication from the Commission — Guidelines on the application of Article 101 of the Treaty on the Functioning of the European Union to technology transfer agreements [2014] OJ C 89/3, paras. 19-40; Guidelines on Vertical Restraints [2010] OJ C 130/1, paras. 86-95; Communication from the Commission — Guidelines on the applicability of Article 101 of the Treaty on the Functioning of the European Union to horizontal co-operation agreements [2011] OJ C 11/1, paras. 112-126, 155-156, 197-199, 229, and 261-262.

609 Guidelines on the assessment of horizontal mergers under the Council Regulation on the control of concentrations between undertakings [2004] OJ C 31/5, para. 10.

610 Communication from the Commission — Guidelines on the applicability of Article 101 of the Treaty on the Functioning of the European Union to horizontal co-operation agreements [2011] OJ C 11/1, paras. 194-199.

to the specific situations with a fairly detailed account of how to define relevant purchasing markets[611].

311. The Notice on Market Definition divides the relevant market methodology in a product and geographic dimension. Once this is done, competition authorities should assess two types of competitive constraints for determining the relevant market: demand and supply substitution, the key analytical aspects for determining a relevant market[612]. The following subsections analyze these constraints from a buyer power perspective.

a. Demand substitution: Buyer's SSNIP test

312. Demand substitution constitutes the most immediate, important and effective disciplinary constraint on the pricing and market strategy of a buyer or seller of a good[613], as also acknowledged by the General Court in *Telefónica and Telefónica de España v Commission*[614]. As the starting point of the methodology for defining the relevant product market, its function is to determine which available products are seen by the consumers as interchangeable to satisfy a need[615]; an example would be whether or not limes compete with lemons in the citrus fruit market.

313. For buyer power cases, a re-interpretation of this concept is what I denominate the *'reverse demand substitution'*[616] and which describes the ability of suppliers to switch from one buyer to another as a response to a decrease in the relative purchasing price for their output[617]. This interpretation of the reverse demand substitution was employed by the Commission in *Rewe/Meinl* when it was stated that: "[t]he position is different, however, when it comes to defining procurement markets. Here, the critical factors are the producers' flexibility in changing output and the alternative outlets open to them"[618]. In addition to the switching factor due to a price decrease, the reverse demand substitution

---

611 Van Bael and Bellis, [2005], p. 146-147.

612 Potential competition, the third competitive constraint indicated by the Notice on Market Definition is generally not taken into account at this stage of the process of market definition but rather later on when the market power assessment is made. See: Commission Notice on the definition of relevant market for the purposes of Community competition law [1997] OJ C 372/5, para. 14; Bishop and Walker, [2010], para. 4-011.

613 Van Bael and Bellis, [2005], p. 135.

614 Judgment of 29 March 2012, *Telefónica and Telefónica de España v Commission*, T-336/07, ECR, EU:T:2012:172, para. 113; see also: Commission Notice on the definition of relevant market for the purposes of Community competition law [1997] OJ C 372/5, para. 13. For an economic discussion on demand substitution see: Bishop and Walker, [2010], para. 4-011; Niels, Jenkins and Kavanagh, [2011], p. 31-37.

615 Baker (2007), p. 132; Säcker, [2008], p. 30.

616 Term coined by the author.

617 See also: Ritter and Braun, [2004], p. 395; also suggesting the application of a reverse of the demand substitutability test see: Faull and Nikpay, [1999], para. 6.321; Bundeskartellamt '*Summary of the Final Report of the Sector Inquiry into the Food Retail Sector*' (2014), p. 6.

618 Commission Decision of 3 February 1999 relating to proceedings under Council Regulation (EEC) No 4064/89 (Case No IV/M.1221 - *Rewe/Meinl*) OJ L 274/1, para. 76.

should take into account the switching costs of suppliers to find alternative buyers, as remarked by the Bundeskartellamt[619].

314. Furthermore, according to the Guidelines on Horizontal Agreements, the reverse demand substitution is anchored on the concept of substitutability as "the suppliers' alternatives are decisive in identifying the competitive constraints on purchasers"[620]. Substitutability exists according to the CJEU in *Hoffmann-La Roche v Commission* when "there is a sufficient degree of interchangeability between all the products forming part of the same market in so far as a specific use of such products is concerned"[621]. The substitutability of a good ought to be assessed depending on the case; in seller-side cases it has to be assessed from a consumer's perspective as settled by the EU in *United Brands v Commission*[622] as well as by the Commission in the Notice on Market Definition[623]. In a buyer power case, therefore, substitutability ought to be defined *from a supplier's perspective* and it will determine not which products are substitutes but instead which distribution channels are substitutes amongst each other[624].

315. Consequently, the reverse demand substitution defines which other buyers compete with the undertaking under investigation for the acquisition of a specific input[625]. In other words, if buyers are plentiful and suppliers have other distribution channels to resort to, there is no compulsion to surrender to the buyer power of a specific purchaser[626]. For example, in a market for the purchase of beef, reverse demand substitution represents all the different sales channels a buyer has to offer its goods. These could be food retailers (super-

---

619 Bundeskartellamt '*Summary of the Final Report of the Sector Inquiry into the Food Retail Sector*' (2014), p. 6.

620 Communication from the Commission — Guidelines on the applicability of Article 101 of the Treaty on the Functioning of the European Union to horizontal co-operation agreements [2011] OJ C 11/1, para. 198.

621 Judgment of 13 February 1979 in *Hoffmann-La Roche v Commission*, C-85/76, EU:C:1979:36, para. 28 in fine; the same wording has been ratified recently by the General Court and the CJEU in several occasions; see also: Judgment of 15 December 2010, *CEAHR v Commission*, T-427/08, ECR, EU:T:2010:517, para. 67.

622 Judgment of 14 February 1978 in *United Brands v Commission*, C-27/76, EU:C:1978:22, paras. 12-35, wherein the CJEU decided that from the consumer's point of view bananas constitute a significantly different product market from other fruits.

623 "A relevant product market comprises all those products and/or services which are regarded as interchangeable or substitutable *by the consumer*, by reason of the products' characteristics, their prices and their intended use", Commission Notice on the definition of relevant market for the purposes of Community competition law [1997] OJ C 372/5, para. 7 (emphasis added); and recently ratified by the General Court in Judgment of 29 March 2012, *Telefónica and Telefónica de España v Commission*, T-336/07, ECR, EU:T:2012:172, para. 113; and Judgment of 28 April 2010, *Amann & Söhne and Cousin Filterie v Commission*, T-446/05, ECR, EU:T:2010:165, para. 59; see also: Lawrence Wu and Simon Baker, 'Applying the Market Definition Guidelines of the European Commission' 19 European Competition Law Review (1998) 273; Füller in Hirsch, Montag and Säcker, [2008], p. 438-439; For common mistakes defining which products are substitutes among each other see: Niels, Jenkins and Kavanagh, [2011], p. 27-29.

624 Commission Notice on the definition of relevant market for the purposes of Community competition law [1997] OJ C 372/5, para. 17 (in fine); Carstensen 'Buyer Power and the Horizontal Merger Guidelines: Minor Progress on an Important Issue' (2012), p. 782.

625 Van Bael and Bellis, [2005], p. 146; Cosmo Graham, *EU and UK Competition Law* (Pearson Education Limited 2010), p. 25.

626 Galbraith, [2010], p. 116. Stressing the importance of alternative purchasers in buyer power cases, see: Ritter and Braun, [2004], p. 35.

markets), restaurants, hotels or even direct end consumers. However, these alternative buyers might not be direct competitors in the downstream market. Thus, reverse demand substitution does not determine which other buyers compete as a retailer with the buyer under investigation because they might use the acquired input for different outputs[627].

316. The Notice on Market Definition and the Commission's practice reveal that the main factors assessed when determining demand substitution are three: product characteristics, its intended use and price[628]. Nevertheless and from a buyer-oriented perspective, the fact that distribution channels share similar characteristic or are intended for a similar use is not a necessary condition for the distribution channels to be considered as demand substitutes with respect to each other, as clarified by the Notice on Market Definition[629]. Whether the products satisfy its consumer's needs will be determined by deciding if they are substitutes from a supplier's perspective[630]. For example, whether the supplier has been required to meet a specific need for a buyer or there is a technical specification precluding them from selling the output to other buyers with other needs[631]. Additionally, the price indicator employed – prevailing or but-for price – is relevant in determining the reverse side substitution as it permits the application of the *Buyer's SSNIP test*.

---

627 Carstensen 'Buyer Power and the Horizontal Merger Guidelines: Minor Progress on an Important Issue' (2012), p. 810.

628 "An analysis of the product characteristics and its intended use allows the Commission, as a first step, to limit the field of investigation of possible substitutes", Commission Notice on the definition of relevant market for the purposes of Community competition law [1997] OJ C 372/5, para. 36; see also: Van Bael and Bellis, [2005], p. 136-138; Oinonen, [2010] p. 244; cf with the opinion of Ten Kate and Niels who suggest that demand substitution must take into account three factors: internal substitution, external substitution and demand reduction. Following this proposal and adapting it to a buyer power scenario, internal substitution measures the likelihood that suppliers of products within the relevant market resort to different buyers in the same product market pursuant to a decrease in the purchasing price. External substitution would measure the ease with which suppliers will switch to the production of another product due to the decrease in purchasing price. Lastly, supply reduction would measure the degree to which suppliers stop producing the product that suffered the decrease in purchasing price without switching its production to another good or service, ten Kate and Niels (2009), p. 312-313.

629 Commission Notice on the definition of relevant market for the purposes of Community competition law [1997] OJ C 372/5, para. 36.

630 This was the case for the comparison between tampons and sanitary towels, which were deemed not substitutes despite having the same purpose, in Commission Decision of 21 June 1994 declaring a concentration to be compatible with the common market and the functioning of the EEA Agreement (IV/M.430 - *Procter & Gamble/VP Schickedanz (II)*) [1994] OJ L 354/32, para. 42.

631 Ritter and Braun, [2004], p. 35.

317. To assess the reverse demand substitution, the Notice on Market Definition employs the SSNIP test[632], which is mostly demand-side oriented[633]. For buyer power cases, however, it suggests the application of the *Buyer's SSNIP test*[634]. The Notice on Market Definition states that:

> [t]he equivalent analysis (SSNIP test) is applicable in cases concerning the concentraiton [sic] of buying power, where the starting point would then be the supplier and the price test serves to identify the alternative distribution channel or outlets for the supplier's product. In the application of these principles, careful account should be taken of certain particular situations as described within paragraphs 56 or 58[635].

318. Further, Paragraph 17 of the Notice on Market Definition suggests applying the *Buyer's SSNIP test* by adopting the supplier's point of view. The methodology then requires decreasing in a small and permanent manner the purchasing price level to test whether there are alternative distribution channels or outlets that would acquire the supplier's goods[636]. With this price decrease, the degree of reverse demand substitution can be analyzed[637]. A similar methodology is also adopted in the Guidelines on Horizontal Agreements, which suggest measuring demand substitution by examining the suppliers' reaction

---

632 SSNIP stands for "small but significant and non-transitory increase in price". The SSNIP test was introduced in 1982 in the US with the Horizontal Merger Guidelines. The SSNIP test remains in force in the last version of the US Horizontal Merger Guidelines [2010], p. 8-13; in the EU the test developed by the Commission is slightly different: "a hypothetical small (in the range of 5% to 10%) but permanent relative price increase in the products and areas being considered", Commission Notice on the definition of relevant market for the purposes of Community competition law [1997] OJ C 372/5, para. 17; see also the OECD report on the differences between the test in: OECD 'Policy Roundtables: Market Definition' (2012), p. 30-31.

633 "The discussion above [referring to the general discussion on market definition] is predicated on markets defined on the supply side. However, it is also possible to define markets on the demand side, that is, in terms of what is being bought", Jones and Sufrin, *EU Competition Law: Text, Cases and Materials* [2014], p. 81.

634 The Buyer's SSNIP test is a name adopted by the author as it clearly defines what the methodology is. Other authors have adopted a different denomination, for example Kokkoris that adopts the SSNDP (Small but Significant Non-Transitory Decrease in Prices) in Kokkoris (2006) and Kokkoris and Day (2009), which is in turn based on the previous work by Commission and others (2000).

635 Commission Notice on the definition of relevant market for the purposes of Community competition law [1997] OJ C 372/5, para. 17 (in fine).

636 Commission Notice on the definition of relevant market for the purposes of Community competition law [1997] OJ C 372/5, para. 17.

637 Commission Notice on the definition of relevant market for the purposes of Community competition law [1997] OJ C 372/5, para. 17; a similar point is made by Blair and Harrison when stating that "[i]f buyers respond quickly to the efforts of another buyer to depress prices by increasing purchases when prices fall, they must be included as part of the defendant's market", Blair and Harrison, [2010], p. 63. Also in the same line is the methodology proposed by Kokkoris of the SSNIP test which assesses "whether suppliers would refuse to supply a buyer in the presence of a permanent five to ten percent reduction in the price the buyer would pay for the suppliers' products, so as the price reduction to be unprofitable for the buyer", in Kokkoris (2006), p. 147; see also the proposal by Chen who describes the hypothetical monopsonist test as "[a] relevant market is defined as the smallest group of products and the smallest geographic area in which a sole profit-maximizing buyer (a 'hypothetical monopsonist') would impose and sustain a significant and non-transitory price decrease below its normal level" and focusing on the ability of the seller to find alternative buyers in Chen 'Buyer power: Economic Theory and Antitrust Policy' (2007), p. 29.

to a small but non-transitory (as opposed to permanent) price decrease[638], as one alternative used for defining relevant purchasing markets, without any express reference to other options.

319. The application of the *Buyer's SSNIP test* will ask whether, after a non-transitory decrease in the range of five to ten percent in purchasing prices, sellers are able to switch to other buyers and make the decrease in price non-profitable for the buyer[639]. It will not be profitable if suppliers are able to find alternative buyers or switch production to another good or service[640]. If buyer's substitution is enough to make the price decrease unprofitable then additional buyers and geographical areas are included in the relevant market and the price decrease test is applied to them[641]. Competition authorities will continue adding buyers or areas until the set of buyers and the geographic area is such that a small, non-transitory decrease in relative prices would be profitable for a hypothetical monopsonist[642].

320. Importantly, under the *Buyer's SSNIP test*, the *relevant market might be composed of buyers belonging to different downstream markets* as the input acquired can have different uses[643]. Or, as Chen points out, relevant upstream markets are not necessarily aligned with the relevant downstream markets as they can be quite differentiated regarding the products included[644]. For example, the product market for purchasing fresh oranges might include juice and ice-cream producers that compete for the input but are not competitors in the downstream market. Also, it must be taken into account that generally there are more buyers than suppliers of a good or service – because the same good can be used for different means or user types – and, therefore, the evaluation concerning the amount of buyers in a market should bear this in mind. For these reasons, it is necessary that competition authorities do not evaluate competing buyers focused solely on those that are downstream competitors at the same time[645]. Otherwise, the market definition will not adequately reflect

---

638 The wording employed by the Commission in the Notice on Market Definition speaks of "permanent" and "lasting change". In contrast with the wording used in the Communication from the Commission — Guidelines on the applicability of Article 101 of the Treaty on the Functioning of the European Union to horizontal co-operation agreements [2011] OJ C 11/1, para. 198; non-transitory is understood as a period of usually one or two years whereas permanent is understood as a long-term price variation. See: Niels, Jenkins and Kavanagh, [2011], p. 45-46.

639 Commission Notice on the definition of relevant market for the purposes of Community competition law [1997] OJ C 372/5, para. 17.

640 Van Bael and Bellis, [2005], p. 146.

641 Similarly, but from a seller's perspective: Crocioni (2002), p. 335; ten Kate and Niels (2009), p. 301.

642 Commission Notice on the definition of relevant market for the purposes of Community competition law [1997] OJ C 372/5, para. 17; for a similar explanation see: Kokkoris (2006), p. 148; Graham, [2010], p. 26.

643 Canadian contribution in OECD '*Policy Roundtables: Monopsony and Buyer Power*' (2009), p. 143.

644 Chen 'Buyer power: Economic Theory and Antitrust Policy' (2007), p. 30.

645 See also the opinion of Carstensen when referring to substitutability from an input perspective in Carstensen 'Buyer Cartels Versus Buying Groups: Legal Distinctions, Competitive Realities, and Antitrust Policy' (2010), p. 19.

which undertakings compete in which markets. Unfortunately, the Notice on Market Definition does not take this situation into account.

321. Additionally, the price level to be applied in the *Buyer's SSNIP test* varies depending on the case at hand. In general, the *prevailing market price* would be the starting point, particularly for concentration cases. In instances of unilateral behaviour, however, the prevailing price might have been determined in the absence of effective competition, as discussed in the cellophane fallacy[646]. In these cases, the price level that should be taken into account is the price that would have existed under a competitive market, which is difficult in practice.

322. In this sense, the Notice on Market Definition seems to consider the prevailing price as the competitive and applicable price level for buyer power cases in general, but in doing so it may overlook the *reverse cellophane fallacy*[647]. The reverse cellophane fallacy theory claims that if the prevailing price is taken into account by using estimated demand elasticities, instead of making the market too broad, the market definition becomes too narrow and "the potential for the exercise of market power is likely to be overstated"[648]. This occurs, for example, if the prevailing price is too low, making other goods (or distribution channels) appear to be weaker substitutes when they are really not[649]. Therefore, in buyer power cases the reverse cellophane fallacy may lead to the erroneous conclusion that a buyer that pays a low price has substantial market power when in reality this is not so.

323. Furthermore, the Notice on Market Definition remarks that when determining demand substitution special attention should be paid to secondary markets and chains of substitution[650]. The examples given by the Notice on Market Definition are not related to buyer power cases although this does not imply that these effects cannot occur in buyer power scenarios.

646 Commission Notice on the definition of relevant market for the purposes of Community competition law [1997] OJ C 372/5, para. 19; discussing the cellophane fallacy in some detail see: George A. Hay, 'Market Power in Antitrust' 60 Antitrust Law Journal (1991-1992) 807.

647 Luke M. Froeb and Gregory J. Werden, 'The Reverse Cellophane Fallacy in Market Delineation' 7 Review of Industrial Organization (1992) 241; discussing the reverse cellophane fallacy in regulated markets see: Debra J. Aron and David E. Burnstein, 'Regulatory Policy and the Reverse Cellophane Fallacy' 6 Journal of Competition Law and Economics (2010) 973; see also: Jerry A. Hausman and J. Gregory Sidak, 'A Consumer-Welfare Approach to the Mandatory Unbundling of Telecommunications Networks' 109 The Yale Law Journal (1999) 417.

648 Froeb and Werden (1992), p. 241.

649 Aron and Burnstein (2010), p. 975-976.

650 Commission Notice on the definition of relevant market for the purposes of Community competition law [1997] OJ C 372/5, paras. 17 and 56-58; for an economic discussion of aftermarkets, see: Niels, Jenkins and Kavanagh, [2011], p. 87-89.

324. Secondary markets or aftermarkets (not to be confused with two-sided markets)[651] present the dilemma of determining whether the main product and its spare parts or consumables are part of the same market or constitute different markets, as car windscreens would be for cars[652]. When carrying out buyer power analysis of secondary markets, therefore, it is necessary to take into account the "constraints on substitution imposed by conditions in the connected markets"[653], such as, for example, compatibility issues. A buyer power example of a secondary purchasing market would be when a large buyer acquires specialized industrial machinery with a long lifespan from a provider at a competitive price. The supplier, rather small in comparison to the buyer, commits its total production capacity to satisfy the demand of machinery spares and replacement parts for the large buyer, becoming dependent on that buyer and having an inelastic supply curve. To exploit the supplier, the large buyer would exert its market power on the spare and replacement parts market by paying a purchasing price below competitive levels. If the market is broadly defined including the industrial machinery and the spare and replacement parts, the buyer would appear to have less buyer power than if the market definition is made with the spare and replacement parts market as the focus.

325. Lastly, chains of substitution are problematic as they might lead to the definition of a relevant market where the product or geographic areas at the market limits are not substitutes for each other[654]. The example provided by the Notice on Market Definition defines the geographic market when transport costs are a significant issue as the pricing of the goods might be constrained by the chain substitution effect, leading to a definition of a different market[655].

b. Supply substitution – supply buyer substitution

326. Supply substitution is the second competitive constraint assessed when determining the relevant market according to the Notice on Market Definition, and

---

651 Two-sided markets, nevertheless, are important for buyer power cases, in particular regarding buyer power in public procurement regulated markets in the case of central purchasing bodies, as pointed out by Sánchez Graells in Sánchez Graells, *Public Procurement and the EU Competition Rules* [2011], p. 54-55. A two-sided market is when two distinct groups of customers have inter-related demand and the groups impose positive externalities. One example of such a two-sided market is newspapers that sell advertisement space and information; another example is credit cards connecting retailers and consumers, as discussed in Judgment of 30 June 2016, *CB v Commission*, T-491/07, ECR, EU:T:2012:633, and appealed before the CJEU in Judgment of 11 September 2014 in *CB v Commission*, C-67/13 P, EU:C:2014:2204; for a description of the basic economics of two-sided markets see, *inter alia*, Carlton (2007), p. 25-26; Bishop and Walker, [2010], paras. 3.042-3.045; OECD 'Policy Roundtables: Market Definition' (2012); Niels, Jenkins and Kavanagh, [2011], p. 89; American Bar Association, *Market Definition in Antitrust* [2012], p. 437-469. See also: Gauss and Oldale, [2013], paras. 1.109-1.112.

652 Van Bael and Bellis, [2005], p. 148-149.

653 Commission Notice on the definition of relevant market for the purposes of Community competition law [1997] OJ C 372/55, para. 56.

654 Commission Notice on the definition of relevant market for the purposes of Community competition law [1997] OJ C 372/5, para. 57.

655 Kokkoris (2006), p. 146.

the CJEU's case law derived from *Continental Can*[656] and *Michelin I*[657]. Supply substitution defines the capacity of other suppliers (or buyers) to switch to the production (or purchasing) of the monopolized good in the short term without incurring significant additional costs or risks in response to small and permanent changes in relative prices[658]. Consequently, in a buyer power case, supply substitution – which I refer to as supply buyer substitution – *would measure the ability of non-current buyers of an input that due to the price decrease now decide to purchase it.*

327. This means that supply buyer substitution measures a different variable than selling-side supply substitution and this is not its reverse[659]. Supply buyer substitution would measure the response of other buyers that were not originally purchasing the good and which, in response to the reduction of the purchasing price, decide to acquire the input, but not take into account that other suppliers would be producing the same input. This purchasing behaviour is a reaction to the perceived new profit maximizing opportunity[660], and the additional purchases will discipline the behaviour of the buyer under investigation as new buyers become competitors for the underpriced input. An example illustrates this effect: buyer "A" located in the region of Cognac in France is a monopsonist buyer of the grape Ugni Blanc for the production of the liquor Cognac[661]. Due to a non-transitory decrease in the purchasing prices of Ugni Blanc, buyer "B", a red wine producer also located in Cognac, decides to acquire Ugni Blanc to also start producing Cognac. Owing to its expertise in the production of grape-based alcoholic beverages, geographic location and spare capacity, "B" can effectively and immediately start buying grapes for Cognac production, thus being a supply-sided constraint vis-à-vis "A".

328. As in the case of supply substitution, buyer substitution should not be overestimated when assessing competitive pressure from other buyers[662].

656 Judgment of 21 February 1973 in *Europemballage Corporation and Continental Can Company v Commission*, C-6/72, EU:C:1973:22, para. 33 and ss, where the CJEU consider that potential competitors were able to switch their facilities to the production of cans to determine a market for light metal packaging.

657 "[...] an examination limited to the objective characteristics only of the relevant products cannot be sufficient: the competitive conditions and the structure of supply and demand on the market must also be taken into consideration", Judgment of 9 November 1983 in *Michelin v Commission*, C-322/81, EU:C:1983:313, para. 37; Judgment of 21 October 1997, *Deutsche Bahn v Commission* T-229/94, ECR, EU:T:1997:155, para. 37.

658 Commission Notice on the definition of relevant market for the purposes of Community competition law [1997] OJ C 372/5, paras. 20-23; see also: Van Bael and Bellis, [2005], p. 138-139; Bishop and Walker, [2010], para. 4-012; Niels, Jenkins and Kavanagh, [2011], p. 68-74; for a US antitrust law perspective, see Hovenkamp, [2005], p. 108-113.

659 Cf with Kokkoris who seems to use a traditional definition of supply substitution in buyer power cases in Kokkoris (2006), p. 147.

660 Crocioni (2002), p. 355.

661 The CJEU dealt with a buyer power-related case in Judgment of 30 January 1985 in *BNIC v Clair*, C-123/83, EU:C:1985:33, in which the main issue dealt with fixing minimum purchasing prices to limit the buyer power of purchasers of white grapes. For the analysis of this case see chapter 10, section II. Cognac is variety of brandy produced in the Cognac region of France from specific grapes, among them the Ugni Blanc. Cognac is a denomination of origin and protected since 1909 in France.

662 See for supply substitution: Niels, Jenkins and Kavanagh, [2011] p. 71-74.

Additionally, buyer substitution is a less immediate constraint and assessment tool when compared to reverse demand substitution and requiring less of an analysis of additional factors to be taken into account[663].

329. However, unlike demand substitution, supply substitution is future oriented[664]. When assessing it, it is necessary to grant it adequate importance to avoid making the market definition too narrow or too broad, as remarked by Oinonen[665]. If supply substitutability is not taken into account or its impact minimized, the market definition may become too narrow as potential sources of competitive constraint are disregarded. On the other hand, if too much emphasis is placed on supply substitution, the market definition may become too broad as, depending on the market, many undertakings could begin to acquire the goods. This latter concern is especially important in buyer power cases as traditionally there are more buyers than sellers in a given market and a non-traditional buyer of a good may desire to upon seeing the reduction in the input's purchasing price.

330. These inherent problems of supply substitution have led to some critical voices concerning its appropriateness when performing the buyer's market definition. Baker, in the sphere of US antitrust, argues that supply substitution should not be taken into account at the stage of market definition but instead later because "it can be both difficult and confusing to ask one analytical step, market definition, to account for two economic forces, demand and supply substitution"[666]. In contrast, in EU competition law, the Commission's practice and the Notice on Market definition assess supply substitutability in the market definition phase[667]. Part of the reasoning behind this is that, as argued by Motta, "there is no reason to delay the moment at which substitutes on the supply side are considered. Immediate consideration of the existing competitive constraints will save time and help the investigation"[668].

331. To minimize risks concerning the assessment of supply substitution in buyer power cases, the Notice on Market Definition and the Courts remark that it would only be taken into account whenever the switching effects are "equivalent to those of demand substitution in terms of effectiveness and immedia-

663 Commission Notice on the definition of relevant market for the purposes of Community competition law [1997] OJ C 372/5, para. 14.

664 Säcker, [2008], p. 37.

665 Oinonen, [2010], p. 257-258.

666 Baker (2007), p. 134.

667 Oinonen, [2010], p. 263.

668 Motta, *Competition Policy: Theory and Practice* [2004], p. 104.

cy"[669]. Absent the factors of timeliness and effectiveness, supply substitution will be considered only when dealing with the market power assessment. The General Court clarified in *Clearstream v Commission* that timely and effective means that "suppliers are able to switch production to the relevant products and market them in the short term without incurring significant additional costs or risks in response to small and permanent changes in relative prices"[670]. To be effective, buyer substitution would require fulfilling several variables, among others, the market should have sufficient spare production capacity and flexibility, lack of barriers to expansions, buyers should have flexible contractual commitments with their current sellers, little risk of defensive or retaliative strategies and no need to significantly adjust tangible and intangible assets[671]. Also, supply substitution would be timely if it is within six months or up to one year, as suggested by Motta[672]. Consequently, supply substitution will be irrelevant if the supplier's ability to change its production does not affect the involved undertaking's position in the market[673].

C. Shortcomings of the current buyer-oriented methodology

332. As it stands in EU competition law, my evaluation of the *Buyer's SSNIP test* reveals some deficiencies that ought to be remarked upon when it comes to future policy chances. Some of my criticisms address, and stem from, the SSNIP test methodology in general and not only the *Buyer's SSNIP test.* In the following paragraphs, I, however, address the problems I identified from a buyer's perspective so that competition authorities are aware of them and take them into consideration when dealing with a buyer power market definition pursuant to the *Buyer's SSNIP test.*

333. The Notice on Market Definition takes a simplistic and uni-dimensional approach to buyer power definition as it only contemplates defining the upstream market while neither requiring nor suggesting an additional market definition in the downstream market[674]. In failing to do so, the analysis does not consider the competitive effects of buyer power in the downstream market and only looks at the effects upstream. Not looking at downstream market effects is at odds with the implementation or use of a broader standard to buyer power

669 Judgment of 29 March 2012, *Telefónica and Telefónica de España v Commission*, T-336/07, ECR, EU:T:2012:172, para. 113. See also: Commission Notice on the definition of relevant market for the purposes of Community competition law [1997] OJ C 372/5, paras. 20-21; Füller in Hirsch, Montag and Säcker, [2008], p. 438-439; Säcker considers that supply substitutability also includes current competitors in Säcker, [2008] p. 37.

670 Judgment of 9 September 2009, *Clearstream v Commission,* T-301/04, ECR, EU:T:2009:317, para. 50.

671 Commission Notice on the definition of relevant market for the purposes of Community competition law [1997] OJ C 372/5, para. 20; Kokkoris (2006), p. 147; Säcker, [2008], p. 38-39.

672 Motta, *Competition Policy: Theory and Practice* [2004], p. 103.

673 Füller in Hirsch, Montag and Säcker, [2008], p. 444.

674 The same opinion was given by the now extinct Competition Commission and Office of Fair Trading of the UK in the UK's Contribution in OECD '*Policy Roundtables: Monopsony and Buyer Power*' (2009), p. 231.

anti-competitive harm and the ordoliberal concern of protecting competition as such. Furthermore, a pure upstream market analysis also disregards the direct end consumer harm, which, as it will be discussed in Parts VI and V of this study, are the center of concern for US antitrust and, to a lesser extent, the Commission.

334. The Commission's buyer power market definition methodology may lead to situations in which the relevant market found is narrower than the real one. As a consequence, the buyer under investigation may appear to have more market power than it actually does. This effect occurs as the Commission's *Buyer's SSNIP test* inquires whether a hypothetical purchasing undertaking would make more profit if the purchasing prices were 5-10 percent lower than the current level, and not if a hypothetical monopsonist would reduce the purchasing price by the same amount, as it is done in US antitrust[675]. Furthermore, the Notice on Market Definition does not indicate whether the reduction in purchasing prices should be performed in terms of one price, some prices or all prices in the candidate market[676]. Daljord, Sørgard and Thomassen suggest that this should be done on a case-by-case assessment depending on the market's characteristics[677].

335. Also, the application of a decrease in purchasing price in the range of 5-10 percent by a hypothetical monopsonist may well have a greater impact on the supplier than when compared to an increase in price for end consumers, especially if the supply curve is highly inelastic, and because large buyers might represent a higher proportion of the sales of a supplier than is the case when end consumers act individually. Therefore, as it is discussed when it comes to dealing with unfair purchasing prices, a lesser decrease in purchasing prices might still have a strong effect on the quantity supplied and the search for alternative buyers by the seller, if the suppliers depend on the buyer. Think, for example, of the agriculture sector. A purchasing price decrease by a supermarket chain of 4 percent can still have a powerful effect on the supplier's response to the change in price because the farmer will usually face a very inelastic demand curve (for instance, the commodities it sells perish quickly if not properly refrigerated or seasonal factors)[678]. Also, the supermarket may be a necessary trading partner and/or because the profit margins are quite small. This concern has been expressed in somewhat analogous terms by the Commission by reference to the "threat point" which is discussed in detail in

675 A similar criticism from a demand-side oriented perspective is found in: Bishop and Walker, [2010], para. 4-006.

676 Øystein Daljord, Lars Sørgard and Øyvind Thomassen, 'The SSNIP Test and Market Definition with the Aggregate Diversion Ratio: A Reply to Katz And Shapiro' 4 Journal of Competition Law and Economics (2008) 263.

677 Ibid. p. 263.

678 David L. Baumer, Robert T. Masson and Robin Abrahamson Masson, 'Curdling the Competition: An Economic and Legal Analysis of the Antitrust Exemption for Agriculture' 31 Villanova Law Review (1986), 187.

the section dealing with market power assessment[679]. The threat point was defined as the ratio of purchases that a buyer represents for a seller upon which the loss of this client will endanger the supplier's operability and which has been deemed to exist whenever a buyer represents 22% of the sales of a supplier, as discussed by the Commission in several merger cases[680].

336. An additional shortcoming is that the market definition resulting from the *Buyer's SSNIP test* may be composed of a smaller number of undertakings, both on the supply side and on the demand side, than when compared to a relevant market with final consumers[681]. Consequently, the undertakings' market share will be rather large and the HHI level will tend to be concentrated, in either the supplier's side, the demand, or both. This is a factor that should be kept in mind when assessing the undertaking's market power and which should not be over or underestimated. Furthermore, the case law concerning buyer power abuse or dealing with countervailing buyer power as an efficiency defense can be misleading because in some of these cases the market shares and concentration thresholds were very high, which may erroneously lead one to think that buyer power cases are always represented by very high market shares indexes[682]. For example, in the countervailing buyer power cases of *Imperial Chemical Industries v Commission*[683], *Irish Sugar v Commission*[684] and *Tomra and Others v Commission*[685], there were very high levels of market concentration and market shares.

---

679 See chapter 5, section §IV.C.a. Also referring to the threat point concerning the *Carrefour/Promodès* Decision see, Ezrachi and Ioannidou (2014), p. 81.

680 Non-opposition to a notified concentration (Case COMP/M.1684 — *Carrefour/Promodès*) [2000] OJ C 164/5, French public version, paras. 52-55; Commission Decision of 3 February 1999 relating to proceedings under Council Regulation (EEC) No 4064/89 (Case No IV/M.1221 - *Rewe/Meinl*) OJ L 274/1, para. 101.

681 Bundeskartellamt '*Buyer Power in Competition Law - Status and Perspectives*' (2008), p. 5.

682 Cf with the concentration thresholds in the Guidelines on the assessment of horizontal mergers under the Council Regulation on the control of concentrations between undertakings [2004] OJ C 31/5, paras. 19-21, where two scenarios are distinguished: first, concentrations below 1,000 HHI do not merit extensive analysis (unconcentrated markets); second, it is unlikely to identify horizontal competition concerns in a merger with a post-merger HHI between 1 000 and 2 000 and a delta below 250, or a merger with a post-merger HHI above 2 000 and a delta below 150 (moderately concentrated markets).

683 In this case the HHI was of 8,150 and the undertaking's market share was 90%, which indicates an almost monopsonistic position by Imperial Chemical Industries in Judgment of 25 June 2010, *Imperial Chemical Industries v Commission*, T-66/01, ECR, EU:T:2010:255; and Commission Decision of 19 December 1990 relating to a proceeding under Article 85 of the EEC Treaty (IV/33.133-A: *Soda-ash - Solvay, ICI*) [1991] OJ L 152/1, para 1.

684 In *Irish Sugar v Commission* the market shares and HHI were also very high, ranging between 90% and 88% of the market and 8100 and 7225 HHI; see: C-497-99 P - *Irish Sugar v Commission*, EU:C:2001:393 E.C.R. [2001] I-05333; T-228-97 - *Irish Sugar v Commission,* EU:T:1999:246 E.C.R. [1999] II-02969; and Commission Decision of 14 May 1997 relating to a proceeding pursuant to Article 86 of the EC Treaty (IV/34.621, 35.059/F-3 - *Irish Sugar plc*) [1997] OJ L 258/1.

685 In *Tomra and Others v Commission* the HHI varied considerably, ranging from 5625 up to a maximum of 9025 in accordance with the provided figures and the market share ranged from 70% to 95%; see, Judgment of 19 April 2012 in *Tomra and Others v Commission*, C-549/10 P, EU:C:2012:221; Judgment of 9 September 2010, *Tomra Systems and Others v Commission*, T-155/06, ECR, EU:T:2010:370; and Summary of Commission Decision of 29 March 2006 relating to a proceeding under Article 82 of the Treaty establishing the European Community and Article 54 of the EEA Agreement against Tomra Systems ASA, Tomra Europe AS, Tomra Systems BV, Tomra Systems GmbH, Tomra Butikksystemer AS, Tomra Systems AB and Tomra Leergutsysteme GmbH (Case COMP/E-1/38.113 — *Prokent/Tomra*) [2008] OJ C 219/11, para. 11. The full version of the Decision can be accessed at: http://ec.europa.eu/competition/antitrust/cases/dec_docs/38113/38113_250_8.pdf

337. In contrast with this tendency, unilateral substantial buyer power has said to arise in the presence of relatively low concentration and market shares levels. In *British Airways v Commission* the CJEU confirmed that British Airways was a dominant undertaking with a market share of 39.7% of the total tickets sold by travel agents in the downstream market[686]. *British Airways v Commission* is a breakthrough in cases of dominance in EU competition law in general due to the low market share threshold, and also because in most buyer power cases the market share percentage of the dominant undertaking has been higher. However, British Airways was found to be a necessary trading partner and also enjoyed substantial downstream market power, which may be one of the factors why it was considered to be a dominant undertaking. Also, in the merger assessments of *Carrefour/Promodès,* and *Rewe/Meinl,* substantial relative buyer power was said to exist between a buyer and a supplier when the former represented 22% of the supplies; yet, in both this cases, as I discuss in chapter 8, the concentrations were cleared pursuant to commitments.

338. Additionally, the Canadian Competition Bureau has pointed out that the relevant product market stemming from the *Buyer's SSNIP test* may include products that, from the buyer's perspective, are unrelated or not substitutes, and if this would be the case, it would be contrary to the case law[687]. This raises the question of whether the substitutability of products in buyer power investigations should be defined through the relevant use given to it by the buyer or the supplier[688]. Traditionally, when facing a decrease in purchasing price, suppliers may switch their production toward another good or service, which does not entail incurring substantive costs[689]. For example, a citrus farmer may start to produce mandarins instead of oranges. The problematic aspect of this would be that the market definition outcome will include both mandarins and oranges in the relevant product market, which is incorrect from a buyer's perspective.

339. In my view, to answer this problem the substitutability/interchangeability of goods in the upstream product market should be assessed from the *supplier's* perspective and not from the buyer's perspective, while also taking into consideration "the

686 Judgment of 17 December 2003, *British Airways v Commission* of 17 December 2003, T-219/99, ECR, EU:T:2003:343; Judgment of 15 March 2007 in *British Airways v Commission*, C-95/04 P, EU:C:2007:166.

687 Canadian contribution in OECD '*Policy Roundtables: Monopsony and Buyer Power*' (2009), p. 144-145; Cf with C-27/76 - *United Brands v Commission*, EU:C:1978:22 E.C.R. [1978] 00207, para. 22; C-6/72 - *Europemballage Corporation and Continental Can Company v Commission*, EU:C:1973:22 E.C.R. [1973] 00215, para. 32.

688 Füller in Hirsch, Montag and Säcker, [2008], p. 441.

689 Canadian contribution in OECD '*Policy Roundtables: Monopsony and Buyer Power*' (2009), p. 144-145.

structure of supply and demand on the market, and competitive conditions"[690]. This shift in the perspective in terms of the substitutability was made even clearer in *CEAHR v Commission*, where it was stated that "[t]he interchangeability or substitutability is not assessed solely in relation to the objective characteristics of the products and services at issue, but the competitive conditions and the structure of supply and demand on the market must also be taken into consideration"[691]. This interpretation is further supported by means of analogy to seller cases in which it is the end consumer who judges the substitutability/interchangeability between products, as settled by the CJEU in *United Brands v Commission*[692], as well as by the Notice on Market Definition[693].

340. Furthermore, the simplified *Buyer's SSNIP test* has been criticized by the former UK Office of Fair Trading because if a supplier is forced to price below competitive levels this would imply that "the supplier would not earn a normal profit over the long term and so would be *better off leaving the industry*"[694]. This criticism reveals two shortcomings of the methodology. First, a mere upstream market definition only captures monopsony effects and not bargaining power effects. Second, the Notice on Market Definition is not explicit when it comes to stating if the decrease in the purchasing price is to be above or below the competitive level. The differences are well illustrated by the previous quote: if it is set below the competitive levels, the supplier will be forced out of the business to avoid losses; if it is still within competitive levels, then the supplier will remain in the industry.

341. Additionally, my analysis shows that applying the current approach of the *Buyer's SSNIP test* requires determining what the current or competitive purchasing price is, which is a challenging exercise, particularly regarding the latter aspect. Also, the difficulty increases in buyer power cases because prices in intermediate markets are usually not readily available to end consumers

---

690 "For this purpose, therefore, an examination limited to the objective characteristics only of the relevant products cannot be sufficient: the competitive conditions and the structure of supply and demand on the market must also be taken into consideration", in Judgment of 9 November 1983 in *Michelin v Commission*, C-322/81, EU:C:1983:313, para. 37; Judgment of 21 October 1997, *Deutsche Bahn v Commission* T-229/94, ECR, EU:T:1997:155, para. 54.

691 Judgment of 15 December 2010, *CEAHR v Commission*, T-427/08, ECR, EU:T:2010:517, para. 67; see also: Judgment of 17 December 2003, *British Airways v Commission* of 17 December 2003, T-219/99, ECR, EU:T:2003:343, para. 91.

692 Judgment of 14 February 1978 in *United Brands v Commission*, C-27/76, EU:C:1978:22, para. 12-35, wherein the CJEU decided that from the consumer's point of view the product market for bananas constitutes a significantly different product market from other fruits.

693 "A relevant product market comprises all those products and/or services which are regarded as interchangeable or substitutable *by the consumer*, by reason of the products' characteristics, their prices and their intended use", Commission Notice on the definition of relevant market for the purposes of Community competition law [1997] OJ C 372/5, para. 7 (emphasis added); and recently ratified by the General Court in Judgment of 29 March 2012, *Telefónica and Telefónica de España v Commission*, T-336/07, ECR, EU:T:2012:172, para. 113; and Judgment of 28 April 2010, *Amann & Söhne and Cousin Filterie v Commission*, T-446/05, ECR, EU:T:2010:165, para. 59.

694 Office of Fair Trading, *The Competitive Effects of Buyer Groups*, para 1.77 (emphasis added).

or the general public, even when they are not protected under confidentiality clauses[695]. This would be particularly relevant in cases of private litigation, as it happens in the US, because neither the supplier nor the buyer have incentives to reveal their price or costs to competitors and will indeed use confidentiality clauses to protect prices. Also, in other cases, and as remarked by Carstensen, transactions are entered into as one-on-one sales where buyer and seller have some flexibility to determine prices *ad hoc*[696]. However, this difficulty would be less in cases of public enforcement as agencies have right to access this confidential information, diminishing the risks for not finding adequate price levels.

342. Finally, the purchasing market definition ought to consider that purchasing contracts in some industries, such as manufacturing input markets, are typically of long duration, as opposed to the majority of contracts among sellers and final consumers, which are typically (although not always) a one-time deal. Consequently, this has to be factored in when determining an appropriate "non-transitory" or "permanent" period when performing the *Buyer's SSNIP test*[697].

D. The hypothetical monopsony test: the OECD alternative

343. The OECD has proposed a methodology for market definition that centers its attention on monopsony cases[698]. The proposed methodology — the *hypothetical monopsonist test* — is drafted in general terms, providing guidance in terms of agreement, dominance and merger cases. In my view, the *hypothetical monopsonist test* is a more detailed, refined and modern methodology than the one which is proposed in the Notice on Market Definition by the Commission. The differences, however, are not many.

344. The *hypothetical monopsonist test* identifies the "smallest set of products in the smallest geographic area such that a hypothetical monopsonist of those products in that area would be able to depress prices by a small but significant and non-transitory amount"[699]. Therefore, it is similar to the standard hypothetical monopolist test[700].

---

695 Joe Harrington, "The Current State of the Theory of Collusion: Unexplained Phenomena and Unexplored Directions" (BECCLE Competition Policy Conference).

696 Carstensen 'Buyer Cartels Versus Buying Groups: Legal Distinctions, Competitive Realities, and Antitrust Policy' (2010), p. 19.

697 American Bar Association, *Market Definition in Antitrust* [2012], p. 55-56.

698 OECD '*Policy Roundtables: Monopsony and Buyer Power*' (2009), p. 34-42.

699 Ibid, p. 34.

700 For a thorough discussion on the hypothetical monopolist test see *inter alia*: Gregory J. Werden, 'The 1982 Merger Guidelines and the Ascent of the Hypothetical Monopolist Paradigm' 71 Antitrust Law Journal (2003) 253; Malcolm B. Coate and Jeffrey H. Fischer, 'A Practical Guide to the Hypothetical Monopolist Test for Market Definition' 4 Journal of Competition Law and Economics (2008), 1031; Bishop and Walker, [2010], p. 111-124; Niels, Jenkins and Kavanagh, [2011], p. 37-56.

345. In this test, the product market is defined as the productive assets over which a buyer could exercise monopsony power as it determines the smallest group of goods that can be profitably monopsonized by a hypothetical monopsonist by withholding demand to lower purchasing prices below competitive levels[701]. To do so, the key lies in recognizing the existence of alternative channels for the seller, in consistency with *Buyer's SSNIP test* discussed above[702]. The more alternative buyers there are, the less monopsony power the undertaking has. For bargaining power cases the OECD does not provide an explicit methodology for defining the relevant market; however, the hypothetical monopsonist test can be employed as well to measure the existence and extent of bargaining power in its measurement. I discuss this in more detail in chapter 5.

346. The methodology would indicate that a buyer necessarily has limited monopsony power when it is proven that the sellers can easily find other buyers. The OECD distinguishes 3 cases:

i) Other buyers that acquire the input for different uses than the undertaking under investigation;

ii) Other buyers located in different geographic areas that acquire the input for similar uses as the undertaking under investigation;

iii) And lastly, other buyers for whom the assets can be used to make a different input[703].

347. The OECD also suggests applying two different price levels when carrying out the test. If the case is retrospective, the price level used would be the competitive one. If, on the other hand, the case is prospective then the price level used would be the current price, unless it is reasonable to expect that the price for the input is going to rise[704]. This clarification concerning the price levels to be used constitutes an improvement compared to the vague rule on price levels set in the Notice on Market Definition[705]. Importantly, the OECD does not suggest what the range of the price decrease should be, arguably due to the different approaches in the EU and US competition methodologies.

348. In sum, the *hypothetical monopsonist test* proposed by the OECD constitutes an improvement to the *Buyer's SSNIP test* suggested in the Notice on Market Definition. The fact that the test is expressly oriented to monopsony cases does not mean it cannot be applied to bargaining power ones. However, the test and its results would not indicate if the buyer power exerted is monop-

---

701 OECD '*Policy Roundtables: Monopsony and Buyer Power*' (2009), p. 34.

702 Ibid, p. 34.

703 Ibid, p. 34.

704 Ibid, p. 34

705 Commission Notice on the definition of relevant market for the purposes of Community competition law [1997] OJ C 372/5, para. 19.

sony or bargaining power; what it does is to define the boundaries in which the undertaking's conduct is to be analyzed. Lastly, despite its specificity, the *hypothetical monopsonist test* does not expressly indicate the need to perform a dual relevant market definition, as I propose.

E. Buyer's market definition in some Member States

349. Some NCAs of the EU Member States have also engaged in efforts to refine the existing tools regarding buyer's market definition. In the following section, I briefly discuss the proposals put forth by the German Bundeskartellamt and the former UK Office of Fair Trading.

a. Ability of suppliers to switch to alternative sale opportunities

350. The Bundeskartellamt has proposed a structural approach regarding the definition of relevant purchasing markets that is centered on the analysis of the ability of suppliers to switch to alternative sale opportunities, which is in line with, and appears to be inspired by, the Commission's and the OECD's methodologies. This buyer oriented market definition "focuses on the products the supplier is offering or would be able to offer *without any significant problems*. With these products in view it has to be asked which (alternative) sales channels could be services in an economically viable manner"[706]. The Bundeskartellamt approach, however, does not explicitly contemplate the application of a *Buyer's SSNIP test*; although, in determining whether the supplier would be able to offer its products without any significant problems it seems to apply it. Lastly, an aspect not covered by this proposal, concerns the level of prices to be used as a basis of the test, which is not specified, nor is it identified with the decrease in percentage that will be used.

b. A dualistic approach to buyer markets

351. In the UK, the Guidance Notice on Market Definition of the former Office of Fair Trading sets the methodology applicable when determining the relevant market in an investigation[707]. The Notice does not contain any direct mention of how to determine relevant buying markets, although it follows the Commission Notice on Market Definition and builds upon it[708], I interpret this as meaning that the Buyer's SSNIP test is the pertinent one to be applied.

---

706 Bundeskartellamt '*Buyer Power in Competition Law - Status and Perspectives*' (2008), p. 5 (emphasis added).

707 Office of Fair Trading, 'Market Definition: Understanding Competition Law' (2004), the now Competition and Markets Authority makes the disclaimer, however, that the Guidance Notice was retained unammended and, therefore, does not reflect the changes in the case law, legislation or practice.

708 Office of Fair Trading, 'Market Definition: Understanding Competition Law' (2004); also stressing the common ground between the guidelines, see Graham, [2010], p. 23.

352. Nevertheless, the UK's contribution in the OECD Roundtable on Monopsony and Buyer Power of 2009 provides further and more detailed information regarding buyer market definition for both monopsony and bargaining power[709]. The contribution rightly points out that measuring and defining markets for buyer power cases is not straightforward. As most buyer power theories of harm[710] involve an undertaking with market power upstream and downstream, the proposal suggests that it might "be necessary to *define and analyse markets at a number of different levels* in the supply chain"[711]. This solution appears to condition the dualistic approach to the existence of a theory of harm that involves competitive issues in both markets. Although this is a step in the right direction, in my view there is no need to make such a pre-condition as all buyer power problems will have some downstream implication, as discussed in chapter 2, sections §V and §VI.

353. Also, this methodology distinguishes between three different scenarios when defining the relevant market in buyer power cases. Firstly, in the case of countervailing buyer power, buyer power is seen as "a potential, benign, constraint on the exercise of supplier market power [i.e. countervailing buyer power], buyer power will be assessed within the supply market of concern"[712]. Examples of such supply market concerned definitions are found in EU competition law practice, and I discuss this in detail in chapter 9 turning to cases such as *Nestlé/Perrier*[713] and *Enso/Stora*[714]. However, in these types of cases, the assessment of countervailing buyer power is made at the market power assessment and not at the relevant market definition stage. Secondly, *when buyer power is seen as abusive*, the markets to be defined will depend on whether the abusive behaviour is *exclusionary* or *exploitative*. If exploitative, the methodology stresses that the "[d]ownstream markets would be defined in the normal way using the hypothetical monopolist test and then the degree of potential buyer power is assessed in this context"[715]. If the conduct is exclusionary, it may be necessary to define several markets, depending on which the exclusion takes place in. Lastly, if buyer power is exercised in one market but has consequences on another, for example due to leverage[716], then assessment must be made in both these markets[717].

---

709 See the UK's Contribution, jointly prepared by the now extinct Competition Commission and Office of Fair Trading, in OECD '*Policy Roundtables: Monopsony and Buyer Power*' (2009), p. 229-243.

710 For a general discussion on theories of harm and EU competition law see: Hans Zenger and Mike Walker, *Theories of Harm in European Competition Law: A Progress Report* (Jacques Bourgeois and Denis Waelbroeck eds, Bruylant 2013) available at http://ssrn.com/abstract=2009296.

711 UK Contribution, jointly prepared by the now extinct Competition Commission and Office of Fair Trading, in OECD '*Policy Roundtables: Monopsony and Buyer Power*' (2009), p. 229 (emphasis added).

712 Ibid, p. 239.

713 Commission Decision of 22 July 1992 relating to a proceeding under Council Regulation (EEC) No 4064/89 (Case No IV/M.190 - *Nestlé/Perrier*) [1992] OJ L 356/1.

714 Commission Decision of 25 November 1998 declaring a concentration to be compatible with the common market and the functioning of the EEA Agreement (Case No IV/M.1225 - *Enso/Stora*) [1999] OJ L 254/9.

715 UK Contribution, jointly prepared by the now extinct Competition Commission and Office of Fair Trading, in OECD '*Policy Roundtables: Monopsony and Buyer Power*' (2009), p. 239.

716 For a discussion of leveraging buyer market power see chapter 6, section §VII.

717 OECD '*Policy Roundtables: Monopsony and Buyer Power*' (2009).

354. This proposed UK approach to buyer power market definition is case-by-case oriented and dependent on which effects are presumed by the theory of harm and used as a starting point, along with the need to carry out several market definitions, both of these factors constituting positive improvements. However, the contribution does not provide a detailed account of the process itself pertaining to defining the relevant market from a buyer's perspective. Additionally, this approach might be criticized for being too case specific and for compromising legal certainty, as it is based on theories of harm as a starting point. I believe, nevertheless, that this proposal does not compromise legal certainty if the three alternatives are properly understood and applied in a consistent manner. Furthermore, the employment of a theory of harm to guide the design of the case is common practice among competition authorities and, therefore, not a source of real concern.

F. Buyer's market definition in US Antitrust law

355. The US Horizontal Merger Guidelines of 2010 were first developed in 1982 and introduced the hypothetical monopolist test into the arena of competition law, in order to determine the relevant market[718]. They are drafted for merger assessments, nonetheless, the US courts and literature have also found them relevant in clarifying the methodology for cartel and monopolization cases[719]. As in EU competition law, these Guidelines are not binding on the Courts but are helpful in providing an analytical framework to evaluate the case[720]. Due to their importance, and the comparisons I draw to buyer power aspects of certain US antitrust issues I discuss them in brief.

a. Market definition in US Antitrust law: some generalities

356. The US Horizontal Merger Guidelines incorporate a thorough methodology regarding market definition and clarify that carrying a market definition in merger cases does not need to be the first step in the assessment[721], thereby breaking with more than 50 years of precedent, as remarked by Coate and Fischer[722]. Instead, the antitrust agencies may resort to assessing competitive effects in a direct manner.

---

718 For an overview of the main changes introduced by the 2010 Horizontal Merger Guidelines see: Richard A Feinstein, '2010 Revisions to the US Horizontal Merger Guidelines' 7 Competition Law International (2011) 6.

719 For a similar opinion on the relevance of the Horizontal Merger Guidelines in monopolization cases see: Hovenkamp, [2005], p. 129; Einer Elhauge and Damien Geradin, *Global Competition Law and Economics, 2nd Edition* (Hart Publishing Ltd 2011), p. 304-317.

720 American Bar Association, *Market Definition in Antitrust* [2012] 6; *State v. Kraft General Foods, Inc., 926 F. Supp. 321* (S.D.N.Y. 1995), para. 359. See also: Hovenkamp, [2005], p. 129-134.

721 U.S. Department of Justice and Federal Trade Commission, Horizontal Merger Guidelines (2010), p. 7; American Bar Association, *Market Definition in Antitrust* [2012], p. 7-8.

722 Malcolm B. Coate and Jeffrey H. Fischer, 'Is Market Definition still Needed After all these Years' (2014) p. 1.

357. Like the EU Notice on Market Definition, the relevant market assessment is made through the hypothetical monopolist test, and also entails a product and geographic market dimension[723]. Unlike the Notice on Market Definition, however, the US Horizontal Merger Guidelines only take into consideration demand substitution as a constraint factor, defined as the customer's ability to substitute one product for another in response to an increase in price or a corresponding non-price change, such as reduction in quality or service[724]. Supply substitutability will only be considered at the market power assessment stage as part of the identification of market participants and possible entrants, regardless of whether the entry is timely and effective[725].

b. Buyer's market definition in US Antitrust law

358. An entire Section of the US Horizontal Merger Guidelines is devoted to dealing with mergers of competing buyers (Section 12)[726]. To assess buyer market power, the US Horizontal Merger Guidelines adopt "essentially the framework [...] for evaluating whether a merger is likely to enhance market power on the selling side of the market"[727]. As with the Notice on Market Definition and the OECD's hypothetical monopsonist test, the US Horizontal Merger Guidelines focus is on determining whether there are alternatives available to sellers when facing a decrease in the price paid by the *hypothetical monopsonist*[728]. Also, the US Horizontal Merger Guidelines do not expressly distinguish between monopsony power effects or bargaining power effects and neither does it provides a thorough analysis as when compared to selling-oriented methodology[729]. However, like all other methodologies, it can be applied in both cases.

359. Analogous to the standard seller-side methodology, the hypothetical monopsonist test is applied as part of the product and geographic market analysis. When it is conducted, the market shares of the merging parties are calculated, and the market power is then assessed. Buyer market power will not be a significant concern when suppliers have "numerous attractive outlets for their goods or services"[730]. On the contrary, should this not be the case, then the creation of buyer power is *"likely to lessen competition in a manner harmful to sellers"*[731].

---

723 For a thorough discussion of the test in US antitrust law, see: Areeda, Hovenkamp and Solow, [1995], p. 284-307.

724 US Department of Justice and Federal Trade Commission, Horizontal Merger Guidelines [2010], p. 7.

725 Gavil, Kovacic and Baker, [2008], p. 492.

726 U.S. Department of Justice and Federal Trade Commission, Horizontal Merger Guidelines [2010], p. 32; for a detailed analysis of this section see Carstensen 'Buyer Power and the Horizontal Merger Guidelines: Minor Progress on an Important Issue' (2012).

727 U.S. Department of Justice and Federal Trade Commission, Horizontal Merger Guidelines [2010], p. 32.

728 U.S. Department of Justice and Federal Trade Commission, Horizontal Merger Guidelines [2010], p. 33.

729 Carstensen 'Buyer Power and the Horizontal Merger Guidelines: Minor Progress on an Important Issue' (2012), p. 781.

730 U.S. Department of Justice and Federal Trade Commission, Horizontal Merger Guidelines [2010], p. 33; Feinstein (2011), p. 9.

731 U.S. Department of Justice and Federal Trade Commission, Horizontal Merger Guidelines [2010], p. 33 (emphasis added).

360. To summarize, the US Horizontal Merger Guidelines provide a similar, albeit more detailed, approach as that of the Notice on Market Definition when defining the relevant buying market in a partial manner. It proposes performing a *hypothetical monopsonist test* to determine the market power solely upstream capturing mostly monopsony effects[732]. As with the Commission's Notice, no additional downstream relevant market analysis is suggested, which leads to an incomplete picture of the effects of buyer power cases, which, to me, is a deficiency.

V. Conclusions concerning the relevant market

361. This chapter has illustrated the importance of *revisiting traditional views concerning purchasing market definition* due to the particularities of purchasing markets that distinguish them from standard selling-side cases. My contribution shows that *relevant buying markets are different from selling side markets because the incentives, dynamics and economics of purchasing respond to different factors, which require specific methodologies* and reinterpretation of traditional concepts when defining relevant markets.

362. Therefore, I submitted that buyer power cases and their relevant market assessments should be anchored on a *dualistic market definition methodology* for all buyer power cases, and not limited to a selection of them. The dualistic approach allows for the measurement of both monopsony and bargaining power, covering buyer power effects as a whole in the upstream and downstream markets. Moreover, this proposal *goes one step further than the traditional reverse approach advocated by the Notice on Market Definition because the latter lacks detail and a one side-approach is simplistic*. This implies that, for the market definition and the subsequent assessment of the undertaking's market power, the analysis must be made in both the upstream and downstream markets in which the undertaking conducts its economic activity.

363. A dualistic approach fully captures the buyer power implications pursuant to conduct that might be perceived as anti-competitive. The dual approach's function when defining relevant markets is to serve as the starting point to assess the competitive effects of the behaviour of an undertaking vis-à-vis its suppliers (upstream) and rival buyers, and vis-à-vis end consumers and rival buyers that compete as retailers (downstream). Thus, *it grants a complete*

732 See also the literature review carried out by Carlton, Coleman and Israel concerning the US Horizontal Merger Guidelines and the fact that most authors speak about it capturing monopsony cases by that it can be used for buyer power in general: Carlton, Coleman and Israel, [2015], p. 537-539.

overview of the exploitative and exclusionary effects of buyer power in all related markets. Moreover, it has been shown that not only the literature and the soft law instruments issued by the Commission, but also the EU case law increasingly support the adoption of this dualistic approach, particularly concerning the assessment of concentrations[733], but also in the case of dominance with buyer power implications in downstream markets.

364. Regarding the relevant market definition, I submit that a mere reversal of the SSNIP test – the *Buyer's SSNIP test* – and the current methodologies adopted in the Commission's soft law is insufficient. Instead, certain adjustments and re-interpretations of traditional concepts such as demand substitution and buyer substitution should be made. In this chapter, I analyzed the standing methodologies adopted in the Commission's soft law and other institutions, at both the national and international level. The analysis shows that there has been a *gradual development towards a dualistic approach* from the traditional and insufficient reverse side approach anchored on a pure upstream market definition, towards a more integrative one, as is reflected in the Merger Control Regulation, the OECD and, importantly, some influential NCAs. However, the development at the EU level of the methodology for defining relevant purchasing market is still insufficient and requires adjustment. These authoritative sources modernize the previous state of the soft law and are a good step in the right direction towards a dualistic approach to buyer power cases. Nevertheless, most of them are still too timid, as they only tend to capture half of the picture, by only focusing on the upstream market definition, or applying dualistic definitions in some but not all cases.

365. Therefore, in buyer power investigations, the market definition should resort to a dualistic approach that involves several aspects. Firstly and most importantly, the market definition must be done in both markets where the undertaking carries out its economic activity. In the upstream market where it purchases its goods and exerts buyer market power vis-à-vis its suppliers or with a foreclosure effect regarding competing buyers. Furthermore, an additional market definition should be made in the downstream market to fully capture the downstream competitive effects of buyer market power vis-à-vis end consumers, having greater relevance when the involved undertakings also compete as retailers. For the upstream market, I have shown that competition authorities should resort to more than a mere reverse application of selling-oriented methodologies. To do so, two important factors should be assessed differently than in selling side cases. With regard to demand substitution, the assessment should be focused on the concepts of *reverse demand substitution* to determine the ability of suppliers to switch to alternative buyers in case the purchasing price decreases. With regard to *supply buyer substitution*, it should

733 Council Regulation (EC) No 139/2004 of 20 January 2004 on the control of concentrations between undertakings (the EC Merger Regulation) [2004] OJ L 24/1, Article 2.1.(a) and (b) (emphasis added).

be assessed if other buyers that were not originally purchasing the good decide to acquire the input in response to the reduction of the purchasing price.

366. Also, I analyzed some problems faced by the current methodology as well as the dualistic approach regarding buyer market definitions that should be kept in mind when carrying out the assessment. For example, the fact that a decrease in purchasing prices in buyer markets might have a larger impact than in selling ones, or that purchasing markets might be defined more narrowly than they should, making the undertaking more powerful, or concerning which perspective to take into account to assess the substitutability/ interchangeability of goods in a buyer power case.

367. In the chapter I also discussed how to re-interpret the assessment when defining buying relevant markets. The changes proposed do not require a complete change of the existing methodologies nor proclaiming that buyer market definitions are entirely different and disconnected from selling-oriented cases. What these revisions conclude is that it is necessary to take into account buyer power dynamics and adopt a dualistic approach to the assessment. Further, my suggestions for a change in the methodologies and incorporating a dualistic approach also finds support, steadily but decisively, in the EU soft law as well as in other MS with important examples in Germany and the UK. However, I think that the move towards it should be more decisive. This is an area in which I acknowledge that more academic and administrative development is necessary and in which my dualistic approach and observations are an additional step in that direction.

368. In sum, an additional downstream market definition is required to properly assess the market power and competitive effects of the buying undertaking's behaviour. A pure upstream market focus is insufficient. Thus, in this chapter, I have highlighted the need for resorting to such a dualistic approach, despite its shortcomings, when defining relevant buyer markets because it is better-suited tool than the mere reverse SSNIP test or methodologies focusing on the upstream market and/or monopsony effects, exclusively.

5

BUYER MARKET POWER ASSESSMENT

I. Introduction

369. Once the relevant product and geographic markets have been defined, competition authorities will assess the market power of the involved undertaking(s) to determine the economic effects of the investigated conduct. In this chapter, I discuss the assessment of buyer market power from an *active perspective*, in opposition to the *passive* measurement in cases of *countervailing buyer power*, which is discussed in much more detail in chapter 9 as a neutralizing force of seller market power. In this chapter I look into *how is buyer power assessed* and *when does substantial buyer power (but not necessarily dominance) arise?*

370. I put forward that the measurement of market power in buyer-side cases also ought to follow the dualistic approach to buyer market definition to fully capture the specificities of the exercise of buyer power and its repercussions in the upstream and downstream markets. This is done by taking into account the competitive structure of the buying and retailing markets and interpreting the relation between them as suggested by the Commission[734]. Also, another important finding of this chapter is that substantial buyer power seems to arise in lower market share thresholds when compared to selling side cases, at least in terms of bilateral relations; i.e.: between a specific buyer and a supplier, due to the existence of dependence, and which is decisive factor when studying unfair purchasing practices, discussed in chapter 8.

---

734 Communication from the Commission — Guidance on the Commission's enforcement priorities in applying Article 82 of the EC Treaty to abusive exclusionary conduct by dominant undertakings [2009] OJ C 45/7, para. 12.

371. To structure my analysis, I have drafted this section as follows. In section §II I discuss market power and its assessment at large. This is followed by an analysis of the specificities of buyer market power assessment in a dualistic manner in section §III. I then deal, in section §IV, with the methodology and tools employed in EU competition law to measure the amount of market power a buyer has: market shares, market concentration, unavoidable trading partners and dependence, and gate-keeping. These assessment tools are quantitative indicators that guide the decision-making body in determining whether or not an undertaking possesses market power. In my discussion, I evaluate them from a buyer-oriented perspective and follow the dualistic approach to market definition. This is followed, in section §V, with a discussion of direct methodologies for assessing buyer market power, while section §VI concludes with a discussion of the chapter's findings.

II. Market power assessment

372. The market power assessment phase allows for the measurement of an undertaking's market power and is carried out once the relevant market has been defined; consequently, its accuracy relies on the appropriateness of such market definition[735].

373. Market power, in the neoclassical economics sense, is the capacity of an undertaking to profitably sustain prices above – or below, in buyer power cases[736] – competitive levels, or restrict output or quality by charging a price above – or below – marginal costs[737]. In more practical terms and following Hay's definition, market power expresses the idea of the "potential for consumers to suffer injury through the actions of a single firm or a group of firms acting in concert"[738]. Therefore, there are three main elements connected to market power:

i) its exercise will reduce output or input;
ii) the price increase or decrease must be profitable in a medium and short term;
iii) market power is usually exercised relative to the benchmark of effective competition[739].

374. Additionally, market power can be possessed by selling and buying undertak-

735 Posner, [1976], p. 125; Hyman and Kovacic (2004), p. 26.

736 Highlighting the need for the increase or decrease of prices remain profitable, see: Posner and Landes (1980), p. 937.

737 Office of Fair Trading, 'Assessment of Market Power: Understanding Competition Law' (December 2004). A similar definition is proposed in Bishop and Walker, [2010], para. 3-001. See also: Areeda, Hovenkamp and Solow, [1995], p. 109; Hovenkamp, [2005], p. 80; Niels, Jenkins and Kavanagh, [2011], p. 116.

738 Hay (1991-1992), p. 808.

739 Bishop and Walker, [2010], p. 53-61.

ings without changing its nature, what changes is the way that is exercised: by increasing or lowering prices below the competitive levels, respectively.

375. In opposition to the neo-classical concept, Monti identifies three other definitions of market power[740]. A first alternative definition inquires whether the undertaking has a greater commercial strength than others in the market, such as in the case of economic dependence regarding buyer power[741]. A second definition, inspired in post-Chicago economics, conceptualizes market power as the ability of an undertaking to devise strategies that harm rivals (exclusionary power) to then profitably raise or decrease prices (exploitative power). Lastly, market power can be defined as a jurisdictional concept, for example, when using market share thresholds to create safe harbors precluding the application of EU competition rules, such as the *de minimis* doctrine or the block exemption regulations[742]. In this study, I employ the neo-classical definition of market power unless otherwise stated.

376. Furthermore, undertakings have *different degrees of market power* (including bargaining power)[743], with monopoly and monopsony power being the extreme case for selling and buying cases, respectively[744]. As no real market is perfectly competitive, all undertakings have a certain degree of market power[745], even if this may imply that they are pricing below average costs[746]. This is important because the fact that a buyer has some degree of buyer power does not imply that the undertaking is dominant, as remarked by Posner and Landes[747], and which is a requirement for the application of Article 102 TFEU.

377. In this chapter, the center of my discussions is the assessment of buyer market power and I will not deal with the assessment of selling market power, even though my proposal for the dualistic approach to buyer market definition includes also doing an assessment of the undertaking's selling market power, both because it is outside of my research scope and because it is well discussed in the literature.

---

740 Monti, [2007], p. 124-127; and the same idea but proposed as four concepts of dominance see: Giorgio Monti, 'The Concept of Dominance in Article 82' 2 European Competition Journal (2006) 31, p. 31. For the discussion of different definitions of market power in US antitrust law see, *inter alia*: American Bar Association, *Market Power Handbook: Competition Law and Economic Foundations* [2012], p. 1-11.

741 For the discussion of economic dependence as a market power assessment tool, see infra in chapter 5, section IV.A.d.

742 See: Communication from the Commission — Notice on agreements of minor importance which do not appreciably restrict competition under Article 101(1) of the Treaty on the Functioning of the European Union (De Minimis Notice), [2014] OJ C 291/1, paras. 2 and 12. See also the Judgment of 13 December 2012 in *Expedia*, C-226/11, EU:C:2012:795, paras. 23-29 in which the CJEU considers it as non-binding neither for the NCAs nor the courts of the Member States.

743 Hay (1991-1992), p. 813-814; Christopher Cook and Ruchit Patel, *Abuse of Dominance under Article 102 TFEU*, Vol. 5 (F. Enrique González-Díaz and Robbert Snelders eds, Claeys and Casteels 2013), para. 2.84; Kirkwood (2014), p. 54.

744 Thomas D. Morgan, *Cases and Materials on Modern Antitrust Law and its Origins* (4th edn, West Publishing Company 2009), p. 75. Van den Bergh and Camesasca, [2006], p. 75.

745 Monti, [2007], p. 124.

746 Hay (1991-1992), p. 813.

747 Posner and Landes define monopoly power as a high degree of market power in Posner and Landes (1980), p. 937. For a discussion on the need of this distinction see: Hay (1991-1992), p. 818-819.

III. Buyer market power: dual market power assessment

378. Following my dualistic approach proposal to buyer market definition, the buyer power assessment must also be made in the two markets in which the undertaking under investigation carries out its economic activity as a buyer and seller, respectively. This dualistic approach to buyer market power is also shared by other authors like Faull and Nikpay, who, in quite similar terms referring to joint purchasing agreements argue that "[a]ny effects on competition must be assessed on two categories of market. First, the market or markets with which the joint purchasing arrangement is directly concerned, that is, the relevant purchasing market or markets. Secondly, the selling market or markets, that is, the market or markets downstream where the parties to the joint purchasing agreements are active as sellers"[748]. The dual approach, however, applies to all buyer power cases and not to some of them.

379. Adopting a dualistic approach implies that the market power assessment considers the case particularities and captures its effects on all the related markets. Therefore, the assessment ought to determine if in addition to buyer power the undertaking enjoys significant selling power to then analyze the competitive effects of the behaviour in both markets. If the assessment of buyer market power only factors the effects in the upstream market, the analysis would only take into account welfare effects upstream and the wealth transfer between the supplier and buyer and the rival buying undertakings, but it would not capture any welfare effects in the downstream market vis-à-vis end consumers and rival buyers that act as retailers. Then, to assure consistency with a broad standard for buyer power anti-competitive harm intervention and capture effects in all related markets, a dual approach is necessary. Hence, I submit that the buyer market power assessment must measure the undertaking's purchaser buyer power and its seller power and then analyze the relation between them and the final outcome of the competitive effects[749].

380. This, however, should not be interpreted as implying that a dual analysis also requires dual dominance or substantive market power in both markets to trigger competition intervention. It is sufficient for a buyer to have substantial market power in the upstream market to be considered dominant, or for when its market power is sufficient to have current or future anti-competitive effects; therefore, for substantial buyer power to exist there is no need for

748 Faull, Nikpay and Taylor, [2014], para. 7.364; see also: Faull and Nikpay, [1999], para. 6.320.

749 Somewhat similar but regarding the valuation of the economic welfare effects of buyer power was the idea expressed in European Commission and others (2000), p. 4.

additional downstream market power. The existence of the latter is an additional factor for the assessment of conduct's impact but not a requirement[750].

381. One of the chapter's findings is *that buyer (bargaining) power may be effectively exerted at lower levels of market power in comparison to seller side from a buyer with respect to its suppliers, especially if there is an asymmetrical relation between them*[751]. Nevertheless, that buyer power can effectively be exercised at lower thresholds and may have competitive effects (particularly in a bilateral manner) *does not imply that buyer power dominance exists at lower thresholds* when compared to selling side dominance. What it does imply is that buyer power may be used 'exploitatively' vis-à-vis individual suppliers at a lower level because they might be economically dependent on the buyer. This has been confirmed, for example, in the Commission's practice regarding the finding of a "threat point"[752] in some large food retailer mergers or in the case of *relative dominance* or *dependence*, as discussed in detail in chapter 8 dealing with unfair purchasing practices[753].

382. The main reason accounting for how substantial buyer power is able to arise on lower market share thresholds when compared to seller side power and create competitive concerns – even if not always caught by EU competition rules – is that the buyer is the 'decider' of the transaction[754]. This is particularly the case concerning bargaining power[755]. By being the one setting the pace, the buyer has more negotiation/power strength, even if the supplier is also large, as confirmed by the Bundeskartellamt[756].

---

750 "*Peraltro, appare opportuno porre in evidenza che l'art. 3 della legge n. 287/90, che vieta l'abuso di posizione dominante, già contempla la possibilità di intervenire nei confronti di un'impresa la quale, benché non dotata di una posizione dominante nella vendita dei propri prodotti, tuttavia detenga una posizione dominante dal lato della domanda nei confronti dei propri fornitori, in assenza di alternative economicamente significative per questi ultimi*", ("Moreover, it is appropriate to highlight that Article 3 of the Law n. 287/90 that forbids the abuse of a dominant position, contemplates the possibility of intervening against the actions of an undertaking which, even if it does not have dominance with regard to the sales of goods as a retailer, has a dominant position with regard to its suppliers in the upstream market, in the absence of economically meaningful alternatives for the latter" (author's translation), in Opinion of June 20, 1995 of the Autorità Garante della Concorrenza e del Mercato, *Subfornitura Industriale* (1995).

751 Also supporting this see: Faull and Nikpay, [1999], para. 6.338; American Antitrust Institute [2008], p. 104; Carstensen 'Buyer Power and the Horizontal Merger Guidelines: Minor Progress on an Important Issue' (2012), p. 782.

752 Non-opposition to a notified concentration (Case COMP/M.1684 — *Carrefour/Promodès*) [2000] OJ C 164/5, French public version, paras. 52-55; Commission Decision of 3 February 1999 relating to proceedings under Council Regulation (EEC) No 4064/89 (Case No IV/M.1221 - *Rewe/Meinl*) [1999] OJ L 274/1, para. 101.

753 Bundeskartellamt '*Summary of the Final Report of the Sector Inquiry into the Food Retail Sector*' (2014), p. 13.

754 Carstensen 'Buyer Power and the Horizontal Merger Guidelines: Minor Progress on an Important Issue' (2012), p. 783.

755 Doyle and Inderst (2007), p. 215; Carstensen 'Buyer Cartels Versus Buying Groups: Legal Distinctions, Competitive Realities, and Antitrust Policy' (2010), p. 6.

756 Bundeskartellamt '*Summary of the Final Report of the Sector Inquiry into the Food Retail Sector*' (2014), p. 14. However, if the supplier enjoys a strong product, then its seller power raises even vis-à-vis strong buyers because the buyer also is dependent on the supplier, a situation discussed with dealing with mutual dependence below.

383. Additionally, I have identified a *substantive difference in the levels of market power needed to effectively exercise monopsony and bargaining power*. Effective monopsony power exercised during a non-transitory period requires that the buyer possesses a substantially large degree of market power that is akin to or greater than being dominant in the market, a position also shared by the American Antitrust Institute[757]. This, however, is not shared by Carstensen, who claims that "monopsony arises at lower market shares and so is more pervasive" (than seller power)[758]. I disagree with this with regard to monopsony power. In my view, monopsony power and the withholding effect can only exist profitably and for a substantial period of time if an undertaking is vastly dominant and where there are significant entry barriers to the purchasing market. The case law, economics of monopsony power and its sources, as discussed in chapter 2 of this study, corroborate this.

384. Contrarily, substantial bargaining power can be exercised effectively at lower thresholds, and even in the absence of dominance, with or without anti-competitive effects[759], for instance whenever a supplier depends on a buyer, as confirmed by the Commission's finding in food retailing cases where when a buyer represented 22% of the profits of a supplier, that supplier depends on the buyer and said buyer had substantial buyer power vis-à-vis that party[760]. Nonetheless, the fact that a party is dependent on a buyer does not mean that the buyer as a whole has a dominant position because dominance is an *erga omnes* concept. An undertaking is dominant in the market vis-à-vis all suppliers and other retailing competitors; thus, it is not sufficient to conclude that a buyer is dominant because it has substantial buyer power in relation to some but not most of its suppliers. When that happens then the undertaking enjoys a *relative dominant position,* a concept that exists in some national legislations, as discussed in chapter 8, section §IV of this study, but not in EU competition law. The discussion regarding up to what extent and how situations that arise from the unilateral exercise of buyer market power of an undertaking that is not dominant in the traditional EU competition law terms is carried out in chapter 8, dealing with the imposition of unfair purchasing practices.

---

757 American Antitrust Institute [2008], p. 104.

758 Carstensen 'Buyer Power and the Horizontal Merger Guidelines: Minor Progress on an Important Issue' (2012), p. 799.

759 Also suggesting that substantial buyer power may arise in the presence of relatively small market shares see Doyle and Inderst (2007), p. 215.

760 Non-opposition to a notified concentration (Case COMP/M.1684 — *Carrefour/Promodès*) [2000] OJ C 164/5, French public version, para. 52 (translation by the author). See also mentioning this 22% threshold as part of the "threat point" theory Ezrachi and Ioannidou (2014), p. 81; and Këllezi [2008], p. 70-71, who links the threat point to dependence.

IV. Measuring the buying undertaking's market power

385. Buyer power arises from different sources, as discussed in chapter 2, and the extent of it is measured by means of different assessment tools, regardless of whether it is monopsony or bargaining power. In this section, I analyze the five assessment tools that case law and authoritative sources have identified as the most relevant in the determination of buyer market power, namely: market shares, market concentration, alternative supply sources, gate-keeping role, and dependence. These factors in conjunction represent by and large the synthetization of buyer power sources. These assessment tools are not exclusive to buyer market power measurement and are also frequently used for seller-side cases.

386. In my opinion, in the assessment phase of buyer power, competition authorities do not require making a distinction between monopsony and bargaining power cases, in contrast to some that suggest this distinction is made in this competition stage[761]. In my view, the distinction regarding whether a conduct involves monopsony or bargaining power is fundamental, but should be made before the assessment of buyer power whenever determining the sources and behavioural forms. This is because buyer power sources *explain* buyer market power's origin, whereas these assessment tools *quantify* its degree. However, and as held through this study, what should be distinguished from the outset is whether the market power exercised is in the form of monopsony effect or bargaining power effect. That which determines whether the effect is one of monopsony or of bargaining power is not the existence of buyer power, but the characteristics of the behaviour. Furthermore, there is no need to make a distinction between bargaining and monopsony power at the assessment stage because the assessment tools I discuss below can be indistinctively applied to both types of buyer power.

A. Market shares

387. Market shares are a useful first indication but not a precise proxy for market power, as repeatedly clarified by the CJEU, for both buyer and seller side cases[762]. The larger the market shares of a buyer in the upstream market, the more

761 OECD '*Policy Roundtables: Monopsony and Buyer Power*' (2009), p. 42; Office of Fair Trading, *The Competitive Effects of Buyer Groups*.

762 Judgment of 13 February 1979 in *Hoffmann-La Roche v Commission*, C-85/76, EU:C:1979:36, paras. 39-41; Judgment of 30 January 2007, *France Télécom v Commission*, T-340/03, ECR, EU:T:2007:22, para. 100. Also expressed in the Communication from the Commission — Guidance on the Commission's enforcement priorities in applying Article 82 of the EC Treaty to abusive exclusionary conduct by dominant undertakings [2009] OJ C 45/7, para. 13. Also applicable in concentration cases as stated in the Guidelines on the assessment of horizontal mergers under the Council Regulation on the control of concentrations between undertakings [2004] OJ C 31/5, para. 14; see also a US antitrust law perspective Ernest Gellhorn, Stephen Calkins and William E. Kovacic, *Antitrust Law and Economics in a Nutshell* (Thomson/West 2004), p. 132-140; American Bar Association, *Market Power Handbook: Competition Law and Economic Foundations* [2012], p. 93.

likely it is that it has substantial buyer market power[763]. Econometric findings by the Bundeskartellamt confirm this intuition: the greater the purchasing volumes of an undertaking, the larger the impact on negotiated conditions and, thus, its buyer power[764]. Therefore, market shares above 50% act as a rebuttable presumption of (buyer) market power in accordance with the AKZO presumption[765], but not of prices above (or below) marginal costs[766], and help competition authorities by serving as a screening device[767] to determine the existence of substantial market power and dominance[768].

388. In a dualistic approach to buyer power cases, the market shares of the investigated undertaking(s) will be calculated both in the upstream and downstream market[769]. Importantly, in the upstream market, the market share computation should include all buyers and not only those buyers that also compete downstream with the involved undertaking[770]. For example, in the case of a purchasing market for oil, the computation must include buyers that acquire oil to process it into gasoline and buyers that acquire oil and process it as plastic[771].

389. The Notice on Market Definition defines the Commission's methodology for market share computation and bases it on the sales of the products in the relevant area[772]. In a buyer power case, this would be represented by the proportion of the relevant product acquired by the involved undertaking[773]. In practice, this is calculated through companies' estimates, and industry studies carried out by consultants or trade associations. If the data is not available, then the Commission requests the information directly from the undertak-

---

763 See chapter 2, sections §III and §IV for buyer power sources. Similarly, see: Guidelines on Vertical Restraints [2010] OJ C 130/1, para. 116; European Commission and others (2000), p. 9; Doyle and Inderst (2007), p. 215; Ezrachi and De Jong (2012), p. 258.

764 Bundeskartellamt '*Summary of the Final Report of the Sector Inquiry into the Food Retail Sector*' (2014), p. 10.

765 Judgment of 3 July 1991 in *AKZO v Commission*, C-62/86, EU:C:1991:286, para. 60; Hay (1991-1992), p. 822; see also: Faull and Nikpay, [1999], para. 6.314. Cf with Carlton's critical view of market share's suitability, who claims that "the definition of a market and the use of market shares and changes in market shares are at best crude first steps to begin an analysis. I would use them to eliminate frivolous antitrust cases when shares are low, but would use them cautiously for anything else", in Carlton (2007), p. 3.

766 Werden (2014), p. 4.

767 Carlton (2007); Monti, [2007], p. 124-127.

768 Judgment of 13 February 1979 in *Hoffmann-La Roche v Commission*, C-85/76, EU:C:1979:36, para. 39; similarly, see: Hay (1991-1992), p. 821; Areeda, Hovenkamp and Solow, [1995], p. 243; Motta, *Competition Policy: Theory and Practice* [2004], p. 117; Cook and Kerse, [2009] 235, p. 235; Niels, Jenkins and Kavanagh, [2011], p. 124.

769 Monti, [2007], p. 143.

770 Chen 'Buyer Power: Economic Theory and Antitrust Policy' (2007), p. 18.

771 Carstensen 'Buyer Cartels Versus Buying Groups: Legal Distinctions, Competitive Realities, and Antitrust Policy' (2010), p. 19.

772 Commission Notice on the definition of relevant market for the purposes of Community competition law [1997] OJ C 372/5, para. 53. Market shares can be calculated regarding sales, quantity, amount of suppliers, capacity, etc. Hovenkamp points out that other data can be used in the computation of market shares, such as revenue, units of output manufactured, units of output sold, capacity or a mix of these variables. If markets are competitive, using any of these indicators will tend to give the same result; see: Hovenkamp, [2005], p. 122.

773 European Commission and others (2000), p. 19.

ing(s) investigated. Other indicators, however, can be used to provide useful information for the calculation and valuation of market share, such as: capacity, the number of players in bidding markets, units of fleet as in aerospace, or the reserves held in case sectors such as mining[774].

390. Important shortcomings must be borne in mind, with regard to market share analysis[775]. Firstly, as market shares are directly derived from the market definition, any flaws in the determination of the latter will impact the outcome of the market share estimation. Secondly, the market shares interpretation must be made in its relative context and not *in abstracto*, reflecting the circumstances of the case[776]. Thirdly, market share analysis does not involve the assessment of barriers to exit or entry because it is a static exercise and therefore, lacking depth concerning future competition. Fourthly, and as noted by Hay, market share analysis is retrospective, whereas market power is dynamic because "the degree of market power enjoyed by a firm depends on how much business it will lose to rivals *if* it attempts to raise prices above competitive levels"[777].

a. *Standard thresholds*

391. Concerning the application of Article 102 TFEU, the CJEU has established in *AKZO v Commission* that a finding of 50% market share constitutes a rebuttable presumption for the existence of dominance[778]. The Commission has stated that dominance is unlikely if the undertaking's market share is below 40%, unless specific circumstances make competitor's constraint ineffectively[779]. However, in *British Airways v Commission,* a buyer power case, dominance was found with a market share below 40%, which I discuss at length in the subsequent section[780].

392. In concentration cases, market shares are used for determining whether the concentration could lead to a significant impediment of effective competi-

---

774 Commission Notice on the definition of relevant market for the purposes of Community competition law [1997] OJ C 372/5, para. 54.

775 Raising these issues see, *inter alia*: Hay (1991-1992), p. 821-822; Oinonen, [2010], p. 169-170; Niels, Jenkins and Kavanagh, [2011], p. 123-124.

776 Judgment of 13 February 1979 in *Hoffmann-La Roche v Commission*, C-85/76, EU:C:1979:36, paras. 40-41; see also: Communication from the Commission — Guidance on the Commission's enforcement priorities in applying Article 82 of the EC Treaty to abusive exclusionary conduct by dominant undertakings [2009] OJ C 45/7, para. 14.

777 Hay (1991-1992), p. 821-822.

778 Judgment of 3 July 1991 in *AKZO v Commission*, C-62/86, EU:C:1991:286, para. 60. Contrast this with the US antitrust case law that holds that it is doubtful that market shares as high as 60% or 70% are enough to determine monopolization cases, see: *United States v. Alcoa*, 148 F.2d 416 (2nd Cir. 1945).

779 Communication from the Commission — Guidance on the Commission's enforcement priorities in applying Article 82 of the EC Treaty to abusive exclusionary conduct by dominant undertakings [2009] OJ C 45/7, para. 14; see also for concentration cases a similar view on the applicable thresholds in the Guidelines on the assessment of horizontal mergers under the Council Regulation on the control of concentrations between undertakings [2004] OJ C 31/5, para. 17.

780 Judgment of 15 March 2007 in *British Airways v Commission*, C-95/04 P, EU:C:2007:166; Judgment of 17 December 2003, *British Airways v Commission* of 17 December 2003, T-219/99, ECR, EU:T:2003:343, para. 211; Commission Decision of 14 July 1999 relating to a proceeding under Article 82 of the EC Treaty (IV/D-2/34.780 - *Virgin/British Airways*) [2000] OJ L 30/1, para. 41.

tion, particularly, but not exclusively, due to the creation or strengthening of a dominant position[781]. Hence, competition risks can be triggered even absent dominance, and some buyer power cases, particularly at the national level as I discuss in chapter 8, confirm that buyer power may trigger competition concerns even in relatively low market shares scenarios or when a buyer is powerful vis-à-vis its suppliers in a bilateral situation. The Commission takes into consideration market shares of the merging firms, pre and post-merger to evaluate the impact of the operation. The practice in buyer power cases shows that mergers between two or more buyers may significantly impede competition, if no proper commitments are entered into, even if the parties have substantially less than 40% of market share post-merger vis-à-vis its suppliers, as happened in the mergers of *Kesko/Tuko*[782], *Rewe/Meinl*[783] and *Carrefour/Promodès*[784].

393. Additionally, market shares are also used as an indicator for delineating 'safe harbors' inside of which agreements and concentrations are deemed as falling outside of the prohibitions because of their non-significant effect on trade between MS[785]. Concerning the latter, the Commission has held that even object agreements among undertakings that have a combined market share of 5% of the relevant market are not capable of appreciably affecting trade between MS and falling outside Article 101(1) TFEU,[786] even if agreements restrictive by object do not benefit of the De Minimis Notice regardless of the market shares of the parties to it.[787] In the case of anti-competitive agreements by their effects the Commission in its De Minimis Notice has stated that an agreement will not appreciably affect competition if: i) it is entered into by competing undertakings with an aggregate market share not exceeding 10% of the relevant market; and ii) it is entered into by non-competing parties, none of which not exceed a market share of 15% in its respective relevant market[788]. For concentrations there is a rebuttable presumption that operations in which the combined under-

---

781 Council Regulation (EC) No 139/2004 of 20 January 2004 on the control of concentrations between undertakings (the EC Merger Regulation) [2004] OJ L 24/1, Article 2.3; Bundeskartellamt 'Summary of the Final Report of the Sector Inquiry into the Food Retail Sector' (2014), p. 17.

782 Commission Decision of 20 November 1996 declaring a concentration to be incompatible with the common market (Case No IV/M.784 - *Kesko/Tuko*) Council Regulation (EEC) No 4064/89 [1997] OJ L 110/53, taken from the unabridged version.

783 Commission Decision of 3 February 1999 relating to proceedings under Council Regulation (EEC) No 4064/89 (Case No IV/M.1221 - *Rewe/Meinl*) [1999] OJ L 274/1; Guidelines on the assessment of horizontal mergers under the Council Regulation on the control of concentrations between undertakings [2004] OJ C 31/5, para. 17.

784 Non-opposition to a notified concentration (Case COMP/M.1684 — *Carrefour/Promodès*) [2000] OJ C 164/5, French public version, paras. 52-55.

785 Judgment of 9 July 1969 in *Voelk v Vervaecke*, C-5/69, EU:C:1969:35, 5/7.

786 Commission Notice — Guidelines on the effect on trade concept contained in Articles 81 and 82 of the Treaty [2004] OJ C 101/81, para. 52.

787 Communication from the Commission — Notice on agreements of minor importance which do not appreciably restrict competition under Article 101(1) of the Treaty on the Functioning of the European Union (De Minimis Notice), [2014] OJ C 291/1.

788 Communication from the Commission — Notice on agreements of minor importance which do not appreciably restrict competition under Article 101(1) of the Treaty on the Functioning of the European Union (De Minimis Notice), [2014] OJ C 291/1, para. 8.

takings' market share does not exceed 25% either in the common market or in a substantial part of it are not liable to impede effective competition[789].

b. Thresholds under buyer power cases

394. Concerning buyer power, and *in particular bargaining power*, the case law and the Commission's practice reveal that bargaining power may raise competitive concerns under lower market share thresholds than when compared to seller side cases. However, as discussed above, this does not imply that effective buyer market power implies dominance, although it may indicate that buyers enjoy a preferential bilateral position vis-à-vis their suppliers, which allows them to effectively exercise their buyer power. This appears to be the situation for all spheres of competition law: agreements, dominance and concentration cases.

395. Thus, *bargaining power can be exercised without the undertaking being dominant*, as pointed out by the literature[790]. This implies that an *undertaking may enjoy substantial market power with relatively low market shares*. The conundrum posed by this situation is that a non-dominant buyer may *unfairly* exercise buyer market power that against its suppliers. If it were dominant would be captured by EU competition laws, but as the buyer is not dominant, its purchasing conduct falls outside of the scope of EU competition law in most occasions, as I discuss in chapter 8[791]. In the case of monopsony, however, the ability to withhold demand profitably with relatively little market shares does not seem to hold in practice based on its economic requirements. In other words, it is unlikely that monopsony power may exist in the absence of dominance. Therefore, the assessment and evaluation of buying side market shares should reflect these particularities.

396. Concerning dominance and as mentioned *supra*, in the exceptional[792] case of *British Airways v Commission*, the CJEU confirmed the General Court's Judgment that an undertaking with a market share of 39.7% in the downstream market of the sale of airline tickets, and also a high but undisclosed market share in the upstream market of the purchasing of travel agencies services may be in a situation of dominance with respect to its competitors[793].

---

789 Council Regulation (EC) No 139/2004 of 20 January 2004 on the control of concentrations between undertakings (the EC Merger Regulation) [2004] OJ L 24/1, recital 32.

790 Kirkwood 'Buyer Power and Exclusionary Conduct: Should Brooke Group Set the Standards for Buyer-Induced Price Discrimination and Predatory Bidding?' (2004-2005), p. 637-639; Chen 'Buyer Power: Economic Theory and Antitrust Policy' (2007), p. 31; Buttà and Pezzoli (2014), p. 165.

791 See also: raising this concern and suggesting that a possible solution should be the implementation of unfair competition law in Pera; see also highlighting the little room for application of abuse of dominance in buyer power cases and the adoption of *ad-hoc* solutions: Buttà and Pezzoli (2014).

792 As noted by Whish and Bailey and confirmed by my research on buyer power matters, the decision represents "the first (and only) occasion on which an undertaking with a market share of less than 40 per cent has been found by the commission to be in a dominant position under Article 102", in Whish and Bailey, [2015], p. 193.

793 Judgment of 15 March 2007 in *British Airways v Commission*, C-95/04 P, EU:C:2007:166; Judgment of 17 December 2003, *British Airways v Commission* of 17 December 2003, T-219/99, ECR, EU:T:2003:343, para. 211; Commission Decision of 14 July 1999 relating to a proceeding under Article 82 of the EC Treaty (IV/D-2/34.780 - *Virgin/British Airways*) [2000] OJ L 30/1, para. 41.

397. The main issue of the case, which I discuss concerning buyer power leveraging in chapter 6, section §VII, was the granting of supra-competitive bonuses to travel agents based on the volume of airline tickets sold to clients by British Airways and whether or not this was an abuse of its dominant position in the service of air passenger transportation. The General Court found that a market share even as low as 39.7% for the air ticket sales handled by IATA as a travel agency coordinator was still enough to find British Airways a dominant undertaking, by assessing the large market shares of British Airways as a purchaser of travel agency services and as a provider of air transport, as well as comparing "the ratio between the market share held by the undertaking concerned and that of its nearest rivals"[794]. The General Court reasoning seems to factor in a dualistic approach to buyer market power and market power leveraging because even though the dominance of British Airways was to be assessed in its condition as a purchaser of services[795], the "economic strength which BA derives from its market share is farther reinforced by the world rank it occupies in terms of international scheduled passenger-kilometres flown, the extent of the range of its transport services and its hub network"[796], all characteristics of British Airways as a seller in the downstream market and not in the upstream market as a buyer.

398. Because of its strength in both the upstream and downstream market and, thus, *substantial market power in both markets*, the General Court concluded that:

> BA is therefore wrong to deny that it is an obligatory business partner of travel agents established in the United Kingdom and to maintain that those agents have no actual need to sell BA tickets. BA's arguments are not capable of calling into question the finding, in recital 93 of the contested decision, that BA enjoys a particularly powerful position in relation to its nearest rivals *and* the largest travel agents[797].

399. A buyer oriented interpretation of *British Airways v Commission* offers a good explanation as to why the CJEU confirmed the finding of dominance at such lower threshold levels when compared to the standard dominance presumptions for seller-side cases[798]. Whenever a buyer of travel agency services also possesses substantial seller market power regarding air passenger transportation it has dual market power, upstream and downstream fitting the hourglass shape. When

---

794 Judgment of 17 December 2003, *British Airways v Commission* of 17 December 2003, T-219/99, ECR, EU:T:2003:343, para. 210.

795 Judgment of 17 December 2003, *British Airways v Commission* of 17 December 2003, T-219/99, ECR, EU:T:2003:343, para. 191.

796 Judgment of 17 December 2003, *British Airways v Commission* of 17 December 2003, T-219/99, ECR, EU:T:2003:343, para. 212.

797 Judgment of 17 December 2003, *British Airways v Commission* of 17 December 2003, T-219/99, ECR, EU:T:2003:343, para. 217 (emphasis added).

798 Judgment of 3 July 1991 in *AKZO v Commission*, C-62/86, EU:C:1991:286, para. 60.

an undertaking fits the hourglass shape, the competitive risks posed by buyer power are increased as the buyer exerts buyer and seller market power concomitantly, one reinforcing the other. An analysis of the case indicates that both the Commission and the Courts were concerned with the foreclosing effect that buyer power through fidelity-enhancing rebates had in the downstream market, in addition to the risks of anti-competitive effects among travel agents' competition. This connection between market power in the upstream and downstream markets was caused by the leveraging of it: if British Airways offered conditions to its travel agents that were so attractive, the travel agents were mainly going to sell airline tickets to end consumers of British Airways rather than those of its competitors. By British Airways being able to control this distribution channel of sales by capturing the supply of travel agency services to airlines, it was able to strengthen its dominance in the downstream market as an airline carrier.

400. However, should *British Airways v Commission* be interpreted as indicating that in buyer power cases dominance arises at lower market share thresholds than seller side cases? An analysis of the conduct illustrates that it fitted a rather unusual circumstance with a very specific market structure. Also, due to the lack of further case law reaffirming this position, it is difficult to conclude if this constitutes an isolated decision, whether buyer power dominance can be found on lower market share thresholds, or if other circumstances of the case, such as the stringent and formalistic approach the Courts have with regard to rebates had an influence in it.

401. In my view, a conservative approach to the finding of dominance at such low market share thresholds should be adopted, even if by doing so the Commission and the Courts recognized the likelihood and broader extent of the anti-competitive effects generated by an hourglass undertaking exerting buyer market power. The correct interpretation of this considerably low market share threshold has to be restrictive and not be applied to all seller cases or all buyer power cases. The 40% market share threshold applied in *British Airways v Commission* may in principle be a *reference for buyer power cases where the investigated undertaking also possesses substantial downstream market power*. In those cases in which a buyer does not possess substantial downstream market power, I argue that, in the absence of guidance from the case law, the contrast to other buyer power with very high market shares[799], and based on buyer power economics, finding a buyer to be dominant with a market share as low as 40% would lead to instances of over-enforcement, particularly concerning bargaining power.

799 Such is the example of *Irish Sugar v Commission*, where Irish Sugar was found to have abused its dominance as purchaser of water transport services by demanding its suppliers not offer sugar transportation services to its competitors. In this case, Irish Sugar enjoyed a very large market share in the Irish market for sugar, of 90% and 88% throughout the period of investigation. Commission Decision of 14 May 1997 relating to a proceeding pursuant to Article 86 of the EC Treaty (IV/34.621, 35.059/F-3 - *Irish Sugar plc*) [1997] OJ L 258/1, partially ratified by the General Court in Judgment of 7 October 1999, *Irish Sugar v Commission*, T-228/97, ECR, EU:T:1999:246.

402. This conservative approach to a lower dominance threshold as the rule of thumb for all buyer power cases appears also to be the Commission's view when arguing that its "experience suggests that dominance is not likely if the undertaking's market share is below 40% in the relevant market"[800].

403. Nevertheless, this approach regarding the finding of dominance and the application of competition law has been partially challenged by statutory national law provisions establishing *relative dominant positions* and, especially by recent modifications of national competition laws specifically designed to address an imbalance in the food retailing industry, as I discuss in further detail in chapter 8[801]. These national competition policy choices that trigger the application of dominance under low market share thresholds as allowed by Article 3.2 of the Regulation 1/2003 do not find support in the EU case law and are not followed by the majority of MS.

404. From a comparative perspective, the contrast with US antitrust law of adopting very low market share thresholds for finding absolute or relative dominance is striking; in the US the case law has clarified that cases of monopolization/ monopsonization can only arise if the market shares are around 70% but not below[802]. Thus based on a simple market share analysis approach, US antitrust law appears to focus on sanctioning monopsony practices while leaving most bargaining power issues (especially in instances of relative dominance) less attended by antitrust rules, whereas in EU competition law both bargaining power and monopsony power appear to be under a tighter scrutiny.

405. In addition to dominance thresholds, market shares are also used regarding the creation or strengthening of substantial buyer market power through concentrations that may significantly impede effective competition and the creation of buyer power through buyer agreements among undertakings.

406. Regarding concentration cases, the Commission's practice, particularly in the case of food-retailing, sheds some light on what proportion of the supplier's sales may be sufficient for a buyer to exercise *significant buyer power* that may lead to a significant impediment to competition and a situation of *economic dependence* for its supplier[803]. In this context, economic dependence of a supplier to a buyer does not necessarily imply that the buyer is dominant in the purchasing market. Dependence should be regarded as a relative concept

---

800 Communication from the Commission — Guidance on the Commission's enforcement priorities in applying Article 82 of the EC Treaty to abusive exclusionary conduct by dominant undertakings [2009] OJ C 45/7, para. 14.

801 For a detailed discussion of these lower thresholds applicable to the food retailing sector see chapter 8, section §VI.A.

802 *United States v. Alcoa*, 148 F.2d 416 (2nd Cir. 1945).

803 Economic dependence is discussed as a buyer market power assessment tool in chapter 5, section §IV.C.b and chapter 8.

that describes an asymmetrical relation between two parties where the economic viability of the dependent party is tied to the existence of the commercial relationship[804], whereas dominance is an objective concept that does not require a bilateral relation[805].

407. In *Rewe/Meinl*[806] *and Carrefour/Promodès*[807], these two concentration assessments regarding food retailing were declared compatible thanks to the submission of commitments that palliated the buyer-power related anti-competitive concerns[808]. In the case of *Carrefour/Promodès*, it was concluded that the merged undertaking, that would have had 25-35% of market share in the downstream market[809], could exercise upstream buyer power if it were able to reach a "threat point" [*taux de 'menace'*][810]. This threat point, calculated at 22% of the profits earned by a supplier pursuant to a series of sector and case specific surveys, was said to create a situation in which the supplier would be dependent on a buyer as the "loss of a customer (with that market share) would threaten the very existence of their business"[811]. The Commission concluded that, when a buyer exceeds such a threshold in the turnover of one of its suppliers, the latter is found to be in a de facto situation of "economic dependence"[812].

408. Importantly, and a factor that may easily be overlooked, is that this 22% does not represent the undertaking's market shares in the purchasing market but instead *represents the ratio of sales that a buyer signifies for a particular buyer*. However, this situation was not isolated concerning a single supplier of a single product (which qualifies as an individual market) but happened in at least ten of the markets affected by the merger[813]. In practice, this may imply that even a buyer with a small total purchasing market share may still have *relative*

---

804 European Commission '*Tackling Unfair Trading Practices in the Business-to-Business food supply chain*' (2014), p. 11.

805 Pera, p. 17; see also suggesting a similar idea but distinguishing between buyer power and bargaining power – which in reality is dependence: European Competition Network (2012), para. 73.

806 "The Commission asked producers above what proportion of turnover, with a given customer could not be switched to other sales channels without difficulty. It transpired that on average 22% of turnover is the say, of one branded goods producer who makes 'must figure above which a customer can be replaced only at carry'/products, as Rewe/Billa and Meinl risk losing the cost of very heavy financial losses, if at all", Commission Decision of 3 February 1999 relating to proceedings under Council Regulation (EEC) No 4064/89 (Case No IV/M.1221 - *Rewe/Meinl*) OJ L 274/1, para. 101.

807 Non-opposition to a notified concentration (Case COMP/M.1684 — *Carrefour/Promodès*) [2000] OJ C 164/5, French public version, paras. 52-55.

808 See also: discussing the buyer power aspects of these two cases: van Doorn, p. 163-164.

809 Non-opposition to a notified concentration (Case COMP/M.1684 — *Carrefour/Promodès*) [2000] OJ C 164/5, French public version, para. 60.

810 See also discussing the existence of this "*taux de menace*" for this case: Këllezi [2008], p. 82.

811 Non-opposition to a notified concentration (Case COMP/M.1684 — *Carrefour/Promodès*) [2000] OJ C 164/5, French public version, para. 52 (translation by the author); see also: mentioning this 22% threshold as part of the "threat point" theory Ezrachi and Ioannidou (2014), p. 81 and Këllezi [2008], p. 70-71, who link the threat point to dependence.

812 Non-opposition to a notified concentration (Case COMP/M.1684 — *Carrefour/Promodès*) [2000] OJ C 164/5, French public version, para. 52 (translation by the author); see also: supporting this, Doyle and Inderst (2007), p. 213.

813 van Doorn, p. 164.

buyer power vis-à-vis a particular supplier but not *general* buyer power. Yet and at least for concentration assessments, relative buyer power may be an issue that can, along with other circumstances, imply that the operation may not be compatible with the internal market.

409. In connection to food retailing and buyer market shares that may indicate substantial buyer market power vis-à-vis suppliers, the literature suggests even lower thresholds. For instance, Pera has suggested other indicative figures: if the shares are between 20% and 10%, buyers have a "strong negotiating power to retailers", and below 10% "there would not be an asymmetric situation"[814]. Also, in the UK the now extinct UK Competition Commission suggested adopting a supplier's turnover of only 8% to represent the threat point.[815] This 8% ceiling appears to be quite low and, as Dobson remarks, this threshold limit was chosen without the report providing any explanation[816].

410. In the US in an exceptional and much criticized case, an even stricter approach was applied also concerning a concentration in the food-retailing sector. In *United States v Von's Grocery Co*, the US Supreme Court held that a merger between two retailers who controlled only 7.5% of the food retailing market was a violation of §7 of the Clayton act, as the firms were the most successful in food retailing and were in a market characterized by the decline of the existence of small retailers and the significant absorption of small firms by larger ones[817]. The US Supreme Court based its findings on the fact that §7 of the Clayton act had "sought to preserve competition among small businesses by halting a trend toward concentration in its incipiency, and, thus, the courts must be alert to protect competition against increasing concentration through mergers especially where concentration is gaining momentum in the market" [818]. Therefore, even such low market shares were able to generate sufficient buyer power that can be used in an exclusionary way to the detriment of rival buyers. This decision, not surprisingly, has been subject to stern criticism as an example of excessive interventionism that characterized US antitrust law enforcement prior to the '1970s Revolution' and the influence of the Chicago School[819]. Because of the shift in antitrust enforcement priorities, the case is still good law as cas-

814 Pera.

815 UK Competition Commission (2000), paras. 2.588 to 2.596.

816 Dobson [2009], p. 119.

817 *United States v. Von's Grocery Co.*, 384 U.S. 270 (1966), p. 274-279.

818 *United States v. Von's Grocery Co.*, 384 U.S. 270 (1966), p. 276-277.

819 See for example the strong wording used by Justice Stewart when dissenting from the Judgment by the majority of the Court when holding that: "[t]he sole consistency that I can find is that, in litigation under § 7, the Government always wins" in Dissenting Opinion by Justice Stewart in *United States v. Von's Grocery Co.*, 384 U.S. 270 (1966), at 301. See also criticizing the decision from a buyer power perspective: Joshua Wright, 'Von's Grocery and the Concentration-Price Relationship in Grocery Retail' 48 UCLA Law Review (2001) 743; Richard Scheelings and Joshua D Wright, 'Sui Generis: An Antitrust Analysis of Buyer Power in the United States and European Union' 39 Akron Law Review (2006) 207; see also the opinion of Wright suggesting that this case is probably one of the "worst Antitrust decisions that is good law" in Joshua Wright, 'What is the Worst Antitrust Decision That is Good Law?' (2008) <http://truthonthemarket.com/2008/07/22/what-is-the-worst-antitrust-decision-that-is-good-law/>

es under such low thresholds are no longer prosecuted, as remarked by FTC Commissioner Wright[820]. However, and despite the shift, *Von's Grocery* shows that in buyer power merger assessments the creation of supplier's dependence (and buyer induced exclusion) raises competition concern on both sides of the Atlantic, despite the existence of low market shares as a buyer.

411. These suggested relative low thresholds for concentration cases derived from Commission's practice reinforce the proposition that substantial *relative* buyer market power (i.e. between one buyer and its supplier) may arise with lower market shares than when compared to seller power because of the special conditions of purchasing markets. I, however, am critical of suggesting that the Commissions' threshold of 22% should be used as a general presumption of expected anticompetitive effects in buyer concentration cases. There are several reasons for this. In none of them, the low market share threshold implied that the involved undertakings' concentration would lead to a significant impediment of effective competition; in fact the two merger cases, where 22% of supplier's profit from a single buyer was used as a reference were declared compatible pursuant commitments. Secondly, these decisions are connected to a narrow sector, food retailing, where the undertakings participating tend to have substantial market power both upstream and downstream market, fitting the hourglass description, and the sample is very small, with only two cases. Additionally, these are non-binding Commission Decisions neither ratified nor dismissed by the Courts. Furthermore, this ratio of 22% does not represent the undertaking's total market share in the purchasing market but just a ratio of sales-purchases between a buyer and a specific supplier; thus it is a relative measure of buyer power but not absolute. Lastly, adopting such threshold levels regardless of the upstream and downstream market competitive circumstances may lead to erroneous results. In other words, these thresholds have to be compared with the suppliers' own market shares and determine whether or not there is a disparity in the ratio of purchases-profit represented by a buyer to a seller.

412. This cautious approach to buyer market shares also has a basis in the EU case law. In *Cementbouw Handel & Industrie v Commission*, the General Court concluded that the proportion of sales a buyer represents taken as an isolated factor does not necessarily imply that the buyer has substantial (countervailing) buyer power even if this seller accrues on its own 20-30% of the seller's turnover. This absence of substantial (countervailing) buyer power was due to the existence of other buyers that "organised in buyer groups [were] capable of obtaining supplies in significant volumes, towards which CVK could if necessary steer its production"[821]. If a seller has other alternative buyers to turn to, the bargaining power of its current customers is reduced and therefore there is no dependence among the parties.

413. Lastly, *concerning agreements among buying undertakings*, the Commission in its

820 Wright, 'What is the Worst Antitrust Decision That is Good Law?'.

821 Judgment of 23 February 2006, *Cementbouw Handel & Industrie v Commission,* T-282/02, ECR, EU:T:2006:64, para. 233.

Guidelines on Horizontal Co-Operation Agreements has also established a dual market share threshold that acts as an *iuris tantum* presumption that the parties to the agreement lack substantial anti-competitive buyer market power. Also, and unlike the food retailing cases, the market shares are considered in relation to the general markets and not the *relative* buyer power between the purchasing parties and a single supplier.

414. According to the Guidelines on Horizontal Co-Operation Agreements, if the parties to the agreement have a combined market share threshold not exceeding 15% on the purchasing market, as well as a combined market share not exceeding 15% on the selling market (or markets), it is unlikely that substantial buyer market power exists and also, even if it does, it is also likely that the conditions for the application of Article 101(3) TFEU will be met[822]; i.e.: the purchasing agreement is an example of efficient bargaining power. If one of the market shares thresholds is above 15%, the Commission's view is that this "does not automatically indicate that the joint purchasing arrangement is likely to give rise to restrictive effects on competition"[823]; instead a case-by-case assessment ought to be made[824].

415. Recapitulating the use of market shares as buyer power threshold indicators, the case law and Commission' practice reveals that in buyer power cases the dualistic approach has been followed on occasions as the market shares are computed in the upstream and downstream markets, albeit with lack of full consistency regarding this practice. Also, it confirms that substantial buyer power may arise even if the market share is relatively low in comparison to seller-side cases (i.e. below 30% of the sales of its supplier)[825]. In the particular situation of dominance, the case law indicates that a buying undertaking may abuse its dominance as a buyer if its market share threshold is above 39.7%. As I discussed, I do not think this conclusion should be the same for seller side cases nor buyer power in general, and that is why the interpretation of *British Airways v Commission* must be restrictive. Regarding concentrations, the Commission has taken into account in its assessment as indication of anticompetitive effects the existence of substantial relative market power

---

822 Communication from the Commission — Guidelines on the applicability of Article 101 of the Treaty on the Functioning of the European Union to horizontal co-operation agreements [2011] OJ C 11/1, para. 208; see also suggesting the adoption of a 15% threshold for the safeguarding of buyer alliances in US antitrust law Carstensen 'Buyer Cartels Versus Buying Groups: Legal Distinctions, Competitive Realities, and Antitrust Policy' (2010), p. 44.

823 Communication from the Commission — Guidelines on the applicability of Article 101 of the Treaty on the Functioning of the European Union to horizontal co-operation agreements [2011] OJ C 11/1, para. 209.

824 In contrast, in US antitrust law, with respect to joint purchasing arrangements among health care providers, it is suggested that a much higher threshold is adopted when stating that the "Agencies will not challenge, absent extraordinary circumstances, any joint purchasing arrangement among health care providers where two conditions are present: (1) the purchases account for less than 35 percent of the total sales of the purchased product or service in the relevant market; and (2) the cost of the products and services purchased jointly accounts for less than 20 percent of the total revenues from all products or services sold by each competing participant in the joint purchasing arrangement", US Department of Justice and Federal Trade Commission *Statements of Antitrust Enforcement Policy in Health Care*, Washington D.C. (1996). For a critical view of this threshold see: Carstensen 'Buyer Cartels Versus Buying Groups: Legal Distinctions, Competitive Realities, and Antitrust Policy' (2010).

825 Pera, p. 14.

based on the 'threat point' benchmark but, ultimately, cleared the operations pursuant commitments. Finally, and as remarked by Doyle and Inderst, when determining the *prima facie* existence of buyer power through market shares thresholds *"this should not be done in isolation from the potential theory of harm that would be (subsequently) applied"*[826]; otherwise the use of isolated thresholds may lead to incorrect results.

c. *Market share valuation*

416. Once the market shares have been calculated it is necessary to interpret them. As held in *Hoffmann-La Roche v Commission*, the valuation of market shares is one of the most important factors when assessing the market power of an undertaking[827]. Market share valuation is a dynamic exercise that shall be made on a case-by-case basis and its importance varies from market to market, in according to the structure of these, as well as whether they have been held for some time by the same undertaking[828]. Echoing this, the Commission has stated that the valuation of market shares shall be made "in the light of the *relevant market conditions*, and in particular of the *dynamics of the market* and of the extent to which products are differentiated"[829].

417. For buyer power cases, this entails that the assessment of market shares ought to incorporate the specific buying market dynamics and conditions to fully capture buyer power effects in the upstream and downstream markets and as discussed *supra*[830]. Hence, a case-by-case approach to value market shares should be adopted by competition authorities by factoring the sources of buyer market power, market conditions and the size of the markets shares, and not purely using threshold indicators. Also, I suggest that the valuation should compare the buyer's market shares with its competitors and suppliers in the upstream and downstream markets[831], as a buying undertaking is more likely

---

826 Doyle and Inderst (2007), p. 215 (italics in the original).

827 Judgment of 13 February 1979 in *Hoffmann-La Roche v Commission*, C-85/76, EU:C:1979:36, para. 39 *in fine*.

828 Judgment of 13 February 1979 in *Hoffmann-La Roche v Commission*, C-85/76, EU:C:1979:36, paras. 40-41; see also: in this same line American Bar Association, *Market Power Handbook: Competition Law and Economic Foundations* [2012], p. 104-105.

829 Communication from the Commission — Guidance on the Commission's enforcement priorities in applying Article 82 of the EC Treaty to abusive exclusionary conduct by dominant undertakings [2009] OJ C 45/7, para. 14 (emphasis added); see also the work of Chen when stating that "[a] large retailer may not be able to obtain below-normal prices from a supplier if it has to compete aggressively against other retailers for the supplier's products. The key to the existence of buyer power, therefore, is not the relative size, but whether there is vigorous competition, either actual or potential, for the supplier's products", in Chen 'Buyer Power: Economic Theory and Antitrust Policy' (2007), p. 30.

830 Also of this opinion is Kokkoris, who states that: "[b]uyer concentration can provide an indication of the buyer power, but cannot be definitive. The structure of the buyer and the seller markets must also be taken into account", in Kokkoris (2006), p. 148.

831 European Commission DG Competition *Discussion Paper on the Application of Article 82 of the Treaty to Exclusionary Abuses*, Brussels (2005), para. 31; see: the opinion of Monti who openly criticizes the interpretation of the Commission of the case law by narrowing exceptional circumstances to the market shares of rivals in Monti 'The Concept of Dominance in Article 82' (2006), p. 49.

to be dominant if its suppliers and competitors are relatively weak[832]. By doing so, and contrasting the market shares and welfare effects in both markets, all buyer power effects are taken into consideration, as advocated by the dualistic approach. Additionally, I propose that when assessing the markets shares of the investigated buying undertaking, in addition a valuation of the relative selling power of suppliers in the upstream market should also be taken into account. If suppliers are relatively powerless, there is further evidence of the existence of buyer power.

B. Market concentration

418. Another widely used market power assessment tool are the indexes of market concentration[833]. They offer information concerning the relative size and strength of the market participants helping determining the extent of an undertaking's market power[834]. Market concentration is directly linked to market shares as it is calculated by the sum of the squares of the market share of the undertakings that purchase or sell a good in the relevant market, thus giving proportionately greater weight to the larger market share[835], in accordance to the Herfindahl-Hirschman Index (HHI)[836]. The HHI is obtained by summing the squares of the individual market shares of all firms included in the formula and expressed as HHI =

$$\sum_{i=1}^{N} s_i^2 .$$

419. Market concentration measures how concentrated a market is, which is particularly useful when assessing the compatibility of a proposed merger[837] because it allows determination of the likelihood of coordinated (tacitly or ex-

832 Office of Fair Trading (2004), p. 7.

833 See also briefly analyzing buyer concentration as a measure to determine the extent of buyer power: Faull and Nikpay, [1999], paras. 6.315-6.316.

834 Hovenkamp, [2005], p. 518; Niels, Jenkins and Kavanagh, [2011], p. 128.

835 Janusz A. Ordover and Robert D. Willig, 'The 1982 Department of Justice Merger Guidelines: An Economic Assessment' 71 California Law Review (1983) 535; U.S. Department of Justice and Federal Trade Commission, Horizontal Merger Guidelines [2010], para. 18.

836 Guidelines on the assessment of horizontal mergers under the Council Regulation on the control of concentrations between undertakings [2004] OJ C 31/5, para. 16; see also: Gavil, Kovacic and Baker, [2008], p. 500-501.

837 Different market concentrations ranges have been proposed by NCAs for concentration assessment using the HHI index. For example the US HMG consider a market unconcentrated when the HHI is below 1,500; the market will be moderately concentrated markets if the HHI is between 1,500 and 2,500, and lastly the market will be highly concentrated if the HHI is above 2,500. The equivalent thresholds are slightly lower in the EU: i) concentrations below 1,000 HHI do not merit extensive analysis (unconcentrated markets); ii) it is unlikely to identify horizontal competition concerns in a merger with a post-merger HHI between 1,000 and 2,000 and a delta below 250, or a merger with a post-merger HHI above 2,000 and a delta below 150 (moderately concentrated markets). Despite the fact that neither the Notice on Market Definition nor the Guidance Notice on Article 102 TFEU make explicit references to market concentration, this parameter is used in the analysis of dominance cases as well in this study; see also: Cook and Kerse, [2009], p. 236.

plicitly) behaviour[838]. The rationale is that, the more concentrated the market, the easier it will be for firms to coordinate their behaviour and reap monopoly/monopsony profits[839]. In dominance cases, on the other hand, an elevated market concentration may indicate the existence of a dominant position or the possibility of a collective dominant position[840].

420. However, market concentration does not indicate whether or not the market is competitive[841], even if concentration levels are high, as noted by Hyman and Kovacic[842]. Non-coordinated oligopsonist markets may be fiercely competitive if the leading undertakings are of equivalent size and equally efficient[843]. However, when one firm is much larger than the others, this is likely to be conducive to 'price leadership' as noted by Hovenkamp[844]. For buyer power cases, nevertheless, it seems unlikely that a phenomenon such as purchasing price leadership may arise, as this would imply that the large buyer must pay a lower price for the input. Were this to happen then the smaller buyers, in paying slightly more, would deprive the larger buyer of the input.

421. In EU competition law, market concentration indexes have been seldom employed. Yet, the General Court found them to be of use in helping determine the existence of substantial buyer power, as held in *Cementbouw Handel & Industrie v Commission*, where it stated that the "degree of concentration of buyers on the market means that their limited number may be capable of reinforcing their bargaining power vis-à-vis the supplier"[845]. Lastly, a factor that should be taken into account for buyer power cases when evaluating market concentration is that, even in relatively unconcentrated markets, it may

---

838 Oinonen, [2010], p. 158; also this is the opinion of Kokkoris and Shelanski regarding buyers' markets in Kokkoris and Shelanski, [2014], p. 427.

839 Oinonen, [2010], p. 158-159.

840 The topic of collective dominance and its regulation by means of either or Article 102 TFEU or the EU Merger Control Regulation is one of the most controversial aspects of EU competition law and plenty of literature abounds in this field of the law. For further reading see, *inter alia*: Barry J. Rodger, 'The Oligopoly Problem and the Concept of Collective Dominance: EC Developments in the Light of U.S. Trends in Antitrust Law and Policy' 2 Columbia Journal of European Law (1995-1996) 25; Giorgio Monti, 'The Scope of Collective Dominance under Article 82 EC' 38 Common Market Law Review (2001) 131; Warren S Grimes, 'The Sherman Act's Unintended Bias Against Lilliputians: Small Players' Collective Action as a Counter to Relational Market Power' 69 Antitrust Law Journal (2001), 195; Sigrid Stroux, 'Collective Dominance under the Merger Regulation: A Serious Evidentiary Reprimand for the Commission' 27 European Law Review (2002) 736; Dehtmers (2005); Simon Baxter and Frances Dethmers, 'Collective Dominance under EC Merger Control - After Airtours and the Introduction of Unilateral Effects is there Still a Future for Collective Dominance?' 27 European Competition Law Review (2006) 148; Nicolas Petit, *Oligopoles, Collusion Tacite et Droit Communautaire de la Concurrence* (Bruylant 2008); Ronny Gjendemsjø, *Oligopolproblemet: Om Anvendelsen av TFEU Artikkel 101 og 102 på Koordinerte Priser i et Oligopol* (Universitetet i Bergen 2011); Elhauge and Geradin, [2011], p. 960-981; Nazzini, [2011], p. 359-388; Whish and Bailey, [2015], p. 607-618.

841 Bishop and Walker, [2010], p. 70.

842 Hyman and Kovacic (2004), p. 26.

843 Hovenkamp, [2005], p. 518; see also the criticism to the value of market concentration measures in Gavil, Kovacic and Baker, [2008] p. 505-506.

844 Hovenkamp's proposition is made with a selling undertaking in mind, rather than a buyer undertaking, in Hovenkamp, [2005], p. 518.

845 Judgment of 23 February 2006, *Cementbouw Handel & Industrie v Commission*, T-282/02, ECR, EU:T:2006:64, para. 232.

be possible to exercise bargaining power (although arguably not monopsony power).

C. Unavoidable trading partner and dependence

422. Two of the most important buyer market power measurement tools are the *concepts of unavoidable trading partner* and *dependence*. By and large, if a buyer constitutes an unavoidable trading party for its suppliers then the latter will be in a situation where their economic viability depends on maintaining the buyer as a client, even if the competitive conditions are not particularly profitable. In the absence of any contractual relation to that buyer, the supplier will have to leave the market in the long run[846]. In this section, I discuss these two assessment tools from a buyer-oriented perspective. This discussion sets the background for the last two tools with which to measure buyer market power: gate-keeping and alternative supply sources, which are intrinsically related to the doctrines covered here.

a. *Unavoidable trading partner*

423. The doctrine of an unavoidable trading partner, established by the CJEU in *Hoffmann-La Roche v Commission*, has played a particularly relevant role in the assessment of buyer market power[847]. The CJEU defined that an undertaking is an unavoidable trading partner when it "has a very large market share and has held it for some time"[848]. When an undertaking is an unavoidable trading partner, at least from a seller-perspective, customers are forced to obtain part of their demand from the dominant undertaking. Thus, suppliers of an unavoidable trading partner may also be dependent on it because they are forced to sell to it[849]. However, the unavoidable trading partner doctrine, in contrast with the dependence doctrine, is an *erga omnes* and objective privileged position. In other words, when an undertaking is an unavoidable trading partner it is vis-à-vis the generality of its suppliers and customers, unlike the case of dependence, which is a relative concept.

---

846 Cf with the view that "[a]t most, the consideration that a company may be an 'unavoidable trading partner' will assist the Commission in identifying the relevant parameters – outside market shares – that are relevant for a finding of dominance in the particular industry under examination (e.g., barriers to entry linked to a must stock brand, barriers to entry raised by the control of essential assets, etc.), i.e. the factors that make customers dependent upon the allegedly dominant player", Damien Geradin and others, *The Concept of Dominance in EC Competition Law* (College of Europe 2005), p. 13-14.

847 Judgment of 13 February 1979 in *Hoffmann-La Roche v Commission*, C-85/76, EU:C:1979:36, para. 41. Ratified more recently in Judgment of 12 June 2014, *Intel v Commission*, T-286/09, ECR, EU:T:2014:547, paras. 91-93.

848 Judgment of 16 March 2000 in *Compagnie Maritime Belge Transports and Others v Commission*, C-395/96 P, EU:C:2000:132, para. 132.

849 Këllezi [2008], p. 75.

424. Being an unavoidable trading partner grants the undertaking a "non-contestable" share, against which competitors are not able to "compete for the full supply of a customer, but only for the portion of the demand exceeding the non-contestable share", as recently confirmed by the General Court in *Intel v Commission*[850]. This is, "the portion of a customer's requirements which can realistically be switched to an undertaking's competitor in a dominant position in any given period".[851] Therefore, unavoidable trading partners have a freedom of action that is akin to, or even greater than, that of a dominant undertaking[852].

425. In order to determine if an undertaking is an unavoidable trading partner, Advocate General Kokott has remarked that is necessary to carry out a market shares comparison of said undertaking with other market participants either *in the upstream and downstream market*[853], an opinion which is in line with the dualistic approach to buyer market power. In addition to this, I submit that, from a buyer power perspective, the analysis must determine whether suppliers are dependent on the buyer *because* it constitutes an unavoidable trading partner[854], which implies that suppliers are willing to concede better terms to the buyer in order to retain the opportunity to sell to it owing to buyer's significance to the supplier[855]. Such a position of an unavoidable buying trading partner might be earned as a result of advertising, marketing and/or product differentiation, having a 'must stock' product,[856] or being a necessary distribution mechanism to reach end consumers.

---

850 Judgment of 12 June 2014, *Intel v Commission*, T-286/09, ECR, EU:T:2014:547, para. 92. According to Jessen, an unavoidable trading partner has been found in most of the relevant rebate cases: Anders Fløjstrup Jessen, *The Effect-Based Approach to Rebates: Is the Theory of Raising Rival's Costs the Answer?* (2015), p. 13; see also: Joshua D. Wright, 'Simple but Wrong or Complex but More Accurate? The Case for an Exclusive Dealing-Based Approach to Evaluating Loyalty Discounts' (Bates White's 10th Annual Antitrust Conference).

851 Judgment of 12 June 2014, *Intel v Commission*, T-286/09, ECR, EU:T:2014:547, para. 92.

852 "Very large market shares are in themselves, and save in exceptional circumstances, evidence of the existence of a dominant position. An undertaking which has a very large market share and holds it for some time, by means of the volume of production and the scale of the supply which it stands for – without those having much smaller market shares being able to meet rapidly the demand from those who would like to break away from the undertaking which has the largest market share – is by virtue of that share in a position of strength which makes it an unavoidable trading partner and which, because of this alone, secures for it, at the very least during relatively long periods, that freedom of action which is the special feature of a dominant position", Judgment of 25 June 2010, *Imperial Chemical Industries v Commission*, T-66/01, ECR, EU:T:2010:255, para. 265. An identical and previous formulation is found in Judgment of 17 December 2009, *Solvay v Commission*, T-57/01, ECR, EU:T:2009:519, para. 277.

853 "Because of its much higher market share, a dominant undertaking is normally, so far as *other market participants* are concerned, an unavoidable trading partner", Opinion of Advocate General Kokott of 23 February 2006 in Judgment of 15 March 2007 in *British Airways v Commission*, C-95/04 P, EU:C:2006:133, para. 52.

854 Commission Decision of 14 July 1999 relating to a proceeding under Article 82 of the EC Treaty (IV/D-2/34.780 - *Virgin/British Airways*) [2000] OJ L 30/1, para. 32. Also commenting on this aspect of the case, see: Këllezi [2008], p. 78-79.

855 Office of Fair Trading *Assessment of Market Power: Understanding Competition Law*, London (2004), p. 24; see also: Doyle and Inderst (2007), p. 213; International Competition Network *Unilateral Conduct Workbook Chapter 3: Assessment Of Dominance* The Hague, Netherlands (2011), para. 106.

856 Summary of Commission Decision of 13 May 2009 relating to a proceeding under Article 82 of the EC Treaty and Article 54 of the EEA Agreement (Case COMP/C-3/37.990 — Intel) [2009] OJ C 227/13.

426. If a buying undertaking is an unavoidable trading partner, its suppliers will also be dependent on it[857]. The reverse also holds true, if the supplier is the unavoidable trading partner then the buyer loses its relative bargaining power. This was the case in *GE/Honeywell*, where the Commission considered that the exercise of buyer power vis-à-vis a dominant seller was limited by the imbalance in the commercial relationship because GE was an unavoidable trading partner[858]. The same was point raised in *Syniverse/Mach*, where the merged entity would become an *unavoidable trading partner* making it "unlikely that customers can resist its attempts to increase prices or decrease quality in NRTRDE"[859], rendering the exercise of countervailing buyer power insufficient. This merger was ultimately declared compatible due to the divestiture of essentially the entirety of Mach's DC and NRTRDE businesses. Recently, in *Intel* the Commission argued that as Intel was a necessary trading partner and its argumentation of countervailing buyer power "ignores the fundamental element in its relationship with OEMs, namely the fact that it is an unavoidable trading partner for them: OEMs depend on Intel for what is the most important single hardware component in their computers. As such, Intel is a must-stock brand"[860]. Thus, buyers were not able to neutralize the behaviour of Intel as they were dependent on it and they lacked buyer power[861].

427. Thus, the fact that a buyer is an unavoidable trading partner will confer upon it substantial buyer power vis-à-vis all suppliers. Also if a supplier is an unavoidable trading partner then the buyers will see their ability to exercise buyer power curtailed.

b. Dependence

428. Dependence is another assessment tool employed to determine whether a buyer enjoys substantial buyer power *vis-à-vis a particular supplier*. Consequently, the state of dependence is a *relative* concept as a supplier may be dependent regard-

857 Also considering that an unavoidable trading partner creates vertical dependence see: Jan Bernd Nordemann, 'Buying Power and Sophisticated Buyers in Merger Control Law: The Need for a More Sophisticated Approach' 16 European Competition Law Review (1995) 270, p. 273; see in respect to merger cases: Ulrich Schwalbe and Daniel Zimmer, *Law and Economics in European Merger Control* (Oxford University Press 2009), p. 154.

858 Commission Decision of 3 July 2001 declaring a concentration to be incompatible with the common market and the EEA Agreement Case COMP/M.2220 — *General Electric/Honeywell* [2004] OJ L 48/1, para. 227. See the commentary of the case by Ezrachi and Ioannidou (2014), p. 91-92.

859 Summary of Commission Decision of 29 May 2013 declaring a concentration compatible with the internal market and the functioning of the EEA Agreement (Case COMP/M.6690 — *Syniverse/Mach*) [2014] OJ C 60/7, para. 54.

860 Summary of Commission Decision of 13 May 2009 relating to a proceeding under Article 82 of the EC Treaty and Article 54 of the EEA Agreement (Case COMP/C-3/37.990 — *Intel*) [2009] OJ C 227/13, taken from the unabridged version, para. 886.

861 Summary of Commission Decision of 13 May 2009 relating to a proceeding under Article 82 of the EC Treaty and Article 54 of the EEA Agreement (Case COMP/C-3/37.990 — *Intel*) [2009] OJ C 227/13, taken from the unabridged version, para. 894. See criticizing the argumentation by the commission Cook and Patel, [2013] para 2.83.

ing a buyer (or group of joint buyers), albeit not necessarily to others[862]. For the market power assessment, dependence is an important factor because its existence reveals the ability of a buyer to obtain better terms and conditions from a supplier. Therefore, its existence is a source of buyer market power and it can help in determining how large or important it is with respect to a single supplier: *the more dependent a supplier or a group of them, the more buyer market power an undertaking has*. Also, and as I discuss in greater detail in chapter 8, dependence is not only an indicator or measurement tool of buyer market power, but a problem in itself that can be exploited by imposing 'unfair purchasing conditions'[863].

429. A supplier may be in a state of dependence with respect to its buyer (or vice versa), which grants the non-dependent party the ability to exercise substantial bargaining power with regard to the other. In that sense, dependence is also relative because its degree of intensity varies from relation to relation, as confirmed in *Kesko/Tuko*[864].

430. In the case of buyer power, as described by Galbraith, dependence puts "the seller in a state of uncertainty as to the intentions of a buyer who is indispensable to him"[865]. Therefore, its existence will be a strong indicator of substantial bargaining power and, consequently, its assessment is one of the most relevant elements to consider when measuring the degree of buyer power enjoyed by an undertaking, as noted by Këllezi[866].

431. An example may illustrate the concept: if a provider of sugar cane in a MS sells 85% of its sugar production to a single processing undertaking with very large market shares as a seller in the downstream market, the fact that this buyer threatens to switch to alternative suppliers or simply stop buying sugar may lead to the supplier's financial failure[867].

---

862 Also supporting the notion that dependence is a relative concept in opposition to dominance see: Bundeskartellamt '*Buyer Power in Competition Law - Status and Perspectives*' (2008), p. 6; using the term "relative economic dependence"; see: Oinonen (2014). See also discussing dependence and buyer power: Ioannis Lianos and Claudio Lombardi, *Superior Bargaining Power and the Global Food Value Chain. The Wuthering Heights of Holistic Competition Law?* (2016), p. 21-24.

863 See also raising this point: Këllezi [2008], p. 55.

864 Commission Decision of 20 November 1996 declaring a concentration to be incompatible with the common market (Case No IV/M.784 - *Kesko/Tuko*) Council Regulation (EEC) No 4064/89 [1997] OJ L 110/53, taken from the unabridged version, para. 150. See also: Ezrachi and Ioannidou (2014), p. 79.

865 Galbraith, [2010], p. 108.

866 Këllezi [2008], p. 78-79 and 82.

867 This example is loosely model on Judgment of 10 July 2001 in *Irish Sugar v Commission*, C-497/99 P, EU:C:2001:393. Also stressing that losing a contract may imply the loss of financial viability, Dobson and Inderst (2008), p. 340.

432. Furthermore, dependence rises among buyers and sellers, and sellers and buyers, as illustrated in *IMS Health*[868], and *JCI/FIAMM*, where buyers were dependent on the supply of batteries but the suppliers were not dependent on these purchases, as this sub-market accounted for only a third of the total turnover of the battery business[869]. Nevertheless, dependent buyers are less frequent because in buying markets the supplier is generally far more dependent on its customers than vice versa[870].

433. Importantly, dependence *may exist even if an undertaking is not dominant and/or not an unavoidable trading partner*, nor that a concentration would necessarily lead to a significant impediment of effective competition[871], as confirmed in the merger cases *Rewe/Meinl,* and *Carrefour/Promodès,* where the Commission approved the concentrations followed by the submission of commitments that alleviated the competitive risks posed by the operation, despite the existence of buyer dependence that was said to exist based on the 'threat point' of 22%[872]. The commitments addressed the buyer dependence

868 "[...] account must be taken of the fact that a high level of participation by the pharmaceutical laboratories in the improvement of the 1 860 brick structure protected by copyright, on the supposition that it is proven, *has created a dependency by users* in regard to that structure, particularly at a technical level. In such circumstances, it is likely that those laboratories would have to make exceptional organisational and financial efforts in order to acquire the studies on regional sales of pharmaceutical products presented on the basis of a structure other than that protected by the intellectual property right. The supplier of that alternative structure might therefore be obliged to offer terms which are such as to rule out any economic viability of business on a scale comparable to that of the undertaking which controls the protected structure", Judgment of 29 April 2004 in *IMS Health, C*-418/01, EU:C:2004:257, para. 29 (emphasis added).

869 Summary of Commission Decision of 10 May 2007 declaring a concentration compatible with the common market and the functioning of the EEA Agreement (Case COMP/M.4381 — *JCI/FIAMM*) [2009] OJ C 241/12; taken from the unabridged version, paras. 407-413. This degree of dependence was satisfied in the Commission's view for example by recourse to the threats made by one of the parties to FIAT, one of its battery buyers, of stop deliveries if the higher purchasing prices were not accepted.

870 Dobson (2004-2005), p. 531.

871 Cf with Këllezi who argues that in dominance cases "the central point was nevertheless the examination of the economic dependence of a number of suppliers, which affirms the importance of the analysis of the bilateral relationships between the new entity and its customers: in merger control, a dominant position can be found if the new entity will be capable of behaving independently of its customers, even if it cannot be held capable of ignoring its competitors but only enjoys a more comfortable position than they do. The Commission's approach, finally, shows that under 'exceptional circumstances', – the most important of which is the presence of economically dependent customers – even (very) low market shares may indicate the existence of a dominant position", in Këllezi [2008], p. 82.

872 "Lors de son enquête, la Commission a demandé aux fournisseurs d'indiquer à partir de quel pourcentage de leur chiffre d'affaires ils considéraient que la perte d'un client représenterait une menace pour l'existence même de leur entreprise. La moyenne des réponses obtenues fait apparaître un seuil de 22%. Ce seuil de 22% avait été également retenu dans l'affaire Rewe/Meinl18. Il convient de noter que les réponses recueillies auprès des fournisseurs font apparaître des différences selon les groupes de produits considérés. Par exemple, en moyenne, les fournisseurs du groupe 'liquides' ont ainsi indiqué que la perte d'un client représentant plus de 24% de leur chiffre d'affaires risquait de mettre en péril la survie de leur entreprise. Pour les fournisseurs d'épicerie sèche, ce taux de menace se situe aux alentours de 22%. D'une manière générale, les taux mentionnés par les fournisseurs se situent aux alentours de 20-22%. Les données obtenues de l'enquête doivent bien évidemment être nuancées (pour certains groupes de produits, le nombre de réponses obtenues est en effet trop faible pour constituer un échantillon représentatif). A priori, on pourrait en déduire que lorsqu'un distributeur dépasse un tel seuil dans le chiffre d'affaire d'un de ses fournisseurs, ce dernier se retrouve de facto en situation de 'dépendance économique'", in Non-opposition to a notified concentration (Case COMP/M.1684 — *Carrefour/Promodès*) [2000] OJ C 164/5, French public version, para. 52; see also: Commission Decision of 3 February 1999 relating to proceedings under Council Regulation (EEC) No 4064/89 (Case No IV/M.1221 - *Rewe/Meinl*) OJ L 274/1, para. 101, where it was held that "[t] he Commission asked producers above what proportion of turnover, with a given customer could not be switched to other sales channels without difficulty. It transpired that on average 22% of turnover is the say, of one branded goods producer who makes 'must figure above which a customer can be replaced only at carry'/products, as Rewe/Billa and Meinl risk losing the cost of very heavy financial losses, if at all." See suggesting this threshold: College of Europe and Centre for European Policy Studies (2012), p. 62.

indirectly as it was ordered to divest some stores that represented alternative buyers for the suppliers who would have been less dependent on the single entity. Nevertheless, the existence of dependence has been said to pose sufficient anticompetitive risks to block a merger among buyers only when the supplier depended on at least 50% of its profit from a single buyer, as it occurred in *Kesko/Tuko*[873] which I discuss in detail in chapter 8, section §IV.C.

434. The issue, then, is determining how and why dependence takes place. There are several factors to take into account and which may vary from case to case[874]. The main factor is the proportion a buyer represents for a seller. The larger the proportion a buyer represents for the total sales of a seller (and in accordance its profitability), the more powerful the buyer becomes[875], as confirmed by the case law in *Cementbouw Handel & Industrie v Commission*[876]. With regard to the proportion of sales or a buyer's importance to a supplier, dependence measures the relative economic harm that each party will suffer in the event that there is failure to reach an agreement[877]. As expressed in *KE KELIT v Commission* "the bonds of economic dependence existing between participants in an agreement is [sic] liable to affect their freedom of initiative and decision, the existence of those bonds does not make it impossible to refuse to consent to the agreement which is proposed to them"[878]. The more dependent a party is on another, the more it will be willing to cede part of its profits to secure the contract[879]. For this reason, the financial capacity of both undertakings plays a role that ought to be assessed by competition authorities[880].

---

873 The Commission considered that the concentration would create an entity with too high a degree of buyer power creating a dependency of suppliers to the buyer, and also imposing too high entry barriers for potential competition. Commission Decision of 20 November 1996 declaring a concentration to be incompatible with the common market (Case No IV/M.784 - *Kesko/Tuko*) Council Regulation (EEC) No 4064/89 [1997] OJ L 110/53, taken from the unabridged version.

874 See for example under French Law that dependence – which also requires a degree of dominance – is triggered under four accumulative conditions: notoriety of the brand, ratio of sales, importance of the buyer's market share in the market and lack of business partner alternatives as discussed by Nollet in Luce Nollet, 'France: Anti-Competitive Practices' 24 European Competition Law Review (2003) N116, and in length in chapter 8, section §VI.C.

875 Carstensen 'Buyer Cartels Versus Buying Groups: Legal Distinctions, Competitive Realities, and Antitrust Policy' (2010), p. 30.

876 Judgment of 23 February 2006, *Cementbouw Handel & Industrie v Commission*, T-282/02, ECR, EU:T:2006:64, para. 233; Doyle and Inderst (2007), p. 213; OECD '*Policy Roundtables: Monopsony and Buyer Power*' (2009), p. 40; Carstensen 'Buyer Cartels Versus Buying Groups: Legal Distinctions, Competitive Realities, and Antitrust Policy' (2010), p. 30.

877 Dobson (2004-2005), p. 533.

878 Judgment of 20 March 2002, *KE KELIT v Commission*, T-17/99, ECR, EU:T:2002:73, para. 48. See discussing dependence between a parent company and its subsidiary: Judgment of 12 July 1979 in *BMW Belgium v Commission*, C-32/78, EU:C:1979:191, para. 36. Also clarifying that dependence is not a valid argument to claim that an undertaking was to be involved in a cartel see: Judgment of 27 September 2012, *Ballast Nedam Infra v Commission*, T-362/06, ECR, EU:T:2012:492, para. 104.

879 See also supporting this the Opinion of Advocate General Tesauro of 16 June 1994 in Judgment of 15 December 1994 in *Gøttrup-Klim and Others Grovvareforeninger v Dansk Landbrugs Grovvareselskab*, C-250/92, EU:C:1994:249 [1994], section 18, I – 5658. Similarly, see: Alla Pozdnakova, 'Buyer Power in the Retail Trading Sector: Evolving Latvian Regulation' 30 European Competition Law Review (2009) 387.

880 Kokkoris and Day (2009), p. 187.

435. Also, dependence can be measured in terms of the innovation and adjustments costs that a supplier has entered into to satisfy the specific needs of a buyer, which may not be useful for other parties, or where there may be no other buyers, as remarked by Lianos and Lombardi and the former UK Office of Fair Trading[881].

436. Other factors to consider regarding the existence and extent of dependence are the existence of exclusive supply agreements, charging structures that are not obviously related to the cost structure of the goods specified[882], the lack of substitutes for the supplier[883] or if other supply sources are eliminated[884], the fact that supplier owns well-known brands or 'must stock' products as remarked in *Nestlé/Perrier*[885], the contractual relation length as stressed in *Enso/Stora*[886], or when the buyer is a necessary trading partner because of its privileged position upstream and downstream, as discussed in by the Commission in *Virgin/British Airways* and ratified by the General Court[887].

437. However, a state of dependence or *'rapport captif'* does not necessarily imply, at least in the case of a cartel member, that the supplier is not able to allocate their products to a different buyer, in accordance to *Car Glass*[888]. This means that the degree of dependence is reduced or negated by entering into a collusive outcome with the aim to "circumvent their customers by colluding" with other suppliers[889]. Thus, dependent suppliers will be incentivized to either enter into a selling alliance or forming a cartel to reduce their dependence and create opposing seller bargaining countervailing power against a powerful buyer, a topic that I discuss in chapter 2, which is discussed in the US antitrust by Kirkwood[890].

---

881 Lianos and Lombardi, p. 22. See also: Office of Fair Trading, *The Competitive Effects of Buyer Groups*, para. 7.6.

882 European Commission and others (2000), 19; Kokkoris and Day (2009), p. 179.

883 As decided in a French National case *Décision n° 05-D-44 du 21 juillet 2005 relative à des pratiques mises en œuvre par le groupe La Provence (anciennement dénommé Le Provençal) dans le secteur de la publicité dans la presse quotidienne régionale à Marseille,* Autorité de la Concurrence, para. 24, available at: http://www.autoritedelaconcurrence.fr/pdf/avis/05d44.pdf.

884 Commission Decision of 22 July 1992 relating to a proceeding under Council Regulation (EEC) No 4064/89 (Case No IV/M.190 - *Nestlé/Perrier*) [1992] OJ L 356/1, para. 89. German Federal Court, *Rossignol* [1975], BGH NJW 1976, 801, translation in English available at: https://law.utexas.edu/transnational/foreign-law-translations/german/case.php?id=1488.

885 Commission Decision of 22 July 1992 relating to a proceeding under Council Regulation (EEC) No 4064/89 (Case No IV/M.190 - *Nestlé/Perrier*) [1992] OJ L 356/1, para. 83.

886 Commission Decision of 25 November 1998 declaring a concentration to be compatible with the common market and the functioning of the EEA Agreement (Case No IV/M.1225 - *Enso/Stora*) [1999] OJ L 254/9, where it was found that Enso's trading partnership with a supplier had lasted for more than 40 years.

887 Commission Decision of 14 July 1999 relating to a proceeding under Article 82 of the EC Treaty (IV/D-2/34.780 - *Virgin/British Airways*) [2000] OJ L 30/1, paras. 32 and 47; "[i]t necessarily follows that those agents substantially depend on the income they receive from BA in consideration for their air travel agency services", Judgment of 17 December 2003, *British Airways v Commission* of 17 December 2003, T-219/99, ECR, EU:T:2003:343, para. 216.

888 Summary of Commission Decision of 12 November 2008 relating to a proceeding under Article 81 of the Treaty establishing the European Community and Article 53 of the EEA Agreement (Case COMP/39.125 — *Car glass*) [2009] OJ C 173/13, taken from the unabridged version, para. 441.

889 Summary of Commission Decision of 12 November 2008 relating to a proceeding under Article 81 of the Treaty establishing the European Community and Article 53 of the EEA Agreement (Case COMP/39.125 — *Car glass*) [2009] OJ C 173/13, taken from the unabridged version, para. 437.

890 Kirkwood (2014).

438. It could also be that, due to particular circumstances of the case, *both parties are dependent on each other in a state of 'mutual interdependence'*. In these situations of 'mirror market structure', parties are unable to play off each other because their bargaining power is neutralized. This was the case in *Enso/Stora*, where the Commission found a symmetrical market structure upstream and downstream that created a relation of 'mutual interdependence' between the merging entities and the largest purchaser[891]. The mutual dependence was caused by the long-term relationship, and the unlikeliness of switching commercial parties, and the proportion of sales and purchases they represented to each other. This element of mutual dependence was seen as an indication of sufficient countervailing buyer power to neutralize any risks of post-merger exercise of pernicious market power by the merging entity. The existence of 'mutual interdependence' was later reviewed by the Courts in *Imperial Chemical v Commission*[892], where the plaintiff unsuccessfully alleged that there was 'mutual interdependence' because of a perception of a community of shared interests between itself and its customers[893]. The General Court dismissed the countervailing buyer power argument[894] based on the fact that the applicant did not support it with evidence and did not show that its customers were "able to counterbalance its market power"[895]. Thus, there was no interdependence, but rather dependence from the buyers to the seller.

c. Relation between the unavoidable trading partner doctrine and dependence

439. Furthermore, the buyer power Commission's practice and the case law shows that there is a link between the fact that an undertaking is an unavoidable purchasing trading partner and its suppliers' dependence on it, as discussed in *Irish Sugar v Commission*[896], and *Virgin/British Airways*[897], and as confirmed by the General Court in *British Airways v Commission*[898]. The connection between these two factors, therefore, further helps in determining the extent of the un-

---

891 Commission Decision of 25 November 1998 declaring a concentration to be compatible with the common market and the functioning of the EEA Agreement (Case No IV/M.1225 - *Enso/Stora*) [1999] OJ L 254/9.

892 Judgment of 25 June 2010, *Imperial Chemical Industries v Commission*, T-66/01, ECR, EU:T:2010:255.

893 See also the discussion of interdependence between oligopsonist competitors, which was a central issue in the assessment of the Airtours concentration by the General Court in Judgment of 28 June 2004, *Airtours v Commission*, T-342/99, ECR, EU:T:2002:146; see also Judgment of 31 March 1998 in *France and Société commerciale des potasses and de l'azote and Entreprise minière and chimique v Commission*, Joined cases C-68/94 and C-30/95 EU:C:1998:148.

894 Judgment of 25 June 2010, *Imperial Chemical Industries v Commission*, T-66/01, ECR, EU:T:2010:255, paras. 276-277.

895 Judgment of 25 June 2010, *Imperial Chemical Industries v Commission*, T-66/01, ECR, EU:T:2010:255, para. 277.

896 Commission Decision of 14 May 1997 relating to a proceeding pursuant to Article 86 of the EC Treaty (IV/34.621, 35.059/F-3 - *Irish Sugar plc*) [1997] OJ L 258/1, para. 17.

897 Commission Decision of 14 July 1999 relating to a proceeding under Article 82 of the EC Treaty (IV/D-2/34.780 - *Virgin/British Airways*) [2000] OJ L 30/1, paras. 32 and 47.

898 Judgment of 17 December 2003, *British Airways v Commission* of 17 December 2003, T-219/99, ECR, EU:T:2003:343, para. 217.

dertaking's buyer market power and upon the existence of an undertaking that is an unavoidable trading partner it follows that suppliers are dependent on it.

D. Gate-keeping

440. Linked to the unavoidable trading partner doctrine is the ability of a buyer to enhance its market power if it is able to *act as a gate-keeper by controlling access to the downstream market*[899]. A gate-keeper or 'bottleneck' structure[900] exists when the buyer possesses a privileged position for the distribution of goods or services in the upstream or downstream markets. Thanks to this ability to control access to markets, and as held by the US Federal Trade Commission (FTC):

> a retailer is so important a part of the retail market that its refusal to carry a product will, by itself, make it too costly for the supplier to effectively enter. The supplier may be held below minimum efficient scale in manufacturing, or may be unable to advertise efficiently in the mass media. In those circumstances the buyer stands as a gatekeeper to the retail marketplace[901].

441. Gate-keeping, therefore, is present in retailing industries or where distributors of goods to end consumers play an important role, as clarified and by the UK Competition Commission[902] and the Bundeskartellamt[903].

442. Because of these characteristics, gate-keeping is more likely to exist in specific markets in which to reach end consumers firms require an intermediary undertaking, such as food retailing. Also, gate-keeping appears if the product sold is not in demand in any other markets but only demanded by a particular one. For example, in the case of raw materials gatekeeping is less likely to occur because the same input can be used in several industries, as is the case with oil employed in energy production and plastics.

---

899 Faull and Nikpay, [1999], para. 6.334; Grimes 'Buyer Power and Retail Gatekeeper Power: Protecting Competition and The Atomistic Seller' (2004-2005); Doyle and Inderst (2007), p. 213; Dobson and Inderst (2008), p. 340; Pozdnakova (2009), 388. Undertakings may also be gatekeepers as well as sellers, particularly if they have the control of IP rights as confirmed in Commission Decision of 11 October 2000 declaring a concentration to be compatible with the common market and the EEA Agreement (Case No COMP/M.1845 — *AOL/Time Warner*) [2001] OJ L 268/28, para. 25.

900 Bottleneck positions are frequently invoked in cases dealing with refusals to deal or essential facilities. For literature dealing with this in the EU see, *inter alia*: Gregory J Werden, 'The Law and Economics of the Essential Facility Doctrine' 32 Saint Louis University Law Journal (1987-1988) 433; Phillip Areeda, 'Essential Facilities: An Epithet in Need of Limiting Principles' 58 Antitrust Law Journal (1989) 841; Hans Henrik Lidgard, 'Unilateral Refusal to Supply: an Agreement in Disguise' 6 European Competition Law Review (1997) 352; Christopher Stothers, 'Refusal to Supply as Abuse of a Dominant Position: Essential Facilities in the European Union' 22 European Competition Law Review (2001) 256; Valentine Korah, 'The Interface Between Intellectual Property and Antitrust: The European Experience' 69 Antitrust Law Journal (2002) 801; Csongor István Nagy, 'Refusal to Deal and the Doctrine of Essential Facilities in US and EC Competition Law: a Comparative Perspective and a Proposal for a Workable Analytical Framework' 32 European Law Review (2007) 664.

901 U.S. Federal Trade Commission, (2001), p. 58.

902 Competition Commission - UK (2008), para. 9.7.

903 Bundeskartellamt '*Summary of the Final Report of the Sector Inquiry into the Food Retail Sector*' (2014), 12, which refers to this phenomenon as "bottleneck".

443. Gate-keeping, however, may also be exercised by buyers not under the scope of application of EU competition law and not part of the retailing markets, such as the instance of contracting authorities under the scope of public procurement. These entities act as administrators of business opportunities by regulating the entrance into public procurement markets, and thus, being a market controller and having a potential for competition distortion, as noted by Sánchez Graells[904].

444. Furthermore, for a buyer to be a gate-keeper it must possess downstream market power (also fitting the hourglass shape), as noted by the OECD[905], otherwise, its presence would not be required or significant to distribute goods to end consumers. This would be the case of a buyer acting as a reseller and who is key to allowing market penetration of the supplier's product, as occurs in food retailing[906]. Therefore, its market power downstream is leveraged and this enhances its upstream market power further, justifying a dualistic approach to these types of cases. Additionally, if the undertaking acts as a gate-keeper, the analysis of market power downstream is even more important than its market power upstream as a buyer, because of the effects on competition as such and a broader standard regarding buyer power anti-competitive harm[907].

445. The role of an undertaking as gate-keeper has been subject to scrutiny in several instances by the Commission, particularly when dealing with retailing concentrations[908]. In *Procter & Gamble/Gillette*, the Commission found that powerful buyers that control access to the end consumer "perform an important 'gatekeeper' function for suppliers since they serve as a 'one-stop-shop' for the parties' products[909]. If a retailer refused to carry a brand of the parties, the brand would risk disappearing from the customers' awareness"[910]. Therefore, if the buyer acts as a gate-keeper, its suppliers will be constrained to keep the commercial relation with it – even to the extent of accepting less favorable conditions – to avoid incurring significant losses pertaining to the product in the end market, as a reaction to end consumers not obtaining the 'must stock' good.

446. Furthermore, in the food retailing concentration *Kesko/Tuko*, that concluded declaring the operation incompatible with the internal market, gatekeeping

---

904 Sánchez Graells, *Public Procurement and the EU Competition Rules* [2015], p. 58.

905 OECD '*Policy Roundtables: Monopsony and Buyer Power*' (2009), p. 22.

906 Bundeskartellamt '*Summary of the Final Report of the Sector Inquiry into the Food Retail Sector*' (2014), p. 13.

907 Office of Fair Trading, *The Competitive Effects of Buyer Groups*, para. 1.21; OECD '*Policy Roundtables: Monopsony and Buyer Power*' (2009), p. 42.

908 See also raising the issue of buyer power in retailing industries: Gorrie (2006).

909 Also stressing the distribution function played by gate-keeper buyers see: Vogel (1998), p. 11. See also discussing this case and the gate-keeping ability: Ezrachi and Ioannidou (2014), p. 88-89.

910 Non-opposition to a notified concentration (Case COMP/M.3732 — *Procter & Gamble/Gillette*) [2005] OJ C 239/6, public version, para. 125.

was relevant to assess the extent of the undertaking's future buyer power. The Commission found that the "gate-keeper effect," along with the large market shares of the merged entity as buyer and retailer created serious anti-competitive risks, both for upstream and downstream competition[911]. For the suppliers, in this case, it was necessary to achieve an agreement with the proposed party, as the only way to guarantee shelf-space in retail outlets, representing at least 55% of the Finnish market[912], as also remarked by Ezrachi and Ioannidou[913]. Furthermore, as gatekeepers *Kesko/Tuko* would have been an indispensable channel of distribution for suppliers to reach end consumers, reinforcing its buyer market power. Owing to this factor, and the need of suppliers to secure a contract with the gate-keeper (also an unavoidable trading partner), the assessment concluded that suppliers would have been in a position that could have been abused by the proposed entity through exploitative prices (such as those which I discuss in chapter 7). Also, the fact that the proposed concentration would create or reinforce a gate-keeping position was seen as leading to the possibility of a "spiral effect", a type of waterbed effect (as I discussed in chapter 2, section §VI.A), negatively affecting prices among rival buyers[914]. The spiral effect was deemed to generate a situation in which the merged party would have been able to obtain lower purchasing prices than its competitors, allowing them to drive them out of the market and raise barriers to entry[915]. However, the existence of the waterbed and the spiral effects have been questioned by more recent economic literature, which perhaps if known at the time would have changed the outcome or the justification of the assessment.

447. Lastly, in *Unilever/Sara Lee Body Care*, the Commission analyzed, and found as insufficient, the effects of the interaction between food and cosmetic product retailers (supermarkets and drugstores) and their position in the downstream market as gate-keepers[916]. The merging parties argued that the operation would not lead to a price increase because of the countervailing buyer power of its customers that acted not only as buyers but also controlled market access and competitors supplying private label products. In their view,

911 Commission Decision of 20 November 1996 declaring a concentration to be incompatible with the common market (Case No IV/M.784 - *Kesko/Tuko*) Council Regulation (EEC) No 4064/89 [1997] OJ L 110/53, taken from the unabridged version, para. 133. I discuss this case in further detail in chapter 8, section §IV.C.

912 Commission Decision of 20 November 1996 declaring a concentration to be incompatible with the common market (Case No IV/M.784 - *Kesko/Tuko*) Council Regulation (EEC) No 4064/89 [1997] OJ L 110/53, taken from the unabridged version, para. 133.

913 Ezrachi and Ioannidou (2014), p. 79.

914 Commission Decision of 20 November 1996 declaring a concentration to be incompatible with the common market (Case No IV/M.784 - *Kesko/Tuko*) Council Regulation (EEC) No 4064/89 [1997] OJ L 110/53, taken from the unabridged version, para. 153; Ezrachi and Ioannidou (2014), p. 79.

915 Ibid, p. 79.

916 Summary of Commission Decision of 17 November 2010 declaring a concentration compatible with the internal market and the functioning of the EEA Agreement (Case COMP/M.5658 — *Unilever/Sara Lee Body Care*) [2012] OJ C 23/30. See also: Ezrachi [2014], p. 438.

these gate-keeper buyers (supermarkets and drugstores) were able to exercise countervailing buyer power by threatening to *delist* the supplier's secondary brand[917], refusing to stock new variants of the leading brand or reducing the number of stock-keeping units[918]. The Commission rejected these arguments and found that in the post-merger structure, the bargaining power of these gate-keeper buyers would not have been sufficient to mitigate the likelihood of price increases; however, the concentration was approved as the offered commitments sufficiently mitigated the competition concerns[919].

448. From the case law, I conclude that, to determine if a buyer is a gate-keeper and what consequences not securing a contract may entail for suppliers, several factors are to be taken into account:

i) whether the supplier has to access end consumers through inferior sale channels, for example, a weaker distributor[920];

ii) whether the supplier forgoes substantial economies of scale or network effects[921];

iii) if the buyer counts for a large share of the purchases in the upstream market[922];

iv) the existence of much smaller buyers acting in the same market[923];

v) the presence of entry barriers preventing upstream entry and circumventing the powerful buyer by sponsoring new distribution channels.

E. Alternative supply sources

449. Alternative supply sources are the last assessment tool I have identified in the measurement of buyer market power, as confirmed by the case law and other authoritative sources. Measuring alternative supply sources describe whether a party does or does not have substantial *bargaining* power, as suggested by

917 Faull, Nikpay and Taylor, [2014], paras. 5.890-5.891.

918 Commission Decision of 17 November 2010 declaring a concentration compatible with the internal market and the functioning of the EEA Agreement (Case COMP/M.5658 — *Unilever/Sara Lee Body Care*) [2012] OJ C 23/30; taken from the unabridged version, para. 200.

919 Commission Decision of 17 November 2010 declaring a concentration compatible with the internal market and the functioning of the EEA Agreement (Case COMP/M.5658 — *Unilever/Sara Lee Body Care*) [2012] OJ C 23/30, taken from the unabridged, para. 44.

920 Office of Fair Trading, *The Competitive Effects of Buyer Groups*, para. 1.21; Kokkoris and Day (2009), p. 180.

921 Office of Fair Trading, *The Competitive Effects of Buyer Groups*, para. 1.21.

922 Gorrie (2006), p. 218.

923 Office of Fair Trading, *The Competitive Effects of Buyer Groups*, para. 1.21; OECD '*Policy Roundtables: Monopsony and Buyer Power*' (2009), p. 42.

the OECD and the OFT[924]. Also, assessing alternative supply sources is a very useful tool when determining the sufficiency of countervailing buyer power, as clarified by the EU Horizontal Merger Guidelines[925] and a topic covered in chapter 9. Nevertheless, in the case of *monopsony power*, threatening to switch to alternative supply sources is not a particularly important or relevant factor when it comes to determining the extent of buyer market power because the withholding effect will take place regardless of outside options for the buyer. Thus, threatening to acquire input from a different supplier does not capture this effect.

450. If the buyer can credibly threaten to switch, or switch to, "alternative suppliers, sponsor new entry, or self-supply without incurring substantial costs" within a reasonable timeframe[926], it will be a buyer power indicator. In the absence of credible alternative supply sources, buyers may lack substantial buyer power and may even be dependent on the supplier, as it was the case in *Cementbouw Handel & Industrie v Commission*[927]. Therefore, the more alternative supply sources the buyer has, the more bargaining room vis-à-vis its supplier when it comes to obtaining better trading terms, and vice versa, and the more buyer market power it has[928]. This means that alternative supply sources are measured by reference to the buyer's options. Unlike the measurement of demand side substitutability, which I discussed in chapter 4, section §IV.B.a, the analysis is centered on alternative supply sources for the buyer and not alternative buyers for the seller. Also, measuring alternative supply sources is different from buyer substitution in the sense that, for the latter, the capacity of new buyers to timely and effectively start purchasing the input is assessed.

451. The existence of alternative sources has been employed by the Commission and the Courts when measuring the extent of buyer market power, on several occasions. In most of these cases, the analysis of alternative sources of supply is directly linked to the ability of a buyer to exercise countervailing buyer

924 Office of Fair Trading '*Assessment of Market Power: Understanding Competition Law*' (2004), p. 24; Office of Fair Trading, *The Competitive Effects of Buyer Groups*; OECD '*Policy Roundtables: Monopsony and Buyer Power*' (2009), p. 42. See also suggesting that alternative supply and procurement channels are a key element in the assessment of bargaining power models see: Bundeskartellamt '*Summary of the Final Report of the Sector Inquiry into the Food Retail Sector*' (2014), p. 9.

925 A source of buyer power "would be if a customer could credibly threaten to resort, within a reasonable timeframe, to *alternative sources* of supply", Guidelines on the assessment of horizontal mergers under the Council Regulation on the control of concentrations between undertakings [2004] OJ C 31/5, para. 65 (emphasis added).

926 Office of Fair Trading, *The Competitive Effects of Buyer Groups*, para. 1.21; and replicated in OECD '*Policy Roundtables: Monopsony and Buyer Power*' (2009), p. 42. See also this indicator in Network (2011), para. 103.

927 Judgment of 23 February 2006, *Cementbouw Handel & Industrie v Commission*, T-282/02, ECR, EU:T:2006:64, para. 231.

928 See also stressing this, from a suppliers' perspective, how a merge that eliminates alternative buyers increase the buyer power of a powerful firm in Bundeskaterllamt, Case summary from 6 July 2015: Prohibition of acquisition of Kaiser´s Tengelmann outlets by Edeka, B2-96/14 (English version), p. 1, appealed and revoked by the German Federal Minister for Economic Affairs and Energy under § 42 of the German Competition Act based, *inter alia*, on the protection of working positions that would be absorbed by Edeka.

power, as recognized by the EU Horizontal Merger Guidelines[929], and the General Court in *Sun Chemical Group and Others v Commission*[930]. This, however, does not imply that an analogous analysis should not be made when resorting to cases of active use of buyer market power.

452. In *Tomra and Others v Commission*, the Commission expressly remarked that alternative supply sources are one of the two *alternative* conditions for buyer power to exist[931]. However, a broader view was given by the General Court in *Cementbouw Handel & Industrie v Commission*, in expressing that there were more than two conditions for the existence and measurement of buyer market power, but insisting that alternative sources of supply and market concentrations were one of its fundamental sources[932]. The General Court went on by stating that buyer power can be exercised by an undertaking vis-à-vis its suppliers, "if those customers have the ability to resort to credible alternative sources of supply within a reasonable time if the supplier decides to increase its prices or to make the conditions of delivery less favourable"[933]. Therefore, the likelier this is, the greater the buyer market power.

453. In *Irish Sugar v Commission,* a defense claiming countervailing buyer power was rejected by the Commission and ratified by the General Court because, *inter alia*, the customers of Irish Sugar, despite having some degree of buyer power, were said to be dependent of Irish Sugar due to the lack of sufficient alternative supply sources caused by the exclusionary tactics employed by Irish Sugar[934]. The Commission's argumentation links dependence with the lack of alternative supply sources, as the lack of the former strengthens the supplier's dependence vis-à-vis the buyer. The fewer alternative supply sources, the less a buyer can threaten a supplier with switching their purchase orders to a competitor.

---

929 "Countervailing buyer power in this context should be understood as the bargaining strength that the buyer has vis-à-vis the seller in commercial negotiations due to its size, its commercial significance to the seller and its ability to switch to alternative suppliers", in Guidelines on the assessment of horizontal mergers under the Council Regulation on the control of concentrations between undertakings [2004] OJ C 31/5, para. 65.

930 Judgment of 9 July 2007, *Sun Chemical Group and Others v Commission,* T-282/06, ECR, EU:T:2007:203, para. 210.

931 The second condition being "that customers are able to sponsor new entrants", Summary of Commission Decision of 29 March 2006 relating to a proceeding under Article 82 of the Treaty establishing the European Community and Article 54 of the EEA Agreement against Tomra Systems ASA, Tomra Europe AS, Tomra Systems BV, Tomra Systems GmbH, Tomra Butikksystemer AS, Tomra Systems AB and Tomra Leergutsysteme GmbH (Case COMP/E-1/38.113 — *Prokent/Tomra*) [2008] OJ C 219/11, taken from the unabridged version, para. 89. Arguably, the alternative conditions pointed out by the Commission are part of the strategic advantages. Cf with Ezrachi and Ioannidou, who are of the opinion that there are two types of sources of buyer power: i) dominance *or* ii) strategic advantages, in Ezrachi and Ioannidou (2014).

932 Judgment of 23 February 2006, *Cementbouw Handel & Industrie v Commission,* T-282/02, ECR, EU:T:2006:64, para. 232.

933 Judgment of 23 February 2006, *Cementbouw Handel & Industrie v Commission,* T-282/02, ECR, EU:T:2006:64, para. 230.

934 Commission Decision of 14 May 1997 relating to a proceeding pursuant to Article 86 of the EC Treaty (IV/34.621, 35.059/F-3 - *Irish Sugar plc*) [1997] OJ L 258/1, para. 107.

454. Lastly, in *Alrosa v Commission*, the issue of limiting access to alternative supply sources by a dominant purchaser was dealt with by the General Court. The controversy did not deal with alternative sources of supply but, instead, concerned a dominant buyer's conduct in seeking to limit access of other buyers to alternative supply sources to exclude rival buyers (as I discuss in chapter 6, section §III). This is an indirect way of achieving buyer market power because it limits the buyer market power of its rivals.

455. In this case, the Commission adopted a Commitment Decision in which De Beers, at the time the largest rough diamond buyer and supplier in the world[935], agreed not to purchase rough diamonds from Alrosa – also a diamond-buyer and supplier – as the purchasing relation between them reduced access to a "viable source of alternative supply of rough diamonds for potential consumers"[936]. Furthermore, the purchasing from De Beers to Alrosa could hinder the "second biggest competitor from competing fully with De Beers"[937]. The Commission found that this purchasing relation eliminated alternative supply sources (Alrosa) to other diamond-buyers and, therefore, only approved the Decision based on commitments offered by De Beers not to buy from Alrosa so the provision of "third parties with an alternative source of supply" was possible[938]. When reviewing the case the General Court found that if a dominant buyer nullifies supply alternatives for other buyers, these lose any bargaining power they could have and access to input. Hence, if a purchaser in a dominant position "*reserve[s] to itself the whole of Alrosa's production exported outside the CIS [such practice] could, even if the latter consented, constitute an abuse in the context of their relations*"[939]. To prevent such abuse, a suitable alternative for the General Court would have been to prohibit parties from entering into exclusive purchasing agreements or reserving a material part of the purchases for the dominant undertaking, but without necessarily prohibiting all purchases from a party to a supplier indefinitely[940]. On appeal, however, the CJEU reverted the General Court's Judgment as it found that in the case of Commitment Decisions, the extent of the principle of proportionality is substantially lower than in not committed decisions[941].

---

935 De Beers, up to date, is also the largest undertaking in the world market of rough diamond.

936 Commission Decision of 22 February 2006 relating to a proceeding pursuant to Article 82 of the EC Treaty and Article 54 of the EEA Agreement (Case COMP/B-2/38.381 — *De Beers*) [2006] OJ L 205/24, para. 1.

937 Commission Decision of 22 February 2006 relating to a proceeding pursuant to Article 82 of the EC Treaty and Article 54 of the EEA Agreement (Case COMP/B-2/38.381 — *De Beers*) [2006] OJ L 205/24, para. 1.

938 Judgment of 11 July 2007, *Alrosa v Commission*, T-170/06, ECR, EU:T:2007:220, para. 119.

939 Judgment of 11 July 2007, *Alrosa v Commission*, T-170/06, ECR, EU:T:2007:220, para. 127 (emphasis added).

940 Judgment of 11 July 2007, *Alrosa v Commission*, T-170/06, ECR, EU:T:2007:220, para. 128.

941 Judgment of 29 June 2010 in *Commission v Alrosa*, C-441/07 P, EU:C:2010:377.

V. Alternatives to buyer market definition

456. In opposition to the structural and indirect analysis of relevant buying markets and market power assessment, the literature evidences different methods for directly measuring (buyer) market power. There is lack of academic consensus regarding the suitability of direct market power assessment and, from a legal standpoint, none of these methodologies have been endorsed by the legislation, the case law or soft law[942]. In this section, I discuss two methodologies suggested for the direct measurement of buyer market power: the Lerner Index and the Buyer Power Index.

A. The Lerner Index

457. The Lerner Index allows for direct market power assessment in both seller and buyer markets based on the elasticities of supply and demand of an undertaking[943], having an intuitive economic appeal[944]. The Lerner Index represents the price-marginal cost margin and is defined as

$$L = \frac{P - MC}{P}$$

and also equates the inverse of the price elasticity of the demand of the firm and it is represented as

$$L_i = \frac{P_i - MC_i}{P_i} = \frac{-1}{\varepsilon_i}\ ^{945}.$$

458. The Lerner Index provides a measure of market power based on the elasticity of the goods commercialized by the undertaking by determining its residual demand[946]. First, it describes the ability of an undertaking to raise its price above short marginal costs, and secondly that market power is inversely related to the elasticity of demand that an undertaking faces. If the price elasticity is very high, then the price-marginal cost margin will be low and vice versa[947]. In simpler terms, the Lerner Index will indicate how much, as a percentage, the

942 Monti 'The Concept of Dominance in Article 82' (2006), p. 34.

943 The Lerner Index was first developed Abraham Ptachya Lerner, 'The Concept of Monopoly and the Measurement of Monopoly Power' 1 The Review of Economic Studies (1934) 157; Roger J. Van den Bergh and Peter D. Camesasca, *European Competition Law and Economics: A Comparative Perspective* (Intersentia 2001), p. 94-95.

944 Schwalbe and Zimmer, [2009], p. 51. See also: Niels, Jenkins and Kavanagh, [2011], p. 131-132.

945 Bishop and Walker, [2010], para. 3-037.

946 Hovenkamp, [2005], p. 134.

947 Bishop and Walker, [2010], para. 3-037.

demand of good "A" will decrease if the price of it increases by 1%[948]. The more elastic the demand is, the lower the market power of the undertaking will be[949].

459. A *reverse* Lerner Index could be employed to directly assess the market power of a buying undertaking. In this case, the elasticity will determine the change that takes place when the buyer decreases its purchasing price and how this affects the quantity supplied by undertakings in the input market. The less a decrease in price reduces the quantity supplied to the undertaking, the more market power the undertaking has.

460. Despite its simplicity and intuitive appeal, the Lerner Index has not been adopted as the methodology for market definition due to several criticisms. Firstly, estimating the competitive price is complex[950], and so is estimating the marginal cost[951]. Secondly, the Lerner Index indicates the deviation of price from marginal cost at the current output, but not necessarily the deviation from the competitive price[952]. Thirdly, it is considered incorrect to equate marginal costs to the competitive price, and the Lerner Index assumes that high costs preclude dominance while high costs are precisely inherent to monopoly/monopsony power[953]. Fourthly, the Lerner Index only holds true for an undertaking producing a single product but most undertakings produce more than one product. Fifthly, the Lerner Index supposes that firms are choosing their prices to maximize short-term profits instead of long-term profits, and which is usually not the strategy adopted by firms[954]. Lastly, direct market definition might, occasionally, be more accurate but it improves accuracy at the expense of legal certainty[955].

B. Buyer Power Index

461. The Buyer Power Index (BPI) is a methodology for the direct measure of buyer market power, based on the reverse application of the Lerner Index[956], developed by Blair and Harrison[957], and Blair and Lopatka[958]. The BPI describes the deviation between the competitive outcome and the amount purchased by the monop-

---

948 OECD, 'Policy Roundtables: Market Definition' (2012), p. 25.

949 The intuition is simple: if demand decreases little in comparison with the price increase, then the firm is dominant as it pricing conduct has an appreciable effect in the market price.

950 OECD 'Policy Roundtables: Market Definition' (2012), p. 26. Also stressing the difficulty of calculating elasticities see Malcolm B. Coate and Jeffrey H. Fischer, 'Is Market Definition still Needed After all these Years' (2014), p. 13.

951 Motta, *Competition Policy: Theory and Practice* [2004], p. 116; Schwalbe and Zimmer, [2009], p. 57.

952 Areeda, Hovenkamp and Solow, [1995], p. 118-119.

953 Motta, *Competition Policy: Theory and Practice* [2004], p. 116.

954 Bishop and Walker, [2010], para. 3-039.

955 OECD 'Policy Roundtables: Market Definition' (2012), p. 13.

956 Faull and Nikpay, [1999], para. 6.313.

957 Blair and Harrison, [2010], p. 54 to 67.

958 Blair and Lopatka (2008).

sonist based on the *elasticity of supply*[959]. Its creators argue that could represent an attractive tool for measuring buyer power as it "suggest[s] a way of thinking about buying power that is easy to understand and useful in application"[960]. However, its implementation, like the Lerner Index, is not as simple as it sounds.

462. The BPI is anchored on pure monopsony cases where the monopsonist will determine the quantity of goods it aims to buy, where the marginal product curve or value of the marginal product intersects the marginal factor cost (VMP=MFC). This assumption allows the BPI, described by the formula

$$BPI = \frac{1}{\varepsilon'},$$

to "measure… the responsiveness of the quantity supplied to changes in price. As ε rises, the firm's monopsony power declines"[961]. In less technical terms, the more buyer power the undertaking has, the less alternative buyers the sellers will have to offer their products to.

463. The BPI determines the buyer power of a dominant non-monopsonistic buyer, a dominant undertaking that imposes monopsonistic losses, but is not the only buyer. The buying competitors are assumed in this model to take the price that the dominant buyer pays as the market price maker[962]. These fringe buyers will buy input until their demand equals the set price. To maximize its profit, the dominant buyer will adjust its purchases so that it buys a quantity "Q^*_{df} where mfc equals D_{df}, which determines price equal to w^* from the residual supply. As a price of w^*, sellers will provide Q^*, which is equal to the sum of Q^*_f and Q^*_{df}."[963]

464. Therefore, according to the model, the BPI for a dominant buyer is derived in the following expression:

$$BPI = \frac{1}{\varepsilon_{DB}} = \frac{1}{\frac{\varepsilon}{s} + \frac{n(1-s)}{s}} = \frac{s}{\varepsilon + n\,(1-s)}$$

959 Blair and Harrison, [2010] p. 54 to 67; OECD '*Policy Roundtables: Monopsony and Buyer Power*' (2009), p. 32-34; Faull, Nikpay and Taylor, [2014], para. 7.393.

960 Blair and Harrison, [2010], p. 64.

961 Ibid, p. 55.

962 Ibid, p. 56.

963 Ibid, p. 56.

465. The amount of BPI will depend on the overall elasticity of supply (ε) and the elasticity of demand (n) for the fringe competitors as well as the dominant buyer's market share[964].

466. Simplifying the economic discussion, the BPI calculates the market power of a dominant undertaking on two main variables: elasticities and market shares. In the proposed model, if all else remains constant, buyer power will increase as the market share of the dominant firm also increases[965]. I have found that this is both intuitively appealing and also consistent with the case law and practice of buyer power cases discussed regarding the assessment of market shares.

467. In the BPI, the elasticity of supply measures the response on the quantity offered by suppliers when there is a change in purchasing price. The more elastic the supply is, the less the BPI. As "the quantity supplied becomes more responsive to changes in price, the large buyer's power falls. This is because the suppliers can redirect the efforts to other products where prices may be higher"[966]. As the elasticity of *fringe demand* of the smaller buyers, increases, the buying power of the dominant undertaking tends to fall. The intuition behind this is that "any reduction in price implemented by the dominant buyer's curtailed purchases is tempered by the enhanced purchases of the fringe. The more responsive they are to price decreases, the more difficult it is for the dominant buyer to make such a decrease stick"[967]. If all three variables point in the same direction, it is arguably quite easy to determine the existence of substantial buyer power. When the market shares are large, supply is inelastic and fringe demand is also inelastic, then the BPI index is expected to be high[968].

C. Criticism against the BPI

468. In general, most criticisms formulated against the Lerner Index can be applied by analogy to the BPI, as both mechanisms are based on the relation between elasticity and market share[969]. Firstly, as remarked by Faull, Nikpay and Taylor, the BPI applies to monopsony power cases but it is not useful in situations of bargaining power, which limits its practical application unless a major revision is applied to it, making it a very narrow tool[970], which then goes against my proposal of a general dualistic approach to buyer power cases. Secondly, the BPI sacrifices legal certainty in an attempt to promote a case-by-case accuracy. However, the large amount of data that is required

964 Ibid, p. 58.
965 Ibid, p. 58.
966 Ibid, p. 58.
967 Ibid, p. 59.
968 Ibid, p. 67.
969 For the criticism against the Lerner Index see in this same chapter, section §V.A.
970 Faull, Nikpay and Taylor, [2014], para. 7.389.

to determine the BPI of a case makes prediction and planning of future behaviour by undertakings difficult. Thirdly, an accurate assessment of elasticities of supply and demand is a difficult practical exercise, as also remarked by Faull, Nikpay and Taylor[971]. Fourthly, no authoritative legal source (either soft or hard law) suggests or endorses the application of the BPI. Lastly, Blair and Harrison do not provide a hierarchy of importance between the variables to consider. This leads to the question concerning which factor should prevail in case of a discrepancy between them? The balancing order is not clear and a different hierarchy might lead to different outcomes for the very same case.

VI. Conclusion

469. This second chapter dealing with the assessment of buyer power as part of the buyer market power definition builds upon and develops the dualistic market approach suggested in chapter 4. In this chapter I have stressed the fact that *substantial buyer market power* – although not necessarily dominance – *may rise at lower market shares* and concentration levels that are lower than on seller-side cases. This holds true for the exercise of effective bargaining power. However, in the case of monopsony power, a very large amount of buyer power is needed (and, therefore, usually represented by very large market shares as well) for it to be exerted in a non-transitory manner. This ability to exercise effective buyer (bargaining) power at a lower threshold than compared to seller market power has been confirmed by the Commission's practice, the case law and the literature, and is related to the fact that the buyer usually has the ability to dictate the terms of the discussion and – if there are other sources of supply – walk away to take another offer, thereby bestowing the buyer with an advantageous bargaining position. The ability to exert substantial and effective buyer (bargaining) power at lower market share thresholds is also connected to the fact that these buyers may enjoy privileged positions – such as acting as a gate-keeper being relatively dominant or being an unavoidable trading partner – which may imply that suppliers are dependent on them and lead to the imposition of unfair purchasing practices (as I discuss in chapter 8).

470. Concerning the dualistic approach for the *market power assessment*, I submitted that this measurement looks at the undertaking's market power both upstream and downstream, fully capturing the competitive effects of the behaviour in question. By adopting this approach, it is possible to fully assess the undertaking's market power as a buyer and retailer to appropriately determine the welfare implications of the buyer power exercise. This approach, therefore, does not limit itself to assessing buyer market power only in the upstream market – the traditional focus of monop-

971 Ibid, para. 7.393.

sony theory – but it integrates the effects downstream, fully reflecting buyer power effects. By adopting this approach, the assessment takes into account "the *relevant market conditions*, and in particular of the *dynamics of the market* and of the extent to which products are differentiated"[972], in accordance with EU competition law.

471. Also, I inquired what the adequate tools to *assess the market power of a purchasing undertaking* are and concluded that it is possible to resort to the traditional methodologies employed in selling side cases, such as market shares, market concentration, and entry and exit barriers. However, not only is required re-orienting the way that these tool are employed. It is also important to resort to other buyer power specific sources: whether the undertaking is either an unavoidable trading partner and/or suppliers are dependent on it, based on whether the buyer acts as gatekeeper downstream market, and if buyers have alternative supply sources. I also found that even if these measurement tools are connected to the sources of buyer power, they do not determine the existence of buyer power, but rather its degree, something which is not always clearly distinguished by the case law and Commission's practice.

472. I have also discussed the use of market share thresholds for buyer power cases. Concerning dominance, I discussed whether the test for buying undertakings has to be symmetrical to seller-oriented cases. In light of the relatively small amount of relevant case law, with the exception of *British Airways v Commission*[973], it is difficult to give a definitive answer whether under the current state of the law, the abuse of a dominant purchasing position has a lower threshold than abuse of a selling dominant position. In my view, and in accordance with the economics of buyer power, a lower threshold for dominance may be resorted to in exceptional circumstances for those cases where the buyer also enjoys substantial market power in the related downstream market, fitting the hourglass shape due to the higher anti-competitive effects of the conducts in the market. This, nevertheless, should not be interpreted as meaning that whenever there is substantial buyer power in the upstream and the downstream market, there is a presumption that the conduct is in breach of Article 102 TFEU. However, and as I will discuss further in chapter 8, the developments of competition law regulation in some MS, have led to the application of lower thresholds for unilateral buying conduct and also to cover situations like relative dominance or abuse of economic dependence.

473. Furthermore, in addition to the tools for indirect measurement of buyer market power, I discussed two alternatives for the direct measurement of buyer

---

972 Communication from the Commission — Guidance on the Commission's enforcement priorities in applying Article 82 of the EC Treaty to abusive exclusionary conduct by dominant undertakings [2009] OJ C 45/7, para. 14 (emphasis added).

973 Judgment of 17 December 2003, *British Airways v Commission* of 17 December 2003, T-219/99, ECR, EU:T:2003:343; and Judgment of 15 March 2007 in *British Airways v Commission*, C-95/04 P, EU:C:2007:166.

market power: the reverse Lerner Index and the BPI. These indicators could be resorted to as substitutes or complementary tools to reinforce the analysis of the relevant market and the market power assessment. Nonetheless, these tools, from a legal perspective, have not been recognized by the case law, neither as soft law nor strong authoritative sources, nor have they been employed as part of the Commission's practice in buyer power cases this far. Therefore, they should be used with caution.

474. All in all, as a summary of my discussion concerning both buyer market definition and buyer market power assessment, neither the case law, nor the soft law in EU competition law have placed a special emphasis regarding buyer side cases. Furthermore, most of the analysis and methodologies are based on reverse of selling sides practices or are still underdeveloped buyer power oriented approaches. However, the Commission's guidance instruments and the case law have gradually started to recognize the distinction in defining buying markets vis-à-vis selling markets, although in order to satisfactorily incorporate and update the instruments to fully capture a dualistic market definition approach to buyer power cases, work remains to be done. In my view, farther developments are still needed in the realm of EU competition law in order to integrate buyer power specific tools and metrics for determining relevant buyer markets and, most importantly, adopt a dualistic approach to them.

PART IV

EXERTING BUYER POWER. EXCLUSION AND EXPLOITATION

6

EXCLUSIONARY BUYER POWER

I. Introduction to Part IV and buyer power exclusion

475. This Part IV constitutes the core of this study as it deals with the conducts and theories of harm through which buyer power is exerted in the upstream and the related downstream market where the buyer(s) carries out it (or their) economic activity. Therefore, these chapters look at *buyer power from an active perspective* and how it can trigger competition concerns by discussing different conducts that exclude rivals or exploit suppliers. My aim with Part IV is to provide a substantiated answer to the research questions: *In which circumstances or type of cases does buyer power pose competitive risks that ought to be tackled by EU competition law? What do these 'theories of harm' look like and what is the legal regime applicable to such conducts?*

476. This first chapter of Part IV deals with buyer power exclusion and how purchasing behaviours may foreclose rival buyers in the upstream market - or rival retailers in the downstream market – through buyer power exertion vis-à-vis suppliers.

477. Buyer power can be employed anti-competitively by coordinated buyers, or a single buyer[974] to foreclose[975] competitors or prevent entrance of new rivals into the purchasing market to protect and/or expand its market power, distorting the competitive process and market structure[976]. Exclusionary buyer power by a dominant undertaking or through buyer coordination raises issues of harm related to "increased prices, reduced output, product quality or variety, or innovation, market allocation, or anti-competitive foreclosure"[977], due to the effects of the conduct on rival buyers that may also compete as retailers in a horizontal manner, unlike buyer power exploitation which is mostly a vertical issue. Consequently, the regulation of exclusionary buyer power may result in the application, separately or jointly, of both Article 101 and Article 102 TFEU[978], or lead to a concentration among competing buyers to be declared incompatible with the internal market. In this chapter my analysis is concerned with how buyers foreclose rivals in the upstream or downstream markets, I do not discuss, in the case of agreements or tacit collusion the ways in which several buyers would coordinate their behaviour horizontally to foreclose rival buyers. I have excluded this modality of specific foreclosure because there are no relevant cases in EU competition law and because its treatment would be that of a cartel that has the aim of excluding rivals to a necessary input and, therefore, likely to constitute a breach of Article 101(1) TFEU by object, as buyer cartels' have been found to be in general in EU competition law and as I discuss from an exploitative perspective in chapter 7, section §VI.

---

974 Exclusionary buyer power employed by a group of undertakings acting in collaboration from an economic point of view is analytically similar to the behavior of a single dominant firm. In this section, to facilitate discussion and avoid repetition, I center the analysis on the exclusionary effects of buyer power exercise through the analysis of mostly conducts exerted by a dominant undertaking. This, however, does not preclude a group of undertakings for being liable to breach Article 101 TFEU when entering into agreements with a foreclosing effect. For some literature regarding exclusionary conducts in general see, *inter alia*: Eleanor M. Fox, 'What is Harm to Competition? Exclusionary Practices and Anticompetitive Effect' 70 Antitrust Law Journal (2002) 371; John Vickers, 'Abuse of Market Power' 115 The Economic Journal (2005) F244; Neelie Kroes, 'Tackling Exclusionary Practices to Avoid Exploitation of Market Power: Some Preliminary Thoughts on the Policy Review of Article 82' 29 Fordham International Law Journal (2005) 593; Eirik Østerud, *Identifying Exclusionary Abuses by Dominant Undertakings under EU Competition Law: The Spectrum of Tests* (Kluwer 2010); Rousseva, [2010]; John Temple-Lang, 'How can the Problems of Exclusionary Abuses under Article 102 TFEU be Resolved?' 2 European Law Review (2012) 136.

975 Anticompetitive foreclosure is defined by the Commission as "a situation where effective access of actual or potential competitors to supplies or markets is hampered or eliminated as a result of the conduct of the dominant undertaking whereby the dominant undertaking is likely to be in a position to profitably increase prices to the detriment of consumers" in Communication from the Commission — Guidance on the Commission's enforcement priorities in applying Article 82 of the EC Treaty to abusive exclusionary conduct by dominant undertakings [2009] OJ C 45/7, para. 19.

976 Communication from the Commission — Guidance on the Commission's enforcement priorities in applying Article 82 of the EC Treaty to abusive exclusionary conduct by dominant undertakings [2009] OJ C 45/7, para. 6; Barry J Rodger and Angus MacCullogh, *Competition Law and Policy in the EU and UK* (5th edn, Routledge 2015), p. 110.

977 Communication from the Commission — Guidelines on the applicability of Article 101 of the Treaty on the Functioning of the European Union to horizontal co-operation agreements [2011] OJ C 11/1, para. 201.

978 The joint application of both Article 101 and 102 TFEU was confirmed by the General Court in Judgment of 30 September 2003, *Atlantic Container Line and Others v Commission*, joined cases T-191/98, T-212/98 to T-214/98, EU:T:2003:245 E.C.R. [2003] II-03275, para. 1447.

478. Buyer power exclusion has the particularity of being able to generate a *dual effect* as it may foreclose competing undertakings in either the upstream market as rival buyers and/or the downstream market as rival retailers (if in addition to competing for the input, the undertakings compete for the output market). In most instances, however, the exclusion occurs when undertakings compete in both markets as buyers and retailers as the buyer leverages its purchasing power to capture downstream market power in some form akin to input (vertical) foreclosure[979], which also may explain why there seems to be a narrow standing that considers that buyer power exclusion is anti-competitively only upon end consumer harm. However, as I discuss in this chapter, this is not the case in EU competition law because exclusionary buyer power conducts trigger the application of the law even absent consumer harm whenever there is an anti-competitive effect in the upstream market among undertakings that may not compete as retailers and only as buyers, which implies a broader harm standard and which is in line with my interpretation of a dualistic approach to buyer power.

479. In this chapter, I discuss how buyer power can have an exclusionary effect in either the upstream and/or downstream market and which different conducts and theories of harm exist to explain the different exclusionary scenarios. Hence, this chapter answers the research question: *What is the legal treatment granted to behaviours by buyers that may exclude rivals either in an input or output market?*

480. To answer this, I have identified and grouped exclusionary buyer power conducts under different theories of harm which will be subject to detailed discussion in this chapter, even though they may sometimes be indistinguishable in their effects from an economic perspective as they revolve around *increasing a rival's cost*. To do so, I have structured the chapter as follows: firstly, I discuss in section §II *how buyer-induced exclusion works* and its capacity to foreclose rivals in the upstream and/or downstream relevant markets. Then, in section §III, I study how input foreclosure operates by means of exclusive supply obligations. I next address the issue of *overbuying* as a theory of harm where buyers over-acquire (or overpay for) an input to restrict access to rival buyers and increase their costs, in section §VI. This is followed in section §V by an analysis of *concentrations that may lead to vertical foreclosure and have negative vertical effects* on competition. Section §VI deals with *purchasing price discrimination* as an exclusionary mechanism and compares the legal treatment given in EU competition law with the regulation under US

979 Regarding the economics of vertical foreclosure see, *inter alia*: Oliver Hart and Jean Tirole, 'Vertical Integration and Market Foreclosure' Brookings Papers on Economic Activity (1990) 205; Karl M. Meessen, 'The Conflict over Vertical Foreclosure in Competition Policy and Intellectual Property Law: Comment' 160 Journal of Institutional and Theoretical Economics (JITE) / Zeitschrift für die gesamte Staatswissenschaft (2004) 97; Marie-Laure Allain, Claire Chambolle and Patrick Rey, 'Vertical Integration, Innovation and Foreclosure' IDEAS Working Paper Series from RePEc (2010) 1; Roman Inderst and Tommaso Valletti, 'Incentives for Input Foreclosure' 55 European Economic Review (2011) 820; Herbert Hovenkamp, 'Robert Bork and Vertical Integration: Leverage, Foreclosure, and Efficiency' 79 Antitrust Law Journal (2014) 983.

antitrust law under the Robinson-Patman Act. Subsequently, *market power leverage* in an input market to affect downstream competition is discussed in section §VII, in which I analyze *British Airways v Commission*, one of the most relevant buyer power cases and where the Courts found a buyer to be liable pursuant to abusing its dominant purchasing market position. Section §VIII discusses the *'squeeze to buy'* theory of harm in which suppliers' exploitation is carried out with an exclusionary aim, while section §IX examines the application of the *'as efficient buying competitor test'* for buyer power cases, and is followed by a discussion in section §X regarding *which type of harm triggers competition application in exclusionary buyer power cases.* Section §XI concludes the chapter with a discussion of the findings.

II. How does buyer-induced exclusion work?

481. *Exclusionary buyer-induced abuses are the most pernicious and common anti-competitive type of practices*[980] *because they hamper current and future competition*, as remarked by the Commission in *Sovion/Südfleisch*[981], and require a larger degree of intervention from authorities as they are not self-correctable by market forces[982]. They consist in using buyer market power vis-à-vis a supplier to increase the purchasing costs of a rival and put the latter in a competitive disadvantage in the upstream market that may also have an additional downstream market effect. Exclusionary conducts are not self-correctable because whenever an undertaking increases its rival's costs it drives market prices of an input upwards, which would make the entrance of new rival buyers unattractive, as also remarked by Blair and Lopatka[983]. Therefore, it comes to no surprise that exclusionary buyer power conducts are the most concerning type of anticompetitive behaviours and a prioritized area of scrutiny for the Commission[984], and as well as recognized in the US antitrust[985].

---

980 Communication from the Commission — Guidance on the Commission's enforcement priorities in applying Article 82 of the EC Treaty to abusive exclusionary conduct by dominant undertakings [2009] OJ C 45/7, para. 7.

981 For the Commission buyer power (monopsony) may significantly impede competition when "it is likely to lead to a reduction in output of the final products or the *foreclosure of competitors of the merged entity*" in Commission Decision of 21/12/2005 declaring a concentration to be compatible with the common market (Case No COMP/M.3968 - *Sovion/Südfleisch*) according to Council Regulation (EC) No 139/2004 [2005], para. 37 (emphasis added).

982 This has been explicitly recognized and ratified by the Commission through its Communication from the Commission — Guidance on the Commission's enforcement priorities in applying Article 82 of the EC Treaty to abusive exclusionary conduct by dominant undertakings (O.J. 24.2.2009 C45/7).

983 Blair and Lopatka (2008), p. 467.

984 Communication from the Commission — Guidance on the Commission's enforcement priorities in applying Article 82 of the EC Treaty to abusive exclusionary conduct by dominant undertakings (O.J. 24.2.2009 C45/7), para. 20.

985 American Antitrust Institute [2008], p. 97.

482. In general terms, buyer power exclusion aims at making "market entry very difficult or impossible for competitors [other buyers] of the undertaking in a dominant position, and secondly, of making it more difficult or impossible for its co-contractors to choose between various sources of supply or commercial partners", as stressed by the CJEU in *British Airways v Commission*[986]. Unlike buyer power exploitation, the anti-competitive conduct has a primary effect on a competing undertaking (either a buyer in the input market or a retailer in a related downstream market) on a horizontal level, but not vis-à-vis supplier or end consumers on a vertical level.

483. Exclusionary buyer power in an upstream market affects rival buyers by putting them at a disadvantage when acquiring an input by increasing their costs, and which is achieved by using buyer market power against suppliers to that end[987]. Therefore, all buyer-induced exclusionary tactics have a commonality: *their aim and strategy is to raise rivals' costs* to gain upstream and, more importantly, downstream market power, as explained by Salop and Krattenmaker, as well as by Scheelings and Wright[988]. By increasing its rivals' costs, the buyer gains a competitive advantage in the upstream market because if the exclusion succeeds in the medium and long term there would not be any other buyers and it can later exercise exploitative buyer power vis-à-vis suppliers. Additionally, and when the buyer competes with their rivals also as a retailer, it gains an advantage in the downstream market because these retailers cannot compete in terms of price (as their costs are higher), do not have access to sufficient input to efficiently produce an output, or simply completely lack the desired input – a 'must stock' product –, that end consumers desire. In other words, exclusionary buyer power is often used to leverage market power from the upstream market to the downstream (or vice-versa) as occurred in *British Airways v Commission*[989], or by exercising pressure on suppliers that are dependent on the powerful buyer to discriminate other rival purchasers, as discussed in the US in *Toys "R" Us, Inc. v F.T.C*[990].

484. Consequently, exclusionary buyer power tactics *may affect both upstream and downstream markets* – jointly or separately – because of the dualistic nature of buyer power, and also because firm(s) engaged in exclusionary conducts

986 Judgment of 15 March 2007 in *British Airways v Commission*, C-95/04 P, EU:C:2007:166, para. 68.

987 Morten Hviid and Matthew Olczak, 'Raising Rivals' Fixed Costs' 23 International Journal of the Economics of Business (2016) 19.

988 Krattenmaker and Salop (1986); Scheelings and Wright (2006), p. 215. Also generally, see: David T. Scheffman and Richard S. Higgins, 'Raising Rivals' Costs' in Roger D. Blair and D. Daniel Sokol (eds), *The Oxford Handbook of International Antitrust Economics*, vol 2 (Oxford University Press 2015). See also discussing the effectiveness of raising rivals' costs in term of fixed costs: Hviid and Olczak (2016).

989 Commission Decision of 14 July 1999 relating to a proceeding under Article 82 of the EC Treaty (IV/D-2/34.780 - *Virgin/British Airways*) [2000] OJ L 30/1; Judgment of 17 December 2003, *British Airways v Commission* of 17 December 2003, T-219/99, ECR, EU:T:2003:343; Judgment of 15 March 2007 in *British Airways v Commission*, C-95/04 P, EU:C:2007:166.

990 *TOYS "R" US, INC. v. Federal Trade Commission*, 221 F.3d 928 (7th Cir. 2000). Also making a similar statement see: Kirkwood 'Powerful Buyers and Merger Enforcement' (2012), p. 1488 and 1509.

will attempt to increase both their buyer and seller power at the same time[991], which is consistent with the hourglass shape theory discussed in chapter 2. Also, as noted by Hylton, a firm able to exercise market power both upstream and downstream will be further incentivized to engage in exclusionary conduct[992], creating a dangerous circle of anti-competitive behaviours that will be exerted with exploitative effects vis-à-vis suppliers (monopsony power) and end consumers (monopoly power).

485. Now, what kind of costs are increased in cases of buyer power exclusion? In principle the straightforward answer would be the marginal cost of an additional unit of input. However, Hviid and Olczak have recently demonstrated that an exclusionary tactic will aim at increasing marginal costs but can also attempt to increase fixed costs by, for instance, gold-platting legislation "to remove so-called red tape of regulators" in highly regulated industries, or vexious litigation[993]. In my view, Hviid and Olczak's proposal of analyzing both fixed and marginal costs is sound and helpful for understanding buyer power exclusion, particularly because both would be helpful indicators and, additionally, the effects on an increase of a fixed cost (and also sunk), will tend to have a greater effect on the wellbeing of a competitor (or motivate the entry of a newcomer) as fixed costs will not vary as much as marginal costs and, therefore be more likely to enter market conditions in more a permanent fashion.

486. However, determining whenever a conduct that appears exclusionary is unlawful is a difficult task, even if one knows which kind of costs are to be assessed. Behaviours that may seem exclusionary, such as purchasing price discrimination, may be efficiency enhancing and pro-competitive. Thus, as remarked by Østerud, and also Rousseva, there is no single test to determine the lawfulness for all exclusionary conducts, neither for buyer nor seller cases[994]. Regarding exclusionary buyer power, the uncertainty regarding what the legal standard to regulate these conducts should be is even greater due to the lack of cases that can guide and predict the outcome of competition law. This chapter aims at synthetizing and clarifying how buyer-induced exclusion occurs and what constitutes adequate legal treatment applicable to buyer-induced exclusion.

487. Furthermore, buyer-induce exclusion also takes the form of input foreclosure, which is an important form of exerting buyer market power to the detriment of rivals that is employed to raise the rival's costs. Input foreclosure takes place whenever a powerful buyer aims at hampering or eliminating access to a required input to a rival buyer[995], reducing its rival's ability to compete

---

991 See also making a similar claim: van Doorn, p. 129.

992 Hylton, p. 1.

993 Hviid and Olczak (2016), p. 29.

994 Østerud, p. 3; Rousseva, [2010], p. 327-352.

995 See discussing incentives related to input foreclosure on a vertical merger: Inderst and Valletti (2011).

in either the upstream or – more usually – a related downstream market[996]. This input can either be a raw material required for the elaboration of a final product, for example, timber logs employed in paper production; or a finished good, such as processed beef to be resold to end consumers by food retailers. Furthermore, I distinguish between two types of input foreclosure: the type that *increases rivals' costs* (partial foreclosure), and the kind that downright *eliminates access to the input* (total foreclosure). Both types make it harder for competitors to obtain supplies of the input under similar prices as those obtained by the powerful buyer and therefore, render the excluded suppliers less attractive to end consumers – because their sale prices are also pushed upwards – or force them out of the market[997]. However, input foreclosure will be only effective if there is substantial buyer (bargaining) power. Absent substantial buyer power input foreclosure strategies are unlikely to have a significant influence on the upstream trading conditions as suppliers will not be forced to comply with the requirements of the buyer as there are other alternatives of demand[998].

488. My analysis has identified different means through which input foreclosure is carried out and, due to their importance and differences between the conducts, I have opted to analyze them in different modalities: exclusive supply obligations, overbuying, concentrations leading to input foreclosure, purchasing price discrimination, and foreclosure of an input by means of granting supracompetitive bonuses. In the following sections, I discuss these theories of harm, as well as the case of squeeze to buy, as an independent theory that increases rival's costs but does not involve input foreclosure.

III. Exclusive supply obligations

489. In this section, I discuss how a buyer, through the use of exclusive supply obligations, may be capable of foreclosing rival buyers from efficient sources of input. To do so, I discuss these types of vertical relations in the realm of agreements, dominance and concentrations.

---

996 Guidelines on the assessment of non-horizontal mergers under the Council Regulation on the control of concentrations between undertakings [2008] OJ C 265/6, para. 29. See also: Scheelings and Wright (2006), p. 213.

997 Guidelines on the assessment of non-horizontal mergers under the Council Regulation on the control of concentrations between undertakings [2008] OJ C 265/6, para. 31; Scheelings and Wright (2006), p. 216; Schwalbe and Zimmer, [2009], p. 363.

998 Guidelines on the assessment of non-horizontal mergers under the Council Regulation on the control of concentrations between undertakings [2008] OJ C 265/6, para. 35.

490. Through an exclusive supply obligation a buyer agrees with (or forces) its supplier(s) so that the latter shall sell its output only or mainly to the buyer, creating a relation of exclusivity or semi-exclusivity between the parties that may be captured by Article 101(1) TFEU, and/or by Article 102 TFEU, if the buyer is a dominant undertaking[999]. The reverse situation also leads to an exclusive supply obligation: a powerful buyer or group of coordinated buyers may threaten its (or their) suppliers to stop purchasing input from them if they sell to a different buyer[1000]. Furthermore, the literature distinguishes two types of exclusivity supply agreements with exclusionary effects. Firstly, a powerful buyer may impose a 'naked' exclusivity supply obligation to its supplier(s) forcing them to exclusively sell all their production to the powerful buyer, or to refrain from selling to any other party[1001]. Secondly, exclusive supply obligations may be forced upon or agreed by suppliers by granting incentives or 'bonuses'[1002] to ensure that the supplier concentrates most of its sales to a single buyer, for example, by granting some type of preferential purchase conditions[1003].

491. Exclusive supply agreements, however, may also be conducts that enhance and improve competition because they allow for the generation of efficiencies among the cooperating undertakings[1004]. These vertical agreements may incentivize firms to invest in the development of new products (hold up problem)[1005], avoid free riding situations[1006], promote economies of scale for the buyer and supplier alike regarding distribution and administrative expenditure, or guarantee sources of supply[1007]. Because of these benefits and its efficiency-enhancing nature, exclusive supply agreements entered into by non-dominant buyers may benefit from the application of the Block Exemption Regulation if under the required thresholds or, if not, also satisfy the efficiency analysis requirement under Article 101(3) TFEU. In the case of dominant buying undertaking that imposes an exclusive supply obligation on

---

999 "Thus an agreement notified by an undertaking in a dominant position, such as an exclusive supply agreement, may constitute not only an agreement prohibited by Article 85(1) of the Treaty but also an abuse prohibited by Article 86 of the Treaty", Judgment of 30 September 2003, *Atlantic Container Line and Others v Commission*, joined cases T-191/98, T-212/98 to T-214/98, EU:T:2003:245 E.C.R. [2003] II-03275. See also suggesting the exclusionary effect of exclusive supply obligations: Carstensen 'Buyer Power, Competition Policy, and Antitrust: The Competitive Effects of Discrimination Among Suppliers' (2008), p. 307-310.

1000 Blair and Harrison, [2010], p. 163.

1001 Krattenmaker and Salop use the 'naked' term only to denote this second meaning in Krattenmaker and Salop (1986), p. 235.

1002 Using this term to refer to benefits granted by exclusive supply agreements see the Advocate General Kokott's Opinion on 14 April 2011 in Judgment *Solvay v Commission*, C-109/10 P -, EU:C:2011:256, para. 76.

1003 Bellamy and others, [2013], para. 7.065.

1004 See also raising this issue: Østerud, p. 63; Bellamy and others, [2013], para. 7.081.

1005 Bellamy, Child and Roth, [2001], para. 7-076.

1006 Bellamy, Child and Roth, [2001], para. 7-040; Ritter and Braun, [2004], 304.

1007 Faull and Nikpay, [1999], para. 3.186. For a detailed discussion of the economic efficiencies generated by vertical agreements in general see: Korah and O'Sullivan, [2002], p. 1-46. See also for the economics of exclusive dealing: Bishop and Walker, [2010], para. 6-028 and ss; Niels, Jenkins and Kavanagh, [2011], p. 237-238.

its suppliers, it is possible for the plaintiff to demonstrate that the obligation is not anti-competitive if the conduct is objectively justified and efficient pursuant to an analysis under the scope of Article 102 TFEU[1008].

492. Nonetheless, exclusive supply obligations *may raise anti-competitive foreclosing effects* if the buyer uses its buyer power to put its competitors at a disadvantage in two ways. Firstly, it may prevent or hinder access of competing buyers to a necessary input – for example, a particular tailored-made intermediate, good or a well-known trademark. Or/and secondly, a powerful buyer may increase its rivals' costs by securing exclusive supply from the most efficient sellers and, hence, putting an upward pricing pressure on their competitors and leaving them in a less competitive situation in the downstream market regarding end consumers[1009]. Exclusive supply obligations *may also have an exploitative effect* in some cases and may generate monopsony abuses, as I also discuss in chapter 7. Once a supplier is tied through an exclusive supply agreement, the buyer may abuse its buyer power – and even monopsony power as there is a single buyer – to obtain lower selling prices through threats or by withholding demand in an exploitative manner vis-à-vis its exclusive supplier.

493. Furthermore, exclusive supply agreements may foreclose *current* and *future* competing buyers by making market entry very difficult or impossible for other buyers, or by making it more difficult or impossible for its suppliers to choose between various commercial (buying) partners, for instance, by granting loyalty enhancing bonuses, as discussed in *British Airways v Commission*[1010], or because suppliers depend on the buyer for their economic viability, as analyzed in *De Beers*[1011]. Regarding *existing competitors'* exclusive supply is likely to increase rival's costs, particularly if they are smaller than the buyer, for two reasons. First, as remarked by Krattenmaker and Salop, weaker buyers will have to negotiate with less efficient undertakings, driving buyers' costs upwards[1012].

1008 "[…] although the fact that an undertaking is in a dominant position cannot deprive it of its right to protect its own commercial interests if they are attacked, and that such an undertaking must be conceded the right to take such reasonable steps as it deems appropriate to protect those interests", Judgment of 16 September 2008 in *Sot. Lélos kai Sia v. GlaxoSmithKline*, joined cases C-468/06 to C-478/06, EU:C:2008:504 E.C.R. [2008] I-07139, para. 50. See also: Communication from the Commission — Guidance on the Commission's enforcement priorities in applying Article 82 of the EC Treaty to abusive exclusionary conduct by dominant undertakings [2009] OJ C 45/7, para. 28-31.

1009 Krattenmaker and Salop (1986), p. 234; Guidelines on the assessment of non-horizontal mergers under the Council Regulation on the control of concentrations between undertakings [2008] OJ C 265/6, para. 36; Carstensen 'Buyer Power, Competition Policy, and Antitrust: The Competitive Effects of Discrimination Among Suppliers' (2008), p. 307-308.

1010 Judgment of 15 March 2007 in *British Airways v Commission*, C-95/04 P, EU:C:2007:166, para. 68. See also: Communication from the Commission — Guidance on the Commission's enforcement priorities in applying Article 82 of the EC Treaty to abusive exclusionary conduct by dominant undertakings [2009] OJ C 45/7, para. 19.

1011 Commission Decision of 22 February 2006 relating to a proceeding pursuant to Article 82 of the EC Treaty and Article 54 of the EEA Agreement (Case COMP/B-2/38.381 — *De Beers*) [2006] OJ L 205/24; Judgment of 11 July 2007, *Alrosa v Commission*, T-170/06, ECR, EU:T:2007:220, paras. 53-55. This Judgment was appealed and repealed by the CJEU in Judgment of 29 June 2010 in *Commission v Alrosa*, C-441/07 P, EU:C:2010:377.

1012 Krattenmaker and Salop (1986), p. 236.

Second, weaker buyers would also be cut off from a source of supply and will see their bargaining power reduced as there are fewer alternative suppliers and, therefore, buyers are now less able to obtain favorable conditions from the remaining sellers. For *future competitors,* exclusive supply obligations may act as an entry barrier as they will make it more difficult, costly, or even impossible for newcomers to get access to an input due to the lack of available suppliers, which may disincentivize firms from entering the purchasing market.

494. Importantly, buyer induced exclusive supply agreements should not be mistaken with *exclusive supplier agreements imposed by a seller*, even though the Courts and the literature use the terms indistinctively. I have found evidence of this interchangeable use – and rather imprecise terminology – in the buyer-power related dominance cases: *Imperial Chemical Industries v Commission*[1013], *Tomra Systems and Others v Commission*[1014]; the buying related merger of *General Electric v Commission*[1015], and the non-buyer power case *Intel v Commission*[1016]. In a supplier-induced exclusive supply agreement, however, it is the seller and not the buyer that exerts market power vis-à-vis its buyers by limiting or precluding the buyer from choosing a different supplier; thus, in practice, such agreements are another form of selling-side exclusive dealing[1017].

A. Assessment of exclusive supply agreements under Article 101 TFEU

495. Exclusive supply agreements between buyers and sellers may be captured by Article 101(1) TFEU[1018]. However, the general rule applicable to these agreements is that they would benefit from the Block Exemption Regulation if the parties that have entered into it are within the 30% market share threshold in the upstream and downstream markets and if the buyer is also below 30% in the retailing market[1019], even if combined with other non-hardcore vertical restraints[1020], but not if combined with hard-core restrictions, and in partic-

---

1013 See for example using the term 'exclusive supply' to refer to exclusive dealing obligations where a supplier forces its buyer(s) to acquire all input from them in Commission Decision of 13 December 2000 relating to a proceeding under Article 82 of the EC Treaty (COMP/33.133-D: *Soda-ash — ICI*) [2003] OJ L 10/33, further appealed before the General Court under Judgment of 25 June 2010, *Imperial Chemical Industries v Commission*, T-66/01, ECR, EU:T:2010:255.

1014 Judgment of 9 September 2010, *Tomra Systems and Others v Commission*, T-155/06, ECR, EU:T:2010:370.

1015 Judgment of 14 December 2005, *General Electric v Commission*, T-210/01, ECR, EU:T:2005:456.

1016 Judgment of 12 June 2014, *Intel v Commission,* T-286/09, ECR, EU:T:2014:547.

1017 Communication from the Commission — Guidance on the Commission's enforcement priorities in applying Article 82 of the EC Treaty to abusive exclusionary conduct by dominant undertakings [2009] OJ C 45/7, para. 33-36. See discussing exclusivity supply agreements from a seller's perspective: Østerud, p. 63-69; Whish and Bailey, [2015], p. 722-727; Rodger and MacCullogh, [2015], p. 205-206.

1018 In US antitrust law this would be captured under Section 1 of the Sherman Act.

1019 Whish and Bailey, [2015], p. 684.

1020 Article 2.1 and Article 3 of the Commission Regulation (EU) No 330/2010 of 20 April 2010 on the application of Article 101(3) of the Treaty on the Functioning of the European Union to categories of vertical agreements and concerted practices [2010] OJ L 102/1; Guidelines on Vertical Restraints [2010] OJ C 130/1, para. 193.

ular input or output price fixing[1021]. Below such margins, exclusive supply agreements are less prone to competition risks as efficiencies generated would trump any anti-competitive effects, and hence, the reason for the exemption. Outside the Block Exemption Regulation's scope, exclusive supply agreements may be declared lawful if found to satisfy the requirements of Article 101(3) TFEU, which further reinforces my proposal that buyer (bargaining) power tends to be mostly pro-competitive. Therefore, an agreement of exclusive supply entered into or forced by an undertaking with a market share above 30% as either a buyer or retailer is subject to scrutiny[1022].

496. To carry out the competitive analysis of these types of exclusive supply agreements, the Guidelines on Vertical Restraints offer important and detailed guidance[1023]. The assessment is anchored on three main aspects: market shares of buyers and sellers in the upstream and downstream market, length of the contracts, and the type of good that is sold exclusively. In this subsection, I discuss these three assessment elements.

497. According to the Guidelines on Vertical Restraints, the competitive risks that may be generated by an exclusive supply agreement *depend on the position of the buyer in both the upstream and downstream market*. This reasoning is in line with the *dualistic approach* to buyer power cases proposed in this work where the buyer power welfare effects depend on both upstream and downstream conditions. For the Commission, the extent of undertaking's buyer power will determine its ability to force suppliers to enter into exclusive supply agreements. However, the Commission only seems to consider that anti-competitive effects will trigger if the same buyer also has market power in the downstream market when stating that:

> The market share of the buyer on the upstream purchase market is obviously important for assessing the ability of the buyer to 'impose' exclusive supply which forecloses other buyers from access to supplies. The importance of the buyer on the downstream market is however the factor which determines whether a competition problem may arise. If the buyer has no market power downstream, then no appreciable negative effects for consumers can be expected[1024].

498. Although I concur with the Commission's first premise (the capacity to induce exclusive supply), I disagree with the narrow approach that only con-

---

1021 Judgment of 11 September 2008 in *CEPSA*, C-279/06, EU:C:2008:485. For a discussion of this case see: Paolo Giudici, 'The CEPSA Case' 5 European Review of Contract Law (2009) 159.

1022 In the US, the Supreme Court found that exclusive supplying services of movies where distributors of motion pictures had an exclusivity agreement with 40% of theaters for a period over one year was in breach of Section 5 of the Federal Trade Commission Act as an "unfair method of competition" in *Federal Trade Commission v. Motion Picture Advertising Svc. Co., Inc.*, 344 U.S. 392 (1953).

1023 Guidelines on Vertical Restraints [2010] OJ C 130/1, paras. 192-202.

1024 Guidelines on Vertical Restraints [2010] OJ C 130/1, para. 194.

siders downstream effects in competition to be of importance. While it is true that in most cases of buyer power exclusion the buyer competes with its rival buyers also as a retailer, there are also instances in which buyers only compete for an input and not an output. In these situations where competition only exists in the upstream market, the Commission's approach whereby it seems to only intervene in the presence of end consumer harm, runs the risk of being under-inclusive for instances of monopsony power or anti-competitive harm in the upstream market, and failing to fully take into account the dualistic effects of buyer power[1025]. As discussed in chapter 2, section §V, if the buyer faces strong competition downstream it has to pass on the benefits it has received from its suppliers and the exclusivity to its end consumers in the form or higher output and/or lower prices. However, the same cannot be said in the case of monopsony power upstream (or exploitative bargaining power) absent downstream market power, or when rival buyers only compete for the input but not in a downstream market as the output they produce is different. If a monopsonist has secured an exclusive supply deal with its supplier(s) and faces competition in the downstream market, even though it will not be able to exercise downstream market power vis-à-vis end consumers, there will still be a deadweight loss generated in the upstream market due to the withholding effect necessary to decrease a purchasing price vis-à-vis its suppliers. Nevertheless, pure monopsony cases are scarce and, hence, this could explain why the Commission seems to overlook these instances.

499. Furthermore, the Guidelines on Vertical Restraints remark that when the *buyer is dominant in the downstream market* an exclusive supply obligation with this hourglass-shaped undertaking is likely to *become an object restriction* of competition as these agreements "may easily have significant anti-competitive effects"[1026], which draws parallels with the current case law on Article 102 TFEU, discussed below. The Guidelines on Vertical Restraints do not expressly determine what the situation is when the buyer is only dominant in the upstream market, even if it does remark that the buyer market is obviously important to determine the ability to foreclose other buyers to access to supply[1027]. In my view, if the undertaking is dominant in the upstream and downstream markets then, in line with the proposals of the hourglass shape, the risks for anti-competitive foreclosure increase and, therefore, the practice should and is highly likely to be treated as *an object restriction of competition* due to its aim, content and context. If, however, the dominant buying undertaking faces strong downstream competition, this is likely to be an indication that downstream competitors have their own supply sources and are not prone to foreclosure by the dominant undertaking, or that the upstream market

1025 Also suggesting that taking into account pure downstream market power appears as too strict, see: Bellamy, Child and Roth, [2001], para. 7-046.

1026 Guidelines on Vertical Restraints [2010] OJ C 130/1, para. 194.

1027 Guidelines on Vertical Restraints [2010] OJ C 130/1, para. 194.

definition is narrower than the downstream market definition – where the buying side is local whereas the selling side is national or worldwide, for example. If that is the case, exclusivity supply effects on welfare would be counteracted by the competitive pressure of other retailing firms and should be assessed as an *effect based restriction of competition.*

500. Additionally, the *length of an exclusive supply agreement is an indicator of its possible foreclosing effects*. In the case of agreements among non-dominant undertakings, the Commission uses as a rule of thumb a maximum length of five (5) years. If the exclusive supply obligation is above five years, the Guidelines on Vertical Restraints consider that such agreements are not likely to satisfy the requires of Article 101(3) TFEU as the foreclosing effects are likely to trump any efficiencies that an exclusive supply agreement may bring, taking a strict stand. Nevertheless, in certain situations exclusive supply agreements beyond five years may be compatible with EU competition law because of the nature of investments required, market structure and combination with other type of agreements[1028], or due to a transitional period[1029]. In the case of agreements shorter than five years, the rule of thumb is that these agreements would be presumed to be efficient, and, in case of doubt, it is necessary to conduct an *effect-based* analysis to balance the competitive and pro-competitive effects of the agreement[1030]. However, other aspects, for example considerations regarding the recoupment period of a supplier regarding its investment and avoid hold-up problems, as well as the fidelity effects on end-consumers and/or type of buyers, should also be factored in when determining the maximum length of these types of agreements.

501. Lastly, to determine the compatibility of an exclusive supply agreement, the Commission will evaluate the *type of input involved.* If the goods are homogenous or they are an intermediate product, the chances of foreclosure diminish as suppliers can adjust to changes in demand with more ease and there are more opportunities to find substitute products[1031]. If the goods are differentiated, or for final consumers the risk of exclusionary buyer power abuses is higher, particularly if there are entry barriers or the competing buyers are small in comparison to the large buyer, as these smaller buyers will probably lose access to a particularly desired good by end consumers[1032].

1028 See also regarding a preliminary ruling dealing with a twenty years supply obligation agreement which, in reality, was an exclusive dealing obligation imposed by the supplier to the buyer in Judgment of 2 April 2009 in *Pedro IV Servicios*, C-260/07, EU:C:2009:215.

1029 Judgment of 11 September 2008 in *CEPSA*, C-279/06, paras. 60-62.

1030 Guidelines on Vertical Restraints [2010] OJ C 130/1, para. 195.

1031 Guidelines on Vertical Restraints [2010] OJ C 130/1, para. 199.

1032 Guidelines on Vertical Restraints [2010] OJ C 130/1, para. 199.

502. As a conclusion, under EU competition law and based on the Guidelines on Vertical Restraints, exclusive supply agreements are considered to be pro-competitive and efficiency enhancing if entered into by undertakings with a market share below 30% in the upstream and downstream markets, therefore, benefiting from the Block Exemption Regulation. This lenient treatment is in-line with buyer (bargaining) power economics and relevant economic literature dealing with vertical agreements. Even above these thresholds, an exclusive supply agreement is to be treated as an effect-based restriction of competition – unless the undertaking is downstream dominant – and can satisfy the requirements of Article 101(3) TFEU. Such an approach reinforces the idea that buyer power facing strong competition downstream is likely to be efficiency enhancing. However, the current treatment assumes that buyers also compete in the downstream market and does not cover instances where there is only competition for the input market and not the downstream market. Accordingly, the guidance must be re-adjusted for cases in which buyer exclusion may occur regardless of downstream competition.

B. Exclusive supply agreements imposed by a dominant buyer

503. Imposing exclusive supply agreements is not an easy task, even for dominant undertakings, which explains the reduced amount of cases dealing with imposition of buyer-induced exclusive supply agreements[1033]. Suppliers will, unless offered supracompetitive purchasing conditions[1034], resist attempts to be cut off from alternative sources of demand and, therefore, will employ their countervailing selling power to neutralize the buyer power of the purchasing undertaking[1035]. Thus, as suggested by the Commission, exclusive supply agreements by dominant buyers would only tend to occur in cases of "weak suppliers and strong buyers", particularly if suppliers are dependent on the buyer or the buyer is a necessary trading partner.

504. If a dominant buying undertaking imposes exclusive supply agreements on their suppliers, such conduct may be in breach of Article 101(1) TFEU and/or Article 102 TFEU(a)(c) or even (d), depending on the content of the exclusivity agreement and, importantly, the scope its effects. This is, the foreclosing effect must affect a *significant proportion of rival firms* and have a

1033 Also stressing this for selling side cases: Communication from the Commission — Guidance on the Commission's enforcement priorities in applying Article 82 of the EC Treaty to abusive exclusionary conduct by dominant undertakings [2009] OJ C 45/7, para. 34

1034 Communication from the Commission — Guidance on the Commission's enforcement priorities in applying Article 82 of the EC Treaty to abusive exclusionary conduct by dominant undertakings [2009] OJ C 45/7, para. 34.

1035 See making a somewhat similar statement concerning the use of buyer power vis-à-vis suppliers: Bellamy, Child and Roth, [2001], para. 7-045.

duration that is sufficient to generate a competitive disadvantage for rivals[1036]. If the suppliers are dependent on the powerful buyer, this might be because the buyer constitutes a necessary trading partner (as a gatekeeper) for them to reach end consumers, or because there are no other viable purchasing options when it comes to acquiring a necessary amount of volume for the suppliers to be economically viable. If this is the case, the likelihood of the foreclosing effect is increased, as suppliers fear the buyer's retaliation and would accept being tied to a single buyer[1037]. Concerning the duration, a similar approach as with the agreement under Article 101 TFEU applies. The longer the exclusive supply obligation, the more likely the foreclosing effect for both existing and future buying competitors will also be greater[1038].

505. Because of the lack of substantial buyer power cases dealing with exclusive supply, the Commission and the Courts are likely to analogically use the strict treatment provided by the case law, and, to a minor extent if any, the Commission's soft law[1039], in particular, *Suiker Unie and Others v Commission*[1040] and *Hoffmann-La Roche v Commission*, where the CJEU held that:

> An undertaking which is in a dominant position on a market and ties purchasers — even if it does so at their request — by an obligation or promise on their part to obtain all or most of their requirements exclusively from the said undertaking abuses its dominant position within the meaning of Article [102] of the Treaty, whether the obligation in question is stipulated without further qualification or whether it is undertaken in consideration of the grant of a rebate[1041].

506. Furthermore, in *Imperial Chemical Industries v Commission,* a case dealing with selling side exclusivity agreements but with some relevance for the discussion to countervailing buyer as a defense[1042], the General Court held that a dominant undertaking that engages in an exclusivity agreement with its commercial

---

1036 Judgment of 19 April 2012 in *Tomra and Others v Commission*, C-549/10 P, EU:C:2012:221, paras. 37-45, upholding the Judgment by the General Court in Judgment of 9 September 2010, *Tomra Systems and Others v Commission*, T-155/06, ECR, EU:T:2010:370, paras. 238-246; Communication from the Commission — Guidance on the Commission's enforcement priorities in applying Article 82 of the EC Treaty to abusive exclusionary conduct by dominant undertakings [2009] OJ C 45/7, para. 36. Also supporting this position see: Østerud, p. 67-69.

1037 Communication from the Commission — Guidance on the Commission's enforcement priorities in applying Article 82 of the EC Treaty to abusive exclusionary conduct by dominant undertakings [2009] OJ C 45/7, para. 36.

1038 Communication from the Commission — Guidance on the Commission's enforcement priorities in applying Article 82 of the EC Treaty to abusive exclusionary conduct by dominant undertakings [2009] OJ C 45/7, para. 36.

1039 Communication from the Commission — Guidance on the Commission's enforcement priorities in applying Article 82 of the EC Treaty to abusive exclusionary conduct by dominant undertakings [2009] OJ C 45/7, paras. 33-36.

1040 Judgment of 16 December 1975 in *Suiker Unie and Others v Commission*, C-40/73, EU:C:1975:174.

1041 Judgment of 13 February 1979 in *Hoffmann-La Roche v Commission*, C-85/76, EU:C:1979:36, para. 89.

1042 I deal with countervailing buyer power and this case in chapter 9.

partners is in breach of Article 102 TFEU as such exclusivity obligations have a foreclosing effect that is "incompatible with the objective of undistorted competition within the common market, because they are *not based on an economic transaction* which justifies this burden or benefit but are designed to *deprive the purchaser* [or the supplier in buyer power cases] *of or restrict its possible choices of sources of supply and to deny other producers access to the market*"[1043].

507. Therefore, in the absence of specific buying-oriented cases, it is highly likely that the Courts would resort to the reverse application of the precedents regarding seller imposed exclusivity agreements due to the risks of foreclosure for buying cases with them. The only difference between them being which contractual party is the one that has its freedom of choice limited. Such analogical treatment would be justified due to the similarities in the foreclosure effects and the fact that it would grant legal certainty by making the outcome predictable by the parties in the absence of any buyer power specific case law or Commission's practice. Hence, dominant buyers that impose exclusivity supply agreements to their suppliers are likely to be in breach of Article 102 TFEU.

508. This approach was tangentially explored by the Courts in the single example of a conduct imposing exclusive supply obligations by a dominant buyer in *De Beers – Alrosa*[1044]. In this case, the Commission preliminary found that a purchasing scheme between Alrosa and De Beers, the two largest diamond producer companies in the world, based on a buyer induced imposition of exclusive supply from Alrosa to De Beers could foreclose competing buyers of diamonds in the intermediate market.

509. De Beers, an undertaking dominant as a purchaser and retailer (hence *hourglass shaped*), and its competitor Alrosa were both active in the upstream of supply/purchase of rough diamonds and the downstream market of selling processed diamonds. Through the exclusive supply agreement, De Beers would guarantee that Alrosa's production would be sold exclusively to it and, therefore, competing buyers would have been deprived of an efficient supplier. This would have implied an increase in their purchasing costs that could lead to their market foreclosure as they were put at a competitive disadvantage when compared to De Beers. For the Commission, this 'willing-buyer-willing-seller agreement' "had the effect of hindering the maintenance of the degree of competition existing in the market or the growth of that competition and of maintaining De Beers' control over the rough diamonds market" due to its

---

1043 Judgment of 25 June 2010, *Imperial Chemical Industries v Commission*, T-66/01, ECR, EU:T:2010:255, para. 315, quoting Judgment of 13 February 1979 in *Hoffmann-La Roche v Commission*, C-85/76, EU:C:1979:36, para. 90 (emphasis added).

1044 This case is well known due to its impact regarding the application of the proportionally principle in commitment decisions, Commission Decision of 22 February 2006 relating to a proceeding pursuant to Article 82 of the EC Treaty and Article 54 of the EEA Agreement (Case COMP/B-2/38.381 — *De Beers*) [2006] OJ L 205/24; Judgment of 11 July 2007, *Alrosa v Commission*, T-170/06, ECR, EU:T:2007:220; Judgment of 29 June 2010 in *Commission v Alrosa*, C-441/07 P, EU:C:2010:377.

exclusionary effect, and also hindered the ability of Alrosa to compete as a retailer in the downstream market[1045]. Consequently, this exclusionary agreement could be contrary to Article 102 TFEU, even if the exclusive supply was accepted by the seller, as remarked by the General Court[1046]. This exclusive supply agreement, as stressed by Advocate General Kokott, was perceived as though it could "have detrimental consequences for the *market structure* and ultimately also for consumers"[1047], as there is a "danger that by buying up the production of the other producer, the dominant undertaking influences sales and thus ultimately also prices on the relevant market, to the detriment of consumers"[1048].

510. To address the concerns that arose from the 'willing-buyer-willing-seller agreement' and minimize its foreclosing effects, the Commission accepted a unilateral commitment offered by De Beers in which it agreed to gradually decrease the value of purchases of diamonds from Alrosa[1049]. The commitments offered aimed at solving a competition problem in the downstream market, by forcing Alrosa to supply diamonds to other buyers and preventing the existence of an exclusive supply agreement requiring De Beers to not buy rough diamonds from Alrosa in the future; i.e.: restricting the ability of using buyer power to affect downstream market conditions. Therefore, and even if the Courts did not expressly pronounce concerning the legality of the agreement, it can be seen that these type of buyer-imposed agreements by a dominant undertaking do trigger the application of EU competition law.

511. In the US, exclusive supply agreements imposed by a powerful buyer *have been held to be in breach of antitrust law*, in particular §5 of the Federal Trade Commission Act and §15 of the United States Code. In *Toys "R" Us, Inc. v F.T.C,* the 7th Circuit of Appeals upheld a decision by the FTC in which it found that Toys "R" Us – a large retailer specialized in toys – had abused its buyer power by entering into boycotting agreements with toy manufacturers so that these did not sell products to other toy retailers on the condition that the other Toys "R" Us suppliers would do the same[1050]. Rival buyers were

1045 Commission Decision of 22 February 2006 relating to a proceeding pursuant to Article 82 of the EC Treaty and Article 54 of the EEA Agreement (Case COMP/B-2/38.381 — *De Beers*) [2006] OJ L 205/24, para. 30.

1046 Judgment of 11 July 2007, *Alrosa v Commission*, T-170/06, ECR, EU:T:2007:220, para. 127.

1047 Opinion of Advocate General Kokott in Judgment of 29 June 2010 in *Commission v Alrosa*, C-441/07 P, EU:C:2009:555, para. 122.

1048 Opinion of Advocate General Kokott in Judgment of 29 June 2010 in Commission v Alrosa, C-441/07 P, EU:C:2009:555, para. 122.

1049 Commission Decision of 22 February 2006 relating to a proceeding pursuant to Article 82 of the EC Treaty and Article 54 of the EEA Agreement (Case COMP/B-2/38.381 — *De Beers*) [2006] OJ L 205/24, para. 44.

1050 *TOYS "R" US, INC. v. Federal Trade Commission*, 221 F.3d 928 (7th Cir. 2000), 930; Noll (2004-2005), p. 623. See the discussion of the case by Scherer, testifying expert economist on behalf of the Federal Trade Commission, in F.M. Scherer, 'Retailer -Instigated Restraints on Suppliers' Sales: Toys "R" US (2000)' in John E. Kwoka and Lawrence J. White (eds), *The Antitrust Revolution* (Fifth Edition edn, Oxford University Press 2009), 441-455.

foreclosed as Toys "R" Us was able to control the kind of goods that were sold to its rivals (i.e.: those toys not wanted by Toys "R" Us), making them, therefore, less attractive for end consumers of highly differentiated goods[1051]. Such practice aimed at preventing losing its preferential downstream position as a toy retailer vis-à-vis warehouse clubs who benefit from their large storage business model to sell toys at low prices[1052]. Also, these agreements with manufacturers prevented rival buyers from exercising price pressure against Toys "R" US, as retailers in the downstream market were unable to effectively use their buyer power to lower further prices for end consumers[1053]. Furthermore, the exclusive supply and boycott agreement also prevented end consumers from carrying out price comparisons between the goods, as Toys "R" Us forced manufacturers to not sell toys identical to those sold to Toys "R" US to rival buyers[1054]. Consequently, the FTC found that the agreements had led to a reduction of output sales from ten toy manufacturers to warehouse clubs, which caused those buyers to be unable to compete in terms of lower prices, and deprived them of toys desired by end consumers[1055].

512. By the time of the Appeal, Toys "R" Us had a market share of 20% of the whole US toy retailing market, and, in some urban areas, it enjoyed of market shares between 35% and 49%. Because of its strong position as a buyer, the Court of Appeal affirmed that Toys "R" Us enjoyed market power upstream and downstream, like an hourglass shaped undertaking. The Judgment held that "TRU is a critical outlet for toy manufacturers. It buys about 30% of the large, traditional toy companies' total output and it is *usually their most important customer*"[1056]. In other words, suppliers were *dependent* on Toys "R" Us as it represented about 30% of their sales – a situation similar to the "threat point" evaluated by the Commission merger retailing cases – and suppliers were not able to find alternative demand sources[1057]. The Courts of Appeal upheld in full the analysis by the Federal Trade Commission that found such agreements had an exclusionary and boycotting effect that was *per se illegal* under the rule enunciated in *Northwest Wholesale Stationers, Inc. v Pacific Stationery Printing Co*[1058]. Hence, the conduct was not exempt under an efficiency analysis, and the vertical agreements were in breach of the cartel prohibition of the §1 of the Sherman Act[1059].

1051 Toys are not interchangeable goods because their end consumers (kids) generally demand a specific one and do not readily accept alternative substitutes.

1052 *TOYS "R" US, INC. v. Federal Trade Commission*, 221 F.3d 928 (7th Cir. 2000), 931.

1053 Scherer [2009].

1054 Ibid, p. 444.

1055 *TOYS "R" US, INC. v. Federal Trade Commission*, 221 F.3d 928 (7th Cir. 2000), 937. Kirkwood 'Powerful Buyers and Merger Enforcement' (2012), p. 1509.

1056 *TOYS "R" US, INC. v. Federal Trade Commission*, 221 F.3d 928 (7th Cir. 2000), 930.

1057 See chapter 5, section §IV.C, and chapter 8 dealing with supplier dependence and the threat point theory used by the Commission.

1058 *Northwest Wholesale Stationers, Inc. v. Pacific Stationery Printing Co.*, 472 U.S. 284 (1985).

1059 *TOYS "R" US, INC. v. Federal Trade Commission*, 221 F.3d 928 (7th Cir. 2000), 933.

513. By analyzing the treatment in *Toys "R" Us, Inc. v F.T.C.*, a parallel can be traced to cases of exclusive supply agreements imposed by means of anti-competitive agreements among undertakings with a foreclosing effect (boycott), and unjustifiable exclusive supply agreements imposed by dominant buyers. Both regimes prevent large buyers from leveraging their market power as a buyer to foreclose rival buying firms that compete in a related downstream market. However, the approach taken is somewhat different as these buyer-induced agreements qualify under US law as 'agreements' under Section 1 of the Sherman Act and Section 2 of the Sherman Act, and not only as unilateral behaviour.

514. If had a European approach been taken to *Toys "R" Us, Inc. v F.T.C.*, the outcome to the case would probably have been different due to the structure and applicability of EU competition law when compared to US antitrust. Firstly, the application of unilateral behaviour under Article 102 TFEU would *have proven to be impossible or highly unlikely* because the market shares of the buyer in either the upstream or downstream market would have been quite different to the levels required to declare the undertaking dominant. Therefore, it would have been unlikely that the Commission and/or the Courts would have found an abuse of dominant position through unilateral behaviour. Interestingly, though, the US Courts resorted to the issue of dependence, a figure that is adopted by some MS in their national legislation to tackle buyer power abuses below traditional dominance thresholds, and which I discuss in detail in chapter 8.

515. This would then lead to the possibility of finding the agreement anti-competitive under Article 101(1) TFEU. Under such a possibility the case would have to be analyzed as a possible vertical restriction of competition, and in principle theoretically under the scope of the Block Exemption Regulation[1060]. In this sense, it would have to be determined if the suppliers in an aggregate would have had more than 30% of the toy's manufacturer market. If that would not have been the case, then the agreements in *Toys "R" Us, Inc. v F.T.C.*, could have potentially benefited from the Exemption of Article 2.1 of the Block Exemption Regulation, unless it would qualify as a hardcore restriction of competition in accordance to Article 4, which it does not because these exemptions are designed for cases in which it is the buyer the one that

1060 Commission Regulation (EU) No 330/2010 on the application of Article 101(3) of the Treaty on the Functioning of the European Union to categories of vertical agreements and concerted practices [2010] OJ L102/1.

is restricted[1061]. Hence, in principle should the type of agreement as the one discussed in *Toys "R" Us, Inc. v F.T.C.*, have been under the scope of application of the Block Exemption Regulation, the case would have been likely exempted from EU competition law, in an unusual occurrence of a less strict treatment of buyer power than when compared to the US antitrust law. If, on the other hand, the case due to the market shares would not have been under the scope of the Block Exemption Regulation because it exceeded the thresholds, it would be likely to be captured under Article 101(1) TFEU, the assessment the Commission and the Courts may perhaps have found that by Toys "R" Us agreeing with their suppliers not to sell certain type of toys to other retailers it was entering into an agreement restrictive of competition by object.

C. Conclusions regarding exclusive supply

516. From the preceding discussion and the little case law available, it can be concluded that exclusive supply agreements may raise anti-competitive effects due to their ability to foreclose rival buyers and may also serve as a starting point for exploitative buyer power vis-à-vis suppliers. These exclusivity supply obligations can be entered into by means of agreements that may be under the scope of Article 101 TFEU. In these cases of coordination between buyers and suppliers, the main rule is to consider them unproblematic and likely to be efficiency enhancing if the parties are not dominant and have market shares below 30% in the relevant markets - as either buyers or retailers - and if the agreements are under five years' duration and do not deal with particularly tailored goods. However, I have also highlighted that the Commission seems to adopt a narrow approach to competition concerns regarding exclusive supply agreements, as it places its emphasis on situations in which the foreclosure upstream also has effects in the downstream markets. While this is indeed the priority and most cases would comply with this premise, it is also important to remark that pure upstream foreclosure can also take place among non-competing buyers in the downstream market, which should not be disregarded.

517. Concerning dominant buyers that engage in exclusive supply obligations, the case law confirms that these undertakings are likely to be *in breach of Article 102 TFEU*[1062], as such unjustified agreements imposed by a dominant undertaking thwart the competitive process and market structure, foreclosing rival

1061 See for these situations to be exempted under the Block Exemption Regulation Article 4(b) of the Commission Regulation (EU) No 330/2010 on the application of Article 101(3) of the Treaty on the Functioning of the European Union to categories of vertical agreements and concerted practices [2010] OJ L102/1. See also: Commission staff working document - Guidance on restrictions of competition "by object" for the purpose of defining which agreements may benefit from the De Minimis Notice, accompanying communication from the Commission - Notice on agreements of minor importance which do not appreciably restrict competition under Article 101(1) of the Treaty on the Functioning of the European Union (De Minimis Notice), [C(2014) 4136 final], Brussels, 25.6.2014, SWD (2014) 198 final, p. 13.

1062 See the discussion of whether the language employed by the Courts creates a per se prohibition Whish and Bailey, [2015], p. 724. Calling this an "object restriction" see: Østerud, p. 65.

buyers, being contrary to the protection of the suppliers' economic freedom, and, ultimately, to the detriment of end consumers[1063]. These concerns and reasons given by the case law are quite in line with an ordoliberal approach to buyer power, particularly when dealing with the protection of the competitive process, rivalry and market structure. Such a stand of EU competition law may be criticized for not emphasizing the efficiency of the practice sensu stricto, particularly regarding short-term consumer welfare. Nonetheless, as indicated earlier, treating supply agreements as a breach of Article 102 TFEU still allows room for efficiency considerations as part of an objective justification analysis giving room for dominant buying undertakings to justify the existence of exclusive supply obligations. These efficiency remarks would be likely to be accepted if the buyer is dominant in the upstream market but faces strong competition in the downstream market, as the likelihood of foreclosure will then be limited, as discussed when dealing with the assessment under Article 101 TFEU, and the pro-competitive effects of the exclusivity may trump the negative welfare consequences of them.

518. In practice, however, it is likely that if the Commission follows its Enforcement Guidelines on Article 102 TFEU – as it should -, it will adopt a less restrictive approach to buyer induced exclusive supply agreements by dominant undertakings, which is in line with economics dealing with vertical restraints. This will be the case if these conducts do not have a significant distorting impact on the downstream market and consumer welfare (of intermediary and final consumers, and particularly the latter) rather than on protection of suppliers' economic freedom or market structure[1064]. Hence, in my view, it is unlikely to see a sharp increase of exclusive supply cases by dominant buyers being prosecuted or cases where buyers only compete upstream and not downstream, which may risk issues of under-enforcement in buyer power cases, although this is doubtful.

1063 Opinion of Advocate General Kokott in Judgment of 29 June 2010 in *Commission v Alrosa*, C-441/07 P, EU:C:2009:555, para. 122. See remarking the value of protection of the competitive process under Article 102 TFEU and linking it to the British Airways case: Wils (2014), p. 418.

1064 This is the approach used in the case of exclusive selling obligations under the Communication from the Commission — Guidance on the Commission's enforcement priorities in applying Article 82 of the EC Treaty to abusive exclusionary conduct by dominant undertakings [2009] OJ C 45/7, para. 34.

IV. Overbuying

519. 'Overbuying'[1065] is the equivalent – but no mirror[1066]– of predatory pricing when carried out by a buying dominant undertaking or a group of coordinated buyers. Through overbuying, the undertaking will increase the amount it pays for its input above the competitive level in an effort to exclude other buyers from access to it and foreclose them by recourse to a form of vertical foreclosure, as labeled by Hemphill and Wu[1067]. The buyer can do this either by increasing the purchasing price it pays (by overbidding)[1068], or buying more input than necessary (hoarding), as occurred in the US antitrust case of input price bid rigging, *Reid Bros. Logging Co. v Ketchikan Pulp Co* and *American Tobacco v United States.*[1069] Either of these two conducts would increase the buyer's rival's costs if its marginal costs are upward slopping, i.e.: the more input acquired, the higher the cost of the next unit.

520. By overbuying, a predatory buyer incurs in a short-term sacrifice (by raising its costs) in order to obtain a benefit in the medium/long term once competitors have left the market through recoupment by exercising its buyer (monopsony or monopoly) power[1070]. Hence, in cases of overbuying, suppliers are not exploited — quite the contrary, they receive a supra-competitive bonus as they are paid more than the competitive price[1071].

521. Therefore and because of the exclusionary effect of rival undertakings that compete as buyers and sellers alike, overbuying will tend to have a *dual market effect.* In the upstream market, it excludes rival buyers (horizontal effect), and once they exit the market it will allow the buyer to also reap monopsony profits vis-à-vis suppliers (vertical effect). In the downstream market (if un-

---

1065 Using the same term see: Salop (2004-2005). Other authors use the term "predatory bidding" to refer to the same conduct see, *inter alia*: Kirkwood 'Buyer Power and Exclusionary Conduct: Should Brooke Group Set the Standards for Buyer-Induced Price Discrimination and Predatory Bidding?' (2004-2005); van Doorn, p. 101.

1066 See also supporting this claim, *inter alia*: Kirkwood 'Buyer Power and Exclusionary Conduct: Should Brooke Group Set the Standards for Buyer-Induced Price Discrimination and Predatory Bidding?' (2004-2005); Richard O. Zerbe Jr, 'Monopsony and the Ross-Simmons Case: A Comment on Salop and Kirkwood' 72 Antitrust Law Journal (2004-2005) 717; Hylton. Cf with the opinion of the US Supreme Court when stating that "[p]redatory-pricing and predatory-bidding claims are analytically similar" in *Weyerhaeuser Company, v. Ross-Simmons Hardwood Lumber Company, Inc.*, in 127 S. Ct. 1069 (2007), IV A, 8; Salop (2004-2005).

1067 C. Scott Hemphill and Tim Wu, 'Parallel Exclusion' 122 The Yale Law Journal (2013) 1182, p. 1203-1204.

1068 Carstensen 'Buyer Power, Competition Policy, and Antitrust: The Competitive Effects of Discrimination Among Suppliers' (2008), p. 288.

1069 *Reid Bros. Logging Co. v. Ketchikan Pulp Co.*, 699 F.2d 1292 (9th Cir. 1983); *American Tobacco Co. v. United States*, 328 U.S. 781 (1946), see discussing this case: Hemphill and Wu (2013), 1203-1024. See a similar theory of harm for overbuying: Blair and Harrison, [2010], p. 38-39.

1070 Lars Henriksson, 'Predatory Foreclosure and EC Competition Law' 3 Europarättslig tidskrift (2008) 689, p. 689; Hylton, p. 1; Carstensen 'Buyer Power, Competition Policy, and Antitrust: The Competitive Effects of Discrimination Among Suppliers' (2008), p. 288.

1071 Also in this sense see: Kirkwood 'Buyer Power and Exclusionary Conduct: Should Brooke Group Set the Standards for Buyer-Induced Price Discrimination and Predatory Bidding?' (2004-2005), p. 628.

dertakings compete as retailers), if the overbuying has successfully excluded rivals this would grant the undertaking monopoly power vis-à-vis consumers and the ability to exploit them[1072]. Thus, upon successful overbuying the undertaking will have market power upstream as a buyer and downstream as a seller, like the *hourglass shape* concept introduced in this study. However part of the literature argues that whenever a buyer overbuys an input it would (unless it hoards that input) increase its output production, drop its retailing price or increase production to minimize loses, which may lead to a short-term consumer benefit due to the overbuying, as theorized by Salop[1073]. Also, if the overbuying fails, part of the literature and the US case law argue that it will benefit consumers because there is more output in the market and because of this a failed overbuying tactic that does not exclude rival undertakings may benefit in the short run end consumers[1074].

522. An example will illustrate the overbuying effects: Isolation's Supermarket decides to acquire all meat produced from all farmers and slaughterhouses in Isolation Town. It does so by paying a purchasing price (substantially) higher than the current prevailing price in the market, with the intention to exclude Isolation's Butchery from any access to beef (its input) and, therefore, force their exit from the Isolation's beef-retailing market in a couple of months. As there is no competition in the downstream market of beef sale for end consumers, Isolation's Supermarket will, after a few months and following the rival's foreclosure, also increase its retail price to reap supra-competitive profits[1075]. Additionally, as there are no rival buyers, Isolation's Supermarket can now exploit its buyer power vis-à-vis its suppliers and exert exploitative purchasing prices to monopsony or supra-competitive purchasing profits.

523. Consequently, overbuying is a complex exclusionary tactic that may have implications for upstream competition among the buyer and its rivals when competing for an input. Additionally, this type of conduct is likely to distort competition in the downstream market if those rival buyers compete also as retailers, as they are now in a disadvantaged position due to the increase in their purchasing costs, affecting their competitiveness vis-à-vis end consumers.

1072 See also: ibid, p. 653.

1073 Salop (2004-2005), p. 695.

1074 See discussing the positive impact of overbuying: *Weyerhaeuser Company, v. Ross-Simmons Hardwood Lumber Company, Inc.*, in 127 S. Ct. 1069 (2007). Cf with the negative opinion of Zerbe regarding overbuying effects in Zerbe Jr (2004-2005).

1075 Predatory bidding cases have also been few times challenged before the US courts as noted by Kirkwood in Kirkwood 'Buyer Power and Exclusionary Conduct: Should Brooke Group Set the Standards for Buyer-Induced Price Discrimination and Predatory Bidding?' (2004-2005), p. 655.

A. How overbuying operates? Predatory overbuying and raising rival costs overbuying

524. As discussed by Salop, overbuying can be used by a powerful buyer to gain market power in either/or the upstream and downstream markets and then *recoup its losses by exercising monopsony or monopoly power* by means of predatory overbuying, and raising rivals' costs overbuying, the two types of overbuying[1076]. The aim of any of these overbuying modalities is to foreclose rivals so that the buyer becomes a monopsonist and faces no competition in the upstream market, allowing it to depreciate the purchasing price by withholding demand[1077], which may also allow it to gain a competitive advantage in a related downstream market.

525. *'Predatory overbuying'* has its effects primarily in the upstream market, as the buyer will gain market share and market power in the upstream market by limiting or neglecting in whole the access of other buyers to a necessary input. For Salop, once the buyer has excluded its competitors or forced them to permanently decrease their output capacity it will be able to withhold demand and decrease its purchasing costs by exerting monopsony power[1078]; thus the recoupment occurs upstream. However, in my view this would not be the optimal move by a powerful buyer. If it is tempted to withhold demand, the reduction in price may force suppliers out of the market or attract entry of new buyers to the market. Instead, the buyer will probably exert market power by increasing prices downstream as it now faces no competition (if the excluded buyers also compete downstream) as there are no other retailers, being able to recoup by exploiting consumers through high retailing prices. Nevertheless, for Salop these retailing price levels may on occasion be lower than they were before the predatory scheme and, therefore there is no short-term harm to consumers – if a strict end consumer harm standard is adopted[1079]. This theory, however, seems to overlook that quantities sold in the downstream market will be reduced if demand is withheld to recoup losses through monopsony power, which will be welfare detrimental in itself and may lead to higher prices in the downstream market.

526. *'Raising rivals' costs overbuying'*, on the other hand, has its primary effects in the downstream market as the rival buyers that compete also as retailers suffer a cost increase and are forced to raise their retail prices. By having to increase their price vis-à-vis end consumers, this leads them to a situation in which they are at a competitive disadvantage in comparison to the powerful buyer that is able to maintain or increase to a lesser degree its retailing prices than

---

1076 Salop (2004-2005), p. 669.

1077 Blair and Lopatka (2008).

1078 Salop (2004-2005), p. 675.

1079 Ibid, p. 677.

compared to other rivals and, therefore, gain market share downstream[1080]. Under this theory of harm, the exclusion takes place whenever the powerful buyer increases its output price less than its rivals that now see their market position harmed in what Salop calls "price-cost squeeze"[1081]. Unlike predatory overbuying, raising rival's costs overbuying does not imply a permanent rival exclusion but it hinders their competitiveness. As costs raise, the competing buyers will have to either increase their selling prices or reduce their output, which will transfer market share to the powerful buyer engaging in buyer predation. Additionally, as prices of competitors rise, the large buyer may also increase its prices and consumers are then worse off than before the predation.

527. An example of another theory of harm based on raising rivals' costs overbuying that I have identified is the case of the *profit distribution and benefits of producer cooperatives*[1082]. Cooperatives distribute profits among their members in a different way that corporations do among their stakeholders. Furthermore, cooperatives may benefit from special and kinder rules regarding taxation or labor laws that reduce their operative costs and enjoy an advantage when compared with corporations[1083]. Because of these advantages, cooperatives might pay their members a higher price for the input it acquires (for example milk) increasing the overall market price and increasing rivals' costs that, even if as efficient as the cooperative, would not be able to fully compete as their costs have been artificially raised because of the cooperative's internal profit distribution system.

528. For Salop, these *theories of overbuying-caused harm differ in the market they operate (upstream and downstream) and in the consumer harm effect*[1084]. In his view, predatory overbuying, if successful, will rarely harm consumers – thereby adopting a softer stance, whereas in the case of raising rivals' costs overbuying consumer harm is affected because the powerful buyer may be tempted to increase its own retailing prices or reduce output, directly hurting consumers. In my view, however, such distinction and lenient treatment given to predatory overbuying would not hold under EU competition law standards as predation in EU competition law for several reasons. First, and as I will elaborate further in this chapter, exclusionary buyer power conducts are prohibited even absent evidence of direct consumer harm because the EU competition law has as an aim the protection of competition as a process and, to a

---

1080 Hypothetically speaking, the buyer could attempt to more aggressively gain downstream market share by lowering its selling prices and, therefore, carrying out selling side predation, which was the theory of harm suggested by the US Supreme Court in *Weyerhaeuser Company, v. Ross-Simmons Hardwood Lumber Company, Inc.*, in 127 S. Ct. 1069 (2007), and which I discuss below in detail.

1081 Salop (2004-2005), p. 679.

1082 Cooperatives and their relation to buyer power are discussed in depth in chapter 7, section §V.C.

1083 Cf with Fici who argues that cooperatives do not get a preferential treatment but a different treatment because of their special nature in: Antonio Fici, 'An Introduction to Cooperative Law' in Dante Cracogna, Antonio Fici and Hagen Henry (eds), *International Handbook of Cooperative Law* (Springer 2013), p. 7.

1084 Salop (2004-2005), p. 671.

certain degree, the protection of smaller (yet not inefficient) rival buyers and their economic freedom. Second, the case law of EU competition law regarding predatory conduct has been interpreted as not requiring recoupment[1085] for it to be anti-competitive[1086], as discussed in *Tetra Pak v Commission* where the CJEU rejected the recoupment for the specific situation at hand (although not excluding it could be required in other circumstances)[1087], and in *France Télécom v Commission* where the recoupment requirement seems to have been rejected in more absolute terms[1088]. Third, if only attention is paid to the competitiveness of downstream markets, the approach might be under-inclusive whenever the buyers only compete for the input but do not compete as retailers, for instance when the buyers use the same input to produce different outputs. Lastly, Salop's distinction, albeit interesting from a theoretical perspective, will in practice be blurred as both effects combine in a larger upstream and downstream impact.

a. *Naked overbuying and hoarding*

529. Furthermore, there are two other overbuying mechanisms that can be employed by a powerful buyer to exclude its competitors – 'naked overbuying' and 'hoarding' – as forms of carrying out either predatory or increasing rival's costs overbuying. Both naked overbuying and hoarding are practices that by their very nature and object are aimed at reducing, restricting or impeding competition and, therefore, should be considered anti-competitive.

530. Through *naked overbuying* a buyer attempts to exclude its competitors by acquiring an input it does not require, but which it is used by its competitors, in order to produce its output. An example of this was the case of *American Tobacco v United States,* in which producers of cigarettes entered into an agreement to overbid and acquire the less expensive tobacco types even

1085 For a detailed discussion of recoupment in EU competition law: Cyril Ritter, 'Does the Law of Predatory pricing and Cross-Subsidisation Need a Radical Rethink?' 27 World Competition (2004) 613; Michal S. Gal, 'Below-Cost Price Alignment: Meeting or Beating Competition? The France Télécom Case' 28 European Competition Law Review (2007) 382; Rousseva, [2010], p. 160-171; Richard Whish and David Bailey, *Competition law* (Oxford University Press 2012), p. 745-746; Whish and Bailey, *Competition law* [2015], p. 786. Suggesting that recoupment is not an adequate test for predation see: Nazzini, [2011], p. 203-205. Suggesting that scholars have argued for incorporation of recoupment in EU competition law see: Stavros S Makris, 'Applying Normative Theories in EU Competition Law: Exploring Article 102 TFEU' 3 UCL Journal of Law and Jurisprudence (2014) 30, p. 55.

1086 See also stressing that there is no recoupment requirement in EU competition law: Whish and Bailey, *Competition law* [2012], p. 745. See also stressing the divergent policy regarding recoupment from a comparative perspective: Elhauge and Geradin, [2011], p. 1137.

1087 "Furthermore, it would not be appropriate, *in the circumstances of the present case*, to require in addition proof that Tetra Pak had a realistic chance of recouping its losses. It must be possible to penalize predatory pricing whenever there is a risk that competitors will be eliminated." Judgment of 14 November 1996 in *Tetra Pak v Commission*, C-333/94 P, EU:C:1996:436, para. 44 (emphasis added). See interpreting this as implying no actual need for recoupment and therefore a difference with US antitrust law: Graham, [2010], p. 143.

1088 "[…] it *does not follow* from the case-law of the Court *that proof of the possibility of recoupment of losses* suffered by the application, by an undertaking in a dominant position, of prices lower than a certain level of costs *constitutes a necessary precondition* to establishing that such a pricing policy is abusive" in Judgment of 2 April 2009 in *France Télécom v Commission*, C-202/07 P, EU:C:2009:214, para. 110 (emphasis added).

if they did not incorporate such product into their own brands[1089]. The US Supreme Court found that such behaviour was a *per se* violation of antitrust law, in particular Section 1 of the Sherman Act as a boycotting agreement[1090]. *Hoarding*, on the other hand, consists in the overbuying of an input that is used by the undertaking but that will not be used in the short term and, instead will be stored to deny other buyers access to the input and increase their costs, somewhat analogous to the conduct forbidden by the CJEU in *Istituto Chemioterapico Italiano and Commercial Solvents v Commission,* where the supplier of a good refused to deal its product to prevent competition in the downstream market[1091].

B. Objective reasons to overbuy

531. However, not all instances of overbuying will be anti-competitive and would warrant intervention by competition authorities because what may appear as an exclusionary overbuying conduct can instead be an efficiency enhancing purchasing pattern that increases demand for an input. As discussed by the US Supreme Court in *Weyerhaeuser Co. v Ross-Simmons Hardwood Lumber Co., Inc,* there are several legitimate reasons why an undertaking may want to increase its purchases of an input that should not be unduly hindered by excessive regulation intervention. For example, a buyer may decide to acquire more goods than before because it takes a gamble based on the current and expected price of an input, or because it has expanded or intends to expand its output to increase its efficiency[1092], or simply because it has failed to properly calculate the amount of input it requires.

532. Alternatively, input price increases – an element to look for in cases of overbuying – may have occurred because of external circumstances, for example, regarding commodities like oil and gas that vary prices constantly and where the discovery of new techniques or reserves can have a sudden impact on input prices[1093].

C. Is overbuying common in practice?

533. According to my research, anti-competitive overbuying is rare, an opinion also shared by Lopatka, who claims that the fact "[t]hat predatory buying can be a rational anticompetitive strategy in theory does not mean that it is

1089 *American Tobacco Co. v. United States*, 328 U.S. 781 (1946). Discussing the case see: Natalie Rosenfelt, 'The Verdict on Monopsony' 20 Loyola Consumer Law Review (2008) 402, p. 406.

1090 *American Tobacco Co. v. United States*, 328 U.S. 781 (1946), p. 810.

1091 Judgment of 6 March 1974 in joined cases C-6/73 and C-7/73 *Istituto Chemioterapico Italiano and Commercial Solvents v Commission*, EU:C:1974:18, para. 25.

1092 John E. Lopatka, 'Predatory Buying' in Roger D. Blair and D. Daniel Sokol (eds), *The Oxford Handbook of International Antitrust Economics*, vol 2 (Oxford University Press 2015), p. 81.

1093 See also discussing reasons to overbuy an input: Blair and Lopatka (2008), p. 452-453.

prevalent"[1094]. At EU level there have been no competition law sensu stricto cases of overbuying before the Commission or the Courts and in the US only a handful of cases discuss it[1095]. The sole instance dealing with overbuying/ overbidding before the Courts has been a state aid case, *DTS Distribuidora de Televisión Digital v Commission*[1096], where the General Court dismissed an applicant's claim that argued that the Spanish National Broadcaster (RTVE) infringed Article 106(2) by consistently overbidding in the market for the acquisition of exclusive TV program content[1097]. The General Court dismissed such allegations based on lack of evidence and the legal national provisions applicable, but it did not dismiss the fact that overbuying – even if done by the state – may run contrary to the competition provisions of the TFEU *lato sensu.*

534. This lack of cases in EU competition law (and also in US antitrust) provides a good indication that overbuying is rarely a successful exclusionary tactic because there might be little chance of recovery, there may be other substitutes for the purchased goods, or because it requires pockets that are 'too deep' to function[1098]. Also, economic crisis and shifts in macroeconomic trends will make undertakings wary of overbuying an input because if their purchasing patterns or the values of the input or output change drastically, these buyers would be left with an excessive amount of input that is not possible to be sold at a price to sufficiently cover its costs[1099].

535. Despite the lack of cases, in the US, however, overbuying was discussed at length by the US Supreme Court in the seminal case of *Weyerhaeuser Co. v Ross-Simmons Hardwood Lumber Co., Inc,* which I discuss below, due to its importance for buyer power regulation[1100].

1094 Lopatka [2015], p. 87.

1095 *Weyerhaeuser Company, v. Ross-Simmons Hardwood Lumber Company, Inc.*, in 127 S. Ct. 1069 (2007); *American Tobacco Co. v. United States*, 328 U.S. 781 (1946), p. 810; *In re Beef Indus. Antitrust Litig.*, 907 F.2d 510 (5th Cir. 1990); *Reid Bros. Logging Co. v. Ketchikan Pulp Co.*, 699 F.2d 1292 (9th Cir. 1983); *Cargill, Inc. v. Monfort of Colorado, Inc.*, 479 U.S. 104 (1986), which was analyzed as a predatory pricing but not predatory buying case.

1096 Judgment of 11 July 2014, *DTS Distribuidora de Televisión Digital v Commission*, T-533/10, EU:T:2014:629, and under appeal pending decision as C-449/14 P - *DTS Distribuidora de Televisión Digital v Commission.*

1097 Judgment of 11 July 2014, *DTS Distribuidora de Televisión Digital v Commission*, T-533/10, EU:T:2014:629, para. 131.

1098 *Weyerhaeuser Company, v. Ross-Simmons Hardwood Lumber Company, Inc.*, in 127 S. Ct. 1069 (2007), IV B, 10. See also suggesting that predatory buying tends to fail: Kirkwood 'Buyer Power and Exclusionary Conduct: Should Brooke Group Set the Standards for Buyer-Induced Price Discrimination and Predatory Bidding?' (2004-2005), p. 628; Salop (2004-2005), p. 678-697; Blair and Lopatka (2008), p. 468. Cf with Zerbe who argues that there is little data that supports such claim in Zerbe Jr (2004-2005), p. 717.

1099 Think for example of an undertaking that overbuys oil as price drops and expect it to rise again in the short term but the price remains constant. I would like to thank Marco Corradi for bringing up to my attention the argument of macroeconomic crisis and the lower chance for overbuying to be successful.

1100 *Weyerhaeuser Company, v. Ross-Simmons Hardwood Lumber Company, Inc.*, in 127 S. Ct. 1069 (2007).

D. Weyerhaeuser Co. v Ross-Simmons Hardwood Lumber Co., Inc.

536. In *Weyerhaeuser Co. v Ross-Simmons Hardwood Lumber Co., Inc* (Weyerhaeuser), the US Supreme Court dealt in detail with the regulation of overbuying. This judgment is important for buyer power regulation because it sets an international precedent that the European Courts at EU or MS level may resort to when dealing with similar cases in the future. Nevertheless, in my view, and as I discuss in the next section, the case outcome would have been different if dealt with by the Courts. In particular, under EU competition law, the case law does not seem to require recoupment to find the anti-competitiveness of a predatory practice, the Courts apply competition law to conducts that harm the upstream market without requiring direct end consumer harm, and there would not be a requirement of double predation as the US Supreme Court did. This is, exclusionary overbuying affects competition as such without requiring predatory selling[1101]. This shows an important example of the 'Atlantic Divide' between EU and US antitrust regulation in buyer power[1102].

537. The US Supreme Court in Weyerhaeuser, pursuant to a Writ of Certiorari, *concluded that overbuying is analytically similar to predatory pricing* and, therefore, the applicable legal test is the one for predatory selling cases under §2 of the Sherman Act, the *Brooke Group* test[1103], reversing a decision by the Ninth Circuit, which refused to apply such a test. Before analyzing the US Supreme Court Decision, I shall briefly describe the case's facts and the Judgment from the Ninth Circuit.

538. Ross-Simmons Hardwood Lumber Co. (Ross-Simmons), and Weyerhaeuser Co. are two undertakings engaged in the operation of lumber sawmills in the Pacific Northwest of the US. These undertakings acquired timber and alder logs locally (the upstream and local geographic market) as input to then process the wood and produce lumber that was resold as hardwood finished lumber nationally (the output market). The purchasing had three methods:

1101 Judgment of 14 November 1996 in *Tetra Pak v Commission*, C-333/94 P, EU:C:1996:436, para. 44. Henriksson 'Predatory Foreclosure and EC Competition Law' (2008), p. 710; Thomas Eilmansberger, 'Article 82' in Günther Hirsch, Frank Montag and Franz Jürgen Säcker (eds), *Competition law: European community practice and procedure: article-by-article commentary* (Sweet & Maxwell 2008), paras. 2-15-524 to 2-15-525.

1102 For a discussion of the 'Atlantic Divide' and a comparative analysis of the man differences between US antitrust law and EU competition law see: Gifford and Kudrle, [2015].

1103 *Brooke Group Ltd. v. Brown & Williamson Tobacco Corp.*, 509 U.S. 209 (1993). See also reaching a similar conclusion: Blair and Harrison, [2010], p. 166. For a discussion of the Brooke Group Test see: Phillip Areeda and Donald F. Turner, 'Predatory Pricing and Related Practices under Section 2 of the Sherman Act' 88 Harvard Law Review (1975) 697; Phillip Areeda and Donald F. Turner, 'Williamson on Predatory Pricing' 87 The Yale Law Journal (1978) 1337; Kenneth G Elzinga and David E. Mills, 'Trumping the Areeda-Turner Test: The Recoupment Standard in Brooke Group' 62 Antitrust Law Journal (1993-1994) 559; Jonathan B. Baker, 'Predatory Pricing after Brooke Group: An Economic Perspective' 62 Antitrust Law Journal (1993-1994) 585; Kirkwood 'Buyer Power and Exclusionary Conduct: Should Brooke Group Set the Standards for Buyer-Induced Price Discrimination and Predatory Bidding?' (2004-2005); Blair and Lopatka (2008).

i) open bidding market;

ii) contracts with timberland owners;

iii) harvesting by the involved undertaking themselves.

Only the bidding market was subject to complaint by Ross-Simmons[1104].

539. Around the time of the complaint, Weyerhaeuser Co., which entered the sawmill business in 1980, had a market share of about 65% of the alder logs available in the region and had increased the production of hardwood finished lumber due to intensive investment. Furthermore, Weyerhaeuser Co. was (and still is) a large retailer and one the largest owners of private timberland in the world[1105]. On the other hand, Ross-Simmons, a smaller undertaking, had been operating in the region since 1962, and was found to have not engaged in efficiency enhancing investment and saw its market position eroded by its more efficient competitor.

540. From 1998 to 2001, the *prices for alder saw-logs (the input) increased while the prices of hardwood finished lumber (the output) declined.* This price variation led Ross-Simmons to shut down its mill in May 2001, and it went out of business. Following the closure of its operations, Ross-Simmons "blamed Weyerhaeuser for driving it out of business by bidding up input costs, and it filed an antitrust suit against Weyerhaeuser Co., for monopolization and attempted monopolization under §2 of the Sherman Act"[1106]. Ross-Simmons argued that Weyerhaeuser Co. had used its buyer power and 'deep pockets' to engage in predatory overbuying to increase the input price (of logs) to exclude its competitors; i.e.: it increased its rivals' costs by setting a higher purchasing price. As evidence the plaintiff put forth the existence of large market shares by Weyerhaeuser Co., the increase of log prices during the 1998-2001 period, and the declining profits of Weyerhaeuser Co.

541. Before the Court of Appeals of the Ninth Circuit Weyerhaeuser Co., claimed that Ross-Simmons had not fulfilled the extremes required by the *Brooke Group test,* which comprise:

> [f]irst, a plaintiff seeking to establish competitive injury resulting from a rival's low prices must prove that the prices complained of are below an appropriate measure of its rival's costs [...] Second, a plaintiff must demonstrate that the competitor had [...] a dangerous probabilit[y] of recouping its investment in below-cost prices[1107].

1104 *Weyerhaeuser Company, v. Ross-Simmons Hardwood Lumber Company, Inc.*, in 127 S. Ct. 1069 (2007) I, 2.

1105 http://www.weyerhaeuser.com/company/history/

1106 *Weyerhaeuser Company, v. Ross-Simmons Hardwood Lumber Company, Inc.*, in 127 S. Ct. 1069 (2007), I, 2-3.

1107 *Brooke Group Ltd. v. Brown & Williamson Tobacco Corp.*, 509 U.S. 209 (1993), 222-224.

542. The Court of Appeals of the Ninth Circuit declined to apply this test and re-affirmed the District Court of the District of Oregon's decision instructing the jury to determine whether there was an anti-competitive conduct based on whether Weyerhaeuser Co., "*purchased more logs than it needed*, or *paid a higher* price for logs *than necessary*, in order to *prevent* [Ross-Simmons] from *obtaining the logs they needed at a fair price*"[1108]. Thus, the proposed test by the Court of Appeals for predatory buying relies on two aspects:

i) purchasing more logs or paying more than necessary; and

ii) foreclosure that prevents competitors from acquiring an input at a 'fair price'.

543. The Jury found that these two elements (purchasing and pricing effect) were present in the case.

544. The Court of Appeals held that the Brooke Group test did not apply to purchasing side cases because benefits to consumers and competition stimulation do not derive in predatory buying cases as in predatory pricing investigations[1109]. Such a view was grounded on previous case law and the work of Kirkwood, who argued in 2004 that "Brooke Group should not apply to buyer-induced price discrimination" and proposed instead a full-fledged rule of reason approach based on consumer welfare[1110].

545. For the Court of Appeals, predatory bidding will not benefit consumers based on two grounds that are similar to my proposal of the hourglass shape. Firstly, as input prices increase rival buyers are excluded from the market, and once there is no input nor output competition the undertaking would:

> [l]ikely *pay less for its materials while charging consumers a higher price*. The firm would have little incentive to pass on the benefit of lower input prices to consumers when it possessed greater market power and needed to recoup the higher costs it had paid for its materials. Thus, the *overall effect of a predatory bidding scheme would result in harm to consumers*[1111].

546. Secondly, regarding entry of new rivals, the Court of Appeals also remarked that in cases of predatory buying this was unlikely because there were entry barriers in the industry due to the limited annual supply of logs. The Court of Appeal

1108 *Confederated Tribes of Siletz Indians of Ore. v. Weyerhaeuser Co.*, 411 F. 3d 1030, 10 (9th Cir. 2005) at 978a (emphasis added). These standards have been criticized as not being an adequate benchmark for overbuying cases other than naked overbuying and hoarding. See: Salop (2004-2005), p. 714; Blair and Lopatka (2008), p. 456.

1109 *Confederated Tribes of Siletz Indians of Ore. v. Weyerhaeuser Co.*, 411 F. 3d 1030, 10 (9th Cir. 2005), para. 14.

1110 Kirkwood 'Buyer Power and Exclusionary Conduct: Should Brooke Group Set the Standards for Buyer-Induced Price Discrimination and Predatory Bidding?' (2004-2005), p. 625-626.

1111 *Confederated Tribes of Siletz Indians of Ore. v. Weyerhaeuser Co.*, 411 F. 3d 1030, 10 (9th Cir. 2005), para. 16 (emphasis added).

based its reasoning on *Reid Bros. Logging Co. v Ketchikan Pulp Co.* [1112], another overbuying case of wood pulp, where buyers rigged bids to pay higher prices for an input and foreclose another buyer and conduct which was held contrary to §1 of the Sherman Act and which was not overruled by the Supreme Court in Brook Group. A relevant difference among these cases that was not discussed in detail by the Court of Appeal is that in *Reid Bros. Logging Co. v Ketchikan Pulp Co.*, the prohibited conduct was not carried out by a dominant firm, but instead by coordinated undertakings. Under the §1 of the Sherman Act, a buyers' cartel fixing prices or input would qualify as a per se infringement of antitrust law, similar to how a conduct is treated as an object restriction of competition under Article 101 TFEU.

547. Pursuant to a Writ of Certiorari, the US Supreme Court reviewed the Judgment by the Court of Appeals of the Ninth Circuit and held the latter had erred in law by not applying the *Brooke Group* test to overbuying cases by doing a reverse or mirror application of it[1113]. This implies that, according to US Supreme Court in Weyerhaeuser, overbuying would only be illegal if the purchasing undertaking has been able to recoup its losses after predating in the input and the downstream markets and whenever the plaintiff manages to prove consumer harm[1114]. By taking this approach, the US Supreme Court adopted a *lenient and narrow stand to exclusionary buyer power* by emphasizing the impact of buyer power in a related downstream market regardless of the effects in the upstream market, which implies that through such policy there is a tendency to favor the case of false negatives (erroneous acquittals) rather than false positives (erroneous condemnations), and granting more room to buyers with regard to their purchasing patterns[1115].

548. The US Supreme Court held that overbuying constitutes an exclusionary practice through which a powerful buyer "aims to exercise the monopsony power gained from bidding up input prices" to then exert monopsony power through withholding demand once the other competitors have left the market[1116]. It also held that predatory buying and selling are "analytically similar" because of the connection between monopsony and monopoly[1117]. Consequently, both predatory buying and selling require undertakings to incur short-term losses due to the chance to recoup them later on and reap supracompetitive profits[1118].

1112 *Reid Bros. Logging Co. v. Ketchikan Pulp Co.*, 699 F.2d 1292 (9th Cir. 1983), at 1297-98. Rosenfelt (2008), p. 406.

1113 See also criticizing the outcome of the decision of the Court of Appeals in *Confederated Tribes of Siletz Indians of Ore. v. Weyerhaeuser Co.*, 411 F. 3d 1030, 10 (9th Cir. 2005); Salop (2004-2005), p. 709-714. Qualifying it as a "mechanical description" of Brooke Group see: Hylton, p. 3. See also: Lopatka [2015], p. 81.

1114 Kirkwood 'Buyer Power and Exclusionary Conduct: Should Brooke Group Set the Standards for Buyer-Induced Price Discrimination and Predatory Bidding?' (2004-2005), p. 664. Salop (2004-2005), p. 713.

1115 See also stressing the broader scope granted by *Weyerhaeuser* to decision making by buyers: Thomas Donovan and others, 'USA: Monopolisation - Predatory Bidding' 28 European Competition Law Review (2007) N86, p. N87.

1116 *Weyerhaeuser Company, v. Ross-Simmons Hardwood Lumber Company, Inc.*, in 127 S. Ct. 1069 (2007), III, 8.

1117 Also remarking this analytical approach see: Rousseva, [2010], p. 147-148.

1118 *Weyerhaeuser Company, v. Ross-Simmons Hardwood Lumber Company, Inc.*, in 127 S. Ct. 1069 (2007), IV A, 8-9.

549. However, the US Supreme Court reasoned that *predatory buying schemes are rarely applied* because the chances of recoupment are slim[1119] and, thus, rational buyers will rarely overpay for an input[1120], conclusions that are consistent with the findings of this study. Furthermore, it argued that there are many legitimate reasons why overbuying may occur. For instance, due to a managerial error to expand production, to acquire goods before the possibility of an increase in the purchasing price of the good it requires, or prevent future shortages, particularly if the good is seasonal.

550. Additionally, for the Supreme Court, *unsuccessful overbuying may be pro-competitive* as it may spur innovation, for instance, by motivating new suppliers to enter the market (since prices of input are now higher), and benefiting consumers if there is no recoupment[1121]. Furthermore, the Supreme Court observed that overbuying is less harmful to consumers, using a pure short term end consumer harm approach, because "a predatory bidding scheme could succeed with little or no effect on consumer prices because a predatory bidder does not necessarily rely on raising prices in the output market to recoup its losses"[1122]. Recoupment, if possible, would only be obtained in the upstream market through further application of exploitative buyer (monopsony) power vis-à-vis suppliers.

551. Pursuant to these arguments, the US Supreme Court vacated the Judgment of the Court of Appeals and remanded the case to be retried in the light of the Brooke Group test[1123]. The application of this test demands the plaintiff must prove that Weyerhaeuser Co. was overbuying in the upstream market and also selling logs below costs in the *output* market with the capacity to recoup losses by later exercising monopsony power[1124]. Hence, the *US Supreme Court established a double predation test requirement – input and output predation – that may lead to under enforcement of predatory buying cases,* as I discuss below.

1119 Also suggesting that recoupment chances in this case were reduced see: Salop (2004-2005), p. 713.

1120 *Weyerhaeuser Company, v. Ross-Simmons Hardwood Lumber Company, Inc.*, in 127 S. Ct. 1069 (2007), IV B, 10.

1121 *Weyerhaeuser Company, v. Ross-Simmons Hardwood Lumber Company, Inc.*, in 127 S. Ct. 1069 (2007), IV B, 10-11.

1122 *Weyerhaeuser Company, v. Ross-Simmons Hardwood Lumber Company, Inc.*, in 127 S. Ct. 1069 (2007), IV B, 11.

1123 This is the same solution that was suggested by Salop in Salop (2004-2005).

1124 Donovan and others (2007), p. N86; Blair and Harrison, [2010], p. 166; Rousseva, [2010], p. 147-18; Herbert Hovenkamp, *Antitrust* (West ed, 2011), p. 170. See also the opinion of Blair and Lopatka who in their analysis of this case argue that "[u]nder the first prong of our modified rule, the plaintiff would be required to prove that the alleged predator sold its output at a price below marginal costs (or a surrogate) or destroyed input", therefore also incurring in downstream losses in Blair and Lopatka (2008), p. 466.

E. Weyerhaeuser *à la Europée ne:* revisiting the case from an Ordoliberal perspective and EU competition law

552. In this section, I criticize several aspects of the US Supreme Court Decision and aim to provide a "Europeanized" version of the Judgment inspired by an ordoliberal buyer power perspective. In my view, if Weyerhaeuser would have been decided by the Courts, the outcome would have been different because of the different philosophical and legal foundations of EU competition law, as well as the broader approach to buyer power cases when compared to US antitrust. In a nutshell, Weyerhaeuser appears under-inclusive and to be offering a too lenient treatment to instances of abusive overbuying by dominant undertakings inspired by the Chicago School, as noted by Rousseva[1125], making the claim almost impossible to meet the requirements of the test[1126]. Instead, the approach would resemble more the Judgment from the 7th Appeal Circuit and the suggestions by Kirkwood sanctioning overbuying because of its competitive impact also in the upstream market and protection of the competitive structure and the adoption a welfare standard that is broader than a pure end consumer harm standard.

553. In Weyerhaeuser, the US Supreme Court adopted a *narrow view to the concept of buyer power,* overbuying, and buying power competitive harm by requiring the application of the Brooke Group test and only considering monopsony power as a relevant type of buyer power. This approach is incorrect for several reasons.

554. Firstly, and as also remarked by Kirkwood, even before Weyerhaeuser was decided[1127], overbuying is to be carried out by buyers exercising bargaining power and not monopsony power. In fact, overbuying is the *reverse* of monopsony power; firms do not withhold demand but increase demand. Hence, *in an overbuying situation input prices and input quantity increases and not decrease, as it occurs in monopsony cases.* Monopsony may only by exerted after and if overbuying becomes a successful conduct as now there are no rival buyers allowing the predatory undertaking to recoup the loss of profit through demand withholding and setting exploitative purchasing prices.

555. Secondly, and related to *assumptions of output*, the US Supreme Court takes for granted that overbuying will not be a problem because the buyer may have excess capacity and, therefore, by acquiring more input it will produce more output which will reduce prices downstream. While I agree that larger output is beneficial for consumers and would likely lead to lower prices, this

1125 Rousseva, [2010], p. 148.

1126 Also remarking about the demanding nature of the test: American Antitrust Institute [2008], p. 127-128.

1127 Kirkwood 'Buyer Power and Exclusionary Conduct: Should Brooke Group Set the Standards for Buyer-Induced Price Discrimination and Predatory Bidding?' (2004-2005), p. 627.

analysis cannot be devoid of a case-specific study as overbidding may not necessarily result in additional output in all cases; it requires available excess capacity from suppliers and that a supplier is also willing to sell more units. Furthermore, an increase in costs is likely to shift the downstream price curve upwards as well, which will lead to higher prices for end consumers than before the overbuying is initiated. Consequently, taking as a given that buying more input translates into more output does not always hold, and it requires a case-specific assessment based on spare capacity, costs structures and the existence of demand for more output by consumers.

556. Thirdly, in *Weyerhaeuser* the US Supreme Court *assumes that predatory buying takes place only in cases where the parties compete both in the upstream and downstream markets*, as confirmed by Lopatka[1128]. However, if firms only compete for the acquisition of input (timber) but not in the downstream market (because undertaking 'A' sells furniture, whereas undertaking 'B' sells paper) then downstream predation, nor recoupment, is an adequate assessment tool because a comparison is not possible among non-rival retailers[1129]. In a pure buying predation case the powerful buyer wants to exclude rivals from the upstream market, not to leverage market power downstream, *but to gain further buyer power*. Eventually, as rival buyers are squeezed out of the market the powerful buyer is able to exert monopsony power vis-à-vis suppliers due to the lack of rival buyers for the input and additionally, but not necessarily, may also acquire the assets of these excluded rivals at a below competitive price and enter these other downstream markets in which it did not originally competed, in a practice akin to the 'squeeze to buy' theory of harm, discussed in this chapter 6, section §VIII.

557. Fourthly, the *application of the Brooke Group* test could be criticized[1130]. In Weyerhaeuser, the US Supreme Court requires the plaintiff to prove overbuying harm by complying with the downstream predation requirement of the *Brooke Group* test[1131]. This is, *the buying undertaking is – in addition to overbuying an input – additionally selling its output below costs in the downstream market,* including as part of its costs the raise caused by the overbuying. Also, said undertaking also *needs to recoup its losses* by exercising its buyer market power in the form of monopsony power (upstream) or monopoly power (downstream)[1132]. As put by Blair and Lopatka, "[t]he Court requires an exam-

1128 "In the simplest setting for predatory buying, the predator is a dominant firm in the input market; its input competitors do not compete with it in the output market; and it has no monopoly power in the output market. These are the conditions the US Supreme Court assumed prevailed in *Weyerhaeuser*", Lopatka [2015], p. 78.

1129 Also remarking that a downstream comparison is an unworkable test, even for the selling of the same output see: Michael E. Haglund, 'Weyerhaeuser's aftermath: Increased Vulnerability of Resource Based Input Markets to Monopsony' 53 The Antitrust Bulletin (2008) 411, p. 446-451.

1130 See also criticizing the application of the test but concluding that "the Court's decision, with certain qualifications, is sound though imperfect", Blair and Lopatka (2008), p. 416.

1131 See also discussing that not only has to be an overpay in the input market but "the price paid was so high that the outlay for logs forced the defendant's resale price to be below its costs", Hovenkamp, [2011], p. 170.

1132 Ibid, p. 170.

ination of the price and cost of the defendant's output, whereas the predation relates to the defendant's purchase of an input"[1133]. It would be difficult for such a stringent requirement to be met by a plaintiff, leaving cases of overbuying largely unsanctioned, as also remarked by Carstensen[1134]. Likewise, the US Supreme Court failed to properly understand buyer power dynamics, as also remarked by Haglund[1135].

558. On the one hand, the plaintiff must prove that the buyer – with no objective justification – has acquired either substantially more input (or its entirety) that it needed and has paid a higher price than the "competitive price", while incurring in a loss. On the other hand, the second limb of the test demands yet another anti-competitive conduct in the downstream market: to sell output at a price below either average variable costs or prices below average total costs but above average variable costs[1136], (i.e.: traditional selling side predation). The reason behind this strict requirement seems to be the fact that the US Supreme Court felt that overbuying as an anti-competitive conduct is unlikely to happen, whereas buying additional input – for legitimate business reasons or simply because of a mistake – happens often and should not be discouraged.

559. Hence, a successful application of the *Brooke Group* test may be an indicator that the buying undertaking possesses market power in the upstream and downstream markets and fits the hourglass model, and has also carried out predation as a seller. Therefore, the *Brooke Group* test seems tailored to capture the most severe instances of buyer power abuse *but grant large leeway to overbuying by dominant buyers that face a competitive market*. Hence, this theory assumes and is only applicable if and when the downstream markets are competitive. This lenient approach would be compatible with a strict end short consumer welfare or harm standard to buyer power, but not with a broader approach that also factors the competitive structure of the markets upstream and downstream, possible dynamic effects concerning suppliers, or the economic freedom of other rival buyers.

560. In my view, however, despite the fact that there are many reasons why a buyer may legitimately acquire more input, having such a strict predatory buying test that also demands downstream predation *will result in under-inclusion and predatory buying cases not being captured by antitrust and competition law*,

1133 Blair and Lopatka (2008), p. 469.

1134 Carstensen 'Buyer Power, Competition Policy, and Antitrust: The Competitive Effects of Discrimination Among Suppliers' (2008), p. 317.

1135 Haglund (2008), p. 411.

1136 Judgment of 3 July 1991 in *AKZO v Commission*, C-62/86, EU:C:1991:286, paras. 71-72; Judgment of 2 April 2009 in *France Télécom v Commission*, C-202/07 P, EU:C:2009:214, paras. 195-218. See discussing costs levels used in EU competition law: Graham, [2010], p. 140-145; Whish and Bailey, *Competition law* [2012], p. 742-748.

a problem also identified by van Doorn, and Blair and Lopatka[1137]. This is the main problem concerning the applicability of a dual predation test.

561. Also, another argument against the application of the *Brooke Group* test is that buyer that has increased its rivals' costs by overbuying does not need to predate in the downstream market to increase its market share. By simply maintaining previous prices or increasing them less than those of its rivals not requiring to price below costs, it will be able to capture the excess demand and reap supra-competitive profit downstream. Nevertheless, with this I do not discard the fact that downstream predation may not take place, what it means is that it is not, and should not be, a necessary requirement for overbuying to be an anti-competitive concern. A problem with this criticism is that by overbuying the costs of the buyer are increased upstream, which will impact its own costs downstream. Therefore, if the buyer sells at the same price as before or a price below its new marginal downstream costs, it is incurring in downstream predation because it would be pricing below either average variable costs or prices below average total costs but above average variable costs. Hence, unless the buyer increases its retailing prices to reflect the current purchasing upstream costs, there will be some form of selling side predation.

562. An additional reason why the application of the Brooke Group test does not suit overbuying situations is that there is actually no need for recoupment in the downstream market if the exclusion succeeds. The recoupment can take place in the upstream market alone as the buyer has managed to displace rival buyers and is now able to decrease the purchasing prices it pays to generate a supracompetitive profit without requiring any further increase in downstream prices. The recoupment downstream would, in any case, be an additional albeit unnecessary source of profit. A caveat to this argument should be made as it would not hold in case the buyer decides to exert monopsony power upstream and faces downstream competition. If that is the case, the demand withhold would affect its profitability as a seller downstream and see how rival retailers are able to substitute the amount of goods withheld by the monopsony practice. Regarding bargaining power, as there is no demand withhold, if markets are not competitive the buyer would not be incentivized to decrease its retailing prices. But if the downstream market is competitive then passing on the lower prices to end consumers would allow it to increase its market share and, therefore, increase profits.

563. Lastly, Weyerhaeuser follows the Brooke Group Test by assuming that *consumer harm* – sensu stricto – is the *requirement to trigger competition intervention in buyer power cases*. In so doing, the US Supreme Court disregarded

---

1137 van Doorn, p. 156; Blair and Lopatka (2008), p. 448.

granting any protection to competition as such in the upstream market, as well as the economic freedom and competitiveness of weaker (but not necessarily inefficient buyers), and it concentrated its analysis purely on end consumer harm. Blair and Lopatka also seem to criticize this narrow approach to over-buying, when holding that

> the fact that an increase in monopsony power may have little impact on consumers does not mitigate the antitrust concern, because the negative impact on sellers by itself warrants equal antitrust concern, a point oddly unacknowledged by the Supreme Court in its Weyerhauser [sic] decision[1138].

564. This narrow approach concerning competition intervention in buyer power cases by unilateral conduct, in my view, would be inconsistent with the general treatment granted to buyer power cases in EU competition law, and the case law arguing that a violation of EU competition law does not require a "direct link between that practice (the wrongdoing) and consumer prices"[1139]. Consequently, *how would the Courts have decided Weyerhaeuser?*

565. Under EU competition law, the case would have been focused by means of Article 102 as a price predation investigation and, to an extent, using the few and all selling side predation cases as a guiding tool or precedent[1140].

566. In my opinion, the main difference would have been the requirement made by the US Supreme Court of direct end consumer harm in order to intervene in the market. The case law and the EU competition policy foundations as a whole, and for buyer power specifically, have an approach that does not require the evidence of direct end consumer harm to trigger the application of Article 102 TFEU, as expressly confirmed by the case law in *T-Mobile Netherlands and Others*[1141] and also in *TeliaSonera Sverige*[1142]. This is the situation for buyer power because, as held by the CJEU in *British Airways v Commission,* Article 102 TFEU concerning exclusion is not only designed to protect the short-term wellbeing of the end consumer but also to protect the competitive structure and competition as such, as I discuss in detail below,

---

1138 Blair and Lopatka (2008), p. 468.

1139 Judgment of 4 June 2009 in *T-Mobile Netherlands and Others*, C-8/08, EU:C:2009:343, para. 39. See the opinion of Petit who found "unsurprisingly" that the CJEU found that unfair competition applies even absent a direct link between the conduct and end consumer harm in Nicolas Petit, *The IEEE-SA Revised Patent Policy and its Definition of "Reasonable" Rates: A Transatlatic Antitrust Divide?* (2016) 1, p. 14. See also remarking that evidence of end consumer harm is not required to protect competition as a process in Judgment of 6 October 2009 in *GlaxoSmithKline Services and Others v Commission and Others*, Joined cases C-501/06 P, C-513/06 P, C-515/06 P and C-519/06 P, EU:C:2009:610, para. 78

1140 Judgment of 3 July 1991 in *AKZO v Commission*, C-62/86, EU:C:1991:286; Judgment of 2 April 2009 in *France Télécom v Commission*, C-202/07 P, EU:C:2009:214; Judgment of 14 November 1996 in *Tetra Pak v Commission*, C-333/94 P, EU:C:1996:436.

1141 Judgment of 4 June 2009 in *T-Mobile Netherlands and Others*, C-8/08, EU:C:2009:343, para. 36 to 37.

1142 Judgment of 17 February 2011 in *TeliaSonera Sverige*, C-52/09, EU:C:2011:83, para. 22.

and also regarding countervailing buyer power, as I discuss in chapter 9[1143]. This implies that an additional downstream predation (which could exist) is not required to prove the existence of an abuse if upstream predation by itself is proven. The downstream predation, if anything, would be an additional factor confirming the existence of the anticompetitive conduct and its perniciousness as an exclusionary device, but not a pre-requisite.

567. Hence, it is likely that the Courts would have been satisfied if the plaintiff were able to show a substantial harm to competition in the upstream market that was capable of affecting the competitive structure, in this case by excluding a rival from the market without any economic justification. Hence, the test is somewhat similar to the one upheld by the 9th Appeal Circuit, but, in my view, it would not need to determine if the overbuying *prevented* Ross-Simmons from *obtaining the logs they needed at a fair price*[1144]. I think fairness would not have been the standard applied by the courts to determine if there was predation. Instead, the Courts would have resorted to some form of cost analysis to determine the predation in the upstream market.

568. The problem with the existing tests and cost benchmarks employed up to now is that the use of either average variable costs or prices below average total costs but above average variable costs[1145] looks at the predation from a selling side perspective and are not an adequate benchmark for buyer side cases, as also happens with the applicability of the as efficient competitor test and which I discuss below in this chapter's section §IX. They are not good indicators because these costs benchmarks do not measure the efficiency of the undertaking as a buyer but as a seller. Determining what the adequate benchmark to be used would be from an economics perspective entails a complex economic assessment, and the Courts have clarified that the Commission has a broad margin of discretion when deciding which benchmark to use[1146].

569. Lastly, another relevant difference is that, as I mentioned above, under EU competition law the Courts have not required express evidence of the possibility of recoupment[1147]. Therefore, unlike in the US, the existence of recoupment would be a relevant factor regarding the predatory pricing to determine whether it is abusive and/or exclusionary, but it is does not constitute a pre-requisite as in US antitrust law.

1143 Judgment of 15 March 2007 in *British Airways v Commission*, C-95/04 P, EU:C:2007:166, para. 106

1144 *Confederated Tribes of Siletz Indians of Ore. v. Weyerhaeuser Co.*, 411 F. 3d 1030, 10 (9th Cir. 2005), at 978a. These standards have been criticized as not being adequate benchmark for overbuying cases other than naked overbuying and hoarding. See: Salop (2004-2005), p. 714; Blair and Lopatka (2008), p. 456.

1145 Judgment of 3 July 1991 in *AKZO v Commission*, C-62/86, EU:C:1991:286, paras. 71-72; Judgment of 2 April 2009 in *France Télécom v Commission*, C-202/07 P, EU:C:2009:214, para. 195-218.

1146 Judgment of 30 January 2007, *France Télécom v Commission*, T-340/03, ECR, EU:T:2007:22, para. 129.

1147 See chapter 6, section §IV.A for the case law and relevant literature dealing with this topic.

570. Thus, if *Weyerhaeuser* had been litigated before the Courts, the overbuying behaviour would likely have been to be found in breach of Article 102 TFEU, although not anchored on a weak reasoning based on buying more than needed or raising costs beyond a 'fair price', but on the economic analysis of the foreclosure harm to the state of competition in the upstream market by means of an economic analysis of the purchasing conduct, that would not necessarily require demonstrating end consumer harm nor an additional downstream predation.

V. Concentrations leading to input (vertical) foreclosure

A. Horizontal mergers

571. As in the case of past and current unilateral input foreclosure, horizontal and vertical mergers that may exclude rival undertakings may be considered anti-competitive. The general standard employed concerning input foreclosure is that the concentration would be considered incompatible with the SIEC test, even if rivals are not forced to exit the market, as it is only required to demonstrate "that the rivals are disadvantaged and consequently led to compete less effectively"[1148]. However, there is little specific guidance for foreclosure – and in buyer mergers in general – as a consequence of the small amount of buyer-side mergers[1149], which implies that the Commission and the Court are likely to evaluate input foreclosure risks in a way that is analogous to that which is carried out for seller side cases[1150].

572. As discussed in the Horizontal Merger Guidelines, concentrations that create or strengthen buyer power in upstream markets "may significantly impede competition, in particular by creating or strengthening a dominant position", especially if the "merged entity were likely to use its buyer power vis-à-vis its suppliers to foreclose rivals"[1151]. This could be the case, for example, if suppliers were to become, or are, dependent on the merged entity and would be willing to enter into exclusive supply agreements or offer better purchasing conditions than those offered to rival buyers. Thus, input foreclosure in mergers is closely connected with buyer dependence.

1148 Guidelines on the assessment of non-horizontal mergers under the Council Regulation on the control of concentrations between undertakings [2008] OJ C 265/6, para. 29.

1149 Scheelings and Wright (2006), p. 233.

1150 See the Guidelines on the assessment of non-horizontal mergers under the Council Regulation on the control of concentrations between undertakings [2008] OJ C 265/6 for the general assessment for coordinate and non-coordinated foreclosing effects of seller-side mergers.

1151 Guidelines on the assessment of horizontal mergers under the Council Regulation on the control of concentrations between undertakings [2004] OJ C 31/5, para. 61.

573. This theory of harm of input foreclosure in mergers was used as one of the grounds leading to the declaration of incompatibility with the internal market of the *Kesko/Tuko* concentration[1152]. The assessment of the proposed merger between two food retailing chains found that the operation would have created a dominant buying and selling – hourglass shaped – undertaking that would have been in a position to both exploit their suppliers – as discussed in chapter 8, section §IV.C.b – as well as also potentially excluding rival buyers, in particular new entrants from other Member States, hence impacting market integration[1153]. According to the Commission, input foreclosure risks arose due to two circumstances. First, dependent suppliers would be less willing to find and switch to alternative sources of demand (buyers) to prevent retaliation from the dominant buyer (as occurs in cases of unfair purchasing practices that I discuss in chapter 8), and because the new undertaking would be preferred by consumers, for example, because of its widespread distribution. Second, and derived from the exclusionary pressure vis-à-vis rival buyers, the existence of such a large retailer and powerful buyer would have disincentivized new entries into the retailing business due to the lack of access to some of the suppliers[1154].

574. A similar theory of harm *linking dependence of suppliers to input foreclosure* was used by the Commission when reviewing the *Boeing/McDonnell Douglas* concentration among two airplane manufacturers and buyers of spare parts that was declared compatible with the internal market pursuant to commitments[1155]. The Commission held that the proposed concentration "would lead to a large increase in Boeing's buying power vis-à-vis its suppliers," some of which received up to 50% of their total turnover in sales to Boeing and McDonnell Douglas. If those suppliers were to lose such a powerful buyer this would be "very critical for them", meaning that *suppliers were dependent* on the buyer[1156]. As a result of the merger, the buyer power of Boeing would be strengthened and, therefore, this "would increase suppliers' overall reliance on Boeing and might put them in a position where they could not resist prior-

1152 Commission Decision of 20 November 1996 declaring a concentration to be incompatible with the common market (Case No IV/M.784 - *Kesko/Tuko*) Council Regulation (EEC) No 4064/89 [1997] OJ L 110/53. See discussing the case from a purely exploitative perspective see: Scheelings and Wright (2006), p. 234. See also: Faull and Nikpay, [1999], para. 4.154.

1153 Commission Decision of 20 November 1996 declaring a concentration to be incompatible with the common market (Case No IV/M.784 - *Kesko/Tuko*) Council Regulation (EEC) No 4064/89 [1997] OJ L 110/53, taken from the unabridged version, para. 11, upheld by the General Court in Judgment of 15 December 1999, *Kesko v Commission*, T-22/97, ECR, EU:T:1999:327.

1154 Guidelines on the assessment of horizontal mergers under the Council Regulation on the control of concentrations between undertakings [2004] OJ C 31/5, para. 31.

1155 Commission Decision of 30 July 1997 declaring a concentration compatible with the common market and the functioning of the EEA Agreement (Case No IV/M.877 - *Boeing/McDonnell Douglas*) [1997] OJ L 336/16.

1156 Commission Decision of 30 July 1997 declaring a concentration compatible with the common market and the functioning of the EEA Agreement (Case No IV/M.877 - *Boeing/McDonnell Douglas*) [1997] OJ L 336/16, para. 105.

itizing Boeing over Airbus"[1157]. Consequently, Boeing would be in a position to either *secure exclusive supply agreements or induce purchasing price discrimination to the detriment of competing buyers.*

575. Based on the risk of input foreclosure as a side effect of supplier's dependency, the Commission concluded that, "it seems likely that the increase in Boeing's buying power could significantly weaken the competitive position of Airbus and, in turn, strengthen the position of Boeing"[1158]. To offset the input foreclosure risks, Boeing accepted commitments that required it to not exert undue influence on its suppliers by either promising to increase demand or threatening to decrease demand in any way that could lead suppliers to reject requirements from other competitors, while still entitled to select its suppliers and enforce contracts regarding price, delivery, quality and proprietary information[1159].

B. Vertical Mergers

576. Vertical mergers between a buyer and one (or several) of its suppliers may also raise concerns regarding buyer induced input foreclosure. Post-merger, the new entity may be in a position to hamper or eliminate altogether actual or potential rivals' access to a necessary input as it has vertically integrated, thereby putting those rival buyers and business partners of the supplier at a disadvantage, restricting their ability to compete with the newly merged entity, as discussed at length in the Guidelines on the assessment of non-horizontal mergers under the Council Regulation on the control of concentrations between undertakings ("Non-horizontal Mergers Guidelines")[1160].

577. However, *vertical mergers* – like agreements among non-competing undertakings – *do not generally have significant buyer power induced foreclosing effects* and tend to be pro-competitive because they provide room for efficiencies arising from the complementarities of the operations and may reduce transaction and administrative costs[1161]. Hence, it is unlikely that vertical mergers would create substantial risks of input foreclosure that may cause the concen-

---

1157 Commission Decision of 30 July 1997 declaring a concentration compatible with the common market and the functioning of the EEA Agreement (Case No IV/M.877 - *Boeing/McDonnell Douglas*) [1997] OJ L 336/16, para. 106.

1158 Commission Decision of 30 July 1997 declaring a concentration compatible with the common market and the functioning of the EEA Agreement (Case No IV/M.877 - *Boeing/McDonnell Douglas*) [1997] OJ L 336/16, para. 108.

1159 Commission Decision of 30 July 1997 declaring a concentration compatible with the common market and the functioning of the EEA Agreement (Case No IV/M.877 - *Boeing/McDonnell Douglas*) [1997] OJ L 336/16, para. 119.

1160 Guidelines on the assessment of non-horizontal mergers under the Council Regulation on the control of concentrations between undertakings [2008] OJ C 265/6, paras. 31-57. See discussing the economics of input foreclosure in vertical mergers and the Commission's practice: Bishop and Walker, [2010], para. 8-009 to 8-019.

1161 Guidelines on the assessment of non-horizontal mergers under the Council Regulation on the control of concentrations between undertakings [2008] OJ C 265/6, paras. 11-14 and 54-57; Bishop and Walker, [2010], para. 8-011.

tration to significantly impede effect competition. Nevertheless, if the vertical merger leads to a creation of substantial buying power and has the capacity to hinder significantly competition in the downstream market due to foreclosure of rival undertakings, then it would be not compatible with the internal market. Practice and literature, however, confirm that anti-competitive foreclosure in vertical mergers is a rare phenomenon, as I discuss in detail below[1162].

578. Merger-induced vertical input foreclosure takes place whenever a large buyer merges either with several suppliers or with one large supplier to secure the most efficient input source(s). By integrating one of the buyers into the upstream market, an alternative demand source for other suppliers disappears and the former buyer becomes a rival supplier, which alters the purchasing patterns in the market[1163]. Through the integration, the merged entity may limit input access by refusing to supply competitors, and ultimately may increase its rivals' costs in the upstream market, which will confer an advantage in the downstream market on the downstream department of the merged undertaking[1164]. In the purchasing market, the undertaking's upstream department will employ its ability to sell the necessary input to weaken competing buying firms by either charging them higher input prices (purchasing price discrimination, as discussed in chapter 6, section §VI) or simply refusing to supply the good[1165]. To do so, the merged undertaking must have market power in the upstream market (i.e. the place where rival firms buy), as remarked by Non-horizontal Mergers Guidelines and the literature, which links this theory of harm with market power leverage, and which I discuss in this chapter 6, section §VII[1166]. This explains why, for the Commission, the focus of the assessment should be placed on the downstream (output) market and less so on the upstream market, as the merged entity will seek to leverage its buyer market power downstream[1167].

579. In the assessment of possible vertical foreclosure effects pursuant a concentration the Commission pays attention to three key aspects connected to the theories of harm discussed above:

i) the ability to foreclose access to an input upstream;

1162 Also of this opinion and claiming they are "very rare", see: Schwalbe and Zimmer, [2009], p. 369.

1163 Guidelines on the assessment of non-horizontal mergers under the Council Regulation on the control of concentrations between undertakings [2008] OJ C 265/6, para. 37.

1164 See also making a similar remark regarding vertical mergers in general: Schwalbe and Zimmer, [2009], p. 362.

1165 Refusal to supply is a typical example of exclusionary conducts by a dominant seller and, thus, outside of the scope of discussion of this study. For some literature in the topic see: Werden 'The Law and Economics of the Essential Facility Doctrine' (1987-1988); Areeda (1989); Lidgard (1997); Stothers (2001); Korah (2002); Nagy (2007).

1166 Guidelines on the assessment of non-horizontal mergers under the Council Regulation on the control of concentrations between undertakings [2008] OJ C 265/6, para. 35; Schwalbe and Zimmer, [2009], p. 363-364; Bishop and Walker, [2010], para. 8-011. I discuss exclusionary buyer power market leverage in section §VII of this same chapter.

1167 Guidelines on the assessment of non-horizontal mergers under the Council Regulation on the control of concentrations between undertakings [2008] OJ C 265/6, para. 32.

ii) the existence of an incentive to foreclose;

iii) significant impact in the competition downstream market.

580. Pursuant to the merger, the new entity may have acquired the ability to foreclose rivals to input access as it may now decide *to not supply its competitors*, engage in *purchasing price discrimination,* or *degrade the quality of the input sold to rivals*. The foreclosing ability can be done unilaterally or by means of agreements. By itself, the merging undertaking is only able to foreclose rivals if by reducing access to competitors it is able to negatively affect "the overall availability of inputs for the downstream market in the terms of price or quality"[1168]. For example, if the remaining suppliers are less efficient or offer goods not preferred by end consumers in the case of 'must stock' products. If in addition to the merger the new entity secures exclusive supply obligations with other suppliers then the foreclosing effect is larger. However, if there are any alternative sources of supply, foreclosure is unlikely.

581. Additionally, the merging undertaking must also be *incentivized to foreclose competition in the upstream market*. This decision will be made based on whether or not the foreclosure is profitable for both the upstream and downstream divisions of the merged entity[1169]. Foreclosing rival buyers – by not selling any output, for example – will reduce profit as a supplier but will also increase profits as a retailer. Therefore, there is a trade-off to be considered between profitability as a supplier or as a retailer and if the foreclosure would lead to a loss of profits then the merging entity is expected not to engage in it. This was the approach taken by the Commission in *Philips/Intermagnetics,* where anti-competitive foreclosure effects were rejected as it was more profitable for the merged entity to keep on supplying competing downstream undertakings and because buyers would have been able to find alternative sources of supply[1170].

582. Furthermore, a vertical concentration would be incompatible with the internal market if the foreclosure leads to "increased prices in the downstream market thereby significantly impeding effective competition"[1171]. As discussed above, buyers of the merged entity may suffer from a post-merger price increase, which may decrease their competitiveness as retailers in the downstream market. However, not all post-merger price increase would mean that the concentration is incompatible, as the *effects must be substantial* in the sense that not

1168 Guidelines on the assessment of non-horizontal mergers under the Council Regulation on the control of concentrations between undertakings [2008] OJ C 265/6, para. 36.

1169 Guidelines on the assessment of non-horizontal mergers under the Council Regulation on the control of concentrations between undertakings [2008] OJ C 265/6, para. 40.

1170 Non-opposition to a notified concentration (Case COMP/M.4300 — *Philips/Intermagnetics*) [2007] OJ C 123/1, paras. 56-62.

1171 Guidelines on the assessment of non-horizontal mergers under the Council Regulation on the control of concentrations between undertakings [2008] OJ C 265/6, para. 47.

only a small rival should see its costs increased, but rather the *input foreclosure must affect a significant proportion of rival undertakings* and also have a significant price increase[1172]. Furthermore, adverse effects on downstream competition may occur if the input foreclosure is capable of affecting potential entrants in the market because it sells output in discriminatory conditions (partial foreclosure) or refrains from doing so (total foreclosure). Also, if there are no other sources of supply – because other competitors are also integrated or the input is necessary – then foreclosure of entrant undertakings will be significant. Interestingly, despite the fact that the focus of the Commission is on the foreclosure effects on downstream competition and prices, its analysis is centered on granting protection to both end consumers and rival buyers to safeguard the ability of rival firms to compete and the competitive process as such, which attests to a standard going beyond pure end consumer harm towards a broader harm to trigger the applicability of competition law to buyer power cases.

583. Lastly, buyer power is also taken into account regarding the input foreclosure effects of a vertical merger in its passive form as *countervailing buyer power may limit the foreclosing effects of the concentration.* If the merging firm faces a strong buyer upon which it may be dependent, then the risks of foreclosure will diminish as not supplying goods or doing so in less favorable conditions will reduce its profit as a supplier and will strengthen the position of rival suppliers that now have a strong customer[1173].

584. Summing up, in common with most buyer power exclusionary cases, the main concern regarding input foreclosure in horizontal and vertical concentrations is centered on the adverse competitive effects on downstream competition and how input foreclosure affects the competitiveness of rival undertakings in the retail market by hindering access to supply sources or disincentivizing entry of new players. Horizontal input foreclosure is largely caused by the existence of supplier dependence that leads to a fear of retaliation from the buyer as their turnover is critically dependent on keeping such a large business partner[1174], and which is in line with the dualistic approach to buyer power effects proposed in this work and analogous to the input foreclosure treatment discussed under Articles 101 and 102 TFEU. On the other hand, vertical foreclosure arises due to the unwillingness of the merged entity to supply rival buyers or apply discriminatory purchasing prices, possibly affecting the ability of rivals to compete in the downstream market. However, the likelihood

---

1172 Guidelines on the assessment of non-horizontal mergers under the Council Regulation on the control of concentrations between undertakings [2008] OJ C 265/6, para. 48.

1173 Guidelines on the assessment of non-horizontal mergers under the Council Regulation on the control of concentrations between undertakings [2008] OJ C 265/6, para. 51.

1174 "In order to meet the Commission's concerns that Boeing could leverage its supply relationships to discriminate against other manufacturers of large commercial aircraft, Boeing makes the following commitments […]" in Commission Decision of 30 July 1997 declaring a concentration compatible with the common market and the functioning of the EEA Agreement (Case No IV/M.877 - *Boeing/McDonnell Douglas*) [1997] OJ L 336/16, para. 119.

of anti-competitive vertical mergers is small as the conduct will most often not be profit maximizing and, therefore, seen as mostly pro-competitive, as occurs with vertical supply agreements among non-competing undertakings.

VI. Purchasing price discrimination

585. Another way of foreclosing rivals through exerting exclusionary buyer power is resorting to purchasing price discrimination. Price discrimination occurs when buyers (or sellers) pay different prices for the same products under the same conditions and in a manner that does not reflect supply or buying costs in any persistent way[1175]. By and large, price discrimination is pro-competitive as it allows a more efficient distribution of goods and the ability to exert neutralizing seller power. Therefore, most instances of price discrimination are legitimate and efficiency enhancing, as remarked by Bishop and Walker[1176]. This would be the case for instance if price discrimination is based on economies of scale or quantity based discrimination[1177]. Nevertheless, price discrimination in legal terms may also imply that there is a differentiated and discriminatory treatment among undertakings that may trigger the application of competition law. Unjustified and discriminatory purchasing price discrimination with an exploitative[1178] or exclusionary effect is prohibited under Article 102(2) (c) TFEU for buyers and sellers alike absent an objective justification[1179], and whenever it distorts competition either among competing buyers or vis-á-vis suppliers[1180]. Also purchasing price discrimination is forbidden among coordinated undertakings by means of Article 101(1) (d)

1175 Bishop and Walker, [2010], para. 6-028; Jones and Sufrin, *EU Competition Law: Text, Cases and Materials* [2014], p. 396; Whish and Bailey, *Competition law* [2015], p. 802.

1176 Bishop and Walker, [2010], para. 6-028. See the analysis regarding price discrimination's effect on welfare in ibid para. 6-031 to 6-036. Also stressing the positive effects of price discrimination in a buyer power context see: Scheelings and Wright (2006), p. 211.

1177 Judgment of 9 September 2010, *Tomra Systems and Others v Commission*, T-155/06, ECR, EU:T:2010:370; Judgment of 19 April 2012 in *Tomra and Others v Commission*, C-549/10 P, EU:C:2012:221, para. 212.

1178 I deal with exploitative purchasing price discrimination in chapter 7, section §IV.

1179 Such a efficiency argument could be assessed as part of an objective justification analysis under Article 102 TFEU or an objective justification pursuant to Article 106(2) TFEU as discussed in Judgment of 29 March 2001 in *Portugal v Commission*, C-163/99, EU:C:2001:189, paras. 67-78. See also Opinion of Advocate General Jacobs in C-53/03 - *Syfait and Others (GlaxoSmithKline)*, EU:C:2004:673 E.C.R. [2005] I-04609, para. 72. For a thorough discussion of objective justifications defenses in exclusionary abuses see: Albertina Albors-Llorens, 'The Role of Objective Justification and Efficiencies in the Application of Article 82 EC ' 44 Common Market Law Review (2007) 1727; Penelope Papandropoulos, 'How Should Price Discrimination be Dealt with by Competition Authorities?' 3 Concurrences (2007) 34; Østerud, p. 245-299; Rousseva, [2010], p. 259-296.

1180 Judgment of 15 March 2007 in *British Airways v Commission*, C-95/04 P, EU:C:2007:166, para. 144. Under US antitrust law purchasing price discrimination is prohibited by the Robinson-Patman Act and not the Sherman Antitrust Act. The Robinson-Patman Act is a legislative piece more akin to those European national legislations prohibiting unfair purchasing practices and which are discussed in detail in chapter 8. In economics, price discrimination is understood as the situation in which the same exact good is sold at different prices that do not correspond to any cost differences. For some competition economics dealing with price discrimination see: Niels, Jenkins and Kavanagh, [2011], p. 215-223; Bishop and Walker, [2010], para. 6.29-6.36.

TFEU. In both cases, as noted by Akman, the prohibition of price discrimination is interpreted as targeted against rival undertakings but not towards end consumers[1181]. Hence, there is a tension between the economic efficiency generated by price discrimination and the prohibition of legal discrimination (sensu stricto) between parties, which is one of the most discussed aspects of the EU case law[1182], as the Courts have taken a stand that is seen as "extremely hostile"[1183] or old fashioned[1184].

586. Purchasing price discrimination can be done through different practices, such as rebates, predatory pricing schemes and forms of exclusive dealing[1185], and I cover all aspects in detail in this chapter and in chapter 7. In this section, however, I adopt a narrow approach and discuss the situation in which the buyer incentivizes its suppliers so they charge a higher selling price to rival buyers to raise their costs and put them at a competitive disadvantage in a related downstream market. Hence, I will not discuss traditional selling side price discrimination or the effects of rebates[1186], but rather will center on *buyer induced price discrimination* with exclusionary effects on competing buyers.

587. Buyer induced price discrimination occurs when a powerful buyer forces suppliers to sell goods to other buyers at a higher price than those that are offered to it; this implies than this buyer obtains a lower purchasing prices than those offered to its competitors[1187]. In such a way, the purchasing undertaking obtains a competitive advantage over its rivals that may force their market exit, resulting in the foreclosure effect[1188]. Yet, the exercise of buyer (bargaining) power to obtain better terms and conditions based on buyer power will unavoidably result in price discrimination, as the outcome of the negotiation

---

1181 Akman, *The Concept of Abuse in EU Competition Law: Law And Economic Approaches* [2012], p. 232.

1182 See, *inter alia*: Judgment by the General Court in Judgment of 17 December 2003, *British Airways v Commission* of 17 December 2003, T-219/99, ECR, EU:T:2003:343; and Judgment of 15 March 2007 in *British Airways v Commission*, C-95/04 P, EU:C:2007:166; Judgment of 9 September 2009, *Clearstream v Commission*, T-301/04, ECR, EU:T:2009:317; Judgment of 24 October 2002 in *Aéroports de Paris v Commission*, C-82/01 P, EU:C:2002:617; T-504/93 - *Tiercé Ladbroke v Commission*, EU:T:1997:84 E.C.R. [1997 II-00923]; Judgment of 14 February 1978 in *United Brands v Commission*, C-27/76, EU:C:1978:22.

1183 Bishop and Walker, [2010], para. 6-040.

1184 See discussing the economic treatment given to price discrimination (rebates) in *Intel v Commission* and addressing part of this discussion: Wils (2014). See in general: Denis Waelbroeck, 'Michelin II: A Per Se Rule Against Rebates by Dominant Companies?' 1 Journal of Competition Law and Economics (2005) 149; Christian Ahlborn and David Bailey, 'Discounts, Rebates and Selective Pricing by Dominant Firms: A Trans-Atlantic Comparison' 2 European Competition Journal (2006) 101; Damien Geradin and Nicolas Petit, 'Price Discrimination under EC Competition Law: Another Antitrust Doctrine in Search of Limiting Principles?' 2 Journal of Competition Law and Economics (2006) 479; Nicholas Economides, 'Loyalty/Requirement Rebates and the Antitrust Modernization Commission: What is the Appropriate Liability Standard' 54 Antitrust Bulletin (2009) 259; Zenger and Walker, [2013].

1185 Geradin and Petit (2006), p. 479; Graham, [2010], p. 155.

1186 For a discussion concerning the effects of rebates limiting exercise of buyer power and some literature dealing with it see chapter 10.

1187 Blair and Harrison, [2010], p. 167.

1188 Kirkwood 'Buyer Power and Exclusionary Conduct: Should Brooke Group Set the Standards for Buyer-Induced Price Discrimination and Predatory Bidding?' (2004-2005); Kirkwood, *Buyer Power and Healthcare Prices*, p. 7.

depends on the bargaining power of each party[1189], and which is economically justified. Therefore, the issue would be determining when the discrimination has exclusionary (and exploitative)[1190] effects and when such effects are unjustified.

A. How does buyer purchasing price discrimination operate and what are its effects?

588. Unlike in the case of selling side price discrimination – which occurs through rebates or discounts – although a buyer may not directly set exclusionary purchasing price discrimination, it "*induces* a supplier to engage in price discrimination by causing it to grant the buyer a lower price than it charges competing buyers"[1191]. A way of differentiating buyer induced price discrimination with selling side discrimination is that the buyer is the one that has the largest amount of bargaining power and the one 'forcing' or 'motivating' the seller to grant it the price concession. However, the distinction is blurred and probably impractical for most cases, as it is also in the interest of the seller to price discriminate to the benefit of a large buyer to secure more sales than otherwise; hence, the buyer induced discrimination is the flip side of the coin of selling side discrimination.

589. For instance, Isolation's Supermarket will 'convince' the slaughterhouses of Isolation to grant it a preferential price for processed beef, thanks to its buyer power[1192] and, also to charge a non-preferential (and higher) price to its competitors, which may not be economically justified (i.e.: the suppliers' cost curve is flat, the buyer does not buy in large amounts allowing for supplier's economies of scale, or there are no additional distribution costs). Thus, by forcing such a purchasing price discrimination strategy, Isolation's Supermarket is increasing their rivals' costs and possibly forcing exit from the market of some of them. Accordingly and in such a setting, buyer power is usually employed to gain a competitive benefit in the adjacent downstream market, reinforcing its dualistic effect.

590. Furthermore, in some cases buyer market power is leveraged to induce price discrimination of the same entity as a retailer (selling side price discrimination). This was the theory of harm employed in *Irish Sugar v Commission,* where it was found that Irish Sugar, a dominant undertaking as a buyer of raw sugar and retailer of processed sugar, granted its customers of processed

---

1189 See also: Scheelings and Wright (2006), p. 210.

1190 I discuss exploitative purchasing price discrimination in chapter 7, section §IV.

1191 Kirkwood 'Buyer Power and Exclusionary Conduct: Should Brooke Group Set the Standards for Buyer-Induced Price Discrimination and Predatory Bidding?' (2004-2005), p. 629 (emphasis in original).

1192 Also suggesting that the ability to impose price discrimination is a characteristic of having market power: Jones and Sufrin, *EU Competition Law: Text, Cases and Materials* [2014], p. 396.

sugar rebates that were seen to have a discriminatory effect, by charging buyers of sugar that competed with its own processed sugar brand higher prices for industrial sugar[1193]. Thus, pricing discrimination by a dominant buyer in a related market was used to exclude retailing competitors[1194].

591. The effects of buyer induced price discrimination, however, are not particularly straightforward under an efficiency analysis to conclude it is a conduct in breach of Article 101(1) (d) or 102(c) TFEU. *Justified purchasing price discrimination* (for example, based on quantities purchased) will tend to be efficiency enhancing in allocative terms and passed on to consumers, whereas *unjustified purchasing price discrimination* will tend to be inefficient (from a broader welfare perspective) and disrupt the competitive structure, as the efficiency gains of the buyer and perhaps its consumers do not out outweigh the losses of other buyers, suppliers and consumers. Thus, the analysis of purchasing price discrimination is highly counterfactual[1195].

592. More often than not, however, the purchasing *price discrimination is justified in terms of economic efficiency,* even if the difference in price can have an impact on rivals' costs that may also have a foreclosure effect. In such circumstances, for example, whenever the price reduction is based on the amount of quantities purchased (secondary line discrimination)[1196], the price discrimination does not have an anti-competitive effect, even if induced by the buyer and, therefore, not of an abusive nature.

593. Nonetheless, and as I discuss below, there are other types of price discrimination and rebate modalities – those with a loyalty enhancing effect and the residual type of rebates that are conditional and presumed to have anti-competitive effects.

594. Furthermore, even if purchasing price discrimination is a buying conduct it *may have foreclosing effects in the upstream and downstream markets*, as also recently confirmed by the EFTA Court in *Sorpa bs. v The Icelandic Competition Authority,* as the "disadvantage must occur on a market either downstream *or* upstream of the dominated market"[1197]. *In the downstream market,* the powerful buyer receives a discount that lowers its costs and grants it a competitive advantage in the downstream market by reducing its retail prices and, therefore, attracting end consumers to the detriment of rival buyers that compete in the downstream market. If this is the case, *prima facie,* such behaviour would be

1193 Judgment of 7 October 1999, *Irish Sugar v Commission*, T-228/97, ECR, EU:T:1999:246, paras. 150-172.

1194 Jones and Sufrin, *EU Competition Law: Text, Cases, and Materials* [2011], p. 397-398.

1195 O'Donoghue and Padilla, *The Law and Economics of Article 82 EC* [2006], p. 561-562.

1196 Geradin and Petit (2006), p. 483.

1197 Judgment of 22 September 2016 in *Sorpa bs. v The Icelandic Competition Authority (Samkeppniseftirlitið)* E-29/15 [2016], para. 108.

efficiency enhancing as the undertaking employs its bargaining power to obtain better purchasing conditions that are then passed on to consumers, who now acquire more goods at a lower price, having a positive impact on allocative efficiency, *although only if there is competitive pressure in the downstream market.* Absent intense competition in the retailing market, the buyer is not forced to pass on the benefits to end consumers and, as rivals increase their output prices, the powerful buyer can also increase prices and still capture demand[1198].

595. Concerning the upstream market, the effects are more ambiguous. Induced purchasing price discrimination may lead to a *waterbed effect* in the upstream market if suppliers decide to increase their selling prices to other buyers to recoup the lost supracompetitive profits to the powerful buyer[1199]. Consequently, if the rivals increase their costs and retail prices, the powerful buyer may also increase its retail prices to reap additional profit[1200]. However, the reverse effect can also take place if the discount obtained by the large buyer from a seller with oligopoly power (i.e.: charging prices above the competitive level) also generates a *spillover or anti-waterbed effect* as the discount is also obtained, in the same or a smaller scale, by other smaller buyers[1201]. The *spillover effect* would occur whenever the other buyers are aware of the discount obtained by the powerful buyer and demand discounts from their supplier which would theoretically lead to lower purchasing prices, and also lower downstream prices if the downstream market is competitive. Therefore, the exercise of buyer power and price discrimination benefits both the large buyer and other rivals, even if unwanted, because it lowers prices overall. If there is such a *spillover effect* on smaller buyers, then the buyer power application will benefit competing undertakings and consumers alike. This *spillover defense* and effect that could be claimed by the powerful buyer to justify its buying discrimination conduct is efficiency enhancing, and also bearing similarities to the legal treatment granted to countervailing buyer power as a seller-side market power neutralizing force by the Courts, as I discuss in chapter 9. Under the 'comparison test,' to determine the sufficiency of countervailing buyer power to neutralize seller market power, the Courts demand that in addition the neutralizing effects spillover and benefit other smaller buyers than the one exercising the countervailing buyer power.

1198 The economic analysis of purchasing price discrimination follows closely the discussion on the effects of bargaining power in general addressed in chapter 2. See also how Kirkwood distinguishes five different situations in which welfare of competing buyers and consumers can be affected under such circumstances in: Kirkwood 'Buyer Power and Exclusionary Conduct: Should Brooke Group Set the Standards for Buyer-Induced Price Discrimination and Predatory Bidding?' (2004-2005), p. 647-652.

1199 The waterbed effect was discussed in chapter 2, section §VI.A.

1200 Krattenmaker and Salop (1986).

1201 See also: Kirkwood 'Buyer Power and Exclusionary Conduct: Should Brooke Group Set the Standards for Buyer-Induced Price Discrimination and Predatory Bidding?' (2004-2005), p. 645-651. For the discussion of the anti-waterbed effects see chapter, 2, section §VI.B.

596. Contrastingly, if purchasing price discrimination is employed against suppliers with no oligopoly power (i.e.: pricing on the competitive level) then there are no supracompetitive profits to extract and, if any, *the imposition of purchasing price may have exploitative or exclusionary effects,* as discussed in chapters 7 and 8 with regard to *unfairly low purchasing prices and unfair purchasing practices, respectively.*

597. If there is no spillover effect due to the purchasing price discrimination, the effects on consumers and market conditions depend on the case circumstances. If the powerful buyer faces downstream competition – or if it wants to gain market share - it will have to pass on its benefits, in the form of lower retail prices, to its final consumers, who will therefore be benefited, at least in the short term. This is the argument raised by large food retail chains that claim that obtaining preferential purchasing conditions allows them to obtain lower purchasing prices that are passed on to end consumers and being efficiency enhancing.

598. This analysis has shown that discriminatory purchasing prices by a powerful buyer (or a group of coordinated buyers) may have some anti-competitive foreclosure risks that may be captured under either Article 101(1) (d) or Article 102(c) TFEU. However, an economic analysis of these types of practices also reveals that purchasing price discrimination is the natural consequence of bargaining power exercise (the powerful buyer receives a discount due to is bargaining abilities) and, it is usually economically justified and efficient.

599. In the section below I briefly discuss the legal standards used under Article 102(c) TFEU to determine when unilateral price discrimination amounts to an abuse of a dominant position.

B. What is the legal standard used for purchasing price discrimination?

600. In EU competition law, there are no specific examples of cases dealing with exclusionary price discrimination sensu stricto. Hence, the analysis of these types of possibly anti-competitive practices must be carried out following the general approach taken with respect to exclusionary price discrimination selling side conducts. Due to the complexity of the topic and the fact that it is not linked to buyer power exertion itself, I limit my discussion in this section to highlighting the general treatment of exclusionary price discrimination by dominant undertakings in EU competition law in general.

601. As mentioned above, purchasing price discrimination may fall under the scope of application of Article 102(c) TFEU. The first element to show is that there is a "dissimilar condition" with regard to the purchasing prices paid by the buyer,

which, according to Geradin and Petit's interpretation of the case law, implies "dissimilar prices"[1202]. For purchasing prices to be a dissimilar condition, the facts of the case and, therefore, the buyer's characteristics must be based on "equivalent transactions", as required expressly by Article 102 TFEU.

602. This first analysis is where the buyer power of an undertaking plays an important role in justifying the difference in prices paid. The fact that a large buyer is able to acquire a large amount of goods may also allow the supplier to exploit economies of scale, reduce transaction and transportation costs and secure an important sale to a customer. Therefore, the purchases made by a buyer with market power are likely to be different from those made by a buyer with no substantial market power and the counterfactual evidence of the case at hand is very relevant when determining if two purchases are equivalent. Hence, the ability of a buyer to obtain a discount and which it is likely to pass on in the form of lower prices to end consumers if there is downstream competition would be efficiency enhancing and should with "[g]reat caution [...] be the norm when considering the condemnation of price discrimination in such circumstances", as remarked by Papandropoulos[1203]. Because of this, plaintiffs would have to prove that the pricing difference is not generated due to quantities purchased, because such type of discounts or rebates are economically justified and legal.

603. A second requirement imposed by the wording of Article 102 TFEU is that rival buyers of the dominant undertaking must be put at a competitive disadvantage, this being the situation leading to the foreclosure of those buyers[1204]. This would be when rival buyers that see their purchasing costs increased and now are in a worse situation than before.

604. In the case of rebates, the recent case law clarifies what the legal treatment to these types of price discrimination that may have a foreclosing effect is, a topic discussed in the soft law and the literature[1205]. In *Intel v Commission,* the General Court classified rebates according to three large types depending on their effects, particularly regarding exclusion[1206]. This classification of rebate types was later on discussed but not expressly upheld by the CJEU in *Post Danmark*, with the important remark that any type of rebates can be economically justified[1207]. Very recently, however Advocate General Wahl

---

1202 Geradin D and Petit N, 'Price Discrimination under EC Competition Law: Another Antitrust Doctrine in Search of Limiting Principles?' (2006) 2 Journal of Competition Law and Economics 479, p. 486.

1203 Papandropoulos (2007), p. 38.

1204 See also stressing that the foreclosed firms must be rivals of the undertaking investigated: Geradin and Petit (2006), p. 487.

1205 See also Communication from the Commission — Guidance on the Commission's enforcement priorities in applying Article 82 of the EC Treaty to abusive exclusionary conduct by dominant undertakings [2009] OJ C 45/7, para. 37. Wils (2014), p. 406.

1206 Judgment of 12 June 2014, *Intel v Commission,* T-286/09, ECR, EU:T:2014:547, paras. 74-78.

1207 Judgment of 6 October 2015 in *Post Danmark*, C-23/14, EU:C:2015:651, para. 31.

strongly criticized the classification of rebates done by the General Court in *Intel v Commission* in his opinion on the same case, which is now pending for clarification by the CJEU[1208].

605. First, there are quantity rebates, which would be forced on a supplier by its buyer. These types of rebates are generally considered to not create an anti-competitive foreclosure effect because they are linked to the amount of goods purchased in which the buyer acting as a retailer, if there is downstream competition, is entitled to pass on that reduction to the customer in the form of a more favorable tariff[1209]. Hence, the larger discounts obtained by a buyer due to its purchasing size would not in principle be abusive, even if they would increase the rivals' costs or cause the buyer to have lower costs. This is economically sound, as I discussed earlier.

606. Second, there are conditional rebates, in which the price discrimination obtained by the buyer depends on the fulfillment of an additional requirement, for example buying most of the goods from the same seller or reaching a threshold in order to obtain the rebate. These types of exclusivity and loyalty enhancing rebates are deemed in principle anti-competitive because they are not economically justified, have a foreclosure effect on rivals due to the suction effect[1210] of beneficiaries wanting to reach the conditional margins, and restrict the economic freedom of undertakings in choosing their business partners[1211].

607. Thirdly, the case law recognizes a third and residual type of rebates "where the grant of a financial incentive is not directly linked to a condition of exclusive or quasi-exclusive supply from the undertaking in a dominant position, but where the mechanism for granting the rebate may also have a fidelity-building effect", which do not have an explicit exclusivity component, but may be anti-competitive depending on the circumstances, for instance the attainment of individual sales or purchases objectives[1212].

608. The EU case law adopts a formalistic approach to the last two types of conducts, by assuming these are likely to have a potential foreclosure anti-competitive effect. Nevertheless, a dominant undertaking is capable of demonstrating that its rebate scheme is not anti-competitive if it is able to "justify the

---

1208 Opinion of Advocate General Wahl of 20 October 2016 in *Intel Corporation v Commission,* C-413/14 P, EU:C:2016:788, paras. 39-174.

1209 Judgment of 12 June 2014, *Intel v Commission,* T-286/09, ECR, EU:T:2014:547, para. 75; Judgment of 30 September 2003, *Michelin v Commission*, T-203/01, ECR, EU:T:2003:250, para. 58.

1210 Bishop and Walker, [2010], para. 6.038. See also: Communication from the Commission — Guidance on the Commission's enforcement priorities in applying Article 82 of the EC Treaty to abusive exclusionary conduct by dominant undertakings [2009] OJ C 45/7, para. 40.

1211 Judgment of 12 June 2014, *Intel v Commission,* T-286/09, ECR, EU:T:2014:547, para. 77; Judgment of 6 October 2015 in *Post Danmark*, C-23/14, EU:C:2015:651, para. 33.

1212 Judgment of 12 June 2014, *Intel v Commission,* T-286/09, ECR, EU:T:2014:547, para. 78; Judgment of 30 September 2003, *Michelin v Commission*, T-203/01, ECR, EU:T:2003:250, para. 73; Judgment of 15 March 2007 in *British Airways v Commission*, C-95/04 P, EU:C:2007:166, paras. 65 and 67.

use of an exclusivity rebate system, in particular by showing that its conduct is objectively necessary or that the potential foreclosure effect that it brings about may be counterbalanced, outweighed even, by advantages in terms of efficiency that also benefit consumers"[1213].

609. From a buyer power perspective, the two types of rebates that the Courts have identified as having a potential foreclosure effect on rivals are *unlikely to be the type of purchasing price discrimination 'imposed' by a buyer on a seller*. This is the case because the buyer, if it has substantial market power to be dominant, would not make its price discounts conditional on certain targets; instead it would request or impose a uniform rebate on all its purchasing without any kind of additional requirements from its side. Therefore, in my view, one is unlikely to see any of these types of buyer induced purchasing discrimination, which explains the absence of any of these kind of cases in EU competition law, although this does remain a theoretical possibility, and which is likely to be evaluated under the same standards as for selling side cases. What does exist is the payment of supra-competitive bonuses from the buyer to the supplier, as I discuss in the section below, but that is not a discount obtained by the buyer but rather a form of overbuying and compensation for an input, as I discuss regarding *British Airways v Commission* in section §VII of this chapter.

610. This way of approaching rebates and the fact that the case law has tailored the application of exclusive and residual types of rebates explain why authors like Gifford and Kudrle in the US argue that Article 102(c) TFEU

> applies only to large sellers that can meet the criteria for 'dominance' [...] Thus, while Congress ostensibly designed Article 82(c) and the Robinson-Patman Act to prevent buyers from being competitively disadvantaged, the two provisions actually direct their focus in opposite directions. Article 82(c) focuses on the pricing behavior of powerful sellers while the core concern of the Robinson-Patman Act is upon the purchasing behavior of powerful buyers[1214].

611. Although it is true that Article 102(c) TFEU is unlikely to capture buyer induced price discrimination, this does not mean that it could not potentially apply to it. Hence, I think the remarks by Gifford and Kudrle might be too absolute and were probably made to emphasis the differences between EU

1213 Judgment of 12 June 2014, *Intel v Commission*, T-286/09, ECR, EU:T:2014:547, para. 94. See also reiterating this possibility of objective justification and cited by the General Court: Judgment of 13 February 1979 in *Hoffmann-La Roche v Commission*, C-85/76, EU:C:1979:36, para. 90; Judgment of 15 March 2007 in *British Airways v Commission*, C-95/04 P, EU:C:2007:166, para. 85 to 86; Judgment of 27 March 2012 in *Post Danmark*, C-209/10, EU:C:2012:172, para. 40 to 41.

1214 Daniel J. Gifford and Robert T. Kudrle, 'The Law and Economics of Price Discrimination in Modern Economies: Time for Reconciliation?' 43 UC Davis L Rev (2010) 1235.

competition law and the Robinson-Patman Act as an instrument to prevent buyer induced exclusion, which I discuss below.

612. Also, and more recently, the CJEU has confirmed that in order for purchasing price discrimination to constitute an abuse of dominance, this would be the case only to the extent that it has a distorting effect on competition as "charging a single price to customers for whom supply costs differ, cannot of itself suggest that there exists an exclusionary abuse"[1215].

613. Lastly, and of importance for buyer power cases, the CJEU[1216] has confirmed that the effects of exclusionary price discrimination are prohibited, regardless of whether the price discrimination takes place in the upstream market but the foreclosure effects are present in the downstream market, as was confirmed by the General Court in *Irish Sugar v Commission*[1217]. In a buyer case, this would imply, therefore, that the purchasing price discrimination by the buyer could be carried out to eliminate competition from a rival buyer that also acts as a rival retailer, which is consistent with the treatment given to buyer market power leverage, as I discuss below in this chapter's section §VII.

C. The Robinson-Patman Act: exclusionary purchasing price discrimination in US Antitrust law

614. Under US antitrust, competing buyers excluded by buyer induced discrimination may have standing to file a claim based on the Robinson-Patman Act and its prohibition of secondary line discrimination (that one that puts other buyers at a competitive disadvantage pursuant a demand by other buyer to a supplier)[1218]. Unlike EU competition law regulation for single behaviour, the Act applies to any supplier or intermediary buyer *regardless of the involved undertaking's market power* and the market impact of the conduct[1219], taking a very stern stance towards price discrimination by buyers, even stricter than EU competition law, and disregarding any type of economic justification for the buyer induced purchasing price discrimination.

615. The explicit goal of the Robinson-Patman Act, a substantial amendment of the Clayton Act[1220], is to limit the capacity of powerful buyers to exert buyer market power that allows them to obtain preferential purchasing conditions from

1215 Judgment of 27 March 2012 in C-209/10 - *Post Danmark*, EU:C:2012:172, para 30.

1216 Judgment of 6 March 1974 in joined cases C-6/73 and C-7/73 *Istituto Chemioterapico Italiano and Commercial Solvents v Commission*, EU:C:1974:18, para. 25.

1217 Judgment of 7 October 1999, *Irish Sugar v Commission*, T-228/97, ECR, EU:T:1999:246, para. 165.

1218 Primary line discrimination, i.e.: targeted vis-à-vis suppliers is discussed in chapter 7 in section §IV. See also using the term for buyer induced exclusion: Blair and Harrison, [2010].

1219 Herbert Hovenkamp, 'The Robinson-Patman Act and Competition: Unfinished Business' 68 Antitrust Law Journal (2000-2001) 125, p. 128.

1220 Marius Schwartz, 'The Perverse Effects of the Robinson-Patman Act' 31 Antitrust Bulletin (1986) 733, p. 733.

sellers[1221]. Therefore, this Act aims at limiting the use of buyer power and preventing price discrimination on suppliers. To do so, the Act prohibits price discrimination in two ways. First, discrimination by sellers that would sell the same good to two different buyers at different prices (primary line discrimination), for example, by granting rebates or preferential dealing conditions[1222]. Second, buyer induced exclusionary price discrimination as discussed above (secondary line discrimination). In this case *both the buyer and the supplier* are held in breach of Section §2(f) of the Robinson-Patman Act, which makes it look more akin to regulation through Article 101 TFEU than Article 102 TFEU, even if it is the buyer that is the one 'imposing' the discrimination. However, Section §2(f) will only trigger *if there is active participation by the retailer* after being induced or forced by buyer, and it will not be applicable if the seller claims that it is meeting rival's competition or the discrimination is justified, as interpreted by the US Supreme Court in *Great Atlantic & Pacific Tea Co. v FTC*[1223].

616. The Act, unlike the rest of the US antitrust law, *protects the interest of competitors*[1224] without express regard to efficiency concerns[1225], as confirmed by the US Supreme Court in *Jefferson Cty. Pharm. Ass'n v Abbott Labs,* in which the US Supreme Court held that the Act's aim is to protect small businesses over large organizations[1226]. Because of this, the Act "has the distinction of being almost universally unpopular among antitrust scholars" as remarked by Ross[1227] and is said to capture price differences but not price discrimination[1228]. Hansen, for instance, argues that the Robinson-Patman Act is not really an antitrust piece of legislation and that it only is "an antitrust statute in name only"[1229]. Gifford, on the other hand goes further and claims it is an "anachronism [... whose] purpose is inconsistent with the current consensus that the antitrust laws are designed to foster efficiency and thus to add to the total

1221 See also Mezines stressing already in 1969 that the Robinson-Patman Act is an instrument to limit buyer power as: "[o]ne of the primary purposes of the Robinson-Patman Act is to control large-scale buying power so that small consumers will not be unduly prejudiced by their lack of purchasing power" in Basil J Mezines, 'Group Buying--When is it Permitted under the Robinson-Patman Act' 44 New York University Law Review (1969) 729, p. 729.

1222 Hovenkamp 'The Robinson-Patman Act and Competition: Unfinished Business' (2000-2001), p. 128.

1223 *Great Atlantic & Pacific Tea Co. v Federal Trade Commission*, 440 U.S. 69 (1979).

1224 Also stressing that the Act is meant to protect competitors and not economic efficiency: Geradin and Petit (2006), p. 487-488.

1225 Terry Calvani and Gilde Breidenbach, 'An Introduction to the Robinson-Patman Act and its Enforcement by the Government' 59 Antitrust Law Journal (1990) 765, p. 766.

1226 *Jefferson Cty. Pharm. Ass'n v. Abbott Labs.*, 460 U.S. 150 (1983).

1227 Thomas W. Ross, 'Winners and Losers under the Robinson-Patman Act' 27 Journal of Law & Economics (1984) 243, p. 243. Also calling the Act's effect as "perverse" see: Schwartz (1986). Calling the Act as "irritating to almost anyone who is serious about antitrust" see: Hovenkamp 'The Robinson-Patman Act and Competition: Unfinished Business' (2000-2001), p. 125. See criticizing the effects of the Robinson-Patman Act and suggesting that prohibiting purchasing price discrimination increases overall prices: Daniel P. O'Brien and Greg Shaffer, 'The Welfare Effects of Forbidding Discriminatory Discounts: A Secondary Line Analysis of Robinson-Patman' 10 Journal of Law, Economics, & Organization (1994) 296.

1228 Blair and Harrison, [2010], p. 23.

1229 Hugh C. Hansen, 'Robin-Patman Law: A Review and Analysis' 51 Fordham L Rev (1983) 1113, p. 1124.

well-being of society"[1230]. Indeed, a reading of the Act reveals that, *more than being a piece of competition law, it is a piece of unfair competition law*[1231], a topic I discussed when dealing with unfair purchasing practices in chapter 8. This is because the Act adopts an un-economical and strict approach to buyer power purchasing discrimination as it forbids it regardless of the existence of market power by either the buyer inducing the exclusionary treatment of the seller grating the rebate. However, not all sectors of antitrust recommend repealing the act, as is the case of the American Antitrust Institute, albeit it recommends making amendments to it[1232].

617. The wording and the strict approach followed by the Robinson-Patman Act is the result of historical circumstances. It was created due to the pressure and lobby of small buyers against the emergence of chain/department stores in the first decade of the twentieth century[1233]. Traditional businessmen saw how buyers with substantial bargaining power were able to obtain better prices from their suppliers (buyer induced price discrimination) which granted them a competitive advantage in the downstream market, as they were able to pass on the benefits to end consumers by setting lower retailing prices. The proponents of the Robinson-Patman Act saw those better terms and *conditions as 'unfair,' despite the fact that, on occasion, they were obtained by legitimate reasons such as cost differences, economies of scale, and superior efficiency.*

618. Despite its stern approach to buyer-induced price discrimination, the application of the Robinson-Patman Act has increasingly diminished, particularly since the 1970s and the 'US Antitrust revolution', as remarked by Gifford and Kudrle and confirmed in a recent study by Luch *et alia*[1234]. This dis-application of the Act is pursuant to its interpretation by the US Courts and the low priority these types of cases receive from antitrust agencies. Firstly, the Act only applies to sales and purchases of commodities and does not cover sales of services nor leases. Secondly, goods must be of "like grade and quantity" which implies that they must be close substitutes. Because the Act applies only to the sales of "like grade and quantity" from *the same supplier* it only captures conduct affecting intra-brand competition and not competition among different producers

---

1230 Daniel J. Gifford, 'Farewell to the Robinson - Patman Act - The Antitrust Modernization Commission's Report and Recommendation' 53 The Antitrust Bulletin (2008) 481, p. 515-516.

1231 See the opinions of O'Brien and Shaffer stressing the fact that the Robinson-Patman Act aims at precluding unfair exclusionary buyer power tactics when remarking that: "in an effort to protect small business from alleged unfair purchasing practices of larger rivals, and thereby to ensure 'equal competitive opportunity', Congress enacted the Robinson-Patman Act in 1936" in O'Brien and Shaffer (1994), p. 296; and also Abood who stressed the lobby campaign of independent merchants and suppliers against what they saw as unfair purchasing practices in Richard R Abood, 'Differential Pricing of Pharmaceuticals and Retail Competition under the Robinson-Patman Act' 11 American Journal of Law & Medicine (1985), p. 296.

1232 American Antitrust Institute [2008], p. 98.

1233 Calvani and Breidenbach (1990).

1234 Gifford (2008); Gifford and Kudrle (2010), p. 1235; Ryan Luchs and others, 'The End of the Robinson-Patman Act? Evidence from Legal Case Data' 56 Management Science (2010) 2123.

of different goods[1235]. Thirdly, the buyer that is harmed by the foreclosure must prove damage to its business, which, as remarked by Blair & Harrison, is quite difficult in cases of exclusionary buyer power[1236]. Lastly, the Act only applies in instances of interstate sale, limiting its geographical space of application.

a. Exclusionary buyer induced discrimination

619. The Robinson-Patman Act precludes buyer induced price discrimination by making it unlawful for "any person engaged in commerce, in the course of such commerce, knowingly to induce or receive a discrimination in price which is prohibited by this section"[1237]. The type of exclusionary purchasing that is pursued under the Robinson-Patman Act includes conducts in line with those discussed in the section §VII below. For example, buyers must refrain from inducing suppliers to grant discounts that are not justified in terms of costs or meeting competitor's prices or granting promotional services or allowances that are not available to the same extent, or only available to a lesser extent, to competing buyers.

620. As mentioned, purchasing price discrimination will be prohibited regardless of the buyer's market power and even *absent consumer harm and without requiring harm to market-wide competition*[1238]. This was clarified by the US Supreme Court in *Morton Salt* when holding:

> The legislative history of the Robinson-Patman Act makes it abundantly clear that Congress considered it to be an evil that a large buyer could secure a competitive advantage over a small buyer solely because of the large buyer's quantity purchasing ability[1239].

621. Therefore, under the Robinson-Patman Act, obtaining a price reduction due to bargaining power ability of the buyer that may put other rival buyers at a disadvantage because they do not receive the same price reduction would be an infringement of antitrust laws, even if the buyer does not have substantial upstream nor downstream market power. However, despite the triggering of the prohibition absent substantial buyer (bargaining power), and as remarked by Kirkwood, buyer induced exclusionary price discrimination would be unlikely to arise if the buying undertaking lacks some substantial bargaining power vis-à-vis the specific supplier; i.e. the buyer would not be able to obtain

1235 Hovenkamp 'The Robinson-Patman Act and Competition: Unfinished Business' (2000-2001), p. 126.

1236 Blair and Harrison, [2010], p. 167.

1237 15 U.S. Code § 13(f) - Discrimination in price, services, or facilities.

1238 Hovenkamp 'The Robinson-Patman Act and Competition: Unfinished Business' (2000-2001), p. 125; Kirkwood 'Buyer Power and Exclusionary Conduct: Should Brooke Group Set the Standards for Buyer-Induced Price Discrimination and Predatory Bidding?' (2004-2005), p. 634.

1239 *Federal Trade Commission v. Morton Salt Co.*, 334 U.S. 37 (1948), 43.

a discount and prevent the supplier from giving discounts to rival buyers[1240]. Hence, when applying the rule, the lack of substantial market power requirement will be balanced by the economics exerting purchasing price discrimination that require substantial buyer power to operate.

622. As a conclusion, the Robinson-Patman Act treats exclusionary buyer power discrimination under US antitrust law in a more restrictive manner than EU competition law, which, in my view, may be unjustified as it will render as an antitrust violation instances where bargaining power is exerted without a real foreclosing effect to competitive buyers[1241]. As a commonality, both regimes sanction buyer induced purchasing price discrimination because of its exclusionary effects. A large buyer forces suppliers to sell goods (or services in the case of the EU) at higher prices to competing undertakings of the buyer, which raises their costs and makes them less competitive in a connected downstream market or, if do not compete downstream, to have less or worse access to a required input and, therefore, exit either the upstream and downstream market in the long run. However, in the case of EU competition law this would only be unlawful if there is an 'agreement' among some of the buyers forcing such discrimination or if the buying undertaking is dominant. If the exclusion is pursuant to the buying pressure of a dominant undertaking that imposes the discrimination under EU competition law, only the dominant undertaking would be in breach, not the supplier. In contrast, according to the Robinson-Patman Act, no substantial market power is required to trigger the application of the law and, in the case of buyer induced purchasing discrimination with foreclosing effects, both the buyer and the supplier would be held liable under Section 2(f), if the supplier has actively participated in the foreclosing conduct.

623. The *lack of substantial market power requirement and its application even absent consumer and competition harm* makes the Robinson-Patman Act prone to over-enforcement, particularly for situations in which there is no need for competition intervention because the purchasing price discrimination is justified and the natural consequence of bargaining power exertion. Therefore, in my view, an excessively punishing competition policy against buying discrimination absent coordination among undertakings or unilateral conduct by a buyer with substantial buyer market power, is economically *unjustified* if the intention of the act is to protect the competitive process and/or consumer welfare. Further, it is also *disproportionate* even if there is some room for a limited protection of rival buyers to preserve the competitive conditions,

1240 "The firm must have significant market power as a buyer in the form of bargaining power that it can exert against the seller of the input", Kirkwood 'Buyer Power and Exclusionary Conduct: Should Brooke Group Set the Standards for Buyer-Induced Price Discrimination and Predatory Bidding?' (2004-2005), p. 636.

1241 Also supporting this claim, see the opinion of Hovenkamp who argues that: "[i]n sum, to impose Robinson-Patman Act liability when significant buyer power is lacking is to go beyond the concerns of the Congress that passed the statute" in Hovenkamp 'The Robinson-Patman Act and Competition: Unfinished Business' (2000-2001), p.141.

as happens under EU competition law. For these reasons the provisions on exclusionary buyer induced price discrimination of the *Robinson-Patman Act more resemble provisions of unfair competition than competition law* and explain why there has been not only a decline in the application of the law but also why the antitrust agencies have not prioritized its enforcement, as well as why the US Courts have narrowed the Acts interpretation.

VII. Leveraging market power from input to output markets with a foreclosing effect

624. Exclusionary practices such as the one discussed above can be exerted along with, or in connection to, the leverage of market power by an undertaking from one market to another, in this case upstream buying market power towards downstream retailing market power. Leverage, however, is not exclusive to buyer power cases and in general refers to the circumstance in which an undertaking will employ its market power in one market to gain market power in another. Therefore, leverage in itself is not an autonomous conduct but the consequence or effect of another conduct, for example obtaining exclusivity agreements with the best suppliers of an input to strengthen the ability of the buyer to compete as a retailer. Also, leveraging has taken many forms in competition law cases, for example, using the market power of an undertaking in electricity generation to exclude a rival selling light bulbs[1242], or concerning complementary goods to a main product[1243], or using local geographic market power to maintain or strengthen its position in an adjacent market, as discussed by Inderst[1244], and as happens in the case of tying and bundling[1245].

625. Additionally, market power leverage is a rather common abusive conduct, which has been dealt with on several occasions in EU competition law and

---

1242 *Cantor v. Detroit Edison Co.*, 428 U.S. 579 (1976). See commenting this case from a state action doctrine perspective: Schwarz JD, 'The Use of the Antitrust State Action Doctrine in the Deregulated Electricity Utility Industry' (1999) 48 American University Law Review 1449, p. 1460-1462.

1243 *Eastman Kodak Company v. Image Technical Services, Inc., et al.* 504 U.S. 451 (1992).

1244 Roman Inderst, 'Leveraging Buyer Power' 25 International Journal of Industrial Organization (2007) 908.

1245 Also remarking the link between leveraging of market power and tying and bundling in connection with exclusionary rebates see: Nicolas Petit, 'Intel, Leveraging Rebates and the Goals of Article 102 TFEU' 11 European Competition Journal (2015) 26, p. 38-39. See linking buyer power leverage with tying and bundling: Blair and Harrison, [2010], p. 37. For literature discussing tying and bundling practices and its legal treatment see, *inter alia*: Daniel J. Seidmann, 'Bundling as a Facilitating Device: A Reinterpretation of Leverage Theory' 58 Economica (1991) 491; Jean Tirole, 'The Analysis of Tying Cases: A Primer' 1 Competition Policy International (2005) 1; F. Enrique Gonzalez Diaz and Anton Leis Garcia, 'Tying and Bundling under EU Competition Law: Future Prospects' 3 Competition Law International (2007) 13; Einer Elhauge, 'Tying, Bundled Discounts, and the Death of the Single Monopoly Profit Theory' 123 Harvard Law Review (2009) 397; Christian Ahlborn and David S. Evans, 'The Microsoft Judgment and its Implications for Competition Policy Towards Dominant Firms in Europe' 75 Antitrust Law Journal (2009) 887; Erik Hovenkamp and Herbert Hovenkamp, 'Tying Arrangements and Antitrust Harm' 52 Arizona Law Review (2010) 925; Nicolas Petit and Norman Neyrinck, 'Back to Microsoft I and II: Tying and the Art of Secret Magic' 2 Journal of European Competition Law & Practice (2011) 117.

typically as exerted by dominant undertakings. In *Istituto Chemioterapico Italiano and Commercial Solvents v Commission* the CJEU set the foundations for exclusionary (unilateral) market power leverage. The Court held that

> [a]n abuse of a dominant position on the market in raw materials may thus have effects restricting competition in the market on which the derivatives of the raw material are sold and these effects must be taken into account in considering the effects of an infringement, even if the market for the derivative does not constitute a self-contained market[1246].

626. This is true, particularly if "it is further apparent that the undertaking in question held a dominant position on *both markets concerned,*" as held in *Irish Sugar v Commission,* where Irish Sugar had an hourglass shape by virtue of being dominant both in the market of purchasing raw sugar and the retail market of processed sugar in Ireland[1247]. Similarly, under US antitrust law market leverage may be captured by Section 2 of the Sherman Act, as recognized by the US Supreme Court in *Eastman Kodak Company v Image Technical Services, Inc*[1248], and reaffirmed by the Court of Appeals of the Second Circuit in *Virgin Atlantic Airways Limited v British Airways Plc*[1249].

627. In buyer power leveraging cases, *an undertaking will employ its buyer power in the upstream market to affect a downstream market where it acts as a retailer* that has a connection with the input market in which it carried out the foreclosing conduct through the granting of a supracompetitive bonus[1250]. By exercising buyer power vis-à-vis its suppliers and creating a loyalty enhancing effect with respect to them, the powerful buyer may disadvantage rival buyers that also compete in a related downstream. This could be done, for example by securing all input or the most efficient input sources through bonuses which will allow the buyer to gain and exert market power in a now less competitive downstream market allowing the powerful buyer to reap supra-competitive benefits as a retailer[1251]. Consequently, leverage of buyer power increase rivals' costs in a form that is analogue to margin-squeezing

---

1246 Judgment of 6 March 1974 in joined cases C-6/73 and C-7/73 *Istituto Chemioterapico Italiano and Commercial Solvents v Commission*, EU:C:1974:18, para. 22. See also in the same sense when dealing with leveraging of market power and granting discriminatory rebates: Judgment of 7 October 1999, *Irish Sugar v Commission*, T-228/97, ECR, EU:T:1999:246, para. 166; Judgment of 17 December 2003, *British Airways v Commission* of 17 December 2003, T-219/99, ECR, EU:T:2003:343, para. 127.

1247 Judgment of 7 October 1999, *Irish Sugar v Commission*, T-228/97, ECR, EU:T:1999:246, para. 166 (emphasis added).

1248 *Eastman Kodak Company v. Image Technical Services, Inc.*, et al. 504 U.S. 451 (1992), at 483.

1249 *Virgin Atlantic Airways Limited v. British Airways Plc*, 99-9402 (2nd Cir., 2001).

1250 See also remarking that buyer power is used in the upstream market to affect conditions in a related downstream market: Carstensen 'Buyer Power, Competition Policy, and Antitrust: The Competitive Effects of Discrimination Among Suppliers' (2008), p. 309. See also stressing that leveraging market power can affect either the upstream or the downstream activities of a competitor: Judgment of 22 September 2016 in *Sorpa bs. v The Icelandic Competition Authority (Samkeppniseftirlitið)* E-29/15 [2016], paras. 99-118.

1251 Salop (2004-2005); Scheelings and Wright (2006).

practices[1252], because buyer power leverage combines several types of effects and conducts and is exerted by applying them jointly.

628. On most occasions, the leverage of buyer market power is possible because suppliers *are dependent on the powerful buyer* and suppliers fear retaliation of the buyer and succumb to its demands; therefore, the exclusion is also based on the potential risks of buyer power exploitation. For example, Isolation's Supermarket employs its buyer power in the beef purchasing market by granting slaughterhouses a bonus fee or fidelity benefit for entering into an exclusive supply agreement with it. This, on the other hand, forecloses other buyers that now have no access to the beef sold by the slaughterhouses and permits Isolation's Supermarket to use its buyer power to gain downstream market power.

629. Under EU competition law, exclusionary buyer market power leverage is captured by Article 102(b) or (c) TFEU *even if the powerful buyer is not directly competing with its foreclosed rivals in a similar market* but only if the input acquired is necessary for the affected foreclosed undertakings to carry out its own economic activity, as held in *Aéroports de Paris*[1253], and confirmed in *British Airways v Commission* for buyer power cases[1254]. This implies that exclusionary buyer power leveraging conducts are precluded even absent strict downstream consumer harm, if the conduct has a substantial effect in the upstream market. In other words, EU competition law intervenes even if end consumer prices are not affected to protect the competitive process and the market structure. However, it ought to be remarked that this protection of competition as a process is also for the benefit of end consumers of the other market in which the rival carries out its economic activity. By intervening in a market, even if in its subsequent direct downstream market there is no harm end consumer harm, Courts protect the wellbeing of end consumers in the other indirectly affected market where the rival carries its own downstream activity. Therefore, as a whole, such perspective protects competition as such and end consumers, being in line with my discussion on ordoliberalism in chapter 3. Also, leveraging would be precluded by competition law if buyer

1252 See, for instance, the leverage of market power in an upstream and downstream market to foreclose competitors in a related market in Judgment of 10 April 2008, *Deutsche Telekom v Commission*, T-271/03, ECR, EU:T:2008:101, upheld by the CJEU in appeal in Judgment of 14 October 2010 in *Deutsche Telekom v Commission*, C-280/08 P, EU:C:2010:603; Judgment of 17 February 2011 in *TeliaSonera Sverige*, C-52/09, EU:C:2011:83; Judgment of 29 March 2012, *Telefónica and Telefónica de España v Commission*, T-336/07, ECR, EU:T:2012:172, appealed and upheld by the CJEU in Judgment of 10 July 2014 in *Telefónica and Telefónica de España v Commission*, C-295/12 P, EU:C:2014:2062; Commission Decision of 18 July 1988 relating to a proceeding under Article 86 of the EEC Treaty (Case No IV/30.178 *Napier Brown - British Sugar*) [1988] OJ L 284/41.

1253 Judgment of 12 December 2000, *Aéroports de Paris v Commission*, T-128/98, ECR, EU:T:2000:290; upheld in full in Judgment of 24 October 2002 in *Aéroports de Paris v Commission*, C-82/01 P, EU:C:2002:617.

1254 Judgment by the General Court Judgment of 17 December 2003, *British Airways v Commission* of 17 December 2003, T-219/99, ECR, EU:T:2003:343; and Judgment of 15 March 2007 in *British Airways v Commission*, C-95/04 P, EU:C:2007:166.

market power is used to reserve for the buyer, without an objective justification, an auxiliary or derivative activity on a related upstream (input market) to affect and restrict competition in a downstream market where it may or may not be an dominant undertaking, as confirmed by the CJEU in *Tetra Pak v Commission*[1255].

630. Also, buyer power leverage may constitute a breach of US antitrust law, as confirmed by the US Supreme Court in *United States v Griffith*[1256], in which it was found that the leveraging of market power by the owner of the only movie theater in small towns to decrease the purchasing price it paid for the movies and to prevent competitors from obtaining enough first- or second-run films to operate successfully was a violation of the antitrust laws. Because, in accordance to the US Supreme court, "it would be a violation of § 2 of the Sherman Act to use monopoly power in one market to gain a competitive advantage in another, *even without an attempt to monopolize the second market*"[1257]. Nevertheless, the standards have changed pursuant to the US Supreme Court case *Spectrum Sports, Inc. v McQuillan* where it was held that §2 of the Sherman Act "makes the conduct of a single firm unlawful when it actually monopolizes or threatens to do so"[1258]. This approach is narrower than the previous requirement of gaining a competitive advantage and is in line with the *Weyerhaeuser* doctrine that requires an element of double predation in the related downstream market, as discussed above, and adopts a consumer harm approach to buyer power exclusion.

631. In the following sections, I discuss the legal treatment given by EU competition law to a buyer leveraging its market power downstream as discussed at length in *British Airways v Commission.*

A. Input leveraging through supra-competitive bonuses and British Airways v Commission

632. Buyer market power can be leveraged though the granting of fidelity enhancing bonuses to suppliers to obtain a competitive advantage in the downstream market by foreclosing rivals' access to a necessary input or distribution channel, as was the case of *British Airways v Commission*[1259].

1255 Judgment of 14 November 1996 in *Tetra Pak v Commission*, C-333/94 P, EU:C:1996:436, paras. 21-33.

1256 *United States v. Griffith*, 334 U.S. 100 (1948). See also interpreting this case as involving buyer power leverage: Blair and Harrison, [2010], p. 37.

1257 *Virgin Atlantic Airways Limited v. British Airways Plc*, 99-9402 (2nd Cir., 2001), quoting its own precedent in *Berkey Photo, Inc v. Eastman Kodak Co.*, 603 F.2d 263, (2nd Cir. 1979), at 275.

1258 *Spectrum Sports, Inc. v. McQuillan*, 506 U.S. 447 (1993), at 459.

1259 Judgment by the General Court in Judgment of 17 December 2003, *British Airways v Commission* of 17 December 2003, T-219/99, ECR, EU:T:2003:343; Judgment of 15 March 2007 in *British Airways v Commission*, C-95/04 P, EU:C:2007:166.

633. By granting exclusionary and retroactive bonuses, a powerful buyer does not employ its buyer power exploitatively. Quite the contrary, it grants supracompetitive benefits to its suppliers to secure their fidelity when selling their output, which compensates the suppliers for their inability to sell to other buyers and, therefore, said buyer now has no, or fewer, suppliers, which raises its purchasing costs. Such supracompetitive benefits may have the effect of creating a *quasi de facto* exclusive supply obligation that makes it more difficult for other competitors to reach end consumers, for instance by not being able to sell airplane tickets because there are no available travel agents to connect the buyer/supplier with the passengers.

634. This modality of market leveraging was the one employed in *British Airways v Commission*[1260]. In this case the leveraging of buyer market power involved a complex set of conducts that included the payment of supracompetitive bonuses to travel agents in order to obtain an exclusivity or quasi exclusivity effect. The General Court and the CJEU confirmed that the type of supracompetitive bonuses used by British Airways as a buyer were abusive because they were conditional and loyalty enhancing rebates that were not economically justified[1261]. The leverage occurred because buyer power was used to exclude or make difficult the access of other buyers to an upstream services that constituted a necessary distribution mechanism, the travel agents, to reach downstream consumers for the sale of air passenger transport and which, therefore, impacted on the rivals' ability to compete downstream. From the suppliers' perspective, the use of buyer power in the form of supracompetitive bonuses with an exclusionary effect made either entry very difficult to the market of rivals, or "more difficult or impossible for its co-contractors to choose between various sources of supply or commercial partners", as confirmed by the CJEU[1262]. And, then, the granting of exclusionary rebates increased other rivals' costs in the upstream market to be less of a competitive threat in the downstream market, levering market power as a purchaser to benefit its competitiveness as a seller.

635. To clarify, the leverage of buyer market power was an instrument and not the conduct itself that created the foreclosure, these were the loyalty enhancing rebate schemes. Due to the scope of my study, I will center on how buyer power was leveraged, and not deal in extenso with the treatment of rebates under EU competition law. Due to the complexity of the case and the fact that

---

1260 This series of Decisions and Judgments comprehends 3 different legal instruments to be discussed, namely: Commission Decision of 14 July 1999 relating to a proceeding under Article 82 of the EC Treaty (IV/D-2/34.780 - *Virgin/British Airways*) [2000] OJ L 30/1; Judgment by the General Court Judgment of 17 December 2003, *British Airways v Commission* of 17 December 2003, T-219/99, ECR, EU:T:2003:343; and Judgment of 15 March 2007 in *British Airways v Commission*, C-95/04 P, EU:C:2007:166.

1261 Judgment of 17 December 2003, *British Airways v Commission* of 17 December 2003, T-219/99, ECR, EU:T:2003:343, para. 270-299; Judgment of 15 March 2007 in *British Airways v Commission*, C-95/04 P, EU:C:2007:166, para. 57-80.

1262 Judgment of 15 March 2007 in *British Airways v Commission*, C-95/04 P, EU:C:2007:166, para. 68.

I discuss several aspects of it in different parts of this work, I will present a brief summary of the case and then discuss how and what the legal treatment given to buyer power leverage by the Courts was.

a. *British Airways v Commission: long story short*

636. Virgin Atlantic Airways Limited (Virgin) lodged a complaint against certain commercial conducts carried out by British Airways before the Commission as they were said to be contrary to Articles 101 and 102 TFEU. At the time of the complaint, British Airways was a privately owned company incorporated under English law. It was formerly a public undertaking and was privatized in 1987 as part of the liberalization process in the air transport sector[1263]. British Airways is active in the air transport market and, at the time of the Decision, was the largest airline in the United Kingdom with a market share of between 46% in 1992 and 39.7% in 1998, the years in which the discount rebates object of analysis were in force[1264]. In contrast, the main competitors of British Airways, namely five airline undertakings, had much smaller market share, as was noted both by the Commission[1265] and the General Court[1266].

637. Virgin complained that British Airways engaged in commercial practices that constituted an abuse of dominance by offering rebates, upgrades or other incentives to travel agencies by British Airways when purchasing their services[1267]. For Virgin, the strategy of British Airways was to offer supracompetitive commissions to travel agents to incentivize selling (almost exclusively) British Airways tickets to end consumers. At the time of the decision, travel agents constituted a necessary distribution tool for airline tickets and, therefore, a necessary vehicle to end consumers as travel agents represented an average of 80 to 85% of the sales of air tickets in the UK. Only the remaining 15 to 20% were sold directly by the airline's offices or other alternative mechanisms[1268].

638. Said financial incentives were granted through three types of supracompetitive bonuses: marketing agreements, global agreements and a performance reward scheme, rewarding the sale of British Airways tickets to end consumers. The three agreements had a common feature: all of them had a noticeable effect at the margin because of its retroactivity. In this sense, the Commission held that "[i]

1263 For more on the presence of a 'public' element on buyer power cases see chapter 11, section §II.

1264 Commission Decision of 14 July 1999 relating to a proceeding under Article 82 of the EC Treaty (IV/D-2/34.780 - *Virgin/British Airways*) [2000] OJ L 30/1, para. 36.

1265 Commission Decision of 14 July 1999 relating to a proceeding under Article 82 of the EC Treaty (IV/D-2/34.780 - *Virgin/British Airways*) [2000] OJ L 30/1, para. 41.

1266 Judgment of 17 December 2003, *British Airways v Commission* of 17 December 2003, T-219/99, ECR, EU:T:2003:343, para. 211-212.

1267 Commission Decision of 14 July 1999 relating to a proceeding under Article 82 of the EC Treaty (IV/D-2/34.780 - *Virgin/British Airways*) [2000] OJ L 30/1, para. 3-4.

1268 By the time the Decision was issued the sales of air transport tickets by alternative means (i.e.: websites) was still rather small. Both the Commission and the EU judiciary made reference to this issue when analyzing alternative sources of supply.

n each case meeting the targets for sales growth leads to an increase in the commission paid on all tickets sold by the agent, not just on the tickets sold after the target is reached"[1269]. The effect was said to be fidelity inducing because when a travel agent is close to reaching the threshold, it will do all it can to keep selling British Airways tickets, as this will have very large effect on the commission it receives. For a competitor, on the other hand, the rebates make it very costly to compete with British Airways as it will have to "pay a much higher rate of commission [...] to overcome this [the loyalty/fidelity building] effect"[1270]. This characteristic rendered the rebates to be considered both by the Commission and the Courts exclusionary, and the vehicle to leverage the market power downstream. Because the rebates were found to be conditional, having a loyalty-enhancing effect not economically justified, British Airways supracompetitive schemes were found to be anti-competitive under EU competition law[1271].

b. How did British Airways leverage its market power?

639. In the assessment of the case, the Commission, and consequently the Courts, focused the analysis of the rebates on the position of *British Airways as buyer of a service*, and not as a supplier of goods in the downstream market[1272]. As it was pleaded by the Commission "BA is a purchaser in a dominant position on the United Kingdom market for air travel agency services, especially because of the percentage which sales of BA tickets represent in the total of air ticket sales"[1273]. This condition of a buyer of a service was found to be "irrelevant having regard to the definition of the market in question. Article [102 TFEU] applies both to undertakings whose possible dominant position is established, as in this case, in relation to their suppliers and to those which are capable of being in the same position in relation to their customers"[1274]. Hence, the General Court also looked at the conduct from a buyer perspective or, at least, did not challenge the Commission's way of presenting the case.

1269 Commission Decision of 14 July 1999 relating to a proceeding under Article 82 of the EC Treaty (IV/D-2/34.780 - *Virgin/British Airways*) [2000] OJ L 30/1, para. 29. This finding by the Commission was upheld both by the General Court and the CJEU in the respective procedures.

1270 Commission Decision of 14 July 1999 relating to a proceeding under Article 82 of the EC Treaty (IV/D-2/34.780 - *Virgin/British Airways*) [2000] OJ L 30/1, para. 29. See discussing how the fact that British Airways's market share declined was a signal that the input leverage was not effective: Bishop and Walker, [2010], paras. 6-042 to 6-043.

1271 Judgment of 17 December 2003, *British Airways v Commission* of 17 December 2003, T-219/99, ECR, EU:T:2003:343, para. 270-299 Judgment of 15 March 2007 in *British Airways v Commission*, C-95/04 P, EU:C:2007:166, para. 57-80.

1272 A remark concerning this point ought to be made. In *British Airways v Commission* the purchasing of a service or a distribution channel is not identical to the purchase of a physical input. However, in my view the acquisition of a service constitutes a purchasing activity, regardless if such service is acquired in order to carry out a downstream economic activity (the air passenger transport). Also, the case can be seen as a downstream conduct because it implies buying a distribution service that would act as if the undertaking was an integrated firm or that acquires just an agent to carry out part of its business.

1273 Judgment of 17 December 2003, *British Airways v Commission* of 17 December 2003, T-219/99, ECR, EU:T:2003:343, para. 22.

1274 Judgment of 17 December 2003, *British Airways v Commission* of 17 December 2003, T-219/99, ECR, EU:T:2003:343, para. 101.

640. To secure the best access to an input and make it more difficult, or very costly, for rivals to obtain such service, British Airways remunerated suppliers of travel agency services by means of a supracompetitive bonus for the sale of its tickets[1275]. Therefore, British Airways *used its buyer market power by acquiring a distribution service to gain access to a necessary input* and at the same time prevent rival buyers from getting access to it or making it very costly, due to the nature of the rebates, which had a loyalty and retroactive enhancing effect, which had no economic justification as they were not based on quantity. As British Airways was a very important air transportation service provider (with a market share that at its lowest was 39.7%) *suppliers were said to be dependent on the sales or airline tickets and the commissions paid by British Airways created a relation with similar effects as a selling exclusivity for the travel agents*[1276]. Such dependence was the key element in order for British Airways to be able to leverage its buyer market power and obtain an advantage in the retailing market by foreclosing access of competitors to the most efficient travel agents[1277].

641. This dependence existed according to the Commission due to BA's position on the markets for air transport take it an obligatory business partner for travel agents. For the travel agents the sales of British Airways' tickets was their largest source of income[1278], due to the "extremely successful"[1279] position of British Airways as provider of air transport services in the UK. This bargaining strength vis-à-vis travel agents *gave British Airways substantial bargaining power* that could be used to secure a semi-exclusivity relation with the as suppliers of travel agency services that were the vehicle to sell airline tickets at the time. Likewise, for airline companies, *travel agents were a necessary distribution channel to reach each consumers,* as travel agents represented an average of 80% to 85% of the sales of air tickets in the UK at the time and only the remaining 15% to 20% were sold directly to end consumers[1280]. Therefore, a symbiosis existed between airlines and travel agents to sell tickets to end consumers and for travel agents to maximize their profits by the bonuses.

1275 "Payment of the performance reward or the special bonus was subject to travel agents increasing their sales of BA tickets from one year to the next", Judgment of 17 December 2003, *British Airways v Commission* of 17 December 2003, T-219/99, ECR, EU:T:2003:343, para. 10.

1276 Also remarking that this was the exclusionary effect of the rebates and, therefore, foreclosing access to competing buyers see: Østerud, p. 72.

1277 The General Court confirmed that British Airways was a dominant seller even if there was evidence that the market shares of their competitors increased during the years the bonus schemes were implemented in Judgment of 17 December 2003, *British Airways v Commission* of 17 December 2003, T-219/99, ECR, EU:T:2003:343, para. 212-217.

1278 Also remarking the fact that British Airways was an unavoidable trading partner for the travel agents see: Petit 'Intel, Leveraging Rebates and the Goals of Article 102 TFEU' (2015), 33-34. See also stressing the strong position of British Airways vis-à-vis its suppliers: Graham, [2010], p. 162.

1279 Commission Decision of 14 July 1999 relating to a proceeding under Article 82 of the EC Treaty (IV/D-2/34.780 - *Virgin/British Airways*) [2000] OJ L 30/1, para. 91.

1280 See the discussion of necessary trading partner and gatekeeping in chapter 5, section §IV for a reverse explanation of this phenomenon.

642. To secure access to the best travel agents and incentivize them to sell the largest amount of British Airways tickets as possible, British Airways offered them bonuses through three financial incentive programs: through marketing agreements, global agreements and a performance reward scheme. All these incentive agreements rewarded travel agents for their sale of British Airways' air transport tickets to end consumers. The three agreements had a common feature: all of them had a noticeable effect at the margin because of its retroactivity which created a *loyalty enhancing effect* that was deemed capable of *foreclosing rival airline companies*. The Commission held that

> [i]n each case meeting the targets for sales growth leads to an increase in the commission paid on all tickets sold by the agent, not just on the tickets sold after the target is reached[1281].

643. The effect was said to be fidelity inducing because when a travel agent is close to reaching the threshold imposed by British Airways to trigger the compensation, the agent will do all it can to keep selling British Airways tickets, as this will have a large effect on the commission it receives. For a competing buyer, on the other hand, the rebates make it very costly to compete with British Airways as it will have to "pay a much higher rate of commission [...] to overcome this [the loyalty/fidelity building] effect"[1282].

644. In this way, and in quite ordoliberally-sounding terms, the bonuses schemes would foreclose competition and be in breach of Article 102 TFEU when it is proven that they:

> tended to remove or restrict the agents' freedom to sell their services to the airlines of their choice and thereby hinder the access of BA's competitor airlines to the United Kingdom market for air travel agency services[1283].

645. Furthermore, using an argument based on the market power of big vs small undertakings, the General Court held that, as British Airways competitors were small in the downstream market for air transport services, they "were not in a position to attain the United Kingdom a level of revenue capable of constitution a sufficiently broad financial base to allow them effectively to establish a reward scheme similar to BA's in order to counteract the exclusionary effect of the scheme against them"[1284]. The General Court based its decision on the fact that,

---

1281 Commission Decision of 14 July 1999 relating to a proceeding under Article 82 of the EC Treaty (IV/D-2/34.780 - *Virgin/British Airways*) [2000] OJ L 30/1, para. 29. This finding by the Commission was upheld both by the General Court and the CJEU in the respective procedures.

1282 Commission Decision of 14 July 1999 relating to a proceeding under Article 82 of the EC Treaty (IV/D-2/34.780 - Virgin/British Airways) [2000] OJ L 30/1, para. 29..

1283 Judgment of 17 December 2003, British Airways v Commission of 17 December 2003, T-219/99, ECR,EU:T:2003:343, para. 270.

1284 Judgment of 17 December 2003, *British Airways v Commission* of 17 December 2003, T-219/99, ECR, EU:T:2003:343, para. 278..

according to the Commission's findings, the bonus scheme had a foreclosure effect because for a competitor to replace 1000 GBP of the sales for British Airways by a travel agent they would have to offer them a "commission of 17.4% on those tickets to compensate the travel agent for its loss of BA commission revenue", which implies an increase in British Airways' rivals' costs[1285].

646. A similar approach was taken by Advocate General Kokott when remarking that the exclusionary effect of the bonus schemes made it "particularly difficult for competitors of the dominant undertaking to outbid such whole-turnover-based rebates [... because they] *in absolute terms*, regularly weigh more strongly in the balance than anything which even more generous offers from competitors could normally achieve"[1286].

647. This finding of the exclusionary effect of the supracompetitive rebates on other buyers attempting to acquire travel agency services was upheld by the CJEU. The Court reasoned that the leverage of buyer power by granting bonuses schemes to contracting parties can have an exclusionary effect on the competitors of the undertaking as buyers of a necessary input because, "[i]n order to attract the co-contractors of the undertaking in a dominant position, or to receive a sufficient volume of orders from them, *those competitors would have to offer them significantly higher rates of discounts of bonus*", which is another method to raise a rival's costs[1287]. And it confirmed expressly the finding of the General Court regarding that the "rival airlines were not in a position to grant travel agents the same advantages as British Airways, since they were not capable of attaining in the United Kingdom a level of revenue capable of constituting a sufficiently broad financial base to allow them effectively to establish a reward scheme similar to BA's"[1288]. Furthermore, the CJEU also confirmed that the General Court was correct in deciding that the bonuses schemes by British Airways were not objectively justified under a counterbalancing test due to the competitive benefits of the scheme[1289]. Consequently, the General Court and later the CJEU upheld the finding that British Airways had abused its dominant position by granting of loyalty enhancing rebates that had a foreclosure effect on rival airline companies[1290].

648. An analysis of the case law shows that the Courts confirmed the theory of

---

1285 Judgment of 17 December 2003, *British Airways v Commission* of 17 December 2003, T-219/99, ECR, EU:T:2003:343, para. 30.

1286 Opinion of Advocate General Kokott of 23 February 2006 in Judgment of 15 March 2007 in *British Airways v Commission*, C-95/04 P, EU:C:2006:133, para. 52 (emphasis in original).

1287 Judgment of 15 March 2007 in *British Airways v Commission*, C-95/04 P, EU:C:2007:166, para. 75 (emphasis added).

1288 Judgment of 15 March 2007 in *British Airways v Commission*, C-95/04 P, EU:C:2007:166, para. 76.

1289 Judgment of 15 March 2007 in *British Airways v Commission*, C-95/04 P, EU:C:2007:166, para. 84-89.

1290 "Therefore, the Court of First Instance was right to examine, in paragraphs 270 to 278 of the judgment under appeal, whether the bonus schemes at issue had a fidelity-building effect capable of producing an exclusionary effect", Judgment of 15 March 2007 in *British Airways v Commission*, C-95/04 P, EU:C:2007:166, para. 77; Judgment of 17 December 2003, *British Airways v Commission* of 17 December 2003, T-219/99, ECR, EU:T:2003:343, paras. 270-278.

harm used by the Commission concerning the way in which the downstream exclusion operated through the leverage of buyer power by the granting of loyalty enhancing bonuses. This was the case because, by preventing rivals from having better or cheaper access to travel agency services, it made it difficult for them to sale airline tickets to end consumers. The foreclosure effect was created because, due to the fidelity-enhancing nature of the rebates, the rivals would have had to pay a much higher bonus to travel agents so they would sell a ticket from the competitors rather than British Airways. Therefore, the use of buyer power in the upstream market *to affect the downstream market and gain a competitive advantage by securing the best/most efficient distribution channels of its retail products* was found to be, in addition to the rebate system, an abuse of a dominant position, a finding that confirms the *dual market effect of buyer power cases.*

c. A buyer power analysis through the dualistic approach

649. *British Airways v Commission*[1291] constitutes the landmark case concerning input leveraging through supra-competitive bonuses by a dominant buying undertaking in EU competition law, as also remarked by Jones and Sufrin[1292]. Furthermore, it is the sole instance where the anti-competitive behaviour took place in the upstream market as it was through the purchasing that the foreclosure was imposed on other rival buyers/sellers[1293].

650. The case is important not only because it constitutes the sole instance in EU competition law where an exclusionary unilateral conduct has been focused on buyer power analysis, but also because it clearly shows the relation between the effects of the upstream and downstream markets in buyer power cases. This is so because *British Airways v Commission* illustrates how a privileged position or dominance in a market allows the undertaking to exercise market power in another market if they are sufficiently connected, which is not a novel proposal in EU competition law, as it was confirmed in *Istituto Chemioterapico Italiano and Commercial Solvents v Commission*[1294]. This finding of the case law *reinforces the need for a dualistic approach to buyer power conducts.*

1291 Commission Decision of 14 July 1999 relating to a proceeding under Article 82 of the EC Treaty (IV/D-2/34.780 - *Virgin/British Airways*) [2000] OJ L 30/1; Judgment by the General Court Judgment of 17 December 2003, *British Airways v Commission* of 17 December 2003, T-219/99, ECR, EU:T:2003:343; and Judgment of 15 March 2007 in *British Airways v Commission*, C-95/04 P, EU:C:2007:166.

1292 Jones and Sufrin, *EU Competition Law: Text, Cases, and Materials* [2011], p. 286; Jones and Sufrin, *EU Competition Law: Text, Cases and Materials* [2014], p. 323-325 and 469-475.

1293 "The Commission then maintains that BA is a purchaser in a dominant position on the United Kingdom market for air travel agency services, especially because of the percentage which sales of BA tickets represent in the total of air ticket sales carried out in the United Kingdom [...]", Judgment of 17 December 2003, *British Airways v Commission* of 17 December 2003, T-219/99, ECR, EU:T:2003:343, para. 22. See also making a similar statement: van Doorn, p. 154. The case is well known because of its treatment of rebates. The discussion in this section, however, will not be focused on rebates in general but rather on the buyer power related aspects of the case.

1294 Judgment of 6 March 1974 in joined cases C-6/73 and C-7/73 *Istituto Chemioterapico Italiano and Commercial Solvents v Commission*, EU:C:1974:18, para. 22.

651. The case also shows how a powerful buyer, who is also a powerful seller, is more likely to exert anti-competitive effects with its buyer power than powerful buyers without downstream market power; by negatively affecting the ability of rivals to compete in the downstream market, because it has an *hourglass shape*. I make this interpretation based on the fact that the Commission and the Courts took into account the "extremely successful"[1295] position of British Airways as provider of air transport services in the UK, which allowed the applicant to possess a dominant position vis-à-vis travel agents. Therefore, being a strong retailer allowed it to exert pressure on its suppliers, and having access to the best suppliers allowed it to have an even better position as a retailer, due to the undeniable close connection between these markets[1296]. This interconnection of buyer and seller market power explains why the literature tends to discuss the case from a selling side perspective disregarding the buyer power aspects of it focusing on rebate schemes, and why, in the US, the case was brought as a pure selling side case.

652. Furthermore, the analysis of the buyer power effects seems to be anchored on the risks of a buyer having dual market power (upstream and downstream), as by having an hourglass shape, anti-competitive effects of the buying conduct are more likely to be present. Hence, upon the existence of loyalty rebates the General Court adopted an approach in which it seems to have assumed that, because of the characteristics of British Airways as a powerful buyer and seller as "for the purposes of establishing an infringement of Article 82 EC, it is not necessary to demonstrate that the abuse in question had a concrete effect on the markets concerned. It is sufficient in that respect to demonstrate that the abusive conduct of the undertaking in a dominant position tends to restrict competition, or, in other words, that the conduct is capable of having, or likely to have, such an effect"[1297]. Hence, it could be interpreted that the General Court found convincing the fact that an undertaking with an hourglass shape when it carries out an activity that is likely to create a foreclosure effect there is a high likelihood that the conduct would restrict competition. Hence, the form of the undertaking along with the form of the conduct, in this case the loyalty enhancing rebate, created the presumption of the harm, also in line with the ideas of Wils[1298]. This interpretation of the case is not supported by an express wording of the Judgments but could be an alternative and economically sound explanation in accordance to the buyer power economics described in chapter 2, section §V, why dominance (in this situation as a seller) was said to exist at even at relatively low market shares of 39%,

1295 Commission Decision of 14 July 1999 relating to a proceeding under Article 82 of the EC Treaty (IV/D-2/34.780 - *Virgin/British Airways*) [2000] OJ L 30/1, para. 91.

1296 Judgment of 17 December 2003, *British Airways v Commission* of 17 December 2003, T-219/99, ECR, EU:T:2003:343, para. 132.

1297 Judgment of 17 December 2003, *British Airways v Commission* of 17 December 2003, T-219/99, ECR, EU:T:2003:343, para. 293.

1298 Wils (2014).

when compared to other cases of breaches of Article 102 TFEU,[1299] and why the anti-competitive nature of the loyalty enhancing bonuses was presumed.

653. In connection to the dualistic effect and the need for a dualistic approach to buyer power cases, the General Court confirmed that in buyer power leverage there is a *connection between the dominated market and the non-dominated market in which the anti-competitive effects also take place*[1300]. Furthermore, it is settled case law that the abuse of dominance in a market that has its competitive effects in another falls under the scope of application of Article 102 TFEU if those markets are sufficiently related[1301]. In this case, the General Court and the Commission found that the air travel agency market and air transport market to and from the UK were closely connected as "there is a mutual dependence between travel agents and airlines which are not in themselves in a position to market their air transport services effectively"[1302]. Because of the existence of a close connection between the two markets and the ability of buyer power to have dualistic effects of competition it was, therefore, correct for the Commission and Courts to conclude that the abusive leverage of buyer market power with anti-competitive foreclosure effects in a related downstream market could be prohibited by Article 102 TFEU.

654. Moreover, and in line with a broader approach to buyer power, by placing the emphasis on the increase of rival's costs, the General Court and the CJEU granted a limited competitive protection to rival buyers and their ability to compete with the dominant undertaking as buyers and retailers in a related market. Hence, competition law *should protect the competitive structure upstream and downstream and competition as such*, arguments much in line with an ordoliberal approach to buyer exclusion[1303]. Therefore, the legal standard employed by the Courts was to consider buyer power exclusion as anti-competitive if the ability of rival undertakings to effectively compete (as buyers and retailers) was diminished *even absent end consumer harm* (as there was no evidence of a price increase for airline tickets), triggering competition law application upon substantial harm to rivals and the competitive structure.

1299 Cf with Venit who argues that the case lacked of a substantive economic analysis as it treated the rebates as restrictive by nature: Venit (2004), p. 1158-1160 and 1166-1167.

1300 Judgment of 17 December 2003, *British Airways v Commission* of 17 December 2003, T-219/99, ECR, EU:T:2003:343, paras. 127-136.

1301 "An abuse of a dominant position on the market in raw materials may thus have effects restricting competition in the market on which the derivatives of the raw material are sold and these effects must be taken into account in considering the effects of an infringement, even if the market for the derivative does not constitute a self-contained market. The arguments of the applicants in this respect and in consequence their request that an expert's report on this subject be ordered are irrelevant and must be rejected", Judgment of 6 March 1974 in joined cases C-6/73 and C-7/73 *Istituto Chemioterapico Italiano and Commercial Solvents v Commission*, EU:C:1974:18, para. 22.

1302 Judgment of 17 December 2003, *British Airways v Commission* of 17 December 2003, T-219/99, ECR, EU:T:2003:343, para. 95.

1303 See also remarking and criticizing the ordoliberal influence in the decision Venit (2004), p. 1166-167.

655. Even if *British Airways v Commission* acknowledge that buyer power can be abusively leveraged to adversely affect competition, particularly if a buyer is powerful both upstream and downstream in line with the hourglass shape, the Court's approach can be criticized regarding the assessment of the bonuses effects on the markets involved. In this case, the Courts analyzed the leverage effects mostly anchored on the buyer power aspects and consequences on the upstream market but did *not analyze in depth the consequence of the practice in the downstream market where British Airways and Virgin competed as providers of air transport services. This is, the Courts could be criticized by being shy of doing a full dualistic assessment to the case*. As other authors have pointed out, from the Commission's investigation it is clear that, despite the fact that British Airways exercised buyer power vis-à-vis travel agents the market shares of British Airways' competitors still increased[1304]. This could be interpreted in two different ways. One way of interpretation, in line with the case's outcome, is that competition in the downstream market was affected because absent the leverage conduct the competitors would have been in a position to increase further their market shares. An alternative approach would have been claiming that the leverage of buyer market power *was not exclusionary because it was not aimed at foreclosing rivals* – or at least it did not have such an effect – but instead it *aimed at securing the best distribution channels* for British Airways to reach end customers without having an adverse nor unjustified effect in competition. This approach could be further backed up as there appears to be no evidence in the case of a price increase vis-à-vis end consumers in the form of higher airline transport tickets, which implies that British Airways internalized the costs of the supracompetitive bonuses granted to airline travel agents. However, this can also be criticized by the implicit Court's reasoning that even if no direct end consumer harm had occurred, there was still harm to the competitive structure and the ability of the rivals of the dominant undertaking to compete, thereby also creating downstream harm in the medium and long run. Also, it could be interpreted from the case that, if were not for the supracompetitive bonus scheme, the market shares of the competitors in the downstream market would have increased much further than they did, due to the existence of the loyalty enhancing rebates.

656. Lastly, an aspect that was not dealt with by the Courts or the Commission concerning the foreclosure effects of the rebates was the decision-making power of end consumers when determining which airline service provider to acquire tickets from. In principle, and despite the commission paid by British Airways, the passengers were able to determine which airline they should choose. However, it could have also been the case that travel agents were reluctant to provide passengers with information about different travel options

---

1304 Graham, [2010], p. 162; Ariel Ezrachi, *EU Competition Law: An Analytical Guide to the Leading Cases* (Hart 2012, 3rd edn), p. 209; Whish and Bailey, *Competition law* [2012], p. 734.

or routes and downplayed other competitors with the interest of selling only, or mostly, British Airways tickets. From the Commission's report, nevertheless, there were no indications of these types of practices, nor of customers frequently requesting alternative options.

657. All in all, *British Airways v Commission* constitutes the most important case in EU competition law dealing with buyer power exclusion and its line of thought appears to be based on the concerns of buyer power leverage to affect competition in a related downstream market where the powerful buyer also enjoys substantive downstream market power. The General Court and CJEU's stands were centered on the way in which through granting supracompetitive benefits to a supplier a buyer could create a relation of semi-exclusive supply that would have foreclosed rival's access to a necessary distribution mechanism to reach end consumers, increasing their costs. The perspective of the Courts in this case, appears to be that they have indeed resorted to a milder dualistic approach to the analysis of buyer power, as they centered its analysis more on upstream competition than downstream. Also, the Courts showed a preference for the *protection of competition as a process and guaranteeing the wellbeing of upstream market conditions* by granting a limited protection to rival buyers of a dominant undertaking by prohibiting supra-competitive bonus schemes that would affect their ability to acquire an input and compete downstream. Consequently, the case adopted a broader approach to buyer power as it triggered the application of EU competition law absent evidence of direct end and short-term consumer harm if there was evidence of substantial upstream harm to the competitive process.

d. Virgin vs British Airways: the US Antitrust law version

658. *Virgin Atlantic Airways Limited v British Airways Plc* is a clear-cut example of the differences regarding the treatment given to buyer power cases (and rebates in general) between US and EU competition regulation[1305]. Unlike the Commission, the plaintiff Virgin initiated a private antitrust claim against the anti-competitive behaviour of British Airways as a retailer and offeror of air passenger transportation. Both in the first instance and the Court of Appeals of the Second Circuit, it was found that the alleged behaviour of British Airways was not proven to be anti-competitive because "Virgin failed to show how British Airways' competition harmed consumers", as "[t]he Sherman Act and other antitrust laws are designed to protect competition, not individual competitors"[1306]. Therefore, the standard applied assumes that exclusionary buyer power must directly affect downstream competition and harm consumers, taking a narrower stance to buyer power harm.

1305 *Virgin Atlantic Airways v. British Airways Plc*, 69 F.Supp. 2nd 571 (1999); appealed and upheld in its entirety in *Virgin Atlantic Airways Limited v. British Airways Plc*, 99-9402 (2nd Cir., 2001). See also stressing the different outcome but without analyzing the different approach: Elhauge and Geradin, [2011], p. 1137; Whish and Bailey, *Competition law* [2012], p. 734.

1306 *Virgin Atlantic Airways Limited v. British Airways Plc*, 99-9402 (2nd Cir., 2001).

659. The way of focusing the case was also very different. Instead of focusing its arguments on a theory of harm anchored on exclusionary leverage of buyer market power, Virgin argued that British Airways was a powerful retailer of air passenger transport and that it used its downstream market power to engage in downstream predation practices by offering 'loyalty programs' for its individual and corporate clients that allow these to obtain a rebate according to how much they flew with this airline company. These practices, along with British Airways' dominant presence in the routes to and from the UK to the US impeded, according to Virgin, new routes being opened that could compete. Also, before the Court of Appeals Judgment Virgin claimed that British Airways had leveraged its buyer power by granting incentive agreements to travel agencies. The Court of Appeals dismissed *in limine litis* such claims - and the appeal altogether – as Virgin failed to prove that British Airways:

> (1) possessed monopoly power in one market; (2) used that power to gain a competitive advantage over Virgin another distinct market; and (3) caused injury by such anticompetitive conduct [...]. In other words Virgin would have to demonstrate that British Airways' use of alleged monopoly power via its incentive agreements "threaten[ed] the [second] market with higher prices or reduced output or quality associated with the kind of monopoly that is ordinarily accompanied by a large market share[1307]

660. Hence, as Virgin was unable to provide evidence that buyer market power leveraging had any effects in the downstream conditions (increase of prices vis-à-vis end consumers), the Court of Appeals decided to dismiss the appeal and issued a summary judgment.

B. Where do we stand in buyer market power leverage?

661. To conclude, *British Airways v Commission* confirms that the exclusionary application of buyer power through leveraging is captured as a breach of EU competition law (particularly if exerted by a dominant undertaking)[1308]. *Leverage buyer market power through the granting of retroactive bonuses* allows a powerful buyer to foreclose rivals' from a necessary input that will either impede them from acquiring it (total foreclosure) or mean that they obtain it at higher cost or through inferior sales channels, increasing their costs and making them less attractive as retailers. This grants the buyer an advantage in the upstream market as a buyer and an additional advantage as a retailer if parties compete in a downstream market. Not all types of rebates

1307 *Virgin Atlantic Airways Limited v. British Airways Plc*, 99-9402 (2nd Cir., 2001) quoting III Phillip E. Areeda et al., Antitrust Law ¶ 652).

1308 See also stressing the anticompetitiveness by nature of retroactive rebates pursuant to the recent CJEU case law: Sunny S. H. Chan, 'Post Danmark II: Per Se Unlawfulness of Retroactive Rebates Granted by Dominant Undertakings' 37 European Competition Law Review (2016) 43.

nor bonuses, however, would be anti-competitive, as the case law shows that only those that have a fidelity enhancing effect and that are not economically justified are anti-competitive.

662. Buyer market power leveraging can potentially constitute an abuse of a dominant position when it, in combination with the practice used to cause the foreclosure effect (for example a loyalty reverse rebate), adversely affects the competitive structure in the upstream and/or downstream markets, even absent end consumer harm. However, leveraging seems to be insufficient to constitute in itself an infringement of competition because it has to be accompanied by the conduct that causes the leveraging effect. In the case of *British Airways v Commission,* leveraging was found abusive because it was done through granting an exclusionary and abusive loyalty-enhancing rebate that was unjustified. Therefore, the legal standard to be applied in leverage cases to determine its anti-competitiveness seems to be coupled with the type of conduct that generated the leveraging effect. What can be said of leveraging itself is that the Courts adopt a broader approach in terms of finding the anti-competitiveness of leveraging in buyer power cases because it can be found to be abusive even absent end consumer harm. Therefore, the case law can be interpreted as showing how the Courts have an interest in protecting competition as a process, the ability of rival buyers (and retailers) to compete with the powerful firm without being subject to an unjustified economically disadvantage, and in a way, the economic freedom of these rivals. Additionally, unlike US antitrust law, leveraging of buyer market power will trigger the application of EU competition law, even if parties do not compete in a related downstream market. Also, EU competition law will preclude an undertaking from leveraging market power even if it has no presence in the downstream market but the input in the upstream market is necessary for the rival buyer to carry out its economic activity.

VIII. Squeeze to buy

663. *Squeeze to buy*[1309] is a hybrid practice in which exploitative and exclusionary effects of buyer power jointly operate to the benefit of the buying(s) undertaking(s) and to the detriment of its suppliers, rival buyers and end consumers alike. As a hybrid practice like margin squeeze[1310], squeeze combines exploitative and foreclosure effects that affect different parties and markets in different ways as suppliers are abused through exploitative pricing and a subsequent forced take-over. Therefore, unlike in the previous theories of harm, the exclusion effects take place on a vertical level to force the exit of suppliers, but not rival buyers or sellers.

664. In a squeeze to buy scheme a powerful buyer (or a group of coordinate buyers) would employ its market power by paying an exploitatively low purchasing price[1311] – or just barely covering the costs – forcing its supplier to either leave the market or accept a take-over offer under less favorable conditions than absent the exploitative practice. In this scenario, the powerful buyer is not interested in reaping supracompetitive monopsony profits but rather in acquiring at a lower price the assets of a supplier to vertically integrate, in an analogue and reverse scenario as discussed in *Istituto Chemioterapico Italiano and Commercial Solvents v Commission*[1312].

665. An example will illustrate this theory of harm. Isolation's Supermarket possesses an excellent market position in the processed beef retailing business after it has managed to exclude Isolation's Butchery through overbuying. Now that it dominates the downstream market it wishes to expand in the supply market by acquiring its beef providers. To avoid paying the market price of the assets or shares of Isolation's three slaughterhouses, Isolation's

---

1309 Term coined by the author. I would like to thank Sebastian Peyer for his suggestion about a theory of harm like this for buyer power cases.

1310 For some literature dealing with margin and price squeeze and its hybrid nature as an anticompetitive conduct, as well as whether the practice is in reality or not a competition concern see, *inter alia*: Damien Geradin and Robert O'Donoghue, 'The Concurrent Application of Competition Law and Regulation: The Case of Margin Squeeze Abuses in the Telecommunications Sector' 1 Journal of Competition Law and Economics (2005) 355; Dennis W. Carlton, 'Should "Price Squeeze" be a Recognized Form of Anticompetitive Conduct?' 4 Journal of Competition Law and Economics (2008) 271; E. Hovenkamp and H Hovenkamp, 'The Viability of Antitrust Price Squeeze Claims' 51 Arizona Law Review (2009) 273; Alberto Heimler, 'Is a Margin Squeeze an Antitrust or a Regulatory Violation?' 6 Journal of Competition Law and Economics (2010) 879; John B Meisel, 'The Law and Economics of Margin Squeezes in the US Versus the EU' 8 European Competition Journal (2012) 383; Barak Y. Orbach and Raphael Avraham, 'Squeeze Claims: Refuslas to Deal, Essential Facilities and Price Squeezes' in Roger D. Blair and D. Daniel Sokol (eds), *The Oxford Handbook of International Antitrust Economics*, vol 2 (Oxford University Press 2015).

1311 I discuss buyer power exploitation through low purchasing prices in chapter 7, section §III.

1312 In this case, the dominant firm refused to supply an input required for the production of a good to a competing undertaking to gain market power in the downstream market and exclude undertakings from competing and selling their goods to end consumers. Judgment of 6 March 1974 in joined cases C-6/73 and C-7/73 *Istituto Chemioterapico Italiano and Commercial Solvents v Commission*, EU:C:1974:18. See discussing this case from an angle linked with the ordoliberal concern of protecting market structures: Gormsen 'Article 82 EC: Where are we Coming from and Where are we Going to?' (2006), p. 12-15.

Supermarket has decided to exert exploitative buyer power to force the exit of the beef suppliers. The strategy is to pay a beef-purchasing price below the marginal costs of the most efficient of its suppliers in a take-it-or-leave-it offer (but not below the competitive level). By setting such low purchasing price the supplier "do(es) not have a sufficient profit margin on the processing to remain competitive on the market for the processed product"[1313]. To remedy such a situation, the slaughterhouses – absent other demand sources - are forced to either heavily invest to reduce its production costs or exit the market and carry out a different economic activity that would be profitable for its shareholders. Some months after the exploitative prices are set by Isolation's Supermarket, two of the slaughterhouses approach the board of directors with a communication stating they have decided to leave the business and close their operations as beef producers and are offering Isolation's Supermarket a preferential deal in case they are interested in purchasing their assets.

666. However, the squeeze to buy theory of harm, despite its intuitive appeal has hurdles for it to be a credible competition problem as hybrid theories tend to be. A powerful buyer might impose a purchasing price sufficiently low for a supplier to not be able to fully cover its costs, pushing it out of the market, or accepting a low takeover bid. Nevertheless, unlike in the case of exploitatively low purchasing prices, the purchasing price is compared to the particular supplier's cost structure and it does not have to be below the competitive level as an exploitative price. This is so, because *this relative threshold is sufficient to create the squeeze to buy scenario*. If the relative suppliers' costs is resorted to as the applicable legal standard to trigger the application of the law, and the purchasing price paid is above the competitive costs, then considering this practice anti-competitive due to foreclosure risks would in some instances excessively protect rival undertakings and the economic freedom of inefficient suppliers. If, on the other hand, the standard resorted to for the determination of whether the price has a foreclosure effect is the competitive level, then competition intervention would be warranted because there are two violations: first, the price is exploitatively low, as discussed in chapter 7, section §III, which would in itself constitute an abuse under Article 102 TFEU not requiring the takeover, and, second, the conduct has a foreclosure effect and it is abusive because it restricts the rival's economic freedom unjustifiably and distorts the upstream market structure.

667. Therefore, it is difficult to predict whether the Courts in Europe – and to a minor degree in the US – would find conducts such as the squeeze to buy

---

1313 Judgment of 30 November 2000, *Industrie des poudres sphériques v Commission*, T-5/97, ECR, EU:T:2000:278, para. 178. See, however, the change in criterion to trigger competition application in cases of margin squeeze when the General Court held that the anticompetitiveness lies between the prices an undertaking charges for its wholesale access and its retail prices in Judgment of 10 April 2008, *Deutsche Telekom v Commission*, T-271/03, ECR, EU:T:2008:101, paras. 166-168. See the upheld appeal in Judgment of 14 October 2010 in *Deutsche Telekom v Commission*, C-280/08 P, EU:C:2010.

purchasing behaviour anti-competitive if the prices offered are not below the competitive levels (which is a difficult standard to apply), or more likely by taking as reference the marginal or average costs of an efficient supplier. If they do, the competition intervention would risk preventing efficient purchasing behaviour. Though, if they do not, then these exclusionary conducts could perhaps trigger medium to long-term competition concerns with regard to the upstream market structure, dynamic efficiency due to lack of incentives to invest, or entry into a supply market and significantly impede effective competition in either the upstream and downstream market.

668. However, would squeeze to buy be likely to be condemned by the Courts under EU competition law? In my view, if the effects are widespread on the upstream market and not only a few marginal and inefficient suppliers are squeezed out, and if the buyer is a dominant undertaking, then squeeze to buy practices could be captured under the scope of Article 102(a) TFEU, if the prices are exploitative and unfairly low, which is unlikely to happen, as I discuss in chapter 7, Section §VII. However, if that is the case there would not be any need for a theory of harm such as squeeze to buy. An alternative approach, based on *Istituto Chemioterapico Italiano and Commercial Solvents v Commission*[1314], would be that competition intervention would take place at the moment when the take-over is evaluated by competition authorities and then determine the terms in which was carried out and find out any possible harm. A problem with this merger-based approach is that the harm has already taken place and would not represent a significant impediment to effective competition in the future. Therefore, even if under EU competition law there is some concern regarding the protection of the undertaking's economic freedom and a broader standard is employed in buyer power cases without requiring evidence of downstream end consumer harm, I think it is unlikely that squeeze to buy scenarios would be found anti-competitive by the Courts as an autonomous theory of harm.

1314 Judgment of 6 March 1974 in joined cases C-6/73 and C-7/73 *Istituto Chemioterapico Italiano and Commercial Solvents v Commission*, EU:C:1974:18.

IX. 'As efficient buying competitor test' for price related abuses?

669. The Commission in its Enforcement Guidelines on the Application of Article 102 TFEU has suggested applying the *As Efficient Competitor Test* (AECT) to determine whenever the exclusion of competitors by a dominant undertaking is abusive and not the outcome of competition[1315]. A thorough discussion of the test is outside the scope of this study. However, in this section I discuss and criticize its application from a buyer side perspective and why the reverse application of the AECT may not be an adequate policy in EU competition law for buyer power cases, and, in particular, for rebates, position in line with the buyer power case law in *British Airways v Commission*[1316].

670. In short, the AECT aims at determining if the conduct of an undertaking is anti-competitive and has a foreclosure effect by taking as a reference another firm that is as efficient as the dominant undertaking. The Commission would only intervene whenever the conduct under analysis has already been, or is capable of, hampering competition from that as 'efficient competitor'[1317]. The judicial reception of the AECT has been mixed. In cases of predatory pricing[1318] and margin squeeze[1319] it has been endorsed by the Courts, whereas concerning rebates it has recently been clarified in *Post Danmark II* that the AECT is one of the many tools available to determine whether a rebate could have an exclusionary and illegal nature[1320].

1315 Communication from the Commission — Guidance on the Commission's enforcement priorities in applying Article 82 of the EC Treaty to abusive exclusionary conduct by dominant undertakings [2009] OJ C 45/7, para. 23. For some literature discussing the AECT see, *inter alia*: Vickers (2005); Giorgio Monti, 'Article 82 EC: What Future for the Effects-Based Approach?' 1 Journal of European Competition Law & Practice (2010) 2; Damien Geradin, 'The Decision of the Commission of 13 May 2009 in the Intel case: Where is the Foreclosure and Consumer Harm?' 1 Journal of European Competition Law & Practice (2010) 112; Giulio Federico, 'The Antitrust Treatment of Loyalty Discounts in Europe: Towards a more Economic Approach' Journal of European Competition Law & Practice (2011) 1; Nazzini, [2011], p. 221-256; Wils (2014).

1316 The General Court and the CJEU held in *British Airways v Commission* that in the case of rebates there is no need of applying the AECT test as some rebates may be anticompetitive due its nature and without requiring assessment of their effects in either consumers nor competitors. See also criticizing with strong arguments the AECT for rebates: Wils (2014), p. 428-432.

1317 Communication from the Commission — Guidance on the Commission's enforcement priorities in applying Article 82 of the EC Treaty to abusive exclusionary conduct by dominant undertakings [2009] OJ C 45/7, para. 23.

1318 Judgment of 3 July 1991 in *AKZO v Commission*, C-62/86, EU:C:1991:286; Judgment of 14 November 1996 in *Tetra Pak v Commission*, C-333/94 P, EU:C:1996:436.

1319 Judgment of 14 October 2010 in *Deutsche Telekom v Commission*, C-280/08 P, EU:C:2010:603; Judgment of 17 February 2011 in *TeliaSonera Sverige*, C-52/09, EU:C:2011:83; Judgment of 29 March 2012, *Telefónica and Telefónica de España v Commission*, T-336/07, ECR, EU:T:2012:172, appealed and upheld by the CJEU in Judgment of 10 July 2014 in *Telefónica and Telefónica de España v Commission*, C-295/12 P, EU:C:2014:2062.

1320 Judgment of 6 October 2015 in *Post Danmark*, C-23/14, EU:C:2015:651, paras. 63-74. See also Opinion of Advocate General Kokott in Judgment of 6 October 2015 in *Post Danmark*, C-23/14, EU:C:2015:343, para. 56-75.

671. The AECT is designed with selling cases in mind where firms compete in a downstream market offering their output to other consumers (final or intermediaries) and with an exclusive focus on price, but not on variety or quality. As such, the test measures the capacity of a hypothetical competitor to produce a similar or like output as efficiently as the dominant undertaking under investigation, by taking as reference if that hypothetical would have similar or lower costs and sale prices than the dominant undertaking, as explicitly remarked by the Commission[1321]. Therefore, the AECT does not take into account the efficiency of current rivals. The assessment is carried out measuring the efficiency of the foreclosed undertakings as producers of an output (and the Guidelines use average avoidable cost and long-run average incremental cost) but not when buying. Thus, its reverse application is challenging.

672. If the test is reversed, I distinguish two different alternatives on how it could be applied. First, the AECT could assess which firm is more efficient by focusing the costs test *in the output market*; i.e. how the firm behaves in the downstream market as a seller but not a buyer. If that is the case, then the AECT is just applied in a regular way to buyer cases. The problem with this methodology would be that to find that the undertaking has engaged into an exclusionary conduct *it must have substantial seller market power in the downstream market in addition to having substantial buyer power*. Hence, this test would be analogue to the double predation requirement as established in *Weyerhaeuser* and risks being under-inclusive[1322]. Additionally, the test might be under-inclusive because a reverse application presumes that the upstream and downstream markets are a reverse of each other and would not determine if there is foreclosure in cases where the rivals only compete for the input but not the downstream market. If firms do not compete in the downstream market, then their cost structure and sale prices are not comparable and, therefore, the test cannot be easily applied.

673. Additionally, the analysis could be based on *who acquires cheaper the input* – that is, ultimately, the most efficient buying firm. However, purchasing input at low prices does not exclude competitors and may have the opposite effect. If a buyer offers a higher purchasing price then the suppliers of the desired input will shift the sale to the new buyer that pays a higher amount, either because it values the input more or because it has less buyer power (and is thus less efficient). If a

---

1321 "In order to determine whether even a hypothetical competitor as efficient as the dominant undertaking would be likely to be foreclosed by the conduct in question, the Commission *will examine economic data relating to cost and sales prices*, and in particular whether the dominant undertaking is engaging in below-cost pricing", Communication from the Commission — Guidance on the Commission's enforcement priorities in applying Article 82 of the EC Treaty to abusive exclusionary conduct by dominant undertakings [2009] OJ C 45/7, para. 25 (emphasis added).

1322 *Weyerhaeuser Company, v. Ross-Simmons Hardwood Lumber Company, Inc.*, in 127 S. Ct. 1069 (2007). See also remarking that with the Weyerhaeuser requirement of the Brooke Group test "the Supreme Court immunized pricing behavior from antitrust scrutiny and substantially increased the potential for a dominant buyer to exercise monopsony power to the detriment of its smaller competitors, input sellers generally, and ultimately consumers" in Haglund (2008), p. 440.

higher purchasing price is paid that implies that the firm has higher costs and it can be assumed that such higher costs would be transferred in the form of higher output prices for end consumers. Hence, a buyer that pays more will be able to capture all sources of supply and this is not because it is an efficient buyer. This would, for example, be the case for an agricultural cooperative that, due to its internal profit distribution mechanisms, is able to pay more to its members than a more efficient buyer that could pay less but if it does would not be able to acquire input. Therefore, the more efficient buyer is unable to compete with a less efficient dominant undertaking for the acquisition of input — these are some factors to take into account if a reverse application of the test is suggested. For these reasons, an application based on who acquires the input cheaper would not be an adequate application of the AECT to buyer power cases.

674. Furthermore, a reverse application of the AECT places the emphasis on triggering the application of EU competition law in the presence of direct end consumer harm despite the fact that it is designed to determine when a conduct is anti-competitive because it has a foreclosing effect vis-à-vis competing undertakings. This happens because the test looks at how efficient the firm is regarding its costs and the sales of output vis-à-vis end consumers who will benefit from acquiring the end product from the most efficient/cheapest source. If this is the case then there is little room for welfare considerations of other buyers[1323], particularly if they are not part of the same downstream market, the protection of competition as a process and the undertaking's economic freedom being contrary to the broader approach taken in EU competition law concerning buyer power exclusion, which takes these factors into account and intervenes even absent consumer harm if upstream competition has been substantially affected.

675. Therefore, in my view a reverse application of the AECT test for buyer power cases as it stands *risks being under-inclusive* and/or inadequate, in particular concerning the granting of supracompetitive benefits. Consequently, and following the recent case law concerning its use as an assessment tool as discussed CJEU in *Post Danmark II*[1324] and the General Court in *Intel v Commission,*

1323 See also the opinion of Monti who argues that the application of the AECT in selling side cases already shows little concern for weaker (but not necessarily inefficient firms) in Monti, 'EU Competition Law from Rome to Lisbon - Social Market Economy' [2013], p. 48.

1324 "The Court has also held that, in order to establish whether such a practice is abusive, that practice must have an anti-competitive effect on the market, but the effect does not necessarily have to be concrete, and it is sufficient to demonstrate that there is an anti-competitive effect which may potentially exclude competitors who are at least as efficient as the dominant undertaking (...). It follows that only dominant undertakings whose conduct is likely to have an anti-competitive effect on the market fall within the scope of Article 82 EC. In that regard, the assessment of whether a rebate scheme is capable of restricting competition must be carried out in the light of all relevant circumstances, including the rules and criteria governing the grant of the rebates, the number of customers concerned and the characteristics of the market on which the dominant undertaking operates", Judgment of 6 October 2015 in *Post Danmark*, C-23/14, EU:C:2015:651, paras 66-68. See also the Opinion of Advocate General Kokott in Judgment of 6 October 2015 in *Post Danmark*, C-23/14, EU:C:2015:343, in particular paras 56-75. See also: Judgment of 12 June 2014, *Intel v Commission,* T-286/09, ECR, EU:T:2014:547, paras. 140-166, in which the General Court considered that in rebate cases there is no obligation to carry out the AEC to determine if a conduct is exclusionary or not, especially because the Commission Guidelines are not binding for Courts.

the use of the AECT to determine the exclusionary nature of a buying conduct should be approached with caution, always taking into account the specificities of buyer power cases and its dual impact in competition. Consequently, this is an area ripe for further academic research and in particular for economic methodologies oriented to determining when exclusion exists in buyer power cases.

X. Which type of harm triggers competition law application in exclusionary cases?

676. In this section I discuss two different approaches concerning what kind of consumer harm must be proven by a plaintiff or a competition authority in order to trigger the application of competition laws to exclusionary cases and the implications of such choice. To do so, I synthesize the approaches adopted by the Courts – choosing a broader approach that does not require evidence of direct end consumer harm – and the US antitrust Courts – choosing a narrow approach requiring such evidence – with the exception of the Robinson-Patman Act. In this discussion I evaluate these approaches and contrast them with ordoliberalism.

677. This analysis is of particular relevance to unilateral conduct (dominance and mergers), as well as agreements that restrict competition by effect, but less so for agreements where the objective is to foreclose rival buyers because these types of collusive behaviour are captured because they constitute a serious breach to the rivalry process without requiring any existence of effects (either upstream or downstream) as their pernicious is presumed. In a nutshell, if for buyer power exclusion, a pure end consumer harm standard is to be applied – as occurred in *Weyerhaeuser* – and antitrust liability would only exist whenever the purchasing behaviour has an effect on the welfare conditions of consumers in a downstream market. Therefore, absent direct end consumer harm, competition law would not prohibit a conduct if there is only harm in the upstream market among rival buyers or suppliers[1325]. However, if a broader welfare standard applies that seeks protection of not only end consumers but also competition as an economic process and economic freedom of suppliers and rival buyers, or as the EFTA Court recently held from a seller side perspective in *Sorpa bs. v The Icelandic Competition Authority (Samkeppniseftirlitið)*, competition intervention against anti-competitive exclusion is triggered to "prohibits (sic) a dominant undertaking from distorting competition on an upstream or downstream market, in other words between suppliers or customers

1325 This was also the argument used by British Airways before the CJEU and which was overruled in Judgment of 15 March 2007 in *British Airways v Commission*, C-95/04 P, EU:C:2007:166, para. 103.

of that undertaking"[1326], then such approach would intervene in an exclusionary case absent evidence of direct consumer harm with the aim of preventing it in the long run, analogous to what Petit calls the *incipiency theory*[1327].

678. An example simplifying but also illustrating the differences is helpful. If a narrow end consumer harm standard is employed by the Courts the fact that Isolation's Supermarket decides to overbuy all the available meat in Isolation from all farmers to foreclose the local butcher shops in town, rival buyers would not warrant competition intervention unless that 'buy-out' has a short term negative effect on end consumer prices. Therefore, Isolation's Supermarket would need to also raise downstream end consumer prices for its behaviour to be anti-competitive, regardless of whether the local butchers are pushed out of the market and all the end consumer demand is captured by Isolation's Supermarket[1328]. The second alternative where competition law applies not requiring direct end consumer harm, would reach a different outcome. The overbuying conduct would be prohibited because rival buyers have been foreclosed in an unjustified manner and the competitive structure in the upstream market would have been substantially affected. This would be sufficient because it is presumed that the harm to competition in the medium and long term would harm end consumers because it allowed Isolation's Supermarket to become a monemporist (monopsonist and monopolist). Also, this broader approach would capture conducts with a foreclosure effect in which the buyers only compete upstream, but not downstream, thus it is a more inclusive approach than the end consumer harm one.

679. In connection with this I would like to stress that the fact that adopting a *legal standard that triggers the application of EU competition law even absent evidence direct consumer harm does not imply that there is an inconsistency to a dualistic approach to buyer power cases*. If only an upstream market perspective is taken into account, then the effects of buyer power in the downstream market (whether there is direct or indirect harm to direct or indirect consumers) would be completely disregarded, which is contrary to the idea of protecting competition as a process because it is protected in the interest of the consumer in the medium and long run, as I explain under the welfare standard advocated by ordoliberalism in chapter 3, section §VI.C., which is also contrary to the case law. In connection with this, the fact that upstream consumer harm is sufficient to trigger the application of EU competition law is precisely because the aim is to guarantee a competitive environment and the maximization of allocative and dynamic efficiencies in both sides of the market to the ultimate benefit of consumers.

1326 Judgment of 22 September 2016 in *Sorpa bs. v The Icelandic Competition Authority (Samkeppniseftirlitið)* E-29/15 [2016], para. 109.

1327 Petit, *The IEEE-SA Revised Patent Policy and its Definition of "Reasonable" Rates: A Transatlatic Antitrust Divide?*

1328 In this example I assume that all consumers of the foreclosed butchers are not consumers of Isolation's Supermarket. If that is not the case, then there is some consumer harm to 'other consumers' part of a different but related downstream market.

680. Furthermore, adopting a harm standard that is broader than pure end downstream consumer harm does not mean that competition law would not intervene if there is existence of that harm; in fact, in my opinion, in cases of direct end consumer harm competition authorities must intervene. What it means is that not only that short term harm to end consumers triggers the application of the law, but also harm in the upstream market that might impact consumers in the medium and long term. And, in order to determine the possibility or existence of the current or future end consumer harm, a dualistic approach is needed by looking at the buyer power effects downstream.

681. My research has identified that under EU competition law the second alternative applies; that of a *broader welfare standard that applies to buyer power exclusion* even absent consumer harm, as it was the case in *British Airways v Commission* where there was no evidence of an increase in the prices of air transportation services for end consumers.

A. Precluding buyer exclusion absent consumer harm – the broader view

682. Precluding unilateral or concerted exclusionary buyer power behaviour even absent evidence of direct end consumer harm seeks to protect the competitive process by guaranteeing that upstream competition and rivalry among buyers is undistorted. Therefore, under this approach, competition law would be triggered if the buying conduct has a substantial restrictive effect on upstream competition, without requiring direct end consumer harm or that buyers compete both as purchasers and retailers. Such a position implies that exclusionary and unjustified buyer power exertion will be condemned in the upstream market with the goal of protecting competition as a process, protecting the competitive structure and protecting the legitimate interest of efficient rival buyers that see their market access and economic freedom affected by the buyer induced exclusion.

683. This protection to competition structure and economic freedom – and indirectly to rival buyers –is granted not to safeguard inefficient buyers but rather *to preserve a healthy competitive environment and to allow other firms potentially as efficient* – or more – as the dominant one *to thrive*. Paraphrasing Jones in his analysis of the goals of US antitrust law, protection of rivalry among competing buyers absent short term end consumer harm is important because it promotes competitive markets and in the end economic efficiency[1329]. Hence, protection should be granted to existing and entrant undertakings so that they have the opportunity to be as efficient, or more so, as the

1329 Jones (1989), p. 91

dominant undertaking[1330]. If, however, the dominant undertaking is allowed to foreclose these rivals then those options would not exist. A disclaimer must be made, nevertheless. Granting protection to the competitive process in the upstream market and to a certain extent also protecting the rival undertakings' economic freedom is not equivalent to the protection of other inefficient firms that, as the Commission points out, might be forced out of the market as part of the competitive process as a mechanism towards achieving efficiency[1331], as I discussed in chapter 3 under ordoliberalism.

684. This proposition of a *broader welfare standard for buyer power exclusion* that seeks to *protect the competitive process* as such, and consequently, in the medium and long run, also the wellbeing of consumers thanks to a healthy competitive environment, has grounds in the EU case law and the Commission policy, as I discuss below[1332].

685. For instance, the Non-horizontal Mergers Guidelines when dealing with input foreclosure clarify that a merger would raise anti-competitive concerns even if the outcome does not force rival buyers to exit the market because this would cause "consumer harm" being the benchmark of whether the merger "would lead to higher prices for consumers"[1333]. The use of the terms by the Commission, however are misleading. When the Commission speaks of consumers it means that "[i]n the context of competition law, *the concept of 'consumers'* encompasses *intermediate and ultimate consumers"*[1334]. In the context of buyer power *exclusion, those 'consumers' are no other than rival buyers that are affected because the exclusion increases their costs* and therefore affects their ability to compete and also affects the competitive structure and competition as such.

686. Even clearer is the position of the CJEU in *British Airways v Commission,*

1330 See also stressing that in exclusionary abuses there must be protection for weaker competitors against methods other than competition on the merits: Rodger and MacCullogh, [2015], p. 110.

1331 Communication from the Commission — Guidance on the Commission's enforcement priorities in applying Article 82 of the EC Treaty to abusive exclusionary conduct by dominant undertakings [2009] OJ C 45/7, para. 6.

1332 This policy is not exclusive to exclusionary buyer power cases but a part of the EU exclusionary competition policy as a whole. As early as in Judgment of 13 February 1979 in *Hoffmann-La Roche v Commission*, C-85/76, EU:C:1979:36, the CJEU, in quite ordoliberal terms, held that the relevant effect of exclusionary abuses is the impact on market structure that leads to a weakening of competition because it has the "effect of hindering the maintenance of the degree of competition still existing in the market or the growth of that competition", para 91. A similar an even clearer approach of applying a broader welfare standard was held in Judgment of 17 February 2011 in *TeliaSonera Sverige*, C-52/09, EU:C:2011:83, when holding that: "[t]he function of those rules [Article 102 TFEU] is precisely to prevent competition from being distorted to the detriment of the public interest, individual undertakings and consumers, thereby ensuring the well-being of the European Union", para 42.

1333 Guidelines on the assessment of non-horizontal mergers under the Council Regulation on the control of concentrations between undertakings [2008] OJ C 265/6, para. 31.

1334 Council Regulation (EC) No 139/2004 of 20 January 2004 on the control of concentrations between undertakings (the EC Merger Regulation) [2004] OJ L 24/1, Article 2.1(b); Guidelines on the assessment of non-horizontal mergers under the Council Regulation on the control of concentrations between undertakings [2008] OJ C 265/6, para. 16 (emphasis added).

where it confirmed that dominant buyers would be in breach of Article 102 TFEU even if their conduct does not generate short-term end consumer harm, but in case their conduct has the effect of restricting competition by unjustifiably increasing its rivals' costs, pushing them outside of the market, or making them less attractive for end consumers[1335]. The CJEU, in terms much in line with an ordoliberal policy for buyer power and largely following Advocate General Kokott's Opinion[1336], held that:

> [...] Article [102 TFEU] is aimed not only at practices which may cause prejudice for consumers directly, but also at those which *are detrimental to them through their impact on an effective competition structure* [...][1337].

687. This was also the position of the General Court when it held that "Article [102 TFEU] is aimed at penalizing even an objective detriment to the structure of competition itself [...], BA's argument that there is no proof of damage caused to consumers by its reward schemes cannot be accepted"[1338].

688. Therefore, it confirmed that the General Court was entitled "[...] *not to examine whether BA's conduct had cause prejudice to consumers* within the meaning of subparagraph (b) the second paragraph of Article [102 TFEU], but to examine [...] whether *the bonus scheme at issue had a restrictive effect on competition* and to conclude that the existence of such effect had been demonstrated by the Commission in the contested decision"[1339].

689. This broader approach to buyer power exclusion was also explicitly adopted by Advocate General Kokkott in this case, going further explaining the reasons why buyer power exclusion and abuse of dominant buying undertakings should be prohibited with the aim of protecting the competitive process

1335 Judgment of 15 March 2007 in *British Airways v Commission*, C-95/04 P, EU:C:2007:166, para. 103-108. See also reaching a similar conclusion: Victoria Daskalova, 'Consumer Welfare in EU Competition Law: What Is It (Not) About?' 11 The Competition Law Review (2015) 133, p. 157. Also stressing this point from a buyer power perspective when stating that "it is important to note that the British Airways case that has been concisely discussed above provides for an important indication that the European Commission does not take the position that consumer harm is a necessary requirement for a violation of Article 102 TFEU. That is, the Commission specifically held in British Airways that proof of consumer harm is no necessary requirement in the enforcement of Article 102 TFEU. The decision by the European Commission was moreover upheld by the General Court and the European Court of Justice", in van Doorn, p. 157. See in general terms remarking that consumer harm is not required for the finding of an exclusionary abuse: Østerud, p. 43.

1336 Opinion of Advocate General Kokott of 23 February 2006 in Judgment of 15 March 2007 in *British Airways v Commission*, C-95/04 P, EU:C:2006:133, para. 67-84.

1337 Judgment of 15 March 2007 in *British Airways v Commission*, C-95/04 P, EU:C:2007:166, para. 106 (emphasis added). See also Nazzini that corroborates this interpretation of the CJEU's Judgment that consumers are protected if the market structure and competition as such is protected in: Nazzini, [2011], p. 14 and more specifically p. 138-139. See also: Jones and Sufrin, *EU Competition Law: Text, Cases, and Materials* [2011], p. 50.

1338 Judgment of 17 December 2003, *British Airways v Commission* of 17 December 2003, T-219/99, ECR, EU:T:2003:343, para. 311.

1339 Judgment of 15 March 2007 in *British Airways v Commission*, C-95/04 P, EU:C:2007:166, para. 106-107 (emphasis added).

and rival buyers affected by the foreclosure effects of a conduct. In Advocate General Kokkott's view the application of Article 102 TFEU is to "protect *existing competition* in a market, weakened by the presence of the dominant undertaking"[1340]. For the Advocate General, the purpose of Article 102 TFEU must be to prevent competition as a process from being distorted and, therefore, competition law:

> [it]... is not designed only or primarily to protect the immediate interests of individual competitors or consumers, but to protect the *structure of the market* and thus *competition as such (as an institution)*, which has already been weakened by the presence of the dominant undertaking on the market. In this way, consumers are also indirectly protected. Because where competition as such is damaged, disadvantages for consumers are also to be feared[1341].

690. Exclusionary buyer power is captured by Article 102 TFEU "as soon as it *runs counter to the purpose* of protecting competition in the internal market from distortions" and not only whenever it has concrete effects on market participants[1342]. What needs to be proven is the *likelihood* of the exclusionary conduct to hinder the maintenance or development of competition in the market, proving that bonus schemes "are *capable* of making it difficult or impossible for that undertaking's competitor to have access to the market and its business partners to choose between various sources of supply"[1343]. Hence, and in the current state of the law, "Article [102 TFEU] applies not only to conduct which can *directly* prejudice consumers, but also to conduct which can prejudice them *indirectly* in that it is detrimental to a state of effective competition"[1344], a position which happens to be quite in line with the ordoliberal policy regarding competition harm that triggers the intervention of the law.

691. Lastly, Zerbe suggests adopting a *total welfare standard* where the position of other buyers and suppliers is expressly considered in cases of buyer power exclusion, which is another form of a broad harm standard, even broader than the one resorted to by EU competition law. Under this approach, an exclusionary buying conduct that can be detrimental for consumers may be deemed legal if the aggregated effect is welfare enhancing (supplier/buyer surplus out-

---

1340 Opinion of Advocate General Kokott of 23 February 2006 in Judgment of 15 March 2007 in *British Airways v Commission*, C-95/04 P, EU:C:2006:133, para. 44 (emphasis in original).

1341 Opinion of Advocate General Kokott of 23 February 2006 in Judgment of 15 March 2007 in *British Airways v Commission*, C-95/04 P, EU:C:2006:133, para. 68 (emphasis in original).

1342 Opinion of Advocate General Kokott of 23 February 2006 in Judgment of 15 March 2007 in *British Airways v Commission*, C-95/04 P, EU:C:2006:133, para. 69 (emphasis in original).

1343 Opinion of Advocate General Kokott of 23 February 2006 in Judgment of 15 March 2007 in *British Airways v Commission*, C-95/04 P, EU:C:2006:133, para. 71 (emphasis in original).

1344 Opinion of Advocate General Kokott of 23 February 2006 in Judgment of 15 March 2007 in *British Airways v Commission*, C-95/04 P, EU:C:2006:133, para. 86 (emphasis in original).

weighs consumer surplus)[1345], thus harm to competitors could be sufficient to trigger competition intervention or vice versa.

B. The US Antitrust law narrow approach: protection only present consumer harm

692. A narrow approach to buyer power exclusion implies that there will be competition law intervention whenever there is consumer harm in a related downstream market. This is a less intervening approach favored by those advocating that competition law's aim is seeking end consumer welfare or preventing end consumer harm, and it is the standard adopted by the US Supreme Court in *Weyerhaeuser* and preferred by the adherents to the Chicago School as a competition policy. Therefore, *buyer power exclusion is only illegal under the rule of reason approach if there is consumer harm*. Furthermore, this also may imply that the conduct would be deemed lawful in case it benefits end consumers but forecloses or harms competitors, as the goal is the promotion and protection of consumer welfare end not protecting competition as such[1346].

693. Part of the literature in US antitrust law also supports this stricter consumer harm approach. For instance, Scheelings and Wright argue that "[a] basic lesson of the economics of vertical restraints, and exclusionary conduct in general, is that antitrust analysis *need only be concerned with the welfare of the final consumer*"[1347] and therefore, reject the adoption of a broader approach to buyer power exclusion cases. Also, Salop remarks that "[o]f course, the overriding concern of antitrust is the impact of the overbuying conduct on consumers, not competitors or suppliers"[1348] and, thus, in cases of buyer power exclusion "[t] he consumer welfare reason of rule standard would require evidence of harm to competition (i.e., consumers), not just harm to competitors"[1349].

694. In Europe, this narrower standard seems to find support in some of the Commission's guidance documents by means of promoting consumer welfare as the goal of EU competition law and also for buyer power exclusion, for instance by resorting to the '*as efficient buying competitor test*' as a mirror of the selling side approach. Also in the same vein is the guidance given by the Commission regarding its assessment dealing with exclusive supply obligation imposed through vertical agreements, in which the position of the buyer in the downstream market seems to be the sole source of concern, while the competitive conditions in the upstream market are downplayed. However, as discussed, this approach is un-

---

1345 Zerbe Jr (2004-2005).

1346 *Kartell v. Blue Shield of Massachusetts*, 749 F.2d 922 (1st Cir. 1984). See discussing this case from an exploitative perspective chapter 7, section §III.

1347 Scheelings and Wright (2006), p. 212 (emphasis in original).

1348 Salop (2004-2005), p. 677.

1349 Ibid, p. 704.

der-inclusive for buyer power cases and the adequacy of the test (even for selling side cases) has been recently questioned by the CJEU in *Post Danmark II*[1350].

a. The broader approach to buyer power exclusion in the Robinson-Patman Act: protecting small buyers

695. Nevertheless, and somewhat surprisingly, in the US antitrust law *an even a broader approach to exclusion in buyer power* cases is adopted by the Robinson-Patman Act regarding purchasing price discrimination[1351]. As remarked by Kirkwood, buyer power exclusion is precluded with the aim of protecting smaller buyers, regardless of the efficiency of the conduct[1352]. Indeed, the US Supreme Court in *Morton Salt* held that: "[t]he legislative history of the Robinson-Patman Act makes it abundantly clear that *Congress considered it to be an evil that a large buyer could secure a competitive advantage over a small buyer solely because of the large buyer's quantity purchasing ability*"[1353]. Thus, buyer power exclusion or exploitation is prohibited under the Robinson-Patman Act, even absent consumer harm, if there is harm to "a small buyer" that would be foreclosed or be put at a disadvantage. Also, in these cases there will be no need to prove an impact on market-wide competition, only to the foreclosed buyer[1354]. Hence, the Robinson-Patman Act goes much further than EU competition law when dealing with buyer power exclusion because it triggers absent consumer harm, regardless of the impact of the exclusion and also regardless of whether buyer imposing the exclusion has any substantial market power. Therefore, the Robinson-Patman Act and its wording resemble more an "unfair competition law" clause than a competition law provision, as I discuss in chapter 8.

696. However, this broader approach to US buyer power exclusion is not representative of current US law because, as discussed in chapter 6, section §VI, the Robinson-Patman Act is a piece of legislation that is not actively enforced by the antitrust authorities and has a very limited room, if any, when it comes to application in private litigation cases[1355].

1350 Judgment of 6 October 2015 in *Post Danmark*, C-23/14, EU:C:2015:651, paras 66-68. See also the Opinion of Advocate General Kokott in Judgment of 6 October 2015 in *Post Danmark*, C-23/14, EU:C:2015:343, in particular paras 56-75. See also: Judgment of 12 June 2014, *Intel v Commission*, T-286/09, ECR, EU:T:2014:547, paras. 140-166.

1351 The Robinson-Patman Act is the amendment introduced to §2 of the The Clayton Antitrust Act of 1914 (Pub.L. 63–212, 38 Stat. 730, enacted October 15, 1914, codified at 15 U.S.C. §§ 12–27, 29 U.S.C. §§ 52–53).

1352 Kirkwood 'Buyer Power and Exclusionary Conduct: Should Brooke Group Set the Standards for Buyer-Induced Price Discrimination and Predatory Bidding?' (2004-2005), p. 631-635; Hovenkamp, [2011], p. 324.

1353 *Federal Trade Commission v. Morton Salt Co.*, 334 U.S. 37 (1948), 43 (emphasis added).

1354 Kirkwood 'Buyer Power and Exclusionary Conduct: Should Brooke Group Set the Standards for Buyer-Induced Price Discrimination and Predatory Bidding?' (2004-2005), p.633.

1355 Luchs and others (2010).

C. What are the differences between the approaches?

697. Choosing one of the standards regarding the type of harm to be required to trigger the application of competition law in buyer power exclusion has important consequences because opting for either one or the other, in some cases, would lead to different outcomes and would condemn some purchasing conducts that under a different standard would not be illegal.

698. In my view, if the approach taken is based on pure downstream consumer harm then it will be under-inclusive because it will only capture those instances where buyers are rivals in the same input and output markets, unless the competition authorities take into account the end consumer harm in a market in which the buyer does not participate but its rival does, this is something not explicitly taken into account in EU competition law. If pure purchasing harm is irrelevant, then buyers may exclude rivals without directly and in the short term increasing their selling costs (they could even offer a lower end consumer price), which will lead to an increase in further market concentration[1356].

699. If a broader welfare approach is employed, then exclusion that takes places in an upstream market where firms compete as buyers but that does not involve competition as retailers will also be captured, as well as the foreclosure effects of anti-competitive conducts without any immediate harm to end consumers. These instances of exclusion should also be captured because the buyer will foreclose rivals from the upstream market to gain more buyer (monopsony) power, potentially creating a loss in welfare even if there is no direct comparable consumer harm (end consumers for the competing rivals are not the same), and affecting the upstream competitive structure.

700. I submit that this broader standard for buyer power exclusion requiring no end consumer welfare harm is adequate because it aims at protecting competition as such, the competitive process and grants a limited and justified protection to the economic freedom of market participants so that they can be as efficient as or more than a buying undertaking exerting the foreclosure[1357]. A broader approach to buyer exclusion does not necessarily imply that it will protect inefficient rivals through decisions lacking economic "depth" and "revea[ling] a bias towards protecting competitors irrespective of whether they are efficient or not", as argued by Rousseva[1358]. Instead, as Carstensen puts it from an antitrust perspective, by adopting a broader and more inclusive welfare standard for exclusionary buyer power and therefore "retaining workably competitive

1356 Haglund (2008), p. 440.

1357 Also stressing that this broader approach but with an emphasis on supplier welfare, see the opinion of Haglund who claims that one of the purposes of US antitrust law because it aims at protecting "the competitive process, which includes sellers victimized by cartels or monopsony, just as it protects consumers from monopoly" in ibid, p. 441.

1358 Rousseva, [2010], p. 187.

buying markets, many of the problems involved in focused analysis of specific buyer conduct can be avoided"[1359].

701. This section has shown that this preferred broader approach to buyer power exclusion, particularly regarding dominance cases is the one endorsed by the Courts. This reinforces one of the proposals and findings of this study: *buyer power abuse law triggers the application of EU competition law beyond strict consumer harm*. Buyer power exclusion has been found to trigger EU competition law application absent evidence of direct consumer harm, as well as in cases in which the buyers compete only for the input but not downstream, because the buyer induced foreclosure exclusion has a negative competitive impact on the competitive process, which has an indirect effect on end consumers.

XI. Conclusions

702. This chapter has shown that buyer induced exclusion is the most important problem concerning abuse of buyer power, as also recognized by the Commission[1360]. Not only does the buyer power induced exclusion have repercussions in the upstream purchasing market where buyers compete for an input regardless if they compete downstream. In most cases, however, the foreclosure is made with the aim of having an additional impact on the competitive conditions in the downstream market if the undertakings compete as retailers of the input vis-à-vis consumers. In such scenario the buyer gains an advantage as a buyer to eventually exercise monopsony power against suppliers and monopoly power vis-à-vis final consumers. Therefore, *buyer power exclusion has a dualistic effect in upstream and downstream markets* as supported by the case law, the Commission's practice, and examples of buyers competing in related markets.

703. I analyzed different theories of harm involving buyer power exclusion and have shown that all of them have in common that their aim is to *disadvantage rival buyers by increasing their costs* which will make it either impossible for these competing buyers to gain access to an input (total foreclosure) or more expensive (partial foreclosure). To do so, I discussed the theories of harm leading to *input foreclosure* through exclusive supply obligations, overbuying or mergers that may lead to equivalent effects. Also, I discussed instances in which *purchasing price discrimination* may amount to an infringement of

---

1359 Carstensen 'Buyer Power, Competition Policy, and Antitrust: The Competitive Effects of Discrimination Among Suppliers' (2008), p. 331.

1360 Communication from the Commission — Guidance on the Commission's enforcement priorities in applying Article 82 of the EC Treaty to abusive exclusionary conduct by dominant undertakings [2009] OJ C 45/7, para. 20.

competition and how US antitrust law takes a surprisingly stern stance regarding the protection of rival buyers in this regard through the Robinson-Patman Act. Furthermore, I discussed how buyer power can be used through *leveraging practices* so that a powerful buyer can affect the competitive capability in a related downstream market through *the granting of supra competitive and fidelity enhancing bonuses.* Finally, the last theory of harm explored is the situation of *squeeze to buy* as an exploitative practice with the aim of preparing for a take-over under a lower purchasing price absent the conduct.

704. An important finding regarding buyer conducts with foreclosure effects is that on most occasions buyer power exertion is connected to a strong position in the market as a retailer, as occurred in *British Airways v Commission.* If a buyer is dominant as a retailer this will generally put its suppliers (particularly if they are atomized) in a dependent position. The dependence is not used to exploit the suppliers, as a monopsonist would do, but instead to exclude rivals through their suppliers by imposing input foreclosure tactics or by securing the most efficient supply sources. Therefore, *exclusionary buyer power cases tend to deal with abuses of bargaining power but not with demand withholding* (monopsony power) as purchasing prices are usually not lowered below the competitive level, nor are suppliers exploited.

705. Also, this chapter has shown that buyer power exclusion happens in different ways and with different aims, and in some instances the foreclosure is even economically efficient, for example concerning exclusive supply agreements. Sometimes the foreclosure aims to exclude rival buyers from being able to exercise monopsony power upstream as there are no other buyers and, additionally, if they compete downstream as retailers, to leverage their buying power to gain a competitive advantage in the downstream market by raising rivals' costs and making them less attractive to end consumers. However, despite these commonalities there is no standard test to be applied in buyer exclusion and most cases will require an evaluation of the circumstances of the case and the effect of the behaviour, either on a superficial level if the behaviour due to is object or nature seems *prima facie* anti-competitive, or in a more detailed manner if its effects may reveal that it creates an anti-competitive foreclosure.

706. Finally, I discussed two policy issues regarding buyer power exclusion. First, I evaluated whether the reverse application of *the 'as efficient buying competitor test'* is an adequate tool to capture buyer induced exclusion. I sustain that as the test stands it risks *being under enforcing and not appropriate for buyer power cases*, therefore I suggest adopting further the test for buyer power realities and consider this an area ripe for the development of further methodologies. Secondly, and regarding *which welfare standard applies to buyer power exclusion,* this chapter has shown that under EU competition law the approach goes beyond triggering the application of EU competition rules

only whenever the exclusion also has direct end consumer harm as competition intervention is warranted to protect competition as such, the competitive upstream market structure and grant some limited protection to the economic freedom of rival buyers. This *more interventionist (and justified) approach* regarding buyer power exclusion captures cases where buyers compete in the input and output markets as well as those instances where buyers only compete in the input but not the output market. On the other hand, narrower approaches like the one resorted to in the US concerning unilateral foreclosure and those advocating for end consumer as the goal of competition law represent a more 'hands-off' approach and subordinate competition intervention in buyer power exclusion cases to an eventual downstream consumer harm centered around the protection of end consumers in the short term, as shown in *Weyerhaeuser* and as supported by part of the literature. In my view, however, such an approach is flawed because of risks of under-enforcement and because it fails to grasp the different dynamics of buyer power exclusion.

7

EXPLOITATIVE BUYER POWER

I. Introduction

707. The exploitation of buyer power implies imposing purchasing conditions to the detriment of suppliers and the benefit of the buyer, which are typically but not exclusively in the form of very low purchasing prices[1361]. In this chapter I discuss the different behaviours through which a buyer may exploit its market power vis-à-vis suppliers to obtain a "monopsony" or excessive profit as a buyer, therefore transferring said profit from the supplier to the buyer. My analysis starts with a discussion of unilateral conduct followed by concerted exercise of buyer power because, even though the buyer power economics is rather similar for both unilateral and concerted behaviour, the legal treatment is different.

708. Concerning unilateral behaviour, I submit that anti-competitive buyer power exploitation through monopsony pricing (i.e.: below the competitive level) is not a real concern because it rarely arises (if at all)[1362], due to the fact that, from an economics perspective, it is a conduct that is unlikely to be held for a long period of time. *The same cannot be said when it comes to coordinated behaviour*, however. The stance taken regarding coordinated purchasing varies depending on whether the agreement involves a *buyers' cartel* or a *buying alliance*. In the case of buyers' cartels that fix purchasing prices or quotas, the approach given by EU competition law is to consider these types of agreements as anti-competitive by object, as they aim to erode the natural

1361 For a discussion of the concept of exploitation see: Akman, *The Concept of Abuse in EU Competition Law: Law And Economic Approaches* [2012], p. 6.

1362 Also stressing that the "case law on abuse of buying power is relatively scarce" see: Frederic Jenny, 'International Report' in Pierre Kobel, Pranvera Këllezi and Bruce Kilpatrick (eds), *Antitrust in the Groceries Sector & Liability Issues in Relation to Corporate Social Responsibility* (Springer Berlin Heidelberg 2015), p. 31.

rivalry competitive process, even if it may lead to lower purchasing prices. In the case of a buying alliance, used to create bargaining power in an efficiency-enhancing manner, the legal treatment is to consider them pro-competitive and, if anything, to assess them as effect-based restrictions of competition. Therefore, there are discrepancies concerning the exploitative treatment to buyer power.

709. To study buyer power exploitation and the different ways in which to exert it, I have organized this chapter as follows. In section §II I discuss how buyer power exploitation works (if it does) from an economic perspective and whether self-correction is an alternative for these types of cases. This is followed by an analysis concerning unilaterally imposing "unfairly low purchasing prices" and its treatment under Article 102 TFEU. In section §III, I propose that the traditional United Brands test must be reinterpreted for buyer power cases and suggest resorting to the supplier's profit curve as a better benchmark to determine when a purchasing price is unfair and abusive. Section §IV continues the discussion concerning unilateral behaviour and discusses price discrimination that may exploit suppliers and which may also create disadvantages for them with respect to other suppliers. Then, in section §V, I analyze the case of centralized purchasing and cooperatives as a form to group and maximize the efficiency of buyer power but also for exploitative purposes. This section serves as an introduction to the discussions concerning agreements among buyers and the analysis regarding the differences between buyer cartels and buying alliances, which I carry out in section §VI. In section §VII I discuss how undertakings – both for unilateral and coordinated behaviours – may present efficiency defenses to justify their purchasing conduct and, therefore, show that the practice was not exploitative. In section §VIII I discuss the type of harm and in which relevant market it should be present to trigger EU competition law intervention in exploitative buyer power cases. Finally, section §IX concludes.

II. How does low purchasing price exploitation work, if it does?

710. The most intuitive form of exploitation of buyer power occurs *when a buyer underpays its supplier below the competitive level for the input it acquires,* which implies a transfer of profits from supplier to buyer[1363]. The exploitative effect is usually connected with a previous exclusionary practice by undertakings that make the scenario ripe for exploitation as there is less competition[1364]. However, pure exploitative practices can exist without the involvement of prior exclusion of rival buyers. Nevertheless, despite its intuitive appeal and the fact that buyer power has traditionally been linked to monopsony price exploitation, in my view, and as is corroborated by the economic theory and the (absence of) case law, it is unlikely that buyer exploitation by means of prices below the competitive level and the supplier's marginal costs will take place, either unilaterally or collectively. Therefore, it is unsurprising that very few cases dealing with buyer power exploitation exist[1365]. In the following, I aim to explain how purchasing price exploitation works, if it does, and what the risks associated with it are, as an introduction for the remainder of the chapter.

711. Excessively low purchasing prices is the textbook effect of monopsony. By withholding purchases the buyer is able to pay a price that is *below the marginal cost of production and the competitive level*. This price imposition can either be done unilaterally by a dominant undertaking or jointly if it is the result of competitor's agreement among rival buyers. If a very low purchasing price is imposed and buyers do not have other sources of demand they will be in principle obliged to sell their output to the sole buyer who extracts a monopsony profit from the trade. This generates a *transfer of wealth from the supplier to the buyer* which has no direct effect on a pure direct end consumer surplus perspective[1366]. If the supplier refuses to accept the monopsony price

1363 O'Donoghue and Padilla, *The Law and Economics of Article 102 TFEU* [2013], p. 841. See also making a similar statement from a seller's perspective: Robles Martín-Laborda, *Exploitative Prices in European Competition Law*, p. 2. For further literature: Massimo Motta and Alexandre de Streel, 'Excessive Pricing in Competition Law: Never say Never?' in Konkurrensverket - Swedish Competition Authority (ed), *The Pros and Cons of High Prices* (2007), p. 20; Carstensen 'Buyer Cartels Versus Buying Groups: Legal Distinctions, Competitive Realities, and Antitrust Policy' (2010), p. 30; F. Enrique González-Díaz and John Temple Lang, *The Concept of Abuse*, Vol. 5 (F. Enrique González-Díaz and Robbert Snelders eds, Claeys and Casteels 2013).

1364 OECD *Policy Rountables: Excessive Prices,* Paris (2011), p. 26.

1365 See also stressing the lack of cases dealing with exploitative purchasing prices: Motta and de Streel [2007], p. 16; Jones and Sufrin, *EU Competition Law: Text, Cases, and Materials* [2011] 538. For example, the OECD report on excessive prices does not even have a section on excessively low purchasing prices in its 468 pages, see: OECD '*Policy Rountables: Excessive Prices*' (2011).

1366 Also raising this issue for buyer power cases see: John B. Kirkwood and Robert H. Lande, 'The Fundamental Goal of Antitrust: Protecting Consumers, Not Increasing Efficiency' 84 Notre Dame Law review (2008-2009) 191; Carstensen 'Buyer Cartels Versus Buying Groups: Legal Distinctions, Competitive Realities, and Antitrust Policy' (2010), p. 21. See suggesting that even within a consumer welfare standard there ought to be protection to smaller suppliers in John B. Kirkwood, 'The Essence of Antitrust: Protecting Consumers and Small Suppliers from Anticompetitive Conduct' 81 Fordham Law Review (2013) 2425.

its options are limited and will tend to exit the upstream market as it is no longer economically viable[1367]. Therefore, exploitative purchasing prices can result in exclusionary tactics in the long run with some similitude to cases of margin squeeze, as noted by Robles Martín-Laborda[1368]. In addition to these static effects, exploitative purchasing practices can also have a *negative impact on dynamic efficiency* as suppliers will exit the market or may refuse to carry out investments, as stressed by Faull and Nikpay[1369]. These impacts on dynamic efficiency, such as triggering the exit of suppliers from the upstream market, disincentivizing entry of new suppliers or buyers, affecting innovation and variety are a competition concern when the exploitation is carried out by a dominant purchasing undertaking, as captured under Article 102 TFEU and as I discuss in chapter 7, section §III.

712. Like monopoly pricing, when the quantities purchased by a buyer are reduced from its normal purchasing pattern in order to obtain the price reduction, there is an efficiency loss that triggers competition intervention, as discussed in the concentration appraisal in *Sovion/Südfleisch*[1370]. In this Decision, the Commission evaluated possible buyer power effects pursuant to a proposed concentration by two entities engaged in the purchasing and slaughtering of pigs and cattle for human consumption and proposed two theories of harm. One of them being the *reduction of purchases typical of monopsony power* and the other the risk of competitors' foreclosure in the input market (topic discussed in chapter 6)[1371]. However, despite recognizing monopsony pricing as a theory of harm, it dismissed the allegations, as I discuss in this chapter's, section §III.

713. Furthermore, exploitative purchasing prices affect mostly smaller suppliers, as noted by Kirkwood and Carstensen[1372]. I distinguish between two situations here. One situation where the suppliers are inefficient and their costs of production are above the competitive level. Harm to those suppliers is not anti-competitive because the market would be better without them in the first place. Nevertheless, there are other suppliers that might be small yet able to produce with costs that are equal or slightly below the competitive level. These small,

1367 See also remarking that buyer power exploitation may lead to supplier squeeze, particularly if these are SMEs in Alexander Italianer, 'The Object of Effects' (CRA Annual Brussels Conference – Economic Developments in Competition Policy), p. 6.

1368 See also: Robles Martín-Laborda, 'La Cadena Alimentaria: Cuando el Poder de Mercado lo Tiene el Comprador'.

1369 Faull and Nikpay, [1999], para. 6.328.

1370 Commission Decision of 21/12/2005 declaring a concentration to be compatible with the common market (Case No COMP/M.3968 - *Sovion/Südfleisch*) according to Council Regulation (EC) No 139/2004 [2005].

1371 Commission Decision of 21/12/2005 declaring a concentration to be compatible with the common market (Case No COMP/M.3968 - *Sovion/Südfleisch*) according to Council Regulation (EC) No 139/2004 [2005], paras. 37 and 44.

1372 Carstensen 'Buyer Power, Competition Policy, and Antitrust: The Competitive Effects of Discrimination Among Suppliers' (2008); Kirkwood 'The Essence of Antitrust: Protecting Consumers and Small Suppliers from Anticompetitive Conduct' (2013).

yet still competitive suppliers[1373], are the ones most likely to be anti-competitively affected by buyer power exploitation because the price reduction below the competitive level will erode any chance of profitability; instead, larger and more efficient suppliers with lower costs would not be that affected because even if their profitability would be reduced they are not producing at a 'minus'.

714. However, and in contrast to what happens concerning excessive pricing, the effects of low purchasing prices are not necessarily welfare detrimental *if* quantities purchased are not reduced, a proposal not shared by Akman that seems to equate buyer exploitation with monopsony price[1374]. This is not the case because exertion of bargaining power that reduce prices *towards* the competitive level and does not adversely affect quantity are not welfare detrimental and may be welfare beneficial, from both a total and a consumer welfare perspective.

715. Therefore, from a welfare perspective, buyer power exploitation involves a wealth transfer from the supplier to the buyer that, depending on the downstream conditions, can be passed on to consumers in the form of lower final retailing prices[1375]. This is an important difference with selling-side excessive pricing which is always welfare detrimental and in which there is no passing on of any efficiencies. If the purchasing price reduction is passed on to end consumers and there is no demand withholding, then the buyer exploitation is likely not to be 'exploitative' and it is an efficiency enhancing exercise to the benefit of end consumers, as also remarked by O'Donoghue and Padilla[1376]. If, on the other hand, the prices paid are exploitative and set below the competitive level and the supplier's marginal costs then suppliers are not duly compensated for their goods and are exploited by the buyers[1377].

716. However, the price reductions obtained by powerful buyers are not always passed onto consumers and would be kept by the buyers, therefore not increasing welfare from a consumer perspective and only increasing their own (buyer) welfare. This would happen if the unilateral buyer is also a powerful retailer, as shown by the hourglass shape facing no real downstream competi-

---

1373 Kirkwood 'The Essence of Antitrust: Protecting Consumers and Small Suppliers from Anticompetitive Conduct' (2013), p. 2426.

1374 Cf with the view of Akman who claims that "there is no fundamental distinction between the economic analysis and mechanism of buyer power and seller power", even though it makes a reference to O'Donoghue and Padilla who explain that there is a difference when it comes to the welfare effects and wealth transfer in Akman, *The Concept of Abuse in EU Competition Law: Law And Economic Approaches* [2012], p. 193 and see note 22.

1375 Communication from the Commission — Guidelines on the applicability of Article 101 of the Treaty on the Functioning of the European Union to horizontal co-operation agreements [2011] OJ C 11/1, para. 194. See also supporting this interpretation O'Donoghue and Padilla, *The Law and Economics of Article 102 TFEU* [2013], p. 841.

1376 See also making a similar analysis: O'Donoghue and Padilla, *The Law and Economics of Article 82 EC* [2006], p. 639-641.

1377 Kirkwood 'The Essence of Antitrust: Protecting Consumers and Small Suppliers from Anticompetitive Conduct' (2013), p. 2427.

tion, or those instances in which buyers coordinate their behaviour upstream and downstream to erode competition between them, as discussed in *Raw Tobacco Italy*[1378].

717. Hence, and based on the economics of buyer power, in my view, an excessive fear concerning its exploitation by means of setting exploitative and below the competitive level purchasing pricing and withholding demand is unwarranted, even if done by a dominant undertaking. As I discuss in chapter 2, section §III.C, monopsony cases rarely happen because monopsony purchasing is not the most profitable buying tactic. Also, exploitative purchasing price is not rational because in so doing the buyer squeezes its suppliers (even if not all of them, at least marginal suppliers) away from business. As confirmed in the analysis by the OFT in *BetterCare II:*

> in principle, charging excessively low purchase prices could constitute an abuse of a dominant position, the OFT considers that it is only likely to do so in exceptional circumstances. In the absence of barriers to exit by suppliers from the relevant market, a purchaser which paid excessively low prices would be unable to obtain supply beyond the short term even if it was a monopsonist[1379].

718. Consequently, a powerful buyer (both a monopsonist and one enjoying substantial buyer power) will not be actively seeking to eliminate alternative sources of supply because by doing so it grants further seller market power to the remaining suppliers and loses some of its buyer power. The case law discussed in this chapter confirms this argumentation, as there have been only two instances in which such possibility has been argued and in none of them the decision-making body found the theory of harm to be sufficiency substantiated[1380].

719. The situation shifts, however, if the *exploitation of buyer power occurs by means of coordination among undertakings*. Buyer cartels fixing purchasing prices, quotas or other buying modalities do so with the intention of maximizing the profits of the cartel members, and reducing competition between them in the upstream and downstream markets[1381], while not passing on the benefits of lower purchasing prices to end consumers. Therefore, even if setting low purchasing prices may perhaps decrease end consumer prices in the short

---

1378 Commission Decision of 20 October 2005 relating to a proceeding under Article 81(1) of the EC Treaty (Case COMP/C.38.281/B.2 — *Raw tobacco Italy*) [2006] OJ L 353/45, para. 280 to 282. See for a somewhat similar view but regarding monopsony effects exclusively: Blair and Harrison, [2010], p. 79.

1379 CA98/09/2003 *BetterCare Group Ltd/North & West Belfast Health & Social Services Trust* [2003], para. 56.

1380 Judgment of 28 March 1985 in *CICCE v Commission*, C-298/83, EU:C:1985:150; Commission Decision of 21/12/2005 declaring a concentration to be compatible with the common market (Case No COMP/M.3968 - *Sovion/Südfleisch*) according to Council Regulation (EC) No 139/2004 [2005].

1381 Communication from the Commission — Guidelines on the applicability of Article 101 of the Treaty on the Functioning of the European Union to horizontal co-operation agreements [2011] OJ C 11/1, para. 201.

term, coordination among firms that has the object of eliminating, impeding or restricting competition is forbidden because the normal competitive process of rivalry is vitiated, which it is the protective goal of Article 101 TFEU. Additionally, another reason for which competition intervention happens in cases of coordination of buyer power is that purchasing agreements might have exclusionary effects by foreclosing the access to suppliers for new entrants[1382]. Furthermore, this stricter treatment concerning agreements among buyers, even if the coordination fixes lower purchasing prices for end consumers, can be explained from the perspective of the remedies available to NCAs. In the case of an agreement among buyers, it is necessary to terminate, sanction and prohibit the coordination, although individual and un-coordinated purchasing is not prohibited. Whereas regarding a dominant undertaking what must be changed is the conduct: for example, it is no longer allowed to pay a purchasing price below the competitive level for the input it requires.

720. However, not all coordination among purchasing firms is anti-competitive. As I will discuss, buying alliances that are formed in the upstream markets to generate buyer (bargaining) power by pooling purchases while not exchanging sensitive information and keeping intense downstream competition are pro-competitive as they tend to lower purchasing prices towards the competitive level and pass on these benefits to end consumers. This explains why there is a benevolent treatment in EU competition law when discussing buying alliances, and, in most cases, these types of behaviours may only constitute competition infringements by effect and tend to be exempt because of their efficiency effects under a 101(3) TFEU analysis.

A. Self-correction in buyer power cases?

721. This discussion leads to the question of whether buyer power exploitation can be self-corrected by the market's own competitive forces, as it is the preponderant theory regarding selling side price exploitation[1383]. According to this self-correcting force, exploitative conducts will be neutralized by the market itself as new players enter it to reap the supracompetitive profits extracted by the monopolist by selling the same goods at a lower price. Despite its appeal, not all economists agree with this self-correcting theory and seems not to not hold true in all scenarios[1384]. Therefore, based on this line of thinking, the Commission has considered cases of excessive pricing to be beyond its enforcement priorities regarding dominance, although may intervene if the proper functioning

1382 Communication from the Commission — Guidelines on the applicability of Article 101 of the Treaty on the Functioning of the European Union to horizontal co-operation agreements [2011] OJ C 11/1, para. 203.

1383 See, for example, the opinion of Robles Martín Laborda when arguing that: "[t]herefore, even if competition law promotes consumer welfare rather than total welfare, dominant firms should be free to charge prices at the level they choose, as supra-normal profits will attract new competitors", in Robles Martín-Laborda, *Exploitative Prices in European Competition Law*, p. 12.

1384 OECD '*Policy Rountables: Excessive Prices*' (2011), p. 10.

of the market cannot be otherwise adequately ensured[1385], for example in the presence of high and non-transitory entry barriers into the market[1386].

722. *However, how self-correctable are exploitative buyer power cases?* In buyer power exertion instances, market self-regulation is apparently not as straightforward as it is in a seller-oriented scenario. In this case, firms obtain a lower purchasing price thanks to its buyer power. If the prices are excessively low, new suppliers will not be incentivized to enter the market because they will not obtain supracompetitive profits, nor will other buyers enter the upstream market because when they do the low prices will be increased and not decreased. These newcomer buyers, though, will be able to profit from entry due to the abnormally low prices to a greater or lesser extent depending on the competitive conditions in the downstream market in which they operate as a retailer but not as a buyer. Hence, new entrant buyers – that act in the same vein as to buyer substitution discussed in chapter 4[1387] – will be a competitive constraint for the excessively low purchasing prices having the ability to regulate the market[1388]. Therefore, it is a combination of the *competitive downstream and upstream market conditions that will largely dictate the possibility of entry of new buyers in the upstream market as a buyer.*

723. Consequently, albeit self-regulation concerning buyer power exploitation is possible, it might not always occur and, thus, competition law intervention is warranted and justified. Hence, if self-regulation is not the always possible, what is the legal treatment given by EU competition law to buyer power exploitation? This is the focus of the remainder of the chapter.

1385 See also the Communication from the Commission — Guidance on the Commission's enforcement priorities in applying Article 82 of the EC Treaty to abusive exclusionary conduct by dominant undertakings [2009] OJ C 45/7, para. 7.

1386 OECD '*Policy Rountables: Excessive Prices*' (2011), p. 12. See *inter alia* for tests when to intervene in cases of excessive pricing: David S. Evans and A. Jorge Padilla, 'Excessive Prices: Using Economics to Define Administrable Legal Rules' 1 Journal of Competition Law and Economics (2005) 97; O'Donoghue and Padilla, *The Law and Economics of Article 82 EC* [2006]; Motta and de Streel [2007]; Bishop and Walker, [2010] para 6.014-6.019; Niels, Jenkins and Kavanagh, [2011], p. 268-282.

1387 See chapter 4, section §IV.B.

1388 See from a seller oriented perspective a similar argument by the OECD in OECD '*Policy Rountables: Excessive Prices*' (2011), p. 9-10.

III. Unilaterally imposing unfairly low purchasing prices

724. Imposition of unfairly low purchasing prices is the most intuitive type of buyer power exploitation. In this section I discuss *how a single undertaking may exploit their buyer power* vis-à-vis suppliers through the imposition of unfairly low purchasing prices below *the competitive level*. However, despite its intuitive appeal, my research concludes that these instances are very rare, as corroborated by Faull and Nikpay[1389]. This confirms that cases of unilateral monopsony power rarely happen in practice and that buyers do not attempt to squeeze their suppliers until reaching a point that drives them out of the market, as argued in this study, and, therefore, monopsony does not represent a real competitive concern.

725. According to Article 102(a) TFEU a dominant buying undertaking abuses its dominant position when it imposes *unfairly* lower prices, as it also does in terms of selling side exploitation. This prohibition takes place regardless of whether or not the buyer also abuses its position in the downstream market; i.e. the abuse is autonomous and can be triggered even when there is no abuse in the downstream market or consumer harm. Furthermore, the application of Article 102 TFEU requires an *element of fairness,* as the prices have to be both excessively low and unfair, which is a requirement that does not exist concerning purchasing price fixing by buyers' cartels.

726. As I demonstrate in this section, not only unfairly low purchasing prices rarely happen in practice: its regulation by the Courts is practically non-existent and it remains in general very modest for selling side cases[1390]. Regarding buyer power, the lack of case law and legal guidance is even scarcer, as there are no cases in which these issues have been dealt with in detail[1391]. Only in *CICCE*

1389 Faull, Nikpay and Taylor, [2014], para. 4.882.

1390 See: Judgment of 29 February 1968 in *Parke, Davis & Co. v Probel and Others*, C-24/67, EU:C:1968:11; Judgment of 18 February 1971 in *Sirena v Eda*, C-40/70, EU:C:1971:18; Judgment of 13 November 1975 in *General Motors v Commission*, C-26/75, EU:C:1975:150; Judgment of 14 February 1978 in *United Brands v Commission*, C-27/76, EU:C:1978:22; Judgment of 13 July 1989 in *Tournier*, C-395/87, EU:C:1989:319; Judgment of 4 May 1988 in *Bodson v Pompes funèbres des régions libérées*, C-30/87, EU:C:1988:225; Commission Decision of 23 July 2004 in case no. COMP/A.36.568/D3 – *Scandlines Sverige AB v Port of Helsingborg* [2004], para. 226 to 228; and Commission Decision of 23 July 2004 in case no. COMP/A.36.570/D3 – *Sundbusserne v Port of Helsingborg* [2004], para. 207 to 208. Also stressing this point see, *inter alia*, Pinar Akman and Luke Garrod, 'When are Excessive Prices Unfair' 7 Journal of Competition Law & Economics (2011) 403; Jones and Sufrin, *EU Competition Law: Text, Cases, and Materials* [2011], p. 538; Ioannis Kokkoris and Marcus Glader, *Excessive Pricing*, Vol. 5 (F. Enrique González-Díaz and Robbert Snelders eds, Claeys and Casteels 2013), para 10.5.

1391 Also having found no case in which there was a condemnation of excessively low purchasing prices see: Akman, *The Concept of Abuse in EU Competition Law: Law And Economic Approaches* [2012], p. 192-193; O'Donoghue and Padilla, *The Law and Economics of Article 102 TFEU* [2013].

v Commission[1392] for dominant firms, and in *Sovion/Südfleisch*[1393] with respect to concentrations, was the topic partially addressed. In the US the scenario is similar; there are few cases in which unfairly low prices (monopsony prices) have been subject to analysis by the US Courts, such as the exceptional case of *Kartell v Blue Shield of Massachusetts*[1394], which I discuss below. On other occasions, some party claimed before the US courts the existence of exploitatively low purchasing practices but the courts did not deal with the claims, as it occurred in *West Penn Allegheny Health System, Inc. v UPMC; Highmark, Inc*[1395]. Lastly, most instances of unilateral excessive pricing are related to or exist because of the existence of a legal monopoly[1396].

727. The main rule concerning excessive pricing and scenarios where it is contrary to Article 102(a) TFEU is based on the United Brands test. In *United Brands v Commission*, the CJEU held that a price becomes 'unfair' when it is set higher (or lower for buyer power cases) than that which would result from effective competition[1397]. The Court, though, did not provide specific guidance as to what 'unfair' means. It did, however establish a reference for determining when a price is unfair, the CJEU clarified that the "price [...] is excessive because it has no reasonable relation to the economic value of the product [purchased]"[1398]. Thus, *United Brands v Commission* established a two-tier test[1399] for determining when a price is unfair from a seller side perspective:

> [...] whether the difference between the costs actually incurred and the price actually charged is excessive, and, it [sic] the answer to this question is in the affirmative, whether a price has been imposed which is either unfair in itself or when compared to competing products[1400].

1392 Judgment of 28 March 1985 in *CICCE v Commission*, C-298/83, EU:C:1985:150. See commenting this case: Faull and Nikpay, [1999], para. 3.306; Jones and Sufrin, *EU Competition Law: Text, Cases, and Materials* [2011], p. 538; Whish and Bailey, *Competition law* [2015], p. 766.

1393 Commission Decision of 21/12/2005 declaring a concentration to be compatible with the common market (Case No COMP/M.3968 - *Sovion/Südfleisch*) according to Council Regulation (EC) No 139/2004 [2005].

1394 *Kartell v. Blue Shield of Massachusetts*, 749 F.2d 922 (1st Cir. 1984).

1395 *West Penn Allegheny Health Sys., Inc. v. UPMC*, No. 09-4468 (3rd Cir. 2010). For some discussion of the case see: Kirkwood, *Buyer Power and Healthcare Prices*, p. 34; Bruce D. Sokler and Farrah Short, 'Third Circuit Revives Conspiracy Claims against Hospital and Insurer' (2010) <https://www.mintz.com/newsletter/2010/Advisories/0801-1210-NAT-AFR/web.html>

1396 See: Judgment of 20 March 2002, *UPS Europe v Commission*, T-175/99, ECR, EU:T:2002:78.

1397 Judgment of 14 February 1978 in *United Brands v Commission*, C-27/76, EU:C:1978:22, paras. 248-249. For a discussion of fairness under Article 102 TFEU, ordoliberal influence and the case law see: Akman, *The Concept of Abuse in EU Competition Law: Law And Economic Approaches* [2012], p. 146-184.

1398 Judgment of 14 February 1978 in *United Brands v Commission*, C-27/76, EU:C:1978:22, para. 250.

1399 Supporting the two tier test see, *inter alia*, Robles Martín-Laborda, *Exploitative Prices in European Competition Law*, p. 3-4; OECD '*Policy Rountables: Excessive Prices*' (2011), p. 11; Akman and Garrod (2011); Gal, 'Abuse of Dominance - Exploitative Abuses' [2013], p. 401; Cf with the one tier test interpretation given in Motta and de Streel [2007].

1400 Judgment of 14 February 1978 in *United Brands v Commission*, C-27/76, EU:C:1978:22, para. 252.

728. The first limb of the test measures the difference between the costs for producing the good and the selling price and whether or not the sale leads to an excessive profit[1401]. The second limb consists in determining whether or not the price is unfair by comparing the good with identical products produced by another undertaking, or substitutes ones, or comparing the prices charged by the undertaking in the relevant market with competing products to determine if the price is exploitative and illegal because of the exercise of abusive market power or due to efficiency[1402]. Importantly, the CJEU recognized that this test is not the only option for assessing whether or not prices are excessive. This leaves the Commission and NCAs with certain margins of discretion[1403], as occurred in *Scandlines Sverige AB v Port of Helsingborg* and *Sundbusserne v Port of Helsingborg*[1404], which is particularly important for excessive purchasing prices as discussed infra.

729. Furthermore, excessive pricing can be forbidden even in the absence of end consumer harm. As remarked by Robles Martín-Laborda, in case of selling side conducts the Courts have found unlawful the imposition of exploitative selling prices that affect other undertakings acting in intermediate markets, without a requirement of evidence of end consumer harm[1405]. An analogical interpretation of this for buyer power cases leads to the conclusion that, concerning exploitative purchasing prices, EU competition law intervention is warranted whenever buyer exploitation affects suppliers with the aim to protect competition as a process and the market from consumer harm in a broad sense, not only due to consumer welfare considerations, which may appear consistent with an ordoliberal approach[1406], and also with the approach to exclusionary conducts. Therefore, for buyer power exploitation, no harm is required to trigger the application of the prohibition of excessively low prices.

1401 European Commission, 'Contribution of the European Union in OECD Policy Rountables: Excessive Prices' in OECD (ed), *Policy Rountables: Excessive Prices* (OECD 2011) 317, p. 317; Akman and Garrod (2011), p. 404.

1402 European Commission, 'Contribution of the European Union in OECD Policy Rountables: Excessive Prices' [2011], p. 317; OECD '*Policy Rountables: Excessive Prices*' (2011), p. 11.

1403 Judgment of 14 February 1978 in *United Brands v Commission*, C-27/76, EU:C:1978:22, para. 253. In practice NCAs tend to apply not only a different methodology, but several to a same case. See supporting this approach: Motta and de Streel [2007]; OECD '*Policy Rountables: Excessive Prices*' (2011), p. 12.

1404 Commission Decision of 23 July 2004 in case no. COMP/A.36.568/D3 – *Scandlines Sverige AB v Port of Helsingborg* [2004], para. 226 to 228; and Commission Decision of 23 July 2004 in case no. COMP/A.36.570/D3 – *Sundbusserne v Port of Helsingborg* [2004], para. 207 to 208. For some discussion on how these cases deviate from the United Brands test see, *inter alia*: G.J. Werden, 'Monopoly Pricing and Competition Policy: Divergent Paths to the Same Destination' in Barry E. Hawk (ed), *Annual Proceedings of the Fordham Competition law Institute* (Juris Publishing, Inc 2009); OECD '*Policy Rountables: Excessive Prices*' (2011), p. 56; Akman and Garrod (2011), p. 424 to 426.

1405 Robles Martín-Laborda, *Exploitative Prices in European Competition Law*, p. 8.

1406 See the opinion of Robles Martín Laborda who explains that for exploitative selling prices "the prohibition would be in line with some of the proposals of the ordoliberal ideology, which strongly influenced the prohibition of abuse of a dominant position in Article 102 TFEU (initially Article 86 EEC)." But for whom this interpretation is wrong as the incorporation into the Treaties was not prompted by the German delegation but rather the French delegation, in ibid, p. 9-11.

A. The case law on unfairly low purchasing prices

730. In the case law and the Commission's practice there have been two instances in which the possibility of a breach of EU competition law by means of excessively low purchasing practices has been discussed to a certain extent. In this section I analyze these cases, while also briefly touching upon the scenario involving MS dealing with these types of practices and the US antitrust.

731. In *CICCE v Commission*, the Comité des Industries Cinématographiques des Communautés Européennes (CICCE), representative of film makers, claimed before the Commission that three public French television companies (the TV companies) were imposing unfairly low license fees for broadcast copyright content administered by the applicant as a collecting society[1407]. These TV companies were organized in the form of '*service public*'[1408] and enjoyed a dominant purchasing position due to it being granted by means of a legislative measure[1409].

732. CICCE claimed before the French NCA, and later before the CJEU, that the TV companies abused their dominant purchasing position to impose film license fees that were deemed to be abnormally low[1410], basing its claim also on a non-binding opinion of the French NCA that had reached said conclusion[1411]. For CICCE, the fees paid by the TV companies were "so low as to bring about an unbalanced distribution of amortization between the cinemas [...] and the television [and also therefore] one third of television programmes were paid for with between 3% and 6% of the aggregate budget [...]"[1412].The procedure before the French NCA was discontinued because it was not possible to determine by using a single average value of license fees if an abuse of a dominant purchasing position had taken place. The evidence should have been presented film by film and not by a general presumption of the average values of the license fees, or based on the budget earmarked for the purchasing of licenses for films. Against this rejection, CICCE lodged an application for the declaration of its voidness before the CJEU.

733. The CJEU found that the decision to discontinue with the investigation was

1407 Judgment of 28 March 1985 in *CICCE v Commission*, C-298/83, EU:C:1985:150, para. 2. See briefly discussing this case and stressing the difficulty of proving excessive pricing practices: Faull and Nikpay, [1999], para. 3.305-3.306.

1408 *Loi n° 74-696 du 7 août 1974 relative à la radiodiffusion et à la télévision*, last modified in 14 May 2014.

1409 The companies involved were: i) Société nationale de la télévision française 1 (TF 1) a public undertaking at the time of decisión and privatized 2 years after the rendering of the Judgment by the CJEU; ii) Société nationale de la télévision en couleur Antenne 2 (A 2) a public undertaking at the time and still part of the state-owned France Telévisions group; and iii) Société nationale des programmes France Régions (FR 3) also a public undertaking at the time and still part of the state-owned France Telévisions group.

1410 Opinion of the Advocate General Lenz of 16 January 1985, in Judgment of 28 March 1985 in *CICCE v Commission*, C-298/83, EU:C:1985:16 [1985], p. 1106-1107.

1411 Opinion of the Advocate General Lenz of 16 January 1985, in Judgment of 28 March 1985 in *CICCE v Commission*, C-298/83, EU:C:1985:16 [1985], in Judgment of 28 March 1985 in *CICCE v Commission*, C-298/83, EU:C:1985:16 [1985], p. 1108. Article 50 of Regulation reproduced almost identically Article [102] TFEU.

1412 Opinion of the Advocate General Lenz of 16 January 1985, in Judgment of 28 March 1985 in *CICCE v Commission*, C-298/83, EU:C:1985:16 [1985], p. 1108.

lawful and correct, demanding from the applicant the "need to prove the alleged abuse by reference to actual cases involving specific films rather than by reference to the average licence fee paid for all the films for which the television companies acquired broadcasting rights"[1413]. From the evidence available the CJEU confirmed that the license fees were not consistent but varied from film to film[1414]. The CJEU, although not explicitly[1415], gave acquiescence and did not reverted the Commission's finding that "an undertaking in a dominant position imposes *unfair purchase prices may constitute an abuse within the meaning of Article [102] of the Treaty*"[1416]. However, the CJEU dismissed the case and dealt neither with determining whether or not the prices were abusive, nor the suggestion of Advocate General Lenz that a reverse application of the *United Brands v Commission* test be performed.

734. Advocate General Lenz applied the test to determine whether the purchasing prices paid were effectively unfairly low. He did this through two steps. In terms of the first limb, he concluded that films are heterogeneous goods[1417], and, therefore, went on to state that "the size of that budget item (the movie price) says nothing conclusive about its use: where it is used only to pay for a relatively small number of films a fair price is quite possible paid for each film"[1418]. Thus, movies are different goods and it is difficult to compare them. Then, Advocate General Lenz applied the second limb of the test and compared the prices paid in France for the films' licenses with the prices pair in other Member States, demonstrating that "all other countries recorded lower fees, with the sole exception of [...] Germany, where the average fee [...] was somewhat higher than France"[1419]. The test, despite not being endorsed, is interesting because it proposed a methodology to review unfairly low purchasing prices, which I review in chapter 7, section III.B.

735. *CICCE v Commission,* therefore, clarifies that unfairly low exploitative purchasing prices may account for a breach of Article 102(a) TFEU and the as-

1413 Judgment of 28 March 1985 in *CICCE v Commission*, C-298/83, EU:C:1985:150, para. 24; see also stressing the fact that the CJEU rejected the allegation by lack of sufficient evidence Faull, Nikpay and Taylor, [2014], para. 4.883.

1414 Judgment of 28 March 1985 in *CICCE v Commission*, C-298/83, EU:C:1985:150, para. 26.

1415 See also noting that the Court did not dispute the Commission's assertion, O'Donoghue and Padilla, *The Law and Economics of Article 102 TFEU* [2013], p. 843.

1416 Judgment of 28 March 1985 in *CICCE v Commission*, C-298/83, EU:C:1985:150, para. 22 (emphasis added).

1417 Of the same view was the Advocate General Lenz when he stated that "it is plain that films are very *heterogeneous* products and consequently very different values". Opinion of the Advocate General Lenz, in C-298/83 - *CICCE v Commission*, EU:C:1985:16 [1985], p. 1114 (emphasis in original).

1418 Opinion of the Advocate General Lenz of 16 January 1985, in Judgment of 28 March 1985 in *CICCE v Commission*, C-298/83, EU:C:1985:16 [1985], p. 1114.

1419 Opinion of the Advocate General Lenz of 16 January 1985, in Judgment of 28 March 1985 in *CICCE v Commission*, C-298/83, EU:C:1985:16 [1985], p. 1115. The comparison of prices among MS was discussed by the CJEU in Judgment of 21 February 1973 in Judgment of 14 February 1978 in *United Brands v Commission*, C-27/76, EU:C:1978:22, para. 258 and ratified in Judgment of 13 July 1989 in *Tournier*, C-395/87, EU:C:1989:319, para. 46.

sessment must be made case-by-case[1420]. Secondly, the CJEU did not deal with how to determine when a price is unfairly low, which leaves uncertainty regarding the legal standard to be applied for these cases but confirms the very rare occurrence of exploitative purchasing practices[1421].

736. Additionally, regarding the risk of future unilateral imposition of unfairly low purchasing prices, the assessment of the Commission in *Sovion/Südfleisch*[1422] sheds some light on this, albeit to a limited extent. In this case, the Commission evaluated and dismissed the argument that the proposed concentration would have led to situations in which the new buyer would have been able to exercise exploitatively low prices by withholding demand. In the assessment, the Commission found that the proposed concentration posed no real risks of supplier exploitation through low purchasing prices or demand withholding because, even in areas where the concentration would have increased the purchasing market shares dramatically, suppliers would have been able to find alternative buyers (slaughterhouses) with sufficient spare capacity to purchase the meat. Consequently, the merging parties would have been unable to withhold demand to decrease the purchasing price of meat[1423]. Also, the Commission found that there was no serious risk of exploitative low prices due to other factors such as the transparent pricing system, the increase in the size of pig farms (which allow them to exercise selling countervailing power), the capacity to easily switch to other slaughterhouses, the competitive pressure exercised by traders purchasing livestock and, lastly, the buyer power of food retailers which will constrain the buyer power of slaughterhouses[1424]. Consequently, the Commission found that the proposed concentration posed no risks concerning exploitation of buyer (monopsony) power and, after evaluating other effects, declared the concentration compatible with the internal market[1425]. However, the fact that the Commission evaluated the likelihood of imposition of future exploitatively low prices renders theoretically possible that a concentration that may significantly impede effective competition in an upstream market because of exploitation of suppliers.

737. On a national level, the UK NCA also dealt with complaints regarding unilateral abusive purchasing prices in *The Association of British Travel Agents and*

1420 Judgment of 28 March 1985 in *CICCE v Commission*, C-298/83, EU:C:1985:150, paras. 22 and 26.

1421 Faull and Nikpay, [1999], para. 3.306.

1422 Commission Decision of 21/12/2005 declaring a concentration to be compatible with the common market (Case No COMP/M.3968 - *Sovion/Südfleisch*) according to Council Regulation (EC) No 139/2004 [2005].

1423 Commission Decision of 21/12/2005 declaring a concentration to be compatible with the common market (Case No COMP/M.3968 - *Sovion/Südfleisch*) according to Council Regulation (EC) No 139/2004 [2005], paras 38-46.

1424 Commission Decision of 21/12/2005 declaring a concentration to be compatible with the common market (Case No COMP/M.3968 - *Sovion/Südfleisch*) according to Council Regulation (EC) No 139/2004 [2005], paras 47-52.

1425 Commission Decision of 21/12/2005 declaring a concentration to be compatible with the common market (Case No COMP/M.3968 – *Sovion/ Südfleisch*) according to Council Regulation (EC) No 139/2004 [2005], para. 95.

British Airways[1426]. The Decision found that even, if British Airways had reduced booking payments to travel agents, it did not infringe Section 18 of the UK Competition Act by setting low purchasing prices for the acquisition of travel agent services. The travel agents argued that the new payment fee – *recoupment fee* – was so low that it did not allow travel agents to cover their costs[1427]. It was held, nevertheless, that even if the prices were not sufficient to cover the costs, the travel agents would have been able to recoup these losses by charging a mark-up or service fee added to the ticket price for end consumers[1428]. Because the suppliers could recover its costs through the end consumer, like any other retailer, there was no buyer power exploitation. Concerning the additional cost, the UK NCA clarified that for consumers and their wellbeing, the important factor was the end ticket price and not the fees paid to the carrier or travel agent[1429]. Therefore, provided that the final price for the ticket would be the same or lower than before the reduction of the payment for the travel agency services, the fact that the supplier charges a new fee would not be detrimental[1430]. This, reasoning, however, seems to disregard the fact that the new fee imposed by the travel agents to cover their costs in the form of a service fee would increase the final end consumer prices unless British Airways had also reduced their prices as the result of the lower purchasing prices paid for the travel agency services.

738. In contrast to EU competition law, where *unilaterally* imposing unfairly low purchasing prices is a conduct that can be prohibited by Article 102 TFEU or the Merger Control Regulation, in the US antitrust law the regulation of excessive unilateral pricing is the opposite. As a general rule, US antitrust law does not intervene in cases of exploitation of buyer power through excessively low prices as "U.S. courts tak[e] the position that merely charging profit-maximization monopoly prices is not an antitrust violation"[1431], as clarified by the US Supreme Court case law[1432]. Concerning exploitative purchasing prices, this has been ratified in US antitrust in *Kartell v Blue Shield of Massachusetts,* where the Court of Appeals of the First Circuit adopted a pure end-consumer harm perspective and held that US antitrust law only intervenes in pricing matters on special circumstances[1433], it concluded that low

1426 CA98/19/2002 *The Association of British Travel Agents and British Airways plc* [2002].

1427 CA98/19/2002 *The Association of British Travel Agents and British Airways plc* [2002], para. 1.

1428 CA98/19/2002 *The Association of British Travel Agents and British Airways plc* [2002], para. 2.

1429 CA98/19/2002 *The Association of British Travel Agents and British Airways plc* [2002], para. 32

1430 CA98/19/2002 *The Association of British Travel Agents and British Airways plc* [2002], para. 33.

1431 Elhauge and Geradin, [2011], p. 404.

1432 The US Supreme Court goes as far to say that "[t]he opportunity to charge monopoly prices at least for a short period is what attracts "business acumen" in the first place; it induces risk taking that produces innovation and economic growth. To safeguard the incentive to innovate, the possession of monopoly power will not be found unlawful unless it is accompanied by an element of anticompetitive conduct", in *Verizon Communications Inc., v. Law Offices of Curtis v. Trinko, LLP,* 540 U.S. 398 (2004). See also: *United States v. Trans-Missouri Freight Ass,* 166 U.S. 290 (1987); *United States v. Aluminim co. of America,* 148 F.2d 416 (2nd Cir. 1945). See also: Motta and de Streel [2007], p. 16; Elhauge and Geradin, [2011], p. 404; see supporting in general that exploitative prices for buyer and seller side cases should not be prohibited under Article 102 TFEU: Robles Martín-Laborda, *Exploitative Prices in European Competition Law*, p. 15.

1433 *Kartell v. Blue Shield of Massachusetts*, 749 F.2d 922 (1st Cir. 1984), 929.

purchasing prices did not constitute a violation of antitrust law, even if the buyer is a monopsonist[1434].

739. In my view, such a different approach to buyer power exploitation through excessively low purchasing prices in EU and US antitrust is anchored on the goals and competition policy grounds of each jurisdiction. EU competition law adopts a broader approach to buyer power competition intervention because it seeks to safeguard competition as such and the wellbeing of market structure. As setting unfairly low purchasing prices may lead to suppliers exiting the market, this will negatively impact the freedom of choice, diversity and, importantly, the economic freedom of market players, ideas which are also consistent with ordoliberal theory. In the US, on the other hand, the approach to buyer power is a narrow one, warranting exploitation only whenever there is end consumer harm and the economic foundations of the case law are grounded on the postulates of the Chicago School and the self-regulating mechanism of the market in exploitative cases. This, like buyer power as a whole, is a topic ripe for future pure comparative legal research between the jurisdictions.

B. United Brands test for excessive purchasing prices: a profit curve test

740. The United Brands test is the legal standard employed in EU competition law for determining whether a price is abusive and therefore prohibited by Article 102(a) TFEU. Its reverse application, as suggested by Advocate General Lenz in his opinion in *CICCE v Commission*[1435], is the logical starting point for buyer power cases. In this section, I use the United Brands test and discuss the application of a methodology to determine when a purchasing price is unfairly low and exploitative.

741. In my view, the methodology to be employed must review the two limbs of the United Brand test and adjust them to buyer power economics in order to be an adequate legal standard for unilateral excessively low purchasing pricing. Furthermore, in my proposal I do not require the dominant buyer to in addition decrease the price below the suggested levels to also reduce the quantities, as is required by O'Donoghue and Padilla's model, which I understand as a logical consequence of applying a pure monopsony power perspective to purchasing price exploitation[1436]. If an abuse of dominance regarding purchasing price exploitation would necessarily involve a withholding effect, this implies that Article 102 TFEU would not capture the abuse

1434 *Kartell v. Blue Shield of Massachusetts*, 749 F.2d 922 (1st Cir. 1984), 928. See also: Blair and Harrison, [2010], p. 72.

1435 Opinion of the Advocate General Lenz of 16 January 1985, in Judgment of 28 March 1985 in *CICCE v Commission*, C-298/83, EU:C:1985:16 [1985].

1436 O'Donoghue and Padilla, *The Law and Economics of Article 102 TFEU* [2013], p. 841.

of bargaining purchasing power; only monopsony power would be under its scope. While I fully agree with the fact that exploitative monopsony power should be captured by Article 102(a) TFEU, it should also be the case for exploitative and abusive bargaining power because, even if it is unlikely, the exercise of bargaining power may also comply with the test requirements and be exploitatively abusive. Therefore, the lack of a withholding requirement does not compromise the test but rather adequately broadens its scope to capture all forms of buyer power abuse.

a. The test's first limb

742. The first limb of the test dealing with the difference between the production costs and the purchasing price offered by the buyer is the most relevant part of the analysis. It must be determined whether the price offered for the purchasing of goods makes *the profit curve of the supplier negative and below the competitive level; if it does, then the price is unfairly low*. Consequently, any price paid by the buying undertaking that it is either competitive and/or does not make the profit curve negative would be lawful and not abusive. Therefore, the industry's competitive level acts as an indicator and precondition to determine whether there might be an instance of unfair pricing, followed also by a case-by-case cost assessment. Finding this competitive level, however, and as I discuss below in the limitations of this methodology, is a difficult exercise in practice.

743. Here lies the main difference with the traditional United Brands test: in a perfectly competitive market, the optimal price would be the intersection between demand and supply so that none of the parties makes any extraordinary profits and are able to cover their costs[1437]. A supplying undertaking will choose as its optimal production-point, the output for which the difference between revenue and cost is the greatest[1438]. This occurs whenever *marginal revenue equals marginal costs*, regardless of the market power of the firm; i.e.: firms determine their production output based on their marginal costs. The profitability of an undertaking varies and has a margin from the least to the most profitable extreme. In the lower end, profitability is negative because the income does not cover fixed or variable costs until output reaches a point in which revenue increases faster than costs and the difference become positive.

744. In this scenario, the excessively low prices would be imposed when the buyer forces the supplier to sell goods when the marginal costs of producing one additional unit are higher than its revenue; selling the units is unprofitable because the revenue it obtains is insufficient to cover its production costs. This

---

1437 Costs in economics, unlike other sciences like business administration or accounting include already a profit. See also: Pindyck and Rubinfeld, [2009], p. 222; OECD '*Policy Rountables: Excessive Prices*' (2011), p. 12.

1438 Pindyck and Rubinfeld, [2009], p. 276.

could be done by acquiring less input than required –withholding demand – while perhaps being able to decrease purchasing prices without restricting purchases, due to other type of bargaining strategies, such as offering a take or leave it contract to a farmer with rapidly perishable goods, or by demanding extraordinary contractual conditions. Additionally, for the prices to be exploitatively and unfairly low, *this price paid must be below the competitive price level*; otherwise, the exploitative analysis will run the risk of over enforcement, as inefficient suppliers that have higher costs than the competitive level will be unduly protected[1439]. For this reason, to avoid protecting inefficient suppliers, I suggest also adopting the competitive production cost of the market as a proxy.

745. In order to force an undertaking to sell its goods below its costs and also below the competitive level, if a monopsony approach is employed to buyer power exploitation, there must be a demand withholding conduct. This would imply, nevertheless, that only exploitative purchasing prices can exist if the supply curve of the seller is upward-sloping and which would disregard any possibilities of exploitatively low purchasing prices in industries with a flat or downward sloping supply curve, for which I think the requirement of demand withholding is excessive and under-inclusive. Alternatively, the price could be decreased without withholding demand, but by threatening not to purchase, for instance using a take-it-or-leave it offer and or switching suppliers, therefore, not necessarily resorting to a monopsony practice and not requiring an inelastic supply curve.

746. However, courts should not use marginal costs as the guiding parameter in all cases as there might be instances in which marginal costs would not truly reveal the real expenses of a firm to produce output. Such cases would include, for example, whenever the supplier has to incur high fixed costs, is a new entrant, or needs to recoup costs incurred because of an important investment or costs incurred for R&D, or where the specific type of transaction is not known in advance; i.e.: whenever there is a hold-up problem[1440]. In such situations, an average cost would more accurately represent the 'costs' a supplier would need to cover to continue selling a good to a buyer in a repeated game[1441].

1439 The competitive price level is a benchmark to be used in both monopsony and bargaining power cases of exploitative buyer power not only to prevent protection of inefficient buyers, but because the monopsony model itself requires purchasing prices to be lowered below it.

1440 A hold up problem is when parties would be better off if they decided to collaborate to determine their input/output but refrain from doing so to avoid granting more bargaining power to its counterpart. The hold-up problem usually leads to underinvestment and, therefore, loss of efficiency. For some literature discussing the hold-up problem in industrial organization and buyer power see: Dieter Bos and Christoph Lulfesmann, 'The Hold-up Problem in Government Contracting' 98 Scandinavian Journal of Economics (1996) 53; Faruk Gul, 'Unobservable Investment and the Hold-Up Problem' 69 Econometrica (2001) 343; Robert A Skitol, 'Concerted Buying Power: Its Potential for Addressing the Patent Holdup Problem in Standard Setting' 72 Antitrust Law Journal (2004-2005) 727; Stephanie Lau, Information and Bargaining in the Hold-Up Problem (The RAND Corporation 2008) 266; J. Gregory Sidak, 'Patent Holdup and Oligopsonistic Collusion in Standard-Setting Organizations' 5 Journal of Competition Law and Economics (2009) 123; Eva I. Hoppe and Patrick W. Schmitz, 'Can Contracts Solve the Hold-Up Problem? Experimental Evidence' 73 Games and Economic Behavior (2011) 186.

1441 Average costs will tend to be lower than marginal costs until a point in which marginal costs surpass average costs due to being an additional unit being much more expensive compared to previous ones.

747. Recapitulating, to satisfy the first limb of the test a purchasing price would qualify as being unfairly low if in the price comparison two requirements are met: first, the price should be below the competitive level, and, second, the price should not cover the supplier's marginal (or average costs). If the price charged is on or above the competitive level but below the previous purchasing price, the purchasing price imposed by the buyer would be competitive and would only negatively impact inefficient suppliers with higher-than competitive costs. Therefore, prices would be unfair and exploitative whenever they are reduced below the competitive level and also make the suppliers' profit negative because the purchase price is insufficient to cover the supplier's costs. Furthermore, prices would not be exploitatively abusive if they allow the supplier to sell in the long run its goods in a quantity that is able to satisfy the effective demand by buyers and end consumers, without leading to an inefficient outcome by employing less than ideal resources[1442]. Lastly, prices may be also considered unfairly low if the payment makes the profit curve of the seller negative, unless a *recoupment fee* is charged, but the final price remains the same or lower for end consumers, if a similar approach as the UK Courts is taken[1443]. However, the charging of a recoupment fee would not be admissible when it implies that the final consumer price would be higher or when it is not possible to do such charging because the supplier has no control over the downstream prices, which would be in the majority of cases. My proposal for a test can be understood by looking at the following graph:

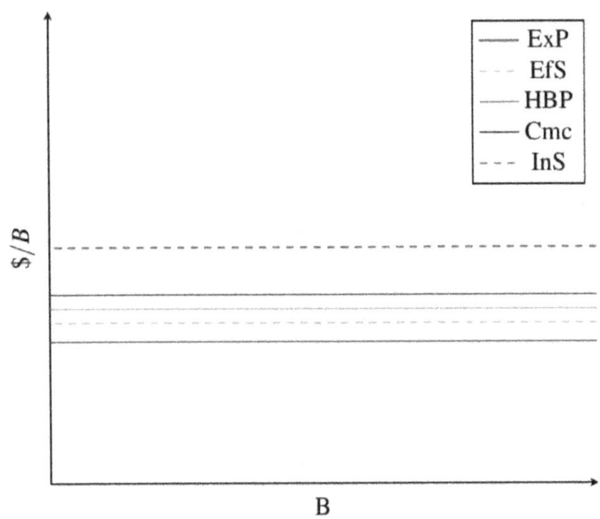

Figure 5: Exploitative purchasing prices

1442 OECD '*Policy Rountables: Excessive Prices*' (2011), p. 25.

1443 CA98/19/2002 *The Association of British Travel Agents and British Airways plc* [2002].

> In this case, the flattening of the supplier's profit curve because of low purchasing prices up to the limit in which it breaks even (profit = 0) will not be abusive (EfS). It will only become abusive when the profit curve is forced to: i) reduce the quantity purchased so that profits are negative; or ii) not reduce quantity purchased by force the supplier to sell below costs, making profit negative and when such price paid is also below the competitive level (ExP).
>
> **Legend:**
>
> ExP = exploitative purchasing price; EfS = efficient supplier's costs;
>
> CmC = competitive industry cost; InS = inefficient supplier's costs;
>
> HBP = hypothetical business partner

b. *The test's second limb*

748. The second limb, entailing a comparison of costs between the purchased good and other similar ones, appears to be less controversial and admits a reverse application of the United Brands test in cases where adequate substitutes exist without any major adjustments[1444]. For example, it would be possible to compare the purchasing price for the same or a substitutable input in other geographic markets, such as in the case of licenses for works under copyright protection, or the fees charged in a MS for the same work compare to those in another MS, as suggested by Advocate General Lenz in *CICCE v Commission*[1445].

c. *Possible shortcomings of the proposed methodology*

749. This suggested profit-curve based test to identify when a purchasing price is exploitatively low is not without deficiencies, which I acknowledge need for further refinement for the competition authorities to consider applying it.

750. The most important shortcoming is the use of the industry's competitive cost as a proxy for supplier efficiency. Determining what is the competitive cost of production of a specific good is a very difficult exercise that may prove almost impossible in certain cases due to lack of sufficient data. However, not resorting to a sort of industry-wide proxy would trigger the application of Article 102(a) in cases in which suppliers are not competitive and inefficient and any kind of buyer pressure would result anti-competitive. Such a broad approach would imply granting an undue protection to suppliers to the detriment of competition as such because efficient purchasing behaviour is precluded and upstream un-

---

1444 See remarking this issue from a seller side perspective: Robles Martín-Laborda, *Exploitative Prices in European Competition Law*, p. 5.

1445 Opinion of the Advocate General Lenz of 16 January 1985, in Judgment of 28 March 1985 in *CICCE v Commission*, C-298/83, EU:C:1985:16 [1985], p. 1115.

dertakings would not be required to invest to decrease their costs and improve their quality. Hence, an excessive protection of the suppliers' economic freedom would run contrary to the protection of competition as such from an ordoliberal perspective. Alternatively, other indicators – for example, the industries' historical costs, or an efficient producer benchmark – could be used as additional proxies. This, contrastingly, is not the case regarding selling side price exploitation because there is no need to determine costs of other producers, only of the dominant undertaking exerting monopoly power. Second, it is difficult to calculate the investigated firms' profit and cost and, unless a profit-curve average is used, then the profitability of the sale must be carried out seller by seller. This difficulty leads to errors of either under or over enforcement that have an impact on welfare conditions, as discussed in length by Gal[1446]. Also, the test defines when a price is excessively low but does not answer a related problem that I discussed in chapter 6, section §VIII when dealing with the theory of harm: "squeeze to buy". Therefore, this profit-based test does not determine if prices below costs but above the competitive level can be exploitative if the aim is to squeeze suppliers out of the market to then acquire them.

IV. Exploitative purchasing price discrimination

751. Articles 101(1) (d) and 102(c) TFEU preclude undertakings, coordinately or unilaterally, from "applying dissimilar conditions to equivalent transactions with other trading parties, thereby placing them at a competitive disadvantage", which reduce the chances of equal opportunity when they compete among themselves[1447]. This implies that, under EU competition law, discrimination with exclusionary (against other buyers)[1448] and exploitative effects (against suppliers) by buyers is prohibited[1449]. The general literature regarding exclusionary price discrimination – in particular rebates from a seller perspective – is vast and outside of the scope of this section, which focuses on purchasing exploitative cases exclusively,[1450] and which I have also dealt in chapter 6, section §VI from a buyer power angle.

752. In the US, the Robinson-Patman Act prohibits buyers' induced price discrimination by making it illegal for any buyer (*not necessarily dominant*) "know-

1446 Gal, 'Abuse of Dominance - Exploitative Abuses' [2013], p. 414-421.

1447 Wils (2014), p. 418.

1448 I have discussed in detail in chapter 6, section §VI, the theories of harm and legal regulations concerning price discrimination by means of paying a supracompetitive bonus to a supplier of a good.

1449 See also distinguishing purchasing price discrimination and foreclosure: Papandropoulos (2007).

1450 The literature dealing with price discrimination, both from and economic and legal perspective is abundant. See, *inter alia*: Bellamy, Child and Roth, [2001], para. 9-083 to 9-087; Papandropoulos (2007); Gifford and Kudrle (2010); Bellamy and others, [2013], para. 10.091 to 10.100.

ingly to induce or receive discrimination in price which is prohibited"[1451]. This provision, however, has been toned down by the US Supreme Court in *Great Atlantic & Pacific Tea Co., Inc. v FTC* as, to infringe the Robinson-Patman Act under buyer induced discrimination it also is required that the seller is engaging in seller discrimination[1452]; i.e.: pure buying pressure would not suffice to trigger the application of the provision.

753. The differences concerning price discrimination between EU competition law and US antitrust have also spurred interesting debate concerning whether buyer induced exploitative price discrimination is condemned in EU competition law. As mentioned in chapter 6, section §VI, Gifford and Kudrle argue that under EU competition law, buyer power discrimination is not captured by Article 102(c) TFEU for dominant buyers unlike the Robinson-Patman Act does in the US[1453]. While this premise perhaps might find support in the lack of exclusionary cases, it does not with regard to buyer induced exploitative discrimination as the EU case law does prohibit a dominant undertaking from doing so as I discuss below. Furthermore, concluding that buying side exploitative discrimination is not covered by EU competition law would lead to under-enforcement risks, disregard for the wellbeing of competition as such[1454], put in jeopardy the economic freedom of market participants and, ultimately, make the application of Article 102 TFEU discriminatory and selective. The Commission's practice, and as endorsed by the Courts in *British Airways v Commission,* illustrates that price discrimination cases can be focused from a buying or seller side perspective and both being under the scope of Article 102 TFEU.

754. In this current section, I discuss how buyers can use their purchasing power to discriminate among different suppliers and exploit them by abusing of their dependent position in order to pay a purchasing price that is lower than what is paid to other suppliers that are not in a weak bargaining position. This constitutes a reverse form of *primary line discrimination*[1455], in opposition to secondary line discrimination that implies the grant of different bonuses for the purchase of a good, which I discuss in chapter 6, section §VI[1456]. Exploitation occurs as a buyer of a service might take advantage of the dependence of its suppliers on it and offer lower prices (or bonuses) for this, compared to anoth-

---

1451 15 U.S. Code § 13(f).

1452 *Great Atlantic & Pacific Tea Co. v Federal Trade Commission*, 440 U.S. 69 (1979).

1453 "Although the Robinson-Patman Act directs most of its provisions against the discriminating sellers, its premise is that buying power is misused at the purchaser level. By contrast, Article 82(c) applies only to large sellers that can meet the criteria for "dominance" as used in the EC Treaty" in Gifford and Kudrle (2010), p. 1276.

1454 Wils (2014), p. 414.

1455 Using primary line discrimination to deal with exclusionary behavior and secondary line discrimination referring to exploitative discrimination see: Gifford and Kudrle (2010), p. 1263-1266 and 1272.

1456 See also using secondary line discrimination as based on the amount of units acquired: Geradin and Petit (2006), p. 483. I discussed exclusionary discrimination by means of granting supracompetitive bonuses in chapter 6, section §VI.

er seller that is not dependent and that would receive a better commission by segregating suppliers based on their supply elasticity[1457]. In other words, those suppliers are 'locked-in' as buyers of a good might be vis-à-vis the buyer(s) and succumb to the low and exploitative offered purchasing price[1458].

755. In the case of unilateral behaviour, the intuition is simple: the buyer would underpay a supplier regarding the price paid for the same goods in similar conditions to a different supplier. In so doing, it extracts supracompetitive profits from that specific supplier, which, at the same time, is left in a worse competitive situation vis-à-vis rival suppliers,[1459] as confirmed in *British Airways v Commission,* which I discuss immediately below[1460]. In the case of coordinated agreements, the situation is more complicated and, due to the specificities of the concept of agreement in EU competition law, buyer or seller exploitative discrimination is unlikely to arise, as stressed by Gifford and Kudrle[1461], and as confirmed due the lack of cases of a horizontal or vertical nature. However, Gifford and Kudrle's interpretation of the case law seems to go beyond the concept of agreement under EU competition law[1462], and, in my view, would only be correct concerning sales to end consumers, but not concerning contracts between suppliers and intermediary buyers[1463].

756. My study of this theory of harm and the case law dealing with it shows that buyer power exploitative discrimination is directly linked with buyer power exclusionary discrimination. In the case of the exploitation, the harm is on the supplier, whereas regarding exclusion the harm is to rival buyers of the undertaking(s) exercising the discrimination. Despite this theoretical distinction, both effects usually take place within the same conduct and are evaluated jointly, as occurred in *British Airways v Commission* where it was found that a buyer is in breach of Article 102(2) (c) TFEU by offering different rebate schemes that are applied to identical amounts of revenues generated by the suppliers, as this puts some suppliers at a *competitive disadvantage*[1464].

1457 Hovenkamp, [2011], p. 320.

1458 Whish and Bailey, *Competition law* [2012], p. 760.

1459 See discussing persistent and sporadic price discrimination: Hovenkamp, [2011], p. 319.

1460 Judgment of 17 December 2003, *British Airways v Commission* of 17 December 2003, T-219/99, ECR, EU:T:2003:343, para. 240.

1461 Gifford and Kudrle (2010), p. 1273.

1462 See discussing the unilateral element in vertical agreements: Okeoghene Odudu, *The Boundaries of EC Competition Law: The Scope of Article 81* (Oxford University Press 2006), Chapter 4; Albertina Albors-Llorens, 'Horizontal Agreements and Concerted Practices in EC Competition Law: Unlawful and Legitimate Contacts Between Competitors' 51 The Antitrust Bulletin (2006) 837; Gjendemsjø, [2011]; Whish and Bailey, *Competition law* [2012], p. 105-110.

1463 Guidelines on Vertical Restraints [2010] OJ C 130/1, para. 25.

1464 Judgment of 17 December 2003, *British Airways v Commission* of 17 December 2003, T-219/99, ECR, EU:T:2003:343, paras. 133-141. Also remarking that the abuse was buyer power induced vis-à-vis travel agents and contrary to Article 102(c) TFEU, see: Rousseva, [2010], p. 180 and 202; and Jones and Sufrin, *EU Competition Law: Text, Cases, and Materials* [2011], p. 389 and p. 538-548; Whish and Bailey, *Competition law* [2015], p. 805. See discussing discrimination under Article 102 TFEU and two different ways to look at it: Temple-Lang J, 'The Principle of Essential Facilities in European Community Competition Law - The Position Since Bronner' (2000) 1 Journal of Network Industries 375, p. 390-391.

757. In *British Airways v Commission,* the General Court confirmed that suppliers and buyers can be mutually interdependent as firms need the collaboration of the other to market their products effectively, as input and output markets are independent but related economic activities representing distinct markets[1465]. In this case, however, the dominance in the market of air transport passenger services by British Airways put its suppliers of travel agency services in a dependent situation as travel agents "substantially depend on the income they receive from BA in consideration for their air travel agency services"[1466], particularly because British Airways was also an obligatory business partner[1467]. Therefore, the General Court found that dependent suppliers from a powerful buyer *can be subject to buyer power exploitation whenever they are offered discriminatory low purchasing prices by remunerating identical services in different ways.* Additionally, as travel agencies compete between each other and depend on the bonuses paid by the powerful buyer, the competition between them is distorted due to the discrimination in purchasing prices as well as with regard to their relation to other airline companies. Consequently, it was held that:

> [i]n those circumstances, the Commission was right to hold that BA's performance reward schemes constituted an abuse of BA's dominant position on the United Kingdom market for air travel agency services, in that they produced discriminatory effects within the network of travel agents established in the United Kingdom, thereby inflicting on some of them a competitive disadvantage within the meaning of subparagraph (c) of the second paragraph of Article 82 EC[1468].

758. The CJEU confirmed this finding of the General Court as it held that Article 102(2) (c) TFEU "prohibits any discrimination on the part of an undertaking in a dominant position which consists in the application of dissimilar conditions to equivalent transactions with other trading partners, thereby placing them at a competitive disadvantage"[1469]. The test, therefore, requires finding discrimination sensu stricto and the placing of suppliers at a disadvantage because they compete among each other[1470]. In the analysis of British Airways' conduct the CJEU confirmed that the payment for the travel agency services

---

1465 Judgment of 17 December 2003, *British Airways v Commission* of 17 December 2003, T-219/99, ECR, EU:T:2003:343, paras 89-100.

1466 Judgment of 17 December 2003, *British Airways v Commission* of 17 December 2003, T-219/99, ECR, EU:T:2003:343, para. 216.

1467 Judgment of 17 December 2003, *British Airways v Commission* of 17 December 2003, T-219/99, ECR, EU:T:2003:343, para. 217.

1468 Judgment of 17 December 2003, *British Airways v Commission* of 17 December 2003, T-219/99, ECR, EU:T:2003:343, para. 240.

1469 Judgment of 15 March 2007 in *British Airways v Commission*, C-95/04 P, EU:C:2007:166, para. 133.

1470 This test is similar to the conditions required under US antitrust law for a secondary-line violation of the Robinson-Patman Act concerning buyer induced discrimination. However, in this case, the Robinson-Patman Act would not have been triggered because it does not apply to sales (or purchases) of services, only goods. See also: Hovenkamp, [2011], p. 324-330.

to some of them *was discriminatory and exploitative* because the rewards paid lead to situations in which different travel agents would receive, for the same amount of ticket sales, different remunerations based on whether they reached their sales target. Thus, the CJEU took a quite formalistic and strict approach to the definition of discriminatory conditions centered on a comparison of amounts and identity of subjects.

759. Furthermore, the CJEU held that discriminatory purchasing practices are exploitative and abusive "as soon as the behavior of the undertaking in a dominant position tends, having regard to the whole of the circumstances of the case, to lead to a distortion of competition between business partners"[1471]. To determine whether the conduct put the discriminated suppliers at a disadvantage in this case, the CJEU evaluated how travel agents competed with each other based on offering attractive seats to consumers, and their financial resources. As the rebates had a direct impact on the financial resources of the agents and their ability to offer the best services possible, the CJEU confirmed that the General Court was entitled to decide on the basis of the reward structure and without any detailed analysis to conclude that the competitive conditions among suppliers of a dominant buyer were affected and some of them were put at a disadvantage.

760. Hence, adopting a rather formal and strict stand towards discriminatory and disadvantaging trading conditions and perhaps excessively protective of suppliers, the CJEU confirmed that purchasing price discrimination – and bonus schemes granted by a dominant buyer – are abusive depending the underlying factors of the case, such as for example obtaining a benefit set on reaching specific sales objectives not based on quantities nor fidelity discounts in the meaning of *Hoffmann-La Roche*[1472]. For British Airways, the CJEU confirmed that purchasing price discrimination based on bonus schemes in upstream markets runs contrary to Article 102(2)(c) TFEU whenever the bonus:

> [...] tends to remove or restrict the buyer's [*rectius* seller] to choose his sources of supply, to bar competitors from access to the market, to apply dissimilar conditions to equivalent transactions with other trading parties or to strengthen the dominant position by distorting competition[1473].

761. Thus, if a dominant undertaking imposes discriminatory purchasing practices that lead to a distortion of competition among suppliers – ones that are bene-

---

1471 Judgment of 15 March 2007 in *British Airways v Commission*, C-95/04 P, EU:C:2007:166, para. 145. See also referring to this Judgment of 22 September 2016 in *Sorpa bs. v The Icelandic Competition Authority (Samkeppniseftirlitið)* E-29/15 [2016], para. 109.

1472 This is, granting rebates based on an exclusive or quasi exclusive supply agreement, Judgment of 15 March 2007 in *British Airways v Commission*, C-95/04 P, EU:C:2007:166, para. 60-80.

1473 Judgment of 15 March 2007 in *British Airways v Commission*, C-95/04 P, EU:C:2007:166, para. 67.

fitted to the detriment of others creating a *disadvantage* – it would be found as infringing Article 102 TFEU for abuse of its purchasing power[1474]. In this case, the disadvantage is very clear because the travel agent gets remunerated by the buyer for its services and then sells to end consumers the airline tickets, in a two-sided market setup[1475]. Those travel agents that have received fewer bonuses than others for the same amount of sales are at a disadvantage as they would need to increase their retailing prices to obtain the same level of profits when compared to those obtaining the supracompetitive bonus. Hence, the Judgment in British Airways, tacitly, appears to take this into account to determine the existence of a competitive disadvantage.

762. Therefore, the rationale of the decision seems to be based on a protection of the economic freedom and competitive conditions among suppliers to a powerful buyer.

763. Summing up, according to the little case law concerning buyer power discriminatory exploitation, Article 102(c) TFEU would be applied prohibiting a dominant buyer from discriminating among its suppliers if two conditions are met. First, there must be discrimination sensu stricto in the sense that some suppliers are paid less than others for the similar goods sold in similar circumstances due to their weak bargaining position vis-à-vis the powerful buyer. Additionally, this differentiated and lesser payment for the same goods must also lead these suppliers to be at a competitive disadvantage with regard to other suppliers, and which is likely to exist if the supplier sells goods in a downstream market to end consumers, such as a distributor. If, on the other hand the suppliers only compete vis-à-vis the intermediary buyers (like a producer of wood would do with respect to furniture manufacturers), then differences in prices paid by buyers to suppliers may be justified by the balance of bargaining power among the parties without it existing a competitive disadvantage not leading to exploitative price discrimination. This competitive disadvantage, nonetheless, may exist if the price difference is not objectively justified (for example by purchasing volumes) and when it is discriminatory in line with the first limb of the test because that supplier is less able, for instance, to invest when compared to a better-paid supplier. No cases, however, in EU law have dealt with this for which it remains an unclear area of the law. Therefore, this dual requirement and legal standard seems to grant protection to some weaker suppliers vis-à-vis a strong buyer based on the protection of economic freedom and the competitive process in the upstream market, in line with, but also going beyond, ordoliberal competition policy ideas.

764. This approach to buyer power discriminatory exploitation can be criticized

---

1474 Østerud, 116; Jones and Sufrin, *EU Competition Law: Text, Cases, and Materials* [2011], p. 547.

1475 For a short discussion of two-sided markets and some relevant literature see chapter 4, section §IV.B, footnote 651.

because the legal standard applied by the CJEU relies perhaps excessively on a formalistic approach to the protection of economic freedom without an in-depth analysis of the justification or otherwise of the discrimination. The analysis and the legal standard adopted by the CJEU is centered on the creation of a disadvantage by applying dissimilar purchasing conditions among different suppliers, but not on whether there could be grounds for a differentiated treatment justifying the conduct. However, the Courts did take into account the fact that for the same sales different remuneration schemes were applied to different suppliers, which constitute discrimination sensu stricto. *A contrario* interpretation would imply that supracompetitive bonuses that are not conditional and economically justified would not exploit suppliers by leaving some of them at a competitive disadvantage.

V. Centralized purchasing and cooperatives, between cartels and dominance

765. Centralized purchasing is a common commercial practice that is carried out both by undertakings acting jointly or by single firms that agglutinate all the purchases from their different departments with the aim of creating buyer power, generating economies of scale and reducing transactional costs. Additionally, centralization allows obtaining other benefits, such as the creation of economies of scale for both the buyer and the seller as well as minimization of administrative costs. Therefore, it comes as no surprise that centralized purchasing – that does not involve demand withholding – is often associated with the pro-competitiveness of buying alliances or individual centralized purchasing, and it is brought as a pro-competitive argument whenever an undertaking's buying conduct is evaluated. Due to these positive economic effects, centralized purchasing is a phenomenon that has now been incorporated into public procurement markets, particularly with the impulse given to demand aggregation techniques and central purchasing bodies, a topic which I have explored extensively elsewhere[1476].

766. Cooperatives, on the other hand, are societal forms that allow their members/users to join efforts to carry out an economic activity through the cooperative that grants them benefits derived from their own work and the group's effort as a whole. Cooperatives are active in industries where buyer power plays an

1476 Herrera Anchustegui 'Centralizing Public Procurement and Competitiveness in Directive 2014/24' (2015); Sánchez Graells and Herrera Anchustegui, 'Impact of Public Procurement Aggregation on Competition. Risks, Rationale and Justification for the Rules in Directive 2014/24' [2016]; Ignacio Herrera Anchustegui, 'Division into Lots and Demand Aggregation – Extremes Looking for the Correct Balance?' in GS Ølykke and A Sánchez-Graells (eds), *Reformation or Deformation of the EU Public Procurement Rules in 2014* (Cheltenham, Edward Elgar Publishing 2016).

important role, for instance in the case of agriculture, and are vehicles used to agglutinate both buyer power and reap centralization benefits, and also to oppose buyer power when the sales are made through the cooperative and not individually.

767. In this section, I discuss the rationale for purchasing centralization, economies of scale and cooperatives as agglutinates of buyer power. These two forms of buyer market power pooling, in particular in the case purchasing centralization and the generation of economies of scale are not forms of abuse of buyer market power with an exploitative effect, but efficiency reasons that can justify a purchasing conduct and which serve to the understanding of the pro-competitiveness of buying alliances and centralization conducts.

A. Rationale for purchasing centralization – economies of scale

768. The economic rationale behind centralized purchasing is the ability to accumulate buyer market power by pooling several buyers' purchases (or re-arranging demand within a single undertaking)[1477]. By agglutinating demand, the joint purchasing leads to economies of scale and a reduction of transaction costs[1478].

769. Demand is pooled by means of a purchasing agreement among buyers or when in the case of a single buyer all departments consolidate their purchasing in a single unit[1479]. Centralizing and agglutinating demand grants the buyer a more favorable negotiation position vis-à-vis the suppliers and allow it to exert the buyer market power generated to improve the supply conditions offered by its seller(s)[1480].

770. Furthermore, purchasing centralization permits the formation of *economies of*

1477 James Chard, Gustaf Duhs and John Houlden, 'Body Beautiful or Vile Bodies? Central Purchasing in the UK' Public Procurement Law Review (2008) NA26. Bundeskartellamt '*Summary of the Final Report of the Sector Inquiry into the Food Retail Sector*' (2014), 10. See also: Alberto Vaquero García, 'Compras Agregadas y Eficiencia Económica' in Patricia Valcárcel Fernández (ed), *Compra conjunta y demanda agregada en la contratación del sector público Un análisis jurídico y económico* (Thomson-Aranzadi 2016), p. 211-215.

1478 Also supporting this view that aggregated procurement techniques achieve "economies of scale" see Office of Fair Trading *Assessing the Impact of Public Sector Procurement on Competition,* (2004) para 1.43 to 1.51; Hamer (2014). See also Recital (59) of Directive 2014/24/EU of the European Parliament and of the Council of 26 February 2014 on public procurement and repealing Directive 2004/18/EC [2014] OJ L 94/65.

1479 Judgment of 20 January 2011 in *General Química and Others v Commission*, C-90/09 P, EU:C:2011:21, para. 37-43. See discussing the concept of single economic entity: Okeoghene Odudu and David Bailey, 'The Single Economic Entity Doctrine in EU Competition Law' 51 Common Market Law Review (2014) 1721.

1480 Argument raised by the French Republic in Judgment of 3 April 2003, *Petrolessence and SG2R v Commission*, T-342/00, ECR, EU:T:2003:97, para. 92-93.

scale[1481] for the purchaser (and in some circumstances also for the supplier)[1482] by fostering operational efficiency and reducing administrative and transaction costs, as recognized by the case law and literature[1483].

a. *How do the economies of scale in centralized purchasing work? What are the effects?*

771. In microeconomic terms, and because of the scale of its operational efficiency[1484], centralized purchasing allows buyer(s) to reduce the overall costs of their purchasing compared to the situation where the undertaking(s) would have carried out individual purchases. This occurs as a higher purchasing capacity reduces the average costs paid by a buyer and vice versa for a supplier[1485], as explicitly recognized by the Commission when remarking that economies of scale "normally accompany high volume purchases," as held in *DaimlerChrysler v Commission*[1486].

1481 For an economic discussion on the concept of economies of scale see, *inter alia*: George J. Stigler, 'The Economies of Scale' 1 Journal of Law & Economics (1958) 54; Paul R. Krugman, 'Increasing Returns, Monopolistic Competition, and International Trade' 9 Journal of International Economics (1979) 469; Pindyck and Rubinfeld, [2009], p. 245; Niels, Jenkins and Kavanagh, [2011], p. 136-137. For a discussion of economies of scale generated by centralization of purchases see in particular: Office of Fair Trading '*Assessing the Impact of Public Sector Procurement on Competition*' (2004), para 1.43 to 1.51; Katri Karjalainen, 'Challenges of Purchasing Centralization: Empirical Evidence from Public Procurement' (Helsinki School of Economics 2009); Karolis Šerpytis, Vytautas Vengrauskas and Zinaida Gineitienė, 'Evaluation of Financial effects of Public Procurement Centralisatiom' 90 Ekonomika (2011) 87; Sigma, *Central Purchasing Bodies* (Brief, 2011), p. 4; Hamer (2014), p. 201. See also recital (59) of Directive 2014/24/EU of the European Parliament and of the Council of 26 February 2014 on public procurement and repealing Directive 2004/18/EC [2014] OJ L 94/65.

1482 This would be the case when the supplier is able to sell in bulk, increase its output and reduce its transaction costs.

1483 Judgment of 12 June 2014, *Intel v Commission*, T-286/09, ECR, EU:T:2014:547, para. 75. For some selected works on operational efficiency in the public sector, see: Peter Smith and David Mayston, 'Measuring Efficiency in the Public Sector' 15 Omega, International Journal of Management Science (1987) 181; John Ruggiero, 'On the Measurement of Technical Efficiency in the Public Sector' 90 European Journal of Operational Research (1996) 553; Lars Anwandter and Teofilo Jr. Ozuna, 'Can Public Sector Reforms Improve the Efficiency of Public Water Utilities?' 7 Environment and Development Economics (2002) 687; Hannu Rantanen and others, 'Performance Measurement Systems in the Finnish Public Sector' 20 International Journal of Public Sector Management (2007) 415; António Afonso, Ludger Schuknecht and Vito Tanzic, 'Public Sector Efficiency: Evidence for new EU Member States and Emerging Markets' 42 Applied Economics (2010) 2147.

1484 See the Commission's opinion also highlighting the importance of large operational scales in Judgment of 14 April 2011, *Visa Europe and Visa International Service v Commission*, T-461/07, ECR, EU:T:2011:181, para. 147.

1485 Faull and Nikpay, [1999], para. 1.37.

1486 Judgment of 15 September 2005, *DaimlerChrysler v Commission*, T-325/01, ECR, EU:T:2005:322, para. 134.

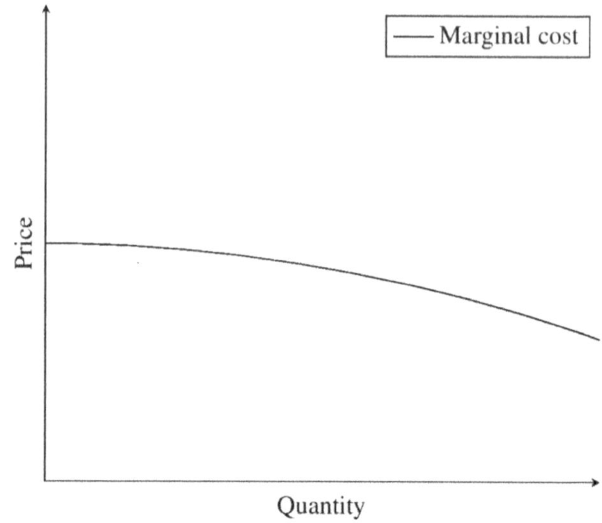

Figure 6: Buying Economies of Scale

772. Two examples will help to illustrate how centralized purchasing generates economies of scale in practice. In the case of a purchasing alliance, several undertakings agree to delegate to a common entity/division the purchasing of all input required by all parties which will later on distribute the purchased goods among the members, as it occurred in the *National Sulphuric Acid Association* Decision[1487].

773. On the other hand, a single economic entity could assign all purchases it carries out through all its different departments to a central single purchasing office. This initiative, for instance, is being currently used in the field of public procurement where contracting authorities agglutinate their demand on a single buyer, the central purchasing body, which carries purchases for or on behalf of them[1488]. In EU competition law, interestingly, in a few occasions centralized purchasing by a single undertaking has also been under scrutiny, while also serving to recognize the efficiency of centralized purchasing, as well as its ability to enhance anti-competitive buyer power effects.

774. The case law has recognized these positive effects expressly. For instance, in *Car Glass,* car manufacturers individually centralized glass purchases for all their own affiliated trademarks to achieve two economic and efficiency en-

1487 Commission Decision of 9 July 1980 relating to a proceeding under Article 85 of the EEC Treaty (IV/27.958 *National Sulphuric Acid Association*) [1980] OJ L 260/24.

1488 Article 37 of Directive 2014/24/EU of the European Parliament and of the Council of 26 February 2014 on public procurement and repealing Directive 2004/18/EC [2014] OJ L 94/65.

hancing benefits[1489]. First, purchasing centralization allowed buyers to, even in the presence of a suppliers' cartel, to play-off their sellers against each other which help them to obtain lower prices based on the volume of sales and incentivizes cartel members to 'cheat'[1490]. Second, purchase centralization allowed a powerful buyer to extend its geographic market and reach larger deals, for instance by purchasing for all its subsidiaries[1491].

775. Furthermore, centralized purchasing may also generate economies of scale for suppliers under certain conditions. If the centralization of purchases allows a supplier to sell to the joint purchasing entity larger amounts of goods, in particular *homogenous* ones, this will enable it to reduce its average production costs as noted by Albano and Sparro[1492]. Additionally, centralization of purchases produces benefits aimed at the reduction of transactional and administrative costs as a single entity is carrying out all purchasing routines. This has been confirmed in the case law by the Opinion of Advocate General Jacobs who held that "institutionalised management cooperation [...] allows the companies involved to achieve significant economies of scale [...] is generally procompetitive"[1493].

776. Economies of scale are, however, limited[1494]. This means that a point is reached in both the purchasing and supplying curves — the "minimum efficient scale" — and no further benefits can be reaped[1495]. This occurs because after reaching a certain point in the production or purchasing curves, the average costs cannot decrease any further and increase instead. Also, the minimum efficient scale has been used to explain market concentration issues and why, under certain circumstances, "more companies in a market does not necessarily lead to a better market outcome"[1496].

1489 Summary of Commission Decision of 12 November 2008 relating to a proceeding under Article 81 of the Treaty establishing the European Community and Article 53 of the EEA Agreement (Case COMP/39.125 — *Car glass*) [2009] OJ C 173/13, taken from the unabridged version, para. 437. Confirmed by the General Court in Judgment of 17 December 2014, *Pilkington Group and Others v Commission*, T-72/09, EU:T:2014:1094, para. 109. Appealed and dismissed in its entirety as Judgment of 7 September 2016 in *Pilkington Group and Others v Commission*, C-101/15, EU:C:2016:631.

1490 Summary of Commission Decision of 12 November 2008 relating to a proceeding under Article 81 of the Treaty establishing the European Community and Article 53 of the EEA Agreement (Case COMP/39.125 — *Car glass*) [2009] OJ C 173/13, taken from the unabridged version, para. 441.

1491 Summary of Commission Decision of 12 November 2008 relating to a proceeding under Article 81 of the Treaty establishing the European Community and Article 53 of the EEA Agreement (Case COMP/39.125 — *Car glass*) [2009] OJ C 173/13, taken from the unabridged version, para. 33.

1492 Gian Luigi Albano and Marco Sparro, 'Flexible Strategies for Centralized Public Procurement' 1 Review of Economics and Institutions (2010), p. 4. See also: Faull and Nikpay, [1999] para. 1.37; Herrera Anchustegui 'Centralizing Public Procurement and Competitiveness in Directive 2014/24' (2015).

1493 Opinion of Advocate General Jacobs of 28 January 1999 in Judgment in *Albany*, C-67/96, EU:C:1999:28, para. 265.

1494 Also arguing that economies of scale might get exhausted see the Commission's arguments in Judgment of 9 March 2015, *Deutsche Börse v Commission*, T-175/12, EU:T:2015:148, para. 311.

1495 Schmalensee (1981); Faull, Nikpay and Taylor, [2014], para. 1.43-1.49.

1496 Faull and Nikpay, [1999] para. 1.40; Faull, Nikpay and Taylor, [2014], para. 1.44.

777. Also, economies of scale and the ability to reinforce buyer market power may increase its pernicious effects, or may tie a buyer to a supplier. This was the case regarding the purchasing patterns and rebates system discussed in *Tomra and Others v Commission,* where the Courts analyzed the effects of the purchases of bottle-recycling machines by means of "central purchasing organisations such as Superunie and ICA/Hakon"[1497]. Tomra, as discussed in detail in chapter 9, alleged that their customers had countervailing buyer power, despite these allegations the Courts did not evaluate whether centralized purchasing had an effect on the countervailing ability. Instead, to dismiss an allegation of lack of exclusivity enhancing effect of the rebates, the General Court reasoned that centralized purchasing had the effect of tying purchasers further to the seller as it were easier to attain the rebates offered if all members of the purchasing organization acquired goods through the centralized purchasing entity[1498], therefore revealing a negative aspect of centralized purchasing. Also, in the General Court's view, a system of centralized purchasing had an effect *extra-partes* as it also influenced the purchasing behaviour of independent retailers and reinforced the rebates' effect[1499].

B. Centralized purchasing and economies of scale under an efficiency analysis

778. Based on its efficiency-enhancing ability, economies of scale generated through centralized purchasing are raised as pro-efficiency arguments under Article 101(3) TFEU[1500], Article 102 TFEU[1501], or in concentration operations[1502]. In the following I discuss how and what the legal assessment of the benefits of centralized purchasing is, with a particular emphasis on unilateral behaviour.

779. Centralization of purchases and economies of scale are one of the most fre-

---

1497 Judgment of 9 September 2010, *Tomra Systems and Others v Commission*, T-155/06, ECR, EU:T:2010:370; Judgment of 19 April 2012 in *Tomra and Others v Commission*, C-549/10 P, EU:C:2012:221.

1498 Judgment of 9 September 2010, *Tomra Systems and Others v Commission*, T-155/06, ECR, EU:T:2010:370, paras. 55 to 67.

1499 Judgment of 9 September 2010, *Tomra Systems and Others v Commission*, T-155/06, ECR, EU:T:2010:370, para. 63.

1500 To name just but a few of the many examples dealing with economies of scale in collusion cases as an efficiency defense: Judgment of 11 September 2014 in *CB v Commission*, C-67/13 P, EU:C:2014:2204, para. 84; Opinion Advocate General Wahl in Judgment of 11 September 2014 in *CB v Commission*, C-67/13 P, EU:C:2014:1958, para. 71; Judgment of 17 September 2007, *Microsoft v Commission*, T-201/04, ECR, EU:T:2007:289, para. 1000; Judgment of 22 March 2011, *Altstoff Recycling Austria v Commission*, T-419/03, ECR, EU:T:2011:102, para. 23. See also stressing this from a centralized purchasing perspective: Wollmann [2008], para. 2-2-109.

1501 For some examples dealing with economies of scale in dominance cases: Judgment of 27 March 2012 in *Post Danmark*, C-209/10, EU:C:2012:172, para. 10 and 11; Opinion of Advocate General Mengozzi in Judgment of 27 March 2012 in *Post Danmark*, C-209/10, EU:C:2011:342, paras. 52 and 105; Judgment of 29 March 2012, *Telefónica and Telefónica de España v Commission*, T-336/07, ECR, EU:T:2012:172.

1502 Judgment of 4 July 2006, *easyJet v Commission*, T-177/04, ECR, EU:T:2006:187, paras. 86 and 87; Judgment of 6 July 2010, *Ryanair v Commission*, T-342/07, ECR, EU:T:2010:280, paras. 122-124; 261-272; and 427 to 431; Judgment of 3 April 2003, *BaByliss v Commission*, T-114/02, ECR, EU:T:2003:100, para. 360; Judgment of 3 April 2003, *Petrolessence and SG2R v Commission*, T-342/00, ECR, EU:T:2003:97.

quently employed arguments to support the efficiency and compatibility of buying alliances or to justify the existence of a buyers' cartel. In the case of coordinated behaviour, for economies of scale to be considered as an efficiency enhancing, at least some of the benefits accrued by them ought to be passed to consumers, according to Article 101(3) TFEU and the Opinion of Advocate General Léger in *Wouters and Others*[1503]. The case law, however, remains silent regarding whether the economies of scale should also benefit the supplier by generating selling side benefits thanks to the increase in purchasing quantities. In my view, such a requirement would be an additional factor to consider but not a necessary element, as it is not required by Article 101(3) TFEU.

780. In the case of single behaviour, powerful firms have argued that their centralized purchasing conduct allowed them to generate efficient economies of scale either in the upstream market or a related downstream market and that, consequently, this should be taken into account in an object justification analysis or the assessment of a concentration. This has been confirmed in *Intel v Commission* and previously in *Michelin v Commission*[1504], where the General Court recognized that quantity rebates may be a reflection of efficiency gains obtained through economies of scale and may be an efficiency defense under Article 102 TFEU[1505]. This was subsequently restated in the buyer power related case of *Tomra and Others v Commission*[1506]. The existence of economies of scale, however, does not deprive an undertaking of its liability under Article 102 TFEU if it decides to impose below cost pricing predatory pricing - as discussed by the General Court in *France Télécom v Commission*[1507]. *A contrario* interpretation of this passage implies that the reverse would hold true in cases of exploitation of buyer power; exploitative buying in connection with economies of scale where a price is paid that is below the competitive level and below the supplier's marginal costs would be contrary to Article 102 TFEU, as discussed in this chapter's section §III. Hence, the benefits of centralized purchasing can also be used to extract supracompetitive profits[1508]. Nevertheless, a reverse application of such test would require using the supplier's and not the buyer's costs as a reference.

781. In relation to unilateral buyer power cases, there are four instances in which centralized purchasing and its benefits regarding buying economies of scale have been scrutinized by the Courts. In three of them, the argument was raised

---

1503 Opinion of Advocate General Léger of 10 July 2001 in Judgment of 19 February 2002 in *Wouters and Others*, C-309/99, EU:C:2001:390, para. 119.

1504 Judgment of 30 September 2003, *Michelin v Commission*, T-203/01, ECR, EU:T:2003:250, paras. 99 to 110.

1505 Judgment of 12 June 2014, *Intel v Commission,* T-286/09, ECR, EU:T:2014:547, para. 75.

1506 Judgment of 9 September 2010, *Tomra Systems and Others v Commission*, T-155/06, ECR, EU:T:2010:370; Judgment of 19 April 2012 in *Tomra and Others v Commission*, C-549/10 P, EU:C:2012:221, para. 212.

1507 Judgment of 30 January 2007, *France Télécom v Commission*, T-340/03, ECR, EU:T:2007:22, para. 217.

1508 The reverse of predatory selling, predatory buying (i.e.: paying more for an input) is analyzed in chapter 6, section §IV.

under abuse of dominance cases, namely *Tomra and Others v Commission*[1509], *British Airways v Commission*[1510], and *Imperial Chemical Industries v Commission*[1511]. One of them involved a concentration assessment and risk of creating a collective dominant position in *Airtours v Commission*[1512]. Yet, in none of these cases were the economies of scale generated by the large buyer part of the substantive discussion, nor did they have much weight in the analysis of the competitive effects of the conducts.

782. In *British Airways v Commission*, in an attempt to justify its rebate policy, the defendant recognized and the CJEU used as an argument that there was no relation:

> [...] between, on the one hand, the possible economies of scale achieved by virtue of BA tickets sold after the attainment of the sales objectives and, on the other hand, the increases in the commission rates granted to United Kingdom travel agents in consideration for exceeding those objectives[1513].

783. From this wording, it may be concluded that, for the CJEU in cases regarding buyer power leveraging or exploitation, economies of scale would be relevant if they are connected with the conduct that is under scrutiny and has taken place in the related market. In this case, the economies of scale argument was not upheld because British Airways was not able to prove that obtaining economies of scale in the air transport service would lead to paying a larger commission rate to travel agents to sell further tickets. Therefore, there must be a relation between the economic benefit, the conduct and the economies of scale generated. *A contrario* argumentation of this passage could also imply that economies of scale will only be relevant when its achievement generate an economic effect in the related market.

784. Also, in *Imperial Chemical Industries v Commission* and *Tomra and Others v Commission,* economies of scale were invoked as a justification regarding rebates granted by a dominant undertaking. In *Tomra and Others v Commission* the General Court concluded that quantity rebates, even if conceded by a dominant undertaking, can and should be justified if granted because of reasons of economic efficiency and economies of scale – i.e. if the buyer acquires large quantities of the goods[1514]. In *Imperial Chemical Industries v Commission,* the CJEU, following the Commission's assessment, found that the rebates granted by this dominant buyer and seller were not the reflec-

---

1509 Judgment of 9 September 2010, *Tomra Systems and Others v Commission*, T-155/06, ECR, EU:T:2010:370; Judgment of 19 April 2012 in *Tomra and Others v Commission*, C-549/10 P, EU:C:2012:221.

1510 Judgment of 15 March 2007 in *British Airways v Commission*, C-95/04 P, EU:C:2007:166.

1511 Judgment of 25 June 2010, *Imperial Chemical Industries v Commission*, T-66/01, ECR, EU:T:2010:255.

1512 Judgment of 28 June 2004, *Airtours v Commission*, T-342/99, ECR, EU:T:2002:146, para. 211.

1513 Judgment of 15 March 2007 in *British Airways v Commission*, C-95/04 P, EU:C:2007:166, para. 83 and 29.

1514 Judgment of 9 September 2010, *Tomra Systems and Others v Commission*, T-155/06, ECR, EU:T:2010:370; Judgment of 19 April 2012 in *Tomra and Others v Commission*, C-549/10 P, EU:C:2012:221, para. 212.

tion of "efficiency gains or economies of scale"[1515]. Interestingly, in this case, Imperial Chemical – which claimed the existence of countervailing buyer power by its clients – did not argue that its own economies of scale could also lead to economies of scales for its clients.

785. Lastly, in *Airtours v Commission,* a case dealing with a collective dominant position and in which countervailing buyer power was brought up as a defense, economies of scale were also discussed. The discussion, however, did not deal with buyer power related issues but instead the inability of small and not vertically integrated travel services suppliers to "make the same economies of scale and scope as the larger operators"[1516].

786. Interestingly, in none of these cases where economies of scale were invoked did the large buyers claim that in addition to their own economic benefits generated by centralized purchasing there were also economic benefits generated for their suppliers in the form of selling economies of scale and reduction costs, which is an efficiency effect that economic literature recognizes. It is very likely that in none of these cases would their behaviour have generated a spillover effect to the economies of scale of suppliers that could be quantified.

787. At a national level, I have also found instances where centralized purchasing and its derived economies of scale have been taken into account in connection with buyer power exploitation and unfair purchasing practices, the latter is discussed in chapter 8. In Germany, the Bundeskartellamt has recently stated in the merger *Edeka- Kaiser's Tengelmann* that large buyers are "able to make use of its economies of scale by asking to be granted special conditions, which the Bundeskartellamt considers as abusive conduct to the detriment of suppliers and smaller competitors" and contrary to the prohibition of *Anzapfverbot,* which I discuss in chapter 8, section §VI.B[1517]. This sort of exploitative use of economies of scale, however, has not been claimed at the EU level, nor is there a provision similar to the *Anzapfverbot* in EU competition law that seeks to protect small and medium undertakings from relative dependence to larger firms.

788. In sum, purchasing economies of scale generated because of centralized purchasing techniques or large purchases are commonly used efficiency arguments by undertakings that have been said to be in breach of EU competition law to different extents of success. Therefore, purchasing economies of scale are factored in when determining if an agreement between buyers may satisfy the conditions required under Article 101(3) TFEU, serve as an objective justifica-

---

1515 Judgment of 25 June 2010, *Imperial Chemical Industries v Commission*, T-66/01, ECR, EU:T:2010:255, para. 222, see also paras. 298 and 303.

1516 Judgment of 28 June 2004, *Airtours v Commission*, T-342/99, ECR, EU:T:2002:146, para. 211.

1517 Bundeskaterllamt, Case summary from 6 July 2015: Prohibition of acquisition of Kaiser´s Tengelmann outlets by Edeka, B2-96/14 (English version), p. 4, appealed and revoked by the German Federal Minister for Economic Affairs and Energy under § 42 of the German Competition Act based, *inter alia*, on the protection of working positions that would be absorbed by Edeka.

tion assessment under Article 102 TFEU in the case of individual behaviour, or whenever a concentration is being evaluated and future competition is assessed. In the case of purchasing agreements and buying alliances, purchasing economies of scale often succeed in justifying the agreement or as a precondition for the disapplication of EU competition law by means of the Block Exemption Regulation. However, purchasing (or selling) economies of scale that may justify individual current or future behaviour have less probability of success.

C. Cooperatives as agglutinates of buyer and countervailing power

789. Like centralized purchasing arrangements, cooperatives, as an organizing form grouping different buyers/sellers/workers, play an important role concerning the creation of purchasing alliances and buyers' cartels, as discussed in this chapter's section §VI[1518]. In buyer power related cases, cooperatives are usually not the buyer but the entity that groups smaller farmers that claim to be exploited by large food retailers. As remarked by Reich, small farmers tend to agglutinate in cooperatives "[t]o countervail the power of the marketing firms and improve their lots"[1519]. This allows them to join efforts, jointly commercialize their products and derive benefits from the pooling of sales and purchases[1520].

790. A cooperative is a societal form different from for-profit corporations and not for-profit legal entities, whereby it is necessary to discuss and then evaluate their impact in buyer power and the competitiveness of these entities.

791. A cooperative has a 'mutual purpose'. It is created to benefit its members, and the economic activities it carries out are precisely fitted to serve this purpose[1521]. Therefore, a cooperative is primarily a horizontal agreement that also contains vertical elements[1522]. Furthermore, cooperatives, unlike a traditional corporation, require their members to have a "double quality": they are beneficiaries of the cooperative but also users[1523]. This means that the members must contribute by means of direct effort in the activities, for example in a farmer's cooperative, by running a farm and transferring the goods it produces to the cooperative. This also implies that the members of a cooperative have a "fidelity duty" to supply their goods or obtain their goods from the cooperative, as remarked by Faull and Nikpay[1524]. The benefits for their members/us-

1518 See also linking cooperatives with joint purchasing and buyer power creation: Faull, Nikpay and Taylor, [2014], para. 7.362.

1519 Arie Reich, 'The Agricultural Exemption in Antitrust Law: A Comparative Look at the Political Economy of Market Regulation' 42 Texas International Law Journal (2007) 843, p. 846.

1520 Fici [2013], p. 24.

1521 Ibid, p. 23.

1522 Faull, Nikpay and Taylor, [2014], para. 7.363.

1523 Fici [2013], p. 26.

1524 Faull and Nikpay, [1999], para. 6.295.

ers will be generated whenever the cooperative sells those goods to, for example, a large food retailer and the profits are then distributed among members.

792. The cooperative allows its members to join efforts and set prices and selling conditions that, if done by a group of non-cooperatively affiliated farmers, would have probably triggered the application of EU competition law as an agreement between undertakings[1525]. However, this does not mean that cooperatives are not under the scrutiny of EU competition law, as *cooperatives constitute associations of undertakings,* because farming constitutes an economic activity and single farmers also constitute undertakings themselves, as the buyer power case law shows below in this chapter's section §VI[1526], even if the application of competition law to agriculture is limited[1527]. In the US, producer cooperatives related to agriculture are partially exempted from the application of US antitrust law by means of Article 6 of the Clayton Act and, more importantly by the Capper-Vollstead Act of 1922, except whenever the cooperative engages in exclusionary conducts or restraints of trade vis-à-vis competitors[1528].

793. Furthermore, cooperatives agglutinate market power in *two different ways that are relevant for this buyer power study*. From a negative perspective, suppliers can integrate into the form of a cooperative to create *countervailing selling power* to improve their bargaining position vis-à-vis retailers to prevent the imposition of UPPs as they negotiate as a group and are, therefore, less prone to be dependent on the buyer, as I discuss in chapter 8. From a positive perspective, suppliers' *cooperatives create buyer power by agglutinating all the purchases* from their members/users, for example when purchasing cheese colorant for the preparation of yellow cheese of fertilizer to cultivate[1529].

1525 For a similar opinion from a US antitrust law perspective: Reich (2007), p. 847-848. See discussing the role of cooperatives in agriculture and its competition effects Opinion of Advocate General Tesauro of 16 June 1994 in Judgment of 15 December 1994 in *Gøttrup-Klim and Others Grovvareforeninger v Dansk Landbrugs Grovvareselskab*, C-250/92, EU:C:1994:249, section 18, I – 5658.

1526 See also applying competition law to the agreements entered into by the members of a cooperative and the agreements between the cooperative and other undertakings: Judgment of 14 May 1997 in *VGB and Others v Commission*, T-77/94, EU:T:1997:70; appealed and upheld in Judgment of 30 March 2000 in *VBA v VGB and Others*, C-266/97 P, EU:C:2000:171. Mario Monti, *The Relationship Between CAP and Competition Policy - Does EU Competition Law Apply to Agriculture?* (Helsinki Fair Trade edn, 2003); Ritter and Braun, [2004], p. 708; Whish and Bailey, *Competition law* [2015], p. 1116-117.

1527 Agriculture has a special regime pursuant to Articles 38 to 44 of the TFEU including in Article 42 a provision stating that "[t]he provisions of the Chapter relating to rules on competition shall apply to production of and trade in agricultural products only to the extent determined by the European Parliament and the Council". The level of applicability of EU competition law to agriculture is regulated by the Regulation (EU) No 1308/2013 of the European Parliament and of the Council establishing a common organization of the markets in agricultural products [2013] (OJ L 347/671), Articles 206-210. See also: Reich (2007); Whish and Bailey, *Competition law* [2015], p. 1018-1021.

1528 7 U.S. Code Chapter 12 - Associations of Agricultural Products Producers, § 291-292. For a discussion of the Act and US antitrust law see: Christine A. Varney, 'The Capper-Volstead Act, Agricultural Cooperatives, and Antitrust Immunity' December 2010 The Antitrust Source (2010) 1; Donald M. Barnes and Christopher E. Ondeck, 'The Capper-Volstead Act: Opportunity Today and Tomorrow' (1997) <http://www.uwcc.wisc.edu/info/capper.html>; Hovenkamp, [2011], p. 339.

1529 Judgment of 25 March 1981 in *Coöperatieve Stremsel- en Kleurselfabriek v Commission*, C-61/80, EU:C:1981:75; Judgment of 15 December 1994 in *Gøttrup-Klim and Others Grovvareforeninger v Dansk Landbrugs Grovvareselskab*, C-250/92, EU:C:1994:413.

794. The special nature of cooperatives, their ability to agglutinate buyer power as a buying alliance, its use as countervailing seller power mechanisms to oppose the buyer power of large retailers, and a special treatment in some legal areas (for example, tax law, labor law, special rules regarding corporations and to a minor extent competition law), might grant cooperatives an advantage when exercising their (buyer) market power when compared to non-cooperative undertakings and which may also carry competition risks related to buyer power exploitation and exclusion[1530].

795. For example, in New Zealand, the milk sector and its competitiveness has been impacted in a negative way because of the existing cooperative milk structure by Fonterra[1531], a dominant cooperative owned by more than 15,000 milk producers. According to a recent study Fonterra "in the years 2005 to 2009 enjoyed a world market share of 45% for butter, 35% for whole-milk powder, 27% for skimmed milk powder, 19% of all cheese sales and 50%, or more, for milk protein concentrate and casein"[1532]. Pursuant to buying related allegations the New Zealand Commerce Commission elaborated a report in 2016, which confirmed that the competitiveness in the milk sector was affected by Fonterra's purchasing and selling behaviour, particularly regarding competition in the factory gate market which is very limited. Furthermore, the report concluded that without the current regime restraining Fonterra's market power, then Fonterra "would be able to increase the price of raw milk it sells to other domestic processors, referred to in this report as independent processors (IPs). This would likely result in higher prices for dairy products in downstream domestic markets"[1533]. Thus, the preferential position of Fonterra as a cooperative grouping producers of milk was seen as having an impact of rival processors of milk – and indirect purchasers of milk. Additionally, the report also raised issues concerning the ability of Fonterra to exert buyer market power in an anti-competitive manner and concluded that Fonterra:

> also has buyer side market power in the purchase of raw milk at the farm gate. Buyer side market power gives Fonterra the ability to depress the price paid to farmer suppliers for raw milk below competitive levels. However, we do not think that Fonterra would exercise this market power against its farmers despite its ability to do so[1534].

796. In other words, the report concluded that Fonterra would not use its buyer pow-

---

1530 See also raising a similar argument about the effects of cooperatives in competition: Faull and Nikpay, [1999], para. 6.295.

1531 http://www2.fonterra.com/our-co-op.

1532 http://www.agrifuture.com/fileadmin/agrifuture/binary/summer11/af_0211_22-25.pdf

1533 Commerce Commission of New Zealand *Review of the State of Competition in the New Zealand Dairy Industry,* (2016), para. X6.

1534 Ibid, para. X7.

er to exploit the suppliers of milk which is to be expected because these suppliers are the members of Fonterra as a cooperative. Therefore, by reducing the purchasing prices it pays as a buyer to exploit its monopsony power, it would be underpaying its own members which runs counter to the cooperative spirit as the payment of a purchasing price below the competitive levels would imply a reduction in the profitability and production levels of the farmers integrating it.

797. Yet, as the report shows, particularly in the agricultural sector, cooperatives may trigger exploitative issues as both buyers and retailers that are half way between single conducts by dominant undertakings and purchasing alliances, and which are accentuated by the particularities of the cooperatives' societal form. I, however, acknowledge that this is an area that is ripe for further academic research that due to its specificity, sector focus and requirement of additional legal and economic tools, I do not discuss in further depth.

VI. Agreements imposing purchasing conditions

798. Buyers acting in coordination may pool their forces through joint purchasing agreements to increase their buyer power leading to situations that can be positive or negative for welfare depending on the way the carry out their activity and the aim pursued by its members[1535].

799. I distinguish between two types of joint purchasing agreements and I attempt to differentiate these. On the one hand, those that operate as *buyers' cartels* that aim at pooling buyer power to reduce competition among their members in the upstream and downstream markets, abuse their buyer power vis-à-vis suppliers and/or facilitate collusion in the downstream market where they act as retailers[1536]. On the other hand, *buying alliances*[1537] that aim at pooling buyer power to improve their bargaining ability vis-à-vis suppliers and obtain the benefits of a joint purchasing enterprise by achieving economies of scale[1538],

1535 See also stressing the ambiguous effect on welfare regarding strategic joint purchasing behavior: Faull and Nikpay, [1999], para. 6.297; Faull, Nikpay and Taylor, [2014], para. 7.362.

1536 Communication from the Commission — Guidelines on the applicability of Article 101 of the Treaty on the Functioning of the European Union to horizontal co-operation agreements [2011] OJ C 11/1, para. 201.

1537 The term "buying alliance" appears to be the most widely used at least in EU competition literature, see for example using this term: Ioannis Kokkoris, 'Purchase Price Fixing: A Per Se Infringement?' 28 European Competition Law Review (2007) 473; Ezrachi, *EU Competition Law: An Analytical Guide to the Leading Cases* [2012], p. 120, 135-137; Ezrachi 'Buying Alliances and Input Price Fixing: In Search of a European Enforcement Standard' (2012). On the other hand, other authors use the term "buying groups" to refer to these buyers' association mechanism, see: Carstensen 'Buyer Cartels Versus Buying Groups: Legal Distinctions, Competitive Realities, and Antitrust Policy' (2010).

1538 "An economy of scale exists whenever the cost of some input decliens as volume increases. *The result of economies of scale is that the cost of production decreases on a per unit basis as the amount being produced increases*", Hovenkamp, [2011], p. 90 (emphasis in original).

obtaining lower purchasing prices, reducing transaction costs and/or buying larger quantities of input[1539]. Both types share a commonality, as discussed by Advocate General Jacob's in *Albany*: the larger the amount of participants in the cartel or alliance, the larger the accumulated buyer power[1540]. However, there is a striking difference between them which is also reflected in their legal treatment. Buyers' cartels are anti-competitive devices made to eliminate competition between their members as buyers, exploit suppliers, and may also be a recourse for reducing competition intensity in downstream markets and, therefore, are regarded as object restrictions of competition. Buying alliances are mostly efficiency enhancing and enjoy a presumption of legality, being treated as possible infringements of competition by effect, depending on their impact in upstream and/or downstream competition[1541].

800. The Guidelines on Horizontal Agreements identify several theories of harm or competitive concerns raised by purchasing agreements in general leading to exploitative and/or exclusionary effects on competition in either the upstream and/or downstream, an idea that is also supported in this work when discussing the dualistic effect of buyer power. As a main rule, and also for buyer power exercise as a whole, purchasing alliances may raise anti-competitive risks of a general nature such as "increased prices, reduced output, product quality or variety, or innovation, market allocation, or anti-competitive foreclosure of other possible purchasers"[1542]. Furthermore and as a particularized theory of harm for concerted behaviour, *purchasing agreements may be used to reduce competition among purchasers to coordinate their behaviour, particularly regarding price competition in the downstream market* in part now generated by the commonality of costs and exchange of information[1543]. This also implies that joint purchasing agreements may be used to exclude other buyers' access to the most efficient suppliers[1544] or to reduce technological innovation if the buyers select the same supplier[1545]. Additionally, the Commission fears that when the purchasing agreement pools substantial buyer power *and* downstream market power, the buyer power benefits may not be passed to the

1539 Ritter and Braun, [2004], p. 233; Hans-Theo Normann, Jürgen Rösch and Luis Manuel Schultz, 'Do Buyer Groups Facilitate Collusion?' 109 Journal of Economic Behavior & Organization (2015), p. 73.

1540 "By contrast, sectoral funds have an obvious interest in maintaining a high level of affiliation. More affiliated persons means, for example, greater economies of scale as regards administrative costs, more buying power on the investment markets and a more advantageous spreading of risks" in Opinion of Advocate General Jacobs of 28 January 1999 in Judgment in *Albany*, C-67/96, EU:C:1999:28, para. 452.

1541 Communication from the Commission — Guidelines on the applicability of Article 101 of the Treaty on the Functioning of the European Union to horizontal co-operation agreements [2011] OJ C 11/1, para. 194.

1542 Communication from the Commission — Guidelines on the applicability of Article 101 of the Treaty on the Functioning of the European Union to horizontal co-operation agreements [2011] OJ C 11/1, para. 200.

1543 Communication from the Commission — Guidelines on the applicability of Article 101 of the Treaty on the Functioning of the European Union to horizontal co-operation agreements [2011] OJ C 11/1, para. 201. Faull, Nikpay and Taylor, [2014], paras. 7.367-7.368.

1544 Communication from the Commission — Guidelines on the applicability of Article 101 of the Treaty on the Functioning of the European Union to horizontal co-operation agreements [2011] OJ C 11/1, para. 203.

1545 Carstensen 'Buyer Cartels Versus Buying Groups: Legal Distinctions, Competitive Realities, and Antitrust Policy' (2010), p. 33.

consumer, a concern that is in line with the hourglass shape argument[1546]. With regard to exploiting suppliers, the Commission acknowledges that if parties "have a significant degree of market power on the purchasing market [buying power] there is a risk that they may force suppliers to reduce the range or quality of products they produce"[1547], which is a concern regarding the withholding effect of monopsony power.

801. However, the Guidelines on Horizontal Agreements also set a "safety zone" when indicating that a buying agreement is unlikely to raise competition concerns if the parties belonging to it have a combined market share not exceeding 15% on the purchasing market or markets as well as a combined market share not exceeding 15% on the selling market or markets, because it is unlikely that substantial buyer market power exists[1548]. Therefore, the Commission recognizes that a buying agreement can be both anti-competitive and efficient, depending on its form, aims and content. What is unclear from the Guidelines on Horizontal Agreements is whether a buyers' cartel may benefit from this safety zone presumption. From the wording employed[1549], though, it can be concluded that this *presumption of substantial market power existence* applies for both buyers' cartels and buying alliances alliance, but the analysis of the competitiveness of the agreements based on its effects likely to render a different outcome.

802. Furthermore, the Guidelines on Horizontal Agreements *do not expressly differentiate a buying alliance from a buyers' cartel*, although they offer some indications concerning which circumstances are likely to make a purchasing agreement a buyers' cartel fixing purchasing conditions and an object restriction of competition[1550]. The main indicator of a collusive purchasing agreement is when its design facilitates coordination on the retailing market, which can be carried out if the outcome allows parties to achieve a high degree of common-

---

1546 Communication from the Commission — Guidelines on the applicability of Article 101 of the Treaty on the Functioning of the European Union to horizontal co-operation agreements [2011] OJ C 11/1, para. 201.

1547 Communication from the Commission — Guidelines on the applicability of Article 101 of the Treaty on the Functioning of the European Union to horizontal co-operation agreements [2011] OJ C 11/1, para. 202. See also raising this point Carstensen 'Buyer Cartels Versus Buying Groups: Legal Distinctions, Competitive Realities, and Antitrust Policy' (2010), p. 30.

1548 Communication from the Commission — Guidelines on the applicability of Article 101 of the Treaty on the Functioning of the European Union to horizontal co-operation agreements [2011] OJ C 11/1, para. 208. Cf with the more lenient approach in US antitrust law in which a buying alliance has been deemed as being in a "safety zone" if the group represents less than 35% of sales in the *downstream* market in US Department of Justice and Federal Trade Commission '*Statements of Antitrust Enforcement Policy in Health Care*' (1996).

1549 "However, in most cases it is unlikely that market power exists if *the parties to the joint purchasing arrangement* have a combined market share not exceeding 15 % on the purchasing market or markets as well as a combined market share not exceeding 15 % on the selling market or markets. In any event, if the parties' combined market shares do not exceed 15 % on both the purchasing and the selling market or markets, it is likely that the conditions of Article 101(3) TFEU are fulfilled", being a purchasing agreement a general category that engulfs both buying alliances and buyers' cartels, Communication from the Commission — Guidelines on the applicability of Article 101 of the Treaty on the Functioning of the European Union to horizontal co-operation agreements [2011] OJ C 11/1, para. 208 (emphasis added).

1550 Communication from the Commission — Guidelines on the applicability of Article 101 of the Treaty on the Functioning of the European Union to horizontal co-operation agreements [2011] OJ C 11/1, para. 205.

ality of costs[1551]. This can also be facilitated if there is an exchange of sensitive or confidential information among the parties[1552]. Also, a collusive outcome is likely to happen if parties have a significant proportion of their variable costs in the downstream market where they compete against each other, as in the retail sector[1553]. This is the case because their costs as buyers are similar which means that their downstream prices would tend to be also very similar.

803. Thus, the lack of more precise indications concerning the differences between collusive and non-collusive purchasing agreements and their legal treatment justifies discussing these aspects in detail, as I do in the following sections.

A. Buyers' cartel fixing purchasing conditions

804. In accordance with Article 101.1(a) TFEU any agreement that imposes purchasing prices or other purchasing conditions, regardless of whether they are exploitative or not, constitutes a violation of competition law[1554]. Therefore, a joint purchasing agreement that fixes prices, limits output or allocates markets for the parties *is a buyers' cartel* and *not a buying alliance*[1555], and which in accordance with the limited Commission's practice it accrues to an object restriction of competition, as I discuss below[1556]. Additionally, in a buyers' cartel their members become price makers and not price takers to the detriment of their suppliers, who are forced to sell their input at prices lower than they would have been absent the coordination[1557].

a. What are and how buyers' cartels operate and affect competition?

805. Exploitative price-fixing buyers' cartels - like sellers' cartels – are conceived to increase their members' profits. This is done by eliminating competition among them and agglutinating purchasing power that can be used exploitatively vis-à-vis suppliers by reducing the purchasing price the cartel pays

---

1551 Communication from the Commission — Guidelines on the applicability of Article 101 of the Treaty on the Functioning of the European Union to horizontal co-operation agreements [2011] OJ C 11/1, para. 213; Faull, Nikpay and Taylor, [2014], para. 7.388.

1552 Communication from the Commission Guidelines on the applicability of Article 101 of the Treaty on the Functioning of the European Union to horizontal co-operation agreements [2011] OJ C11/1, para. 215 and para. 224 example 4.

1553 Communication from the Commission — Guidelines on the applicability of Article 101 of the Treaty on the Functioning of the European Union to horizontal co-operation agreements [2011] OJ C 11/1, para. 214.

1554 Communication from the Commission — Guidelines on the applicability of Article 101 of the Treaty on the Functioning of the European Union to horizontal co-operation agreements [2011] OJ C 11/1, para. 205 to 206.

1555 See the definition of a cartel by the Commission in Commission Notice on Immunity from fines and reduction of fines in cartel cases [2006] OJ C 298/17, para. 1; Faull, Nikpay and Taylor, [2014], para. 7.375.

1556 Commission Decision of 20 October 2004 relating to a proceeding under Article 81(1) of the EC Treaty (Case COMP/C.38.238/B.2) — *Raw tobacco — Spain* [2007] OJ L 102/14; Commission Decision of 20 October 2005 relating to a proceeding under Article 81(1) of the EC Treaty (Case COMP/C.38.281/B.2 — *Raw tobacco Italy*) [2006] OJ L 353/45, taken from the unabridged version.

1557 Blair and Harrison, [2010], p. 157.

when compared to the situations in which buyers competed for an input. In addition to exploiting suppliers, purchasing price fixing may also have related effects, such as exclude other buyers from the market, reduce output by restricting purchases and negatively affect variety and innovation[1558]. A buyers' cartel may additionally have *exploitative effects in the downstream market* as its members can use the cartel to restrict competition as retailers and facilitate collusion in the output market[1559]. Exclusionary buyers' cartels, however, do not usually involve a price decrease but the opposite, they tend to involve overpaying for an input as it discussed in the US antitrust law case *Reid Bros. Logging Co. v Ketchikan Pulp Co.* analyzed in chapter 6, section §IV[1560].

806. Traditionally, buyers' cartels are formed by undertakings part of private or competitive markets. Nevertheless, it is also possible for public buyers under the scrutiny of public procurement law to coordinate their purchasing behaviour and exert their buyer market power. As noted by Sánchez Graells, this could occur, for example, when public purchases are made by few entities aggregating demand through central purchasing bodies or other institutional collaborative forms, like dynamic purchasing systems or framework agreements, or by agglutinating demand through *ad hoc* forms of collaboration, if harmonization or cost-saving policies are implemented by public policy makers[1561]. Also, the more demand aggregation is fostered, the more likely public buyers will be incentivized to collude as private buyers would[1562]. However, coordination in these types of markets among buyers might be harder to achieve because of 'jurisdictional' limitations: i.e.: each contracting authority is only competent to acquire goods in its own region and political pressure from different parties may make coordination among different entities less likely.

807. In addition to fixing purchasing prices, buyers' cartels are usually accompanied by other types of practices or contractual clauses as noted by Doyle and Han[1563], and as confirmed in *Raw Tobacco Italy,* such as purchasing quotas[1564]. These additional clauses are aimed at preventing cartel members from 'cheating' and obtaining their purchases outside of the cartel and, thus, get an even lower input price. Among

---

1558 Communication from the Commission — Guidelines on the applicability of Article 101 of the Treaty on the Functioning of the European Union to horizontal co-operation agreements [2011] OJ C 11/1, para. 210. See also: Carstensen 'Buyer Cartels Versus Buying Groups: Legal Distinctions, Competitive Realities, and Antitrust Policy' (2010), p. 21.

1559 Chris Doyle and Martijn A Han, 'Cartelization Through Buyer Groups' 44 Review of Industrial Organization (2014) 255, p. 257.

1560 *Reid Bros. Logging Co. v. Ketchikan Pulp Co.*, 699 F.2d 1292 (9th Cir. 1983), at 1297-98.

1561 Sánchez Graells, *Public Procurement and the EU Competition Rules* [2015], p. 75.

1562 For a discussion on demand aggregation in the Directive 2014/24 see, *inter alia*: Hamer (2014); Herrera Anchustegui 'Centralizing Public Procurement and Competitiveness in Directive 2014/24' (2015); Sánchez Graells and Herrera Anchustegui, 'Impact of Public Procurement Aggregation on Competition. Risks, Rationale and Justification for the Rules in Directive 2014/24' [2016]; Vaquero García [2016].

1563 Doyle and Han (2014), p. 270-271.

1564 Commission Decision of 20 October 2005 relating to a proceeding under Article 81(1) of the EC Treaty (Case COMP/C.38.281/B.2 — *Raw tobacco Italy*) [2006] OJ L 353/45.

these stability clauses the agreements typically accompany provisions such as exclusive dealing clauses, minimum purchase quotas, and rebate schemes.

808. Alternatively, or along with these additional clauses, buyers may instead of fixing purchasing prices opt to *divide markets horizontally creating 'monopsony' markets for each cartel member*. The effect of the cartel is also exploitative because competition is eliminated in the designated geographic market and the legal treatment follows a similar approach as input price fixing; they are forbidden by Article 101(1) (c) TFEU[1565], and found to be object restrictions of competition by the Commission's practice and by analogy to selling side cases[1566].

b. Cartels fixing purchasing prices as object restrictions of competition

809. The anti-competitive nature of buyers' cartels fixing purchasing price as either object or effect restrictions of competition is an element that this far has not been clarified by the case law. However, and as I mentioned above, in my view, cartels fixing purchasing prices ought to be considered as *object restrictions of competition even absent substantial buyer power*[1567]. This proposal is based on several grounds: the anti-competitive nature of the conduct, the Commission's practice, the Opinion of Advocate General Jacobs in *AOK-Bundesverband and Others*[1568], the literature and the analog case law for selling side cases. In the following, I discuss why buyers' cartels fixing purchasing prices should be treated as object restrictions.

810. The most obvious and important reason to treat buyers' cartels fixing purchasing prices as object restriction is the *blatant anti-competitive nature of these practices*[1569]. The aim of these agreements is to disrupt the competitive price formation, which is the core of competition as a process under an ordoliberal competition policy, and which adversely affects the competition structure upstream and downstream. As purchase price fixing alters the dynamic of price formation it follows that this type of coordination "can be regarded, by their very nature, as being harmful to the proper functioning of normal competi-

1565 The same approach is followed in the US as noted by Blair and Harrison in Blair and Harrison, [2010], p. 162-163.

1566 See, *inter alia*: Judgment of 17 October 1972 in *Vereeniging van Cementhandelaren v Commission*, C-8/72, EU:C:1972:84, paras. 19-25; Judgment of 11 July 1989 in *Belasco and Others v Commission*, C-246/86, EU:C:1989:301, para. 10-15; Judgment of 15 July 1970 in *Chemiefarma v Commission*, C-41/69, EU:C:1970:71.

1567 See also supporting this interpretation of the Commission's practice: Ezrachi 'Buying Alliances and Input Price Fixing: In Search of a European Enforcement Standard' (2012), p. 58.

1568 Opinion of Advocate General Jacobs of 22 May 2003 in Judgment of 16 March 2004 in *AOK-Bundesverband and Others*, joined cases C-264/01, C-306/01, C-354/01 and C-355/01, EU:C:2003:304 [2003].

1569 See also stressing that "[h]orizontal price fixing would be regarded by most people as the most blatant and undesirable of restrictive trade practices", Whish and Bailey, *Competition law* [2012], p. 522.

tion"[1570], and which is presumed to have anti-competitive effects which makes unnecessary to demonstrate any actual or likely anti-competitive effects on the market[1571]. Hence, if anything, purchasing price fixing prima facie constitutes a prime example of a hardcore object restriction of competition.

811. The nature of buyers' cartel fixing purchasing practices as object restrictions of competition has been explicitly declared by the Commission in two decisions: *Raw Tobacco Spain*[1572], and *Raw Tobacco Italy*[1573], both related to agricultural markets[1574].

812. In *Raw Tobacco Spain*[1575] the Commission found two infringements in a sellers' vs. buyers' cartels that were involved in the production and purchasing of raw tobacco, respectively[1576]. Concerning the buyers' cartel the Commission found that an agreement among four major Spanish processors of raw tobacco through an inter-professional organization had the object or effect of fixing the (maximum) average delivery price for each variety of raw tobacco (all qualities) and to share out the quantities of each variety of raw tobacco that were to be bought.

1570 Commission staff working document - Guidance on restrictions of competition "by object" for the purpose of defining which agreements may benefit from the De Minimis Notice, accompanying communication from the Commission - Notice on agreements of minor importance which do not appreciably restrict competition under Article 101(1) of the Treaty on the Functioning of the European Union (De Minimis Notice), [C(2014) 4136 final], Brussels, 25.6.2014, SWD (2014) 198 final, p.3.

1571 Judgment of 11 September 2014 in *CB v Commission*, C-67/13 P, EU:C:2014:2204, para. 51.

1572 Commission Decision of 20 October 2004 relating to a proceeding under Article 81(1) of the EC Treaty (Case COMP/C.38.238/B.2) — *Raw tobacco — Spain* [2007] OJ L 102/14, taken from the unabridged version, para. 275.

1573 Commission Decision of 20 October 2005 relating to a proceeding under Article 81(1) of the EC Treaty (Case COMP/C.38.281/B.2 — *Raw tobacco Italy*) [2006] OJ L 353/45, Article 1, and para. 285. See also discussing this case from a buyer's oriented perspective: Petit, *The IEEE-SA Revised Patent Policy and its Definition of "Reasonable" Rates: A Transatlatic Antitrust Divide?*, p. 15-16. See also: Kokkoris 'Purchase Price Fixing: A Per Se Infringement?' (2007), p. 483-484; Whish and Bailey, *Competition law* [2012], p. 528; Ezrachi [2014], p. 149.

1574 These two cases, *Raw tobacco Spain* and *Raw tobacco Italy* have in common with *French beef – France Coop de Bétail* (case which I discuss concerning buyer power limitation in chapter 10) that they constitute the three buyer power cases in EU competition law in which the Commission imposed a fine to undertakings in the agricultural sector, as pointed out by van Doorn, in van Doorn, p. 141, which reinforces the argument put forth in this study that food retailing and agricultural markets are susceptible of exercise of buyer power. This is also confirmed by the relatively significant amount of cases dealing with buying cartels in the production of milk, for example in Greece, Bulgaria and Lithuania as discussed in European Competition Network (2012), paras. 97.101, p. 53- 55. In Greece, the NCA found that the five largest diary companies had entered into a cartel fixing purchasing prices for raw milk, allocated supply sources and exchanged price information. The Greek NCA found that these breaches were object restrictions of competition and set a fine of more than €78 million. In Bulgaria, the NCA fined a group of dairies in 2007 after an investigation also determining the fixation of purchasing prices and exchange of information in a buyer cartel on the basis of pure national law. Also, these diaries operated in a downstream cartel by imposing a minimum price for white cheese, which reinforces the argument presented in this study concerning the hourglass shape and the capacity of powerful buyers to affect downstream markets.

1575 Commission Decision of 20 October 2004 relating to a proceeding under Article 81(1) of the EC Treaty (Case COMP/C.38.238/B.2) — *Raw tobacco — Spain* [2007] OJ L 102/14, taken from the unabridged version, para. 275. See also considering this case as a buyers' cartel: Kokkoris 'Purchase Price Fixing: A Per Se Infringement?' (2007), p. 483; Whish and Bailey, *Competition law* [2015], p. 563; van Doorn, p. 141-142.

1576 Commission Decision of 20 October 2004 relating to a proceeding under Article 81(1) of the EC Treaty (Case COMP/C.38.238/B.2) — *Raw tobacco — Spain* [2007] OJ L 102/14, taken from the unabridged version, para. 2.

813. The Commission found that the tobacco buyers had agreed to fix each year the (maximum) average delivery price of each variety of raw tobacco from 1996 to 2001, and additionally, from 1999 to 2001 to share out the quantities of each variety of raw tobacco to be bought and set price brackets per quality grade of each variety of raw tobacco and additional conditions[1577]. The Commission held that fixing by a (maximum) average delivery price of each of the raw tobacco varieties the processors managed to align as closely as possible the final prices paid to the producers, and reduce them for their own benefit to a level below that which would result from the free interplay of competition[1578]. Price fixing was deemed to be an object restriction of competition as there was "no need to take account of the actual effects of an agreement once it appears that its aim is to prevent, restrict or distort competition within the common market", even though preliminary evidence found that input prices stabilized and fell at least in 1998[1579]. Therefore, even if the cartel reduced the prices paid for the input (like bargaining power would), the cartel was prohibited.

814. A similar approach finding purchase price fixing as an object restriction of competition is *Raw Tobacco Italy*[1580]. In this case, the Commission declared an agreement among four major Italian processors of raw tobacco fixing the trading conditions for the purchase of raw tobacco in Italy as *an object restriction of competition under Article 101(1) (a) TFEU*[1581]. The agreement, which lasted more than 6 years, included several clauses which, *inter alia*, set common purchase prices to be paid to tobacco producers, allocated quantities of supply and demand and coordinated purchasing behaviour[1582]. The tobacco processors' agreement *not only affected competition upstream by fixing purchasing prices but served to coordinate surplus and pricing policies in the downstream market*[1583], further increasing the competitive harm as if the buyer/seller cartel would integrate the undertakings in the form of *an hourglass shaped buyer*. Concerning purchasing price fixing, the cartel members agreed on setting a

1577 Commission Decision of 20 October 2004 relating to a proceeding under Article 81(1) of the EC Treaty (Case COMP/C.38.238/B.2) — *Raw tobacco — Spain* [2007] OJ L 102/14, taken from the unabridged version, para. 276.

1578 Commission Decision of 20 October 2004 relating to a proceeding under Article 81(1) of the EC Treaty (Case COMP/C.38.238/B.2) — *Raw tobacco — Spain* [2007] OJ L 102/14, taken from the unabridged version, para. 301.

1579 Commission Decision of 20 October 2004 relating to a proceeding under Article 81(1) of the EC Treaty (Case COMP/C.38.238/B.2) — *Raw tobacco — Spain* [2007] OJ L 102/14, taken from the unabridged version, para. 314. Also stressing the fact that the case was an object restriction of competition Kokkoris 'Purchase Price Fixing: A Per Se Infringement?' (2007), p. 483.

1580 Commission Decision of 20 October 2005 relating to a proceeding under Article 81(1) of the EC Treaty (Case COMP/C.38.281/B.2 — *Raw tobacco Italy*) [2006] OJ L 353/45.

1581 Commission Decision of 20 October 2005 relating to a proceeding under Article 81(1) of the EC Treaty (Case COMP/C.38.281/B.2 — Raw tobacco Italy) [2006] OJ L 353/45, Article 1, and para. 285.

1582 Commission Decision of 20 October 2005 relating to a proceeding under Article 81(1) of the EC Treaty (Case COMP/C.38.281/B.2 — *Raw tobacco Italy*) [2006] OJ L 353/45, taken from the unabridged version, para. 1 and 238.

1583 Commission Decision of 20 October 2005 relating to a proceeding under Article 81(1) of the EC Treaty (Case COMP/C.38.281/B.2 — *Raw tobacco Italy*) [2006] OJ L 353/45, taken from the unabridged version, para. 240 to 255.

maximum price limit to pay at delivery depending on the quality and variety of tobacco[1584]. This was done by single transactions between tobacco producers and buyers as well as on bids for tobacco auctions, taking the form of bid-rigging[1585]. However, other times it was agreed that processors would buy as a centralized buyer at an agreed price as confirmed by the Decision[1586].

815. In some important passages for the legal treatment of buyers' cartels as object restrictions of competition, the Commission held that purchase price fixing had *a dual effect in the upstream and downstream market*, confirming the need for a dualistic approach in buyer power cases, as price fixing caused a detriment to suppliers and the imposition of joint purchasing prices and quotas affected consumers directly in the downstream market when holding that:

> (280) [...] The impact of this aspect of the infringement on competition was *significant as purchase price is a fundamental aspect of the competitive conduct* of any undertaking operating in a processing business and is also, by definition, capable of affecting the behaviour of the same companies in any other market in which they compete, including downstream markets. [...]
>
> (281) By fixing volume quotas and allocating suppliers, the processors were prevented from competing for market shares and might have gradually succeeded in preventing or limiting the increase of purchase prices [...]. In other words, allocation of suppliers is a strategy to prevent price increases as a supplier allocated to a specific processor would not be able to sell to other processors and would find itself price-constrained by its allocated processor. In addition, by fixing purchasing quotas, the processors limited and controlled the suppliers' production and the production of their competitors.
>
> (282) By doing so, the processors' purchasing cartel had the potential to affect the producers' willingness to generate output and thus reduce global tobacco production to the ultimate detriment of consumers[1587].

1584 Commission Decision of 20 October 2005 relating to a proceeding under Article 81(1) of the EC Treaty (Case COMP/C.38.281/B.2 — *Raw tobacco Italy*) [2006] OJ L 353/45, taken from the unabridged version, para. 243.

1585 Commission Decision of 20 October 2005 relating to a proceeding under Article 81(1) of the EC Treaty (Case COMP/C.38.281/B.2 — *Raw tobacco Italy*) [2006] OJ L 353/45, taken from the unabridged version, para. 252. For some discussion on bid rigging in buyer cartels, see: Blair and Harrison, [2010] p. 2-3 and 86-88.

1586 Commission Decision of 20 October 2005 relating to a proceeding under Article 81(1) of the EC Treaty (Case COMP/C.38.281/B.2 — *Raw tobacco Italy*) [2006] OJ L 353/45, taken from the unabridged version, para. 248.

1587 Commission Decision of 20 October 2005 relating to a proceeding under Article 81(1) of the EC Treaty (Case COMP/C.38.281/B.2 — *Raw tobacco Italy*) [2006] OJ L 353/45, taken from the unabridged version, para. 280 to 282 (emphasis added).

816. Therefore, the Commission concluded that the agreements between tobacco processors had "by their *very nature the object to restrict competition* within the meaning of Article [101] (1) as they shelter processors and producers of raw tobacco in Italy from full exposure to market forces"[1588]. This was irrespective of whether the agreement created or strengthened buyer power for the tobacco producers[1589]. Also, the Commission stressed the fact that purchasing price fixing may also have an impact on the output decision of suppliers and therefore imply or generate some degree of scarcity. Interestingly, the Commission dismissed some allegations claiming that the cartel and price fixing was entered into to counteract other wrongdoings and market power by intermediaries in the tobacco industry, which appears to confirm that in EU competition law the creation of illegal buyer power would not be allowed even if to oppose illegal market power[1590]. Lastly, the Commission concluded that there were neither relevant arguments nor effects that could exempt the agreement under Article 101(3) TFEU[1591].

817. An interesting case that also helps to illustrate the anti-competitive nature of buyers' cartels by object is *AOK-Bundesverband and Others*[1592]. In this case the CJEU resorted not to apply competition law to that an agreement among groups of sickness funds fixing maximum amounts corresponding to the upper limit of the price of medicinal products is outside of the scope of application of competition law because *these bodies do not constitute undertakings*[1593], largely based on their exclusively social function based on the principle of solidarity and which implies that purchasing was not an economic

---

1588 Commission Decision of 20 October 2005 relating to a proceeding under Article 81(1) of the EC Treaty (Case COMP/C.38.281/B.2 — *Raw tobacco Italy*) [2006] OJ L 353/45, taken from the unabridged version, para. 285 (emphasis added).

1589 The Decision does not have any relevant analysis if the agreement created or strengthened substantial buyer power.

1590 "Serious infringements of Article [101] (1) of the Treaty, such as those described in this Decision, cannot be justified by the aim to counteract third parties' allegedly illegal conduct. It is clearly not the task of undertakings to take steps contrary to Article [101] (1) of the Treaty to counteract behaviour which, rightly or wrongly, they regard as illegal and/or contrary to their own interests", in Commission Decision of 20 October 2005 relating to a proceeding under Article [101](1) of the EC Treaty (Case COMP/C.38.281/B.2 — *Raw tobacco Italy*) [2006] OJ L 353/45, para. 289.

1591 Commission Decision of 20 October 2005 relating to a proceeding under Article 81(1) of the EC Treaty (Case COMP/C.38.281/B.2 — *Raw tobacco Italy*) [2006] OJ L 353/45, taken from the unabridged version, para. 292.

1592 Judgment of 16 March 2004 in *AOK-Bundesverband and Others*, joined cases C-264/01, C-306/01, C-354/01 and C-355/01, EU:C:2004:150.

1593 Judgment of 16 March 2004 in *AOK-Bundesverband and Others*, joined cases C-264/01, C-306/01, C-354/01 and C-355/01, EU:C:2004:150, ruling of the Court page I – 2548, and para. 55. In the US Kirkwood has recently suggested granting the Federal Government some negotiation capacity to concentrate purchases of medicines as part of the Medicare program to generate public buyer power. See: Kirkwood, *Buyer Power and Healthcare Prices*.

activity[1594]. However, the Opinion of Advocate General Jacobs suggested considering purchase price fixing as an object restriction[1595].

818. As the Court found these sickness funds to not be undertakings, it did not discuss whether the purchase price fixing constituted an infringement of competition, although it did not overrule such possibility. Nonetheless, the Opinion of Advocate General Jacobs did refer to this issue who held that:

> It seems clear to me that, whether or not the funds are, as a matter of national law, the purchasers of medicinal products, they are *engaged in a fixing of trading conditions within the meaning of Article [101](1)(a) when they coordinate, by setting fixed amounts, the maximum level of contribution* which they will make towards the cost of those products. The respondents are also correct, in my opinion, to characterise such a practice as *fixing the purchase price* for medicinal products[1596].

819. Advocate General Jacobs concluded that "an agreement or decision on the part of buyers to fix the purchase price on a given market *must be understood to have as its object to restrict competition*"[1597], having the "*potential to suppress the price of purchased* products to *below the competitive level*, with negative consequences for the *supply side* of the relevant market"[1598], which is in my view a clear reference to the exploitative effects of buyer market pow-

1594 The CJEU based its reasoning on the fact that the sickness funds were not in competition to each other and operated in the management of the social security system based on a solidarity scheme and fulfilled an exclusively social function, being entirely non-profitmaking and the funds had to provide the same services/prices to all their beneficiaries irrespective of their own contribution. See: Judgment of 16 March 2004 in *AOK-Bundesverband and Others*, joined cases C-264/01, C-306/01, C-354/01 and C-355/01, EU:C:2004:150, paras. 52-55. Concerning the principle of solidarity see: Judgment of 17 February 1993 in *Poucet and Pistre v AGF and Cancava*, joined cases C-159/91 and C-160/91, EU:C:1993:63, para. 15 and 18; and Judgment of 22 January 2002 in *Cisal*, C-218/00, EU:C:2002:36, para. 43 to 46; Judgment of 5 March 2009 in *Kattner Stahlbau*, C-350/07, EU:C:2009:127. Also some literature dealing with this principle see, *inter alia*: Catherine Barnard, 'EU Citizenship and the Principle of Solidarity' in Michael Dougan and Eleanor Spaventa (eds), *Social welfare and EU law* (Hart Pub. 2005); Timothy Stoltzfus Jost, Diane Dawson and André den Exter, 'The Role of Competition in Health Care: A Western European Perspective' 31 Journal of Health Politics, Policy and Law (2006) 687; Malcom Ross, 'Promoting Solidarity: From Public Services to a European Model of Competition?' 44 Common Market Law Review (2007) 1057; Nina Boeger, 'Solidarity and EC competition law' 32 European Law Review (2007) 319; Markus Krajewski, Ulla Neergaard and Johan van de Gronden, *The Changing Legal Framework for Services of General Interest in Europe: Between Competition and Solidarity* (Asser 2009); Sánchez Graells, *Public Procurement and the EU Competition Rules* [2011], p. 133-134.

1595 Opinion of Advocate General Jacobs of 22 May 2003 in Judgment of 16 March 2004 in *AOK-Bundesverband and Others*, joined cases C-264/01, C-306/01, C-354/01 and C-355/01, EU:C:2003:304 [2003]. See also confirming this interpretation: Ezrachi [2014], p. 149.

1596 Opinion of Advocate General Jacobs of 22 May 2003 in Judgment of 16 March 2004 in *AOK-Bundesverband and Others*, joined cases C-264/01, C-306/01, C-354/01 and C-355/01, EU:C:2003:304 [2003], para. 68 (emphasis added).

1597 Opinion of Advocate General Jacobs of 22 May 2003 in Judgment of 16 March 2004 in *AOK-Bundesverband and Others*, joined cases C-264/01, C-306/01, C-354/01 and C-355/01, EU:C:2003:304 [2003], para. 70 (emphasis added).

1598 Opinion of Advocate General Jacobs of 22 May 2003 in Judgment of 16 March 2004 in *AOK-Bundesverband and Others*, joined cases C-264/01, C-306/01, C-354/01 and C-355/01, EU:C:2003:304 [2003], para. 70. See also supporting this interpretation: Ezrachi, *EU Competition Law: An Analytical Guide to the Leading Cases* [2012] p. 134; and Ezrachi 'Buying Alliances and Input Price Fixing: In Search of a European Enforcement Standard' (2012), p. 56.

er. Nevertheless, Advocate General Jacobs concluded that even if the fixing of maximum purchasing prices is captured by Article 101(1)(a) TFEU as an object restriction if competition law were to be applied, it was not in this case based on the State action doctrine or the application of Article 106(2) TFEU exemption. Neither of these solutions was ultimately adopted by the CJEU in an exceptional case of not following the Opinion of the Advocate General, but reaching a similar conclusion.

820. A different reading of the case shows two problems that are outside the scope of this study and related to exploitative abuses of buyer market power. Firstly as highlighted by Sánchez Graells, the current definition of economic activity and, consequently, the concept of undertaking is narrow and overlooks all procuring entities that do not carry out a subsequent downstream economic activity[1599] or carry out their purchases in a solidarity system fulfilling an exclusively social function, being excluded from the application of competition law[1600]. This means that buyer cartels by contracting authorities are permitted even if their market effects are as pernicious as cartels by undertakings. Secondly, despite recognizing the competition problems generated by the exercise of buyer power by the state in procurement markets, the current legal regime limits itself to exclude the application of competition law and does not offer alternatives to control or palliate this problem[1601]. These are issues that I acknowledge as ripe for further research.

821. Furthermore, the legal treatment of buyers' cartels fixing prices as object restrictions of competition finds good support on an uncontroversial and straightforward analogic interpretation of seller side cases, as also supported by Advocate General Jacobs who held that "[i]n my view, therefore, they [buyers' cartels] should be subject to the same strict control applied by Community competition law to supply cartels"[1602]. Indeed, the case law has found that price fixing is an object restriction of competition as confirmed in *Vereeniging van Cementhandelaren v Commission*[1603], *Belasco and Others v Commission*[1604], or *Chemiefarma v Commission*[1605], as some examples. An

1599 Judgment of 4 March 2003, *Fenin v Commission*, T-319/99, ECR, EU:T:2003:50, para. 36; Judgment of 11 July in *FENIN v Commission*, C-205/03 P, EU:C:2006:453, para. 26; Judgment of 12 December 2006, *SELEX Sistemi Integrati v Commission*, T-155/04, ECR, EU:T:2006:387, para. 65; Judgment of 26 March 2009 in *Selex Sistemi Integrati v Commission*, C-113/07 P, EU:C:2009:191, para. 102 and 114.

1600 Sánchez Graells, *Public Procurement and the EU Competition Rules* [2011], p. 115-187.

1601 For a discussion on the law and economics of buyer power in public procurement markets through aggregated purchasing see: Sánchez Graells and Herrera Anchustegui, 'Impact of Public Procurement Aggregation on Competition. Risks, Rationale and Justification for the Rules in Directive 2014/24' [2016].

1602 Opinion of Advocate General Jacobs of 22 May 2003 in Judgment of 16 March 2004 in *AOK-Bundesverband and Others*, joined cases C-264/01, C-306/01, C-354/01 and C-355/01, EU:C:2003:304 [2003], para. 70.

1603 Judgment of 17 October 1972 in *Vereeniging van Cementhandelaren v Commission*, C-8/72, EU:C:1972:84, paras. 19-25.

1604 Judgment of 11 July 1989 in *Belasco and Others v Commission*, C-246/86, EU:C:1989:301, para. 10-15.

1605 Judgment of 15 July 1970 in *Chemiefarma v Commission*, C-41/69, EU:C:1970:71.

analogic mirror application of the object nature to naked purchase price fixing is justified because, like in seller cases, purchase price fixing disrupts the core mechanism of price formation.

822. Also, in the literature there is consensus concerning the character of object restrictions of these types of concerted buyer conducts, as remarked by Whish and Bailey[1606], but not a per se infringement as suggested by Kokkoris[1607]. The distinction is important and the use of per se is misleading in EU competition law, because even if an agreement is qualified as an object restriction of competition it may theoretically satisfy the requirements of Article 101(3) TFEU[1608]. Also, as Ezrachi puts it, considering purchasing price fixing as an object restriction of competition "does not determine the outcome of the analysis, but rather its starting point"[1609].

823. Furthermore, most buyers' cartels fixing purchasing prices are not only object restrictions of competition but also constitute hardcore horizontal agreements and, therefore, are outside of the scope of application of the research and development block exemption regulation[1610], and the specialization block exemption regulation[1611]. Furthermore, in accordance with the case law[1612] object restrictions of competition do not benefit from the *De Minimis* exemption[1613].

824. Lastly, in the US an even stricter general approach to buyers' cartels as per se violation of antitrust law has been adopted for some cases[1614], as confirmed in

1606 Whish and Bailey, *Competition law* [2012], p. 604.

1607 Kokkoris refers to this as object restriction but also as a "per se infringement", in my opinion erroneously in Kokkoris 'Purchase Price Fixing: A Per Se Infringement?' (2007). An alternative view could be that the use of per se in his article resembles the idea of "object" restriction, but this is still inaccurate.

1608 Judgment of 15 July 1994 in *Matra Hachette v Commission*, T-17/93, EU:T:1994:89 [1994], para. 85.

1609 Blair and Harrison, [2010], p. 113; Ezrachi 'Buying Alliances and Input Price Fixing: In Search of a European Enforcement Standard' (2012), p. 58.

1610 Article 5 of the Commission Regulation (EU) No 1217/2010 of 14 December 2010 on the application of Article 101(3) of the Treaty on the Functioning of the European Union to certain categories of research and development agreements [2010] OJ L 335/36.

1611 Article 4 of the Commission Regulation (EU) No 1218/2010 of 14 December 2010 on the application of Article 101(3) of the Treaty on the Functioning of the European Union to certain categories of specialization agreements 2010] OJ L 335/43.

1612 Judgment of 13 December 2012 in *Expedia*, C-226/11, EU:C:2012:795, para. 35 to 37.

1613 Communication from the Commission — Notice on agreements of minor importance which do not appreciably restrict competition under Article 101(1) of the Treaty on the Functioning of the European Union (De Minimis Notice), [2014] OJ C 291/1, paras. 2 and 13.

1614 15 U.S. Code § 1 - Trusts, etc., in restraint of trade illegal; penalty, formerly § of the Sherman Act. See also: *United States v. Crescent Amusement Co.*, 323 U.S. 173 (1944); *Swift & Co. v. United States*, 196 U.S. 375 (1905); *Knevelbaard Dairies v. Kraft Foods, Inc.*, 232 F.3d 979 (9th Cir. 2000); *United States v. Romer*, 148 F.3d 359 (4th Cir. 1998); *Reid Bros. Logging Co. v. Ketchikan Pulp Co.*, 699 F.2d 1292 (9th Cir. 1983). See: Rosenfelt (2008), p. 405; Carstensen 'Buyer Cartels Versus Buying Groups: Legal Distinctions, Competitive Realities, and Antitrust Policy' (2010); Hovenkamp, [2011], p. 98; Kirkwood 'Collusion to Control a Powerful Customer: Amazon, E-Books, and Antitrust Policy' (2014). See also *Vogel v. American Society of Appraisers*, 744 F.2d 598, (7th Cir. 1984), 601 where the Seventh Circuit held that "buyer cartels, the object of which is to force the prices that suppliers charge the members of the cartel below the competitive level, are illegal per se.".

Mandeville Island Farms, Inc. v American Crystal Sugar Co[1615] and *National Macaroni Manufacturers*[1616], and receive an analog treatment to sellers' cartels[1617]. The per se standard used for buyers' cartels fixing purchasing prices was confirmed by the Supreme Court in *Mandeville Island Farms, Inc. v American Crystal Sugar Co*[1618] where it held that:

> It is clear that the agreement is the sort of combination condemned by the Act, even though the price-fixing was by purchasers, and the persons specially injured under the treble damage claim are sellers, not customers or consumers[1619].

825. Nevertheless, the US case law shows that courts are reluctant to find all agreements fixing purchasing prices as per se illegal and have allowed in occasions agreements to be evaluated under the rule of reason approach, as was the case in *US v Brown University*[1620]. In this case involving fees for the admission of students into prestigious colleges it was held that "the district court was obliged to more fully investigate the procompetitive and noneconomic justifications proffered by MIT than it did when it performed the truncated rule of reason analysis. Accordingly, we will remand this case to the district court with instructions to evaluate Overlap using the full-scale rule of reason analysis outlined above"[1621].

826. Also, the same treatment under a rule of reason approach was taken in *Balmoral Cinema v Allied Artist Pictures* where an agreement among owners of movie theaters not to compete when bidding for which movies to acquire was declared lawful by the Sixth Circuit Court of Appeals[1622], in a decision that in my view is grounded on poor economics. The reasoning behind the Sixth Circuit Court of Appeals decision was that the purchasing cartel could have had the result of reducing the prices paid by the movie-owners and which could translate into lower ticket prices for movie tickets, adopting a mistaken consumer welfare standard that equates low purchasing prices upstream with low retailing prices without taking into account the withholding effect of such agreement nor the downstream market competitiveness[1623]. This decision would not hold under the EU buyer power treatment to buyers' cartel

---

1615 *Mandeville Island Farms, Inc. v. American Crystal Sugar Co.*, 334 U.S. 219 (1948). See also commenting the case from a welfare perspective Jones (1989).

1616 I discuss the case when dealing with imposition of purchasing quotas below: *National Macaroni Manufacturers Association v. Federal Trade Commission*, 345 F2.d 421 (7th Cir. 1965).

1617 Blair and Harrison, [2010], p. 157.

1618 *Mandeville Island Farms, Inc. v. American Crystal Sugar Co.*, 334 U.S. 219 (1948). See also commenting the case from a buyer and welfare perspective: Jones (1989); American Antitrust Institute [2008], p. 121.

1619 *Mandeville Island Farms, Inc. v. American Crystal Sugar Co.*, 334 U.S. 219 (1948), 236.

1620 *United States v. Brown University*, 5 F. 3d 658 (3rd Cir.1993).

1621 *United States v. Brown University*, 5 F. 3d 658 (3rd Cir.1993), 678.

1622 *Balmoral Cinema Inc., v Allied Artist Pictures Corp.*, 855 F.2d 313 (6th Cir. 1989).

1623 *Balmoral Cinema Inc., v Allied Artist Pictures Corp.*, 855 F.2d 313 (6th Cir. 1989). See also criticizing the decision, Roger D. Blair and Jeffrey L. Harrison, 'Antitrust Policy and Monopsony' 76 Cornell Law Review (1991) 297, p. 300.

that hinders price competition for an input. Instead, such agreements would be considered as object restrictions of violation despite the dubious possibility of obtaining lower retailing prices for end consumers. Also, under current US antitrust law the standard used by the Court of Appeals would not be upheld, as courts would not accept lower purchasing prices as an argument to accept the validity of an agreement among buyers.

827. Finally, and connected to the per se treatment of buyer cartels, a similar approach was the one adopted in Germany until the 7th Amendment of the German Competition Act, which now considers purchase price fixing as an object restriction[1624].

c. *Is there a difference between monopsony power cartels and bargaining power cartels?*

828. Buyer cartels are considered *object restrictions of competition*, even if the immediate effect they might have is to reduce the purchasing prices paid by buyers and which may also lead to lower input prices to end consumers, particularly in the cartel does not decrease demand to reduce the prices it pays for an input. Also, this qualification as object remains even if the cartel does not have direct effects on the downstream competition which would be, in any case, an aggravating factor. This begs the question of *why a cartel that decreases prices is prohibited by competition law* and whether there is a *difference between monopsony and bargaining power cartels.*

829. In the case of a buyers' cartel that exerts monopsony power the answer is straight forward because due to the demand withholding the amounts of goods purchased decline creating a scarcity effect that leads to the use of fewer resources than needed and which affects negatively consumers and suppliers alike due to the welfare loss and the existence of less input, which may also lead to higher purchasing prices or fewer consumers capable of acquiring the good. Thus, any monopsonist buyers' cartel should be a restriction of competition both by object and effect, unless the four cumulative conditions of Article 101(3) TFEU are fulfilled, which is unlikely (and arguably impossible), as pointed out by the Commission[1625], and the literature[1626].

1624 Bundeskartellamt '*Buyer Power in Competition Law - Status and Perspectives*' (2008), p. 8-9.

1625 Communication from the Commission - Guidelines on the application of Article 81(3) of the Treaty [2004] OJ C 101/97, para. 46; and Communication from the Commission — Guidelines on the applicability of Article 101 of the Treaty on the Functioning of the European Union to horizontal co-operation agreements [2011] OJ C 11/1, para. 246.

1626 Also reaching a similar conclusion, see: Garth Lindrup (ed) *Butterworth's Competition Law Handbook*, vol II (12th edn, Lexis Nexis 2006), p. 555, when stating: "a joint purchasing agreement under which the participants agree not to purchase above certain maximum prices is liable to distort the structure of demand in the market, to be prohibited by Article 81(1) and to be ineligible for exemption under Article 81(3)"; Carstensen 'Buyer Power, Competition Policy, and Antitrust: The Competitive Effects of Discrimination Among Suppliers' (2008), p. 323. See also Kokkoris 'Purchase Price Fixing: A Per Se Infringement?' (2007), p. 478.

830. However, if the buyers' cartel does not resort to demand withholding tactics but to decrease the intensity of competition among its members and therefore obtain lower purchasing prices without restricting demand should the treatment be different? The Commission's practice is clear in affirming that fixing purchasing conditions constitute an object restriction of competition without requiring a decrease in units acquired. Therefore, cartels that do not resort to demand withholding are also captured by Article 101 TFEU. Nonetheless, these types of agreements among buyers may exceptionally have positive effects that under an analysis of Article 101(3) TFEU may successfully comply with the four cumulative conditions.

831. Nevertheless, this does not imply that coordinated bargaining power that fixes purchasing prices should be treated as an effect restriction of competition. *Input price fixing is de lege lata and ought to be de lege ferenda an object restriction of competition* both for monopsony power and bargaining power because the creation of cartels by themselves is contrary to the protection of competition as a process[1627] and freedom to compete as understood in ordoliberal terms, because cartels precisely bypass the competitive process[1628]. Furthermore, buyer cartels in general have pernicious effects also for allocative and dynamic efficiency because as buyers do not compete among themselves they would not be incentivized to invest[1629]. Additionally, this qualification of object restrictions of competition in my view should be kept regardless of the buyers' cartel effects in downstream competition; i.e.: if the cartel in addition to altering upstream conditions also distorts downstream competition.

832. My proposal for a uniform treatment to sellers' cartels is based on the following. Firstly, from the reading both literal and teleological of Article 101(1)(a) TFEU it is clear that the clause does not distinguish between upstream or downstream price fixing. Secondly, EU competition law practice supports this interpretation and has recognized that purchase price fixing by itself constitutes an object restriction of competition without distinguishing among types of buyers' cartels. Thirdly, that a conduct is an object restriction it does not imply that it might not fulfill the requirements of Article 101(3) TFEU which would be the instrument to assess the likelihood of beneficial effects of the agreement. Fourthly, considering that buyer cartels and its qualification as object restriction depend on downstream competition harm goes contrary to the broader and general legal standard used by the Courts in buyer power cases as restrictions of competition in the upstream market may also by themselves alone have the object of distorting competition. Lastly, this approach

1627 Judgment of 6 October 2009 in *GlaxoSmithKline Services and Others v Commission and Others*, Joined cases C-501/06 P, C-513/06 P, C-515/06 P and C-519/06 P, EU:C:2009:610, para. 63.

1628 See also case law from the US in which the Ninth Circuit Court of Appeals decided that buyer cartels fixing prices, even if passing benefits to end consumers in the form of lower retail prices, were contrary to the Sherman Act in *Knevelbaard Dairies v. Kraft Foods, Inc.*, 232 F.3d 979 (9th Cir. 2000).

1629 van Doorn.

of creating no distinctions between buyer cartels is also accepted in some MS, particularly in Germany where the German Competition Act finds purchasing price fixing as an object restriction irrespectively of its type but allows for the exemption of the agreement under efficiency considerations[1630].

833. This solution of finding all buyer cartels as object restriction is not shared by all the literature. Ezrachi suggests distinguishing between two main situations to determine when a buyers' cartel is an object restriction, *depending on its effects on downstream competition.* Firstly, he argues that purchasing price fixing should be an object restriction for all cases in which there is collusion both upstream and downstream and that the trigger of such treatment is the retail price fixing[1631]. The second scenario distinguishes between agreements that create buyer power and agreements that execute buyer power (and not distinguishing between monopsony or bargaining power like I do). Under this perspective when undertakings enter into an agreement creating buyer power for fixing purchasing prices but not as part of wider and transparent activities it should constitute an object restriction[1632]. On the other hand, if the input price fixing is a by-product of other open and transparent legitimate activities, then buyer power is not created by executed and, therefore, should be assessed under an effect restriction approach[1633].

834. Such approach, as acknowledged by Ezrachi, is not problem-free, yet I argue is more complicated as foreseen. This perspective implies an assessment of activity by activity of the buying cartel and subordinating the gravity of the infringement and its legal treatment on the existence of downstream consumer harm. Furthermore, the approach is problematic because it assumes some element of intent in the behaviour for determining when purchasing price fixing is likely to be anti-competitive. Additionally, Ezrachi's distinction appears to run *in contrario* to Commission's practice dealing with purchase price fixing and the analog selling side case law that interprets these practices as an object restriction under the scope of Article 101(1) TFEU, regardless of downstream consumer harm. Also, in my view, this approach confuses the origin of buyer power with the pooling of buyer power; individual buyer power exists before the cartel, what the cartel does is to pool it and allow the buyers to exert it with a substantial effect. Hence, implying that cartels fixing purchasing prices as a stand-alone activity create buyer power is erroneous.

1630 Act Against Restraints of Competition in the version published on 15 July 2005 (Bundesgesetzblatt (Federal Law Gazette) I, page 2114; 2009 I, p. 3850), as last amended by Article 3 of the Act of 26 July 2011 (Federal Law Gazette I, page 1554). See also supporting this approach: Bundeskartellamt '*Buyer Power in Competition Law - Status and Perspectives*' (2008), p. 10.

1631 Ezrachi 'Buying Alliances and Input Price Fixing: In Search of a European Enforcement Standard' (2012), p. 63.

1632 Ibid, p. 64.

1633 Ibid, p. 64.

835. Another distinction concerning buyers' cartel has been suggested by Kokkoris. In his view, EU competition law should consider purchasing price fixing as a per se infringement of competition irrespectively if the behaviour involves a withholding effect or not[1634]. This position appears too radical and not consistent with EU competition law as there are no behaviours that are per se prohibited. However, if Kokkoris' use of the term per se accounts for object restrictions then his interpretation of the Commission's practice and the case law and proposals are not much different from my perspective discussed above.

B. Imposing maximum purchasing quotas as object restrictions

836. A different way to distort competition among buyers and exploit buyer power is by imposing purchasing quotas through a buyers' cartel[1635]. By restricting the amount of goods a buyer is free to purchase, if the supply curve is upward sloping the prices paid for the input are artificially lowered. This is the consequence of the withholding effect of monopsony power[1636]. Furthermore, by artificially narrowing the quantities purchased this negatively impact the availability of the goods in the downstream market, affecting consumers in the form of fewer goods and higher prices than under competitive trading conditions. Therefore, the effect is equivalent as imposing a ceiling of maximum purchasing prices which explains why these types of *agreements should also be treated as restriction of competition by object* as they distort the competitive price formation, based on quite similar arguments as the ones I used above for purchasing price fixing.

837. The Commission's practice also helps illustrating that this by object treatment is the correct and desired approach to buyers setting purchasing quotas by finding such practices in breach of Article 101(1), (b) and (c) TFEU. Also, the few Decisions by the Commission confirm that setting purchasing quotas is usually an additional measure taken by a buyers' cartel fixing prices to prevent cheating, as occurred both in *Aluminium imports from Eastern Europe*[1637], and *Raw Tobacco Spain*[1638].

838. In *Aluminium imports from Eastern Europe,* the Commission decided that the fixing of purchasing quotas eliminated the freedom to individually ne-

1634 Kokkoris 'Purchase Price Fixing: A Per Se Infringement?' (2007), p. 477. Kokkoris also argues that selling price fixing is "per se anticompetitive", ibid, p. 478.

1635 Ritter and Braun, [2004], p. 169.

1636 See also raising this point: Blair and Harrison, [2010], p. 70-71.

1637 Commission Decision of 19 December 1984 relating to a proceeding under Article 85 of the EEC Treaty (IV/26.870 - *Aluminium imports from eastern Europe*) [1985] OJ L 92/1, 11.2. See discussing this case also from a buyer power perspective: Kokkoris 'Purchase Price Fixing: A Per Se Infringement?' (2007), p. 481.

1638 Commission Decision of 20 October 2005 relating to a proceeding under Article 81(1) of the EC Treaty (Case COMP/C.38.281/B.2 — *Raw tobacco Italy*) [2006] OJ L 353/45, taken from the unabridged version, para. 246.

gotiate purchasing quantities and this was found to be restrictive of competition, which I interpret as accounting for an object restriction[1639]. In a similar approach as the one held in *Raw Tobacco Spain*, a case previously discussed, the agreement between tobacco processors in addition to the setting of a maximum purchasing quantity included a second restrictive practice consisting in sharing the quantities of raw tobacco that each processor was able to buy in the cultivation contracts signed with each producer group the agreement aimed at "'limit or control production' and 'share markets or sources of supply'" constituting an object restriction of competition under Article 101 (b) and (c) TFEU[1640].

839. An analogous stern approach to fixing purchasing quotas is followed in US antitrust law, as confirmed in the case of *National Macaroni Manufacturers Association v Federal Trade Commission*[1641]. In this case, the parties to a purchasing agreement controlled the production of a downstream good – pasta (macaroni) – by colluding regarding the amount of durum wheat to be used in its recipe as an answer to a critically bad crop season. To avoid the increase in total purchasing costs, the macaroni recipe was modified to contain only 50% durum wheat instead of the traditional 100%. This manipulation of production and limiting of purchasing was qualified by the Seventh Circuit as a per se violation of the Federal Trade Commission Act[1642].

C. Buying alliances

840. Buying alliances, unlike buyers' cartels, tend to *improve the competitive conditions and be efficiency enhancing* as they might lead to lower prices for end consumers, larger output, increase in quality and innovation and overall better market conditions[1643]. A buying alliance will also benefit its members by allowing them to reduce the purchasing price[1644] they pay for goods based

---

1639 Commission Decision relating to a proceeding under Article 85 of the EEC Treaty IV/26.870 - *Aluminium imports from Eastern Europe,* 11.2. See discussing this case also from a buyer power perspective: Kokkoris 'Purchase Price Fixing: A Per Se Infringement?' (2007), p. 481.

1640 Commission Decision of 20 October 2004 relating to a proceeding under Article 81(1) of the EC Treaty (Case COMP/C.38.238/B.2) — *Raw tobacco — Spain* [2007] OJ L 102/14, taken from the unabridged version, para. 303 to 304 and 314.

1641 *National Macaroni Manufacturers Association v. Federal Trade Commission,* 345 F2.d 421 (7th Cir. 1965). See also briefly discussing the case: Kokkoris 'Purchase Price Fixing: A Per Se Infringement?' (2007), p. 485.

1642 *National Macaroni Manufacturers Association v. Federal Trade Commission,* 345 F2.d 421 (7th Cir. 1965), 427; Rosenfelt (2008).

1643 For an analysis of the price and non-price effects of bargaining power see chapter 2, sections §V and §VI. Also stressing the pro-competitiveness of buyer alliances that foster bargaining power: Communication from the Commission — Guidelines on the applicability of Article 101 of the Treaty on the Functioning of the European Union to horizontal co-operation agreements [2011] OJ C 11/1, para. 194; European Commission *Green Paper on Unfair Trading Practices in the Business-to-Business Food and Non-Food supply Chain in Europe,* Brussels (2013). See also: Wollmann [2008], para. 2-2-104-105.

1644 Carstensen 'Buyer Cartels Versus Buying Groups: Legal Distinctions, Competitive Realities, and Antitrust Policy' (2010), p. 28-30.

on volume[1645], and decrease administrative, transportation, storage and operation costs, through the creation of economies of scale thanks to the pooling of buyer market power[1646]. Also, unlike buyers' cartels that fix prices, buying alliances tend to act as price takers instead of price makers, which implies that they in principle *do not distort the competitive price formation*; rather they improve the terms and conditions in which goods are bought in the upstream market and exert competitive pressure on suppliers[1647] to pass on their supra-competitive profits, acting as countervailing buyer power as remarked by the CJEU in *Gøttrup-Klim and Others Grovvareforeninger v Dansk Landbrugs Grovvareselskab*[1648], following the Opinion of Advocate General Tesauro[1649]. However, a buying alliance should not degenerate in a scheme for coordinating conducts downstream that will lead to erosion of rivalry among the alliance's players as remarked by the Guidelines on Horizontal Agreements, becoming an anti-competitive agreement[1650].

841. Furthermore, buying alliances are complex agreements that may imply vertical and/or horizontal coordination as remarked by the Commission[1651]. The horizontal level is the relation among buyers themselves and the focus of this section. On the other hand, the vertical level deals with the relation between the buyers and their supplier(s), which is carried out in accordance with the rules of the Block Exemption Regulation on Vertical Restraints and the Guidelines on Vertical Restraints.

842. Because of these implications in horizontal and vertical levels buying alliances are also seen as partial and *de facto* concentrations among undertakings[1652], or may constitute a previous step towards a future merger because, as suggested by Carstensen, the alliance "acts to gain the efficiencies of a joint enterprise" (in a scenario akin to a partial upstream merger)[1653]. By improving

---

1645 Bundeskartellamt '*Summary of the Final Report of the Sector Inquiry into the Food Retail Sector*' (2014), p. 4.

1646 European Commission '*Green Paper on Unfair Trading Practices in the Business-to-Business Food and Non-Food supply Chain in Europe*' (2013), p. 3. For a discussion of economies of scale generated by buyer power related practices see in chapter 7, section §V.

1647 European Competition Network (2012), para. 98. See also discussing the legitimacy of sellers cartels to oppose a strong buyer Kirkwood 'Collusion to Control a Powerful Customer: Amazon, E-Books, and Antitrust Policy' (2014).

1648 Judgment of 15 December 1994 in *Gøttrup-Klim and Others Grovvareforeninger v Dansk Landbrugs Grovvareselskab*, C-250/92, EU:C:1994:413, para. 32; Bellamy and others, [2013], para. 2.141.

1649 Opinion of Advocate General Tesauro of 16 June 1994 in Judgment of 15 December 1994 in *Gøttrup-Klim and Others Grovvareforeninger v Dansk Landbrugs Grovvareselskab*, C-250/92, EU:C:1994:249 [1994], section 18, I – 5658.

1650 Communication from the Commission — Guidelines on the applicability of Article 101 of the Treaty on the Functioning of the European Union to horizontal co-operation agreements [2011] OJ C 11/1, para. 201.

1651 Communication from the Commission — Guidelines on the applicability of Article 101 of the Treaty on the Functioning of the European Union to horizontal co-operation agreements [2011] OJ C 11/1, para. 195.

1652 Summary of Commission Decision of 17 December 2008 declaring a concentration compatible with the common market and the functioning of the EEA Agreement (Case COMP/M.5046 — *Friesland Foods/Campina*) [2009] OJ C 75/21, taken from the unabridged version.

1653 Carstensen 'Buyer Cartels Versus Buying Groups: Legal Distinctions, Competitive Realities, and Antitrust Policy' (2010), p. 13.

the purchasing conditions and setting a transparent and unified buying mechanism undertakings effectively integrate purchasers in a similar, but not identical and more limited way, to a single entity operating in the upstream market and which may result in a consolidation in the market that sets a pre-merger scenario[1654]. This, however, does not mean that all alliances will end up in market concentration upstream.

843. Additionally, most buying alliances act as a centralized purchasing device, such as the buying groups described by Lianos and Lombardi[1655], as an agreement among different cooperatives, or a cooperative itself, for example as in the concentration case of *Friesland Foods/Campina*[1656], and which I discussed in this chapter's section §V. Furthermore, the purchasing patterns of the buying alliances vary from case to case but, in general, in a buying alliance scheme there is *central agent* that carries out the negotiations for the alliance members and acquires the input in a consolidated manner. This central agent then resells or distributes the purchases among the members of the alliance as it occurred in *National Sulphuric Acid Association,* a case I discuss below and which was exempted under Article 101(3) TFEU[1657].

844. Also, buying alliances tend to be formed by small and medium undertakings to generate buyer market power by pooling demand[1658], and oppose a large supplier as predicted by Galbraith's countervailing power theory[1659], which is confirmed by a Commission report[1660]. It is notorious the example of buying alliances in the agricultural sector in which farmers join forces to acquires inputs such as seeds, petroleum, fertilizers, farming equipment, etc.[1661]. Also, buying alliances in the food retailing market are increasingly common but not a new phenomenon as the first buying alliances already existed back in the 1930s[1662].

845. However, there are also cases in which the buying alliances are formed also by medium and larger firms, an increasingly common practice, particularly

---

1654 Bundeskartellamt '*Summary of the Final Report of the Sector Inquiry into the Food Retail Sector*' (2014), p. 16.

1655 Lianos and Lombardi, p. 19.

1656 Summary of Commission Decision of 17 December 2008 declaring a concentration compatible with the common market and the functioning of the EEA Agreement (Case COMP/M.5046 — *Friesland Foods/Campina*) [2009] OJ C 75/21. See discussing also this case: Ezrachi and Ioannidou (2014), p. 80-81.

1657 Commission Decision of 9 July 1980 relating to a proceeding under Article 85 of the EEC Treaty (IV/27.958 *National Sulphuric Acid Association*) [1980] OJ L 260/24.

1658 Doyle and Han (2014), p. 256; Whish and Bailey, *Competition law* [2015], p. 640.

1659 *American Capitalism* in Galbraith, [2010].

1660 European Commission, *The Economic Impact of Modern Retail on Choice and Innovation in the EU Food Sector* (2014), p. 53.

1661 See also stressing the existence of buying alliances in agricultural markets to neutralize opposing market power: Opinion of Advocate General Tesauro of 16 June 1994 in Judgment of 15 December 1994 in *Gøttrup-Klim and Others Grovvareforeninger v Dansk Landbrugs Grovvareselskab*, C-250/92, EU:C:1994:249 [1994], section 18, I – 5658.

1662 European Commission, *The Economic Impact of Modern Retail on Choice and Innovation in the EU Food Sector* (2014), p. 52.

in the retail sector as discussed by Director General Italianer[1663]. According to the Commission, buyers join forces to "increase their bargaining power to obtain better deals in the procurement market" and that should not be seen as a negative form of collaboration[1664]. For example, in the case of Germany larger buyers acting as food retailers "tend to pool their demand in purchasing cooperations" including the market leaders: Edeka, Rewe[1665], Bünting and Bartels Langness[1666].

846. Lastly, there are cases of *asymmetrical alliances*, with one large buyer and many smaller buyers. In these instances it is usually the largest partner who "negotiates on behalf of all the companies' participation in the purchasing operation"[1667]. However, the parties that tend to benefit the most in these asymmetrical alliances are the smaller buyers because they would obtain benefits thanks to the aggregated buyer power and which go beyond what they could have obtained alone[1668]. Nevertheless, in practice, there might be instances in which the large buyer may not always pass in full the benefits of the purchasing alliances.

a. Buying alliances as efficient purchasing agreements and only likely to constitute effect based restrictions of competition

847. Buying alliances are in principle compatible with EU competition law and only liable of breaching Article 101 TFEU under an *effect based assessment*, as also remarked by Korah and O'Sullivan[1669], albeit this legal standard is not explicitly confirmed by the Courts due to the absence of relevant case law. This more lenient approach is consistent with the procompetitive nature of buying alliances that exert bargaining power to neutralize seller market power and the fact that, unlike a buyers' cartel, the aim of the alliance is not to reduce competition among their members or fix upstream purchasing conditions, but rather to increase efficient competition among buyers and sellers, without compromising competition between its members.

848. Consequently, buying alliances may benefit from a safe harbor and are presumed competitive if the parties belonging to it have a combined market share in both the upstream and downstream markets where they operate be-

1663 Italianer, *The Devil is in the Retail*, p. 4.

1664 Ibid, p. 4.

1665 For example, Edeka in Germany represents between 25-30% of the market shares in food retailing and Rewe on its part represents 15-20% of the market. The other large retail supermarket chain, but not part of a buying alliance, the Schwarz Gruppe (LIDL and Kaufland) represent 20-25% taken together: Bundeskartellamt '*Sektoruntersuchung: Lebensmitteleinzelhandel*' (2014), Table 1, p. 78.

1666 Bundeskartellamt '*Summary of the Final Report of the Sector Inquiry into the Food Retail Sector*' (2014), p. 4.

1667 Ibid, p. 5.

1668 Ibid, p. 11.

1669 Korah and O'Sullivan, [2002], p. 47.

low 15%[1670]. Falling outside this safe harbor does not imply that the buying alliance becomes a cartel, but that a more detailed assessment is to be carried out[1671]. Additionally, the Commission has clarified that even if a buying alliance in some way affects the way purchasing prices are set (in this case it lowers them for the members) buying alliances could benefit from the De Minimis Notice[1672], and which implies that these types of purchasing coordination *do not qualify as an object restriction of competition for the Commission.*

849. Concerning the legal basis for considering buying alliances as eventual anti-competitive agreements because of their effects the limited Commission's practice gives some indications. As I mentioned above, buying alliances tend to be formed by small undertakings which render them unlikely to raise significant anti-competitive effects in the market as it was confirmed in *EEIG Orphe*[1673]. In this case the horizontal purchasing agreement was found to not have a significant effect on competition because it only allowed seven small and medium size pharmaceuticals to join efforts by creating a purchasing alliance and a common trademark that would permit them to be able to compete against larger firms.

850. Also, the procompetitive effects of the purchasing alliance were taken into account by the Commission in the assessment of a proposed concentration in *Friesland Foods/Campina*[1674]. In this case and unlike in *EEIG Orphe,* the buying alliance grouped a very substantial amount of buyers, but even then, the Commission assessed how the purchasing was carried out to determine the effects, instead of assuming that the collaborative purchasing had an anti-competitive nature. In the assessment of *Friesland Foods/Campina* the Commission found that a concentration among milk purchaser cooperatives leading up to a purchasing position with 70-80% market share would act as a buying alliance and, regardless of its size, still generate pro-competitive

---

1670 Communication from the Commission — Guidelines on the applicability of Article 101 of the Treaty on the Functioning of the European Union to horizontal co-operation agreements [2011] OJ C 11/1, para. 208.

1671 Communication from the Commission — Guidelines on the applicability of Article 101 of the Treaty on the Functioning of the European Union to horizontal co-operation agreements [2011] OJ C 11/1, para. 209; Faull, Nikpay and Taylor, [2014], para. 7.379.

1672 "In the context of joint purchasing agreements (that is to say, a number of competitors openly coming together to make joint purchases on the market), where the parties agree on the purchasing price that their 'joint purchasing arrangement' may pay to its suppliers for the products subject to the supply contract", Commission staff working document - Guidance on restrictions of competition "by object" for the purpose of defining which agreements may benefit from the De Minimis Notice, accompanying communication from the Commission - Notice on agreements of minor importance which do not appreciably restrict competition under Article 101(1) of the Treaty on the Functioning of the European Union (De Minimis Notice), [C(2014) 4136 final], Brussels, 25.6.2014, SWD (2014) 198 final, p. 7.

1673 EEIG Orphe, Report on Competition Policy 1990 (Vol XX) 80, point 102. See discussing this case: Nick Gardner, *A Guide to United European Union Competition Policy* (3rd edn edn, Palgrave MacMillan 2000), p. 128; Richard S. Markovits, *Economics and the Interpretation and Application of U.S. and E.U. Antitrust Law*, Vol. II Economics-Based Legal Analyses on Mergers, Vertical Practices and Joint Ventures (Springer ed, Springer 2014), p. 609-610; Faull, Nikpay and Taylor, [2014], para. 7.398.

1674 Summary of Commission Decision of 17 December 2008 declaring a concentration compatible with the common market and the functioning of the EEA Agreement (Case COMP/M.5046 — *Friesland Foods/Campina*) [2009] OJ C 75/21.

effects[1675]. This large buying position could have negatively impacted the raw milk purchasing market. However, the fact that the *buyers were organized as a purchasing alliance not exerting monopsony power* along with the fact that the parties were grouped in the form of a cooperative, agreed to form a Dutch milk fund, and its statutes allowed farmers to leave the merged entity was sufficient to accept the creation of a purchasing alliance through the merger[1676].

851. Lastly, another legal ground to consider buying alliances as eventual effect based restrictions of competition is the treatment under a rule of reason approach under US antitrust law[1677], and the recognition by the US Courts of their efficiency-enhancing nature. This was the case in *Northwest Wholesale Stationers v Pacific Stationary and Printing* when the US Supreme Court clarified that a buyers' cooperative allows its members "to achieve economies of scale in purchasing and warehousing that would otherwise be unavailable"[1678], recognizing the efficient character of most buyer alliances as these types of agreements "are not a form of concerted activity characteristically likely to result in predominantly anti-competitive effects"[1679].

b. *Competitive risks generated by buying alliances*

852. Despite the fact that buying alliances are usually seen as pro-competitive agreements this does not mean that these forms of buying coordination may not raise upstream and downstream competition concerns. Therefore, buying alliances are and should be under competition law scrutiny as potential restrictions of competition by their effects under Article 101(1) TFEU. Furthermore, a buying alliance might devoid into a buyer's cartel, which is a matter of debate concerning licensing of essential patents under standard setting organizations[1680]. Also buying alliances can have anti-competitive effects vis-à-vis suppliers (exploitative) but also among their members themselves and rival buyers (exclusionary). Consequently, it is important to determine which type of anti-competitive risks can be generated by these types of horizontal cooperation agreements among buyers as I discuss in this section.

1675 Summary of Commission Decision of 17 December 2008 declaring a concentration compatible with the common market and the functioning of the EEA Agreement (Case COMP/M.5046 — *Friesland Foods/Campina*) [2009] OJ C 75/21, taken from the unabridged version, para. 99; Ezrachi and Ioannidou (2014), p. 80-81.

1676 Summary of Commission Decision of 17 December 2008 declaring a concentration compatible with the common market and the functioning of the EEA Agreement (Case COMP/M.5046 — *Friesland Foods/Campina*) [2009] OJ C 75/21, taken from the unabridged version, paras. 1841 and 1894-1898.

1677 See also remarking the rule of reason approach used in this case: Jones (1989), p. 80-81.

1678 *Northwest Wholesale Stationers, Inc. v. Pacific Stationery Printing Co.*, 472 U.S. 284 (1985).

1679 *Northwest Wholesale Stationers, Inc. v. Pacific Stationery Printing Co.*, 472 U.S. 284 (1985), at 295.

1680 See discussing whether such organizations facilitate collusion among buyers: Petit, *The IEEE-SA Revised Patent Policy and its Definition of "Reasonable" Rates: A Transatlatic Antitrust Divide?*; Sidak (2009); J. Gregory Sidak, *Letter from J. Gregory Sidak to the Hon. Renata B. Hesse Regarding the Business Review Letter for the Institute of Electrical and Electronics Engineers (IEEE) Concerning Proposed Bylaw Amendments Affecting FRAND Licensing of Standard-Essential Patents* (January 28, 2015), https://www.criterioneconomics.com/proposed-ieee-bylaw-amendments-affecting-frand-licensing-of-seps.html

853. The most important risk is that a buying alliance may become a device to *co-ordinate their members' conduct in the upstream purchasing market* beyond the limits imposed by collaborative legal purchasing or, more importantly, *to reduce competition in the related downstream market*[1681]. This would occur, for example, if the buying alliance coordinates behaviour in the downstream market and eliminates retailing competition among its members.

854. Additionally and linked to the former, the assessment of the alliance's effects must pay attention to *both its operations in the upstream and the downstream market*. As noted by Doyle and Han, buying alliances may look as pro-competitive devices if the assessment is made regarding the setting of input prices, but they might not for example if they involve practices such as slotting allowances fees[1682]. Therefore, the analysis of buying alliances should include a careful examination of the practices in both upstream and downstream markets in line with the dualistic approach adopted regarding the analysis of buyer power in this study.

855. Also, buying alliances entail risks concerning *exchanges of information,* and whether its members benefit in different ways from the alliance, and if this can be used to the detriment of smaller buyers in the retailing market benefit, particularly if the alliance is asymmetrical (i.e. some or one very large member and many small ones). As discussed in a report from the Bundeskartellamt in food retailing, in cases of asymmetrical buying alliances it is usually the largest partner the main negotiator and this grants it with the ability to obtain sensitive information concerning its competitors downstream[1683]. The transfer of confidential information among members facilitates collusion in the upstream and downstream markets, becoming a device more akin to a cartel than a buying alliance[1684], as also remarked in the economic literature[1685]. If information is exchanged among members, in addition to the general risks of coordination, the larger buyer may also use the knowledge it has regarding the purchasing patterns of smaller buyers to then exclude them from the downstream market and leverage its buyer market power to affect downstream market conditions. Also, exclusion among members can take place because the large buyer often decides what input is acquired reducing the independence of decision making by smaller buyers parts of the alliance. Therefore, an asymmetric alliance can have intra-members exclusionary effects.

1681 See also discussing the degeneration of buying alliances into anticompetitive devices: Lianos and Lombardi, p. 20.

1682 Doyle and Han (2014), p. 271.

1683 Bundeskartellamt '*Summary of the Final Report of the Sector Inquiry into the Food Retail Sector*' (2014), p. 5.

1684 Also suggesting that this type of alliance must be "carefully examined" by the competition authorities see: ibid, p. 18; Communication from the Commission — Guidelines on the applicability of Article 101 of the Treaty on the Functioning of the European Union to horizontal co-operation agreements [2011] OJ C 11/1, para. 213.

1685 Normann, Rösch and Schultz (2015), p. 82.

D. Distinguishing a buying alliance from a buyers' cartel and its consequences

856. The Commission defines buying alliances as "an association of undertakings formed by a group of retailers for the joint purchasing of products" on its Guidelines for Horizontal Agreements[1686]. On the other hand, I defined buyers' cartel in chapter 7, section §VI.A as a purchasing agreement that fixes prices, limits output or allocates markets for the parties with the aim of restricting competition between them in the upstream market and also likely to be in the related downstream market(s), in line with the Commission's definition of a cartel[1687]. From these definitions based on the Commission's soft law, the difference appears on whether the purchasing agreement may lead to a collusive outcome by facilitating the coordination of the parties' behaviour on the downstream market.[1688] Nevertheless, this distinction is of little help because it does not really contribute with a clear-cut answer: it bases the difference on a case-by-case-assessment and leaves the classification, somewhat, to the intention of the parties[1689]. Also, buying alliances may degenerate into buyers' cartels even if not originally created with such purpose. However, such degeneration should not be taken for granted as discussed by Normann et alia, who find that buying alliances do not necessarily facilitate collusion in any of the involved markets[1690]. Therefore, the question is *what really differentiates a buying alliance from a buyers' cartel and what elements should be taken into account when making the distinction?*

857. The simplest and perhaps more important distinction, which surprisingly can be overlooked, is the content of the agreement by the buying parties. If the parties had agreed to fix prices, set purchasing quotas, distribute territories among its members or agree not to compete as buyers and/or retailers, then the agreement qualifies as a cartel. If, on the other hand, the members agree to pool their buyer power through a central agent that carries out the purchases on their behalf without this implying a diminishment in their rivalry in the upstream and/or downstream markets, then the agreement qualifies as an alliance. In this assessment the authorities have to take into account the expression of the will of the parties and determine what is the content and the context of the agreement.

1686 Communication from the Commission — Guidelines on the applicability of Article 101 of the Treaty on the Functioning of the European Union to horizontal co-operation agreements [2011] OJ C 11/1, para. 196.

1687 See also the Commission's definition of a cartel as "agreements and/or concerted practices between two or more competitors aimed at coordinating their competitive behaviour on the market and/or influencing the relevant parameters of competition through practices such as the fixing of purchase or selling prices or other trading conditions, the allocation of production or sales quotas, the sharing of markets including bid-rigging, restrictions of imports or exports and/or anti-competitive actions against other competitors" in Commission Notice on Immunity from fines and reduction of fines in cartel cases [2006] OJ C 298/17, para. 1.

1688 Communication from the Commission — Guidelines on the applicability of Article 101 of the Treaty on the Functioning of the European Union to horizontal co-operation agreements [2011] OJ C 11/1, para. 213.

1689 This is also noted by Ezrachi who argues that the Guidelines provide with a "hazy benchmark" in Ezrachi 'Buying Alliances and Input Price Fixing: In Search of a European Enforcement Standard' (2012), p. 48.

1690 Normann, Rösch and Schultz (2015), p. 82.

858. Further, a buying alliance has as its most distinguishing feature the fact that is a purchasing agreement that *does not have as its object or effect fixing purchasing prices or imposing other purchasing conditions, neither to limit competition among its members, particularly as retailers*. A buying alliance, therefore and additionally, creates *competitively enhancing bargaining power and not monopsony power*. Hence a first indication of the difference anchored on the upstream behaviour would be *determining the purchasing patterns of the buying agreement*. If there is an indication of demand withholding, then the agreement exerts monopsony power to exploit suppliers as it reduces the purchasing price below the competitive level. This is difficult to determine in practice; however, examples of historical purchasing patterns of the involved undertakings before entering into the purchasing agreement could be used as indicators.

859. Another indicator is the way the *prices are negotiated* between the suppliers and the buyers. Unlike a buyers' cartel, buying alliances operate not by fixing purchasing prices or setting purchasing quotas. Hence, indicia of take-it-or-leave-it offers or unwillingness to negotiate prices by the cartel members can be also taken into account to differentiate between the purchasing conducts.

860. Also, a distinctive feature *is the way buying alliances operate internally when carrying out purchases,* in accordance with what the content of the agreement is. Buying alliances tend to operate by means of a central agent that has to coordinate the purchases for all members and execute them in a transparent and independent manner to avoid becoming a cartel device[1691]. This agent carries out the purchases on behalf of the alliance and possesses a character of a permanent body and with strategies oriented to a long-term collaboration[1692]. Therefore, the buying alliance and its system should minimize the risk of exchange of sensitive information when the administering organ of the alliance is the one receiving but not passing on the information[1693], which is an important anti-competitive concern regarding buying alliances as I discussed in chapter 7, section §VI.C.a. A buying cartel, on the other hand, is not transparent and members do not require having an independent purchaser and are likely to share information regarding their purchasing patterns to coordinate conducts in the downstream market, if they 'compete' as retailers. Also, unlike some buyers' cartels, buying alliances integrate their purchasing

1691 Commission Decision of 9 July 1980 relating to a proceeding under Article 85 of the EEC Treaty (IV/27.958 *National Sulphuric Acid Association*) [1980] OJ L 260/24. Also raising the transparency element as a difference between cartels and alliances see: Ezrachi 'Buying Alliances and Input Price Fixing: In Search of a European Enforcement Standard' (2012), p. 60.

1692 Bundeskartellamt '*Summary of the Final Report of the Sector Inquiry into the Food Retail Sector*' (2014), p. 4; Suchan Chae and Paul Heidhues, 'Buyers' Alliances for Bargaining Power' 13 Journal of Economics & Management Strategy (2004) 731, p. 731.

1693 Communication from the Commission — Guidelines on the applicability of Article 101 of the Treaty on the Functioning of the European Union to horizontal co-operation agreements [2011] OJ C 11/1, para. 215 and para. 224 example 4.

operation and restrict the ability of their members to unilaterally carry out their buying activity[1694], as also confirmed by a study by the German NCA[1695].

861. This central and transparent purchasing modality was relevant for the Commission to determine the pro-competitive nature of a purchasing agreement and qualify it as a buying alliance in *National Sulphuric Acid Association*[1696]. In this case involving the joint purchasing of sulphur and the limitation of freedom of their members, the Commission studied the purchasing rules agreed by the members to show how the pool was a buying alliance and not a cartel[1697]. The price paid by the members (and *not the price paid by the pool to their suppliers*) for their sulphur within the pool was agreed by a committee; the quantities and type of sulphur to be purchased were affixed 6 months in advanced; the sulphur acquired by the pool was resold to the members on a non-profit basis; each member of the pool had to acquire a minimum of 25% of its sulphur input through the pool and if not, then would be considered as no longer member of it. In other words, the pool did not impose purchasing prices but instead acted like a centralized purchasing agent for all its members[1698].

a. Conclusions regarding the distinction

862. Recapitulating, the key normative element that distinguishes a buying alliance from a buyers' cartel is that *the former should be treated as agreements that tend to be pro-competitive and ought to be considered only as possible effect restrictions of competition law under Article 101(1) TFEU, and not object restrictions like the latter*[1699]. Thus, the analysis of buying alliances is more lenient, and if anything, it has to assess the market effects of the conduct both in quantity, price and quality dimensions as suggested by the Bundeskartellamt[1700]. A somewhat similar approach is also taken in US antitrust law as the Supreme Court has considered that buying alliances are not to

---

1694 Carstensen 'Buyer Cartels Versus Buying Groups: Legal Distinctions, Competitive Realities, and Antitrust Policy' (2010), p. 14-17.

1695 Bundeskartellamt '*Summary of the Final Report of the Sector Inquiry into the Food Retail Sector*' (2014), p. 4.

1696 Commission Decision of 9 July 1980 relating to a proceeding under Article 85 of the EEC Treaty (IV/27.958 *National Sulphuric Acid Association*) [1980] OJ L 260/24.

1697 Also claiming that the buying pool was "transparent" see: Ezrachi 'Buying Alliances and Input Price Fixing: In Search of a European Enforcement Standard' (2012). Also stressing that the lowering of the purchasing obligation was an element for the pool to be deemed lawful: Faull and Nikpay, [1999], para. 6.340. See also: Ezrachi [2014], p. 151-152.

1698 Commission Decision of 9 July 1980 relating to a proceeding under Article 85 of the EEC Treaty (IV/27.958 *National Sulphuric Acid Association*) [1980] OJ L 260/24, para. 26.

1699 This also appears to be the position of the Commission when arguing that "[j]oint purchasing arrangements which do not have as their object the restriction of competition must be analyzed in their legal and economic context with regard to their actual and likely effects on competition", in Communication from the Commission — Guidelines on the applicability of Article 101 of the Treaty on the Functioning of the European Union to horizontal co-operation agreements [2011] OJ C 11/1, para. 207.

1700 Bundeskartellamt '*Summary of the Final Report of the Sector Inquiry into the Food Retail Sector*' (2014), p. 19.

be assessed under a per se rule like most buyer cartels, but under the rule of reason standard instead[1701].

863. Furthermore, even if a buying alliance is found to be anti-competitive due to its effects according to the assessment carried out in Article 101(1) TFEU, they are much more likely to fulfil the cumulative conditions of Article 101(3) TFEU as the limited case law and Commission's practice demonstrates[1702], unlike in the case of a buyers' cartel. This is even more the case if the buying alliance has an upstream market share of less than 15%[1703]. This likelihood of fulfilling the efficiency requirements of Article 101(3) TFEU is so because, like bargaining power in general, if there is competition downstream, lower wholesale prices are passed on to consumers[1704]. Also, a buying alliance is unlikely to raise serious competitive effects if the parties to it have little market power because coordination is rather unlikely or ineffective[1705]. Therefore, buying alliances that agglutinate or pool buyer power but lack downstream market power as retailers are unlikely to raise competition concerns – particularly concerning end consumers. If, on the other hand, the buying alliance has also downstream market power (like an hourglass-shaped undertaking) then it is likely that the cost commonality will also serve to eliminate downstream competitiveness. Lastly, unlike buyers' cartels, buying alliances may benefit from the application of the *De Minimis* doctrine if the agreement does not have a significant impact in competition[1706].

E. Buying agreements and restrictions to competition among its own members

864. Another aspect that has received attention in the Commission's practice and the case law is how becoming a member of a buying alliance *limits the individual capacity of its members to purchase independently or outside of the alliance,* and whether this amounts to a restriction of competition. The re-

1701 *United States v. Topco Associates, Inc.*, 405 U.S. 596 (1972); *Northwest Wholesale Stationers, Inc. v. Pacific Stationery Printing Co.*, 472 U.S. 284 (1985).

1702 Commission Decision of 9 July 1980 relating to a proceeding under Article 85 of the EEC Treaty (IV/27.958 *National Sulphuric Acid Association*) [1980] OJ L 260/24; Judgment of 25 March 1981 in *Coöperatieve Stremsel- en Kleurselfabriek v Commission*, C-61/80, EU:C:1981:75.

1703 Communication from the Commission — Guidelines on the applicability of Article 101 of the Treaty on the Functioning of the European Union to horizontal co-operation agreements [2011] OJ C 11/1, para. 208. Also confirming this interpretation: Bundeskartellamt '*Summary of the Final Report of the Sector Inquiry into the Food Retail Sector*' (2014), p. 19.

1704 Doyle and Han (2014), p. 256.

1705 Communication from the Commission — Guidelines on the applicability of Article 101 of the Treaty on the Functioning of the European Union to horizontal co-operation agreements [2011] OJ C 11/1, para. 221 example 1; Faull, Nikpay and Taylor, [2014], paras. 7-385-7.390.

1706 Commission staff working document - Guidance on restrictions of competition "by object" for the purpose of defining which agreements may benefit from the De Minimis Notice, accompanying communication from the Commission - Notice on agreements of minor importance which do not appreciably restrict competition under Article 101(1) of the Treaty on the Functioning of the European Union (De Minimis Notice), [C(2014) 4136 final], Brussels, 25.6.2014, SWD (2014) 198 final, p. 7.

strictiveness of a buying concerning the economic freedom of its members has been taken into account to determine if these cooperation agreements can be restrictive of competition, or if restrictive, whether they can satisfy the requirements of Article 101(3) TFEU. Therefore, this assessment and my analysis of the cases do not deal with the effects of the alliance with regard to external parties, but with *the intra- competition limitations imposed to the members of the alliance*. Also, these cases do not constitute 'buying alliance cases' as they are traditionally interpreted by the literature[1707], in the sense that they do not deal with buyer power exploitation. However, in my view, provisions that restrict or prohibit purchasing outside of the alliance - also known as network effects[1708]- increase further the alliance's buyer power and may allow it to exploit suppliers or even develop into a buyers' cartel, for which they are also relevant considering buyer power exploitation.

865. In *National Sulphuric Acid Association* the Commission found that the *intra-*effects[1709] and activities by a transparent buying alliance that centralized the purchasing and the conditions for at least 25% of the sulphur requirements by its members were under the scope of Article 101(1) TFEU. However, it declared it inapplicable because of the pro-competitive efficiencies derived from the buying alliance pursuant to an assessment under Article 101(3) TFEU[1710]. The members of the buying pool jointly acquired sulphur for internal consumption or to be sold in the downstream market as sulphuric acid[1711]. As discussed above, the buying system was carried out through a central agent that determined the prices paid by the member internally, the quantities and type of sulphur to be purchased. Furthermore, the rules required that each member had to acquire a minimum of 25% of its sulphur input through the pool and if not, then it would be considered as no longer member of it. In the assessment of this constraint, the Commission found that the rules of the pool had the *effect* of restricting competition "*between the members* of the Pool"[1712] but not between the pool and the suppliers. The restriction was internal because by becoming a member, the buyers were not able to negotiate

---

1707 See referring to some of these cases as examples of joint purchasing agreements and not exclusive purchasing obligations: Kokkoris 'Purchase Price Fixing: A Per Se Infringement?' (2007); Ezrachi 'Buying Alliances and Input Price Fixing: In Search of a European Enforcement Standard' (2012); Whish and Bailey, *Competition law* [2015], p. 641-642.

1708 Bundeskartellamt '*Summary of the Final Report of the Sector Inquiry into the Food Retail Sector*' (2014), p. 19-20.

1709 Part of the literature seems to omit this fact when analyzing the case. Such is the example of Kokkoris who briefly discusses it and concludes that "the Commission did not find that joint purchasing was itself a direct infringement of Art 81(1)" but appears to overlook the fact that the case was about intra effects and not extra effects of the pool in Kokkoris 'Purchase Price Fixing: A Per Se Infringement?' (2007), p. 486.

1710 Commission Decision of 9 July 1980 relating to a proceeding under Article 85 of the EEC Treaty (IV/27.958 *National Sulphuric Acid Association*) [1980] OJ L 260/24, Article 1. See also discussing this case from a buyer power perspective: Faull, Nikpay and Taylor, [2014], paras. 7.399-7.406.

1711 Commission Decision of 9 July 1980 relating to a proceeding under Article 85 of the EEC Treaty (IV/27.958 *National Sulphuric Acid Association*) [1980] OJ L 260/24, para. 4 to 5.

1712 Commission Decision of 9 July 1980 relating to a proceeding under Article 85 of the EEC Treaty (IV/27.958 *National Sulphuric Acid Association*) [1980] OJ L 260/24, para. 31 (emphasis added).

better terms with suppliers on an individual basis if within the 25% quota[1713]. After having determined that this could constitute an effect restriction of competition among the members of the pool and a restriction to each member's economic freedom[1714], the Commission evaluated the *intra*-effects of the buying alliance and found that, as a whole, the internal rules helped in making the agreement to be as a whole pro-competitive pursuant to an assessment of the cumulative conditions of Article 101(3) TFEU, reinforcing the efficiency enhancing effects of buying alliances[1715].

866. Later, in *Coöperatieve Stremsel- en Kleurselfabriek v Commission* the CJEU confirmed a Commission's Decision declaring Article 101(3) TFEU inapplicable to a cooperative agreement producing rennet of animal origin and coloring agents for cheese, rendering the buying alliance unlawful because it was too restrictive of their member's freedom[1716]. This was the case because the statutes restricted excessively the members' economic freedom of choosing where and from whom to acquire the input, as also noted by Faull and Nikpay[1717]. According to the buying alliance rules, the cooperative members were obliged to purchase all quantities of rennet and coloring exclusively from the cooperative otherwise a fine were to be imposed and/or they could be expelled[1718]. The Commission Decision held that the *intra* purchasing obligation of members to acquire from the cooperative had the effect of restricting competition among themselves, reinforced by the fine and expulsion threat. When analyzing if the agreement could benefit from Article 101(3) TFEU the Commission found that the third and fourth cumulative conditions were not fulfilled because the obligation was not proportionate and it eliminated competition among the members in the Netherlands[1719]. The CJEU confirmed that the provision constituted an exclusive purchasing obligation[1720] for the members of the cooperative that had "clearly as their object to prevent members from obtaining supplies from other suppliers"[1721], and therefore, was in breach of Article 101(1) TFEU and confirmed that the Commission was right

1713 Commission Decision of 9 July 1980 relating to a proceeding under Article 85 of the EEC Treaty (IV/27.958 *National Sulphuric Acid Association*) [1980] OJ L 260/24, para. 33 to 34.

1714 Faull, Nikpay and Taylor, [2014], para. 7.404; Faull and Nikpay, [1999], para. 6. 333 and 6.340.

1715 Commission Decision of 9 July 1980 relating to a proceeding under Article 85 of the EEC Treaty (IV/27.958 *National Sulphuric Acid Association*) [1980] OJ L 260/24, para. 39 to 50.

1716 See also indicating that in this case the buyer's agreement was not compatible with EU competition law: Korah and O'Sullivan, [2002], p. 47. See discussing this case but not dealing with the CJEU Judgment: Faull, Nikpay and Taylor, [2014], para. 7.400.

1717 Faull and Nikpay, [1999], para. 6.339.

1718 Judgment of 25 March 1981 in *Coöperatieve Stremsel- en Kleurselfabriek v Commission*, C-61/80, EU:C:1981:75, para. 3.

1719 Judgment of 25 March 1981 in *Coöperatieve Stremsel- en Kleurselfabriek v Commission*, C-61/80, EU:C:1981:75, 853 to 854.

1720 Also raising the fact that the joint purchasing agreement was anticompetitive because of the exclusive purchasing obligation see: Ritter and Braun, [2004], p. 243.

1721 Judgment of 25 March 1981 in *Coöperatieve Stremsel- en Kleurselfabriek v Commission*, C-61/80, EU:C:1981:75, para. 12.

when declaring Article 101(3) TFEU not applicable because the limits of the obligation were not indispensable for the attainment of the benefits[1722].

867. In *Gøttrup-Klim and Others Grovvareforeninger v Dansk Landbrugs Grovvareselskab*[1723] the CJEU dealt again with the restriction of the member's economic freedom within a buying alliance on a different legal basis. In this case, the alliance's rules prohibited multi-cooperative participation (i.e.: members could not belong to more than one alliance) and found that the restriction of competition was allowed because it was an ancillary restraint that allowed for the buying alliance to achieve its competitive objective[1724]. The case was prompted because after a change in the alliance's statutes. The amendments stipulated that none of its members could compete in the sale or buy of fertilizers or plant protection products and prohibited their members from participating in other forms of organized cooperation[1725]. The cooperatives claimed that such provision accounted for the infringements or Article 101 and 102 TFEU and brought and action before the national courts.

868. The CJEU highlighted the pro-competitive nature of cooperative purchasing agreements as "a voluntary association of persons established in order to pursue common commercial objectives"[1726], able to oppose selling market power and improve the competitive conditions[1727]. Then, it proceeded to assess the need for such strict rules and their adequacy in the light of the alliance's objective[1728]. The CJEU stressed that restricting dual membership was allowed as an *ancillary restraint of intra-competition* because belonging to two cooperatives makes "each association less capable of pursuing its objectives for the benefit of the rest of its members, especially where the members concerned, as in the case in point, are themselves cooperative associations with a large number of individual members"[1729]. Following this assessment the CJEU concluded that a statute banning a member from having a dual cooperative membership "does not, therefore, necessarily constitute a restriction

---

1722 Judgment of 25 March 1981 in *Coöperatieve Stremsel- en Kleurselfabriek v Commission*, C-61/80, EU:C:1981:75, para. 18.

1723 Judgment of 15 December 1994 in *Gøttrup-Klim and Others Grovvareforeninger v Dansk Landbrugs Grovvareselskab*, C-250/92, EU:C:1994:413.

1724 Also remarking that this case deals with purchasing alliances but not discussing in detail the alternative solution found by the CJEU of ancillary restraints see: van Doorn, p. 143. See also: Faull and Nikpay, [1999], para. 2.99; Whish and Bailey, *Competition law* [2015], p. 136. See also a somewhat similar interpretation by Kokkoris who sees the case as a discussion of the clause of the agreement but not purchasing price fixing in: Kokkoris 'Purchase Price Fixing: A Per Se Infringement?' (2007), p. 486 to 487.

1725 Judgment of 15 December 1994 in *Gøttrup-Klim and Others Grovvareforeninger v Dansk Landbrugs Grovvareselskab*, C-250/92, EU:C:1994:413, para. 7.

1726 Judgment of 15 December 1994 in *Gøttrup-Klim and Others Grovvareforeninger v Dansk Landbrugs Grovvareselskab*, C-250/92, EU:C:1994:413, para. 30.

1727 Judgment of 15 December 1994 in *Gøttrup-Klim and Others Grovvareforeninger v Dansk Landbrugs Grovvareselskab*, C-250/92, EU:C:1994:413, para. 32; Bellamy and others, [2013], para. 2.141.

1728 Judgment of 15 December 1994 in *Gøttrup-Klim and Others Grovvareforeninger v Dansk Landbrugs Grovvareselskab*, C-250/92, EU:C:1994:413, para. 31.

1729 Judgment of 15 December 1994 in *Gøttrup-Klim and Others Grovvareforeninger v Dansk Landbrugs Grovvareselskab*, C-250/92, EU:C:1994:413, para. 33.

of competition within the meaning of Article [101] (1) of the Treaty and may even have beneficial effects on competition"[1730]; while recognizing that such a provision may also have adverse effects in competition if barring members from acquiring goods from other suppliers[1731]. Hence, the compatibility of the agreement depended on a proportionality assessment[1732] limiting the measure to what is necessary to ensure that the cooperative functions properly[1733].

869. In this sense, the Judgment can be read as an extension of the *ancillary restraint doctrine*[1734], as banning dual membership and the ability to compete with the cooperative while being a member is a necessary restriction of competition that is justified by the aim it seeks to achieve and is proportional to that end. Therefore, the assessment made was based on determining not if the buying alliance itself was an efficient agreement but rather if the restriction was necessary for the implementation of the buying alliance[1735]. Hence, even if the provision in the statutes restricted competition it was not captured by Article 101(1) TFEU as the provision was to ensure the functioning of the cooperative which had a legitimate commercial purpose, as remarked by the literature[1736].

870. In my opinion *Gøttrup-Klim and Others Grovvareforeninger v Dansk Landbrugs Grovvareselskab* must be given a restrictive interpretation as it should not be resorted to as a device that lawfully allows the restriction of competition among members of a buying alliance as a general rule. As r

1730 Judgment of 15 December 1994 in *Gøttrup-Klim and Others Grovvareforeninger v Dansk Landbrugs Grovvareselskab*, C-250/92, EU:C:1994:413, para. 34.

1731 Judgment of 15 December 1994 in *Gøttrup-Klim and Others Grovvareforeninger v Dansk Landbrugs Grovvareselskab*, C-250/92, EU:C:1994:413, para. 35.

1732 Judgment of 11 July 1985 in *Remia v Commission*, C-42/84, EU:C:1985:327. Also suggesting the adoption of a proportionality assessment in the case: Whish and Bailey, *Competition law* [2012], p. 129.

1733 Judgment of 15 December 1994 in *Gøttrup-Klim and Others Grovvareforeninger v Dansk Landbrugs Grovvareselskab*, C-250/92, EU:C:1994:413, para. 35. This case law was subsequently ratified by the CJEU also dealing with ancillary restraints in cooperatives in Judgment of 12 December 1995 in *Dijkstra and Others v Friesland (Frico Domo) Coöperatie and Others*, C-319/93, EU:C:1995:433; and Judgment of 12 December 1995 in *Oude Luttikhuis and Others v Verenigde Coöperatieve Melkindustrie Coberco*, C-399/93, EU:C:1995:434, para. 14 to 18.

1734 "[...] the concept of an 'ancillary restriction' covers any restriction which is directly related and necessary to the implementation of a main operation" in Judgment of 18 September 2001, *M6 and Others v Commission*, T-112/99, ECR, EU:T:2001:215, para. 104; Judgment of 30 June 1966 in *Société Technique Minière v Maschinenbau Ulm*, C-56/65, EU:C:1966:38; Judgment of 11 July 1985 in *Remia v Commission*, C-42/84, EU:C:1985:327. See also: Commission Notice on restrictions directly related and necessary to concentrations [2005] OJ C 56/24. For some literature on the topic see, *inter alia*: Robert H. Bork, 'Ancillary Restraints and the Sherman Act' 15 Section of Antitrust Law (1959) 211; Jeffrey L. Harrison, 'Price Fixing, the Professions, and Ancillary Restraints: Coping With Maricopa County' 4 University of Illinois Law Review (1982) 925; F. Enrique González Díaz, 'The Notion of Ancillary Restraints Under EC Competition Law' 19 Fordham International Law Journal (1995) 951; Gregory J. Werden, 'The Ancillary Restraints Doctrine' (54th Antitrust Law Spring Meeting); Whish and Bailey, *Competition law* [2015], p. 136-142.

1735 Communication from the Commission - Guidelines on the application of Article 81(3) of the Treaty [2004] OJ C 101/97, para. 30-31; Ezrachi, *EU Competition Law: An Analytical Guide to the Leading Cases* [2012], p. 100.

1736 Jones and Sufrin, *EU Competition Law: Text, Cases, and Materials* [2011], p. 228-230; Whish and Bailey, *Competition law* [2012], p. 129; Ezrachi 'Buying Alliances and Input Price Fixing: In Search of a European Enforcement Standard' (2012), p. 59.

marked by Advocate General Tesauro, the case and its circumstances were very "specific to the agricultural sector" and, therefore, its interpretation should be limited as well[1737]. In other words, buying alliances should not be used as instruments to limit the ability of their members to compete in and outside of the cooperative/buying alliance, and only in exceptional cases an ancillary restraint could be accepted under Article 101(1) TFEU, following a proportionality assessment. Otherwise, the buying alliance risks eliminating competition among its members and excessively restricting its members' economic freedom.

871. In sum, these cases show that buying alliances even if they might be pro-competitive in most occasions with regard to the relation of their members with their suppliers and end consumers are also devices that may restrict the buying ability of their own members. Most of the times these restrictions of competition would be unproblematic and required to attain the alliance's goal and others it might be too restrictive rendering the agreement incompatible with Article 101 TFEU, adding an additional component to the competitive analysis of purchasing agreements.

VII. Defenses and efficiency justifications regarding buyer power exploitation

872. In this section, I discuss the possible defenses undertakings that are investigated due to a risk of buyer power exploitation may resort to in case the behaviour is efficient. The section builds upon the general treatment of these types of defenses for exploitative buyer power cases in all competition law areas and, in particular, the differences concerning competition effects of bargaining and monopsony power exertion. In the case of monopsony power, it would be unlikely that any purchasing conduct would be efficient because monopsony always produces a deadweight welfare loss due to the demand withholding. In the case of bargaining power exertion, the chances of a conduct being considered justified due to being it pro-competitive are higher due to its efficiency-enhancing nature.

1737 Opinion of Advocate General Tesauro of 16 June 1994 in Judgment of 15 December 1994 in *Gøttrup-Klim and Others Grovvareforeninger v Dansk Landbrugs Grovvareselskab*, C-250/92, EU:C:1994:249 [1994], section 18, I – 5658. See also: C-26/76 - *Metro v Commission*, EU:C:1977:167 [1977] 01875.

A. Single conduct efficiency analysis: objective justification under Article 102 TFEU and concentration cases

873. Regarding *unilateral behaviour,* the doctrine of objective justification according to which "[...] although the fact that an undertaking is in a dominant position [this] cannot deprive it of its right to protect its own commercial interests if they are attacked, and that such an undertaking must be conceded the right to take such reasonable steps as it deems appropriate to protect those interests"[1738]. This defense allows for a conduct that seems to exploit suppliers, for instance by paying an 'unfairly low purchasing price', be proven not abusive and, therefore, not be caught by Article 102 TFEU. Concerning buyer power exploitation, an argument that may be put forth by a dominant undertaking is that the price paid is not unfairly low because, even if the purchasing price does not cover the supplier's costs, because the price paid is above the competitive level, even if it is a lower purchasing price than the one prevailing in the market. This could happen in an industry where there has not been very aggressive purchasing behaviour and suppliers have traditionally extracted supra-competitive prices, for example, in a market that was protected by a statutory selling price regulation (like a public utility such as electricity generation) where buyers were not allowed to exercise their buyer power. However, if the price regulation is eliminated, a dominant buyer in the region, for instance the largest electricity buyer, may 'impose' prices that the formerly competition-protected suppliers consider unfair because they are lower than the previous price, which was considered to be 'competitive' but which, in reality, was not so because it was a higher price than would have been the case if competition among suppliers had been intensified.

874. Also, *regarding concentrations* that may lead to future exploitative practices and, therefore, a significant impediment to effective competition, the involved undertakings may claim that the merger generates efficiencies that justify the operation and it compatible, as recognized by Recital 29 and Article 2.1. (b) of

1738 Judgment of 16 September 2008 in *Sot. Lélos kai Sia v. GlaxoSmithKline*, joined cases C-468/06 to C-478/06, EU:C:2008:504 E.C.R. [2008] I-07139, para. 50. See also: Communication from the Commission — Guidance on the Commission's enforcement priorities in applying Article 82 of the EC Treaty to abusive exclusionary conduct by dominant undertakings [2009] OJ C 45/7, para. 28-31. For some literature on the topic see, *inter alia*: Paul-John Loewenthal, 'The Defence of "Objective Justification" in the Application of Article 82 EC' 28 World Competition (2005); Albors-Llorens 'The Role of Objective Justification and Efficiencies in the Application of Article 82 EC ' (2007); Østerud; Rousseva, [2010]; Tjarda Van der Vijver, 'Objective Justification and Article 102 TFEU' 35 World Competition (2012) 55; Whish and Bailey, *Competition law* [2015], p. 221-222.

the Merger Control Regulation[1739], and the Horizontal Merger Guidelines[1740]. These efficiencies may counteract the possible anti-competitive exploitative effects in an operation among buyers and could be represented by any type of a substantiated efficiency claim[1741]. Somewhat similar to the conditions required by Article 101(3) TFEU, the Horizontal Merger Guidelines and the Commission's practice require these efficiencies to comply with three cumulative requirements. First, the concentration should benefit consumers who shall not be in a worse situation than before the merger, which in this case following a dualistic approach to buyer power would be the situation of the end consumers in the downstream markets. This would mean that the parties should demonstrate that their ability to exert bargaining power over suppliers allows them to pass on the lower prices to end consumers, or that the creation of buyer power incentivizes suppliers to invest in new products or technology to regain bargaining power vis-à-vis their buyer and avoid the buyer power exertion[1742]. Furthermore, these benefits to consumers must also be substantial and timely, which implies that the later they happen, the less substantial they would be. Secondly, the concentration must also generate buying-specific efficiencies, for example purchasing economies of scale that would not have been achieved to a similar extent by less anti-competitive alternative, for example by constituting a purchasing alliance instead of concentrating several buying undertakings into one[1743]. Thirdly and lastly, the efficiencies must be verifiable in the sense that it is possible to foresee they will materialize and offset the possible anti-competitive and exploitative effects of the merger based on an economic counterfactual assessment[1744].

1739 Council Regulation (EC) No 1/2003 of 16 December 2002 on the implementation of the rules on competition laid down in Articles [101] and [102] of the Treaty [2003] OJ L 1/1.

1740 Guidelines on the assessment of horizontal mergers under the Council Regulation on the control of concentrations between undertakings [2004] OJ C 31/5, paras. 76-88. See also some literature dealing with efficiencies in merger regulation: Joseph Farrell and Carl Shapiro, 'Scale Economies and Synergies in Horizontal Merger Analysis' 68 Antitrust Law Journal (2001) 685; William J. Kolasky and Andrew R. Dick, 'The Merger Guidelines and the Integration of Efficiencies into Antitrust Review of Horizontal Mergers' 71 Antitrust Law Journal (2003) 207; David Spector, 'Horizontal Mergers, Entry, and Efficiency Defences' 21 International Journal of Industrial Organization (2003) 1591; Johan N. M. Lagerlöf and Paul Heidhues, 'On the Desirability of an Efficiency Defense in Merger Control' 23 International Journal of Industrial Organization (2005) 803; Schwalbe and Zimmer, [2009], p. 318-356; Manfred Neumann, 'Efficiency Defense in EU and US Horizontal Merger Control if Costs are Endogenous' 17 German Economic Review (2015) 48.

1741 Guidelines on the assessment of horizontal mergers under the Council Regulation on the control of concentrations between undertakings [2004] OJ C 31/5, paras. 76-77.

1742 Guidelines on the assessment of horizontal mergers under the Council Regulation on the control of concentrations between undertakings [2004] OJ C 31/5, paras. 80-81.

1743 Guidelines on the assessment of horizontal mergers under the Council Regulation on the control of concentrations between undertakings [2004] OJ C 31/5, para. 85.

1744 Guidelines on the assessment of horizontal mergers under the Council Regulation on the control of concentrations between undertakings [2004] OJ C 31/5, paras. 86-88.

B. Assessing purchasing agreements under Article 101(3) TFEU

875. Additionally, the parties to a joint purchasing agreement may claim that even if the agreement is deemed a as restriction competition by object or effect it would satisfy the requirements of Article 101(3) TFEU because of the efficiencies it may generate. As mentioned before, a purchasing alliance will tend to be pro-competitive and, therefore is in principle not to be captured by Article 101(1) TFEU and, if it is, it is likely to satisfy the requirements of Article 101(3) and render Article 101(1) TFEU inapplicable. In the case of buyers' cartels, on the other hand, especially if they are an object restriction of competition because the cartel fixes purchasing prices or quotas, it would be unlikely that they would benefit from an efficiency exemption. Nevertheless, in both cases, factors specific to the case can be assessed on a case-by-case basis in the light of the four cumulative conditions of Article 101(3) TFEU.

876. Joint purchasing agreements can be efficiency enhancing if they foster the creation of buyer (bargaining) power and are used to maximize the benefits of a joint enterprise by leading to reductions in the purchasing price, reductions of transaction, storage and transportation costs and facilitate purchasing economies of scale[1745]. This could be the case even if the joint purchasing agreement also involves an exclusive selling obligation that improves overall production and distribution of goods conditions, as was discussed in the case of distribution of films because the joint purchasing allowed more films to be broadcasted than compared to its absence[1746]. Also, buyer (bargaining) power might have non-price related positive effects by creating incentives to suppliers to innovate promoting technical progress, produce an anti-waterbed effect for buyers not part of the alliance and promote variety, as discussed in chapter 2, section §VI.

877. Furthermore, the undertakings must prove that the agreement was indispensable in order to generate the efficiencies. This condition will not be fulfilled when it is possible proving that the purchasing agreement includes provisions that go beyond what is necessary to generate the efficiencies due to the pooling of buyer power and creation of purchasing economies of scale. The assessment to determine if the buying alliance was the indispensable measure to create the sufficient purchasing volume has to be done on a case-by-

1745 Communication from the Commission — Guidelines on the applicability of Article 101 of the Treaty on the Functioning of the European Union to horizontal co-operation agreements [2011] OJ C 11/1, para. 217; Ritter and Braun, [2004] p. 235. Purchasing economies of scale are finite as discussed recently in Albert Sánchez Graells, *Some Bold Thoughts about the (Distant?) Future of Public Procurement in the EU* (2015).

1746 Commission Decision of 15 September 1989 relating to a proceeding under Article 85 of the EEC Treaty (IV/31.734 - *Film purchases by German television stations*) [1989] OJ L 284/36, para. 49 to 56.

case basis, as recognized by the Guidelines for Horizontal Agreements[1747]. In *Métropole Télévision v Commission,* the General Court found that the exemption given by the Commission to a joint purchasing of TV broadcasting rights was based on a misinterpretation of Article 101(3) TFEU due to the lack of sufficient analysis of economic data and because of only basing its decision on the fulfillment of a particular public mission[1748].

878. As a third assessment element, a joint purchasing agreement can be efficiency enhancing whenever it fosters the creation of *bargaining power that also benefits end consumers* as the lower purchasing prices grant a fair share of the resulting benefits to end consumers. As discussed in chapter 2, section §V, this is more likely to be the case when the parties to the buying agreement do not possess substantial market power in the downstream market. If they, in addition to substantial buyer power, possess retail power, the efficiencies might not be passed on in accordance with the hourglass shape proposal[1749]. On the other hand, if the joint purchasing agreement exercises *monopsony power* the purchasing conduct will always imply a welfare loss that may or not additionally increase downstream prices to end consumers[1750]. This is because of the withholding effect that will lead to the use of an inefficient amount of resources and has an upward pressure on price.

879. Lastly, if the purchasing agreement eliminates substantial competition both *intra* and *extra partes* to the agreement, it will not benefit from the exemption. As recognized by the Guidelines for Horizontal Agreements, and in line with the dualistic approach to buyer power that I advocate[1751], this competitive analysis must include competition among the members and those non-members of the agreement in both the upstream and downstream markets, particularly because purchasing agreements may have both exploitative effects (for suppliers and/or end consumers) as well as exclusionary (for other buyers in the upstream market).

1747 Communication from the Commission — Guidelines on the applicability of Article 101 of the Treaty on the Functioning of the European Union to horizontal co-operation agreements [2011] OJ C 11/1, para. 218.

1748 Judgment of 11 July 1996, *Métropole Télévision v Commission*, joined cases T-528/93, T-542/93, T-543/93 and T-546/93, ECR, EU:T:1996:99, paras. 118 to 123. See also: Ritter and Braun, [2004], p. 236.

1749 Also supporting this see: Ezrachi 'Buying Alliances and Input Price Fixing: In Search of a European Enforcement Standard' (2012), p. 68.

1750 See also raising this issue but instead of referring to monopsony power to buyer power in general: ibid, p. 68.

1751 Communication from the Commission — Guidelines on the applicability of Article 101 of the Treaty on the Functioning of the European Union to horizontal co-operation agreements [2011] OJ C 11/1, para. 219.

VIII. Which types of harm and standard are used for exploitative cases?

880. The analysis of the law, the Commission's practice and the case law regarding exploitation of buyer power does not provide any explicit answers regarding which type of harm and which type of welfare standard are employed by the EU institutions to trigger the application of competition law to buyer power exploitation. From my research, however, it appears to be the case that EU competition law *does not adopt a pure short-term consumer welfare standard, nor does it require end consumer harm to trigger the application of the law*. Rather, it tends to factor other issues that are not directly related to the immediate well-being of the consumer, for example by triggering the application of EU competition law whenever there is a substantial distortion of the competitive market structure upstream due to exploitation of suppliers, or when their economic freedom is compromised, even granting some limited protection to the position of small suppliers, for instance by allowing elimination of competition in cases of cooperative buying. This standing is consistent with the one applied to exclusionary buyer power cases as discussed in the previous chapter. In more practical terms, for instance, if a pure consumer harm standard would be chosen, hardcore buyers' cartel that fix upstream prices or quotas but have no impact on end consumer prices would be legal[1752]. Nonetheless, they are considered object restrictions of competition in EU competition law, and also in occasions being found as per se prohibitions in US antitrust law as discussed in *Mandeville Island Farms, Inc. v American Crystal Sugar Co*[1753].

881. An example will illustrate the point. Take for instance an asymmetrical buying agreement entered into by Isolation's Supermarket and the other two local butchers in Isolation town agreeing to not compete for beef and, therefore, decrease the price currently paid for it to farmers without raising end consumer prices (and without diminishing the quantity purchased). In this case, as prices and quantities in the downstream market remain the same consumers are – strictly speaking - not worse off in the immediate term. The harm and the distortion to competition have only taken place in the upstream market because there is a transfer of profit between suppliers and buyers, because now suppliers are worse off than if the buyers would be competing against each other for the input which may for their exit from the market and puts them at a competitive disadvantage vis-à-vis other farmers. However, as a broader harm and welfare standard is adopted, the agreement would trigger competition intervention even absent consumer harm because it impacts up-

1752 See making a similar point from the US antitrust law perspective: Dennis W. Carlton, 'Does Antitrust Need to Be Modernized?' 21 The Journal of Economic Perspectives (2007) 155, p. 158.

1753 *Mandeville Island Farms, Inc. v. American Crystal Sugar Co.*, 334 U.S. 219 (1948). See also commenting the case from a welfare perspective: Jones (1989); Blair and Lopatka (2008), p. 417-419.

stream competitive conditions and the agreement disrupts the rivalry process between the buyers. The same applies when the exploitation is carried out by a single undertaking if it imposes unfairly low purchasing prices that push input prices below the competitive level. Exploitative harm in the upstream market is sufficient to trigger the application of Article 102 TFEU or declare a merger incompatible with the internal market. However, if prices are pushed below the competitive level it is likely that the input decreases due to demand withholding or the lack of interest to supply by sellers and, therefore, there are fewer amounts of goods available pushing upwards the prices in the downstream markets due to scarcity. If, on the other hand, a strict short term consumer harm and/or welfare standard is resorted to, then Isolation's Supermarket coordinated behaviour or single conduct imposing an unfairly low purchasing price that does not have an adverse effect on direct end consumer prices would not merit competition intervention.

882. In EU competition law, by and large, Articles 101(1) and 102 TFEU as well as the Merger Control Regulation and its interpretation by the Courts adopt a broader perspective than a pure short term consumer harm and consumer welfare standard when dealing with exploitation of buyer power, which implies that competition law is triggered absent end consumer harm, also to promote the protection of competitive conditions in the upstream market.

883. The case law and the Commission's practice clarifies that for buyers' cartels, and their treatment as object restrictions of competition regardless of their impact and even in the absence of substantial buyer power, end consumer harm has does not need to be demonstrated for the conduct to be in breach of Article 101(1) TFEU[1754]. Therefore, the NCAs are not required to prove the existence of end consumer harm: either that the agreement has the object of distorting competition or such effect, and the existence of a type of harm – either to suppliers or other competitors of the buyer.

884. This lack of a direct end consumer harm to trigger the application of EU competition law is not exclusive to buyer power cases and rather the general rule concerning anti-competitive agreements. As confirmed by the CJEU in *T-Mobile Netherlands and Others*, "in order to find that a concerted practice has an anti-competitive object, *there does not need to be a direct link between that practice and consumer prices*"[1755], because "Article [101 TFEU], like the other competition rules of the Treaty, is designed to protect not only the immediate interests of individual competitors or consumers but also *to protect the structure of the*

1754 See also stressing this point the opinion of Albæk who argues that a buyer's cartel if the downstream market is competitive can result in lower final prices to end consumers and still be contrary to competition law in Albæk [2013], p. 86-87.

1755 Judgment of 4 June 2009 in *T-Mobile Netherlands and Others*, C-8/08, EU:C:2009:343, para. 39 (emphasis added).

market and thus competition as such"[1756]. This same broad standing regarding the type of harm required and the protective nature of competition law with regard to 'competition as such' was later on reaffirmed by the CJEU in *GlaxoSmithKline Services and Others v Commission and Others* in almost identical terms[1757], and confirming that is not necessary to prove that an "agreement entails disadvantages for final consumers as a prerequisite for a finding of anti-competitive object"[1758].

885. It is settled case law that an agreement that is anti-competitive by object, such as in the case of a buyers' cartel that fixes prices or purchasing quotas, competition law intervenes without requiring evidence of end consumer harm to protect the interests of individual competitors and as well consumers and the competitive market structure as such. This is so even if one of the explicit conditions required by Article 101(3) TFEU to be satisfied is that end consumers obtain a fair share of the benefits generated by the agreement, which *de facto* demands some improvement to consumer welfare[1759]. This requirement, however, does demand evidence of end consumer harm for a breach of Article 101(1) TFEU to exist; what it does is helping to demonstrate that some conducts that restrict competition are more efficient than the harm the caused, including an analysis of end consumer conditions.

886. Concerning Article 102 TFEU, an ordoliberally inspired provision, as remarked by Akman[1760], it is well known that it does not include an exception clause because

> there is no exception to the principle in Community competition law prohibiting abuse of a dominant position. Unlike Article [101] of the Treaty, Article [102] of the Treaty does not allow undertakings in a dominant position to seek to obtain exemption for their abusive practices [...]. Furthermore, according to the case-law, dominant undertakings have a special responsibility not to allow their conduct to impair genuine undistorted competition on

---

1756 Judgment of 4 June 2009 in *T-Mobile Netherlands and Others*, C-8/08, EU:C:2009:343, para. 38 (emphasis added).

1757 "First of all, there is nothing in that provision to indicate that only those agreements which deprive consumers of certain advantages may have an anti-competitive object. Secondly, it must be borne in mind that the Court has held that, like other competition rules laid down in the Treaty, Article 81 EC aims to protect not only the interests of competitors or of consumers, but also the structure of the market and, in so doing, competition as such. Consequently, for a finding that an agreement has an anti-competitive object, it is not necessary that final consumers be deprived of the advantages of effective competition in terms of supply or price. It follows that, by requiring proof that the agreement entails disadvantages for final consumers as a prerequisite for a finding of anti-competitive object and by not finding that agreement had such an object, the Court of First Instance committed an error of law", Judgment of 6 October 2009 in *GlaxoSmithKline Services and Others v Commission and Others*, Joined cases C-501/06 P, C-513/06 P, C-515/06 P and C-519/06 P, EU:C:2009:610, paras. 63-64.

1758 Judgment of 6 October 2009 in *GlaxoSmithKline Services and Others v Commission and Others*, Joined cases C-501/06 P, C-513/06 P, C-515/06 P and C-519/06 P, EU:C:2009:610, para. 64.

1759 Also raising this issue and linking it with ordoliberalism see: Gormsen, [2010], p. 50-51. See also: Lianos [2013], p. 26-27.

1760 Akman, *The Concept of Abuse in EU Competition Law: Law And Economic Approaches* [2012], p. 151.

> the common market [...]. Consequently, there can be no exceptions to the prohibition of abuse by dominant undertakings[1761].

887. Unlike the case of Article 101(3) TFEU an abuse of dominance is not 'justified'. It either does or does not exist from an objective perspective. As confirmed by the CJEU, this lack of a '102(3) TFEU' provision does not, however, imply that efficiencies and trade-offs generated by the behaviour cannot be taken into account to determine whether or not the undertaking has abused its dominant position, as confirmed by the CJEU in the buyer power case *British Airways v Commission*[1762], and, more recently, in *Post Danmark II,* when the CJEU argued that "it is nevertheless open to a dominant undertaking to provide justification for behavior liable to be caught by the prohibition set out in Article [102 TFEU]"[1763]. The CJEU confirmed that the General Court was right to examine whether the granting of reverse rebates had an objective economic justification. Such an assessment in accordance to the CJEU must:

> be made on the basis of the whole of the circumstances of the case [...]. It has to be determined whether the exclusionary effect arising from such a system, which is disadvantageous for competition, may be counterbalanced, or outweighed, by advantages in terms of efficiency which also benefit the consumer. If the exclusionary effect of that system bears no relation to advantages for the market and consumers, or if it goes beyond what is necessary in order to attain those advantages, that system must be regarded as an abuse[1764].

888. Thus, the CJEU takes into account for the existence of an abuse of a dominant position that a conduct might not be abusive if the granting of rebates is outbalanced by efficiency and competitive advantages that may also benefit the consumer and improve market conditions[1765]. This could mean, therefore, that consumer harm has a role to play in dominance cases.

889. However, regarding exploitative end purchasing prices, the text of the provision in Article 102(a) TFEU introduces *an element of fairness* not to be found expressly regarding discriminatory trade conditions in Article 102(c) TFEU[1766]. This brings forth the question of whether the fairness element *also demands a benefit for suppliers.*

1761 Judgment of 30 September 2003, *Atlantic Container Line and Others v Commission*, joined cases T-191/98, T-212/98 to T-214/98, EU:T:2003:245 E.C.R. [2003] II-03275, para. 1109.

1762 Judgment of 15 March 2007 in *British Airways v Commission*, C-95/04 P, EU:C:2007:166, para. 85.

1763 Judgment of 6 October 2015 in *Post Danmark*, C-23/14, EU:C:2015:651, para. 47.

1764 Judgment of 15 March 2007 in *British Airways v Commission*, C-95/04 P, EU:C:2007:166, para. 86.

1765 See also: Gormsen, [2010] p. 52-53.

1766 Interestingly, in the US, purchasing price discrimination as regulated under the Robinson-Patman Act has an explicit reference to a "taste for fairness" although this provision has been applied less and less since the 1970s.

890. In this sense, if solely end consumer harm is employed when determining whether a purchasing price is unfairly low, the behaviour will only be anti-competitive when the reduction in the purchasing price has a negative impact on the end consumer because of a reduction in quantities purchased: the withholding problem. This appears to be the position of O'Donoghue and Padilla, who argue that prices will only be unfairly low if there is a reduction of quantities purchased[1767]. If, on the other hand, competition law has concern for some degree of 'fairness', protection of economic freedom, the wellbeing of small suppliers and considers that, even absent end consumer harm, the transfer of wealth that occurs between buyers and suppliers if *unfair* will trigger competition intervention, in an '*à la Kirkwood*'[1768] consumer welfare standard, or what from an ordoliberal perspective I call an aggregate consumer welfare standard, following a broader perspective to competition harm[1769].

891. If this concern for suppliers and fairness is factored in, this would mean that competition law would intervene and protect the competitive conditions whenever there are anti-competitive effects *in the downstream market but also when there are anti-competitive effects purely in the upstream market between suppliers and buyers. However, this should not be interpreted as implying that EU competition law, because of this element of 'fairness', should protect inefficient suppliers from buyer power exertion.* This aspect is important because the case law concerning exploitative pricing conducts, neither in the selling nor the buying side, introduce moral or ethical elements nor other requirements concerning fairness with the exception of a 'gap' between production costs and prices charged. Therefore, and in line with these factors, to avoid protection of inefficient firms and over-application of rules concerning single undertaking behaviour, competition authorities should resort to parameters such as employing the competitive price level as a legal standard, as I submitted in chapter 7, section §III, and carefully determine when some degree of suppliers' protection does not amount to the safeguarding of inefficient firms. In such light, some degree of protection to suppliers and, indirectly, to competing rival buyers can be interpreted as a way to safeguard suppliers from buyer power exploitative conducts, the protection of competitive conditions in all markets and, to a certain degree, the protection of the economic freedom of the agents too. Unlike Ezrachi, in my view this is not the result of "a shift in focus from the downstream market to the upstream one, and a closer look

---

1767 O'Donoghue and Padilla, *The Law and Economics of Article 102 TFEU* [2013], p. 843.

1768 "The most basic purpose of antitrust law is to protect consumers from such behavior. A closely related goal is to protect small suppliers like farmers and ranchers from price fixing by large buyers. When buyers with market power agree to depress the prices they pay small, competitive suppliers, they exploit them in the same way that colluding sellers exploit consumers. They take the suppliers' wealth without providing them with countervailing benefits", Kirkwood 'The Essence of Antitrust: Protecting Consumers and Small Suppliers from Anticompetitive Conduct' (2013), p. 2426. Cf with a previous paper of the same author in Kirkwood and Lande (2008-2009).

1769 See chapter 3, section §IV.C for the discussion of the ordoliberal welfare standard in buyer power cases. Also recognizing the influence of ordoliberalism in the welfare standard incorporated in Article 102 and its case law see: Gormsen, [2010], p. 39-48; Cole (2015).

at the effects on suppliers and other competitors"[1770], which is a valid interpretation, but rather a continuation of the welfaristic tradition by the Courts of protecting competition as such in the market as a whole, akin to the idea of "*vollständiger Wettbewerb*", a concept some link with ordoliberalism[1771].

892. Therefore, and integrating the findings for both concerted and unilateral behaviour this extended focus on buyer power exploitation and intervention absent end consumer harm occurs for three fundamental reasons. Firstly, in EU competition law there is a goal of protecting the competitive structure and competition as such[1772], which also implies that EU competition law is also "designed to protect [...] the immediate interests of individual competitors or consumers"[1773]. In accordance with the goals of competition law of protecting competition as a process, a broader standard for the required harm in buyer power exploitation must be resorted to. This implies that, to a certain degree and to avoid the (upstream) competitive structure being substantially disrupted, there must be a limited protection to interests and wellbeing of suppliers with regard to the anti-competitive and exploitative purchasing prices of buyers. This explains why buyers' agreements and the unilateral imposition of low purchasing prices are sanctioned even if they may lower prices for end consumers in the short term. In other words, the interest of suppliers are protected to avoid that the upstream market conditions and the competitiveness of input markets are adversely affected in terms of market concentration, suppliers being squeezed out of the market, reduced variety, decreased innovation and impacting both static and dynamic welfare in the medium and long run. This approach of safeguarding the competitive process that requires some protection of the suppliers' interest and, therefore, the intervention of EU competition without requiring evidence of direct end consumer harm, *is in line with my ordoliberal approach to buyer power cases*. Secondly, if a pure end consumer harm standard is applied, cases of abusive bargaining power will be outside of the scope of application of competition law because the prices may remain the same as before and quantity will not diminish regardless of the 'unfair' wealth transfer among suppliers and buyers or that buyers do not compete between each other any longer as well as the negative effect to the upstream competition structure. Thirdly and following this previous argument, the wording used in Article 102 TFEU, i.e. 'unfair', implies that there

---

1770 Ezrachi 'Buying Alliances and Input Price Fixing: In Search of a European Enforcement Standard' (2012), p. 58.

1771 See the discussion of ordoliberal ideas in chapter 3. Supporting such approach to competition in both the upstream and downstream market as an ordoliberal concern, but confusing this with 'competition as if' see: Gormsen, [2010], p. 46-47. See also arguing that, in general, Article 102 TFEU has goals others than pure consumer welfare and efficiency: Wils (2014).

1772 Judgment of 4 June 2009 in *T-Mobile Netherlands and Others*, C-8/08, EU:C:2009:343, para. 37; Judgment of 6 October 2009 in *GlaxoSmithKline Services and Others v Commission and Others*, Joined cases C-501/06 P, C-513/06 P, C-515/06 P and C-519/06 P, EU:C:2009:610, para. 63.

1773 Judgment of 4 June 2009 in *T-Mobile Netherlands and Others*, C-8/08, EU:C:2009:343, para. 38.

is an element of commercial fairness – or non-economic goals[1774] – involved not only for end consumers but also pertaining to the economic freedom of market participants. The use of the word "unfair" gives room for an interpretation allowing competition intervention even absent inefficiency in order to deter morally offensive conduct[1775], and even this "taste for fairness"[1776] can be quantified and monetized in terms of welfare[1777]. Thus, disregarding the problem arising from the 'unfair' – *rectius* disproportionate – profit transfer problem creates a wealth distribution problem that may be inconsistent with the postulates of a social market economy advocated by Article 3 TEU[1778].

893. Thus, my interpretation of the law, the Commission's practice and the case law in the exploitation of purchasing prices for both Article 101 and 102 TFEU, and the control of concentrations confirms that EU competition law does not follow a pure end consumer harm nor end consumer welfare standard for exploitative buyer power cases. Instead, it follows a balance that takes into account the well-being of consumers, in conjunction with other goals such as protecting competition as such in the upstream and downstream markets, taking into account and safeguarding to some extent the economic freedom of the market participants and the wellbeing of small/medium (albeit not inefficient) suppliers, wherein economic static efficiency may be trumped for some proportionate degree of contractual fairness and the wellbeing of competitive conditions for suppliers and rivals, that would lead to a medium to long term efficiency to the benefit of consumers. By protecting these other goals, "consumers are also indirectly protected. Because where competition as such is damaged, disadvantages for consumers are also to be feared", as stated by Advocate General Kokott in a rather ordoliberal vein in *British Airways v Commission*[1779]. Consequently, my finding is that, regarding exploitative buyer power, EU competition law adopts a broader harm standard concerning buyer power exploitation that is also in line with an ordoliberal approach to buyer power by balancing consumer surplus with the goal of protecting competition as a process and economic freedom of all market participants.

1774 See the work of Townley when dealing with non-efficiency arguments in EU competition law, particularly regarding Article 101 TFEU in Townley, [2009]. See the interpretation of ordoliberal ideas in conjunction with fairness, and idea I do not share, Gormsen 'The Conflict Between Economic Freedom and Consumer Welfare in the Modernisation of Article 82 EC' (2007), p. 334, and Gormsen, [2010], p. 42.

1775 *Cooper Indus. v. Leatherman Tool Grp.*, 532 U.S. 424, 439.

1776 This expression is coined by Kirkwood in Kirkwood 'The Essence of Antitrust: Protecting Consumers and Small Suppliers from Anticompetitive Conduct' (2013).

1777 Herbert J. Hovenkamp, 'Antitrust Policy After Chicago' 84 Michigan Law Review (1985) 213; Kirkwood 'The Essence of Antitrust: Protecting Consumers and Small Suppliers from Anticompetitive Conduct' (2013).

1778 For my interpretation of the social market economy in the TEU see: Ignacio Herrera Anchustegui, 'The Social Market Economy and the European Union' in Nina Vladimirovna Anischuk and Mykhailo Katsyn (eds), *Історико-правовий вимір інтеграційного процесу у новий та новітній час (Historical and Legal Views on the Integration Process During the Modern and Contemprorary Era)* (2016) 74.

1779 Opinion of Advocate General Kokott of 23 February 2006 in Judgment of 15 March 2007 in *British Airways v Commission*, C-95/04 P, EU:C:2006:133, para. 68. Also stressing that this statement "replicates ordoliberal thinking" see: Gormsen, [2010], p. 89.

IX. Conclusion

894. In this chapter, I discussed the ways in which buyers can exploit their buyer power vis-à-vis suppliers in the upstream market through the imposition of purchasing conditions, unilaterally or through concerted behaviour. The chapter has put forward that *buyer power exploitation is less likely to be self-correctable* by market forces, as is the case with supplier side exploitation, because of the different dynamics of buyer power. Therefore, EU competition law intervention is warranted and its role should be determining which type of practices buyers can exploit their suppliers and assessing whether these conducts indeed amount to exploitation and competition infringement and distinguishing them from purchasing conducts that – like in the case of bargaining power – are efficiency enhancing and part of the countervailing power of buyer power vis-à-vis seller market power.

895. Concerning dominant buyers, buyer power can be exploited through setting 'unfairly low purchasing prices' – which I define as prices below the competitive level that, additionally, do not cover the suppliers' marginal costs – like a monopsonist would do in a standard microeconomic model. However, as I discussed in chapter 2 and as confirmed by the absence of cases in EU competition law, exerting buyer power in an exploitative manner through unilaterally imposed *exploitatively low purchasing prices rarely occurs*. In cases where it does, the pertinent question is: *What test is to be applied to determine whether a price is unfairly low*? I submit, in line with Advocate General Lenz in *CICCE v Commission*[1780], a buyer power version of the *United Brands v Commission* test to determine when a price is "unfairly low". In this proposal, I use as indicators of exploitative purchasing prices the supplier's marginal cost as a first element and then the market's competitive price as a second benchmark. If the prices paid by the dominant undertaking are insufficient to cover production costs, suppliers will be forced outside of the market and, if they are and also if the price paid is lower than the competitive level, then the conduct is abusive. This double cost standard allows for the protection of efficient suppliers and avoids excessive regulation that may hinder efficient buying conducts because it does not protect suppliers that are not competitive enough. The proposed test, however, is highly counterfactual and a guiding tool that requires further development by the literature and the Courts.

896. Also, my discussion concerning unilateral behaviour has extended to purchasing price discrimination that exploits suppliers and creates a situation in which some of them are in a disadvantage position vis-à-vis other suppliers that have not been exploited. The Commission's practice and case law shows that EU

1780 Opinion of the Advocate General Lenz of 16 January 1985, in Judgment of 28 March 1985 in *CICCE v Commission*, C-298/83, EU:C:1985:16 [1985].

competition law grants protection to those discriminated buyers and takes a strict and formal approach to purchasing discrimination anchored on perhaps an excessive protection of the supplying undertakings' economic freedom that may thwart efficient purchasing behaviours, which is akin to the general treatment of price discrimination in selling side cases of unilateral conduct.

897. With regard to concerted conducts, the chapter discussed the rationale of pooling buyer power to create economies of scale and how this can be done through different types of coordination, including the case of cooperatives and purchasing alliances. Furthermore, I distinguished two main forms of exerting buyer power coordination with quite different outcomes and legal treatment. EU competition law distinguishes between *buyers' cartels and buying alliances*. Buyers' cartels are agreements among purchasers of goods to alter the competitive process of price formation and directed at imposing purchasing prices, maximum purchasing quotas, or dividing markets. These concerted practices are held by the Courts *as object restrictions of competition* – regardless of whether they exert bargaining or monopsony power – because of their detrimental effect on the competitive process *even absent consumer harm*. Furthermore, due to their perniciousness, competition authorities should prosecute buyers' cartels as a priority enforcement in buyer power, an opinion also shared in the US by the American Antitrust Institute[1781]. In the case of buying alliances, nonetheless, the treatment given is, and should be, different. Buying alliances tend to be a legitimate form of buyer (bargaining) power exertion that do not anti-competitively distort the price formation among undertakings. Consequently, if buying alliances are used to *generate neutralizing bargaining power and create economies of scale, their impact in welfare will be positive, as long as those benefits* obtained through the increase buyer power *are also passed on to end consumers* in the form of lower purchasing prices. This is not to say, however, that all buying alliances are pro-competitive and should be exempted from the application of competition law absent any kind of effect based evaluation. The proposal, instead, is to *approach buying alliances under an effect based approach* within Article 101 TFEU. However, and as discussed in the chapter, determining what constitutes a buying alliance and a buyers' cartel is a difficult exercise because what at first sight might look like a transparent alliance where purchasing prices are not fixed and competition among buyers in the upstream and downstream markets exists, might degenerate into a buyers' cartel that sets purchasing prices, which seems to be a growing trend in Europe as remarked by the Bundeskartellamt[1782].

1781 American Antitrust Institute [2008], p. 97.

1782 Bundeskartellamt *'Sektoruntersuchung: Lebensmitteleinzelhandel'* (2014).

898. Furthermore, undertakings that have been accused of exploiting anti-competitively their buyer power can resort to efficiency defenses for unilateral and concerted behaviours and show that their conduct was either not abusive or that it was efficient. This is the case regarding the doctrine of objective justification with regard Article 102 TFEU and the efficiency analysis concerning concentrations pursuant to Article 2.1. (b) of the Merger Control Regulation. Concerning coordinated behaviour, the same applies; both regarding buyer cartels and buying alliances, the parties to such agreements may claim that the conduct is not unlawful as it satisfies the requirements for the application of Article 101(3) TFEU. With respect to buyer cartels the conditions required and the Commission's practice and case law shows that it will be rare, not to say impossible, for these types of agreements to satisfy the four cumulative conditions regardless of whether the cartel reduces purchasing prices or not. In the case of buying alliances it is more likely that these forms of buyer coordination may be exempted from the prohibition of Article 101(1) TFEU because, by their very nature, they tend to have pro-competitive effects that outweigh any anti-competitive effects and which tend to be of an ancillary nature for the achievement of the buying alliance.

899. Finally, this chapter also discussed what the welfare and harm standard that applies to buyer power exploitative cases is. The answer is that a strict end consumer harm standard is under-inclusive and it also is not the adopted approach under EU competition law regarding buyer power exploitation. In fact, that the Courts and the Commission apply competition law even absent evidence of direct end consumer harm towards the protection of upstream market conditions, some degree of economic freedom of the suppliers, and to protect competition as a process, a posture that is also in line with the ordoliberal standard proposed concerning buyer power cases in general and the dualistic approach to buyer power cases advocated in this study.

8

EXPLOITATIVE BUYER POWER: UNFAIR PURCHASING PRACTICES*

I. Introduction

900. A powerful buyer, alone or in agreement with other buyers, may exploit its buyer power vis-à-vis its supplier(s) by imposing 'unfair' trading conditions, in particular Unfair Purchasing Practices (UPPs). Examples of UPPs, like slotting allowances, requirements to contribute to advertisements, etc., involve *a transfer of risk or profit from the seller to the buyer that is not duly compensated or objectively justified and may prohibited* under Articles 101(1) and 102 TFEU, the Merger Control Regulation, or under the scope of stricter national rules for unilateral behavior in accordance with Article 3(2) of Regulation 1/2003, and which escape the Unfair Commercial Practice Directive's scope[1783]. However,

---

* This chapter builds upon a previous version that has been published as Ignacio Herrera Anchustegui, 'Buyer Power Exploitation: Unfair Purchasing Practices' in Fernando Cachafeiro, Rafael García Pérez and Marcos A. López Suárez (eds), *Derecho de la Competencia y Gran Distribución Comercial* (Thomson-Reuters Aranzadi 2016) p. 349-421.

1783 Directive 2005/29/EC of the European Parliament and of the Council of 11 May 2005 concerning unfair business-to-consumer commercial practices in the internal market and amending Council Directive 84/450/EEC, Directives 97/7/EC, 98/27/EC and 2002/65/EC of the European Parliament and of the Council and Regulation (EC) No 2006/2004 of the European Parliament and of the Council ('Unfair Commercial Practices Directive') [2005] OJ L 149/22. For some literature dealing with the Directive's application and derived case law see: Malek Radeideh, *The Principle of Fair Trading in EC Law: Information and Consumer Choice in the Internal Market* ([s.n.] 2004); Christian Handig, 'The Unfair Commercial Practices Directive – A Milestone in the European Unfair Competition Law?' European Business Law Review (2005) 1117; Geraint G. Howells, Hans- W. Micklitz and Thomas Wilhelmsson, *European Fair Trading Law: The Unfair Commercial Practices Directive* (Ashgate Pub. Co. 2006); Rossella Incardona and Cristina Poncibò, 'The Average Consumer, the Unfair Commercial Practices Directive, and the Cognitive Revolution' 30 J Consum Policy (2007) 21; Deborah L. Parry, *The Yearbook of Consumer Law 2009* (Ashgate 2008); Chris Willett, 'Fairness and Consumer Decision Making under the Unfair Commercial Practices Directive' 33 J Consum Policy (2010) 247; Georgios Anagnostaras, 'The Unfair Commercial Practices Directive in Context: From Legal Disparity to Legal Complexity?' 47 Common Market Law Review (2010) 147; Peter Shears, 'Overviewing the EU Unfair Commercial Practices Directive: Concentric Circles' European Business Law Review (2012) 497; Jules Stuyck, 'The Court of Justice and the Unfair Commercial Practices Directive' 52 Common Market Law Review (2015) 721.

more often than not, *UPPs are outside the scope of application of EU competition law* and regulated in the different MS under unfair competition laws or relative dominance provisions which aim at addressing issues of market imbalances but not explicitly designed to deal with issues of market efficiency or wide market power abuse, such as EU competition law does. An example of these alternative approaches to deal with UPPs outside of EU competition law at the Community level is the creation of a voluntary and food-retailing specific proposal to regulate UPPs within the framework of the Supply Chain Initiative, as discussed in section §VI of this chapter. This legislative overlapping creates a complex patchwork of rules addressing UPPs that may apply jointly or separately, particularly at national level[1784], and a gray area of the application (or not) of EU competition law to buyer power issues[1785].

901. UPPs have grasped most of the attention in literature concerning abuse of buyer power, particularly when dealing with food retailing, and have been portrayed by the literature, politicians and lobby groups, along with monopsony power, as the negative side of buyer power[1786]. The link of UPPs with buyer power seems to have led some to the erroneous belief, particularly among lawyers, that buyer (bargaining) power is a generally negative expression of market power, and policy makers and politicians to demand more competition law control over UPPs, as done by the European Parliament[1787], in part motivated by the dichotomy between strong vs. weak undertakings[1788], or large companies vs. small producer agricultural cooperatives[1789].

902. In this chapter, I submit that arguably the most "feared" aspect of buyer power is on most occasions neither a sensu stricto competition concern nor an EU competition law problem because UPPs tend to lack a substantial market-wide impact on competition, nor are they an expression of a market power

---

1784 Also remarking the myriad of legal solutions given to UPPs within and outside competition law see: Jenny [2015], p. 4.

1785 A similar expression was used by a report from by European Commission, *Study on the Legal Framework Covering Business-To-Business Unfair Trading Practices in the Retail Supply Chain* (2014), p. 36, and another report by the Finnish NCA dealing with abuses in the food retailing industry and which has been summarized in European Competition Network (2012), para. 254. See for a discussion of the relation between competition law and unfair competition law: Faull and Nikpay, [1999], para. 3.307-3.311; Franz Jürgen Säcker, 'Basic Principles' in Günther Hirsch, Frank Montag and Franz Jürgen Säcker (eds), *Competition law: European community practice and procedure : article-by-article commentary* (Sweet & Maxwell 2008), para. 1-1-034 to 1-1-06; Eilmansberger [2008], para. 2-15-226 to 2-15-246.

1786 Tribunal Vasco de Defensa de la Competencia (April 2009), p. 5.

1787 European Parliament *Imbalances in the Food Supply Chain,* Brussels (19 January 2012). Also remarking the political impact of UPPs see: Jenny [2015].

1788 This issue of bargaining power imbalance between large buyers and small suppliers was addressed back in 1936 in the US through the Robinson-Patman Act that prohibits any type of buyer induced purchasing price discrimination in order to protect small suppliers from hard bargaining.

1789 For a general discussion on the types of cooperatives see: Fici [2013], p. 24-25. Also in the US, the issue of cooperatives and the abuse of powerful buyers vis-à-vis small farmers has been noted since 1952 when it was held that "[i]ndividual farmers, lacking adequate storage facilities and dependent upon a rapid turnover of harvested crops to meet operating expenses, occupy an extremely disadvantageous bargaining position in disposing of overabundant production to much larger, highly concentrated purchasers", in 'Cooperatives and the Antitrust Laws' 27 Indiana Law Journal (1952) 430, p. 430. See also: Reich (2007), p. 486.

problem[1790]. Instead, the impact of UPPs tends to be a *bilateral issue involving contractual imbalances among parties to a commercial relationship and problems of profit distribution*[1791].

903. However, these issues of profit distribution, contractual fairness and the impact of UPPs on suppliers in the medium and long term *may have an adverse effect in competition and become a competition law problem.* The UPP effects on these variables may lead to the creation of barriers to entry and exit in the upstream market, market concentration and, predominantly affecting dynamic efficiency in terms of innovation, variety and investments by the suppliers. Furthermore, the imposition of UPPs may also affect the *competition among rival suppliers* in a horizontal level pursuant to purchasing price discrimination, as those that are exploited through them are at a disadvantage when compared to others that are not. Also, UPPs can eventually have *adverse effects on end consumers*, for example in terms of less variety of goods, different or specialized retailers that are substituted by large and standardized ones or lesser quality on the products they acquire. These are economic law problems that can be exceptionally addressed under EU competition law in case the UPPs are exerted by a dominant undertaking, a buyer's cartel or a vertical agreement, or arising pursuant a concentration, but much more likely to be issues captured by *non-core EU competition law* in most cases[1792].

904. In fact, this chapter shows how solutions to UPPs have arisen in most MS under national laws to address these problems, for instance by resorting to their regulation under unfair competition laws, sectoral laws, or national competition laws setting stricter rules for unilateral behaviour that either diminish the thresholds to determine purchasing dominance, or creating figures of 'relative dominant positions'[1793], or abuse of dependence to regulate the conduct of individual buyers with substantial market power[1794]. The question is whether these types of solutions are an adequate remedy to UPPs or whether they could lead to overregulation, prohibition of efficiency enhancing purchasing conducts, and the application of remedies not tailored to address issues of contractual imbalance[1795]. However, the trend that uses national competition law to regulate UPPs remains a minority one and it has been developed almost exclusively to *tackle problems in food retailing, a socially and politically*

1790 Cf with Lianos and Lombardi who argue that situations of superior bargaining power are a competition issue if observed with detachment from neoclassical theories and a holistic approach to markets is taken, Lianos and Lombardi, p. 7-8.

1791 For a discussion on welfare distribution issues in US antitrust law see: Herbert J. Hovenkamp, *Distributive Justice and Consumer Welfare in Antitrust* (2011) 1.

1792 See also for a similar approach: European Commission, *Study on the Legal Framework Covering Business-To-Business Unfair Trading Practices in the Retail Supply Chain* (2014), p. 114.

1793 Ibid, p. 116.

1794 Also stressing this fact see: ibid, p. 36.

1795 Also remarking the fact that rules that aim to promote competition and ensure fairness at the same time "are often contradictory" see: Jenny [2015], p. 6. Cf with Lianos and Lombardi.

sensitive topic because of the protection of both end consumers and the agricultural producers[1796].

905. Consequently, in this chapter, *I discuss what the nature of UPPs is and how can they be used to exploit buyer power vis-à-vis suppliers*. I argue that despite the exploitative character of UPPs most of the time these types of practices *will fall outside of EU competition law because they do not represent, by and large, a market power problem with substantive impact on allocative nor dynamic efficiency, as they have little impact on the competitive structure and, instead, have effects mostly concerning fairness and contractual balance*. This, nevertheless, does not mean that UPPs might not also be a competition problem; what it means is that EU competition law is triggered whenever the effects of UPPs substantially and adversely impact the upstream competitive structure, competition as a process and allocative and dynamic efficiency in the medium and long term. Therefore, if it is proven that UPPs have this anti-competitive effect in the market, then EU competition law would be triggered to tackle this buyer power abuse, as I discuss in section §IV. At the same time, this also means that, to solve problems that tend to remain within the sphere of profit distribution (without affecting market efficiency) and contractual fairness, other regulatory mechanisms – particularly at the national level – are better suited to address these exploitative buying conducts.

906. Accordingly, I inquire *what type of regulation is better suited to regulate these practices, when the EU competition law applies to UPPs,* and analyze what the *current practice in the national law of some MS* is. The outcome of this analysis shows that MS do not follow a common path to address UPPs issues and that there is a growing trend towards (over)regulation of food retailing. The results of the increasing regulation, however, do not correlate with an increase in cases being denounced before NCAs or the Commission at the EU level, which shows that, perhaps, UPPs are not as pernicious as they are portrayed, or that suppliers fear retaliation by their powerful buyers in case they file complaints against the imposition of UPPs.

907. To answer these questions, the chapter is organized as follows: In section §II I discuss the concept of UPPs and describe some of the most common practices found in different markets. Section §III discusses what the market impact of UPPs is, followed in section §IV with an analysis of whether and when UPPs are under the scope of application of EU competition law. My

---

1796 A similar concern was expressed by the Basque NCA when dealing with the food retailing in Spain and the impact on the welfare of suppliers and end consumers when holding that: "the Spanish procurement market is studied and it is concluded that members of the distribution oligopoly are exercising their buyer power in the supply market in detriment to free competition and consumers." In Tribunal Vasco de la Competencia (April 2009), p. 137. See also suggesting that most buyer power cases deal with food retailing but without distinguishing between an *inter partes* or an *erga omnes* approach: Faull and Nikpay, [1999], para. 3.110. See also recently analyzing the effects of bargaining power in food retailer and its effects vis-à-vis suppliers: Lianos and Lombardi.

analysis demonstrates that, by and large, UPPs are outside of the scope of application of EU competition law and because of this they tend to be a contractual fairness and profit distribution problems that usually have no adverse effects on the market's competitiveness. In section §V, I discuss the need to address UPPs by means of other types of economic regulation due to the reduced scope of EU competition law applicability. In section §VI, I review the alternative solutions to UPPs adopted in most MS and other non-EU/EEA jurisdictions and classify them into four different regulatory types. In section §VII I discuss the EU Supply Chain Initiative as a method of self-enforcing good business practices within the EU whenever the impact has a cross-border nature. Finally, section §VIII concludes the chapter with a discussion of the findings and future suggestions.

II. Unfair purchasing practices: definition and modalities

908. UPPs are a sub-type of unfair trading practices that are imposed by a buyer to a seller. Generally speaking, unfair trading practices constitute behaviours that are contrary to the idea of 'fairness' in a commercial transaction[1797]. The Commission has defined unfair practices as behaviours that "grossly deviate from good commercial conduct and are contrary to good faith and dealing"[1798]. A trading condition will be unfair whenever one of the parties employs its superior bargaining power to demand from its counterpart a transfer of wealth *without providing offsetting benefits* or proper retribution, as remarked by Kirkwood[1799], or it could be unfair because the benefits are not objectively justified; characteristics which are shared by all unfair practices[1800]. Furthermore, unfair trading conditions and UPPs surge pursuant to the imbal-

---

1797 Fairness, distributive and philosophical discussions aside, is understood in the competition (*lato sensu*) context as "any act of competition contrary to honest trade practices in industrial or commercial manners" according to Article 10bis (2) of the Paris Convention, Paris Convention for the Protection of Industrial Property of March 20, 1883, as revised at Brussels on December 14, 1900, at Washington on June 2, 1911, at The Hague on November 6, 1925, at London on June 2, 1934, at Lisbon on October 31, 1958, and at Stockholm on July 14, 1967, and as amended on September 28, 1979. See also: European Commission *Report from the Commission to the European Parliament and the Council on Unfair Business-to-Business Trading Practices in the Food Supply Chain,* Brussels (2016), p. 2; paragraph 2 of the UK Groceries Supply Code of Practice and the principle of "fair dealing", and also using the term "unfair" when referring to payment delays conducts by large buyers vis-à-vis suppliers see: Groceries Code Adjudicator, Investigation into Tesco Plc, 26 January 2016, public version available online at: https://www.gov.uk/government/uploads/system/uploads/attachment_data/file/494840/GCA_Tesco_plc_final_report_26012016_-_version_for_download.pdf

1798 European Commission *Green Paper on Unfair Trading Practices in the Business-to-Business Food and Non-Food supply Chain in Europe,* Brussels (2013), p. 3.

1799 Kirkwood 'The Essence of Antitrust: Protecting Consumers and Small Suppliers from Anticompetitive Conduct' (2013), p. 2448. Also remarking the unfair transfer of benefits see: Competition Commission - UK *The Supply of Groceries in the UK Market Investigation,* London (2008), para. 95.

1800 Bundeskartellamt *Summary of the Final Report of the Sector Inquiry into the Food Retail Sector,* (2014), p. 18.

ance of bargaining power among parties to a transaction as recognized by the Supply Chain Initiative[1801], or "inequality of bargaining power," as labeled by Akman[1802], connected with dependence, and which take place within the "business-to-business" relation[1803].

909. Pursuant to the general definition of unfair practices, I conceptualize UPPs as those 'unfair' and exploitative requirements imposed by a buyer on its suppliers due to the existence of a bargaining power imbalance that deviates from "good commercial conduct and [which] are contrary to good faith and fair dealing"[1804]. This would be the case of the buyer demanding some specific benefit without an objective justification and/or without a proper retribution[1805]. Therefore, it comes as no surprise that some of these unfair purchasing conditions are perceived by politicians and society as unethical buying behaviours that should be addressed beyond pure welfare considerations. Furthermore, I submit that *UPPs are vertical types of purchasing practices* and *the effects* between buyers and suppliers are the *expressions of bargaining power exercise but rarely of monopsony power as UPPs do not involve underbuying a good* (withholding effect) but instead shift commercial risks or transfer costs[1806]. Thus, UPPs are not a form of pure exercise of monopsony power but instead an exercise of unequal bargaining power between parties to a commercial transaction.

910. UPPs arise in general because there exists a *large disproportion of bargaining power* and information among the parties in which the buyer has a privileged position that allows it to abuse its supplier, particularly if it depends on the

---

1801 European Commission '*Report from the Commission to the European Parliament and the Council on Unfair Business-to-Business Trading Practices in the Food Supply Chain*' (2016), p. 4; a recent study by the European Competition Network shows how from all cases of anticompetitive practices in the food retailing sector at least 20% of them were accrued due to dominance and in particular the imposition of unjustified contractual obligations, European Competition Network (2012), para. 10. In the UK 35% of suppliers claim to have been subject to payment delays practices by suppliers, Groceries Code Adjudicator, Investigation into Tesco Plc, 26 January 2016, public version available online at: https://www.gov.uk/government/uploads/system/uploads/attachment_data/file/494840/GCA_Tesco_plc_final_report_26012016_-_version_for_download.pdf, para. 7.5

1802 Akman, *The Concept of Abuse in EU Competition Law: Law and Economic Approaches* [2012].

1803 European Commission '*Green Paper on Unfair Trading Practices in the Business-to-Business Food and Non-Food supply Chain in Europe*' (2013), p. 3.

1804 Ibid, p. 3.

1805 Decision B2-58/09 *Edeka Konditionenforderungen - Verstoß gegen das "Anzapfverbot"*, 3 July 2014 by the Bundeskartellamt. Summary available at: http://www.olg-duesseldorf.nrw.de/behoerde/presse/Presse_aktuell/20151118_PM_Edeka/index.php; Bundeskartellamt (2014), 17. See also: Case summary from 6 July 2015: Prohibition of acquisition of Kaiser´s Tengelmann outlets by Edeka, B2-96/14 (English version), appealed and revoked by the German Federal Minister for Economic Affairs and Energy under § 42 of the German Competition Act based, *inter alia*, on the protection of working positions that would be absorbed by Edeka.

1806 European Commission '*Green Paper on Unfair Trading Practices in the Business-to-Business Food and Non-Food supply Chain in Europe*' (2013), p. 21. See also supporting this: Kirkwood 'Buyer Power and Exclusionary Conduct: Should Brooke Group Set the Standards for Buyer-Induced Price Discrimination and Predatory Bidding?' (2004-2005), p. 625 and 637.

buyer[1807], as explicitly recognized in Regulation 261/2012[1808], and partially discussed in chapter 5, section §IV.C when dealing with buyer power assessment. From this follows that *dependence* can both be an indication of substantial market power and can be also a situation in which suppliers are prone to be exploited by a powerful buyer by means of imposing UPPs.

911. Nevertheless, these *'unfair' practices may be examples of "hard bargaining" that would not lead to any anti-competitive effect* but towards more efficiency that benefits consumers in the form of lower prices and higher quantities of goods[1809]. In other words, the difficulty of suppliers to earn profit may not be because of the exploitative or unfair exercise of buyer power but instead because of a healthy exercise of competitive pressure by a buyer, as noted by van Doorn[1810], or because the suppliers are not particularly efficient. This same view was expressed recently by the Düsseldorf Court of Appeals when revoking a decision by the German NCA concerning abuse of dominance when holding that practices that look like UPPs are nothing but *hard bargaining between contractual parties* where demands are exchanged and profit is distributed in a process of offers and counteroffers[1811]. Furthermore, a price or practice might appear to be unfair for a particular supplier because *it is not an efficient undertaking* and, therefore, the low prices paid or the strict requirements imposed by the buyer would be met and would be neither exploitative nor unfair if exercised vis-à-vis an efficient supplier. This could be the case in agricultural markets where producers, such as in some areas of Spain, are still small farmers that run a business that due to its size is not able to optimize production and/or generate economies of scale, and has higher production costs than, for instance, a much larger farm[1812]. Thus, there is a thin line between when a prac-

1807 Carstensen 'Buyer Power, Competition Policy, and Antitrust: The Competitive Effects of Discrimination Among Suppliers' (2008), p. 271.

1808 "However, in many cases the concentration of supply is low, which results in an imbalance in bargaining power in the supply chain between farmers and dairies. This imbalance can lead to unfair commercial practices", Regulation (EU) No 261/2012 of the European Parliament and of the Council of 14 March 2012 amending Council Regulation (EC) No 1234/2007 as regards contractual relations in the milk and milk products sector [2012] OJ L 94/38, Recital (5); European Commission *Tackling Unfair Trading Practices in the Business-to-Business food supply chain,* Strasbourg (2014), p. 2; European Commission '*Green Paper on Unfair Trading Practices in the Business-to-Business Food and Non-Food supply Chain in Europe*' (2013), p. 3 and 5.

1809 Bundeskartellamt '*Summary of the Final Report of the Sector Inquiry into the Food Retail Sector*' (2014), p. 2.

1810 van Doorn, p. 171-177.

1811 Düsseldorf Appellate Court in Decision of 18 November 2015 *EDEKA/Plus-Übernahme* revoking a Decision B2-58/09 *Edeka Konditionenforderungen - Verstoß gegen das "Anzapfverbot"*, 3 July 2014 by the Bundeskartellamt. Summary available at: http://www.olg-duesseldorf.nrw.de/behoerde/presse/Presse_aktuell/20151118_PM_Edeka/index.php. See the discussion of this case in "Sobre el abuso de dependencia económica en la cadena alimentaria: el asunto EDEKA" in the blog "Competencia y Regulación" of Prof. Robles Martín-Laborda, available at: http://derechocompetencia.blogspot.com.es/2015/12/sobre-el-abuso-de-dependencia-economica.html.

1812 This, for example, appears to be the case in the Spanish region of Galicia where suppliers group themselves in very small cooperatives and the size of each farm/producer is so small that does not allow them group seller power – or buyer power to acquire their required input –, generate economies of scale, and drive their operational costs upwards. This is particularly striking in the case of milk production where farmers feed cows not with natural grass, but with bought cereals which increase their costs. I would like to thank Fernando Cachafeiro from bringing up this situation to my knowledge.

tice is unfair and imposed by a strong buyer and when it is accepted through bilateral negotiations by both parties because both undertakings are efficient.

912. Hence, and connected to the difficulty of defining from an economic perspective when a contractual of purchasing requirement is 'unfair', other approaches could be resorted to. For instance, a more 'economic approach' would be to determine if a practice is *not unfair* but rather if the UPP is *inefficient and undesirable from a welfare maximization perspective* by inquiring whether parties that enter into UPPs are not maximizing the contract welfare and making the contractual relation less efficient. If the UPP causes the contract to be less efficient, for example, because it implies a reduction on purchases or because parties would have entered a different type of contract, then the UPP is *inefficient*, whether or not it is 'unfair'. If this approach is adopted then competition authorities dealing with UPPs would have to first determine whether the UPP has made the contract less efficient and then evaluate if there is additionally a fairness problem represented by an imbalance of profit distribution originating from the parties' bargaining position. Therefore, under this approach, UPPs would only be sanctionable whenever, in addition to being unfair, they also represent a source of concern regarding value creation and economic efficiency. This approach, however, has not yet been endorsed by the Courts or the Commission's practice, as I discuss further in this chapter.

A. UPPs as exploitative and vertical related practices

913. UPPs are primarily *exploitative buyer practices of a vertical nature,* accordingly, they are also known as *buyer-led vertical restraints*[1813]. The rules dealing with UPPs aim at "eliminating competition restraints that occur within or because of the relationship between undertakings active in two different stages of the market," as remarked by Këllezi[1814]. Therefore, UPPs primarily have an impact in the buyer-supplier relation as the buyer obtains an 'unfair' profit. However, UPPs may also impact the competitive relation among suppliers – those not subject to the conduct and those affected by it – as well as competitive conditions downstream and vis-à-vis the end consumer, as confirmed by the UK Competition Commission, for instance by affecting variety, market concentration or entry of new players[1815]. Hence, UPPs have an *impact on three levels vis-à-vis three different target groups*: suppliers that are exploited; competing buyers that might be foreclosed, and consumers that may also be exploited by the UPPs, directly or indirectly[1816], in line with the *dualistic effect of buyer power exertion.*

1813 American Antitrust Institute [2008], p. 112.

1814 Këllezi [2008], p. 83.

1815 UK Competition Commission (2000), p. 103. See also stressing the multidimensionality of UPPs' effects: Jenny [2015], p. 9.

1816 Also highlight the levels of impact of UPPs see: Tribunal Vasco de la Competencia (April 2009), p. 5.

914. In this chapter, my focus lies on the exploitative nature of UPPs vis-à-vis suppliers and I do not discuss the horizontal effects of UPPs concerning competition among suppliers[1817], the impact of private labels, or the UPPs consequences vis-à-vis consumer, as these scenarios fall outside of my study's scope, but I do recognize that these are areas ripe for further investigation as a side-effect of buyer power related practices.

915. UPPs surge on verticals relations between suppliers and buyers because if the bargaining power differences are so large that the supplier is in a dependent position, the buyer will be able to unilaterally impose terms on its weaker suppliers to transfer economic profit whenever they are negotiating their commercial transaction. Therefore, the UPPs are generally set through contractual clauses – or pre-contractual negotiations[1818] – that have *the aim of exploiting suppliers* by transferring risks, reducing information exchange, imposing payments for additional services[1819], unilateral modifications of contract conditions among others[1820].

916. However, not all instances of UPPs are caused by an express interest in exploiting suppliers. Practice shows that conducts that have analog consequences to UPPs are sometimes carried out not in explicit exercise of exploitative buyer power but owing to poor administration and communication standards on behalf of large buyers, as was found to be the case in the recent *Tesco* investigation in the UK[1821]. This, nonetheless, does not imply that the exploitative effect should be outside of a regulatory scope or that it does not requires a remedy.

917. In addition to their vertical nature, although UPPs are not an exclusive food retailing phenomenon, this is the market most seriously affected by such practices because of the peculiar and dichotomist structure of big buyers represented by supermarket chains and small sellers represented by farmers and food producers, and the existence of buyer dependence.

1817 My discussion regarding buyer power exploitation and the disadvantage to suppliers with respect to others is found in chapter 7, section §IV.

1818 European Commission '*Green Paper on Unfair Trading Practices in the Business-to-Business Food and Non-Food supply Chain in Europe*' (2013), p. 6.

1819 Like in the case of shelf space, which was subject to a study by the Norwegian NCA in 2005 and in which it concluded that if competition downstream was fierce then those fees would be passed on to consumers as lower prices. Also, if these types of fees were to be banned they would be replaced by other unfair condition practices, such as volume rebates or bonuses on sales in European Competition Network (2012), para. 255.

1820 For example, the UK Competition Commission found in 2008 at least 52 unfair trading practices which could be employed by buyers and suppliers alike in the food retailing market: Competition Commission - UK (2008). See also for additional modalities of unfair trading practices: European Commission '*Tackling Unfair Trading Practices in the Business-to-Business food supply chain*' (2014); European Commission '*Green Paper on Unfair Trading Practices in the Business-to-Business Food and Non-Food supply Chain in Europe*' (2013), also see the list of unfair trade conditions related to access to retailers (buyer power induced) and contractually related as suggested by the European Parliament in European Parliament Resolution on the Imbalances in the Food Supply Chain [2012], P7_TA(2012)0012, para. 10. See also listing a comprehensive list UPPs in Tribunal Vasco de la Competencia (April 2009), p. 167-70.

1821 Groceries Code Adjudicator, Investigation into Tesco Plc, 26 January 2016, public version available online at: https://www.gov.uk/government/uploads/system/uploads/attachment_data/file/494840/GCA_Tesco_plc_final_report_26012016_-_version_for_download.pdf, p. 5.

a. UPPs and dependence

918. As discussed above, UPPs arise because of the difference in bargaining power among the parties to a bilateral relation. If such difference in buyer (bargaining) power among suppliers and buyers is sufficiently large it may lead to a *relation of dependence* where suppliers may become easy prey allowing them to extract additional profits without proper compensation[1822]. Dependence arises because the buyer represents a substantial portion of the business of the retailer or because there is no possibility to switch to alternative buyers[1823], as in some industries the buyer represents an important and sometimes necessary distribution network for the supplier's goods to reach end consumers in a way that allows production to reach a scale in which it is efficient, an idea also supported by Berasategi[1824]and Carstensen[1825]. If a dependent supplier refuses to accept the UPPs, there is a possibility that the buyer will not conclude the contract, which restricts access to the supplier to the downstream market and may drive it out of business if there are no alternative distribution channels[1826], especially because these modalities of contracts tend to be offered in a 'take-it-or-leave-it' situation[1827]. Hence, UPPs will *more likely be exerted if suppliers depend on a particular buyer,* which explains the existence of provisions dealing with the abuse of economic dependence under national competition laws that tackle UPPs, as I discuss below.

919. In EU competition law, the issue of dependence and UPPs has played a role when evaluating three concentration operations in food retailing, and, at the national level, it constitutes one of the main pillars for the application of competition-like rules dealing with contractual balancing and relative dominance provisions. As I discuss below, however, dependence is in principle a concept with an *inter-partes* reach as a supplier might depend on one buyer, in opposition to dominance, but not another. Nonetheless, dependence can be generalized if the buyer is a dominant undertaking because the vast majority of its suppliers will depend on it and, therefore, its effects stop being a merely inter-partes situation to become an effect *erga omnes*.

1822 Also raising the issue of supplier dependence see Groceries Code Adjudicator, Investigation into Tesco Plc, 26 January 2016, public version available online at: https://www.gov.uk/government/uploads/system/uploads/attachment_data/file/494840/GCA_Tesco_plc_final_report_26012016_-_version_for_download.pdf, para. 37.

1823 European Commission '*Green Paper on Unfair Trading Practices in the Business-to-Business Food and Non-Food supply Chain in Europe*' (2013), p. 7. Robles Martín-Laborda, 'La Cadena Alimentaria: Cuando el Poder de Mercado lo Tiene el Comprador'.

1824 Berasategi argues that large food retailers act as a bottleneck or quasi essential facilities and, therefore, proposes employing a system based on FRAND similar to essential patents for food retailing in Berasategi, p. 118-153.

1825 Carstensen 'Buyer Power, Competition Policy, and Antitrust: The Competitive Effects of Discrimination Among Suppliers' (2008).

1826 European Commission '*Green Paper on Unfair Trading Practices in the Business-to-Business Food and Non-Food supply Chain in Europe*' (2013), p. 6.

1827 Kirkwood 'Powerful Buyers and Merger Enforcement' (2012), p. 1485; Carstensen 'Buyer Power and the Horizontal Merger Guidelines: Minor Progress on an Important Issue' (2012), p. 775.

B. Modalities of unfair purchasing practices

920. As mentioned above, UPPs can take many different forms and any listing of them will be indicative as these practices vary from commercial transaction to commercial transaction and are tailored for each specific relation[1828]. In most cases, UPPs are imposed in the contractual negotiation phase, although they can also be imposed in a retroactive manner in the post-contractual phase and may take the form of pricing and non-pricing related demands[1829].

921. Among the *price/payment* types, there are: imposition of unfairly low purchasing prices; delayed payments[1830]; listing charges; slotting allowances; atypical payments; additional payment requirements (e.g. listing charges, slotting allowances, retro-active discounts, or joint marketing contributions); or data input errors leading to overcharges, for example[1831].

922. Regarding the *non-price related UPPs,* these group different conducts that either restrict the ability of the supplier to find alternative buyers, shift risks, or grant the buyer some unwarranted competitive advantage. Among these there are: refusals to buy or threats to delist products[1832]; imposition of buying or not buying goods or services from a third party designated by the buyer (for instance transportation services); conditional purchasing behaviour (e.g. exclusive supply obligations or reciprocal buying); most-favored customer clauses; deliberate risk shifting (such as enforced sale-or-return or delayed payments)[1833]; duty to transfer sensitive information on prices; preferential treatment given to private label goods; requirements to produce own branded goods and private label goods; marketing contributions; category captaincy; or setting of minimum quality standards as a requirement for purchasing all the production.

1828 For examples of business to business unfair trading conditions see, *inter alia*: Supply Chain Initiative *Vertical Relationships in the Food Supply Chain: Principles of Good Practice,* (2011); European Commission '*Green Paper on Unfair Trading Practices in the Business-to-Business Food and Non-Food supply Chain in Europe*' (2013), p. 7-8 and 17-22. See also the 52 different practices found by the Competition Commission - UK (2008), p. 30; the Portuguese report by the Autoridade da Concorrência, *Final Report on Commercial Relations Between the Large Retail Groups and their Suppliers* (2010); or the Spanish NCA report listing 18 practices in the food retailing sector in Comisión Nacional de la Competencia, *Informe sobre las Relaciones entre Fabricantes y Distribuidores en el Sector Alimentario* (2011).

1829 European Commission '*Green Paper on Unfair Trading Practices in the Business-to-Business Food and Non-Food supply Chain in Europe*' (2013), p. 6.

1830 Judgment of 11 July in *FENIN v Commission*, C-205/03 P, EU:C:2006:453; Judgment of 4 March 2003, *Fenin v Commission*, T-319/99, ECR, EU:T:2003:50; Groceries Code Adjudicator, Investigation into Tesco Plc, 26 January 2016, public version available online at: https://www.gov.uk/government/uploads/system/uploads/attachment_data/file/494840/GCA_Tesco_plc_final_report_26012016_-_version_for_download.pdf

1831 Groceries Code Adjudicator, Investigation into Tesco Plc, 26 January 2016, public version available online at: https://www.gov.uk/government/uploads/system/uploads/attachment_data/file/494840/GCA_Tesco_plc_final_report_26012016_-_version_for_download.pdf

1832 Faull, Nikpay and Taylor, [2014], para. 5.890-5.891.

1833 European Commission, *Study on the Legal Framework Covering Business-To-Business Unfair Trading Practices in the Retail Supply Chain* (2014), p. 32.

III. Market Impact of UPPs

923. As mentioned in this chapter's introduction, UPPs are portrayed as exploitative buyer power conducts that transfer profit from suppliers to buyers without proper compensation. However, a different approach would be to see UPPs as nothing but hard bargaining between buyers and suppliers to neutralize seller market power and therefore, approach the contractual conditions to an efficient distribution of wealth among the parties and towards the competitive price level. Hence, there is not a clear picture regarding the competitive impact of UPPs from a competition law perspective. In other words, it is clear that UPPs can lead to issues of contractual unbalance and disequilibria that need some form of redress from an 'unfair competition law' or contract law perspective. Nonetheless, *do UPPs raise any market impact that goes beyond purely bilateral profit distribution problems?* In this section, I discuss their impact on competition and in particular the viability of suppliers; impact on innovation and variety; and impact on end consumers in the form of higher prices. The impact of UPPs on these variables paves the way to the discussion regarding whether and to what extent UPPs are a competition problem. However, a thorough econometric analysis of UPPs' impact in all these areas is outside the study's scope and is an area ripe for future multidisciplinary research owing to the lack of sufficient and conclusive data[1834].

924. Yet, this does not mean there is no data available in this field. In the last decade, there have been reports entrusted by the EU institutions and NCAs to discuss the impact of UPPs, with a special emphasis on food retailing. In particular, the 2014 report entitled: The Economic Impact of Modern Retail on Choice and Innovation in the EU Food Sector[1835] (the 2014 Innovation Report) has been instrumental in clarifying whether modern retailing undertakings and their purchasing behaviour may have negative effects on the EU food market. Another recent study by the Commission[1836] also discussed the potential impact of UPPs, further backed up by Jenny's findings concerning the effect of UPPs in food retailing and the fact that they are not a competition problem even though market concentration has been high or is increasing[1837]. This section builds on those reports and buyer power economics to discuss UPPs effects in the market.

1834 Econometrics is the application of statistical analysis to economic data to provide some empirical answers to research questions.

1835 European Commission, *The Economic Impact of Modern Retail on Choice and Innovation in the EU Food Sector* (2014).

1836 European Commission, *Study on the Legal Framework Covering Business-To-Business Unfair Trading Practices in the Retail Supply Chain* (2014), p. 116-117.

1837 Jenny [2015], p. 16-17.

A. Suppliers' viability

925. UPPs may have an impact on the *viability of suppliers* in the medium and long run; if a buyer squeezes its suppliers by demanding extraordinary conditions that are not properly compensated there will be a point in which, if the buyer over-squeezes, the supplier will exit the market in a situation similar to a BATNA (Best Alternative to a Negotiated Agreement)[1838]. This would happen when its exit option is more advantageous than remaining in the supply market, for instance by stopping food production and selling the farmland. This argument of UPPs forcing suppliers out of the market was the basis for a complaint made by the Spanish Federation of Food and Drinks against a supermarket buying alliance: small producers will be subject to abuse and may have to exit the suppliers' market[1839]. In this exploitation scenario UPPs effects are the transferring of profits from a supplier to the buyer that, in principle, do not affect market conditions or allocative efficiency, and nor is it a competition law concern; it only has an effect on the profitability of the transaction for each party. This exploitative and 'squeezing' argument is remarkably similar to the monopsony effects I discussed in chapter 2, section §V.A, and which I consider unlikely to occur in practice. In fact, this concern regarding the exploitative nature of UPPs as a monopsony-like behaviour is tempered because of its self-destructive nature.

926. A powerful buyer will be incentivized to impose UPPs to reap extraordinary buying (monopsony) profits but will not exercise them indefinitely or it will be cut off from suppliers and have no access to an input, as these suppliers would be unable to cover their costs and, consequently, would exit the market. If aggressive purchasing happens then perhaps a few, inefficient suppliers will be forced to exit the market (the marginal suppliers) but not all will. This is because even after 'paying the UPP' they will still be able to sufficiently cover their costs and, as some suppliers may have left the market, they will strive to capture that market share that is free to be absorbed, which in turn will grant them more bargaining power to oppose the powerful buyer.

927. However, if the exploitative impact has a wide effect on a substantial group of suppliers that are forced to exit the market, the UPPs would not only trigger issues of wealth distribution, but also of market structure, and competition as a process. Additionally, if an important group of suppliers are forced to exit the market this would increase market concentration and may also have an adverse effect on product variety, which would lead to less inter-brand competition and increase in prices for end consumers, as suggested by the Report

1838 "Best Alternative to a Negotiated Agreement", idea firstly developed by Fisher and Ury in Roger Fisher, William Ury and Bruce Patton, *Getting to Yes: Negotiating Agreement Without Giving in* (Penguin Books 2011). Also using the BATNA argument see: European Commission, *Study on the Legal Framework Covering Business-To-Business Unfair Trading Practices in the Retail Supply Chain* (2014), p. 25.

1839 See my commentary regarding this case in: http://derechocompetencia.blogspot.no/2015/12/el-acuerdo-dia-eroski-alianza.html.

on Unfair Practices[1840]. Also, this could lead to lower intra-community trade as undertakings will be less incentivized to carry out their activities in other MS. This negative effect on market concentration may be reflected in modern food retailing where there is a "clear trend towards greater retailer's concentration" – i.e. the buyers – and among suppliers also, where the 2014 Innovation Report found that *"[a]t national level, supplier concentration increased for* 20 of the 23 product categories and 13 of 14 of the sample Member States"[1841]. Likewise, UPPs have the effect of fostering concentration on the suppliers' market as producers engage in buying alliances or merge to create neutralizing seller market power and oppose the strong buyer[1842]. Hence, UPPs may have a detrimental concentration effect on both sides of the retailing market.

928. Furthermore, if there is an exploitative widespread effect on suppliers', *dynamic efficiency in the medium and short term may be affected* and, therefore, competition law intervention warranted, as the aggressive conduct of the buyer will determine the interest of suppliers to exit or enter the market and invest. Consequently, UPPs can have a detrimental effect on competition as such because the distributive unfairness would have a long-term consequence on incentives to remain in the markets.

929. However, the data seems to suggest and support that *UPPs do not appear to have a major role regarding supplier's viability*, at least concerning modern food retailing. The 2014 Innovation Report shows how in the period 2004-2012, the number of brand suppliers available in supermarkets increased – even during the post financial crisis scenario – across all EU MS ranging from 1.7% in Italy to 6.4% in Spain[1843]. A critical observation regarding this interpretation can be made, however: the study speaks about the amount of brand suppliers (which may be interpreted as the amount of trademarks available) but not necessarily the trademark holders; i.e. it is possible that despite there now being more different trademarks available for the same type of good (assuming that the trademarks identify perfect substitutes), the trademarks may be owned by the same or even fewer undertakings than in the pre-2004 scenario. Also, the report does not discuss what the proportion of the growth of private labels is (i.e. goods sold and manufactured for, or on behalf of, the supermarket chain)[1844].

1840 European Commission, *Study on the Legal Framework Covering Business-To-Business Unfair Trading Practices in the Retail Supply Chain* (2014), p. 116-117.

1841 European Commission, *The Economic Impact of Modern Retail on Choice and Innovation in the EU Food Sector* (2014), p. 32 (emphasis in original).

1842 Ibid, 32. See also: Jenny [2015], p. 5.

1843 European Commission, *The Economic Impact of Modern Retail on Choice and Innovation in the EU Food Sector* (2014).

1844 For some literature discussing private labels see: Gorrie (2006), p. 217; Ezrachi and Bernitz [2009]; Ezrachi (2010); Doyle and Murgatroyd (2011), p. 631; Ezrachi and De Jong (2012), p. 257; Möschel (2014), p. 29. See also in Germany a decision by the Bundeskartellamt where there was concern regarding loss of competition in the private label sector pursuant to a proposed concentration in Case summary from 6 July 2015: Prohibition of acquisition of Kaiser´s Tengelmann outlets by Edeka, B2-96/14 (English version), p. 1. Appealed and revoked by the German Federal Minister for Economic Affairs and Energy under § 42 of the German Competition Act based, *inter alia*, on the protection of working positions that would be absorbed by Edeka.

B. Variety and Innovation

930. Regarding variety, the 2014 Innovation Report indicates that, despite a concentration trend among supermarket retailers, *the imposition of UPPs has not decreased the variety of goods available for end consumers*. The report shows that "[c]hoice in alternative products, measured at a local level, has increased on average by 5.1% annually from 2004 to 20012"[1845]. The growth happened across all MS of the EU with a minimum average of 3.2% in Italy and a maximum of 8.3% in Poland, and across all categories of goods and even sizes available of goods[1846]. It also showed how the introduction of private labels has a positive impact on consumer's choice and variety, particularly if the private label is a 'premium type'[1847].

931. Concerning *innovation,* there are two arguments that contradict each other concerning the effect of UPPs and bargaining power as a whole, which I discuss in general terms in chapter 2, section §III.F. On the one hand, and as remarked by the Report on Unfair Practices, "UTPs lead to the transfer of risk and the appropriation of most of the surplus from the transaction by the stronger party, this might affect the resources available to weaker parties for R&D and innovation"[1848]. Therefore, there might be risks of a hold-up problem. On the other hand, the counter argument is based on the fact that a supplier that has imposed UPPs will be instead incentivized to innovate to gain bargaining power vis-à-vis its supplier and break the relation of economic dependence. In the case of food retailing, the 2014 Innovation Report shows a trend towards innovation for both suppliers and buyers dealing with food distribution, even amidst the financial crisis of the late 2000s[1849]. This could very well indicate that even in the presence of some UPPs, both suppliers and producers keep their incentives to innovate higher to either maintain or gain bargaining power. If this is the case, UPPs are not likely to have a detrimental effect on market innovation.

C. End-consumer conditions

932. What about the effect of UPPs on end consumers? This is perhaps the most complex question to answer concerning their impact, but one of fundamental importance. End consumers are actively seeking to pay lower end prices, which motivates undertakings to employ their bargaining power to their full capacity. Therefore, it is in their best interest that bargaining over profits is

1845 European Commission, *The Economic Impact of Modern Retail on Choice and Innovation in the EU Food Sector* (2014), p. 26.

1846 Ibid, p. 26.

1847 Ibid, p. 34 and 53-54.

1848 European Commission, *Study on the Legal Framework Covering Business-To-Business Unfair Trading Practices in the Retail Supply Chain* (2014), p. 116. Also remarking the negative effect on innovation of UPPs see: Jenny [2015], p. 31.

1849 European Commission, *The Economic Impact of Modern Retail on Choice and Innovation in the EU Food Sector* (2014), p. 28-30.

efficient and made as competitively as possible to leave nothing on the table (i.e. extraordinary profits for either suppliers or retailers). Thus, hard bargaining in the upstream market that does not involve monopsony practices (withholding) tends to benefit end consumers in the form of lower prices and/or higher output, as lower purchasing prices and/or better conditions are passed on to end consumers[1850].

933. According to the Commission's data, there is no evidence that exercise of UPPs has an adverse effect on end prices paid by consumers, at least in the short-medium term[1851]. Also, the report by the European Competition Network found that imposition of unfair trading practices from a buyer to a supplier "do not involve anti-competitive practices implying harm for consumers and, consequently, do not fall under the scope of EU nor most of national competition rules of Member States"[1852]. In my opinion, this could be the indication of two variables that may or may not be linked. On the one hand, it shows the limited competition effects of UPPs – if not imposed by a dominant undertaking – on prices and therefore, strengthens the argument that these behaviours could be subject to other types of regulatory treatment than competition law. Secondly, in markets such as retailing, if they are highly competitive downstream, the exercise of buyer (bargaining power) is mostly efficiency enhancing as the benefits are passed on to end consumers in the form of lower prices, more variety and better products and services.

934. Also, it is possible that UPPs will impact consumers "in the medium and long term from lower product quality, a decline in innovation activity, less product diversity and the risk of price increases caused by lower competition intensity"[1853], as stressed by the Bundeskartellamt. In my view, this argument may hold if the UPP is exercised by a buyer that has substantial buyer power and the effect of the practices spills over the market and not when the UPP has a reduced scope and only affects a small group of suppliers.

935. Therefore, it can be concluded that the end consumers' behaviour and interest seem to reinforce the large retailer's bargaining against suppliers, which may explain why large buyers impose conditions that may appear unfair to their suppliers but that lead to lower prices in the downstream market.

1850 Jenny [2015], p. 31.

1851 European Commission '*Tackling Unfair Trading Practices in the Business-to-Business food supply chain*' (2014), p. 12. For a monitoring tool of food prices through Europe the European Food Prices Monitoring Tool is a helpful indication, also includes Norway and Iceland as EEA Members: http://appsso.eurostat.ec.europa.eu/nui/submitViewTableAction.do.

1852 For a somewhat similar argument and going as far as saying that because there is no consumer harm there is no EU competition law intervention, a position I disagree with, see: European Competition Network (2012), para. 254.

1853 Decision B2-58/09 Edeka Konditionenforderungen - Verstoß gegen das "Anzapfverbot", 3 July 2014 by the Bundeskartellamt. Summary available at: http://www.olg-duesseldorf.nrw.de/behoerde/presse/Presse_aktuell/20151118_PM_Edeka/index.php.

IV. Are unfair purchasing practices an EU competition problem?

936. The most important competition policy question regarding UPPs is whether these practices are a competition problem and, if so, under which circumstances should competition intervention be warranted to address their anti-competitive effects? This section, therefore, aims to answer the research question of *when are UPPs under the scope of application of EU competition law and why?*[1854]

937. There are three avenues to answer this query. Firstly, a *de lege ferenda*, an approach that absolutely dismisses the application of EU competition law to UPPs. This extreme position is contrary to the state of the law, which would be prone to excessive under enforcement and would also be contrary to the protection of certain competition goals. In my research, however, I have not found any advocates of such an extreme approach.

938. A second alternative my proposal supporting a nuanced and limited application of EU competition law to UPPs whenever they have adverse effects on the competitive structure and competition as such, based on their market impact. This is anchored both in the goals of EU competition law as recognized by the Courts concerning buyer power, and the interpretation of the applicability of EU competition law as it stands to UPPs, hence it is a *de lege lata* perspective, partially influenced by my ordoliberal approach to buyer power. As discussed in this contribution, EU competition law has a limited scope of application when dealing with UPPs because they do not tend to represent market-wide problems. Also, there are better suited pieces of legislation at the EU or national level to address UPPs and their economic impact.

939. As a general rule, the more the UPPs will impact market conditions and competition as such, the more there is solid ground to require EU and/or national competition law intervention, as would be the case if the buyer that imposes them is a dominant undertaking or a buyers' cartel. However, when UPPs are imposed by non-dominant undertakings or uncoordinated buyers it becomes unclear whether UPPs will have a negative impact on welfare or efficiency. Furthermore, competition law should apply to UPPs whenever these become a market power problem that affects prices, innovation, variety and consumer welfare, but not when UPPs affect bilateral relations of a contractual fairness nature[1855]. This perspective finds support also in the recent studies carried out by the Commission, as well as economic literature and competition policy[1856].

1854 A similar question was made by the former Director-General of the Directorate General Competition Alexander Italianer in Italianer, *The Devil is in the Retail*, p. 3.

1855 Lianos and Lombardi, p. 5.

1856 European Commission, *Study on the Legal Framework Covering Business-To-Business Unfair Trading Practices in the Retail Supply Chain* (2014); European Commission, *The Economic Impact of Modern Retail on Choice and Innovation in the EU Food Sector* (2014); Italianer.

940. However, this reduced scope for competition law to issues related to UPPs is not shared by all the literature and has been challenged by Lianos and Lombardi, advocates of a third way proposing the full application of competition law to UPPs. These authors argue that competition law still has a role to play regarding superior bargaining issues, even if the problems tackled are outside the accepted economic efficiency aspects protected and addressed by competition laws. In their view, competition law should intervene against imposition of UPPs if a "holistic competition law model" is adopted that detaches from neoclassical economic theory and resorts to:

> the global value chain approach, developed by political economists and economic sociologists, [as it] provides the appropriate theoretical framework in order to better understand the interaction between suppliers and retailers in the food sector and enable us, on this basis, to design competition law interventions[1857].

941. Additionally, they argue that this is possible, as legislators and NCAs do not seem too negative when it comes to applying competition law to these problems.

942. This innovative approach by Lianos and Lombardi that grants a broader scope to competition law tackling UPPs, in my view goes too far from the moderate solution I support for several reasons. First, Lianos and Lombardi argue that there is a need to substitute the current approach anchored on neoclassical price theory models to the application of EU competition law for a "holistic approach". This would presuppose that the competition law construct, both in the EU and the US antitrust law, would require a complete turnabout and that use of industrial organization and neoclassical microeconomics is the wrong approach. It goes without saying that this would meet resistance from most of academics, practitioners, judges and NCAs, as there is a general consensus that neoclassical theory provides the most reliable and trustworthy explanations to economic phenomena affecting the market because, precisely, the market as we understand it is theorized from a neoclassical perspective. Also from a methodological perspective, the use of sociology and political economy as suggested by Lianos and Lombardi would be inconsistent with an understanding of market dynamics, as these disciplines do not center their attention on the study of (private) markets, price creation or industrial organization theory. These disciplines see markets from a wide and top-down approach that is unable to warrant sufficient legal certainty regarding specific conducts and can only provide indications regarding economic policy theories from a macroeconomic perspective, which does not necessarily fit the nuances of competition law and competition economics.

1857 Lianos and Lombardi, p. 8.

943. Furthermore, Lianos and Lombardi argue that a "holistic approach" to competition law should capture UPPs even if they are not competition law problems sensu stricto. The difficulty I find with this approach is that competition law provisions and remedies are neither appropriate nor tailored to redress issues related to bilateral contractual relations, distribution of profits and contractual fairness. Their provisions and its application are, and should be, applied to maximize economic efficiency, the wellbeing of the markets and competition as such. By contrast, other solutions, such as unfair competition or contract law are much better suited to regulate these conducts, as this is the majoritarian view of the legislation and the doctrine, as I discuss in this chapter. Furthermore, and from an ordoliberal perspective, such a holistic interpretation of competition law, even if designed to protect the market structure, forgets that competition first and foremost should foster economic efficiency so that other regulatory regimes distribute the wealth in a more effective and overreaching manner. Additionally, the proposal of these authors anchored on their idea of global value chains appears to be more a case of a different method to look at UPPs rather than a different regulatory approach. In fact, it is not clear in their paper how this method should be applied under the current legal regime, nor are there any authoritative legal sources supporting it.

944. Lastly, their argument that NCAs and legislators are less negative to the application of competition law to UPPs contradicts the findings of this research, as most reports by NCAs argue the contrary. Competition law has very limited room for resolving UPP derived issues. Also, the argument that legislators are less negative to the application of competition laws to UPPs can be motivated by the strong political and social impact of UPPs in society and the lobby, particularly by agricultural sectors, and not necessarily because legislators think it is an economically optimal solution[1858].

945. Going back to my proposal of a moderate approach to UPPs under competition law, this suggestion is justifiable as adequate because competition law is designed to address issues relative to the abuse of market power and market efficiency but not of bilateral bargaining power unbalance[1859]. Therefore, EU competition law is not only insufficient to regulate UPPs because it does not apply in most cases[1860], but, and more importantly, because EU competition law is not an adequate remedy for most instances of UPPs with no widespread market effects, as these tend to be mostly issues of profit distributions and contractual balance, while not necessarily of wealth maximization. In a nutshell, whenever the UPPs' effect is only *inter partes*, these instances are usually regulated by means of 'unfair competition laws' or '*concurrence*

1858 Ibid, p. 5-6.

1859 Also suggesting a similar argument see: European Commission, *Study on the Legal Framework Covering Business-To-Business Unfair Trading Practices in the Retail Supply Chain* (2014), p. 40.

1860 Ibid, p. 17.

déloyale' provisions. Consequently, if UPPs are an issue of 'fairness' or *bona fide* in commercial practices but not a market power problem sensu stricto, then this is an unfair competition issue and not a competition issue[1861], and, as remarked by Bishop and Walker, a problem not usually dealt with by micro-economics[1862]. If the problem is a contractual imbalance, the solutions to be found are closer to traditional 'contract law-like' provisions, and, therefore, another set of economic rules should apply, including consumer protection laws if the UPPs affect end consumers vis-à-vis retailers. In particular, part of the literature has proposed using other sub-types of economic law, like unfair competition laws, as better regulatory instruments[1863], or the application of national broad competition law provisions, like the case of relative dominance or abuse of dependence[1864].

946. On the other hand, UPPs will be a *competition problem when they develop into a market power problem* by affecting overall market conditions, hindering competition, economic efficiency and welfare[1865]. This would be the case when they are imposed by a dominant buying undertaking on all or most of its suppliers, by a large buying alliance or cartel, or are expected to arise pursuant a concentration that may significantly impede competition, because in these circumstances UPPs would have adverse effects on price, innovation, variety and the competitive process. If this is the case then EU competition law applies and should apply to address these efficiency issues, as was held by the CJEU in *Schutzverband gegen Unwesen i.d. Wirtschaft v Rocher* when holding that instances of unfair competition may degenerate in restrictions of competition[1866]. On the other hand, UPPs will not trigger competition law when there is no substantial restriction to competition or whenever they do not adversely affect the competitive process as such.

947. However, the differences between these legal spheres in practice are quite blurred and requires on a case-by-case assessment to properly determine what set of rules govern the wrongdoing, depending on the practice effects. In my view, the key lies in the fact that competition law addresses market problems

---

1861 Frauke Henning-Bodewig, *Unfair Competition Law: European Union and Member States* (Kluwer Law International 2006), p. 1. See also suggesting that fairness should not be the ultimate aim of EU competition law because the difficulty in defining what is fair, Nazzini, [2011], p. 21- 24.

1862 Bishop and Walker, [2010], para. 6-044.

1863 See: Pera and Bonfitto (2011), p. 414; Pera; Antonio Buttà and Andrea Pezzoli, 'Buyer Power and Competition Policy: From Brick-and-Mortar Retailers to Digital Platforms' 41 Economia E Politica Industriale (2014) 159; European Competition Network (2012), para. 26; O'Donoghue and Padilla, *The Law and Economics of Article 102 TFEU* [2013], p. 846-847.

1864 See the discussion on national implementation of rules on abuse of dependence and unfair trading practices in section §VI of this chapter.

1865 Also supporting this view see: van Doorn, p. 174.

1866 "As for the protection of fair trading, and hence of competition, it is important to note that correct price comparisons, prohibited by a rule of law of the kind at issue, cannot in any way distort the conditions of competition. On the other hand, a rule which has the effect of prohibiting such comparisons may restrict competition" in Judgment of 18 May 1993 in *Schutzverband gegen Unwesen i.d. Wirtschaft v Rocher*, C-126/91, EU:C:1993:191, para. 22.

affecting the overall market, whereas unfair competition rules seem to tackle issues concerning bilateral relations[1867], or, as put by Henning-Bodewig, "the competitive relation *between* the parties"[1868]. Therefore, these relations and connections between competition and contractual (related) law as different avenues for addressing UPPs demonstrate the complexity in dealing with these types of possibly exploitative buying conducts.

A. Why are UPPs often outside EU competition law?

948. As discussed above, most cases of UPPs occur outside the scope of application of EU competition law because of their limited market-wide impact, if not imposed by a dominant undertaking, a buyers' cartel, or pursuant a buyers' concentration. In this section, I discuss the economic and policy reasons supporting my proposal that most cases of UPPs should be addressed by means of regulations other than EU competition law, given that it is not only insufficient due to its limited room for applicability, but also because it is, in my view, not the most adequate tool to tackle UPPs. However, I also discuss when and how EU competition law may apply to cases of UPPs.

a. Limited market impact

949. Most UPPs are not captured by competition laws because these practices do not reflect market power market failures but rather problems regarding contractual imbalances and wealth distribution among parties to a contract. Therefore, UPPs *do not tend to have a substantial negative impact on competition and welfare, particularly concerning innovation and variety, as discussed in the previous section*[1869]. Hence, UPPs by and large represent a *contractual disequilibrium inter-partes*[1870] rather than having an *erga omnes* effect in market conditions, as most instances of anti-competitive conducts do, which explains why *inter partes* legislation like contract law, unfair competition laws or relative dominance clauses are better suited to deal with these problems.

950. A similar approach has been adopted by the Commission and some NCAs. For instance, the Commission expressed that EU competition law does not deal with most instances of unfair trading practices "unless those entail malfunctioning of the market due to existence of market power"[1871]. Likewise,

1867 Italianer, *The Devil is in the Retail*, p. 6. Cf with the narrower approach by Henning-Bodewig in Henning-Bodewig, [2006], p. 1 and 7-8.

1868 Henning-Bodewig, [2006], p. 1.

1869 European Commission, *The Economic Impact of Modern Retail on Choice and Innovation in the EU Food Sector* (2014). Also stressing that a national level is rare for UPPs to have a "detrimental impact on economic welfare" see: Faull and Nikpay, [1999], para. 6.338.

1870 Also suggesting that unfair trading practices have a connection with contractual equilibrium see: European Commission '*Green Paper on Unfair Trading Practices in the Business-to-Business Food and Non-Food supply Chain in Europe*' (2013), p. 6.

1871 Ibid, p. 12.

the Portuguese NCA stressed in a report that: "[t]he concerns identified by the PCA on the basis of this market study do not come strictly within the scope of prohibited practices as per competition law, a finding that is in line with similar studies undertaken in other countries of the European Union"[1872].

b. Goals protected

951. Directly linked to the argument above, EU competition law's scope is too narrow to solve or intervene in most instances of UPPs because EU competition law aims at protecting the competitive process, and promoting economic efficiency and maximization of welfare[1873]. In other words, EU competition law sensu stricto does not deal with broader issues such as contractual fairness and protection of the weaker party to a contractual relation, even though these concerns may also be addressed through national competition laws if an MS so desires, as confirmed in Article 3(3) of Regulation 2003/1 when stating that EU competition provisions do not "preclude the application of provisions of national law that predominantly pursue an objective different from that pursued by Articles [101] and [102] of the Treaty"[1874]. Furthermore, at the EU level there are indications that rules protecting consumers/clients absent market power abuse are outside of competition law, sensu stricto. For example, regulations that address purely *inter partes* relations are the Directive on Consumer's rights[1875], the Directive on unfair terms[1876], and the special sector regulation in the case of the Technology Transfer Block Exemption Regulation regarding licensing terms[1877].

952. Also, from an economic-oriented perspective, the regulation of UPPs is complex due to the overall effects in the market and the nature of economic transactions. For neo-classical economics contracts would only be voluntarily entered into – assuming the rationality of parties and their profit maximizing interest – when both parties will be better off than their BATNA[1878]. If

1872 Concorrência (2010), p. 6.

1873 van Doorn, p. 174. For a discussion of the relation between competition law and unfair competition law from a procedural perspective see: Thomas M. J. Möllers and Andreas Heinemann, 'Outlook: The Link Between Unfair Competition Law and Antitrust Law' in Thomas M. J. Möllers and Andreas Heinemann (eds), *The Enforcement of Competition Law in Europe* (Cambridge University Press 2008).

1874 Council Regulation (EC) No 1/2003 of 16 December 2002 on the implementation of the rules on competition laid down in Articles [101] and [102] of the Treaty [2003] OJ L 1/1.

1875 Directive 2011/83/EU of the European Parliament and of the Council of 25 October 2011 on consumer rights, amending Council Directive 93/13/EEC and Directive 1999/44/EC of the European Parliament and of the Council and repealing Council Directive 85/577/EEC and Directive 97/7/EC of the European Parliament and of the Council [2011] OJ L 304/64.

1876 Council Directive 93/13/EEC of 5 April 1993 on unfair terms in consumer contracts [1993] OJ L 95/29. Amended by Directive 2011/83/EU of the European Parliament and of the Council of 25 October 2011 on consumer rights, amending Council Directive 93/13/EEC and Directive 1999/44/EC of the European Parliament and of the Council and repealing Council Directive 85/577/EEC and Directive 97/7/EC of the European Parliament and of the Council [2011] OJ L 304/64.

1877 Commission Regulation (EU) No 316/2014 of 21 March 2014 on the application of Article 101(3) of the Treaty on the Functioning of the European Union to categories of technology transfer agreements [2014] OJ L 93/17.

1878 Also discussing the BATNA in UPPs see: Lianos and Lombardi.

there is a better alternative than the one proposed, the supplier would resort to a different buyer and will not accept the agreement containing UPPs, or invest its resources elsewhere. In the words of Friedman, a transaction will be "economically ethical" if it "is provided that the transaction is bi-laterally voluntary and informed"[1879]. While a transfer of wealth without compensation may take place between the powerful buyer and its weaker supplier, competition law does not intervene to protect the profitability of one of the parties, particularly if one of them is inefficient. If it did, then competition law would, indeed, be an instrument for the protection of rivals devoid of its objective of making the market as efficient as it could be to the interest of consumers[1880].

c. *Fairness and intent*

953. Another aspect why EU competition law does not deal explicitly with unfair purchasing practices can be explained by the element of intent, the requirement of fairness[1881], and the doctrines of 'duress' and 'undue influence' in common law systems as raised by Akman[1882]. In the case of unilateral abusive conducts under competition law scrutiny, the illegality of them does not involve any element of intent; the breach is objective, and even in cases of agreements only the coordination has to be proven, but not the willfulness of affecting competition. Once it has happened, competition law is triggered even if the party did not aim to restrict competition. In cases of imposing unfair trading practices by a purchaser, there is a willful/intent element that may be relevant to determine the 'fairness' of the conduct. The powerful buyer is aware of its stronger bargaining power and that it is likely that its supplier is a dependent party and, thus willfully imposes a certain practice or demands some kind of benefit without appropriate compensation[1883].

954. Also, laws dealing with unfair trading practices and contractual fairness aim at remedying contractual imbalances and banning certain practices to avoid a party from exploiting its superior bargaining power, rather than regulating the behaviour in the market[1884]. Thus, these rules are not aimed at addressing issues of inefficiency but at restoring fairness to the commercial transaction[1885].

1879 Milton Friedman and Rose D. Friedman, *Capitalism and freedom* (University of Chicago Press 1962), p. 55.

1880 European Competition Network (2012); Italianer.

1881 Henning-Bodewig, [2006], p. xv-xvi.

1882 Akman, *The Concept of Abuse in EU Competition Law: Law and Economic Approaches* [2012], p. 169-174.

1883 See also remarking this element of willfulness and knowledge of the illegitimate pressure under the economic duress and undue influence doctrines ibid, p. 170-174.

1884 College of Europe and Centre for European Policy Studies, *The Impact of National Rules on Unilateral Conduct that Diverge from Article 102 of the Treaty of the Functioning of the European Union* (2012), p. 22.

1885 Këllezi [2008], p. 84.

d. *Not an area of enforcement priority*

955. Furthermore, UPPs are not an enforcement priority, even if they might be under the scrutiny of EU competition law, as, for the Commission, vertical and exploitative issues are not of major importance when compared to conducts affecting competition among rivals. Therefore, these kinds of practices are of lower enforcement (or no) priority because they can:

> only arise if there is insufficient competition at one or more levels of trade, that is, if there is some degree of market power at the level of the supplier or the buyer or at both levels. Vertical restraints are generally less harmful than horizontal restraints and may provide substantial scope for efficiencies[1886].

956. Thus, UPPs are much less likely to be an area of competition priority, unless there is a change in the current competition policy, which is highly unlikely and not desirable[1887].

e. *Lack of cross-border impact*

957. Lastly, the majority of unfair purchasing obligations will lack a cross-border or community dimension that affects the internal market because the purchasing markets are narrow in geographic scope, even more so if we are talking about UPPs exercised against farmers or local food producers. Therefore, the lack of an effect on trade between MS[1888] precludes the application of EU competition law and leaves the matter to the national laws pursuant to the subsidiarity principle, which also explains the lack of substantive cases dealing with UPPs at the EU level.

1886 Guidelines on Vertical Restraints [2010] OJ C 130/1, para. 6.

1887 "Not every case of unfairness is a matter for competition law. We won't prioritize cases that are not really about competition", Margrethe Vestager, *Setting Priorities in Antitrust* (European Commission 1 February 2016).

1888 Commission Notice — Guidelines on the effect on trade concept contained in Articles 81 and 82 of the Treaty [2004] OJ C 101/81. For a thorough discussion of the cross-border element in EU competition law see, *inter alia*: Mihail Danov, Florian N. T. Becker and Paul Beaumont, *Cross-Border EU Competition Law Actions*, Vol. 4 (Hart 2013); Mihail Danov and Florian Becker, 'Governance Aspects of Cross-Border EU Competition Actions: Theoretical and Practical Challenges' 10 Journal of Private International Law (2014) 359. See discussing the cross-border element from and the applicability of EEA competition law: Christian N.K. Franklin, Halvard Haukeland Fredriksen and Ingrid M.H. Barlund, *Private Enforcement and Collective Redress in European Competition Law - National report for Norway* (2016).

B. When are UPPs under the scope of EU competition law?

958. UPPs may or may not be outside of the scope of application of EU competition law, as explicitly recognized in Recital (9) of Regulation 1/2003[1889] and a recent Commission's report[1890]. In the following, I discuss the scope of application of EU competition law for UPP cases under Article 101, Article 102 TFEU and the Merger Control Regulation[1891].

959. In the case of *concentrations, what is evaluated is the likelihood of the imposition of unfair purchasing practices* by the new entity that may significantly impede competition, *particularly when the suppliers are dependent on a buyer*, as discussed in this chapter and chapter 5, section §IV.C. Therefore, the exam is not an ex-ante but rather a potential ex-post situation which accounts for the limited availability of the EU concentration control to deal with UPPs, as I analyze below.

960. Regarding Article 101 TFEU, UPPs will be under its scope when they are imposed pursuant to an agreement or a concerted practice among buyers – either in the form of a buyer cartel or a buying alliance[1892].

961. In accordance with the broad definition of an agreement in EU competition law[1893], UPPs that include a concurrence of wills as the faithful expression of the parties' intention qualify as an agreement[1894]. In principle, it does not matter whether the supplier is forced into the agreement; what matters is the fact that the parties accepted to be in a commercial relationship: i.e. the supplier accepted the contract containing the UPP. In accordance with this general ap-

1889 "Articles 81 and 82 of the Treaty have as their objective the protection of competition on the market. This Regulation, which is adopted for the implementation of these Treaty provisions, does not preclude Member States from implementing on their territory national legislation, which protects other legitimate interests provided that such legislation is compatible with general principles and other provisions of Community law. In so far as such national legislation pursues predominantly an objective different from that of protecting competition on the market, the competition authorities and courts of the Member States may apply such legislation on their territory. Accordingly, Member States may under this Regulation implement on their territory national legislation that prohibits or imposes sanctions on acts of unfair trading practice, be they unilateral or contractual. Such legislation pursues a specific objective, irrespective of the actual or presumed effects of such acts on competition on the market. This is particularly the case of legislation which prohibits undertakings from imposing on their trading partners, obtaining or attempting to obtain from them terms and conditions that are unjustified, disproportionate or without consideration", Council Regulation (EC) No 1/2003 of 16 December 2002 on the implementation of the rules on competition laid down in Articles [101] and [102] of the Treaty [2003] OJ L 1/1, Recital (9).

1890 European Commission '*Green Paper on Unfair Trading Practices in the Business-to-Business Food and Non-Food supply Chain in Europe*' (2013), p. 10 and 13.

1891 Also stressing that UPPs are covered by competition when they are the outcome of an agreement or exerted by a dominant firm see Tribunal Vasco de la Competencia (April 2009), p. 167.

1892 For a discussion of regulating food retailing markets through oligopoly theories anchored on concerted practices or collective dominance see: ibid, p. 5 and 48-53 and making reference to the concerted practices case Judgment of 14 July 1972 in *SA française des matières colorantes (Francolor) v Commission*, C-54/69, EU:C:1972:75.

1893 Marian Paschke, 'Anti-Competitive Practices (Agreements, Decisions, Concerted Practices)' in Günther Hirsch, Frank Montag and Franz Jürgen Säcker (eds), *Competition law: European community practice and procedure: article-by-article commentary* (Sweet & Maxwell 2008), para. 2-1-010.

1894 Judgment of 26 October 2000, *Bayer v Commission*, T-41/96, ECR, EU:T:2000:242, para. 69. Upheld by the CJEU in Judgment of 6 January 2004 in *BAI and Commission v Bayer*, C-2/01 P, EU:C:2004:2.

proach, UPPs imposed by a single buyer would be considered vertical agreements. Therefore as vertical agreements, most types of UPPs would be covered by the Block Exemption Regulation, unless the parties belonging to it are above the 30% market share threshold in both the upstream and downstream markets or they constitute a 'hardcore' restriction of competition pursuant to Article 4[1895]. Some UPP conducts that are likely to benefit from the Block Exemption Regulation would be, for example, slotting allowances, requirements to contribute with the payment of advertisement, and transferring certain types of contractual risks such as transportation, among others. However, if the UPPs in a vertical agreement are considered to be in breach of Article 101(1) TFEU, it is important to remark that only the buyer that 'forced' the agreement should be fined by the competition authorities to prevent a double exploitation of the supplier.

962. However, some UPPs, even if as part of a vertical relation would, in reality, constitute 'unilateral conduct'[1896] because by their nature they do not constitute an agreement. As clarified by the CJEU in *BAI and Commission v Bayer*, these practices do not fulfill the requirements to constitute an agreement because

> such an agreement cannot be based on what is only the expression of a unilateral policy of one of the contracting parties, which *can be put into effect without the assistance of others*. To hold that an agreement prohibited by Article [101(1)] of the Treaty may be established simply on the basis of the expression of a unilateral policy aimed at preventing parallel imports would have the effect of confusing the scope of that provision with that of Article [102] of the Treaty[1897].

963. Conducts such as delisting, refusing to renew a contract or unilaterally terminating an agreement would be unilateral because they are analogous to a refusal to deal. The problem with these 'unilateral conducts' within an agreement is that they would not be captured under Article 101(1) TFEU but only captured by Article 102 TFEU if the buyer is dominant, which would be an unusual case.

964. Therefore, it is likely that most types of vertically imposed UPPs would not be under the scope of Article 101(1) TFEU due to the Block Exemption Regulation or because the conduct is unilateral as it does not require the intervention of the supplier to cause its effects.

1895 Commission Regulation (EU) No 330/2010 on the application of Article 101(3) of the Treaty on the Functioning of the European Union to categories of vertical agreements and concerted practices [2010] OJ L 102/1.

1896 See discussing these aspects of the concept of an agreement: Paschke [2008], para. 2-1-029 to 2-1-037; Gjendemsjø, [2011]; Whish and Bailey, *Competition law* [2015], p. 110-120.

1897 Judgment of 6 January 2004 in *BAI and Commission v Bayer*, C-2/01 P, EU:C:2004:2, para. 101 (emphasis added).

965. From a dominance perspective, UPPs are typically the outcome of individual conduct and in accordance with Article 102 TFEU UPPs will be under its application scope if the undertaking that imposes them is dominant or whenever there is a collective dominant position, as remarked by the Basque NCA and Berasategi when dealing with food retailing[1898]. However, studies and the case law show that very rarely do dominant undertakings impose anti-competitive UPPs or have been found to impose them, even at a national level, as confirmed by a Commission's Report (Report on Unfair Practices)[1899], including those countries in which the level of absolute dominance has been lowered, such as in Finland, Latvia or Lithuania, which I discuss below, because the buyers are not dominant under the national nor EU thresholds[1900].

966. If a buyer is dominant, the imposition of UPPs may amount to an abuse, even if such conduct would not warrant intervention and would not be seen as abusive if entered into by a non-dominant undertaking[1901], which is particularly relevant in the case of UPPs. This is so because *conducts by a dominant undertaking are presumed to have a significant effect on the market erga omnes because the structure of competition on the market has already been weakened*, and because practices by dominant undertakings are by their "very nature, liable to give rise to not insignificant restrictions of competition"[1902]. This also includes UPPs because it is presumed that such conducts as applied by the dominant buyer across all the upstream market will have a market-wide impact that goes beyond the relation of a single buyer-single seller.

967. If a dominant undertaking exploits its suppliers through UPPs, the application of competition law would be warranted because these purchasing conducts would be likely to have an impact on the market overall[1903], even if such effect in the market is not concrete, being sufficient to prove that the abuse has an exploitative (or exclusionary) effect[1904]. Thus, if the anti-competitive effect is proven, the effect is appreciable because the undertaking is a dominant one

---

1898 Tribunal Vasco de la Competencia (April 2009); Berasategi. However, this approach of regulating supermarket retailing is focused on its selling side aspect rather on the purchasing side.

1899 European Commission, *Study on the Legal Framework Covering Business-To-Business Unfair Trading Practices in the Retail Supply Chain* (2014), p. 119.

1900 The countries with the highest level of concentration in food retailing in Europe are (percentages represent the cumulative market share of the 3 largest firms): Denmark 89%; Finland 88%; Sweden 79,6%; Ireland 71.7% and Estonia 59%. In all other MS of the EU the 3 largest firms are below 50% market share. Source: European Commission, *Study on the Legal Framework Covering Business-To-Business Unfair Trading Practices in the Retail Supply Chain* (2014), Figure 1, 40.

1901 Frédéric de Bure, *Other Abuses*, Vol. 5 (F. Enrique González-Díaz and Robbert Snelders eds, Claeys and Casteels 2013), para. 11.53.

1902 Judgment of 6 October 2015 in *Post Danmark*, C-23/14, EU:C:2015:651, para. 73.

1903 This same solution is the one adopted by several national legislations, among them the French, Italian Portuguese (and the former Spanish) Competition Act when dealing with abuses of dependence by a dominant undertaking and which I discuss below.

1904 Judgment of 17 February 2011 in *TeliaSonera Sverige*, C-52/09, EU:C:2011:83, paragraph 64. Cf with the more strict approach taken by the CJEU regarding the lack of a minimum requirement of the seriousness of an anticompetitive rebate scheme in Judgment of 6 October 2015 in *Post Danmark*, C-23/14, EU:C:2015:651, paras. 63-74.

and because it is assumed that the UPPs will be applied to a substantial group (or all) of the suppliers[1905]. However, the examination of the anti-competitiveness of the practice is not automatic nor per se as the EU case law has clarified that the determination of whether a contract condition is unfair depends on the "specific circumstances of the case" and the effect of the particular clause or measure[1906]. Hence, not all UPPs that look 'unfair' would be anti-competitive, even if imposed by a dominant buyer.

968. Several arguments back the application of EU competition law to UPPs imposed by a dominant undertaking. If an undertaking is dominant, it is subordinated to the *doctrine of special responsibility* as developed by the Courts, which limits the economic freedom of dominant undertakings, as their sole existence is deemed to have weakened the competitive structure[1907]. Furthermore, if a dominant undertaking imposes UPPs, it is under a presumption that their effects will go beyond a mere contractual issue and will have an impact on the overall market trading conditions. Additionally, Article 102 TFEU and EU competition law in general adopt a broader approach to buyer power triggering the application of the law to protect the competitive process and, indirectly, suppliers and competitors from being exploited unjustifiably and anti-competitively by dominant buyers, as discussed by Advocate General Kokott in *British Airways v Commission*, which implies that competition intervention will be triggered in a case of UPPs, even absent short term end consumer harm[1908]. Lastly, the requirement of dominance for the application of EU competition law to unilateral behaviour to UPPs is a screening device to avoid dealing with conducts that may have rather limited market impact. This threshold avoids overregulation, the employment of remedies not suited to deal with contractual imbalances and avoids excessive administrative burden for the Commission.

969. Interestingly, and from an applicability perspective, albeit at a national level, Robles Martín-Laborda argues that competition law will be applicable to UPPs whenever the dominant undertaking carrying out the behaviour withholds demand (monopsony). If there is no demand withholding but exercise of bargaining power, in his view, unfair competition laws apply[1909]. I, however, do not think this is an appropriate distinction concerning the applicability of EU

1905 See also of the same opinion Pablo Ibanez Colomo, 'Streetmap v Google: Lessons for Pending Article 102 TFEU Cases (Including Google Itself)' (17th February, 2016) <http://chillingcompetition.com/2016/02/17/streetmap-v-google-lessons-for-pending-article-102-tfeu-cases-including-google-itself/>.

1906 Judgment of 10 July 1990, *Tetra Pak v Commission*, T-51/89, ECR, EU:T:1990:41, paras. 23-24. See also: Judgment in of 11 April 1989 in *Ahmed Saeed Flugreisen and Others v Zentrale zur Bekämpfung unlauteren Wettbewerbs*, C-66/86, EU:C:1989:140.

1907 Judgment of 13 February 1979 in *Hoffmann-La Roche v Commission*, C-85/76, EU:C:1979:36.

1908 The protective aspect of Article 102 TFEU was subject of discussion in the Opinion of Advocate General Kokott of 23 February 2006 in Judgment of 15 March 2007 in *British Airways v Commission*, C-95/04 P, EU:C:2006:133, para. 69.

1909 Robles Martín-Laborda, 'La Cadena Alimentaria: Cuando el Poder de Mercado lo Tiene el Comprador'.

competition law to UPPs imposed by dominant buyers as it disregards possible anti-competitive effects by bargaining power conducts, which is the most common scenario and may lead to under enforcement risks, even if bargaining power will be mostly procompetitive. Allowing a dominant undertaking that abuses its bargaining power to escape competition law application and only resort to unfair competition rules appears contrary to the definition of dominance and the established scope of application of EU competition rules.

970. A question regarding dominance applicability, nevertheless, remains: *To capture UPPs under Article 102 TFEU, in which market should the undertaking be dominant?* In the case that it is required for the undertaking to be dominant in both the upstream and downstream market, there is a high risk of under enforcement of cases as firms are seldom dominant in both. In my view, the answer should be that dominance is required *in either the upstream or the downstream market* anchored on the protection of market structure and competition as a process. If the undertaking is dominant in the upstream market as a buyer, there is no doubt that UPPs arise directly from its privileged market position and, therefore, UPPs may be captured by Article 102 TFEU. If the undertaking is dominant only in the downstream market but not in the upstream market, the imposition of UPPs should still be captured under the current EU competition law by analogy to the treatment given to buyer power market leverage, which I discussed in chapter 6, section §VII, if the conduct is able to use market power in a market to affect another[1910]. As with market power leverage, the fact that the undertaking is not dominant in the market in which it imposes UPPs is not an impediment to capture the conduct of a buyer that employs its seller market power to impose trading conditions to suppliers. In this case, the retailers' aim is to not only strengthen its already dominant position downstream but to also increase its market power as a buyer and extract supracompetitive profits from its suppliers. Furthermore, this argument is also anchored on the fact that if the buyer is dominant as a retailer this means that it is likely to constitute an important – if not necessary – distribution channel for suppliers to reach end consumers and be able to effectively commercialize its products.

C. Are there any UPP cases in EU competition law?

971. Following the previous discussion on the applicability of EU competition law to exploitative UPPs, in this section, I analyze the few cases in which UPPs have been subject to scrutiny under EU competition law. My research shows

1910 See somewhat related the views of Doherty for cases regarding essential facilities and the criterion of eliminating competition the case where an undertaking must be dominant in an upstream market and also be dominant or have a strong position in the downstream market for an abuse to take place whenever refusing access to the essential facility in Barry Doherty, 'Just what are Essential Facilities?' 38 Common Market Law Review (2001) 397, p. 425. See also the Opinion of Advocate General Jacobs in Judgment of 28 May 1998 in *Bronner*, C-7/97, EU:C:1998:264, para. 58.

that UPPs have exceptionally been an EU competition law concern, with a mere five instances in which they have been subject of scrutiny. These being: the case of *FENIN v Commission*[1911]; three merger assessments dealing with creation of a position that could trigger UPPs based on a situation of economic dependence[1912], and one case of exploitative purchasing price discrimination based on dependence by a dominant buyer, as occurred in *British Airways v Commission* and as is discussed in chapter 7, section §IV[1913]. This trend also holds true for national cases, as confirmed by a 2014 Commission's report, as buyers imposing UPPs do not qualify as a dominant undertaking, even if they might be strong[1914] and therefore, 'core' competition law provisions are "almost never met in practice in the EU 28"[1915].

a. FENIN v Commission: a case of UPPs?

972. In *FENIN v Commission,* a well-known case due to its impact on the definition of 'economic activity', the claimant Fenin filed an action against the purchasing behaviour of the Spanish State while operating its national health system, as in its view the latter had unjustifiably delayed the payments for input acquired from its suppliers. According to Fenin, the Spanish State had a dominant position as a buyer and provider of healthcare in Spain and abused it by taking an average of 300 days to pay for the input acquired from its suppliers, including Fenin. Furthermore, Fenin claimed that these *payment delays* were discriminatory and exploitative because other suppliers were paid much faster[1916]. Consequently, Fenin claimed before the Commission that the Spanish Government had engaged in UPPs when it argued that:

> [t]he abusive exploitation, individually or collectively, of the dominant position derives from [...], secondly, the *requirement of additional performance and obligation that*, due to their nature and the commercial customs, *do not have any relation with the contract object such as, for example, payment of extraordinary fees to celebrate hospital anniversaries, purchasing of outdated machinery as precondition for entering into new sup-*

1911 Judgment of 11 July in *FENIN v Commission*, C-205/03 P, EU:C:2006:453; Judgment of 4 March 2003, *Fenin v Commission*, T-319/99, ECR, EU:T:2003:50.

1912 Commission Decision of 20 November 1996 declaring a concentration to be incompatible with the common market (Case No IV/M.784 - *Kesko/Tuko*) Council Regulation (EEC) No 4064/89 [1997] OJ L 110/53, taken from the unabridged version; Commission Decision of 3 February 1999 relating to proceedings under Council Regulation (EEC) No 4064/89 (Case No IV/M.1221 - *Rewe/Meinl*) OJ L 274/1.

1913 Judgment of 17 December 2003, *British Airways v Commission* of 17 December 2003, T-219/99, ECR, EU:T:2003:343; Judgment of 15 March 2007 in *British Airways v Commission*, C-95/04 P, EU:C:2007:166.

1914 European Commission '*Report from the Commission to the European Parliament and the Council on Unfair Business-to-Business Trading Practices in the Food Supply Chain*' (2016), p. 3.

1915 European Commission, *Study on the Legal Framework Covering Business-To-Business Unfair Trading Practices in the Retail Supply Chain* (2014), p. 17.

1916 Judgment of 4 March 2003, *Fenin v Commission*, T-319/99, ECR, EU:T:2003:50, para. 1.

ply contracts; and thirdly, imposing maximum purchasing prices going against the innovative development of the sector[1917].

973. In short, Fenin claimed that the Spanish Government had exerted 'classic' examples of UPPs: payment delays; extraordinary contributions required from a supplier; complementary obligations to enter into a new supply agreement, and discriminatory treatment[1918].

974. Despite these allegations, neither the Decision nor the Judgments analyzed whether the alleged UPPs imposed by a dominant undertaking accrued to an abuse of dominance. Instead, the Commission, the General Court and the CJEU dismissed the complaint filed by Fenin because in their view the bodies of the Spanish healthcare service were not acting as undertakings, as pure purchasing does not constitute an economic activity in itself. Its qualification as 'economic' depends on the use of the purchased goods in the downstream market[1919].

975. Nevertheless, if the Courts had found that such practices were imposed by a *dominant undertaking* carrying out an economic activity by purchasing, the outcome of the case would have been different. In such a scenario, I submit that *FENIN v Commission* would have clarified that whenever UPPs are imposed by a dominant undertaking they may be captured under Article 102(a) TFEU as imposing "other unfair trading conditions". Alternatively, UPPs such as those allegedly imposed in this case could be captured under or Article 102(b) TFEU due to the hindrance of innovation and triggering hold up problems for suppliers by fixing maximum purchasing prices, or be contrary to Article 102(c) TFEU as the UPPs were imposed selectively among suppliers putting some of them at a disadvantage vis-à-vis rival suppliers. Also, it could be captured by Article 102(d) TFEU because it made the contract acceptance dependent on supplementary obligations not connected with the contract.

1917 EU Commission Case IV.F.1/36.834-FENIN, document number SG(99) D/7040 (in Spanish and translation by the author), para. 12 (emphasis added).

1918 See also briefly discussing this case as an example of unfair commercial practices: Jones and Sufrin, *EU Competition Law: Text, Cases, and Materials* [2011], p. 549-550. Cf with Whish and Bailey that refer to the case as a monopsonistic case, however probably meaning a large buyer case instead of demand withholding case in Whish and Bailey, *Competition law* [2015], p. 188.

1919 For literature discussing the case concerning the concept of 'economic activity' and the concept of undertaking see, *inter alia*: Jennifer Skilbeck, 'Just When is a Public Body an "Undertaking"? Fenin and BetterCare Compared' 4 Public Procurement Law Review (2003) NA 75; K.P.E. Lasok, 'When is an Undertaking not an Undertaking?' 25 European Competition Journal (2004) 383; Victoria Louri, 'The FENIN Judgment: The Notion of Undertaking and Purchasing Activity. Case T-319/99, Federación Nacional de Empresas de Instrumentación Científica, Médica, Técnica y Dental v. Commission [2003] ECR II-00357' 32 Legal Issues of Economic Integration (2005) 87; Ronit Kreisberger, 'FENIN: Immunity from Competition Law Attack for Public Buyers?' 6 Public Procurement Law Review (2006) NA 214; Wulf-Henning Roth, 'Case C-205/03 P, Federación Española de Empresas de Tecnología Sanitaria (FENIN) v. Commission, Judgment of the Grand Chamber of 11 July 2006, [2006] ECR I-6295' 44 Common Market Law Review (2007) 1131; Markus Krajewski and Martin Farley, 'Non-Economic Activities in Upstream and Downstream Markets and the Scope of Competition Law After FENIN' 32 European Law Review (2007) 111; Alison Jones, 'The Boundaries of an Undertaking in EU Competition Law' 8 European Competition Journal (2012) 301; Sánchez Graells, *Public Procurement and the EU Competition Rules* [2015], p. 135-142.

976. Two reasons support this alternative interpretation of *FENIN v Commission* and which were covered in the previous section §IV.B. Firstly, when UPPs are imposed by a dominant undertaking to a substantial proportion of its suppliers, there is a presumption that the effect goes beyond a contractual imbalance and becomes a market power problem because the imposition of them on suppliers affects a substantial proportion of market conditions and alters the competitive structure. Secondly, dominant undertakings have a special responsibility with regard to the competitiveness of the markets, and which implies that they are precluded from carrying out certain conducts that affect not only end consumers, but also suppliers and the market overall, and which could also explain why competition law applies to these type of cases.

977. Regrettably, the CJEU opted to decide the case by dealing with the nature of the buyer involved rather than to determine if the claims were substantiated and the imposition of these conditions were indeed exploitative of suppliers.

b. *Risk of UPPs pursuant to a merger leading suppliers in a dependent position*

978. The risk of imposition of UPPs pursuant to a concentration among buyers has been discussed in three food retailing mergers as the concentration of two buyers could leave suppliers being dependent on the new entity and therefore, prone to suffer UPPs and significantly impede effective competition[1920]. However, the final impact of possible exertion of UPPs by the merged undertaking was only relevant in one of these cases, which reinforces the limited influence of UPPs in the applicability of EU competition law.

979. *Carrefour/Promodès, Rewe/Meinl* and *Kesko/Tuko* have in common that whenever a buyer reaches a point equivalent or higher to the *"taux de menace"*[1921], in which said buyer represents 22% of the profits of the supplier, then suppliers may be dependent on it, as argued by the Commission[1922]. A dependent supplier is easy prey for a buyer to demand UPPs as its economic viability may rest on the existence of the contractual relationship and thus, losing that buyer would render its economic activity unprofitable due to a lack

1920 The cases in which suppliers' dependence was taken as a factor to determine the buyer power of a proposed merger are: Non-opposition to a notified concentration (Case COMP/M.1684 — *Carrefour/Promodès*) [2000] OJ C 164/5, French public version; Commission Decision of 3 February 1999 relating to proceedings under Council Regulation (EEC) No 4064/89 (Case No IV/M.1221 - *Rewe/Meinl*) OJ L 274/1; Commission Decision of 20 November 1996 declaring a concentration to be incompatible with the common market (Case No IV/M.784 - *Kesko/Tuko*) Council Regulation (EEC) No 4064/89 [1997] OJ L 110/53, taken from the unabridged version.

1921 In this case the proportion of sales a buyer represents for a supplier, and which lead to this threat point was of 22%. Non-opposition to a notified concentration (Case COMP/M.1684 — *Carrefour/Promodès*) [2000] OJ C 164/5, [2000], French public version, para. 52.

1922 See also discussing these three cases under the optic of buyer power exploitation in Tribunal Vasco de la Competencia (April 2009), p. 58-60 and 140-145.

of sufficient alternatives to capture the large buyer's demand[1923]. Since for food suppliers large food retailers (supermarkets) are by far the most important sales channel for foodstuffs to reach end consumers, the seller depends on securing the contract with the buyer[1924]. Therefore, the risk of supplier dependence in these cases whereby the new buyer could represent at least 22% of the turnover of most of its suppliers was seen as a threat that could significantly impede competition in the upstream and downstream markets and led the Commission to declare the *Kesko/Tuko* concentration incompatible, along with other downstream competitive concerns. In the cases of *Rewe/Meinl* and *Carrefour/Promodès,* the UPP threat was not sufficient to declare the incompatibility of the concentration. In the following, I discuss these cases in detail.

980. In *Rewe/Meinl,* the Commission declared the merger between two food retailers located in Austria compatible despite the risks of future imposition of UPPs due to the adoption of purchasing strategy commitments[1925]. The concentration operation was deemed as having the ability to affect competition upstream and downstream because the large buyer would also be a large retailer, as remarked by Ezrachi and Ioannidou[1926], an argument that echoes the hourglass shape theory[1927].

981. The Commission assessed the competitive conditions anchored on the market structure of a supplier side that is "much less concentrated than the demander side" in a big vs. small argument[1928], where suppliers depend on the buyer as a distribution mechanism to reach end consumers[1929]. Furthermore, it found that with the concentration the new entity would have increased its shares in the upstream and downstream markets which would reinforce the dependence of the suppliers on *Rewe/Billa* as a customer and, therefore, strengthened its already strong position in the upstream and downstream market[1930]. According to the data available, the proposed entity would have represented four large market shares (at least 25% in the less dependent sector for suppliers) of turnover for the suppliers and reinforced their dependence on the new entity as a

1923 Ibid, p. 141.

1924 Commission Decision of 3 February 1999 relating to proceedings under Council Regulation (EEC) No 4064/89 (Case No IV/M.1221 - *Rewe/Meinl*) OJ L 274/1, para. 94-97.

1925 See commenting this case: Ezrachi [2014], p. 434-435.

1926 Ezrachi and Ioannidou (2014).

1927 Commission Decision of 3 February 1999 relating to proceedings under Council Regulation (EEC) No 4064/89 (Case No IV/M.1221 - *Rewe/Meinl*) OJ L 274/1, para. 71.

1928 Commission Decision IV/M.1221 — *Rewe/Meinl* [1999] OJ L274/1, paras. 89-90. See recently raising the big vs. small argument: European Commission '*Report from the Commission to the European Parliament and the Council on Unfair Business-to-Business Trading Practices in the Food Supply Chain*' (2016), 2.

1929 Commission Decision of 3 February 1999 relating to proceedings under Council Regulation (EEC) No 4064/89 (Case No IV/M.1221 - *Rewe/Meinl*) OJ L 274/1, para. 98-99.

1930 Commission Decision of 3 February 1999 relating to proceedings under Council Regulation (EEC) No 4064/89 (Case No IV/M.1221 - *Rewe/Meinl*) OJ L 274/1, para. 98-99.

customer[1931]. Furthermore, the amount of suppliers that were dependent on the new entity constituted a *considerable proportion of them*; i.e. not only a few marginal suppliers could be affected but most suppliers, which reinforces the idea that UPPs only raise competition concern when they affect a substantial portion of the suppliers in the upstream market[1932].

982. Also, from the investigation, it was revealed that suppliers were dependent on the buyer whenever the latter accrued to 22% of their turnover. From a survey, the Commission found that it "transpired that on average 22% of turnover is the figure above of which a customer can be replaced only at the cost of very heavy financial losses, if at all"[1933]. As the buyers' market was so concentrated, losing a major customer would leave the suppliers *with no viable alternative to sell the proportion of goods they were selling or export their goods* owing to the high investment costs they would incur in doing so and the estimated timespan of four or five years before a satisfactory export level would be reached. This lack of alternative buyers, is in my view, an important point of the Decision, as UPPs could only be credibly exerted if finding alternative demand sources for suppliers would be impossible or too costly; otherwise, if there were alternative buyers, the supplier would not have to accept the imposition of the UPPs.

983. However, despite these risks of the imposition of UPPs, the Commission accepted a series of commitments offered by the parties that mitigated the dependence risks as the merging parties would remain independent in determining their purchasing patterns for an unlimited period[1934]. Consequently, this "sharply reduced market share increase in the distribution market (which) will mean that the dependence of suppliers on Rewe/Billa as buyers in the product categories referred to in recital 99 will be hardly any greater"[1935]. Also, as Meinl would remain an independent buyer then suppliers could resort to it as an alternative demand source in case they were exploited by the undertaking resulting from the operation.

984. A similar approach to dependence and risks of UPP imposition by a powerful buyer were evaluated in *Carrefour/Promodès,* a concentration that was de-

1931 Commission Decision of 3 February 1999 relating to proceedings under Council Regulation (EEC) No 4064/89 (Case No IV/M.1221 - *Rewe/Meinl*) OJ L 274/1, para. 99.

1932 Commission Decision of 3 February 1999 relating to proceedings under Council Regulation (EEC) No 4064/89 (Case No IV/M.1221 - *Rewe/Meinl*) OJ L 274/1, para. 100.

1933 Commission Decision of 3 February 1999 relating to proceedings under Council Regulation (EEC) No 4064/89 (Case No IV/M.1221 - *Rewe/Meinl*) OJ L 274/1, para. 101.

1934 Commission Decision of 3 February 1999 relating to proceedings under Council Regulation (EEC) No 4064/89 (Case No IV/M.1221 - *Rewe/Meinl*) OJ L 274/1, para. 118; Ezrachi [2014], p. 435.

1935 Commission Decision of 3 February 1999 relating to proceedings under Council Regulation (EEC) No 4064/89 (Case No IV/M.1221 - *Rewe/Meinl*) OJ L 274/1, para. 123.

clared compatible following the acceptance of divestiture commitments[1936]. In this case the proposed concentration also raised concerns because the suppliers would be dependent on the new entity in the upstream market. Following the reasoning and using the threat point theory as in *Rewe/Meinl*, the Commission argued that a supplier would be in a *dependent position* to the buyer if this latter reached the 'threat point' and therefore, the supplier would be exposed to a risk of being exploited[1937]. However, in the assessment of the case, the risks of UPPs imposed by the creation of strengthening of a dominant position were less than in the *Rewe/Meinl* case as the parties agreed to structural commitments including the sale of shares in another supermarket chain to reduce extended risks of upstream dependence[1938].

985. Only in the case of *Kesko/Tuko* was the risk of dependence of suppliers to be exploited through UPPs a major concern and did it play a role when declaring the concentration incompatible with the internal market as it created or strengthened a dominant purchasing and retailing position, and ordering its divestiture as the concentration had been already implemented[1939]. However, unlike in the previous cases, the market share thresholds which the merged entity would have achieved as a buyer and as a retailer were substantially higher and there were serious concerns regarding downstream competition and end consumer prices. Particularly because "[f]ollowing the acquisition of Tuko, Kesko would hold a market share of at least 55 % of the Finnish market for retail of daily consumer goods"[1940], likely to create strengthen or create a dominant position in the retail market, and also being a dominant undertaking in the cash and carry market.

986. Unlike in the *Rewe/Meinl* and *Carrefour/Promodès* where the dependence levels were close to 25-35%, *suppliers in Finland would have been dependent on the merged entity for a proportion of about 50-75% of their total sales in Finland,* almost three times more than in these other cases, which considerably increases the degree of dependence of suppliers to the new buyer[1941]. This dependence, in particular, affected medium and small-sized suppliers, for which it was of "vital importance [...] to maintain sales through Kesko at

---

1936 Non-opposition to a notified concentration (Case COMP/M.1684 — *Carrefour/Promodès*) [2000] OJ C 164/5, French public version.

1937 Non-opposition to a notified concentration (Case COMP/M.1684 — *Carrefour/Promodès*) [2000] OJ C 164/5, French public version, para. 52.

1938 Ezrachi and Ioannidou (2014), p. 81-82.

1939 Commission Decision of 20 November 1996 declaring a concentration to be incompatible with the common market (Case No IV/M.784 - *Kesko/Tuko*) Council Regulation (EEC) No 4064/89 [1997] OJ L 110/53, taken from the unabridged version.

1940 Commission Decision of 20 November 1996 declaring a concentration to be incompatible with the common market (Case No IV/M.784 - *Kesko/Tuko*) Council Regulation (EEC) No 4064/89 [1997] OJ L 110/53, para. 136.

1941 Commission Decision of 20 November 1996 declaring a concentration to be incompatible with the common market (Case No IV/M.784 - *Kesko/Tuko*) Council Regulation (EEC) No 4064/89 [1997] OJ L 110/53, taken from the unabridged version, para. 150.

the present level"[1942] and were therefore more likely to succumb to the imposition of UPPs by the powerful buyer-retailer absent alternative demand sources. Furthermore, the dependence was aggravated as post-merger suppliers would not have a similar possibility to switch to alternative buyers because the rest of buyers would only accrue 40% of the market demand, which was insufficient to produce goods at a sustainable level. Also, additional retail capacity was found to only be possible in the medium or even long term, which would have implied that those suppliers would not have been able to sell their goods[1943]. Lastly, the ability of the merged entity to compete with suppliers through its own private label was seen as further pressure in the upstream market that made suppliers more prone to be exploited through UPPs[1944].

987. However, the main reason for the declaration that the merger was incompatible with the internal market was the combination of suppliers' dependence with *risks in distorting competition in the downstream market,* as before the merger one of the parties was already a dominant undertaking. Therefore, the increased buyer power due to the concentration would have allowed the new entity to increase its competitive advantage by leveraging market power and foreclose downstream rival retailers that also competed as upstream buyers due to the combination of dual substantial market power. This circumstance was aggravated further as other retailers in Finland had some commercial ties with the merged entity which did not allow them to sufficiently deter possible end consumer price increases.

988. In connection to the former downstream market concern, both in the case of *Carrefour/Promodès*[1945] and *Kesko/Tuko*[1946], the Commission also factored in the existence of the 'spiral effect'[1947]. The spiral effect was found to be an additional concern that generates exclusionary risks to rival buyers that compete

---

1942 Commission Decision of 20 November 1996 declaring a concentration to be incompatible with the common market (Case No IV/M.784 - *Kesko/Tuko*) Council Regulation (EEC) No 4064/89 [1997] OJ L 110/53, taken from the unabridged version, para. 150.

1943 Commission Decision of 20 November 1996 declaring a concentration to be incompatible with the common market (Case No IV/M.784 - *Kesko/Tuko*) Council Regulation (EEC) No 4064/89 [1997] OJ L 110/53, taken from the unabridged version, para. 151.

1944 Commission Decision of 20 November 1996 declaring a concentration to be incompatible with the common market (Case No IV/M.784 - *Kesko/Tuko*) Council Regulation (EEC) No 4064/89 [1997] OJ L 110/53, taken from the unabridged version, para. 152. See also stressing the relevance of private labels in increasing suppliers' pressure: Ezrachi and Ioannidou (2014); Faull, Nikpay and Taylor, [2014], para. 5.888.

1945 Non-opposition to a notified concentration (Case COMP/M.1684 — *Carrefour/Promodès*) [2000] OJ C 164/5, French public version, para. 45-46.

1946 The Commission considered that the concentration would create an entity with too high degree of buyer power creating a link of dependence of suppliers to the buyer, and also imposing too high entry barriers for potential competition. Commission Decision of 20 November 1996 declaring a concentration to be incompatible with the common market (Case No IV/M.784 - *Kesko/Tuko*) Council Regulation (EEC) No 4064/89 [1997] OJ L 110/53, taken from the unabridged version.

1947 For a discussion of the spiral effect and its economic consequences, see chapter 2, section §VI.A.

in the downstream market, as well as creating barriers of entry[1948]. The spiral effect focused on the ability of a powerful buyer-retailer to gain downstream market share by offering better end consumer prices and raising their rivals' costs. Therefore, the more the buyer gains downstream market power, the less chances its competitors have of offering better conditions to end consumers, for which they might end up being foreclosed, and in the long run being able to exploit end consumers. However, economic theory disputes this theory of harm because a powerful and efficient buyer may use its buyer power to lower its costs and improve (reduce) its retailing price to capture consumer demand, to the benefit of end consumers through low prices, as noted by Dobson[1949].

989. Lastly, an alternative reading to these cases is the position of Këllezi, who argues that the finding of anti-competitive risks under such low market share thresholds was not prompted by unilateral future behaviour nor by risks of UPP exploitation. Rather, in her view, the risk was due to the possibility of collusion as the concentrations increased downstream concentration and could have generated a collusive response from other supermarket chains[1950].

990. In conclusion, and in line with the prospective nature of concentration clearance, *the concern in these mergers was the ability of the new entity to impose UPPs on a substantial part of its dependent suppliers.* This risk of supplier exploitation was also coupled with the fact that suppliers did not have a sufficient buying alternative and that the *concentration would have adversely affected the competitive conditions upstream and downstream*. From the cases it can also be concluded that if the situation of economic dependence would arise only regarding a *single* supplier, or few suppliers, or there were other alternative sources of demand, these risks of future UPPs would not warrant competition intervention. This would be the case where such possible future breaches of contractual fairness would have a limited market impact, and because there can also be other regulatory means available to the harmed suppliers under national laws. Also, pure dependence of most suppliers without additional anti-competitive concerns – as in the case of *Kesko/Tuko* regarding some degree of downstream consumer harm, or substantial impact on the upstream market structure – is likely to be insufficient to render a concentration incompatible with the internal market. Hence, also regarding concentrations, the room for applicability of EU competition law to tackle possible cases of UPPs anchored on the idea of suppliers' dependence is limited.

1948 See discussing the spiral effect and its effects on competition: Overd (2001), p. 250; Office of Fair Trading, *The Competitive Effects of Buyer Groups* para 1.74; Bundeskartellamt '*Buyer Power in Competition Law - Status and Perspectives*' (2008), p. 3; Tribunal Vasco de la Competencia (April 2009), p. 139; Dobson [2009], p 122; Ezrachi and De Jong (2012), p. 258.

1949 Dobson [2009], p. 122-123.

1950 For these two cases Këllezi argues that economic dependence can be a factor considered in merger control. However, I would not go as far as claiming that in these cases the dependence lead to a conclusion that the undertakings were dominant as it could be interpreted from her Table 2 which refers to "[d]ominant position in the EC and market shares" in Këllezi [2008], p. 76 and 81.

D. A glance at US Antitrust law

991. In the US, "unfair competition" and UPPs receive treatment within and outside antitrust law. In general, "unfair competition rules" are a matter of state law and not federal law. The exception to this being Section 5 §45 of the Federal Trade Commission Act, which declares that "[u]nfair methods of competition in or affecting commerce, and unfair or deceptive acts or practices in or affecting commerce, are hereby declared unlawful"[1951]. The vague wording of the provision is a catch all device as the Supreme Court has held that Section 5 "registers violations of the Clayton and the Sherman Acts" as well as the Robinson-Patman Act[1952].

992. Section 5 "enables the FTC to proscribe behavior beyond conduct prohibited by the other federal antitrust statutes" that *fall outside core antitrust law issues*[1953]. Section 5, therefore, is analogous to European rules of "unfair competition laws" or national competition regulation going beyond EU competition law for unilateral behaviour. This provision, nevertheless, is a jurisdictional device that grants the FTC administrative competence rather than a substantial piece of legislation of prohibited conducts as it does not list any forbidden conduct[1954]. Furthermore, the FTC has employed it on very few occasions since 1914, which has diminished the practical value of Section, as remarked by Kovacic and Winerman[1955].

993. Another piece of legislation that deals with 'unfair' practices within US antitrust law is the Robinson-Patman Act, which I have analyzed in chapters 6 and 7[1956]. The Robinson-Patman Act, however, does not protect suppliers from the imposition of UPPs because it only applies to selling side discrimination (primary line discrimination) or to cases in which the discrimination is the result of buyer-induced pressure (secondary line discrimination). Therefore, it offers little protection to suppliers that feel they are 'unfairly' treated by powerful buyers.

1951 Section 5(a)(1) § 45 The Federal Trade Commission Act of 1914, last amended and incorporating the U.S. SAFE WEB Act amendments of 2006, codified under Title 15, Chapter 2, Section of the U.S.C.

1952 *Times-Picayune Publishing Co. v. United States*, 345 U.S. 594, at 609 (1953). See also: Neil W Averitt, 'The Meaning of Unfair Methods of Competition in Section 5 of the Federal Trade Commission Act' 21 Boston College Law Review (1979-1980) 227, p. 237.

1953 William E. Kovacic and Marc Winerman, 'Competition Policy and the Application of Section 5 of the Federal Trade Commission Act' 76 Antitrust Law Journal (2010) 929, p. 929.

1954 Section 5 §45 Federal Trade Commission Act Incorporating U.S. SAFE WEB Act amendments of 2006, available at https://www.ftc.gov/sites/default/files/documents/statutes/federal-trade-commission-act/ftc_act_incorporatingus_safe_web_act.pdf. For some literature discussion Section 5 of the Federal Trade Commission Act see, *inter alia*: Averitt (1979-1980); Richard A. Posner, 'The Federal Trade Commission: A Retrospective' 72 Antitrust Law Journal (2005) 761; Herbert Hovenkamp, 'The Federal Trade Commission and the Sherman Act' 62 Florida Law Review (2010) 871; Kovacic and Winerman (2010).

1955 Kovacic and Winerman (2010), p. 933-934.

1956 See also discussing the Robinson-Patman Act as a piece of legislation seeking the fairness with regards to small buyers and suppliers: American Antitrust Institute [2008], p. 130.

994. Lastly, in Federal US antitrust law the Packers and Stockyards Act grants sectoral coverage against UPPs regarding the purchasing of beef and poultry[1957]. The Act prohibits any buyer of livestock, meats, meat food products, or livestock products in unmanufactured form, or any live poultry dealer, from imposing conducts akin to European UPPs, and also from engaging in other practices typically covered by US antitrust and the Clayton Act[1958]. For example, the Packers and Stockyards Act expressly prohibits buyers from "[e]ngag[ing] in or us[ing] any unfair, unjustly discriminatory, or deceptive practice or device"[1959], or "subject[ing] any particular person or locality to any undue or unreasonable prejudice or disadvantage in any respect"[1960].

995. The wording of the Packers and Stockyards Act resembles European national legislation dealing with *unfair practices*, rather than being a part of core antitrust legislation, as also remarked by Hovenkamp when holding that the Act's provisions "are simple tort-like provision, not monopoly or antitrust-like provisions"[1961]. However, despite its clear wording, the US Courts have *refused to apply these provisions dealing with UPPs absent significant consumer harm* which implies that these unfair competition law provisions have been reinterpreted as antitrust provisions with consumer welfare as a goal[1962]. Therefore, through the case law rules originally designed with the intention to tackle UPPs and protect the wellbeing of small suppliers have been narrowed down in its scope and made applicable only upon end consumer harm, following the narrower and, in my view, under-inclusive standard that exists in the US regarding buyer power in general and in particular to UPPs when compared to the European regime.

996. This narrowed scope of application was applied in *Terry v Tyson Farms, Inc* where the Sixth Circuit Court of Appeals refused to apply the provisions of the Packers and Stockyards Act when a large buyer – but not dominant undertaking – underweighted chicken to pay a lower purchasing prices, and unilaterally terminated purchasing of poultry contracts to counteract the organization of chicken growers to organize cooperatives[1963]. The Court of Appeals concluded that absent market-wide harm to competition affecting end consumers the provisions (a) and (b) of the Statute did not apply, restricting therefore the protection of suppliers vis-à-vis UPPs under US Federal Law.

1957 The Packers and Stockyards Act of 1921, codified under Section 7 U.S.C. sections 181 to 229b. For a discussion of the law see: http://nationalaglawcenter.org/wp-content/uploads/assets/articles/obrien_producermarketing_ch8.pdf. See also: Carstensen 'Buyer Power, Competition Policy, and Antitrust: The Competitive Effects of Discrimination Among Suppliers' (2008), p. 274.

1958 Herbert Hovenkamp, *Does the Packers and Stockyards Act Require Antitrust Harm?* (2011), p. 1

1959 7 U.S.C. § 192(a).

1960 7 U.S.C. § 192(b).

1961 Hovenkamp, *Does the Packers and Stockyards Act Require Antitrust Harm?*, p. 3.

1962 Ibid, p. 6.

1963 *Terry v. Tyson Farms, Inc.*, 604 F.3d 272 (6th Cir. 2010).

V. Need for regulation

997. In any case, it must be stressed that even if UPPs may usually be outside of EU competition law this does not imply that these exploitative practices do not require legal intervention to be corrected both at the national and EU level, or most likely at the national level in which national law is applied and extraordinarily EU competition law as well, as confirmed by European Competition Network[1964]. On the contrary, national and European legislation having a wider set of protected goals[1965], which aim to "fill the alleged lacuna in the supra-national European Law"[1966], confirms that UPPs are, and should be, under the scrutiny of some type of economic regulation; whether this be competition laws sensu stricto or another type of legislation, such as unfair competition laws or specific sectoral regulation. *The issue is one of determining which regulatory avenue is better suited to tackle issues regarding UPPs.*

998. The fact that UPPs' effects tend to mostly impact contractual fairness and profit distribution between parties with a reduced effect on allocative efficiency does not mean that suppliers should be left unprotected against behaviours of buyers that are contrary to ethical business practices. This is so not only due to the moral component of the action, but because a widespread use of UPPs can, in the long run and from a dynamic efficiency perspective, adversely affect the competition conditions by compromising the viability and profitability of suppliers, conditioning entry and exit conditions from the market, and also unduly restricting the market participant's economic freedom.

999. In my view, *it is the role of rules like unfair competition laws or tort-like provisions, and not stricter pure competition laws, to deal with UPPs at either the national level or the EU level* (if there is a possibility for harmonization,

---

1964 The report concluded that most instances in which NCAs dealt with claims of competition breaches in retailing markets and UPPs there was little application of EU competition law. From the 36 cases it analyzed in only 2 occasions EU competition law was solely applied by national NCAs and Courts, and in only 8 cases EU and national competition law were applied concomitantly. In contrast, in 26 cases only national law was applied, European Competition Network (2012), para. 62. In fact, in 16 instances the law applied went beyond the limits imposed by Article 102 TFEU and was stricter as I discuss below setting lower limits to control unilateral behavior by strong buyers as "In this context it is important to note the distinction between buyer power and unequal bargaining power. Unequal bargaining power exists whenever one party to a proposed contract, be it either the supplier or the buyer, can 'drive a hard bargain'; that is, can impose upon the other contracting party terms and conditions that are deemed unfavourable by that other party. Unequal bargaining power and resulting contractual imbalances do not necessarily imply a competition infringement in most cases. Such issues may be, where appropriate, addressed by other policy tools, such as contract and unfair commercial practices law. Buyer power, by contrast, exists if a market is concentrated to such an extent that a particular buyer has not only power over a particular supplier but over suppliers in general. From the perspective of EU competition law, the power of a buyer over its suppliers can constitute a problem, for instance, if this position is used to foreclose (potential) rivals to the detriment of consumers. However, buyer power can also be to the benefit of consumers, for instance, by acting as a countervailing power that exerts competitive constraints on a powerful supplier or by creating purchase efficiencies that are passed on to consumers" ibid, para. 73.

1965 See discussing the different width of goals protected by competition laws in a national and EU level: Rodger and MacCullogh, [2015], p. 14-18.

1966 Scheelings and Wright (2006), p. 235.

which seems unlikely due to the different legal traditions among the MS). These contract or tort provisions are a better solution than core competition laws because they are designed for handling contractual imbalance issues and wealth distribution problems as well as having remedies available that are better suited to the redress of contractual balances, a proposition that is consistent with an ordoliberal competition policy approach. As expressed by Böhm, Eucken and Grossmann-Doerth:

> [f]ree competition must not be stopped on the erroneous grounds of alleged unfair practice. On the other hand, it must not be allowed to degenerate into truly unfair competition either. How the line is to be drawn between unfair and permissible competition, whether competition is restricted, whether competition is efficient or obstructive, whether or not price-cutting contradicts the principle of the system-all these issues can only be decided by investigations conducted by economists into the various stats of the market. The collaboration of [law and economics], which in this respect still leaves much to be desired is clearly essential[1967].

1000. For ordoliberalism there is a tension between free competition and unfair competition practices, between market efficiency and the idea of fairness and the economic freedom of suppliers that are dependent on their buyers[1968]. Therefore, and in line with the idea of protection of the competitive order in a broad sense, it is the duty of the state or the EU to regulate the adverse effects of UPPs through competition regulation (*lato sensu*); to draw the line dividing which buying conducts are anti-competitive because they represent a market power problem from those that are typical of a contractual imbalance that exploit suppliers and restrict the market freedom of inefficient and efficient market participants and which should be regulated by other type of rules[1969]. This distinction is important because employing the wrong regulatory instruments to address UPPs may lead to a situation where it is detrimental to the competitive order by over-enforcing rules designed to tackle market power problems and not to remedy issues of contractual balance.

1001. Under EU law, other regulatory avenues outside EU competition law have been developed to partially address UPPs and unfair trading practices in gen-

---

1967 Böhm, Eucken and Grossman-Doerth [1989], p. 24-25.

1968 This uneasy mix between competition and fairness is not only exclusive to EU competition law. In US antitrust law fairness was an important component of the application of the law until the 'antitrust revolution of the 1970s' when fairness is substituted for the protection of consumer welfare. For a thorough discussion of fairness in US antitrust law and price discrimination see: Gifford and Kudrle (2010), p. 1255-1259.

1969 See discussing the idea of fairness and protection of economic freedom as concerns of ordoliberalism and the concepts of "unfair competition" and "competition" sensu stricto and that ordoliberalism protects competitors and not competition: Akman, *The Concept of Abuse in EU Competition Law: Law and Economic Approaches* [2012], p. 151-152.

eral, such as the Unfair Commercial Practice Directive[1970]. This piece of legislation, however, has a narrow scope of application covering only "unfair business-to-consumer commercial practices [...] before, during and after a commercial transaction in relation to a product"[1971]. *Thus, the relation among undertakings in any spectrum of the commercial chain are excluded from its scope*. Other alternatives employed at the EU level are the Late Payment Directive[1972], applicable to transactions among undertakings, or sectoral specific regulation, for instance in the case of the milk/dairy sector[1973].

1002. Nevertheless, *there is no indication that in the future the EU institutions will support adoption of community legislation dealing with UPPs from a buyer-supplier perspective* as confirmed in 2014 and again in 2016 by the Commission[1974]. Two arguments justify this approach. Firstly, it would be difficult to find a harmonized legal landscape to tackle UPPs because of the myriad of national regulatory avenues adopted due to the quite distinct legal approaches of MS to unfair practices based on their legal roots. Furthermore, and in accordance with Article 3 of Regulation 1/2003, MS have discretion to enact not only stricter rules regarding unilateral behaviour but also to adopt instruments that complement competition law to address economic issues that do not necessarily affect market-wide conditions. Therefore, alternative solutions tailored for each MS appear to be a better solution than a harmonized EU regulation.

1003. Due to this lack of EU legislation tailored to address UPPs and the little room for applicability of EU competition law, all European countries have developed mechanisms based on the idea of 'fairness' to govern commercial activ-

1970 Directive 2005/29/EC of the European Parliament and of the Council of 11 May 2005 concerning unfair business-to-consumer commercial practices in the internal market and amending Council Directive 84/450/EEC, Directives 97/7/EC, 98/27/EC and 2002/65/EC of the European Parliament and of the Council and Regulation (EC) No 2006/2004 of the European Parliament and of the Council ('Unfair Commercial Practices Directive') [2005] OJ L 149/22. For some literature dealing with the Directive's application and derived case law see: Radeideh, [2004]; Handig (2005); Howells, Micklitz and Wilhelmsson, [2006]; Incardona and Poncibò (2007); Parry, [2008]; Willett (2010); Anagnostaras (2010); Shears (2012); Stuyck (2015).

1971 Directive 2005/29/EC of the European Parliament and of the Council of 11 May 2005 concerning unfair business-to-consumer commercial practices in the internal market and amending Council Directive 84/450/EEC, Directives 97/7/EC, 98/27/EC and 2002/65/EC of the European Parliament and of the Council and Regulation (EC) No 2006/2004 of the European Parliament and of the Council ('Unfair Commercial Practices Directive') [2005] OJ L 149/22, Article 3.1.

1972 Articles 1 and 3 of Directive 2011/7/EU of the European Parliament and of the Council of 16 February 2011 on combating late payment in commercial transactions [2011] OJ L 48/1.

1973 Regulation (EU) No 261/2012 of the European Parliament and of the Council of 14 March 2012 amending Council Regulation (EC) No 1234/2007 as regards contractual relations in the milk and milk products sector [2012] OJ L 94/38.

1974 European Commission '*Tackling Unfair Trading Practices in the Business-to-Business food supply chain*' (2014); European Commission '*Report from the Commission to the European Parliament and the Council on Unfair Business-to-Business Trading Practices in the Food Supply Chain*' (2016), p. 3.

ities and contractual balance within and/or parallel to competition laws[1975], with up to 20 MS that have recently introduced legislation exclusively to deal with UPPs[1976]. These regulatory formulas outside EU competition law, and arguably suited to meet the needs of each national market *are better equipped to tackle imposition of UPPs by non-dominant undertakings or practices that do not have an overall and substantial effect in the market,* particularly if they do not aim at applying core competition laws nor remedies, unless such application is warranted because of a widespread and substantial effect of the UPPs in the market.

1004. In the following section, I discuss how MS deal with UPPs in their national legislation by classifying the solutions into four categories, depending on the legal strategy adopted to tackle UPPs.

VI. Alternative solutions to UPPs under national law

1005. An analysis of the regulation of UPPs in the MS shows that this is a matter open to national discretion where each national legislator adopts an alternative suited to its legal historical roots and market dynamics[1977]. This explains why on the national level there is a "piece meal" approach to UPPs, as labeled by Henning-Bodewig[1978]. However, all these different regulatory avenues concerning UPPs share a commonality, they "are often used to curb the negotiating power of large-scale retailers", as stressed by Jenny[1979].

1006. These different approaches and legal backgrounds explain why some MS, particularly those anchored on a continental law tradition, regulate UPPs as part of their competition act, others as part of laws on unfair competition, commercial or civil codes. On the other hand, common law countries usually place them as part of the common-law torts while jointly or alternatively adopting codes of self-regulatory conduct in specific sectors. However, this divide between continental and common law approaches is slowly fading as MS engage in a 'mix and match' of regulatory solutions to deal with UPPs.

1975 Henning-Bodewig, [2006], xv. For an analysis of the legal treatment of UPPs within the food retailing sector from a worldwide perspective see: Pierre Kobel, Pranvera Këllezi and Bruce Kilpatrick (eds), *Antitrust in the Groceries Sector & Liability Issues in Relation to Corporate Social Responsibility* (Springer Berlin Heidelberg 2015).

1976 European Commission '*Report from the Commission to the European Parliament and the Council on Unfair Business-to-Business Trading Practices in the Food Supply Chain*' (2016), p. 2.

1977 Dennis Corgill, 'United States of America' in Frauke Henning-Bodewig (ed), *International handbook on unfair competition* (Beck Hart Nomos 2013), p. 1.

1978 Henning-Bodewig, [2006], xvi.

1979 Jenny [2015], p. 9.

All these national legislative solutions, with the exception of 'competition laws *sensu stricto*' address UPPs in line with tort-law or contract law-like remedies tailored to deal with issues of contractual unbalance and not abuse of market power. Therefore, these solutions outside competition laws are in my view better suited for dealing with issues of contractual fairness, whereas competition law remedies are better suited to addressing the well-functioning of the market and addressing market power market failures, although not necessarily in line with the idea of business ethics.

1007. I classify these solutions into four different categories, which I discuss below by briefly analyzing the national legislation of some MS. Firstly, competition law provisions regarding dominance in food retailing that are stricter and adopt lower dominance thresholds than Article 102 TFEU in accordance with Article 3.2 of the Regulation 1/2003. Secondly, competition law rules or provisions dealing with abuse of dependence or relative dominance, also stricter than Article 102 TFEU. Thirdly, rules dealing with UPPs through 'unfair competition law-like' provisions in either standard unfair competition laws, specific laws addressing food retailing, or general legislative instruments like commercial or civil codes. And fourthly, I discuss the soft-law alternatives of regulation by means of a code of conduct or other *soft law* measures[1980]. In practice, however, these categories are not isolated but connected with each other, as MS are increasingly choosing to regulate UPPs by a mixture of these legislative solutions.

A. Lower thresholds or special dominance provisions as part of competition law – the food retailing sector

1008. A few MS have included within their competition law provisions tailored to address the imposition of UPPs by large buyers in the food retailing sector. This solution adopts special dominance thresholds below the traditional standards triggering the application of competition law against powerful buyers (that act as retailers) in the food retailing sector and that may be able to exploit their buyer market power vis-à-vis suppliers. This approach, however, risks taking a simplistic approach to buyer power and UPPs based on 'market share' thresholds which may lead to over enforcement of competition law with respect to situations that are better addressed by other regulatory means and involve the application of remedies that may be inadequate to solve contractual unbalancing. Furthermore, these threshold solutions sometimes impose a presumption of dominance outside of the market context or the conduct's characteristics which sets a rigid and un-economically informed standard for large food retailing buyers that might not be justified. On the other hand, this

1980 European Competition Network (2012), para. 254.

trend corroborates that bilateral buyer market power surges with regard to specific suppliers at lower market share thresholds, as discussed in chapter 5.

1009. In **Finland**, the Competition Act amended in 2014 introduced a special provision establishing that, in the case of food retailers, an undertaking with 30% market share in the downstream and/or upstream market is *a dominant undertaking*:

> Definitions
>
> In the context of this Act [...],
>
> Dominant position in daily consumer goods trade
>
> An undertaking or an association of undertakings with a minimum of 30 per cent market share in the Finnish daily consumer goods retail trade shall be deemed to occupy a dominant position in the Finnish daily consumer goods market. This includes both the retail and procurement markets[1981].

1010. The provision not only lowers the threshold required for dominance under Finnish law but it goes beyond this by establishing a *non-rebuttable presumption* that an undertaking with 30% market share in food retailing is automatically dominant. Establishing a *jure et de jure* presumption that allows for no counterevidence appears excessive and non-proportional, and may lead to an over-enforcement of Finnish competition law or, at least, an over employment of public resources to investigate cases in food retailing that do not have an overall market impact. To date, however, this provision has not been yet invoked before the Finnish NCA and/or in private litigation.

1011. The **Latvian** competition law also includes a specific provision dealing with abuses of dominance in the retail trade (at any level) aimed at precluding buyers from abusing dependent suppliers and imposing UPPS[1982]. In this sense, Section 13(2) of the Latvian Competition Act holds that:

> (2) A market participant or several market participants are in a dominant position in retail trade if, considering their buying power for a sufficient period of time and the suppliers' dependence in the relevant market, they have the capacity of directly or indirectly applying or imposing unfair and unjustified provisions, conditions or payments upon suppliers and may hinder, restrict or distort competition in any relevant market in the ter-

1981 Section 4a of the Competition Act (No 948/2011), available (in English) at http://www.kkv.fi/en/facts-and-advice/competition-affairs/legislation-and-guidelines/competition-act/; and the official Finnish version available at: http://www.finlex.fi/fi/laki/ajantasa/2011/20110948. See discussing this provision Oinonen (2014), p. 97.

1982 See also discussing this provision: Pozdnakova (2009).

> ritory of Latvia. Any market participant who is in a dominant position in retail trade are [sic] prohibited from abusing such dominant position in the territory of Latvia[1983].

1012. According to the Latvian NCA such a powerful buyer is *not able to behave independently* from its customers or competitors (traditional dominance) but is *capable of exerting UPPs* vis-à-vis most of its suppliers (relative dominance)[1984]. Therefore, this Latvian solution incorporates a rule dealing with economic dependence but *only applicable to food retailing*[1985], a difference to the general applicability of relative dominance provisions as adopted in other MS, as I discuss below. However, unlike the Finish or Lithuanian solutions, the Latvian provision does not apply when reaching a specific market share or even proportion of sales a buyer represents to a supplier.

1013. In **Lithuania**, dominance is presumed if the market share is at least 40% *with the exception of an economic entity engaged in retail*, in which the threshold is lower[1986]. In the case of food retailing markets, according to Article 3 of the Lithuanian Competition Law:

> Unless proved otherwise, an economic entity engaged in retail trade with the market share of not less than 30 per cent shall be considered to enjoy a dominant position within the relevant market. Unless proved otherwise, each of a group of three or a smaller number of economic entities engaged in retail trade with the largest shares of the relevant market, jointly holding 55 per cent or more of the relevant market shall be considered to enjoy a dominant position[1987].

1014. Thus, Lithuanian law has a similar approach as that of Finland, with the important difference that in the Lithuanian case the presumption is rebuttable, to limit the abuse of exploitative buyer power vis-à-vis suppliers. In addition, it has a special provision regarding collective dominance in food retailing that is not contemplated in any other legislation, and which has not been to this date enforced.

1015. However, it is necessary to remark that these rules that set lower or special dominance thresholds for firms involved in food retailing respond to specific

1983 Latvian Competition Law, lastly amended in 2009, Section 13(2), electronically available in its English version at: http://www.kp.gov.lv/en/abuse-of-dominant-position. European Commission, *Study on the Legal Framework Covering Business-To-Business Unfair Trading Practices in the Retail Supply Chain* (2014), p. 57.

1984 Ibid, p. 57.

1985 College of Europe and Studies (2012), p. 61-62.

1986 Also discussing the legal Lithuanian regime for dominance: ibid, p. 35-37.

1987 Law on Competition 23 March 1999 No Viii-1099 (As last amended on 22 March 2012 No XI-1937), English version found at the Competition Council of the Republic of Lithuania at http://kt.gov.lt/en/index.php?show=antitrust&antitrust_doc=law_competition.

market circumstances in the Baltic area which may explain, albeit in my view fail to justify, this specific and rather strict and over-enforcing solution to trigger the applicability of competition law to UPPs. Food retailing markets in these countries are very concentrated with few and large active players (three or four in most cases).

1016. Furthermore, these measures reinforce the idea that the buyer power effects of an undertaking that is not only a powerful buyer, but also a reseller with substantial market power downstream, tend to be more pernicious to competitive conditions. This is so because the exertion of buyer power can have repercussions in both upstream and downstream markets and may adversely impact end consumers of food products, a quite inelastic segment of purchases.

1017. Nonetheless, in my view, setting lower thresholds, as low as 30% market share for a buying undertaking to be considered dominant, might be excessively low and an inadequate competition policy, even if it is true that buyer market power tends to arise in situations with lower market share thresholds. Prohibitions of abuse of dominance are designed to keep under control the exercise of market power of particularly large undertakings which tend to have at least 40% of market share and in general market shares of 50% or more – indeed in the US those numbers are even higher and up to 80%. Additionally, these types of provisions are prone to over-enforcement due to the 'form based' tests that are used with regard to dominance abuses in general, therefore increasing the risks of false positives. Hence, adopting the same type of prohibition of unilateral conducts and imposition of competition remedies may imply an excessive restriction of the undertaking's economic freedom, the prohibition of efficiency-enhancing bargaining power conducts, and/or which may lead to instances of unjustified and disproportional application of competition law rules not suited to the problems at stake. Thus, in my view, the adoption of lower thresholds to apply competition law rules for unilateral behaviour should be approached with caution.

B. Economic Dependence and UPPs under national competition law

1018. Other MS address UPPs through the idea of 'relative dominant positions' or the abuse of dependence, as sub-types of abuse of unilateral behaviour that tend to be below the traditional market dominance thresholds. Relative dominance and dependence describe situations where one of the parties to a relation has a much larger degree of bargaining power that allows it to exploit its other commercial partners, and is anchored on the idea of 'big and strong vs small and weak' undertakings. Both relative dominance and dependence appear on lower buyer market power thresholds, when compared to traditional dominance cases, and are conditions belonging to an *inter partes* situation;

i.e. undertaking "A" is relatively dominant with respect to undertaking "B", but not necessarily with undertaking "C".

1019. At the EU level, I have shown how risks of imposition of UPPs and buyer market power assessment take into consideration whether a *supplier is dependent on a buyer,* and the Commission has found that an indicator is when the buyer represents 22% of the supplier's turnover in cases concerning a merger among buyers as discussed above[1988]. At the national level, however, my investigation found no replication of this or any other market share threshold to determine the existence of relative dominance or dependence, as the assessment is done on a case-by-case basis. What it revealed, however, was that most of these provisions are designed to capture unilaterally imposed UPPs at lower market shares and less wide market conditions than EU competition law rules regarding unilateral behaviour. Nonetheless, other countries trigger the application of competition law rules to issues of economic dependence or relative dominant positions *only if the effect of the UPP affects a substantial part of the market and the competitive structure*. This implies that these rules would trigger under almost the same requirements than traditional dominance or as I discussed in my proposal for the application of EU competition law to UPPs. Therefore, these types of provisions dealing with relative dominance and dependence seek to protect smaller or weaker suppliers from the exertion of buyer power by large (but not dominant) undertakings, in a gray area between competition law and unfair competition law.

1020. In **Austria**, traditional dominance is presumed under lower thresholds than when compared to EU competition law[1989], and it is linked to the concept of relative dominance[1990]. According to §4.3 of the Austrian Competition Act, an undertaking is in a *relative dominant* position *if it has a superior market position* with regard to its customers or suppliers and such condition is said to be particularly present if these undertakings are *dependent on the other party to avoid serious economic disadvantages*[1991]. The provision is not drafted to specifically address buyer exploitation, but to cover any type of abuses of imbalances of bargaining power among parties to a contract having a wider scope.

1988 Commission Decision of 3 February 1999 relating to proceedings under Council Regulation (EEC) No 4064/89 (Case No IV/M.1221 - *Rewe/Meinl*) OJ L 274/1, para. 101.

1989 Firms are presumed dominant if they have 30% market share and alternatively, by comparing its market shares with those of its rivals on a 5% difference base, § 4.2 of the Austrian Bundesgesetz gegen Kartelle und andere Wettbewerbsbeschränkungen (Kartellgesetz 2005 – KartG 2005) (zuletzt geändert durch das Bundesgesetz BGB1. I. Nr. 2/2008), (author's translation).

1990 Also confirming this interpretation see European Commission, *Study on the Legal Framework Covering Business-To-Business Unfair Trading Practices in the Retail Supply Chain* (2014), p. 44.

1991 § 4.3 of the Austrian Bundesgesetz gegen Kartelle und andere Wettbewerbsbeschränkungen (Kartellgesetz 2005 – KartG 2005) (zuletzt geändert durch das Bundesgesetz BGB1. I. Nr. 2/2008), (author's translation).

1021. In addition to these rules, part of the Austrian Competition Act, Austrian national legislation, addresses imbalances of bargaining power by non-competition-like rules under the Improvement of Local Supplies and Competitive Conditions Act[1992]. These rules adopt the form of tort/contract law-like solutions that are applicable to imposition of UPPs on specific sectors.

1022. In **France** the abuse of economic dependence and imposition of unfair trading practices are governed within the Commercial Code. However, it ought to be noted that competition law sensu stricto is also integrated under French Law in the Commercial Code under the Book IV entitled *"De la liberté des prix et de la concurrence"*[1993]. According to Article L420-2 of the French Commercial Code, it is forbidden to abuse a *relative* dominant position by a single undertaking or a group of them with regard to the *state of economic dependence* vis-à-vis its other trading partners[1994]. Nevertheless, this type of abuse will be prohibited when they are *likely to affect the functioning or the structure of competition*[1995]. Therefore, this provision resembles more a state of general dependence to a traditionally dominant undertaking than a case or relative dominance despite its wording[1996], as the prohibition would not apply if the effect is reduced to be purely *inter partes* and without affecting competition as such[1997]. According to Nollet, there are several cumulative conditions that must be complied with to trigger the prohibition of economic dependence:

> notoriety of the supplier's brand; importance of the supplier's market share; significance of the supplier's market share in the sales figures of the company in question, provided this market share is not the result of a deliberate choice by the corporate customer; difficulty for the company to find other suppliers of equivalent products[1998].

1992 Bundesgesetz vom 29. Juni 1977 zur Verbesserung der Nahversorgung und der Wettbewerbsbedingungen, available (in German) at: https://www.ris.bka.gv.at/GeltendeFassung.wxe?Abfrage=Bundesnormen&Gesetzesnummer=10002393.

1993 French Commercial Code, Legislative Section, Book IV Article L410-1 to L470-8.

1994 "Est en outre prohibée, dès lors qu'elle est susceptible d'affecter le fonctionnement ou la structure de la concurrence, l'exploitation abusive par une entreprise ou un groupe d'entreprises de l'état de dépendance économique dans lequel se trouve à son égard une entreprise cliente ou fournisseur. Ces abus peuvent notamment consister en refus de vente, en ventes liées, en pratiques discriminatoires visées au I de l'article L. 4426 ou en accords de gamme", French Commercial Code, Legislative Section, Book IV Article L420-2. Also remarking that this provision regulates in exclusive manner the issue of economic dependence see: College of Europe and Studies (2012), p. 50-53. See for a discussion of the provision: OECD *France - The Role of Competition Policy in Regulatory Reform,* (2003), para. 46-47.

1995 See also remarking this fact that the UPP must affect market wide conditions: OECD '*France - The Role of Competition Policy in Regulatory Reform*' (2003), para. 46.

1996 See also briefly discussing the consequences of this wording: Këllezi [2008], p. 63.

1997 See also suggesting that "[t]he provision is intended to repress the practice of unbalanced contracts implemented by an undertaking or group of undertakings, who dominate in one or more markets but hold a dominant position in the market as a whole" in College of Europe and Studies (2012), p. 51.

1998 Nollet (2003), p. N 116. See also highlighting these same conditions: European Commission, *Study on the Legal Framework Covering Business-To-Business Unfair Trading Practices in the Retail Supply Chain* (2014), p. 46, referencing to Nollet; and Këllezi [2008], p. 64.

1023. Due to the difficulty in meeting these cumulative conditions, it is unsurprising that there have been few cases of abuse of dependence before the French NCA and Courts[1999].

1024. **Germany** is an important country when it comes to the analysis of dependence and relative positions as it was the first country to introduce dependence provisions in its competition law, back in 1973[2000]. Paragraphs §19 and 20 of the Act against Restraints of Competition address the issue of dominance and prohibits *abuse of superior bargaining power* for both buyers and sellers alike under a 'relative dominance clause'[2001]. Furthermore, the provision establishes that buyer induced dependence arises when:

> [...] a supplier of a certain kind of goods or commercial services *shall be presumed to depend* on a purchaser within the meaning of sentence 1 if this purchaser regularly obtains from this supplier, in addition to discounts customary in the trade or other remuneration, special benefits which are not granted to similar purchasers[2002].

1025. These special benefits would be special purchasing conditions only granted to the powerful buyer and not other rivals.

1026. According to this provision, prohibition of abuse of dominance and discriminatory practices:

> shall also apply to undertakings and associations of undertakings to the extent that *small or medium-sized enterprises* as suppliers or purchasers of certain type of goods or commercial services *depend on them* in such a way that sufficient and reasonable possibilities of resorting to other undertakings do not exist (relative market power)[2003]

1027. Thus, in German law there are two types of dominance and abuse of dependence:

1999 European Commission, *Study on the Legal Framework Covering Business-To-Business Unfair Trading Practices in the Retail Supply Chain* (2014), p. 46-47.

2000 Ibid, p. 47-48; Këllezi [2008], p. 61; College of Europe and Studies (2012), p. 53; Gormsen 'Article 82 EC: Where are we Coming from and Where are we Going to?' (2006), p. 14, footnote 49.

2001 Also remarking this see: KJ Cseres, 'The Impact of Regulation 1/2003 in the New Member States' 6 The Competition Law Review (2010), p. 152-153; College of Europe and Studies (2012), p. 43.

2002 §20.1. of the Act Against Restraints of Competition (2014) last amended by Article 5 of the Act of 21.07.2014 (Federal Law Gazette I, p.1066) (emphasis added).

2003 §20.1. of the Act Against Restraints of Competition (2014) last amended by Article 5 of the Act of 21.07.2014 (Federal Law Gazette I, p.1066) (emphasis added).

i) abuse of dependence by dominant buyers with an *erga omnes* effect[2004];

ii) abuse of dependence by non-dominant buyers with an *inter partes* effect and which requires a lower threshold of buyer market power to be applied[2005].

1028. In the first case, a provision known as *Anzapfverbot,* the German Competition Act, forbids dominant undertakings from hindering other undertakings (buyers or suppliers) in an unfair manner either when settling purchasing or selling prices or treating them different "from similar undertakings without any objective justification"[2006].

1029. However, for the second situation called "*relative Marktmacht*", as opposed to the traditional 'absolute market power' cases[2007], the case law of dependence in Germany clarifies that dependence may occur even "where not in a market-dominating position, an enterprise can hold such a strong position in the market that it can disrupt the markets in a manner which para. 26 II GGWB intended to prevent and to combat"[2008]. Thus, relative dependence may exist even if competition in the market as a whole is not significantly affected[2009]. This applies to both cases of unfair hindrance (*Behinderungsverbot*) or discrimination (*Diskriminierungsverbot*) below traditional market power levels[2010]. Thus, these two provisions are triggered in narrower circumstances and in which neither traditional dominance under German law nor EU competition law would apply[2011].

1030. In **Italy** the competition act applies whenever a dominant undertaking is *abusing its supplier's dependence and significantly affecting competition and market conditions*[2012]. Therefore, competition law will apply if the UPPs have

---

2004 The Commission employs the term "relative dominant position" in European Commission, *Study on the Legal Framework Covering Business-To-Business Unfair Trading Practices in the Retail Supply Chain* (2014), p. 44.

2005 Also suggesting that the dominance level is lower see: Këllezi [2008], p. 61; College of Europe and Studies (2012), p. 53. Cf with the Report of the 2015 Conference of the Ligue Internationale du Droit de la Concurrence by Pinar Akman, *Question A: Abuse of a Dominant Position and Globalization* (2015), p. 4 who remarks that in these legislations there is no requirement of dominance and "go over and beyond the prohibition found in Article 102 TFEU". For a discussion of the types of dependence in German Competition Law, including buyer related dependence see: Këllezi [2008], p. 62.

2006 §20.1. of the Act Against Restraints of Competition (2014) last amended by Article 5 of the Act of 21.07.2014 (Federal Law Gazette I, p.1066). For a discussion of the application of this provision in food retailing market see: Bundeskartellamt '*Summary of the Final Report of the Sector Inquiry into the Food Retail Sector*' (2014), p. 17-18.

2007 European Commission, *Study on the Legal Framework Covering Business-To-Business Unfair Trading Practices in the Retail Supply Chain* (2014), p. 47.

2008 German Federal Court, *Rossignol* [1975], BGH NJW 1976, 801, translation in English available at: https://law.utexas.edu/transnational/foreign-law-translations/german/case.php?id=1488. For a discussion of the case see: College of Europe and Studies (2012), p. 54-55.

2009 European Commission, *Study on the Legal Framework Covering Business-To-Business Unfair Trading Practices in the Retail Supply Chain* (2014), p. 49.

2010 Ibid, p. 48.

2011 College of Europe and Studies (2012), p. 57.

2012 ibid, p. 61.

a market-wide impact on competition and in such cases it allows the Italian NCA to *ex officio* investigate abuse of economic dependence when it is *"relevant for the protection of the competition and the market"*, in a solution akin to the Portuguese competition law that I discuss below, and to a lesser degree to the German provision dealing with economic dependence[2013].

1031. In **Portugal** the Competition Law Act[2014] also regulates *economic dependence* under the scope of traditional competition law but with the caveat *that it does so only if it affects market wide competition.* The prohibition is established in Article 12 — independently from abuse of dominance (Article 11) — and it prohibits:

> one undertaking or more undertakings to abuse the economic dependence under which any of its supplier or customer may find itself as a result of the fact that any equivalent alternative is not available, to the extent that *such a practice affects the way the market or competition operate*[2015].

1032. Despite the provision's wording, the Portuguese Supreme Court interpreted it as implying that dependence might occur in both *vertical and horizontal relations*, which seems to be contrary to its text and the trend in the other MS[2016]. This interpretation broadens the scope of the provision and may lead to an over enforcement of UPPs among competitors in a horizontal market in a logic that is hard to grasp. However, as I have discussed, UPPs are imposed on a vertical level and, therefore, it is unlikely and unnecessary to expand UPP protection in a horizontal manner.

1033. Furthermore, according to the Portuguese legislation, abuses of economic dependence will only be prosecuted under competition law when the conduct has an *impact in the market or competition overall* but not when there only is a contractual imbalance. Consequently, abuse of dependence is no longer a pure *inter partes* effect but becomes *erga omnes,* adversely impacting upstream and/or downstream market conditions. This requirement of wide

---

2013 "2. Dopo il comma 3 dell'articolo 9 della legge 18 giugno 1998, n. 192, è aggiunto il seguente:

"3-bis. Ferma restando l'eventuale applicazione dell'articolo 3 della legge 10 ottobre 1990, n. 287, l'Autorità garante della concorrenza e del mercato può, qualora ravvisi che un abuso di dipendenza economica abbia rilevanza per la tutela della concorrenza e del mercato, anche su segnalazione di terzi ed a seguito dell'attivazione dei propri poteri di indagine ed esperimento dell'istruttoria, procedere alle diffide e sanzioni previste dall'articolo 15 della legge 10 ottobre 1990, n. 287, nei confronti dell'impresa o delle imprese che abbiano commesso detto abuso"." Article 11.2 of the Legge 57/2001, "Disposizioni in materia di apertura e regolazione dei mercati" published in the Gazzetta Ufficiale n. 66 of March 20, 2001 that modified Article 9.3 of the Legge 18 giugno 1998, n. 192.

2014 Law No 19/2012 of 8 May, repealing Laws No 18/2003 of 11 June and No 39/2006 of 25 August, and makes the second amendment to Law No 2/99 of 13 January, available in English at: http://www.concorrencia.pt/vEN/News_Events/Noticias/Documents/Lei19_2012_En.pdf.

2015 Article 12 of Law No 19/2012 of 8 May, repealing Laws No 18/2003 of 11 June and No 39/2006 of 25 August, and makes the second amendment to Law No 2/99 of 13 January (emphasis added).

2016 European Commission, *Study on the Legal Framework Covering Business-To-Business Unfair Trading Practices in the Retail Supply Chain* (2014), p. 53.

market impact demands a higher threshold of market power from the buying undertaking and the capacity to create buyer dependence in a large number of suppliers, which is a concept closer to the traditional abuse of dominance, and which steers away from pure relative dominance situations. Thus, it is likely that this provision on dependence would rarely be applied by the Portuguese NCA absent traditional dominance[2017].

1034. The Portuguese provision on dependence and its predecessor, however, have been subject to criticism and a recommendation was made that it ought not to be included in the last legislative reform due to risks of competition law over-enforcement or the application of non-suitable remedies to address issues of a more *inter partes* nature[2018]. Nevertheless, the 2012 Competition Law Act kept the provision with the aim of protecting smaller undertakings in particular vis-à-vis stronger buyers in the retail sector[2019].

1035. Lastly, the Portuguese Competition Act also forbids "any unjustified break, total or partial, in established commercial relations, bearing in mind previous commercial relations, recognized practices in that particular economic activity and the contractual conditions that have been set down" as part of the dependence prohibition[2020]. As remarked by Gorjao-Henriques and Sousa Ferro, these conducts would be prohibited even if they result from negligence following a strict application standard[2021].

2017 This provision has never been enforced or applied in the finding of a breach of the competition act by the Portuguese Competition Authority. See: Miguel Gorjao-Henriques and Miguel Sousa Ferro, 'P/CPortugal/Commentary' in *Competition Law in Western Europe and the USA* (Wolters Kluwer 2010), para. 57; College of Europe and Studies (2012), p. 64.

2018 Ibid, p. 63-64.

2019 Ibid, p. 63.

2020 Article 12.2.b) of Law No 19/2012 of 8 May, repealing Laws No 18/2003 of 11 June and No 39/2006 of 25 August, and makes the second amendment to Law No 2/99 of 13 January.

2021 Gorjao-Henriques and Sousa Ferro [2010], para. 55.

1036. Lastly, at least three countries — Cyprus[2022], Hungary[2023], and Romania[2024] — adopted very similar legislations to the ones discussed in detail above tackling UPP's imposition through their national competition laws based on rules dealing with economic dependence.

C. UPPs on specific legislative instruments – unfair competition rules

1037. Other countries regulate the imposition of UPPs and the abuse of economic dependence by buyers through legislation *outside competition law,* usually by resorting to unfair competition laws, or sectoral regulation with a particular emphasis on food retailing.

1038. In the **Czech Republic** the Act on Significant Market Power in the Sale of Agricultural and Food Products and Abuse thereof regulates imposition of UPPs derived from dependence or superior bargaining power in the food market[2025]. The act applies to abuse of buyer (bargaining) power by purchasers whenever "the supplier becomes dependent on the buyer with regard to a possibility to supply own goods to consumers, and in which the buyer may im-

---

2022 The Cypriot Competition Act also addresses the issue of economic dependence under its Article 6(2) – dealing with abuse of dominance – and in particular, the imposition of unfair trading practices. (Article 6.2 of the Cypriot Protection of Competition Laws of 2008 and 2014 available in English at: http://www.competition.gov.cy/competition/competition.nsf/All/41E291273015085EC2257E6D002F0ACB/$file/OLC-COMP-Law%202008+2014-ENGLISH-FINAL.pdf?OpenElement).The rule covers practices addressed against customers, suppliers, produces, representatives, distributors or business partners and has been enforced only 11 times over a period of 21 years and always prompted by a private claim, which is an indication of the priority given to these types of cases by Cypriot authorities and/or the lack of market harm pursuant to UPPs. One of the cases dealing with UPPs dealt with complains of abuse of the economic dependence of suppliers to a yoghurt processing cooperative that unilaterally terminated a purchasing contract for raw milk vis-à-vis a dairy farmer and which threatened the farmer to be driven out of business, see further in European Union, *Roundtable on Competition Issues in Food Chain Industry -- Note by the European Union--* (2013), para. 32; European Competition Network (2012), para. 99.

2023 In Hungary, the Hungarian Competition Law Act (The Competition Act (Act LVII of 1996), lastly amended in April 2010, available in English at: http://www.gvh.hu/en/legal_background/rules_for_the_hungarian_market/competition_act) also regulates dependence abuses by dominant undertakings in its Article 21.b) and c). These provisions only apply if the undertaking is dominant and if said undertaking has, for example, refused to create or maintain business relations without justification. Article 21 a), d) and j) of the Hungarian Competition Law Act may also apply to situations of "abuse of superior bargaining position" which attempt to limit the imposition of unfair trading practices in general and UPPs in particular. See further: European Commission, *Study on the Legal Framework Covering Business-To-Business Unfair Trading Practices in the Retail Supply Chain* (2014), p. 50,

2024 The Romanian Competition Act precludes dominant undertakings to abuse "of the state of economic dependence of another undertaking towards such an undertaking or undertakings and which does not have an alternative solution under equivalent conditions, as well as breaking contract relations for the sole reason that the partner is refusing to submit to certain unjustified commercial conditions" (Article 6.1.f) of the Law of Competition 21 of April 10th 1996, last reformed in 14 of February, 2012, available in English at: http://www.consiliulconcurentei.ro/uploads/docs/concurenta/LEGEA_CONCURENTEI_Nr_21_eng_rev_1.pdf). The provision is general and not limited to pure retailing sectors and covers all trading partners, and it adopts a 'relative dominance' approach as it requires the conduct and situation to be addressed specifically to a partner not requiring a market impact as a whole. The provision, however, has had a limited applicability and has been invoked in very few occasions. Also, a 2012 Commission's report remarks that only ten (10) cases have been brought forth under this provision in College of Europe and Studies (2012), p. 65.

2025 Act No. 395/2009 of 9 September 2009 on Significant Market Power in the Sale of Agricultural and Food Products and Abuse thereof, available in English at: http://www.uohs.cz/download/Legislativa/legislativa_EN/2009_395_EN.pdf; Commission, *Study on the Legal Framework Covering Business-To-Business Unfair Trading Practices in the Retail Supply Chain* (2014), p. 55-56.

pose unilaterally beneficial trade conditions on the supplier", which may lead to situations of over enforcement[2026]. The Act goes even further and remarks that "[a]n abuse of significant market power towards suppliers is prohibited" but without making a distinction of the type of supplier that faces an UPP[2027]. Also, the Act employs a rebuttable presumption that a buyer has significant market power if it has a turnover above 5 billion CZK, although the determination must be made on a case-by-case basis[2028]. Lastly, *ratione materiae* the Act distinguishes between and applies to six categories of buyer market power abuse: invoicing; general business conditions; infringement of conditions agreed between suppliers and retailers; non-observance of sale conditions; exercising prohibited practices to buyers, and other prohibited customs between retailers and suppliers[2029].

1039. In **France**, in addition to the rules on relative dependence as part of the Competition Law Section of the French Commercial Code, the Code under the Chapter II of the Book IV regulates in addition *unfair commercial practices* that a buyer may impose to its suppliers by means of Article L442-6, which forbids certain practices for suppliers and buyers[2030]. These rules have been designed to tackle the issue of "*marges arrières*", practices which aim at "changing the prices effectively paid from those shown on the invoice at time of delivery" and which have arisen with the increase of market power of the "5 or 6 largest distributors and retailers of consumer goods"[2031]. The rationale behind this provision is not the protection of competition as such, but instead *protecting small and medium enterprises from the abuse of larger companies* and, therefore, addressing the issue of unfairness in contracting.[2032] As remarked by an OECD Report, these provisions dealing with unfair commercial practices apply as a general prohibition against formal discrimination[2033]. Hence, unlike the competition provisions, there is no need to prove existence or dependence, nor market power[2034].

1040. In **Greece** *economic dependence* is regulated by Article 18.1. of the Act on Unfair Competition. This unfair competition provision aims at protecting in-

---

2026 Article 3(1) of Act No. 395/2009 of 9 September 2009 on Significant Market Power in the Sale of Agricultural and Food Products and Abuse thereof.

2027 Article 4 of Act No. 395/2009 of 9 September 2009 on Significant Market Power in the Sale of Agricultural and Food Products and Abuse thereof.

2028 European Commission, *Study on the Legal Framework Covering Business-To-Business Unfair Trading Practices in the Retail Supply Chain* (2014), p. 56.

2029 Article 4 of Act No. 395/2009 of 9 September 2009 on Significant Market Power in the Sale of Agricultural and Food Products and Abuse thereof. For a discussion on the procedural aspects of the act in a critical way see: College of Europe and Studies (2012), p. 47-50.

2030 French Commercial Code, Legislative Section, Book IV Article L442-6.

2031 OECD '*France - The Role of Competition Policy in Regulatory Reform*' (2003), para. 47.

2032 College of Europe and Studies (2012), p. 53.

2033 OECD '*France - The Role of Competition Policy in Regulatory Reform*' (2003), para. 46.

2034 College of Europe and Studies (2012), p. 51 making reference to a report by the General Directorate for Competition Policy, Consumer Affairs and Fraud Control.

dividual traders from unfair practices that go against "good moral" customs and applies regardless of the existence of market power[2035]. On the other hand, the current Greek Competition Law Act (modeled after Articles 101 and 102 TFEU) does not contain any provisions dealing with abuse of economic dependence by a dominant party[2036]. The reason given by the Greek legislator to not include a regulation of dependence was that its abuse is an issue of protection of individuals but not of competition or markets[2037].

1041. **Hungary** constitutes a special case. The Act CLXIV of 2005[2038] establishes a concept labeled "abuse of significant market power"[2039] targeting abuses of buyer (bargaining) power below traditional dominance levels[2040], which resembles relative dominance provisions[2041]. The Act prohibits imposition of an extensive amount of conducts that qualify as UPPs such as: unjustifiably discriminating against suppliers; unjustifiably restricting suppliers access to sales opportunities; imposing unfair conditions on suppliers; unjustifiably altering contract terms, to the detriment of the suppliers; charging fees one-sidedly to suppliers; threatening with termination of the agreement (delisting).

1042. In **Italy** *abuse of dependence* is regulated outside of the scope of traditional competition and unfair competition laws through the 1998 Law on Subcontracting and which applies absent market power requirements[2042]. The Law on Subcontracting regulates economic dependence following a unique approach through contract law provisions unlike most other MS of a civil tradition[2043]. Its Article 9 deals with "abuse of economic dependence" and prohibits a buyer or a supplier to abuse of the dependence of its counter-

---

2035 Article 1 of the Law 146/1914 of January 27, 1914, on Unfair Competition, available in English at: http://www.wipo.int/wipolex/en/text.jsp?file_id=127658. European Commission, *Study on the Legal Framework Covering Business-To-Business Unfair Trading Practices in the Retail Supply Chain* (2014), p. 49.

2036 Law 3959/2011 - "Protection of Free Competition", English text available at: http://www.epant.gr/img/x2/categories/ctg391_3_1418031420.pdf.

2037 College of Europe and Studies (2012), p. 57.

2038 Hungarian Act CLXIV of 2005 on Trade /competition law related provisions of the Act, available in English at: http://www.gvh.hu/en/legal_background/rules_for_the_hungarian_market/other_statutes_relating_to_the_activity_of_the_gvh/act_on_trade_/4341_en_act_clxiv_of_2005_on_trade.html

2039 "[S]ignificant market power' refers to a market situation as a consequence of which the dealer becomes or has become a contracting partner for the supplier which the latter is unable to reasonably evade at forwarding its goods and services to the customers and which is able, due to the size of its share in the turnover, to influence regionally or all over the country market access of a product or a group of products", §2 of the Act CLXIV of 2005 on Trade /competition law related provisions of the Act.

2040 College of Europe and Studies (2012), p. 34.

2041 European Commission, *Study on the Legal Framework Covering Business-To-Business Unfair Trading Practices in the Retail Supply Chain* (2014), p. 50.

2042 Legge 18 giugno 1998, n. 192, "Disciplina della subfornitura nelle attività produttive", pubblicata nella Gazzetta Ufficiale n. 143 del 22 giugno 1998, available (in Italian) at: http://www.parlamento.it/parlam/leggi/98192l.htm. For a detailed discussion of the Italian regulation of economic dependence in the law and the case law see: Valeria Falce, *The Italian Regulation Against the Abuse of Economic Dependence* (2015), p. 1. See also: College of Europe and Studies (2012), p. 60-61.

2043 European Commission, *Study on the Legal Framework Covering Business-To-Business Unfair Trading Practices in the Retail Supply Chain* (2014), p. 51.

part[2044]. According to the law, dependence is defined as a situation in which an undertaking is able to determine in an excessive imbalance the rights and duties with other undertaking as part of a commercial relation[2045]. In particular, the law on subcontracting prohibits refusing to sell or *purchase,* imposing unfair or excessive contractual conditions or a termination of a contract without sufficient reasons.

1043. In **Lithuania**, in addition to the special competition law provision for dominance in food retailing, the Law on Prohibition of Unfair Business-To-Consumer Commercial Practices governs the behaviour of large food retailers and prohibits them from employing their buyer power 'unfairly' vis-à-vis suppliers[2046]. Specifically, it precludes food retailers from entering into UPPs and misleading practices more akin to trademark, origin or consumer protection. To date, the UPP provisions have been only applied in a case against a food retailer (Maxima Lt, Uab) that was deemed to have "significant market power" and breached the rules concerning "terms on return of goods"[2047].

1044. In **Portugal**, as a complement to the rules concerning relative dominance in the Competition Act, UPPs are also regulated by the Decree-Law 166/2013 related to Unilateral Practices Restricting Trade. Under this regulation UPPs are forbidden regardless of a market power threshold as the Decree-Law aims at remedying contractual imbalances and protecting small suppliers from large buyers[2048]. The Decree-Law prohibits, *inter alia*, discriminatory prices or terms of sale, sales at loss, and has received some criticism[2049]. Unlike the provision on dependence, the law on unfair trading practices has been enforced privately on some occasions before courts and the NCA[2050].

1045. In **Slovakia** the regulation of UPPs follows a similar approach as in the Czech Republic. There are no specific provisions dealing with dependence on the competition act, instead, they are regulated in a sectoral way by means of the Unfair Trade in Foodstuff Act[2051]. This act replaced other laws dealing with

---

2044 Article 9.2 of Legge 18 giugno 1998, n. 192, "Disciplina della subfornitura nelle attività produttive", pubblicata nella Gazzetta Ufficiale n. 143 del 22 giugno 1998.

2045 "È vietato l'abuso da parte di una o più imprese dello stato di dipendenza economica nel quale si trova, nei suoi o nei loro riguardi, una impresa cliente o fornitrice. Si considera dipendenza economica la situazione in cui un'impresa sia in grado di determinare, nei rapporti commerciali con un'altra impresa, un eccessivo squilibrio di diritti e di obblighi. La dipendenza economica è valutata tenendo conto anche della reale possibilità per la parte che abbia subito l'abuso di reperire sul mercato alternative soddisfacenti", Article 9.1 of Legge 18 giugno 1998, n. 192, "Disciplina della subfornitura nelle attività produttive.

2046 Law on Prohibition of Unfair Business-To-Consumer Commercial Practices 21 December 2007 No X-1409, available in English at: http://kt.gov.lt/en/index.php?show=advertising&adv_doc=law_pub.

2047 Competition Council of the Republic of Lithuania, 'Competition Council Imposes a fine of 40 000 Ltl on Maxima Lt, Uab' (2014) <http://kt.gov.lt/en/index.php?show=news_view&pr_id=1303>.

2048 College of Europe and Studies (2012), p. 64.

2049 Gorjao-Henriques and Sousa Ferro [2010], para. 7. See also: College of Europe and Studies (2012), p. 64.

2050 College of Europe and Studies (2012), p. 64; Gorjao-Henriques and Sousa Ferro [2010], para. 7.

2051 Act No. 140/2010 Coll. on Unfair Terms in Business Contracts between Reseller and Supplier of Goods that are Foodstuffs.

contractual imbalances between buyers and suppliers in the retailing industry to give a fairer balance to suppliers facing powerful buyers[2052]. To prevent the imposition of UPPs, the Act limits the ability of large buyers to exercise bargaining power and improves the position of suppliers by making some contractual practices illegal and void. The act lists more than thirty 'unfair' contract terms, including practices such as:

> pecuniary consideration by supplier to the reseller for services that have not been provided, immediate termination of contract without giving a notice period and grounds for such termination [...], sale of goods at a price below the purchase price [allowed in some cases][2053].

1046. Interestingly, the Unfair Trade in Foodstuff Act goes beyond prohibiting certain practices and encourages retailers and suppliers to enter *into ethical codes* regulating their conduct in an effort to shift from mere hard law to soft-law enforcement of unfair competition practices and a solution adopted in other Member States, which I discuss below[2054].

1047. In **Spain** UPPs and unfair contractual terms are regulated by specialized laws whenever the exercise of buyer power does not impose a reduction in demand of goods (monopsony power)[2055] by a dominant buyer or have an impact on the market overall. These laws are the Unfair Competition Act[2056] and the sectoral Act on Better Functioning for the Food Retailing Markets[2057]. Previously, however, *the former Spanish Competition Act regulated explicitly the imposition of UPPs practices by a dominant undertaking*[2058]. Nevertheless, the latest reform to the Spanish Competition Act revoked this prohibition as the legislator found that UPPs did not require a specific provision and were better addressed through specific instruments such as unfair competition laws.

2052 Zuzana Turayova, 'Slovakia's Unfair Terms in Business Contracts between Resellers and Suppliers of Foodstuffs' e-Competitions N 31177 Concurrences (2010). See also discussing the Act in quite similar terms in College of Europe and Studies (2012), p. 65-67. This was the case of the former Act No. 172/2008 Coll. on Unfair Terms in Commercial Contracts, repelled by the Unfair Trade in Foodstuff Act.

2053 Turayova (2010).

2054 College of Europe and Studies (2012), p. 66; Turayova (2010).

2055 Robles Martín-Laborda, 'La Cadena Alimentaria: Cuando el Poder de Mercado lo Tiene el Comprador'.

2056 Ley 3/1991, de 10 de enero, de Competencia Desleal, Boletín Oficial del Estado núm. 10, de 11/01/1991, available at (in Spanish): http://www.boe.es/buscar/act.php?id=BOE-A-1991-628.

2057 Ley 12/2013, de 2 de agosto, de medidas para mejorar el funcionamiento de la cadena alimentaria, Boletín Oficial del Estado núm. 185, de 3 de agosto de 2013, páginas 56551 a 56581 (31 págs.), available at (in Spanish): http://www.boe.es/diario_boe/txt.php?id=BOE-A-2013-8554.

2058 Article 6(2)(f) and (g) of Act 52/1999, of 28 December, amending Act 16/1989, of 17 July, of Competition, available at (in Spanish): https://www.boe.es/boe/dias/1999/12/29/pdfs/A45778-45787.pdf.

1048. The Spanish Unfair Competition Act prohibits in its Article 16 the abuse of economic dependence and discrimination, and has a scope of application aiming to remedy contractual imbalances in a gray area between "internal commerce" and "consumer protection," as clarified in its recitals[2059]. The prohibition against discriminatory treatment only applies to non-justified differentiated treatment vis-à-vis consumers (hence it will *not apply to buyers with regard to suppliers*)[2060]. However, the prohibition of economic dependence applies to both "clients and suppliers that do not have an equivalent alternative to carry out their commercial activity"[2061]. Furthermore, the Unfair Competition Act establishes a *juris tantum* presumption of dependence whenever a supplier "in addition to the customary discounts or conditions, must grant its buyer in a regular manner additional benefits that are not granted to similar buyers"[2062]. If the abuse of economic dependence leads to a *substantial distortion of competition affecting the public interest* – even absent dominance – *then the Spanish Competition Authority is the competent authority,* reinforcing the argument put forth in this chapter that UPPs are, and should be, covered by competition law if they have a market-wide impact[2063].

1049. The Unfair Competition Act includes a list of prohibited UPPs such as: forbidding buyers to terminate contracts without a previous written notification at least six months in advance, unless there are serious grounds for termination; or obtaining better terms and conditions (lower purchasing prices, modalities, additional fees, etc.) that were not originally established in the contract under duress[2064].

1050. Furthermore, the Act on Better Functioning for the Food Retailing Markets is a new sectoral instrument enacted in 2013 which aims at addressing buyer power imbalances in food retailing, in particular because of the "vulnerable character" of the agricultural supply side, its "high atomization level" and opposing retailers that have two commercial channels[2065], in a way which resembles the history of the Robinson-Patman Act in the US[2066]. The preamble of the Act stresses that, on the one hand, there is a food distribution channel that is:

2059 Recital Section IV of Ley 3/1991, de 10 de enero, de Competencia Desleal.

2060 Article 16.1 of Ley 3/1991, de 10 de enero, de Competencia Desleal.

2061 Article 16.2 of Ley 3/1991, de 10 de enero, de Competencia Desleal (author's translation).

2062 Article 16.2 of Ley 3/1991, de 10 de enero, de Competencia Desleal (author's translation).

2063 Article 3 of the Ley 15/2007, de 3 de julio, de Defensa de la Competencia. Moreover, Article 2 of this Law is the one defining abuse of dominance. European Commission, *Study on the Legal Framework Covering Business-To-Business Unfair Trading Practices in the Retail Supply Chain* (2014), p. 54.

2064 Article 16.3 of Ley 3/1991, de 10 de enero, de Competencia Desleal (author's translation).

2065 Article 2 of the Ley 12/2013, de 2 de agosto, de medidas para mejorar el funcionamiento de la cadena alimentaria.

2066 Recital Section I of the Ley 12/2013, de 2 de agosto, de medidas para mejorar el funcionamiento de la cadena alimentaria.

very concentrated in undertakings with large and medium sales locations and offering a wide array of goods and that, normally, belong to large groups of distribution and concentrate demand in specific sale point which *confers great bargaining power vis-à-vis their suppliers*[2067].

1051. Whereas on the other hand, the other distribution channel is represented by small and specialized shops, usually a family-owned business, and spread around the country in the form of traditional market shops or small establishments. The law remarks that the asymmetries in bargaining power conditions the relations among suppliers and buyers in a vertical and horizontal level that it aims to address.

1052. The Act's objective is controlling buyer power exercise to allegedly promote efficiency and competitiveness of food retailing markets by reducing the contractual imbalances among the market players[2068]. Nevertheless, these two goals may counteract each other if the positive effects of bargaining power for end consumers are compromised by limiting the capacity of buyers to neutralize any seller market power. To do so, Article 9 of the Act requires contracts among suppliers and buyers to *comply with some minimum (or maximum) standards* restricting the parties' contractual freedom in an ex-ante regulation method that is analog to solutions applied to consumer protection, as well as forbidding an extensive group of purchasing practices. Among these are included the modification or requirement of commercial payments not foreseen, exchange of sensitive information and handling of trademarks.

1053. Lastly, like in the case of Slovakia, the Act on Better Functioning for the Food Retailing Markets also requires the creation of a "Code of Conduct"[2069] to regulate "good practices" that was finally approved in 2015 and draw inspiration from the UK solution, as discussed in the following section[2070]. The Code is binding for those parties that agree to adhere to it, according to Article 15.4, and its content is based on the prohibitions in the law, also providing an alternative dispute mechanism in case of conflicts between the parties[2071].

2067 Recital Section I of the Ley 12/2013, de 2 de agosto, de medidas para mejorar el funcionamiento de la cadena alimentaria. Also stressing the increasing concentration issue in food suppliers market in Germany see: Bundeskartellamt '*Summary of the Final Report of the Sector Inquiry into the Food Retail Sector*' (2014), p. 3.

2068 Article 3 of the Ley 12/2013, de 2 de agosto, de medidas para mejorar el funcionamiento de la cadena alimentaria.

2069 Title III of the Ley 12/2013, de 2 de agosto, de medidas para mejorar el funcionamiento de la cadena alimentaria.

2070 http://www.magrama.gob.es/es/prensa/codigobuenaspracticasmercantiles_tcm7-403866_noticia.pdf.

2071 Article 16 of the Ley 12/2013, de 2 de agosto, de medidas para mejorar el funcionamiento de la cadena alimentaria.

D. Soft Law alternatives? The case of the 'codes of conduct'

1054. Other countries, with the UK at the forefront in the EU/EEA, have decided to apply soft-law or self-enforcing mechanisms to deal with UPPs outside their competition law, and sometimes as a complement to sectoral regulation. The idea of self-regulation through a code of conduct comes from countries with a Common Law background with Australia as the first country to implement it by means of the Retail Grocery Industry Code of Conduct enacted in 2000, which has been replaced on several occasions, the latest one being 2015 with the Food and Grocery Code of Conduct[2072]. In this section, however, I analyze the UK code of conduct as a European example of this alternative regulatory path due to its importance in modeling the content of other codes in different jurisdictions.

1055. The UK promulgated the Groceries Supply Code of Practice (the Code)[2073] in 2009 pursuant a Groceries Market Investigation. The Code is administered by the Groceries Code Adjudicator Act of 2013 that created a Groceries Code Adjudicator, a body that administers it as an investigator-arbitrator and imposes sanctions whenever it is breached by its parties. The Code aims:

> to address the *adverse effect on competition arising from the exercise of buyer power by grocery retailers with respect to their direct suppliers of groceries*"[2074].
>
> And in the words of the Code's Adjudicator "the purpose of the Code is to ensure that the UK's largest supermarkets *treat their direct suppliers fairly*[2075].

1056. The Code applies to "Designated Retailers," which are undertakings with a turnover exceeding £1 billion in the UK market for retail supply, or listed in an annex[2076]. Hence it applies to large buyers but not to smaller or local ones. These Designated Retailers "must not enter into or perform any Supply Agreement unless that Supply Agreement incorporates the Code and does not contain any provisions that are inconsistent with the Code"[2077].

2072 Competition and Consumer (Industry Codes—Food and Grocery) Regulation 2015, Select Legislative Instrument No. 16, 2015 and available at: https://www.comlaw.gov.au/Details/F2015L00242. The Code is "voluntary" but "legally enforceable" instrument that aims to "deliver more contractual certainty in trading relations between suppliers and supermarkets, encourage the better sharing of risk and reduce inappropriate use of market power across the value chain" Australian Food & Grocery Council *Food and Grocery Industry Code of Conduct,* (2015).

2073 Groceries Supply Code of Practice, published on 4 August 2009 by the Department for Business, Innovation & Skills and the Groceries Code Adjudicator.

2074 Groceries Code Adjudicator, Investigation into Tesco Plc, 26 January 2016, public version available online at: https://www.gov.uk/government/uploads/system/uploads/attachment_data/file/494840/GCA_Tesco_plc_final_report_26012016_-_version_for_download.pdf, para. 51, last visited 27 January 2016 (emphasis added).

2075 Groceries Code Adjudicator, Investigation into Tesco Plc, 26 January 2016 (emphasis added).

2076 Competition Commission, The Groceries (Supply Chain Practices) Market Investigation Order 2009, Part 2, Article 4 (1).

2077 Competition Commission, The Groceries (Supply Chain Practices) Market Investigation Order 2009, Part 2, Article 4 (2).

1057. To prevent UPPs, the Code sets some *minimum requirements*, such as the duty to provide information to suppliers and have contracts in written form[2078]. And, furthermore, it contains an extensive list of prohibited practices. Among them: fair dealing and keeping buyer-supplier relations based on good faith and without duress; rules on variations on supply and terms of supply; obligations to pay within a "reasonable time after the date of the Supplier's invoice"[2079]; not requiring the supplier to pay for the buyer's costs regarding advertisement[2080]; prohibition of direct and indirect setting of slotting allowances; and strict rules on de-listing a supplier from a retailer's stock.

1058. The Code's *enforcement* is based on an alternative dispute resolution system regulated in its Section 5. Retailers and suppliers "must negotiate in good faith" to reach an agreement and if there is a dispute among them, the case ought to be brought before a Code Compliance Officer that will act as a mediator between the parties. If the complaint is not resolved, then the supplier (but not the buyer) can submit an arbitration request before the Ombudsman in accordance with the Rules of the Chartered Institute of Arbitrators. The Code Adjudicator's decision is "binding and final" for the parties and may only be appealed under specific grounds regulated in the UK Arbitration Act. Regarding fees and expenses, the Code favors suppliers in all cases, except when the arbitrator decides that the supplier's claim was "vexatious or wholly without merit"; otherwise, all costs have to be to be borne by the retailer.

1059. Since its adoption in 2009 there has been a single investigation dealing with a breach of the Code and imposition of UPPs. On January 26, 2016 the Groceries Code Adjudicator found that Tesco Plc, the largest retailing supermarket chain in the UK, with about 28% market share in 2015[2081], had breached the Code due to the payment delays regarding non-goods payments or in case of disagreement[2082]. Tesco was also investigated for possibly demanding from suppliers slotting allowances to secure better positioning of their goods; yet, the Adjudicator found no evidence to declare the Code's breach in this regard. Despite the finding of the "serious Code's breach" the Adjudicator was in no position to impose a financial penalty because of the entry into force of administrative Order granting this power. It was decided, however, to issue five

2078 Competition Commission, The Groceries (Supply Chain Practices) Market Investigation Order 2009, Part 2, Article 4 (2).

2079 Such a rule (or the absence of it) was precisely the main issue under discussion in Judgment of 11 July in *FENIN v Commission*, C-205/03 P, EU:C:2006:453; Judgment of 4 March 2003, *Fenin v Commission*, T-319/99, ECR, EU:T:2003:50.

2080 "Shrinkage means losses that occur after Groceries are delivered to a Retailer's premises and arise due to theft, the Groceries being lost or accounting error", Schedule 1 of the Groceries (Supply Chain Practices) Market Investigation Order 2009.

2081 http://www.statista.com/statistics/279900/grocery-market-share-in-the-united-kingdom-uk/; http://www.theguardian.com/business/2015/sep/22/tesco-asda-morrisons-sales-slump-despite-cut-prices-supermarkets.

2082 Groceries Code Adjudicator, Investigation into Tesco Plc, 26 January 2016.

recommendations for Tesco to follow to address the uncertainties and limit the pernicious effects of the payment delays[2083].

1060. As mentioned above, the UK example of regulating UPPs through codes of conduct has been followed by other MS, such as Spain and Slovakia and proposed but rejected in the case of Norway. In my opinion, the adoption of Codes of Conduct to regulate UPPs as an alternative form of regulation may keep spreading through Europe, in particular, if the enforcement of the Code in the UK is perceived as a success story.

1061. However, a question concerning the adoption of codes of conduct remains: *should these soft law approaches involve the imposition of fines and hard remedies?* In my view, the use of soft enforcement mechanisms that impose behavioural remedies and ensure that the decision receives sufficient publicity, without resorting to fines, may be an adequate and sufficiently deterrent measure in countries where there is a tradition of relying on self-regulation and common law approaches[2084]. The same, might not necessarily work in other legal cultures and a "hard enforcement approach" might be required. I, however, find the idea of a softer approach within a Code of Conduct system a better alternative than the imposition of fines or other administrative sanctions for several reasons. The lack of fines will incentivize retailers to self-report possible breaches to the Code; making the decision public will have an impact on the retailer's goodwill and thus, customers' preferences when shopping for food. Also, the imposition of fines may backfire as food retailers might be tempted to recoup their losses by either tightening their purchasing practices or increasing end consumer's prices. Nevertheless, for very serious cases, or if the soft approach proves to be insufficient, then fines might be required[2085].

2083 I have discussed the details and implications of this case in an invited blog entry at the Competition Policy Blog of the Centre for Competition Policy, University of East Anglia in Unfair purchasing practices and the Groceries Code of Conduct: the Tesco investigation. Available at: https://competitionpolicy.wordpress.com/2016/02/01/unfair-purchasing-practices-and-the-groceries-code-of-conduct-the-tesco-investigation/.

2084 Making a similar remark see: Jenny [2015], p. 4.

2085 "Unfair purchasing practices and the Groceries Code of Conduct: the Tesco investigation". Available at: https://competitionpolicy.wordpress.com/2016/02/01/unfair-purchasing-practices-and-the-groceries-code-of-conduct-the-tesco-investigation/

VII. The EU and the Supply Chain Initiative

1062. Pursuant to the political pressure and interest in regulating fairness within the commercial relations in the food supply chain at the EU level, the Commission's High Level Forum for a Better Functioning of the Food Supply Chain developed the Supply Chain Initiative (SCI)[2086]. The SCI follows a similar soft law approach like codes of self-regulation, as parties to the SCI will *voluntarily adhere to it and commit themselves in not entering into UPPs and setting ethical standards* when dealing to avoid abuses of bargaining power, and when these purchasing practices have a cross-border dimension. By 2016, over a thousand (1,155) undertakings in the retail, wholesale and manufacturing business had registered as parties to the SCI since its implementation in 2013[2087]. However, as the Commission reported, farmers and SMEs are underrepresented in the SCI partially due to lack of awareness and support.

1063. In the SCI framework, the stakeholders implemented a set of "principles of good practices" that "provide a framework for doing business that respects contractual freedom and ensures competitiveness, trust and continuity, all required for business development, innovation and the three pillars of sustainability"[2088]. These principles are rooted in three main aspects: first, the interest of end consumers; second, protection of the contractual freedom – or respect to each undertaking's economic freedom from an ordoliberal perspective; and third, an obligation of fair dealing. At the same time, these pillars are operationalized by 7 principles of best practices:

i) contracts must be in written form;

ii) unilateral contractual chances are limited;

iii) parties must comply to their agreements;

iv) parties should respect rules regarding information confidentiality;

v) and should also respect competition rules regarding exchanging sensitive information;

vi) both parties should assume their commercial risks to a transaction;

vii) parties should not resort to threats to obtain an advantage or transfer risks or costs[2089].

2086 European Commission '*Report from the Commission to the European Parliament and the Council on Unfair Business-to-Business Trading Practices in the Food Supply Chain*' (2016), p. 8.

2087 Ibid, p. 8-9.

2088 Supply Chain Initiative (2011), p. 2.

2089 Ibid, p. 3.

1064. Additionally, the SCI lists a series of forbidden non-exhaustive and rather general UPPs which coincide with the different modalities discussed in this chapter's section §II.B.

1065. The SCI also adopts an alternative dispute resolution mechanism where parties to it can raise complaints in cases where a principle has been breached under a contractual relation under five modalities[2090]: the commercial track or within the company itself; contract options; an internal dispute resolution; mediation or arbitration; or, finally, jurisdictional methods[2091]. The remedies adopted as part of the dispute settlement are decided on a case-by-case basis and parties are obliged to commit to them.

1066. Lastly, the SCI is complemented at the MS level by means of "national platforms" entrusted with the task of promoting knowledge regarding the SCI among undertakings engaged in food retailing and supporting its members. However, so far only Belgium, the Netherlands and Finland have created such platforms[2092].

VIII. Conclusions

1067. In this chapter, I discussed buyer power exploitation through the imposition of UPPs. My analysis shows that the regulation of these types of 'unfair' purchasing *conducts lies in a gray area between competition and unfair competition laws* as they are connected to fairness, contractual imbalances and matters of distributive justice and tend not to be issues of market power exercise sensu stricto, despite the fact that their widespread exertion can negatively impact the upstream competitive structure and dynamic efficiency. Therefore, it is not clear whether, when and how much scope of applicability EU competition law has when dealing with the imposition of UPPs, particularly regarding cases of unilateral behaviour.

1068. I showed that UPPs arise from an *unbalance in bargaining power* between the parties in a commercial relation and are linked to the abuse of buyer power vis-à-vis dependent suppliers. Therefore, UPP regulation tends to seek the protection of supplier welfare and fairness in the exercise of buyer power but not necessarily address aspects related to market power abuse, economic efficiency, or end-consumer welfare. Because of this, legal intervention against UPPs seeks to redress issues of contractual balancing and distribution of profits between contractual parties having a clear *protecting role with regard to*

2090 Supply Chain Initiative *Rules of Procedure for the Governance Group*, (2013).

2091 http://www.supplychaininitiative.eu/faq#8

2092 European Commission (2016), p. 11.

weaker suppliers facing a powerful buyer, and which is not always consistent with the improvement of market efficiency or end consumer welfare, explaining the limited role of EU competition law.

1069. From a welfare perspective, UPPs by and large are an issue of profit distribution in which the buyer, thanks to its bargaining power, obtains supracompetitive benefits that are extracted from the supplier without an appropriate retribution. These types of issues connected with profit distribution to a contract are purely bilateral aspects, and an economic problem that is not a concern for EU competition law. However, UPPs can *become a competition law problem* affecting the upstream competitive conditions in allocative and dynamic terms, for example by eliminating incentives for suppliers to remain or enter the market or invest. This could be the case whenever the UPPs are imposed in a way that affects the market as a whole, for instance when they are imposed by a dominant buyer to most of its suppliers, pursuant a concentration or due to agreements concluded with a powerful, yet not dominant buyer.

1070. Hence, as a profit distribution issue, UPPs may affect the financial viability of suppliers as their unjustified exploitation may force them to exit the input market and, consequently, have a detrimental effect on consumers in the long term. Furthermore, the generalized exploitation of suppliers by a dominant buyer may reduce choice, variety, and quantities offered in downstream markets, adversely impacting the competitive structure in the upstream market as well as end consumers. However, the existing data regarding the welfare effects of UPPs is not conclusive regarding the 'squeeze-out' effect on suppliers from the upstream market, at least in the short and medium term. The same ambiguous outcome regarding UPP effect appears regarding variety, innovation and end-consumer conditions. Consequently, a purchasing conduct that might appear 'unfair' can actually be welfare enhancing.

1071. Therefore, *while it is clear that abusive UPPs appear as practices that from a moral standpoint as 'unfair' (but not necessarily inefficient) and portraying a negative aspect of buyer (bargaining) power, it is less clear whether they constitute a core competition problem for which EU competition law is the adequate tool.*

1072. I submitted that EU competition law will rarely and should rarely apply to cases dealing with the imposition of UPPs, as the very few cases confirm. As I put forth, UPPs will be captured by the current regime if they are imposed by a buyers' cartel or are the outcome of a concerted practice under Article 101(1) TFEU. Regarding the exertion of UPPs within a vertical agreement, I have also shown that, unless the UPP constitutes a hardcore restriction of competition, it would likely be under the scope of the Block Exemption Regulation. Also, some of these UPPs even if part of a vertical agreement would be 'unilateral' in the sense that the supplier is not needed to generate the effect. These factors, along with the lack of prioritization of vertical restrains by NCAs make it unlikely that most UPPs would be under the scope of Article 101(1) TFEU. Consequently, UPPs if under EU competition law, would be mostly addressed by rules designed to tackle unilateral behaviour, therefore requiring the buyer to be a dominant undertaking – either in the upstream or the downstream market as it could have been the case in *FENIN v Commission*, if the Courts would have found the purchasing to constitute an economic activity[2093]. However, risks of future imposition of UPPs also could trigger the application of EU competition law pursuant to a buyers' concentration that may lead to (most or all) the suppliers becoming dependent on the powerful buyer, as was discussed in *Carrefour/Promodès, Rewe/Meinl* and *Kesko/Tuko*. Nevertheless, in these cases the risks of imposition of UPPs was only deemed relevant enough, along with concerns for downstream competition, to declare the concentration of *Kesko/Tuko* incompatible with the internal market. Therefore, in any of the different competition law areas there is limited room for intervention in cases of UPPs.

1073. This *reduced room for the application of EU competition law, however, does not imply that UPPs are not a problem needing regulation* within a broad ordoliberally influenced competition policy, at either the EU level or the national level, because of their possible adverse effects. On the EU level, I have discussed the limited applicability of the current instruments that exist to regulate unfair practices, as well as the position of the Commission in arguing that regulation of UPPs from a buyer-supplier perspective is better suited for national regulation than applying a harmonized non-core competition law regime. At the national level, I have analyzed how MS have adopted different alternatives within, although mostly outside, their national competition laws to tackle UPPs and particularly in the last decade. My analysis distinguished four different modalities: adopting *lower dominance thresholds for food retailing* within their competition laws; regulating UPPs through rules related *to relative dominant positions and abuse of dependence*; contract and tort-law like solutions based on *'unfair competition laws' or sectoral regulation*; and lastly the adoption of *soft law instruments as codes of conduct*. Hence, the European map is anything but standardized and many different regulatory avenues tackle UPPs leading to somewhat similar outcomes: protecting small suppliers vis-à-vis large buyers and having a strong component of fairness and distributive justice.

1074. Despite this increasing trend towards the regulation of UPPs, partly pursuant to political and social pressure, my research found that instances of UPPs are rare, both at the EU as well as the national level. This lack of abundant cases, despite the 'popularity' of UPPs, can have several explanations. Firstly, one option is that UPPs are not really an issue of efficiency or market power

2093 Judgment of 11 July in *FENIN v Commission*, C-205/03 P, EU:C:2006:453; Judgment of 4 March 2003, *Fenin v Commission*, T-319/99, ECR, EU:T:2003:50.

abuse and suppliers complain against them not because they are exploited but because they are not paid as much as they would like to be or are required to assume risks that they normally would not be willing to take if they were in a stronger bargaining position. Furthermore, if the UPPs are seen as a way to countervail seller market power and pass on the benefits to end consumers, then authorities will perceive them to be consumer welfare enhancing because end-consumer prices are lowered and efficient. Another answer is that as exploitative abuses are considered to be less pernicious and self-correctable, EU institutions and NCAs do not consider UPPs an enforcement priority. Also, another possibility is that UPPs are not denounced by suppliers as they *fear retaliation* from buyers they depend on, an explanation also supported by the Commission[2094]. Therefore, in case of a complaint the buyer can simply terminate any kind of commercial relation and perhaps drive the supplier out of business. Alternatively, it could well be that suppliers that complain due to imposition of UPPs happen to be not very efficient and thus, have higher costs that may not be necessarily justified, as other providers could take their place.

1075. In sum, UPPs are an example of *exploitative vertical buyer power practices* that in most cases are not a market power problem but rather an issue of contractual imbalance as it is not clear, or at least it *seems that UPPs have a limited market-wide impact on the competitive conditions in the upstream and downstream related markets,* as shown by the recent Commission studies. Because of this, there is little room for the application of EU competition law to UPPs, as put forward in this chapter and recently clarified by the Commission[2095]. This, therefore, is an area ripe for further sectoral research from a welfare perspective, both in terms of allocative and dynamic efficiency. Again, the key seems to lie in guaranteeing that the powerful buyer does not "pocket" this supracompetitive profit and passes it on to end consumers, without distorting in an adverse manner the competitive conditions in the upstream market, in either static nor dynamic terms. If that is the case, then EU competition law intervention is required to control the anti-competitive exercise of buyer power by buyers' cartels, dominant buyers or as the outcome of a proposed concentration among buyers. This moderate approach to the scope of application of EU competition law to UPPs is also in line with the broader application of EU competition law to buyer power as it offers a degree to the competitive process and, consequently, some limited and justified protection to suppliers, the undertaking's economic freedom and captures instances of anti-competitive harm, even absent evidence of direct end consumer harm. However, as shown, the room for applicability of EU competition law to UPPs is narrow as other regulatory and better avenues are available at the national level.

2094 European Commission '*Report from the Commission to the European Parliament and the Council on Unfair Business-to-Business Trading Practices in the Food Supply Chain*' (2016), p. 6 and 10.

2095 Italianer, *The Devil is in the Retail*.

PART V

BUYER POWER FROM A SELLER'S PERSPECTIVE: COUNTERVAILING BUYER POWER AND BUYER POWER LIMITATION

9

COUNTERVAILING BUYER POWER

I. Introduction

1076. Countervailing buyer power (CBP), along with UPPs, is arguably the sub-topic of buyer power that has received the most attention in literature on EU competition law[2096]. Despite this 'popularity' its importance as a factor in the decision making by the Commission or the Courts is rather limited because the employed sufficiency test is rather strict, as I discuss in this chapter. CBP acts as a *competitive constraint mitigating or nullifying the market power effects by a supplying undertaking*[2097], serving as a defense argument as its existence prevents an undertaking from behaving independently from its buyer and, therefore, being dominant or significantly impeding effective competition in the future[2098]. CBP, then, neutralizes seller market power making the suppliers lose a fraction of it and distributing profits and welfare among the remaining participants[2099]. Consequently, in these cases *it is the seller and not the buyer that is the one that claims the existence of buyer power*, hence I entitled Part V 'Buyer Power from a Seller's Perspective'[2100].

1077. In this chapter, I analyze CBP from a general perspective in light of the case law, the Commission's practice, and other authoritative sources across all ar-

2096 Cook and Kerse have stated that CBP is a factor regularly considered by the EU Commission but that it rarely alleviates significant competition concerns, the analysis of the case law done in this study confirms this assertion, Cook and Kerse, [2009], p. 250-251.

2097 Motta, *Competition Policy: Theory and Practice* [2004], p. 121-122.

2098 Communication from the Commission — Guidance on the Commission's enforcement priorities in applying Article 82 of the EC Treaty to abusive exclusionary conduct by dominant undertakings [2009] OJ C 45/7, para. 18; Guidelines on the assessment of horizontal mergers under the Council Regulation on the control of concentrations between undertakings [2004] OJ C 31/5, para. 64-67; Kokkoris and Day (2009), p. 176.

2099 American Antitrust Institute [2008], p. 105.

2100 Also addressing this buyer power topic from a supplier's perspective in the case of mergers see: Carlton, Coleman and Israel [2015], p. 540-546.

eas of EU competition law. My goal is to contribute to the existing literature by *defining what CBP is in EU competition law and under which circumstances it is a sufficient force to neutralize seller market power*. To answer these questions I have structured the chapter as follows. In section §II I define the concept of CBP from a legal perspective. I employ a narrow approach to CBP by defining it as a specific expression of bargaining power that acts as an extraordinary circumstance precluding an undertaking from behaving independently of its customers or from significantly impeding competition by neutralizing seller market power. In section §III I review and discuss the most relevant characteristics that define CBP, followed, in section §IV, by a detailed analysis of the treatment of CBP by the Commission's Guidance Notices and soft law instruments, according to its level of detail and importance. The remainder of the chapter deals with the analysis of CBP in the case law and the Commission's practice. In section §V I discuss the treatment of CBP in EU competition law, its sources and which circumstances hinder a buyer from exerting sufficient CBP. In section §VI I discuss the applicability of CBP as an argumentative defense and identify a test employed by the Courts to determine the sufficiency of CBP, and also discuss how the test has developed over time. In section §VII I discuss how, and to what extent, the case law has required that CBP has a broader protective effect by creating a 'spillover effect' that demands that the neutralizing benefits favor not only the powerful buyer but also smaller buyers in their situation vis-à-vis the seller whose market power is being neutralized. Then, in section §VIII I discuss whether the Courts and the Commission are under any obligation to *ex officio* analyze the existence and extent of CBP in a competition case. Lastly, section §IX concludes the chapter.

II. Defining countervailing buyer power: a narrow approach

1078. CBP is a form of countervailing power, as theorized by Galbraith in 1952 in *American Capitalism*[2101]; however, following the EU case law, I define CBP in a *narrow manner*[2102]. I submit that CBP in EU competition law represents the bargaining strength of a buyer vis-à-vis its supplier in a manner which allows the former to neutralize the exercise of selling market power, fully or partially in an upstream market, and is therefore sufficient to prevent the seller from behaving independently of its competitors and *customers/buyers*, hence

2101 Galbraith, [2010].

2102 Also using a narrow approach to CBP see: Catherine Corbett, Reena das Nair and Simon Roberts, 'Countervailing Power, Bargaining Power and Market Definition: A Reflection on two Mergers'. Also stressing the element of neutralizing sufficiency: Faull and Nikpay, [1999], para. 4.152 and Faull, Nikpay and Taylor, [2014], para. 5.877.

neither being dominant or able to significantly impede effective future competition[2103]. Consequently, CBP can exist both in the assessment of *ex-ante* and *ex-post* selling conducts. In simpler terms, the buyer(s) force(s) the seller to behave in a competitive – or as competitive as possible – manner by neutralizing its (or their) seller power through the exercise of buyer market power. This neutralization prevents the seller from increasing selling prices, reducing the quality of the goods or making conditions of delivery less favorable, as confirmed by the CJEU in *AstraZeneca v Commission*[2104]. Therefore, for CBP to exist there must be a substantial degree of market power on both sides of the market (which oppose each other), described as a bilateral power situation by Faull and Nikpay[2105]. To determine when CBP is sufficient, the case law, the Commission's practice, and the guidance notices have developed a 'comparison test' that assesses the neutralizing buyer market power and determines its sufficiency. This test has evolved from a mere contrasting of market shares among parties to a more accurate and complex comparison of several factors.

1079. An example helps illustrate the concept[2106]. The undertaking "Engine Jet Producer" is involved in the manufacture of aircraft engines. Due to its commercial success, the capacity to innovate and its reputation, it has legally acquired a large market share that amounts to 75% of the market for the provision of jet engines. In normal conditions such an extraordinarily large market share would serve as a strong indicator that Engine Jet Producer is able to behave independently from its competitors and buyers and could impose high prices for jet engines, or engage in other types of abusive selling conditions. There are two main buyers of jet engines from Engine Jet Producer: the undertakings "European Aircrafts" and "Fly-away". European Aircrafts and Fly-away are fierce rivals in the design and manufacture of commercial planes and together account for more than 85% of the purchases of jet engines in the EU. Due to their importance as buyers for Engine Jet Producer, European Aircrafts and Fly-away 'keep in check' the behaviour of the seller. This importance and countervailing ability as buyers is derived from their large size and strategic value for suppliers, the fact that no other purchasers have the capacity to acquire even half the amount of jet engines that European Aircrafts or Fly-away

2103 Judgment of 9 July 2007, *Sun Chemical Group and Others v Commission*, T-282/06, ECR, EU:T:2007:203, para. 210; Judgment of 13 February 1979 in *Hoffmann-La Roche v Commission*, C-85/76, EU:C:1979:36, para. 41; Faull, Nikpay and Taylor, [2014], para. 5.879; OECD '*Policy Roundtables: Monopsony and Buyer Power*' (2009), p. 60.

2104 "AZ was able to maintain much higher market shares than those of its competitors while charging prices higher than those charged for other PPIs was a relevant factor showing that AZ's behaviour was not, to an appreciable extent, subject to competitive constraints from its competitors, its customers and, ultimately, consumers" in Judgment of 6 December 2012 in *AstraZeneca v Commission*, C-457/10 P, EU:C:2012:770, para. 181. See also: Nazzini, [2011], p. 358.

2105 Faull and Nikpay, [1999], para. 6.326 and 6.330.

2106 This example is loosely modeled after the Commission Decision of 3 July 2001 declaring a concentration to be incompatible with the common market and the EEA Agreement Case COMP/M.2220 — *General Electric/Honeywell* [2004] OJ L 48/1. In this case, however, the Commission concluded that purchasers of aircraft engines lacked sufficient CBP and decided to declare the concentration incompatible with the relevant market.

individually buy each year, and the fact that Engine Jet Producer has neither the interest nor capacity to enter into the airplane design nor production business. If Engine Jet Producer threatens to raise the prices of engines, European Aircrafts and/or Fly-away would stop purchasing them and look for an alternative supplier or may even decide to enter into the jet engine manufacturing business themselves. The buyers exercise CBP because they neutralize the market power of Engine Jet Producer as a seller.

1080. Not all authors adopt a narrow definition to CBP, nor do the Commission's guidance notices[2107]. For instance, the Commission defines CBP as the "bargaining strength that the buyer has vis-à-vis the seller in commercial negotiations due to its size, its commercial significance to the seller and its ability to switch to alternative suppliers"[2108]. Other authors[2109] also use the term to represent the benign sign of buyer (bargaining) power in opposition to monopsony power. In my view, their understanding is synonymous to the concept of countervailing power by Galbraith[2110]. This broader usage, however, faces two difficulties: firstly, it equates CBP with bargaining power, and, secondly, it assumes that CBP takes place automatically. I discuss these issues below.

1081. Firstly, and for the sake of precision, I employ the term CBP not as an equivalent to the theory of *countervailing power* by Galbraith, nor as equivalent to bargaining power in general, arising between two contractual parties. Instead, I employ the term within its legal meaning, pertaining to the appraisal of the existence of opposed market power. In my view, Galbraith's theory is broader than CBP, the latter being a specific expression of bargaining purchasing power. This legal approach to the definition of CBP implies that this market power is an efficiency defense restraining the existence of unchallenged market power. Also, unlike bargaining power in general, CBP requires a much higher threshold to exist and be *sufficient*; i.e., it has to be enough to preclude dominance or prevent a significant impediment of competition by the opposed supplier[2111]. This neutralization level is much higher than bargaining power in general because it may neutralize either very little or very much of opposing seller market power. Therefore, CBP is a degree of bargaining buyer power that must be sufficient to neutralize dominant seller market power, as it is

2107 See for example Chen who uses the term countervailing power as synonym of bargaining power in Chen 'Buyer power: Economic Theory and Antitrust Policy' (2007); also Kirkwood uses the term countervailing power to refer to what is understood in this study as bargaining power, see Kirkwood 'Powerful Buyers and Merger Enforcement' (2012).

2108 Guidelines on the assessment of horizontal mergers under the Council Regulation on the control of concentrations between undertakings [2004] OJ C 31/5, para. 64.

2109 Kokkoris (2006); Kokkoris and Day (2009); Robert O'Donoghue and Jorge Padilla, *The Law and Economics of Article 102 TFEU* (2nd edn, Hart Publishing 2013), p. 166-167; Kokkoris and Shelanski, [2014].

2110 Galbraith, [2010] p. 97-135; for a commentary on Galbraith's work in the context of merger analysis see: Facey and Brown, [2013], p. 239-241.

2111 Also raising the issue of sufficiency see: Bellamy and others, [2013], para 10.020.

employed by the Commission in its Decisions when it repeatedly discusses either the *sufficiency* or the limited character of CBP[2112].

1082. Regarding the second assumption, that while indeed CBP allows for the neutralization of dominance by a selling undertaking, it should not be implicitly assumed that CBP will *automatically restrain abuse of dominance*. This is so because CBP will be exercised "only to the extent that it serves their own – buyers' – interests", as stressed by Hovenkamp[2113], or when the buyers' actions will not be subject to free-riding by competitors, as decided in *Prokent-Tomra*[2114]. Therefore, and assuming a profit-maximization rationale, buyers will neutralize the seller market power of a strong seller only when doing so is more profitable than benefiting from the dominance structure in the seller's market. This could happen, for example, if parties decide to coordinate their purchasing and selling behaviour and behave like in a bilateral monopoly scenario[2115]. If buyers coordinate the conduct with the seller then the consequences could be worse than pure selling market power as the firms could behave like monemporist exerting upstream and downstream market power in a coordinated fashion.

1083. Furthermore, and part of this narrow approach, my study found that there is a tension concerning the measurement and the degree of CBP's effect and whether for CBP to exist it must affect a bilateral situation (buyer-seller) or has to affect competition as a whole. The case law and the Commission's practice remark that CBP, if defined through its measurement, constitutes a relative concept that defines the relation of bargaining power between a seller and a specific buyer[2116]. On the other hand concerning its effects and sufficiency as a neutralizing factor, the exercise of CBP must have a general impact on the competitive conditions as it has to neutralize the market power of the seller vis-à-vis the strongest buyer and also produce a 'spillover effect'[2117], as I discuss in detail in this chapter's section §VIII. This spillover effect implies that CBP cannot only have a limited effect between the supplier and its largest buyer(s), but it also ought to benefit (albeit not to the same degree) other smaller buyers;

2112 See: Commission Decision of 17 October 2001 declaring a concentration to be incompatible with the common market and the functioning of the EEA Agreement (Case COMP/M.2187 — *CVC/Lenzing*) [2004] OJ L 82/20, para. 192-194 and 213-223; Commission Decision of 3 April 2001 declaring a concentration to be compatible with the common market and the functioning of the EEA Agreement (Case COMP/M.2139 — *Bombardier/ADtranz*) [2002] OJ L 69/50, para. 81.

2113 Hovenkamp, *Federal Antitrust Policy: The Law of Competition and its Practice* [2005], p. 544.

2114 Summary of Commission Decision of 29 March 2006 relating to a proceeding under Article 82 of the Treaty establishing the European Community and Article 54 of the EEA Agreement against Tomra Systems ASA, Tomra Europe AS, Tomra Systems BV, Tomra Systems GmbH, Tomra Butikksystemer AS, Tomra Systems AB and Tomra Leergutsysteme GmbH (Case COMP/E-1/38.113 — *Prokent/Tomra*) [2008] OJ C 219/11; taken from the unabridged version, para. 89.

2115 For the discussion of bilateral monopoly see chapter 2, section §III, footnote 74.

2116 Judgment of 14 December 2005, *General Electric v Commission*, T-210/01, ECR, EU:T:2005:456, para. 277; Judgment of 23 February 2006, *Cementbouw Handel & Industrie v Commission*, T-282/02, ECR, EU:T:2006:64, para. 230.

2117 Commission Decision of 25 November 1998 declaring a concentration to be compatible with the common market and the functioning of the EEA Agreement (Case No IV/M.1225 - *Enso/Stora*) [1999] OJ L 254/9, para. 96.

hence the effect cannot be solely *inter partes* but also produce a limited *erga omnes* effect that neutralizes the undertaking's seller market power.

III. Countervailing buyer power characteristics

1084. There are several characteristics that are topical to CBP. Firstly, it may exist regardless of whether its effect is actual or potential. As confirmed by the General Court in *Cementbouw Handel & Industrie v Commission,* CBP would neutralize seller market power if the buyers forces a seller to either limit its increase in current prices or to refrain from increasing prices in the future[2118]. Furthermore, in the case of CBP assessment in concentrations, the assessment is always forward looking, anchored on the *post-merger market structure,* as held in JCI/FIAMM, whereas in the case of agreements or dominance the exam tends to be focused on the actual effect[2119]. Also, in *CVC/Lenzing*, the Commission stressed that in the pre-merger scenario the buyers "regard their current bargaining power as balanced, the vast majority expect it to be rather weak if the notified operation goes ahead", therefore, the risks of eliminating the existing CBP were taken into consideration as a consequence of the merger[2120].

1085. Secondly, the measurement of CBP is a relative concept[2121]. This implies that a customer may have sufficient CBP vis-à-vis a supplier whereas another buyer does not, as confirmed in *General Electric v Commission*[2122]. Thus, the fact that a buyer has CBP does not imply that other undertaking's customers do. Hence, the assessment and measurement must be made buyer-by-buyer. The same, however, cannot be said of the extent of its effect, which, in the light of the case law, the Commission's practice and the EU Horizontal Merger Guidelines has to have a limited *erga omnes* or spillover effect.

1086. Thirdly, CBP is usually, but not exclusively, exercised by customers that are not physical end consumers (i.e.: natural persons), as confirmed in *Airtours v*

2118 Judgment of 23 February 2006, *Cementbouw Handel & Industrie v Commission,* T-282/02, ECR, EU:T:2006:64, para. 232.

2119 Summary of Commission Decision of 10 May 2007 declaring a concentration compatible with the common market and the functioning of the EEA Agreement (Case COMP/M.4381 — *JCI/FIAMM*) [2009] OJ C 241/12, taken from the unabridged version.

2120 Commission Decision of 17 October 2001 declaring a concentration to be incompatible with the common market and the functioning of the EEA Agreement (Case COMP/M.2187 — *CVC/Lenzing*) [2004] OJ L 82/20, para. 214.

2121 See also stating that "[b]uyer power is not an absolute concept, however, and it is important to consider the degree of buyer power and whether it operates as an effective constraint on the ability of the supplier to exert market power", in Bellamy and others, [2013], para 10.141

2122 "It is sufficient to find here, as the Commission does, that the buyer power refereed to in the decisions in question *existed vis-à-vis companies other than the applicant and in respect of other products*", in Judgment of 14 December 2005, *General Electric v Commission*, T-210/01, ECR, EU:T:2005:456, para. 277 (emphasis added); Judgment of 23 February 2006, *Cementbouw Handel & Industrie v Commission,* T-282/02, ECR, EU:T:2006:64, para. 230.

Commission by the General Court[2123]. End consumers purchase individually, and therefore possess little CBP, do not pool their purchases like a buying alliance or a large undertaking would. More importantly, they may represent an insignificant proportion of the sales if taken in isolation, as confirmed by the Commission in *Slovak Telekom*[2124]. Nevertheless, the fact that a buyer may not exercise sufficient CBP does not imply that it would not be able to react to a price increase by shifting to a different supplier or stop purchasing the good, if such possibilities exist[2125]. Also, the case law and the Commission's practice confirm that it is more likely that large and sophisticated buyers will possess CBP than smaller firms in a fragmented industry[2126].

1087. Fourthly, CBP is a relevant factor to *prevent or minimize the risks of the creation of collective dominance or to impede collusion among sellers*[2127]. In these assessments it ought to be considered whether CBP can prevent or limit coordination among undertakings by *creating incentives to deviate from the agreement* by offering a different purchasing price to providers that allows them to reap extra profits, as discussed in *Airtours v Commission*[2128], and further confirmed in the *Sony/BMG* Decisions and subsequent Judgments[2129], *MCI WorldCom/Sprint*[2130], and *Korsnäs/AD Cartonboard*[2131], as I discuss below.

1088. A similar distortive argument was used in *Carglass*[2132], where CBP and the existence of dual sourcing from the buyers disrupted the *collusive agreement among the selling parties*. However, and as remarked by the General Court in the annulment action, the existence of CBP power *did not prevent the agree-*

2123 Judgment of 28 June 2004, *Airtours v Commission*, T-342/99, ECR, EU:T:2002:146, para. 262.

2124 Summary of Commission Decision of 15 October 2014 relating to a proceeding under Article 102 of the Treaty on the Functioning of the European Union and Article 54 of the EEA Agreement (Case AT.39523 — *Slovak Telekom*) [2015] OJ C 314/7, taken from the unabridged version, para. 336.

2125 Judgment of 28 June 2004, *Airtours v Commission*, T-342/99, ECR, EU:T:2002:146, para. 274.

2126 Judgment of 9 July 2007, *Sun Chemical Group and Others v Commission*, T-282/06, ECR, EU:T:2007:203, para. 210. Guidelines on the assessment of horizontal mergers under the Council Regulation on the control of concentrations between undertakings [2004] OJ C 31/5, para. 65. For a discussion on sophisticated buyers see: Nordemann (1995).

2127 Also raising this issue see: Peder Christensen and Valerie Rabassa, 'The Airtours Decision: Is there a new Commission Approach to Collective Dominance?' 22 European Competition Law Review (2001) 227.

2128 Judgment of 28 June 2004, *Airtours v Commission*, T-342/99, ECR, EU:T:2002:146.

2129 This case involves two Commission Decisions, an annulment action before the General Court and an appeal before the CJEU. The involved legal instruments are, in order of its date: i) Commission Decision of 19 July 2004 declaring a concentration to be compatible with the common market and the functioning of the EEA Agreement (Case No COMP/M. 3333 - *Sony/BMG*) [2004] OJ L 62/30; ii) Judgment of 13 July 2006 in *Impala v Commission*, T-464/04, EU:2006:16; Judgment of 10 July 2008 in *Bertelsmann and Sony Corporation of America v Impala,* C-413/06 P, EU:2008:392; and iv) Commission Decision declaring a concentration compatible with the common market and the functioning of the EEA Agreement (COMP/M.3333 — *Sony/BMG*), [2007], taken from the unabridged version.

2130 Commission Decision of 28 June 2000 declaring a concentration incompatible with the common market and the EEA Agreement (Case COMP/M.1741 — *MCI WorldCom/Sprint*) [2003] OJ L 300/1, para. 302.

2131 Commission Decision of Non-opposition to a notified concentration M.4057 — *Korsnäs/Assidomän Cartonboard* [2006] OJ C 209/12, taken from the unabridged version.

2132 Summary of Commission Decision of 12 November 2008 relating to a proceeding under Article 81 of the Treaty establishing the European Community and Article 53 of the EEA Agreement (Case COMP/39.125 — *Car glass*) [2009] OJ C 173/13.

ment to constitute an object restriction of competition in breach of Article 101(1) TFEU, even though it might have limited the implementation of a cartel that had not been yet implemented[2133].

1089. Concerning tacit collusion and the distortive role played by CBP, in *Sony/BMG,* CBP was raised as one of the elements that may neutralize the creation or strengthening of a collective dominant position. The final outcome of the case concluded that the proposed merger was compatible with the relevant market partially because the CBP acted as an incentive to deviate from a tacit collusive scheme[2134]. However, the assessment of CBP as a mechanism to break up the tacit collusion was not fully carried out in the first assessment of the concentration[2135] and was one of the reasons why the General Court annulled the Commission's decision[2136]. Upon this, the Commission was asked to assess CBP as an instability factor against collective dominant positions and the special role played by iTunes[2137]; in particular that the buyer power of iTunes led music providers to charge iTunes a lower wholesale price than that charged other buyers, and not due to some form of coordination among the suppliers of online music[2138]. Furthermore, iTunes' purchasing behaviour and CBP was a *deterrent mechanism for the tacit collusion* because its strength as a buyer allowed it to reject any wholesale price differentiation for single tracks, generating a "balance of power" between the music suppliers and iTunes. This, along with the lack of transparency and limited credible retaliation, led the Commission to conclude that no collective dominant position was being created nor strengthened as result of the operation. In such light CBP creates incentives to deviate from tacit collusion because it grants the buyer the ability to "negatively affect the ability to reach a coordinated effect," in particular by offering incentives to deviate from the agreement[2139]. This happens when the buyer represents a substantial portion of sales, even if the purchasing price it is willing to pay is below the coordinate price but above "the marginal cost of supply, firms will have a considerable incentive to accept the buyer's offer". The Commission therefore recognizes that *buyer power,* and in particular CBP, acts as a *destabilizing factor* in collusive cases.

2133 Judgment of 17 December 2014, *Pilkington Group and Others v Commission*, T-72/09, EU:T:2014:1094, paras. 287-289. Appealed and dismissed in its entirety as Judgment of 7 September 2016 in *Pilkington Group and Others v Commission*, C-101/15, EU:C:2016:631.

2134 Article 1 of the Commission Decision declaring a concentration compatible with the common market and the functioning of the EEA Agreement COMP/M.3333 — *Sony/BMG*, [2007].

2135 For the Commission, however, there was no need to evaluate the existence of CBP as it concluded that one of the cumulative conditions for the existence of a collective dominant position – price transparency – was not present, in Judgment of 13 July 2006 in *Impala v Commission*, T-464/04, EU:2006:16, para. 505.

2136 Judgment of 13 July 2006 in *Impala v Commission*, T-464/04, EU:2006:16, para. 490.

2137 Commission Decision declaring a concentration compatible with the common market and the functioning of the EEA Agreement COMP/M.3333 — *Sony/BMG*, [2007], taken from the unabridged version, paras. 96-98.

2138 Commission Decision declaring a concentration compatible with the common market and the functioning of the EEA Agreement COMP/M.3333 — *Sony/BMG*, [2007], taken from the unabridged version, para. 115.

2139 Commission Decision declaring a concentration compatible with the common market and the functioning of the EEA Agreement COMP/M.3333 — *Sony/BMG*, [2007], taken from the unabridged version, para. 146.

1090. Also, the existence and ability of CBP to destabilize tacit collusion was assessed in *MCI WorldCom/Sprint* where the Commission recognized that as "customers could foster the emergence of other leading players by contracting with the existing smaller competitors", CBP prevented the collusive outcome and among other considerations, it decided not to pursue its objection of collective dominance related to the market for provision of global telecommunications services[2140]. Additionally, in *Korsnäs/AD Cartonboard,* the Commission found that the presence of CBP reduced the risks of customer sharing among the merging party and its competitor, as the buyer could play off the suppliers by agreeing to acquire from one of them the sale of the whole production and the buyer's demand, as in this case there was spare capacity and costs that would have not been increased much further[2141].

1091. Fifthly, and lastly, *the origin of the CBP – public or private - is irrelevant* for its effectiveness. In *GE/Instrumentarium* the Commission found that no sufficient CBP could be exercised against the merged entity by contracting authorities under the scope of public procurement law (mainly public hospitals). However, the Commission did not rule out the possibility that public buyers can also exercise it[2142]. Also, in *AstraZeneca v Commission,* Advocate General Mazák dismissed the possibility that a public (monopsonist) buyer of prescription medicines could mitigate the seller power of a dominant undertaking[2143]. Nonetheless, the origin and nature of the CBP may limit its effectiveness, particularly if the buyer is subject to regulations limiting its freedom of contractual choice, even if the public buyer is a central purchasing body[2144].

2140 Commission Decision of 28 June 2000 declaring a concentration incompatible with the common market and the EEA Agreement (Case COMP/M.1741 — *MCI WorldCom/Sprint*) [2003] OJ L 300/1, para. 302.

2141 Commission Decision of Non-opposition to a notified concentration M.4057 — *Korsnäs/Assidomän Cartonboard* [2006] OJ C 209/12, paras. 71 and 73.

2142 Commission Decision of 2 September 2003 declaring a concentration to be compatible with the common market and the functioning of the EEA Agreement (Case COMP/M.3083 — *GE/Instrumentarium*) [2004] OJ L 109/1, para. 118.

2143 Opinion of Advocate General Mázak in Judgment of 6 December 2012 in *AstraZeneca v Commission*, C-457/10 P, EU:C:2012:293, para. 117-127.

2144 For some literature concerning centralized purchasing and the ability of buyers to agglutinate countervailing buyer power see, *inter alia*, Chard, Duhs and Houlden (2008); Albano and Sparro (2010); Herrera Anchustegui 'Centralizing Public Procurement and Competitiveness in Directive 2014/24' (2015); Sánchez Graells, Public Procurement and the EU Competition Rules [2015]; Sánchez Graells and Herrera Anchustegui, 'Impact of Public Procurement Aggregation on Competition. Risks, Rationale and Justification for the Rules in Directive 2014/24' [2016].

IV. Countervailing buyer power in the Commission Guidelines

1092. Unlike with the majority of buyer power topics, the Commission has devoted sections in its soft law instruments to describe the assessment, application and its policy concerning CBP for cases under Arts. 101 and 102 TFEU, and horizontal concentrations. Because of Commission's unusual interest in the topic and the detailed treatment given to CBP, I discuss these instruments in this section. Also, this discussion paves the way for the remainder of the chapter as the guidelines incorporate and have further advanced the legal treatment given by the Courts concerning CBP. Of particular importance for the analysis of CBP are the EU Horizontal Merger Guidelines from 2004, which summarize the "comparison test" and were used as the basis for the drafting of the successive guidelines with respect to Article 101 and Article 102 TFEU[2145].

A. Countervailing buyer power assessment in concentration cases

a. EU Horizontal Merger Guidelines

1093. The 2004 EU Horizontal Merger Guidelines devote an important section to CBP as a competitive constraint imposed on a merging supplier by its customers, as discussed at length in its Section V[2146]. According to 2004 EU Horizontal Merger Guidelines, CBP and its effectiveness on constraining the behaviour of the merged undertaking ought to be weighed up when performing the competitive assessment of the proposed concentration[2147]. Furthermore, the EU Horizontal Merger Guidelines embraces the 'comparison test' developed by the case law and the Commission's practice and advocates carrying it out as part of the assessment of the concentration albeit without providing further guidance regarding its application.

1094. The EU Horizontal Merger Guidelines define CBP in a very general manner akin to bargaining power "as the bargaining strength that the buyer has vis-à-vis the seller in commercial relations," having its origin in three main factors

---

2145 Also stressing the importance of the EU Horizontal Merger Guidelines for the assessment of CBP see: Ezrachi and Ioannidou (2014). For a brief analysis of countervailing buyer power in the EU Horizontal Merger Guidelines see: Sylvie Maudhuit and Trevor Soames, 'Changes in EU merger control: Part 2' 26 European Competition Law Review (2005) 75.

2146 Schwalbe and Zimmer, [2009], p. 153. See a brief discussion of CBP in the EU Horizontal Merger Guidelines: Whish and Bailey, *Competition law* [2015], p. 919-920.

2147 Guidelines on the assessment of horizontal mergers under the Council Regulation on the control of concentrations between undertakings [2004] OJ C 31/5, para. 10-11.

or sources[2148], which have been identified by the case law in *Sun Chemical Group and Others v Commission* and *Irish Sugar v Commission* and incorporated into the Guidelines[2149]. These sources are:

i) size[2150];

ii) commercial significance[2151];

iii) the ability of buyers to switch to alternative suppliers[2152], vertically integrate, or sponsor upstream expansion or entry[2153].

1095. Concerning the buyer's size, for the Commission, CBP is more likely to arise if buyers are large and sophisticated as opposed to small and ordinary buyers[2154]. Also, CBP may be exercised by refusing to buy goods, or particularly "in the case of durable goods, delaying purchases"[2155], as I discussed regarding the ability to exercise monopsony power in chapter 2, section §III.A, and regarding exploitative purchasing prices in chapter 7, section §III.B. This, however, does not imply that the buyer has to be dominant, nor does it need to have particularly large market shares to exert sufficient CBP. This observation in the EU Horizontal Merger Guidelines is consistent with bargain-

2148 The sources of CBP and its assessment are linked to the sources and assessment of buyer market power in general as CBP is a sub-type of it. My general analysis concerning the sources and assessment of buyer power has been covered in chapters 2, 4 and 5.

2149 Guidelines on the assessment of horizontal mergers under the Council Regulation on the control of concentrations between undertakings [2004] OJ C 31/5, para. 64. These CBP sources were ratified by the General Court in Judgment of 9 July 2007, *Sun Chemical Group and Others v Commission*, T-282/06, ECR, EU:T:2007:203, para. 210. See also Judgment of 7 October 1999, *Irish Sugar v Commission*, T-228/97, ECR, EU:T:1999:246.

2150 Guidelines on the assessment of horizontal mergers under the Council Regulation on the control of concentrations between undertakings [2004] OJ C 31/5, para. 64. See also in *Irish Sugar v Commission* where the General Court dismissed the plea of lack of independence from customers because the market share of the two largest customers was not large enough to counterbalance the market dominance by Irish Sugar, Judgment of 7 October 1999, *Irish Sugar v Commission*, T-228/97, ECR, EU:T:1999:246, para. 97. Economists have expressed doubts on the importance of market shares and size as a genuine source of CBP, for example, see: Bishop and Walker, [2010], para. 7-046.

2151 Guidelines on the assessment of horizontal mergers under the Council Regulation on the control of concentrations between undertakings [2004] OJ C 31/5, para. 64. See the general discussion on the issue of commercial dependence in chapters 5 and 8.

2152 Guidelines on the assessment of horizontal mergers under the Council Regulation on the control of concentrations between undertakings [2004] OJ C 31/5, para. 64. See also: Commission Decision of 25 November 1998 declaring a concentration to be compatible with the common market and the functioning of the EEA Agreement (Case No IV/M.1225 - *Enso/Stora*) [1999] OJ L 254/9, paras. 90 and 94. See also *Valeo/ITT* wherein the Commission found that the presence of few but large clients – major car manufacturers- able to switch suppliers was a competitive constraint of sufficient magnitude to neutralize the important increase of market share of Valeo as a spare parts supplier, Commission Decision of 30/07/1998 declaring a concentration to be compatible with the common market (Case No IV/M.1245 - *Valeo/ITT Industries*) [1998] OJ C 288/5, public version, para. 26.

2153 Tetra Pak was deemed to have "the option of developing new capacity with other existing or new suppliers, should the parties attempt to exercise market power" and, thus, have every incentive to seek to exercise its CBP vis-à-vis the merged entity between Enso and Stora, Commission Decision of 25 November 1998 declaring a concentration to be compatible with the common market and the functioning of the EEA Agreement (Case No IV/M.1225 - *Enso/Stora*) [1999] OJ L 254/9, para. 91. See also the commentary of this aspect of the case in Baker and Lofaro (2000), p. 188.

2154 Supporting this approach of sophistication over market power see: Nordemann (1995); Ezrachi and Ioannidou (2014), p. 84.

2155 Guidelines on the assessment of horizontal mergers under the Council Regulation on the control of concentrations between undertakings [2004] OJ C 31/5, para. 65.

ing power economics and the fact that buyer market power arises, and has a substantial effect, in lower market share levels than when compared with seller market power[2156], as discussed in chapters 4 and 5. In this sense, the Guidelines also recognize that pure market shares are not enough to grant CBP in the absence of other factors[2157].

1096. Additionally, according to the Guidelines the third source of CBP – alternative supply sources – only ought to be taken into consideration if the threat is *credible* and possible to be executed *within a reasonable time frame*[2158]. Albeit not expressly mentioned in the EU Horizontal Merger Guidelines but connected to this source, spare capacity is also a relevant indicator, as competitors might be unable to meet the demand of customers, as discussed in *Enso/Stora* and *SCA/Metsä Tissue*[2159].

1097. Although not considering it as a source, the Commission suggests taking into account whether there are *particular incentives of buyers to use their buyer power*, reinforcing the idea that CBP does not operate automatically[2160]. A positive incentive to CBP was found to exist for Tetra Pak in case the merger Enso/Stora had happened, as it would use its buyer power to neutralize seller market power and prevent price increases after the concentration[2161]. However, the EU Horizontal Merger Guidelines stress that there might be lack of incentives to exercise buyer power whenever the benefits of new entrants can be reaped by other customers by free-riding the investments[2162].

1098. Concerning the analysis of the sufficiency of CBP to offset the adverse effects of a concentration on competition, the EU Horizontal Merger Guidelines provide little guidance as to what situations and how the comparison test should be applied. Instead, they only suggest that CBP will be a sufficient constraint

---

2156 Bishop and Walker, [2010] para. 7-046-7048. See chapter 5, section §IV.A for the discussion of the market share thresholds used in buyer power cases.

2157 In this sense, the proposed definition of CBP appears to include both monopsonistic buyers and buyers enjoying bargaining power, despite the fact that the welfare outcome of the exercise of CBP by these two types of buyers may be dissimilar. This, in turn, opens the question on whether a monopsonistic CBP should receive the same treatment as a bargaining CBP.

2158 Guidelines on the assessment of horizontal mergers under the Council Regulation on the control of concentrations between undertakings [2004] OJ C 31/5, para. 65.

2159 Commission Decision of 25 November 1998 declaring a concentration to be compatible with the common market and the functioning of the EEA Agreement (Case No IV/M.1225 - *Enso/Stora*) [1999] OJ L 254/9, para. 94; Commission Decision of 31 January 2001 declaring a concentration to be incompatible with the common market and the functioning of the EEA Agreement (Case COMP/M.2097 *SCA/Metsä Tissue*) [2001] OJ L 57/1, para. 89; Schwalbe and Zimmer, [2009], p. 153. See also stressing the importance of capacity in the *Enso/Stora* case: Motta, *Competition Policy: Theory and Practice* [2006], p. 122.

2160 Guidelines on the assessment of horizontal mergers under the Council Regulation on the control of concentrations between undertakings [2004] OJ C 31/5, para. 66.

2161 Commission Decision of 25 November 1998 declaring a concentration to be compatible with the common market and the functioning of the EEA Agreement (Case No IV/M.1225 - *Enso/Stora*) [1999] OJ L 254/9, para. 91. See also discussing this: Monti 'The Concept of Dominance in Article 82' (2006), p. 36-38.

2162 Guidelines on the assessment of horizontal mergers under the Council Regulation on the control of concentrations between undertakings [2004] OJ C 31/5, para. 66. See also: Schwalbe and Zimmer, [2009] p. 154.

to the merging party market power when it is present in a sufficient degree to offset the potential effects of a merger[2163].

1099. From a negative perspective however, they indicate when CBP will be *insufficient* to offset adverse effects derived from a merger in two circumstances. Firstly, CBP will be insufficient if it would only preclude the merging entity from raising prices or diminishing trading conditions with respect to a specific segment of customers with a particularly substantial bargaining strength[2164]. This means that CBP ought to have at least a partial *erga omnes* effect. This also implies that the treatment of CBP recognizes, as buyer power in general does, as one of its aims the protection of the competitive structure, as well as protecting smaller (yet not inefficient) weaker buyers, and has a concern regarding waterbed effects on rival buyers, as I discuss in further detail in section §VIII of this chapter. Secondly, effective CBP must exist pre and post-merger, otherwise it would be ineffective[2165]. If as a consequence of the merger, a credible alternative of supply is removed, the CBP will be diminished and buyers will be harmed[2166]. In my view, this implies that assessment of CBP in merger cases has to be done in the pre and post-merger scenarios, as its absence or substantial diminishment post-merger, even if it exists pre-merger, will mean that it does not sufficiently offset potential adverse effects.

b. Non-horizontal Mergers Guidelines

1100. The "Non-horizontal Mergers Guidelines"[2167] largely follow the CBP's treatment in the EU Horizontal Merger Guidelines by simply referring to them when assessing buyer power in different vertical scenarios: the overall impact of competition in vertical mergers[2168]; customer foreclosure in vertical mergers[2169]; and the foreclosing effect of conglomerate mergers[2170]. In all these cases, the Commission suggests assessing the existence of CBP as a mitigating factor without providing any further indications[2171].

2163 Guidelines on the assessment of horizontal mergers under the Council Regulation on the control of concentrations between undertakings [2004] OJ C 31/5, para. 67.

2164 Guidelines on the assessment of horizontal mergers under the Council Regulation on the control of concentrations between undertakings [2004] OJ C 31/5, para. 67.

2165 Guidelines on the assessment of horizontal mergers under the Council Regulation on the control of concentrations between undertakings [2004] OJ C 31/5, para. 67.

2166 Elhauge and Geradin, [2011], p. 1034.

2167 Guidelines on the assessment of non-horizontal mergers under the Council Regulation on the control of concentrations between undertakings [2008] OJ C 265/6.

2168 Guidelines on the assessment of non-horizontal mergers under the Council Regulation on the control of concentrations between undertakings [2008] OJ C 265/6, para. 51.

2169 Guidelines on the assessment of non-horizontal mergers under the Council Regulation on the control of concentrations between undertakings [2008] OJ C 265/6, para. 76.

2170 Guidelines on the assessment of non-horizontal mergers under the Council Regulation on the control of concentrations between undertakings [2008] OJ C 265/6, para. 114.

2171 Also indicating that in these cases the presence of CBP may indicate that harm to consumers may be unlikely see: Alex Petrasincu, 'The European Commission's New Guidelines on the Assessment of Non-Horizontal Mergers - Great Expectations Disappointed' 29 European Competition Law Review (2008) 221.

B. Countervailing buyer power in the Guidance Notice on Article 102 TFEU

1101. The Commission's Guidance Notice on Article 102 TFEU takes into account CBP as part of the "constraints imposed by the bargaining strength of the undertaking's customers [countervailing buyer power]"[2172] when assessing whether an undertaking enjoys a dominant position[2173]. In its assessment the Guidance Notice on Article 102 TFEU builds upon the methodology and considerations discussed in the EU Horizontal Merger Guidelines, with some minor modifications or updates.

1102. Concerning the CBP sources, the Guidance Notice on Article 102 TFEU lists the same three as discussed above with regard to the EU Horizontal Merger Guidelines. Namely:

i) customer's (buyer) size;

ii) its commercial significance for the dominant undertaking;

iii) its ability to quickly switch to competing suppliers, promote new entry or to vertically integrate and credibly threaten to do so[2174].

1103. Regarding size the Guidance Notice on Article 102 TFEU makes an explicit reference to the Judgment of *Irish Sugar v Commission* by the General Court, in which a defense of CBP was rejected[2175] as it was determined that the dominant seller was not successful in "demonstrating that the Commission erred by not regarding its alleged lack of independence vis-à-vis its customers as an exceptional circumstance"[2176]. However, from the Judgment it can be interpreted that the General Court considered that even a very large buyer, such as Irish Sugar with over 90% of the market share could be constrained in its behaviour even by small buyers. In this case, nonetheless, "the share of sales of the two largest customers does not counterbalance the dominant position of Irish Sugar"[2177].

2172 Communication from the Commission — Guidance on the Commission's enforcement priorities in applying Article 82 of the EC Treaty to abusive exclusionary conduct by dominant undertakings [2009] OJ C 45/7, para. 12.

2173 Witt (2010), p. 223.

2174 Communication from the Commission — Guidance on the Commission's enforcement priorities in applying Article 82 of the EC Treaty to abusive exclusionary conduct by dominant undertakings [2009] OJ C 45/7, para. 18. These sources are somewhat based on the ideas expressed in the Commission's Discussion paper on the application of Article [102] TFEU of 2005 where it stated that "[t]he presence of strong buyers can only serve to counter a finding of dominance if it is likely that in response to prices being increased above the competitive level, the buyers in question will pave the way for effective new entry or lead existing suppliers in the market to significantly expand their output so as to defeat the price increase", in European Commission, DG Competition (2005), para. 41.

2175 Communication from the Commission — Guidance on the Commission's enforcement priorities in applying Article 82 of the EC Treaty to abusive exclusionary conduct by dominant undertakings [2009] OJ C 45/7, footnote 5. Reference is made to Judgment of 7 October 1999, *Irish Sugar v Commission*, T-228/97, ECR, EU:T:1999:246, para. 97-104.

2176 Judgment of 7 October 1999, *Irish Sugar v Commission*, T-228/97, ECR, EU:T:1999:246, para. 94-96.

2177 Judgment of 7 October 1999, *Irish Sugar v Commission*, T-228/97, ECR, EU:T:1999:246, para. 98, ratifying the CBP assessment carried out by the Commission Decision of 14 May 1997 relating to a proceeding pursuant to Article 86 of the EC Treaty (IV/34.621, 35.059/F-3 - *Irish Sugar plc*) [1997] OJ L 258/1, para. 108.

1104. Unfortunately, the Guidance Notice on Article 102 TFEU, like the other soft law notices, does not offer much guidance on how the CBP assessment through the comparison test ought to be made. Nevertheless, it states that CBP will be an effective competitive constraint if it may deter or defeat an attempt by an undertaking to profitably increase prices[2178]. On the other hand, it will not be an effective constraint if it only ensures "that a particular or limited segment of customers is shielded from the market power of the dominant undertaking"[2179], reiterating the concern over the protection of arguably weaker buyers and market structure expressed in the EU Horizontal Merger Guidelines.

1105. Additionally, countervailing power is considered by the Guidance Notice on Article 102 TFEU whenever discussing the imposition of exclusive purchasing agreements. In this case, though, countervailing power is used in a *broad manner* and not in the same form as CBP as defined in this chapter. By 'countervailing power' the Commission refers to the need for a dominant undertaking to compensate a buyer when it comes to entering into an exclusive purchasing deal "for the loss in competition resulting from the exclusivity" in the form of countervailing benefits[2180]. Therefore, the rebate (discount) constitutes a limitation of the buyer's ability to resort to other suppliers, as I discuss in chapter 10, section §IV.

C. Countervailing buyer power and *countervailing benefits* in the assessment of cases under the scope of Article 101 TFEU

1106. The Commission refers to CBP in three instruments dealing with the application of Article 101 TFEU, namely, the Guidelines on the application of Article 101(3) TFEU, the Guidelines on Vertical Restraints of 2010, and the Guidelines on Horizontal Agreements of 2011. However, in most of these the use of the term countervailing (buyer) power is much broader than the meaning I employ and the way it is used in the soft law for unilateral behaviour as discussed above. With regard to Article 101 TFEU, the Commission refers to the ability of buyers to act as a competitive constraint in the assessment of agreements between non-directly competing undertakings, in particular in the case of single branding and exclusive supply agreements. In this perspective,

---

2178 Communication from the Commission — Guidance on the Commission's enforcement priorities in applying Article 82 of the EC Treaty to abusive exclusionary conduct by dominant undertakings [2009] OJ C 45/7, para. 18.

2179 Communication from the Commission — Guidance on the Commission's enforcement priorities in applying Article 82 of the EC Treaty to abusive exclusionary conduct by dominant undertakings [2009] OJ C 45/7, para. 18.

2180 Communication from the Commission — Guidance on the Commission's enforcement priorities in applying Article 82 of the EC Treaty to abusive exclusionary conduct by dominant undertakings [2009] OJ C 45/7, para. 34.

countervailing power is factored when assessing whether an agreement may benefit from the application of Article 101(3) TFEU after a prior determination of its restrictive nature and impact,[2181] which I expand upon in chapter 10, section §V in the discussion of *countervailing benefits*. The lack of a detailed analysis of CBP under Article 101 TFEU is, on the other hand, logical because CBP would act in any case as an element to prevent coordination (as was discussed above regarding tacit collusion) and may also be used exceptionally to claim that a sellers' agreement might not be anti-competitive as its market power effects are neutralized by a powerful buyer.

a. *Guidelines on Horizontal Agreements*

1107. The Guidelines on Horizontal Agreements of 2011 expressly mention CBP as a mitigating efficiency defense in three circumstances. Firstly, as one of the factors to assess when determining the existence and extent of seller market power of the parties involved in an agreement that might be considered restrictive of competition by effect[2182]. Secondly, CBP is weighed up when deciding if an information exchange is genuinely public. If information is publicly exchanged, CBP may act as a constraint decreasing the likelihood of a collusive outcome, as customers would be able to jeopardize the expected outcome from the collusive behaviour[2183]. Thirdly, it is applicable when adopting a "countervailing *seller* power" approach, a scenario that I discuss in detail in chapter 10, section §V. In these cases, countervailing power of sellers is taken into account when assessing purchasing agreements. In this evaluation, the Commission considers that when a purchasing agreement is outside of the safe harbor of market shares[2184], the exercise of *countervailing power by suppliers* vis-à-vis the buyers of the agreement may in effect preclude the agreement from giving rise to restrictive effects in competition[2185]. Hence, it acts as a defense mechanism for deeming the agreement a pro-competitive one.

b. *Guidelines on Vertical Restraints of 2010*

1108. The Guidelines on Vertical Restraints of 2010 consider countervailing (bargaining power) in a broad manner as a relevant constraint limiting the effects

---

2181 Guidelines on the application of Article [101](3) TFEU [2004] OJ C 101/97, para. 12.

2182 Communication from the Commission — Guidelines on the applicability of Article 101 of the Treaty on the Functioning of the European Union to horizontal co-operation agreements [2011] OJ C 11/1, para. 45.

2183 Communication from the Commission — Guidelines on the applicability of Article 101 of the Treaty on the Functioning of the European Union to horizontal co-operation agreements [2011] OJ C 11/1, para. 94.

2184 In principle, it is unlikely that a purchasing agreement by parties that have a combined market share not exceeding 15% on the purchasing – upstream- and selling – downstream- market, respectively, may have restrictive effects on competition. Communication from the Commission — Guidelines on the applicability of Article 101 of the Treaty on the Functioning of the European Union to horizontal co-operation agreements [2011] OJ C 11/1, para. 208.

2185 Communication from the Commission — Guidelines on the applicability of Article 101 of the Treaty on the Functioning of the European Union to horizontal co-operation agreements [2011] OJ C 11/1, para. 209.

of *single branding agreements*[2186], and acting as *countervailing benefits* that compensate the buyer for its inability to find alternative suppliers. These countervailing benefits, therefore, do not preclude the parties to a selling agreement from behaving independently like CBP does, and instead constitute a measurement to determine whether the buyer is sufficiently compensated and whether or not the exclusive purchasing obligation is abusive nor anti-competitive.

1109. The same broad approach to countervailing power is employed by the Commission when analyzing *exclusive supply agreements*[2187], and using the countervailing power of *suppliers* as a relevant competitive constraint, as large suppliers will not easily permit being cut off from alternative buyers. If suppliers are weak and thus lack countervailing *seller* power, then the risk of foreclosure due to the exclusive supply agreement increases[2188]. This happens because if the buyer is too powerful then other buyers will not be able to obtain the input from the supplier[2189]. On the other hand, if suppliers are strong and enjoy countervailing power then exclusive supply is said to be found in combination with non-competing clauses.

c. Guidelines on the application of Article 101(3) TFEU

1110. Lastly, the ability of buyers to exert competitive pressure on the parties to an agreement in a broad manner is also discussed by the Guidelines on the application of Article 101(3) TFEU. In particular, the Guidelines are relevant when assessing whether or not an agreement eliminates competition with respect to a substantial part of the products concerned. In such cases, and as part of the entry barrier assessment, the Commission resorts to the ability to bring new sources of competition into the market[2190], as this pressure may indicate that CBP is exercised by sponsoring entry, therefore further preventing the restriction of competition.

D. Critical remarks to the Commission's soft law

1111. According to the Commission's Guidelines, CBP precludes (an) undertaking(s) from behaving (to an appreciable extent) independently or from significantly impeding competition in the market by exerting seller market power. Despite the scant guidance, the assessment according to the soft law is to be

2186 Single branding agreements limit the ability to exercise buyer market power as "the buyer is obliged or induced to concentrate its orders for a particular type of product with one supplier", Guidelines on Vertical Restraints [2010] OJ C 130/1, para. 129.

2187 Exclusive supply agreements are understood as those "that have as their main element that the supplier is obliged or induced to sell the contract products only or mainly to one buyer, in general or for a particular use", Guidelines on Vertical Restraints [2010] OJ C 130/1, para. 192.

2188 Guidelines on Vertical Restraints [2010] OJ C 130/1, para. 198.

2189 Bellamy, Child and Roth, [2001] para 7.040; Bellamy and others, [2013], para. 7.065.

2190 Guidelines on the application of Article [101](3) TFEU [2004] OJ C 101/97, para. 115 (v).

carried out through the comparison test, which entails determining whether it will impose a sufficient buyer-side constraint to the provider such that it is capable of offsetting the anti-competitive effects of the conduct.

1112. Interestingly, CBP is discussed across all areas of EU competition law, albeit it is only with respect to unilateral behaviour (present or future) that the discussion is more detailed, and rightly so, with considerably lesser importance in the case of assessment of agreements. Furthermore, the treatment of CBP across the different soft law instruments and areas of competition law is largely similar, which indicates that the Commission adopts a homogenous treatment of CBP for all aspects of EU competition law, rather than adopting a casuistic approach to it, a position that is welcomed. The welfare effects of CBP will tend to be similar regardless of whether the case deals with dominance, an agreement or a concentration. However the specific assessment ought to take into consideration the particular market structure and specificities of each case, to determine whether it is *sufficient* to neutralize the other's side market power. From a legal perspective, a homogenous approach to CBP is also desirable as it fosters predictability and legal certainty. Nevertheless, in my view, what differs in the treatment is the threshold that CBP must reach to offset the anti-competitive effects generated by the dominant position, concentration operation or agreement among undertakings, a topic not directly addressed by the soft law. This differentiated threshold also appears to be the approach taken by the Courts, as will be discussed infra in this chapter's section §VI.

1113. Additionally, the soft law focuses on stating the sources of countervailing buyer and clarifying under which circumstances CBP is deemed as sufficient. Although, they do not provide a defined methodology regarding how all these factors are to be assessed and compared vis-à-vis the market power of the selling undertaking. Two reasons may explain this. First, the Commission tacitly recognizes that the Courts are the organs entrusted in setting legally binding standards, such as the elements to factor in the comparison test and determining when CBP is sufficient to offset negative effects on competition derived from the undertaking's seller market power. Second, not formally embracing any assessment methodology for the comparison test grants a margin of discretion to NCAs to develop their own, at least in the case of 'pure' national cases. This room for limited diversity, still tied to the legal test set by the Courts, allows for further improvement of the economic assessment of CBP[2191].

1114. Lastly, the soft law coincides in indicating that CBP will not sufficiently offset potential adverse effects derived from the seller's market power when it only shields a particular set of customers from it. In other words, CBP must have a

2191 See advocating for some room for limited diversity on the application of EU competition law see: Christopher Townley, 'Co-Ordinated Diversity: Revolutionary Suggestions for EU Competition Law (and for EU Law too)' King's College London Dickson Poon School of Law, Legal Studies Research Paper Series 2014-13 (2013) 1.

spillover effect on other buyers. Consequently, there appears to be a requirement for CBP to improve purchasing market conditions as a whole and not simply that of a sole buyer, adopting a broader and more demanding approach to determine the sufficiency of CBP[2192]. This reaffirms an interest of EU competition law for the protection of the competitive structure in the markets, as well as concern for possible waterbed effects affecting weaker buyers[2193].

V. Countervailing buyer power in the case law and Commission's practice: sources and hindrances

1115. The remainder of this chapter discusses how CBP has been dealt with by the Courts, through the analysis of different concepts and key issues that concern it, to determine what the legal treatment given to these different aspects of CBP by the Courts is, in a holistic manner. This first section deals with the origin of CBP and the assessment of these sources. From another perspective, I also discuss hindrances or impediments for buyers to exercise CBP.

A. Sources of countervailing buyer power

1116. The EU case law and Commission's practice confirms that CBP originates from different non-exhaustive sources that depend on the circumstances at hand, as reiterated by the General Court in *Cementbouw Handel & Industrie v Commission*[2194], and more recently by the Commission in *Car Glass*[2195]. By and large, the sources identified by the Courts are those that have been incor-

2192 Judgment of 21 March 2002, *Shaw and Falla v Commission*, T-131/99, ECR, EU:T:2002:83, para. 163.

2193 A similar concern was expressed by the Commission when stating "[…] given the fact that dominance is assessed in relation to a market, it is not sufficient that certain strong buyers may be able to extract more favourable conditions from the allegedly dominant undertaking than their weaker competitors" in European Commission, DG Competition (2005), para. 41.

2194 Judgment of 23 February 2006, *Cementbouw Handel & Industrie v Commission*, T-282/02, ECR, EU:T:2006:64, para. 232.

2195 "Bargaining power apart, other reasons for the "rapport captif" referred to by Saint-Gobain result from i) the absence of carglass suppliers on the determination of a certain number of economic key parameters such as the renewal politics of the range of models of cars (e.g. design, technical specifications, and frequency of renewals/restyling of car models), marketing issues, volumes, and prices (including in particular the decision by car manufacturers to apply a target price for a target volume requested at the stage for the RFQ; ii) the transfer of a significant amount of commercial risk which is partly imposed on the carglass suppliers; iii) totally one-way transparent market exclusively seen from the car manufacturers point of view (they receive all the detailed information from the carglass suppliers), in particular as regards the breakdown of prices in an RFQ; iv) it was not in the carglass supplier's interest to engage in price collusion as this would imply implementing further capacity which would increase heavy investments only to see itself loosing [sic] the business to another supplier. Even if the result is achieved and the bid is won/contract supply is renewed, the car manufacturers may have a strategic interest not to give more business to that particular glass supplier in order to maintain a balance between his glass suppliers; v) the margin of manoeuvre that the glass supplier has is very limited as car manufacturer may change several things regarding a model all the time". Summary of Commission Decision of 12 November 2008 relating to a proceeding under Article 81 of the Treaty establishing the European Community and Article 53 of the EEA Agreement (Case COMP/39.125 — *Car glass*) [2009] OJ C 173/13, taken from the unabridged version, para. 441, footnote 672.

porated in the Commission's Guidance Notices, which I discuss in detail below. These are: alternative supply sources and demand shifting, buyer's size, commercial significance of the buyer for the supplier, and price differentials.

a. Alternative supply sources and demand shifting

1117. The capacity to find *credible* alternative supply sources or shift demand in a "reasonable time" is the *most important source of CBP according to the case law, the Commission's practice and the literature*[2196], and also constitutes a part of the traditional element to determine the existence of dominance, even absent CBP.

1118. Shifting demand and, therefore, resorting to additional supply sources represents the ability of the buyer to channel its demand through other sellers. The more options there are, the less the seller is able to behave independently from its buyer. This shifting of demand can take several forms, as clarified by the General Court in *Sun Chemical Group and Others v Commission,* that go beyond just changing a supplier, as I discuss below[2197]. However, there are circumstances where, even if there are other suppliers it is not always possible to switch demand due to infrastructural reasons, as occurred in *Slovak Telekom*, where the lack of alternative offers to the local loop infrastructure for telecommunications made entry into the market of other suppliers highly unlikely[2198]. Also, the ability to switch to alternative supplies (in this case docking ports) and spare capacity was a factor to consider to determine the sufficiency of CBP in *Hutchison/RCPM/ECT*, in which CBP was not sufficient, but the concentration was accepted pursuant to commitments[2199].

1119. Furthermore, the General Court has given further advice concerning the general assessment when determining if CBP arises from alternative supply sources in *Cementbouw Handel & Industrie v Commission*[2200]. The General Court held that CBP has its origin and "compensate[s] for the supplier's market power if those customers have the ability to resort to credible alternative sources of supply within a reasonable time if the supplier decides to increase its prices or to make the conditions of delivery less favourable"[2201]. Therefore, the presence of

---

2196 Also making reference to these sources see: Johan Karlsson, 'Clearance of near-duopoly' 27 European Competition Law Review (2006) 514; Cook and Patel, [2013] para 2.79.

2197 Judgment of 9 July 2007, *Sun Chemical Group and Others v Commission,* T-282/06, ECR, EU:T:2007:203.

2198 Summary of Commission Decision of 15 October 2014 relating to a proceeding under Article 102 of the Treaty on the Functioning of the European Union and Article 54 of the EEA Agreement (Case AT.39523 — *Slovak Telekom*) [2015] OJ C 314/7, taken from the unabridged version, paras. 289-291.

2199 Commission decision of 3 July 2001 declaring a concentration to be compatible with the common market and the functioning of the EEA Agreement (Case COMP/ JV.55 — *Hutchison/RCPM/ECT*) 1723) [2003] OJ L 223 1/31, para. 120.

2200 Judgment of 23 February 2006, *Cementbouw Handel & Industrie v Commission,* T-282/02, ECR, EU:T:2006:64.

2201 Judgment of 23 February 2006, *Cementbouw Handel & Industrie v Commission,* T-282/02, ECR, EU:T:2006:64, para. 230.

credible alternative supply sources confers CBP if there is "a strong probability that the supplier is forced to limit any increase in prices or indeed to refrain from increasing prices", as stressed by the General Court[2202]. This should be interpreted as implying that the ability to switch demand and, thus, CBP, may be either *actual or potential.* Additionally, in *Cementbouw Handel & Industrie v Commission,* the General Court clarified that, unlike the Commission held[2203], not simply large buyers but indeed *any* buyer can resort to alternative supply sources to generate CBP, therefore the ability to switch demand is not dependent on the size of the buyer, but it is an alternative factor for the origin of CBP.

1120. In *Sun Chemical Group and Others v Commission,* the General Court dealt with the way in which buyers may find alternative supply sources. For instance, this could happen if the buyer shifts purchases to other sellers, credibly threatens to vertically integrate into the upstream market[2204], is able to sponsor upstream expansion or entry[2205], or could resort to *in-house* production of the input even if said product is not identical to that which is supplied by the seller[2206]. In this case, production in house and vertical integration were of particular importance as the General Court concluded that the capacity to resort to in-house production "allows [buyers] to discipline their suppliers to a certain extent"[2207], even if it implies transferring just a substantial part of their requirements should it amount to a "significant proportion of the merged entity's production"[2208].

1121. Moreover, the case law and Commission's practice also indicates that shifting demand can be effective even if not all of it is transferred to another supplier, particularly depending on the capacity of production or the specificity of the product. In *Enso/Stora,* the Commission concluded that losing a large volume of (but not all) purchases from a large buyer would mean that "the parties would

2202 Judgment of 23 February 2006, *Cementbouw Handel & Industrie v Commission,* T-282/02, ECR, EU:T:2006:64, para. 232.

2203 According to the Commission countervailing buyer power is the "*ability of large customers* [...] to resort to credible alternatives within a reasonable time if the supplier decides to increase its price or to make the conditions of delivery less favourable", Judgment of 23 February 2006, *Cementbouw Handel & Industrie v Commission,* T-282/02, ECR, EU:T:2006:64, para. 186 (emphasis added).

2204 Judgment of 9 July 2007, *Sun Chemical Group and Others v Commission,* T-282/06, ECR, EU:T:2007:203, para. 194. See also: Ezrachi [2014], p. 437.

2205 Judgment of 9 July 2007, *Sun Chemical Group and Others v Commission,* T-282/06, ECR, EU:T:2007:203, paras. 191 and 210; Commission Decision of 25 November 1998 declaring a concentration to be compatible with the common market and the functioning of the EEA Agreement (Case No IV/M.1225 - *Enso/Stora*) [1999] OJ L 254/9; Commission Decision of Non-opposition to a notified concentration M.4057 — *Korsnäs/Assidomän Cartonboard* [2006] OJ C 209/12, taken from the unabridged public version, para. 46.

2206 Judgment of 9 July 2007, *Sun Chemical Group and Others v Commission,* T-282/06, ECR, EU:T:2007:203, para. 194. In this case, the General Court accepted as a source of CBP the capacity to produce a different type of rosin resin.

2207 Judgment of 9 July 2007, *Sun Chemical Group and Others v Commission,* T-282/06, ECR, EU:T:2007:203, para. 213.

2208 Judgment of 9 July 2007, *Sun Chemical Group and Others v Commission,* T-282/06, ECR, EU:T:2007:203, para. 215.

have to find other customers in order to fill the capacity"[2209], thus referring to customers that may not yet exist. A similar conclusion was reached in *Korsnäs/AD Cartonboard* where it was concluded that buying enough orders to fill the capacity of one cardboard-processing machine was sufficient to generate CBP[2210]. This is explained by the fact that in certain industries a decrease in the utilization of installed machinery may have a large and detrimental impact on the cost structure of the supplier undertaking, as remarked by Baker and Lofaro[2211]. Therefore partial shifts in demand can be sufficient to discipline the seller.

1122. Also, the Courts have recognized *second supplier strategies* as an additional and important source of CBP, as the Commission found that car glass (car windscreens) buyers enjoyed countervailing buyer power that allowed them to reduce or thwart the actions of a sellers' cartel if they could obtain their supplies from an additional supplier[2212]. In *Carglass*[2213] the dual sourcing strategy allowed car manufacturers to partially neutralize the efforts of the cartel members as the allocation agreements were not always successful. This Commission's finding was ratified by the General Court on the annulment action, as it held that CBP and the dual sourcing ran contrary "to the collusive practices of the cartel participants and the fact that those counterstrategies had allowed them to thwart some decisions taken in the context of that cartel"[2214]. Also, a dual sourcing strategy was claimed to generate CBP in *CVC/Lenzing*, but the claim was rejected as only a handful of buyers resorted to this strategy, along with other indicators of the absence of CBP[2215].

1123. Concerning the *timeliness* of the demand shift, the case law and Commission's practice show a trend that has *shifted from requiring a short term to a reasonable time* in certain circumstances. In *Enso/Stora*, the Commission argued that if suppliers are unable to find alternative buyers in *the short term*, this means that the

2209 Commission Decision of 25 November 1998 declaring a concentration to be compatible with the common market and the functioning of the EEA Agreement (Case No IV/M.1225 - *Enso/Stora*) [1999] OJ L 254/9, para. 90.

2210 Commission Decision of Non-opposition to a notified concentration M.4057 — *Korsnäs/Assidomän Cartonboard* [2006] OJ C 209/12, taken from the unabridged public version, para. 50.

2211 Baker and Lofaro (2000), p. 188.

2212 Summary of Commission Decision of 12 November 2008 relating to a proceeding under Article 81 of the Treaty establishing the European Community and Article 53 of the EEA Agreement (Case COMP/39.125 — *Car glass*) [2009] OJ C 173/13, taken from the unabridged version, para. 677.

2213 Summary of Commission Decision of 12 November 2008 relating to a proceeding under Article 81 of the Treaty establishing the European Community and Article 53 of the EEA Agreement (Case COMP/39.125 — *Car glass*) [2009] OJ C 173/13, taken from the unabridged version.

2214 Judgment of 17 December 2014, *Pilkington Group and Others v Commission*, T-72/09, EU:T:2014:1094, para. 285. Appealed and dismissed in its entirety as Judgment of 7 September 2016 in *Pilkington Group and Others v Commission*, C-101/15, EU:C:2016:631.

2215 Commission Decision of 17 October 2001 declaring a concentration to be incompatible with the common market and the functioning of the EEA Agreement (Case COMP/M.2187 — *CVC/Lenzing*) [2004] OJ L 82/20, para. 213.

buyer has some or more CBP[2216]. In *Irish Sugar v Commission,* the General Court rejected a claim of the existence of CBP because the largest buyers of an undertaking had no capacity to turn to other alternative supply sources, even *in the short term,* due to the existence of community export and import quotas on sugar[2217].

1124. However, the switching timeliness may vary depending on the circumstances of the case and it may not always be possible, or indeed necessary for the shift to be conducted in the short term[2218]. This was the issue in *CVC/Lenzing,* where the Commission found that short-term switching of suppliers was not feasible because each buyer had particular specifications that the supplier must comply with and adapt its equipment to[2219]. Therefore, the buyer was locked-in to a specific supplier for more than a short term[2220]. The intuition is that the longer it takes to switch to alternative suppliers the less powerful the threat is. However, there are situations in which the switch, even if not done in a short term, would still generate CBP, for example if the shift to a different supplier would entail that the current seller would have to de-utilize 'tailored' machinery of specialized service that involves high sunk costs, or if having a different buyer would require costs to suit the production to their specific needs, the threat to switch demand *even if within more than a short term would still be credible.* This criticism was noted by the Courts in *Cementbouw Handel & Industrie v Commission* when the General Court held that the shift in demand would be a credible threat and generating CBP even if done "within a reasonable time"[2221]. This change in criteria under these special circumstances is corroborated by looking at other versions of the Judgment. In both the French and Spanish version, the wording used by the General Court is the same "*dans un délai raisonnable*" and "*en un plazo razonable*", respectively.

1125. Synthetizing, the ability of buyers to shift to alternative supply sources (in all its different forms) constitutes the most important source for CBP to exist. This however does not imply that it is the only source, as the Commission

2216 Commission Decision of 25 November 1998 declaring a concentration to be compatible with the common market and the functioning of the EEA Agreement (Case No IV/M.1225 - *Enso/Stora*) [1999] OJ L 254/9, para. 90.

2217 Judgment of 7 October 1999, *Irish Sugar v Commission*, T-228/97, ECR, EU:T:1999:246, para. 97.

2218 Baker and Lofaro (2000), p. 188-189.

2219 Commission Decision of 17 October 2001 declaring a concentration to be incompatible with the common market and the functioning of the EEA Agreement (Case COMP/M.2187 — *CVC/Lenzing*) [2004] OJ L 82/20, para. 213.

2220 Commission Decision of 17 October 2001 declaring a concentration to be incompatible with the common market and the functioning of the EEA Agreement (Case COMP/M.2187 — *CVC/Lenzing*) [2004] OJ L 82/20, para. 222.

2221 "First of all, it should be observed that, as the Commission maintained in its written submissions, without being challenged by the applicant, the buyer power of a supplier's customers may compensate for the supplier's market power if those customers have the ability to resort to credible alternative sources of supply within a reasonable time if the supplier decides to increase its prices or to make the conditions of delivery less favourable", in Judgment of 23 February 2006, *Cementbouw Handel & Industrie v Commission,* T-282/02, ECR, EU:T:2006:64, para. 230.

erroneously held in *SCA/Metsä Tissue* when stating that "*buyer power* [*rectius*: CBP] *can only by exercised* if the buyer has an *adequate choice of alternative suppliers*"[2222]. Furthermore, the case law clarifies that shifting to an alternative source of supply takes different forms besides just finding a new seller. Also, there is further guidance concerning the timeliness of the switch in demand. A first criterion was resorted to, which required change to be in the short term, and a more recent criterion that accepts the timeliness, even if within a reasonable time. Therefore, the standard seems to vary depending on the factors of the case but the longer time it takes to switch to other suppliers, the less threatening the demand shift will be and the lower the CBP of the buyer vis-à-vis the supplier.

b. *Buyer size*

1126. Buyer size and market share in the upstream market are other indicators of the existence of CBP, which the General Court qualifies as one of the "very relevant sources"[2223]. If buyers are large, for example an electricity distribution company with respect to an energy producer[2224], and, in addition, they have a gate-keeping position, as occurred in the merger of *Procter & Gamble/Gillette*, then it is very likely that they will have large CBP[2225]. Also, intuitively appealing, larger buyers, such as supermarket chains, "have more negotiating power than smaller retailers and are able to negotiate discounts which are not available to smaller retailers"[2226], as held by the Commission in *The Coca-Cola Company/Carlsberg A/S,* but without necessarily implying that obtaining discounts or exerting some degree of buyer market power is equivalent to sufficient CBP vis-à-vis a powerful seller, especially if the latter has a must stock product. However, the Commission's practice illustrates that, in specific circumstances and in the presence of other factors, small buyers may exercise substantial CBP, as occurred in *Enso/Stora*[2227] and *Korsnäs/AD Cartonboard,* cases discussed in detail infra

2222 Commission Decision of 31 January 2001 declaring a concentration to be incompatible with the common market and the functioning of the EEA Agreement (Case COMP/M.2097 *SCA/Metsä Tissue*) [2001] OJ L 57/1, para. 86 (emphasis added). In my view taking such a strict view that CBP can *only* be exercised if there is an adequate choice of alternative suppliers might be stretching too far the importance of this source. CBP can be exercised, as recognized by the Commission in *Enso/Stora*, in the case the sponsoring entry of *new* suppliers or even in the case of in-house production of the input.

2223 Judgment of 23 February 2006, *Cementbouw Handel & Industrie v Commission,* T-282/02, ECR, EU:T:2006:64, EU:T:2006:64 E.C.R. [2006] II-00319, para. 232.

2224 See briefly discussing CBP in the electricity markets: Pierce RJ, 'Antitrust Policy in the New Electricity Industry' (1996) 17 Energy Law Journal 29, p. 50.

2225 Non-opposition to a notified concentration (Case COMP/M.3732 — *Procter & Gamble/Gillette*) [2005] OJ C 239/6, public version, para. 120-133. See also commenting this case and discussing the important and large size of retailers exerting countervailing buyer power: Ezrachi and Ioannidou (2014), p. 88-89. See also: Areeda, Hovenkamp and Solow, [1995], Volume IIA, ¶404c7.

2226 Commission Decision of 11 September 1997 declaring a concentration to be compatible with the common market and the functioning of the EEA Agreement (Case No IV/M.833 - *The Coca-Cola Company/Carlsberg A/S*) [1998] OJ L 145/41, para. 81.

2227 Commission Decision of 25 November 1998 declaring a concentration to be compatible with the common market and the functioning of the EEA Agreement (Case No IV/M.1225 - *Enso/Stora*) [1999] OJ L 254/9.

in this chapter's section §VIII.A[2228]. In these cases, smaller buyers were able to place purchasing orders that utilized the capacity of a machine that, if left unused, would have constituted a high unemployed cost for the supplier[2229].

1127. In *Sun Chemical Group and Others v Commission,* the General Court confirmed that market size and buyer side concentration are a very relevant source of CBP. If the buying market structure is concentrated this may "be capable of reinforcing [the buyer's] bargaining power vis-à-vis the supplier"[2230]. Also, the larger a customer is, the more CBP it will have, particularly if "demand is concentrated on a very limited number of large customers", conferring upon them "considerable negotiating power" that is capable of neutralizing opposite seller market power[2231]. In *Cementbouw Handel & Industrie v Commission,* the General Court also took into account market concentration and it confirmed the Commission's argument that a high degree of market concentration of buyers – and consequently that they have relatively large market shares – "means that their limited number may be capable of reinforcing their bargaining power vis-à-vis the supplier"[2232].

1128. In *Carglass* the sheer size and purchasing structure of car manufacturers – along with alternative supply sources – was a decisive factor for the Commission to acknowledge the existence of some degree of CBP vis-à-vis the members of a cartel supplying car-glass pieces[2233]. The Commission found that car-glass purchasers "enjoyed countervailing buyer power which enabled them to devise counterstrategies, such as the systematic use of second supplier strategies, which allowed them in some cases to reduce or thwart the coordinated actions"[2234]. CBP, therefore, was present as the car manufacturing market had four buyers that represented more than 60% of the market shares for cars and car glass[2235]. Also, in addition to the car manufacturer's size, the fact that their purchasing pattern was centralized for all their own and

---

2228 Commission Decision of Non-opposition to a notified concentration M.4057 — *Korsnäs/Assidomän Cartonboard* [2006] OJ C 209/12, taken from the unabridged public version, para. 47-53.

2229 Commission Decision of Non-opposition to a notified concentration M.4057 — *Korsnäs/Assidomän Cartonboard* [2006] OJ C 209/12, taken from the unabridged public version, para. 50.

2230 Judgment of 23 February 2006, *Cementbouw Handel & Industrie v Commission,* T-282/02, ECR, EU:T:2006:64, para. 232.

2231 Judgment of 9 July 2007, *Sun Chemical Group and Others v Commission,* T-282/06, ECR, EU:T:2007:203, para. 213.

2232 Judgment of 23 February 2006, *Cementbouw Handel & Industrie v Commission,* T-282/02, ECR, EU:T:2006:64, para. 232.

2233 Summary of Commission Decision of 12 November 2008 relating to a proceeding under Article 81 of the Treaty establishing the European Community and Article 53 of the EEA Agreement (Case COMP/39.125 — *Car glass*) [2009] OJ C 173/13.

2234 Summary of Commission Decision of 12 November 2008 relating to a proceeding under Article 81 of the Treaty establishing the European Community and Article 53 of the EEA Agreement (Case COMP/39.125 — *Car glass*) [2009] OJ C 173/13, taken from the unabridged version, para. 677.

2235 Summary of Commission Decision of 12 November 2008 relating to a proceeding under Article 81 of the Treaty establishing the European Community and Article 53 of the EEA Agreement (Case COMP/39.125 — *Car glass*) [2009] OJ C 173/13, taken from the unabridged version, para. 29.

affiliated brands, this reinforced their bargaining power and allowed them to secure EEA-wide deals[2236].

1129. Although buyer's size and its market share is an indicator of the existence of CBP, the same cautious approach concerning oversimplification of its meaning, as I discuss in chapter 5 when talking about buyer market power assessment, should prevail. Even in the presence of large market shares of buyer concentration, CBP may not exist or the buyers might not be incentivized to exert it[2237]. Therefore, in my view, ability to switch supply is a more importance source of CBP. This view, however, is not shared by O'Donoghue and Padilla, who argue that market concentration is "the most important factor in assessing the extent to which a market is likely to be influenced" by CBP[2238].

1130. In any case, the assessment of the origin and extent of CBP should consider the buyer's size and the concentration in the market and also take into account commercial significance of the buyer to the seller.

c. *Commercial significance of the buyer to the seller: ratio of business*

1131. Another key source of CBP as identified by the case law and the Commission's practice is the proportion of profits that a buyer represents for a seller. This ratio of sales is also an indicator of the ability of a buyer to exert buyer market power on a supplier that is dependent on it, as I discussed in chapter 8, section §IV.C, when discussing three cases of mergers in food retailing.

1132. In *Enso/Stora* the fact that Tetra Pak as a buyer acquired more than 50% of its liquid packing board from the merging entities and that this amount represented "the output of several board machines and about [more than 50 %]* of the parties' total output for the EEA" market was seen as an important source of CBP[2239].

1133. Also, in *Irish Sugar v Commission,* the proportion of sales a buyer represents was taken into account by the General Court when a claim of existence of CBP was rejected. The applicant argued that it was not dominant because the ratio of profits and sales with respect to its two largest customers precluded it from behaving independently. The General Court held that these customers did not have

2236 Summary of Commission Decision of 12 November 2008 relating to a proceeding under Article 81 of the Treaty establishing the European Community and Article 53 of the EEA Agreement (Case COMP/39.125 — *Car glass*) [2009] OJ C 173/13, taken from the unabridged version, paras. 29 and 33. See in chapter 7, section §V a discussion of centralized purchasing.

2237 Also supporting that even if a buyer is 'big' it might not possess CBP and also making reference to these sources see: Karlsson (2006), p. 516; Carlton and Israel (2011), p. 134.

2238 O'Donoghue and Padilla, [2013], p. 167.

2239 Commission Decision of 25 November 1998 declaring a concentration to be compatible with the common market and the functioning of the EEA Agreement (Case No IV/M.1225 - *Enso/Stora*) [1999] OJ L 254/9, para. 90.

this level of commercial strength arguably due to their low ratio compared to Irish Sugar (Irish Sugar had ca. 90% of the sugar supply market but the public version does not show the market shares nor does it show the ratio of the buyers)[2240] and because the buyers had no access to alternative sources of supply[2241].

1134. In *Cementbouw Handel & Industrie v Commission* the commercial significance of the buyer for the seller was also taken into account. As it was decided that despite the relatively concentrated market in which five buyers of construction materials amounted to 60 to 80% of the sales of the undertaking under investigation, this factor in itself was insufficient to prove the existence of CBP. This was because "no single customer accounts for a substantial part of CVK's turnover"[2242]. This confirms that mere size alone is insufficient. Size has to be related to the proportion of sales the buyer represents. The larger the ratio, the closer the seller is to becoming dependent on the buyer's absent other undertakings that it could resort to sell their goods.

1135. Lastly, in *Imperial Chemical Industries v Commission,* the General Court also stressed the influence of the ratio and commercial significance of a buyer for a particular supplier as a source of CBP when it held that "the applicant stated that its four largest customers represented about 50% of its sales. However, it gives no details regarding the respective share [ratio buyer-supplier] of each of those four customers"[2243]. The General Court decided that since the applicant failed to provide the details of this ratio buyer-supplier, it was unable to determine if they represented a substantial part of the turnover of the undertaking and dismissed the allegation.

1136. From the reading of these cases and the wording used referring to "no single customer", doubt arises concerning whether for CBP to exist the buyer has to act alone or if the ratio of sales of a group of coordinated buyers can be taken into account. In my view, the answer should be affirmative in the sense that Courts and NCAs should also consider whether the ratio of pooled demand by a buying alliance as a whole is sufficient to generate joint CBP, and should not estimate the existence of it based on which proportion each of the members represents, and also because, for the supplier (if the alliance buys as a joint entity and is transparent), it is not possible to distinguish which proportion of purchases is represented by which member of the alliance. If, on the other hand, the interpretation given is that the ratio assessed must be measured on a purchaser by purchaser basis then the ability of the buying alliance to pool

2240 Commission Decision of 14 May 1997 relating to a proceeding pursuant to Article 86 of the EC Treaty (IV/34.621, 35.059/F-3 - *Irish Sugar plc*) [1997] OJ L 258/1, para. 21.

2241 Judgment of 7 October 1999, *Irish Sugar v Commission*, T-228/97, ECR, EU:T:1999:246, para. 97.

2242 Judgment of 23 February 2006, *Cementbouw Handel & Industrie v Commission,* T-282/02, ECR, EU:T:2006:64, para. 233.

2243 Judgment of 25 June 2010, *Imperial Chemical Industries v Commission*, T-66/01, ECR, EU:T:2010:255, para. 277.

CBP would be artificially reduced for no good reason, making the sufficiency or existence of CBP more restrictive than it should be. Therefore, the proportion of sales, in cases of buying alliances, should be computed as a whole and not with respect to each member. This, however, seems unproblematic for future cases, as the Commission's practice has not rejected this possibility explicitly or implicitly.

d. Price differentials

1137. Price differentials are another source employed in the assessment of CBP. They represent the difference between two different goods, or between the same good when bought by different buyers. These price differentials have been resorted to as an origin of CBP in *CVC/Lenzing* where the Commission employed them to determine whether "the price level of VSF for tampons (particularly of Acordis' speciality fibre Galaxy, but also of standard fibres for tampons) is above the price level for commodity VSF [...]*. *Such a price differential would not be likely if customers actually had sufficient countervailing buyer power"*[2244]. Therefore, the indication of a difference in price between two similar products from different sellers could be interpreted as a signal of the absence of sufficient CBP.

B. Hindrances to countervailing buyer power

1138. The case law and the Commission's practice also illustrate certain situations that constrain the possible exercise of CBP. As in the case of sources, there is no exhaustive list of what these hindrances are, but the following circumstances provide a good indication of when CBP can be limited or negated. In the following paragraphs I discuss how to assess these limitations.

1139. In *Syniverse/Mach*, the Commission found that the *low probability of entry of new suppliers* in the market hinders the ability of buyers to exercise CBP and concluded that in the market for near real-time roaming data exchange, the concentration would significantly impede competition. In my view this must be interpreted as, if CBP were to be sufficient then it would have likely precluded the merged entity from impeding competition in such a market. Despite the absence of CBP, the merger was ultimately declared compatible with the internal market[2245].

1140. In *Tomra and Others v Commission*, the General Court and the CJEU ratified the Commission's finding that buyers might not be willing to exercise their

---

2244 Commission Decision of 17 October 2001 declaring a concentration to be incompatible with the common market and the functioning of the EEA Agreement (Case COMP/M.2187 — *CVC/Lenzing*) [2004] OJ L 82/20, para. 215 (emphasis added).

2245 Summary of Commission Decision of 29 May 2013 declaring a concentration compatible with the internal market and the functioning of the EEA Agreement (Case COMP/M.6690 — *Syniverse/Mach*) [2014] OJ C 60/7, paras. 79-97.

CBP, for example by sponsoring entry of new suppliers, if its investments can be subject to *free riding by its own competitors*. As held by the Commission "[m]oreover, such behaviour would have been prone to free riding, as building up a competitor would have resulted in a public good. Consequently, there was no substantial countervailing buyer power which would have been able to challenge Tomra's dominance in any of the markets concerned".[2246] Therefore, if sponsoring entry can be prone to free riding then the powerful buyer would not be incentivized to engage in the financing. This additionally reinforces the fact that CBP does not automatically takes place, as the buyer may choose to not exert it if it would not be the most optimal business strategy to maximize its profits.

1141. Also, the Commission has used *brand recognition* and the existence of a 'must stock product' as an argument to diminish the strength of CBP, as occurred in *SCA/Metsä Tissue*[2247]. In this case, the merging entity would have controlled 80-90% of the sales of toilet paper and the brands with the strongest brand recognition in the geographical market. Therefore, when buyers even as powerful as food retailing stores face a supplier with a 'must stock' product, their bargaining power diminishes, as they are not in a position to retaliate by switching to another supplier because losing access to this desired input would negatively impact its sales in the downstream market.

1142. Brand recognition was also an important factor in *The Coca-Cola Company/ Carlsberg A/S* to determine that even large buyers that obtain discounts from a powerful supplier do not have sufficient CBP because these buyers saw the goods sold by the involved undertakings as 'must stock' brands that they are not able to obtain from other suppliers and, consequently, "they are not able to find other suppliers for their CSD requirements to such an extent that it could remove the dominance of the parties"[2248]. Despite the finding that "little [rectius

2246 Summary of Commission Decision of 29 March 2006 relating to a proceeding under Article 82 of the Treaty establishing the European Community and Article 54 of the EEA Agreement against Tomra Systems ASA, Tomra Europe AS, Tomra Systems BV, Tomra Systems GmbH, Tomra Butikksystemer AS, Tomra Systems AB and Tomra Leergutsysteme GmbH (Case COMP/E-1/38.113 — *Prokent/Tomra*) [2008] OJ C 219/11, para. 89. See also where this argument was not appealed by Tomra: Judgment of 19 April 2012 in *Tomra and Others v Commission*, C-549/10 P, EU:C:2012:221; Judgment of 9 September 2010, *Tomra Systems and Others v Commission*, T-155/06, ECR, EU:T:2010:370. For some literature regarding the free rider problem see in an antitrust perspective, *inter alia*: Richard A. Posner, 'The Chicago School of Antitrust Analysis' 127 University of Pennsylvania Law Review (1979) 925, p. 927-931; Sanford J. Grossman and Oliver D. Hart, 'Takeover Bids, The Free-Rider Problem, and the Theory of the Corporation' 11 The Bell Journal of Economics (1980) 42; Victor P Goldberg, 'Free Rider Problem Imperfect Pricing and the Economics of Retailing Services' 79 Northwestern University Law Review (1984-1985) 736; Z Neeman, 'The Freedom to Contract and the Free-Rider Problem' 15 Journal of Law, Economics, and Organization (1999) 685; Niels, Jenkins and Kavanagh, [2011], p. 315-318.

2247 Commission Decision of 31 January 2001 declaring a concentration to be incompatible with the common market and the functioning of the EEA Agreement (Case COMP/M.2097 *SCA/Metsä Tissue*) [2001] OJ L 57/1, para. 87.

2248 Commission Decision of 11 September 1997 declaring a concentration to be compatible with the common market and the functioning of the EEA Agreement (Case No IV/M.833 - *The Coca-Cola Company/ Carlsberg A/S*) [1998] OJ L 145/41, para. 81.

insufficient] countervailing buyer power exists"[2249], it was confirmed that "in the overall market for CSDs, TCCC's market share, the strength of its brand, the barriers to entry for competitors and *the lack of countervailing buyer power*, lead the Commission to conclude that TCCC is dominant on the CSD market at the brand level"[2250], the concentration was compatible with the internal market following some commitments that included divestitures of the undertakings.

1143. Furthermore, in *JCI/FIAMM* the Commission found that the *internal purchasing organization* of an undertaking and internal managerial interest may limit the effective exercise of CBP. The assessment found that buyers were not able to leverage their buyer power into other goods to affect the terms and conditions concerning starter batteries[2251]. This inability to affect the purchasing price was because buyers employed separate purchasing internal units for batteries and other automotive components, and diluted their buyer power by not acquiring goods from the same supplier as a whole, even if the separation was due to the specificity of the goods to be acquired. Also, the purchasing structure and the behaviour of the managers had an impact as these would not purchase aggressively or to reduce the profitability of its section to increase the overall turnover of the undertaking[2252]. While on occasion separation of purchases within the same entity would be required and justified, the argument that managers decide not to exercise buyer power because their own division will suffer at the expense of overall profit is much weaker as it represents a problem of internal coordination and, arguably, bad management which is difficult to accept as a valid argument for the lack of exercise of CBP. However, it is still a fact that NCAs should also consider in their assessment, for the sake of thoroughness, particularly if it is proven and in dominance cases as opposed to mergers.

1144. In *GE/Instrumentarium,* the Commission found that CBP (and buyer power) may be limited by the fact that a *public buyer ought to comply with tender rules when entering into public contracts under the scope of public procurement rules*. A public buyer (or buyers) may see its (or their) ability to exercise CBP diminished for four reasons. Firstly, price may not be the most relevant factor when employing the most economically advantageous offer award cri-

2249 Commission Decision of 11 September 1997 declaring a concentration to be compatible with the common market and the functioning of the EEA Agreement (Case No IV/M.833 - *The Coca-Cola Company/Carlsberg A/S*) [1998] OJ L 145/41, para. 81.

2250 Commission Decision of 11 September 1997 declaring a concentration to be compatible with the common market and the functioning of the EEA Agreement (Case No IV/M.833 - *The Coca-Cola Company/Carlsberg A/S*) [1998] OJ L 145/41, para. 82 (emphasis added).

2251 Summary of Commission Decision of 10 May 2007 declaring a concentration compatible with the common market and the functioning of the EEA Agreement (Case COMP/M.4381 — *JCI/FIAMM*) [2009] OJ C 241/12, taken from the unabridged version, para. 407-413.

2252 Summary of Commission Decision of 10 May 2007 declaring a concentration compatible with the common market and the functioning of the EEA Agreement (Case COMP/M.4381 — *JCI/FIAMM*) [2009] OJ C 241/12, taken from the unabridged version, para. 412.

teria[2253]. Secondly, the Commission's investigation revealed that only large suppliers were generally able to meet the technical requirements set by hospitals when purchasing equipment, thus limiting demand switching. Thirdly, the inherent nature of public tenders hinders buyers from exercising CBP as "once tenders are organised in order to meet the hospitals' needs, the actual purchase cannot realistically be delayed for a substantial period of time"[2254]. Fourthly buyer's demand was highly fragmented as the Commission considers each tender as an individual market (unless aggregated procurement techniques are employed)[2255].

1145. Also in connection with the ability of public buyers to exert CBP, in *AstraZeneca v Commission* the CJEU confirmed that even a "monopsonist" public buyer may on occasion not be able to sufficiently exercise CBP with regard to medicinal products issued on prescription due to the *innovative character of the good*[2256], mainly because these new drugs have an inelastic demand, as also remarked by Advocate General Mázak[2257]. Thus, despite the buyer's size and its condition of sole buyer in Germany, AstraZeneca was able "to obtain from the public authorities a higher price as against existing products and 'metoo' products"[2258]. Additionally, both the CJEU and the General Court confirmed that CBP exertion was hindered due to the structure of the tenders and the public financing. In the judgment, the CJEU reaffirmed that a buyer might not be able to exercise sufficient CBP if its *purchasing schemes restrict it from doing so*. This was the case because, besides demand being inelastic, end consumers do not pay the full amount of the value of the good as it is financed by the national social security systems[2259]. Therefore, end consumers will be less incentivized to obtain a lower price or a different product and instead obtain the better or more innovative goods. As end consumers were not price sensitive, this reduced the constraint of the buyer on the powerful seller. This argument by the CJEU and General Court is also consistent with my own research with regards to exercise of public buyer power under

---

2253 Commission Decision of 2 September 2003 declaring a concentration to be compatible with the common market and the functioning of the EEA Agreement (Case COMP/M.3083 — *GE/Instrumentarium*) [2004] OJ L 109/1, para. 206 and 120. In my view, this is partially correct and the outcome depends directly on the weightings attributed to each award criterion where the good's price can be the most important factor.

2254 Commission Decision of 2 September 2003 declaring a concentration to be compatible with the common market and the functioning of the EEA Agreement (Case COMP/M.3083 — *GE/Instrumentarium*) [2004] OJ L 109/1, para. 208.

2255 For a discussion on aggregated procurement strategies see: Sánchez Graells and Herrera Anchustegui, 'Impact of Public Procurement Aggregation on Competition. Risks, Rationale and Justification for the Rules in Directive 2014/24' [2016].

2256 Judgment of 6 December 2012 in *AstraZeneca v Commission*, C-457/10 P, EU:C:2012:770, para. 170-182. See also: Judgment of 1 July 2010, *AstraZeneca v Commission*, T-321/05, ECR, EU:T:2010:266, para. 255-269.

2257 Opinion of Advocate General Mázak in Judgment of 6 December 2012 in *AstraZeneca v Commission*, C-457/10 P, EU:C:2012:293, para. 124.

2258 Judgment of 1 July 2010, *AstraZeneca v Commission*, T-321/05, ECR, EU:T:2010:266, para. 179, and paras. 256-260.

2259 Judgment of 6 December 2012 in *AstraZeneca v Commission*, C-457/10 P, EU:C:2012:770, para. 180.

the scope of public procurement laws[2260]. Public buyers do not set purchasing prices as a normal undertaking would do, as their demand is derived by end consumers in most cases and constrained by the application of public procurement rules and public market particularities, as confirmed by the General Court in *AstraZeneca v Commission*[2261].

1146. Lastly, in *Slovak Telekom,* a case discussing margin squeeze practices contrary to Article 102 TFEU, the Commission remarked that end consumers, despite there being many of them, are unable to exercise any appreciable countervailing buyer power against a dominant undertaking as "[e]ach individual customer in the retail mass-market for broadband services represents only a insignificant share of the total sales"[2262] The same occurs, for example, in food retailing markets where end consumers – individually – are unable to exercise any countervailing buyer power because their purchasing power is atomized and, therefore, unless it is pooled, it is not sufficient. Also, in *Slovak Telekom* it was considered a hindrance for the exercise of CBP that the dominant undertaking that claimed its existence was vertically integrated and enjoyed a dominant position in the downstream market that prevented its competitors from "exercis[ing] sufficient pressure or influence on STæs decisions in the wholesale market for access to ULL"[2263].

2260 Herrera Anchustegui 'Centralizing Public Procurement and Competitiveness in Directive 2014/24' (2015); Sánchez Graells and Herrera Anchustegui, 'Impact of Public Procurement Aggregation on Competition. Risks, Rationale and Justification for the Rules in Directive 2014/24' [2016].

2261 "The Court observes however that, since prices are influenced by decisions of public authorities as regards reimbursement levels or maximum prices, *those prices are not the result of normal market forces*. It is not therefore possible to argue that the level of a price set in such a context is competitive, since it has been set in the absence of competitive mechanisms for ascertaining where such a competitive level lies", Judgment of 1 July 2010, *AstraZeneca v Commission*, T-321/05, ECR, EU:T:2010:266, para. 265 (emphasis added).

2262 Summary of Commission Decision of 15 October 2014 relating to a proceeding under Article 102 of the Treaty on the Functioning of the European Union and Article 54 of the EEA Agreement (Case AT.39523 — *Slovak Telekom*) [2015] OJ C 314/7, taken from the unabridged version, para. 336.

2263 Summary of Commission Decision of 15 October 2014 relating to a proceeding under Article 102 of the Treaty on the Functioning of the European Union and Article 54 of the EEA Agreement (Case AT.39523 — *Slovak Telekom*) [2015] OJ C 314/7, taken from the unabridged version, para. 291.

VI. Countervailing buyer power as a defense and its success

1147. CBP is an extraordinary circumstance that represents an "effective constraint on any exercise of market power"[2264], preventing a seller from behaving independently from its buyers[2265], in particular by deterring or defeating an attempt to profitably increase prices[2266], and neutralizing seller market power in any type of competition case. Traditionally, but not exclusively, as shown in this chapter, the Commission's practice and the EU case law have dealt with it in the sphere of dominance[2267] and concentration[2268] instances. Therefore, CBP is a defensive[2269] argument used by selling undertakings to mitigate their own seller market power and challenge the anti-competitive claims against their conduct. Also, CBP not only protects buyers, but ultimately end consumers, reinforcing the dualistic effect of buyer power in both the upstream and downstream markets[2270].

1148. Concerning dominance cases, CBP plays a role as *an extraordinary circumstance precluding dominance* in accordance with *Hoffmann-La Roche v Commission*[2271]. Thus, the selling undertaking invoking the existence of one or more buyers with sufficient CBP claims that is no longer dominant because it is not able to behave independently with regard to them. Despite being invoked on several occasions, the CBP defense has never been successful as a factor precluding dominance under Article 102 TFEU cases because neither the Commission nor the Courts have found it to sufficiently exist. These have been the Judgments related to *Irish Sugar v Commission*[2272];

2264 Judgment of 25 June 2010, *Imperial Chemical Industries v Commission*, T-66/01, ECR, EU:T:2010:255, para. 247. Also considering CBP as a defense in Swedish national see: Henriksson, *Swedish National Report: The Grocery Retail Market in Sweden: Is Antitrust Efficiently Handling this Market?* (2013), p. 14.

2265 Judgment of 28 June 2004, *Airtours v Commission*, T-342/99, ECR, EU:T:2002:146, para. 208.

2266 Communication from the Commission — Guidance on the Commission's enforcement priorities in applying Article 82 of the EC Treaty to abusive exclusionary conduct by dominant undertakings [2009] OJ C 45/7, para. 18. See also Guidelines on Vertical Restraints [2010] OJ C 130/1, para. 116. From a comparative perspective, see: Facey and Brown, [2013], p. 244.

2267 Communication from the Commission — Guidance on the Commission's enforcement priorities in applying Article 82 of the EC Treaty to abusive exclusionary conduct by dominant undertakings [2009] OJ C 45/7, para. 12 and 18.

2268 Guidelines on the assessment of horizontal mergers under the Council Regulation on the control of concentrations between undertakings [2004] OJ C 31/5, para. 64-67.

2269 For a discussion on the use of the term "defense" concerning efficiencies in abuse of dominance cases see: Gormsen, [2010], p. 54-57.

2270 Summary of Commission Decision of 17 December 2008 declaring a concentration compatible with the common market and the functioning of the EEA Agreement (Case COMP/M.5046 — *Friesland Foods/Campina*) [2009] OJ C 75/21, taken from the unabridged version, para. 274. See also: Ezrachi [2014], p. 438.

2271 Judgment of 13 February 1979 in *Hoffmann-La Roche v Commission*, C-85/76, EU:C:1979:36, para. 41.

2272 Commission Decision of 14 May 1997 relating to a proceeding pursuant to Article 86 of the EC Treaty (IV/34.621, 35.059/F-3 - *Irish Sugar plc*) [1997] OJ L 258/1, confirmed by the General Court in Judgment of 7 October 1999, *Irish Sugar v Commission*, T-228/97, ECR, EU:T:1999:246.

Imperial Chemical Industries v Commission[2273]; and *Tomra and Others v Commission*[2274]. Similarly, in the Commission's practice no dominant seller has sufficiently demonstrated that its position was neutralized by CBP itself or conjunction with other circumstances. What has occurred in these cases is that there is a degree of buyer market power enjoyed by some buyers that is *insufficient* to neutralize the dominance, therefore, not existing CBP as such.

1149. Contrastingly, CBP has been a more relevant argument in terms of offsetting the adverse effects of a proposed concentration and thus declaring its compatibility with the internal market. This was the state of affairs in the landmark case *Enso/Stora,* whereby CBP constituted the main reason to determine the compatibility of the merger due to the existence of a mirror structure in the buying and selling side and mutual dependence between buyers and sellers, as I discuss below[2275]. However, most often CBP has played a minor role, albeit occasionally being significant, in contributing in the outcome of a case as a "deal maker"[2276]. In fact, CBP has been invoked many times by the parties but has been considered an insufficient constraint for the clearance of the concentration.

1150. Regarding Article 101 TFEU cases, my research shows that there has been no case in which CBP has been relevantly invoked either by a group of buyers or a group of sellers to neutralize the negative effects of a selling-side coordinated agreement. In *Car Glass*, a cartel that accounted for an object restriction of competition in the supply of car glass, the defendants claimed that the stability and implementation of the cartel was limited due to the countervailing power of its customers[2277]. Both the Commission and the General Court accepted the the-

2273 Commission Decision of 19 December 1990 relating to a proceeding under Article 85 of the EEC Treaty (IV/33.133-A: *Soda-ash - Solvay, ICI*) [1991] OJ L 152/1, confirmed by the General Court in Judgment of 25 June 2010, *Imperial Chemical Industries v Commission*, T-66/01, ECR, EU:T:2010:255.

2274 Summary of Commission Decision of 29 March 2006 relating to a proceeding under Article 82 of the Treaty establishing the European Community and Article 54 of the EEA Agreement against Tomra Systems ASA, Tomra Europe AS, Tomra Systems BV, Tomra Systems GmbH, Tomra Butikksystemer AS, Tomra Systems AB and Tomra Leergutsysteme GmbH (Case COMP/E-1/38.113 — *Prokent/Tomra*) [2008] OJ C 219/11; confirmed by both the General Court and the CJEU in Judgment of 9 September 2010, *Tomra Systems and Others v Commission*, T-155/06, ECR, EU:T:2010:370; and Judgment of 19 April 2012 in *Tomra and Others v Commission*, C-549/10 P, EU:C:2012:221, respectively.

2275 Commission Decision of 25 November 1998 declaring a concentration to be compatible with the common market and the functioning of the EEA Agreement (Case No IV/M.1225 - *Enso/Stora*) [1999] OJ L 254/9.

2276 Commission Decision of 22 July 1992 relating to a proceeding under Council Regulation (EEC) No 4064/89 (Case No IV/M.190 - *Nestlé/Perrier*) [1992] OJ L 356/1; Commission Decision of 14 May 1997 relating to a proceeding pursuant to Article 86 of the EC Treaty (IV/34.621, 35.059/F-3 - *Irish Sugar plc*) [1997] OJ L 258/1; Summary of Commission Decision of 29 March 2006 relating to a proceeding under Article 82 of the Treaty establishing the European Community and Article 54 of the EEA Agreement against Tomra Systems ASA, Tomra Europe AS, Tomra Systems BV, Tomra Systems GmbH, Tomra Butikksystemer AS, Tomra Systems AB and Tomra Leergutsysteme GmbH (Case COMP/E-1/38.113 — *Prokent/Tomra*) [2008] OJ C 219/11, para. 11, summarized version; Commission Decision of Non-opposition to a notified concentration M.4057 — *Korsnäs/Assidomän Cartonboard* [2006] OJ C 209/12, taken from the unabridged public version; Commission Decision of 3 April 2001 declaring a concentration to be compatible with the common market and the functioning of the EEA Agreement (Case COMP/M.2139 — *Bombardier/ADtranz*) [2002] OJ L 69/50.

2277 Summary of Commission Decision of 12 November 2008 relating to a proceeding under Article 81 of the Treaty establishing the European Community and Article 53 of the EEA Agreement (Case COMP/39.125 — *Car glass*) [2009] OJ C 173/13, taken from the unabridged version, para. 677.

oretical argument that CBP could be used to neutralize the adverse effects of an agreement on competition but held that in an agreement that is anti-competitive by object (such as this one fixing selling conditions, establishing selling quotas and setting prices), the existence of some countervailing buyer power does not preclude the agreement from having at its aim to distort competition[2278]. This reasoning is sound, as the cartel has been created precisely to negate, as much as possible, the countervailing buyer power effects and, thus, increase profits of sellers. Hence, the aim was to eliminate any countervailing bargaining power in the market to exploit buyers and reap supracompetitive benefits.

1151. From a theoretical perspective, however, CBP may be used as an argument by a group of buyers to justify the existence of a buying alliance and, therefore, the competitiveness of a purchasing agreement as it outweighs the restrictive effects on competition[2279]. In accordance with Article 101(3) TFEU, this would be the case if the creation of CBP would be indispensable to the attainment of certain objectives and does not afford the undertakings possibility of substantially eliminating competition[2280]. However, countervailing *seller* power has proven to be an important factor when determining if a conduct satisfies the requirements of Article 101(3) TFEU, in particular regarding exclusivity supply agreements[2281].

1152. Lastly, I have identified two arguments to explain why CBP has very limited success as a defense in EU competition law. Most instances where CBP has been used as an efficiency defense were unsuccessful because at times the claims were weak and/or frivolous, particularly concerning dominance cases. In these circumstances the analysis is succinct and superficial because it is evident that CBP is not sufficiently present. The other reason that explains why CBP as an efficiency defense is unlikely to be successful has to do with the large threshold demanded to neutralize opposing seller power, which regarding concentrations is lower than in dominance cases and partially explains why CBP is a more likely useful defense in such type of cases.

2278 Judgment of 17 December 2014, *Pilkington Group and Others v Commission*, T-72/09, EU:T:2014:1094, paras. 287-289. Appealed and dismissed in its entirety as Judgment of 7 September 2016 in *Pilkington Group and Others v Commission*, C-101/15, EU:C:2016:631. Summary of Commission Decision of 12 November 2008 relating to a proceeding under Article 81 of the Treaty establishing the European Community and Article 53 of the EEA Agreement (Case COMP/39.125 — *Car glass*) [2009] OJ C 173/13, taken from the unabridged version, para. 694.

2279 Communication from the Commission — Guidelines on the applicability of Article 101 of the Treaty on the Functioning of the European Union to horizontal co-operation agreements [2011] OJ C 11/1, para. 20.

2280 Judgment of 18 September 2001, *M6 and Others v Commission*, T-112/99, ECR, EU:T:2001:215, para. 74.

2281 Commission Decision of 16 June 1999 relating to a proceeding pursuant to Article 81 of the EC Treaty (Case IV/36.081/F3 — *Bass*) [1999] OJ L 186/1, subject of an annulment action before the General Court and decided as Judgment of 21 March 2002, *Joynson v Commission*, T-231/99, ECR, EU:T:2002:84.

VII. Assessment of countervailing buyer power: 'the comparison test'

A. Introduction and thresholds required for its sufficiency

1153. Once the origin and the type of case at hand have been assessed, the Courts, the Commission and NCAs have to determine whether CBP is sufficient to neutralize opposing seller market power. To do so, the case law, the Commission's practice and its guidelines have suggested employing a 'comparison test'[2282] that determines if the degree of CBP can offset the market power on the selling side. In other words, the test determines if CBP is sufficient to preclude an undertaking from being dominant, the agreement having an anti-competitive effect, or significantly impeding effective competition regarding a concentration operation[2283]. Therefore, CBP has to reach certain thresholds depending on the type of case, and its sufficiency is carried out through the 'comparison test', as I discuss in this section.

1154. In the *case of dominance*, CBP must be sufficiently large to be considered an exceptional circumstance that may preclude the existence of dominance, as stated in *Hoffmann-La Roche v Commission*[2284] and ratified in *AKZO v Commission*[2285]. To be sufficiently large to qualify as an exceptional circumstance it must neutralize the ability of a seller to exert market power vis-à-vis its buyers, whereupon it may "constitute a significant counterweight to the contractual power of large [suppliers] and make way for more effective competition"[2286], as supported by the case law in *Irish Sugar v Commission*[2287], and *Gøttrup-Klim and Others Grovvareforeninger v Dansk Landbrugs Grovvareselskab*[2288]. Thus in dominance cases the sufficiency of CBP must reach a threshold in which it is found sufficient to *neutralize dominance*, and which it is a stern requirement.

1155. In the *case of concentrations*, CBP would be a sufficient exceptional circumstance whenever it is capable of precluding a merged undertaking from *significantly impeding effective competition as a result of the creation or strengthening*

2282 Term coined by the author.

2283 As stated by the Commission: "[...] in an assessment of dominance the question is whether there is sufficient CBP to neutralize the market power of the parties"; Commission Decision of 11 September 1997 declaring a concentration to be compatible with the common market and the functioning of the EEA Agreement (Case No IV/M.833 - *The Coca-Cola Company/Carlsberg A/S*) [1998] OJ L 145/41, para. 81.

2284 Judgment of 13 February 1979 in *Hoffmann-La Roche v Commission*, C-85/76, EU:C:1979:36, para. 41

2285 Judgment of 3 July 1991 in *AKZO v Commission*, C-62/86, EU:C:1991:286, para. 60.

2286 Judgment of 15 December 1994 in *Gøttrup-Klim and Others Grovvareforeninger v Dansk Landbrugs Grovvareselskab*, C-250/92, EU:C:1994:413, para. 32.

2287 Judgment of 7 October 1999, *Irish Sugar v Commission*, T-228/97, ECR, EU:T:1999:246, paras 93-104.

2288 Judgment of 15 December 1994 in *Gøttrup-Klim and Others Grovvareforeninger v Dansk Landbrugs Grovvareselskab*, C-250/92, EU:C:1994:413, para. 32.

of a dominant position[2289]. The threshold, then, is no longer based on the creation or strengthening of a dominant position as it was under Article 2.(2) the Merger Control Regulation of 1989 and which would coincide with cases under Article 102 TFEU,[2290] but appears to be less demanding and lower. Therefore, if the CBP is capable of preventing the undertaking from significantly impeding effective competition, then the concentration may be considered compatible with the internal market, in accordance to Article 2(2) of the Merger Control Regulation[2291].

1156. Also, as confirmed by the General Court in *Airtours v Commission,* CBP is a competitive constraint that ought to be taken into account as being capable of "counteracting the creation of a collective dominant position"[2292]. In these cases of collective dominance arising from a merger the threshold required seems to be less than under unilateral merger standard. Upon interpreting the case law, and in particular *Airtours v Commission,* I conclude that CBP may be sufficient to prevent a collective dominant position post-merger if it is capable of "counteracting the creation of a dominant position" by disturbing the coordination and which, in the case of an oligopoly, is sufficient to neutralize the joint market power as parties can no longer coordinate their behaviour as if they were a single entity[2293]. This would be whenever CBP is strong enough to create sufficient incentives to the suppliers to deviate from a coordinated conduct and fight off their competitor in the market to reap the profits.

1157. In the *case of agreements under the scope of Article 101 TFEU,* the CBP test ought to determine whether the effects of the agreement are pro-competitive due to the existence of opposing market power and, consequently, may satisfy the requirements of Article 101(3) TFEU, barring the application of Article 101(1) TFEU. In my view, this is the lowest threshold that must be reached by CBP, as it has to be sufficient enough to, among other factors, make the efficiencies of the agreement offset its anti-competitive effects. However, as discussed above, CBP would not eliminate the classification of an agreement as anti-competitive by object, and in such circumstances and the stringent requirements of Article 101(3) TFEU, it would be unlikely that the parties to it benefit from the existence of CBP.

1158. In the remainder of this section, I discuss how the comparison test has been applied and developed by analyzing the case law and the Commission's practice.

2289 Whish and Bailey, [2015], p. 906-907.

2290 "A concentration which does not create or strengthen a dominant position as a result of which effective competition would be significantly impeded in the common market or in a substantial part of it shall be declared compatible", Article 2(2) Council Regulation (EEC) 4064/89 on the control of concentrations between undertakings [1989] OJ L 395.

2291 Council Regulation (EC) No 139/2004 of 20 January 2004 on the control of concentrations between undertakings (the EC Merger Regulation) [2004] OJ L 24/1, Article 2.2.

2292 Judgment of 28 June 2004, *Airtours v Commission*, T-342/99, ECR, EU:T:2002:146, para. 277.

2293 Judgment of 28 June 2004, *Airtours v Commission*, T-342/99, ECR, EU:T:2002:146, para. 277.

B. The 'comparison test' and its evolution

1159. As discussed before, the comparison test is applied by the Courts and the Commission consistently across all areas of EU competition as the key lies in determining whether CBP can offset the potential *adverse effect in competition of the market power by the undertaking*(s) under investigation[2294]. What varies across the areas is the threshold required for its sufficiency, while the nature of the assessment remains the same. To determine this, the comparison test *contrasts several sources or indicators of the existence and the degree of CBP vis-à-vis the market power of the undertaking* that claims the existence of this competitive constraint[2295].

1160. In the initial development of the state, both the Commission and the Courts conducted a straightforward and simplified comparison of the market shares, concentration and structure of the undertakings under investigation, as occurred in *Nestlé/Perrier*[2296], *The Coca-Cola Company/Carlsberg A/S*[2297], and *Irish Sugar v Commission*[2298]. The test, nevertheless, has evolved to become a more in-depth analysis of the competitive constraints imposed on a supplier by its buyer(s) *beyond symmetry*. This evolution and departure from a comparison of market shares or market concentration is a welcomed development because the previous practice overlooked the dynamics of buyer power, the fact that, in certain circumstances, CBP can be exercised sufficiently even by small buyers, and that bargaining power can effectively be exerted under lower market share and concentration thresholds than seller market power comparatively[2299]. However, practice shows that the thoroughness of the analysis depends on case circumstances and both the Commission and the Courts are ready to dismiss without further elaboration in cases which after a preliminary market share comparison the degree of asymmetry is large between the involved undertakings' market shares. In the following, I discuss the evolution of the test in the case law and the Commission's practice.

1161. In *Nestlé/Perrier*, the first occasion where the comparison test was applied, the Commission found that the ten largest customers of Nestlé represented

---

2294 Guidelines on the assessment of horizontal mergers under the Council Regulation on the control of concentrations between undertakings [2004] OJ C 31/5, para. 67. Cf with the view of Van Bael and Bellis who claim that buyers are deemed to have enough countervailing power when its market share is greater than that of the supplier and/or there exist low barriers or consequences to the changing of a supplier, Van Bael and Bellis, [2005], p. 809.

2295 For a different perspective on the assessment of CBP (and arguably it sources) see O'Donoghue and Padilla, [2013], p. 167-169.

2296 Commission Decision of 22 July 1992 relating to a proceeding under Council Regulation (EEC) No 4064/89 (Case No IV/M.190 - *Nestlé/Perrier*) [1992] OJ L 356/1.

2297 Commission Decision of 11 September 1997 declaring a concentration to be compatible with the common market and the functioning of the EEA Agreement (Case No IV/M.833 - *The Coca-Cola Company/Carlsberg A/S*) [1998] OJ L 145/41, para. 81.

2298 Commission Decision of 14 May 1997 relating to a proceeding pursuant to Article 86 of the EC Treaty (IV/34.621, 35.059/F-3 - *Irish Sugar plc*) [1997] OJ L 258/1, para. 106 to 113.

2299 Bishop and Walker, [2010], para. 7-048.

63.7% of its turnover, granting them certain buyer power[2300]. However, it also remarked that:

> concentration of these buyers is much less important than the concentration of the supply side [...]. While 82% by value and 75% by volume (for still mineral waters over 90 %) of the supply side would be in the hands of only two suppliers which can easily engage in anticompetitive parallel behaviour [...], the demand side is composed of a much greater number of independent companies, none of which exceeds 15% of the total water turnover of all three /two suppliers[2301].

1162. After conducting a comparison of the market share and market concentration ratios, the Commission concluded that the demand side "is composed of a number of buyers which are not equally strong and which cannot be aggregated to conclude that they may constrain the market power of the three, and after the merger, only two national suppliers"[2302].

1163. An analysis of the criteria used by the Commission reveals that the CBP analysis was rather simplistic and perhaps too strict, as the Commission could have gone a step further and discussed whether, even though the demand side was smaller, its buyer power could have been deterrent enough to prevent post-merger coordination between the new entity and the other national supplier in the event of concerns of possible collective dominance. In such circumstances, and as stated above, it is likely that the threshold demanded for CBP to be sufficiently neutralizing would have been lower, as the requirement would have been to sufficiently disturb coordination by creating incentives to detach from the coordinated behaviour.

1164. Later, in *Irish Sugar v Commission,* the comparison test was carried out by the Commission and the General Court to dismiss the allegation made by Irish Sugar that its buyers were in a position to preclude it from behaving independently as a seller of processed sugar. The Commission's assessment was based also on comparing the concentration of buyers to the concentration on the supply side[2303]. It was concluded that:

> [...] despite the presence of two large customers, the demand side is composed of a number of buyers which are not equally

2300 Commission Decision of 22 July 1992 relating to a proceeding under Council Regulation (EEC) No 4064/89 (Case No IV/M.190 - *Nestlé/Perrier*) [1992] OJ L 356/1, paras. 77 to 78.

2301 Commission Decision of 22 July 1992 relating to a proceeding under Council Regulation (EEC) No 4064/89 (Case No IV/M.190 - *Nestlé/Perrier*) [1992] OJ L 356/1, para. 78.

2302 Commission Decision of 22 July 1992 relating to a proceeding under Council Regulation (EEC) No 4064/89 (Case No IV/M.190 - *Nestlé/Perrier*) [1992] OJ L 356/1, para. 78.

2303 Commission Decision of 14 May 1997 relating to a proceeding pursuant to Article 86 of the EC Treaty (IV/34.621, 35.059/F-3 - *Irish Sugar plc*) [1997] OJ L 258/1, para. 108.

strong and which cannot be aggregated to conclude that they may constrain the market power of the supplier with over 90% of the market. The share of sales of the two largest customers does not counterbalance the dominant position of Irish Sugar[2304].

1165. Therefore, the test in *Irish Sugar v Commission* resembled the previous experience in *Nestlé/Perrier* without going any further than the comparison of market shares.

1166. Additionally, in *The Coca-Cola Company/Carlsberg A/S,* the Commission held that CBP did not exist because "the concentration ratio on the supply-side is much higher than on the buyer side", along with the fact that the suppliers had 'must-stock brands' that the buyer would not have been able to obtain elsewhere. These two factors lead to the conclusion that even if buyers were large, they had insufficient CBP[2305]. Consequently, the symmetry analysis was accompanied by further discussion of CBP buyer sources and hindrances, as I discussed in chapter 9, section §V.

1167. Furthermore, in *Enso/Stora,* a landmark Commission's decision where CBP was the *main factor* in order to declare the compatibility of the concentration[2306], *the comparison test was further developed and thoroughly applied*, as also noted by Baker and Lofaro[2307]. Following the precedent of *Nestlé/Perrier,* the Commission once again used the comparison test to determine the sufficiency of CBP to neutralize the possible anti-competitive effects of a merger between two cardboard producers in *Enso/Stora*[2308].

1168. In *Enso/Stora,* the Commission first performed a comparison of the market shares, concentration and market structure of the involved merging suppliers and the customers. In so doing, it concluded that, due to *the unique symmetrical market circumstances,* the involved parties were in a situation of economic *mutual dependence* that kept in check the market behaviour of both buyers and sellers[2309]. The merging parties, Enso and Stora, were engaged in the production of different types of paper and cardboard, in particular liquid packaging board (LPB). In the LPB market both parties enjoyed a combined

2304 Commission Decision of 14 May 1997 relating to a proceeding pursuant to Article 86 of the EC Treaty (IV/34.621, 35.059/F-3 - *Irish Sugar plc*) [1997] OJ L 258/1, para. 108.

2305 Commission Decision of 11 September 1997 declaring a concentration to be compatible with the common market and the functioning of the EEA Agreement (Case No IV/M.833 - *The Coca-Cola Company/ Carlsberg A/S*) [1998] OJ L 145/41, para. 81.

2306 Faull and Nikpay, [1999], para. 4.151; Ezrachi and Ioannidou (2014), p. 86.

2307 Arguing that the *Enso/Stora* decision was a step forward from the mere comparison of concentration/ thresholds, see: Baker and Lofaro (2000), p. 189-190.

2308 Commission Decision of 25 November 1998 declaring a concentration to be compatible with the common market and the functioning of the EEA Agreement (Case No IV/M.1225 - *Enso/Stora*) [1999] OJ L 254/9.

2309 Commission Decision of 25 November 1998 declaring a concentration to be compatible with the common market and the functioning of the EEA Agreement (Case No IV/M.1225 - *Enso/Stora*) [1999] OJ L 254/9, para. 86. See also stressing the symmetry element: Ezrachi and Ioannidou (2014), p. 86.

market share of between 50% and 70%, with two smaller rivals, Korsnäs and AssiDomän, with individual market shares of 10% to 20%[2310]. Under the applicable regime at the time, a concentration between Enso and Stora would have prima facie created a dominant position, as the merged entity would have a market share that has been traditionally found sufficient to create a situation of dominance[2311]. However, regarding CBP, the buying market for LPB also had few buyers and was dominated by a single large buying undertaking, Tetra Pak, which enjoyed a market share of 60% to 80% of market demand, and two smaller buyers Elopak and SIG Combibloc, with about 10% and 20% market share each[2312]. In concentration terms, this implies that the supplier side had a HHI minimum of 3,000 and maximum of 5,125, whereas the demand side had a HHI minimum of 3,800 and maximum of 6,800, not identical but rather similar.

1169. By comparing the market structures, concentrations and shares, the Commission reached the conclusion that:

> after the merger the structure of the supply-side *will mirror* the structure of the demand-side of the market for liquid packaging board, with one large supplier and two smaller suppliers facing one large buyer and two smaller buyers[2313].

1170. Additionally, the assessment analyzed the *supply-demand relationship between the parties,* taking into account the *commercial significance of the buyer to the seller*, and concluded that the parties were mutually dependent because contracts in the LPB market are of long duration and suppliers and buyers reach agreements to suit their specific product needs, which requires investment from the supplier to specialize its production. The Commission also evaluated the ratio of sales a buyer represents for a supplier[2314], the fact that if Tetra Pak were to shift demand, the merged entity would not be able to find other suitable buyers to fill the now spare capacity in the short term[2315], as well as the capacity of Tetra Pak to sponsor entry or financially support other LPB suppliers. Lastly, in the compari-

---

2310 Commission Decision of 25 November 1998 declaring a concentration to be compatible with the common market and the functioning of the EEA Agreement (Case No IV/M.1225 - *Enso/Stora*) [1999] OJ L 254/9, para. 74.

2311 Judgment of 3 July 1991 in *AKZO v Commission*, C-62/86, EU:C:1991:286, para. 60

2312 Commission Decision of 25 November 1998 declaring a concentration to be compatible with the common market and the functioning of the EEA Agreement (Case No IV/M.1225 - *Enso/Stora*) [1999] OJ L 254/9, para. 84.

2313 Commission Decision of 25 November 1998 declaring a concentration to be compatible with the common market and the functioning of the EEA Agreement (Case No IV/M.1225 - *Enso/Stora*) [1999] OJ L 254/9, para. 84 (emphasis added).

2314 Commission Decision of 25 November 1998 declaring a concentration to be compatible with the common market and the functioning of the EEA Agreement (Case No IV/M.1225 - *Enso/Stora*) [1999] OJ L 254/9, para. 90.

2315 Commission Decision of 25 November 1998 declaring a concentration to be compatible with the common market and the functioning of the EEA Agreement (Case No IV/M.1225 - *Enso/Stora*) [1999] OJ L 254/9, para. 90.

son test, the ability of Tetra Pak to *resort to alternative suppliers or sponsor entry* if needed, along with its raw buyer power, was deemed sufficient to neutralize the risks of the creation or strengthening of a dominant position pursuant to the merger and, therefore, declaring the merger compatible with the market[2316].

1171. Closely linked to the *Enso/Stora* Decision, the Commission once again reviewed a *symmetrical market situation* in *Korsnäs/AD Cartonboard,* which involved the same market and participants, declaring the concentration compatible with the market. Also, and as noted by Karlsson, in *Korsnäs/AD Cartonboard* the Commission further developed the comparison test by factoring in market shares, market concentration, sale ratios, and dependency as I discuss below[2317]. Korsnäs and AD Cartoboard were undertakings involved in the production of LPB, competing directly with the now merged StoraEnso. The merging parties accounted for ca. 40% of the total supply of the EEA market, with StoraEnso enjoying a market share of 50-60%, as the other supplier. Despite the fact that this concentration would eliminate one independent source of supply it was *declared compatible due to the CBP exercised by Tetra Pak.* As a buyer, Tetra Pak enjoyed a market share of 40-60% of all purchases of LPB in the EEA, representing 80 to 100% of the LPB sales of both merging parties[2318]. Furthermore, Tetra Pak adopted a multi-supplier strategy as it acquired goods from three suppliers: 20-40% from AD Cartonboard and 10-30% from Korsnäs as merging parties, and the remaining 40-60% from Stora/Enso. Based on these figures, the Commission concluded that "there is no doubt that Tetra Pak enjoys a *significant degree of countervailing buyer power* with respect to all LPB suppliers [including the merged entity and StoraEnso], as suppliers are heavily *dependent* upon Tetra Pak for a *large share of their respective sales* and profitability in relation to their LPB activities"[2319]. Furthermore, Tetra Pak was deemed to be less dependent on its suppliers and able to exert sufficient CBP because, even after the merger, it would be capable of securing competitive LPB supplies by playing them off each other by having multi-supply sources and also avoiding the establishment of a collective dominance by the LPB suppliers. Lastly, the Commission also evaluated the possibility of the merger leading to a situation analogous to a bilateral monopoly in which buyers and sellers could coordinate their behaviour. However, the assessment concluded that it was not possible to coordinate vertically due to the incentives created by CBP, which would make all participants play each other off[2320].

2316 Faull, Nikpay and Taylor, [2014], para. 5.889.

2317 Karlsson (2006).

2318 Commission Decision of Non-opposition to a notified concentration M.4057 — *Korsnäs/Assidomän Cartonboard* [2006] OJ C 209/12, taken from the unabridged public version para. 44.

2319 Commission Decision of Non-opposition to a notified concentration M.4057 — *Korsnäs/Assidomän Cartonboard* [2006] OJ C 209/12, taken from the unabridged public version, para. 46 (emphasis added).

2320 Commission Decision of Non-opposition to a notified concentration M.4057 — *Korsnäs/Assidomän Cartonboard* [2006] OJ C 209/12, unabridged public version, para. 66 to 81. I briefly discussed bilateral monopoly and indicated relevant literature in chapter 2, section §III and footnote 74.

1172. Both *Enso/Stora* and *Korsnäs/AD Cartonboard* represent a successful finding of CBP to neutralize the negative effects of a merger and are a step forward in the application of the comparison test due to the thoroughness of the analysis and its sophistication. At the same time, this level of refinement can be explained because the *prima facie* observations – symmetry in market shares – was successfully achieved, unlike in the precedent of *Nestlé/Perrier.* This also can be understood as saying that a fully-fledged comparison test would be made when there are strong *prima facie* indications of the existence of some degree of CBP. Nevertheless, it is important to remark that this preliminary assessment should not solely rest on an evaluation of symmetry, but has to consider all relevant CBP sources as a whole, as leaving the application of a thorough test upon symmetry disregards the economics of CBP. Hence, in my criterion the preliminary assessment should not be restrictive and, in fact, in case of doubt of even the possible existence of to a reasonable degree, regarding CBP, a fully-fledged analysis ought to be undertaken to safeguard the procedural and substantive rights of the undertaking involved, regardless of the expenditure of human and economic resources by the NCAs and Courts.

1173. Later, in *Tomra and Others v Commission,* the General Court and the CJEU ratified a Commission Decision that found that Tomra had breached Article 102 TFEU, due to the grant of exclusionary rebates that prevented market entry of competitors, kept them small by limiting their growing possibilities, and eliminated them by means of acquisition[2321]. Tomra alleged the existence of CBP to neutralize its dominance and the Commission, making a *prima facie* assessment, found that "a comparison of the demand and the supply structure in the individual countries does not suggest that customers are able to outweigh Tomra's strong position on the supply side"[2322]. Even in markets that were highly concentrated, for example in the Nordic countries, the shares of the largest retailer where comparatively much smaller than they were in the Tomra situation. This very large difference between the sellers and the buyer helps when it comes to determining that there was no possibility of credible CBP as, additionally, there were no credible supply alternatives and the buyers had no incentive to sponsor new entrants, as the business of reverse vending machines was an ancillary activity for food retailers[2323].

2321 Summary of Commission Decision of 29 March 2006 relating to a proceeding under Article 82 of the Treaty establishing the European Community and Article 54 of the EEA Agreement against Tomra Systems ASA, Tomra Europe AS, Tomra Systems BV, Tomra Systems GmbH, Tomra Butikksystemer AS, Tomra Systems AB and Tomra Leergutsysteme GmbH (Case COMP/E-1/38.113 — *Prokent/Tomra*) [2008] OJ C 219/11, para. 11, summarized version.

2322 Summary of Commission Decision of 29 March 2006 relating to a proceeding under Article 82 of the Treaty establishing the European Community and Article 54 of the EEA Agreement against Tomra Systems ASA, Tomra Europe AS, Tomra Systems BV, Tomra Systems GmbH, Tomra Butikksystemer AS, Tomra Systems AB and Tomra Leergutsysteme GmbH (Case COMP/E-1/38.113 — *Prokent/Tomra*) [2008] OJ C 219/11, taken from the unabridged version, para. 88.

2323 Summary of Commission Decision of 29 March 2006 relating to a proceeding under Article 82 of the Treaty establishing the European Community and Article 54 of the EEA Agreement against Tomra Systems ASA, Tomra Europe AS, Tomra Systems BV, Tomra Systems GmbH, Tomra Butikksystemer AS, Tomra Systems AB and Tomra Leergutsysteme GmbH (Case COMP/E-1/38.113 — *Prokent/Tomra*) [2008] OJ C 219/11, taken from the unabridged version, para. 89.

1174. One final and important aspect of the comparison test is the issue of the efficacy of CBP from a *temporary perspective and the overall market conditions*. In my view, in the assessment of CBP it has to be taken into account that the neutralization of the seller market power has to go beyond the short-term basis and extend into at least the medium term[2324]. This is the case according to the Commission's practice, at least regarding mergers, when it has been explicitly stated that the CBP assessment must be made "in the context of the post-merger market structure"[2325]. This policy choice of requiring CBP to be effective in the medium and long run with regard to the purchasing competition conditions has two implications that in my view are consistent with an ordoliberally oriented competition policy. Firstly, it implies that competition law ought to make sure that CBP is able to neutralize seller market power beyond the immediate situation to prevent abuses of market power in the longer run that would hurt the competitive process. Secondly, and related to the former, the exercise of CBP may also take into account the situation of weaker (but not inefficient) buyers and whether the benefits from the CBP spillover to them as I discuss below[2326].

VIII. Protecting weaker buyers: the spillover effect

1175. Once the assessment of the existence of CBP has been carried out, the Commission's practice and its Guidance Notices require an additional step to determine the sufficiency of CBP, as I discuss in this section. According to this second aspect of the test, the exertion of CBP has to benefit not only the powerful buyer that has it but it also must have a *positive spillover effect, analogous to the anti-waterbed effect*[2327]. This means that for CBP to be sufficient, the effects must also benefit weaker buyers that do not possess the same degree of countervailing power as the buyer exerting CBP, as the neutralization effect should benefit the competitive process as a whole and not only the position of a powerful buyer, as remarked by Hughes[2328], thereby granting

---

2324 Of a different opinion is Nazzini, who claims that the prevention should be long term, Nazzini, [2011], p. 355.

2325 Summary of Commission Decision of 10 May 2007 declaring a concentration compatible with the common market and the functioning of the EEA Agreement (Case COMP/M.4381 — *JCI/FIAMM*) [2009] OJ C 241/12, taken from the unabridged version, para. 402.

2326 Commission Decision of 22 July 1992 relating to a proceeding under Council Regulation (EEC) No 4064/89 (Case No IV/M.190 - *Nestlé/Perrier*) [1992] OJ L 356/1, para. 78 *in fine* (emphasis added). Also, the Commission expressed its concern over the protection of weaker buyers when stating that "it is not sufficient that certain strong buyers may be able to extract more favourable conditions from the allegedly dominant undertaking than their weaker competitors" and even suggesting defining "separate relevant markets for, respectively, strong and weak buyers", in European Commission, DG Competition (2005), para. 41.

2327 The anti-waterbed effect implies that the exercise of buyer power benefits the powerful buyer and other buyers by reducing the overall purchasing price in the market. I discuss this effect in chapter 2, section §VI.B.

2328 Paul Hughes, 'Business strategy and EC competition law - Two Systems Separated by a Common Language' International Company and Commercial Law Review (2009) 387.

some limited protection to smaller buyers. The protection is granted because CBP would not be sufficient if the buyer power would put rival buyers at a disadvantage compared to the powerful buyer *and* prone to seller side exploitation from the powerful supplier. In this sense, the spillover effect can be understood as a way to prevent or diminish the risk of weaker buyers becoming victim to a waterbed-effect-like situation in which the supplier concedes a better price to the powerful buyer but increases its prices vis-à-vis the rest, as I discussed in chapter 2, section §VI.A. Therefore, the spillover effect *prevents exploitation of buyers by a powerful seller,* as well as protects buyers from being at a now greater competitive disadvantage regarding the powerful buyer exerting the CBP and *minimizes the risks of buyer power induced foreclosure*, leading to further market concentration and the risks associated with it.

1176. This protection for smaller buyers, however, is not shared by all the literature; as Carlton, Coleman and Israel argue, "[i]f there exist a reasonably large number of large buyers, such that the downstream market would remain competitive even without price constraints from the smaller buyers, then there is little cause for concern", because welfare overall remains the same or improves even if the weaker/smaller buyers are worse off. Though, as the Commission's practice shows, this more welfaristic proposal has not been endorsed in EU competition law[2329].

1177. In addition to proving that CBP must be sufficient vis-à-vis a specific buyer exerting the competitive pressure, the seller claiming the existence of CBP has the burden to demonstrate the existence of the spillover effect. In my view, although the requirement of an additional spillover effect raises the bar when it comes to proving the sufficiency of CBP, it is justified finding anchorage in the overall buyer power treatment under EU competition law taking a broader approach to competitive harm. This is so because, by requiring a spillover effect, the logic is that buyer power is beneficial if it maintains or improves the upstream competition conditions as a whole for the protection of the competitive structure. This approach and additional requirement for the CBP sufficiency is consistent with an ordoliberal buyer power competition policy.

1178. The existence of this spillover effect is uncontroversial and has been recognized in the literature. For example, Bishop and Walker hold that "when assessing buyer power, it is important to confirm that it will protect small buyers as well as large buyers"[2330]. Also Monti when commenting on the *Enso/Stora* Decision highlighted that for the Commission CBP is effective if "all buyers are able to exercise power so that the dominant firm is unable to price discriminate, offering low prices to the powerful buyers and high prices to the weak"[2331]. More recently, Ezrachi and Ioannidou remarked that "even where the customers appear willing

2329 Carlton, Coleman and Israel [2015], p. 545.

2330 Bishop and Walker, [2010], para. 3-032.

2331 Monti 'The Concept of Dominance in Article 82' (2006), p. 37.

to switch to alternative suppliers, if the exercise of buyer power will benefit only these customers, to the detriment of smaller customers and consumers, countervailing buyer power cannot be found"[2332]. Cook and Patel go even further and claim that, "the strong buyer[s] should not only protect themselves, but effectively protect the entire market"[2333]. In even stronger terms, Faull and Nikpay indicate that "[f]or buyer power to be accepted as the countervailing factor to the exercise of market power on the part of the supplier, it must benefit all customers in the market"[2334]. Also this concern for the protection of smaller buyers is also present in the literature dealing with US and Canadian Antitrust[2335].

1179. Additionally, an aspect that is important to explore is that, even though the spillover effect appears counterintuitive and unprofitable for the supplier it is not necessarily so. A supplier is, or should be, interested in preserving a degree of competition among its buyers so that it can have alternative sources of demand granting to it bargaining power vis-à-vis the most powerful of its buyers, as was discussed by the Commission in *Enso/Stora* and which I address below. If CBP benefits a single buyer and gives that buyer an even stronger position, then the seller will be worse off when negotiating a new contract. Thus, the supplier claiming the existence of CBP in a specific case will also be interested when designing its selling strategies to make sure that the benefits of CBP do not benefit only the large buyer but also other ones.

A. The spillover effect in the Commission's practice

1180. The first decision to recognize and require the spillover effect is *Nestlé/Perrier* in which the Commission explicitly stated that:

> In the enforcement of the competition rules, the Commission *must also pay attention to the protection of the weaker buyers*. Even if some buyers might have a certain buying power, in the absence of sufficient competition pressure on the market, it can not be excluded that Nestle and BSN apply different conditions of sale to the various buyers[2336].

1181. Therefore, the Commission also considered the position in which smaller buyers would have been if CBP had been declared sufficient with respect to

2332 Ezrachi and Ioannidou (2014), p. 85.

2333 Cook and Patel, [2013], para 2.81.

2334 Faull, Nikpay and Taylor, [2014], para. 5.892.

2335 In US antitrust law, a merger and CBP is "to be evaluated by its impact on all buyers, however, not just on the larger more sophisticated ones", as pointed out by Hovenkamp in Hovenkamp, *Federal Antitrust Policy: The Law of Competition and its Practice* [2005], p. 544. Similarly, in Canadian Antitrust, CBP held by only some customers may not be sufficient to prevent all anticompetitive effects of a merger, particularly if sustained price discrimination between different customers groups is feasible, Facey and Brown, [2013] p. 242.

2336 Commission Decision of 22 July 1992 relating to a proceeding under Council Regulation (EEC) No 4064/89 (Case No IV/M.190 - *Nestlé/Perrier*) [1992] OJ L 356/1, para. 78 (emphasis added).

a large buyer, and what the effects of the concentration on the competitive conditions beyond the short term would be.

1182. Later, in *Enso/Stora* the protection of smaller or weaker buyers was central in the assessment of the sufficiency of CBP to declare the compatibility of the merger[2337]. From the facts and the Commission's assessment, it was clear that Tetra Pak in its condition of carton purchaser was able to beneficiate from CBP vis-à-vis the merging parties of *Enso/Stora*. The Commission, nevertheless, was concerned with the effects of the merger regarding the position and competitiveness of two smaller players vis-à-vis the new entity, as the merger would weaken their relative buyer power and could involve difficulties in switching supplier in the short term, therefore leaving them prone to exploitation[2338]. However, the Commission found that the CBP exercised by Tetra Pak "will [...] to a certain extent, *spill over to Elopak and SIG Combibloc* as well"[2339] because the merging parties, to counteract the very strong bargaining position of Tetra Pak, would be incentivized to guarantee the presence of these smaller buyers in the market in order to have alternative demand sources[2340]. In my view, the Commission's assessment of the spillover effect is intuitively correct and in line with buyer power economics. The spillover effect in this case occurred not because after the merger the smaller parties would have CBP or more bargaining power, but rather because it was in the interest of *Enso/Stora* to offer them supply conditions that would guarantee its market presence so that the merged entity would not be dependent on the purchases of a single buyer. Alternatively, another way of explaining the spillover is the fact that the price reductions obtained by Tetra Pak would also have been demanded by the smaller buyers, particularly due to the sunk costs in operating the machines. Also, from *Enso/Stora* it can be concluded that the spillover effect not only is required to protect smaller buyers but that a supplier would avoid becoming dependent on a large buyer by offering attractive purchasing conditions to smaller/weaker buyers, therefore benefiting the competitive conditions as a whole.

1183. Like in *Enso/Stora,* the protection of other smaller buyers in the self-interest of the supplier was also factored in by the Commission in *Korsnäs/AD Cartonboard,* where it was found that after the merger of the cardboard producers, the second and third buyers in size also had some degree of "buyer

2337 See also highlighting the discussion of benefits to all buyers: Faull, Nikpay and Taylor, [2014], para. 5.897.

2338 Commission Decision of 25 November 1998 declaring a concentration to be compatible with the common market and the functioning of the EEA Agreement (Case No IV/M.1225 - *Enso/Stora*) [1999] OJ L 254/9, para. 94.

2339 Commission Decision of 25 November 1998 declaring a concentration to be compatible with the common market and the functioning of the EEA Agreement (Case No IV/M.1225 - *Enso/Stora*) [1999] OJ L 254/9, para. 96 (emphasis added).

2340 Also stressing the 'spillover effect' of Tetra Pak's CBP without explaining any further how the spillover operates see: Ezrachi and Ioannidou (2014), p. 86. See the views of Baker and Lofaro who argue that these smaller buyers, if switching to sources of supply, would have had substantial bargaining power vis-à-vis the merging entity in Baker and Lofaro (2000), p. 189.

power vis-à-vis LPB suppliers as they place orders large enough to fill the capacity of a board machine", even if they were much smaller in comparison to the largest buyer[2341]. In this case the Commission concluded that the merging entity was in no position to discriminate against these weaker buyers – which implies a negation of possible waterbed effects – as this:

> [...] would clearly be counter-productive in medium to long term for LPB suppliers as it would affect smaller converter's competitiveness and would ultimately put them at risk of being foreclosed from the market. This in turn would leave the LPB suppliers with a monopsonistic buyer [Tetra Pak][2342].

1184. Thus, exerting exploitative seller power vis-à-vis these weaker buyers would have been against the interest of the merging entity because squeezing of them out of the market would have left the seller facing a single and more powerful buyer, and due to the costs of having a board machine out of production.

1185. In *SCA/Metsä Tissue,* a merger declared incompatible with the internal market, the Commission also argued that weaker buyers would be under a worse situation with respect to the merged entity and could be subject to anti-competitive price discrimination through arbitrage as the supplier would have been able to raise prices above the pre-merger level to weaker buyers[2343]. In this case, unlike in *Korsnäs/AD Cartonboard,* there were no special spare capacity circumstances, nor a single and very powerful buyer that would have prevented the merging entity from price discriminating vis-à-vis weaker buyers. Therefore, "*even if the largest customers* would be able to exercise some countervailing buyer power *this would not protect smaller customers*, and the new entity would *still be able to raise prices above the pre-merger level*"[2344] From the wording used by the Commission, my interpretation is that the exercise of *CBP must protect or at least not put weaker or smaller undertakings in a worse-off situation than the pre-merger levels with respect to weaker buyers*. In other words, the Commission took into consideration risks of possible waterbed effects that would have weakened the competitiveness of smaller buyers. From a total welfare perspective, however, the Commission did not analyze whether the increase in price to the weaker buyers may be neutralized by the discounts that may be achieved by the large buyers, which reinforces its interest in preserving a sufficient amount of players in the market to protect future competition.

2341 Commission Decision of Non-opposition to a notified concentration M.4057 — *Korsnäs/Assidomän Cartonboard* [2006] OJ C 209/12, taken from the unabridged public version, para. 50.

2342 Commission Decision of Non-opposition to a notified concentration M.4057 — *Korsnäs/Assidomän Cartonboard* [2006] OJ C 209/12, taken from the unabridged public version, para. 52.

2343 Commission Decision of 31 January 2001 declaring a concentration to be incompatible with the common market and the functioning of the EEA Agreement (Case COMP/M.2097 *SCA/Metsä Tissue*) [2001] OJ L 57/1, para. 88.

2344 Commission Decision of 31 January 2001 declaring a concentration to be incompatible with the common market and the functioning of the EEA Agreement (Case COMP/M.2097 *SCA/Metsä Tissue*) [2001] OJ L 57/1, para. 88 (emphasis added).

1186. In *Bombardier/ADtranz* the lack of buyer (bargaining) power by weaker buyers was an element to conclude that no sufficient CBP existed, even if a large buyer had relative CBP with respect to the supplier. In this case, involving the demand for regional trains in Germany, the Commission concluded that even though Deutsche Bahn Regio AG (a publicly owned undertaking) had CBP due to being the largest buyer, there were other smaller privately owned buyers that lacked buyer market power. Consequently, it concluded that the demand side in regional trains "does not enjoy the same degree of buyer power" and this was a factor to determine that sufficient CBP did not exist to neutralize the competitive risks pursuant to the concentration[2345]. The decision, however, did not make an express assessment of the effects the merger would have produced on these weaker buyers, or the spillover of the CBP of the large buyer, and just dismissed the CBP claim. Nevertheless, from the wording used by the Commission it can be inferred that the position of these weaker buyers was taken into account, either in terms of a spillover effect or the existence of their own CBP. My impression is that the Commission decided not to carry out an assessment of the spillover effect because the prima facie assessment based on a basic comparison led to the conclusion that CBP was unlikely to exist due to the asymmetrical market conditions. Despite the lack of sufficient CBP, and either CBP or a spillover effect on weaker buyers, the concentration was deemed compatible as the Commission was satisfied with a set of commitments that, instead of strengthening the position of the smaller buyers, divested parts of the supplier undertaking. Hence, in this case, the absence of the spillover was not critical for the merger assessment as a whole, but it was for not declaring CBP to be sufficient.

1187. Also, in the soft law the Commission has several times reiterated the need for CBP to have a spillover effect to the benefit of weaker buyers, in several of its policy instruments. In its Discussion Paper on the application of Art [102] TFEU, the Commission stated that:

> [t]he presence of strong buyers can only serve to counter a finding of dominance if it is likely that in response to prices being increased above the competitive level, the buyers in question will pave the way for effective new entry or lead existing suppliers in the market to significantly expand their output so as to defeat the price increase. In other words, *the strong buyers should not only protect themselves, but effectively protect the market*[2346].

1188. This requirement of market protection and, therefore CBP effects spillover to weaker buyers, was reinstated in the EU Horizontal Merger Guidelines when requiring that CBP:

2345 Commission Decision of 3 April 2001 declaring a concentration to be compatible with the common market and the functioning of the EEA Agreement (Case COMP/M.2139 — *Bombardier/ADtranz*) [2002] OJ L 69/50, para. 67.

2346 European Commission, DG Competition (2005), para. 41.

> [...] cannot be found to sufficiently off-set potential adverse effects of a merger if it only ensures that a particular segment of customers, with particular bargaining strength, is shielded from significantly higher prices or deteriorated conditions after the merger[2347].

1189. Despite the recognition of the protection of weaker buyers as part of the CBP by the EU competition law practice and the soft law, none of these Decisions or instruments incorporate any express rationale for the protection of weaker buyers. In my view, the *raison d'être* behind this protection is an interest in protecting the competitive market structure, the freedom to compete, and the wellbeing of small and medium undertakings[2348], as remarked by the literature[2349], which is consistent with the broader approach to buyer power harm used in other EU competition law areas and ordoliberalism.

1190. Put differently, these findings clarify that, at least when it comes to the CBP, EU competition law does not resort to a pure short term end consumer harm[2350]. If that were the case, the protection of weaker buyers would not be a requirement and CBP would be sufficient if consumer prices would ultimately be lower in the short run for end consumers purely based on the benefits obtained by the large buyer. The protection of weaker buyers and the requirement for a limited *erga omnes* effect reveal that the Courts, and surprisingly the Commission acknowledge the need for a more comprehensive approach to competition law as a whole, and buyer power related aspects in particular, by taking into account as part of the assessment competition in the upstream market and not only the benefits of end consumers in the short term.

1191. The problem with granting some limited protection and considering the position of weaker and/or smaller buyers to determine the sufficiency of CBP is that it can become a way to grant undue protection to inefficient firms. Therefore, determining what is the limit of the protection to weaker buyers is an important albeit difficult exercise that warrants a case-by-case assessment. However, and as expressed by Carlton and Israel, a general answer that can be given is that "[i]f there exists a reasonably large number of large buyers, such that the downstream market would *remain highly competitive* even without price constraints from the smaller buyers, then there is little cause for concern"[2351] The key, then, lies in the protection of the market structure and its intrinsic competitiveness for the spillover effect to be sufficient.

2347 Guidelines on the assessment of horizontal mergers under the Council Regulation on the control of concentrations between undertakings [2004] OJ C 31/5, para. 66 (emphasis added).

2348 The TFEU makes explicit reference to the need of fostering and protecting small and medium enterprises in three occasions: Article 153(2)(b); Article 173(1); Article 179(2).

2349 Korah and O'Sullivan, [2002], p. 42-43.

2350 Cf with the position of Kirkwood who argues for the protection of weaker suppliers instead of weaker buyers as part of a consumer welfare standard in US antitrust law in Kirkwood 'The Essence of Antitrust: Protecting Consumers and Small Suppliers from Anticompetitive Conduct' (2013).

2351 Carlton and Israel (2011), p. 135.

IX. Are the Commission and the Courts obliged to assess countervailing buyer power?

1192. A question that is left unaddressed thus far is *whether it is the Commission or the Courts duty to assess the existence of CBP unless its existence is of particular importance for the case*. My analysis of the Commission's practice and the case law confirms that there is no such duty. However, competition law practice does clarify that the *extent of this analysis depends on the particularities of the case*, implying that the degree of thoroughness to be exercised by the decision-maker varies and appears to incorporate a pre-requisite of a *prima facie* examination before performing the full-fledged analysis, as I mentioned before.

1193. The standard in EU competition law appears to be that the one claiming the existence of the CBP is obliged to prove its existence in application of analogy to standard rules of the distribution of the burden of the proof, as confirmed by Directive 1/2003 Article 2[2352], as well as the case law regarding the application of Article 101(3) TFEU to agreements in *GlaxoSmithKline Services and Others v Commission and Others*[2353]. Also, this is consistent with the general principles of distributions of the burden of the proof in EU competition law; the party that claims a circumstance has the burden of the proof to demonstrate its existence and extent. At the same time, the Commission also has a duty to assess particularly relevant circumstances of the case that may include the existence of CBP within the requirements of the principle of good administration[2354]. I discuss the conclusions derived from the case law and the Commission's practice in the following paragraphs.

1194. In *Impala v Commission* the General Court confirmed that the Commission is not obliged to reach a conclusion concerning the existence of sufficient CBP if the conditions for finding collective dominance are not present[2355]. An

---

2352 Council Regulation (EC) No 1/2003 of 16 December 2002 on the implementation of the rules on competition laid down in Articles [101] and [102] of the Treaty [2003] OJ L 1/1.

2353 Judgment of 6 October 2009 in *GlaxoSmithKline Services and Others v Commission and Others*, Joined cases C-501/06 P, C-513/06 P, C-515/06 P and C-519/06 P, EU:C:2009:610, para. 78.

2354 For a doctrinal and general discussion on the principle of good administration in EU (and EU competition) law see, *inter alia*: P. Nikiforos Diamandouros, 'Improving EU Competition Law Procedures by Applying Principles of Good Administration: The Role of the Ombudsman' 1 Journal of European Competition Law & Practice (2010) 379; Johannes Siegfried Schnitzer, 'Regulating Public Procurement Law at Supranational Level: The Example of EU Agreements on Public Procurement' 10 Journal of Public Procurement (2010) 301; Melanie Smith, 'Developing Administrative Principles in the EU: A Foundational Model of Legitimacy?' 18 European Law Journal (2012) 269; Margrét Vala Kristjánsdóttir, 'Good Administration as a Fundamental Right' 9 Icelandic Review of Politics and Administration (2013) 237. For some cases dealing with the principle of good administration in EU competition law see: Judgment of 1 October 2015 in *Electrabel and Dunamenti Erőmű v Commission*, C-357/14 P,EU:C:2015:642, para. 29-31; Judgment of 24 January 2013 in *3F v Commission*, C-646/11 P, EU:C:2013:36, para. 58-75; see also the Opinion of Advocate General Kokott in Judgment of 29 June 2010 in *Commission v Alrosa*, C-441/07 P, EU:C:2009:555, para. 220.

2355 Judgment of 13 July 2006 in *Impala v Commission*, T-464/04, EU:2006:16, paras. 188 and 505.

interpretation a contrario implies that if the Commission would have found that the concentration was likely to lead to the creation or strengthening of a collective dominant position, then it would have had to evaluate the existence and sufficiency of CBP. In the Judgment the General Court confirmed that the Commission's analysis "involving collective dominance calls for close examination in *particular of the circumstances* which, in each individual case, *are relevant* for assessing the effects of the concentration on competition in the reference market"[2356]. Therefore, as CBP was not relevant, it explains why the General Court did not discuss the need to evaluate CBP, even if it was part of applicant's plea.

1195. In *Imperial Chemical Industries v Commission,* the General Court more clearly stated that "*even if* the Commission *ought to* have taken the countervailing power of customers into account, the applicant has not shown that its customers were able to counterbalance its market power"[2357], confirming that the Commission has a duty to assess CBP when it is of relevance for the case. In this case as the applicant did not prove that the customers were able to exercise CBP and simply claimed it without proving it, the General Court dismissed the allegations.

1196. Also, in *Sun Chemical Group and Others v Commission,* the General Court held that if CBP is to be assessed the sophistication of the analysis depends on the circumstances of the case, in particular the industry structure and seller strategies as carried out in *Enso/Stora*[2358]. It held that:

> [f]urthermore, whilst the facts in Enso/Stora may have required, due to an exceptional market structure, *sophisticated analyses* of the industry structure and strategies that buyers could undertake to curb price increases post-merger, it is clear from the foregoing that *this does not apply to the present case*. In the light of the above findings, the Court considers that the Commission could not be required, in the circumstances of this case, to carry out a more detailed examination of the countervailing buyer power of the merging parties' customers[2359].

2356 Judgment of 13 July 2006 in *Impala v Commission*, T-464/04, EU:2006:16, para. 522 (emphasis added), making reference to Judgment of 31 March 1998 in *France and Société commerciale des potasses and de l'azote and Entreprise minière and chimique v Commission,* Joined cases C-68/94 and C-30/95 EU:C:1998:148, para. 222; and Judgment of 28 June 2004, *Airtours v Commission*, T-342/99, ECR, EU:T:2002:146, para. 63.

2357 Judgment of 25 June 2010, *Imperial Chemical Industries v Commission*, T-66/01, ECR, EU:T:2010:255, para. 277.

2358 Commission Decision of 25 November 1998 declaring a concentration to be compatible with the common market and the functioning of the EEA Agreement (Case No IV/M.1225 - *Enso/Stora*) [1999] OJ L 254/9.

2359 Judgment of 9 July 2007, *Sun Chemical Group and Others v Commission*, T-282/06, ECR, EU:T:2007:203, para. 216 (emphasis added).

1197. This position of carrying out a detailed assessment only if it is of importance for the case was supported by Advocate General Kokott in *Solvay v Commission* when addressing whether the Commission is obliged to state reasons concerning the existence (or not) of CBP. The Advocate General concluded that the institution carrying out the assessment is "not required [...] to define its positions on matters which are *plainly of secondary importance or to anticipate potential objections*"[2360]. This claim was not dealt with by the CJEU in its Judgment, as it was found that arguments backing the appeal relative to the access to the administrative file were well founded and sufficient to set aside the General Court's Judgment[2361].

1198. Contrasting with the previous case law, in *SIV and Others v Commission* the General Court criticized the Commission as it found that in its assessment of an allegedly collective dominance situation it had not submitted relevant evidence, nor it had "even attempted to gather the information necessary to weigh up the economic power of the three producers against that of Fiat, which could cancel each other out"[2362]. The lack of CBP analysis was one of the reasons why the General Court set aside the finding of the collective dominant position, as remarked by Faull and Nikpay[2363]. A way to interpret this requirement is that since the Commission had claimed the existence of a collective dominant position, it had to prove its existence and also the other relevant factors that could have had an impact on it, such as opposing CBP.

1199. Lastly, concerning object restrictions of competition under Article 101(1) TFEU the Commission has clarified that it is not obliged to assess CBP defenses or its sufficiency as held in *Candle Waxes*[2364] *and in Bananas*[2365]. In *Candle Waxes* the Commission concluded that even if the existence of buyer power in general may be a reason to enter into a seller's cartel, the existence of countervailing buyer power "not be relied upon to negate the existence of an infringement itself"[2366]. This was later on confirmed in *Bananas* when the Commission held that countervailing buyer power in itself cannot justify the infringement of Article 101 TFEU[2367].

2360 Opinion of Advocate General Kokott on 14 April 2011 in Judgment *Solvay v Commission*, C-109/10 P, EU:C:2011:256, para. 66.

2361 Judgment of 25 October 2011 in *Solvay v Commission*, C-109/10 P, EU:C:2011:686, para. 73.

2362 Judgment of 10 March 1992, *SIV and Others v Commission*, joined cases T-68/89, T-77/89 and T-78/89, EU:T:1992:38, para. 366. Also remarking that the General Court reproached the Commission's lack of analysis see, Bellamy, Child and Roth, [2001], para. 9-058; O'Donoghue and Padilla, [2013], p. 167.

2363 Faull, Nikpay and Taylor, [2014], para. 4.217.

2364 Summary of Commission Decision of 1 October 2008 relating to a proceeding under Article 81 of the Treaty establishing the European Community and Article 53 of the EEA Agreement (Case COMP/C.39181 — *Candle Waxes*) [2009] OJ C 295/17, taken from the unabridged version, para. 322.

2365 Summary of Commission Decision of 15 October 2008 relating to a proceeding under Article 81 of the EC Treaty (Case COMP/39.188 — *Bananas*) [2009] OJ C 189/12, taken from the unabridged version, para. 282.

2366 Summary of Commission Decision of 1 October 2008 relating to a proceeding under Article 81 of the Treaty establishing the European Community and Article 53 of the EEA Agreement (Case COMP/C.39181 — *Candle Waxes*) [2009] OJ C 295/17, taken from the unabridged version, para. 322.

2367 Summary of Commission Decision of 15 October 2008 relating to a proceeding under Article 81 of the EC Treaty (Case COMP/39.188 — *Bananas*) [2009] OJ C 189/12, taken from the unabridged version, para. 282, partially ratified in Judgment of 14 March 2013, *Fresh Del Monte Produce v Commission*, T-587/08, EU:T:2013:129, and on appeal as Judgment of 24 June 2015 in *Fresh Del Monte Produce v Commission and Commission / Fresh Del Monte Produce*, C-293/13 P, EU:C:2015:416, in which the fine was reduced.

X. Conclusions

1200. In this chapter, I have analyzed CBP as one of the sub-expressions of buyer power and defined in a narrow manner the competitive constraint exercised by a buyer(s) vis-à-vis a seller that is sufficient to neutralize the exercise of seller market power. CBP, therefore, acts as an efficiency defense for selling side firms that claim that they are unable to substantially exercise market power that otherwise would have allowed them to behave independently from their buyers and other competitors, significantly impede effective future competition or that an agreement between suppliers was not anti-competitive.

1201. I have also shown the origins and characteristics of CBP. With regard to its characteristics, I demonstrated that its effect may be actual or potential, also a relative concept between a buyer and a supplier, having the ability also to prevent coordination among sellers and which can be exercised by any type of buyers, but which unorganized end consumers would not exercise sufficiently.

1202. Concerning the sources, I have shown that the case law and the soft law have identified a non-exhaustive list of them, including but not limited to the ability to shift demand to alternative suppliers, relative size and concentration, ratio of purchases/profit represented by a buyer to a seller and price differentials. Also, against these sources, other case circumstances that may hinder the ability of buyers to exercise CBP must be assessed. This implies that the assessment of the existence and sufficiency of CBP must be made on a case-by-case basis.

1203. This analysis is carried out through a *comparison test* that seeks to determine if CBP is sufficient to offset the opposed seller market power and that follows the assessment of sources of it. According to the test, if seller market power is sufficiently neutralized by the CBP and it has a spillover effect improving the overall conditions in the market, then it would be sufficient and effective. Importantly, this comparison test *ought not* to be made by a pure contrasting of market shares or market concentration, as substantial CBP may rise in lower market thresholds than seller market power, which may lead to erroneous conclusions. Nevertheless, a market share and market concentration can be a good first indicator of the level of symmetry (or lack thereof) providing a rebuttable presumption of the existence of CBP.

1204. My analysis has also shown that the Commission and the Courts employ a consistent approach regarding the application of the test across all areas of EU competition law, which, in my view, is adequate. The consistency appears to be due to the understanding of the economics behind bargaining power, but as there are no explicit remarks in this sense it is not possible to confirm that the consistent treatment is due to this. What is different, nevertheless, is the threshold required for CBP to be sufficient depending on the type of case at hand. For dominance cases, it must be sufficient at least to preclude an undertaking from behaving dominantly in a market; in the case of the assessment of a concentration, it must be sufficient to prevent the merging entities from significantly impeding effective competition, and, concerning agreements among undertakings, it may be invoked as part the assessment of the efficiency of the agreement in the application of Article 101(3) TFEU.

1205. Furthermore, my analysis of the Commission's practice, the case law and the application of the comparison test shows that despite CBP being frequently invoked by parties, in only a handful of cases has it been found to be capable of overriding the competitive concerns of seller market power. To date, CBP has not been a relevant defense in a dominance case. Concerning concentrations, its invocation has been slightly more successful and on occasions has been either the fundamental aspect to declare the compatibility of the concentration, although more often it has been an additional factor in non-opposing the merger.

1206. Additionally, I have found that EU competition law demands for CBP to be sufficient also to be capable of shielding or protecting from the exercise of seller market power not only the large buyer exerting it, but also smaller/weaker buyers, having a *spillover effect*. This implies three important consequences. Firstly, it increases the threshold required for CBP to be sufficient as it not only has to neutralize seller power with respect to the buyer exerting it, but it also has to be beneficial to other buyers. Secondly, the CBP treatment is in line with the general buyer power competition policy in EU competition law that adopts a broader standard to harm seeking the protection of the competitive structure and preserving a sufficient amount of buyers and sellers to generate sufficient competitive pressure to keep markets competitive in the long run. This additional concern for the protection of weaker (yet not inefficient buyers) is also consistent with an ordoliberal competition policy regarding buyer power as protecting competition as such, and, to a certain extent, the protection of the economic freedom to compete. Thirdly, in requiring this spillover effect the Commission acknowledges that the exercise of CBP and buyer power in general may have ambiguous effects on other buyers in addition to suppliers, i.e.: the waterbed and anti-waterbed effect. The positive aspect of the spillover effect can be understood as, the exercise of CBP by a large buyer might generate positive consequences for other smaller buyers in the market vis-à-vis a powerful seller in the form of discounts or other preferential conditions. This occurs also because the seller would not risk becoming dependent on a single buyer and, therefore, would rather ensure that other buyers remain in the market. At the same time, the spillover effect, as has been applied by the Commission, seems to indicate that the exercise of CBP in certain circumstances may put smaller buyers in a weaker situation than before vis-à-vis their supplier. Because of this, they can be victims of seller power exploitation and, they should receive some degree of protection to avoid them being excluded from the market, thus, altering the competitive structure upstream. Which of these two antagonist effects is dominant depends on the circumstances of the case and awaits clarification by the Courts on whether the spillover assessment should be made in all cases or only if CBP is likely to sufficiently exist.

1207. Additionally, my study found that under EU competition law in general terms there is no obligation for neither the Commission nor the Courts to *ex officio* assess the existence and sufficiency of CBP in all cases. The rule of thumb is that CBP should be assessed thoroughly whenever it is particularly relevant for the case and when it has been invoked and supported with relevant and admissible evidence by one of the involved parties.

1208. Lastly, an aspect that I did not directly address in my discussion of CBP but find ripe for further methodological discussion is the issue of *during which stage of the competitive analysis CBP should be assessed*. Should it be during the assessment of the relevant market or outside of it? The Commission's practice and also the limited national case law discussed in this study shows that authorities tend to evaluate CBP most of the time apart from the evaluation of the relevant market. This is usually done in a separate section of the decision and normally prompted by the defendant. However, as I discussed in chapter 5 when dealing with the assessment of buyer market power, CBP is at times considered and/or mixed with the existence of alternative supply sources and dependence. Therefore, competition authorities could evaluate the existence of CBP already at the market definition stage instead of at a later time, which may occasionally save time and resources at the administrative level.

1209. In sum, CBP is one of the most relevant and analyzed buyer power topics for good reasons. It is frequently invoked by parties before the Courts, albeit to very little success. Furthermore, its legal treatment is consistent and follows a progressive development of the comparison test, granting the parties relative legal predictability despite the fact that the assessment ought to be carried out on a case-by-case basis. An unanswered question remains, though: Will the theoretical possibility that a dominant undertaking see its market power neutralized by (one or more) buyer(s) become a practical reality in the scope of Article 102 TFEU? Only time and the circumstances of the cases, if ever, will tell.

10

LIMITING BUYER POWER

I. Introduction

1210. Buyer power may be limited by undertakings, either acting individually, coordinated or even through the intervention of the state of its organs, when the behaviour of these entities seeks to restrict the ability of a buyer to exert its market power vis-à-vis its suppliers. This can be done, for instance, by imposing minimum purchasing prices, limiting supply, granting some discount (rebate), a countervailing benefit, or imposing a legislative or administrative restriction. The first two of these restrictive of practices, as shown by the EU case law, tend to be imposed by association of undertakings or sellers' cartels as the consequence of sectoral crisis related to agriculture. Rebates, on the other hand, are the mechanisms employed by powerful – dominant – sellers to prevent buyers from seeking alternative trading partners and create a relation of quasi exclusivity purchasing. Countervailing benefits are usually employed as compensation mechanisms for the loss of buyer power in exclusive supply agreements. And lastly, legislative measures aim to address what is usually a structural problem in a specific market.

1211. All these conducts *constrain buyer power exercise as they limit the buyer's capacity to negotiate better terms and conditions*, by setting a floor price limit, or disincentivizing buyers to find alternative sources of supply. Therefore, they do not imply the exercise of buyer power but its limitation and constitute tactics used by suppliers to weaken the bargaining position of the buyer. Hence, I analyze *buyer market power limitation from a seller's point of view*. Due the scope of this work, I discuss these behaviours from a buyer power limitation perspective only, without dealing in length with the particularities of some of them, especially regarding the granting of rebates by dominant undertakings[2368].

1212. My aim in this chapter is to analyze *why and how suppliers attempt to limit buyer power* exercise and *whether such restrictions of the buyer's economic freedom constitute a competition law infringement.* To answer these issues I have structured the chapter on the analysis of four mechanisms to (unduly) restrict buyer market power. First, in section §II, I discuss the imposition of minimum purchasing prices. This is followed in section §III, by the study of schemes designed to limit the quantities supplied by setting production quotas and preventing buyers from benefiting from economies of scale. In section §IV, I discuss how the grant of rebates can also be used to compensate and/or restrict the ability of buyers to seek alternative supply sources if imposed by a dominant undertaking. In section §V, I address the granting of countervailing benefits in the case of vertical agreements, such as exclusive branding. Section §VI concludes with a summary of the findings and synthetizing under which circumstances limiting buyer power constitutes a competition law breach.

II. Imposing minimum purchasing prices

1213. Setting minimum purchasing prices restricts or eliminates the ability of buyers to exercise buyer market power as sellers impose a limit from which it is not possible to negotiate further. For example, if suppliers decide to set a common selling price 'P = X' per unit, the buyer, even if it could have obtained a lower price by increasing its demand due to its bargaining power, would not be able to pay a price of 'P = X-1'. Hence, the buyer is forced to accept the price dictated by the sellers. These types of practices are, and should be, prohibited because, by their very object or nature, they restrict the competitive price formation, the buyer's economic freedom and competition as a process by guaranteeing a supra-competitive profit for the seller. Furthermore, by setting minimum prices this indirectly fixes retailing prices and reduces the buyer's incentives to lower the price vis-à-vis final consumers[2369].

2368 There is plenty of literature dealing with the treatment of rebates and well known case law in EU competition law. For some recent literature dealing specifically with these issues see, *inter alia*: Hans Zenger, 'Loyalty Rebates and the Competitive Process' 8 Journal of Competition Law and Economics (2012) 717; Paul Nihoul, 'The Ruling of the General Court in Intel: Towards the End of an Effect-based Approach in European Competition Law?' 5 Journal of European Competition Law & Practice (2014) 521; Richard Whish, 'Intel v Commission: Keep Calm and Carry on!' Journal of European Competition Law & Practice (2014) 1; Wils (2014); Brian Sher, 'Intel: General Court Rewinds the Clock on Rebates' (2014) <http://www.nabarro.com/insight/briefings/2014/june/intel-general-court-rewinds-the-clock-on-rebates/>; Geradin (2015); Petit 'Intel, Leveraging Rebates and the Goals of Article 102 TFEU' (2015); Nicolas Petit, 'Rebates and Article 102 TFEU: The European Commission's Duty to Apply the Guidance Paper' 2 Competition Law & Policy Debate (2016) 4; Chan (2016).

2369 Guidelines on Vertical Restraints [2010] OJ C 130/1, para. 48 and 223. See also: Ehlers [2008], para 2.3.046.

1214. Imposing minimum purchasing prices restricts a buyer's ability to exert buyer market power in several ways. A price limit *precludes buyers to decrease the purchasing price they pay* either by monopsony and bargaining power, which guarantees a supracompetitive profit proportion to the supplier that would not have existed under normal competitive conditions. Also, it *may negatively affect the quantity purchased by buyers* as they lack incentives to buy larger amounts if the supply curve is downwards slopping. This could also lead to scarcity of goods and consequently have an upward effect on prices as well as under-utilizing goods leading to a loss on allocative efficiency. Additionally, it undermines the incentives of buyers to compete in the downstream market and *facilitates downstream collusion*[2370]. Furthermore, price limits may have a *foreclosing effect in the upstream market for smaller buyers,* who, if prices are too high, will not be able to compete with financially stronger purchasers[2371]. Lastly, it may negatively impact innovation and investment by buyers to improve their products or distribution channels due to the inability to benefit from the exercise of their buyer power[2372].

1215. Setting minimum purchasing prices can be done in several ways. For instance by imposing price ceilings (naked price fixing), setting selling ranges or decreasing sales percentages, along with other factors[2373]. Moreover, purchasing price fixing is often accompanied by other restrictions of competition also aimed at limiting buyer power, such as imposing maximum sale quotas, as occurred in a Bulgaria when the NCA found that a union of poultry breeders had entered into a cartel from 2002 until 2007 to set minimum prices and production quotas on an example of object restriction of competition[2374].

A. Legal treatment to the imposition of minimum purchasing prices

1216. Concerning unilateral behaviour, Article 102(a) TFEU prohibits the imposition of "unfair purchase or selling prices or other unfair trading conditions". Therefore, the fixing of a purchasing price by a dominant undertaking would be anti-competitive if it is both 'unfair' and exploitative. As I discussed in chapter 7, section §III, in EU competition law there have been very few instances in which an exploitative/unfair pricing behaviour has been deemed as anti-competitive. The fixing of a minimum price limit would have an analog effect as imposing an exploitatively high purchasing price because the seller extracts

2370 Guidelines on Vertical Restraints [2010] OJ C 130/1, para. 224.

2371 Judgment of 30 January 1985 in *BNIC v Clair*, C-123/83, EU:C:1985:33, p. 417; Guidelines on Vertical Restraints [2010] OJ C 130/1, para. 224.

2372 Guidelines on Vertical Restraints [2010] OJ C 130/1, para. 224.

2373 Bellamy and others, [2013], para 5.039.

2374 European Competition Network (2012), para. 121; the decision by the NCA was upheld before the Supreme Administrative Court, http://www.novinite.com/articles/120369/24+Bulgarian+Firms+Fined+-for+Forming+'Poultry'+Cartel.

a supracompetitive profit that is higher than the price it would have obtained absent ceiling and in normal price competition[2375]. My research confirms that such practices are rare because a supplier would be able to conduct this type of conduct only if there are no possible alternative providers, which is unlikely to happen, particularly in markets where buyer power plays a role, such as those of raw materials or retailing because there are several undertakings offering the same or a similar good. Furthermore, this is corroborated by the absence of cases of this type in which a dominant undertaking imposes a minimum purchasing price with the aim of restricting its buyers' ability to exercise buyer power.

a. Object restrictions of competition

1217. In the case of *agreements among suppliers to fix minimum purchasing* prices, these conducts are expressly prohibited by Article 101(1) (a) TFEU, which, according to the case law and the Commission's practice, constitute *object restrictions of competition,* as I discuss below[2376]. These cases also have in common that undertakings coordinated their behaviour to mitigate adverse circumstances related to sectoral agricultural crisis and in which the state or an association of undertakings intervened.

1218. The first confirmation that *imposition of minimum purchasing prices constitutes an object restriction of competition* was in connection to two interrelated cases dealing with the production and distribution of Cognac, and involving the activities of the same association of undertakings, the Bureau National Interprofessional du Cognac (BNIC)[2377]. Since 1945 the retail prices of processed Cognac were fixed by public authorities setting minimum purchasing prices. These prices were imposed in meetings held among the members of BNIC. However, the price fixing measures became "unnecessary after 1967, as from then until 1973 and 1974 demand far outstripped supply"[2378]. Nevertheless, in 1976 and then in 1978-1980, BNIC *adopted decisions fixing minimum purchasing prices for sale of Cognac in casks* and bottles determined according to several criteria[2379].

2375 Bellamy, Child and Roth, [2001], para. 9-073.

2376 Judgment of 30 January 1985 in *BNIC v Clair*, C-123/83, EU:C:1985:33, para. 22; Judgment of 3 July 1985 in *Binon v AMP*, C-243/83, EU:C:1985:284; Judgment of 13 December 2006, *FNCBV and Others v Commission*, joined cases T-217/03 and T-245/03, EU:T:2006:391, para. 83 and 85, making reference to Judgment of 30 January 1985 in *BNIC v Clair*, C-123/83, EU:C:1985:33, para. 22. See also: Wollmann [2008], para 2.2.032.

2377 Judgment of 30 January 1985 in *BNIC v Clair*, C-123/83, EU:C:1985:33; Commission Decision of 15 December 1982 relating to a proceeding under Article 85 of the EEC Treaty (IV/29.883 - *AROW/BNIC*) [1982] OJ L 379/1. See also considering these cases as purchase price fixing: Ezrachi 'Buying Alliances and Input Price Fixing: In Search of a European Enforcement Standard' (2012), p. 55; Ezrachi, *EU Competition Law: An Analytical Guide to the Leading Cases* [2012], p. 134. Cf with Kokkoris that sees the case as part of a purchase price fixing instead of a limitation of buyer power in Kokkoris 'Purchase Price Fixing: A Per Se Infringement?' (2007), p. 480-481.

2378 Commission Decision of 15 December 1982 relating to a proceeding under Article 85 of the EEC Treaty (IV/29.883 - *AROW/BNIC*) [1982] OJ L 379/1, para. 15.

2379 These decisions were made pursuant to national law which stated that in case parties fail to comply with the agreement contracts of cognac sales were automatically void and may imply the payment of compensation. Article 4 Law No 75.600 of 10 July 1975 on the organization of agriculture, supplemented and amended by Law No 80.502 of 4 July 1980.

1219. Based on these decisions, the Commission initiated an investigation in *AROW/BNIC*[2380]. The Commission concluded that BNIC was an association of undertakings[2381] and its price fixing measures constituted decisions of undertakings, even if they were adopted and approved under state conferred legislation[2382]. Furthermore, the Commission found that the agreement fixing prices had the *object and effect of restricting competition in the market by preventing free price formation* among contractual parties and appreciable affected trade between MS, in breach of Article 101(1) (a) TFEU[2383]. Additionally, the Commission asserted that BNIC had *forced Cognac shippers willing to sell the product at a lower price to raise their prices*[2384], and shielded suppliers from buyer market power. Consequently, the Commission declared that these measures had breached Article 101(1) TFEU and imposed a fine to BNIC.

1220. The legal treatment of purchasing price fixing as an object restriction was later confirmed by the CJEU in *BNIC v Clair*. This time BNIC complained before the national courts that Mr. Clair, a Cognac dealer, bought cognac from various wine-growers at prices lower than the inter-trade price, which prompted a reference for a preliminary ruling[2385]. In its assessment, the CJEU - largely following the Opinion of Advocate General Slynn[2386] - concluded that the decisions between the wine growers and dealers constituted agreements by an association of undertakings[2387]. Furthermore, it declared that *an agreement as this setting minimum purchasing and selling prices by its very nature constitutes an object restriction of competition*[2388], and prohibited under Article 101 TFEU.

1221. The Commission's intervention in *BNIC v Clair* is also interesting as it went further in the buyer power discussion than the CJEU[2389], making remarks that support my claim that purchasing ceilings limit unduly buyer market power. It held that *price ceilings restricted competition among suppliers willing to sell at lower prices,* which could have a negative impact on consumers as retailers would not be willing to reduce their own output prices. These suppliers willing

---

2380 Commission Decision of 15 December 1982 relating to a proceeding under Article 85 of the EEC Treaty (IV/29.883 - *AROW/BNIC*) [1982] OJ L 379/1, para. 23.

2381 Commission Decision of 15 December 1982 relating to a proceeding under Article 85 of the EEC Treaty (IV/29.883 - *AROW/BNIC*) [1982] OJ L 379/1, para. 51.

2382 Commission Decision of 15 December 1982 relating to a proceeding under Article 85 of the EEC Treaty (IV/29.883 - *AROW/BNIC*) [1982] OJ L 379/1, para. 53.

2383 Commission Decision of 15 December 1982 relating to a proceeding under Article 85 of the EEC Treaty (IV/29.883 - *AROW/BNIC*) [1982] OJ L 379/1, para. 58 to 60.

2384 Commission Decision of 15 December 1982 relating to a proceeding under Article 85 of the EEC Treaty (IV/29.883 - *AROW/BNIC*) [1982] OJ L 379/1, para. 62.

2385 Judgment of 30 January 1985 in *BNIC v Clair*, C-123/83, EU:C:1985:33, p. 405.

2386 Advocate General Slynn Opinion of 2 October 1984 in Judgment of 30 January 1985 in *BNIC v Clair*, C-123/83, EU:C:1984:300 00391.

2387 Judgment of 30 January 1985 in *BNIC v Clair*, C-123/83, EU:C:1985:33, para. 26.

2388 Judgment of 30 January 1985 in *BNIC v Clair*, C-123/83, EU:C:1985:33, para. 22.

2389 Judgment of 30 January 1985 in *BNIC v Clair*, C-123/83, EU:C:1985:33, p. 417.

to sell below the fixed price wanted to do so because it was *still profitable for them*, possibly because they were more efficient than other suppliers. Secondly, the Commission argued that setting price ceilings (minimum or maximum) could resort in weaker buyers being squeezed out of the market as they are unable to pay the minimum required, in an argument somewhat resembling a waterbed-like effect, and, which as I discuss in chapter 2, section §VI, is disputed by modern buyer power economics. Thirdly, these restrictions had an upward rising effect on downstream prices for Cognac as there was a limitation on the ability of exercising buyer (bargaining) power. As parties had no possibility of negotiation, the room for a more efficient contractual outcome is lost in inefficiencies generated by the price ceiling preventing lower purchasing prices to be passed on to end consumers in the form of lower retailing prices.

1222. Also in *French beef – France Coop de Bétail* the Commission, and later on the Courts, confirmed that *setting minimum purchasing prices constitutes an object restriction of competition* under Article 101(1)(a) TFEU. In this case the price limit was imposed in connection to the crisis generated in the beef industry because of the "mad cow disease"[2390] and the drastic drop in the prices for meat during 2000[2391]. However, despite this price decrease in the upstream wholesale beef markets, the prices for end consumers remained largely the same before the crisis or even increased, partly owed to the extra costs to control the mad cow disease[2392], or maybe because supermarkets were not necessarily passing the price reductions to end consumers[2393]. Due to the wholesale price drop, six federations of cattle farmers agreed to fix minimum purchase price for certain categories of cattle and suspending imports of beef into France[2394]. The agreement was concluded with the acquiescence of the French government, which even encouraged it[2395], and the agreement was intended to last until 30 November 2001 but parties had the intent to continue with its application[2396].

2390 Bovine Spongiform Encephalopathy.

2391 Commission Decision of 2 April 2003 relating to a proceeding pursuant to Article 81 of the EC Treaty (Case COMP/C.38.279/F3 — *French beef*) [2003] OJ L 209/12, para. 14.

2392 Commission Decision of 2 April 2003 relating to a proceeding pursuant to Article 81 of the EC Treaty (Case COMP/C.38.279/F3 — *French beef*) [2003] OJ L 209/12, para. 15.

2393 This last point is interesting because it also illustrates a problem of buyer market power when exerted by a buyer that has an hourglass shape. There are two possible explanations to why even if upstream wholesale prices of beef decrease 20% end consumer prices remain stable or even increased. As suggested by the Commission, distributors had to incur in extra expenses to assure that the meat was not contaminated with the mad cow disease. Alternatively or jointly, if competition at the food retailing level was weak supermarkets could have been able to keep the supra competitive profits derived from buyer power exertion without having to pass the lower prices to end consumers.

2394 Commission Decision of 2 April 2003 relating to a proceeding pursuant to Article 81 of the EC Treaty (Case COMP/C.38.279/F3 — *French beef*) [2003] OJ L 209/12, para. 1.

2395 Commission Decision of 2 April 2003 relating to a proceeding pursuant to Article 81 of the EC Treaty (Case COMP/C.38.279/F3 — *French beef*) [2003] OJ L 209/12, para. 150 to 156.

2396 Commission Decision of 2 April 2003 relating to a proceeding pursuant to Article 81 of the EC Treaty (Case COMP/C.38.279/F3 — *French beef*) [2003] OJ L 209/12, para. 41.

1223. The Commission assessed this decision by an association of undertakings and held that the agreement *had the object* and effect of imposing minimum prices for the purchase of culled cows in France and ran contrary to Article 101(1)(a) TFEU[2397]. The case was later on subject to an annulment action before the General Court and then appealed before the CJEU[2398]. The General Court confirmed that *agreements that direct or indirect fixing minimum purchasing prices constitute an object restriction of competition*[2399], while also dismissing that competition law ought not to automatically apply to agricultural markets because of their special characteristics, a remark important for buyer power cases[2400]. On appeal, the CJEU confirmed that the General Court and the Commission were correct in holding that the agreement was an object restriction of competition and, consequently, the General Court "was not bound to research the actual effects on competition of the measures adopted by that agreement"[2401].

1224. Lastly, in *Raw Tobacco Spain*[2402], a dispute involving a buyers' vs sellers' cartels in which minimum and maximum prices for raw tobacco were fixed, the Commission found that such practices fixing price brackets per quality grade and additional purchasing conditions *constituted an object restriction of competition.* The suppliers' cartel was formed to neutralize the buyer power of cigarette manufacturers and force the buyers to acquire goods at the same prices and conditions during part of the life of the agreement. Additionally, the agreement also included non-naked price purchasing modalities such as setting an "average minimum price per producer" and the "average minimum price per group". The Commission found that such *an agreement limiting prices restricted the interplay of competition* and aimed at "impos[ing] on the processors conditions for selling raw tobacco that were as favourable as possible to their own interests", and therefore, was an object restriction of competition[2403].

2397 Commission Decision of 2 April 2003 relating to a proceeding pursuant to Article 81 of the EC Treaty (Case COMP/C.38.279/F3 — *French beef*) [2003] OJ L 209/12, para. 125 and 127.

2398 Judgment of 13 December 2006, *FNCBV and Others v Commission*, joined cases T-217/03 and T-245/03, EU:T:2006:391; Judgment of 18 December 2008 in *Coop de France bétail and viande v Commission*, joined cases C-101/07 P and C-110/07, EU:C:2008:741.

2399 Judgment of 13 December 2006, *FNCBV and Others v Commission*, joined cases T-217/03 and T-245/03, EU:T:2006:391, para. 83 and 85, making reference to Judgment of 30 January 1985 in *BNIC v Clair*, C-123/83, EU:C:1985:33, para. 22.

2400 Judgment of 13 December 2006, *FNCBV and Others v Commission*, joined cases T-217/03 and T-245/03, EU:T:2006:391, para. 86.

2401 Judgment of 18 December 2008 in *Coop de France bétail and viande v Commission*, joined cases C-101/07 P and C-110/07, EU:C:2008:741, para. 88.

2402 Commission Decision of 20 October 2004 relating to a proceeding under Article 81(1) of the EC Treaty (Case COMP/C.38.238/B.2) — *Raw tobacco — Spain* [2007] OJ L 102/14. See my analysis of this case with regard to buyer power exploitation in chapter 7, section §VI.B.

2403 Commission Decision of 20 October 2004 relating to a proceeding under Article 81(1) of the EC Treaty (Case COMP/C.38.238/B.2) — *Raw tobacco — Spain* [2007] OJ L 102/14, taken from the unabridged version, para. 330.

1225. All these cases confirm that *fixing minimum purchasing prices* – as all horizontal direct price fixing conducts – *constitute an object restriction of competition* and are prohibited under Article 101(1) TFEU because they disrupt the normal price formation and limit the ability to exercise buyer market power. This is a sound approach because these forms of price coordination have the aim to distort competition as such by precluding the purchasing prices be decreased due to the ability of a buyer to obtain better terms and conditions through buyer market power exertion. This implies that prices would be higher for the buyer and for end consumers as well. Hence, the purchasing conduct is inefficient and it only benefits the suppliers who reap a supracompetitive profit.

1226. Moreover, in the case of agreements fixing minimum purchasing prices, and also applicable to unilateral conduct in connection to the general broad standard regarding buyer power harm, these conducts are prohibited *even if these price limitations do not adversely impact those paid by the end consumers*, as clarified in *T-Mobile Netherlands and Others*[2404]. However, in the case of fixing minimum purchasing prices this does not mean that the condition of end consumers is irrelevant or not affected. Instead, what it means is that in these cases it is inferred that end consumer harm exists because the price limit hinders the buyers to pass on any price reduction to end consumers achieved thanks to its buyer market power.

1227. In this sense, in *T-Mobile Netherlands and Others*, a case dealing with fixing of prices paid to dealers concerning post-paid telephone subscriptions, the CJEU expressly recognized that "contrary to what the referring court would appear to believe, in order to find that a concerted practice has an anti-competitive object, there does not need to be a direct link between that practice and consumer prices"[2405]. Furthermore, the CJEU remarked that declaring price fixing prohibited absent consumer harm was the consequence that competition law's aim is "not only the immediate interests of individual competitors or consumers but also to protect the structure of the market and thus competition as such"[2406], echoing the Opinion of Advocate General Kokott.[2407] This statement from the CJEU reinforces and it is consistent with *the overall broad harm standard applicable to buyer power in other areas of EU competition law protecting the upstream competitive structure and competition as such*[2408]. Furthermore, it is also in line with the ordoliberal concern of safeguarding the

---

2404 Judgment of 4 June 2009 in *T-Mobile Netherlands and Others*, C-8/08, EU:C:2009:343. See also the opinion of Ezrachi in similar terms in Ezrachi 'Buying Alliances and Input Price Fixing: In Search of a European Enforcement Standard' (2012).

2405 Judgment of 4 June 2009 in *T-Mobile Netherlands and Others*, C-8/08, EU:C:2009:343, para. 39.

2406 Judgment of 4 June 2009 in *T-Mobile Netherlands and Others*, C-8/08, EU:C:2009:343, para. 38.

2407 Opinion of Advocate General Kokott on 19 February 2009 in *T-Mobile Netherlands and Others*, C-8/08, EU:C:2009:110, para. 58.

2408 Judgment of 6 October 2009 in *GlaxoSmithKline Services and Others v Commission and Others*, Joined cases C-501/06 P, C-513/06 P, C-515/06 P and C-519/06 P, EU:C:2009:610, para. 78; Ezrachi 'Buying Alliances and Input Price Fixing: In Search of a European Enforcement Standard' (2012), p. 58.

competitive process as a whole to prevent competition being distorted even absent short term end consumer harm.

1228. Lastly, setting minimum purchasing prices is prohibited even if the agreement has not been implemented. In accordance to the case law, once the agreement has been entered into it is captured by Article 101 TFEU without requiring its implementation nor adverse effects in the market[2409].

B. Price fixing justifications and the legal consequences

1229. A question that arises from the reading of the case law is whether fixing minimum purchasing prices may be justified to palliate adverse circumstances faced by suppliers. The economic intuition is that if buyers are not able to decrease further their purchasing costs they will not be able to pass to consumers a fair share of the benefits of their buyer power in the form lower final prices. This, however, does not preclude undertakings from requesting that an agreement that imposes minimum purchasing price may be exempted if it satisfies the conditions imposed by Article 101(3) TFEU[2410], or under the objective justification in Article 102 TFEU for unilateral conducts. Nonetheless, in both cases and due to its welfare detrimental nature it would be quite remote the possibility that minimum purchasing prices may satisfy the requirements imposed by Article 101(3) TFEU as they are unlikely to fulfill its cumulative conditions[2411], as confirmed by the Commission's soft law[2412], and in analogy the same would apply for an efficiency analysis under Article 102 TFEU.

1230. Furthermore, naked agreements fixing minimum purchasing prices also constitute hardcore horizontal agreements and, therefore, are outside of the scope of application of the research and development block exemption regulation[2413], and the specialization block exemption regulation[2414]. Furthermore, in

---

2409 Judgment of 12 July 2001, *Tate & Lyle and Others v Commission*, T-202/98, ECR, EU:T:2001:185, para. 103; Summary of Commission Decision of 15 October 2008 relating to a proceeding under Article 81 of the EC Treaty (Case COMP/39.188 — *Bananas*) [2009] OJ C 189/12, taken from the unabridged version, para. 284 and 292; partially ratified by the General Court in Judgment of 14 March 2013, *Fresh Del Monte Produce v Commission*, T-587/08, EU:T:2013:129, and appealed before as Judgment of 24 June 2015 in *Fresh Del Monte Produce v Commission and Commission / Fresh Del Monte Produce*, C-293/13 P, EU:C:2015:416,where the fine was reduced.

2410 Judgment of 15 July 1994 in *Matra Hachette v Commission*, T-17/93, EU:T:1994:89 [1994], para. 85.

2411 Wollmann [2008], para. 2-2-037; Whish and Bailey, *Competition law* [2012], p. 529.

2412 Communication from the Commission - Guidelines on the application of Article 81(3) of the Treaty [2004] OJ C 101/97, para. 46; and Communication from the Commission — Guidelines on the applicability of Article 101 of the Treaty on the Functioning of the European Union to horizontal co-operation agreements [2011] OJ C 11/1, para. 246. See also: Guidelines on Vertical Restraints [2010] OJ C 130/1, para. 47; Bellamy and others, [2013] para 5.058.

2413 Article 5 of the Commission Regulation (EU) No 1217/2010 of 14 December 2010 on the application of Article 101(3) of the Treaty on the Functioning of the European Union to certain categories of research and development agreements [2010] OJ L 335/36.

2414 Article 4 of the Commission Regulation (EU) No 1218/2010 of 14 December 2010 on the application of Article 101(3) of the Treaty on the Functioning of the European Union to certain categories of specialisation agreements 2010] OJ L 335/43.

accordance to the case law[2415] object restrictions of competition do not benefit from the *De Minimis* exemption[2416]. Hence, receiving a similar treatment as buyers' cartels fixing prices as I discussed in chapter 7, section §VI.A.

1231. Despite of this, the case law shows that whenever there is an imposition of minimum purchasing prices these practices are pursuant to an interest in protecting suppliers facing difficult conditions, for example in the case of excess capacity due to changes in the market structure[2417], as the result of an economic crisis[2418], or to protect supplier economically dependent of buyers, particularly in the agriculture sector[2419], and in general as an instrument of public policy[2420]. Because of this, the sellers' part of the cartel have claimed that their conduct is not anti-competitive under an efficiency assessment or that no fine should be imposed.

1232. In *AROW/BNIC,* BNIC claimed that fixing minimum purchasing prices was a policy oriented "to maintain the traditional quality of cognac, and to assure the consumer that there will be no artificial reduction in prices to the detriment of the characteristics of the product"[2421]. The Commission rejected the measure's justification on quality reasons as imposing minimum purchasing prices "is both pointless and ineffective for that purpose"[2422], implying that there were no efficiencies benefiting either the final consumer or competition as a process.

1233. Later, in *BNIC v Clair,* BNIC again tried justifying the imposition of minimum price as these intended to avoid "prices to depend on supply and demand would lead to a collapse which wine-growers could not withstand" and lead them to financial failure[2423]. The CJEU's preliminary ruling did not deal with this justification expressly, but it held that EU competition law applies regard-

2415 Judgment of 13 December 2012 in *Expedia*, C-226/11, EU:C:2012:795, para. 35 to 37.

2416 Communication from the Commission — Notice on agreements of minor importance which do not appreciably restrict competition under Article 101(1) of the Treaty on the Functioning of the European Union (De Minimis Notice), [2014] OJ C 291/1, paras. 2 and 13.

2417 Judgment of 20 November 2008 in *Beef Industry Development and Barry Brothers*, C-209/07, EU:C:2008:643.

2418 Judgment of 15 October 2002 in *Limburgse Vinyl Maatschappij and Others v Commission*, joined cases C-238/99 P, C-244/99 P, C-245/99 P, C-247/99 P, C-250/99 P to C-252/99 P and C-254/99 P, EU:C:2002:582, EU:C:2002:582 E.C.R. [2002] I-08375, para. 488. See also: Commission Decision of 17 December 1980 relating to a proceeding under Article 85 of the EEC Treaty (IV/29.869 - *Italian cast glass*) [1980] OJ L 383/19; see Wollmann who call this "structural crisis cartels" in Wollmann [2008], para. 2.2.046.

2419 Judgment of 30 January 1985 in *BNIC v Clair*, C-123/83, EU:C:1985:33; Commission Decision of 2 April 2003 relating to a proceeding pursuant to Article 81 of the EC Treaty (Case COMP/C.38.279/F3 — *French beef*) [2003] OJ L 209/12.

2420 Townley, [2009].

2421 Commission Decision of 15 December 1982 relating to a proceeding under Article 85 of the EEC Treaty (IV/29.883 - *AROW/BNIC*) [1982] OJ L 379/1, para. 21.

2422 Commission Decision of 15 December 1982 relating to a proceeding under Article 85 of the EEC Treaty (IV/29.883 - *AROW/BNIC*) [1982] OJ L 379/1, para. 69.

2423 Judgment of 30 January 1985 in *BNIC v Clair*, C-123/83, EU:C:1985:33, p. 408.

less whether these products are of economic importance for the producer's viability, even if they were dependent in price[2424].

1234. In *French beef – France Coop de Bétail* the existence of a sectoral crisis due to the mad cow disease did not render the agreement compatible with EU competition law pursuant to an assessment under Article 101(3) TFEU. While the Commission recognized that the beef industry was facing "a serious crisis" that lead to imposing EU-wide measures, a crisis, however, "cannot in itself preclude the anti-competitive nature of an agreement" as decided by the CJEU in *Limburgse Vinyl Maatschappij and Others v Commission*[2425]. Nevertheless, it can be taken into account if an exemption under Article 101(3) TFEU is requested, or more likely towards the reduction of a fine[2426]. In its assessment, the Commission found that the first two legs of the efficiency test were not satisfied as it did not improve distribution nor allowed consumers to share benefits[2427]. The circumstances of the crisis, however, were taken into account as a *mitigating circumstance, which led to a reduction of 60% of the fines*. On the annulment action before the General Court the argument was used and the fine was reduced even further up to 70% compared to the original amount[2428].

1235. Furthermore, an alternative allegation to justify the imposition of purchasing prices by sellers different from sectoral crisis could be that fixing minimum purchasing prices is not anti-competitive if the prices *countervail the buyer power of a dominant undertaking*, idea that has been suggested by Kirkwood under very narrow circumstances[2429]. The logic here is that the creation of a 'selling alliance' will generate seller market bargaining power to neutralize a buyer and prevent the buyer from reaping supracompetitive profits and, *in particular monopsony power*.

1236. In my view, though, *two wrongs do not necessarily make a right*, as confirmed by the Commission in *Bananas* were it was held that limiting buyer power

---

2424 Judgment of 30 January 1985 in *BNIC v Clair*, C-123/83, EU:C:1985:33, para. 15.

2425 Judgment of 15 October 2002 in *Limburgse Vinyl Maatschappij and Others v Commission*, joined cases C-238/99 P, C-244/99 P, C-245/99 P, C-247/99 P, C-250/99 P to C-252/99 P and C-254/99 P, EU:C:2002:582, EU:C:2002:582 E.C.R. [2002] I-08375, para. 487; quoted by the Commission in Commission Decision of 2 April 2003 relating to a proceeding pursuant to Article 81 of the EC Treaty (Case COMP/C.38.279/F3 — *French beef*) [2003] OJ L 209/12, para. 130.

2426 Judgment of 15 October 2002 in *Limburgse Vinyl Maatschappij and Others v Commission*, joined cases C-238/99 P, C-244/99 P, C-245/99 P, C-247/99 P, C-250/99 P to C-252/99 P and C-254/99 P, EU:C:2002:582, EU:C:2002:582 E.C.R. [2002] I-08375, para. 488.

2427 Commission Decision of 2 April 2003 relating to a proceeding pursuant to Article 81 of the EC Treaty (Case COMP/C.38.279/F3 — *French beef*) [2003] OJ L 209/12, para. 130.

2428 Judgment of 13 December 2006, *FNCBV and Others v Commission*, joined cases T-217/03 and T-245/03, EU:T:2006:391, para. 90.

2429 Kirkwood 'Collusion to Control a Powerful Customer: Amazon, E-Books, and Antitrust Policy' (2014).

is not a legitimate ground for justifying an anti-competitive agreement[2430]. Imposing minimum purchasing prices shields suppliers from the exercise of monopsony power, but it may lead to a bilateral monopoly structure worsening the competitive conditions if suppliers and buyers coordinate their conduct and, even if they not, fixing purchasing prices leads to inefficiencies in allocative and dynamic terms. However, if that is not the case, this could be a factor to consider in the assessment. Nevertheless, the existence of seller market power implies that suppliers will reap parts of the profits and which is likely to have a negative impact on end consumer prices as now the costs of the buyer can be higher. Therefore, this proposal of fostering seller market power seems to be counter-intuitive with obtaining lower purchasing prices, albeit it might be beneficial for consumers as it may allow suppliers to invest and develop better products.

1237. To conclude this section, the argument employed by sellers regarding the efficiency or need for neutralizing buyer market power by fixing purchasing prices may, on very specific and limited occasions (perhaps almost just theoretically) comply with the precepts required by Article 101(3) TFEU for the exemption or an objective justification analysis under Article 102 TFEU. Nevertheless, the Commission's practice and the case law confirm this is not the case. In most instances, setting minimum purchasing prices to protect suppliers has not been found sufficient to declare the price fixing as efficient[2431]. What has been considered by the Courts and the Commission's practice, nevertheless, is that extraordinary circumstances that led to the imposition of these purchasing prices and therefore have may be taken into account as mitigating factors when setting fines, as it occurred in *FNCBV and Others v Commission* (*French beef – France Coop de Bétail*), in case the requirements of Article 101(3) TFEU are not fulfilled[2432].

2430 "The Commission also notes that once the anti-competitive object of the arrangements has been established, it is not relevant whether the trade in issue was, as certain addressees claim, subject to a significant "buying power", and the existence of any buying power could not justify the infringement found in the present decision", Summary of Commission Decision of 15 October 2008 relating to a proceeding under Article 81 of the EC Treaty (Case COMP/39.188 — *Bananas*) [2009] OJ C 189/12, taken from the unabridged version, para. 282.

2431 Commission Decision of 2 April 2003 relating to a proceeding pursuant to Article 81 of the EC Treaty (Case COMP/C.38.279/F3 — *French beef*) [2003] OJ L 209/12; Ritter and Braun, [2004], p. 174.

2432 Judgment of 13 December 2006, *FNCBV and Others v Commission*, joined cases T-217/03 and T-245/03, EU:T:2006:391; ratified in Judgment of 18 December 2008 in *Coop de France bétail and viande v Commission*, joined cases C-101/07 P and C-110/07, EU:C:2008:741. See also: Judgment of 6 April 1995, *Baustahlgewebe v Commission*, T-145/89, EU:T:1995:66, paras. 121-122, partially upheld in Judgment of 17 December 1998 in *Baustahlgewebe v Commission*, C-185/95 P, EU:C:1998:608.

C. Formation of 'legal' sellers' cartels pursuant EU regulation

1238. The EU has implemented sectoral specific legislative measures to limit the buyer power of large retailers vis-à-vis small and fragmented suppliers of raw milk, allowing sellers to jointly negotiate milk selling prices and other contractual conditions[2433]. These legislative measures were imposed as a result of a selling price collapse for milk during 2008-2009, and also due to the *large disequilibria concerning bargaining power of the parties,* which lead to producers of milk being in quite delicate financial situations[2434], or to counter the creation of buyer's cartels in the milk industry[2435]. Thus, this regulation seems to address conducts that are exploitative in the line of UPPs, a topic I discussed in detail in chapter 8.

1239. In connection with the former, the EU has adopted Regulation 261/2012, which explicitly allows for "dairy farmers or their associations *to jointly negotiate contract terms, including price, for some or all of its members' production, with a dairy*"[2436]. These sellers' cartels' aim at improving farmers' conditions vis-à-vis powerful buyers and are *exempted from the temporal application of EU competition* rules pursuant to Article 42 of the TFEU, in particular the application of Article 101(1) TFEU[2437]. The legislative aim is to address the bargaining power unbalance and allow sellers to join their efforts and neutralize the buyer market power of milk retailers (supermarkets and dairy companies). This extraordinary exemption from the application of EU competition law is subject to two limitations. Firstly, it is a legislative answer to a sectoral crisis and, secondly, it must be limited in time, but long enough to have a "full effect"[2438].

2433 Regulation (EU) No 261/2012 of the European Parliament and of the Council of 14 March 2012 amending Council Regulation (EC) No 1234/2007 as regards contractual relations in the milk and milk products sector [2012] OJ L 94/38.

2434 Regulation (EU) No 261/2012 of the European Parliament and of the Council of 14 March 2012 amending Council Regulation (EC) No 1234/2007 as regards contractual relations in the milk and milk products sector [2012] OJ L 94/38, Recitals (3), (5), (10) and (14).

2435 There are reports of several cases dealing with buyers' cartels for the purchase of raw milk in Greece, Bulgaria and Lithuania that, due to their scope, have not been evaluated in a EU level. For more on this see: European Competition Network (2012), paras. 97-101.

2436 Regulation (EU) No 261/2012 of the European Parliament and of the Council of 14 March 2012 amending Council Regulation (EC) No 1234/2007 as regards contractual relations in the milk and milk products sector [2012] OJ L 94/38, Recital (14) (emphasis added).

2437 Regulation (EU) No 261/2012 of the European Parliament and of the Council of 14 March 2012 amending Council Regulation (EC) No 1234/2007 as regards contractual relations in the milk and milk products sector [2012] OJ L 94/38, Article Art 1(5), modifying Article 177(a) of Regulation No 1234/2007.

2438 Regulation (EU) No 261/2012 of the European Parliament and of the Council of 14 March 2012 amending Council Regulation (EC) No 1234/2007 as regards contractual relations in the milk and milk products sector [2012] OJ L 94/38, Recital (21).

1240. Furthermore, cartel members can only benefit from the exemption of the application of competition law if two cumulative and restrictive conditions are complied with[2439]. First, the agreement has to be notified to the Commission. Secondly, and upon notification, the Commission must determine if the agreement is compatible with the Regulation's requirements[2440]. These milk-related agreements would not be compatible with the internal market if they:

i) lead to market division;

ii) affect the market's operation;

iii) are likely to create competition distortions and are not essential to achieve the objectives pursued;

iv) *fixed purchasing and/or selling prices*;

v) create discrimination or eliminate competition with regard to a substantial proportion of the products[2441].

1241. Thus, even if Regulation 261/2012 allows for the formation of selling side agreements to jointly negotiate vis-à-vis large milk buyers like some sort of 'selling alliance', it expressly forbids selling price fixing. However, even if price fixing is not allowed under the Regulation – which is in line with the approach to price fixing under EU competition law – allowing sellers to join efforts and negotiate jointly alters the competitive price formation. Also, it restricts the ability of buyers to exert bargaining power by setting static ways to determine the purchasing price of milk based on factors such as market indicators, volume derived, quality, and composition of raw milk[2442]. Therefore, Regulation 261/2012 has a *protectionist and fairness component* to the price determination of raw milk, which is connected with the concern regarding buyer power exertion in the food retailing markets, as discussed I chapter 8, particularly due to its political sensitivity.

2439 See also stressing the stringent character of the exemption Whish and Bailey, *Competition law* [2012], p. 936-937.

2440 Regulation (EU) No 261/2012 of the European Parliament and of the Council of 14 March 2012 amending Council Regulation (EC) No 1234/2007 as regards contractual relations in the milk and milk products sector [2012] OJ L 94/38, Article 1(5), modifying Article 177(a) of Regulation No 1234/2007.

2441 Regulation (EU) No 261/2012 of the European Parliament and of the Council of 14 March 2012 amending Council Regulation (EC) No 1234/2007 as regards contractual relations in the milk and milk products sector [2012] OJ L 94/38, Article 1(5), modifying Article 177(a) of Regulation No 1234/2007.

2442 Regulation (EU) No 261/2012 of the European Parliament and of the Council of 14 March 2012 amending Council Regulation (EC) No 1234/2007 as regards contractual relations in the milk and milk products sector [2012] OJ L 94/38, Article 1(8).2, introducing Article 185(f) of Regulation No 1234/2007.

D. Conclusions regarding imposition of minimum purchasing prices

1242. Summing up, conducts imposing minimum purchasing prices are considered both regarding Article 101(1) TFEU and Article 102(a) TFEU as infringements of EU competition law. In the case law, the instances in which this modality of buyer power limitation have been analyzed, has always been in connection to agreements fixing prices, which have been qualified *as object restrictions of competition*. A strict legal standard for both unilateral and concerted behaviours regarding fixing purchasing prices is economically coherent and legally proportional because these conducts disrupt the competitive price formation process, and unduly restrict the buyers' economic freedom to negotiate prices that can be lower and, therefore, be passed on to consumers. Furthermore, these conducts are entered into through inter-professional agreements with the participation of associations of undertakings and occasionally the approval of the state and pursuant to a sectoral crisis in agriculture. Also, because of these sectoral crises, the EU has decided to legalize the creation of 'suppliers' cartels' in the raw milk industry, allowing them to negotiate prices jointly, but not to directly set minimum purchasing prices.

1243. Furthermore, fixing minimum purchasing prices may theoretically benefit from an efficiency defense under either Article 101(3) or Article 102 TFEU. However, this is very unlikely to happen due to the economic effects of the conduct. Nevertheless, the fact that purchasing price fixing has usually been resorted to as the consequence of a sectoral crisis in the agricultural sector and with the acquiescence of the state has played a mitigating role when determining the fines to be imposed, as confirmed by the Commission and the Courts' practice.

III. Supply limitation

1244. An alternative measure that limits the exercise of buyer market power vis-à-vis suppliers is the imposition of maximum purchasing quotas. These types of practices have an analogous effect as fixing minimum purchasing prices because they aim at neutralizing the competitive price formation and the ability of buyers to obtain better terms and conditions based on the quantities of goods acquired (i.e. quantity rebates). As remarked by the Commission in *Italian Cast Glass,* supply limitation agreements intend to stabilize supplier's production and "protect the prices of [supplier's] products from the effects of consumer demand"[2443]. Therefore, supply limitation like purchase price fixing has an upward increasing pressure on purchasing prices because of scarcity

2443 Commission Decision of 17 December 1980 relating to a proceeding under Article 85 of the EEC Treaty (IV/29.869 - *Italian cast glass*) [1980] OJ L 383/19, part II A, section 4.

effects[2444]. Also, limiting supply means that there are fewer available goods for resale (unless a substitute can replace the shortage), which increases prices for end consumers and prevents marginal end buyers from acquiring the good. Because of their effect in competition, these types of practices can be captured by either of Article 101(1)(b) TFEU and Article 101(1)(c) TFEU, and the case law has clarified the constitute object restrictions of competition[2445] or, alternatively in case of unilateral behaviour, by Article 102(b) TFEU[2446]. As in the case of minimum purchasing prices, in the case law and Commission's practice, there are only examples of coordinated behaviour.

1245. In *Pabst & Richards/BNIA* the Commission evaluated the compatibility of a decision of undertakings that *set production quotas limiting supply* imposed by the Bureau National Interprofessionnel de l'Armagnac (BNIA)[2447], an association of undertakings representing parties involved in the production of Armagnac[2448]. The supply limitation was allegedly justified as a measure to guarantee Armagnac's quality and prevent "suspicious" imports to Germany bearing a false age indication sold at "abnormally low prices"[2449]. This meant that buyers, particularly in Germany, were no longer able to purchase bulk Armagnac with a specific age grade. Upon this measure, an investigation was initiated by the Commission based, *inter alia*, on the fact that the supply limitation had the effect of "reduc[ing] supply artificially and raised prices so appreciably that the purchase of age grade 5 was no longer a profitable venture"[2450]. After determining that the order was a decision by an association of undertakings and dismissing an allegation that the measures were adopted in the exercise of public powers[2451], the Commission held that this measure was *disproportional to achieve quality control* and was not imposed by administrative authorities, thus qualifying as a private commercial decision[2452]. Furthermore, the limitation of supply affected trade between MS by precluding distribution agree-

---

2444 Whish and Bailey, *Competition law* [2015], p. 568-569; Commission Decision of 26 July 1976 relating to a proceeding under Article 85 of the EEC Treaty (IV/28.980 - *Pabst & Richarz/BNIA*) [1976] OJ L 231/24, part I para. 2.

2445 Judgment of 15 July 1970 in *Chemiefarma v Commission*, C-41/69, EU:C:1970:71.

2446 Van Bael and Bellis, [2005], p. 413; Wollmann [2008], para 2.2.041; Bellamy and others, [2013], para. 5.060.

2447 Commission Decision of 26 July 1976 relating to a proceeding under Article 85 of the EEC Treaty (IV/28.980 - *Pabst & Richarz/BNIA*) [1976] OJ L 231/24.

2448 Armagnac is a type of grape brandy produced in the French region of Armagnac. Commission Decision of 26 July 1976 relating to a proceeding under Article 85 of the EEC Treaty (IV/28.980 - *Pabst & Richarz/BNIA*) [1976] OJ L 231/24, para. 1 and 3. The production of Armagnac involves three stages of production of the liquor; then bottled by the producer, cooperative or distiller and marketed under their label or else sold in bulk. If sold in bulk to a distributor this latter is the one bottling and label the final good.

2449 Commission Decision of 26 July 1976 relating to a proceeding under Article 85 of the EEC Treaty (IV/28.980 - *Pabst & Richarz/BNIA*) [1976] OJ L 231/24, part I, para. 6.

2450 Commission Decision of 26 July 1976 relating to a proceeding under Article 85 of the EEC Treaty (IV/28.980 - *Pabst & Richarz/BNIA*) [1976] OJ L 231/24, part I, para. 6.

2451 Commission Decision of 26 July 1976 relating to a proceeding under Article 85 of the EEC Treaty (IV/28.980 - *Pabst & Richarz/BNIA*) [1976] OJ L 231/24, part II, para. 1.

2452 Commission Decision of 26 July 1976 relating to a proceeding under Article 85 of the EEC Treaty (IV/28.980 - *Pabst & Richarz/BNIA*) [1976] OJ L 231/24, part II, para. 1.

ments to be entered into[2453]. The Commission concluded that *restricting supply of Armagnac constituted an object restriction that had the aim of artificially reducing supply in the market to increase purchasing prices* paid by the buyers to Armagnac suppliers[2454]. As the effects of the measure were so obvious, the Commission found no need to carry out any further assessments either in the upstream or downstream markets. However, the Commission could have analyzed whether the other measures less restrictive of competition could have been efficient, for instance to contribute in the quality control of the products or maybe to protect suppliers against purchasing price exploitation, if any.

1246. Later, in *Italian Cast Glass* a case dealing with a collective dominant position[2455], the Commission found that suppliers of car glass had entered into agreements that had *the object of restricting competition by fixing a maximum sale quota and sharing markets* in breach of Article 101(1) (b)[2456]. The agreement imposed sales quotas (and therefore buying restrictions) to protect suppliers from "effects of consumer demand"[2457] and as a stability factor for the cartel, as in cases of a quota breach, a retribution mechanism to the benefit of the rest of the members was activated. The quota system prevented or limited *the exercise of buyer power* by car manufacturers (hence powerful buyers) *and set prices unilaterally.* The decision also evaluated if the agreement could satisfy the conditions of Article 101(3) TFEU and concluded that the four cumulative requirements were not present, because the agreement shielded from competition more than half of all the Italian production of cast glass[2458]. On appeal, the General Court overturned this aspect of the decision because of the absence of sufficient evidence, but did not object to the finding that supply limitation infringes competition by object[2459].

2453 Commission Decision of 26 July 1976 relating to a proceeding under Article 85 of the EEC Treaty (IV/28.980 - *Pabst & Richarz/BNIA*) [1976] OJ L 231/24, part II, para. 3.

2454 Commission Decision of 26 July 1976 relating to a proceeding under Article 85 of the EEC Treaty (IV/28.980 - *Pabst & Richarz/BNIA*) [1976] OJ L 231/24, part II, para. 2.

2455 Commission Decision of 17 December 1980 relating to a proceeding under Article 85 of the EEC Treaty (IV/29.869 - *Italian cast glass*) [1980] OJ L 383/19, partially annulled in Judgment of 10 March 1992, *SIV and Others v Commission*, joined cases T-68/89, T-77/89 and T-78/89, EU:T:1992:38.

2456 See also discussing briefly the case as limitation of goods and market sharing: Faull and Nikpay, [1999], para. 6.19; Whish and Bailey, *Competition law* [2012], p. 535.

2457 Commission Decision of 17 December 1980 relating to a proceeding under Article 85 of the EEC Treaty (IV/29.869 - *Italian cast glass*) [1980] OJ L 383/19, part II A, section 4.

2458 Commission Decision of 17 December 1980 relating to a proceeding under Article 85 of the EEC Treaty (IV/29.869 - *Italian cast glass*) [1980] OJ L 383/19, part II B, section 1.

2459 Judgment of 10 March 1992, *SIV and Others v Commission*, joined cases T-68/89, T-77/89 and T-78/89, EU:T:1992:38. See also: Whish and Bailey, *Competition law* [2012], p. 535.

1247. In *Zinc Producer Group* the Commission found that parties to a resale price fixing agreement had *also agreed to impose a limitation in supply of quantities sold*[2460]. Again, the fixing of supply quotas was accessory to the main anti-competitive conduct. The Commission determined that the agreement and these clauses constituted an object restriction of competition[2461].

1248. At the national level the same conclusion was reached by the Dutch NCA when an agreement among a decision by the fishermen's association that fixed the amount of shrimps it could be sold and set minimum purchasing prices to protect suppliers from large buyers was also held liable of breaching the Dutch Competition Act[2462].

1249. As noted from the cases above, supply limitation agreements are usually adopted as complements to other anti-competitive behaviours, such as price fixing, but rarely in isolation as they act as a security mechanism for the cartel member's to guarantee that parties would not 'cheat' the collusive agreement[2463]. Additionally, the Commission's practice in general for agreements imposing quotas clarifies that it is not necessary that all suppliers comply with them, as the mere existence of the agreement constitutes a breach of Article 101(1) TFEU[2464].

A. Efficiency assessment for supply limitation agreements

1250. Like in the case of setting minimum purchasing prices, the imposition of supply quotas may be caused due to a sectoral crisis, for example to minimize overcapacity to achieve a better balance between supply and demand as remarked by Wollmann, and which was discussed by the CJEU Commission in *Beef Industry Development and Barry Brothers*[2465].

1251. In the preliminary ruling *Beef Industry Development and Barry Brothers*[2466] the CJEU discussed whether issues of excess capacity and the creation of a

---

2460 Commission Decision of 6 August 1984 relating to a proceeding under Article 85 of the EEC Treaty (IV/30.350 - *Zinc Producer Group*) [1984] OJ L 220/27, para. 67 to 71.

2461 Commission Decision of 6 August 1984 relating to a proceeding under Article 85 of the EEC Treaty (IV/30.350 - *Zinc Producer Group*) [1984] OJ L 220/27, para. 71.

2462 This case was the first opportunity upon with the Dutch NCA imposed a fine for infringement of EU laws (and not pure national law) and setting fines up to €13.8 million to cartel members. Decision No. 2269/326 [2013]. For a summary of the decision in English see: https://www.acm.nl/en/publications/publication/5980/NMa-Fines-Shrimp-Wholesalers-and-Shrimp-Fishery-Industry-Due-to-Price-Agreements/.

2463 Graham, [2010], p. 357.

2464 Commission Decision of 13 July 1994 relating to a proceeding under Article 85 of the EC Treaty (IV/C/33.833 - *Cartonboard*) [1994] OJ L 243/1.

2465 Wollmann [2008], para. 2.2.042; Judgment of 20 November 2008 in *Beef Industry Development and Barry Brothers*, C-209/07, EU:C:2008:643.

2466 Judgment of 20 November 2008 in *Beef Industry Development and Barry Brothers*, C-209/07, EU:C:2008:643.

'crisis cartel'[2467] could be factors to consider regarding the exemption of the conduct under an efficiency analysis based on Article 101(3) TFEU. The case dealt with an agreement among suppliers of beef to limit production due to excess capacity and industry changes, prompted by the lower beef consumption among Irish consumers. Due to the shifts in demand, the suppliers decided to restructure the beef industry through buyouts and payments of compensation, therefore limiting the supply of beef vis-à-vis buyers.

1252. The CJEU found that agreements limiting supply constitute *an object restriction of competition*; however it held that such *restructuring arrangements may be exempted on the basis Article 101(3) TFEU*[2468]. Despite this theoretical possibility, the CJEU made it quite clear that as the agreement included clauses restricting competition by object (non-competition clauses and compensation to the suppliers exiting the market) the existence of a sectoral crisis justifying a reduction of sale quotas could "be relevant for the purposes of the examination of the four requirements which have to be met under Article [101] (3)", and which is for the national court to assess[2469].

B. Conclusions regarding supply limitation

1253. As with purchasing price fixing, limiting supply is treated by EU competition law *as an object restriction of competition* under Article 101(1) TFEU and can be assumed that under Article 102 TFEU it would also be found to be an abuse of dominance by a selling undertaking. My analysis shows that these anti-competitive provisions are usually found in connection with another type of anti-competitive conducts, as they act as a cartel stabilizing device. Furthermore, the case law clarifies that these behaviours are likely to be anti-competitive, even if they have received the acquiescence of the state or are imposed pursuant to a sectoral crisis. In cases of sectoral crisis, and as discussed regarding *Beef Industry Development and Barry Brothers*, at most, these considerations can be taken into account as part of an efficiency defense under Article 101(3) TFEU or Article 102 TFEU to prevent over-production of an undesired good. However, the case law indicates that these types of conducts restricting the ability to exert buyer power are unlikely to satisfy the efficiency analysis requirements.

2467 Tjarda Van der Vijver, 'The Irish Beef Case: Competition Authority v Beef Industry Development Society and Barry Brothers (Carrigmore) Meats (C-209/07), European Court of Justice' 30 European Competition Law Review (2009) 198.

2468 Judgment of 20 November 2008 in *Beef Industry Development and Barry Brothers*, C-209/07, EU:C:2008:643, para., 39. See also the Opinion Advocate General Trstenjak in Judgment of 20 November 2008 in *Beef Industry Development and Barry Brothers*, C-209/07, EU:C:2008:467, paras. 55 to 59, and 86.

2469 Judgment of 20 November 2008 in *Beef Industry Development and Barry Brothers*, C-209/07, EU:C:2008:643, para. 39.

IV. Rebates removing or restricting the buyer's freedom to choose supply sources

1254. Suppliers, particularly if enjoying substantial market power, may grant rebates to buyers to limit their freedom to choose alternative trading partners. In this section, I discuss how or if the granting of rebates may (unduly) restrict the capacity of buyers to exercise their buyer power, and as a side effect, foreclose rival retailers to get access to the buyers that receive such discounts. The latter effect is at the center of the extensive discussion of rebates in EU competition law, which is the central reason why conditional rebates granted by a dominant undertaking are likely to be considered anti-competitive. In this section, I will not discuss the treatment granted to rebates from a seller perspective but only to the rebates' ability to restrict the freedom of choice of a buyer and, consequently, neutralize (or compensate) its ability to exercise buyer power. Also I examine whether rebates restrict the ability of a buyer to find alternative sources of supply or instead compensate the buyer for the less of such possibility.

1255. Granting rebates or discounts[2470] is a common business practice that consist in the offering a lower purchasing price to a buyer that acquires a relatively large quantity of goods from a particular supplier (quantity rebates)[2471], or because it reaches certain targets agreed by the parties on a contract (conditional rebates). Therefore, rebates are a form of price discrimination that can be lawful or prohibited depending on whether it has been granted by a dominant undertaking and if the rebate has an unjustified and anti-competitive foreclosure and/or exploitative effect, as I discussed in chapters 6, section §VI, and chapter 7, section §IV from a buyer power perspective. If, on the other hand, the rebates are granted by an undertaking without substantial market power then EU competition law sees these pricing practices as not generating a sufficient degree of competitive concern.

1256. Also, and recapitulating the discussion concerning the general legal treatment to rebates granted by a dominant undertaking in chapter 6, section §VI, the Courts have classified them into three forms with different legal approaches: quantity rebates, fidelity or loyalty enhancing rebates, and rebates not directly linked to a condition of exclusive or quasi-exclusive supply from the

2470 Rebates and discounts are used most of the time interchangeably in the literature despite not being exactly the same. A discount implies an immediate reduction of price of an item compared to a price list whereas a rebate implies a refund later paid by the supplier.

2471 See also Communication from the Commission — Guidance on the Commission's enforcement priorities in applying Article 82 of the EC Treaty to abusive exclusionary conduct by dominant undertakings [2009] OJ C 45/7, para. 37.

undertaking in a dominant position but where the mechanism for granting the rebate may also have a fidelity-building effect[2472].

1257. The EU case law links the granting of rebates by dominant selling undertakings with possible foreclosure and exploitative effects that, depending on the form of the rebate, can even, by virtue of its very nature, be capable of restricting competition and prohibited due to the application of dissimilar conditions to equivalent transactions[2473], limiting the ability of buyers to freely determine who they acquire goods from[2474]. The question, however, is: *Do rebates really limit buyer market power or, instead, compensate it?*

A. Do rebates restrict buyer power exercise?

1258. From an economics perspective, *rebates have a dual effect.* On the one hand, they secure or help in securing demand for a supplier because they incentivize a buyer to acquire more goods or acquire only from a specific supplier, which may lead to a quasi-exclusivity demand obligation that limits the buyer's ability to choose suppliers. In addition, but from a seller's perspective, conditional rebates can have foreclosure effects on new suppliers entering the market as there are 'tied buyers'[2475], diminish shares shifting, or reduce the capacity of current competitors to extent their market share[2476].

1259. From a buyer's perspective, the granting of a rebate – even if requested by the buyer[2477] – "*tends to remove or restrict the buyer's freedom* to choose his sources of supply," as held by the CJEU in *Michelin I*[2478]. This is the source of

2472 Judgment of 12 June 2014, *Intel v Commission,* T-286/09, ECR, EU:T:2014:547, para. 74 to 78. Cf with the Opinion of Advocate General Wahl of 20 October 2016 in *Intel Corporation v Commission,* C-413/14 P, EU:C:2016:788, paras. 39-174. Also, contrast this rather formal approach with the 'more economic approach' proposed by the Commission regarding the "as efficient competitor test" in Communication from the Commission — Guidance on the Commission's enforcement priorities in applying Article 82 of the EC Treaty to abusive exclusionary conduct by dominant undertakings [2009] OJ C 45/7, paras. 41 to 46. For some literature addressing this controversial topic see, *inter alia*: Alfonso Lamadrid, 'Breaking news- The Intel Judgment is out: the European Commission wins' (12 June 2014) <http://chillingcompetition.com/2014/06/12/breaking-news-the-intel-judgment-is-out-the-european-commission-wins/>; Charles Rivers Associates, 'Intel and the future of Article 102' (June 2014) <http://ecp.crai.com/ecp/assets/Intel_and_the_future_of_Article_102.pdf> ; Wils (2014); Geradin (2015); Italianer, 'The Object of Effects'. See also: Bishop and Walker, [2010], para. 6.028.

2473 Judgment of 12 June 2014, *Intel v Commission,* T-286/09, ECR, EU:T:2014:547, para. 80 to 93. See the opinion of Director General Italianer who draws a thin distinction between object and effect in Article 101 TFEU and nature and effect in Article 102 TFEU in Italianer, 'The Object of Effects'.

2474 Judgment of 9 November 1983 in *Michelin v Commission*, C-322/81, EU:C:1983:313, para. 73.

2475 This explains why Gormsen argues that the treatment of rebates derives from the regulation of exclusivity agreements in Liza Lovdahl Gormsen, 'Can Consumer Welfare Convincingly be Said to be an Objective of Article 102 when the Methodology Relies on an Inference of Effects?' in Caroline Heide-Jørgensen and others (eds), *Aims and Values in Competition Law* (DJØF Publ. 2013), p. 185.

2476 See also Communication from the Commission — Guidance on the Commission's enforcement priorities in applying Article 82 of the EC Treaty to abusive exclusionary conduct by dominant undertakings [2009] OJ C 45/7, para. 19; Bishop and Walker, [2010], para. 6.037.

2477 Judgment of 13 February 1979 in *Hoffmann-La Roche v Commission*, C-85/76, EU:C:1979:36, para. 89.

2478 Judgment of 9 November 1983 in *Michelin v Commission*, C-322/81, EU:C:1983:313, para. 73 (emphasis added).

competition concerns for buyer power because it means that the buyer would not purchase from other suppliers, limiting its own economic freedom (albeit most likely willingly, as I discuss below) and because it makes it more difficult for rival suppliers to reach to customers. In the US, at least in the pre-Antitrust Revolution of the '70s, the US Supreme Court also recognized that restricting the economic freedom and choice of undertakings could potentially be contrary to US antitrust law in *Silver v New York Stock Exchange*[2479]. By restricting a buyer's freedom to determine from which supplier to buy, its capacity to successfully exercise buyer power is also diminished as it is less incentivized to seek alternative supply sources.

1260. However, such restriction of the buyer's economic freedom *is in reality a retribution by the supplier to the buyer* so that the latter either accepts buying more goods from the former and/or being in a de facto exclusive supply situation. Therefore, its buyer power is exercised and compensated by the seller through the grant of the rebates, in analogy to the benefits granted in the case of exclusive purchasing, as I discuss below[2480]. Seen from the perspective of the buyer, rebates will tend to be an economically rational conduct by the seller and to the benefit of the former, which compensates the fact that the purchaser does not resort to other supply sources. Furthermore, the grant of the rebate is the way in which buyer market power reduces purchasing prices and 'neutralizes' seller market power. The price reduction is to the benefit of the buyer that sees its purchasing costs decrease and may also benefit end consumers if the reductions are passed on in the form of lower end consumer prices.

1261. The relation between the loss of the buyer's economic freedom pursuant to the rebate and the interest of the buyer to receive a discount is properly understood if the relative bargaining power of the parties is assessed. If the stronger party is the seller, the buyer, if sufficiently compensated by the rebate[2481], will be more likely to accept the 'loss' of its relative buyer power and restrict its choice of supply. In this scenario *the compensation granted by the rebate is as large or larger than the outside option of the buyer* (its BATNA). This is, the discount it would obtain from exercising its buyer power vis-à-vis this or a different supplier. Thus, even if the rebate may have a foreclosure effect for rival suppliers, it benefits the interests of the buyer. If the buyer has the competitive edge in the negotiation, then it will be able to ask for a larger rebate and/or other favorable conditions without this necessarily implying that it will enter into an exclusive purchasing relation. The stronger the buyer is,

---

2479 "Since the antitrust laws serve, among other things, to protect competitive freedom, i.e., the freedom of individual business units to compete unhindered by the group action of others" in *Silver v. New York Stock Exchange* 373 U.S. 341 (1963), 359-360. See a discussion of the goals of US antitrust law and the analysis of this Judgment in Jones (1989).

2480 Communication from the Commission — Guidance on the Commission's enforcement priorities in applying Article 82 of the EC Treaty to abusive exclusionary conduct by dominant undertakings [2009] OJ C 45/7, para. 34. See also: Guidelines on Vertical Restraints [2010] OJ C 130/1, para. 129 and 137.

2481 See Graham who argues that this perspective is in line with the Chicago School in Graham, [2010], p. 156.

the more difficult it would be for a supplier to preclude it from seeking other supply sources and obtaining better terms and conditions from the rivals of the supplier. A powerful buyer would only agree to acquire most or all goods from the same supplier if its outside option is less attractive than the rebate, which means that its loss on economic freedom is sufficiently compensated by means of better purchasing conditions.

1262. However, the granting of a rebate may also limit the ability or willingness of a buyer to exercise *countervailing buyer power*. In *Tomra and Others v Commission,* it was held that Tomra abused its dominant position as a supplier, *inter alia*, by granting loyalty enhancing rebates to its customers to exclude competition from other suppliers of Reverse Vending Machines (RVM)[2482]. As discussed in chapter 9, section §VII, Tomra unsuccessfully argued that it was not able to behave independently from its buyers because these had sufficient countervailing buyer power to neutralize its market power as a seller of RVMs. Although it was not directly addressed by either the Commission or the Courts, one argument that could explain the insufficient countervailing buyer power of the buyers of RVM, in addition to a size comparison as was done in this case, was the nature of the granting of loyalty enhancing rebates. These rebates and their exclusivity effect could have over-compensated the loss of the buyer's freedom to resort to alternative sources of supply because of the retribution paid by the dominant firm was larger. This could mean that buyers were not incentivized to exert countervailing buyer power or resort to outside options. If seen as such, the rebate had a dual purpose/effect: excluding other suppliers of RVM by limiting the freedom of buyers to shift their demand, and reduce their ability to neutralize the supplier's seller power as there were few supplying options and sponsoring entry or self-sourcing was not a realistic possibility.

1263. Summing up, although the EU case law argues that rebates *tend to remove or restrict the buyer's freedom* to choose his sources of supply, this restriction is usually a *compensation for the loss of its ability to resort to alternative suppliers* and it is in the *self-interest of the buyer*. However, for that to happen, the rebate must represent an economic advantage as good as or better than the buyer's outside option (which would be resorting to other suppliers). This effect to the benefit of the buyer prevents other suppliers from having access to this source of demand, which is why rebates might have a foreclosure effect with regard to sellers. On the other hand, if the *rebate compensation is not large enough then the buyer will rather resort to an alternative source of*

2482 Summary of Commission Decision of 29 March 2006 relating to a proceeding under Article 82 of the Treaty establishing the European Community and Article 54 of the EEA Agreement against Tomra Systems ASA, Tomra Europe AS, Tomra Systems BV, Tomra Systems GmbH, Tomra Butikksystemer AS, Tomra Systems AB and Tomra Leergutsysteme GmbH (Case COMP/E-1/38.113 — *Prokent/Tomra*) [2008] OJ C 219/11; Judgment of 9 September 2010, *Tomra Systems and Others v Commission*, T-155/06, ECR, EU:T:2010:370; Judgment of 19 April 2012 in *Tomra and Others v Commission*, C-549/10 P, EU:C:2012:221.

supply in exercise of its economic freedom. Hence, the limitation of a buyer's economic freedom through rebates can be seen as a compensation for the exercise of its buyer power and in the self-interest of buyers.

1264. However, from a legal perspective, the fact that buyers see their ability to exercise buyer market power diminished and compensated by the rebate, even if it implies a loss in their economic freedom, is not the main reason why the granting of conditional and unjustified rebates by dominant undertaking. In fact, rebates that are agreed between sellers and buyers (being the buyer sufficiently compensated) *can be and are anti-competitive because of the foreclosing effect it has on rival suppliers, but not solely because of the effects on the buyer*. In other words, the main theory of harm in which the prohibition of rebates is grounded is *the ability to foreclose rival suppliers from being able to attract demand from buyers* and, therefore, the restriction of buyer's economic freedom appears as a secondary and less important consideration in this respect.

V. Countervailing benefits in exclusive branding and exclusive purchasing obligations

1265. Similarly, as occurs with rebates in general, countervailing benefits in exclusive branding and exclusive purchasing obligations are incentives granted by suppliers to create an exclusivity relation with a specific buyer. Single branding agreements comprise contracts in which "the buyer is obliged or induced to concentrate its orders for a particular type of product with one supplier"[2483], while an exclusive purchasing obligation is a sub-type of single branding agreements, as remarked by Whish and Bailey[2484]. These types of contracts constitute vertical agreements that will benefit from the Block Exemption Regulation if the share of each of the parties is less than 30%[2485] and the duration is less than five years[2486]. However, not all purchasing agreements would be within the scope of application of the Block Exemption Regulation

2483 Guidelines on Vertical Restraints [2010] OJ C 130/1, para. 129.

2484 Whish and Bailey, *Competition law* [2012], p. 637.

2485 Article 3, Commission Regulation (EU) No 330/2010 of 20 April 2010 on the application of Article 101(3) of the Treaty on the Functioning of the European Union to categories of vertical agreements and concerted practices [2010] OJ L 102/1.

2486 Article 5.1(a), Commission Regulation (EU) No 330/2010 of 20 April 2010 on the application of Article 101(3) of the Treaty on the Functioning of the European Union to categories of vertical agreements and concerted practices [2010] OJ L 102/1.

and their effects in competition law should be assessed on a case-by-case basis[2487]. This is because these types of agreements, particularly if entered into by many buyers with a large supplier, may lead to anti-competitive foreclosure of other suppliers that are unable to get sources of demand, preventing the entry or expansion of other undertakings and reducing variety or choice of different goods[2488].

1266. Furthermore, these of agreements limit the ability of buyers to resort to other suppliers, as rebates do, although not based on quantities or conditional benefits; instead they constitute a naked exclusivity obligation. However, buyers with bargaining power would not allow themselves to be cut off from the supply of the competing goods or services when entering into these agreements with a supplier unless *they receive some form of compensation*[2489]. The intuition behind this is that the powerful buyer will see its product variety diminished at the expense of arguably cheaper input costs. This form of compensation is granted by the seller through *countervailing benefits,* which are price or non-price concessions in favor of the buyer so that the latter agrees to concentrate its orders for a particular good or service from a single supplier[2490].

1267. The existence of these countervailing benefits, granted by the supplier to the buyer as a compensation for accepting the exclusive purchasing, is taken into account by the Courts and the Commission as additional factors to determine the likelihood of the agreement having anti-competitive effects, particularly regarding intra and inter-brand competition. In the remainder of this section, I discuss the nature of countervailing benefits and its assessment from a buyer's perspective.

A. What are countervailing benefits?

1268. *Countervailing benefits*[2491] are a form of compensation granted by sellers to buyers due to the loss of the latter's ability to seek alternative supply sources by accepting an exclusive purchasing obligation, or being forced into them by a supplier undertaking. These benefits are taken into account to determine the anti-competitiveness of a single branding agreement because they help to determine the effects regarding intra-brand competition, as only certain goods

---

2487 "The Court observes, as a preliminary point, that the exclusivity clause does not require retailers to sell only HB products in their sales outlets. Consequently, that clause is not, in formal terms, an exclusive purchasing obligation whose object is to restrict competition on the relevant market," in Judgment of 23 October 2003 in *Van den Bergh Foods v Commission*, T-65/98, EU:T:2003:281, para. 80; Whish and Bailey, *Competition law* [2012], p. 638.

2488 Guidelines on Vertical Restraints [2010] OJ C 130/1, para. 137 *in fine*.

2489 Guidelines on Vertical Restraints [2010] OJ C 130/1, para. 137.

2490 Guidelines on Vertical Restraints [2010] OJ C 130/1, para. 129 and 137.

2491 Graham calls these benefits "incentive schemes" in Graham, [2010] 407, p. 407. See also calling them "reciprocal benefits": Jones and Sufrin, *EU Competition Law: Text, Cases, and Materials* [2011], p. 663.

from the same company can be acquired[2492], and, more obviously, because it forces buyers not to buy and resell or expose goods from other suppliers, as it was required in *Joynson v Commission*[2493].

1269. If a supplier attempts to impose an exclusive purchasing obligation it must grant

> the reseller *certain economic and financial benefits*, such as the grant of loans on favourable terms, the letting of premises for the operation of a public house and the provision of technical installations, furniture and other equipment necessary for its operation. In *consideration for those benefits*, the reseller normally undertakes, for a predetermined period, to obtain supplies of the products covered by the contract only from the supplier[2494].

1270. These benefits take several forms but usually are linked to lower rental prices to be paid by tenants to a beer producer, quality-related in the form of valued added services such as discount on glassware, gas, supply, banking insurance, insurance and paint[2495], or for instance capital maintenance and repairs of fixtures and fittings[2496], as well as benefiting from the "group's purchasing power in relation to the insurance of the premises"[2497].

1271. The evaluation of these benefits, along with the agreement's content as a whole, determine whether the single branding obligation is compatible with the internal market and has a positive effect in the distribution of a good, by sufficiently compensating the buyers and, in some cases, also having an overall positive effect in the market, as remarked by the General Court in *Shaw and Falla v Commission*[2498].

1272. Hence, countervailing benefits are evaluated to determine if an agreement is indeed anti-competitive or may satisfy the requirements of Article 101(3) TFEU – as occurred in *Scottish and Newcastle*[2499] – or whether a single dominant undertaking may benefit from an objective justification under Article 102 TFEU, although this latter possibility is highly unlikely due to the obvious

2492 Commission Decision of 16 June 1999 relating to a proceeding pursuant to Article 81 of the EC Treaty (Case IV/36.081/F3 — *Bass*) [1999] OJ L 186/1, para. 43.

2493 Commission Decision of 16 June 1999 relating to a proceeding pursuant to Article 81 of the EC Treaty (Case IV/36.081/F3 — *Bass*) [1999] OJ L 186/1, para. 119.

2494 Judgment of 28 February 1991 in *Delimitis v Henninger Bräu*, C-234/89, EU:C:1991:91, para. 10 (emphasis added).

2495 Commission Decision of 16 June 1999 relating to a proceeding pursuant to Article 81 of the EC Treaty (Case IV/36.081/F3 — *Bass*) [1999] OJ L 186/1, para. 76.

2496 Commission Decision of 16 June 1999 relating to a proceeding pursuant to Article 81 of the EC Treaty (Case IV/35.992/F3 - *Scottish and Newcastle*) [1999] OJ L 186/28, para. 79.

2497 Commission Decision of 16 June 1999 relating to a proceeding pursuant to Article 81 of the EC Treaty (Case IV/35.992/F3 - *Scottish and Newcastle*) [1999] OJ L 186/28, para. 81.

2498 Judgment of 21 March 2002, *Shaw and Falla v Commission*, T-131/99, ECR, EU:T:2002:83, para. 163.

2499 Commission Decision of 16 June 1999 relating to a proceeding pursuant to Article 81 of the EC Treaty (Case IV/35.992/F3 - *Scottish and Newcastle*) [1999] OJ L 186/28.

foreclosure effects triggered by an exclusive supply purchasing obligation[2500], as confirmed in *Hoffmann-La Roche v Commission*[2501].

1273. To determine the sufficiency of the countervailing benefits and its effects on the buyer's economic freedom in cases related to vertical agreements, the Courts, in a series of cases dealing with beer distribution, applied a '*countervailing benefits test*'. The analysis has the aim "to determine whether the improvements of distribution brought about by the standard leases could materialize notwithstanding the existence of price differentials for tied leases", as remarked by the General Court[2502]. Also, and from a buyer's perspective, the test also determines if the countervailing benefits compensate the buyer for "the loss in competition resulting from the exclusivity" and limit the loss in intra-brand and inter-brand competition[2503]. Therefore, the countervailing effect neutralizes the negative consequences imposed by the exclusivity and non-competition obligations by rewarding buyers that lose their ability to seek alternative suppliers and also benefit beer distribution as a whole[2504].

1274. Lastly, despite the name that may lead to confusions and the existence of a comparison test with countervailing buyer power, a concept I discussed in chapter 9, *countervailing benefits do not act as a direct market power neutralizer, but instead act as a compensation for the loss of commercial freedom of a buyer*.

B. How are countervailing benefits assessed in vertical agreements?

1275. As mentioned, the Courts have evaluated countervailing benefits in connection with the analysis of the competitive effects of single branding agreements in cases related to beer distribution. In this section, I discuss how the countervailing benefits were assessed in each of them.

2500 As remarked by Whish and Bailey, there is little but unequivocal case law dealing with exclusive purchasing agreements granted by dominant undertakings and which appears to be a prohibition almost per se or by nature, Whish and Bailey, *Competition law* [2012], p. 683-684.

2501 "An undertaking which is in a dominant position on a market and ties purchasers — even if it does so at their request — by an *obligation or promise on their part to obtain all or most of their requirements exclusively from the said undertaking abuses its dominant position* within the meaning of Article [102] of the Treaty, whether the obligation in question is *stipulated without further qualification* or whether it is undertaken in consideration of the grant of a rebate", Judgment of 13 February 1979 in *Hoffmann-La Roche v Commission*, C-85/76, EU:C:1979:36, para. 89 (emphasis added). See also the same wording in Judgment of 17 December 2009, *Solvay v Commission*, T-57/01, ECR, EU:T:2009:519, para. 365; Judgment of 25 June 2010, *Imperial Chemical Industries v Commission*, T-66/01, ECR, EU:T:2010:255, para. 315.

2502 Judgment of 21 March 2002, *Joynson v Commission*, T-231/99, ECR, EU:T:2002:84, para. 150.

2503 See also Communication from the Commission — Guidance on the Commission's enforcement priorities in applying Article 82 of the EC Treaty to abusive exclusionary conduct by dominant undertakings [2009] OJ C 45/7, para. 34.

2504 See also raising this point concerning the convenience for the buyer to accept the countervailing benefits despite losing its supply options in Communication from the Commission — Guidance on the Commission's enforcement priorities in applying Article 82 of the EC Treaty to abusive exclusionary conduct by dominant undertakings [2009] OJ C 45/7, para. 34.

1276. In *Delimitis* the CJEU for the first time dealt *in extenso* with the compatibility of agreements related to beer distribution containing non-compete obligations and minimum purchasing quantities clauses and countervailing benefits[2505]. The CJEU concluded that exclusive purchasing obligations – even if mostly pro-competitive and covered by the Block Exemption Regulation[2506] – between breweries and its lessees may be incompatible with Article 101 TFEU under two cumulative conditions. First, the agreements might make it difficult for competitors to enter the market or increase their market share to gain access to the national market for beer distribution. Second, the individual agreement must make a significant contribution to the sealing-off effect generated by the totality of these types of agreements in the market[2507].

1277. However, the agreements can benefit from an efficiency exemption if they *grant sufficient countervailing benefits* to the tied buyers in compensation for the suppression of its contractual freedom and the loss of its buyer power. In so doing, the CJEU introduced in *Delimitis* a comparison test between the granted benefits and the effects of the exclusive purchase obligation to determine whether these favorable conditions for the reseller are gained in practice, and as required at the time by Article 8(2) of Regulation 1984/83[2508].

1278. Building on the *Delimitis,* the Commission and the General Court reviewed exclusive purchasing agreements and the assessment of the countervailing benefits going further and developing the methodology employed to determine its sufficiency.

1279. In *Joynson v Commission,* the Commission and the General Court reviewed the legality of exclusive purchasing agreements that were declared incompatible with Article 101(1) TFEU and did not fulfill the requirements of the efficiency defense under Article 101(3) TFEU between Bass PLC – "Bass" – and its lessees operating public houses in the United Kingdom[2509]. As part of the lease, Bass incorporated an exclusive purchasing and non-competition clause (beer tie). This beer tie obliged Bass tenants to acquire their beer in an almost exclusive manner from

---

2505 Judgment of 28 February 1991 in *Delimitis v Henninger Bräu*, C-234/89, EU:C:1991:91. See also: Korah and O'Sullivan, [2002], p. 290-291.

2506 Articles 3 and 5 of the Commission Regulation (EU) No 330/2010 of 20 April 2010 on the application of Article 101(3) of the Treaty on the Functioning of the European Union to categories of vertical agreements and concerted practices [2010] OJ L 102/1.

2507 Judgment of 28 February 1991 in *Delimitis v Henninger Bräu*, C-234/89, EU:C:1991:91, para. 27. For the cumulative effects on competition of these type of agreements see: Judgment of 12 December 1967 in *Brasserie De Haecht v Wilkin Janssen*, C-23/67, EU:C:1967:54, p. 415.

2508 Judgment of 28 February 1991 in *Delimitis v Henninger Bräu*, C-234/89, EU:C:1991:91. Commission Regulation (EEC) No 1984/83 of 22 June 1983 on the application of Article 85 (3) of the Treaty to categories of exclusive purchasing agreements [1983] OJ L 173/5. In the Opinion of Advocate General Van Gerven if a beer exclusive supply agreement does not include a "more favourable terms" clause falls outside the application of Regulation 1984/83, see: Opinion of Advocate General Van Gerven of 11 October 1990 in Judgment of 28 February 1991 in *Delimitis v Henninger Bräu*, C-234/89, EU:C:1990:358.

2509 Commission Decision of 16 June 1999 relating to a proceeding pursuant to Article 81 of the EC Treaty (Case IV/36.081/F3 — *Bass*) [1999] OJ L 186/1.

Bass, even if the purchasing conditions to acquire goods from other parties were more favorable. When analyzing the countervailing benefit effects the General Court confirmed that *a comparison has to be made* in order to determine whether the improvements for beer distribution generated by the exclusive purchasing are able to materialize despite the price differential lost by the exclusive buyer[2510].

1280. As in *Delimitis*, the beer ties could benefit beer distribution but also cause negative price differentials to the tenant's detriment as these would be *unable to exercise their buyer power* by losing alternative supply sources, particularly regarding lower whole purchasing prices than those obtained by non-tied pubs[2511]. To determine whether the tenants were sufficiently compensated, the Commission did a comparison test assessing "*the trade-off between the detrimental price differential 'lost' by the pubs with the quantification of the benefits*"[2512]. If the benefits sufficiently compensated, the "'average' lessee was therefore in a position to compete on a 'level playing field' with its trade counterpart"[2513]. If so, then, the exclusive purchasing agreement may satisfy the requirements of Article 101(3) TFEU. Pursuant to an annulment action, the General Court further developed the methodology and it held that the trade-off is to be evaluated by means of a *comparison test* through which "a specific comparison had to be made between the position of Bass tied lessees and that of individual free trade operators"[2514]. To carry out the test, countervailing benefits ought to be calculated by comparing the trade-off between the price differentials 'lost' by the purchaser object to an exclusive purchasing agreement when compared to non-tied purchasers and the countervailing benefits granted by the supplier[2515].

1281. In *Shaw and Falla v Commission,* the General Court went one step further by assessing which undertakings should be part of the comparison. With this it took a restrictive approach as it dismissed arguments to broaden the type of beer-selling places and evaluate the different benefits these types of undertakings receive. The General Court clarified that the comparison ought to be made with undertakings that operate at "the same level of distribution as Whitbread's tied lessees, so that a reliable comparison may be made with those lessees"[2516]. Thus, other kinds of beer retailers, such as pub companies, managed houses and clubs should not need to be taken into account when defining the comparison group based on an argument of *collective bargaining power.* Non-tied pubs

---

2510 Judgment of 21 March 2002, *Joynson v Commission*, T-231/99, ECR, EU:T:2002:84, para. 150.

2511 Commission Decision of 16 June 1999 relating to a proceeding pursuant to Article 81 of the EC Treaty (Case IV/36.081/F3 — *Bass*) [1999] OJ L 186/1, para. 177-179.

2512 Commission Decision of 16 June 1999 relating to a proceeding pursuant to Article 81 of the EC Treaty (Case IV/36.081/F3 — *Bass*) [1999] OJ L 186/1, para. 186; Bellamy and others, [2013], para. 7.156.

2513 Commission Decision of 16 June 1999 relating to a proceeding pursuant to Article 81 of the EC Treaty (Case IV/36.081/F3 — *Bass*) [1999] OJ L 186/1, para. 186.

2514 Judgment of 21 March 2002, *Joynson v Commission*, T-231/99, ECR, EU:T:2002:84, para. 150.

2515 Bellamy and others, [2013], para. 7-154.

2516 Judgment of 21 March 2002, *Shaw and Falla v Commission*, T-131/99, ECR, EU:T:2002:83, para. 69.

had to buy on an individual basis vis-à-vis the beer supplier, whereas tied pubs negotiated "collectively for the whole pub company or brewery. It follows that the amounts of beer order are much greater (...), and the discounts given by Whitbread on those collective orders are consequently higher than those given on order from individual free house operators"[2517]. Hence, the scope of the benefits of tied leases, who purchased collectively was broader and therefore the assessment should have not included independent pub owners.

1282. Additionally, a reading of the case law seems to suggest that the sufficiency of the countervailing benefits goes beyond a mere retribution to the buyers tied but also *requires an improvement regarding the overall distribution chain*, as remarked in *Shaw and Falla v Commission,* in an analogue to the *spillover effect in cases of countervailing buyer power,* as I discussed in chapter 9, section §VIII. The General Court required this additional element because as *the context of the exemption of the lease agreements was general, the countervailing benefits were to be also generally assessed* taking into account the effect "on the functioning of the market, and hence on the situation of the tied lessees taken as a whole, not on each lessee considered in isolation"[2518]. Thus, the countervailing benefits have to produce an *overall* market benefit, regardless of whether it may or may not have a different scope concerning individual beneficiaries[2519].

1283. Lastly, the case law confirms that in the assessment of the countervailing benefits, it is irrelevant whether these originated in pre-established contractual obligations or were voluntarily granted by the supplier "once it was certain that they were actually made available only to tied lessees and were quantifiable"[2520].

C. Conclusions regarding countervailing benefits

1284. Countervailing benefits represent, like rebates, a different type of compensation a supplier must offer to a buyer so that the latter accepts having restricted its ability to exercise buyer power by precluding the buyer from switching to alternative sources of supply. Despite the terminology used, these countervailing benefits are not equivalent to the concept of countervailing buyer power because they do not aim at neutralizing seller market power, sensu stricto. However, they do have in common that to determine whether the conduct is anti-competitive, a comparison test must be made between the tradeoffs of accepting the exclusive obligation or being able to freely negotiate with other suppliers. If the tradeoff is sufficient, then this is a factor to take into account

2517 Judgment of 21 March 2002, *Shaw and Falla v Commission*, T-131/99, ECR, EU:T:2002:83, para. 70.

2518 Judgment of 21 March 2002, *Shaw and Falla v Commission*, T-131/99, ECR, EU:T:2002:83, para. 163.

2519 Also of the same opinion is Townley when stating "[o]ne should look at the overall impact of all the notified agreements, in their economic context, as opposed to examining the impact on individual members of the group in isolation", in Townley, [2009], p. 189.

2520 Judgment of 21 March 2002, *Joynson v Commission*, T-231/99, ECR, EU:T:2002:84, para. 150.

when determining the adverse effects on inter and intra-brand competition. This comparison takes into account the many and varied types of compensatory benefits vis-à-vis the detrimental price differential 'lost' by the pubs, but also requires, that, the exclusive supply obligation has an overall positive effect in the distribution of the good in the market overall, which resembles the spillover effect of countervailing buyer power.

1285. Lastly, unlike the cases of imposing minimum purchasing prices or limiting supply, the granting of a countervailing benefit, even if it limits a buyer from exerting its buyer power will be, by itself, unlikely to be deemed as an anti-competitive practice. In fact, it is the reverse: the countervailing benefits may allow an exclusive purchasing agreement to be exempted from being prohibited by Article 101(1) TFEU, as shown by the case law.

1286. However, the legal treatment to the same type of exclusive dealing under an objective justification analysis within Article 102 TFEU is quite different, as there is no evidence that neither the Courts nor the Commission resort to the analysis of countervailing benefits to justify the imposition of exclusive supply obligations. In fact, the case law dealing with exclusive dealing is very strict because it is assumed that the likelihood of anti-competitive foreclosure effects are much higher than in the case of 'vertical agreements'. Therefore, it is unlikely that the granting of some form of compensation to buyers would sufficiently address the concern created over the competitive conditions of rival buyers, and would be adequate to justify the conduct over an objective analysis justification within the application of Article 102 TFEU, as it happens with the granting of rebates with an anti-competitive foreclosure effect.

VI. Conclusions

1287. In this chapter I have discussed buyer power from a reverse angle when compared to the rest of this study. Instead of analyzing how buyer power is exerted, I have shown four different mechanisms through which sellers aim at limiting the exercise of buyer power. EU competition law protects the exercise of buyer power against interferences regarding the competitive setting of prices and the economic freedom of buyers, a position echoed under US antitrust law, particularly when dealing with boycotting agreements that are treated as per se violations[2521].

1288. Regarding the imposition of minimum purchasing prices and limiting supply, the aim is to prevent suppliers from having to transfer part of their profit

2521 Jones (1989), p. 89.

to the buyers by artificially and anti-competitively intervening in the natural price formation. These two anti-competitive conducts have in common that their *object or nature is to restrict competition* and are, therefore, likely to be held liable from infringing either Article 101(1) TFEU or Article 102(b) TFEU. The case law and the Commission's practice further clarify that these two types of practices seldom occur and when they do these tend to be the outcome of *an agreement among agricultural suppliers* and, more often than not, pursuant to a decision by an association of undertakings. The reason why these suppliers' cartels arise in agricultural markets can be explained due to the likelihood that these sellers were or are dependent on the buyers and joined forces to neutralize the imposition of arguably 'exploitative' practices. Also, I have shown that pursuant to the case the law and the Commission's practice, undertakings that fix purchasing prices or set selling quotas are unlikely to benefit from an efficiency defense under either Article 101(3) or Article 102 TFEU because the extent of the conduct's anti-competitive effects is clear and the probability of procompetitive effects is remote[2522]. However, the fact that there is a sectoral crisis or that buyers are in a weaker position may be taken into account when setting the fines as an attenuating circumstance.

1289. Also, the chapter has shown the exceptional case of *lawful sellers' cartels* in the *market for raw milk.* This specific and rare piece of legislation allows milk producers to jointly negotiate prices to counteract the buyer power of large retailers while being temporarily excluded from the application of EU competition law. Nevertheless, Regulation 261/2012 sets rather strict requirements for this waiver to apply, which also begs the question of whether such a solution has any impact when it comes to the price negotiation of raw milk purchases and, furthermore, whether such an interventionist approach might be detrimental for the wellbeing of end consumers in the form of higher final purchasing prices.

1290. When buyer power is restricted through *unilateral behaviour suppliers resort to rebates,* instead of fixing prices or purchasing quotas, to hinder the ability of buyers to freely determine with whom to carry out their purchases. More than simply restricting the buyer's freedom, the aim of rebates is to compensate the buyer for its loss of buyer power, as if the buyer is able to obtain better contractual conditions elsewhere, it will require a further and better discounts from the supplier. Yet, rebates restrict the ability of buyers to seek alternative supply sources, in particular if the buyer is weak in relation to the seller and, is over-compensated, because its outside option of negotiating with a third party as that alternative will be less profitable. This concern regarding the limitation of the buyers' freedom is a secondary and linked theory of harm to the risk of anti-competitive foreclosure effects that conditional rebates have

2522 *Northwest Wholesale Stationers, Inc. v. Pacific Stationery Printing Co.*, 472 U.S. 284 (1985), 294.

over rival suppliers, because these benefits restrict their ability to find sources of demand. In other words, conditional rebates by dominant undertakings are prohibited mainly due to their foreclosure effects on rival buyers and less so because they limit the buyer's economic freedom. This is also the case when dealing with *exclusive purchasing obligations imposed by dominant undertakings,* which are highly likely to be anti-competitive by nature due to their foreclosure effects rather than the buyer's economic freedom restriction.

1291. Also, I analyzed how, in the cases of exclusive vertical purchasing agreements, a supplier will compensate its buyer for the loss of the ability of the latter to exert buyer power, in particular regarding the price differential it would obtain if not tied under an exclusive purchasing obligations. These countervailing benefits have been factored in when determining the compatibility of exclusive purchasing agreements in beer retailing with Article 101 TFEU and whether, as a whole, the agreement improves the distribution of beer in the market under an efficiency analysis pursuant to Article 101(3) TFEU. Despite their name, the countervailing benefits test assesses the limitation of buyer power but not the countervailing of opposing seller market power, as CPB would do. Also, I have shown how these benefits are assessed through a comparison test and which sorts of factors are taken into account.

1292. Lastly, in *none of these four modalities in which buyer power limitation was found to be a breach of EU competition law was end consumer harm a deciding factor*. Conducts fixing purchasing prices, limiting supply, granting exclusionary rebates, or creating exclusive purchasing obligations are prohibited under EU competition to protect the natural formation of prices in the market – the core of the competitive process as such under an ordoliberal perspective – and to safeguard the economic freedom of buyers, which reinforces this study's conclusion that buyer power regulation in EU competition law takes a broader stance than one simply centered on pure end consumer harm.

PART VI

CONCLUSIONS OF THIS STUDY

11

FINAL CONCLUSIONS

I. Introduction

1293. Echoing the introduction of this study, my aim has been to determine the legal treatment that is afforded to buyer power by EU competition law as expressed in the judgments and decisions by the Courts, the Commission and policy makers. Hence, this work aims at clarifying *what the EU competition law regulation of buyer power is,* from a *de lege lata* perspective.

1294. In pursuance of this goal, *my aim has been to identify, synthetize, clarify, discuss, evaluate, and compare the EU competition regulation of buyer power in a holistic manner across all areas of EU competition law*. Moreover, I carried out this legal analysis based on an economically informed legal analysis integrated into the legal discussion anchored on state of the art microeconomics and I have employed ordoliberalism as a benchmarking tool to determine the degree of similarity of EU regulation of buyer power with this competition policy school of thought. Additionally, I have contrasted the regulation of buying conducts under EU competition law with equivalent cases in US antitrust law, and, to a far lesser extent, to some MS, to determine similarities and differences. A pure comparative buyer power study is an area ripe for further research.

1295. In this conclusion, I identify the findings of my study through a synthesis of my general and chapter findings, and discuss what, in my view, the future of buyer power looks like in terms of competition enforcement, policy making and future research.

II. General findings

1296. Buyer power has been, and remains, something of a secondary and rare topic within EU competition law. I put forth four reasons that provide an explanation regarding why buyer power has received little competition enforcement and academic scholarship. First, *anti-competitive buyer power cases are rare*. On the one hand, monopsony power exertion seldom occurs because it is not the most profit-maximizing purchasing behaviour and it may force suppliers to exit the market, leaving the buyer without input sources. On the other hand, anti-competitive instances of buyer power are rare because *bargaining power tends to be efficiency enhancing and, therefore, it improves and increases welfare*. If the buyer conduct is efficient and improves welfare, suppliers will be unwilling to bring forth a case without merit as competition authorities will not condemn the behaviour because it does not negatively affect competition. Second, because of the rarity of buyer power cases, competition authorities have not prioritized them compared to other anti-competitive conducts, as occurs in the EU, with regard to the Commission's enforcement priorities. This lack of enforcement importance is also connected with the view of some competition authorities – mainly the US antitrust law agencies and, to a much lesser degree, the Commission – and academics that only see buyer power as a competition problem whenever there is evidence of direct end consumer harm, as discussed in *Weyerhaeuser*. Therefore, and as a third reason, *absent evidence of direct end consumer harm, competition authorities may be less tempted to initiate proceedings against a buying conduct that may be anti-competitive but only regarding upstream competition, affecting suppliers or rival buyers*. This narrow approach is something I have argued against through the study. My criticism is grounded on the fact that such a stringent perspective disregards the EU competition law goals of protecting competition as a process by focusing purely on the downstream aspects of buyer power cases. Such a restrictive view overlooks that by protecting competition as such and the competitive process substantial harm to the competitive upstream structure will also negatively impact upon the wellbeing of end consumers in the medium and long-term. Consequently, this narrow approach to buyer power harm should not be adopted as it entails under-enforcement risks and acts contrary to the protection of the competitive process and a dualistic approach to buyer power conducts. Lastly, a fourth reason that may explain the lack of buyer power cases is that *up to now there is scant legal guidance available regarding conducts that may constitute buyer power abuses* and suppliers and rival buyers may be less willing to bring forth claims because of the uncertainties and difficulty in determining whether the conduct would be anti-competitive.

1297. This limited amount of anti-competitive buyer power cases observed in practice also applies regarding *unfair purchasing practices,* behaviours that are said to be exerted by large buyers in the food retailing sector and which have attracted significant societal and political attention. I have also shown that unfair purchasing practices by and large do not constitute a competition law problem because they *tend to have limited adverse welfare effects from a static or dynamic efficiency perspective, not having a substantial impact in competition as a process in either the upstream or the downstream markets.* Instead, what takes place is a redistribution of profits between suppliers and buyers on a bilateral level based on the bargaining power of the parties, which is better regulated by means of other types of legislation suited to deal with contractual balancing.

1298. Furthermore, I have shown why *treating buyer power fully economically and symmetrical to monopoly power is not the correct approach*, nor is the way in which the Courts apply the law to it. This is an undesirable one because buyer power economics and its effects are not symmetrical to monopoly power. My research confirms that EU competition law is not applied nor designed in buyer power cases to be fully symmetrical – albeit also not that different treatment – when compared to analogue selling side conducts. Adopting a purely symmetrical approach to selling side cases would disregard the particularities of buyer (and especially bargaining) power effects, its dualistic nature in the upstream and downstream markets and that buyer power cases have triggered, and will trigger, competition intervention absent end consumer harm, the countervailing nature of buyer power, and the fact that bargaining power can, and tends to be, efficiency enhancing, unlike monopoly power. However, *this does not imply that I advocate for a complete reshaping of EU competition law relating to buyer power cases,* nor that in the absence of buyer power precedents, selling side cases cannot be used to analogically guide the application of the law with the proper adjustments to buyer power realities. Using analogue selling side cases as guidance is justified as it would preserve the inner logic of EU competition policy as a whole, and would provide undertakings further legal certainty and a greater ability to predict to some degree the legality of a conduct.

1299. Furthermore, and connected to the former, buyer power cases can be divided into two large categories: those involving demand withholding (monopsony effect) and those involving price reduction by other means (bargaining power). *Concerning monopsony power, both the economics and the legal regime applicable are straight-forward*: monopsony conducts are anti-competitive because they generate a societal deadweight loss to allocative efficiency and may also have detrimental effects on end consumers if the buyer also has downstream market power. Thus, for monopsony cases, their evaluation and legal treatment is rather unsophisticated. Nevertheless, monopsony seldom arises, as confirmed in this study, as instances of demand-withholding do not occur often and when they do so these conducts have been found to be naked and obvious restrictions of competition. Therefore, *the legal and economic discussion should be centered on bargaining power* cases and conducts because they occur more often, do not have straight-forward answers, and require more detailed legal and economic analysis.

1300. Within the scope of this distinction of buyer power cases, I have found that *EU competition law in general seems to treat buyer power in a coherent and rather homogenous way across all its areas, as the Courts and the Commission do not make unjustified or unobserved distinctions among the different cases, nor when compared to equivalent seller side cases*. In other words, buyer power cases are treated consistently despite the fact that the conducts may arise in different competition law areas. For example, a buyer actively countervails the seller power of a unilateral undertaking, but it may also do so regarding future behaviour pursuant a concentration among sellers, or the fact that monopsony power can be exerted by a single undertaking or a buyers' cartel. *This does not mean, however, that buyer power regulation has to be identical in all areas of EU competition law.* Single and coordinated behaviours differ by nature and what might be forbidden as a unilateral conduct for a dominant undertaking could be allowed for a non-dominant one, and what is forbidden in an agreement might not be for unilateral conduct, as the legal and policy treatment distinguish between them. Furthermore, even if the Courts and the Commission do not make an express distinction between monopsony and bargaining power by 'labeling the conducts,' the case law does indeed implicitly recognize that monopsony and bargaining power are different sub-types of buyer power with different economic implications in the *ratio decidendi*. This is quite palpable in several types of conducts. For example, *concerning bargaining power,* buying alliances are seen as a pro-competitive and enjoy a presumption of legality, as well as the benevolent approach to countervailing buyer power; whereas in the case of monopsony power, buyers' cartels, exploitatively low purchasing practices, and restrictions on purchasing quantities, are under a rebuttable presumption of anti-competitiveness and it is up to the involved undertakings to prove that the effects are not anti-competitive, which is highly unlikely.

1301. This *coherent and homogenous treatment of buyer power in EU competition law is the appropriate approach* for several reasons. First, *applying different unjustified legal regulations to the same economic problems* concerning, for example, buyer power exclusion or exploitation *is economically unsound and discriminatory* as the legal regime would treat equivalent circumstances in different ways. Second, applying a uniform and coherent treatment to buyer power regardless of the competition area in which the conduct takes place generates *internal cohesion of the legal system*; at the same time, this *guarantees predictability and legal certainty* which allows undertakings to evaluate whether their purchasing conduct conforms with EU competition law. Third, there are no economic nor legal arguments that support a different buyer power treatment based solely on the specific area of the law to be applied; what does find support in the economics literature is distinguishing whether the conduct involves a monopsony or bargaining power effect and the fact that its competitive analysis is different.

1302. However, the extent of this coherent and homogenous treatment is limited and has not been tested for consistency because most of the theories of harm analyzed in this study have been addressed, if at all, only once or few times by the Courts and others only by the Commission's practice. Consequently, there have been limited opportunities for the Courts to re-assess their previous judgment on analogue cases; when that has occurred the case law shows that there is an overall consistency. Nevertheless, it also shows that a more specific and detailed assessment of cases involving coordinate behaviour and countervailing buyer power exist when compared to other buyer power topics. Yet, there seems to be little room for a radical re-structuring of the ongoing buyer power treatment as a whole.

1303. An aspect of the case law that can be criticized concerning the regulation and legal treatment of buyer power is the lack of sophisticated and explicit economic discussions concerning buyer power effects (and the dichotomy between monopsony and buyer power) in contrast to the far more economically explicit judgments of US courts. This lack of 'economic explicit jargon' by the Courts is not exclusive to buyer power cases; on the contrary it is a general characteristic of EU competition law, and can be explained by the nature of the judicial revisions of the courts and the European legal traditions.

1304. Additionally, I submitted that buyer power cases have to be *analyzed from a dualistic perspective*. This is so because buyer power has effects both in the upstream market where the purchasing activity takes place vis-à-vis suppliers and rival buyers, and in the downstream market where the buyer acts as a retailer having effects on end consumers and rival sellers (that may or may not be rival buyers). This dualistic approach requires carrying out a dualistic market definition and taking into account the buying conduct's effects in both markets to fully capture the competition impact it has.

1305. In connection to the former, I demonstrated that buyer power is at its most pernicious *whenever the undertaking involved has market power both as a buyer and retailer as an hourglass-shaped* undertaking, as confirmed by buyer power economics, the Commission's practice and the case law. As a buyer in the upstream market, the undertaking will exert its market power vis-à-vis suppliers to obtain a price reduction, and, as it has substantial seller market power, it is not pressured by competition as a retailer to pass on the buyer power benefits to end consumers. Hence, and as a general indicator, *whenever buyer market power is exerted by an undertaking that has concurrent buyer and seller market power, then buyer power abuse is more likely and more pernicious*. On the other hand, if the undertaking has buyer market power but faces stern downstream competition, it is much more likely that the obtained price reductions as a buyer will be passed on to end consumers as a result of the competitive pressure. The pressure exerted by downstream competitors explains why US antitrust law and the Commission center their attention on cases where short-term downstream end consumer harm takes place. However, this does not imply that buyer power may not be pernicious absent end consumer harm as rival buyers may not compete as retailers or simply because buyer power may negatively impact the competitiveness of the market in the upstream market exclusively. Building on this, the fact that an undertaking has substantial market power as a buyer and as a retailer is a preliminary indication that the exercise of buyer power in a market may lead to competition issues, as also remarked by the Commission[2523] and Chen[2524] in their buyer power models.

1306. Moreover, the dualistic approach and the perniciousness of buyer market power is also linked with the finding that *EU competition law is triggered even in the absence of end consumer harm in buyer power cases*. Therefore, and as clarified by the Courts, competition intervention will take place whenever buyer power has a *substantial and detrimental effect on the competitive process and competition as such* in the upstream market, even absent evidence of direct end consumer harm because the exertion of buyer market power has already substantially affected competition among buyers and suppliers, or among buyers themselves. This broader harm standard is found under EU Competition and US antitrust law concerning the treatment of buyers' cartels fixing purchasing conditions, and cartels that unduly restrict a buyer's market power and its economic freedom (by setting minimum purchasing prices, for example). In this case, the broader approach is justified because the cartel in itself is an agreement to thwart the competitive process. However, when it comes to unilateral behaviour, present or future (in the case of concentrations), the stance is quite different. In the US antitrust law, as shown by *Weyerhaeuser*, the approach to triggering the application of the law is narrow as the US Supreme Court requires direct end consumer harm to sanction the unilateral conduct of a buyer when attempting to exclude its competitors. This narrow approach to buyer power cases risks under-enforcing and denying protection to the competitive process in the upstream market or between undertakings that only compete as buyers but not as retailers.

1307. The broader approach to buyer power harm has the advantage of being more inclusive and *captures better the complex buyer power dynamics in the markets involved* than a policy stance of intervening exclusively whenever there is short-term end consumer harm. This buyer power intervention stand *takes into account the competitive interests of all market players and not solely end*

2523 European Commission and others (2000), p. 19.

2524 Chen 'Buyer power: Economic Theory and Antitrust Policy' (2007), p. 32-37.

consumers anchored on the idea that detriment to upstream competition and competition as such will lead to harm in the downstream markets in the long run. Also, by protecting the competitive process and the undertaking's economic freedom, EU competition law grants a limited protection to the economic interest of other firms, as it explicitly occurs concerning countervailing buyer power. In my view, this wider approach to the economic protection of the well-being of the market is anchored in the regulatory and political history of EU competition law and the policy goals in which has been built, that *inter alia*, seek to protect a system of undistorted competition[2525], grant importance to the parties' economic freedom, and the ordoliberal influence arising therefrom. Such a perspective also finds support beyond the EU dimension in the work of Carstensen who argues that "[b]y retaining workably competitive buying markets, many of the problems involved in focused analysis of specific buyer conduct can be avoided"[2526]. This protective and more interventionist approach is not exclusive to buyer power regulation but common to EU competition law in general, as recently confirmed in *CB v Commission,* which concluded that restrictions of competition are prohibited when they reveal "a sufficient degree of harm to competition", and not requiring direct end consumer harm[2527].

1308. The problem with this broader approach, and common to instances dealing with vertical restraints[2528], is that, in the interest of protecting the competitive market structure and the undertaking's economic freedom, the intervention may efficient behaviours and affect static and dynamic efficiency due to over-enforcement. Therefore, the extent and the adequacy of the protection of economic freedom and other participants' economic interests must be approached with caution. In connection with these criticisms, the broader approach to harm in buyer power cases has been timidly challenged by some of the Commission's guidelines that place the burden of triggering competition law whenever there is downstream consumer harm. This attitude, likely influenced by the 'more economic approach', has not been endorsed by the Courts and is evidence of the general policy tension regarding EU competition law goals between these institutions.

1309. In connection with these findings, I also embarked on an analysis of whether the EU *buyer power treatment is in line with ordoliberal competition policy?* This question prompted me to devise a framework with which to contrast the legal treatment to buyer power, and to make value and policy judgments concerning the outcomes and the choices made by the Courts and the

2525 Protocol No 27 on the Internal Market and Competition of the Treaty on the Functioning of the European Union, consolidated version [2012] OJ C 326/47.

2526 Carstensen 'Buyer Power, Competition Policy, and Antitrust: The Competitive Effects of Discrimination Among Suppliers' (2008), p. 331.

2527 Judgment of 11 September 2014 in *CB v Commission*, C-67/13 P, EU:C:2014:2204, para. 53 and 58.

2528 Scherer [2009], p. 445.

Commission. My findings are that the current *EU buyer power regulation anchored on its dualistic and broader harm approach seems to be compatible with ordoliberal competition,* as discussed in chapter 3. There are several factors that support such a finding, among them the emphasis placed by the Courts concerning competition intervention even absent evidence of direct end consumer harm, the protection of the competitive process, a limited protection for the wellbeing of other buyers in countervailing buyer power cases, prohibition of unilateral purchasing exploitation vis-à-vis suppliers and the prohibition of unduly and disproportionally restricting the economic freedom of other undertakings. This correlation, however, does not necessarily imply causation; i.e.: I do not claim that the EU buyer power regulation is purely inspired by ordoliberalism because proving or refuting such claim requires a different methodology and approach than the one I used in this study.

1310. In contrast, my analysis of the US antitrust regulation of buyer power, shows that ordoliberal-like ideas have had far less influence and that there has been a shift from an 'old' interventionist and protective regime towards a 'new' buyer power approach focused on pure end consumer harm. The 'old' case law and laws like the Robinson-Patman Act have a competitors-protective emphasis, and the protection to the upstream process and intervention absent consumer harm goes even further than what EU competition law does. However, with the 'Antitrust Revolution' and the influence of the Chicago School from the 1970s onwards, the stance to buyer power has become narrower, particularly regarding unilateral conducts. Pursuant these developments US antitrust law intervention is limited to circumstances where there is presence of direct end consumer harm, in particular for unilateral behaviours. The risks with this approach are that it might be under-enforcing and that it disregards all cases in which buyers do not compete as retailers in the same downstream market.

1311. Also, I identified that potential anti-competitive buyer power arises more frequently in markets with *specific characteristics*. Among them, a high level of demand side concentration; atomization of suppliers; related to processing of raw material or foodstuffs; cases where the buyer is an important distribution mechanism; and markets in which retailers seek to integrate upstream. This makes industries such as *food retailing or those that process raw materials* good examples. However, buyer (bargaining) power arises in any type of commercial relationship, and authorities should resist the temptation to limit their scrutiny to specific industrial sectors or market structures.

1312. Furthermore, my analysis also confirms that *the most pernicious and problematic buyer power forms of abuse are related to exclusionary harm* rather than exploitative buyer power conducts. In my view, the Commission should follow its current approach to selling side cases by placing an enforcement emphasis on exclusionary buyer power conducts for three fundamental reasons. Firstly, buyer power exclusion is not self-correctable or as self-correctable as buyer power exploitation may be[2529], which requires intervention of competition authorities to prevent issues of barriers of entry or market foreclosure. Secondly, buyer power exclusion tends to follow a strategy in which the buyer excludes a rival from the upstream market to directly affect its ability to compete in the downstream market as a retailer, causing therefore harm in both markets and which is likely to have a much shorter negative impact effect on end consumers. Lastly, buyer power exploitation sensu stricto, where one buyer is capable of squeezing suppliers out of the market, is not the most economically rational purchasing behaviour. This is so, as the buyer may eventually either lose all supply sources or grant more seller market power to the few remaining suppliers, tilting the bargaining power balance in their favor, as well as generating more profit if it acquires larger input quantities at a lower price.

1313. Moreover, I identified that *buyer power problems may also be connected with previous and current state/public ownership*. In some of the cases discussed, the involved undertakings were once, or still are, publicly owned, or qualified as contracting authorities under the scope of the application of EU public procurement law (and thereby, in principle shielded from the application of EU competition law). This occurred, for example, concerning the Spanish Ministry of Health in *FENIN v Commission,* the German medicine purchasing system in *AOK Bundesverband*, British Airways as a former publicly-owned airline carrier in the UK, Irish Sugar as a former state monopoly for the purchase and resale of sugar in Ireland, and, as recently occurred in Norway, concerning an alleged but dismissed possible buyer power abuse by Statoil[2530]. Therefore, exercise of public buyer power in recently liberalized sectors may also be an area where competition authorities should maintain a vigilant eye.

1314. Lastly, and as a policy issue flowing from the previous findings, if buyer (bargaining) power tends to be welfare increasing because it has the ability to neutralize seller market power fully or partially, *should buyer power be actively encouraged by competition policy?*

1315. As has been discussed in this work, buyer (bargaining) power tends to improve welfare if it is able to neutralize seller market power, reduce purchasing prices and pass on these benefits to end consumers in the form of cheaper products, better quality and greater variety and innovation. However, this is not the case for monopsony power as it is always inefficient and creating welfare loss due

---

2529 My discussion concerning whether buyer power exploitation is as self-correctable as in seller side cases is in chapter 7.

2530 https://www.regjeringen.no/no/aktuelt/utreder-konkurranseforholdene-i-petroleumsnaringen/id2508080/. The final report was issued on October 1, 2016 and some information in English about is available at http://konkurransetilsynet.no/en/news/news-archive/2016/the-petroleum-industry-buyer-power-can-be-good-for-competition-and-consumers, and the full report (in Norwegian) is available at: http://konkurransetilsynet.no/globalassets/filer/aktuelt/vedlegg-til-nyheter/utredning—petroleumsnaringen-og-kjopermakt.pdf.

to demand withholding. The answer concerning monopsony is simple: despite the fact that it reduces purchasing prices it should not be encouraged because it is an anti-competitive practice with negative welfare effects.

1316. On the other hand, bargaining power tends to be efficiency enhancing but can also be used to exploit suppliers or exclude rivals, as has been demonstrated in this study. Consequently, active intervention that encourages the creation of bargaining power could be potentially dangerous and distort the competitive balance. Also, fostering bargaining power to the benefit of large firms may raise issues concerning increased market concentration, possibilities of regarding the creation of bilateral monopolies, discrimination, and possible instances of illegal state aid. What it is likely is that bargaining power will continue to naturally grow to oppose seller market power and that the new academic knowledge will allow competition authorities to adequately assess bargaining power extension and distinguish pro-competitive from anti-competitive buying conducts. What may occur, and is occurring, is that governmental intervention is being observed in certain markets – for instance regarding the bargaining power of small agricultural producers or cooperatives – and that regulations and policies foster the creation of (buyer or seller) bargaining power to the benefit of small and medium enterprises in these socially sensitive sectors.

III. Chapter-specific findings

1317. I discussed the economics of buyer power and demonstrated that, unlike monopoly, *buyer power is an umbrella term covering two different types of buying conducts with different economic effects,* as analyzed in detail in chapter 2. On the one hand, *monopsony power* is indeed the analogue figure of monopoly power as it describes how a buyer is able to decrease an input's purchasing price below the competitive level by withholding demand (i.e.: purchasing less of it) to reap supracompetitive profits. The monopsony effects are quite straight-forward: withholding demand always generates static and allocative efficiency loss as fewer resources than optimal are employed and a profit transfer takes place from suppliers to the monopsonist. Furthermore, and depending on the competitiveness in the downstream market, monopsony power can have further pernicious effects for downstream consumers as prices are pushed upwards if the monopsonist buyer can also exert downstream market power and/or there are no substitutes for the goods withheld. On the other hand, the economic effects of bargaining power are not so straight-forward, as this purchasing behaviour can be either pro or anti-competitive from a static and dynamic efficiency perspective. Bargaining power is efficiency enhancing because the price reduction obtained by the buyer is not based on demand withholding but on resorting to its negotiation abilities to reduce the purchase price towards the competitive level. Thus, bargaining power is pro-competitive because it countervails opposing seller market power shifting prices towards the competitive level (but not below it), increases the amount of goods acquired, may incentivize innovation by rival buyers and suppliers, and may pass the price reductions to end consumers if the downstream market is competitive. However, bargaining power can also be employed anti-competitively to exploit and exclude suppliers or rival buyers, especially if the powerful buyer also holds market power as a retailer. Therefore, bargaining power is a hybrid concept from a welfaristic perspective. Additionally, for both monopsony and bargaining power, I submitted that whenever a buyer exerting monopsony or bargaining power also enjoys market power as a retailer it possesses the *hour-glass shape* and its ability to leverage market power from (or to) the purchasing market to the retail market may raise further competition concerns and this may have a direct impact in the prices paid by end consumers. Lastly, because of the ambiguous welfare effects of bargaining power it is not possible to say that buyer (bargaining) power is economically equivalent to monopoly power and no straight-forward answer can be given to cases as the outcome will depend on the conduct at hand, the undertaking's bargaining power extent, and the competitive conditions in the upstream and downstream markets.

1318. Following the buyer power economics discussion, I found that one of the main buyer power competition implications is its ability to have dual competition effects in the upstream and downstream markets where the buyer carries out its economic activity, having a direct impact on how the relevant market is defined in buyer power cases, as discussed in chapters 4 and 5. Defining relevant buying markets is different from selling side cases because it requires the adoption of a *dualistic approach to market definition and buyer market power assessment to fully capture the buyer market power effects on suppliers, rival buyers and end consumers*. This dualistic approach involves assessing the undertaking's relevant purchasing market upstream as a buyer as well as the relevant downstream market power as a seller. A dual market definition allows competition authorities to better determine the existence of competitive harm and fully appreciate the buyer power effects on competition as a whole. If the market definition analysis is carried out solely in the purchasing upstream market, the competitive effects of buyer power on end consumers would not be fully assessed, and the same is true vice versa. Furthermore, adopting a dualistic approach to buyer-oriented market definition is consistent with a policy that triggers competition law intervention whenever the competitive process is harmed either upstream or downstream and not exclusively whenever there is direct short term end consumer harm.

1319. Furthermore, defining relevant buying markets goes *beyond applying a reverse methodology to the selling-side product market definition,* and a reassessment of the methodology and variables applied when carrying out the *Buyer's SSNIP test* has been proposed. This buyer market definition methodology implies a re-focusing of the *concepts of demand and supply substitution* and *defining the relevant market upstream and downstream*. This dual definition approach has been gradually accepted by the Commission as well as the NCAs of some MS, such as the UK and Germany. However, the endorsement and refinement of these methodologies still require further legal guidance by the Commission as the little available there is it is insufficient and underdeveloped. This re-tailoring of buyer's market definition is not solely a European concern. Other countries and institutions have, since the mid-2000s, started to re-think and apply market definition techniques for purchasing markets in a different manner. For example, in the US with the Horizontal Merger Guidelines, in Canada with its Merger Guidelines, or at the OECD level with its proposal of a hypothetical monopsonist test.

1320. Following the dualistic buyer market definition proposal, *I have also answered the question concerning how and under what circumstances buyer power arises,* in chapter 5. One of my findings is that substantial buyer market power (but not dominance) is capable of arising at lower market share thresholds than when compared to selling side cases because, in most transactions, the buyer is the one that 'decides' in the operation, as originally highlighted by Carstensen[2531]. However, this idea must be further refined. Substantial buyer power arises at lower thresholds when compared to selling side cases and *has the ability to affect the relationship between a supplier and a buyer in a bilateral manner because the former may be dependent on the latter*. Nevertheless, the fact that a supplier is dependent on a buyer does not imply that all or most suppliers depend on it and that the buyer may behave independently from its suppliers and competitors. Therefore, what is of importance is the market power of the buyer vis-à-vis all suppliers, rival buyers, and end consumers as a retailer.

1321. To properly evaluate the undertaking's market power, and following the dualistic approach to buyer power, the assessment of buyer market power must be made as a buyer and also as a retailer. My analysis focused solely on the determination of buyer market power as a purchaser in the upstream market, as the downstream analysis of market power has been the topic of extensive discussion and is outside the scope of this study. I identified and discussed the buyer-specific assessment tools to measure an undertaking's buyer power: market shares, market concentration, dependence, unavoidability, the buyer's role as a gate-keeper, and alternative supply sources. Lastly, the chapter also discussed the Buyer Power Index as a direct source for quantifying market power, as proposed by Blair and Harrison and how, despite its attractiveness, this methodology anchored on the use of demand elasticity is not adequate in practice.

1322. Part III of this study embarked on a *discussion of buying conducts that may raise anti-competitive concern* and may trigger competition intervention. For

2531 Carstensen 'Buyer Power and the Horizontal Merger Guidelines: Minor Progress on an Important Issue' (2012).

this purpose, I identified theories of harm and types of conducts from a holistic perspective, deviating from an 'article-based' approach, as previously carried out by van Doorn[2532]. This allowed me to discuss similar buying conducts and their legal regulation from different angles, explain their economic underpinnings, contrast them, and avoid repetition of legal and economic arguments. In so doing, I grouped buying conducts from an *active perspective* into three types: *exclusionary buying conducts, exploitative buying conducts, and exploitative and unfair buying conducts*.

1323. Exclusionary buyer power tactics are the most pernicious forms of anti-competitive buyer power exertion, warranting a major degree of intervention by competition authorities, as they involve the *use of buyer power in the upstream market to foreclose rivals that compete in either the upstream market as a buyer and/or the downstream market as a retailer,* as discussed in chapter 6. Therefore, exclusionary buyer power has horizontal and vertical competition effects. The buyer will aim to *exclude its rivals by increasing their costs*. This can be done in several ways: by entering into exclusive supply obligations with the most or most efficient suppliers and leaving available to rivals other suppliers not as efficient. Nevertheless, *not all exclusive supply obligations are anti-competitive nor are they treated as such* as they can also lead to efficiencies as some of these agreements may benefit from the Block Exemption Regulation. Overbuying is another exclusionary tactic, which involves acquiring more input than necessary, thereby increasing the purchasing price paid to prevent rivals from acquiring it and forcing them to exit the upstream market, but also being able to affect them in the downstream market as retailers. Overbuying instances are rare The US seminal case of *Weyerhaeuser* was discussed *in extenso* due to its importance. In *Weyerhaeuser,* the US Supreme Court adopted a narrow approach to buyer power exclusion, by only intervening upon the existence of direct consumer harm. In my opinion, this narrow approach to buyer power harm may be under enforcing in those situations in which buyers do not compete as retailers, and it reveals a lack of concern for the protection of upstream market conditions that in the medium and long run may affect the wellbeing of downstream consumers. I also discussed mergers in which possible input rival foreclosure was perceived as an anticompetitive concern. Then, I analyzed the treatment given to exclusionary buying discrimination and the Robinson-Patman Act, as an example of US legislation applicable to such conducts, and which seeks protection of rival buyers and not economic efficiency. This discussion set the basis for the analysis of exclusionary leveraging of buyer market power through which a buying undertaking exerts its purchasing power to affect competition in a related market, as discussed *in extenso* in *British Airways v Commission* by the Courts. This case shows that dominant buyers may abuse their dominant position by grant-

2532 van Doorn.

ing supracompetitive rebates with a loyalty-enhancing component that incentivizes suppliers to sell their goods or services exclusively or mostly to the dominant undertaking. The Courts sanctioned the undertaking's conduct even absent evidence of direct end consumer harm and chose a broader intervention in a standard not anchored on end consumer harm but rather whenever the competitive structure in the upstream market is affected, in contrast to the narrower approach of the US Supreme Court in *Weyerhaeuser*. Additionally, I discussed the hybrid theory of harm of 'squeeze to buy', where the buyer pays an exploitatively low purchasing price, followed by a take-over offer to the supplier which is forced to sell its business at a lower price than in a competitive setting. The chapter concludes with two discussions concerning the difficulty and unsuitability of the 'as efficient buyer test' for exclusionary abuses, and how EU competition law intervenes in exclusionary buyer power cases even absent evidence of direct end consumer harm if the conduct has a substantive detrimental effect on the competitive structure upstream, and the contrast to the position under US antitrust law.

1324. In chapter 7, I analyzed buyer power exploitation as a *vertical exercise of buyer market power vis-à-vis suppliers that consists of imposing purchasing prices, quotas, distributing geographical markets, or setting purchasing patterns which extract supracompetitive rents from suppliers to buyers*. However, and despite its intuitive appeal, buyer power economics show that imposing exploitative purchasing prices below the competitive level for a long period of time is unlikely to be an effective tactic. Therefore, my analysis confirms that *pure exploitative practices, especially unilateral, are rare*, which is confirmed by the small amount of existing case law. Also, other conducts that may appear exploitative might not be; lowering purchasing prices towards the competitive level has a countervailing effect that transfers supracompetitive profits kept by suppliers. My analysis discussed unilateral exploitation by imposing unfairly low purchasing prices below the competitive level, revisiting the *United Brands* test and proposing a buyer-oriented standard anchored on the supplier's marginal cost and the competitive purchasing price. Furthermore, I discussed how unilateral market power can be used to exert exploitative purchasing price discrimination among suppliers and the strict stance of Courts concerning these types of practices, as confirmed in *British Airways v Commission.* This approach seeks to prevent discrimination among suppliers and to protect the level playing field among rivals, but it might also be criticized from a welfaristic perspective as over protective. Additionally, I evaluated the efficiency and rationale of centralized purchasing structures as buying and collaborative behaviours, as well as cooperatives as agglutinates of buyer power. This was followed by a discussion concerning buyer power exploitation through buyers' coordination and the distinction *between buyer cartels* that seek to impose restrictions on price competition among buyers and reduce rivalry in the downstream markets by exerting monopsony or exploitative bargaining power, *and buying alliances* that seek to agglutinate buyer power to oppose seller market power and bring purchasing prices towards the competitive level. *Buyer cartels constitute object restrictions of competition,* whereas *buying alliances enjoy a presumption of legality and may be considered an effects-based restriction of competition.* I concluded the chapter with an analysis concerning the harm required to trigger competition intervention in exploitative cases. The case law shows that for concerted behaviour, both the EU and US Courts, will intervene in the absence of end consumer harm to sanction naked buyers' cartels. However, there is a trend lead by the Commission relating to concerted and unilateral conduct which narrows, centers and seeks to trigger the enforcement of EU competition law on instances where the supplier exploitation may have direct end consumer harm or it is used as a tool to decrease competition among rival undertakings in the downstream market.

1325. I have identified additional forms of buyer power exploitation through the imposition of *unfair* purchasing conditions, as discussed in chapter 8. These conducts involve a transfer of profits from suppliers to buyers without adequate compensation, which are commonly linked to practices of large food retail chains. In this chapter, I inquired *if and when these unfair purchasing practices are a competition law issue or, alternatively, whether these types of exploitative practices should be addressed by other means of economic regulation,* as they are generally problems of profit distribution within a contract but not market-wide efficiency. My main finding is that *unfair purchasing practices are usually not a competition concern,* but may be under EU competition law scrutiny. This would be the case whenever they are imposed by a dominant buyer, may arise pursuant a buyer's concentration, or are imposed by a buyers' cartel or through a vertical agreement, because they may have an adverse effect on market-wide competition or because their imposition creates competition distortion among rival buyers and also among suppliers. When these circumstances materialize and there is substantial harm to competition as a process and existing or potential harm to dynamic efficiency, then EU competition law as it stands ought to intervene. However, these instances have been very rare, as confirmed by my case analysis. Nonetheless, unfair purchasing practices have generated a great deal of social and political commotion as they are seen as an example of *exploitation of small suppliers* that *may depend on their buyers* for their economic viability. Because of this and the fact that legal systems tend to *protect fairness in contractual relations,* most MS have adopted *different legislative measures to limit the imposition of unfair purchasing practices* within, although mostly outside of, EU competition law; solutions which I have categorized and evaluated. Lastly, I discussed the EU strategies employed against the imposition of unfair purchasing practices outside competition law, such as the EU Supply Chain Initiative.

1326. In Part V I analyzed buyer power from a seller's perspective by evaluating the legal treatment of countervailing buyer power as a neutralizer of seller market power, and how buyer power can be anti-competitively limited by suppliers. In chapter 9 I inquired as to *what countervailing buyer power is, how is it measured and what the effect of countervailing buyer power is*. Countervailing buyer power is a form of bargaining power invoked as a defense based on the inability of suppliers to behave independently from their customers/buyers, therefore being unable to exert seller market power. Accordingly, *my approach to countervailing buyer power is narrow, as I require a degree of sufficiency to offset opposing seller market power*. Furthermore, from the Commission's practice and the case law, I have identified *the existence of a 'comparison test' that seeks to determine the sufficiency of the countervailing buyer power* to adequately neutralize the market power of the selling undertaking. The test has been developed in concentration and dominance cases following a similar approach and tested in several cases, but with only a handful of instances in which the sufficiency was met, and exclusively with regard to concentrations. Furthermore, I have identified a requirement adopted pursuant to the Commission's practice and incorporated within the soft law that requires from countervailing buyer power to, in addition to neutralizing seller market power vis-à-vis a powerful buyer, *generate a positive spillover effect on weaker buyers*. The grounds for this requirement is the *interest in protecting the competitive structure in the upstream market* – although it might also protect rivals – and avoid pernicious waterbed effects on weaker buyers.

1327. Lastly, in chapter 10, *I inquired in which ways sellers may anti-competitively limit buyer power exertion*. My study shows that coordination among suppliers to limit buyer power by setting purchasing ceilings or quotas infringes competition by object, as corroborated by the case law. In other instances, these price limitations arose because of sectoral crises or pursuant to national regulation shielding suppliers from the vagaries of the market. These crises were used as arguments to reduce the fines or even allow some degree of selling side coordination, as occurs concerning the sale of raw milk. In the case of unilateral conduct, a supplier would seek to neutralize buyer power by means of granting a rebate to the buyer and lowering the prices this latter has to pay. In this section, I discussed *whether rebates restrict the buyer's economic freedom*, or *compensate the buyer sufficiently for the loss of buyer power through price purchasing reductions*. Only whenever the rebate substantially over-compensates the loss of economic freedom to choose alternative suppliers (creating an unjustified loyalty enhancing effect) can it have anti-competitive foreclosure effects, where this risk of foreclosure of rival suppliers is the main reason for its illegality and, to a lesser extent, the loss of buyer market power or the buyer's economic freedom. Otherwise, sanctioning suppliers by compensating buyers for their 'loss' of buyer power would hinder the neutralizing characteristics of buyer power and prevent reductions in purchasing price that may also benefit end consumers.

IV. An EU buyer power doctrine?

1328. The question that remains as a synthetization of this study is whether a consolidated EU competition law buyer power doctrine exists. Despite the limited case law and legislation expressly dealing with buyer power, I have identified several principles that guide the application of EU competition law to control the exercise of buyer market power across all competition law areas.

1329. EU competition law applies and oversees the exercise of market power by buyers in all its areas: agreements, unilateral behaviours, and concentrations. Furthermore, buyer market power would be under competition law scrutiny regardless of whether the conduct would be exclusionary or exploitative. Even in the realm of unfair purchasing practices, EU competition law has a narrow scope of application, rarely capturing these practices, as confirmed by the Commission's practice and the case law. This narrower approach concerning unfairly exploitative practices is justified and the toolbox is still sufficient, as most of these conducts have a limited market-wide impact in terms of static and dynamic efficiency. Therefore, the EU competition law tools contained in the Treaties are adequate and sufficiently comprehensive enough to address all anti-competitive exertions of buyer market power.

1330. Also, buyer power is under the scope of EU competition law in its two forms, monopsony and bargaining power, even if the Courts do not explicitly make a distinction between them. However, from the treatment given by the Courts and the Commission to the type of exerted buyer power it is evident that there is an implicit distinction between monopsony and bargaining power cases. Further it is established in the Commission's practice and the case law that certain exertions of buyer power such as buying alliances and countervailing buyer power are efficiency enhancing and constitute acceptable and desirable behaviours in contrast to monopsony exertion. Moreover, despite the fact that the Courts do not engage in explicit economic discussions concerning the nature of buyer power practices, the language used in the judgments reveals an understanding of buyer power economics, particularly – although not exclusively - in the more recent ones, albeit not always, which is more influenced by an economic analysis of the cases and a less formalistic or economic-freedom based stance.

1331. Furthermore, EU competition law adopts a wide approach to buyer power as its abuse is condemned even absent evidence of direct end consumer harm or downstream market effects. It is sufficient that competition as such, and to a lesser extent the economic freedom of rival buyers and suppliers, are adversely affected by the buyer's conduct in the upstream market to trigger competition law intervention. This stance is uncontroversial concerning cartels that exert buyer market power but more contested concerning possible anti-competitive buying alliances and, in particular, the unilateral behaviour of dominant undertakings or pursuant to a concentration. Regarding unilateral conduct, examples such as US antitrust and some of the recent Commission's soft law instruments adopt a narrower stand and intervene only in the presence of short term downstream end consumer harm. While it is true that whenever an undertaking has upstream and downstream market power the likelihood of anti-competitive effects generated by buyer power is higher, particularly regarding its effects on consumers, only triggering competition law intervention in the presence of short term downstream harm is under-inclusive. And more importantly, this is not in line with the legal standard adopted by the Courts because it fails to sufficiently protect the competitive process from buyer power harm. On the other hand, the broader standard concerning competition harm adopted by the Courts runs the risk of over-enforcement and, therefore, this is a something that should be taken into account by the Commission and the Courts to minimize false positives errors in as much as possible.

V. On the future of buyer power

1332. Buyer power has received little attention so far from legal scholars and competition authorities because anti-competitive cases are rare and it involves looking at competition law from 'the other side of the fence'; i.e.: from a buyer's and not a seller's perspective. In this final section, I discuss three aspects that I consider relevant concerning the future of buyer power.

1333. From an *enforcement perspective*, I do not expect a surge of many buyer power related cases in the near future, *although I do foresee an increase in the attention and importance afforded to buyer power* for four main reasons. First, retailing markets are set to become more concentrated due to the advancement of modern retailing business models, the prevalence of large multinational firms, and franchising. The more concentrated the purchasing markets, the more room for buyer power exertion for both pro-competitive bargaining power practices and buyer power exploitation and exclusion. Second, since the early 2000s, the amount of economic and legal research concerning buyer power has increased substantially. This new knowledge may assist in the process of detecting anti-competitive buyer power instances that were not considered as such before. Third, mergers involving powerful buyers and upstream integration will continue to be assessed and the Commission and NCAs will further scrutinize buyer power implications in both upstream and downstream markets. Fourth, buyer power interest will also spur in markets where demand is publicly-driven due to the increase in purchasing centralization techniques and the welfare concern regarding the competitiveness of public procurement in Europe.

1334. From a competition policy perspective, I anticipate *a shift in the way NCAs, policy makers, and the legal audience will look at buyer power issues*. In this contribution, I have shown that bargaining power is the most common form of buyer power and it is also mostly efficiency enhancing as it neutralizes seller market power and increases welfare. Furthermore, a general evaluation to the limited legal regime applicable to buyer power in EU competition law is positive. The EU competition law regulation is mostly coherent, consistent, economically informed, and possesses sufficient tools to tackle all anti-competitive buyer power instances. However, the EU buyer power regime may appear over-enforcing to some when compared to US antitrust law due to its broader approach to buyer power harm. I, nevertheless, think that this broader approach is appropriate as it fully captures buyer power dynamics and is also consistent with the general EU competition law policy on competition harm and the understanding that to achieve end consumer welfare in the medium and long term there is a need to protect upstream competition and competition as a process.

1335. Therefore, I expect authorities, academics and practitioners to change the generally negative perspective to buyer power and shift away from the myth that buyer power is always detrimental because it is only monopsony power. Instead, the 'new approach to buyer power', as remarked by the Bundeskartellamt[2533], should be focused on those instances of anti-competitive bargaining power, with a particular emphasis on buyer power exclusion.

1336. Lastly, in order to contribute to the full understanding of buyer power and give further guidance to authorities, policy makers, and Courts regarding how to enforce competition law in buyer power cases and improve the current legal regime, I have identified several areas that may be ripe for future economic and legal research.

1337. The monopsony power economics are a well-researched phenomenon that requires little further academic work. The same, however, cannot be said of bargaining power and, in particular, *its effects on dynamic efficiency*. As I highlighted in chapter 2, the economic literature is ambiguous when dealing with the bargaining power effects on innovation, investment, variety, quality effects, and the *waterbed and spiral effects*. With regard to the latter two, further economic clarification is needed because these effects are often invoked by the parties and have been used by the Commission and the Courts, albeit sometimes without sufficient precision or scientific rigor. Another area ripe for research is the effects of buyer power and *private labels* in dynamic and static efficiency and retail markets. Is the rise of private labels and the participation of large buyers as producers and retailers a source of compe-

2533 Bundeskartellamt *'Summary of the Final Report of the Sector Inquiry into the Food Retail Sector'* (2014), p. 9.

tition concern in the downstream and upstream markets? Is product variety negatively affected?

1338. Also, I have shown that EU competition law adopts a broad approach to buyer power harm and competition intervention as Courts have declared the behaviour illegal absent consumer harm with the intent to protect competition as such, and, to a certain extent, to the benefit of other undertakings in the upstream market. Nonetheless, what is left unresolved and ripe for future research is *whether there is room for protection of rival buyers and suppliers, and, if so, how much room for protection them is legitimate and required under EU competition law?*

1339. Also, I identified as another area for further research the *interaction between cooperatives and the creation, exertion and limitation of buyer power*, especially when compared to 'traditional undertakings'. Cooperatives are horizontal and vertical agreements that group small producers (in agriculture, but also other buyer power sensitive markets) that may generate and also prevent buyer power exertion. These cooperative groups enjoy certain non-competition law benefits (tax, labor and societal rules) that grant them a competitive edge when compared to other undertakings and enable them to 'over-pay' for their input, which may lead to instances of unjustified buyer power exclusion, as has been investigated in New Zealand regarding milk production.

1340. Connected to the former, I believe there to also be room for further research concerning the *sectoral regulation of buyer power in agriculture*. In my research, I have identified that these markets are characterized by large purchasing agents (supermarket chains, large food producers/distributors) vis-à-vis small producers (farmers or independent good producers), which makes them suitable for buyer power exploitation. In my research, I briefly discussed the limited special sectoral regulation that permits certain types of sellers' cartels to oppose buyer power, both in Europe and the US. However, there is room for further analysis of the adequacy of these measures.

1341. Lastly *the area of EU wide regulation of UPPs within and outside EU competition law* is another buyer power aspect also ripe for academic research, particularly concerning the policy measures (or lack thereof) adopted by the Commission, and possible EU-wide solutions to tackle unfair purchasing practices.

1342. All in all, I hope that the analysis and findings put forward by this study will contribute towards a 'new approach to buyer power', both in terms of the case law and future academic research.

BIBLIOGRAPHY

Abood RR, 'Differential Pricing of Pharmaceuticals and Retail Competition under the Robinson-Patman Act' 11 American Journal of Law & Medicine [1985], 293

Adams M, 'Doing What Doesn't Come Naturally. On the Distinctiveness of Comparative Law' in Van Hoecke M (ed), *Methodologies of legal research: which kind of method for what kind of discipline?* (Hart 2011)

Afonso A, Schuknecht L and Tanzic V, 'Public Sector Efficiency: Evidence for new EU Member States and Emerging Markets' 42 Applied Economics [2010], 2147

Ahlborn C and Bailey D, 'Discounts, Rebates and Selective Pricing by Dominant Firms: A Trans-Atlantic Comparison' 2 European Competition Journal [2006], 101

Ahlborn C and Evans DS, 'The Microsoft Judgment and its Implications for Competition Policy Towards Dominant Firms in Europe' 75 Antitrust Law Journal [2009], 887

Akman P, 'Searching for the Long-Lost Soul of Article 82 EC' 29 Oxford Journal of Legal Studies [2009]

——, *The Concept of Abuse in EU Competition Law: Law and Economic Approaches* (Hart 2012)

——, *Question A: Abuse of a Dominant Position and Globalization* (2015)

Akman P and Garrod L, 'When are Excessive Prices Unfair' 7 Journal of Competition Law & Economics [2011], 403

Albano GL and Sparro M, 'Flexible Strategies for Centralized Public Procurement' 1 Review of Economics and Institutions [2010], 1

Albors-Llorens A, 'Horizontal Agreements and Concerted Practices in EC Competition Law: Unlawful and Legitimate Contacts Between Competitors' 51 The Antitrust Bulletin [2006], 837

—, 'The Role of Objective Justification and Efficiencies in the Application of Article 82 EC' 44 Common Market Law Review [2007], 1727

Albæk S, 'Consumer Welfare in EU Competition Policy' in Heide-Jørgensen C and others (eds), *Aims and values in competition law* (DJØF Publ. 2013)

Allain M-L, Chambolle C and Rey P, 'Vertical Integration, Innovation and Foreclosure' IDEAS Working Paper Series from RePEc [2010]

American Antitrust Institute, 'The New Kid on the Block: Buyer Power' in Foer AA (ed), *The Next Antitrust Agenda: The American Antitrust Institute's Transition Report on Competition Policy to the 44th President of the United States* (American Antitrust Institute 2008)

American Bar Association, *Market Definition in Antitrust* (American Bar Association ed, 2012)

—, *Market Power Handbook: Competition Law and Economic Foundations* (ABA Section of Antitrust Law ed, 2012)

Anagnostaras G, 'The Unfair Commercial Practices Directive in Context: From Legal Disparity to Legal Complexity?' 47 Common Market Law Review [2010], 147

Anwandter L and Ozuna TJ, 'Can Public Sector Reforms Improve the Efficiency of Public Water Utilities?' 7 Environment and Development Economics [2002], 687

Areeda P, 'Essential Facilities: An Epithet in Need of Limiting Principles' 58 Antitrust Law Journal [1989], 841

Areeda P, Hovenkamp H and Solow J, *Antitrust Law: An Analysis of Antitrust Principles and their Application* vol IIB (3rd edn, Wolters Kluwer 1995)

Areeda P and Turner DF, 'Predatory Pricing and Related Practices under Section 2 of the Sherman Act' 88 Harvard Law Review [1975], 697

—, 'Williamson on Predatory Pricing' 87 The Yale Law Journal [1978], 1337

Aron DJ and Burnstein DE, 'Regulatory Policy and the Reverse Cellophane Fallacy' 6 Journal of Competition Law and Economics [2010], 973

Australian Food & Grocery Council, *Food and Grocery Industry Code of Conduct* (2015)

Autoridade da Concorrência (Portugal), *Final Report on Commercial Relations Between the Large Retail Groups and their Suppliers* (2010)

Autorità Garante della Concorrenza e del Mercato (Italy), *Subfornitura Industriale* (1995)

Averitt NW, 'The Meaning of Unfair Methods of Competition in Section 5 of the Federal Trade Commission Act' 21 Boston College Law Review [1979-1980], 227

Baker JB, 'Predatory Pricing after Brooke Group: An Economic Perspective' 62 Antitrust Law Journal [1993-1994]

—, 'Market Definition: An Analytical Overview' 74 Antitrust Law Journal [2007], 129

Baker S and Lofaro A, 'Buyer power and the Enso/Stora decision' 21 European Competition Law Review [2000], 187

Barbier de la Serre E, 'Standard of Review in Competition Law Cases: Posten Norge and Beyond' in EFTA Court (ed), *The EEA and the EFTA Court: Decentred Integration* (Hart Publishing 2014)

Barnard C, 'EU Citizenship and the Principle of Solidarity' in Dougan M and Spaventa E (eds), *Social welfare and EU law* (Hart Pub. 2005)

Barnes DM and Ondeck CE, 'The Capper-Volstead Act: Opportunity Today and Tomorrow' (1997) <http://www.uwcc.wisc.edu/info/capper.html>

Battigalli P, Fumagalli C and Polo M, 'Buyer power and quality improvements' 61 Research in Economics [2007], 45

Baudenbacher C, 'The Implementation of Decisions of the ECJ of the EFTA Court in Member States' Domestic Legal Orders.' 40 Texas International Law Journal [2005], 383

— (ed) *The Handbook of EEA Law* (Springer 2015)

Baumer DL, Masson RT and Masson RA, 'Curdling the Competition: An Economic and Legal Analysis of the Antitrust Exemption for Agriculture' 31 Villanova Law Review [1986], 183

Baxter S and Dethmers F, 'Collective Dominance under EC Merger Control - After Airtours and the Introduction of Unilateral Effects is there Still a Future for Collective Dominance?' 27 European Competition Law Review [2006], 148

Bedre-Defolie Ö and Caprice S, *Merger Efficiency and Welfare Implications of Buyer Power* (2011)

Behrens P, 'The "Consumer Choice" Paradigm in German Ordoliberalism and its Impact upon EU Competition Law' 1/14 Europa-Kolleg Hamburg Discussion Paper Series [2014], 1

Bellamy C and others, *European Union Law of Competition* (7th ed. edited by Vivien Rose, David Bailey. edn, Oxford University Press 2013)

Bellamy C, Child GD and Roth PM, *European Community Law of Competition* (Sweet & Maxwell 2001)

Bengoetxea J, *The Legal Reasoning of the European Court of Justice: Towards a European Jurisprudence* (Clarendon Press 1993)

Bengoetxea J, MacCormick N and Sorian LM, 'Integration and Integrity in the Legal Reasoning of the European Court of Justice' in De Búrca G and Weiler JHH (eds), *The European Court of Justice*, vol. 10/1 (Oxford university press 2001)

Berasategi J, *Supermarket Power: Serving Consumers or Harming Competition* (2014)

Bernheim BD and Whinston MD, *Microeconomics* (McGraw-Hill Irwin 2008)

Bishop S and Walker M, *The Economics of EC Competition Law: Concepts, Application and Measurement* (Sweet & Maxwell 2010)

Blair RD and Harrison JL, 'Antitrust Policy and Monopsony' 76 Cornell Law Review [1991], 297

—, *Monopsony in Law and Economics* (Cambridge University Press 2010)

Blair RD and Lopatka JE, 'Predatory Buying and the Antitrust Laws' 2 Utah Law Review [2008], 415

Blair RD and Sokol DD, 'The Rule of Reason and the Goals of Antitrust: An Economic Approach' 78 Antitrust Law Journal [2012], 471

Boeger N, 'Solidarity and EC competition law' 32 European Law Review [2007], 319

—, 'Book Review: The Regulation of the State in Competitive Markets in the EU by Erika Szyszczak' 33 European Law Review [2008]

Bonefeld W, 'Freedom and the Strong State: On German Ordoliberalism' 17 New Political Economy [2012], 633

—, 'German Neoliberalism and the Idea of a Social Market Economy: Free Economy and the Strong State' Journal of Social Sciences [2012], 139

Bork RH, 'Ancillary Restraints and the Sherman Act' 15 Section of Antitrust Law [1959], 211

—, *The Antitrust Paradox: A Policy at War With Itself* (1978)

Bos D and Lulfesmann C, 'The Hold-up Problem in Government Contracting' 98 Scandinavian Journal of Economics [1996], 53

Bovis C, *The Law of EU Public Procurement* (2nd ed., Oxford University Press 2015)

Brodley JF, 'The Economic Goals of Antitrust: Efficiency, Consumer Welfare, and Technological Progress' 62 New York University Law Review [1987], 1020

Bundeskartellamt (Germany), *Buyer Power in Competition Law - Status and Perspectives* (2008)

—, *Sektoruntersuchung: Lebensmitteleinzelhandel* (2014)

—, *Summary of the Final Report of the Sector Inquiry into the Food Retail Sector* (2014)

Burkett JP, *Microeconomics: Optimization, Experiments, and Behavior* (Oxford University Press 2006)

Buttà A and Pezzoli A, 'Buyer Power and Competition Policy: From Brick-and-Mortar Retailers to Digital Platforms' 41 Economia E Politica Industriale [2014], 159

Böhm F, 'Rule of Law in a Market Economy' in Peacock A and Willgerodt H (eds), *Germany's Social Market Economy: Origins and Evolution* (MacMillan 1989)

—, 'The Non-State ("Natural") Laws Inherent in a Competitive Economy' in Stützel, W. et alia (ed), *Standard Texts on the Social Market Economy* (1992)

Böhm F, Eucken W and Grossman-Doerth H, 'The Ordo Manifesto of 1936' in Peacock A and Willgerodt H (eds), *Germany's Social Market Economy: Origins and Evolution* (MacMillan 1989)

Calvani T and Breidenbach G, 'An Introduction to the Robinson-Patman Act and its Enforcement by the Government' 59 Antitrust Law Journal [1990], 765

Capps CS, 'Buyer Power in Health Plan Mergers' 6 Journal of Competition Law and Economics [2009], 375

Carlos Arrebola, Mauricio AJ and Portilla HJ, *An Econometric Analysis of the Influence of the Advocate General on the Court of Justice of the European Union* (2016)

Carlton DW, 'Does Antitrust Need to Be Modernized?' 21 The Journal of Economic Perspectives [2007], 155

—, 'Market Definition: Use and Abuse' 3 Competition Policy International [2007], 3

—, 'Should "Price Squeeze" be a Recognized Form of Anticompetitive Conduct?' 4 Journal of Competition Law and Economics [2008], 271

Carlton DW, Coleman M and Israel M, 'Buyer Power in Merger Review' in Blair RD and Sokol DD (eds), The Oxford Handbook of International Antitrust Economics, vol 1 (Oxford University Press 2015)

Carlton DW and Israel M, 'Proper Treatment of Buyer Power in Merger Review' 39 Review of Industrial Organization [2011], 127

Carlton DW and Perloff JM, *Modern Industrial Organization* (Pearson/Addison Wesley 2005)

Carstensen PC, 'Buyer Power and Merger Analysis–The Need for Different Metrics' (Workshop on Merger Enforcement held by the Antitrust Division and the Federal Trade Commission) [2004]

—, 'Buyer Power, Competition Policy, and Antitrust: The Competitive Effects of Discrimination Among Suppliers' 53 The Antitrust Bulletin [2008], 271

—, 'Buyer Cartels Versus Buying Groups: Legal Distinctions, Competitive Realities, and Antitrust Policy' 1 William & Mary Business Law Review [2010], 1

—, 'Buyer Power and the Horizontal Merger Guidelines: Minor Progress on an Important Issue' 14 University of Pennsylvania Journal of Business Law [2012], 775

—, 'Emerging Issues in Buyer Power Analysis' 3 Agriculture and Food Committee e-Bulleting, American Bar Association [2012], 2

Chae S and Heidhues P, 'Buyers' Alliances for Bargaining Power' 13 Journal of Economics & Management Strategy [2004], 731

Chan SSH, 'Post Danmark II: Per Se Unlawfulness of Retroactive Rebates Granted by Dominant Undertakings' 37 European Competition Law Review [2016], 43

Chard J, Duhs G and Houlden J, 'Body Beautiful or Vile Bodies? Central Purchasing in the UK' Public Procurement Law Review [2008], NA26

Charles Rivers Associates, 'Intel and the future of Article 102' (June 2014) <http://ecp.crai.com/ecp/assets/Intel_and_the_future_of_Article_102.pdf>

Chen Z, 'Monopoly and Product Diversity: The Role of Retailer Countervailing Power' 04-19 Carleton Economic Papers [2004], 1

—, *Monopoly and Product Diversity: The Role of Retailer Countervailing Power* (2006, revised version)

—, 'Buyer power: Economic Theory and Antitrust Policy' 22 Research in Law and Economics [2007], 17

Chimienti V, 'The Abuse of Dominance in the new Albanian Competition Act' 26 European Competition Law Review [2005], 151

Christensen P and Rabassa V, 'The Airtours Decision: Is there a new Commission Approach to Collective Dominance?' 22 European Competition Law Review [2001], 227

Church J and Ware R, *Industrial Organization: A Strategic Approach* (McGraw-Hill 2000)

Clark JM, *Competition as a Dynamic Process* (The Brookings Institution 1961)

Coate MB and Fischer JH, 'A Practical Guide to the Hypothetical Monopolist Test for Market Definition' 4 Journal of Competition Law and Economics [2008], 1031

—, 'Is Market Definition still Needed After all these Years' [2014]

Cole M, 'Ordoliberalism and its Influence on EU Tying Law' 36 European Competition Law Review [2015], 255 **College of Europe, Centre for European Policy Studies**, *The Impact of National Rules on Unilateral Conduct that Diverge from Article 102 of the Treaty of the Functioning of the European Union* (2012)

Comisión Nacional de la Competencia (Spain), *Informe sobre las Relaciones entre Fabricantes y Distribuidores en el Sector Alimentario* (2011)

Commerce Commission of New Zealand, *Review of the State of Competition in the New Zealand Dairy Industry* (2016)

Competition Commission (UK), *Supermarkets: A report on the Supply of Groceries from Multiple Stores in the United Kingdom* (2000)

—, *The Supply of Groceries in the UK Market Investigation* (2008)

Competition Council of the Republic of Lithuania, 'Competition Council Imposes a fine of 40 000 Ltl on Maxima Lt, Uab' (2014) <http://kt.gov.lt/en/index.php?show=news_view&pr_id=1303>

Condon D, 'Monopsony Power and the Market for Clergy: Some Evidence from the Census' 42 The Quarterly Review of Economics and Finance [2002], 889

Cook C and Patel R, *Abuse of Dominance under Article 102 TFEU*, vol 5 (González-Díaz FE and Snelders R eds, Claeys and Casteels 2013)

Cook CJ and Kerse CS, *EC Merger Control* (Sweet & Maxwell 2009)

Cooter R and Ulen T, *Law & Economics* (Pearson 2008)

'Cooperatives and the Antitrust Laws' 27 Indiana Law Journal [1952], 430

Corbett C, Nair Rd and Roberts S, 'Countervailing Power, Bargaining Power and Market Definition: A Reflection on two Mergers'

Corgill D, 'United States of America' in Henning-Bodewig F (ed), *International handbook on unfair competition* (Beck Hart Nomos 2013)

Craig P and De Búrca G, *EU Law: Texts, Cases and Materials* (Oxford University Press 2011)

Crocioni P, 'The Hypothetical Monopolist Test: What it can and cannot tell you' 23 European Competition Law Review [2002], 354

Cseres K, 'The Impact of Regulation 1/2003 in the New Member States' 6 The Competition Law Review [2010], 145

Cyndecka MA, 'The Applicability and Application of the Market Economy Investor Principle' (2015)

Daljord Ø, Sørgard L and Thomassen Ø, 'The SSNIP Test and Market Definition with the Aggregate Diversion Ratio: A Reply to Katz And Shapiro' 4 Journal of Competition Law and Economics [2008], 263

Danish, Finnish, Greenlandic, Icelandic, Norwegian and Swedish Competition Authorities, *Nordic Food Markets - A Taste for Competition* (2005)

Danov M and Becker F, 'Governance Aspects of Cross-Border EU Competition Actions: Theoretical and Practical Challenges' 10 Journal of Private International Law [2014], 359

Danov M, Becker FNT and Beaumont P, *Cross-Border EU Competition Law Actions*, vol. 4 (Hart 2013)

Daskalova V, 'Consumer Welfare in EU Competition Law: What Is It (Not) About?' 11 The Competition Law Review [2015], 133

De Bure F, *Other Abuses*, vol 5 (González-Díaz FE and Snelders R eds, Claeys and Casteels 2013)

De Conninck J, 'Behavioural Economics and Legal Research' in Van Hoecke M (ed), *Methodologies of legal research: which kind of method for what kind of discipline?* (Hart 2011)

Dehtmers F, 'Collective Dominance under EC Merger Control - After Airtours and the Introduction of Unilateral Effects is there still a Future for Collective Dominance?' 26 European Competition Law Review [2005], 638

Demsetz H, 'Barriers to Entry' 72 The American Economic Review [1982], 47

Department of Justice and Federal Trade Commission (US), *Statements of Antitrust Enforcement Policy in Health Care* (1996)

—, *Horizontal Merger Guidelines* (2010)

De Witte B, Muir E and Dawson M, *Judicial Activism at the European Court of Justice* (Edward Elgar 2013)

Diamandouros PN, 'Improving EU Competition Law Procedures by Applying Principles of Good Administration: The Role of the Ombudsman' 1 Journal of European Competition Law & Practice [2010], 379

Dobson PW, 'Exploiting Buyer Power: Lessons from the British Grocery Trade' 72 Antitrust Law Journal [2004-2005], 529

——, 'Relationship Between Buyer and Seller power in Retailing: UK Supermarkets' in Lyons B (ed), *Cases in European competition policy: the economic analysis* (Cambridge University Press 2009)

Dobson PW and Chakraborty R, 'Buyer Power in the U.K. Groceries Market' 53 The Antitrust Bulletin [2008], 333

Dobson PW and Inderst R, 'Differential Buyer Power and the Waterbed Effect: Do Strong Buyers Benefit or Harm Consumers?' 28 European Competition Law Review [2007], 393

——, 'The Waterbed Effect: Where Buying and Selling Power Come Together' 331 Wisconsin Law Review [2008], 331

Doherty B, 'Just what are Essential Facilities?' 38 Common Market Law Review [2001], 397

Donovan T and others, 'USA: Monopolisation - Predatory Bidding' 28 European Competition Law Review [2007], N86

Doyle C and Han MA, 'Cartelization Through Buyer Groups' 44 Review of Industrial Organization [2014], 255

Doyle C and Inderst R, 'Some Economics on the Treatment of Buyer Power in Antitrust' 28 European Competition Law Review [2007], 210

Doyle C and Murgatroyd R, 'The Role of Private Labels in Antitrust' 7 Journal of Competition Law and Economics [2011], 631

Dutt A and Wilber C, *Economics and Ethics: An Introduction* (Palgrave Macmillan UK 2010)

Ebner A, 'The Intellectual Foundations of the Social Market Economy' 33 Journal of Economic Studies [2006], 206

Economides N, 'Loyalty/Requirement Rebates and the Antitrust Modernization Commission: What is the Appropriate Liability Standard' 54 Antitrust Bulletin [2009], 259

Ehlers J, 'Vertical Restraints' in Hirsch G, Montag F and Säcker FJ (eds), *Competition Law: European Community Practice and Procedure* (Thomson - Sweet & Maxwell 2008)

Eilmansberger T, 'Article 82' in Hirsch G, Montag F and Säcker FJ (eds), *Competition law: European community practice and procedure: article-by-article commentary* (Sweet & Maxwell 2008)

Elhauge E, 'Tying, Bundled Discounts, and the Death of the Single Monopoly Profit Theory' 123 Harvard Law Review [2009], 397

Elhauge E and Geradin D, *Global Competition Law and Economics, 2nd Edition* (Hart Publishing Ltd 2011)

Elzinga KG and Mills DE, 'Trumping the Areeda-Turner Test: The Recoupment Standard in Brooke Group' 62 Antitrust Law Journal [1993-1994], 559

Estevan de Quesada C, 'Competition and Transparency in Public Procurement Markets' 5 Public Procurement Law Review [2014]

Eucken W, 'Técnica, Concentración y Ordenación de la Economía' in Beltrán L (ed), *La Economía de Mercado*, vol I (1950)

—, *Grundsätze der Wirtschaftspolitik* (Mohr Siebeck 1952)

—, 'El Problema Político de la Ordenación' in Beltrán L (ed), *La Economía de Mercado*, vol I (Sociedad de Estudios y Publicaciones 1963)

—, 'What Kind of Economic and Social System' in Peacock A and Willgerodt H (eds), *Germany's Social Market Economy: Origins and Evolution* (MacMillan 1989)

European Commission, 'Contribution of the European Union in OECD Policy Roundtables: Excessive Prices' in OECD (ed), *Policy Rountables: Excessive Prices* (OECD 2011)

—, *Green Paper on Unfair Trading Practices in the Business-to-Business Food and Non-Food supply Chain in Europe* (2013)

—, *The Economic Impact of Modern Retail on Choice and Innovation in the EU Food Sector* (2014)

—, *Study on the Legal Framework Covering Business-To-Business Unfair Trading Practices in the Retail Supply Chain* (2014)

—, *Tackling Unfair Trading Practices in the Business-to-Business food supply chain* (2014)

—, *Market Definition in a Gloablised World* (2015)

—, *Report from the Commission to the European Parliament and the Council on Unfair Business-to-Business Trading Practices in the Food Supply Chain* (2016)

European Commission and others, *Buyer Power and its Impact on Competition in the Food Retail Distribution Sector of the European Union* (2000)

European Commission, Directorate General for Competition, *Discussion Paper on the Application of Article 82 of the Treaty to Exclusionary Abuses* (2005)

European Competition Network, *ECN Activities in the Food Sector* (2012)

European Parliament, *Imbalances in the Food Supply Chain* (19 January 2012)

—, "Public procurement package: getting the best value for money". Press Release – Competition – 05/09/2013 on http://www.europarl.europa.eu/news/en/news-room/content/20130903IPR18507/html/Public-procurement-package-getting-the-best-value-for-money

European Union, *Roundtable on Competition Issues in Food Chain Industry -- Note by the European Union--* (2013)

Evans DS and Padilla AJ, 'Excessive Prices: Using Economics to Define Administrable Legal Rules' 1 Journal of Competition Law and Economics [2005], 97

Ezrachi A, 'Unchallenged Market Power? The Tale of Supermarkets, Private labels and Competition Law' 33 World Competition [2010], 257

—, 'Buying Alliances and Input Price Fixing: In Search of a European Enforcement Standard' 8 Journal of Competition Law and Economics [2012], 47

—, *EU Competition Law: An Analytical Guide to the Leading Cases* (Hart 2012 3rd edn)

—, *EU Competition Law: An Analytical Guide to the Leading Cases* (Hart 2014 4th edn)

Ezrachi A and Bernitz U (eds), *Private Labels, Brands and Competition Policy: The Changing Landscape of Retail Competition* (Oxford University Press 2009)

Ezrachi A and De Jong K, 'Buyer power, private labels and the welfare consequences of quality erosion' 33 European Competition Law Review [2012], 257

Ezrachi A and Ioannidou M, 'Buyer Power in European Union Merger Control' 10 European Competition Journal [2014], 69

Ezrachi A and Williams M, 'Competition Law and the Regulation of Buyer Power and Buyer Cartels in China and Hong Kong' 9 Asian Journal of Comparative Law [2013], 295

Facey B and Brown C, *Competition and Antitrust Laws in Canada* (Lexis Nexis 2013)

Falce V, *The Italian Regulation Against the Abuse of Economic Dependence* (2015)

Farley M and Pourbaix N, 'The EU Concessions Directive: Building (Toll) Bridges between Competition Law and Public Procurement?' Journal of European Competition Law & Practice [2014]

Farrell J and Shapiro C, 'Scale Economies and Synergies in Horizontal Merger Analysis' 68 Antitrust Law Journal [2001], 685

Faull J and Nikpay A, *The EC Law of Competition* (Oxford University Press 1999)

Faull J, Nikpay A and Taylor D, *The EU Law of Competition* (3rd ed., Oxford University Press 2014)

Federal Trade Commission (US), *Report on the Federal Trade Commission Workshop on Slotting Allowances and Other Marketing Practices in the Grocery Industry* (2001)

Federico G, 'The Antitrust Treatment of Loyalty Discounts in Europe: Towards a more Economic Approach' Journal of European Competition Law & Practice [2011]

Feinstein RA, '2010 Revisions to the US Horizontal Merger Guidelines' 7 Competition law International [2011]

Felice F and Vatiero M, 'Ordo and European Competition Law' <http://www.siecon.org/online/wp-content/uploads/2013/09/Felice-Vatiero.pdf>

Fici A, 'An Introduction to Cooperative Law' in Cracogna D, Fici A and Henry H (eds), *International Handbook of Cooperative Law* (Springer 2013)

Fisher R, Ury W and Patton B, *Getting to Yes: Negotiating Agreement Without Giving in* (Penguin Books 2011)

Foucault M and others, *The Birth of Biopolitics: Lectures at the Collège de France, 1978-1979* (Palgrave Macmillan 2008)

Fox EM, 'What is Harm to Competition? Exclusionary Practices and Anticompetitive Effect' 70 Antitrust Law Journal [2002], 371

—, 'Against Goals' 81 Fordham Law Review [2013], 2157

Frank RH and Glass AJ, *Microeconomics and Behavior* (McGraw-Hill 1999)

Franklin CNK, Fredriksen HH and Barlund IMH, *Private Enforcement and Collective Redress in European Competition Law - National report for Norway* (2016)

Fredriksen HH, 'The EFTA Court 15 Years On' 59 Int Comp Law Quart [2010], 731

Fredriksen HH and Franklin CNK, 'Of Pragmatism and Principles: The EEA Agreement 20 Years On' 52 Common Market Law Review [2015], 629

Friedman M and Friedman RD, *Capitalism and freedom* (University of Chicago Press 1962)

Froeb LM and Werden GJ, 'The Reverse Cellophane Fallacy in Market Delineation' 7 Review of Industrial Organization [1992], 241

Gabrielsen TS and Johansen BO, 'Buyer Power and Exclusion in Vertically Related Markets' 38 International Journal of Industrial Organization [2015], 1

Gal MS, 'Below-Cost Price Alignment: Meeting or Beating Competition? The France Télécom Case' 28 European Competition Law Review [2007], 382

—, 'Abuse of Dominance - Exploitative Abuses' in Lianos I and Geradin D (eds), *Handbook on European competition law: enforcement and procedure* (Edward Elgar Pub. Ltd. 2013)

Galbraith JK, *The Affluent Society & Other Writings 1952-1967: American Capitalism; The Great Crash, 1929; The Affluent Society; The New Industrial State.* (The Library of America 2010)

Gardner N, *A Guide to United European Union Competition Policy* (Third Edition edn, Palgrave MacMillan 2000)

Gauss N and Oldale A, *Market Definition*, vol 5 (González-Díaz FE and Snelders R eds, Claeys and Casteels 2013)

Gavil A, Kovacic W and Baker J, *Antitrust Law in Perspective: Cases, Concepts and Problems in Competition Policy* (2nd edn, Thomson West 2008)

Gellhorn E, Calkins S and Kovacic WE, *Antitrust Law and Economics in a Nutshell* (Thomson/West 2004)

Geradin D, 'The Decision of the Commission of 13 May 2009 in the Intel case: Where is the Foreclosure and Consumer Harm?' 1 Journal of European Competition Law & Practice [2010], 112

—, 'Loyalty Rebates after Intel: Time for the European Court of Justice to Overrule Hoffman-La Roche' 11 (forthcoming) Journal of Competition Law & Economics [2015]

Geradin D and others, *The Concept of Dominance in EC Competition Law* (College of Europe 2005)

Geradin D and O'Donoghue R, 'The Concurrent Application of Competition Law and Regulation: The Case of Margin Squeeze Abuses in the Telecommunications Sector' 1 Journal of Competition Law and Economics [2005], 355

Geradin D and Petit N, 'Price Discrimination under EC Competition Law: Another Antitrust Doctrine in Search of Limiting Principles?' 2 Journal of Competition Law and Economics [2006], 479

Gerber DJ, 'Constitutionalizing the Economy: German Neo-Liberalism, Competition Law and the "New" Europe' 42 The American Journal of Comparative Law [1994], 25

—, *Law and Competition in Twentieth Century Europe: Protecting Prometheus* (Oxford University Press 2001)

Gifford DJ, 'Farewell to the Robinson - Patman Act - The Antitrust Modernization Commission's Report and Recommendation' 53 The Antitrust Bulletin [2008], 481

Gifford DJ and Kudrle RT, 'The Law and Economics of Price Discrimination in Modern Economies: Time for Reconciliation?' 43 UC Davis L Rev [2010], 1235

—, *The Atlantic Divide in Antitrust: An Examination of US and EU Competition Policy* (University of Chicago Press 2015)

Ginsburg DH and Fraser EM, 'The Role of Economic Analysis in Competition Law' in McEwin RI (ed), *Intellectual property, competition law and economics in Asia* (Hart 2011)

Giudici P, 'The CEPSA Case' 5 European Review of Contract Law [2009], 159

Gjendemsjø R, *Oligopolproblemet: Om Anvendelsen av TFEU Artikkel 101 og 102 på Koordinerte Priser i et Oligopol* (Universitetet i Bergen 2011)

Goldberg VP, 'Free Rider Problem Imperfect Pricing and the Economics of Retailing Services' 79 Northwestern University Law Review [1984-1985], 736

Goldschmidt N and Berndt A, 'Leonhard Miksch (1901–1950) A Forgotten Member of the Freiburg School' 64 American Journal of Economics and Sociology [2005], 973

González-Díaz FE and Lang JT, *The Concept of Abuse*, vol 5 (González-Díaz FE and Snelders R eds, Claeys and Casteels 2013)

González Díaz FE, 'The Notion of Ancillary Restraints Under EC Competition Law' 19 Fordham International Law Journal [1995], 951

Gonzalez Diaz FE and Leis Garcia A, 'Tying and Bundling under EU Competition Law: Future Prospects' 3 Competition Law International [2007]

Gorjao-Henriques M and Sousa Ferro M, 'P/CPortugal/Commentary' in *Competition Law in Western Europe and the USA* (Wolters Kluwer 2010)

Gormsen LL, 'Article 82 EC: Where are we Coming from and Where are we Going to?' 2 The Competition Law Review [2006], 5

—, 'The Conflict Between Economic Freedom and Consumer Welfare in the Modernisation of Article 82 EC' 3 European Competition Journal [2007], 329

——, *A Principled Approach to Abuse of Dominance in European Competition Law* (Cambridge University Press 2010)

——, 'Can Consumer Welfare Convincingly be Said to be an Objective of Article 102 when the Methodology Relies on an Inference of Effects?' in Heide-Jørgensen C and others (eds), *Aims and values in competition law* (DJØF Publ. 2013)

Gorrie A, 'Competition Between Branded and Private Label Goods. Do Competition Concerns Arise when a Customer is also a Competitor?' 27 European Competition Law Review [2006], 217

Graham C, *EU and UK Competition Law* (Pearson Education Limited 2010)

Gray JC, *The Nature and Sources of the Law* (2nd Edition edn, The MacMillan Company 1927)

Grimes WS, 'The Sherman Act's Unintended Bias Against Lilliputians: Small Players' Collective Action as a Counter to Relational Market Power' 69 Antitrust Law Journal [2001], 195

——, 'Buyer Power and Retail Gatekeeper Power: Protecting Competition and The Atomistic Seller' 72 Antitrust Law Journal [2004-2005], 563

Grosskettler HG, 'Designing an Economic Order. The Contribution of the Freiburg School' in Walker DA (ed), *Perspectives on the History of Economic Thought*, vol II (1989)

Grossman SJ and Hart OD, 'Takeover Bids, The Free-Rider Problem, and the Theory of the Corporation' 11 The Bell Journal of Economics [1980], 42

Gul F, 'Unobservable Investment and the Hold-Up Problem' 69 Econometrica [2001], 343

Haglund ME, 'Weyerhaeuser's aftermath: Increased Vulnerability of Resource Based Input Markets to Monopsony' 53 The Antitrust Bulletin [2008], 411

Hamer CR, 'Regular Purchases and Aggregated Procurement: The Changes in the new Public Procurement Directive Regarding Framework Agreements, Dynamic Purchasing Systems and Central Purchasing Bodies' 4 Public Procurement Law Review [2014], 201

Handig C, 'The Unfair Commercial Practices Directive – A Milestone in the European Unfair Competition Law?' European Business Law Review [2005], 1117

Hansen HC, 'Robin-Patman Law: A Review and Analysis' 51 Fordham L Rev [1983], 1113

Harbord D and Hoehn T, 'Barriers to Entry and Exit in European Competition Policy' 14 International Review of Law and Economics [1994], 411

Harrington J, "The Current State of the Theory of Collusion: Unexplained Phenomena and Unexplored Directions" (BECCLE Competition Policy Conference)

Harris RG and Jorde TM, 'Antitrust Market Definition: An Integrated Approach' 72 California Law Review [1984], 3

Harrison JL, 'Price Fixing, the Professions, and Ancillary Restraints: Coping With Maricopa County' 4 University of Illinois Law Review [1982], 925

Hart O and Tirole J, 'Vertical Integration and Market Foreclosure' Brookings Papers on Economic Activity [1990], 205

Hartwich OM, *Neoliberalism: The Genesis of a Political Swearword* (The Centre for Independent Studies (CIS) 2009)

Hausman JA and Sidak JG, 'A Consumer-Welfare Approach to the Mandatory Unbundling of Telecommunications Networks' 109 The Yale Law Journal [1999], 417

Hay GA, 'Market Power in Antitrust' 60 Antitrust Law Journal [1991-1992]

Hayek FA, 'Competition as a Discovery Procedure' in *New Studies in Philosophy, Politics, Economics and the History of Ideas* (University of Chicago Press 1978)

Heide-Jørgensen C, 'The Relationship Between Article 101(1) TFEU and Article 101(3) TFEU' in Heide-Jørgensen C and others (eds), *Aims and values in competition law* (DJØF Publ. 2013)

Heimler A, 'Is a Margin Squeeze an Antitrust or a Regulatory Violation?' 6 Journal of Competition Law and Economics [2010], 879

Hemphill CS and Wu T, 'Parallel Exclusion' 122 The Yale Law Journal [2013], 1182

Henning-Bodewig F, *Unfair Competition Law: European Union and Member States* (Kluwer Law International 2006)

Henriksson L, 'Predatory Foreclosure and EC Competition Law' 3 Europarättslig tidskrift [2008], 689

—, *Swedish National Report: The Grocery Retail Market in Sweden: Is Antitrust Efficiently Handling this Market?* (LIDC Congress, 2013)

—, *Countervailing Buyer Power in EU Antitrust Analysis* (October 17, 2012)

Herrera Anchustegui I, 'Centralizing Public Procurement and Competitiveness in Directive 2014/24' 4 European Law Reporter [2015], 119

—, 'Competition Law Through an Ordoliberal Lens' 2 Oslo Law Review [2015], 139

—–, 'The Social Market Economy and the European Union' in Anischuk NV, Katsyn M (ed), *Историко-правовий вимір інтеграційного процесу у новий та новітній час (Historical and Legal Views on the Integration Process During the Modern and Contemprorary Era)* (2016)

—–, 'Buyer Power Exploitation: Unfair Purchasing Practices' in Cachafeiro F, García Pérez R and López Suárez MA (eds), *Derecho de la Competencia y Gran Distribución Comercial* (Thomson-Reuters Aranzadi 2016)

—–, 'Division into Lots and Demand Aggregation – Extremes Looking for the Correct Balance?' in Ølykke G and Sánchez-Graells A (eds), *Reformation or Deformation of the EU Public Procurement Rules in 2014* (Cheltenham, Edward Elgar Publishing 2016)

Hildebrand D, *The Role of Economic Analysis in EU Competition Law: The European School* (Fourth Edition edn, Kluwer Law International 2016)

Hirsch G, Montag F and Säcker FJ, *Competition Law: European Community Practice and Procedure: Article-by-Article Commentary* (Sweet & Maxwell 2008)

Hoffman M and Rumsey M, *International and Foreign Legal Research: A Coursebook* (2nd ed., BRILL 2012)

Hole O, *Price Setting in the Swedish Grocery Market: Monopoly and Monopsony Market Forces* ([O. Hole] 2008)

Hoppe EI and Schmitz PW, 'Can Contracts Solve the Hold-Up Problem? Experimental Evidence' 73 Games and Economic Behavior [2011], 186

Hoppmann E, 'Workable Competition - The Development of an Idea on the Norm for the Policy of Competition' 13 Antitrust Bulletin [1968], 61

Hovenkamp E and Hovenkamp H, 'The Viability of Antitrust Price Squeeze Claims' 51 Arizona Law Review [2009], 273

—–, 'Tying Arrangements and Antitrust Harm' 52 Arizona Law Review [2010]

Hovenkamp H, 'The Robinson-Patman Act and Competition: Unfinished Business' 68 Antitrust Law Journal [2000-2001], 125

—–, *Federal Antitrust Policy: The Law of Competition and its Practice* (3rd edn, Thomson/ West 2005)

—–, 'The Federal Trade Commission and the Sherman Act' 62 Florida Law Review [2010], 871

—–, *Antitrust* (West ed, 2011)

—–, *Does the Packers and Stockyards Act Require Antitrust Harm?* (2011)

—, 'Robert Bork and Vertical Integration: Leverage, Foreclosure, and Efficiency' 79 Antitrust Law Journal [2014], 983

Hovenkamp HJ, 'Antitrust Policy After Chicago' 84 Michigan Law Review [1985], 214

—, *Distributive Justice and Consumer Welfare in Antitrust* (2011)

Howells GG, Micklitz H-W and Wilhelmsson T, *European Fair Trading Law: The Unfair Commercial Practices Directive* (Ashgate Pub. Co. 2006)

Hughes P, 'Business strategy and EC competition law - Two Systems Separated by a Common Language' International Company and Commercial Law Review [2009], 387

Hviid M and Olczak M, 'Raising Rivals' Fixed Costs' 23 International Journal of the Economics of Business [2016], 19

Hylton KN, *Weyerhaeuser, Predatory Bidding, and Error Costs* (2008)

Hyman DA and Kovacic WE, 'Monopoly, Monopsony, and Market Definition: An Antitrust Perspective on Market Concentration Among Health Insurers' 23 Health Affairs [2004], 25

Ibanez Colomo P, 'Streetmap v Google: Lessons for Pending Article 102 TFEU Cases (Including Google Itself)' (17th February, 2016) http://chillingcompetition.com/2016/02/17/streetmap-v-google-lessons-for-pending-article-102-tfeu-cases-including-google-itself/

Incardona R and Poncibò C, 'The Average Consumer, the Unfair Commercial Practices Directive, and the Cognitive Revolution' 30 J Consum Policy [2007], 21

Inderst R, 'Contract Design and Bargaining Power' 74 Econ Lett [2002], 171

—, 'Leveraging Buyer Power' 25 International Journal of Industrial Organization [2007], 908

Inderst R and Valletti T, 'Incentives for Input Foreclosure' 55 European Economic Review [2011], 820

Inderst R and Wey C, 'How Strong Buyers Spur Upstream Innovation' 524 DIW Berlin: Discussion Papers [2005], 1

—, 'Buyer Power and Supplier Incentives' 51 European Economic Review [2007], 647

International Competition Network, *Unilateral Conduct Workbook Chapter 3: Assessment Of Dominance* (2011)

Institute of Medicine, National Academy of Sciences, and National Academy of

Engineering, *Facilitating Interdisciplinary Research* (The National Academies Press 2004)

Italianer A, European Commission, *The Interplay Between Law and Economics* (8 December 2010)

—, *The Devil is in the Retail* (2 October 2014)

—, 'The Object of Effects' (CRA Annual Brussels Conference – Economic Developments in Competition Policy) [2014]

Jacobson JM, 'Monopsony 2013: Still Not Truly Symmetric' December 2013 The Antitrust Source [2013]

Jacobson JM and Dorman GJ, 'Joint Purchasing, Monopsony and Antitrust' XXXVI The Antitrust Bulletin [1991], 1

Jenny F, 'International Report' in Kobel P, Këllezi P and Kilpatrick B (eds), *Antitrust in the Groceries Sector & Liability Issues in Relation to Corporate Social Responsibility* (Springer Berlin Heidelberg 2015)

Jessen AF, *The Effect-Based Approach to Rebates: Is the Theory of Raising Rival's Costs the Answer?* (2015)

Johansen BO, *Buyer Power, Welfare and Public Policy* (University of Bergen 2012)

Jones A, 'The Boundaries of an Undertaking in EU Competition Law' 8 European Competition Journal [2012], 301

Jones A and Sufrin B, *EU Competition Law: Text, Cases, and Materials* (Oxford University Press 2011)

—, *EU Competition Law: Text, Cases and Materials* (Oxford University Press 2014)

Jones WK, 'Concerted Refusals to Deal and the Producer Interest in Antitrust' 50 Ohio State Law Journal [1989], 73

Jost TS, Dawson D and den Exter, 'The Role of Competition in Health Care: A Western European Perspective' 31 Journal of Health Politics, Policy and Law [2006], 687 to 703

Kamecke U, 'The Proper Scope of Government Viewed from an Ordoliberal Perspective: The Example of Competition Policy: Comment' 157 Journal of Institutional and Theoretical Economics (JITE) [2001], 23

Kaplow L, 'Market Definition' in Blair RD and Sokol DD (eds), The Oxford Handbook of International Antitrust Economics, vol 1 (Oxford University Press 2015)

Kaplow L and Shavell S, *Fairness Versus Welfare* (Harvard University Press 2002)

Karayigit MT, 'Under the Triangle Rules of Competition, State Aid and Public Procurement: Public Undertakings Entrusted with the Operation of Services of General Economic Interest' 30 European Competition Law Review [2009], 542

Karjalainen K, 'Challenges of Purchasing Centralization: Empirical Evidence from Public Procurement' (Helsinki School of Economics 2009)

Karlsson J, 'Clearance of near-duopoly' 27 European Competition Law Review [2006], 514

Kathuria V, 'A Conceptual Framework to Identify Dynamic Efficiency' 11 European Competition Journal [2015], 319

Këllezi P, 'Abuse below the Threshold of Dominance? Market Power, Market Dominance, and Abuse of Economic Dependence' in Mackenrodt M-O, Gallego BC and Enchelmaier S (eds), *Abuse of Dominant Position: New Interpretation, New Enforcement Mechanisms?* (Springer 2008)

Kelsen H, *General Theory of Law and State*, vol 1 (Reissued. edn, Russell & Russell 1961)

Kerber W and Vanberg V, 'Constitutional Aspects of Party Autonomy and Its Limits - The Perspective of Constitutional Economics' in Grundmann S, Kerber W and Weatherhill S (eds), *Party Autonomy and the Role of Information in the Internal Market* (2001)

Kirkwood JB, 'Buyer Power and Exclusionary Conduct: Should Brooke Group Set the Standards for Buyer-Induced Price Discrimination and Predatory Bidding?' 72 Antitrust Law Journal [2004-2005], 625

—, 'Powerful Buyers and Merger Enforcement' 92 Boston University Law Review [2012], 1485

—, 'The Essence of Antitrust: Protecting Consumers and Small Suppliers from Anticompetitive Conduct' 81 Fordham Law Review [2013]

—, 'Collusion to Control a Powerful Customer: Amazon, E-Books, and Antitrust Policy' 69 University of Miami Law Review [2014], 1

—, *Buyer Power and Healthcare Prices* (2015)

Kirkwood JB and Lande RH, 'The Fundamental Goal of Antitrust: Protecting Consumers, Not Increasing Efficiency' 84 Notre Dame Law review [2008-2009], 191

Klump R and Wörsdörfer M, 'On the Affiliation of Phenomenology and Ordoliberalism: Links between Edmund Husserl, Rudolf and Walter Eucken' 18 The European Journal of the History of Economic Thought [2011], 551

Kobel P, Këllezi P and Kilpatrick B (eds), *Antitrust in the Groceries Sector & Liability Issues in Relation to Corporate Social Responsibility* (Springer Berlin Heidelberg 2015)

Kokkoris I, 'The Concept of Market Definition and the SSNIP Test in the Merger Appraisal' 26 European Competition Law Review [2005], 209

—, 'Buyer Power Assessment in Competition Law: A Boon or a Menace?' 29 World Competition [2006], 139

—, 'Purchase Price Fixing: A Per Se Infringement?' 28 European Competition Law Review [2007], 473

Kokkoris I and Day L, 'Buyer Power in UK Merger Control' 30 European Competition Law Review [2009], 176

Kokkoris I and Glader M, *Excessive Pricing*, vol 5 (González-Díaz FE and Snelders R eds, Claeys and Casteels 2013)

Kokkoris I and Shelanski H, *EU Merger Control: A Legal and Economic Analysis* (Oxford University Press 2014)

Kolasky WJ and Dick AR, 'The Merger Guidelines and the Integration of Efficiencies into Antitrust Review of Horizontal Mergers' 71 Antitrust Law Journal [2003], 207

Korah V, 'The Interface Between Intellectual Property and Antitrust: The European Experience' 69 Antitrust Law Journal [2002], 801

Korah V and O'Sullivan D, *Distribution Agreements under the EC Competition Rules* (Hart Publishing 2002)

Kovacic WE and Winerman M, 'Competition Policy and the Application of Section 5 of the Federal Trade Commission Act' 76 Antitrust Law Journal [2010], 929

Krajewski M and Farley M, 'Non-Economic Activities in Upstream and Downstream Markets and the Scope of Competition Law After FENIN' 32 European Law Review [2007], 111

Krajewski M, Neergaard U and van den Gronden J, *The Changing Legal Framework for Services of General Interest in Europe: Between Competition and Solidarity* (Asser 2009)

Krattenmaker TG and Salop SC, 'Anticompetitive Exclusion: Raising Rivals' Costs to Achieve Power over Price' 96 The Yale Law Journal [1986], 209

Kreisberger R, 'FENIN: Immunity from Competition Law Attack for Public Buyers?' 6 Public Procurement Law Review [2006], NA214

Kristjánsdóttir MV, 'Good Administration as a Fundamental Right' 9 Icelandic Review of Politics and Administration [2013], 237

Kroes N, 'Tackling Exclusionary Practices to Avoid Exploitation of Market Power: Some Preliminary Thoughts on the Policy Review of Article 82' 29 Fordham International Law Journal [2005], 593

—, 'The European Commission's Enforcement Priorities as Regards Exclusionary Abuses of Dominance - Current Thinking' 4 Competition Law International [2008], 4

Krugman PR, 'Increasing Returns, Monopolistic Competition, and International Trade' 9 Journal of International Economics [1979], 469

Kultti K, 'About Bargaining Power' 69 Economic Letters [2000], 341

Lagerlöf JNM and Heidhues P, 'On the Desirability of an Efficiency Defense in Merger Control' 23 International Journal of Industrial Organization [2005], 803

Lamadrid A, 'Breaking news- The Intel Judgment is out: the European Commission wins' (12 June 2014) <http://chillingcompetition.com/2014/06/12/breaking-news-the-intel-judgment-is-out-the-european-commission-wins/>

Lasok KPE, 'When is an Undertaking not an Undertaking?' 25 European Competition Journal [2004], 383

Lau S, *Information and Bargaining in the Hold-Up Problem* (The RAND Corporation 2008)

Lehiaren Defentsarako Euskal Auzitegia / Tribunal Vasco de Defensa de la Competencia (Basque Country, Spain), *Distribution of Daily Consumer Goods: Competition, Oligopoly and Tacit Collusion* (April 2009)

Lenel HO, 'Evolution of the Social Market Economy' in Peacock A and Willgerodt H (eds), *German Neo-Liberals and the Social Market Economy*, vol I (MacMillan 1989)

Lerner AP, 'The Concept of Monopoly and the Measurement of Monopoly Power' 1 The Review of Economic Studies [1934], 157

Lewis D, 'Chilling Competition', Competition Tribunal South Africa

Lianos I, 'Some Reflections on the Question of the Goals of EU Competition Law' in **Lianos I and Geradin D** (eds), *Handbook on European competition law: enforcement and procedure* (Edward Elgar Pub. Ltd. 2013)

—, 'Some Reflections on the Question of the Goals of EU Competition Law' 3/2013 CLES Working Paper Series [2013]

Lianos I and Lombardi C, *Superior Bargaining Power and the Global Food Value Chain. The Wuthering Heights of Holistic Competition Law?* (2016)

Lidgard HH, 'Unilateral Refusal to Supply: an Agreement in Disguise' 6 European Competition Law Review [1997], 352

Lindberg R, 'Buying Exclusion in EU Competition Rules — Assessing Reasons and Consequences' 7 European Competition Journal [2011], 433

Lindrup G (ed) *Butterworth's Competition Law Handbook*, vol II (12th edn, Lexis Nexis 2006)

Loewenthal P-J, 'The Defence of "Objective Justification" in the Application of Article 82 EC' 28 World Competition [2005], 455

Lopatka JE, 'Predatory Buying' in Blair RD and Sokol DD (eds), The Oxford Handbook of International Antitrust Economics, vol 2 (Oxford University Press 2015)

Louri V, 'The FENIN Judgment: The Notion of Undertaking and Purchasing Activity. Case T-319/99, Federación Nacional de Empresas de Instrumentación Científica, Médica, Técnica y Dental v Commission [2003] ECR II-00357' 32 Legal Issues of Economic Integration [2005], 87

Lowe P, 'Consumer Welfare and Efficiency – New Guiding Principles of Competition Policy?' (13th International Conference on Competition and 14th European Competition Day)

Luchs R and others, 'The End of the Robinson-Patman Act? Evidence from Legal Case Data' 56 Management Science [2010], 2123

Lutz FA, 'Objeciones al Orden de la Competencia' in Beltrán L (ed), *La Economía de Mercado*, vol I (Sociedad de Estudios y Publicaciones 1963)

—, 'Observations on the Problem of Monopolies' in Peacock A and Willgerodt H (ed), *Germany's Social Market Economy: Origins and Evolution* (MacMillan 1989)

Maier-Rigaud F, 'On the Normative Foundations of Competition Law – Efficiency, Political Freedom and the Freedom to Compete' in Zimmer D (ed), *The goals of competition law* (Edward Elgar 2012)

Makris SS, 'Applying Normative Theories in EU Competition Law: Exploring Article 102 TFEU' 3 UCL Journal of Law and Jurisprudence [2014], 30

Mario M, , *The Relationship Between CAP and Competition Policy - Does EU Competition Law Apply to Agriculture?* (Helsinki Fair Trade edn, 2003)

Markovits RS, *Economics and the Interpretation and Application of U.S. and E.U. Antitrust Law*, vol II Economics-Based Legal Analyses on Mergers, Vertical Practices and Joint Ventures (Springer ed, Springer 2014)

Maudhuit S and Soames T, 'Changes in EU merger control: Part 2' 26 European Competition Law Review [2005], 75

Meessen KM, 'The Conflict over Vertical Foreclosure in Competition Policy and Intellectual Property Law: Comment' 160 Journal of Institutional and Theoretical Economics (JITE) / Zeitschrift für die gesamte Staatswissenschaft [2004], 97

Meisel JB, 'The Law and Economics of Margin Squeezes in the US Versus the EU' 8 European Competition Journal [2012], 383

Meza S and Sudhir K, 'Do Private Labels Increase Retailer Bargaining Power?' 8 QME-Quant Mark Econ [2010], 333

Mezines BJ, 'Group Buying--When is it Permitted under the Robinson-Patman Act' 44 New York University Law Review [1969], 729

Monti G, 'The Scope of Collective Dominance under Article 82 EC' 38 Common Market Law Review [2001], 131

—–, 'The Concept of Dominance in Article 82' 2 European Competition Journal [2006], 31

—–, *EC Competition Law* (Cambridge University Press 2007)

—–, 'Article 82 EC: What Future for the Effects-Based Approach?' 1 Journal of European Competition Law & Practice [2010], 2

—–, 'EU Competition Law from Rome to Lisbon - Social Market Economy' in Heide-Jørgensen C and others (eds), *Aims and Values in Competition Law* (DJØF Publ. 2013)

Morgan TD, *Cases and Materials on Modern Antitrust Law and its Origins* (4th edn, West Publishing Company 2009)

Motta M, *Competition Policy: Theory and Practice* (Cambridge University Press 2004)

—–, *Competition Policy: Theory and Practice* (Cambridge University Press 2006)

Motta M and de Streel A, 'Excessive Pricing in Competition Law: Never say Never?' in Konkurrensverket - Swedish Competition Authority (ed), *The Pros and Cons of High Prices* (2007)

Munro C, 'Competition Law and Public Procurement: Two Sides of the Same Coin?' 6 Public Procurement Law Review [2006], 352

Müller-Armack A, 'The Social Market Economy as an Economic and Social Order' 36 Review of Social Economy [1978], 325

Mäger T and Paul TB, 'The Interaction of Public and Private Enforcement – The

Calculation and Reconciliation of Fines and Damages in Europe and Germany' in Hüschelrath K and Schweitzer H (eds), *Public and Private Enforcement of Competition Law in Europe: Legal and Economic Perspectives* (Springer 2014)

Möllers TMJ and Heinemann A, 'Outlook: The Link Between Unfair Competition Law and Antitrust Law' in Möllers TMJ and Heinemann A (eds), *The Enforcement of Competition Law in Europe* (Cambridge University Press 2008)

Möschel W, 'Competition Policy from an Ordo Point of View' in Peacock A and Willgerodt H (eds), *German Neo-Liberals and the Social Market Economy*, vol I (MacMillan 1989)

—, 'Market Definition with Branded Goods and Private Label Products' 35 European Competition Law Review [2014], 29

Nagy CI, 'Refusal to Deal and the Doctrine of Essential Facilities in US and EC Competition Law: a Comparative Perspective and a Proposal for a Workable Analytical Framework' 32 European Law Review [2007], 664

Nazzini R, *The Foundations of European Union Competition Law: The Objective and Principles of Article 102* (Oxford University Press 2011)

Neeman Z, 'The Freedom to Contract and the Free-Rider Problem' 15 Journal of Law, Economics, and Organization [1999], 685

Neumann M, *Competition Policy: History, Theory and Practice* (Edward Elgar 2001)

—, 'Efficiency Defense in EU and US Horizontal Merger Control if Costs are Endogenous' 17 German Economic Review [2015], 48

Nicholls WH, *A Theoretical Analysis of Imperfect Competition with Special Application to the Agricultural Industries* (Iowa State College Press 1941)

Niels G, Jenkins H and Kavanagh J, *Economics for Competition Lawyers* (Oxford University Press 2011)

Nihoul P, 'The Ruling of the General Court in Intel: Towards the End of an Effect-based Approach in European Competition Law?' 5 Journal of European Competition Law & Practice [2014], 521

Noll RG, '"Buyer Power" and Economic Policy' 72 Antitrust Law Journal [2004-2005], 589

Nollet L, 'France: Anti-Competitive Practices' 24 European Competition Law Review [2003], N116

Nordemann JB, 'Buying Power and Sophisticated Buyers in Merger Control Law: The Need for a More Sophisticated Approach' 16 European Competition Law Review [1995], 270

Normann H-T, Rösch J and Schultz LM, 'Do Buyer Groups Facilitate Collusion?' 109 J Econ Behav Organ [2015], 72

O'Brien DP and Shaffer G, 'The Welfare Effects of Forbidding Discriminatory Discounts: A Secondary Line Analysis of Robinson-Patman' 10 Journal of Law, Economics, & Organization [1994], 296

O'Donoghue R and Padilla AJ, *The Law and Economics of Article 82 EC* (Hart 2006)

—, *The Law and Economics of Article 102 TFEU* (2nd edn, Hart Publishing 2013)

Odudu O, *The Boundaries of EC Competition Law: The Scope of Article 81* (Oxford University Press 2006)

—, 'The Wider Concerns of Competition Law' 30 Oxford Journal of Legal Studies [2010], 599

Odudu O and Bailey D, 'The Single Economic Entity Doctrine in EU Competition Law' 51 Common Market Law Review [2014], 1721

OECD, *Policy Roundtables: Buying Power of Multiproduct Retailers* (1999)

—, *France - The Role of Competition Policy in Regulatory Reform* (2003)

—, *Policy Roundtables: Monopsony and Buyer Power* (2009)

—, *Policy Rountables: Excessive Prices* (2011)

—, 'Policy Roundtables: Market Definition' [2012]

Office of Fair Trading (UK), *Research Paper 16: The Welfare Consequences of the Exercise of Buyer Power* (1998)

—, *Assessing the Impact of Public Sector Procurement on Competition* (2004)

—, *Assessment of Market Power: Understanding Competition Law* (2004)

—, 'Market Definition: Understanding Competition Law' [2004]

—, *The Competitive Effects of Buyer Groups* (2007)

—, *Competition in Mixed Markets: Ensuring Competitive Neutrality* (2010)

Oinonen M, *Does EU Merger Control Discriminate Against Small Markets Companies?: Diagnosing the Argument with Conclusions* (Kluwer Law International 2010)

—, 'The New 30% Rule: A Viable Solution to Detrimental Buyer Power in the Finnish Grocery Retail Sector?' 10 European Competition Journal [2014], 97

Orbach BY, 'The Antitrust Consumer Welfare Paradox' 7 Journal of Competition Law & Economics [2010], 133

Orbach BY and Avraham R, 'Squeeze Claims: Refuslas to Deal, Essential Facilities and Price Squeezes' in Blair RD and Sokol DD (eds), The Oxford Handbook of International Antitrust Economics, vol 2 (Oxford University Press 2015)

Ordover JA and Willig RD, 'The 1982 Department of Justice Merger Guidelines: An Economic Assessment' 71 California Law Review [1983], 535

Osterdal LP, 'Bargaining Power in Repeated Games' 49 Mathematical Social Sciences [2005], 101

Overd A, 'Buyer Power' 22 European Competition Law Review [2001], 249

Padilla J, 'The Role of Economics in EU Competition Law: From Monti's Reform to the State Aid Modernization Package' 2-2016 Concurrences Review [2016]

Papandropoulos P, 'How Should Price Discrimination be Dealt with by Competition Authorities?' 3 Concurrences [2007], 34

Parker J and Majumdar A, *UK Merger Control* (Hart 2011)

Parry DL, *The Yearbook of Consumer Law 2009* (Ashgate 2008)

Paschke M, 'Anti-Competitive Practices (Agreements, Decisions, Concerted Practices)' in Hirsch G, Montag F and Säcker FJ (eds), *Competition law: European community practice and procedure: article-by-article commentary* (Sweet & Maxwell 2008)

Patel KK and Schweitzer H (eds), *The Historical Foundations of EU Competition Law* (Oxford University Press 2013)

Peacock A and Willgerodt H, 'German Liberalism and Economic Revival' in Peacock A and Willgerodt H (eds), *Germany's Social Market Economy: Origins and Evolution* (MacMillan 1989)

——, 'German Neo-Liberals and the Social Market Economy' in Peacock A and Willgerodt H (eds), *German Neo-Liberals and the Social Market Economy*, vol I (MacMillan 1989)

——, 'Overall View of the German Liberal Movement' in Peacock A and Willgerodt H (eds), *German Neo-Liberals and the Social Market Economy*, vol I (MacMillan 1989)

Pera A, 'Assessment of Buyer Power in Recent Investigations and Mergers' (2010)

Pera A and Bonfitto V, 'Buyer Power in Anti-trust Investigations: A Review' 32 European Competition Law Review [2011], 414

Petit N, *Oligopoles, Collusion Tacite et Droit Communautaire de la Concurrence* (Bruylant 2008)

——, 'Intel, Leveraging Rebates and the Goals of Article 102 TFEU' 11 European Competition Journal [2015], 26

——, *The IEEE-SA Revised Patent Policy and its Definition of "Reasonable" Rates: A Transatlatic Antitrust Divide?* (2016)

——, 'Rebates and Article 102 TFEU: The European Commission's Duty to Apply the Guidance Paper' 2 Competition Law & Policy Debate [2016], 4

Petit N and Neyrinck N, 'Back to Microsoft I and II: Tying and the Art of Secret Magic' 2 Journal of European Competition Law & Practice [2011], 117

Petrasincu A, 'The European Commission's New Guidelines on the Assessment of Non-Horizontal Mergers - Great Expectations Disappointed' 29 European Competition Law Review [2008], 221

Pindyck RS and Rubinfeld DL, *Microeconomics* (Pearson Prentice Hall 2009)

Pliakos A and Anagnostaras G, 'Mediaprint Zeitungs- und Zeitschriftenverlag GmbH & Co. KG v. Österreich-Zeitungsverlag GmbH' 48 Common Market Law Review [2011], 1313

Posner RA, *Antitrust Law: An Economic Perspective* (University of Chicago Press 1976)

——, 'The Chicago School of Antitrust Analysis' 127 University of Pennsylvania Law Review [1979], 925

——, 'The Federal Trade Commission: A Retrospective' 72 Antitrust Law Journal [2005], 761

Posner RA and Landes WM, 'Market Power in Antitrust Case' 94 Harvard Law Review [1980], 937

Pozdnakova A, 'Buyer Power in the Retail Trading Sector: Evolving Latvian Regulation' 30 European Competition Law Review [2009], 387

Quirk JP, *Intermediate Microeconomics* (Science Research Associates 1987)

Radeideh M, *The Principle of Fair Trading in EC Law: Information and Consumer Choice in the Internal Market* ([s.n.] 2004)

Raff H and Schmitt N, 'Buyer Power in International Markets' 79 Journal of International Economics [2009], 222

Rantanen H and others, 'Performance Measurement Systems in the Finnish Public Sector' 20 International Journal of Public Sector Management [2007], 415

Reich A, 'The Agricultural Exemption in Antitrust Law: A Comparative Look at the Political Economy of Market Regulation' 42 Texas International Law Journal [2007], 843

Ritter C, 'Does the Law of Predatory pricing and Cross-Subsidisation Need a Radical Rethink?' 27 World Competition [2004], 613

—, 'A New Look at the Role and Impact of Advocates-General — Collectively and Individually' 12 Columbia Journal of European Law [2006]

Ritter L and Braun WD, *European Competition Law: A Practitioner's Guide* (3rd edn, Kluwer Law International 2004)

Robles Martín-Laborda A, *Exploitative Prices in European Competition Law* (2015)

—, 'La Cadena Alimentaria: Cuando el Poder de Mercado lo Tiene el Comprador' (2015)

Rodger BJ, 'The Oligopoly Problem and the Concept of Collective Dominance: EC Developments in the Light of U.S. Trends in Antitrust Law and Policy' 2 Columbia Journal of European Law [1995-1996], 25

—, 'Competition Policy, Liberalism and Globalization: A European Perspective' 6 Columbia Journal of European Law [2000]

Rodger BJ and MacCullogh A, *Competition Law and Policy in the EU and UK* (5th edn, Routledge 2015)

Rodrigues J, *Buyer Power and Pass-Through of Large Retailing Groups in the Portuguese Food Sector* (2006)

Rose I and Ngwe C, 'The Ordoliberal Tradition in the European Union, Its Influence on Article 82 EC and the IBA's Comments on the Article 82 EC Discussion Paper' 3 Competition Law International [2007], 8

Rosenfelt N, 'The Verdict on Monopsony' 20 Loyola Consumer Law Review [2008], 402

Ross M, 'Promoting Solidarity: From Public Services to a European Model of Competition?' 44 Common Market Law Review [2007], 1057

Ross TW, 'Winners and Losers under the Robinson-Patman Act' 27 Journal of Law & Economics [1984], 243

Roth W-H, 'Case C-205/03 P, Federación Española de Empresas de Tecnología Sanitaria (FENIN) v. Commission, Judgment of the Grand Chamber of 11 July 2006, [2006] ECR I-6295' 44 Common Market Law Review [2007], 1131

Rousseva E, *Rethinking Exclusionary Abuses in EU Competition Law* (Hart 2010)

Ruffle BJ, *Buyer Countervailing Power: A Survey of the Theory and Experimental Evidence* (2005)

Ruggiero J, 'On the Measurement of Technical Efficiency in the Public Sector' 90 European Journal of Operational Research [1996], 553

Rüstow A, 'Zwischen Kapitalismus und Kommunismus' in Goldschmidt N and Wohlgemuth M (eds), *Grundtexte zur Freiburger Tradition der Ordnungsökonomik* (Mohr Siebeck 2008)

Röpke W, *A Humane Economy* (Third Edition edn, ISI Books 1998)

Salop SC, 'Anticompetitive Overbuying by Power Buyers' 72 Antitrust Law Journal [2004-2005], 669

Sánchez Graells A, *Public Procurement and the EU Competition Rules* (Hart 2011)

—, *Public Procurement and the EU Competition Rules* (2nd edn, Hart 2015)

—, *Some Bold Thoughts about the (Distant?) Future of Public Procurement in the EU* (2015)

Sánchez Graells A and Herrera Anchustegui I, 'Impact of Public Procurement Aggregation on Competition. Risks, Rationale and Justification for the Rules in Directive 2014/24' in Valcárcel Fernández P (ed), *Compra conjunta y demanda agregada en la contratación del sector público Un análisis jurídico y económico* (Thomson-Aranzadi 2016)

—, 'Revisiting the Concept of Undertaking from a Public Procurement Law Perspective - A Discussion on EasyPay and Finance Engineering' 37 European Competition Law Review [2016], 93

Sauter W and Schepel H, *State and Market in European Union Law: The Public and Private Spheres of the Internal Market Before the EU Courts* (Cambridge University Press 2009)

Scheelings R and Wright JD, 'Sui Generis: An Antitrust Analysis of Buyer Power in the United States and European Union' 39 Akron Law Review [2006], 207

Scheffman DT and Higgins RS, 'Raising Rivals' Costs' in Blair RD and Sokol DD (eds), The Oxford Handbook of International Antitrust Economics, vol 2 (Oxford University Press 2015)

Scheffman DT and Spiller PT, 'Buyers' Strategies, Entry Barriers, and Competition' 30 Economic Inquiry [1992], 418

Scherer FM, 'Retailer -Instigated Restraints on Suppliers' Sales: Toys "R" US (2000)' in John E. Kwoka J and White LJ (eds), *The Antitrust Revolution* (Fifth Edition edn, Oxford University Press 2009)

Scherer FM and Ross D, *Industrial Market Structure and Economic Performance* (Houghton Mifflin 1990)

Schinkel MP and Tuinstra J, 'Imperfect Competition Law Enforcement' CeNDEF Working Paper No 04-07 [2004]

Schmalensee R, 'Economies of Scale and Barriers to Entry' 89 Journal of Political Economy [1981], 1228

Schnitzer JS, 'Regulating Public Procurement Law at Supranational Level: The Example of EU Agreements on Public Procurement' 10 Journal of Public Procurement [2010], 301

Schultz WJ, *The Moral Conditions of Economic Efficiency* (Cambridge University Press 2001)

Schwalbe U and Zimmer D, *Law and Economics in European Merger Control* (Oxford University Press 2009)

Schwartz M, 'The Perverse Effects of the Robinson-Patman Act' 31 Antitrust Bulletin [1986], 733

—, 'Should Antitrust Assess Buyer Market Power Differently than Seller Market Power?' (DOJ/FTC Workshop on Merger Enforcement)

Schweitzer H, 'Competition Law and Public Policy: Reconsidering an Uneasy Relationship. The Example of Art. 81' LAW 2007/30 EUI Working Papers [2007]

—, 'Recent Developments in EU Competition Law (2006–2008): Single-Firm Dominance and the Interpretation of Article 82' 5 European Review of Contract Law [2009], 175

Seidmann DJ, 'Bundling as a Facilitating Device: A Reinterpretation of Leverage Theory' 58 Economica [1991], 491

Senden L, *Soft Law in European Community law*, vol 1 (Hart 2004)

Šerpytis K, Vengrauskas V and Gineitienė Z, 'Evaluation of Financial effects of Public Procurement Centralisatiom' 90 Ekonomika [2011], 104

Shea J, 'Do Supply Curves Slope Up?' 108 The Quarterly Journal of Economics [1993], 1

Shears P, 'Overviewing the EU Unfair Commercial Practices Directive: Concentric Circles' European Business Law Review [2012], 497

Sher B, 'Intel: General Court Rewinds the Clock on Rebates' (2014) <http://www.nabarro.com/insight/briefings/2014/june/intel-general-court-rewinds-the-clock-on-rebates/>

Sheth JN and Sharma A, 'Supplier Relationships: Emerging Issues and Challenges' 26 Industrial Marketing Management [1997], 91

Sidak JG, 'Patent Holdup and Oligopsonistic Collusion in Standard-Setting Organizations' 5 Journal of Competition Law and Economics [2009], 123

——, *Letter from J. Gregory Sidak to the Hon. Renata B. Hesse Regarding the Business Review Letter for the Institute of Electrical and Electronics Engineers (IEEE) Concerning Proposed Bylaw Amendments Affecting FRAND Licensing of Standard-Essential Patents* (January 28, 2015)

Sigma, *Central Purchasing Bodies* (Brief, 2011)

Skilbeck J, 'Just When is a Public Body an "Undertaking"? Fenin and BetterCare Compared' 4 Public Procurement Law Review [2003], NA75

Skitol RA, 'Concerted Buying Power: Its Potential for Addressing the Patent Holdup Problem in Standard Setting' 72 Antitrust Law Journal [2004-2005], 727

Slynn G, 'They Call it 'Teleological.' (Interpreting Law by Looking at the Design and Purpose of the Legislature)' 7 Denning Law Journal [1992], 225

Smith M, 'Developing Administrative Principles in the EU: A Foundational Model of Legitimacy?' 18 European Law Journal [2012], 269

Smith P and Mayston D, 'Measuring Efficiency in the Public Sector' 15 Omega, International Journal of Management Science [1987], 181

Smits JM, *What is Legal Doctrine? On the Aims and Methods of Legal-Dogmatic Research* (2015)

Snyder F, 'Soft Law and Institutional Practice in the European Community' in Martin S (ed), *The Construction of Europe: Essays in Honour of Emile Noël* (Springer Netherlands 1994) <http://dx.doi.org/10.1007/978-94-015-8368-8_10>

Sokler BD and Short F, 'Third Circuit Revives Conspiracy Claims against Hospital and Insurer' (2010) <https://www.mintz.com/newsletter/2010/Advisories/0801-1210-NAT-AFR/web.html> accessed 4th February 2016

Somma A, 'Private Law as Biopolitics: Ordoliberalism, Social Market Economy, and the Public Dimension of Contract' 76 Law and Contemporary Problems [2013]

Spector D, 'Horizontal Mergers, Entry, and Efficiency Defences' 21 International Journal of Industrial Organization [2003], 1591

Stefan O, 'European Union Soft Law: New Developments Concerning the Divide Between Legally Binding Force and Legal Effects' 75 Modern Law Review [2012], 879

——, *Soft Law in Court: Competition Law, State Aid and the Court of Justice of the European Union*, vol 81 (Kluwer 2013)

Steiner RL, 'Vertical Competition, Horizontal Competition and Market Power' 53 The Antitrust Bulletin [2008], 251

Stenbacka R and Tombak M, 'Make and Buy: Balancing Bargaining Power' 81 Journal of Economic Behavior & Organization [2012], 391

Stigler GJ, 'The Economies of Scale' 1 Journal of Law & Economics [1958], 54

Stothers C, 'Refusal to Supply as Abuse of a Dominant Position: Essential Facilities in the European Union' 22 European Competition Law Review [2001], 256

Streit ME, 'Economic Order, Private Law and Public Policy - The Freiburg School of Law and Economics in Perspective' 148 Journal of Institutional and Theoretical Economics (JITE) [1992], 675

Stroux S, 'Collective Dominance under the Merger Regulation: A Serious Evidentiary Reprimand for the Commission' 27 European Law Review [2002], 736

Stuyck J, 'The Court of Justice and the Unfair Commercial Practices Directive' 52 Common Market Law Review [2015], 721

Supply Chain Initiative, *Vertical Relationships in the Food Supply Chain: Principles of Good Practice* (2011)

——, *Rules of Procedure for the Governance Group* (2013)

Szyszczak E, *The Regulation of the State in Competitive Markets in the EU* (Hart 2007)

Säcker FJ, 'Basic Principles' in Hirsch G, Montag F and Säcker FJ (eds), *Competition law: European community practice and procedure: article-by-article commentary* (Sweet & Maxwell 2008)

——, *The Concept of the Relevant Product Market: Between Demand-Side Substitutability in Supply-Side Substitutability in Competition Law* (Peter Lang 2008)

Temple-Lang J, 'How can the Problems of Exclusionary Abuses under Article 102 TFEU be Resolved?' 2 European Law Review [2012], 136

Ten Kate and Niels G, 'The Relevant Market: A Concept Still in Search of a Definition' 5 Journal of Competition Law and Economics [2009], 297

Thurow LC, *Galbraith, John Kenneth*, vol II (Eatwell J, Milgate M and Newman P eds, The MacMillan Press Limited 1987)

Tirole J, 'The Analysis of Tying Cases: A Primer' 1 Competition Policy International [2005],

Townley C, *Article 81 EC and the Public Policy* (Hart 2009)

——, 'Co-Ordinated Diversity: Revolutionary Suggestions for EU Competition Law (and for EU Law too)' King's College London Dickson Poon School of Law, Legal Studies Research Paper Series 2014-13 [2013]

——, 'Is there (Still) Room for Non-Economic Arguments in Article 101 TFEU Cases?' in Heide-Jørgensen C and others (eds), *Aims and values in competition law* (DJØF Publ. 2013)

Tridimas T, 'The Court of Justice and Judicial Activism. (European Community)' 21 European Law Review [1996], 199

Tumlir J, 'Franz Böhm and the Development of Economic-Constitutional Analysis' in Peacock A and Willgerodt H (eds), *German Neo-Liberals and the Social Market Economy*, vol I (MacMillan 1989)

Turayova Z, 'Slovakia's Unfair Terms in Business Contracts between Resellers and Suppliers of Foodstuffs' e-Competitions N 31177 Concurrences [2010]

University of Oxford, Faculty of Law, *OSCOLA: Oxford University Standard for the Citation of Legal Authorities* (Fourth Edition edn, Faculty of Law, University of Oxford 2012)

Van Bael I and Bellis J-F, *Competition Law of the European Community* (4th edn, Kluwer Law International 2005)

Van den Bergh RJ and Camesasca PD, *European Competition Law and Economics: A Comparative Perspective* (Intersentia 2001)

——, *European Competition Law and Economics: A Comparative Perspective* (Sweet & Maxwell 2006)

Van der Vijver T, 'The Irish Beef Case: Competition Authority v Beef Industry Development Society and Barry Brothers (Carrigmore) Meats (C-209/07), European Court of Justice' 30 European Competition Law Review [2009], 198

——, 'Objective Justification and Article 102 TFEU' 35 World Competition [2012], 55

Van Doorn FAH, 'The Law and Economics of Buyer Power in EU Competition Policy' (Eleven International Publishing 2015)

Van Miert K, 'The Future of European Competition Policy' (1998) <http://ec.europa.eu/competition/speeches/text/sp1998_042_en.html> accessed 6/11/2014

Vanberg V, 'Freiburg School of Law and Economics' in Newman P (ed), *The New Palgrave Dictionary*, vol 2 (1998)

——, 'Consumer Welfare, Total Welfare and Economic Freedom – On the Normative Foundations of Competition Policy' 09 Freiburger Diskussionspapiere zur Ordnungsökonomik [2009]

Vaquero García A, 'Compras Agregadas y Eficiencia Económica' in Valcárcel Fernández P (ed), *Compra conjunta y demanda agregada en la contratación del sector público Un análisis jurídico y económico* (Thomson-Aranzadi 2016)

Varian HR, *Intermediate Microeconomics: A Modern Approach* (W.W. Norton & Co. 2006)

Varney CA, 'The Capper-Volstead Act, Agricultural Cooperatives, and Antitrust Immunity' December 2010 The Antitrust Source [2010], 1

Venit JS, 'Article 82: The Last Frontier - Fighting Fire With Fire?' 28 Fordham International Law Journal [2004], 1157

Vestager M, *Setting Priorities in Antitrust* (European Commission 1 February 2016)

Vickers J, 'Abuse of Market Power' 115 The Economic Journal [2005], F244

——, 'Market Power in Competition Cases' 2 European Competition Journal [2006]

Vogel L, 'Competition Law and Buying Power: The Case for a New Approach in Europe' 19 European Competition Law Review [1998], 4

——, *European Competition Law* (Law Lex 2012)

Von Mises L, *Human Action* (4th edn, 1996)

Vranken JB, 'Methodology of Legal Doctrinal Research: A Comment on Westerman' in Van Hoecke M (ed), *Methodologies of legal research: which kind of method for what kind of discipline?* (Hart 2011)

Waelbroeck D, 'Michelin II: A Per Se Rule Against Rebates by Dominant Companies?' 1 Journal of Competition Law and Economics [2005], 149

Walton SRR, 'Wal-Mart, Supplier-Partners, and the Buyer Power Issue' 72 Antitrust Law Journal [2004-2005], 509

Wang S-S, Rojas C and Lavoie N, 'Buyer Market Power and Vertically Differentiated Retailers' (2010) <http://people.umass.edu/resec/workingpapers/documents/ResEcWorkingPaper2010-1.pdf>

Waterman D, 'Local Monopsony and Free Riders' 8 Information Economics and Policy [1996], 337

Woods L and Watson P, *Steiner & Woods EU Law* (11th Edition edn, Oxford University Press 2012)

Werden GJ, 'The Law and Economics of the Essential Facility Doctrine' 32 Saint Louis University Law Journal [1987-1988], 433

—, 'The 1982 Merger Guidelines and the Ascent of the Hypothetical Monopolist Paradigm' 71 Antitrust Law Journal [2003], 253

—, 'The Ancillary Restraints Doctrine' (54th Antitrust Law Spring Meeting)

—, 'Monopsony and The Sherman Act: Consumer Welfare in a New Light' 74 Antitrust Law Journal [2007], 707

—, 'Monopoly Pricing and Competition Policy: Divergent Paths to the Same Destination' in Hawk BE (ed), *Annual Proceedings of the Fordham Competition law Institute* (Juris Publishing, Inc 2009)

—, 'The Relevant Market: Possible and Productive' April 2014 Antitrust Law Journal Online [2014], 1

Westerman PC, 'Open or Autonomous? The Debate on legal Methodology as a Reflection of the Debate on Law' in Van Hoecke M (ed), *Methodologies of legal research: which kind of method for what kind of discipline?* (Hart 2011)

Whish R, 'Intel v Commission: Keep Calm and Carry on!' Journal of European Competition Law & Practice [2014]

Whish R and Bailey D, *Competition law* (Oxford University Press 2012)

—, *Competition law* (8th ed., Oxford University Press 2015)

Willett C, 'Fairness and Consumer Decision Making under the Unfair Commercial Practices Directive' 33 J Consum Policy [2010], 247

Williamson OE, 'Economies as an Antitrust Defense: The Welfare Tradeoffs' 58 The American Economic Review [1968], 18

Wils W, 'The Judgment of the EU General Court in *Intel* and the So-Called More Economic Approach to Abuse of Dominance' 37 World Competition [2014], 405

—, 'The Judgment of the EU General Court in Intel and the So-Called More Economic Approach to Abuse of Dominance' 37 World Competition [2014], 405

Wiseman J, 'Social Policy and the Social Market Economy' in Peacock A and Willgerodt H (eds), *German Neo-Liberals and the Social Market Economy*, vol I (MacMillan 1989)

Witt AC, 'The Commission's Guidance Paper on Abusive Exclusionary Conduct - More Radical than it Appears?' 35 European Law Review [2010], 214

Wollmann H, 'Horizontal Restraints of Competition' in Hirsch G, Montag F and Säcker FJ (eds), *Competition Law: European Community Practice and Procedure* (Thomson - Sweet & Maxwell 2008)

Wright JD, 'Von's Grocery and the Concentration-Price Relationship in Grocery Retail' 48 UCLA Law Review [2001]

—, 'What is the Worst Antitrust Decision That is Good Law?' (2008) <http://truthonthe-market.com/2008/07/22/what-is-the-worst-antitrust-decision-that-is-good-law/> accessed March 4th, 2016

—, 'Simple but Wrong or Complex but More Accurate? The Case for an Exclusive Dealing-Based Approach to Evaluating Loyalty Discounts' (Bates White 10th Annual Antitrust Conference)

Wu L and Baker S, 'Applying the Market Definition Guidelines of the European Commission' 19 European Competition Law Review [1998], 273

Wyatt D and Dashwood A, *Wyatt and Dashwood's European Union Law* (6th ed. Alan Dashwood ... [et al.]. edn, Hart 2011)

Young B, 'Supermarket Buyer Power' Competition Law Insight [2013], 13

Zenger H, 'Loyalty Rebates and the Competitive Process' 8 Journal of Competition Law and Economics [2012], 717

Zenger H and Walker M, *Theories of Harm in European Competition Law: A Progress Report* (Bourgeois J and Waelbroeck D eds, Bruylant 2013)

Zerbe Jr RO, 'Monopsony and the Ross-Simmons Case: A Comment on Salop and Kirkwood' 72 Antitrust Law Journal [2004-2005], 717

Zweynert J, 'How German is German Neo-Liberalism?' 26 Review of Austrian Economics [2013], 109

Østerud E, *Identifying Exclusionary Abuses by Dominant Undertakings under EU Competition Law: The Spectrum of Tests* (Kluwer 2010)

Concurrences Review

Concurrences is a print and online quarterly peer reviewed journal dedicated to EU and national competitions laws. It has been launched in 2004 as the flagship of the Institute of Competition Law in order to provide a forum for academics, practitioners and enforcers. The Institute's influence and expertise has garnered interviews with such figures as Christine Lagarde, Bill Kovacic, Emmanuel Macron and Margarethe Vestager.

CONTENTS

More than 15,000 articles, print and/or online. Quarterly issues provide current coverage with contributions from the EU or national or foreign countries thanks to more than 1,500 authors in Europe and abroad. Approximately 1/3 of the contributions are published in English, 2/3 in French, as the official language of the General Court of justice of the EU; all contributions have English abstracts.

FORMAT

In order to balance academic contributions with opinions or legal practice notes, Concurrences provides its insight and analysis in a number of formats:

- Forewords: Opinions by leading academics or enforcers
- Interviews: Interviews of antitrust experts
- On-Topics: 4 to 6 short papers on hot issues
- Law & Economics: Short papers written by economists for a legal audience
- Articles: Long academic papers
- Case Summaries: Case commentary on EU and French case law
- Legal Practice: Short papers for in-house counsels
- International: Medium size papers on international policies
- Books Review: Summaries of recent antitrust books
- Articles Review: Summaries of leading articles published in 45 antitrust journals

BOARDS

The Scientific Committee is headed by Laurence Idot, Professor at Panthéon Assas University. The International Committee is headed by Frederic Jenny, OECD Competition Comitteee Chairman. Boards members include Bruno Lasserre, Mario Monti, Howard Shelanski, Richard Whish, Wouter Wils, etc.

ONLINE VERSION

Concurrences website provides all articles published since its inception, in addition to selected articles published online only in the electronic supplement.

WRITE FOR CONCURRENCES

Concurrences welcome spontaneous contributions. Except in rare circumstances, the journal accepts only unpublished articles, whatever the form and nature of the contribution. The Editorial Board checks the form of the proposals, and then submits these to the Scientific Committee. Selection of the papers is conditional to a peer review by at least two members of the Committee. Within a month, the Committee assesses whether the draft article can be published and notifies the author.

The Institute of Competition Law

The Institute of Competition Law is a publishing company, founded in 2004 by Dr. Nicolas Charbit, based in Paris and New-York. The Institute cultivates scholarship and discussion about antitrust issues though publications and conferences. Each publication and event is supervised by editorial boards and scientific or steering committees to ensure independence, objectivity, and academic rigor. Thanks to this management, the Institute has become one of the few think tanks in Europe to have significant influence on antitrust policies.

AIM

The Institute focuses government, business and academic attention on a broad range of subjects which concern competition laws, regulations and related economics.

BOARDS

To maintain its unique focus, the Institute relies upon highly distinguished editors, all leading experts in national or international antitrust: Bill Kovacic, Mario Monti, Eleanor Fox, Barry Hawk, Laurence Idot, Fred Jenny, etc.

AUTHORS

3,800 authors, from 85 jurisdictions.

PARTNERS

- Universities: University College London, King's College London, Queen Mary University, Paris Sorbonne Panthéon-Assas, etc.
- Law firms: Allen & Overy, Cleary Gottlieb Steen & Hamilton, DLA Piper, Hogan Lovells, Jones Day, Norton Rose Fulbright, Skadden Arps, White & Case, etc.

EVENTS

More than 300 events since 2004 in Brussels, London, New York, Paris, Singapore, Washington, DC, Hong Kong, and Chicago.

ONLINE VERSION

Concurrences website provides all articles published since its inception.

PUBLICATIONS

The Institute publishes Concurrences Review, a print and online quarterly peer-reviewed journal dedicated to EU and national competitions laws. e-Competitions is a bi-monthly antitrust news bulletin covering 85 countries. The e-Competitions database contains over 19,900 case summaries from 21,500 authors.

www.ingramcontent.com/pod-product-compliance
Lightning Source LLC
Chambersburg PA
CBHW071406230926
51846CB00001B/17
* 9 7 8 1 9 3 9 0 0 7 2 4 7 *